Transactional Intellectual Property: From Startups to Public Companies

Transactional Intellectual Property: From Startups to Public Companies

A Successor to Intellectual Property in Business Organizations: Cases and Materials

FOURTH EDITION

Richard S. Gruner
PROFESSOR OF LAW
JOHN MARSHALL LAW SCHOOL

Shubha Ghosh
CRANDALL MELVIN PROFESSOR OF LAW
DIRECTOR, TECHNOLOGY COMMERCIALIZATION LAW PROGRAM &
SYRACUSE INTELLECTUAL PROPERTY LAW INSTITUTE
SYRACUSE UNIVERSITY COLLEGE OF LAW

Jay P. Kesan
PROFESSOR OF LAW AND H. ROSS & HELEN WORKMAN RESEARCH SCHOLAR
DIRECTOR, PROGRAM IN INTELLECTUAL PROPERTY AND TECHNOLOGY LAW
UNIVERSITY OF ILLINOIS COLLEGE OF LAW

CAROLINA ACADEMIC PRESS
Durham, North Carolina

LCCN: 2018944088
ISBN: 978-1-5310-0746-1
eISBN: 978-1-53100-747-8

Carolina Academic Press, LLC
700 Kent Street
Durham, North Carolina 27701
Telephone (919) 489-7486
Fax (919) 493-5668
www.cap-press.com

Printed in the United States of America

Dedication

For Marie—R.S.G.

For Soma—S.G.

For my parents, maternal grandmother and maternal uncles—J.P.K.

Preface

Intellectual property (IP) is a pervasive concern in modern society. Individuals regularly utilize diverse items—from computer software to pharmaceutical drugs—that are the products of innovation and subject to intellectual property protection. Businesses have developed new operating models based on extensive use of intellectual property and transfers of the embodiments of such property to their customers. Law schools and business schools are expanding their course offerings concerning intellectual property and its business implications. Academic journals in many disciplines publish articles on the impact of intellectual property and related laws in those fields. The popular press is filled with news stories on intellectual property laws, legal reform of those IP laws, and lawsuits over infringing software, hardware, books, and movies.

Despite all this attention, the concept of intellectual property is far from well understood. Many people, including leading scholars, question whether intellectual property is really property. Others struggle to reconcile intellectual property's right to exclude with the restrictions on exclusionary conduct in antitrust law. Another focus of attention is on how intellectual property laws further and/or hinder progress in particular industries, such as biotechnology, software, and the entertainment industries, both in the United States and worldwide.

Into these debates, we introduce the following casebook, *Transactional Intellectual Property: From Startups to Public Companies*. This text is a successor to our previous casebook *Intellectual Property in Business Organizations: Cases and Materials*. Our perspective is unique and central to the modern role of intellectual property. We propose that intellectual property should be studied and understood in its business context. This approach helps to resolve many of the current policy questions and substantive uncertainties surrounding intellectual property laws. Like other business assets, such as securities, intellectual property has aspects of property. Furthermore, when viewed in business contexts, intellectual property's role in markets and industries can be more systematically appreciated and analyzed. Given its importance in modern society as a whole, there is a surprisingly limited amount of scholarship focused on intellectual property as a business asset and its role in business organizations. A few scholars have addressed intellectual property in these contexts, and their work is cited in many places in our book. We hope that this casebook will stimulate further study of how businesses use intellectual property and how intellectual property law shapes markets and the structure of business activities.

The focus of our casebook reflects our professional and academic interests as attorneys and law professors. We have brought our own combined expertise in economics, engineering, and law, developed through our experience in law firms and in industry, to bear in assembling cases, statutes, regulations, and articles written by practitioners and professors in the fields of business organizations, commercial law, taxation, and intellectual property. The materials are designed to present a wide-ranging picture of the different roles that intellectual property plays in various stages of business activity, ranging from business formation and initial ownership structuring processes, to bankruptcies, mergers, and acquisitions, to public stock offerings and other advanced business transactions. Students using these materials will gain a rich exposure to the place of intellectual property in the contemporary marketplace that will inform their subsequent contexts and their understanding of intellectual property policy.

The topics of business organizations and intellectual property can each be intimidating to students. Putting the two together may be doubly intimidating. We hope that by bringing intellectual property and business organizations together, we can illuminate both fields and make each more understandable for students. In law school settings, we believe these materials will be useful as a basis for a survey course introducing students to the fields of intellectual property and business transactions. If used in more depth, this casebook can also serve as the basis for a capstone course for students who may have taken other intellectual property and business courses and are seeking a practical and applied course that focuses on important aspects of the relationship between intellectual property and various business organizations with differing scope, size, and focus. In order to facilitate usage of this casebook in courses without requiring any prior knowledge of intellectual property, we have included an Appendix that provides a brief introduction to different intellectual property regimes for the uninitiated. In choosing and organizing the materials, we have been sensitive to the multiple needs of different types of students and law school and business school professors. We have also sought to assemble materials that demonstrate how intellectual property interests figure in contemporary business and legal environments. By using this text to provide students with illustrations of the business significance of intellectual property, we also hope that professors in both law schools and business schools will make use of these materials in other courses on intellectual property, business transactions, and technology management.

Because of the salience of intellectual property, it is important that we recognize and study how to conduct business transactions involving intellectual property. While other intellectual property materials have largely focused on litigation involving intellectual property, our book provides a unique and comprehensive overview of transactional lawyering and management decision-making regarding intellectual property. Whether you approach these materials as an instructor or as a student, we hope that we are able to give you a deeper appreciation of the richness of intellectual property and its importance in shaping modern technology, industry, and business organizations.

The writing of this casebook was a truly collaborative enterprise. We each learned a great deal about the fundamental character of intellectual property issues from the authors of the materials used in our text as well as from reviewing the work of our co-authors. We also benefited from the generosity and expertise of the many colleagues, students, and staff members who contributed to the completion of this text at various stages. We particularly wish to thank Professor John R. Allison, Professor Ronald J. Mann, and Professor Peter Yu, who provided insightful comments on early chapters and the original proposal that was the seed for this casebook.

Richard Gruner benefited from repeated instances of research support from the Whittier Law School and especially appreciates the support of Dean Neil Cogan for the research activities leading to the completion of this text. He is deeply grateful for the dedicated, detailed, and unflagging assistance with manuscript changes provided by Karl Friedrich and Henrietta Johnson. He is also indebted to Christian Lopez, Whittier Law School Class of 2005, and Gloria D. Sefton, Whittier Law School Class of 2006, for their extensive efforts in identifying potentially useful sources and in reviewing drafts of chapters.

Shubha Ghosh benefited from the efforts of students and staff of two institutions as well as from support from Dean Nils Olsen of The University at Buffalo, SUNY, Law School. He would like to thank Michelle Oswald of Southern Methodist University Dedman School of Law and Sandy Conti of The University at Buffalo, SUNY, Law School for tremendous secretarial support. He would also like to thank several student research assistants and readers: Ruth Freeburg, University at Buffalo, SUNY, Law School Class of 2005; Harven DeShield, University at Buffalo, SUNY, Law School Class of 2007; Christine Petersen, Southern Methodist University Dedman School of Law Class of 2005; and James Taber, Southern Methodist University Dedman School of Law Class of 2008. Each of these students took an extraordinary amount of time and effort to proofread and comment on drafts of individual chapters. Syracuse University College of Law has provided a supportive environment for teaching from the materials in this book and for working on this newest edition. Thanks to the Crandall Melvin chair for supporting this work and other scholarship, to Dean Hannah Arterian for making the support possible, and to current dean, Craig Boise, for continuing the support that has allowed me to maintain my productivity as a teacher and scholar.

Jay Kesan would like to thank his colleagues at the University of Illinois College of Law for their steadfast commitment to both teaching and scholarly endeavors. He is grateful to Roman Perchyts, University of Illinois of Law Class of 2018, Elizabeth Deshaies, University of Illinois College of Law Class of 2014 and Patty Pisut, University of Illinois College of Law Class of 2006 for their dedicated and responsive assistance with various tasks during the course of completing different editions of this book. He would also like to thank Kevin Brown, University of Illinois College of Law Class of 2004, for his assistance during the early stages of this effort.

Richard S. Gruner, Los Angeles, California
Shubha Ghosh, Syracuse, NY
Jay P. Kesan, Champaign, Illinois
March 2018

Contents

Transactional Intellectual Property: From Startups to Public Companies

Introduction

This casebook focuses on the legal problems of businesses that develop and utilize intellectual property in their founding, financing, operation, expansion, transfers of ownership, and termination. The legal issues presented in this text are important to law students in both substantive and practical terms. These issues are substantively important because they turn on fundamental policy questions underlying intellectual property and business organization law that remain unresolved and that will have a bearing on a broad range of important intellectual property and business organization controversies. At the same time, intellectual property issues in business organizations are practically important because they correspond to areas of highly active legal practice where law students will need special training and have ample opportunities to apply it.

The text addresses the distinctive roles played by intellectual property at three stages of business development: the start-up phase (where intellectual property often plays key roles in business formation and venture capital financing), the mid-life phase (where intellectual property is often an important factor in going public or selling a business through a merger into a larger concern), and the mature company phase (where successful firms must deal with problems such as preventing abuses of dominant intellectual property positions and remaining competitive in complex high tech markets despite being innovators in only small components of those markets).

The text is designed for law students in advanced classes concerning intellectual property, business organizations, and the law of science and technology as well as for students in intellectual property survey courses. It will also be suitable for business school students in classes with a substantial focus on legal problems of developing businesses. A strong background in intellectual property law is not assumed. Rather, background material on important intellectual property standards is provided in an appendix to the text. In addition, detailed notes are included with the readings on particular intellectual property laws and legal issues mentioned in the materials.

The readings in the text revolve around the problems faced by a hypothetical company, the Digital Ignition Systems Corporation (Digital Ignition). The concerns that face this company as it develops serve as the background or backstory for problems raised in the text regarding specific intellectual property issues. Individual chapters in the book focus on particular types of intellectual property problems encountered at different stages of this company's history. Additional factual accounts elaborating on some of the incidents mentioned in the following overview of Digital

Ignition's history are presented in each chapter to highlight particular contexts and intellectual property problems faced by businesses as they develop.

The Saga of Digital Ignition: Intellectual Property and Business Growth in a Start Up Company

Digital Ignition Systems Corporation (Digital Ignition) was established in Salem, Oregon, in 1980. The company was founded by Y.L. See to develop and manufacture computer-based ignition systems for automotive engines. These ignition systems monitor the conditions inside an automotive engine, analyze those conditions through a specialized computer system and associated software, initiate the injection of fuel into the cylinders of the engine, and precisely control the timing of the ignition of fuel in each cylinder in relation to the position of the cylinder components and the fuel and oxygen content of the cylinder. By using these systems, automobile owners gain significant engine power and fuel conservation benefits over engines with prior ignition systems.

Dr. See received a doctorate in computer science in 1970 from the Nevada Institute of Technology, a prestigious university. From 1970–1975, he worked as a designer of engine parts for the International Motors Corporation, a multinational corporation engaged in the design, manufacturing, and marketing of diverse types of automobiles and automotive equipment. Dr. See worked as part of a design group that specialized in the design of electronic ignition systems for automobile engines.

Frustrated by the unwillingness of engineers at International Motors to pursue improved ignition system designs based on new types of computer analyses of engine operating conditions, Dr. See left International Motors in 1975 to form a consulting business aimed at helping designers of race car engines improve the designs and performance of their ignition systems. While engaged in this consulting business, he discovered a computer processing method, which, when applied to electronic ignition designs, produced substantially better engine performance and gas mileage results than prior ignition system designs. In 1980, Dr. See obtained several United States patents covering aspects of his new ignition system designs. Separate patents were obtained for: (1) the computer software implementing his new ignition system control method, (2) an ignition system device incorporating the software and an associated computer and designed to operate in accordance with the method, and (3) the method of information processing in the ignition system itself.

After having obtained these patents, Dr. See formed Digital Ignition to commercialize his designs. His company initially had five financial backers. All of these backers were co-owners of the company along with Dr. See. The five backers included Thomas Carlise, a Salem investment counselor, two former college professors who were also planning to serve as salaried product designers for Digital Ignition, a local dentist, and a member of Dr. See's family.

Digital Ignition's engineers worked for a year to produce a commercially viable ignition system based on Dr. See's designs. Their efforts focused on producing a modified version of an International Motors brand ignition system, altered to incorporate Dr. See's patented software and to operate in accordance with his patented method. Dr. See and fellow executives at Digital Ignition developed a business plan calling for the manufacturing of ignition system units based on this new design and the marketing of these units to builders of race cars and other high performance vehicles sold to select consumers at premium prices. Following a review of this business plan, Future Ventures, LLP, a venture capital partnership in Palo Alto, California, agreed to invest $10 million in Digital Ignition in exchange for a substantial percentage of stock ownership in the company.

Digital Ignition proceeded to manufacture and sell ignition systems in accordance with its initial business plan for three years. Its ignition systems received a considerable amount of favorable publicity when several race car drivers and owners cited the systems as a significant factor in their racing success.

Given the favorable public attention their ignition systems were receiving and having gained substantial experience in the operation and manufacturing of these systems, Digital Ignition's engineers developed a version of the company's ignition equipment that was suitable for retrofitting on standard model cars sold by International Motors and other manufacturers. Installation of the new Digital Ignition system as a substitute for a car's original ignition system was easily accomplished by a car owner or mechanic and significantly improved a car's performance and gas mileage. Demand for these plug compatible substitutes for original equipment ignition systems was brisk, and Digital Ignition's revenues and profits grew rapidly. However, Digital Ignition found that its manufacturing and marketing capabilities were not sufficient to keep up with the new levels of consumer demand for its products.

Digital Ignition's executives considered two options to respond to this identified but unmet demand for its products: (1) a merger with a larger concern having sufficient manufacturing and financial resources to expand the company's production and marketing efforts and (2) a public offering of Digital Ignition stock that would raise sufficient funds for the company to expand its production and marketing.

Company managers approached International Motors and several other large automobile parts manufacturers concerning a possible merger. The objective of these discussions with the larger companies was to obtain a buyout price in a merger that would compensate Digital Ignition's founders and initial investors for their efforts in bringing the company to its present stage of business success and positive public reputation. A merger partner acquiring Digital Ignition would effectively acquire several key assets allowing the partner to expand on the business opportunity identified and partially developed by Digital Ignition. Key assets that would come under the control of the merger partner included Digital Ignition's patents, its product production and marketing facilities, and its customer lists and other marketing and production know how and trade secrets. Of these, the company's primary assets to be transferred in the merger were its patents giving it practical control over the market for ignition systems based on Dr. See's designs for approximately ten more years.

International Motors initially expressed interest in such a merger and Digital Ignition's lawyers drafted a proposed merger agreement. However, merger discussions between the companies ultimately fell through because International Motors refused to pay what Digital Ignition's executives thought was a sufficiently high cash price. Executives for International Motors felt that Digital Ignition did not provide sufficient proof of the probable validity and scope of the company's patents to justify a higher price.

Digital Ignition's executives then shifted their primary attention to a possible public offering of the company's stock. Lawyers for the company spent a considerable amount of time resolving two issues related to this public offering: (1) how should the scope and value of the company's intellectual property interests be evaluated and described in pre-offering discussions with investment bankers and in further public disclosures required by securities laws and (2) what types of risks of patent invalidity or other sources of weakness in the company's intellectual property interests would need to be disclosed in connection with its public offering? The company ultimately filed a registration statement with the SEC and completed its public offering in 1990, raising a total of $40 million in the process. However, sales of the company's products were poor during the two years following the public offering. The price of the company's stock dropped by 50%, motivating several shareholders to file federal and state securities law suits against the company and several of its senior officers. The plaintiffs claimed that the company's disclosures at the time of the public offering overstated management's understanding of the commercial advantages provided by Digital Ignition's intellectual property interests and omitted mention of known risks regarding Digital Ignition's business plans. These suits were ultimately settled through modest payments to the shareholder plaintiffs.

Eventually, Digital Ignition's sales of plug-compatible ignition systems substituting for original equipment systems were highly successful and the company and its ignition systems gained a positive reputation among a widespread portion of the public. Company executives sought to capitalize on Digital Ignition's favorable public reputation in four ways: (1) developing new products and gaining further patents to extend the duration of its control over key technologies in the area of ignition systems, (2) licensing its patented technology to other companies, (3) offering new products under the trademark Digital Ignition, and (4) attempting to market further unpatented products in conjunction with its popular patented components.

In new product development, Digital Ignition sought to produce patentable ignition system improvements and advanced products that would maintain its technological dominance over this narrow area of the automotive products market and allow the company to continue to maintain its image as a product innovator in the eyes of consumers. The company sought to produce advanced products in the ignition equipment field that were unavailable from other sources by both developing and patenting improvements in its own initial products and by obtaining exclusive licenses to produce and sell products incorporating certain patented advances discovered by several other small, innovative companies.

At the same time as it acquired farther intellectual property rights from other concerns, Digital Ignition also attempted to maximize the value of its own patents and other trade secret rights by licensing other parties to make and sell products and sell products based on Digital Ignition's patented designs and transferring related trade secret know how to these licensees. International Motors, by now regretting that it had not acquired rights to Digital Ignition's products through the previously proposed merger, sought to obtain an exclusive license to include products based on Digital Ignition's designs in newly manufactured International Motors vehicles. As part of the resulting license agreement, Digital Ignition agreed not to license any other car manufacturer to include products based on Digital Ignition's designs in newly manufactured vehicles. However, Digital Ignition retained the right to continue to manufacture and sell ignition systems based on its patented designs for use as plug-compatible replacement parts substituting for original equipment ignition systems in diverse types of cars.

International Motors enjoyed a significant increase in auto sales following the addition to its cars of ignition systems based on Digital Ignition's designs. The success of the company coupled with the apparent inability of other new car manufacturers to offer automobiles with similar ignition systems caused several of the other manufacturers to complain to the Federal Trade Commission (FTC) regarding Digital Ignition's licensing practices. The FTC initiated an investigation of Digital Ignition to determine if its licensing practices constituted an unfair trade practice in violation of federal laws.

A further problem arose when Digital Ignition developed and patented an improved ignition system five years after its original license agreement with International Motors. The improved design incorporated and extended Digital Ignition's original patented design. Digital Ignition contended that its licensing agreement with International Motors did not require it to license the new patent to International Motors. However, since the licensing agreement provided that the right to produce and sell ignition systems conforming to the original patented design could not be transferred to any new car manufacturer other than International Motors, Digital Ignition was practically precluded from licensing its new patent to any other company because it could not validly authorize any other company to produce the ignition system features covered by the original patent that were also incorporated in the new design. Negotiations between Digital Ignition and International Motors regarding a license to the new patent broke off after the parties failed to reach an agreement on royalty terms.

Impressed by the positive image of Digital Ignition among automobile owners, the company sought to capitalize on the use of the Digital Ignition trademark. It sought to manufacture and market its own line of automobile repair products under this trademark, to license other manufacturers to market automotive products under this trademark, and to license further manufacturers to market tee shirts, hats, and other clothing items bearing this trademark.

Digital Ignition also sought to use its success in marketing its initial patented products to expand its sales of related, non-patented products. It developed and sold a new version of its patented ignition system that could only be bought in conjunction with cables that were included in the product packaging. Previous Digital Ignition products had not been packaged with such cables, but the company asserted in its product marketing literature that the new design of its product was particularly sensitive to the use of the proper cables and that, to ensure consumer satisfaction, the new design was being sold only in conjunction with the bundled cables. Both consumers and independent cable sellers raised complaints about this new marketing practice of Digital Ignition, asserting that it improperly precluded free competition for sales of the relevant cables.

This brief overview identifies the many important roles that intellectual property and related legal problems can play in a company like Digital Ignition. The readings in this text address some, but not all, of these key developments in the founding and growth of Digital Ignition. In addition, further legal problems that the company encounters in developing and marketing its intellectual property are examined in particular chapters. Collectively, these problems represent critically important challenges faced by many companies in our modern economy and correspondingly significant opportunities for attorneys to aid businesses as problem solvers regarding intellectual property assets and infringement threats.

Typical Legal Problems in an IP-Based Business

The overview of Digital Ignition's business history illustrates a number of the typical legal problems faced by an IP-based business. These problems, many of which will be addressed at length in the text, revolve around such questions as:

(1) What types of IP are created and protectable when a new business (such as Digital Ignition) revisits and adds new technology to the products of an older business (such as automotive products produced by International Motors Corporation and many other car companies)?

(2) When does the transfer of an engineer or other employee from one company to another illegitimately transfer IP as well as employment?

(3) Where new IP is developed in a company, how can its possible roots in the work of another company be traced and when will the other company have rights to control the new IP and its use?

(4) What are the business management advantages of different types of IP protections concerning newly created IP?

(5) Where investors and business managers with different technical and business sophistication come together in shared ownership and management

of a company, what types of disclosures about technological and business risks do securities laws require to be made to the often less well-informed investors?

(6) What interests do venture capitalists and other sources for funding of IP-based businesses have in IP protections and how can these aspects of IP protections be maximized by companies seeking funding?

(7) How can a company with some initial success in using its IP to gain funding and to establish preliminary business operations extend and improve its IP to increase its future success?

(8) How is IP handled in a merger or other corporate acquisition and how will parties seeking to acquire a company evaluate that company's IP in connection with such an acquisition?

(9) What types of scrutiny of IP should precede an initial public offering (IPO) of stock in an IP-based business and what disclosures about IP must be filed with securities regulators in connection with such an IPO?

(10) Once a company grows large, how may antitrust laws impose special restrictions on how the company can use its IP in future business activities?

(11) For well-established companies, what means are available to systematically reduce the risk of infringement of IP held by other concerns and to reduce the business consequences of unanticipated IP infringement?

(12) For well-established companies, what means can be used (both internally and with outside partners) to maximize the value of the IP that the companies produce, control, or use?

Functions of Intellectual Property in Business Activities

One of the key objectives of this casebook is to illustrate the functions of IP in businesses and the types of legal issues and activities of attorneys that surround these different types of IP functions. IP plays at least four different types of important functions in business settings.

IP as a Business Product

IP newly generated by a business can be a fundamentally important business product. From movie companies to pharmaceutical drug manufacturers, diverse types of businesses develop and market products that are based on newly created IP. While product production activities (such as the manufacturing of pills or other pharmaceutical drugs) may create elements of product value by delivering IP to consumers, the real value in many business products (and in the businesses that produce the products) lies in the new discoveries and creative products protected by the companies' IP.

Absent the promise of IP protections providing exclusive opportunities to market and realize the commercial value of their creative products, many businesses would see little advantage in spending large amounts on creative projects and would tend to adjust existing practices in relatively uncreative ways to produce proven older products at the lowest prices possible, rather than producing new ones through greater creative efforts.

Selling products containing innovative IP is not the only way that companies can capture the value of newly created IP. One additional way to realize the value of newly created IP is to license others to use the IP in exchange for a royalty payment or to assign the full set of IP rights protecting an advance to another party in exchange for compensation. Yet another, more elaborate way to realize the value of newly created IP is to sell a company or major business unit containing the IP to another party. This is often beneficial because the transfer can include the IP plus the personnel and resources needed to use the IP effectively, potentially producing a higher value and compensation than a transfer of the IP standing alone.

IP as a Business Input

Where IP is not homegrown within a company, it can still be acquired from another party as a key input to business activities. Important IP such as commercially significant trade secrets may instruct company personnel on how to accomplish some business task. Rights to use a cartoon character may provide the basis for a new marketing campaign featuring TV commercials and print ads with the character. Rights to use a famous trademark (such as the Pepsi logo) may provide the basis for a line of clothing with the logo prominently displayed on various types of garments. In these settings, rights to use otherwise restricted IP provide the bases for new business activities and new profit making opportunities.

Access to IP held by others is particularly valuable where the acquired IP enables the recipient to make better use of other assets already held by the recipient. The combination of existing assets (which may include complementary IP already held by the recipient) and the acquired IP can create synergy effects and increased value that could not exist without the acquired IP. In some cases, complementary IP acquisitions may flow in both directions in an IP acquisition transaction, as when two parties each controlling key patented technologies cross license their technologies, thereby giving both parties full access to the pool of technology represented by both their patents.

IP as a Constraint on Activities of Others

Because they typically enable IP owners to exclude others from the use of IP without permission, IP rights can be means to limit the IP-related activities of competitors to the IP owners and of other unauthorized IP users. Injunctions in IP suits provide means to force parties to stop unauthorized uses of IP, while damage recoveries provide means to offset gains that may have realized in the past from unauthorized use of IP.

Rights to exclude others from unauthorized use of IP also have business planning implications. Parties that are sure that they will be the only parties who will be able to employ IP will often take this into account in their planning and back their exclusive use of IP with major commitments of complementary resources. For example, confidence that they will be the only party to market a product with a patented feature might encourage a company to invest in the manufacturing processes and marketing efforts needed to gain consumer acceptance of the new product and to produce and distribute sufficient units of the product to get that product into consumers' hands.

IP of Others as Constraints on Business Conduct

Constraints imposed through IP interests held by other parties can operate as significant business restrictions, potentially limiting a company from offering a particular type of popular product or product feature if that product or feature is controlled by IP rights held by others and appropriate permission to produce and sell the product or feature cannot be obtained from the IP rights holders. Care in the designing of new products, services, or business practices is often needed to avoid intersecting with the IP rights of others and thereby setting up potential business disruptions and losses when these rights are enforced.

Early detection of potentially conflicting IP rights can provide businesses with favorable options to proceed. A business may be able to avoid a practice or product design that would conflict with IP rights if undertaken or adopted in the future. This type of modified conduct (which is more easily adopted at early stages of planning business practices and product designs) will avoid placing future business activities under the control of IP rights holders. Another option is to acquire rights to use the IP in question, with negotiations for such an acquisition undertaken from a position of strength since the company has not yet committed to use the IP and can simply walk away from unfavorable terms offered for a license or other type of IP acquisition. On the other hand, late recognition by business managers that their company's practices (which may be the objects of considerable resource commitments) are already in conflict with the IP rights of another party may place the company in an extremely bad position. A company in this sort of fix must either stop its related activities to avoid further IP misuse (thereby wasting its resource commitments concerning these activities) or acquire the needed IP under disfavorable terms dictated by the IP owner because the acquiring party has so much at stake in getting the IP and continuing the company's related activities.

Why IP and Business Law
Interactions are Problematic

Business practices involving IP development and use create a number of especially difficult problems under a variety of business laws. Heightened problems related to interactions between IP and certain business law requirements are central topics in this text. Unusual and often difficult business law issues in connection with IP tend to arise in the following areas.

Building New Types of Businesses

IP can create the basis for unprecedented types of businesses, requiring the rethinking of many business law doctrines and issues. For example, patented Internet searching and site indexing methods developed by Google form the basis for that company's very new and very different type of business. The nature of this firm's IP-based business model (and the further ways that Google uses the IP of other companies in advertising products and producing income) raise new types of business problems and related types of business law concerns.

Establishing New Business Techniques

IP can provide new means for operating old types of businesses. For example, IP embedded in new software has facilitated computer-based updates of numerous business practices in fields from accounting to sales presentations. The ways that IP may be misused or produce harmful consequences has grown with the increased use of IP-based practices in diverse business settings. The increased usage of IP also expands the circumstances where the IP and its use may need to be evaluated and described (as in required descriptions to investors of key business practices).

Shifting Methods of Measuring and Realizing Business Value

New types of businesses or business methods based on IP have raised corresponding problems in evaluating the value of businesses and reporting on such value in legally significant contexts. IP valuation problems arise in many types of legally significant transactions, from stock sales, to mergers, to tax liability reporting. The centrality of IP in many businesses sometimes leads to misstatements about the nature or validity of IP in fraudulent statements about the value of businesses. Even where misstatements are made without an intent to deceive, materially misleading descriptions of IP and its business implications may still figure in legal controversies such as claims based on misstatements about IP that are insufficient to meet disclosure requirements of securities laws applicable to publicly traded companies.

Changing Legal Standards

As technology has rapidly changed the nature of IP and how we use it, many new legal standards have grown up in the IP field and in surrounding business law settings. These new standards help to define when IP use is actually misuse and grounds for a remedy. However, the new standards may also specify when IP usage or ownership has implications concerning business law issues. Changing standards concerning both IP and business laws have produced new uncertainties about the range of legitimate activities that companies can undertake and to more and more instances of inadvertent IP misuse and unexpected liability.

Unexpected Business Risks

Because the business activities that create and use IP are changing, the business risks associated with IP creation and use are not well understood. For businesses that create and use IP, uncertainties about the operating risks they will encounter sometimes leads to unexpected business failures as well as to tendencies to make overly optimistic statements about the likelihood of business success in legally significant representations to other parties. For outsiders investing in or relying on IP-based businesses, unexpected risks in the operations of IP-based businesses may lead to poorly-informed investment decisions or to reliance on IP-based businesses for performance that the businesses will not be able to complete. The chances for misplaced reliance on the future performance of an IP-based business are particularly high where the parties on opposite sides of a transaction have different levels of knowledge about particular IP and its business significance, with one party well understanding and accommodating the risks associated with the IP and the other unknowingly accepting the risks because they fall outside of that party's business experience.

New Means for Risk Spreading

As business managers have gained experience with IP, new business methods have developed to spread the business risks associated with IP development and use. Different forms of insurance have helped companies bear the expense of unexpected IP infringement liability and of IP enforcement costs. In some instances, risk spreading methods have spawned whole new types of businesses. For example, the business of a non-practicing entity (NPE) or patent troll (that is, a patent holder that does not expect to produce patented items but that acquires patents and seeks profits solely from enforcement of patent rights to gain licensing royalties) is aimed at shifting the patent enforcement function and associated risks out of the hands of the prior patent owners and into the hands of the NPE. A patent owner transferring a patent to a NPE gives up the risks of patent enforcement in exchange for immediate compensation for his or her patent. The NPE takes on the risks of enforcement and backs enforcement with new resources and specialized enforcement efforts, with the expectation of gaining (on average) more than the entity has paid for the relevant patent. This business model offers new means for risk shifting and patent liquidity (by making a market for immediate transfers of patents from innovators and other patent owners), but does so at the price of increased litigation and heightened patent licensing costs for product producers. These sorts of new risk shifting devices have raised significant new legal issues and business problems as they have affected ever broader and more important types of IP.

Lawyering Skills for Assisting IP-Based Enterprises

The exercises and questions in this text are aimed at giving students experience with some of the lawyering skills that are particularly important in counseling and otherwise assisting IP-based businesses and organizations. Skills concerning IP litigation and dispute resolution processes are very important in assisting IP-based companies with disputes involving large damage amounts and potentially devastating injunctive relief. However, transactional lawyering skills of various types are often even more important in assisting IP-based businesses with planning and implementing actions to build and realize the value of their IP generation and use. Executives in IP-based businesses frequently need to plan for effective development and use of IP (and to plan for ways to avoid the misuse of IP of others as much as possible) and are accordingly particularly interested in forward-looking advice and assistance from their IP and business lawyers. Hence, lawyering techniques which emphasize business planning in light of IP considerations are highly valuable in counseling IP-based businesses and organizations.

Some of the lawyering skills emphasized in this text include the following.

Reading Cases as Planning Tools

The cases reprinted in this text are good sources of information about legal standards in the same way that cases in other courses provide information on the legal standards of importance in those courses. However, the cases here should also be considered in a different way and for a different purpose. Each case serves as a case study in how one or more parties created legal problems and tried to resolve them. By turning back the clock and considering the situations confronting the parties in each case at a stage when the parties could have acted differently, the ways to avoid or minimize similar controversies and problems in the future can be explored, making each case a starting point for planning lessons and learning.

Two types of planning can be considered in this way. First, the cases in the text can be used to evaluate how to resolve a dispute once the facts leading to the dispute are already set in stone and the only uncertain point is what relief or other response to apparent liability will occur. By considering the basis of asserted liability in each case and the business context in which it is being asserted, the means used to resolve the dispute in that case and the alternatives that the parties might have used to reach a better resolution can be considered. In this way, the cases serve as means to better plan and explore dispute resolution alternatives and the avoidance of business disruptions due to already completed misconduct or misuse of IP.

Second, the cases can be used to study preventive practices for avoiding IP liability and misuse altogether. This type of evaluation (involving techniques of preventative lawyering) involves examining the facts of each case and going back even further in time to the point before which IP misuse occurred. By considering why IP misuse occurred (and why it remained undetected to the point where it created a significant threat of liability), the means to prevent similar IP misuse and concealment in the future can be considered. Planning for these types of liability prevention techniques emphasizes systematic management actions (such as articulating standards for IP use, training employees, and monitoring regularly undertaken practices) to prevent IP misuse and to maximize the legal protection of valuable new IP. By using the facts of the cases as the starting points for assessments of management practices that would have either prevented the types of IP problems present in the cases or that would have detected these problems at earlier stages when they could have been dealt with in less damaging ways, cases in this text can facilitate valuable discussions of the lawyering skills that will best aid business executives in planning ongoing IP management practices in IP-based enterprises.

Collaborating with Business Executives and Business Law Specialists

Many modern business decisions are influenced by combinations of IP features, other types of legal considerations, and further business management factors. Complete consideration of decisions turning on factors like these requires contributions by and effective collaborations between the holders of IP, business law, and business management expertise. Consequently, the means for IP specialists, other business law specialists, and business executives to work together effectively are critically important skills in helping executives in IP-based businesses to reach decisions that maximize the value of IP and IP-based activities in these businesses.

In the problems presented in the text, the roles of IP specialists in resolving the problems and the ways that IP specialists typically work with other specialists are emphasized for several reasons. First, this focuses students on their future contributions as IP lawyers—that is, on the completion of distinctive IP-related analyses that should be their first considerations in working on complex business problems because, as IP specialists, they bring IP knowledge and expertise to the resolution of these problems that might otherwise be overlooked. Second, an appreciation of the expertise being contributed by other specialists will suggest areas where IP specialists should ask questions of others or defer to the analytic criteria or frameworks established by others. Third, by reviewing cases illustrating settings where business executives and other organizational managers have had personal interests and agendas that diverged from those of their organizations, IP specialists can better identify settings where parties they are working with may not be fully meeting their organizational duties and, therefore, not fulfilling their normal roles as collaborators, such that the IP specialists may wish to consult with other organizational leaders.

Providing Executives with IP-Based Risk Information

As companies rely increasingly on IP and the business opportunities that depend on IP protections, the nature of IP-related business risks has grown tremendously. This means that several kinds of IP-based risk information need to be considered by business executives in order for them to make well-informed business decisions and to shape future activities in IP-based businesses to maximize the potential for business success and minimize risks of company losses.

A number of types of business developments may raise important IP-based business risks that should be taken into account by corporate managers and that will require extensive advice to such managers by IP specialists. The unexpected presence of unlicensed IP interests of another party may threaten large losses if enforcement of the unanticipated IP means that a company cannot continue with activities that have already received major commitments of resources. The unexpected invalidity of the company's own IP interests may mean that it will not have the exclusive opportunity to commercialize certain products and may realize reduced corporate profits accordingly. Changes in the law may strengthen or weaken the implications of IP for a company and its business practices and plans, leading to new types of business risks. Changes in company activity may cause the company to produce new IP or to encounter the IP of others in new ways, each with new IP-based business risks. IP specialists play increasingly important functions in shaping the management decisions of IP-based businesses by identifying changing risks like these and in working effectively with business managers to analyze these risks in ways that help the managers take these risks into account in making business management decisions.

Considering IP as a Source of Value in Business Operations

In recent years, a variety of companies have come to view their production of new IP as an important source of new business assets and profits. Just as the creation of new products sometimes leads to new sales opportunities, the production of new IP can create new IP transfer or licensing opportunities and new revenue streams. IP lawyers can sometimes assist their clients by thinking like entrepreneurs and addressing the creation of new IP as a new business growth opportunity.

The skills needed by lawyers in advising business executives on the use of IP as a business asset and profit source are somewhat different from the skills normally used by lawyers in assessing the strength of IP rights or litigation matters. The profit potential associated with the enforcement of IP rights (and the profit that might be realized by foregoing such enforcement in exchange for IP licensing revenues) depends on multiple IP-related factors, including the strength of potential legal claims based on IP interests, the scope of potential litigation costs, and the types of IP licensing or IP transfer revenues that are likely to be generated by different types of IP enforcement. Overall, advice on these sorts of topics is aimed at projecting and estimating the business results that can be obtained from enforcement of a business's present and future IP rights.

Working with Executives on Systematic IP Management Practices

Careful planning of a business's generation and use of IP and of the prevention of misuse of the IP of others can have important impacts on business performance. IP specialists can aid clients in planning for IP use and preventing IP misuse by focusing on systematic management programs for addressing IP production and use in business organizations. These sorts of IP management programs—built on the same management techniques that companies use to address other important aspects of business performance such as product safety or financial reporting—involve careful attention to such steps as standard setting, employee education, reporting on corporate performance, audits of key aspects of performance, and evaluations and business practice reforms following incidents of poor performance. All of these steps are needed in a complete management program to maximize the benefits of IP use in a company. IP specialists can play key roles in helping company managers to implement IP management programs by coupling the specialists' knowledge of IP rights and interests with further advice on how to use standard corporate management techniques to maximize these rights and interests.

Beyond the implications of IP management practices in maximizing the value of IP and IP-related business activities, the adequacy of IP management actions can have liability implications outside of IP law. For example, where corporate officers mismanage the creation or enforcement of highly valuable IP rights, these individuals may breach their duties as corporate officers leading to personal liability for resulting losses to their company. These sorts of implications of poor management of IP rights and interests heighten the importance of systematic attention to corporate programs for maximizing the creation and use of valuable IP rights and for preventing the infringement of IP rights of other parties.

These business impacts suggest the importance of IP in modern business management. This text is aimed at aiding students (both law students and business school students) in future endeavors to guide businesses toward the effective generation and use of IP.

Chapter 1

Creating and Protecting
the Business Model

Problem

You are working as an associate in a law firm and are given a case file for Dr. See, a computer scientist who plans to form a new company named Digital Ignition. The case file indicates that Dr. See has received several patents to cover his software-based ignition system, which provides better engine performance and gas mileage. The file also indicates that Dr. See will be meeting with several potential investors in a few weeks and is in the process of putting together a business plan to present to the investors. You are asked to review the plan in order to identify potential intellectual property issues raised by the business plan that Dr. See would like to address before his meeting.

Focus of the Chapter

The following reading materials provide a useful checklist of what to consider in advising Dr. See about his plan and his meeting. Specific topics to keep in mind include recognizing the value of intellectual property, putting a dollar estimate on this value, identifying pitfalls to protecting intellectual property and structuring licensing, and becoming aware of tax issues. As you work through the readings, think about the ways in which you would advise start-up companies on how to identify and manage their intellectual property resources. The materials are divided into subsections addressing the following four issues:

a. Identifying what can be protected as intellectual property;

b. Valuing intellectual property assets, once identified;

c. Avoiding forfeiture of intellectual property rights; and

d. Identifying tax issues raised by intellectual property licenses.

As you work through these readings, think about how these four issues might arise and intersect in the course of starting up a new business.

Readings

A. Capturing Value through Intellectual Property

Jon E. Hokanson & Sa'id Vakili, Intellectual Property Issues for the Technology Startup Company

Los Angeles Lawyer, February 2000, at p. 21*

. . . .

When starting up a technology company, there are so many details to consider that intellectual property questions are often overlooked. The consequences of this oversight can be considerable: greatly increased expenditures or, even worse, unrecoverable loss of valuable rights that could have been secured by taking simple, relatively inexpensive actions at an earlier date. It is therefore important for a startup, at an early stage, to identify the key issues and milestones in the life of its intellectual property and recognize the measures that should be taken to protect its valuable intellectual property rights in a cost-effective manner.

In technology companies, intellectual property issues tend to cluster around three basic areas: utility patents, trademarks used in interstate commerce, and copyrights. While each of these areas is governed by its own statutes and rules, in real life the challenge of securing these rights often cuts across two or even all three of the categories.

A technology company often begins its life with the single objective of exploiting an invention. Even for startups with a broader business plan, a critical first step is to identify any subject matter that may qualify for patent protection. . . .

Once the protectable subject matter has been identified and a decision to seek patent protection has been made, it is often best to file a provisional patent application. The costs of preparing and filing the application are relatively low and depend on the degree of complexity of the invention and the extent to which the inventors are able to provide a full written description of exactly how to make and use the invention.

A provisional patent application is generally considered to be the most cost-effective means of securing the earliest priority right to the invention, which is important for several reasons. First and most important, an early provisional application minimizes the amount of "prior art" that may be used to prevent a patent from being issued. Put another way, the longer that a company waits to file a provisional patent application, the greater will be the developments in the field that will affect the consideration of the patent application.

In addition, an early priority right can become critical when filing for a patent . . . , because most countries [— including the United States under most circumstances —] are governed by the first-to-file rule. Under this principle, if two or more applications are filed for the same invention, the patent is awarded to the application having the earliest priority right. . . .

It is usually best to file a provisional patent application as soon as the inventor knows how to make and use the invention. At the very least, the patent application should be filed prior to any offer for sale, public disclosure, public use, or sale of the invention. Failure to file a patent application prior to any of these events may reduce the available patent rights in certain countries and even prevent a valid patent from issuing.

This dire result is a consequence of a patent rule known as absolute novelty, which is operative in many countries. In order to obtain patent protection in absolute-novelty countries, a patent application must be on file prior to any disqualifying public disclosure, public use, or sale of the invention. The nuances and specific definitions of these rights-losing-events vary from country to country, and a patent attorney should be consulted regarding potential loss of rights in any specific country and under any particular set of circumstances. A failure to file an application on a timely basis prior to making the invention public will prevent the company from obtaining valid patent rights in most countries . . . .

. . . .

The second critical component of a patent rights strategy is to provide a full and complete written description of how to make and use the invention for which the patent is sought. Startups (and mature companies rushing to bring a product to market) too often leave the patenting process to the last minute or consider it only as an afterthought. Then, faced with a deadline under which valuable patent rights will be lost if an application is not filed, a barely adequate, or in some cases an inadequate description of the invention is prepared and filed.

The consequence of having a legally adequate but less than complete written description of the invention is that the maximum scope of patent protection available from the application will not truly match the scope of the invention, and will thus be less than could have been obtained. For example, a legally adequate application might omit a certain claim, which would then give competitors a head start in developing a competing product.

In the worst case, a less-than-complete application might not even be legally adequate. . . . If the U.S. Patent and Trademark Office discovers such inadequacy during its consideration of the application, it may refuse to grant a patent. Even if the Patent Office does not discover the inadequacies and issues a patent, the patent is not secure. If the patent later becomes the subject of litigation, it is likely that the inadequacies will then be exposed, the likely result of which is that a federal court will invalidate the patent.

The additional cost of providing a full and enabling disclosure, compared to an inadequate or barely adequate disclosure, would typically be in the hundreds of dollars or, at most, a few thousand dollars. On the other hand, if the patent application is rejected, the cost of challenging a patent examiner's decision at the Patent Office Board of Appeals, or eventually on appeal to the U. S. Court of Appeals for the Federal Circuit, would be measured at several thousand to potentially tens of thousands of dollars. If the patent is ultimately invalidated in litigation because of a failure to provide an enabling disclosure of the invention and/or to detail the best mode of carrying out the invention, the cost would run at least many tens of thousands to hundreds of thousands of dollars, considering the cost of obtaining the patent, paying the maintenance fees, and defending the validity of the patent in litigation. In some cases, the cost of losing the patent on an invention could be measured in the millions of dollars.

Trademark Rights

Acquisition of federal trademark rights is invariably less risky and less costly if an organized, intelligent approach is made at or near the beginning of the lifetime of a new product, rather than waiting until the product's launch date or even beyond. Once a decision is made to market an invention, the company should begin to select candidates for marks that will be used to identify the product or service in interstate commerce. At this stage, two considerations are paramount:

1) Whether the company can adopt and use the mark in interstate commerce free from the legitimate assertion of rights by another.

2) Whether the company can obtain a federal trademark registration (and in some instances corresponding foreign trademark registrations) for the mark.

As an initial step, a relatively inexpensive computer database search should be made from records available at the U.S. Patent and Trademark Office. The objective of this search is to eliminate bad candidates and thereby save costs that might otherwise be spent on the clearance of marks that are not likely to win approval. Once this initial clearance search is complete, it is wise to conduct a full search beyond the Trademark Office database and include the databases of all state registries, common law databases, and Internet domain names. In situations in which the product is destined for global distribution, it is also worthwhile to commission searches in foreign countries . . . .

Copyright

Copyright registration is a relatively inexpensive form of legal protection available to a technology startup company. On the other hand, the financial consequences of not obtaining appropriate copyright protections are typically not as high as the costs that accompany the failure to obtain patent and trademark protection. Companies often use copyright as a complementary form of protection for promotional materials, manuals, and, most importantly, computer software.

Copyrightable subject matter is referred to as a "work of authorship," and registration may be obtained once the work of authorship has been reduced to a tangible medium, such as a printed page, computer file, and the like. The cost of registration at the U.S. Copyright Office varies, but typically runs only several hundred dollars, including the government filing fee and the associated costs of preparing and filing the application.

Two major benefits accrue from the early filing of an application for registration of copyright if an infringement is discovered and spawns litigation. In a lawsuit brought on a registered copyright, the copyright owner has the ability to obtain 1) statutory damages, without the need to comply with costly discovery requests or offer evidence to prove the damage amounts, and 2) an award of attorney's fees and costs. On the other hand, failure to register the copyright in a timely manner may result, as a practical matter, in not being able to enforce the copyright against infringements.

For technology companies, an important element in copyright registration is to ensure that the documentation reflects the company's ownership of the copyrights, rather than the individual who created those works. This is especially true when the employment relationship between the company and the individual who created the work is unclear. Except for "work made for hire," ownership of the copyright as a matter of law belongs, in the first instance, to the human beings who authored the work rather than to the company who may have paid those humans for creating it. Whereas the cost of obtaining documentation that clearly identifies the company's ownership of the work is typically trivial if completed in conjunction with or prior to the authoring of the work, these costs can become devastatingly high if the work becomes valuable and the company cannot establish through proper documentation that it owns the copyright to the work. As always, if a dispute can only be resolved through litigation, the costs to obtain or prove ownership may reach into the hundreds of thousands of dollars, with typical presumptions working in favor of the human author as opposed to the company. This increases the risk that the company ultimately will not be determined to be the owner of the copyright.

Intellectual property issues often arise in the life of a startup company in the context of company patents, trademarks, and copyrights. Employees and consultants who participate in product development can claim an ownership or co-ownership right to the company's intellectual property unless a written agreement clearly provides that the ownership of the intellectual property right is held by the company.

An employee's claim of right to a company's intellectual property can be devastating in situations in which a company product or trade name becomes a valuable asset. Typically, employee claims of ownership can be prevented by an employee agreement assigning all intellectual property rights to the employer. Because such agreements involve the surrender of prospective employee rights, they need to be drafted in compliance with applicable state labor laws. When dealing with consultants or other independent contractors, the company should have a written agreement providing that the company retains ownership of all intellectual property.

Victoria A. Cundiff, How a Startup Company Can Put Its Intellectual Property at Risk

Practicing Law Institute,

PATENTS, COPYRIGHT, TRADEMARKS AND LITERARY PROPERTY COURSE HANDBOOK SERIES

No. G0-00CW (September, 2000)*

While there may be as many ways to jeopardize intellectual property rights as there are new startup companies, here are some of the most common mistakes, and some solutions.

1. Start up the new company while working for the old.

Starting a successful new company requires good ideas, intense commitment, and the willingness to take risk. Many entrepreneurs try to put off the risk-taking by staying in a salaried job for as long as possible. This approach can lead to a lawsuit—and even to the loss of intellectual property developed for the new company.

While the law is clear that one can prepare to start a new business and can even prepare to compete while working for one employer, the law is equally clear that actually starting a new job or competing while employed is a breach of fiduciary duty. The employee has a duty of undivided loyalty to his or her employer.

What this means, in practical terms, is that an employee who is supposed to be developing software for a current employer should not be developing software for a new company, even at home and even after hours. Otherwise, the soon-to-be former employer may have a viable claim that it owns the software, particularly if the software relates in any way to work the employee was supposed to be doing while on salary or was created using property of the former employer. *See, e.g., Health Care Affiliated Services, Inc. v. Lippany,* 701 F. Supp. 1142 (W.D. Pa. 1988). Even if that claim ultimately fails, time and money spent litigating the issue with the prior employer can quickly drain startup capital.

Further, while working for one company, the employee should not be soliciting its employees or customers to move to a new company. *See, e.g., Duane Jones v. Burke,* 306 N.Y. 172, 117 N.E.2d 237 (1954). The employee needs to quit first and, unless contractually prohibited from doing so, recruit later. The employee should not be soliciting new customers on behalf of the new company, either, since the claim could readily be made that by so doing, the employee was diverting a business opportunity that should have been shared with the employer.

Finally, the employee should not permit work to get the new company up and running to interfere with his or her work for the employer. Doing so may lead to a claim that the employee must repay the salary received during the period of overlap. *See, e.g., Maritime Fish Products, Inc. v. World-Wide Fish Products, Inc.*, 100 A.D.2d 81, 474 N.Y.S.2d 281 (1st Dep't.), *app. dism'd*, 63 N.Y.2d 675 (1984).

2. Wait to search and register trademarks or domain names until just before a public announcement or product release.

Many entrepreneurs conceive of clever, memorable names they plan to use once their business gets started. That name dominates their thinking, their presentations to investors and potential employees, and their graphics and product design. When they finally get around to conducting a trademark search, however, they may discover that some else has already registered, or is using, the very name they had counted on for similar goods or services. While that earlier registration may be the result of mis-appropriation—the registrant learned the entrepreneur's intended trademark and pirated it for its own use—more often the problem is simply that someone else independently thought of, and protected, the same name first.

To prevent the attendant loss of momentum, the entrepreneur should conduct a trademark search as soon as he or she comes up with an appealing name. The greater the commitment to the name, the more comprehensive that search should be. An initial screening of Federally registered trademarks, which can be done free on-line by checking www.uspto.gov, may knock out some proposed marks early on or raise some red flags by showing that others have registered or claim rights in the same or a similar name or logo.

This limited search cannot, however, "clear" a proposed name or logo. In trade-mark law, one gains rights by using the mark, whether or not one seeks a Federal registration. Thus, someone else may have acquired rights in the proposed mark by using it without filing for a Federal registration. A good example is one of the designs for the Coca Cola bottle, which was only registered as a trademark many years after it was first used. *See also BIEC Int'l, Inc. v. Global Steel Services, Ltd.*, 791 F. Supp. 489, 533 (E.D. Pa. 1992).

If the entrepreneur starts using a mark someone else had been using, the "prior user" may be able to put a stop to the new use in the territories where the prior user had used it first. Such "common law" rights enabled the University of Nebraska to stall NBC's proposed national launch of its new stylized "N" logo several years ago, for example. Exacting common law searches conducted by trademark search organizations are necessary to detect such use of proposed marks in commerce by third parties. These searches check telephone directories, trade journals, domain name registrations, state filings, and other resources. Experienced counsel can help interpret those reports so that the fledgling company can more accurately assess whether third parties indeed have a superior claim to a chosen mark.

How can the Company protect the mark it selects? Obtaining a Federal registration can certainly help. Many entrepreneurs believe that they cannot register their own proposed mark until they can prove that they are actually using it. Since 1989, however, the Trademark Office has allowed parties to "reserve" trademarks they hope to use shortly but are not yet using in interstate commerce. By filing an "intent-to-use" application, they can get the trademark approval process underway and, if successful, obtain a Federal registration once they begin using the mark which will be effective as of the date of the intent-to-use application. 15 U.S.C. § 1051(b) (1998). In most instances, an entrepreneur will want to consider this approach, since a Federal registration can generally give the applicant nationwide rights against later, or "junior," users of the mark even if the applicant has not actually used the mark nationwide . . . .

But obtaining a Federal registration is not the only way, or the final step to protect a trademark. Recall that trademark rights come from use. Once the entrepreneur settles on a name, the Company should begin using it in commerce just as soon as it makes business sense to do so. Failing to use the mark can result in forfeiture of rights. "Token" use, such as in shipments to out-of-state friends, however, does not generally establish rights. Lucent Information Management ("LIM") recently learned this in its unsuccessful effort to claim superior rights over Lucent Technologies, Inc., which filed an intent-to-use application and aggressively promoted the mark after LIM had made only a single sale. *Lucent Information Management, Inc. v. Lucent Technologies, Inc.*, 186 F.3d 311 (3d Cir. 1999). Using the mark in a concerted and consistent fashion will both build consumer recognition and help establish legal rights.

3. Ignore trademarks and concentrate solely on domain names.

Many entrepreneurs seek domain name registration the moment they think of a name. If they succeed, they believe they have protected "their trademark" and that others will not be allowed to use similar marks, on-line or elsewhere. This belief confuses domain name rights with trademark rights. The two are related, but are not identical.

Registering a domain name, such as "goodidea.com," simply gives the registrant the right to use that precise name as an Internet address. Obtaining a domain name, however, does not even prevent others from registering similar domain names, such as "good-idea.com." Nor does it stand as a certification that third parties are not already using the name. Apart from seeking some representations from the applicant, the domain name registrar does not make an independent determination of the applicant's right to use a particular name. This means that the party that registers a name as a domain name will not necessarily prevail in an infringement lawsuit if another party has used the name first.

Many readers are familiar with this principle in the context of "cyber pirates" who register domain names incorporating well-known trademarks intending to sell them back to the trademark owner. The pirate who first registers "cocacola.com" will not thereby gain rights superior to those enjoyed by the Coca Cola Company. *See, e.g., Panavision Int'l, L.P. v. Toeppen*, 141 F.3d 1316, 1327 (9th Cir. 1998). But the distinction between domain name rights and trademark rights can also affect the innocent domain name owner who has simply never checked to see if others are using the same or similar name as a trademark . . . .

The lesson? By all means obtain a domain name. But do some research into whether others are using similar names. If so, investigate further. If not, don't simply let the domain name lie dormant and unused. "Trademark protection" does not stop with domain name registration. It begins with careful selection, and is maintained by proper use.

Finally, be aware that registering a name with the Secretary of State, while often a prerequisite to doing business in that state, does not establish trademark rights, either. Only use, and, if appropriate, federal trademark registration, can.

4. Just assume that the Company owns what it pays others to create.

Once they are up and running, many startup companies understandably rely on consultants, part time employees, or "jacks-of-all-trades" who do everything from marketing to raising capital to writing software. Each of these approaches at the very least complicates the question of whether the Company owns the intellectual property it has paid others to create.

Contrary to popular belief, simply paying someone who winds up creating intellectual property does not make the work created a "work-for-hire" belonging to the Company. Nor does the fact that an employee created intellectual property necessarily make that property an asset of the company if it was created outside the scope of the employee's duties or without using company property. Under many circumstances, failing to obtain properly worded written assignment or work-for-hire acknowledgments will leave the Company with only non-exclusive rights in the intellectual property. The parties who created the property will also be able to exploit and license it—with no obligation to pay any proceeds to the Company. Moreover, by the time the lack of assignment agreements becomes apparent, many of the contributors to the intellectual property may have scattered or be unavailable, making it difficult if not impossible to cure the problem.

The conscientious entrepreneur would do well, therefore, to work with counsel to develop and use appropriate assignment agreements and keep careful track of who has contributed to each item of intellectual property developed for the Company. . . .

A related mistake is failing to keep copies of intellectual property created for the Company. If the Company has overwritten the software it wishes to protect, for example, or has failed to keep clear records of how and when its invention was developed, it may not be able to seek a copyright registration or apply for a patent. Moreover, the intellectual property owner who claims that a third party has infringed an early version of its software but does not have a copy of that version to introduce into evidence may face dismissal of the case. Even well-established companies have suffered these consequences of sloppy early record keeping. *See Computer Associates International v. American Fundware, Inc.*, 831 F. Supp. 1516, 1520 (D. Colo. 1993).

The solution? Archive and retain in Company files all material variations of the intellectual property created for the Company. Careful recordkeeping will also make it easier to sell or license intellectual property later on.

5. To generate excitement, freely disclose the Company's plans and intellectual property without a confidentiality agreement.

Entrepreneurs typically need to present their ideas to many people before they can get up and running or take the business to the next level. Bankers, "angels," venture capitalists, strategic alliance partners, and key customers, among others, may all need to investigate the entrepreneur's ideas before they can commit to back them.

But the more people who learn the plan, the more people who can divert it to their own use.

While under certain circumstances courts may be willing to impose a duty of confidentiality on potential investors and others with whom the entrepreneur has shared his or her ideas, counting on these "implied" protections is foolish. Before presenting confidential intellectual property or business plans, or even proposed trademarks, the entrepreneur should get a written commitment that the information will not be used or disclosed except for purposes the entrepreneur specifies, and that all documents, including notes, discussing the disclosures will be returned or destroyed once the specified use ends. (Filing an intent-to-use application should give further protection for the proposed trademark.) Failure to obtain such an agreement in writing has sparked costly litigation between kozmo.com and urbanfetch.com, among others.

Many entrepreneurs fear that insisting that potential financial partners enter into confidentiality agreements will scare them away. It is true that many venture capitalists are so inundated with business plans to which they give only cursory attention that as a matter of policy they will not assume duties of confidentiality with respect to initial submissions from those seeking investment capital.

Once past the initial submission, however, some venture capitalists increasingly view a request for a confidentiality agreement as an indication that the entrepreneur is taking proper measures to protect his or her ideas and, by extension, the value of what the investors are being asked to invest in. Thus requesting a confidentiality agreement before revealing confidential details makes good business sense as well as legal sense. Indeed, at least one venture capital firm has commenced litigation to enforce its own confidentiality rights against its former employees. . . .

The party receiving the disclosure may want to negotiate some limitations on the duties of confidentiality. Many may well be appropriate, such as mechanisms for determining whether the receiving party has already seen or separately developed similar intellectual property, or acknowledgments that the party receiving the disclosures is making no advance commitment to finance the project. But while the entrepreneur may be willing to be flexible as to certain details, he or she must be adamant about limiting and protecting the disclosures he or she does make. This is not an area to compromise. Otherwise, someone else may turn those ideas into the next successful IPO . . . .

The Company needs to be just as careful to insist that its own employees, consultants, and suppliers keep Company secrets under wraps. Some startup companies start out well, carefully developing assignment agreements, confidentiality procedures and policies, non-compete/non-solicitation agreements, and other safeguards. But as time goes on, they get sloppy. They stop legending documentation as confidential. They freely display their breakthroughs to suppliers and potential customers. They "assume" consultants have signed non-disclosure and assignment agreements and "imagine" employees have signed appropriate covenants. They "expect" departing employees to understand their continuing obligations, but stop conducting exit interviews to remind them. Then they are surprised when their expectations are dashed.

Finally, take care not to post secrets on the Company web page. It is amazing how many startup companies post customer lists, employee rosters, joint venture plans and technical papers for all the world — including all the competition — to see.

Establishing proper internal protective measures can help — but only if the Company follows them. Otherwise, their major function is to serve as powerful evidence that the Company did not follow what it knew were reasonable measures to protect its own property. As one court has emphasized, "One who claims that he has a trade secret must exercise eternal vigilance." *Baystate Technologies, Inc. v. Bentley Systems, Inc.*, 946 F. Supp. 1079 (D. Mass. 1996). Investors and intellectual property owners alike should recognize, however, that even well-crafted protective measures are not infallible. Thus entrepreneurs should not overreach in describing the likely efficacy of their confidentiality procedures and agreements. *Cf. Steinberg v. PRT Group, Inc.*, 88 F. Supp. 2d 294 (S.D.N.Y. 2000) (dismissing claim that prospectus misrepresented the nature and importance of its non-compete agreements, concluding that the "subdued description of the non-compete agreements" reflected no more than "general optimism" and holding that company had no obligation to disclose that such agreements are sometimes ignored).

6. Assume the founders and other key employees will stay with the Company forever.

Many startup companies are started by a few friends who spend 120 hour weeks establishing the Company, creating the intellectual property at its heart, and developing its customer base. When these efforts succeed, the Company is often sold to third parties or taken public. What happens to the founders then?

Often they stay on as key employees or full-time consultants. But frequently they leave to pursue new undertakings. The far-sighted company will consider entering early on into agreements that provide for a smooth transition, limit immediate head-to-head competition, and prohibit use of the Company's intellectual property and use and disclosure of its trade secrets. Without such protections in place, a startup company will be far less attractive to investors, including the public. Few announcements scuttle a public offering so quickly as those reporting that the founders are starting NewCo 2000 to market version 2.0 of the Company's intellectual property.

Anticipating key departures is important even if a sale or IPO seems far away. Particularly in the early stages of a company, the loss of a single employee or key consultant to a competitor can endanger the Company. Stock option agreements may entice employees to stay, but what if they do decide to leave? The legal protections available to an employer depend on state law. The contractual safeguards that work for a New York company, for example, may not be enforceable in California. But companies need to work with counsel before departures to plan how to prevent the loss of a key contributor from transferring Company secrets, technology, and business to a competitor.

7. Ignore invasions of Company rights by third parties.

The last thing a company in the process of establishing its business usually wants to do is become embroiled in a lawsuit. Thus, when startup companies detect evidence that others may be adopting similar names or slogans or may be copying the technology, some corporate founders simply shrug and say there's nothing they can afford to do about it. An almost equally common reaction is to threaten to sue the offender for punitive damages and injunctive relief—and then either fail to sue, or sue and devote far too much money and corporate time to the effort.

Deciding what to do about an apparent infringement of the Company's intellectual property rights is a delicate balancing exercise. Every infringement does not warrant a lawsuit. Generally speaking, the courts do not require an intellectual property owner to sue everyone who encroaches upon its rights. But if the owner of a trademark does not protest now when others use substantially similar marks to promote their similar products, it may have to justify its inaction later when it does sue someone else for using marks similar to those ignored in the past.

Or, if a trademark owner has known of an apparent infringement for years but did nothing to challenge it, it may be found to have forfeited its rights against that specific infringer. The trademark owner may become, as one court has said, "the hapless victim of his own lethargy." This problem is by no means limited to startups. The famous French fashion house, Hermés, for example, was recently found to have forfeited its rights to sue a New York firm for handbag copies Hermés had been aware of—but remained silent about—for nearly twenty years. The Court held that even "a single warning letter would have been sufficient to lessen this severe delay." *Hermés Int'l v. Lederer de Paris Fifth Avenue, Inc.*, 50 F. Supp. 2d 212 (S.D.N.Y. 1999).

Thus, even if the Company is not prepared to file a lawsuit, it may still make sense to send protest letters making clear that the Company objects to the infringing activity. The Company should also document internally the reasons it decides not to file suit in particular cases, such as the very limited geographic scope of the infringement, the limited overlap in products, etc. The reasoning that seems logical now may be forgotten, and difficult to explain, in the future. The Company should maintain records of any agreed compromises, as well. Such records can be used in the future to explain how an infringement that does lead to a lawsuit differs from events in the past.

Protest letters should be carefully reviewed with counsel to prevent them from being used by the alleged infringer as the basis for starting a lawsuit in an unfriendly jurisdiction to declare the parties' rights.

One type of misappropriation the intellectual property owner will almost always want to challenge at the outset is use or disclosure of trade secrets. Unlike other forms of intellectual property, a trade secret, once freely disclosed, is as a practical matter, lost forever. *FMC v. Taiwan Tainan Giant Indus. Co.*, 730 F.2d 61, 63 (2d Cir. 1984). Others who learn it without knowledge that it has been misappropriated will generally be free to use it without limitation. While the party disclosing it may well be liable for damages, that fact may be of little comfort, especially if that party has few assets. Thus, at a minimum, a protest letter to the potential discloser and to those likely to receive the disclosure is almost always in order, although it must be carefully drafted and circulation properly controlled to prevent claims of libel. Injunctive relief to "keep the cat in the bag" may also be warranted.

Trade secret owners who believe their valuable secrets have been stolen may also want to consider presenting their claims to the U.S. Attorneys' office for potential prosecution under the Economic Espionage Act, a Federal criminal statute. 18 U.S.C. §§ 1831–1839 (1996). While such actions are not routinely brought and do not lead to financial recovery by the trade secret owner, they may save the secret and punish the thief at minimal cost to the trade secret owner.

8. Ignore protest letters from third parties.

Finally, the entrepreneur needs to be careful not to infringe on the intellectual property rights of others. Following the tips outlined in this article should reduce the risk. Requiring employees and consultants to certify that they are not incorporating the property of others into work they create for the Company and are not using the confidential information of others should also help. But if protest letters come, the startup company, in particular, must pay attention.

Some protest letters are clearly unwarranted or overreaching. Some are sent by third parties who can be easily shown to have inferior, or no, rights to the name or writings or technology. If so, say so—in writing. Many intellectual property lawsuits are filed simply because an initial protest letter was never answered. Ex parte restraining orders are sometimes entered for the same reason. The plaintiff is able to persuade the court that nothing short of a court order will make the accused infringer pay attention and explain the conduct at issue.

Sometimes a protest letter does seem to have substantial merit. Better to try to address it informally than to bog down in litigation. In the case of a trademark dispute, perhaps a license can be worked out permitting use of the name in a specific geographic area or for particular types of goods. Or perhaps the trademark owner could assist the innocent infringer in developing a new mark, or allow some time to phase in the new mark. In the case of a copyright dispute, perhaps certain segments of the computer code could be rewritten in a new version. In the case of potential use or disclosure of a trade secret by a former employee, perhaps the employee could be assigned to new duties which would not put the information at risk.

Not every dispute can be readily resolved, of course. But confronting the risks early on, rather than simply ignoring them, may help prevent a lawsuit or, at the least, a major damages award. By contrast, companies that have simply ignored others' successful claims to intellectual property may find themselves having to pay multimillion dollar damages awards, or even stop selling their products altogether.

Intellectual property can be among a company's most valuable assets, but only if the company works hard to protect it, and to ensure that it does not belong to others. An ongoing partnership with intellectual property counsel can protect the Company when it starts out — and once it becomes a market leader.

Motor City Bagels, LLC. v. American Bagel Co.

United States District Court for the District of Maryland

50 F. Supp. 2d 460 (D. Md. 1999)

Beginning in the fall of 1993, Plaintiff, Joseph Anthony, began researching franchise opportunities as a possible entrepreneurial venture. At that time, Mr. Anthony had an M.B.A. in finance and accounting from the Tuck School of Business Administration at Dartmouth College and had extensive experience in commercial real estate investment and management. By the spring of 1994, Mr. Anthony intensified his evaluation of potential franchise opportunities, focusing particularly on the bagel industry. While researching various bagel franchisors, Mr. Anthony initiated discussions with Chesapeake Bagel Bakery through its sales representative Steve Vierra. After some preliminary discussions on the telephone, Mr. Anthony traveled to McLean, Virginia during the spring of 1994 to meet with Mr. Vierra and to tour a handful of Chesapeake stores in the Washington, D.C. area.

Early in the summer of 1994, Plaintiff, Randall Flinn, teamed with Mr. Anthony in assessing the feasibility of operating a bagel franchise. Mr. Flinn, a friend of Mr. Anthony's from college, had an M.B.A. from the J.C. Kellogg Graduate School of Management and was working as a Senior Product Manager for Teradyne, an Illinois telecommunications concern. By late July 1994, Mr. Anthony and Mr. Flinn received an American Bagel Uniform Franchise Offering Circular, dated August 23, 1993 ("1993 UFOC"), which disclosed information about the Chesapeake Bagel Bakery franchise system, including estimates of initial investment costs experienced by franchisees.

The 1993 UFOC provided an estimate for initial investment costs for Chesapeake Bagel Bakeries, "based on the latest available data," ranging from $240,400 to $304,500. 1993 UFOC at 8. Mr. Anthony and Mr. Flinn used the cost figures provided in the 1993 UFOC as a central assumption in an extensive, written business plan ana-lyzing the viability of owning and operating Chesapeake Bagel Bakery franchises. The plaintiffs used the midpoint in the range provided in the disclosure document, $275,000, to determine the amount of capital required to open an individual store.

Although the plaintiffs used the cost figures from the August 23, 1993 UFOC in drawing up their business plan, American Bagel had actually updated its disclosure information through a revised UFOC, filed in Mr. Anthony's home state of Indiana on April 21, 1994 ("1994 UFOC"). This revised UFOC contained a higher range of estimated initial investment costs than was included in the 1993 UFOC. The 1994 UFOC stated that, "based on the latest available data," start-up costs for individual Chesapeake Bagel Bakery stores ranged between $288,300 and $376,000.

In November 1994, American Bagel mailed Mr. Anthony a second UFOC. The defendants contend that they sent the 1994 UFOC with the revised estimates of ini-tial investment costs. The plaintiffs, however, vehemently deny this assertion, claim-ing that they received a UFOC with the same cost estimates that they had received in July. In any event, Plaintiffs, Mr. Anthony, Mr. Flinn, and Motor City Bagels, L.L.C., signed an Area Franchise Development Agreement ("AFDA") on December 3, 1994 pursuant to which they received the exclusive right, subject to certain terms and con-ditions, to develop Chesapeake Bagel Bakeries in Oakland County, Macomb County, and the city of Grosse Pointe, Michigan. Under the agreement, the plaintiffs had to pay $25,000 at the time of signing, $10,000 prior to December 31, 1994, and an addi-tional $50,000 within forty-five days. That same day, the plaintiffs also entered into two franchise agreements, obligating the plaintiffs to pay license fees of $22,500 and $20,000 by December 31, 1994.

On June 15, 1995, the plaintiffs signed another AFDA pursuant to which they were granted, under certain terms and conditions, the exclusive right to develop Chesa-peake Bagel Bakeries in Washtenaw, Livingston, Clinton, Eaton, and Ingham Coun-ties, Michigan, another franchise agreement, and a promissory note for $10,000 payable to American Bagel. Under the AFDA, the plaintiffs paid to American Bagel $60,000 in franchise fees and the franchise agreement required the plaintiffs to pay an additional $17,500 in license fees.

Allegedly unbeknownst to the plaintiffs, American Bagel had again updated its UFOC between the signing of the first wave of agreements on December 3, 1994, and the second wave on June 15, 1995. On January 25, 1995, the Federal Trade Commis-sion approved the revised offering circular submitted by American Bagel ("1995 UFOC"). In this updated disclosure form, American Bagel had again increased the estimated initial costs that prospective franchisees could expect to spend to a range of $328,800 to $431,000.

Pursuant to the two franchise agreements signed on December 3, 1994, the plain-tiffs opened a Chesapeake Bagel Bakery on December 27, 1995 in Northville, Michigan, and a second one in Troy, Michigan on March 6, 1996. According to the plaintiffs, their start-up costs greatly exceeded the amounts represented by the defendants in the

1993 UFOC. Mr. Anthony estimated that in the Northville store, the plaintiffs spent $425,000 on tenant improvements and equipment, and that franchise fees and expenses associated with training, advertising, and deposits pushed the total cost of the store over $500,000. Similarly, the plaintiffs assert that it cost approximately $400,000 to construct and equip the Troy store, even before accounting for franchise fees, advertising, training, and other sundry start-up expenses.

After Northville and Troy, the plaintiffs failed to open up any additional Chesapeake Bagel Bakery restaurants as required by the Consolidated, Amended and Restated Area Development Agreement, signed by the plaintiffs on August 10, 1996. Mr. Flinn testified at his deposition that the plaintiffs refused to open more stores because they had "been fraudulently induced into signing the contracts and the agreement with [American Bagel] to open these stores through the representation of construction costs that were dramatically lower than the actual costs." The plaintiffs had exhausted their capital in starting up the Northville and Troy restaurants, and the debt burden resulting from the unexpectedly high construction costs was "putting a real strain on the profitability of the stores." Mr. Flinn explained that "at $400,000 to open a store, it's not a viable business. So, yes, we said if it's going to cost us $400,000 to open stores, we are not going to be able to open any additional stores." In addition to not constructing additional stores, the plaintiffs, in November 1996, likewise decided to stop paying various monthly franchise fees to American Bagel and its successor, Defendant, AFC Enterprises, Inc. ("AFC"), arising from the ongoing operations at their Northville and Troy stores.

As a result of this failed business relationship, the plaintiffs filed an eight-count suit against the defendants alleging violations of Indiana franchise law, fraud, negligent misrepresentation, violations of Maryland franchise law, breach of contract, unjust enrichment, and misappropriation of trade secrets. In addition, the plaintiffs seek declaratory judgment against AFC, arguing that the contracts at issue in this case are void ab initio and thus unenforceable. Additional facts will be discussed, as needed, within the framework of the legal issues presented in the individual claims . . . .

. . . .

IX. Misappropriation of Trade Secrets

The plaintiffs have asserted that the defendants' distribution of the business plan, in violation of [its] promise [of confidentiality] to the plaintiffs, constitutes a misappropriation of trade secrets in violation of the Maryland Uniform Trade Secrets Act ("MUTSA"). Md. Com. Law II Code Ann. §§ 11-1201 to 11-1209. At the outset, the Court is unclear as to the basis for applying Maryland law when the alleged misappropriation of the plan actually occurred in Virginia. However, the same analysis would apply under either Virginia or Maryland law as both states have adopted trade secret statutes which closely track the Uniform Trade Secrets Act. In addition, the Maryland legislature has dictated that the MUTSA "be applied and construed to effectuate its general purpose to make uniform the law with respect to" trade secrets among the states that have enacted the Uniform Trade Secrets Act. Md. Com. Law II Code Ann. § 11-1208.

The MUTSA defines "trade secret" as follows:

[I]nformation, including a formula, pattern, compilation, program, device, method, technique, or process, that:

(1) Derives independent economic value, actual or potential, from not being generally known to, and not being readily ascertainable by proper means by, other persons who can obtain economic value from its disclosure or use; and

(2) Is the subject of efforts that are reasonable under the circumstances to maintain its secrecy.

Stated succinctly, "to be protected under Maryland law, information must be secret, and its value must derive from the secrecy. In addition, the owner of the information must use reasonable efforts to safeguard the confidentiality of the information."

As an initial matter, the Court must determine whether the business plan constitutes a "secret" as required under the MUTSA. The Court of Special Appeals of Maryland has noted that a manufacturer's marketing plan did not constitute a protectable trade secret under Maryland law, in part, because it was based on information "readily available from the marketplace." The court specifically observed that the defendants could have obtained the same information in the plaintiff's marketing plan "simply by talking with prospective customers." While the business plan at issue in the case at bar does contain some public information and facts ascertainable from the marketplace, it likewise includes personal insights and analysis brought to bear through diligent research and by marshaling a large volume of information. [A]n attempt to independently duplicate the plaintiffs' efforts in the instant case would be an onerous task.

The United States District Court for the Eastern District of Pennsylvania has recognized that "[t]he fact that individual forms in marketing material or in plaintiff's proposal book were compilations of public information does not itself preclude a finding that the combination of the included elements affords a competitive advantage and is not itself in the public domain." The court continued:

The combination of information in the proposal book reflected market research preformed [sic] by plaintiff and decisions to include and exclude certain elements from a larger pool of data. It is this, rather than the data contained in the individual forms generally known in the self insurance business, which may arguably contain a significant degree of novelty, however, slight, to be excluded from general knowledge, and may qualify the proposal book as a trade secret.

. . . Thus, applying the rationale set forth in these decisions, the Court concludes that the plaintiffs' extensive compilation of information and analysis in their business plan qualifies as a trade secret.

Likewise, the Court finds that the business plan derived value from its secrecy. . . . However, the MUTSA provides that damages caused by misappropriation . . . "may be measured by imposition of liability for a reasonable royalty for a misappropriator's unauthorized disclosure or use of a trade secret." Under this provision, the plaintiffs in the case at bar could argue that they are entitled to monetary damages in the form of royalties as a result of the defendants' unauthorized distribution of their business plan to prospective franchisees. Based on these potential royalty payments, the business plan "[d]erives independent economic value . . . from not being generally known to, and not being readily ascertainable by proper means by" the defendants and prospective Chesapeake franchisees.

The final prong that the plaintiffs must prove in bringing their misappropriation claim is that they took reasonable measures to ensure the secrecy of their business plan. The Fourth Circuit has noted that "[s]ecrecy is a question of fact" to be determined by the circumstances presented in each case. In the case at bar, the plaintiffs drafted an extensive confidentiality agreement that they had "most potential investors sign" when they received a copy of the business plan. The problem for the plaintiffs is that they only produced five executed copies of the confidentiality agreement when they distributed the business plan to over fifteen individuals. When questioned as to whether he recalled ever receiving any confidentiality agreements from other individuals who were given the business plan, Mr. Anthony responded, "I mean I don't remember. I think I probably got—had more of them but maybe not. This might be it." Mr. Anthony's equivocating response to this question reveals that the plaintiffs did not act diligently to protect the secrecy of their business plan. The Supreme Court has observed that the disclosure of a trade secret "to others who are under no obligation to protect the confidentiality of the information" extinguishes the property right in the disclosure. Under this reasoning, the plaintiffs' failure to exact agreements from potential investors to maintain the secrecy of the business plan is inconsistent with recognition of the document as a trade secret under the MUTSA.

In addition, the Court does not find the boilerplate language on the cover of the business plan stating that "[t]his memorandum is for the exclusive use of the persons to whom it is given and is not to reproduced or redistributed" precludes the denial of trade secret status. This sentence appears at the end of a general disclaimer, cautioning investors as to the risks involved in making an investment in the business described in the plan. The language is not highlighted or isolated so as to put one on immediate notice that the plan constitutes a trade secret that the authors of the plan are actively seeking to protect.

Taking the facts as a whole, the Court concludes that the plaintiffs simply did not act reasonably in seeking to ensure the secrecy of their plan. Because the plaintiffs have failed to adduce sufficient proof of this essential element of their misappropriation claim to ward off summary judgment under Anderson and Celotex, and the defendants' motions for summary judgment on this count will be granted.

Notes & Questions

1. A business plan is a document that communicates to investors the key elements of a proposed business. As the *Motor City Bagel* case illustrates, a business plan can be protected by intellectual property, particularly a trade secret. If a business plan consists of information that is not generally known and that would give the owner an advantage over a competitor, trade secret law would protect the plan. The Small Business Administration recommends that a business plan include the following essential elements:

Executive Summary

The executive summary is . . . the most important section of your plan. It provides a concise overview of the entire plan, along with a history of your company. This section tells your reader where your company is and where you want to take it. It's the first thing your readers see; therefore, it is the thing that will either grab their interest and make them want to keep reading or make them want to put it down and forget about it. More than anything else, this section is important because it tells the reader why you think your business idea will be successful.

. . . .

Market Analysis

The market analysis section . . . should illustrate your knowledge about the particular industry your business is in. It should also present general highlights and conclusions of any marketing research data you have collected; however, the specific details of your marketing research studies should be moved to the appendix section of your business plan.

This section should include: an industry description and outlook, target market information, market test results, lead times, and an evaluation of your competition.

. . . .

Company Description

The company description . . . section should include a high-level look at how all of the different elements of your business fit together. The company description section should include information about the nature of your business as well as list the primary factors that you believe will make your business a success.

. . . .

Organization & Management

[The organization and management] section should include: your company's organizational structure, details about the ownership of your company, profiles of your management team, and the qualifications of your board of directors.

. . . .

Marketing & Sales Management

. . . .

Marketing is the process of creating customers, and customers are the lifeblood of your business. In [the marketing and sales management] section, the first thing you want to do is define your marketing strategy. There is no single way to approach a marketing strategy; your strategy should be part of an ongoing business-evaluation process and unique to your company. However, there are common steps you can follow which will help you think through the direction and tactics you would like to use to drive sales and sustain customer loyalty.

. . . .

Service or Product Line

[The service or product line section should] describe your service or product, emphasizing the benefits to potential and current customers. For example, don't tell your readers which 89 foods you carry in your "Gourmet to Go" shop. Tell them why busy, two-career couples will prefer shopping in a service-oriented store that records clients' food preferences and caters even the smallest parties on short notice.

. . . .

Funding Request

The Funding Request . . . section . . . will request the amount of funding you will need to start or expand your business. If necessary, you can include different funding scenarios, such as best- and worst-case scenarios, but remember that later, in the financial section, you must be able to back up these requests and scenarios with corresponding financial statements.

. . . .

Financials

[The financials section] should be developed after you've analyzed the market and set clear objectives. That's when you can allocate resources efficiently. The following is a list of the critical financial statements to include in your business plan packet.

Historical Financial Data

If you own an established business, you will be requested to supply histori-cal data related to your company's performance. Most creditors request data for the last three to five years, depending on the length of time you have been in business.

The historical financial data you would want to include would be your com-pany's income statements, balance sheets, and cash flow statements for each year you have been in business (usually for up to three to five years). Often creditors are also interested in any collateral that you may have that could be used to ensure your loan, regardless of the stage of your business.

Prospective Financial Data

All businesses, whether startup or growing, will be required to supply pro-spective financial data. Most of the time, creditors will want to see what you expect your company to be able to do within the next five years. Each year's documents should include forecasted income statements, balance sheets, cash flow statements, and capital expenditure budgets. For the first year, you should supply monthly or quarterly projections. After that, you can stretch it to quarterly and/or yearly projections for years two through five.

. . . .

Appendix

The Appendix . . . should be provided to readers on an as-needed basis. In other words, it should not be included with the main body of your business plan. Your plan is your communication tool; as such, it will be seen by a lot of people. Some of the information in the business section you will not want everyone to see, but, specific individuals (such as creditors) may want access to this information in order to make lending decisions. Therefore, it is impor-tant to have the appendix within easy reach.

The appendix would include:

- Credit history (personal & business)
- Resumes of key managers
- Product pictures
- Letters of reference
- Details of market studies
- Relevant magazine articles or book references
- Licenses, permits or patents
- Legal documents
- Copies of leases

- Building permits
- Contracts
- List of business consultants, including attorney and accountant

. . . .

United States Small Business Administration, *Essential Elements of a Good Business Plan*, http://www.sba.gov/category/navigation-structure/starting -managing-business/starting-business/writing-business-plan (last visited 8/13/2011).

2. The readings in this section illustrate some of the intellectual property issues that confront a new business. The Cundiff reading is applicable to both high technology and low technology enterprises. The Hokanson & Vakili reading focuses specifically on technology-based businesses, such as in the software and biotechnology sectors. Do the issues confronting high technology and low technology business start-ups differ? If so, how?

3. What could the plaintiffs have done differently in the *Motor City Bagel* case to protect their business plan as a trade secret? Are there tort or contract theories they could have pursued to protect their interests? What would be the likely results?

4. We will discuss forfeiture of intellectual property interests in greater detail below in section C. Notice how entrepreneurs have to be careful about their actions early on to make sure valuable intellectual property is not lost in the future. If you are a business person, at what stage should you consult an attorney? When you first come up with the idea? When you first decide to share the idea with someone else? If you are an attorney, knowledgeable in the fine details of intellectual property law, what should you be aware about from a business perspective?

5. What advice would you give Dr. See about sharing his business plan with potential investors in light of *Motor City Bagels*? In light of the Cundiff and Hokanson & Vakili readings?

B. Valuing Intellectual Property

Ted Hagelin, Valuation of Intellectual Property Assets: An Overview
52 Syracuse Law Review 1133 (2002)*

Introduction

The value of intangible assets relative to the value of physical and financial assets has continuously increased since the early 1980s. In 2000, the market-to-book value for the S&P 500 companies showed that approximately 83.3% of the companies' market values stemmed from intangible assets. For many companies, the ratio of

---

intangible assets to physical and financial assets is considerably higher. The importance of intangible assets has created an urgent need to value these assets in many contexts including intellectual property management, acquisitions, sales, joint ventures, and licensing.

This article will briefly review the three basic valuation methods, then discuss the valuation methods developed for intellectual property and finally present a new valuation method—Competitive Advantage Valuation®.

I. Valuation Methods

There are three basic methods of valuation: the cost method, the market method, and the income method. The cost method of valuation measures the value of an asset by the cost to replace the asset with an identical or equivalent asset. The assumption underlying the cost method of valuation is that the cost to purchase or develop a new asset is commensurate with the economic value that the asset can provide during its life. The market method values an asset based upon comparable transactions between unrelated parties. The income method values an asset based upon the present value of the net economic benefit (net future income stream) expected to be received over the life of the asset.

II. Valuation Methods Developed for Intellectual Property

There are seven commonly used valuation methods developed for use with intellectual property: the 25 Percent Rule, Industry Standards, Ranking, Surrogate Measures, Disaggregation Methods, the Monte Carlo Method, and Option Methods. The 25 percent rule is the most simple, flexible, and often referenced valuation method. Although there are many variations on the 25 percent rule, the most often given definition is that the licensor should receive 25 percent of the licensee's gross profit from the licensed technology. This statement of the 25 percent rule makes clear that its purpose is not the valuation of a technology per se, but rather the apportionment of a technology's value between the licensor and licensee. Discussions of the 25 percent rule generally provide that the percentage split between the licensor and licensee should be adjusted upwards or downwards to take into account the parties' respective investment and risk in the licensed technology.

Valuation of intellectual property by industry standards is another widely used valuation method. The industry standards method, also referred to as the market or comparable technology method, attempts to value an intellectual property asset by reference to royalty rates in similar past transactions. Information on royalty rates is available from a number of different sources such as articles on royalty rates and licensing terms, specific publications, price lists, contracts filed with the Securities and Exchange Commission and court decisions in infringement cases. The industry standards method of valuation is subject to a number of limitations because intellectual property is inherently dissimilar, intellectual property exchanges are motivated by unique strategic considerations, and published royalty rates are often based on broad industry classifications and provided in terms of wide percentage ranges, which might provide little guidance on an appropriate royalty rate for a specific intellectual property asset being valued.

The ranking method of valuation compares the intellectual property asset to be valued to comparable intellectual property assets on a subjective or objective scale. The ranking method is often used in conjunction with the industry standards method to determine a more precise royalty rate within an industry royalty rate range. There are five components to a ranking method: (i) scoring criteria; (ii) scoring system; (iii) scoring scale; (iv) weighting factors; and (v) decision table. These five components are used to calculate a composite score for an asset. That score is then compared to the average score for a comparable intellectual property asset to determine the relative value. The major disadvantages of the ranking method of valuation are the identification of comparable (benchmark) intellectual property asset transactions, the subjectivity of the criteria, and the translation of the composite score into a royalty rate or dollar adjustment. Furthermore, comparability is as much of a challenge in the ranking method as it is in the other methods for the same reasons.

Surrogate measures have been developed to value patents. Surrogate measures do not value patents by reference to profits, industry standards or rankings, but by reference to the patents themselves. The three most common types of surrogate measures are the number of patents issued to a company, payment of patent maintenance fees, and prior art citations. These measures have been shown to correlate, on average, with a firm's market value, suggesting that investors use these measures explicitly or implicitly in making investment decisions. The utility of surrogate measures, however, is limited because they can be inherently misleading, they can be manipulated, and can only be used to value patent portfolios rather than individual patents.

There are two basic types of disaggregation methods—value disaggregation and income disaggregation. Value disaggregation seeks to apportion some fraction of total value to intellectual property assets by setting the value of intangible assets equal to the value of a firm (or a subdivision of a firm) minus the firm's monetary assets (cash, securities, receivables, inventories, prepayments, etc.) and tangible assets (land, buildings, equipment, furniture, vehicles, etc.) to determine the value of the intangible assets. This form of disaggregation is useful to provide perspective on the importance of intangible assets to a firm, but cannot be used value different types of intangible assets or to value individual, or related groups of, intangible assets.

Income disaggregation seeks to apportion some fraction of total earnings of a firm, based upon various factors, to intellectual property assets. Two forms of income disaggregation are the "Technology Factor" method developed for the Dow Chemical Company and the Knowledge Capital Scorecard.

The Monte Carlo method of valuing intellectual property assets is primarily used as a refinement of the income method discussed earlier. Whereas the income method assigns a single value to the variables used in calculating the net present value (NPV) of an asset, the Monte Carlo method assigns a range of values to the variables and the probability of each value. Using the range of values and probabilities, the frequency of specific NPVs are calculated and plotted to provide an indication of the most likely NPV. The benefits of the Monte Carlo method are that it can calculate minimum and maximum NPVs, can associate intermediate NPVs with the probability of their realization, and can determine how different variables affect the uncertainty of the NPV calculation. The challenge in implementing the Monte Carlo method is obtaining the necessary information.

Option methods of valuing intellectual property assets are based on a widely used method for valuing stock options, known throughout the financial industry as the Black-Scholes formula. Under the Black-Scholes formula, the essence of a stock option's value lies in the right to wait and see what happens to a stock's price and to exercise or not exercise the option accordingly. The adaptation of stock option valuation to intellectual property valuation is based on the same "wait and see" value. Option valuation of intellectual property views an investment in intellectual property as an option to develop the intellectual property further, or to abandon the intellectual property, depending upon future technical and market information. The advantages of option valuation are that it avoids exaggerating the risk of investing in intellectual property assets and provides an objective, repeatable means for calculating intellectual property value. The disadvantages of option valuation are its complex mathematics and its requirement of extensive information databases.

III. Competitive Advantage Valuation®

Competitive Advantage Valuation® (CAV) is a new method to value intellectual property assets. The CAV method was developed over a number of years through a series of research projects undertaken in the Technology Transfer Research Center at Syracuse University on behalf of a variety of client organizations. These research projects assessed the commercial potential of many different types of early-stage technologies by analyzing the engineering, marketing, licensing and intellectual property advantages and disadvantages associated with these technologies. When presented with the final research findings, the question most often asked by client organizations was, "So, what's the invention worth?" CAV was developed to answer this question in a simple and direct way.

In comparison to other valuation methods, the CAV method combines a number of unique features. Most importantly, the CAV method is specific. It can be used to value individual intellectual property assets and to determine differences in value within a group of intellectual property assets. The more specific a valuation method is, the more useful it is in managing intellectual property assets. The other unique features of the CAV method are:

> The CAV method is understandable to the broad cross-section of professionals practicing in the fields of licensing and intellectual property management. The easier a valuation method is to understand, the lower the transaction costs of negotiation and the quicker the parties can know whether an agreement can be reached.

The CAV method is repeatable and not dependent upon the subjective choices of individuals or groups. The more repeatable a valuation method is, the easier it is for parties to focus their attention on the variables and value inputs on which they agree or disagree.

The CAV method is affordable in terms of the time and cost of obtaining necessary information and performing the valuation analysis. The more affordable a valuation method is, the more broadly it will be adopted and the more likely it will be standardized.

The CAV method is flexible and can be used to value any type of intellectual property as well as licenses, prospective research and development investments, and pre-market products. The more flexible a valuation method is, the more it can be shared across business divisions and used as a common benchmark.

Finally, the CAV method is scalable. A simple CAV analysis can be performed using built-in default formulas to calculate values and more advanced CAV analyses can be performed using statistical software tools to calculate values. The more scalable a valuation method is, the greater the user's ability to choose the trade-off between the time and cost of the valuation, and the desired degree of accuracy of the result.

The major premise of the CAV method is that intellectual property assets have no inherent value; the value of intellectual property assets resides entirely in the value of the tangible assets which incorporate them. The minor premise of the CAV method is that the value of a given intellectual property asset can best be measured by the competitive advantage which that asset contributes to a product, process, or service. For the purpose of explanation, I will discuss the CAV method with respect to an existing product.

The CAV method is a novel combination of the income and disaggregation approaches to valuation. In its most general form, the CAV method consists of six basic steps:

(1) The intellectual property asset to be valued (IPA) is associated with a product and the product's net present value is calculated.

(2) The product's net present value is apportioned among tangible assets, intangible advantages and intellectual property assets. (There are three groups of intellectual property assets: technical [utility patents, functional software copyrights and technical trade secrets]; reputational [trademarks, service marks and brand names]; and operational [business method patents and proprietary business processes].

(3) The product is associated with competition parameters which can be used to compare the product to substitute products and competition parameter weights are calculated. (There are three groups of competition parameters: technical [price and performance], reputational [recognition

and impression], and operational [cost and efficiency]. Weights are calculated for each parameter group and for individual parameters within each group.)

(4) The IPA is associated with an individual competition parameter and the IPA's competitive advantage relative to substitute intellectual property assets is calculated. (Substitute intellectual property assets are assets which are incorporated in substitute products and associated with the same competition parameter as the IPA.)

(5) The IPA is associated with complementary intellectual property assets and the IPA's competitive advantage relative to complementary intellectual property assets is calculated. (Complementary intellectual property assets are assets which are incorporated in the same product and associated with the same parameter group as the IPA.)

(6) The value of the IPA is calculated by apportioning a share of the product's intellectual property asset value to the IPA based upon the IPA's competitive advantage contribution relative to substitute and complementary intellectual property assets.

If the IPA is associated with multiple products, the IPA's relative competitive advantage contribution to each product is calculated and these contributions are summed to calculate the total value of the IPA. If the IPA is associated with multiple parameters, the IPA's relative competitive advantage contribution for each parameter is calculated and these contributions are summed to calculate the total value of the IPA.

Conclusion

The valuation of intellectual property assets is a trillion dollar problem in today's economy. The success of companies, and indeed the welfare of society, increasingly depend on intellectual property; and intellectual property assets cannot be effectively managed or efficiently transferred without adequate means to value them. Fortunately, a number of new methods to value intellectual property have been developed in recent years. Although each of these methods has certain limitations, together they have provided intellectual property managers a very useful new set of decision-making tools.

As with the valuation of tangible assets, no single method for valuing intellectual property assets will be definitive. Also, as with the valuation of tangible assets, the methods for valuing intellectual property assets will be subject to continuing research and refinement. The development of valuation methodologies has no terminal completion point, but is an ongoing, evolutionary process. The CAV method is proposed as part of this evolutionary process. The CAV method is not a definitive valuation method and further research will be required to refine the method. However, the unique features of the CAV method make it a useful addition to the existing methods. Hopefully, the CAV method will contribute in a small way to increase company values and investor returns.

Hughes Tool Co. v. Dresser Industries, Inc.

United States Court of Appeals for the Federal Circuit

816 F. 2d 1549 (Fed. Cir. 1987)

RICH, CIRCUIT JUDGE.

[The following is a summary of the district court opinion on damages excerpted from the Federal Circuit opinion:]

Although Hughes Tool sought damages based on its lost profits with respect to the TCI journal bearing bits Dresser sold to customers within the United States, the court concluded that Hughes Tool "failed to demonstrate with 'reasonable probability' an approximation of the profits it would have made on the infringing Dresser sales." The court then set out to determine, "under the 'willing buyer—willing seller' rule, what a reasonable royalty" would have been.

In assessing the evidence on the damages issue, the district court found that customer demand for the patented rock bits was strong and that no acceptable non-infringing alternative existed. However, the court also found that Hughes Tool failed to demonstrate the manufacturing and marketing ability to meet the demand for at least part of the period of Dresser's infringement.

Turning specifically to the commercial situation as it existed in 1973, the district court noted that Hughes Tool was experiencing a rising demand for its patented journal bearing bits and that Hughes Tool believed that those bits were more profitable than its sales of certain other tools. Although Hughes Tool had a company policy of not licensing its patented inventions to major competitors, the court did note evidence of forty-five prior licenses and offers of licenses under other patents owned by Hughes Tool at royalty rates of six percent or less. The court did not give much weight to those prior royalty rates, however, because those licenses were for widely diverse products. Similarly, the court acknowledged the existence of one license at four percent to a non-competitor, Gault, and specifically held that it would not consider a fifteen percent license agreement made in 1983 in settlement of litigation with Hughes Tool's competitor, Rock Bit Industries. The court ultimately concluded that Hughes Tool showed no desire to license direct competitors under the '928 patent.

The court also found that Dresser was concerned about a potential loss of fifty to sixty percent of its rock bit market to Hughes Tool; that when Dresser considered beginning to manufacture the patented journal bearing bits itself in 1973, it projected total profits of 60% on sales of the new bits; and that its total profits on all sales the year before had been 7.2%. The district court also noted that Hughes Tool asserted profits of 49–54% on sales of the patented journal bearing insert bits.

The district court found, however, that Hughes Tool did not realize that the demand for rock bits other than sealed journal bearing bits would drop as sharply as it did. In addition, Hughes Tool was aware that its competitors were working diligently to produce competitive rock bits. Finally, the district court found that the '928 patent did not give the new rock bits their essential market value, but rather that the patented O-ring seal was only one of numerous parts that contributed to the overall value of the rock bit.

Although Hughes Tool's expert at trial asserted that 52.8% was a reasonable royalty for both the patents in suit, that assertion was based on the assumption that the patented combination with the O-ring seal was responsible for most of the value of the bit. The district court disagreed, stating that the '928 patent contributed only part of the total value of the bit, and concluded that 25% of the gross sales price would have been a reasonable royalty had the parties negotiated for a license in 1973 . . . .

On May 31, 1985, Dresser appealed the district court's judgment with respect to the validity of the '928 patent and the amount of damages, as well as the district court's denial of its post-trial motions. Hughes Tool filed its cross-appeal on June 13, 1985, seeking review of the district court's failure to award increased damages as well as its failure to award prejudgment interest for the period the '928 patent had temporarily been under the cloud of a district court holding of invalidity.

[The following is the Federal Circuit's opinion on the reasonable royalty rate:]

The district court's award of damages to Hughes calculated as a royalty of 25% of the dollar amount of Dresser's total sales of certain infringing bits is based on a finding of fact with respect to Dresser's projected profits which Dresser asserts is clearly erroneous. The basic predicate for the district court's 25% royalty determination is that Dresser projected "total profits of 60% as a percent of sales." That 60% "profit" figure was then contrasted with Dresser's 1972 actual profits of 7.2% for all of its sales. The 60% profit projection is referenced repeatedly in the court's analysis and is clearly critical to its damage award:

> ". . . the projection of 60% profit in the present case, admitted by Dresser"

> "Hughes's 49% and 54% royalty requests would be 81.6% and 90% of Dresser's projected 60% profits in this case."

> "15% profit" in other Hughes litigation is "considerably lower profit than those projected in the present case."

> "the parties in 1973 projecting 49% [Hughes] to 60% [Dresser] profits."

> "Dresser projected 60% profits on the sale of bits with the '928 seal."

> "Hughes suggests it realized profits of 49% and 54% on its '928 bits sold in the United States and abroad."

> "This figure [25% of sales price] would still have allowed Dresser to realize a large profit on its sales of the bits."

> "Of these various considerations [relevant to setting a reasonable royalty] the expected profit from making and selling the patented invention is the primary consideration."

Before this court Hughes Tool argues: "The magnitude of this 'large profit' of 60% less the royalty award of 25%, left Dresser a 35% profit from sales—as contrasted with its usual profit of 7.2% of sales on all of its products." Hughes's simple arithmetic, however, is a gross distortion of reality.

The evidence of Dresser's projected profitability does not show, as the trial court found and Hughes asserts here, that, in 1973, Dresser was projecting 60% profit on the proposed new product line. Rather, Dresser's projection was a 60% return on the additional investment required to make the bits. Thus, the 60% projection of such return cannot be compared meaningfully with the 7.2% actual profits of 1972.

The evidence . . . on which the district court relied for its finding is set forth below in pertinent part:

> During the year 1973, defendant, Dresser Industries, anticipated that its incremental future sales of Insert Rock Bits with Journal Bearings would provide defendant with profits, on an earnings before tax basis, of not less than 60% of dollar sales of such Rock Bits.
>
> During the year 1973, for the purposes of capital appropriations only, personnel of Defendant at one time forecast that its incremental future sales ascribable to that particular appropriation request of insert Rock Bits with Journal Bearings would provide Defendant with profits, on an earnings before tax basis, of not less than 60% of dollar sales of such Rock Bits.
>
> During its fiscal years 1972 through 1981, defendant, Dresser Industries, was making profits, on a before tax basis, as a percentage of net dollar sales of all of its products and services as set forth below:

YEAR	PROFIT AS % OF NET DOLLAR SALES	NET DOLLAR SALES (Millions)
1972	7.2	906.2
1973	7.1	1,025.2
1974	8.2	1,398.0
1975	11.2	2,011.6
1976	12.2	2,232.2
1977	13.2	2,538.8
1978	12.4	3,054.0
1979	11.8	3,457.4
1980	11.2	4,016.3
1981	11.5	4,614.5

. . . .

The testimony of Dresser's controller, Mr. Munnerlyn, and Hughes Tool's Chief Accounting Officer, Mr. Willis, is consistent with the above evidence that the expected profit on incremental sales would yield a 60% return on incremental investment. There is no evidence to the contrary.

Thus, this case closely parallels *Georgia-Pacific Corp. v. U.S. Plywood-Champion Papers, Inc.*, 446 F.2d 295 (2d Cir.), *cert. denied*, 404 U.S. 870 (1971). The question in *Georgia-Pacific* was the reasonableness of a royalty of $50 per thousand square feet of certain plywood sales. There, the district court (as did the district court here) accepted that a reasonable royalty must be fixed so as to leave the infringer a reasonable profit. To calculate the royalty, the *Georgia-Pacific* trial court erroneously used a figure of $159.41, which represented Georgia Pacific's average "realization" on plywood sales [possibly margin], rather than a figure of $50.00, which represented Georgia Pacific's expected profit on such sales. Thus, the award of a $50.00 royalty, which would leave no profit, was set aside on appeal as excessive.

The royalty of 25% set in this case, being based on a clearly erroneous finding of projected profits of 60% as a percent of sales, is ipso facto arbitrary and must be set aside.

UNILOC USA, Inc. v. Microsoft Corp.

United States Court of Appeals, Federal Circuit

632 F.3d 1292 (Fed. Cir. 2011)

Uniloc USA, Inc. and Uniloc Singapore Private Limited (collectively, "Uniloc") appeal from the decision of the United States District Court for the District of Rhode Island granting Microsoft Corporation's ("Microsoft") motion for judgment as a matter of law ("JMOL") of non-infringement and no willful infringement of asserted claims of Uniloc's U.S. Patent No. 5,490,216 ("'216 patent"), and, in the alternative, granting a new trial on infringement and willfulness. Uniloc USA, Inc. v. Microsoft Corp., 640 F. Supp. 2d 150 (D.R.I. Sept. 29, 2009) ("Uniloc II"). Uniloc also appeals the district court's alternative grant of a new trial on damages.

. . . .

Commercial software manufacturers like Microsoft lose significant sales as a result of the "casual copying" of software, where users install copies of a software program on multiple computers in violation of applicable software license conditions. Uniloc's '216 patent was an early attempt to combat such software piracy. There is no dispute as to the actual functioning of Uniloc's patented invention and Microsoft's accused products . . . .

The jury here awarded Uniloc $388 million, based on the testimony of Uniloc's expert, Dr. Gemini. Dr. Gemini opined that damages should be $564,946,803. This was based on a hypothetical negotiation between Uniloc and Microsoft and the *Georgia-Pacific* factors. *See Georgia-Pacific Corp. v. U.S. Plywood Corp.*, 318 F. Supp. 1116 (S.D.N.Y. 1970). Gemini began with an internal pre-litigation Microsoft document that stated:

> Product Keys are valuable for two major reasons. First, since Product Keys can be used to install a product and create a valid Product ID, you can associate a monetary value to them. An appraisal process found that a Product Key is worth anywhere between $10 and $10,000 depending on usage. Secondly, Product Keys contain short digital signature technology that Microsoft Research created. For these reasons, it is crucial that Product Keys are handled with maximum security.

. . . .

Gemini took the lowest value, $10, and testified that this is "the isolated value of Product Activation." Gemini then applied the so-called "25 percent rule of thumb," hypothesizing that 25% of the value of the product would go to the patent owner and the other 75% would remain with Microsoft, resulting in a baseline royalty rate of $2.50 per license issued. Gemini justified the use of the rule of thumb because it has "been accepted by Courts as an appropriate methodology in determining damages, in [his] experience, in other cases." He then considered several of the *Georgia-Pacific* factors, with the idea being "to adjust this 25% up or down depending on how [the *Georgia-Pacific* factors] favor[] either party." At bottom, he concluded that the factors in favor of Uniloc and Microsoft generally balanced out and did not change the royalty rate. He then multiplied the $2.50 royalty rate by the number of new licenses to Office and Windows products, 225,978,721, to get a final reasonable royalty of $564,946,803. Gemini then "did kind of a check to determine whether that number was reasonable. It's obviously, you know, a significant amount of money. I wanted to check to make sure it was a reasonable number." The "check" was performed by "estimating the gross revenues for the accused products" by multiplying the 225,978,721 licenses by the average sales price per license of $85. The resulting gross revenue value was $19.28 billion. Gemini then calculated that his damages calculation resulted in a royalty rate over the gross revenue of Office and Windows of approximately 2.9%. Gemini presented this information in a demonstrative pie chart to accompany his testimony. In response to Uniloc's attorney's question: "And have you prepared a chart or a graph or a pie chart to show us this comparison?" Uniloc's attorney, Mr. Cronin stated, "Your honor, there's no objection," and Microsoft attorney Mr. Scherkenbach stated, "Right, there is no objection." Gemini then opined that "in my experience, and data I've seen as far as industry royalty rates for software, which are generally above—on average, above 10% or 10, 11%, I felt that this royalty was reasonable and well within that range."

Microsoft had challenged the 25% rule in limine and attempted to exclude Mr. Gemini's testimony. The district court noted that "the concept of a 'rule of thumb' is perplexing in an area of the law where reliability and precision are deemed paramount," but rejected Microsoft's position because the rule has been widely accepted. The district court thus considered the use of the rule of thumb to be reasonable. . . . Microsoft contested Gemini's use of the entire market value rule "check" because Product Activation was not the basis of the consumer demand for Microsoft's Office and Windows products. The district court agreed with Microsoft, and granted a new trial on damages, because the "$19 billion cat was never put back into the bag" and the jury may have "used the $19 billion figure to 'check' its significant award of $388,000,000."

. . . .

1. 25 Percent Rule

Section 284 of Title 35 of the United States Code provides that on finding infringement of a valid patent, damages shall "in no event [be] less than a reasonable royalty for the use made of the invention by the infringer, together with interest and costs as fixed by the court." In litigation, a reasonable royalty is often determined on the basis of a hypothetical negotiation, occurring between the parties at the time that infringement began. *Wang Labs. Inc. v. Toshiba Corp.*, 993 F.2d 858, 869–70 (Fed. Cir. 1993). A reasonable royalty is the predominant measure of damages in patent infringement cases. William C. Rooklidge and Martha K. Gooding, *When Hypothetical Turns to Fantasy: The Patent Reasonable Royalty Hypothetical Negotiation*, BNA Insights Vol. 80:1983, at 701 n. 10 ("*Hypothetical Negotiation*") (citing PriceWaterhouseCoopers, A Closer Look: Patent Litigation Trends and the Increasing Impact of Nonpracticing Entities at 5 (2009)).

The 25 percent rule of thumb is a tool that has been used to approximate the reasonable royalty rate that the manufacturer of a patented product would be willing to offer to pay to the patentee during a hypothetical negotiation. Robert Goldscheider, John Jarosz and Carla Mulhern, *Use Of The 25 Per Cent Rule in Valuing IP*, 37 les Nouvelles 123, 123 (Dec. 2002) ("*Valuing IP*"). "The Rule suggests that the licensee pay a royalty rate equivalent to 25 per cent of its expected profits for the product that incorporates the IP at issue." *Id.* As explained by its leading proponent, Robert Goldscheider, the rule takes the following form:

> An estimate is made of the licensee's expected profits for the product that embodies the IP at issue. Those profits are divided by the expected net sales over that same period to arrive at a profit rate. That resulting profit rate, say 16 per cent, is then multiplied by 25 per cent to arrive at a running royalty rate. In this example, the resulting royalty rate would be 4 per cent. Going forward (or calculating backwards, in the case of litigation), the 4 per cent royalty rate is applied to net sales to arrive at royalty payments due to the IP owner.

Id. at 124. The underlying "assumption is that the licensee should retain a majority (i.e. 75 percent) of the profits, because it has undertaken substantial development, operational and commercialization risks, contributed other technology/IP and/or brought to bear its own development, operational and commercialization contributions." *Id.*

The rule was originally based on Goldscheider's observations of commercial licenses entered into by a "Swiss subsidiary of a large American company, with 18 licensees around the world, each having an exclusive territory." *Id.* The rights transferred were a portfolio of patents and other intellectual property apparently related to the patented products. *Id.* The term of each of these licenses was for three years, with the expectation that the licenses would be renewed. *Id.* at 123. The licensees "faced strong competition," and "were either first or second in sales volume, and probably profitability, in their respective market." *Id.*

According to its proponents, the veracity of the 25 percent rule has been "confirmed by a careful examination of years of licensing and profit data, across companies and industries." John C. Jarosz, Carla S. Mulhern and Michael Wagner, *The 25% Rule Lives On*, IP Law 360, Sept. 8, 2010. Goldscheider published a further empirical study in 2002, concluding that across all industries, the median royalty rate was 22.6 percent, and that the data supported the use of the 25 percent rule "as a tool of analysis." *Valuing IP*, 37 les Nouvelles at 132–33. Additionally, in a 1997 study of licensing organizations, 25 percent of the organizations indicated that they use the 25 percent rule as a starting point in negotiations. Stephen A. Degnan & Corwin Horton, *A Survey of Licensed Royalties*, 32 les Nouvelles 91, 95 (June 1997).

The 25 percent rule has, however, met its share of criticism that can be broadly separated into three categories. First, it fails to account for the unique relationship between the patent and the accused product. *See* Gregory K. Leonard and Lauren J. Stiroh, *Economic Approaches to Intellectual Property Policy, Litigation, and Management*, 949 PLI/Pat 425, 454–55 (Sept.–Nov. 2008) ("[The 25 percent rule] takes no account of the importance of the patent to the profits of the product sold, the potential availability of close substitutes or equally noninfringing alternatives, or any of the other idiosyncrasies of the patent at issue that would have affected a real-world negotiation."); Richard S. Toikka, *Patent Licensing Under Competitive and Non-Competitive Conditions*, 82 J. Pat. & Trademark Off. Soc'y 279, 292–93 (Apr. 2000) (arguing that it fails to "distinguish between monopoly and normal profit . . . . Thus for narrow patents, the rule may be overly generous to the patentee, and for broad patents it may be overly stingy"). Second, it fails to account for the unique relationship between the parties. *See* Ted Hagelin, *Valuation of Patent Licenses*, 12 Tex. Intell. Prop. L.J. 423, 425–26 (Spring 2004) (noting that the rule should not be used in isolation because it fails to "account[] for the different levels of risk assumed by a licensor and licensee"); *Hypothetical Negotiation* at 702 ("[T]he rule is unlikely to have any basis in the accused infringer's industry, in the technology involved in either the patent or the accused product or service, or in the claimed invention's contribution to the infringing product or service."). Finally, the rule is essentially arbitrary and does not fit within the model of the hypothetical negotiation within which it is based. *See* Roy J. Epstein and Alan J. Marcus, *Economic Analysis of the Reasonable Royalty: Simplification and Extension of the Georgia-Pacific Factors*, 85 J. Pat. & Trademark Off. Soc'y 55, 574 (July 2003) ("[The 25% and the 5%] rules of thumb are best understood as special cases [] that may be appropriate to a given situation only by chance."); Roy J. Epstein, Modeling Patent Damages: Rigorous and Defensible Calculations (2003) (paper presented at the AIPLA 2003 Annual Meeting) at 22 available at: http://www.royepstein .com/epstein_aipla_2003_article_website.pdf (last accessed Nov. 19, 2010) (arguing that the 25% rule "shortcut" "is essentially arbitrary. Because it is based on ex post results, it does not necessarily relate to the results of a negotiation that took place prior to the infringement").

The admissibility of the bare 25 percent rule has never been squarely presented to this court. Nevertheless, this court has passively tolerated its use where its acceptability has not been the focus of the case, ... Lower courts have invariably admitted evidence based on the 25% rule, largely in reliance on its widespread acceptance or because its admissibility was uncontested. . . .

This court now holds as a matter of Federal Circuit law that the 25 percent rule of thumb is a fundamentally flawed tool for determining a baseline royalty rate in a hypothetical negotiation. Evidence relying on the 25 percent rule of thumb is thus inadmissible under . . . the Federal Rules of Evidence, because it fails to tie a reasonable royalty base to the facts of the case at issue . . . .

The meaning of [our precedent] is clear: there must be a basis in fact to associate the royalty rates used in prior licenses to the particular hypothetical negotiation at issue in the case. The 25 percent rule of thumb as an abstract and largely theoretical construct fails to satisfy this fundamental requirement. The rule does not say anything about a particular hypothetical negotiation or reasonable royalty involving any particular technology, industry, or party. Relying on the 25 percent rule of thumb in a reasonable royalty calculation is far more unreliable and irrelevant than reliance on parties' unrelated licenses . . . . [T]he 25 percent rule of thumb would predict that the same 25%/75% royalty split would begin royalty discussions between, for example, (a) TinyCo and IBM over a strong patent portfolio of twelve patents covering various aspects of a pioneering hard drive, and (b) Kodak and Fuji over a single patent to a tiny improvement in a specialty film emulsion . . . .

To be admissible, expert testimony opining on a reasonable royalty rate must "carefully tie proof of damages to the claimed invention's footprint in the market place."[citation omitted] This court has sanctioned the use of the *Georgia-Pacific* factors to frame the reasonable royalty inquiry. Those factors properly tie the reasonable royalty calculation to the facts of the hypothetical negotiation at issue. This court's rejection of the 25 percent rule of thumb is not intended to limit the application of any of the *Georgia-Pacific* factors. In particular, factors 1 and 2 — looking at royalties paid or received in licenses for the patent in suit or in comparable licenses — and factor 12 — looking at the portion of profit that may be customarily allowed in the particular business for the use of the invention or similar inventions — remain valid and important factors in the determination of a reasonable royalty rate. However, evidence purporting to apply to these, and any other factors, must be tied to the relevant facts and circumstances of the particular case at issue and the hypothetical negotiations that would have taken place in light of those facts and circumstances at the relevant time.

In this case, it is clear that Gemini's testimony was based on the use of the 25% rule of thumb as an arbitrary, general rule, unrelated to the facts of this case. When asked the basis of his opinion that the rule of thumb would apply here, Gemini testified: "[i]t's generally accepted. I've used it. I've seen others use it. It's a widely accepted rule." Upon further questioning, Dr. Gemini revealed that he had been involved in only four or five non-litigation related negotiations, and had recommended the 25% rule only once in a case involving a power tool. He did not testify that the parties here had a practice of beginning negotiations with a 25%/75% split, or that the contribution of Product Activation to Office and Word justified such a split. He did not base his 25 percent baseline on other licenses involving the patent at issue or comparable licenses. In short, Gemini's starting point of a 25 percent royalty had no relation to the facts of the case, and as such, was arbitrary, unreliable, and irrelevant. The use of such a rule fails to pass muster under [*Daubert v. Merrell Dow Pharmaceuticals, Inc.*, 509 U.S. 579 (1993)] and taints the jury's damages calculation.

This court thus holds that Microsoft is entitled to a new trial on damages.

Notes & Questions

1. Why did the Federal Circuit in *Hughes Tool* reject the special magistrate's decision to use a 60 percent figure for projected profits in determining damages? Does the Federal Circuit offer an alternative approach? If so, what effect would this approach have on damages? Is the analysis in *Hughes Tool* still valid after *Uniloc*?

2. How does a decision like *Hughes Tool* affect negotiations for start-up companies over the licensing of intellectual property? Do you think the decision would lead potential licensors and licensees to adopt more specific terms, such as liquidated damage clauses, to specify a reasonably royalty in terms of breach?

3. The court in *Uniloc* refers with approval to factors for consideration in determining a reasonable royalty that were first described in *Georgia-Pacific Corp. v. U.S. Plywood Corp.*, 318 F. Supp. 1116 (S.D.N.Y. 1970), *judgment modified*, 446 F.2d 295 (2d Cir.), *cert. denied*, 404 U.S. 870 (1971). These factors include:

1. The royalties received by the patentee for the licensing of the patent in suit, proving or tending to prove an established royalty.

2. The rates paid by the licensee for the use of other patents comparable to the patent in suit.

3. The nature and scope of the license, as exclusive or non-exclusive; or as restricted or non-restricted in terms of territory or with respect to whom the manufactured product may be sold.

4. The licensor's established policy and marketing program to maintain his patent monopoly by not licensing others to use the invention or by granting licenses under special conditions designed to preserve that monopoly.

5. The commercial relationship between the licensor and licensee, such as, whether they are competitors in the same territory in the same line of business; or whether they are inventor and promoter.

6. The effect of selling the patented specialty in promoting sales of other products of the licensee; that existing value of the invention to the licensor as a generator of sales of his non-patented items; and the extent of such derivative or convoyed sales.

7. The duration of the patent and the term of the license.

8. The established profitability of the product made under the patent; its commercial success; and its current popularity.

9. The utility and advantages of the patent property over the old modes or devices, if any, that had been used for working out similar results.

10. The nature of the patented invention; the character of the commercial embodiment of it as owned and produced by the licensor; and the benefits to those who have used the invention.

11. The extent to which the infringer has made use of the invention; and any evidence probative of the value of that use.

12. The portion of the profit or of the selling price that may be customary in the particular business or in comparable businesses to allow for the use of the invention or analogous inventions.

13. The portion of the realizable profit that should be credited to the invention as distinguished from non-patented elements, the manufacturing process, business risks, or significant features or improvements added by the infringer.

14. The opinion testimony of qualified experts.

15. The amount that a licensor (such as the patentee) and a licensee (such as the infringer) would have agreed upon (at the time the infringement began) if both had been reasonably and voluntarily trying to reach an agreement; that is, the amount which a prudent licensee — who desired, as a business proposition, to obtain a license to manufacture and sell a particular article embodying the patented invention- would have been willing to pay as a royalty and yet be able to make a reasonable profit and which amount would have been acceptable by a prudent patentee who was willing to grant a license.

Georgia-Pacific, supra, 318 F. Supp. at 1120.

4. The reading by Professor Hagelin identifies three ways to value intellectual property: the cost method, the market method, and the income method. Professor Hagelin discusses these methods as a way to determine royalty rates for licenses. Do these methods have any applicability to the calculation of damages? If so, which one is the most appropriate? How does Professor Hagelin's proposed CAV method compare to these other three in determining damages?

5. Suppose a potential investor in Dr. See's company asks for a valuation of the patents that Dr. See has obtained and any trade secrets he may have. How would you proceed to address the investor's valuation question?

C. Avoiding Forfeitures of Intellectual Property Interests

Patent Act

Conditions for Patentability; Novelty and Loss of Right to Patent

35 USC § 102 (2001)(text as interpreted in the *Pfaff* case below; since amended effective 2013)

A person shall be entitled to a patent unless—

(a) the invention was known or used by others in this country, or patented or described in a printed publication in this or a foreign country, before the invention thereof by the applicant for patent,

or

(b) the invention was patented or described in a printed publication in this or a foreign country or in public use or on sale in this country, more than one year prior to the date of the application for patent in the United States, . . .

Copyright Act

Registration and Infringement Actions

17 USC § 411 (2002)

(a) . . . no action for infringement of the copyright in any United States work shall be instituted until registration of the copyright claim has been made in accordance with this title. In any case, however, where the deposit, application, and fee required for registration have been delivered to the Copyright Office in proper form and registration has been refused, the applicant is entitled to institute an action for infringement if notice thereof, with a copy of the complaint, is served on the Register of Copyrights. The Register may, at his or her option, become a party to the action with respect to the issue of registrability of the copyright claim by entering an appearance within sixty days after such service, but the Register's failure to become a party shall not deprive the court of jurisdiction to determine that issue.

Pfaff v. Wells Electronics, Inc.

United States Supreme Court 525 U.S. 55 (1998)

Justice Stevens delivered the opinion of the Court.

Section 102(b) of the Patent Act of 1952 provides that no person is entitled to patent an "invention" that has been "on sale" more than one year before filing a patent application. We granted certiorari to determine whether the commercial marketing of a newly invented product may mark the beginning of the 1-year period even though the invention has not yet been reduced to practice.

I

On April 19, 1982, petitioner, Wayne Pfaff, filed an application for a patent on a computer chip socket. Therefore, April 19, 1981, constitutes the critical date for purposes of the on-sale bar of 35 U.S.C. § 102(b); if the 1-year period began to run before that date, Pfaff lost his right to patent his invention.

Pfaff commenced work on the socket in November 1980, when representatives of Texas Instruments asked him to develop a new device for mounting and removing semiconductor chip carriers. In response to this request, he prepared detailed engineering drawings that described the design, the dimensions, and the materials to be used in making the socket. Pfaff sent those drawings to a manufacturer in February or March 1981.

Prior to March 17, 1981, Pfaff showed a sketch of his concept to representatives of Texas Instruments. On April 8, 1981, they provided Pfaff with a written confirmation of a previously placed oral purchase order for 30,100 of his new sockets for a total price of $91,155. In accord with his normal practice, Pfaff did not make and test a prototype of the new device before offering to sell it in commercial quantities.

The manufacturer took several months to develop the customized tooling necessary to produce the device, and Pfaff did not fill the order until July 1981. The evidence therefore indicates that Pfaff first reduced his invention to practice in the summer of 1981. The socket achieved substantial commercial success before Patent No. 4,491,377 ('377 patent) issued to Pfaff on January 1, 1985.

After the patent issued, petitioner brought an infringement action against respondent, Wells Electronics, Inc., the manufacturer of a competing socket. Wells prevailed on the basis of a finding of no infringement. When respondent began to market a modified device, petitioner brought this suit, alleging that the modifications infringed six of the claims in the '377 patent.

After a full evidentiary hearing before a Special Master, the District Court held that two of those claims (1 and 6) were invalid because they had been anticipated in the prior art. . . . Adopting the Special Master's findings, the District Court rejected respondent's § 102(b) defense because Pfaff had filed the application for the '377 patent less than a year after reducing the invention to practice.

The Court of Appeals reversed, finding all six claims invalid. 124 F.3d 1429 (C.A. Fed. 1997). Four of the claims (1, 6, 7, and 10) described the socket that Pfaff had sold to Texas Instruments prior to April 8, 1981. Because that device had been offered for sale on a commercial basis more than one year before the patent application was filed on April 19, 1982, the court concluded that those claims were invalid under § 102(b). That conclusion rested on the court's view that as long as the invention was "substantially complete at the time of sale," the 1-year period began to run, even though the invention had not yet been reduced to practice. *Id.* at 1434. The other two claims (11 and 19) described a feature that had not been included in Pfaff's initial design, but the Court of Appeals concluded as a matter of law that the additional feature was not itself patentable because it was an obvious addition to the prior art. Given the court's § 102(b) holding, the prior art included Pfaff's first four claims.

Because other courts have held or assumed that an invention cannot be "on sale" within the meaning of § 102(b) unless and until it has been reduced to practice, *see, e.g., Timely Products Corp. v. Arron*, 523 F.2d 288, 299–302 (C.A.2 1975); *Dart Industries, Inc. v. E.I. du Pont De Nemours & Co.*, 489 F.2d 1359, 1365, n. 11 (C.A.7 1973), cert. *denied*, 417 U.S. 933, 94 S. Ct. 2645, 41 L. Ed. 2d 236 (1974), and because the text of § 102(b) makes no reference to "substantial completion" of an invention, we granted certiorari. 523 U.S. 1003, 118 S. Ct. 1183, 140 L. Ed. 2d 315 (1998).

II

The primary meaning of the word "invention" in the Patent Act unquestionably refers to the inventor's conception rather than to a physical embodiment of that idea. The statute does not contain any express requirement that an invention must be reduced to practice before it can be patented. Neither the statutory definition of the term in § 100 nor the basic conditions for obtaining a patent set forth in § 101 make any mention of "reduction to practice." The statute's only specific reference to that term is found in § 102(g), which sets forth the standard for resolving priority contests between two competing claimants to a patent. That subsection provides:

> "In determining priority of invention there shall be considered not only the respective dates of conception and reduction to practice of the invention, but also the reasonable diligence of one who was first to conceive and last to reduce to practice, from a time prior to conception by the other."

Thus, assuming diligence on the part of the applicant, it is normally the first inventor to conceive, rather than the first to reduce to practice, who establishes the right to the patent.

It is well settled that an invention may be patented before it is reduced to practice. In 1888, this Court upheld a patent issued to Alexander Graham Bell even though he had filed his application before constructing a working telephone. . . . When we apply the reasoning of *The Telephone Cases* [, 126 U.S. 1 (1888),] to the facts of the case before us today, it is evident that Pfaff could have obtained a patent on his novel socket when he accepted the purchase order from Texas Instruments for 30,100 units. At that time he provided the manufacturer with a description and drawings that had "sufficient clearness and precision to enable those skilled in the matter" to produce the device. *Id.*, at 536. The parties agree that the sockets manufactured to fill that order embody Pfaff's conception as set forth in claims 1, 6, 7, and 10 of the '377 patent. We can find no basis in the text of § 102(b) or in the facts of this case for concluding that Pfaff's invention was not "on sale" within the meaning of the statute until after it had been reduced to practice.

III

Pfaff nevertheless argues that longstanding precedent, buttressed by the strong interest in providing inventors with a clear standard identifying the onset of the 1-year period, justifies a special interpretation of the word "invention" as used in § 102(b). We are persuaded that this nontextual argument should be rejected.

[Section] 102 of the Patent Act serves as a limiting provision, both excluding ideas that are in the public domain from patent protection and confining the duration of the monopoly to the statutory term.

We originally held that an inventor loses his right to a patent if he puts his invention into public use before filing a patent application. "His voluntary act or acquiescence in the public sale and use is an abandonment of his right." *Pennock v. Dialogue*, 7 L. Ed. 327, 2 Pet. 1, 24 (1829) (Story, J.). A similar reluctance to allow an inventor to remove existing knowledge from public use undergirds the on-sale bar.

Nevertheless, an inventor who seeks to perfect his discovery may conduct extensive testing without losing his right to obtain a patent for his invention — even if such testing occurs in the public eye. The law has long recognized the distinction between inventions put to experimental use and products sold commercially. In 1878, we explained why patentability may turn on an inventor's use of his product.

> "It is sometimes said that an inventor acquires an undue advantage over the public by delaying to take out a patent, inasmuch as he thereby preserves the monopoly to himself for a longer period than is allowed by the policy of the law; but this cannot be said with justice when the delay is occasioned by a bona fide effort to bring his invention to perfection, or to ascertain whether it will answer the purpose intended. His monopoly only continues for the allotted period, in any event; and it is the interest of the public, as well as himself, that the invention should be perfect and properly tested, before a patent is granted for it. Any attempt to use it for a profit, and not by way of experiment, for a longer period than two years before the application, would deprive the inventor of his right to a patent." *Elizabeth v. American Nicholson Pavement Co.*, 97 U.S. 126, 137, 24 L. Ed. 1000 (1877).

The patent laws therefore seek both to protect the public's right to retain knowledge already in the public domain and the inventor's right to control whether and when he may patent his invention. The Patent Act of 1836, 5 Stat. 117, was the first statute that expressly included an on-sale bar to the issuance of a patent. Like the earlier holding in *Pennock*, that provision precluded patentability if the invention had been placed on sale at any time before the patent application was filed. In 1839, Congress ameliorated that requirement by enacting a 2-year grace period in which the inventor could file an application. 5 Stat. 353 . . . .

Petitioner correctly argues that these provisions identify an interest in providing inventors with a definite standard for determining when a patent application must be filed. A rule that makes the timeliness of an application depend on the date when an invention is "substantially complete" seriously undermines the interest in certainty. Moreover, such a rule finds no support in the text of the statute. Thus, petitioner's argument calls into question the standard applied by the Court of Appeals, but it does not persuade us that it is necessary to engraft a reduction to practice element into the meaning of the term "invention" as used in § 102(b).

The word "invention" must refer to a concept that is complete, rather than merely one that is "substantially complete." It is true that reduction to practice ordinarily provides the best evidence that an invention is complete. But just because reduction to practice is sufficient evidence of completion, it does not follow that proof of reduction to practice is necessary in every case. Indeed, both the facts of *The Telephone Cases* and the facts of this case demonstrate that one can prove that an invention is complete and ready for patenting before it has actually been reduced to practice.

We conclude, therefore, that the on-sale bar applies when two conditions are satisfied before the critical date. First, the product must be the subject of a commercial offer for sale. An inventor can both understand and control the timing of the first commercial marketing of his invention. The experimental use doctrine, for example, has not generated concerns about indefiniteness, and we perceive no reason why unmanageable uncertainty should attend a rule that measures the application of the on-sale bar of § 102(b) against the date when an invention that is ready for patenting is first marketed commercially. In this case the acceptance of the purchase order prior to April 8, 1981, makes it clear that such an offer had been made, and there is no question that the sale was commercial rather than experimental in character.

Second, the invention must be ready for patenting. That condition may be satisfied in at least two ways: by proof of reduction to practice before the critical date; or by proof that prior to the critical date the inventor had prepared drawings or other descriptions of the invention that were sufficiently specific to enable a person skilled in the art to practice the invention. In this case the second condition of the on-sale bar is satisfied because the drawings Pfaff sent to the manufacturer before the critical date fully disclosed the invention . . . . When Pfaff accepted the purchase order for his new sockets prior to April 8, 1981, his invention was ready for patenting. The fact that the manufacturer was able to produce the socket using his detailed drawings and specifications demonstrates this fact. Furthermore, those sockets contained all the elements of the invention claimed in the '377 patent. Therefore, Pfaff's '377 patent is invalid because the invention had been on sale for more than one year in this country before he filed his patent application. Accordingly, the judgment of the Court of Appeals is affirmed.

Notes & Questions

1. This section revisits some of the issues discussed at the beginning of the chapter, particularly the issues relating to identifying ideas and innovations potentially protected by intellectual property law. Rethink the question raised previously: What is the best time to first discuss a business plan with an attorney? Would Pfaff have benefited from working with counsel earlier in the invention and dissemination process? When would intervention have been helpful?

2. How would you advise Dr. See in light of the Supreme Court's decision in *Pfaff*? Notice that Dr. See already has obtained several patents. The problem that may arise as Dr. See speaks with potential investors is that of follow-on inventions. Dr. See must be careful that he does not "give away" potentially patentable inventions as he speaks with the public. How would you advise Dr. See to avoid this problem?

3. Software inventions can be protected by both patent law and copyright law. Patent law protects software as a process when it produces a concrete, tangible, and useful result, but does not protect the written code. Instead, copyright protects the written code, and derivatives, as a literary work, but does not protect any methods or processes. Are patent and copyright complementary? Suppose one of the investors wants to inspect Dr. See's code. How would you advise Dr. See on satisfying this request? Keep in mind that in addition to patent and copyright, trade secret law also protects software.

4. Suppose Dr. See suspects that a former colleague is infringing the copyright in his software. Dr. See has not registered the copyright. Can he bring suit? There is a circuit split on how this situation is handled. The Second Circuit, for instance, will dismiss the complaint if the copyright has not been registered. *See Well-Made Toy Mfg. Corp. v. Goffa Intern Corp.*, 354 F.3d 112 (2d Cir. 2003); *Morris v. Business Concepts Inc.*, 283 F.3d 502 (2d Cir. 2002). Other circuits permit the complaint to be amended once registration has been obtained. *See Syntek Semiconductor Co. Ltd. v. Microchip Technology Inc.*, 285 F.3d 857 (9th Cir. 2002); *Bouchat v. Baltimore Ravens, Inc.*, 228 F.3d 489 (4th Cir. 2000); *Raquel v. Education Management Corp.*, 196 F.3d 171 (3d Cir. 1999). Notice that under the Copyright Act, the copyright owner loses the right to obtain statutory damages and attorney's fees and costs if she fails to register either before the work is published or within three months of publication.

5. Is the *Pfaff* decision still good law after the America Invents Act moving the US patent system to a first inventor to file system? The amended version of 35 U.S.C. § 102(b), which went into effect on March 16, 2013, creates a one year safe harbor for disclosures of an invention made by the inventor or someone who obtained the subject matter disclosed from the inventor. The new version of § 102(a) maintains the "on sale bar" precluding a patent if a sale of an invention was made before the date of filing of a related patent application. Is a sale, under § 102(a), sufficient to create a disclosure under § 102(b)? No court has ruled on this issue, but an argument raised by some practitioners and scholars is that a sale is separately addressed in the statute and should not be treated as a type of disclosure. This interpretation would eliminate the one year safe harbor for the on sale bar. For an analysis of this issue, see the comments by Professor Robert Merges to the USPTO, available at: http://www.uspto.gov/patents/law/comments/r-merges_20121012.pdf.

6. How about intellectual property protection in other countries? Although our primary focus is on the issues confronting intellectual property-related businesses in the United States, it is worth noting that most countries other than the United States adopt an absolute priority rule, meaning that the ability to patent is forfeited

for any disclosure of the invention prior to the date of application. On the other hand, other countries are less formalistic and more flexible when it comes to registration of copyright.

D. Tax and Accounting Issues Raised by Intellectual Property

Joseph Bankman & Ronald J. Gilson, Why Start-Ups?

51 STANFORD LAW REVIEW 289 (1999)*

Assume that we have a risk-neutral, established employer and a group of risk-averse engineers. Each of the engineers is competent at pursuing the employer's ongoing business—normal science—and each has a positive probability of developing an innovation that would give rise to a new business. Neither the engineers nor the employer can identify ex ante which of the engineers actually will develop the innovation. The obvious risk-sharing arrangement is for the employer to hire all the engineers, pay each the mean expected value of the group, and receive in return the engineers' contribution to the employer's ongoing business and all discoveries made by any of them.

Of course, once the uncertainty is eliminated—when the passage of time reveals which engineers have won the innovation lottery—the engineers' attraction to ex ante risk sharing gives way to an incentive for ex post opportunism. The winning engineer wants to keep the discovery for herself. Thus, the risk-sharing arrangement must have some characteristics that protect it from the corrosive effect of learning which engineer wins. And it should be apparent that, whatever the arrangement, it is not perfect. There must be a problem in prospectively transferring ownership of the engineers' discoveries to the employer. If the property rights could be fully specified and transferred ex ante, we would not observe start-ups. Thus, the puzzle is premised on a contracting failure.

However, contracting failure alone is insufficient to account for the existence of start-ups. Even if the employee retains some property right in her discovery, commercializing the idea requires starting a business. In return for some portion of the future earnings from the innovation, other parties still must put up the factors of production the employee lacks: (1) capital; and (2) managerial, manufacturing, and marketing expertise. A conventional solution to this problem is venture capital financing. A venture capital fund contributes capital to the start-up as well as non-capital contributions such as management consulting, monitoring, and reputation, in return for an ownership stake in the start-up. But suppose we recharacterize the venture capital process as an auction. The engineer leaving her position with the

---

employer is selling off a portion of her innovation to the highest bidder. When all else is equal, the employer has advantages — tax, information, and scope — that should result in it consistently winning the auction.

A. The Employer's Tax Advantage

Under current law, the tax treatment of corporate investment depends on the tax history of the organization making that investment. An investment made by a company with sources of past or present income is subject to a symmetrical tax regime: The expenses of the investment are deductible and produce tax savings, while the gains from investment are subject to tax. An investment carried out by a start-up, in contrast, is subject to an asymmetrical tax regime: Gains are fully taxed, but losses may be deducted only against future income. As discussed in more detail below, this difference in tax regime operates in the circumstance of interest here to provide a substantial subsidy for an employer's efforts to develop an employee's innovation internally.

Under Internal Revenue Code (I.R.C.) § 172, a start-up may deduct expenses only against income — expenses in excess of current income (a net operating loss) may generally be carried forward for fifteen years and deducted against future income. In contrast, a company with sources of past or present income from other activities — we will call it an "established company" — may deduct expenses of the start-up activity that exceed start-up activity income as they are incurred: The expenses of the start-up activity are set off against the income from other activities. The significance of the divergent tax treatment of innovation expenses incurred by established companies on the one hand, and start-ups on the other, depends on the timing for tax purposes of expenses and income. For a number of reasons, the consequences of this divergent tax treatment are likely to be particularly important for start-ups.

First, a significant number of start-up companies never earn profits. For these companies, the limitation on deductibility amounts to a permanent loss of the tax benefit. For more successful start-ups that ultimately do earn profits, the combination of staged financing, often involving new investors at each round, and the exercise of employee stock options, likely will result in an identifiable group of five percent shareholders increasing their ownership interests by at least fifty percentage points within a three-year period. This triggers a change of ownership under I.R.C. § 382 which, in turn, sharply restricts the value of the net operating loss. Even companies that reach profitability within the carry forward period and escape the change of ownership limitation still require many years before generating sufficient taxable incomes to take full advantage of early losses. Thus, the tax benefit of the eventual deduction is limited by the loss of value inherent in deferral.

For new ventures carried out by established companies the tax picture is quite different. Such companies face no special limitations on otherwise deductible expenses, and the availability of tax credits and deductions for research and development ensures that most expenses of internally developing an innovation can be immediately offset against income from other activities. Expressed in terms of net present value, the effect of the tax differential is quite stark. Consider, for example, an investment that costs $100 in year one and has the following probability distribution of returns: a 40 percent chance of returning nothing; a 40 percent chance of returning $100 in year ten; and a 10 percent chance of returning $700 in years six through twelve. At a discount rate of 15 percent (quite conservative in light of the 40 to 60 percent rate said to be applied by venture capitalists), the investment has a net present value of approximately $141.

Now assume that the combined state and federal tax rate is 40 percent; that an established company is able to deduct the investment ratably over three years; and that the company is able to gross up the investment by the present value of the tax savings. The investment now shows an after-tax present value of approximately $135. The relatively small reduction in present value as a result of the 40 percent tax reflects that the value of deducting the venture's losses in the first few years offsets most of the future tax on the later occurring venture income. In contrast, a start-up loses the entire deduction on the investments that never generate profit, and loses most of the present value of the deduction for break-even and successful investments. As a result, the after-tax net present value of the investment to the start-up is only $95 — $5 less than its cost, and $40 less than the value of the same investment to an established company.

Our analysis thus far has focused only on the corporate tax. A more complete analysis would also include the tax paid by shareholders of start-ups on the proceeds from the sale of their stock. In general, taking the shareholder-level tax into account would lessen the start-up's disadvantage. For unsuccessful start-ups, the inability to deduct expenses would exacerbate losses on the corporate level and lead to greater losses on the shareholder level; for successful start-ups, the deferral of deduction at the corporate level would reduce gains at the shareholder level. In either event, the result would be a reduction in shareholder-level tax. Tax savings at the shareholder level, however, would be of second-order magnitude. At best, given a 40 percent combined state and federal tax rate, shareholders would recoup only 40 percent of the tax disadvantage experienced by the corporate start-up. In all cases, this partial recoupment of the tax disadvantage would require disposal of the underlying stock. For unsuccessful investments, such recoupment would be hampered by I.R.C. limitations on deduction of capital losses. . . .

Syms Corp. v. Commissioner of Revenue

Supreme Judicial Court of Massachusetts 765 N.E.2d 758 (Sup. Ct. Mass. 2002)

1. Background. Syms is a New Jersey corporation engaged in "off-price" retailing, which is the retail sale of brand name clothing at prices lower than those in department stores. It was founded in 1959 by Sy Syms. It operates two stores in the Commonwealth and therefore is subject to Massachusetts corporate excise tax.

During the years in question, Sy Syms was the chairman of the board of directors and the dominant shareholder, owning fifty-six per cent of the stock and controlling the votes for another twenty-four per cent held in trust for family members. His daughter, Marcy Syms, was the president of the company.

Syms used several marks in its business, including the "Syms" name, a "multiple 'S' logo" that it placed on its own brands of clothing, and the slogan, "An Educated Consumer is Our Best Customer." Prior to December, 1986, Syms owned these marks.

The idea of a trademark holding subsidiary was first brought to the attention of Syms in early 1986 by Irv Yacht, a consultant with a company called Coventry Financial Corporation. Yacht broached this idea in a letter to Syms's chief financial officer, Richard Diamond, in which he promised that he "had a method of saving state taxes." Immediately after their first meeting in the spring of 1986, Yacht and Diamond signed an agreement, which recited that Coventry "has developed a program . . . for reducing [Syms's] income taxes by reorganizing the business activities of [Syms] in certain areas." Yacht's proposal was for Syms to form a Delaware subsidiary, transfer the marks to that subsidiary, and then execute a license agreement under which Syms would continue to use the marks as it had before the transfer (Coventry plan).

Under the license agreement, Syms would pay a large royalty to the subsidiary, thereby generating a deduction for Syms on its State excise taxes. The subsidiary, however, would not pay any State tax on the royalty income because, under Delaware law, corporations that hold intangible assets are exempt from income tax. Syms was to pay Coventry twenty-five per cent of the tax savings realized in the first year, with a declining percentage for the next four years.

In considering whether to engage in the Coventry plan, Syms recognized the risk of a tax audit. In a memorandum to Sy Syms, Diamond wrote, "There have been cases when corporations attempted to do this and did not do it properly and thus had problems in various states. It is everyone[']s feeling that New York is the most sophisticated state in terms of tax audits and most other states will not even realize the impact of the transactions." As a precaution, Syms held part of Coventry's compensation in escrow in case the hoped-for tax savings were disallowed in an audit.

Syms also consulted its trademark attorneys about risks attendant to the transfer of the marks under trademark law, and was advised that the transfer would be valid as a matter of trademark law because "Syms Corp. will own and control the subsidiary. Whether or not the subsidiary is an active entity, its assets (consisting of the trademarks) belong to the parent company. Syms Corp. will, in fact, continue to stand behind the goods and services identified by these marks."

Syms decided to proceed with the Coventry plan and SYL was incorporated in Delaware on December 4, 1986, as Syms's wholly owned trademark holding company. Its board of directors and officers were Sy Syms, Marcy Syms, Richard Diamond, and Edward Jones, a partner in a Delaware accounting firm. SYL and Syms executed a license agreement on December 18, 1986. SYL, acting as the owner of the marks, granted to Syms the right to use the marks nationally for a royalty equal to four per cent of Syms's annual net sales. The marks were transferred from Syms to SYL the next day, December 19, 1986.

For the calendar year 1986, Syms paid SYL a royalty for the marks that consti-tuted four per cent of its annual net sales from October 1, 1986, until the end of December. The 1986 royalty was approximately $2.8 million. In subsequent years, the royalty amount increased from nearly $10 million in 1987 to $12.7 million in 1991. In each of these years SYL received one annual royalty payment from Syms, which it held in Delaware for a few weeks before paying it back to Syms, with inter-est (minus expenses) as a tax-free dividend. SYL's only income came from Syms's annual royalty payments, and its expenses amounted to approximately one-tenth of one per cent of its income.

SYL's corporate "office" consisted of an address rented from Jones's Delaware accounting firm, for an annual fee of $1,200. The accounting firm provided this same service to "a couple of hundred" other corporations that used Delaware subsidiary corporations to hold their intangible assets. Jones was not only a partner of the accounting firm, he was SYL's only employee, serving in a part-time capacity for which he was paid $1,200 per year.

The business operations of Syms did not change after the transfer and license-back of the marks. All of the work necessary to maintain and protect the marks contin-ued to be done by the same New York City trademark law firm that had previously performed those services, and Syms (not SYL) continued to pay all the expenses attendant thereto. All efforts to maintain the good will and thus to preserve the value of the marks were undertaken by Syms, and all advertising using the marks was con-trolled and paid for by Syms or by a wholly owned Syms subsidiary formed solely to do advertising. The choice of which products would be sold under the marks, as well as the quality control of those products, remained the responsibility of the same per-sons who had done that work before the transfer—Sy Syms himself, and the Syms staff of buyers.

2. Sham transaction. Syms does not contest the validity of the "sham transaction doctrine" and the commissioner's authority under that doctrine to disregard, for tax-ing purposes, transactions that have no economic substance or business purpose other than tax avoidance. It is a doctrine long established in State and Federal tax jurisprudence dating back to the seminal case of *Gregory v. Helvering*, 293 U.S. 465, 55 S. Ct. 266, 79 L. Ed. 596 (1935). It works to prevent taxpayers from claiming the tax benefits of transactions that, although within the language of the tax code, are not the type of transactions the law intended to favor with the benefit. "Usually, trans-actions that are invalidated by the doctrine are those motivated by nothing other than the taxpayer's desire to secure the attached tax benefit," and are structured to completely avoid economic risk.

Syms contends that the doctrine does not apply in this case because it had busi-ness purposes, other than tax avoidance, for incorporating SYL and then transfer-ring to it and licensing back the marks which it previously owned. It complains that the board ignored the "uncontroverted" evidence of these other business purposes, and based its decision on the record in another case litigated shortly after this one, and on an across-the-board policy of the "disallowance of deductions for all related trademark protection companies."

The question whether or not a transaction is a sham for purposes of the application of the doctrine is, of necessity, primarily a factual one, on which the taxpayer bears the burden of proof in the abatement process. . . .

The board found that the transfer and license back transaction had no practical economic effect on Syms other than the creation of tax benefits, and that tax avoidance was the clear motivating factor and its only business purpose. The board rejected the other business purposes claimed by Syms during the hearing, finding them to be "illusory, not supported by the evidence, or contrary to the weight of the evidence."

[Syms proffered, and the board rejected, almost a dozen nontax business purposes to support its claim that the transfer and license-back was not intended solely to avoid taxation. For example: Syms's assertion that the transfer would protect the marks from claims of Syms's creditors was rejected by the board, because creditors could reach assets of Syms's wholly owned subsidiary; Syms's claim that the transfer would protect the marks from a hostile takeover was rejected, because Syms could only have achieved that goal by transferring the marks to an independent third party, and with eighty per cent of the stock controlled by the company founder, such a takeover was hypothetical at best; Syms's claim that the transfer would result in better management of the marks was rejected because Syms retained the same responsibilities for managing and maintaining the marks after the transfer; and Syms's assertion that the formation of the subsidiary would enhance Syms's ability to borrow funds was rejected because creditors would have viewed the two entities as intermingled and would not have offered any different financing arrangements, Syms's founder strenuously opposed borrowing money, and the subsidiary never borrowed any money.]

While there may be many important business purposes attendant to the transfer and licensing back of intangible assets within corporate families, to be viable for the purposes claimed by Syms, they must be more than theoretical musings, concocted to provide faint cover for the creation of a tax deduction.

3. Ordinary and necessary expense. General Laws c. 63, § 1 ("[n]et income"), provides that corporations may take business deductions allowable under the Internal Revenue Code (Code). Under the Code, only "ordinary and necessary" business expense deductions are allowable. I.R.C. § 162. Deductions are not permitted if the expense was "created solely for the purpose of effectuating a camouflaged assignment of income." . . . As an alternative ground for the disallowance of Syms's deduction for royalty expense, the board concurred with the commissioner's position that the royalty payments were not an "ordinary and necessary" business expense.

The board found that the value of the marks had been created entirely by Syms, and, even after their transfer and the payment of the royalties, Syms continued to pay the expenses associated with owning them, including the legal expenses incurred in maintaining them. It concluded that, in such circumstances, Syms's royalty payments to SYL for the use of the marks was unnecessary. In effect, Syms was paying twice for their use. The board further reasoned that it was irrelevant that the measure of royalty payments might have been equivalent to what would have been paid in an arm's-length transaction where, as here, the payments were not for services provided by SYL but rather part of a contrived mechanism by which affiliated entities shifted income, tax free, between themselves in a circular transaction for the benefit of Syms.

Syms counters that, having validly transferred the trademarks to SYL in consideration for receipt of SYL stock, it was required to pay royalty fees, and, therefore, they were a necessary business expense. It also argues that there is no requirement that owners add value to assets before allowing their use by another entity, and that the sole test whether the royalty payments are deductible is whether they were made at "arm's length."

These arguments closely mirror those made on the question whether the transfer and license back of the marks constituted a "sham" transaction. The central issue for the court to decide is whether the board's finding that there was no business reason for Syms to incur the expense of millions of dollars in royalties other than to create tax deductions is supported by the record. As we have already concluded, it is. The royalty expense to Syms "resulted not as an ordinary, necessary incident in the conduct of the taxpayer's business, but instead was created solely for the purpose of effectuating a camouflaged assignment of income. It was properly disallowed.

4. Penalties. The board acted within its discretion in refusing to abate penalties levied on Syms. General Laws c. 62C, § 33(f), provides for an abatement of penalties "[i]f it is shown that any failure to file a return or to pay a tax in a timely manner is due to reasonable cause and not due to willful neglect." . . . Here, the board found that the plan was not drafted or reviewed by a competent tax professional on behalf of Syms. An internal company memorandum submitted by Syms indicated that the plan had been "looked at" by "Mann Judd Landau," who believed that it was "within the state tax laws," but that "[t]hey can not give an opinion as to what might occur during a tax audit." On this record, the board was within its discretion to conclude that the taxpayer had not relied on the advice of a competent tax professional, had understood the risks inherent in the tax plan, and, therefore, its failure timely to pay the corporate excise deficiencies resulting from the disallowance of its royalty payment deductions was not due to reasonable cause.

Decision of the Appellate Tax Board affirmed.

Permanent Subcommittee on Investigations of the U.S. Senate, Memorandum: Offshore Profit Shifting and the U.S. Tax Code

May 21, 2013

I. EXECUTIVE SUMMARY

On May 21, 2013, the Permanent Subcommittee on Investigations (PSI) of the U.S. Senate Homeland Security and Government Affairs Committee will hold a hearing that is a continuation of a series of reviews conducted by the Subcommittee on how individual and corporate taxpayers are shifting billions of dollars offshore to avoid U.S. taxes. The hearing will examine how Apple Inc., a U.S. multinational corporation, has used a variety of offshore structures, arrangements, and transactions to shift billions of dollars in profits away from the United States and into Ireland, where Apple has negotiated a special corporate tax rate of less than two percent. One of Apple's more unusual tactics has been to establish and direct substantial funds to offshore entities in Ireland, while claiming they are not tax residents of any jurisdiction. For example, Apple Inc. established an offshore subsidiary, Apple Operations International, which from 2009 to 2012 reported net income of $30 billion, but declined to declare any tax residence, filed no corporate income tax return, and paid no corporate income taxes to any national government for five years. A second Irish affiliate, Apple Sales International, received $74 billion in sales income over four years, but due in part to its alleged status as a non-tax resident, paid taxes on only a tiny fraction of that income.

In addition, the hearing will examine how Apple Inc. transferred the economic rights to its intellectual property through a cost sharing agreement with its own offshore affiliates, and was thereby able to shift tens of billions of dollars offshore to a low tax jurisdiction and avoid U.S. tax. Apple Inc. then utilized U.S. tax loopholes, including the so-called "check-the-box" rules, to avoid U.S. taxes on $44 billion in taxable offshore income over the past four years, or about $10 billion in tax avoidance per year. The hearing will also examine some of the weaknesses and loopholes in certain U.S. tax code provisions, including transfer pricing, Subpart F, and related regulations, that enable multinational corporations to avoid U.S. taxes.

A. Subcommittee Investigation

For a number of years, the Subcommittee has reviewed how U.S. citizens and multinational corporations have exploited and, at times, abused or violated U.S. tax statutes, regulations and accounting rules to shift profits and valuable assets offshore to avoid U.S. taxes. The Subcommittee inquiries have resulted in a series of hearings and reports.[1] The Subcommittee's recent reviews have focused on how multinational corporations have employed various complex structures and transactions to exploit tax loopholes to shift large portions of their profits offshore and dodge U.S. taxes.

---

1. *See, e.g.,* U.S. Senate Permanent Subcommittee on Investigations, "Fishtail, Bacchus, Sundance, and Slapshot: Four Enron Transactions Funded and Facilitated by U.S. Financial Institutions," S.Prt. 107–82 (Jan. 2, 2003); "U.S. Tax Shelter Industry: The Role of Accountants, Lawyers, and Financial Professionals," S.Hrg. 108–473 (No. 18 and 20, 2003); "Tax Haven Abuses: The Enablers, The Tools and Secrecy," S.Hrg 109–797 (Aug. 1, 2006); "Tax Haven Banks and U.S. Tax Compliance," S.Hrg. 110–614 (July 17 and 25, 2008); "Tax Haven Banks and U.S. Tax Compliance: Obtaining the Names of U.S. Clients with Swiss Accounts," S.Hrg. 111–30 (Mar. 4, 2009); "Repatriating Offshore Funds: 2004 Tax Windfall for Select Multinationals," S.Prt. 112–27 (Oct. 11, 2011); and "Offshore Profit Shifting and the U.S. Tax Code—Part 1 (Microsoft and Hewlett-Packard)," S.Hrg.112-*** (Sept. 20, 2012).

At the same time as the U.S. federal debt has continued to grow — now surpassing $16 trillion — the U.S. corporate tax base has continued to decline, placing a greater burden on individual taxpayers and future generations. According to a report prepared for Congress:

"At its post-WWII peak in 1952, the corporate tax generated 32.1% of all federal tax revenue. In that same year the individual tax accounted for 42.2% of federal revenue, and the payroll tax accounted for 9.7% of revenue. Today, the corporate tax accounts for 8.9% of federal tax revenue, whereas the individual and payroll taxes generate 41.5% and 40.0%, respectively, of federal revenue."[2]

Over the past several years, the amount of permanently reinvested foreign earnings reported by U.S. multinationals on their financial statements has increased dramatically. One study has calculated that undistributed foreign earnings for companies in the S&P 500 have increased by more than 400%.[3] According to recent analysis by Audit Analytics, over a five year period from 2008 to 2012, total untaxed indefinitely reinvested earnings reported in 10-K filings for firms comprising the Russell 3000 increased by 70.3%.[4] During the same period, the number of firms reporting indefinitely reinvested earnings increased by 11.4%.

The increase in multinational corporate claims regarding permanently reinvested foreign earnings and the decline in corporate tax revenue are due in part to the shifting of mobile income offshore into tax havens. A number of studies show that multinational corporations are moving "mobile" income out of the United States into low or no tax jurisdictions, including tax havens such as Ireland, Bermuda, and the Cayman Islands.[5] In one 2012 study, a leading expert in the Office of Tax Analysis of the U.S. Department of Treasury found that foreign profit margins, not foreign sales, are the cause for significant increases in profits abroad. He wrote:

"The foreign share of the worldwide income of U.S. multinational corporations (MNCs) has risen sharply in recent years. Data from a panel of 754 large MNCs indicate that the MNC foreign income share increased by 14 percentage points from 1996 to 2004. The differential between a company's U.S. and foreign effective tax rates exerts a significant effect on the share of its income abroad, largely through changes in foreign and domestic profit margins rather than a shift in sales. U.S.-foreign tax differentials are estimated to have raised the foreign share of MNC worldwide income by about 12 percentage points by 2004. Lower foreign effective tax rates had no significant effect on a company's domestic sales or on the growth of

---

2. 12/8/2011"Reasons for the Decline in the Corporate Tax Revenues" Congressional Research Service, Mark P. Keightley, at.1. See also 4/2011"Tax Havens and Treasure Hunts," Today's Economist, Nancy Folbre.

3. 4/26/2011 "Parking Earnings Overseas," Zion, Varsheny, Burnap: Credit Suisse, at 3.

4. 5/1/2013 Audit Analytics, "Foreign Indefinitely Reinvested Earnings: Balances Held by the Russell 3000."

5. See, e.g., 6/5/2010 "Tax Havens: International Tax Avoidance and Evasion," Congressional Research Service, Jane Gravelle, at 15 (citing multiple studies).

its worldwide pre-tax profits. Lower taxes on foreign income do not seem to promote 'competitiveness.'"[6]

One study showed that foreign profits of controlled foreign corporations (CFCs) of U.S. multinationals significantly outpace the total GDP of some tax havens."[7] For example, profits of CFCs in Bermuda were 645% and in the Cayman Islands were 546% as a percentage of GDP, respectively. In a recent research report, JPMorgan expressed the opinion that the transfer pricing of intellectual property "explains some of the phenomenon as to why the balances of foreign cash and foreign earnings at multinational companies continue to grow at such impressive rates."[8]

On September 20, 2012, the Subcommittee held a hearing and examined some of the weaknesses and loopholes in certain tax and accounting rules that facilitated profit shifting by multinational corporations. Specifically, it reviewed transfer pricing, deferral, and Subpart F of the Internal Revenue Code, with related regulations, and accounting standards governing offshore profits and the reporting of tax liabilities. The Subcommittee presented two case studies: (1) a study of structures and practices employed by Microsoft Corporation to shift and keep profits offshore; and (2) a study of Hewlett-Packard's "staggered foreign loan program," which was devised to *de facto* repatriate offshore profits to the United States to help run its U.S. operations, without paying U.S. taxes.

The case study for the Subcommittee's May 2013 hearing involves Apple Inc. Building upon information collected in previous inquiries, the Subcommittee reviewed Apple responses to several Subcommittee surveys, reviewed Apple SEC filings and other documents, requested information from Apple, and interviewed a number of corporate representatives from Apple. The Subcommittee also consulted with a number of tax experts and the IRS.

This memorandum first provides an overview of certain tax provisions related to offshore income, such as transfer pricing, Subpart F, and the so-called check-the-box regulations and look-through rule. It then presents a case study of Apple's organizational structure and the provisions of the tax code and regulations it uses to shift and keep billions in profits offshore in two controlled foreign corporations formed in Ireland. The first is Apple Sales International (ASI), an entity that has acquired certain economic rights to Apple's intellectual property. Apple Inc. has used those rights of ASI to shift billions in profits away from the United States to Ireland, where it pays a corporate tax rate of 2% or less. The second is Apple Operations International (AOI), a 30-year old corporation that has no employees or physical presence, and whose

---

6. 2/2012 "Foreign Taxes and the Growing Share of U.S. Multinational Company Income Abroad: Profits, Not Sales, are Being Globalized," Office of Tax Analysis Working Paper 103, U.S. Department of Treasury, Harry Grubert, at 1.

7. 6/5/2010 "Tax Havens: International Tax Avoidance and Evasion," Congressional Research Service, Jane Gravelle, at 14.

8. 5/16/2012 "Global Tax Rate Makers," JPMorgan Chase, at 2 (based on research of SEC filings of over 1,000 reporting issuers).

operations are managed and controlled out of the United States. Despite receiving $30 billion in earnings and profits during the period 2009 through 2011 as the key holding company for Apple's extensive offshore corporate structure, Apple Operations International has no declared tax residency anywhere in the world and, as a consequence, has not paid corporate income tax to any national government for the past 5 years. Apple has recently disclosed that ASI also claims to have no tax residency in any jurisdiction, despite receiving over a four year period from 2009 to 2012, sales income from Apple affiliates totaling $74 billion.

Apple is an American success story. Today, Apple Inc. maintains more than $102 billion in offshore cash, cash equivalents and marketable securities (cash).[9] Apple executives told the Subcommittee that the company has no intention of returning those funds to the United States unless and until there is a more favorable environment, emphasizing a lower corporate tax rate and a simplified tax code.[10] Recently, Apple issued $17 billion in debt instruments to provide funds for its U.S. operations rather than bring its offshore cash home, pay the tax owed, and use those funds to invest in its operations or return dividends to its stockholders. The Subcommittee's investigation shows that Apple has structured organizations and business operations to avoid U.S. taxes and reduce the contribution it makes to the U.S. treasury. Its actions disadvantage Apple's domestic competitors, force other taxpayers to shoulder the tax burden Apple has cast off, and undermine the fairness of the U.S. tax code. The purpose of the Subcommittee's investigation is to describe Apple's offshore tax activities and offer recommendations to close the offshore tax loopholes that enable some U.S. multinational corporations to avoid paying their share of taxes.

B. Findings and Recommendations

Findings. The Subcommittee's investigation has produced the following findings of fact.

1. **Shifting Profits Offshore.** Apple has $145 billion in cash, cash equivalents and marketable securities, of which $102 billion is "offshore." Apple has used offshore entities, arrangements, and transactions to transfer its assets and profits offshore and minimize its corporate tax liabilities.

2. **Offshore Entities With No Declared Tax Jurisdiction.** Apple has established and directed tens of billions of dollars to at least two Irish affiliates, while claiming neither is a tax resident of any jurisdiction, including its primary offshore holding company, Apple Operations International (AOI), and its primary intellectual property rights recipient, Apple Sales International (ASI). AOI, which has no employees, has no physical presence, is managed and controlled in the United States, and received

---

9. 4/23/2013 Apple Second Quarter Earnings Call, Fiscal Year 2013, http://www.nasdaq.com /aspx/call-transcript.aspx?StoryId=1364041&Title=apple-s-ceo-discusses-f2q13-results-earnings -call-transcript.

10. Subcommittee interview of Apple Chief Executive Officer Tim Cook (4/29/2013).

$30 billion of income between 2009 and 2012, has paid no corporate income tax to any national government for the past five years.

3. **Cost Sharing Agreement.** Apple's cost sharing agreement (CSA) with its offshore affiliates in Ireland is primarily a conduit for shifting billions of dollars in income from the United States to a low tax jurisdiction. From 2009 to 2012, the CSA facilitated the shift of $74 billion in worldwide sales income away from the United States to Ireland where Apple has negotiated a tax rate of less than 2%.

4. **Circumventing Subpart F.** The intent of Subpart F of the U.S. tax code is to prevent multinational corporations from shifting profits to tax havens to avoid U.S. tax. Apple has exploited weaknesses and loopholes in U.S. tax laws and regulations, particularly the "check-the-box" and "look-through" rules, to circumvent Subpart F taxation and, from 2009 to 2012, avoid $44 billion in taxes on otherwise taxable offshore income.

Recommendations. Based upon the Subcommittee's investigation, the Memorandum makes the following recommendations.

1. **Strengthen Section 482.** Strengthen Section 482 of the tax code governing transfer pricing to eliminate incentives for U.S. multinational corporations to transfer intellectual property to shell entities that perform minimal operations in tax haven or low tax jurisdictions by implementing more restrictive transfer pricing rules concerning intellectual property.

2. **Reform Check-the-Box and Look Through Rules.** Reform the "check-the-box" and "look-through" rules so that they do not undermine the intent of Subpart F of the Internal Revenue Code to currently tax certain offshore income.

3. **Tax CFCs Under U.S. Management and Control.** Use the current authority of the IRS to disregard sham entities and impose current U.S. tax on income earned by any controlled foreign corporation that is managed and controlled in the United States.

4. **Properly Enforce Same Country Exception.** Use the current authority of the IRS to restrict the "same country exception" so that the exception to Subpart F cannot be used to shield from taxation passive income shifted between two related entities which are incorporated in the same country, but claim to be in different tax residences without a legitimate business reason.

5. **Properly Enforce the Manufacturing Exception.** Use the current authority of the IRS to restrict the "manufacturing exception" so that the exception to Subpart F cannot be used to shield offshore income from taxation unless substantial manufacturing activities are taking place in the jurisdiction where the intermediary CFC is located.

Notes & Questions

1. The tax treatment of intellectual property is a difficult and technical subject, covered in a class of its own. Our purpose here is to make you aware of some of the

issues and alert you to the need to have clients consult relevant tax counsel for problems that you may identify as a business attorney. For an excellent source on the taxation of intellectual property, see Jeffrey Maine & Xuan Thao-Nguyen, Intellectual Property Taxation (BNA 2003).

2. The reading by Professors Bankman and Gilson raise a startling question: why do entrepreneurs form start-ups as opposed to having all innovation occur within existing companies? What is the tax argument against start-ups? Despite the tax impediments that the professors identify, what are the countervailing benefits of start-ups? A very important tax question that is beyond the scope of this book, but nonetheless worth recognizing, is the relevance of taxation for the choice of business form. Remember that a corporation is a separate entity and is taxed at a different rate and in a different manner from partnerships. One importance difference in manner is that corporation income is paid by the business entity while partnership income passes through to the partners and is taxed at the partner level at the partnership rate. There are also significant differences in deductions and in the treatment of property and service contributions between corporations and partnerships.

3. The *Syms* case illustrates the tax treatment of an intellectual property holding company. Why would someone transfer ownership of intellectual property, or any property for that matter, to a separate entity and then license or lease the property back? Do you see the tax advantages of such an arrangement? Why did the Internal Revenue Service disallow the arrangement as a "sham transaction?" Does the analysis presented in the case make clear what a "sham transaction" is?

4. Delaware has been an attractive jurisdiction for forming subsidiaries to hold intellectual property assets because Delaware law does not tax corporate revenues derived from intellectual property. However, several states have enacted Add-Back legislations that allow state taxation of intellectual property revenues earned by these Delaware subsidiaries. Corporate challenges to these statutes have been mixed with a pro-taxpayer ruling in Massachusetts, and an anti-taxpayer ruling in New York. *See Sherwin-Williams Co. v. Commissioner of Revenue*, 778 N.E.2d 504 (2002); *Sherwin-Williams Co. v. Tax Appeals Tribunal Of The Department Of Taxation and Finance Of The State Of New York*, 12 A.D.3d 112 (N.Y. Sup. Ct. App. Div. 2004). In the New York case, the following testimony was key to the ruling against the taxpayer:

> Shapiro [expert witness for the State] testified that the subsidiaries were unable to add value to the trademarks and that, objectively viewed, the transaction lacked economic substance because there was no reasonable expectation of benefits exceeding costs. He explained that the value of a trademark is principally tied to it being recognized and reflecting the quality and service associated with products bearing that trademark. Thus, according to Shapiro, trademarks cannot be managed "independently of the core branded products and the knowledge that comes from managing those products." He further set forth the reasons for his conclusions that the subsidiaries failed to provide any meaningful quality control, that the arrangement did not

protect against a hostile takeover and that creating the subsidiaries did not advance the goal of limiting liability. 12 A.D.3d at 114.

What lessons can be learned from the New York case? The Massachusetts court concluded that "[b]ecause the record in this case establishes that the reorganization and subsequent transfer and licensing transactions were genuine, creating viable businesses engaged in substantive economic activities apart from the creation of tax benefits for Sherwin-Williams, they cannot be disregarded by the commissioner as a sham regardless of their tax-motivated purpose." 778 N.E.2d at 519. How do you think the Massachusetts court distinguished *Syms*?

5. The *Syms* case deals with trademarks. Would the analysis have been different if patents, copyrights, or trade secrets were at issue? How would you have set up the holding company and licensing arrangements differently in light of the result in *Syms*? In thinking about this question, focus on any relevant differences among the various types of intellectual property.

6. For the purposes of tax planning, a key question is when income from intellectual property licenses will be treated as a return on capital investment and when it will be treated as ordinary income. Tax planners must pay particular attention to the tax treatment (1) of inventions and works made in an employment context and (2) of transfers of intellectual property interests. The following excerpt provides some guidance on the tax treatment of intellectual property transfers:

> Once it has been determined that a bona fide transfer of property took place, the question becomes whether the researcher is entitled to capital gains treatment on the distributions he or she receives. The courts use the same analysis under both the patent and capital asset provisions to determine capital gains treatment (1) whether the property transferred is a recognized patent or a capital asset, (2) if so, whether the transfer constitutes a sale rather than a license arrangement and, (3) if so, whether the holding period for long-term assets is met. When these provisions are met, the income derived is entitled to the capital gains tax rate. However, when these requirements are not met, the payments are classified either as royalty income or income derived from the sales of short-term capital assets, both of which are subject to ordinary income tax rates.

See Edward J. Jennings, *The Taxation and Reporting of Distributions Derived from Licensing Intellectual Property*, 15 TAXATION OF EXEMPTS 207 (Mar/Apr 2004).

7. The final reading is a memo from the Permanent Subcommittee on Investigations on the topic of a tax avoidance device called an *inversion*. As the reading indicates, this device has been used by intellectual property-intensive companies to shift assets and headquarters to non-US jurisdictions, such as Ireland, to avoid U.S. taxes. Defenders of inversions say that they serve to consolidate international ownership of assets and allow multinational companies to take advantage of low tax jurisdictions. One sophisticated theory looks at the benefits derived from corporate taxes paid to the United States, such as the benefits of corporate law, securities law, and intellectual

property law. The author concludes that inversions arise from a disconnect between the benefits of taxes and taxes paid. Tax reform needs to consider the global distribution of benefits from paying corporate taxes across jurisdictions. *See* Inho Andrew Mun, *Reinterpreting Corporate Inversions: Non-Tax Competitions and Frictions*, 126(7) YALE L.J. 1972-2259 (2017).

Critics view inversions as products of a tax loophole that causes the United States Treasury to lose substantial tax revenues. *See* Julie A. Roin, *Inversions, Related Party Expenditures, and Source Taxation: Changing the Paradigm for the Taxation of Foreign and Foreign-Owned Businesses*, 2016 B.Y.U. L. Rev. 1837–1891 (2016). One investigator argues that inversions do not arise solely from differential corporate tax rates across countries, but from multinationals having large cash reserves outside the United States. *See* Jeff Sommer, *Inversions Aren't Only way to Avoid Taxes*, INT'L N.Y. TIMES, Nov. 27, 2015 at 19. From an intellectual property transactions perspective, the interesting question is what role tax considerations should play in the development of an intellectual property portfolio. Should a company seek a large patent portfolio solely for tax purposes? Should the tax code create incentives for this type of patenting and related patent ownership shifting? Arguably, the tax code is distorting the patent system in terms of incentives and the planning decisions of multinational companies.

8. Some of the proposals set forth at the end of the Subcommittee's memo have been promoted by members of Congress. In 2014, Senator Carl Levin (D-MI) and Representative Sander Levin (D-MI) proposed separate bills to treat the overseas corporation resulting from an inversion as a domestic corporation for United States tax purposes if the foreign corporation owned more than 50 percent of the shares of the merged entity and management and business activities continued in the United States. The bills were not enacted. In 2015, the Stop Corporate Inversions Act of 2015 was introduced in the House. The bill would amend the Internal Revenue Code to revise rules for the taxation of inverted corporations (i.e., U.S. corporations that acquire foreign companies to reincorporate in a foreign jurisdiction with income tax rates lower than the United States) to provide that a foreign corporation that acquires the properties of a U.S. corporation or partnership after May 8, 2014, shall be treated as an inverted corporation and thus subject to U.S. taxation if, after such acquisition: (1) it holds more than 50 percent of the stock of the new entity (expanded affiliated group), or (2) the management or control of the new entity occurs primarily within the United States and the new entity has significant domestic business activities.

E. Export Controls Affecting Intellectual Property

NYS Science + Technology Law Center, Export Guidebook (2016) (Excerpts)

http://nysstlc.syr.edu/wp-content/uploads/2017/04/Export-Controls-Guidebook _forweb.pdf*

1. Overview of Export Regulations for Commercial Items

Several sets of regulations control exports of items from the United States. Export controls for commercial items are governed by the Export Administration Regulations (EAR), which are set out in Title 15 of the Code of Federal Regulations, Parts 730 through 774. This manual provides guidance for understanding exports governed by the EAR. Export controls for defense items are governed by the International Traffic In Arms Regulations (ITAR), and other export controls cover other specialized areas. This manual does not cover exports of defense items that are subject to ITAR, or other specialized areas of export controls.

Two federal agencies are involved in control of exports of commercial items. The Bureau of Industry and Security (BIS) administers the classification of exports and the regulatory requirements for each class of exports under the EAR, while the Customs and Border Protection (CBP) division of the Bureau of Census processes exports from the United States and enforces the EAR by inspection of export documents and the associated items being exported.

Exports are defined to include more than products, hence the use of the term "items" instead of products in the title of this manual. Exports are generally defined to include the following activities: 1) shipments of products from the United States to destinations outside of the United States, 2) enabling removal of products from the United States to destinations outside of the United States, and 3) disclosures of information describing technology to any foreign person, whether the disclosure occurs in a foreign country or in the United States. Items therefore refer to products and disclosures of technology. It is important to keep in mind that the regulations described in this manual apply to all three types of activities covered by the definition and that export controls can and do apply to transactions that occur within the United States, as well as the more typical shipment of items from the United States to a foreign destination. Controls that apply to transactions in the United States will be mentioned where appropriate in the manual.

Exports also include "re-exports," which for purposes of this manual can be considered to be a first export of an item from the United States to a first foreign country, coupled with a second export of the same item to a second, different foreign country. The second export is the re-export. For purposes of EAR compliance, both

---

the first and second exports — e.g., the original export and the re-export — must satisfy the terms and conditions of the regulations.

Two general areas of activity that are necessary to handle an export transaction: 1) classifying a contemplated export to determine whether or not an export license is required, and 2) creating export documentation that is necessary to clear exported items through customs and reporting export transactions.

1.1 Classifying an Export to Determine Export License Requirements.

Classification of exports is the means used to determine whether an export can be made without obtaining an export license from BIS or whether a license is necessary. Exports of commercial items are classified into four classes: 1) transactions for which no license is required (NLR transactions), 2) transactions for which a license exception can negate the necessity to obtain an export license, if prescribed conditions are met (LE transactions), 3) transactions for which a specific license from BIS is required (LR transactions), and 4) prohibited export transactions. The approach to handling exports of commercial items outlined in this manual is to first provide guidance on how to determine which classification applies to the contemplated export. This step will determine whether the export is permitted and, if so, whether it is either NLR and requires no license, LE because it meets the conditions to qualify for an applicable licensing exception, or LR and requires application for and obtaining a specific license from BIS.

1.2 Export Clearance through Customs.

All permitted exports of commercial items must be accompanied by a set of export documents that will be used by CBP to evaluate and process the export through customs, and exports also must be reported to CBP. The second activity for handling an export transaction is covered in the manual by providing guidance on the documents that are necessary to create an acceptable set of export documents to enable processing the export through CBP, the information that must be in hand to create this set of documents, and how to report exports to CBP.

Compliance with the export controls set out in the EAR is the responsibility of the U.S. company that sells an item that is exported or engages in an activity that is subject to export controls, to the extent that the U.S. company knows that the purchaser is located in a foreign country or is an agent for a purchaser that is located in a foreign country. The U.S. company in the foregoing situations is designated the U.S. Principal Party in Interest (USPPI), and the USPPI is responsible for compliance with the EAR. The term "routed exports" covers transactions in which a USPPI delivers an item covered by the EAR to a foreign customer or an agent for a foreign customer at a location in the United States and relies on the foreign customer or its agent to arrange the export. The USPPI remains responsible for compliance with the EAR for all routed export transactions.

This manual provides guidance on complying with the EAR and should enable the reader to use the EAR more effectively to process export transactions. The manual, however, does not provide sufficiently detailed information to process export transactions, and reference to the EAR will be necessary in all cases to process actual export transactions.

2. Qualifying as an NLR Export

Classification of an export begins with determining whether or not the export qualifies for NLR status. If the contemplated export qualifies as NLR, no evaluation is necessary regarding whether a license exception is available or the probability of obtaining an export license under the licensing policies of BIS. Determining whether an export qualifies as NLR is a multistep process, based on determining whether the export would violate any one of 10 general prohibitions on exports which are set out in 15 CFR Part 736.2.

The 10 general prohibitions cam be divided into four sets of restrictions as follows: 1) restrictions based on the nature of the item considered for export (prohibitions 1, 2, and 3), 2) restrictions based on the customer to whom the export would be made (prohibitions 4, 5, and 7), 3) restrictions based on the country that is a final destination of the export or a country through which an export shipment is routed (prohibitions 6 and 8), and 4) restrictions based on violating an export license or an export requirement (prohibitions 9 and 10). An export qualifies as NLR only if none of the 10 general prohibitions will be violated by the export.

It will become apparent that evaluating the four sets of export restrictions to determine whether an export license is necessary ultimately involves answering the following five questions. 1) What is being exported? 2) Where is the export going? 3) Who is the customer that will receive the export? 4) What is the business or other activities in which the customer is engaged? 5) How will the customer use the exported item and is that use consistent with the customer's business?

Notes

1. The reading provides a brief introduction to export control rules. If one is transferring technology outside the United States, the transferor must satisfy the export control rules, which are designed to prevent transfer of sensitive technologies overseas. These rules apply regardless of whether the technology is protected by intellectual property laws. Those interested in further details are advised to consult the Department of State website at https://www.state.gov/strategictrade/overview/.

Chapter 2

Organizing and Financing an Intellectual Property Based Start-Up Company

Problem

Part 1

After several years as a successful consultant regarding race car ignition systems and after having obtained several patents regarding new ignition system designs, Dr. See has decided to form a new business (to be called "Digital Ignition Systems Corporation" or "Digital Ignition") in order develop and market products incorporating his patented designs. Dr. See plans to hold a significant ownership share in the new concern, reflecting his contribution of key technologies and his ongoing role in the leadership of the new business. Dr. See has identified five additional individuals who are interested in being initial co-owners of the new business. Some of these co-owners plan to be actively involved in the management and operation of Digital Ignition, while others expect only to be investors. The anticipated roles and financial contributions of the six initial co-owners of Digital Ignition are as follows:

Dr. See will:

- transfer ownership of his patents to Digital Ignition
- invest $100,000
- serve as chief executive officer

Thomas Carlise (an investment counselor) will:

- invest $100,000
- serve as chief financial officer

Mary Sanchez (a college professor of engineering) will:

- serve as chief product engineer
- make no investment

Tom Johnson (another, less-experienced college professor of engineering) will:

- serve as Sanchez's assistant
- also make no investment

Hameed Bukhari (a local dentist and friend of Dr. See's) will:

- contribute $500,000 (in a combination of loans and direct investments of funds, with the fraction of each to be determined)
- play no active management role in the business

Sally Loo (a successful clothing store operator and Dr. See's cousin) will:

- invest $500,000
- play no active management role in the business

Dr. See has come to your law firm for help in setting up Digital Ignition. He is seeking advice on what type of legal entity to select for this business, how the fractional ownership interests in the business might best be allocated given the anticipated activities and contributions of the six initial co-owners, conflicts of interest and fiduciary obligations that may arise among the co-owners once the business is established, and means to generate additional financing for Digital Ignition using loans and, eventually, venture capital financing.

Please provide Dr. See with advice on these questions, with particular attention to how Digital Ignition's present and anticipated intellectual property interests may influence the answers.

Part 2

Soon after the founding of Digital Ignition, the company's senior executives realized that further investment from parties other than the initial owners would be needed to finance the company's operations while it engaged in initial product development and marketing efforts. The goal of this financing would be to bring the company to the stage where it was ready for either an acquisition by another company or for an initial public offering of stock.

To generate this needed financing, Dr. See contacted William Elias, a local dentist with whom See had had some social contacts and who had expressed interest in possibly investing some of his considerable wealth in Digital Ignition. In order to convince Elias to invest in Digital Ignition, See described the assets and business potential of the company in highly favorable terms. See gave Elias a detailed written description of the digital ignition systems technology that See had developed and brought to the company, the patents covering this technology, which were now held by Digital Ignition, the predicted attractiveness of the patented technology to a broad range of automobile owners, and the reasons why Digital Ignition's patents should assure the company of exclusive business opportunities and growth potential related to the marketing of products based on the new technology.

In summarizing the importance of the company's patents to Digital Ignition's future business activities, the documents provided to Elias indicated that "Dr. See and Digital Ignition have developed and patented major advances in automobile ignition system technology that promise to provide car owners with significant increases in automobile gas mileage and performance. We anticipate significant profit potential in future sales to both consumers using ignition systems based on the new technology to retrofit their existing vehicles and to new car manufacturers using the systems in newly manufactured vehicles. As the holder of patents on the key components of this new ignition systems technology, Digital Ignition is in a position to capture the full business potential of this exciting new technology over the life of these patents." Based on these representations and other information about Digital Ignition provided to him in discussions with See, Elias made an investment of $200,000 in Digital Ignition and is now one of the company's major shareholders.

Prior to his discussions with Elias, See told several executives at Digital Ignition that he was concerned about several digital ignition system products being developed and marketed by VF Industries. VF had hired Mary Jones, a former coworker of See's when both served as engine products designers for the International Motors Corporation. VF was developing digital ignition systems to be sold in the same markets that Digital Ignition was targeting for its products. An early version of one of VF's products demonstrated at a trade show appeared to incorporate some of Digital Ignition's patented technology. When See spoke to Elias, he was aware of this possible patent infringement by VF and the potential impact of VF's product sales on Digital Ignition's business prospects, but neither See nor any other Digital Ignition executive had yet evaluated the desirability of a patent infringement suit against VF or the likelihood of Digital Ignition's success in such a suit. Dr. See did not discuss VF's activities with Elias.

Six months after Elias' investment in the company, Digital Ignition filed a patent infringement action against VF, asserting that VF's manufacturing and sales of digital ignition systems were covered by one of Digital Ignition's patents. Digital Ignition sought a preliminary injunction stopping VF from further product development, manufacturing, and marketing activities regarding products incorporating the patented technology. However, in an unexpected ruling, Digital Ignition was denied the preliminary injunction it sought. The district court involved cited what it felt to be two independently sufficient grounds for refusing to grant the preliminary injunction: first, Digital Ignition had not demonstrated a likelihood of success in establishing that VF's products were within the scope of Digital Ignition's patent claims and, second, VF had demonstrated a likelihood of invalidity of the patent in question on the ground that See had failed to properly name a co-inventor in the relevant patent application. The case is still pending and these issues of patent validity and infringement are expected to be more fully litigated at trial.

Elias was outraged upon hearing of the result in this preliminary injunction action. By the time this result was announced, Elias had learned through discussions with other Digital Ignition officers that See had been aware of the possible patent infringement by VF and the potential competitive impacts of the latter's products before Elias had invested in Digital Ignition. Elias thought that See had overstated the strength and significance of Digital Ignition's patents when Elias was considering an investment in the company.

Elias has filed a suit in federal court raising claims for damages under federal and state laws. His federal claims assert that the stock sales to him were accomplished through misleading statements violating SEC Rule 10b-5. Pursuant to these claims, Elias is seeking recovery for the loss in the value of his Digital Ignition stock due to recent publicity about the possible invalidity of the company's patents. In addition, Elias has filed state law claims asserting common law fraud by Digital Ignition officials in connection with Elias' purchase of Digital Ignition stock. Based on this fraud, Elias is seeking to rescind the purchase contract and to recover his $200,000. Because Elias' stock purchase agreement was entered into while he was at his winter home in Florida and many of the key representations at issue were made there, the law of the state of Florida will apply to these fraud claims.

You have been asked to provide a preliminary evaluation of the merits of Elias' suit, paying particular attention to whether it is likely that he will be able to establish that any misstatements made to him in connection with the disputed stock sales transaction involved material information. Please identify the major considerations affecting this aspect of his claims and identify what further information you would like to know in order to conduct a more thorough assessment of this case.

Focus of the Chapter

This chapter considers business formation and financing issues that are especially important to start-up companies with significant intellectual property assets. Section A describes some of the types of business entities that are useful vehicles for developing and commercializing new intellectual property, with emphasis on features of business entities that aid executives in making effective use of intellectual property interests and that prepare the entities for additional investment and growth. Section A also describes some of the common sources for financing of start-up companies seeking to commercialize intellectual property assets. Section B addresses the use of security interests in intellectual property as means to promote lending to companies or to enhance the attractiveness of those companies as they seek venture capital. Section C addresses the impact of securities fraud claims on the financing of intellectual property based companies. Section D explores how corporate law duties of company directors, officers, and shareholders may influence how these individuals build the value of a company's intellectual property assets and increase corporate finances by disposing of these assets.

Readings

A. Commercializing Intellectual Property: Selecting a Business Entity and Obtaining Initial Financing

1. Business Entity Choices

Richard A. Mann et al., Starting from Scratch: A Lawyer's Guide to Representing a Start-up Company

56 Ark. L. Rev. 773 (2004)*

. . . .

Along with protecting intellectual property, establishing a business entity in order to conduct the business is high priority. Business entities considered by entrepreneurs include: (1) sole proprietorships, (2) partnerships and limited partnerships, (3) corporations, and (4) limited liability companies. Each of these entities has advantages as well as disadvantages.

. . . .

B. Sole Proprietorships

The simplest form of business association is the sole proprietorship. A sole proprietorship is an unincorporated business consisting of one person who owns and completely controls the business and is personally liable for all the obligations of the business. The costs in establishing and running a sole proprietorship are minimal; it is formed without any formality. The profits from the business are taxed to the individual owner and filed on the individual's tax returns. The business is freely transferable by sale, gift or will. Finally, the sole proprietorship may have a relatively short life span because the death of the sole proprietor dissolves the sole proprietorship. Typically, the sole proprietorship is used for small family businesses.

C. Partnerships

Broadly speaking, partnerships are either general partnerships or limited partnerships. A general partnership (usually referred to simply as a partnership) is an unincorporated business entity that is formed when two or more persons join together to co-own a business for profit. No formal agreement is necessary to create a general partnership. Thus, if two or more people conduct a business, under normal circumstances a general partnership will result by default. Each partner is personally liable for an unlimited amount of the obligations of the general partnership. The cost to create and run a general partnership depends on the complexity of the ownership arrangement.

A general partnership is not a separate taxable entity. Consequently, the taxation of a general partnership is comparable to a sole proprietorship as the profits and losses "pass-through" to the general partners. Income allocated to the partners is subject to the self-employment tax. The partnership must file an informational return with the Internal Revenue Service (IRS). A general partnership is very flexible in that the management responsibilities can be divided among the partners in virtually any way the partners agree. In the absence of a specific agreement, each partner has an equal right to control of the partnership. Partners may assign their financial interest in the partnership, but the assignee may become a member of the partnership only if all of the members consent. Lastly, under the original UPA, the death, bankruptcy, or withdrawal of a partner dissolves the general partnership. Under the Revised UPA, these dissociations of a partner result in dissolution only in limited circumstances; in many instances, they will result merely in a buyout of the withdrawing partner's interest rather than a termination of the partnership.

In contrast to the informal creation of a general partnership, a limited partnership must be established by filing a certificate of limited partnership with the appropriate state office. The limited partnership is a creation of state statute, and the members of the limited partnership must strictly comply with the state laws. A limited partnership must have at least one general partner and one limited partner. General partners have unlimited personal liability for the partnership's obligations, whereas limited partners have limited liability. The costs of creating and managing a limited partnership will typically be more expensive than a general partnership. Each general partner has an equal right to control of the partnership; limited partners have no right to participate in control. Partners may assign their financial interest in the partnership, but the assignee may become a limited partner only if all of the members consent. Unless otherwise agreed, a limited partnership must dissolve if a general partner dies, goes bankrupt, or withdraws. The limited partnership will survive the death, bankruptcy, or withdrawal of a limited partner. A limited partnership is not a separate taxable entity, so income of the partnership is deemed to be distributed to the partners, similar to a general partnership. Limited partnerships are frequently used to raise capital and to bring together passive investors with managerial talent.

D. Corporations

A corporation has a separate legal existence apart from its owners. A corporation is created by filing articles of incorporation with the appropriate state office. Because each state has adopted its own corporate statutes, the rules governing the creation, internal affairs, and dissolution vary from state to state. A board of directors elected by the shareholders manages the corporation but the board normally delegates to certain officers the oversight of day-to-day activities. Owners are not liable for the actions of the corporation. However, under certain circumstances, state courts will strip away the corporation's protective shield and expose the owners to liability. State courts will "pierce the corporate veil" in extreme cases where shareholders do not follow corporate formalities or intentionally undercapitalize a corporation. The costs of creating and running a corporation may be significant depending upon the complexity of the corporation's organizational documents. A corporation is a more formal entity that requires many administrative tasks such as regular board meetings, shareholder votes, and other corporate governance formalities. The taxation considerations for corporations are also considerable. One tax disadvantage to becoming a corporation is that corporate profits are subject to double taxation: a corporation is taxed as a separate entity, and shareholders are taxed on corporate earnings that are distributed to them. Some corporations, however, are eligible to elect to be taxed as Subchapter S corporations, resulting in flow-through taxation of the shareholders. There are substantial advantages, however, to selecting the corporate form of business. Corporate structures permit the creation of sophisticated financial structures in which variable ownership classes are entitled to different rights and preferences. Also, absent shareholder agreements restricting transfers, an ownership interest is freely transferable. Finally, the corporation's existence can be perpetual.

E. Limited Liability Companies

A limited liability company (LLC) is a relatively new form of business that combines the "pass-through" tax advantages of partnerships while providing limited liability to all its owners. As the name suggests, the owners of a limited liability company are not personally liable for the LLC's obligations. Also, all members of a member-managed LLC may participate in the management of the business. LLC statutes permit LLCs to be managed by one or more managers who may, but need not, be a member. In a member managed LLC, the members have actual and apparent authority to bind the LLC. In a manager-managed LLC, the managers have this authority; while the members have no actual or apparent authority to bind the manager-managed LLC. The ownership interests are transferable and assignable with the consent of the other owners. Depending on the state in which the LLC is organized, the LLC will dissolve on the death, bankruptcy or withdrawal of a member, unless the remaining members take action to prevent the dissolution.

F. Choice of Business Entity Analysis

In [*The UCLA Tax Conference: The Structure of Silicon Valley Start-Ups*, 41 UCLA L. Rev. 1737 (1994),] a 1994 article examining the choice of entity by high-tech start-ups, Professor Joseph Bankman argued that, because of tax advantages, using an entity with pass-through taxation is a better choice than using a corporation. Given that the start-up costs of a high-tech company are tax deductible, his premise was that a partnership structure would allow the inevitable losses in the early stages of the start-up to pass through to each individual partner. These losses could be used to offset income from other sources and reduce the partner's tax liability. On the other hand, if the new entity is a corporation, only the corporation can deduct the losses. As Bankman points out, "[t]he newly-formed company, however, has no material source of present or past income against which to deduct the expense." Yet, Bankman found that most start-ups incorporate and thereby forego many of the tax advantages that partnerships receive. While the theory regarding the value of losses is interesting, as a practical matter, these losses have little if any value to the traditional venture fund supported by institutional investors.

By mid-1996 every state had enacted an LLC statute. LLCs became popular because they combined the best attribute of partnerships, pass-through taxation, with the best attribute of corporations, limited liability. Therefore, some commentators have argued that the LLC is the best initial choice for entrepreneurs. On the other hand, one of the advantages of incorporating is separating equity ownership from control, an attribute not always present with an LLC. LLCs are specifically designed to be more flexible than corporations and can be organized as manager-managed entities. However, venture capitalists appear to be cool to this approach: "Conventional wisdom holds that venture capital firms generally do not invest in limited liability companies."

Not surprisingly, the choice of entity for high-tech start-ups often is driven by their subsequent need for additional money from venture funding. Venture capitalists invest in companies that statistically are likely never to go public. As private company investors, the venture capitalist seeks as much certainty as possible in an investment. In this respect corporations have the advantage because they have many years of case law providing much greater predictability relating to shareholder rights and director duties. Furthermore, even those arguing that the LLC should be the entity of choice, acknowledge that if the start-up ever goes public, the market will require it to incur the costs of restructuring as a corporation. Nevertheless, they contend that the transaction costs associated with a restructuring are less than the tax benefits derived from starting out as an LLC.

In explaining the higher incidence of incorporation over partnership formation, despite the theoretical tax advantages of not incorporating, Bankman suspected that entrepreneurs simply did not value tax savings as a priority. Some entrepreneurs were not even aware of the tax consequences of incorporating. Since Bankman's study, LLCs have become more widely accepted as a viable start-up entity choice. Nevertheless, corporations remain the preferred vehicle for high tech start-ups. The following is an explanation for the persistence of incorporation despite the tax advantages of an LLC:

> To the extent participants in this market continue to choose the corporate form over theoretically available LLC structures, it may be because innovation may not promise sufficient advantages over the customary structure. . . . [V]enture capital firms structure investment relationships through legal forms that create significant rights in firm governance. If these rights are valuable, sophisticated investors are not likely to experiment with organizational innovations that carry uncertain consequences.

[Deborah A. DeMott, *Agency and the Unincorporated Firm: Reflections on Design on the Same Plane of Interest*, 54 WASH. & LEE L. REV. 595, 609, 611 (1997).] In addition to corporate governance issues, most venture capital firms have restrictions in their fund documents that prohibit investing in flow-through entities due to certain adverse income tax consequences to their limited partners. Further, the flow through of losses to pension plans and other tax-exempt entities is in most cases meaningless, so there may be no tax advantage ever under any circumstances. In addition, the body of case law available to interpret stockholder rights, and director duties is well established for corporations but virtually barren for partnerships and LLCs. Finally, venture investors look for methods to enhance cash flow after a start-up reaches profitability. If net operating losses have flowed through to investors, the losses are no longer available to the enterprise. For corporations, the incurred losses are available to shelter future taxable income and support future tax-free growth of the enterprise.

An entrepreneur should weigh the advantages and disadvantages of each business entity, taking into account whether the nature of the entity matches the type of investor that is being targeted. For example, a venture that can be financed by a few high net worth investors may be a candidate for operating as an LLC, but a biotechnology company requiring institutional investors would not typically be a candidate.

. . . .

2. Early Stage Financing Options

Kristopher D. Brown & Graham D. S. Anderson, Financing and Strategic Alliances for the New Media Company

Practising Law Institute, Representing the New Media Company
1999 545 PLI/Pat 709*

[The following reading describes typical financing options for new media companies—companies that are frequently concerned with sales of intellectual property via the Internet and other new media—as well as for other start-up companies with products based on intellectual property.]

I. INTRODUCTION TO FINANCING NEW MEDIA COMPANIES

Every new company eventually requires capital beyond the means of its founders in order to finance its operations. This inevitability creates significant obstacles for the company to overcome including (i) identifying a source of capital, (ii) minimizing the cost of any secured capital, (iii) negotiating a deal to the satisfaction of both parties, and (iv) maintaining a stable flow of capital going forward.

While each obstacle can be overcome through careful planning and diligence efforts by both the company, its lawyers and other advisers, the structure of any new financing will ultimately depend on (i) the amount of capital needed, (ii) the company's operating history (to the extent there is any), (iii) the company's current financial condition, and (iv) the risks associated with the company's business.

Founders of new media companies will generally face the same obstacles as any other start-up. However, because new media companies have, by definition, a limited operating history and are considered fairly risky ventures, simple financing

---

arrangements are few and far between. Therefore, the planning process involved in anticipation of securing third-party financing is all the more important.

A. Formulating a Plan and Assessing Costs

Accepting complexity as a certainty, the founders of a new media company must diligently consider their need for capital and what they would be willing to part with in order to secure this capital. Entrepreneurs too often wait until negotiations have reached a standstill before considering these issues. The result is often that the cost of capital is much higher than what otherwise should have been necessary. It is the responsibility of lawyers to raise these issues early on.

The company must have an acute understanding of its needs going forward to insure that it avoids unnecessary costs. Putting together a detailed and highly specific budget will help to adequately assess the needs going forward. Once the capital requirements are in place, the founders will then be in a position to consider the possible cost of such capital. All third party investors will demand certain concessions in order to mitigate the risk associated with their investment. Such concessions may include (i) control of the company or a percent thereof, (ii) in the case of debt financings, possibly a security interest in the company's assets, (iii) a right to veto certain material corporate transactions, and/or (iv) under certain special circumstances, a right to exit or even take control of the company in the event certain operating goals are not met within a specified time frame. A lawyer should be prepared to advise the company on the pros and cons of each of these terms when working with a company on a financing transaction.

A new media company has much better negotiating leverage with potential investors if it begins its capital raising efforts early on. If a company waits too long to begin trying to identify financing sources, its ongoing costs combined with diminishing financial reserves will put pressure on the company's management to cut any deal they can make with an investor. Accordingly, the average early stage new media company should begin preparing for capital raising activities typically six to twelve months before they anticipate needing the funds. Of course, this is not always possible at the stage where a new media company is first being formed, and lawyers should advise clients seeking to build a new media business that they may be required to finance the operation out of their own pockets for a long period.

For both securities law purposes and to ensure that young companies with limited personnel and other resources are not focusing solely on raising capital to the detriment of building their business, companies also should not be continuously entering into small financing transactions. Instead of raising money on an ad hoc and continuous basis, a company's fund raising activities should be carefully coordinated, with the company first attempting to line up or commit financing sources and then working with its lawyer to finalize the deal with an individual or group of investors. A lawyer should let the company know that this approach is also cheaper for them in terms of his or her time.

Furthermore, the conditions of the new media market amplify the need for a company to adequately consider its position with respect to a financing, i.e., there are now many potential investments and, ultimately, only a finite amount of potential investors. Companies are therefore not only forced to compete with one another in the marketplace, but also for the attention of investors. This situation can increase the cost of capital for new media companies even more than the typical start-up venture.

. . . .

B. Identifying Sources of Capital

Armed with knowledge of both their basic needs and potential concessions, the new media company's founders will be in a good position to know what type of third-party investor to pursue. The traditional sources of capital, i.e., private placements and/or bank lending, are reserved for more established and tested companies and are offered to start-up ventures on an extremely limited basis, and often only with the support (e.g., through a guaranty) by an institutional venture capital firm or strategic partner that is already committed to the company. Nevertheless, there are a number of other options for start-up ventures, and specifically new media companies, to explore.

The major sources of capital for these organizations are detailed below. Generally, they are (i) seed capital for companies looking for small amounts of cash to finance the initial stages of a venture, (ii) venture capital for companies in need of larger amounts of financing for a longer term and willing to give up certain corporate powers, and (iii) strategic alliances for companies looking for an established business partner to mold and shepherd the company into a successful enterprise going forward.

. . . .

II. TRADITIONAL METHODS OF SECURING CAPITAL

A. Bank and Asset Based Lending

Banks are a major source of both short-term and long-term funds. Through borrowing, an entrepreneur is able to acquire the funds she needs to operate her business without giving up control or a piece of any future growth. The principal downside to borrowing is that, in addition to charging interest, banks often require their borrowers to adhere to very strict operating standards to keep the loan in good standing. The pressures of operating in such an environment could outweigh the benefits.

Furthermore, for the start-up company and specifically for the new media company, there are a number of barriers to access to commercial bank loans which must be overcome before a loan will be actually approved. When making a decision as to whether to extend a loan to a small company, banks pay strict attention to the financial history and projections and the management of the business. The bank will also consider the past relationship it has had with the company and its principals.

Unfortunately, since these companies rarely have more than a business plan and budget, qualifying for bank lending is often not possible for a start-up company.

An additional difficulty associated with borrowing money is that banks will often not lend funds without collateral or a recognized institutional investor to secure or guarantee the loan. In fact, banks commonly will require collateral valued at more than two times that of the principal of the loan. Most start-up companies are not able to provide such security. Furthermore, as new media companies typically are not "asset-intensive" businesses, it is difficult to qualify even for the most mature new media company.

The most common solution to the aforementioned difficulties is for the founders of the new media company to take a personal interest in the venture, i.e., a home equity loan (assuming the entrepreneur owns a home) or personal guarantee. The price of such a commitment is of course that should the company fail, the bank will seek to collect as much of its loan as possible and the entrepreneur could lose her home and/or other personal property.

1. National Banking Act

Although many new media companies fail to qualify as borrowers under the stringent criteria of commercial banks, most qualify for direct loans and/or awards from Small Business Investment Companies (SBICs). The structure of SBICs is discussed below, but it is worth mentioning that the National Banking Act, which sets the guidelines for the operation of national banking associations, allows banks to invest 5% of their capital in one or more of these entities. As a result, many national banks, which otherwise are restricted from making equity investments, have formed SBICs to make investments in small businesses. Access to this capital is not as difficult as to actual loans from the bank itself, but as discussed later below, it presents certain other issues for the entrepreneur to consider.

2. Venture Lending

Increasingly, more established new media companies are seeking and obtaining bank debt, either in the form of revolving or term loans to finance certain aspects of their business and operations. Equity is typically used to fund a new media company's highest risk expenses, such as start-up, product development and market entry expenses. A loan or debt, on the other hand, is typically used to fund assets which generate cash, such as products, equipment and facilities, as well as certain lower risk expenses, such as working capital, research and development and administration. Accordingly, as discussed earlier, most early stage new media companies, that are focusing on creating and starting the business, are not appropriate candidates for debt and so do not have access to traditional lenders.

Venture lending, where traditional lending is combined with the grant by a company to the lender of warrants (i.e., rights to buy a proportionate amount of common stock at a specified price) or some other form of equity, is being used more and more to adjust the risk premiums for a lender. New media companies that can obtain venture lending are able to minimize overall equity dilution and diversify sources of capital. In most cases, however, it remains the case that only those new media companies that have already raised some money and are affiliated with institutional venture capital firms can obtain venture loans. Typically, this is because the venture lender will want the new media company to have at least some assets (such as equipment or accounts receivable) that can serve as collateral to secure the loan obligation. Guaranties may also be sought from the venture capital firms affiliated with the company as a condition to any loan.

A lawyer advising a new media company that is seeking to obtain a loan should be familiar with the general legal provisions found in loan documents. Among other terms, the representations, warranties and covenants in such loan documents will need to be carefully analyzed to ensure that they are tailored to the company's business and do not restrict in any material way the company from operating in the normal course. After the loan documents have been entered into, the lawyer should also stay in touch with the client to advise about the importance of not violating certain restrictive and other ongoing covenants contained in such documents. For example, failure in some instances to stay in compliance could cause the company to become in default, triggering the lender's right to seize the company's assets.

3. Venture Leasing

Early stage new media companies will typically lease most of the equipment used in their business (e.g., copiers, telephones, computer systems). Leasing equipment instead of purchasing it outright allows the new media company to limit overall expenditures, helping to ensure that it develops its business in accordance with its budget. Accordingly, for lawyers advising new media companies, it is essential to have at least some basic understanding of equipment or operating leasing issues and the contractual provisions of leases.

Lessors typically present standard form operating leases to start-up new media companies, on a "take-or-leave-it" basis, since a young new media company has very little leverage with which to negotiate and is typically not considered a good credit risk. The lawyer must analyze the lease form presented to the new media company with reference to the company's specific objectives, and with the goal that a demand be made to the lessor to at least modify the standard form to address the company's unique business objectives. It is also critical that the operating lease not be structured in such a way that the new media company will be in violation simply by operating its business in the ordinary course. Most importantly, the lawyer should help the new media company to negotiate the representations, warranties and covenants in the operating lease as they relate to the default provisions.

For most new media companies, it is very difficult to obtain any form of leasing until the company has received at least one or more rounds of venture financing, and has developed a strong relationship with an institutional venture capital firm. In some cases, the lessor may even require that the venture capital firm give it a guaranty as a condition to entering into the operating lease with the new media company. Earlier stage companies (even ones without venture capital firm involvement) may, however, be able to receive such leasing arrangements if they have between $0.5 million to $5 million of non-custom, fungible assets that can be used as collateral, such as personal computer hardware and off-the-shelf software. High end servers and other specialized items, even if owned outright by a new media company, may be too specialized to serve as such collateral.

Increasingly, so-called "venture leasing firms" are seeking warrants or other forms of equity from new media companies in exchange for providing the company with an operating lease. A warrant can serve as "sweetener" to enhance the marketability of the lease. In exchange for the warrant, new media companies will sometimes negotiate to remove all covenants and other restrictive terms from the operating lease. As the number of venture leasing firms has increased in recent years, many such firms appear to be more willing to negotiate such provisions, particularly as they seek to attract the long-term business of good new media customers.

B. Private Placements

Private placements, another traditional source of financing, consist of the offer and sale of equity or debt securities in an offering exempt from both federal and state securities laws. The prime purpose of such an offering is to quickly raise capital without having to contend with the heavy disclosure requirements associated with a public offering.

In order to qualify for any securities law exemption, private placements are normally restricted to wealthy individuals and institutional investors known as accredited investors. The advantage of such an offering is that the company is able to control its cost of capital by setting the terms of the sale and merely selling to those parties willing to buy. In addition, the company is able to avoid the burdensome disclosure requirements required in public offerings. Unfortunately for emerging new media companies, these investors are often not willing to make such an investment in young companies competing within high-risk industries.

As a result of the above, executing a private placement is normally not a viable option for a new media company to pursue. At the early stage of development, a new media company . . . will likely find it difficult to even retain a placement agent to market the securities. Such a company will likely have to raise its initial financing from some of the other sources discussed below.

III. SEED CAPITAL (PRIMARILY EQUITY)

Given the difficulties of raising capital by traditional means, an immediate issue for any new company to face is how it will finance its operations. Although the proposed business plan is still in its formative stage, the entrepreneur must consider this issue. To do so intelligently, the entrepreneur must understand two things: (i) any potential investor will likely evaluate the entrepreneur as much as (and in many cases more than) the business plan she proposes; and (ii) any eventual negotiated deal will likely include the sale of a significant portion of the company.

Investors willing to provide a start-up company with its initial funds, or seed capital, generally trust their ability to evaluate people more than their ability to evaluate an untested business plan. Therefore who the entrepreneur is and how she comes across will play an enormous role in whether any seed capital will ultimately be secured. In addition, the investor will almost certainly demand a significant amount of ownership of the company, usually in the form of common stock. As a common stockholder, the investor can maintain significant control over the affairs of the company and also share in any achieved growth.

Given these truths, the difficult question becomes where to actually find the money. Three sources of seed capital are detailed below.

A. Entrepreneur's Personal Resources

The primary source of third party financing for early stage new media companies is the entrepreneur's "friends and family." Considering that access to seed capital is heavily dependent on the entrepreneur herself, it makes sense that the chief source of capital will be from those with whom she is personally familiar. However, certain potential problems with this form of financing should be considered.

First and foremost, is that the potential pool of funds for most entrepreneurs is limited; i.e., not everyone is related to or friendly with a millionaire. Therefore, a new company will often find that as soon as it secures these funds, it requires more. Second, the costs of any failed enterprise are multiplied when one considers the guilt and emotional pain associated with losing the capital of a loved one. As most start-up companies, including new media companies, are extremely risky investments, there is a strong chance that any invested capital will be lost. As a result, the possibility exists that friends could turn into enemies.

B. Government Sources

A potential way to avoid the pitfalls of "friends and family" money is for a new company to secure its seed capital from the government. Both Federal and various state government agencies fund organizations which help finance small businesses in a variety of ways, including (i) the issuance of a direct financial award (more typical among state organizations), (ii) the extension of a low-rate loan and/or (iii) the guaranty of a commercial bank loan. The federal government's Small Business Administration (the "SBA") is probably the most popular of these organizations.

Most new media companies in search of seed capital will qualify as small businesses by the SBA definition since both their employee base and annual sales are typically small. The most common form of SBA funding is through the guaranty of a commercial loan. In order for the SBA to guaranty a commercial loan, the company must grant a security interest in its assets and, in certain cases, the entrepreneur must also sign a personal guaranty for both the SBA and the lending bank. As a result, the same difficulties previously discussed as relating to bank loans will again be encountered. In addition, these loans are initially offered only in small amounts. However, the potential for additional loans, in higher principal amounts, increases as the company pays off its debt and establishes a favorable credit rating.

As discussed earlier, the SBA also licenses private capital funding organizations known as SBICs. With their own capital and with funds provided by the federal government at favorable rates, SBICs provide capital to small independent businesses, including new media companies. Special SBICs are even formed specifically to provide financing to entrepreneurs who have been denied access to capital because of their race or socio-economic class. The form of financing provided by SBICs is typically debt, but some forms of equity investments are also possible.

. . . .

C. Wealthy Individuals and Other Private Sources (Angels)

Increasingly, new media entrepreneurs are seeking to raise capital in the private sector. A fast-growing source of such money comes from "angel" investors, who in 1998 reportedly provided over $10 billion in seed capital to start-up companies. Angels are typically wealthy individuals, usually former entrepreneurs, who look to grow their fortunes by investing in new start-up ventures. It is estimated that there are approximately 300,000 such people in the United States today. Angels will normally provide capital in the range of few hundred thousand dollars, but sometimes as high as 2 million dollars. In return they will demand various forms of equity including common stock and options for additional shares. As discussed, however, tapping into angel capital is perhaps one of the most burdensome obstacles facing entrepreneurs today.

1. Significant Barriers to Financing

Angel investing is a relatively recent phenomenon that has surfaced to fill a void in the private equity market, notably seed financing for start-up companies. Ten years ago, venture capital organizations filled this void, but insofar as these organizations have significantly larger pools of capital to invest, they no longer make as many small start-up investments. Unfortunately, it is precisely the noninstitutional nature of angel investing that creates the obstacles that entrepreneurs in search of capital must overcome.

First, the angel market is highly fragmented. Angels do not operate as investment companies; they operate as sole proprietorships. The angel usually invests her own capital in one or two investments at a time. Second, most angels restrict their investments to industries they are familiar with or have competed in. Consequently (and unfortunately for new media companies), the more innovative the product or industry, the less chance there will be of finding an angel willing to invest. Third, angels usually like to keep a close personal watch on their investments and as such, they will typically not invest in a company that operates too far away from their home. Again, this poses a difficulty for new media companies which often are located in lesser populated and inexpensive locales.

. . . .

4. Typical Angel Transactions

The most common form of angel financing is equity. Normally, because the founders are usually the only other stockholders, the angel is satisfied to receive common stock in return for his investment. The rights enjoyed by the angel and how great a percentage of the company the angel receives will vary depending on the size of the investment and the maturity of the company.

As mentioned, the typical angel invests his own capital in usually one or two companies. As a result, the angel will feel a personal stake in the company. The entrepreneur should thus expect that the angel will play a significant role in the management of the company. Angels, whether or not in control of the company, will still negotiate a great many rights to assure their ability to closely monitor the day to day operations of their investment. Examples include the right (i) to specifically appoint certain board members, (ii) to approve of certain management appointments and/or (iii) to control a variety of common management functions, including check writing, salary structure and the formulation of the business plan.

5. Cost/Benefit of Angel Capital

The above discussion alludes to some of the many advantages and disadvantages of securing angel financing. The prime advantage of angel capital is that the angel, as a former entrepreneur, is likely to be more understanding of the wants and needs of the company's founders. In addition, as angels are experienced business people, they typically offer a company more than financial assistance; their business sense and personal network of contacts are often great sources of knowledge and capital for the growing company. Finally, because angels are usually investing their own capital they offer more flexibility than do some other more institutional investors. Angel investors are not bound by time windows or performance goals; their capital is truly invested for the long term.

There are certain disadvantages. As discussed, angels are normally more "hands-on" than other private investors. Despite the fact that securing such a partner may not have been what the entrepreneur bargained for, it may be exactly what she gets. In addition, because the angel has negotiated a substantial amount of control over the enterprise, the entrepreneur may experience problems if her vision for the future of the company differs from that of the angel. Finally, as most angel investments are not more than a few hundred thousand dollars, angel capital will only get the company so far. Therefore, although they are willing to keep their money invested for a long time, the company will still have to look for more substantial investors going forward.

Notes & Questions

1. Assuming that venture capital financing is not presently an option, what forms of business entity will best serve a company like Digital Ignition in the short-term as it develops new products and defines its manufacturing and marketing techniques for those products? To what extent are the business entity selection issues confronting Digital Ignition typical of those facing start-ups generally? How does the company's plan to rely on intellectual property protections in commercializing products in a new technology area affect the choice of a desirable business form and ownership structure for Digital Ignition's future activities?

2. What considerations should govern the percentages of ownership interests allo-cated to each of the six initial owners of Digital Ignition? If Digital Ignition is oper-ated as a corporation, what percentage of the corporation's stock should each of the six parties receive? What role should loans from one or more of the initial owners play in funding Digital Ignition's start-up activities? How might preferred stock—which typically gives the holder a right to corporate dividend payments ahead of any payments made to general or "common" stock holders—be used in combination with common stock to adjust the ownership interests of the six co-owners to their investment risk preferences? For example, what would be the implications for the company and for Hameed Bukhari if he were to invest his $500,000 in exchange for preferred or common stock versus loaning Digital Ignition a similar amount? If, as is usually the case, holders of preferred stock do not vote on matters that are con-trolled by a majority vote of the holders of common stock (such as the election of corporate directors or the approval of a merger), how might this affect investors' pref-erences regarding their receipt of preferred versus common stock?

3. Corporate stock options giving the holders the right to purchase stock from a corporation for a specified price can be means to create useful incentives for corpo-rate owners who are also managers or employees of a firm. For example, if a com-pany's stock has a present value of about $10, stock options that are exercisable—that is, can be used to force a sale of stock to the option holder—at $15 per share will encourage the option holders to manage corporate affairs to drive the value of the company's stock above $15 per share. If the company's stock becomes worth, for example, $17 per share, each option to buy at $15 per share has an immediate value of $2 (the difference between the exercise price and the value of the stock at the time of exercise).

Stock options may also be used to ensure that key managers and employees "stick with" a corporate enterprise for a substantial period. This can be accomplished by specifying that stock options received by the key individuals only vest—that is, become exercisable—after the recipient has completed a specified period of service to the company involved.

How might stock options granted to some or all of the six initial owners of Digi-tal Ignition help the company to realize its goals and ensure that these individuals pursue desirable actions on behalf of Digital Ignition?

4. IP-collateralized loans are popular in corporate financing because they offer advantages to both the companies and the financial institutions involved:

> For some major banks like JP Morgan Chase and Bank of America, patent-collateralized lending represents almost 15% of all corporate financing these days. That's because for the companies receiving such loans, it's a way to secure financing at a lower cost of capital without tying up their future rev-enue streams or other corporate assets. For the banks, meanwhile, patents represent assets that they can value and understand from a collateral perspective.

David Pridham, *5 Ways to Turn Your Patents Into Gold* (February 24, 2016), https://www.forbes.com/sites/davidpridham/2016/02/24/5-ways-to-turn-your-patents-into-gold/#73bbff185b70.

5. Angel investors are important sources of early-stage investments in some IP-based start-up companies, but have tended to focus on high-technology companies in specific industries. According to a summary prepared by the federal Securities and Exchange Commission:

> [One report indicates that] angel investments amounted to $24.1 billion in 2014, with approximately 73,400 entrepreneurial ventures receiving angel funding and approximately 316,600 active angel investors. [*See* Jeffrey Sohl, *The Investor Angel Market in 2014: A Market Correction in Deal Size*, Center for Venture Research, May 14, 2015, available at: https://www.unh.edu/unhtoday/news/release/2015/05/14/unh-center-venture-research-us-angel-investor-market-2014-made-market.] In 2014, angel investments were concentrated in software, healthcare, and IT services. The average angel deal size was approximately $328,500. Seed/startup stage deals accounted for 25% and early stage deals accounted for 46%.

Securities and Exchange Commission, Crowdfunding, 80 Fed. Reg. 71388-01 (Nov. 16, 2015) at Sec. III(A)(2)(c).

6. Empirical evidence suggests that the issuance of patents to start-up companies can substantially enhance business financing opportunities and chances for later business success. A study by researchers from the Harvard Business School and the Stern School of Business at New York University identified several types of positive business impacts following the issuance of first patents to start-up companies. The study compared the subsequent fortunes of start-up companies with granted and rejected initial patent applications. The researchers found large business benefits flowing from the issuance of an initial patent:

> Our sample covers all 34,215 first-time patent applications filed by U.S. startups at the USPTO since 2001 that received a final decision by December 31, 2013. Our estimates suggest that [issuance of a first patent] increases the average startup's employment growth over the next five years by 54.5 percentage points. The effect on sales growth — a 79.5 percentage-point increase over five years — is even larger. For the average startup in our sample, these estimates imply that receiving a patent leads to 16 additional employees after five years, and $10.6 million in additional sales cumulated over five years after winning the patent lottery. A first patent grant also increases both the number of subsequent patents the firm is granted (by 49%) and their quality (with the average number of citations per subsequent patent increasing by 26%). Patent approvals appear to have a particularly strong effect on sales growth and follow-on innovation for startups in the [information technology (IT)] sector — a result that contrasts with prior survey

evidence that large IT firms consider patents to be among the least effective mechanisms to ensure the profitability of their R&D investments.

Joan Farre-Mensa, Deepak Hegde & Alexander Ljungqvist, *What Is a Patent Worth? Evidence from the U.S. Patent "Lottery"* (March 14, 2017). USPTO Economic Working Paper 2015-5, https://ssrn.com/abstract=2704028.

The researchers speculated that an initial patent grant provides these large benefits to a start-up company by substantially increasing the company's financing opportunities. They found that a patent grant increased a start-up's chances of securing funding from venture capitalists by 47 percent, and of securing a loan by pledging a patent as collateral by 76 percent during the first three years following the patent decision. They also found that a patent grant more than doubled the odds of a start-up raising funding from public investors through an initial public stock offering. *See id.* at 3–4.

In the specific context of promoting investments in start-up companies by venture capitalists (VCs), initial patents distinguish start-up companies that are likely to have opportunities to pursue their business models and potentially achieve success from similar companies that are mere explorers acting for the benefit of bigger concerns:

> That's because by defining your rights with patents, you show potential investors that you have secured tangible protection for your underlying business model and core innovations — and are thus more likely to succeed in establishing yourself as a viable, growing business.

> Without patent protection for your core innovations, VCs will consider your company to be no more than a free research arm for larger incumbent players — incumbents who will copy your innovations with impunity and eventually drive you from the market using your own inventions.

David Pridham, *5 Ways To Turn Your Patents Into Gold* (February 24, 2016), https://www.forbes.com/sites/davidpridham/2016/02/24/5-ways-to-turn-your-patents-into-gold/#73bbff185b70.

7. Just as granted patents tend to imply enhanced value for corporate patent owners, invalidated patents may correspond to significant reductions in perceived corporate value and drops in associated stock prices. The frequent relationship between losses of patent interests and drops in corporate stock prices has led to stock investment strategies that produce investor gains from IP value losses. Kyle Bass, head of the Hayman Capital Management LP hedge fund, has described a two-part investment approach that may generate investor gains from IP losses. Bass suggested that investment firms could produce profits by (1) initiating a patent validity review while (2) at the same time shorting the shares of the patent owner. Shorting the shares will permit the party with the short ownership position to make money if the shares involved drop in price. With stock owners worrying that the challenged patent will be invalidated (perhaps even before a validity review result is reached), the stock price of the patent owner will tend to drop and investors in short positions may be able to reap corresponding profits. *See* Joseph Walker & Rob Copeland, *New Hedge Fund*

Strategy: Dispute the Patent, Short the Stock, WALL STREET J., April 7, 2015. An empirical study of this investment strategy found that the filing of patent validity challenges did tend to produce statistically significant drops in the stock prices of the patent holders, but indicated that whether these drops were large enough to produce profits by shorting the shares of the patent owners would depend on the transaction costs incurred in carrying out the strategy. *See* Rabea Kruppert, *Dispute the Patent, Ahort the Stock: Empirical Analysis of a New Hedge Fund Strategy*, 50 INT. REV. LAW & ECON. 25, 25–35 (2017).

3. Crowdfunding

Crowdfunding is a rapidly expanding means for funding new business activities and new companies. In one form focusing on the funding of new product development and production, crowdfunding conducted via Internet sites such as Kickstarter allows multiple interested parties to pre-purchase new products (including new IP-based products) and thereby inject funds into enterprises that create and perfect the products. More controversially, crowdfunding can also be a means for widespread investment in new and developing companies, with few of the formal document filings, information disclosures, regulatory oversight, and shareholder protections that have governed large scale public offerings of stock in the United States for many years.

This subsection describes crowdfunding and efforts by the federal Securities and Exchange Commission (SEC) to establish limited protections for crowdfunding investors by regulating aspects of crowdfunding processes and the features of related service providers such as crowdfunding platform operators. As the SEC's commentary below describes, the relatively lightly regulated processes authorized for securities-based crowdfunding in the United States will only support fairly small fundraising campaigns by companies. For more elaborate fundraising via public solicitations of investments, companies will still need to rely on initial public offerings (IPOs) of stock and comply with the elaborate SEC regulations that govern these offerings. IPOs and the legal problems they can pose for IP-intensive businesses are addressed in Chapter 8.

Securities and Exchange Commission, Crowdfunding
80 Fed. Reg. 71388 (November 16, 2015) (Final Rules — Excerpts)

I. Introduction

A. Background

Crowdfunding is a relatively new and evolving method of using the Internet to raise capital to support a wide range of ideas and ventures. An entity or individual raising funds through crowdfunding typically seeks small individual contributions from a large number of people. Individuals interested in the crowdfunding campaign — members of the "crowd" — may share information about the project, cause, idea or business with each other and use the information to decide whether to fund the campaign based on the collective "wisdom of the crowd."

The Jumpstart Our Business Startups Act (the "JOBS Act"), [1 Pub. L. No. 112-106, 126 Stat. 306 (2012),] enacted on April 5, 2012, establishes a regulatory structure for startups and small businesses to raise capital through securities offerings using the Internet through crowdfunding. The crowdfunding provisions of the JOBS Act were intended to help provide startups and small businesses with capital by making relatively low dollar offerings of securities, featuring relatively low dollar investments by the "crowd," less costly. Congress included a number of provisions intended to protect investors who engage in these transactions, including investment limits, required disclosures by issuers, and a requirement to use regulated intermediaries. The provisions also permit Internet-based platforms to facilitate the offer and sale of securities in crowdfunding transactions without having to register with the Commission as brokers.

In the United States, crowdfunding generally has not involved the offer of a share in any financial returns or profits that the fundraiser may expect to generate from business activities financed through crowdfunding. Such a profit or revenue-sharing model—sometimes referred to as the "equity model" of crowdfunding—could trigger the application of the federal securities laws because it likely would involve the offer and sale of a security. Under the Securities Act of 1933 ("Securities Act"), the offer and sale of securities is required to be registered unless an exemption is available. Some observers have stated that registered offerings are not feasible for raising smaller amounts of capital, as is done in a typical crowdfunding transaction, because of the costs of conducting a registered offering and the resulting ongoing reporting obligations under the Securities Exchange Act of 1934 ("Exchange Act") that may arise as a result of the offering. Limitations under existing regulations, including purchaser qualification requirements for offering exemptions that permit general solicitation and general advertising, have made private placement exemptions generally unavailable for crowdfunding transactions, which are intended to involve a large number of investors and not be limited to investors that meet specific qualifications.

Moreover, someone who operates a Web site to effect the purchase and sale of securities for the account of others generally would, under pre-existing regulations, be required to register with the Commission as a broker-dealer and comply with the laws and regulations applicable to broker-dealers. A person that operates such a Web site only for the purchase of securities of startups and small businesses, however, may find it impractical in view of the limited nature of that person's activities and business to register as a broker-dealer and operate under the full set of regulatory obligations that apply to broker-dealers.

B. Title III of the JOBS Act

Title III of the JOBS Act ("Title III") added new Securities Act Section 4(a)(6), which provides an exemption from the registration requirements of Securities Act Section 5 for certain crowdfunding transactions. To qualify for the exemption under Section 4(a)(6), crowdfunding transactions by an issuer (including all entities controlled by or under common control with the issuer) must meet specified requirements, including the following:

- The amount raised must not exceed $1 million in a 12-month period;
- individual investments in all crowdfunding issuers in a 12-month period are limited to:
  - The greater of $2,000 or 5 percent of annual income or net worth, if annual income or net worth of the investor is less than $100,000; and
  - 10 percent of annual income or net worth (not to exceed an amount sold of $100,000), if annual income or net worth of the investor is $100,000 or more; and
- transactions must be conducted through an intermediary that either is registered as a broker-dealer or is registered as a new type of entity called a "funding portal."

In addition, Title III:

- Adds Securities Act Section 4A, which requires, among other things, that issuers and intermediaries that facilitate transactions between issuers and investors in reliance on Section 4(a)(6) provide certain information to investors and potential investors, take other actions and provide notices and other information to the Commission;
- adds Exchange Act Section 3(h), which requires the Commission to adopt rules to exempt, either conditionally or unconditionally, "funding portals" from having to register as a broker-dealer pursuant to Exchange Act Section 15(a)(1);
- mandates that the Commission establish disqualification provisions under which an issuer would not be able to avail itself of the Section 4(a)(6) exemption if the issuer or an intermediary was subject to a disqualifying event; and
- adds Exchange Act Section 12(g)(6), which requires the Commission to adopt rules to exempt from the registration requirements of Section 12(g), either conditionally or unconditionally, securities acquired pursuant to an offering made in reliance on Section 4(a)(6).

. . .

II. Final Rules Implementing Regulation Crowdfunding

[Following a multi-year rule development process, the SEC adopted "Regulation Crowdfunding" containing rules to implement the crowdfunding provisions of federal securities laws.] Regulation Crowdfunding, among other things, permits individuals to invest in securities-based crowdfunding transactions subject to certain thresholds, limits the amount of money an issuer can raise under the crowdfunding exemption, requires issuers to disclose certain information about their offers, and creates a regulatory framework for the intermediaries that facilitate the crowdfunding transactions. As an overview, under the final rules:

- An issuer is permitted to raise a maximum aggregate amount of $1 million through crowdfunding offerings in a 12-month period;

- Individual investors, over the course of a 12-month period, are permitted to invest in the aggregate across all crowdfunding offerings up to:

  - If either their annual income or net worth is less than $100,000, then the greater of:

    — $2,000 or

    — 5 percent of the lesser of their annual income or net worth.

  - If both their annual income and net worth are equal to or more than $100,000, then 10 percent of the lesser of their annual income or net worth; and

- During the 12-month period, the aggregate amount of securities sold to an investor through all crowdfunding offerings may not exceed $100,000.

Certain companies are not eligible to use the Regulation Crowdfunding exemption. Ineligible companies include non-U.S. companies, companies that already are Exchange Act reporting companies, certain investment companies, companies that are disqualified under Regulation Crowdfunding's disqualification rules, companies that have failed to comply with the annual reporting requirements under Regulation Crowdfunding during the two years immediately preceding the filing of the offering statement, and companies that have no specific business plan or have indicated their business plan is to engage in a merger or acquisition with an unidentified company or companies.

Securities purchased in a crowdfunding transaction generally cannot be resold for a period of one year. Holders of these securities do not count toward the threshold that requires an issuer to register its securities with the Commission under Section 12(g) of the Exchange Act if the issuer is current in its annual reporting obligation, retains the services of a registered transfer agent and has less than $25 million in assets.

Disclosure by Issuers. The final rules require issuers conducting an offering pursuant to Regulation Crowdfunding to file certain information with the Commission and provide this information to investors and the relevant intermediary facilitating the crowdfunding offering. Among other things, in its offering documents, the issuer is required to disclose:

- Information about officers and directors as well as owners of 20 percent or more of the issuer;

- A description of the issuer's business and the use of proceeds from the offering;

- The price to the public of the securities or the method for determining the price, the target offering amount, the deadline to reach the target offering amount, and whether the issuer will accept investments in excess of the target offering amount;

- Certain related-party transactions;

- A discussion of the issuer's financial condition; and

- Financial statements of the issuer that are, depending on the amount offered and sold during a 12-month period, accompanied by information from the issuer's tax returns, reviewed by an independent public accountant, or audited by an independent auditor. An issuer relying on these rules for the first time would be permitted to provide reviewed rather than audited financial statements, unless financial statements of the issuer are available that have been audited by an independent auditor.

Issuers are required to amend the offering document during the offering period to reflect material changes and provide updates on the issuer's progress toward reaching the target offering amount.

In addition, issuers relying on the Regulation Crowdfunding exemption are required to file an annual report with the Commission and provide it to investors.

<u>Crowdfunding Platforms.</u> One of the key investor protections of Title III of the JOBS Act is the requirement that Regulation Crowdfunding transactions take place through an SEC-registered intermediary, either a broker-dealer or a funding portal. Under Regulation Crowdfunding, offerings must be conducted exclusively through a platform operated by a registered broker or a funding portal, which is a new type of SEC registrant. The rules require these intermediaries to:

- Provide investors with educational materials;
- Take measures to reduce the risk of fraud;
- Make available information about the issuer and the offering;
- Provide communication channels to permit discussions about offerings on the platform; and
- Facilitate the offer and sale of crowdfunded securities.

The rules prohibit funding portals from:

- Offering investment advice or making recommendations;
- Soliciting purchases, sales or offers to buy securities offered or displayed on its platform;
- Compensating promoters and others for solicitations or based on the sale of securities; and
- Holding, possessing, or handling investor funds or securities.

The rules provide a safe harbor under which funding portals can engage in certain activities consistent with these restrictions.

. . .

[According to the SEC, securities-based crowdfunding practices conforming to the SEC's Regulation Crowdfunding rules and related securities statutes are likely to create significant business funding opportunities but also large implementation challenges. The following discussion describes the SEC's assessment of potential advantages and risks of securities offerings undertaken through crowdfunding processes.]

III. Economic Analysis

B. Analysis of Final Rules

1. Broad Economic Considerations

[O]fferings pursuant to Section 4(a)(6) [of the Securities Act of 1933 governing crowdfunding transactions] will likely represent a new source of capital for many small issuers that currently have difficulty raising capital. Startups and small businesses usually have smaller and more variable cash flows than larger, more established companies, and internal financing from their own business operations tends to be limited and unstable. Moreover, these businesses tend to have smaller asset bases and, thus, less collateral for traditional bank loans. [S]tartups and small businesses, which are widely viewed to have more financial constraints than publicly-traded companies and large private companies, could therefore benefit significantly from a securities-based crowdfunding market. Some small businesses may not qualify for traditional bank loans and may find alternative debt financing too costly or incompatible with their financing needs. While some small businesses may attract equity investments from angel investors or VCs, other small businesses, particularly, businesses at the seed stage may have difficulty obtaining external equity financing from these sources. We believe that the statute, as implemented by the final rules, may increase both capital formation and the efficiency of capital allocation among small issuers by expanding the range of methods of external financing available to small businesses and the pool of investors willing to finance such types of businesses. The extent to which such issuers will use the Section 4(a)(6) offering exemption, however, is difficult to assess.

If startups and small businesses find other capital raising options more attractive than securities-based crowdfunding, the impact of Section 4(a)(6) on capital formation may be limited. Even so, the availability of securities-based crowdfunding as a financing option may increase competition among suppliers of capital, resulting in a potentially lower cost of capital for all issuers, including those that choose not to use securities-based crowdfunding.

For issuers that pursue offerings in reliance on Section 4(a)(6), establishing an initial offering price might be challenging. Offerings relying on Section 4(a)(6) will not involve an underwriter who, for larger offerings, typically assists the issuer with pricing and placing the offering. Investors in offerings relying on Section 4(a)(6) may lack the sophistication to evaluate the offering price. Thus, the involvement of these investors, who are likely to have a more limited capacity for conducting due diligence on deals, may contribute to less accurate valuations.

Moreover, because of the investment limitations in securities-based crowdfunding transactions, there may not be a strong incentive, even assuming adequate knowledge and experience, for an investor to perform a thorough analysis of the issuer disclosures. To the extent that these potential information asymmetries resulting from the lack of a thorough analysis of the disclosures are anticipated by prospective investors, investor participation in offerings made in reliance on Section 4(a)(6) may decline and the associated benefits of capital formation may be lower.

Uncertainty surrounding exit strategies for investors in crowdfunding offerings also may limit the benefits. In particular, it is unlikely that purchasers in crowdfunding transactions will be able to follow the typical path to liquidity that investors in other exempt offerings follow. For instance, investors in a VC-backed startup may eventually sell their securities in an initial public offering on a national securities exchange or to another company in an acquisition. We anticipate that most businesses engaging in offerings in reliance on Section 4(a)(6) will be unlikely to progress directly to an initial public offering on a national securities exchange given their small size, and investors may lack adequate strategies or opportunities to eventually divest their holdings. A sale of the business will require the issuer to have a track record in order to attract investors with the capital willing to buy the business.

Further, the likely broad geographical dispersion of crowdfunding investors may make shareholder coordination difficult. It may also exacerbate information asymmetries between issuers and investors, if the distance between them diminishes the ability for investors to capitalize on local knowledge that may be of value in assessing the viability of the issuer's business. The use of electronic means may mitigate some of these difficulties. Even if an issuer can execute a sale or otherwise offer to buy back or retire the securities, it might be difficult for investors to determine whether the issuer is offering a fair market price. These uncertainties may limit the use of the Section 4(a)(6) exemption.

The potential benefits of the final rules also may depend on how investors respond to potential liquidity issues unique to the securities-based crowdfunding market. It is currently unclear how securities offered and sold in transactions conducted in reliance on Section 4(a)(6) will be transferred in the secondary market after the one-year restricted period ends, and investors who purchased securities in transactions conducted in reliance on Section 4(a)(6) and who seek to divest their securities may not find a liquid market. Assuming a secondary market develops, securities may be quoted on the over-the-counter market or on trading platforms for shares of private companies. Nevertheless, it is possible that secondary trading costs for investors may be substantial, effective and quoted spreads may be wide, trading volume may be low, and price volatility may be high compared to those of listed securities. Illiquidity, to different degrees, remains a concern for other exempt offerings and for registered offerings by small issuers. However, because investors purchasing securities sold in reliance on Section 4(a)(6) may be less sophisticated than investors in other private offerings due to the fact that there are no investor qualification requirements, they may face additional challenges in addressing the impact of illiquidity, either in finding a suitable trading venue or negotiating with the issuer for an alternative liquidity option. The potentially high degree of illiquidity associated with securities purchased in reliance on Section 4(a)(6) may discourage some investors from investing in issuers through such offerings, thus limiting the potential efficiency, competition and capital formation benefits of the final rules.

Even with the mandated disclosures, unsophisticated investors purchasing securities issued in reliance on Section 4(a)(6) may face certain expropriation risks, potentially limiting the upside of their investment, even when they select investments in successful ventures. This can occur if issued securities include certain features (e.g., callable securities or securities with differential control rights) or if issuers conduct insider-only financing rounds or financing rounds at reduced prices (so-called "down rounds") that have the effect of diluting an investor's interest or otherwise diminishing the value of the securities offered and sold in reliance on Section 4(a)(6). Investors purchasing securities issued in reliance on Section 4(a)(6) may not have the experience or the market power to negotiate various anti-dilution provisions, right of first refusal, tag-along rights, superior liquidation preferences and rights upon a change in control that have been developed by institutional and angel investors as protections against fundamental changes in a business. Moreover, the disperse ownership stakes of investors in securities-based crowdfunding offerings may weaken their incentives to monitor the issuer to minimize the risk of expropriation. The ensuing expropriation risk may discourage some investors from participating in offerings made in reliance on Section 4(a)(6), potentially limiting the efficiency, competition and capital formation benefits of the final rules.

The final rules also may have an effect on broker-dealers and finders participating in private offerings. Some issuers that previously relied on broker-dealers and finders to assist with raising capital through private offerings may, instead, begin to rely on the Section 4(a)(6) exemption to find investors. The precise impact of the final rules on these intermediaries will depend on whether (and, if so, to what extent) issuers switch from using existing exemptions to using the exemption provided by Section 4(a)(6) or whether the final rules primarily attract new issuers. The impact of the final rules on registered broker-dealers will also depend on the extent to which broker-dealers participate as intermediaries in the securities-based crowdfunding market. If a significant number of issuers switch from raising capital under existing private offering exemptions to relying on the exemption provided by Section 4(a)(6), this may negatively affect the revenue of finders and broker-dealers in the private offerings market. While this may disadvantage existing private offering market intermediaries, the new competition may ultimately lead to more efficient allocation of capital.

If securities-based crowdfunding primarily attracts new issuers to the market, the impact on broker-dealers and finder revenue may be negligible and the final rules may even have a positive effect on their revenues by revealing more potential clients for them, particularly to the extent that they chose to operate a funding portal. Additionally, greater investor interest in private company investment may increase capital formation, creating new opportunities for broker-dealers and finders that otherwise would have been unavailable.

The final rules also may encourage current participants in the crowdfunding market to diversify their funding models to attract a broader group of companies and to provide additional investment opportunities for investors. For example, donation-based crowdfunding platforms that currently offer investment opportunities in micro-loans generally do not permit donors to collect interest on their investments because of concerns that this activity will implicate the federal securities laws unless an exemption from registration is available. Under the final rules, these platforms may choose to register as funding portals and permit businesses to offer securities that provide investors with the opportunity to obtain a return on investment. This can broaden their user base and attract a group of investors different from those already participating in reward-based or donation-based crowdfunding. It is likely that some registered broker-dealers will find it profitable to enter the securities-based crowdfunding market and operate funding portals as well. Such an entry will increase the competition among intermediaries and likely lead to lower issuance costs for issuers.

However, many projects that are well suited for reward-based or donation-based crowdfunding (e.g., because they have finite lives, their payoffs to investors could come before the project is completed or could be contingent on the project's success, etc.) may have little in common with startups and small businesses that are well suited for an offering in reliance on Section 4(a)(6). As a result, diversification among existing platforms may not always be optimal or preferred, particularly if complying with the final rules proves disproportionately costly compared to the potential amount of capital to be raised.

Notes & Questions

1. Is regulation such as that implemented by the SEC the only way to ensure that potential investors in companies via crowdfunding processes receive complete and accurate information about companies that are the targets of potential investments? What other mechanisms involving the Internet or other means for gathering and distributing information might be used to facilitate crowdfunding while helping to ensure investor protection?

2. Crowdfunding practices are not limited to the types of securities-based crowdfunding (also sometimes referred to as "equity-based" crowdfunding) addressed in the SEC's Regulation Crowdfunding described above. The SEC has summarized the breadth of recent crowdfunding practices as follows:

> A . . . crowdfunding industry report[, Massolution, 2015CF Crowdfunding Industry Report: Market Trends, Composition and Crowdfunding Platforms, available at: http://reports.crowdsourcing.org/index.php?route =product/product&path=0&product_id=54,] defines the current crowdfunding activity in the United States generally as "lending-based," "reward-based," "donation-based," "royalty-based," "equity-based," and "hybrid." . . . [T]he industry report defines reward-based crowdfunding as a model where funders receive a "reward," such as a perk or a pre-order of a product, and it defines donation-based crowdfunding as a model where funders make philanthropic donations to causes that they want to support, with no return on their investment expected. According to the industry report, royalty-based crowdfunding, which involves a percentage of revenue from a license or a usage-based fee for the other parties' right to the ongoing use of an asset, continues to grow.

The industry report indicates that, in 2014, crowdfunding platforms raised approximately $16.2 billion globally, which represented a 167% increase over the amount raised in 2013. These amounts include various types of crowdfunding: lending-based crowdfunding accounted for the largest share of volume (approximately $11.08 billion) followed by equity-based crowdfunding (approximately $1.11 billion), reward-based crowdfunding (approximately $1.33 billion), donation-based crowdfunding (approximately $1.94 billion), royalty-based crowdfunding (approximately $273 million), and hybrid crowdfunding (approximately $487 million). In 2014, North American crowdfunding volume was approximately $9.46 billion, which represented a 145% increase over the amount raised in 2013 (including approximately $1.23 billion in reward-based crowdfunding, approximately $959 million in donation-based crowdfunding, and approximately $787.5 million in equity-based crowdfunding, with the remainder comprised of lending-based, royalty-based, and hybrid models). The industry report further indicates that global equity-based crowdfunding volume grew by 182% in 2014. According to the report, this rapid growth in equity-based crowdfunding has been driven largely by North America and Europe.

The industry report further indicates that, in 2014 the worldwide average size of a funded campaign was less than $4,000 for consumer lending-based, reward-based, and donation-based crowdfunding types. Crowdfunded business loans and equity-based campaigns, however, were substantially higher. In 2014, the global average size of a funded peer-to-business lending-based crowdfunding campaign was $103,618. In 2014, a typical equity-based campaign was larger, with the global average size of $275,461. These figures suggest that the types of ventures financed through equity-based crowdfunding could be different than those financed through other crowdfunding methods. In 2014, the average size of a funded equity-based campaign in North America was $175,000.

Securities and Exchange Commission, Crowdfunding, 80 Fed. Reg. 71388 (November 16, 2015), at Sec. III(A)(3).

3. Crowdfunding has enjoyed considerable popularity as a means to fund creative endeavors and the entities that support these endeavors. Consider the following two examples drawn from the music industry:

Slicethepie utilizes crowdfunding in two ways: First, it utilizes crowdfunding through a "Showcase" process in which artists compete to secure financing [for recording an album] through a . . . patronage model. A fan who invests five pounds sterling or more is entitled to receive a copy of the album upon completion and a few other perks. Second, Slicethepie utilizes crowdfunding through a unique betting "Exchange" system, in which fans can buy, sell, or trade what are known as "Contracts." A maximum of 15,000 Contracts are issued for each album financed through the Showcase process. After an artist begins recording, fans can purchase Contracts for approximately

£1.50. Initial investors from the Showcase process are given one Contract for every £1 invested. These Contracts are good for two years, at which time they are recalled at a price determined by how well the album sold.

. . . .

Sellaband is a German company that was formed in 2006 and is considered the "granddaddy" of the ex ante crowdfunding model. Artists seek to raise $50,000 by selling 5,000 "Parts" to their fans at $10 apiece. During the initial fundraising stage, all investor money is held in an escrow account managed by a third party and regulated under German law. The investor can withdraw individual investments up until the $50,000 goal is reached, at which time the money is transferred to Sellaband to fund the artist's recording project. Sellaband obtains the exclusive right to exploit the master recording rights for 5 years. During that time, the investors and the artist share equally in the net profits derived from sales revenue. Additionally, Sellaband requires that the artist enter into a publishing agreement for all songs recorded. Profits from the exploitation of the compositions are split between the artist (50%), Sellaband (40%), and the Investors (10%).

Ted Kappel, *Ex Ante Crowdfunding and the Recording Industry: A Model for the U.S.?*, 29 Loy. L.A. Ent. L. Rev. 375, 378–79 (2009).

4. A number of crowdfunding Internet sites or "platforms" have been successful in Europe, engaging in rewards-based fund raising (in which contributors receive products or other desirable items as rewards for contributing) or equity-based fund raising (in which investors receive ownership interests or other performance-dependent rights to portions of company profits). The following are some of the leading crowdfunding platforms in Europe:

(1) **Crowdcube (UK)** — Britain's largest equity crowdfunding platform, Crowdcube targets sophisticated investors who understand crowdfunding risks and make their own investment decisions;

(2) **Funding Circle (UK)** — Funding Circle directly connects people and organizations who want to lend, with vetted, credit worthy established businesses who want to borrow;

(3) **OurCrowd (Israel)** — OurCrowd (located in Israel but catering to European investors) is an equity crowdfunding platform aimed at providing venture capital services to accredited investors who invest in Israeli start-up companies;

(4) **Ulule (France)** — Ulule supports project-based and product pre-sale financing to support creative, innovative, or community-minded projects;

(5) **FundedByMe (Sweden)** — Founded in Sweden but with additional offices in Finland, Denmark, Norway, Spain, Germany, Italy, and Singapore, FundedByMe offers both reward-based and equity crowdfunding;

(6) **MyMicroinvest (Belgium)** — This community enables parties to invest in companies via a unique transaction model in which monies raised are invested in a

target company as a single investment once a funding target is met, with investors receiving participation notes and later receiving gains distributed in prorated shares once the single investment is liquidated;

(7) **Symbid (Netherlands)** — Symbid facilitates equity crowdfunding via an investment process in which multiple small investments are bundled and start-ups only have to deal with one shareholder cooperative for each investment bundle;

(8) **KissKissBankBank (France)** — This rewards-based platform assists contributors (termed "Kissbankers") in backing creative and innovative projects;

(9) **Goteo (Spain)** — Goteo is a rewards-based funding platform and collaborative network that assists creative and social service enterprises;

(10) **Seedrs (UK)** — Seedrs facilitates investments in start-ups by conducting due diligence inquiries into particular companies, distributing information to potential investors, and providing post-investment communications from start-ups to investors;

(11) **Booomerang (Denmark)** — Booomerang is a rewards-based crowdfunding platform headquartered in Denmark, but with an additional expansion office in Germany;

(12) **Derev (Italy)** — Derev is aimed at advancing social change and social innovation through crowdfunding, as well as through platform tools that promote activity participation, visibility, feedback and suggestions from interested individuals or communities;

(13) **Companisto (Germany)** — This leading equity-based crowdfunding platform supports several mechanisms for making investments including credit card payments, instant money transfers, and bank transfers;

(14) **Invesdor (Finland)** — Invesdor is an equity-based crowdfunding site that gives companies control over such fundraising features as the parties who can see a company's investment requirements and the nature of parties who can invest;

(15) **Wemakeit.ch (Switzerland)** — This rewards-based crowdfunding site supports numerous projects undertaken by artists and other creative parties.

See Priti Ambani, *Top 15 Crowdfunding Platforms in Europe*, Crowd Sourcing Week, May 30, 2014, http://crowdsourcingweek.com/top-15-crowdfunding-platforms-in-europe/ (last visited 10/27/2017).

4. Venture Capital Financing

This subsection examines the expectations of venture capitalists in financing start-up companies. This section also addresses the impact of venture capitalists' expectations in shaping start-up business enterprises, the initial ownership structures of such enterprises, and the business goals of these enterprises as they look ahead to possible venture capital financing.

Manuel A. Utset, Reciprocal Fairness, Strategic Behavior & Venture Survival: A Theory of Venture Capital-Financed Firms

2002 Wis. L. Rev. 45*

Venture capitalists serve as a major source of capital for young, risky firms with high growth prospects, primarily high-technology firms such as those in the computer, biotechnology, or telecommunications business. They identify, nurture, package, and eventually sell these start-up firms, either through an initial public offering or a private sale to a third party.

. . . .

[I]t is useful to isolate three factors that will affect the actions taken by parties in any long-term venture, such as that between a venture capitalist and an entrepreneur: (1) the extent to which each party has mistaken beliefs about the nature of the transaction; (2) the ability of each party to freely maneuver during the venture, i.e., to take actions that negatively affect the other party; and (3) the ability of each party to exit the venture. The venture capital literature has primarily focused on how venture capitalists structure transactions paying close heed to these three factors. For example, venture capitalists know that they may have mistaken beliefs regarding the viability of the innovation or the abilities of the entrepreneur. Moreover, venture capitalists recognize that an entrepreneur's knowledge and skills—her human capital—will be critical to the venture until the innovation is finished, but will not be as valuable during the marketing and production stages. At those latter stages, the venture will be best run by an individual with well-developed managerial skills.

As a result, venture capitalists structure transactions so as to retain control. Among other things, control gives venture capitalists the ability to freely maneuver during the venture, including the ability to dismiss entrepreneurs when their services are no longer deemed valuable—e.g., entrepreneurs whose managerial skills are sub-par compared to those of professional managers. In addition to retaining control, venture capitalists adopt mechanisms to reduce their costs of exiting the venture and mechanisms that make it very costly for entrepreneurs to exit. Entrepreneurial exit is penalized whether the exit is voluntary or at the hands of the venture capitalist. For example, a fired entrepreneur will lose access to her innovation, will be subject to restrictions on competing employment, and under certain instances will even lose all or part of her equity in the venture.

The existing venture capital literature has analyzed the effects of mistaken beliefs, maneuverability during the venture, and the ability to exit from the point of view of venture capitalists. This Article takes the opposite tack, analyzing the effects of these three factors from the point of view of entrepreneurs. This allows us to bring to the foreground the following three facts that generally hold when an entrepreneur

---

transacts with a venture capitalist: (1) at the time of contracting, the entrepreneur will tend to have substantial mistaken beliefs, a fact that she will recognize as she interacts with the venture capitalist and as onerous provisions in venture capital contracts are triggered; (2) the entrepreneur has the ability to freely maneuver during the venture, given that her human capital is critical to the success of the venture; and (3) there is a high penalty attached to entrepreneurial exit, whether the exit is voluntary or involuntary.

. . . .

I. The Agency Theory of Venture Capital Contracts

Investments in innovation-intensive start-ups are particularly risky, given uncertainties surrounding the innovation process, and potential opportunistic behavior and managerial incompetence on the part of the entrepreneur. Venture capitalists and entrepreneurs enter into a set of highly standardized contracts aimed at reducing the contractual risks faced by venture capitalists. I will use the phrase venture capital contracts to refer to this set of highly standardized written contracts.

Over the years, scholars studying the venture capital process have made a variety of theoretical claims about venture capital contracts using an agency theory approach. Whenever one individual acts on behalf of another, a potential agency problem arises: the agent (the person acting) will undoubtedly have interests incongruous with those of her principal. One would expect that a bona fide, self-interested agent, such as an entrepreneur, would take self-serving actions at the expense of her principal, the venture capitalist. Agency theory provides important insights into the costs of such self-serving actions.

As monitoring costs—that is, informational costs—increase, an agent will be less constrained, allowing her greater freedom to take actions detrimental to the principal. Financing innovation-intensive firms involves numerous informational problems, making the theoretical agency literature a natural starting point. With few exceptions, this literature, following the agency paradigm, has focused on the screening and monitoring difficulties faced by venture capitalists. In keeping with the agency paradigm, the venture capitalist's informational disadvantage vis-a-vis the entrepreneur and the potential for entrepreneurial opportunism are given a central role. Accordingly, this literature focuses on the role of venture capital contracts in reducing venture capitalists' risks arising from informational asymmetries and entrepreneurial opportunism.

A. Contractual Risks Faced by Venture Capitalists

1. Informational Risks

It is fair to assume that at the time of contracting, an entrepreneur has superior information vis-a-vis the venture capitalist regarding the innovation and whether she is a hard worker with the required managerial skills to run the venture. Therefore, before investing in a start-up, a venture capitalist will acquire information about the innovation, such as how feasible and marketable it is, as well as information about the entrepreneur—whether she is the real thing or just a crank, honest or a thief, hard-working or taken to leisure.

During the life of the venture, informational asymmetries continue to be a source of risk to the venture capitalist. A venture capitalist is not involved in the day-to-day managing of the venture and will not have first-hand knowledge of how much time and effort the entrepreneur is dedicating to the venture. This is typical of the delegation implicit in any agency relationship. However, the informational problems in high-tech start-ups are exacerbated by the fact that managerial decision-making requires more than general managerial skills; it also requires an ability to understand, verify, and apply technical information necessary for the managerial decision-making process. The entrepreneur, in managing the venture, will not only have greater access to information related to the ongoing development of the innovation, but will also have a better ability to judge and use that information since she will generally have superior technical knowledge.

2. Risks Related to the Intangible Nature of the Assets in High-Tech Start-Ups

The principal assets of high-tech start-ups, such as the entrepreneur's know-how (her human capital) and intellectual property (e.g., patents and trade secrets), are highly intangible in nature. Firms whose principal assets are intangible are riskier to finance than those with tangible assets, such as manufacturing equipment, since investors can always recuperate some of their investment by selling those tangible assets. Intangible assets like intellectual property are harder to value and sell to third parties.

Reliance on the entrepreneur's human capital exposes a venture capitalist to a "hold-up" risk: after the venture capitalist makes its investment, the entrepreneur can threaten to quit the venture (taking her human capital) unless the venture capitalist agrees to "renegotiate" the bargain to give the entrepreneur a larger portion of the venture's surplus. For example, assume that a venture capitalist invests one million dollars with an entrepreneur to finance the development and marketing of a new drug. This investment is, to some degree, irreversible since it is venture-specific; the venture capitalist will receive less than one million dollars if the entrepreneur quits without developing the drug. Since the value of the venture capitalist's investment depends, in large part, on the entrepreneur remaining in the venture, the entrepreneur has some ability to act opportunistically.

Of course, the venture capitalist will be able to anticipate this behavior and will require some assurances that the entrepreneur will not threaten to quit the venture. However, the venture capitalist's inability to force an entrepreneur to perform against her will means that some other governance mechanisms are needed, such as non-compete agreements or other penalties for exiting the firm inappropriately.

3. Contractual Risks Associated with the Uncertainty Surrounding the Innovation Process

There is a large degree of uncertainty surrounding the financing of high-tech start-ups. This uncertainty is due to a number of factors, including unknowns surrounding the technical viability and market potential of the innovation, the potential for new competitors, as well as the inherent uncertainties surrounding any new venture. Moreover, contracting for innovations and enforcing those contracts is made more difficult by the inherent novelty of innovations, which in some instances may require the development of new ways of perceiving, processing, transferring, and referring to information.

4. Contractual Risks Due to the General Illiquidity of Venture Capital Investments

The relative illiquidity of the venture capitalist's investment produces another contractual risk. As in most close corporations, the venture capitalist's ability to exit by selling its shares is limited. This illiquidity is due to the absence, prior to an initial public offering, of a public market in which the venture capitalist can sell its shares. From the venture capitalist's perspective, the illiquidity problem is exacerbated by the fact that when a venture capitalist attempts to sell its shares it may inadvertently signal to potential buyers that there are undisclosed problems with the venture. This is because a venture capitalist is in a better position to know about the prospect of the venture. Therefore a potential buyer faces the same informational asymmetry problems discussed above in connection with a venture capitalist's initial investment in the venture.

B. Institutions Adopted to Deal with Contractual Risks

In this Section, I describe the principal contractual mechanisms used by venture capitalists to address the four contractual risks described in the prior Section. The agency literature on venture capital contracts describes venture capital contracts as a reaction to these contractual risks. There are two textbook reactions to contractual risks: discounting for the risk and adopting governance structures.

In view of these risks, standard venture capital contracts encompass four principal goals. The first goal is to provide venture capitalists with very high rates of return — usually a ten-fold return of capital over a five-year period. The second goal is to give control of the start-up firm to the venture capitalist. By retaining control over the venture, venture capitalists can change the "rules of the game" and interpret ambiguous rules instead of requiring the intervention of third parties, such as courts or arbitrators. The third goal is to provide a set of high-powered incentive mechanisms aimed at increasing entrepreneurial effort and reducing opportunistic behavior. The final goal is to provide exit mechanisms for venture capitalists.

1. Giving Control Over the Start-Up to the Venture Capitalist

The contractual sources of venture capitalist control are (1) the preferred stock purchase agreement, (2) the terms of the preferred stock, (3) the stockholders' agreement, and (4) employment agreements. By controlling the venture, a venture capitalist can keep a "tight leash" on entrepreneurs, thereby reducing their ability to act opportunistically. Control allows greater access to information needed to monitor entrepreneurs and provides venture capitalists with various mechanisms to discipline errant entrepreneurs, including the ability to fire or demote a managing entrepreneur with little difficulty (other than meeting the provisions of the employment agreement).

A venture capitalist's control over a start-up's board of directors is a critical source of its governance powers. Venture capitalists in most instances negotiate to get outright control of the board. Although the board does not usually run the day-to-day affairs of a company, it is vested with the ultimate power and responsibility of managing the corporation. It selects the officers who will actually manage the corporation (including, in our case, the entrepreneur), sets their salaries, and replaces them when necessary.

Additionally, the stock purchase agreement and stockholders' agreement will contain affirmative and negative covenants, whereby the entrepreneur agrees to take certain actions or to forego taking certain actions, respectively. For example, an entrepreneur may agree to certain affirmative covenants, such as giving the venture capitalist financial statements as well as other types of information. Moreover, an entrepreneur will typically be prohibited from amending the certificate of incorporation, changing the nature of the business, entering into self-dealing transactions, making unauthorized dividend payments, entering into a merger agreement, and selling all or substantially all of its assets.

2. Incentive-Based Mechanisms

Venture capital contracts adopt a variety of incentive mechanisms aimed at better aligning the interests of the entrepreneur with those of the venture capitalist. A principal goal of these incentive mechanisms is to provide an impetus to entrepreneurs to exert the right amount of effort and to dissuade them from acting opportunistically. Under venture capital contracts, the entrepreneur will contribute to the venture her capital, intellectual property, labor, and expertise needed to develop, manufacture, and market the innovation. In return, the entrepreneur retains some of the venture's equity with the expectation that it will provide her with a high rate of return if the venture were to be successful. The higher the intensity of the incentive mechanisms deployed, the greater will be the amount of the venture's risk that is transferred from the venture capitalist to the entrepreneur.

a. Compensation Schemes as High-Powered Incentives

Venture capitalists use compensation schemes to provide entrepreneurs with an incentive to exert the right amount of effort. If a venture capitalist could adequately observe and quantify the effort level of the entrepreneur (and it knew the optimal effort level to be taken), it could then base the entrepreneur's compensation on the amount of effort exerted. However, a venture capitalist cannot fully observe entrepreneurial effort. As a result, an entrepreneur's compensation must be tied to an observable metric, such as the venture's performance, that can act as a proxy for entrepreneurial effort. Stock options can play such a role and, thus, comprise a large part of the compensation package.

Generally, entrepreneurs are paid a salary that is below market with the expectation that the bulk of their compensation will come from appreciation of their base equity holdings and be supplemented by stock options awarded during the venture. The stock options will vest over a period of years, heavily weighed towards the back end. If an entrepreneur leaves the company or is fired (for cause) before the shares have vested, she loses her right to exercise the options.

b. Staged Financing

Unlike banks, which will often disburse borrowed funds in a single transaction, venture capitalists disburse funds over time, in succeeding stages. By staging invest-ments and not pre-committing to financing future stages, venture capitalists, in essence, create a series of call options. At the time each stage arrives, the venture cap-italist will decide—given the current valuation—whether to continue investing in the project or to dissolve the company and salvage what it can. In a sense, staged financing gives venture capitalists an "option to abandon."

According to the venture capital literature, the principal function of staged financ-ing is to reduce the amount of a venture capitalist's investment that is put in jeop-ardy by an entrepreneur's threat to quit the venture. Staged financing also helps reduce a venture capitalist's informational hazard by allowing it to acquire information about the entrepreneur and the innovation before putting too much of its capital at risk.

Several academic observers of the industry have argued that staged financing is the most effective control mechanism available to a venture capitalist. A venture cap-italist can discipline an entrepreneur by threatening not to fund any more stages of the project. The ability to credibly threaten to liquidate the firm at the time of nego-tiating over a stage gives the venture capitalist bargaining leverage. To increase their leverage, venture capitalists often delay their funding until close to the date when the venture's working capital is completely exhausted—what is referred to in the industry as the "burn date." A venture capitalist's leverage is further strengthened by contract provisions giving it a monopoly over future financing. Moreover, even if a venture capitalist allows an entrepreneur to seek additional outside funding, the very refusal by a venture capitalist to provide that additional funding will send neg-ative signals to other potential financiers, making it harder for the entrepreneur to convince third parties to invest in the venture.

c. Power Exerted over the Entrepreneur's Equity Stake

The employment agreement usually provides that if the entrepreneur leaves the venture, she has to, at the option of the venture capitalist, sell back at book value (rather than current market value) any stock she owns. Upon exiting the venture, an entre-preneur will also lose any stock that had been allocated to her—through options, for example—but that had not yet vested. Additionally, the stockholders' agreement will restrict the ability of the entrepreneur to sell her shares.

Venture capitalists make their capital contribution through convertible preferred stock. Like all convertible securities, the preferred stock will have provisions to pro-tect against dilution, in case of stock splits, or issuances of common stock at a lower price than the conversion price. Anti-dilution provisions adjust the conversion price to the price of new shares offered or rights issued. A type of anti-dilution provision often used by venture capitalists is the ratchet-down anti-dilution provision. Such a provi-sion mandates that if even one share is sold at a lower price, the conversion price of all the venture capitalist's preferred stock is adjusted. Once triggered, anti-dilution provisions can wipe out all or most of an entrepreneur's equity stake. Anti-dilution provisions can be used opportunistically, particularly given that the venture capitalist controls the infusion of new capital and the board of directors (which sets the issuance price).

d. Providing Disincentives for Entrepreneur Exit from the Venture

A venture capitalist can increase the entrepreneur's cost of exit by having her sign a non-disclosure agreement. This agreement, which is standard in these transactions, prohibits an entrepreneur from disclosing trade secrets to third parties and requires her to disclose and transfer to the venture any invention or other innovation developed while she was still with the venture. An entrepreneur may also be required to sign an agreement promising not to compete directly with the venture. Although non-compete agreements may be hard to enforce in court, a well-drafted non-disclosure agreement can achieve many of the same results. The entrepreneur's value to other employers (or even as a single proprietor) is significantly reduced by these agreements given the threat of lengthy and expensive litigation. For example, a new employer can be sued for stealing trade secrets, for interfering with an agency relation under agency law, or for tortious interference with a contract.

3. Venture Capitalist Control Over Exit Mechanisms

Venture capital contracts give venture capitalists the ability to liquidate the venture or to sell it through a private sale or initial public offering. Venture capital contracts achieve this through three principal mechanisms: (1) a registration rights agreement, which usually requires that the venture file a registration statement with the Securities and Exchange Commission in order to effectuate an initial public offering; (2) the venture capitalist's voting control over the company's equity and control over the board of directors; and (3) redemption rights — that is, a "put" that forces the venture to buy back the venture capitalist's preferred stock (of course, this is of little use if there are no assets to pay for the redemption). Control over these exit strategies will help alleviate the venture capitalist's liquidity hazard.

. . . .

Ronald J. Mann, Do Patents Facilitate
Financing in the Software Industry?
83 Tex. L. Rev. 961 (2005)*

. . . .

To understand the effect of patents on software development, I focus on small firms, which typically are venture backed. . . . First, I discuss the goals of the venture capital investors, which relate to the likelihood that a [firm with a portfolio of patents] can differentiate itself from its competitors in a reliable way. Second, I

---

analyze the ability of patents to provide that reliable differentiation. Although the discussion evinces pessimism about patents as a mechanism for appropriating the value of innovations in the software industry, it also emphasizes a shift in the efficacy of patents as firms pass through the early stages of growth. To that end, I discuss a number of reasons why patents are not likely to allow such appropriation in the earliest stages of a software firm, before it has revenues or begins shipping a product. Then, I show how once the firm moves beyond infancy—to a stage with revenues or a product—patents can have a variety of beneficial effects. That section provides a framework for relating the evidence drawn from my interviews to the existing analytical literature, teasing out of that pattern a set of direct and indirect positive effects that patents can have in various circumstances.

A. Venture Capitalists and Sustainable Differentiation

The development of software is expensive and time consuming. Thus, it is not common for a successful product to be developed by an individual developer working in his spare time. Rather, most commercial software products are the result of years of effort. That effort, in turn, inevitably requires the expenditure of considerable monetary resources. Of course, young firms can—and normally are expected to—go a considerable way toward developing their concept without using the funds of third parties. At some point, however, the individuals within young firms will exhaust their own resources and the readily available resources of friends and family members.

In most cases, the firm then will turn to institutional investment. One of the most prominent and common sources of that investment is a venture capitalist. Venture capital firms are intermediaries that raise funds from institutional investors (corporate pension plans and the like) and invest those funds in startup companies in technology areas. There is a vast literature on the structure of the venture capital industry, including detailed studies of many aspects of the contract structures that firms use in dealing with their investors and with the portfolio companies in which the firms invest. For the purposes of this project, however, the structure of the venture capitalist is relatively unimportant. What is important is to understand as precisely as possible [are the] characteristics of a portfolio that lead venture capitalists to invest. Although there is little quantitative empirical work on that question, the most obvious role that IP [intellectual property (IP)] protection might play in that process is that the monopoly that IP protection grants on the exploitation of a covered technology could cause investment to flow into the firm that has created the technology. The monopoly supports such a flow of investment—at least in theory—by creating market power that allows the firm to earn supranormal profits by exploiting the technology in question.

The first point to understand about startup companies is that the uniqueness of a firm's product is not likely to be one of the primary issues a potential venture capital investor will analyze in deciding whether to invest in the firm. The investor is likely to examine a large number of plans and invest in only a small number of them—perhaps 6 out of every 1,000. In deciding whether to invest, the investor is likely to start by focusing on issues that validate the firm's competency to execute its concept successfully. For example, investors will be interested in such things as experience in the relevant market and the skills of the management team. One remarked: "Every company of mine that has failed has been [due to] mismanagement of executives, not technical failure." Similarly, even before investors consider whether a firm can protect a market leader position, they will want to know whether the product is one that customers need so desperately that the firm could earn significant revenues from sales of the product.

Still, for firms that have a credible product idea and the expertise to implement it, venture capitalists plainly accept the idea that their goal is to identify firms that will have sufficient market power to earn extraordinary profits. IP protection is important only indirectly, as a tool that might provide that market power. The key is "sustainable differentiation": something special about the particular firm that will enable it to do something that its competitors will not be able to do for the immediate future. The interviews reflect more picturesque terminology—referring to "secret sauce" or "magic dust." But it is clear that the key to a desirable investment opportunity is in the expectation of market power, and all other attributes of the company are indirect predictors of that ultimate goal.

For example, investors commonly referred to lead time or first-mover advantages. The premise is that a portfolio company that truly is the first to provide a sophisticated and functional response to an important problem can expect to earn a supranormal return for years to come. Interestingly enough, that expectation rested on the perception that a firm can maintain a lead on its rivals as long as it keeps improving its technology as quickly as its competitors. I rarely if ever heard investors (as opposed to developers) voice an expectation that portfolio firms obtain and keep a strong market position through "lock-in" or "bandwagon" effects.

That is not to say that IP protection is unimportant. It is clear, however, that different investors have different views about it. Some feel that intellectual property always is important and claim that they never invest without strong patentable technology. Even those investors, however, go on to say that they are not as interested in the IP protection as they are in technology that is sufficiently cutting edge to warrant protection. Others, however, particularly those that emphasize early-stage companies, say IP protection is unimportant for software investments. Still others take a middle position, holding that IP protection matters some, but not all, of the time. Most of those who addressed the subject recognized differing perspectives on the point and argued that those with the other perspectives are misguided. The most likely explanation is that investors are simply implementing different investment models based on their particular expertise.

B. Patents and Sustainable Differentiation

If understanding what venture capitalists want answers the first question, the second question is whether they believe that patents can provide it. This subpart looks quite closely at the various stages of relatively small private firms and suggests that investors and developers discern a balance of interests that shifts as firms grow from the earliest stage, where patents are not often helpful, through intermediate stages to the terminal stage of venture-backed firms (just before an acquisition or IPO), where patents are almost universally viewed as useful.

1. The Basic Problem: Patents and Appropriability. — A basic problem for software firms at all stages is the sense that even with a patent it often is difficult for a firm to "appropriate" the value of its invention. Specifically, my interview subjects agreed that competitors usually could, without infringing a patent, implement most of the aspects of a patented software product. One reason for that problem is the multifarious nature of software innovation, which permits many solutions to any particular problem. Another contributing factor is the poor match between patents and products in the industry: it is difficult to patent an entire product in the software industry because any particular product is likely to include dozens if not hundreds of separate technological ideas. Thus, it may take a number of novel ideas — and patents — to build a defensible barrier around a product. Another problem is that technology tends to develop so rapidly that by the time a patent is issued — and the formal right to exclusivity commences — the technology may be obsolete. Litigation at that point will involve efforts by the patent owner to challenge technology of a subsequent generation to which application of the patent may be less clear. Yet another problem emphasized in my interviews is the problem of detectability — the difficulty of being sure that a competing product infringes a patent.

The problem of appropriating the value of software through patents is not universal. As I discuss below, some patentees manage to obtain patents of sufficient breadth to cover all possible solutions to an important problem. More broadly, some knowledgeable observers attribute the difficulty of appropriation not to the nature of software technology, but to the infancy of the industry. Because the industry is developing so rapidly, some argue, the nature of technology and even of technological developments is so poorly understood that firms do not recognize the value they could appropriate from patents if they pursued them in an informed way. From this perspective, the relatively limited appropriability provided by software patents should be compared not to the relatively high appropriability of hardware patents, but to the even more limited appropriability that software patents provided a decade ago. Those observers expect that in a matter of decades software technology will be as effectively subject to patent protection as the related hardware technology is at this time.

For now, despite those qualifications, the relevant point is that for most firms, most of the time, there is little prospect that the patents they obtain will provide market power that they can use to exclude competitors. That point is underscored by the relative infrequency with which venture-backed software startups obtain patents. For comparative purposes, consider that only about twenty percent of venture-backed software companies have a patent within five years of their first financing (with each of those firms holding, on average, about two patents), while more than half of biotech startups have patents by that time (with each of those firms averaging about seven patents). Thus, even the tenuous exclusivity such patents could provide is usually not a factor for early-stage software startups because so few of them in fact have patents.

The point is further underscored by the statistical relation between the success of venture-backed software startups and their patenting practices. The general theme of the preceding pages is that there are many factors that play into the ability of a startup firm to obtain funding and success and that intellectual property has a low place on the list of factors, if it appears on that list at all. The data I have collected with Tom Sager supports that view — indicating that patenting practices have at best a minuscule ability to predict the success of a venture-backed software startup.

2. Patents and Prerevenue Startups. — In addition to the problem that patents often are not an optimal mechanism for appropriating the value of software innovation, a number of considerations make it particularly difficult for early-stage companies to employ patents effectively. The key points here are the limited efficacy of litigation for those firms, the constraints on resources that make it infeasible to focus on patenting, and the limited value to prerevenue firms of excluding competitors.

a. The Perils of Small-Firm Litigation. — On the first point, even if an early-stage company had a patent, it is unlikely that it would have resources available to enforce the patent through litigation against a competitor. That is particularly true when the competitor is a large firm. One problem is the disparity in litigation resources. One investor emphasized the concern that a large defendant would "rain lawyers on your head and tie you up in court for the next ten years." A somewhat different concern is the likelihood that the large firm might have a patent that the small firm infringes. If so, the lawsuit might simply alert the large firm to the presence of the small firm.

A related concern is that firm culture is degraded when a firm must rely on licensing revenues instead of developing its own product. Interestingly enough, that sentiment was expressed even at firms that rely heavily on licensing revenues. Those firms encouraged efforts to maintain a product-centered culture that emphasizes production of the firm's own products. One executive explained that a cultural risk arises when a company pursues patent litigation and licensing, explaining that such a strategy unfavorably affects the company's needs. "You don't need sales people; you need attorneys. You don't need solutions architects; you need accountants. So you wind up losing the very people who are, who were, and who continue to be constructive . . . and innovative and help you build things and would give us a continuing competitive advantage."

Indeed, the one interviewee whose firm had a major licensing program related that the entire program was entrusted to third-party professionals so that it would not interfere with the focus of the onsite software engineers.

b. Diversion of Focus. — Similarly, many investors and developers emphasized that attention to patents can be damaging to a startup because it has the potential to divert limited time and resources from what is likely to be a highly time-pressured effort to develop a product and convince customers and investors of its worth before the firm runs out of capital resources. One investor explained: "[We] typically find that the companies that focus on just patents don't have the right view of what is important, and they really are therefore not successful in business. And they're usually not around to prosecute their patents." Developers understand the point well. As one said: "Every dollar we spend on [patenting] is a dollar we can't spend on a software engineer." Another, with a patent-leaning background from his days at IBM, commented: "Patentability is something we will pursue, but let's get the product out first."

Thus, a young company is presented with a challenging task. If the nature of the firm's innovation is such that IP is ever likely to be important, it must spend sufficient resources on the protection and development of intellectual property from the earliest days of the company—as an investment in the possibility that the firm might grow to the point at which IP is useful. The firm that fails to protect its IP at the earliest stage is like a desperate ship at sea that empties its drinking water in the hope of evading a faster pursuer: it might survive for the time being, but it may have sown the seeds of its inevitable failure if it survives to a later stage. On the other hand, it must not spend so much that the company fails before it is able to recoup its investment.

Firms have developed a number of strategies for dealing with that problem. Some involve using half measures to protect the IP, such as filing provisional applications or omitting standard practices related to documentation of the work of engineers. Those practices do not directly abandon the IP, but they may make it more costly and difficult to protect it in the future. The bottom line is that even for companies that have begun to earn substantial revenues it often does not seem appropriate to devote the resources necessary to ensure that all of the firm's innovations are patented. Others—it must be said that executives with prior experience at large IP-sensitive firms like IBM or Bell Labs populate this category—seem to relish the discipline of making sure that the IP is pinned down no matter how difficult it may seem to find the time and resources to do so. The difficulty of this strategic choice, coupled with the difficulty in accurately predicting the future prospects for their products and their IP, is a problem about which startup software executives worry constantly.

Investors, of course, are aware of this problem. Their approach typically does not extend to forcing (or even urging) their portfolio companies to seek patent protection. However, they do go to considerable lengths to evaluate the IP that potential portfolio companies have. In a typical process, the venture capitalist (VC) knows most of the reputable patent attorneys in the local community. If one of those attorneys has filed a patent for a potential portfolio company, the VC discusses the patent with that lawyer. If an attorney with whom the VC did not have a preexisting relationship filed the patent application, the VC has the patent studied by an attorney in whom he has confidence. In the context of the interviews, it was clear that the intent of this examination is not purely technical—whether this is a patent likely to be granted—but also a broader exercise to understand what type of market power the patent might (or might not) provide. Indeed, the current practice-oriented literature characterizes examination of market power as central to careful due diligence practices. The practice at first seems to be in tension with the thesis of this section — that patents have little value for the earliest-stage startups. In fact, however, it leads into the point of the next section: the firms that survive their earliest days may reap substantial value from patents.

c. The Limited Benefits of Exclusion. — One final element of the patenting calculus for small firms may seem obvious, but is so important to the overall framework as to warrant brief notice. Because those firms do not yet have a product, they have no opportunity for revenues. Thus, the benefits they reap from excluding competitors are minimal at best. Only if they survive to a later stage — in which they can hope to profit from their own exploitation of that product — will they be able to reap any substantial value from the exclusion of competitors.

3. The Increasing Value of Patents for Later-Stage Startups. — When firms mature to the point of having revenues, the systematic difficulties that plague the efforts of prerevenue startups to obtain and exploit patents dissipate. That does not mean, however, that patents suddenly become a philosopher's stone that will turn their creative endeavors into IPOs. Rather, the underlying problem of appropriability continues to plague most efforts to use patents directly to exclude competitors. Still, my interviews suggest a series of benefits that patents might provide for later-stage software startups. This section describes those benefits by reference to the bodies of existing literature that have offered them as theoretical possibilities.

a. Direct Effects: Protecting a Space for Innovation. — The most important point concerns the direct ability of a software patent to carve out for the firm a space in which it can innovate without competition. I explain above that my interview subjects often complain about how difficult it is to use patents to exclude competitors. Although there is some truth in this complaint, it is an overgeneralization, at least once a firm reaches the stage at which it has designed a product that it can market to customers.

First, it is clear that some firms in the industry obtain a substantial amount of revenues by licensing the use of their patents to competitors that need to use the patented technology in their own products. Indeed, even in my limited sample, three small Austin companies — Applied Science Fiction, Bluecurrent, and Forgent — have obtained substantial revenues from patent licenses. I do not believe that industry wide statistics quantify the size of that market, but it plainly is substantial. Those transactions — and others like them — demonstrate that some software patents are sufficiently robust to allow their holders to appropriate substantial value from the underlying inventions. Licensing transactions are noteworthy given the difficulties small firms face in enforcing patents against large firms. [T]he small firm with a revenue producing product must be quite confident in the value of its technology before it wisely can cross swords with a company like IBM.

More generally, it seems clear that the received wisdom that patents are not useful to appropriate software-related inventions is overstated. Two separate points are important. The first is the distinction between the relative rarity of observed offensive patent use — for out-licensing or litigation — and the use of patents to exclude competitors. The relative rarity of offensive use of patents does not prove that the patents are insufficiently robust to exclude competitors. As discussed in the previous section, there are many reasons why a firm might want to wait until late in its development to advertise the nature of its technology and its proprietary claims to that technology.

A firm can refrain from offensive use of its patents and still derive important value from the patents as an exclusion device. Contrary to the perception that patents tilt the playing field in favor of large incumbent firms to the disadvantage of small firms, patents in this context afford a unique opportunity to the small startup. The patent system grants the small firm an automatic stay of competitive activity that remains in force long enough for the firm to attempt to develop its technology. For large firms, the marginal increase in appropriability that comes from patents may have little benefit: IBM could compete quite successfully against smaller firms even if it did not have patents protecting its product from copycat competitors. For the smaller firm, however, the ability of the implicit threat of patent litigation to prevent incumbents like IBM and Microsoft from taking its technology can be the difference between life and death. As one executive put it: "What's protected me from other people ripping [off our product] has been the specter of patent infringement."

It is instructive to think of the offensive uses of software patents reported in the press. Among the most famous incidents are the successful attempts by small firms — Stac in the mid-1990s and Eolas in 2003 — to force alterations in Microsoft products that arguably infringed patents held by those firms, and the similar attempt by InterTrust to assert rights to digital rights management technology that was important to several Microsoft products. The profits from suing other small firms seem to be so much smaller that it is easy to see why that kind of "horizontal" litigation is apparently less common. I note that the story depicted in the press is consistent with empirical work suggesting that patents held by small firms are more likely to be litigated than patents held by large firms. This also finds strong support in Bronwyn Hall's recent work suggesting that patent rights in complex product industries are more valuable for younger firms than they are for older incumbent firms.

Second, the ability of a patent to appropriate the value of an innovation is often said to vary along several dimensions. One of the most common is the nature of the particular innovation. Thus, it is often thought futile to rely on a patent if the innovation lies in a method of writing software code. At the other end of the continuum, patents that protect an ultimate functionality that the software provides or an algorithm necessary to provide that functionality are more likely to be important in excluding potential competitors. Interestingly, that distinction seems to undermine the conventional wisdom dividing patents along another dimension, in which "process" patents tend to be less valuable than "product" patents. In the software industry, a patent on the product tends to have relatively little value because of the ease of designing a distinct product. A patent on the process that the product implements is much more likely to be valuable, if only because it often is possible for the claimed process to be defined broadly enough to include all practicable methods of competition.

A sectoral variation in patenting appears to be related to those dimensions of analysis. As the empirical data presented in a related paper I authored with Tom Sager demonstrates, there is a strong variation in the rate of patenting by venture-backed firms in different sectors of the software industry. For example, the average number of patents in the dataset was about 0.6 patents per firm. Several sectors, however, had markedly higher rates, including graphics and digital imaging, expert systems and natural language, multimedia, and security. At the same time, some relatively important sectors had unusually low rates of patenting, including email and internet software, applications software, and financial software. That variation is interesting because it can be discerned in a quantitative way even though patents are thought to be less valuable for software than they are for hardware, and even though patents are much less common in the software industry than in some other industries.

This is not a topic on which my interviews produced constructive results. I focused several of my interviews on firms known to me to have commercially valuable patents. Notwithstanding the discussion and empirical evidence above, executives of those firms that expressed a view as to why their patents were valuable generally believed it had nothing to do with the nature of the innovation. Rather, they attributed it to the firm's ability to obtain a patent that staked out a sufficiently large field to cover all plausible variations on the relevant technology. Still, it seems likely that variation is related at least in part to the nature of innovation in different sectors, with higher rates of patenting associated with types of innovation more susceptible to appropriation by patent. However strongly my interview subjects rejected such a distinction, the data powerfully suggest that further inquiry is warranted. For now, my intuition is that the patterns of patenting rates most likely relate to the distinction between product firms (for which patents would be more useful) and service firms (for which patents would be less useful).

Taken together, those two points portray a world in which small firms struggle to innovate, facing the pervasive concern that a competitor might appropriate any useful invention at any time. Given the difficulties those firms face in sustaining differentiation, the possibility that patents can provide shelter for some firms is important. The extent of shelter may be difficult to predict because it depends primarily on the breadth of market protection a patent has by the time it is issued. Furthermore, the frequency of shelter is open to doubt; it plainly was not relevant to most of the firms that I interviewed. The interviews that I discuss above, however, do suggest that shelter is real in the place where its effect would be most important—in the minds of firms doing the innovation. It certainly would be valuable to know more about the frequency with which small firms obtain patents of sufficient strength to use in this way. However, even without quantitative information, it is difficult to believe that this is not a major part of what makes patents and their breadth an item of interest to investors.

b. Indirect Effects. — The most intriguing information from my interviews relates to patent benefits that do not involve direct exploitation of the patents. Those benefits fall into two classes: facilitation of a litigation-free zone through a pattern of cross-licensing; and a set of what I call "information" effects — beneficial effects that patents have on information related to the firm's technology.

(1) Facilitating a Licensing Equilibrium. — As suggested above, many in the industry completely deny any substantial use of patents to exclude competitors. Rather, the most prominent explanation for patents in the interviews was that patents are useful as "barter" in cross-licensing agreements that the firm enters if it reaches a sufficiently mature stage to be a significant player in the industry.

. . . .

(2) Information Effects. — The last set of effects relates to information generated through a firm's participation in the patent system. Moving along the course of a firm's development, these effects fall into three classes: (A) the ability of patents to facilitate the firm's efforts to codify tacit knowledge, (B) the firm's subsequent ability to signal the discipline and technical expertise that allowed it to codify that knowledge, and (C) the use of the patent as a signal of the underlying technology.

. . . .

4. Patents and Large Firms. — Although the bulk of my interviewing base is small venture-backed startups, the interviews and publicly available information do provide enough information to give a good idea of the role that patents play in large firms. Because much of the information is plain from the discussion above, I discuss that topic briefly solely to complete the picture.

First . . . large firms gain relatively little through litigation or the exclusion of competitors from patented spaces because large firms often can compete successfully with small firms without excluding the competitor. The saying that "nobody ever got fired for buying IBM [or Microsoft]" is not baseless, and in a contest between IBM and a small startup, both with equivalent products, IBM (or Microsoft) often will prevail. In contests among large firms, litigation is rare because of cross-licensing of portfolios.

Second, patents provide considerable benefits to large firms by enabling them to participate in cross-licensing agreements that give them the freedom of action to design and deploy products as they wish, without regard to the IP portfolios of competitors. It may be, as I argue above, that large firms that use their portfolios solely for that purpose would be better off without the costs of developing and maintaining those portfolios, but in the existing milieu, each firm has a strong incentive to collect patents for that purpose.

Third, many — though certainly not all — large firms obtain substantial revenues from directly exploiting their patent portfolios. IBM, for example, earns literally billions of dollars each year exploiting its patent portfolio; a significant share of the revenue comes from its software patents. Thus, although different firms have different strategies, the potential for large firms to earn substantial revenues from direct exploitation of patents does exist. Information about the amount of those revenues would be valuable in assessing the net effect of patents, but that data is not readily available.

Beverly A. Berneman, J.D., LL.M., Benjamin, Berneman, and Brom, LLC, Venture Capital Financing for the Development of Intellectual Property Assets: A Marriage of Convenience

Practising Law Institute, Handling Intellectual Property
Issues in Business Transactions 2005

824 PLI/Pat 223 (2005)*

I. INTRODUCTION

For the entrepreneur, [a period encompassing] the development of a new idea can be a heady time. The entrepreneur has a great idea that has marketing potential. But, the entrepreneur needs funding in order to develop the idea. Thus, the excitement of developing an idea can be tempered by the inability to find development financing. When that idea involves different types of patents, copyrights, trademarks and trade secrets, finding financing to develop the idea can be grueling and frustrating.

The financing world offers a wide variety of financing opportunities. The entrepreneur must find the right fit for idea development. Financing schemes range from finding "angels" to obtaining conventional asset based loans.

Within the range of possible financing schemes falls venture capital. Venture capital groups provide financing to riskier and unproven enterprises. Venture capital serves the startup firm in development. In exchange for the needed capital to fund the enterprise, the venture capital investor usually demands stock or subscriptions to acquire stock. Venture capital financing offers many advantages to the entrepreneur such as the availability of funds for assets in development.

Unfortunately, since the recent dot.com debacle, venture capital financing groups have a healthy skepticism when the enterprise has primarily intellectual property assets.

For both entrepreneur and the venture capital group, the pre-relationship due diligence period can be critical. If both parties pay attention to the pre-relationship due diligence, the ultimate relationship will benefit both parties. The entrepreneur and the venture capital group must first find each other and they must engage in an elaborate mating ritual to confirm that they have a future together. Thus, the entrepreneur's future enterprise and the venture capital group can look upon their pre-relationship investigation as a form of courtship and marriage.

As will be discussed below, the phases of meeting, courting, and wedded bliss can provide the entrepreneur's enterprise with financing and the venture group with a successful investment.

II. THE HOMEWORK PHASE

The entrepreneur must strive to make the current status of the enterprise and its future potential attractive to the venture capital group. Before the entrepreneur even begins to search for the perfect venture capital mate, the entrepreneur has to have a good idea of at least three things:

1. What business plan will the enterprise operate under?

2. What assets will the enterprise need to operate?

3. What management organization will help the enterprise accomplish its goals?

The formulation of the business plan and the assets needed to operate often go hand in hand. The entrepreneur should have a clear idea of what the goals of the enterprise will be and how those goals will be accomplished. Once the goals are identified, the role of intellectual property assets can be assessed.

The entrepreneur should identify his assets by conducting his own due diligence that consists of the following:

1. Asset audit where the entrepreneur identifies each of the types of intellectual property assets that will be owned or developed by the enterprise;

2. Value investigation of the intellectual property assets, including researching market impact, the risk of third party development and the risk of infringement; and

3. The asset audit and value identification can and should be as extensive and detailed as the venture capital group's suggested due diligence that will be discussed further below.

The entrepreneur should also take steps to build a strong organization before approaching a venture capital firm. Building a strong reference list will add credibility to the enterprise. Many startup businesses are long on innovation but short on skilled management. The enterprise can address this problem in two primary ways. First, the enterprise should build an active advisory board. This will demonstrate to the venture capital group that the entrepreneur has a strong basis for innovation as well as management. Second the entrepreneur should identify its key personnel and document their relationship to the enterprise through employment agreements and shareholder agreements (where appropriate).

III. THE MATCHMAKING PHASE

While most venture capital groups prefer to invest in an enterprise that has some operating history, a select few will invest in the entirely new venture. Venture capital groups usually concentrate in a specific area such as pharmaceuticals, electronics or biotechnology. Some firms also focus their efforts in certain geographical areas.

Each side must do a lot of "dating" before finding the right match. Venture capital groups receive thousands of business plans each year. They cull out those proposed enterprises that have very little chance of success. On the other side, an entrepreneur will pitch to dozens of venture capital groups before finding a venture capital firm that will fund the enterprise. When the venture capital group has a basic knowledge of the enterprise's industry, the match between venture capital and the enterprise has a better chance for success.

This 'match making' phase involves effort on both sides to find the right fit both in terms of industries and amount of capital needed to fund the enterprise's success. Once the right "match" is found, the parties then enter into phase.

IV. THE COURTING PHASE

During the courting phase, the parties need to learn more about each other to insure that a formal relationship between them will be a comfortable fit. The parties should focus on the exchange of reliable information. The venture capital group will look to the entrepreneur to provide as much information as possible. The more reliable the information from the entrepreneur, the more comfortable the venture capital group will feel during the courting phase. The courting phase is made up of four stages of due diligence.

[These stages of due diligence entail the following types of information gathering steps and analyses:

1) Identifying intellectual property assets that are integral to the function of the enterprise, verifying the ownership of those assets, and ensuring that these assets are free from encumbrances;

2) Reviewing the features and background of the individual intellectual property interests identified in phase 1 to determine the scope of rights associated with these interests and possible grounds for unenforceability of those rights;

3) Verifying key information relied upon in prior phases of due diligence reviews through such investigative techniques as obtaining and evaluating documents used to register interests, searching databases to verify rights, and interviewing key business and technology staff members; and

4) Interpreting the relationship between the confirmed intellectual property interests of the company under scrutiny and the probability of success of the company, taking into account such factors as how those interests are used in the enterprise, how the interests relate to the company's present and projected products, and the expertise and experience of the company's management regarding means to commercialize products based on the type of intellectual property assets held by the company.]

V. THE PRENUPTIAL PHASE

Once due diligence has been completed and the parties determine that they can go forward with the relationship, they enter the prenuptial phase. During this phase, the parties define the structure of their relationship. In a successful venture capital relationship, both parties understand the rules. Thus, the written agreement between the venture capital group and the enterprise should:

1. Define each and every assumption and expectation;
2. Clearly set forth any expectations regarding the progress of research and development and marketing of the enterprises products or services;
3. [Specify the] stages at which funds will be disbursed over time; and
4. Provide disincentives for key personnel to leave the enterprise putting the entire venture at risk.

Once the parties have a written document to describe their relationship, the enterprise can begin using the financing.

VI. THE WEDDING PHASE

Once the venture capital group and the enterprise have reached an agreement, the marriage can be a happy one. However, as with any marriage, both parties must continue to work together in order to keep the relationship functioning. Ongoing disclosures on both sides aid in the progress of the relationship. Both sides should also be aware of and plan for a few situations that may derail the happy relationship.

"Founder's disease" occurs when the entrepreneur, who is good at innovation but not so good at day to day management, becomes discouraged and leaves the enterprise. The parties should have incentives in place to keep the founding entrepreneur in a position where he or she can do the most good.

The possibility of a change in circumstances, such as a change in laws or a shift in projected market conditions may eviscerate the success of the enterprise. If so, the parties should have an exit strategy for the liquidation of the venture.

VII. CONCLUSION

Venture capital financing can be the perfect way to finance the development of an enterprise's intellectual property assets. However, no matter how perfect it is, the experience will not be a successful one unless both the venture capital group and the entrepreneur carefully navigate the road to their ultimate relationship.

As discussed above, the proper due diligence and information exchange can make for a happy marriage between the entrepreneur and the venture capital group.

Notes & Questions

1. What features of Digital Ignition's initial plans for developing its business and related technologies may make the firm unattractive as a candidate for venture capital financing? What aspects of the company's ownership structure may impede further investment by venture capitalists? What weaknesses in the company's present intellectual property interests may concern venture capitalists? What types of intellectual property will Digital Ignition be counting on using that may be freely used by its competitors, leaving the company with little competitive advantage?

2. How can Digital Ignition improve its likelihood of obtaining venture capital financing? What types of legal strategies and steps will be helpful in this regard? How will changes in the company's ownership structure that are likely to attract venture capitalists affect Digital Ignition's initial investors? What types of steps can the company take to clarify the strength and value of its present intellectual property interests? What additional intellectual property interests (or programs to systematically obtain such interests) might be attractive to venture capitalists?

3. Venture capital is an important source of funding for some IP-based startups, but may be available to only a small range of firms. According to the federal Securities and Exchange Commission:

> Startups and small businesses . . . may seek funding from venture capitalists ("VCs") . . . . Entrepreneurs seek VC . . . financing usually after they have exhausted sources of capital that generally do not require the entrepreneurs to relinquish control rights (e.g., personal funds from family and friends).
>
> According to data from the National Venture Capital Association, in calendar year 2014, VCs invested approximately $49.3 billion in 4,361 transactions involving 3,665 companies, which included seed, early-stage, expansion, and late-stage companies. Seed and early-stage deals represented 1.5% and 32.2%, respectively, of the dollar volume of deals and 4.4% and 49.7%, respectively of the overall number of VC deals.
>
> Some startups, however, may struggle to attract funding from VCs because VCs tend to invest in startups with certain characteristics. A defining feature of VCs is that they tend to focus on startup companies with high-growth potential and a high likelihood of going public after a few years of financing. VCs also tend to invest in companies that have already used some other sources of financing, tend to be concentrated in certain geographic regions (e.g., California and Massachusetts) and often require their investments to have an attractive business plan, meet certain growth benchmarks or fill a specific portfolio or industry niche. In addition, when investing in companies, VCs tend to acquire significant control rights (e.g., board seats, rights of first refusal, etc.), which they gradually relinquish as the company approaches an initial public offering. In 2014, according to an industry source, information technology and medical/health/life sciences deals attracted the largest dollar volume of VC financing. According to a 2012 academic study, VCs appear to focus on scale or potential for scale rather than short-term profitability in their selection of targets, and firms that receive VC financing tend to be significantly larger than non-VC firms, based on employment and sales.

Securities and Exchange Commission, Crowdfunding, 80 Fed. Reg. 71388-01 (Nov. 16, 2015) at Sec. III(A)(2)(c).

B. Financing through Security Interests in Intellectual Property

Intellectual property interests can secure loan repayments and thereby further the financing of business activities at various stages of company growth. A security interest in intellectual property allows the holder to claim ownership of the intellectual property upon the occurrence of a specified event such as the failure of a borrower to make required loan payments. Early in the development of a company, security interests in intellectual property may be granted to key lenders in exchange for substantial infusions of operating funds. In later stages of business development, mature companies with valuable intellectual property assets such as film libraries or complex software may obtain loans secured by these assets to accelerate the companies' access to the value of these properties. Through these loans, a company can gain immediate access to the loan proceeds, while spreading and balancing the timing of loan repayments against the pattern of licensing royalties or sale proceeds obtained as slowly realized returns on the assets.

As with security interests generally, security interests in intellectual property are typically established through two sets of steps: initial actions to attach a security interest to a particular intellectual property asset and additional actions to perfect the security interest. Absent successful completion of both these types of steps, a purported security interest in intellectual property may not be enforceable against a party who succeeds to ownership of the intellectual property with no knowledge of the security interest. This means that a party relying on an improperly created security interest to reduce risks associated with repayment of a loan may have her security interest cut off by an assignee of the intellectual property involved, provided that the assignee takes his interest in the intellectual property for value, in good faith, and with no notice of the security interest. A party relying on an improperly created security interest in intellectual property may also have that interest cut off in a bankruptcy proceeding as the intellectual property assets of the bankrupt (including the intellectual property assets affected by the improperly created security interest) are sold off in order to satisfy claims against the bankrupt. *See generally* H. Jason Gold & Christopher M. Mills, "Intellectual Property and Bankruptcy: Protecting Your Investment," Metro. Corp. Couns., March 2004, at 7.

Unfortunately, the actions needed to properly create and perfect enforceable security interests in some types of intellectual property remain in doubt. The main source of uncertainty stem from the interplay of federal and state standards governing the creation and perfection of security interests in intellectual property. In general, the creation of security interests in intellectual property is governed by state law. In most states the relevant statutes are modeled on the provisions of Article 9 of the Uniform Commercial Code (UCC). These provisions treat intellectual property interests as intangible assets and describe how a party can create and perfect enforceable security interests in such assets.

However, many important intellectual property rights—such as rights associated with patents, copyrights, and federally registered trademarks—are products of federal law. The provisions of federal statutes governing the means for recording these federally-created interests may preempt state law provisions regarding the proper means to create and perfect security interests. Courts have reached mixed conclusions about whether Congress, in enacting federal standards for recording intellectual property interests, intended to preempt state standards governing the recording and perfection of security interests.

The court's opinion in *In re Peregrine Entertainment, Ltd.* below describes the UCC's standards for the perfection of security interests in intellectual property and the possible preemption of those standards under federal copyright laws. The impacts of federal standards on the perfection of interests in patents, trademarks, and trade secrets are discussed in the notes following the *Peregrine* case.

In re Peregrine Entertainment, Ltd.

United States District Court for the Central District of California

116 B.R. 194 (C.D. Ca. 1990)

Kozinski, Circuit Judge*

This appeal from a decision of the bankruptcy court raises an issue never before confronted by a federal court in a published opinion: Is a security interest in a copyright perfected by an appropriate filing with the United States Copyright Office or by a UCC-1 financing statement filed with the relevant secretary of state?

I

National Peregrine, Inc. (NPI) is a Chapter 11 debtor in possession whose principal assets are a library of copyrights, distribution rights and licenses to approximately 145 films, and accounts receivable arising from the licensing of these films to various programmers. NPI claims to have an outright assignment of some of the copyrights; as for the others, NPI claims it has an exclusive license to distribute in a certain territory, or for a certain period of time.[1]

In June 1985, Capitol Federal Savings and Loan Association of Denver (Cap Fed) extended to American National Enterprises, Inc., NPI's predecessor by merger, a six million dollar line of credit secured by what is now NPI's film library. Both the security agreement and the UCC-1 financing statements[2] filed by Cap Fed describe the collateral as "[a]ll inventory consisting of films and all accounts, contract rights,

---

*Sitting by designation pursuant to 28 U.S.C. § 291(b) (1982).

1. ... For purposes of presenting the legal issues raised by this appeal, it is sufficient if at least one of the films in NPI's library is the subject of a valid copyright. Cap Fed has stipulated that there is at least one such film, the unforgettable "Renegade Ninjas," starring Hiroki Matsukota, Kennosuke Yorozuya and Teruhiko Aoi, in what many consider to be their career performances.

2. All references are to the California version of the Uniform Commercial Code.

chattel paper, *general intangibles*, instruments, equipment, and documents related to such inventory, now owned or hereafter acquired by the Debtor."[3] Although Cap Fed filed its UCC-1 financing statements in California, Colorado and Utah,[4] it did not record its security interest in the United States Copyright Office.

NPI filed a voluntary petition for bankruptcy on January 30, 1989. On April 6, 1989, NPI filed an amended complaint against Cap Fed, contending that the bank's security interest in the copyrights to the films in NPI's library and in the accounts receivable generated by their distribution were unperfected because Cap Fed failed to record its security interest with the Copyright Office. NPI claimed that, as a debtor in possession, it had a judicial lien on all assets in the bankruptcy estate, including the copyrights and receivables. Armed with this lien, it sought to avoid, recover and preserve Cap Fed's supposedly unperfected security interest for the benefit of the estate.

The parties filed cross-motions for partial summary judgment on the question of whether Cap Fed had a valid security interest in the NPI film library. The bankruptcy

---

3. The UCC-1 [financing statement filed to perfect the security interest] described the collateral as follows:

> All inventory consisting of films and all accounts, contract rights, chattel paper, *general intangibles*, instruments, equipment, and documents related to such inventory, now owned or hereafter acquired by the Debtor, including, but not limited to:
>
> (i) all accounts, contract rights, chattel paper, instruments, equipment, *general intangibles* and other obligations of any kind whether now owned or hereafter acquired arising out of or in connection with the sale or lease of the films, and all rights whether now or hereafter existing in and to all security agreements, leases, invoices, claims, instruments, notes, drafts, acceptances, and other contracts and documents securing or otherwise relating to any such accounts, contract rights, chattel paper, instruments, general intangibles or obligations and other documents or computer tapes or disks related to any of the above; and
>
> (ii) all proceeds of any and all of the foregoing property, including cash and noncash proceeds, and, to the extent not otherwise included, all payments under insurance (whether or not the Secured Party is the loss payee thereof), or any indemnity, warranty or guaranty, payable by reason of loss or damage to or otherwise with respect to any of the foregoing property.

See Memorandum of Decision re Motion for Partial Summary Adjudication (Nov. 14, 1989) at 4 (emphasis added). The security agreement described the collateral in nearly identical language. *See id.* at 3. UCC § 9106 defines "general intangibles" as "any personal property (including things in action) other than goods, accounts, chattel paper, documents, instruments, and money." The official commentary to section 9106, adopted by numerous states (including California), specifically identifies "copyrights, trademarks and patents" as included in the definition of general intangibles. *See United States v. Anderson*, 895 F.2d 641, 647 (9th Cir. 1990) (Kozinski, J., dissenting) (although legislative history generally is a poor source of guidance for statutory interpretation, official commentaries are persuasive).

4. Under UCC § 9103(3)(b), "[t]he law . . . of the jurisdiction in which the debtor is located governs the perfection and the effect of perfection or nonperfection of the security interest" in a general intangible. "A debtor shall be deemed located at the debtor's place of business . . . [or] at the debtor's chief executive office if [it] has more than one place of business. . . ." U.S.C. § 9103(3)(d). Because NPI is a Utah corporation that conducts much of its business in California, Cap Fed apparently deemed filing in both states prudent. Presumably, Cap Fed filed in Colorado because its own headquarters are located in Denver.

court held for Cap Fed. *See* Memorandum of Decision re Motion for Partial Summary Adjudication (Nov. 14, 1989) [hereinafter "Memorandum of Decision"] and Order re Summary Adjudication of Issues (Dec. 18, 1989). NPI appeals.

II

A. *Where to File*

The Copyright Act provides that "[a]ny transfer of copyright ownership or other document pertaining to a copyright" may be recorded in the United States Copyright Office. 17 U.S.C. § 205(a); *see* Copyright Office Circular 12: Recordation of Transfers and Other Documents (reprinted in 1 Copyright L. Rep. (CCH) ¶ 15,015) [hereinafter "Circular 12"]. A "transfer" under the Act includes any "mortgage" or "hypothecation of a copyright," whether "in whole or in part" and "by any means of conveyance or by operation of law." 17 U.S.C. §§ 101, 201(d)(1); *see* 3 *Nimmer on Copyright* § 10.05[A], at 10-43 to 10-45 (1989). The terms "mortgage" and "hypothecation" include a pledge of property as security or collateral for a debt. *See Black's Law Dictionary* 669 (5th ed. 1979). In addition, the Copyright Office has defined a "document pertaining to a copyright" as one that

> has a direct or indirect relationship to the existence, scope, duration, or identification of a copyright, or to the ownership, division, allocation, licensing, transfer, or exercise of rights under a copyright. That relationship may be past, present, future, or potential.

37 C.F.R. § 201.4(a)(2); *see also* Compendium of Copyright Office Practices II ¶¶ 1602–1603 (identifying which documents the Copyright Office will accept for filing).

It is clear from the preceding that an agreement granting a creditor a security interest in a copyright may be recorded in the Copyright Office. Likewise, because a copyright entitles the holder to receive all income derived from the display of the creative work, *see* 17 U.S.C. § 106, an agreement creating a security interest in the receivables generated by a copyright may also be recorded in the Copyright Office. Thus, Cap Fed's security interest *could* have been recorded in the Copyright Office; the parties seem to agree on this much. The question is, does the UCC provide a parallel method of perfecting a security interest in a copyright? One can answer this question by reference to either federal or state law; both inquiries lead to the same conclusion.

1. Even in the absence of express language, federal regulation will preempt state law if it is so pervasive as to indicate that "Congress left no room for supplementary state regulation," or if "the federal interest is so dominant that the federal system will be assumed to preclude enforcement of state laws on the same subject." *Hillsborough County v. Automated Medical Laboratories, Inc.*, 471 U.S. 707, 713, 105 S. Ct. 2371, 2375, 85 L. Ed. 2d 714 (1985) (internal quotations omitted).[6] Here, the comprehensive

---

6. The Copyright Act does expressly preempt state law in respect to the exclusive rights possessed by holders of copyrights under federal law. *See* 17 U.S.C. § 301(a). In *Del Madera Properties v.*

scope of the federal Copyright Act's recording provisions, along with the unique federal interests they implicate, support the view that federal law preempts state methods of perfecting security interests in copyrights and related accounts receivable.

The federal copyright laws ensure "predictability and certainty of copyright ownership," "promote national uniformity" and "avoid the practical difficulties of determining and enforcing an author's rights under the differing laws and in the separate courts of the various States." As discussed above, section 205(a) of the Copyright Act establishes a uniform method for recording security interests in copyrights. A secured creditor need only file in the Copyright Office in order to give "all persons constructive notice of the facts stated in the recorded document." 17 U.S.C. § 205(c).[7] Likewise, an interested third party need only search the indices maintained by the Copyright Office to determine whether a particular copyright is encumbered.

A recording system works by virtue of the fact that interested parties have a specific place to look in order to discover with certainty whether a particular interest has been transferred or encumbered. To the extent there are competing recordation schemes, this lessens the utility of each; when records are scattered in several filing units, potential creditors must conduct several searches before they can be sure that the property is not encumbered. It is for that reason that parallel recordation schemes for the same types of property are scarce as hens' teeth; the court is aware of no others, and the parties have cited none. No useful purposes would be served—indeed, much confusion would result—if creditors were permitted to perfect security interests by filing with either the Copyright Office or state offices.

If state methods of perfection were valid, a third party (such as a potential purchaser of the copyright) who wanted to learn of any encumbrances thereon would have to check not merely the indices of the U.S. Copyright Office, but also the indices of any relevant secretary of state. Because copyrights are incorporeal—they have

Rhodes & Gardner, Inc., 820 F.2d 973 (9th Cir. 1987), the Ninth Circuit adopted the "extra element" test, holding that in order to survive a federal preemption challenge under section 301, a state law must involve rights that are qualitatively different from the exclusive rights established by section 106 of the Copyright Act. _Id._ at 977. The exclusive rights listed in section 106 include the rights to reproduce the copyrighted work, to distribute the work, to prepare derivative works and to display or perform the work. _See_ 17 U.S.C. § 106. Section 301 is inapplicable because here we are concerned not with the creation of the exclusive rights under section 106, but rather their transfer through the creation of a security interest. The transfer of a copyright interest is fundamentally different from the creation of exclusive rights to a work itself, and is governed by separate provisions in the Copyright Act. _See_ 17 U.S.C. §§ 101, 201(d), 205. Therefore, under the rationale of _Del Madera Properties_, the preemptive language of section 301 has no bearing on the issues presented in this case.

7. For a recordation under section 205 to be effective as against third parties, the copyrighted work must also have been registered pursuant to 17 U.S.C. §§ 408, 409, 410. _See_ 17 U.S.C. § 205(c)(2). Of course, registration is also a prerequisite to judicial enforcement of a copyright, except for actions for infringement of copyrights in foreign works covered by the Berne Convention. 17 U.S.C. § 411; _International Trade Management, Inc. v. United States_, 553 F. Supp. 402, 402–03, 1 Cl. Ct. 39 (1982).

no fixed situs — a number of state authorities could be relevant. Thus, interested third parties could never be entirely sure that all relevant jurisdictions have been searched. This possibility, together with the expense and delay of conducting searches in a variety of jurisdictions, could hinder the purchase and sale of copyrights, frustrating Congress's policy that copyrights be readily transferable in commerce.

This is the reasoning adopted by the Ninth Circuit in *Danning v. Pacific Propeller. Danning* held that 49 U.S.C. App. § 1403(a), the Federal Aviation Act's provision for recording conveyances and the creation of liens and security interests in civil aircraft, preempts state filing provisions. According to *Danning,*

> [t]he predominant purpose of the statute was to provide one central place for the filing of [liens on aircraft] and thus eliminate the need, given the highly mobile nature of aircraft and their appurtenances, for the examination of State and County records.

620 F.2d at 735–36. Copyrights, even more than aircraft, lack a clear situs; tangible, movable goods such as airplanes must always exist at some physical location; they may have a home base from which they operate or where they receive regular maintenance. The same cannot be said of intangibles. As noted above, this lack of an identifiable situs militates against individual state filings and in favor of a single, national registration scheme.

Moreover . . . the Copyright Act establishes its own scheme for determining priority between conflicting transferees, one that differs in certain respects from that of Article Nine. Under Article Nine, priority between holders of conflicting security interests in intangibles is generally determined by who perfected his interest first. UCC § 9312(5). By contrast, section 205(d) of the Copyright Act provides:

> As between two conflicting transfers, the one executed first prevails if it is recorded, in the manner required to give constructive notice under subsection (c), *within one month after its execution in the United States or within two months after its execution outside the United States,* or at any time before recordation in such manner of the later transfer. . . .

17 U.S.C. § 205(d) (emphasis added). Thus, unlike Article Nine, the Copyright Act permits the effect of recording with the Copyright Office to relate back as far as two months.

Because the Copyright Act and Article Nine create different priority schemes, there will be occasions when different results will be reached depending on which scheme was employed. The availability of filing under the UCC would thus undermine the priority scheme established by Congress with respect to copyrights. This type of direct interference with the operation of federal law weighs heavily in favor of preemption.

The bankruptcy court below nevertheless concluded that security interests in copyrights could be perfected by filing either with the copyright office or with the secretary of state under the UCC, making a tongue-in-cheek analogy to the use of a belt and suspenders to hold up a pair of pants. According to the bankruptcy court, because either device is equally useful, one should be free to choose which one to wear. With all due respect, this court finds the analogy inapt. There is no legitimate reason why pants should be held up in only one particular manner: Individuals and public modesty are equally served by either device, or even by a safety pin or a piece of rope; all that really matters is that the job gets done. Registration schemes are different in that the *way* notice is given is precisely what matters. To the extent interested parties are confused as to which system is being employed, this increases the level of uncertainty and multiplies the risk of error, exposing creditors to the possibility that they might get caught with their pants down.

A recordation scheme best serves its purpose where interested parties can obtain notice of all encumbrances by referring to a single, precisely defined recordation system. The availability of parallel state recordation systems that could put parties on constructive notice as to encumbrances on copyrights would surely interfere with the effectiveness of the federal recordation scheme. Given the virtual absence of dual recordation schemes in our legal system, Congress cannot be presumed to have contemplated such a result. The court therefore concludes that any state recordation system pertaining to interests in copyrights would be preempted by the Copyright Act.

2. State law leads to the same conclusion. Article Nine of the Uniform Commercial Code establishes a comprehensive scheme for the regulation of security interests in personal property and fixtures. By superseding a multitude of pre-Code security devices, it provides "a simple and unified structure within which the immense variety of present-day secured financing transactions can go forward with less cost and greater certainty." UCC § 9101, Official Comment. However, Article Nine is not all encompassing; under the "step back" provision of UCC § 9104, Article Nine does not apply "[t]o a security interest subject to any statute of the United States to the extent that such statute governs the rights of parties to and third parties affected by transactions in particular types of property."

For most items of personal property, Article Nine provides that security interests must be perfected by filing with the office of the secretary of state in which the debtor is located. *See* UCC §§ 9302(1), 9401(1)(c). Such filing, however, is not "necessary or effective to perfect a security interest in property subject to . . . [a] statute or treaty of the United States which provides for a national or international registration . . . or which specifies a place of filing different from that specified in [Article Nine] for filing of the security interest." UCC § 9302(3)(a). When a national system for recording security interests exists, the Code treats compliance with that system as "equivalent to the filing of a financing statement under [Article Nine,] and a security interest in property subject to the statute or treaty can be perfected only by compliance therewith. . . ." UCC § 9302(4).[9]

---

9. According to the official commentary to section 9302:
   Subsection (3) exempts from the filing provisions of this Article transactions as to which an adequate system of filing, state or federal, has been set up outside this Article and

As discussed above, section 205(a) of the Copyright Act clearly does establish a national system for recording transfers of copyright interests, and it specifies a place of filing different from that provided in Article Nine. Recording in the Copyright Office gives nationwide, constructive notice to third parties of the recorded encumbrance. Except for the fact that the Copyright Office's indices are organized on the basis of the title and registration number, rather than by reference to the identity of the debtor, this system is nearly identical to that which Article Nine generally provides on a statewide basis.[10] And, lest there be any doubt, the drafters of the UCC specifically identified the Copyright Act as establishing the type of national registration system that would trigger the section 9302(3) and (4) step back provisions:

> Examples of the type of federal statute referred to in [UCC § 9302(3)(a)] are the provisions of [Title 17] (copyrights). . . .

---

subsection (4) makes clear that when such a system exists perfection of a relevant security interest can be had only through compliance with that system (i.e., filing under this Article is not a permissible alternative).

. . . .

Perfection of a security interest under a . . . federal statute of the type referred to in subsection (3) has all the consequences of perfection under the provisions of [Article Nine]. UCC § 9302, Official Comment ¶¶ 8, 9.

10. Moreover, the mechanics of recording in the Copyright Office are analogous to filing under the UCC. In order to record a security interest in the Copyright Office, a creditor may file either the security agreement itself or a duplicate certified to be a true copy of the original, so long as either is sufficient to place third parties on notice that the copyright is encumbered. *See* 17 U.S.C. §§ 205(a), (c); 37 C.F.R. § 201.4(c)(1). Accordingly, the Copyright Act requires that the filed document "specifically identif[y] the work to which it pertains so that, after the document is indexed by the Register of Copyrights, it would be revealed by a reasonable search under the title or registration number of the work." 17 U.S.C. § 205(c); *see also* Compendium of Copyright Office Practices II ¶¶ 1604–1612; Circular 12, at 8035-4.

That having been said, it's worth noting that filing with the Copyright Office can be much less convenient than filing under the UCC. This is because UCC filings are indexed by owner, while registration in the Copyright Office is by title or copyright registration number. *See* 17 U.S.C. § 205(c). This means that the recording of a security interest in a film library such as that owned by NPI will involve dozens, sometimes hundreds, of individual filings. Moreover, as the contents of the film library changes, the lienholder will be required to make a separate filing for each work added to or deleted from the library. By contrast, a UCC-1 filing can provide a continuing, floating lien on assets of a particular type owned by the debtor, without the need for periodic updates. *See* UCC § 9204.

This technical shortcoming of the copyright filing system does make it a less useful device for perfecting a security interest in copyright libraries. Nevertheless, this problem is not so serious as to make the system unworkable. In any event, this is the system Congress has established and the court is not in a position to order more adequate procedures. If the mechanics of filing turn out to pose a serious burden, it can be taken up by Congress during its oversight of the Copyright Office or, conceivably, the Copyright Office might be able to ameliorate the problem through exercise of its regulatory authority. *See* 17 U.S.C. § 702.

UCC § 9302, Official Comment ¶ 8; *see* G. Gilmore, *Security Interests in Personal Property* § 17.3, at 545 (1965) ("[t]here can be no doubt that [the Copyright Act was] meant to be within the description of § 9-302(3)(a)").

The court therefore concludes that the Copyright Act provides for national registration and "specifies a place of filing different from that specified in [Article Nine] for filing of the security interest." UCC § 9302(3)(a). Recording in the U.S. Copyright Office, rather than filing a financing statement under Article Nine, is the proper method for perfecting a security interest in a copyright.

. . . .

CONCLUSION

The judgment of the bankruptcy court is reversed. The case is ordered remanded for a determination of which movies in NPI's library are the subject of valid copyrights. The court shall then determine the status of Cap Fed's security interest in the movies and the debtor's other property. To the extent that interest is unperfected, the court shall permit NPI to exercise its avoidance powers under the Bankruptcy Code [allowing the company to disregard the security interest and make an alternate disposition of the intellectual property interests involved].

IT IS SO ORDERED.

Notes & Questions

1. Some federal courts have not followed (or have severely limited) the court's holding in *Peregrine*, ruling instead that filing a security interest in accordance with state law standards is sufficient to perfect a security interest in a copyright. For example, the court in *In re C Tek Software, Inc.,* 117 B.R. 762 (Bankr. D.N.H. 1990) applied state UCC filing requirements to determine whether a security interest in copyrighted software was properly perfected. Taking a less extreme view, the court in *In re World Auxiliary Power Co.,* 303 F.3d 1120 (9th Cir. 2002) limited the sweep of the *Peregrine* rule by holding that a copyright must be registered before a filing with the Copyright Office becomes the exclusive means to perfect a security interest in that copyright. Under this approach, filing a UCC-1 financing statement in the relevant state office would be a sufficient means to perfect a security interest in an unregistered copyright. *See id.* at 1126–29.

2. With respect to patents, federal courts have reached diverse conclusions about the need for federal filings to perfect security interests in patents. Confusion on this point stems from provisions of the Patent Act, which specify means to record and establish the priority of patent assignments over subsequently created interests, but which do not indicate whether these provisions are applicable to security interests in patents. The relevant statutory provisions are as follows:

> Subject to the provisions of this title, patents shall have the attributes of personal property. The Patent and Trademark Office shall maintain a register of interests in patents and applications for patents and shall

record any document related thereto upon request, and may require a fee therefor.

Applications for patent, patents, or any interest therein, shall be assignable in law by an instrument in writing. The applicant, patentee, or his assigns or legal representatives may in like manner grant and convey an exclusive right under his application for patent, or patents, to the whole or any specified part of the United States.

A certificate of acknowledgment under the hand and official seal of a person authorized to administer oaths within the United States, or, in a foreign country, of a diplomatic or consular officer of the United States or an officer authorized to administer oaths whose authority is proved by a certificate of a diplomatic or consular officer of the United States, or apostille of an official designated by a foreign country which, by treaty or convention, accords like effect to apostilles of designated officials in the United States, shall be prima facie evidence of the execution of an assignment, grant or conveyance of a patent or application for patent.

An interest that constitutes an assignment, grant or conveyance shall be void as against any subsequent purchaser or mortgagee for a valuable consideration, without notice, unless it is recorded in the Patent and Trademark Office within three months from its date or prior to the date of such subsequent purchase or mortgage.

35 U.S.C. § 261. The last paragraph of this section clearly specifies that the recording of a patent assignment will cut off a subsequent attempt by the assignor to create a further security interest or "mortgage" involving the same patent. However, this does not resolve the question of whether a security interest is a recordable interest to be treated like a patent assignment for purposes of these provisions.

Many courts have concluded that a security interest was not intended by Congress to be a recordable interest for purposes of the provisions of the last paragraph of this section and that, hence, compliance with federal requirements for filing patent assignments is not required to perfect a security interest in a patent. For example, the court in *In re Cybernetic Services, Inc.,* 239 B.R. 917 (B.A.P. 9th Cir. 1999), *aff'd,* 252 F.3d 1039 (9th Cir. 2001), *cert. denied,* 534 U.S. 1130 (2002), considered whether the provisions of the Patent Act compel a party seeking to perfect a security interest in a patent to file a notice of the interest with the United States Patent and Trademark Office (PTO). The court concluded that, unlike the Copyright Act, the Patent Act does not contain express provisions regarding security interests and liens. While the Patent Act specifies means for filing patent assignments, the Act defines that nature of such assignments and this definition does not appear to encompass security interests or liens. The court concluded that:

A security interest is not an "assignment, grant or conveyance" of a patent. Patent law adheres to strict concepts of title, in order to protect the ownership of new inventions. It therefore distinguishes "assignments" of patents (of which "grants" and "conveyances" are specific types) from all other transfers (which are called "licenses"). William C. Hillman, *Documenting Secured Transactions* 2-19 to 2-20 (1998) (footnotes omitted).

239 B.R. at 921. The court held that, in the absence of clearer language or other indications of Congressional intent to provide for an exclusive means to perfect a security interest in a patent, the Patent Act should not be seen as stating any criteria for the perfection of such an interest and state laws should govern the proper procedure. *See also In re Cybernetic Services, Inc.,* 252 F.3d 1039, 1052 (9th Cir. 2001) (the Patent Act's "text, context, and structure, when read in the light of Supreme Court precedent, compel the conclusion that a security interest in a patent that does not involve a transfer of the rights of ownership is a "mere license" and is not an "assignment, grant or conveyance" within the meaning of 35 U.S.C. §261. And because §261 provides that only an "assignment, grant or conveyance shall be void" as against subsequent purchasers and mortgagees, only transfers of ownership interests need to be recorded with the PTO."), *cert. denied,* 534 U.S. 1130 (2002); *In re Pasteurized Eggs Corp.,* 296 B.R. 283, 291 (Bankr. N.H. 2003) (perfection of a security interest in a patent requires a filing of a financing statement in accordance with UCC standards; recording with the USPTO is insufficient to perfect such a security interest).

In contrast, the court in *Peregrine* argued in dicta that a party seeking to perfect a security interest in a patent would need to file a notice of this interest with the PTO and that courts that have held otherwise have misconstrued the provisions of the UCC recognizing the primacy of federal recording standards. The court in *Peregrine* explained its logic as follows:

> In reaching [the conclusion that federal Copyright Law compels a filing with the Copyright Office in order to perfect a security interest in a copyright], the court rejects *City Bank & Trust Co. v. Otto Fabric, Inc.,* 83 B.R. 780 (D. Kan. 1988), and *In re Transportation Design & Technology Inc.,* 48 B.R. 635 (Bankr. S.D. Cal. 1985), insofar as they are germane to the issues presented here. Both cases held that, under the UCC, security interests in patents need not be recorded in the U.S. Patent and Trademark Office to be perfected as against lien creditors because the federal statute governing patent assignments does not specifically provide for liens:
>
> Applications for patent, patents, or any interest therein, shall be assignable in law by an instrument in writing. The applicant, patentee, or his assigns or legal representatives may in like manner grant and convey an exclusive right under his application for patent, or patents, to the whole or any specified part of the United States.
>
> . . . .
>
> An assignment, grant or conveyance shall be void as against *any subsequent purchaser or mortgagee* for a valuable consideration, without notice, unless

it is recorded in the Patent and Trademark Office within three months from its date or prior to the date of such subsequent purchase or mortgage.

35 U.S.C. § 261 (emphasis added).

According to *In re Transportation*, because section 261's priority scheme only provides for a "subsequent purchaser or mortgagee for valuable consideration," it does not require recording in the Patent and Trademark Office to perfect against lien creditors. *See* 48 B.R. at 639. Likewise, *City Bank* held that "the failure of the statute to mention protection against lien creditors suggests that it is unnecessary to record an assignment or other conveyance with the Patent Office to protect the appellant's security interest against the trustee."[12]

These cases misconstrue the plain language of UCC section 9104, which provides for the voluntary step back of Article Nine's provisions "*to the extent* [federal law] governs the rights of [the] parties." UCC § 9104(a) (emphasis added). Thus, when a federal statute provides for a national system of recordation or specifies a place of filing different from that in Article Nine, the methods of perfection specified in Article Nine are supplanted by that national system; compliance with a national system of recordation is equivalent to the filing of a financing statement under Article Nine. UCC § 9302(4). Whether the federal statute also provides a priority scheme different from that in Article Nine is a separate issue. . . . Compliance with a national registration scheme is necessary for perfection regardless of whether federal law governs priorities. Cap Fed's security interest in the copyrights of the films in NPI's library and the receivables they have generated therefore is unperfected.[14]

---

12. The district court in *City Bank* further held that, if Congress intended to preempt the field of filing and to require perfection in the Patent and Trademark Office, it could have explicitly said so. *See* 83 B.R. at 782. However, under UCC § 9302(3), the proper inquiry is not whether Congress has preempted state law—for Article Nine's provisions clearly could not apply then—but rather whether Congress has established a regulatory scheme governing secured interests that is sufficiently comprehensive to supersede all or part of Article Nine by virtue of section 9104(a).

14. The court also finds two trademark cases, *TR-3 Indus. v. Capital Bank (In re TR-3 Indus.)*, 41 B.R. 128 (Bankr. C.D. Cal.1984), and *Roman Cleanser Co. v. National Acceptance Co. (In re Roman Cleanser Co.)*, 43 B.R. 940 (Bankr. E.D. Mich.1984), *aff'd mem.* (E.D. Mich.1985), 802 F.2d 207 (6th Cir. 1986), to be distinguishable. Both cases held that security interests in trademarks need not be perfected by recording in the United States Patent and Trademark Office. However, unlike the Copyright Act, the Lanham Act's recordation provision refers only to "assignments" and contains no provision for the registration, recordation or filing of instruments establishing security interests in trademarks. *See Li'l' Red Barn, Inc. v. Red Barn System, Inc.*, 322 F. Supp. 98, 107 (N.D. Ind. 1970) (mere agreement to assign mark in the future is not an "assignment" and therefore may not be recorded). The Copyright Act authorizes the recordation of "transfers" in the Copyright Office, and defines transfers as including "mortgages," "hypothecations" and, thus, security interests in copyrights.

In re Peregrine Entertainment Ltd. v. Capitol Federal Savings & Loan of Denver, 116 B.R. 194, 203–04 (C.D. Cal. 1990).

3. The means to perfect security interests in trademarks are somewhat clearer. Common law trademarks established through trademark use and governed by state laws can be the subject of security interests that can be perfected by filing a financing statement in accordance with UCC standards. *See In re Together Dev. Corp.,* 227 B.R. 439 (Bankr. D. Mass. 1998). Because federal trademark laws have been interpreted as establishing a recording system that does not apply to security interests and that, accordingly, does not supersede UCC requirements, security interests in federally registered trademarks can also be perfected by filings in accordance with UCC standards. *See id.*

The role of federal trademark laws in defining the proper means to perfect security interests in federally registered trademarks was examined in detail in *In re TR-3 Industries,* 41 B.R. 128 (Bankr. C.D. Cal. 1984). In that case, TR-3 Industries, Inc., and TR-3 Chemical Corporation borrowed money from a bank and executed security agreements to secure repayment. The agreements granted the bank a security interest in the companies' trademark and trade name TR-3. The bank filed a UCC-1 financing statement in California but did not record the security agreements with the United States Patent and Trademark Office (PTO).

The companies filed for bankruptcy and sought to sell their assets, including rights to the TR-3 mark. To clarify their ability to transfer these rights, the companies sought a ruling from the relevant bankruptcy court confirming that the bank did not have a perfected security interest in the TR-3 mark.

The issue before the court was whether the bank was required to file its security interest with the PTO, in which case its California filing was insufficient to create a perfected interest. The court concluded that:

> 1. Federal trademark laws enacted in the Lanham Act (15 U.S.C. Sections 1051 through 1127) contain no statutory provision for the registration, recording, or filing of any instrument or document asserting a security interest in any trademark, trade name, or application for the registration of a trademark; and

> 2. Congress' goals in passing the Lanham Act did not include providing a method for the perfection of security interests in trademarks, trade names, or applications for the registration of the same or a method for giving notice of the existence of claims of security interests in trademarks, trade names, or related applications for registration.

Id. See also In re 199Z, Inc., 137 B.R. 778 (Bankr. C.D. Cal. 1992) (declining to extend the *Peregrine* rule to trademarks).

4. Trade secrets created prior to 2016, as products of state laws, do not involve the same sorts of potential conflicts between federal and state laws that arise in connection with security interests related to federally defined patents, copyrights, and

trademarks. State laws should unquestionably govern the proper means for perfecting security interests in trade secrets protected under state laws. The enactment of the federal Defend Trade Secrets Act of 2016 (DTSA), 18 U.S.C. § 1836 et seq., may complicate standards regarding the perfection of security interests in federally defined trade secrets as conflicts between the federal standards of the DTSA and state security interest perfection standards are possible.

However, since the value of trade secrets can be destroyed through disclosures and such disclosures typically become more likely over time, the long-term value of trade secrets is often tenuous. This characteristic makes many trade secrets poor candidates for security interests tied to long-term loan payment obligations or other performance duties extending over substantial periods.

C. Misstatements in Financing Transactions

Misstatements about intellectual property assets and their business potential may influence potential corporate shareholders or other sources of corporate financing, leading to various types of fraud claims. Pressures surrounding the attraction of new investors can encourage company founders to overstate or misstate the strength of intellectual property interests. Raising capital for a new venture based on unproven intellectual property and related products or services is often challenging. Investors must be convinced to trust in both the business potential of a company's projected products or services and in the strength of the legal protections that will determine if the company has an exclusive opportunity to commercialize those products or services. To the extent that a particular company's business model depends on a complex chain of steps involving technological developments, new product designs, original marketing efforts, and the assertion of unproven legal protections, the chances that one of the critical steps needed for business success will go astray may appear high to many potential investors, causing substantial numbers of persons to choose investments in more established companies or technological fields.

The readings in this subsection address the features of fraud and misrepresentation claims arising out of high tech activities and related financing efforts. The initial excerpt from the article on "Vaporware" describes the securities fraud standards that govern private claims by injured investors where companies or their executives have misrepresented the characteristics of company operations, products, or legal interests. It considers these standards in the context of misstatements about high-tech start-up companies.

The remaining readings in this subsection are court opinions that discuss the materiality of misrepresentations about the status of intellectual property interests and about the impacts of those interests in protecting valuable product marketing opportunities.

Pommer v. Medtest Corporation concerns a misrepresentation about the scope of patent rights covering a key company asset. A company official made a statement that the company possessed a patent covering its sole substantial asset, a proprietary testing process that the company hoped to market. However, no such patent had issued.

Alna Capital Assocs. v. Wagner analyzes a misstatement concerning efforts to perfect an intellectual property interest. A company president represented that a product incorporating the company's new refrigerant invention was producing substantial profits and that these profits were likely to continue because a patent would soon issue to prevent other parties from marketing similar products. However, the truth was that the initial product was not producing substantial profits and that the Patent and Trademark Office had rejected the company's patent application for the invention because at least four different inventors had previously produced equivalent items.

Gompper v. VISX, Inc. involves an issued patent and a misstatement regarding the status of patent litigation. In a period when the company involved was announcing positive statements about its business and its patent portfolio, company managers were aware of litigation developments in which several of the company's key patents were held invalid and not infringed by an important competitor. Securities holders who were not given this information sued, arguing that company officials put forth the misleading profit projections in order to artificially inflate the company's stock price. The thrust of the complaint was that these statements about projected profits were false or misleading because the defendants knew there was no basis for the company's core patent claims and thus, no basis for the corporate officials' highly positive revenue projections.

1. Standards Governing Securities Fraud

Robert A. Prentice & John H. Langmore, Beware of Vaporware: Product Hype and the Securities Fraud Liability of High-Tech Companies
8 Harv. J.L. & Tech. 1 (1994)*

. . . .

II. THE ELEMENTS OF A SECTION 10(b)/RULE 10b-5 SUIT

Section 10(b) makes it unlawful "[t]o use or employ, in connection with the purchase or sale of any security any manipulative or deceptive device or contrivance in contravention of such rules and regulations as the Commission may prescribe as necessary or appropriate in the public interest or for the protection of investors." Rule 10b-5, of course, is the most significant of those rules and regulations promulgated by the SEC over the years.

A. False Statement or Omission

The first element that must be established by a plaintiff alleging a violation of Section 10(b) and Rule 10b-5 is that the defendant engaged in some form of fraudulent, deceptive or manipulative conduct. The actionability of an outright false statement is fairly easy to understand, but many cases involve more difficult questions. This subsection addresses three of those more difficult issues: (1) What does "misleading" mean? (2) What about inaccurate projections and forecasts? (3) What about misleading omissions rather than positive misstatements?

1. What Does "Misleading" Mean?

The simplest corporate misstatement cases involve obviously false statements, such as "Our new computer responds to voice-activated commands," when it does no such thing. Just as apparent are patently misleading omissions, such as neglecting to disclose that a high percentage of units sold have burst into flame. Both consumers and investors are misled in such instances.

More difficult questions are presented when the information is "soft" — subjective and perhaps forward-looking. When marketing hype is repeated in SEC-mandated disclosures, securities lawyers are typically alert enough to include various disclaimers regarding the risks that vaporware will not be promptly actualized in order to avoid misleading readers. However, securities liability can flow from any public statement and marketing efforts too often go unscrutinized by attorneys.

In the Apple litigation, [*In re Apple Computer Sec. Litig.*, 886 F.2d 1109, 1115 (9th Cir. 1989), *cert. denied*, 496 U.S. 942 (1990),] Apple Computer produced affidavits from several market experts indicating that the vaporware phenomenon is well known, that "when a computer industry product is announced for future availability, the market fully understands that the product is still in the development stage." In other words, Apple was arguing that a preannounced product is merely vaporware, and everyone knows it, and therefore no one could be misled.

However, as the Ninth Circuit stated in response to this argument, "[t]here is a difference between knowing that any product-in-development may run into a few snags, and knowing that a particular product has already developed problems so significant as to require months of delay." A statement that production is progressing smoothly when significant problems have already arisen is obviously misleading. In other words, disclosure of the potential complications that all hardware and software manufacturers may encounter is not required. Disclosure of problems that have already been encountered and undermine previous expressions of optimism is required.

Additionally, statements, although literally true, may be misleading if they make up part of a "mosaic" of information that conveys a misleading impression. Thus, a statement which discloses most relevant facts might still be misleading if it is presented in such a manner that reasonable investors (or consumers) cannot assemble an accurate picture of the whole. This is often termed the "buried facts" doctrine. For example, a company might disclose a good deal of information regarding the features of its new computer and the speed with which the computer performs its tasks, failing to mention the total lack of reliability the computer has demonstrated in internal testing.

In a related vein, half-truths may also be considered misleading. For this reason, as noted above, Rule 10b-5 prohibits companies from "omit[ting] to state a material fact necessary in order to make the statements made, in light of the circumstances under which they were made, not misleading." Thus, if a product press release announced that a company's new line of computers was on schedule to be released on January 1, 1996, but failed to mention that development of the new software needed to operate the computers was behind schedule and would not be ready until July 1, 1996, a misleading half-truth has been told. The hardware is little more than vaporware if there is no software with which to operate it. Disclosure must generally be complete with respect to material facts.

At the same time, the law does not mean that by revealing one fact about a product, one must reveal all other facts that might be interesting to the stock market. One need reveal only such additional facts, if any, that are needed to ensure that what was revealed would not be "so incomplete as to mislead." Thus, a product press release touting a new printer's speed of operation would not necessarily be misleading if it failed to mention that the printer did not have color capacity.

2. What About False and Misleading Projections?

A projection or forecast is not a statement of historical fact. Persons who hear or read a forward-looking statement, perhaps regarding a new computer that is in development, can generally understand that predictions do not always come true. No company must, or could, guarantee the accuracy of its predictions. Therefore, no one expects all vaporware announcements to be realized on schedule.

However, that does not mean that vaporware announcements are never actionable. In the *Apple* case, Apple officers made statements such as "Lisa is going to be phenomenally successful." In fact, Lisa turned out to be a nearly unmitigated flop. The key issue in terms of liability is the good faith and reasonable basis of the prediction, not its ultimate accuracy. As the Ninth Circuit noted in *Apple*:

> A projection or statement of belief contains at least three implicit factual assertions: (1) that the statement is genuinely believed, (2) that there is a reasonable basis for that belief, and (3) that the speaker is not aware of any undisclosed facts tending to seriously undermine the accuracy of the statement. A projection or statement of belief may be actionable to the extent that one of these implied factual assertions is inaccurate.

[886 F.2d at 1113].

Thus, when companies make vaporware announcements about the future availability and projected features of their products, just as when they make financial forecasts regarding gross income or profit margin, securities fraud liability may attach if the statements are not genuinely believed or have no reasonable basis.

In *Apple*, the court found that the company's statements that it had "unequalled strength, experience and expertise," that its new product was "a significant break-through," that "success should continue," and that its forecasting process had been "refined," were generally accurate and certainly believed in good faith. Apple, indeed, was a successful company with a good track record and for a time it believed in its Lisa and Twiggy products, even though they ultimately did not pan out as hoped. Therefore, the trial court held, and its holding was affirmed on appeal, that these statements were not actionable.

Courts generally have been careful to prevent plaintiffs from alleging "fraud by hindsight," a phrase used by the District Court of Massachusetts in dismissing claims arising from a series of infamous vaporware announcements by Lotus Development Corp. In that case, the court held that plaintiffs' claims that the software was not released as scheduled was only a claim of fraud by hindsight: "Especially where, as here, a product is understood to be in development, plaintiffs may not assert merely that, because the product did not come out when projected, plans for an earlier release were false." Again, the true test is the good faith and reasonableness of the company's previous public projections.

On the other hand, if a company predicts an important release date for particular vaporware, and does not publicly revise that date in light of known problems, then the prediction may become actionable. The *Apple* facts discussed above regarding Twiggy's development problems are an obvious example. Another example occurred in *Bharucha v. Reuters Holdings PLC* [810 F. Supp. 37 (E.D.N.Y. 1993)]. When Reuters touted the release of a new product, "Dealing 2000," which was to provide automatic matching facilities for foreign exchange transactions, and predicted that the new product would provide a major new source of revenue in 1990 and 1991, Reuters' ADRs rose from $25-3/4 to $70-5/8. However, when Reuters announced in October, 1990 that problems had occurred and Dealing 2000 would not be introduced for at least six months, Reuters' ADR price dropped to $32-5/8. A subsequent sharehold-ers' complaint alleged that defendant officers knew or should have known that the predicted release date was misleading because the product had experienced devel-opment problems as early as May 1, 1989, and had not even reached the point where it could be released for beta testing. These allegations that the forward-looking state-ments had not been made in good faith enabled the complaint to survive a motion to dismiss.

As noted earlier, the actionability of a disclosed prediction does not turn on whether or not the prediction in fact proves to be inaccurate. This is particularly the case where a projection "bespeaks caution." Under the "bespeaks caution" doctrine, a properly qualified vaporware announcement will not be actionable. However, the adequacy of the caution given will be decided on a case-by-case basis. The caution must be precise rather than broad boilerplate and, obviously, will not immunize forward-looking statements known to be false when made.

For example, the plaintiffs in *In re Storage Technology Corp. Securities Litigation*, [804 F. Supp. 1368 (D. Colo. 1992),] alleged that defendant company had made unduly optimistic claims for its new advanced storage and retrieval computer (the "Iceberg"). Company officers and directors represented that Iceberg had a two- to three-year technological advantage over the competition. These statements naturally excited consumers and investors alike. When problems with Iceberg's production were eventually disclosed, the stock price plunged and plaintiff investors sued under, inter alia, Section 10(b) and Rule 10b-5. Storage Technology defended by claiming that its overly optimistic predictions were mixed with statements of caution. The court denied Storage Technology's motion to dismiss, concluding that its vaporware announcements had not been sufficiently qualified to avoid misleading investors:

> [T]he unmistakable message conveyed by defendants' pre-April 20, 1992 public statements was that Iceberg would be in production by 1992, Storage Technology would enjoy a competitive advantage because it would be the first to reach the market with this new product and Storage Technology would earn large profits in 1992 as a result of Iceberg. Although some of the comments were tempered with caution, I cannot say as a matter of law at this juncture that they are too cautious to be actionable. "Not every mixture with the true will neutralize the deceptive."

[*Id.* at 1373.]

In the case *In re Marion Merrell Dow, Inc. Securities Litigation*, [[1993 Transfer Binder] Fed. Sec. L. Rep. (CCH) ¶ 97,776 (W.D. Mo. Oct. 4, 1993),] plaintiffs evaded a motion to dismiss based on the "bespeaks caution" doctrine because the challenged statements and omissions (relating to adverse effects of defendants' drug) did not contain "repeated specific warnings of significant risk factors." Broad, generic warnings were deemed inadequate to "bespeak caution."

Still, when risk factors are clearly disclosed in a detailed fashion, investors will not be allowed to argue that they were misled when projections known to be contingent fail to materialize. For example, in *In re Convergent Technologies Securities Litigation*, [948 F.2d 507 (9th Cir. 1991),] plaintiff investors complained that Convergent and its officers misled them by concealing from the market certain cost and production problems regarding the company's next generation ("NGEN") workstation product line. Product life cycle decisions are among the most difficult marketers have to make, because in the high technology field new products must continually be developed, but their development always poses technical problems and their marketing often diminishes the sales of the company's predecessor products.

The Ninth Circuit held, inter alia, that the market was not misled regarding the diminished sales of Convergent's earlier workstation product line because "[a]s a general matter, investors know of the risk of obsolescence posed by older products forced to compete with more advanced rivals," and that the risks regarding the development and marketing of NGEN had been particularized and emphasized.

3. What About Mere Omissions of Fact?

Suppose that while a company is in the process of developing a new line of software, its engineers run into several technical roadblocks and it becomes unlikely that they will be able to meet the company's stated performance goals. This is certainly a common if not universal occurrence in high-tech product development, but must the company voluntarily disclose to the market whenever such roadblocks are encountered? In other words, when does a company have the duty to disclose news (usually bad news) to the market?

Of course, if the news is already known to the public or to the plaintiffs, there is no duty to disclose. Further, the general rule is that the simple fact that a company possesses nonpublic, material information does not mean that it automatically has a duty to disclose that information. Absent a duty to disclose, an omission is generally not deemed misleading or deceptive.

According to several recent court decisions, there are three basic situations giving rise to a duty to disclose: (a) when insider trading is occurring, (b) when specific statutes or regulations require disclosure, and (c) when a company should correct "inaccurate, incomplete, or misleading prior disclosures." Each of these will be discussed in turn.

a. Duty to Disclose Arising Because of Insider Trading

The insider trading cases are fairly clear-cut, although they are properly viewed as the major component of a larger subset of cases—those where a fiduciary relationship exists. Assume, for example, that officers of a small computer company that has recently gone public learn that their only product has developed so many technical glitches that it will probably never be anything more than vaporware. If those officers begin unloading their stock in the company without disclosing the technical glitches, an insider trading violation of Section 10(b), actionable by contemporaneous purchasers of the stock, occurs.

Insider trading is often alleged in securities fraud cases arising out of high-tech industries, because many such companies in their formative years reward officers and other employees with stock options. When stock prices drop, plaintiff shareholders often claim that the defendants had been making overly optimistic statements about the company's products or financial prospects in order to buoy the company's stock price for their own personal trading profit. Therefore, for purposes of the corporate disclosure cases discussed in this article, insider trading serves primarily as the wellspring for a duty to disclose by the company and as evidence of scienter, indicating a possible motivation behind misleading statements and omissions.

b. Duty to Disclose Arising from Statute or Regulation

A duty to speak out also arises when SEC rules and regulations require disclosure, as in the filing of annual or quarterly reports. One category of relevant cases deals with projections, forward-looking statements, and other "soft information." A pressing concern for public companies centers on the imposition of liability for not disclosing soft information. What if, for example, a company has a practice of making formal but internal projections as to the date its new products will be issued, and updates these internal projections every quarter? Certainly investors (as well as consumers) would be interested in such projections. Although, as noted earlier, such matters receive certain "safe harbor" protection if they are disclosed, SEC rules and regulations typically do not require that they be disclosed.

On the other hand, despite recent judicial reluctance to widen the corporate duty to disclose, the SEC's 1989 Interpretive Release on Management Discussion and Analysis ("MD&A") seemingly requires disclosure of some forward-looking information, complicating the disclosure picture. Thus, the MD&A disclosure provisions arguably require a company to disclose, for example, major development problems regarding a key product it hopes to produce. SEC action in the MD&A area certainly merits close monitoring by corporate counsel, for the SEC seems to be requiring more in the way of predictive information from companies than are the courts.

Similarly, NYSE-listed companies must consider Exchange Manual Rule ¶ 202.05 which provides that listed companies are "expected to release quickly to the public any news or information which might reasonably be expected to materially affect the market for its securities." Good and bad information about major products (not mere vaporware) would seem to meet these criteria.

c. Duty to Disclose in Order to Correct Prior Disclosures

An understanding of this third category of duty initially requires that a distinction be drawn between historical information and forward-looking information, and between the duty to correct and the duty to update. An examination of three hypothetical scenarios will illustrate the key distinctions drawn by most courts.

Scenario #1: Assume, first, that the McCoy Computer Co. product manager announces at a trade fair that McCoy's engineers have just completed a technological breakthrough enabling McCoy's soon-to-be-released computer to be equally compatible with both IBM-style PCs and Apple-style Macs. Assume that McCoy's officers truly believe this to be true, but six weeks later McCoy's engineers learn that they had overlooked a serious technical problem which will prevent the promised compatibility from occurring. This development means that the trade fair announcement contained an inaccurate statement of historical fact. The misstatement is actionable. Furthermore, McCoy would have an affirmative duty to correct this inaccuracy.

The seminal duty to correct case is perhaps *Ross v. A.H. Robins Co., Inc.*, [465 F. Supp. 904 (S.D.N.Y.), *rev'd on other grounds*, 607 F.2d 545 (2d Cir. 1979), *cert. denied*, 446 U.S. 946 (1980),] in which A.H. Robins made optimistic statements in 1970 and 1971 about the safety, efficacy, and marketability of its intrauterine contraceptive devices. In 1972, an unpublished research report demonstrated that the device was not as safe as previously represented, and Robins was found potentially liable under Section 10(b) and Rule 10b-5 for neither correcting nor modifying its previous statements which had been revealed to be inaccurate statements of historical fact.

Another case involving product marketing is *In re Pfizer, Inc. Securities Litigation*, [[1990–1991 Transfer Binder] Fed. Sec. L. Rep. (CCH) ¶ 95,710 (S.D.N.Y. Dec. 21, 1990),] wherein plaintiffs alleged that Pfizer had been aggressively marketing its Shiley heart valve without disclosing its internal corporate knowledge of serious problems in manufacturing and quality assurance procedures. Pfizer alleged that it had no obligation to disclose its conjecture about these problems or about the tremendous legal liability to which they might give rise as the heart valves failed. The court disagreed, holding that plaintiffs' assertions that Pfizer had known as far back as 1980 that the Shiley heart valve had design flaws but had nonetheless continued to aggressively market and positively describe the valve, adequately stated a claim. Pfizer's marketing claims constituted inaccurate statements of historical fact crying out for correction.

To complicate our first hypothetical scenario slightly, assume that the inaccurate statement of historical fact was contained in a computer magazine article written by an analyst who regularly follows McCoy. Would McCoy have a duty to correct that statement? Inaccurate statements in such sources can affect market price and possibly lead to securities law liability. Companies should not, of course, be generally liable for the statements of third parties and have no duty to police the trade magazines to find inaccuracies that are not attributable to the companies. However, companies are liable for misstatements of their own employees appearing in the trade press and for third parties' misstatements if they have somehow placed their imprimatur upon those misstatements.

Scenario #2: Assume that McCoy's product manager had announced at a January 1993 trade fair that McCoy had sold 10,000 personal computers in 1992, and announced at a January 1994 trade fair that McCoy had sold 20,000 personal computers in 1993. If McCoy really sold these computers, these are accurate statements of historical fact. Assume further that on February 15, 1994, McCoy learns that due to competitive pressures it will probably sell no more than 3,000 personal computers in 1994. No statement needs correction, and most courts would hold that there is no free-standing duty to update an accurate statement of historical fact. In this case, there is no duty to speak, even though the situation, once accurately reported, has changed.

Scenario #3: Assume, finally, that McCoy's product manager states at the January 1994 trade fair that McCoy had sold 10,000 computers in 1992, 20,000 in 1993, and expects to sell 30,000 in 1994. Assume further that this forward-looking statement was made in good faith and with reasonable belief, but on February 15, 1994, McCoy learns that due to competitive pressures it is unlikely that it will sell more than 10,000 units in 1994. Here there is no duty to correct a historical inaccuracy, but a duty to update does exist. A statement, correct at the time, may have a forward connotation upon which readers or listeners may be expected to rely. If it becomes clear that the forward-looking statement was the product of a defective crystal ball, further disclosure may be called for. Thus, companies must update opinions and projections if they have become misleading as a result of intervening events.

In re Convergent Technologies Securities Litigation, [948 F.2d 507 (9th Cir. 1991),] involved several claims of misstatement and omission. One objection was to Convergent's statement that "[o]ur growth in the [first] quarter [of 1983] was the result of increases in shipments to our large OEM customers." Despite plaintiffs' claim that this statement misled investors by implying that the upward trend would continue, the court concluded that no duty to correct arose when Convergent learned that the upward tick in shipments was only temporary because the statement was an accurate statement of historical fact. Nor was there a duty to update, because the statement was not forward-looking.

On the other hand, in *Alfus v. Pyramid Technology Corp.*, [764 F. Supp. 598 (N.D. Cal. 1991),] plaintiffs alleged that defendant corporation fed information to financial analysts for inclusion of the analysts' reports. Those reports were optimistic regarding Pyramid's financial prospects and its MIServer product line, which would purportedly become available in February 1989 and contribute to revenues in the quarter ending in March. These forward-looking statements allegedly were rendered misleading by the fact that the manufacture and initial marketing of the MIServer family of products were plagued by serious and persistent problems causing at least a seven-month delay in their introduction. The court held that because these omissions rendered the previous forward-looking vaporware announcements inaccurate, those announcements should have been updated.

Unfortunately, the duty to update is one of the murkiest areas of federal securities law. Such a duty generally seems to arise when a development occurs that renders a prior forward-looking statement no longer accurate. In other words, a duty to update exists if such a prior statement would be a misstatement or half-truth if it were republished currently. Because a duty to update exists only if forward-looking statements, accurate when made, remain alive and have become false or misleading as a result of subsequent events, it is arguably just a variation of the "duty to correct."

One difficulty often lies in knowing how long a prior statement remains "alive," i.e., how long investors could reasonably rely on the statement. Courts have not set forth clear guidelines regarding the "shelf life" of forward-looking statements. If, for example, on January 1, 1995, the ABC Computer Co. announces that its engineers are working hard on developing software to perform a particular task, may investors reasonably rely on that statement on January 1, 1996? How about January 1, 1997? Because there are no firm answers to these questions, forward-looking statements regarding vaporware (as well as regarding financial conditions) should be made with caution and only with respect to products in the advanced stages of development. To do otherwise, while not necessarily creating Section 10(b)/Rule 10b-5 liability, may create a continuing duty to update.

Another difficulty involves the question of timing. If a company begins to suspect that one of its vaporware products is going to be very late, when must it inform the market? The courts have held that material information may be withheld from the market if there is a good business reason to do so. However, while courts often find good business reasons for the delay of disclosure of "good" information, such as a favorable mineral strike or the obtaining of a major contract, they rarely find a good business reason for the delay of "bad" information, such as the fact that a new product line will not be released on the date previously announced. About the most that can be claimed is a good faith delay sufficient for the company to verify the accuracy of the bad news.

B. Materiality

A second basic element of a Section 10(b)/Rule 10b-5 claim is materiality. The false or misleading statement or omission must be as to a "material" fact in order to be actionable. Matters of only niggling consequence do not affect investment decisions and should not give rise to liability. Classic examples of material facts include major mineral strikes, a substantial dividend reduction, and a large decline in earnings. As discussed earlier, vaporware announcements touting new products aimed at consumers can also influence investors and thereby be material.

Of course, not all product-related misstatements are material. Thus, if a product manager stated that the company's next generation computer would be on the market by July 1 of the following year, when, in fact, she believed that it would not be on the market until July 5 of that year, the inaccuracy would probably be immaterial. Misstatements regarding a line of products accounting for only a small fraction of a company's sales and profits would also most likely not be material.

The difficulty, of course, is drawing the line in that gray area between the obviously material and the obviously immaterial. The Supreme Court has established a test of materiality keyed to whether there is a "substantial likelihood" that a misstated fact had, or disclosure of an omitted fact would have, "significantly altered the 'total mix' of information made available" in the eyes of a reasonable investor. A fact can be material, however, even if it would not have changed the plaintiff's decision on whether to consummate the transaction in question so long as it would have assumed actual significance in a reasonable investor's deliberations.

The Supreme Court has also stated that in some instances materiality is gauged by multiplying the probability that an event will occur by the magnitude of the event. The Supreme Court made its pronouncement in the context of a takeover that was being negotiated but had not yet been consummated, holding that the magnitude of the deal multiplied by the likelihood that it would be consummated might well make it material before negotiations had advanced to the point that the "price and structure" of the transaction had been fixed. It is easy to see the analogy to product development. Information about the development of a particularly significant product could be deemed material before that product was ready for market if there was a reasonable likelihood that it would become ready. Deciding when in the long evolution of a high-tech product the "probability times magnitude" formula provides a conclusion regarding materiality is obviously problematic.

In one case involving a product representation, *Pommer v. Medtest Corp.*, [961 F.2d 620 (7th Cir. 1992),] evidence indicated that the sellers of a company with but a single asset — the intellectual property in a self-administered cervicovaginal cytology testing process — sold the company's stock to a buyer and, in so doing, represented that the process was patented. In fact, it was not patented. Even though the process was ultimately patented two years later, the court concluded that the misstatement was material by applying the Supreme Court's formula:

> West [an attorney owning 26% of Medtest stock] told [buyers] that Medtest had a patent, doubtless recognizing that in selling stock as in other endeavors a bird in the hand is worth two in the bush. Counsel's belief that the process is patentable is a fair distance from a patent. The examiner may disagree or insist that the applicant limit the claims in a way that affects the commercial value of the invention. If we take counsel's belief as signifying an 80% chance that Medtest will obtain a patent on the central claims, still the difference is material. Even a small probability of a bad event may be material, if that event is grave enough.

[*Id.*]

A more concrete indication of materiality than the Supreme Court's "probability times magnitude" formula is, where applicable, actual market response. Given the premise that American securities markets are essentially efficient and respond accurately to new information, a large movement (up or down) of the market in response to a company's news (good or bad) is strong evidence of the materiality of the information. As noted earlier, the announcement that Apple Computer intended to discontinue the development and production of its Twiggy vaporware precipitated a 25% drop in the price of Apple's stock in a single day. This drop indicates that the information was clearly material, although the announcement was made concurrently with public disclosure of a negative report on quarterly earnings.

Similarly, in *In re U.S. Bioscience Securities Litigation*, [806 F. Supp. 1197 (E.D. Pa.1992),] plaintiffs alleged that the company treasurer made a claim that a drug produced by the company might be marketed during the latter half of a specified year, pending FDA approval, knowing that getting the drug to market so quickly was not realistic. When securities analysts learned the truth, they concluded that the news "severely undermined the credibility of both the drug and [Bioscience]." This response by analysts, whose role is critical to providing information upon which investors in public companies make their pricing decisions, was deemed by the trial judge to be evidence of materiality.

"Puffing," the defensive concept that renders overly favorable descriptions of products immaterial in a consumer's fraud suit, is also occasionally successful in an investor's Section 10(b)/Rule 10b-5 suit. For example, an investor sued Commodore International claiming, inter alia, that in press releases Commodore promised that its new product—CDTV (a new interactive compact disc television system for the home)—would do far more than it ultimately did. [*See Vosgerichian v. Commodore Int'l*, 832 F. Supp. 909 (E.D. Pa. 1993).] The trial court dismissed the investor's lawsuit on the same grounds that it might have dismissed a disappointed consumer's fraud suit:

> All of Commodore's statements about CDTV either constitute unactionable "puffing" (CDTV is "revolutionary," it can "change the world," could "be

what VCR's were to the 1980's"), or they are not misleading. Commodore promised only that it would have 50 titles "in (its) introductory phase," not that it would have them immediately. Mr. Gould announced that CDTV represented a "major potential opportunity"—which could only be taken as a doubly qualified advertisement, not any kind of promise at all.

[*Id.* at 916.]

C. Scienter

Although many lower courts once held that mere negligence was sufficient to create a violation of Section 10(b) and Rule 10b-5, the Supreme Court in *Ernst & Ernst v. Hochfelder*, [425 U.S. 185 (1976),] held that in a private cause of action a "mental state embracing intent to deceive, manipulate or defraud" is a necessary element to establishing liability under Section 10(b) and Rule 10b-5. The scienter requirement need not entail a desire to deceive; it may mean only that defendant knowingly made a false statement and appreciated that it would likely mislead investors. As in other areas of the law, securities class action defendants are presumed to intend the natural consequences of their actions.

Although the Supreme Court has never spoken on the issue, most lower courts have held that "recklessness" may be sufficiently condemnable conduct to satisfy the scienter standard. Although courts have not been completely consistent in defining recklessness, one court recently described the concept as:

> [A] highly unreasonable omission, involving not merely simple, or even inexcusable negligence, but an extreme departure from the standard of ordinary care, and which presents a danger of misleading buyers or sellers that is either known to the defendant or is so obvious that the actor must have been aware of it.

[*Hollinger v. Titan Capital Corp.*, 914 F.2d 1564, 1569 (9th Cir. 1990).]

Scienter is a convoluted doctrine that raises difficult problems of both a legal and factual nature. Because plaintiffs cannot read defendants' minds, plaintiffs are typically allowed to establish scienter by inference. But plaintiffs must allege particular facts that give rise to an inference that defendants actually knew (or were reckless in their ignorance) of fraudulent conduct. The Second Circuit, for example, recognizes two primary means for plaintiffs to adequately plead scienter. First, plaintiffs "may allege facts establishing a motive to commit fraud and an opportunity to do so." Second, plaintiffs "may allege facts constituting circumstantial evidence of either reckless or conscious behavior."

In applying these concepts to product hyping, the first means of pleading scienter could be fulfilled by alleging that defendants' motive in prematurely announcing vaporware, as is commonly the case, was to discourage customers from buying competitors' products. It could also be fulfilled by alleging that defendant company officers sought to buoy the company's stock price with overly optimistic product announcements in order to profit personally by the exercise of stock options or other trading in the company's shares. Given the common practice of compensating officers and directors with share ownership, stock options, stock appreciation rights, and the like, plaintiffs often seize upon this "motive and opportunity" to fulfill the scienter requirement. As the Ninth Circuit noted in Apple, "[i]nsider trading in suspicious amounts or at suspicious times is probative of bad faith and scienter."

For example, in *In re RasterOps Corp. Securities Litigation*, [[1993 Transfer Binder] Fed. Sec. L. Rep. (CCH) ¶ 97,790 (N.D. Cal. Aug. 13, 1993),] plaintiffs claimed that the defendant company made misleadingly optimistic vaporware announcements. Plaintiffs survived a motion to dismiss on scienter grounds vis-a-vis individual officer defendants by alleging that defendants suppressed adverse information:

> [S]o that they could (1) protect and enhance their executive positions and the substantial compensation and prestige they obtained thereby; (2) enhance the value of their RasterOps stock holdings and their options to buy RasterOps stock; (3) sell shares of RasterOps stock they owned at inflated prices to obtain large profits; and (4) inflate the reported profits of the Company in order to obtain larger payments under RasterOps' incentive bonus compensation plan and/or via discretionary individual performance bonuses.

[*Id.* at 97,850.]

A second means of adequately establishing scienter in the vaporware context is by use of circumstantial evidence in the form of internal memoranda or the like indicating so many problems in product development that defendants could not have reasonably believed their optimistic product announcements. In Apple, for example, the product press release containing challenged Statements #4 and #5 regarding the Twiggy vaporware, was issued at a time when internal documents showed that Apple's tests indicated slowness and unreliability in Twiggy's information-processing capabilities; when the Apple division in charge of producing Lisa had warned top executives that its current unreliability would probably delay the introduction of Lisa by many months; and when Steven Jobs was expressing "virtually zero confidence" in the division in charge of developing Twiggy. The dissonance between Apple's external optimism and internal pessimism provided sufficient circumstantial evidence of scienter to warrant a jury trial, according to the Ninth Circuit.

Conversely, in *Berliner v. Lotus Development Corp.*, [783 F. Supp. 708 (D. Mass. 1992)], plaintiffs alleged that they bought Lotus stock at an artificially inflated price because Lotus kept announcing that the "1-2-3 Release 3.0" upgrade of its famous software package was about to be released when, in fact, it was nowhere near release. Plaintiffs first attacked a February 25, 1988 announcement that Release 3.0 would be available "late" in the second quarter of 1988, but the complaint alleged no facts or circumstances indicating that the projection was false when made. Absent such facts or circumstances, plaintiffs' allegations were insufficient as mere "fraud by hindsight."

Other pleadings were similarly rejected. On March 18, 1988, Lotus announced that although its senior vice president of software development had resigned, it had not yet changed its plans for introduction of Release 3.0. However, four days later, Lotus announced that the product would be delayed until the fourth quarter of 1988. That projection was repeated on March 29, July 18, August 9, August 12, and August 24. However, on October 7, 1988, Lotus rescheduled the release for the second quarter of 1989. Plaintiffs attempted to raise their claims above the level of fraud by hindsight by pointing to three "circumstances" probative of the falsehood of the later projections. First, plaintiffs alleged that five Lotus vice presidents resigned during the relevant period, but the court found several different reasons for the resignations and deemed them insufficient evidence that Lotus knew Release 3.0 would not meet its projected release dates. Second, plaintiffs alleged that Lotus did not begin beta testing until February 1989, urging the inference that because such testing is a prerequisite to commercial distribution of software, Lotus was reckless in projecting its earlier release dates. The court responded by pointing out that when Lotus announced on August 24, for example, that it was "aiming to" market Release 3.0 "late" in the fourth quarter, four months remained in the year, a period not alleged to be necessarily insufficient to complete beta testing. Finally, plaintiffs advanced a "motive and opportunity" type of argument that Lotus had an incentive to defraud the public in that (a) the company purportedly wished to dissuade customers from purchasing other products, and (b) Lotus insiders sold their Lotus shares during this time period. The court also rejected this third ground (and therefore dismissed the suit), stating in conclusory fashion that the insider sales, which were not alleged to have violated insider trading proscriptions, were not by themselves a sufficient basis for inferring that Lotus had repeatedly misrepresented the product's release date. However, the court never responded to plaintiffs' argument regarding Lotus' motive to dissuade customers from purchasing competitors' products—a motive which, as we have seen, often underlies vaporware announcements.

When, as is usually the case, individual defendants are included in a Section 10(b)/Rule 10b-5 complaint, many courts require very specific pleadings regarding the scienter of each. For example, in *In re Newbridge Network Securities Litigation*, [767 F. Supp. 275 (D. D.C. 1991),] part of the plaintiffs' complaint related to the defendants' alleged misrepresentations and omissions about problems with product quality. Regarding the scienter issue, the court held that where multiple individual defendants are sued, "the complaint must apprise each defendant of his or her participation in the fraud." Plaintiffs met that burden because their complaint specified the statements alleged to be misleading, adequately detailed when, where, and by whom they were made, and identified facts indicating conscious behavior by the individual defendants.

D. Reliance

Reliance by a plaintiff is "essential to a claim under Rule 10b-5 because it 'provides the requisite causal connection between a defendant's misrepresentation and a plaintiff's injury.'" As one court put it, reliance is "the subjective counterpart to the objective element of materiality."

Common law rules required that a plaintiff prove she had actually based decisions upon the defendant's misstatements or omissions. This traditional element of a common law fraud claim requiring a plaintiff to directly read or hear a misstatement and then rely on it has by necessity been altered in causes of action under Section 10(b) and Rule 10b-5.

The first such major alteration arose in *Affiliated Ute Citizens of Utah v. United States*, [406 U.S. 128 (1972),] wherein the Supreme Court held that plaintiffs need not establish reliance in an omission case. In other words, it makes little sense to ask plaintiffs to plead and prove reliance on facts that were hidden from them. Therefore, traditional reliance ("I saw, I read, I relied") need not be proved in omission cases. That the omitted information was material is sufficient to give rise to a presumption of reliance. Two other developments are of particular importance in recent 10b-5 cases.

1. "Fraud-on-the-Market"

In creating the "fraud-on-the-market" theory of reliance, lower courts reasoned that in cases of affirmative misrepresentation, reliance may be presumed even on the part of plaintiffs who did not see, read, or truly rely on misleading documents if they relied on the integrity of the market price. The Ninth Circuit, for example, reasoned that the purchaser of stock "relies generally on the supposition that the market price is validly set and that no unsuspected manipulation has artificially inflated the price, and thus indirectly on the truth of the representations underlying the stock price." This fraud-on-the-market theory equates an investor's reliance on market price with reliance upon statements made to the market. It changes the focus of the inquiry from whether the plaintiffs were misled to whether the market was misled. In *Basic, Inc. v. Levinson*, [485 U.S. 224, 247 (1988),] the Supreme Court accepted the fraud-on-the-market presumption, and the Efficient Capital Market Hypothesis (ECMH) upon which it is based.

Several cases involving statements about products have involved the fraud-on-the-market approach to reliance. One example is *DeVries v. Taylor*, [[1993 Transfer Binder] Fed. Sec. L. Rep. (CCH) ¶ 97,679 (D. Colo. June 28, 1993),] in which Thelma June DeVries (and others) sued Chemex Pharmaceuticals (and its officers and directors) alleging that they had misrepresented numerous aspects of Chemex's business and fraudulently concealed the truth about the development problems of one of its main products, a drug called Actinex. Defendants moved to dismiss on the reliance issue because DeVries candidly admitted that she was unaware of the facts on which the lawsuit was premised, had never read any of the documents allegedly containing misstatements and omissions, and had simply followed her husband Dale's recommendations in buying Chemex stock. On the other hand, Dale had worked in the securities business for 25 years and swore that he had relied on the securities markets to establish a fair price for Chemex stock. Given these facts, the court concluded that DeVries' reliance "on the alleged misrepresentations and omissions can be established via Dale's reliance on the same and the integrity of the marketplace."

Courts have recognized several basic rebuttals to the fraud-on-the-market presumption of reliance in a Section 10(b)/Rule 10b-5 case: (a) proof that the plaintiff did indeed know of the false statement or omission and traded in the stock anyway; (b) proof that the plaintiff would have made the purchase or sale even had she known of the false statement or omission; (c) proof that the market in question was not, in fact, efficient; (d) proof that the market price did not respond to the misrepresentation, indicating that the market was not misled; and (e) proof that "market makers" were privy to the truth in the case of a misrepresentation or omission, and, thus, the market price was not perversely affected by that misrepresentation or omission. This fifth category has evolved into what is currently known as the "truth-on-the-market" defense.

2. "Truth-on-the-Market"

The most interesting aspect of the fraud-on-the-market theory is the "truth-on-the-market" defense that has evolved from it. The essence of this defense is a claim by defendant companies in securities fraud cases that any inaccurate public announcements that they may have made were neutralized by corrections made by other sources that permeated throughout the efficient market. Clearly, if the market knew that a statement made by a corporate defendant was false or misleading, and the market priced the shares accordingly, a plaintiff's presumed reliance on a misleadingly high or low market price is severed. In essence, the company is arguing: "Yeah, we lied, but no one believed us."

Ironically, in vaporware cases the more spectacularly misleading the statement made by the company about its promised products, the more credible is its claim that the market was not defrauded because the truth was well known. This defense was used by Apple in its vaporware case involving Lisa and Twiggy. In *Apple*, the Ninth Circuit applied the truth-on-the-market defense in the following manner:

> The press portrayed Lisa as a gamble, with the potential for either enormous success or enormous failure. At least twenty articles stressed the risks Apple was taking, and detailed the underlying problems producing those risks. Many of the optimistic statements challenged by plaintiffs appeared in those same articles, essentially bracketed by the facts which plaintiffs claim Apple wrongfully failed to disclose. The market could not have been made more aware of Lisa's risks.

[*In re Apple Computer Sec. Litig.*, 886 F.2d 1109, 1116 (9th Cir. 1989).]

In almost the same breath that it recognized the truth-on-the-market defense, the *Apple* court stressed the limits of its holding:

> The investing public justifiably places heavy reliance on the statements and opinions of corporate insiders. In order to avoid Rule 10b-5 liability, any material information which insiders fail to disclose must be transmitted to the public with a degree of intensity and credibility sufficient to effectively counterbalance any misleading impression created by the insiders' one-sided representations.

[*Id.*]

Another product promotion case involving the truth-on-the-market defense is *Ballan v. Upjohn*, [814 F. Supp. 1375 (W.D. Mich. 1992),] in which plaintiffs claimed that in marketing and attempting to secure FDA approval for its drug Halcion, Upjohn hid data showing Halcion's negative side effects. Upjohn also omitted this data from its annual reports, quarterly reports, and other SEC filings. Upjohn argued that the market was well aware of the side-effects of Halcion, but the court denied Upjohn's motion to dismiss, quoting the Ninth Circuit's statement in *Apple* that unqualified exuberance from corporate insiders would typically be weighed heavily by the market and would not be overcome by "information [that] has received only brief mention in a few poorly-circulated or lightly-regarded publications." To prevail with the truth-on-the-market defense, defendant companies must prove that the corrective statements from other sources "credibly entered the market." The court also cited *In re Seagate Technology II Securities Litigation*, [802 F. Supp. 271 (N.D. Cal. 1992),] for the proposition that where the evidence of what the market knew consists of competing volumes of contradictory analysts' reports and contradictory articles published in the popular press, the truth-on-the-market defense is not established. Because the *Ballan* court could not "discern whether information concerning the side-effects of Halcion was credibly made available to the market by other sources," it could not summarily rule for defendants on the reliance issue.

E. Causation

The causation element of a Section 10(b)/Rule 10b-5 claim is closely related to the reliance element. Indeed, for many years most courts were willing to assume that evidence of materiality plus reliance gave rise to a presumption of causation. After all, materiality is defined as the type of information which might well affect an investor's decision whether to invest. The Supreme Court itself, in *Affiliated Ute Citizens of Utah v. United States*, [406 U.S. 128 (1972),] pronounced that the "obligation to disclose and [the] withholding of a material fact established the requisite element of causation in fact." The ease of establishing reliance in both omission cases (through the *Ute* analysis) and in most misrepresentation cases (through the fraud-on-the-market theory) largely eliminated the causation requirement in securities fraud cases for a few years.

However, in a recent development of great benefit to defendants, many courts have split the causation requirement into two distinct elements, transaction causation and loss causation, and have required plaintiffs to establish both.

"Transaction causation" is a requirement of causation in fact which is largely a restatement of the reliance element, demanding that plaintiffs show that a securities violation directly caused them to enter into the challenged transaction. Plaintiffs must show that "but for" the fraud, they would not have entered into the transaction which ultimately resulted in a loss.

The more problematic causation aspect for plaintiffs is "loss causation," a concept that generally requires plaintiffs to show, additionally, that defendants' fraud proximately caused their economic loss. Loss causation acts to limit the damages stemming from a securities fraud and "in effect requires that the damage claimed be one of the foreseeable consequences of the misrepresentation." A strict application of this approach allows defendants to concede that they misrepresented but still escape liability if plaintiffs' economic losses were caused by other factors.

A leading case establishing the loss causation element is *Bastian v. Petren Resources Corp.*, [892 F.2d 680 (7th Cir.), *cert. denied*, 496 U.S. 906 (1990)]. Plaintiffs had the misfortune of investing in an oil and gas venture in 1981, the peak year for oil prices, before a steady decline caused virtually all of the oil and gas limited partnerships formed in that year to lose money. Plaintiffs claimed that they would not have invested in defendants' particular oil and gas limited partnership had they known certain facts about defendants' honesty or lack thereof. However, plaintiffs steadfastly refused to provide the court with evidence as to the cause of their loss. Because the court was convinced that plaintiffs, had they known the truth regarding defendants, would simply have invested in a different oil and gas limited partnership and lost their money anyway, it denied recovery on grounds that plaintiffs had failed to establish loss causation:

> If the alternative oil and gas limited partnerships to which these plaintiffs would have turned had the defendants leveled with them were also doomed, despite competent and honest management, to become worthless, the plaintiffs were not hurt by the fraud; it affected the place but not the time or amount of their loss.
>
> . . . .
>
> . . . No social purpose would be served by encouraging everyone who suffers an investment loss because of an unanticipated change in market conditions to pick through offering memoranda with a fine-tooth comb in the hope of uncovering a misrepresentation. Defrauders are a bad lot and should be punished, but Rule 10b-5 does not make them insurers against national economic calamities.

[*Id.* at 684–85.]

The promulgation of a high standard for establishing the separate element of loss causation has been strongly criticized as "an insuperable barrier to recovery." Fortunately for plaintiffs, some courts presume both transaction and loss causation if the plaintiff proves the elements of the fraud-on-the-market theory.

Causation has been an issue in several product promotion cases. Demonstrating transaction causation is not too onerous because of its coextensiveness with reliance. Loss causation is often more difficult to prove because of the many factors that might affect a stock's price. For example, on May 12, 1983, Fortune Systems announced that it was having problems with its new computer product which were causing it to lose orders and customers. Fortune's stock price dropped dramatically in wake of the announcement. Plaintiff shareholders attempted to recover for, inter alia, a stock price drop that had occurred in the two months preceding the announcement, claiming that the adverse product information had caused that loss. However, the court was convinced that defendant's evidence showed that other factors, including adverse stock market conditions, caused the pre-May 12 drop. [*See In re Fortune Sys. Sec. Litig.*, 680 F. Supp. 1360 (N.D. Cal. 1987).]

Plaintiffs fared better in *Ballan v. Upjohn Company*, [814 F. Supp. 1375 (W.D. Mich. 1992),] the case involving the drug Halcion discussed above. The following claims were deemed sufficient to allege loss causation:

> [Plaintiffs] have alleged that due to defendants' intentional and reckless concealment of true test results from regulatory agencies, Halcion, during the class period, became Upjohn's second biggest sales item. Plaintiffs have further alleged that Upjohn, in the face of charges regarding adverse reactions to Halcion, falsely denied those charges. Plaintiffs have alleged that Upjohn, when faced with the withdrawal of Halcion from the United Kingdom, falsely stated that there was no scientific or medical evidence that warranted such withdrawal. Plaintiffs claim to have purchased Upjohn securities at artificially inflated prices and were damaged when the market price of Upjohn stock fell at the end of the class period. . . . Plaintiffs have alleged that the drop in the value of Upjohn's stock was not due to the approaching patent expiration date of some sleeping drugs.

[*Id.* at 1384–85 (citations omitted).]

Similarly, in *Fujisawa Pharmaceutical Co. Ltd. v. Kapoor*, [814 F. Supp. 720 (N.D. Ill. 1993),] loss causation was adequately alleged when defendants sold all of the stock of Lyphomed Co. to plaintiff without disclosing that Lyphomed had filed false applications and information with the FDA in connection with Lyphomed's quest for FDA approval of new generic drugs. Defendants moved to dismiss for failure to allege loss causation, citing Bastian as precedent. The court denied the motion, responding:

> As [defendant] Kapoor's sole authority on loss causation, Bastian is a poor choice. The relationship between the plaintiffs' loss and the alleged fraud is much clearer in the present case. The Complaint alleged that Fujisawa would not have purchased Lyphomed had it known the truth about Lyphomed's shoddy testing and the ANDA [Abbreviated New Drug Application] filings. It can also be inferred from the Complaint that Fujisawa's loss, in the form of the FDA restrictions and recalls, is a direct result of Kapoor's fraudulent statements and omissions which artificially inflated the price of Lyphomed stock and induced Fujisawa to purchase the company.

[*Id.* at 727 (citations omitted).]

F. Purchase or Sale "In Connection with"

Because Section 10(b) prohibits fraud "in connection with a purchase or sale" of securities, plaintiffs must demonstrate (a) that a purchase or sale occurred, (b) that the alleged fraud occurred in connection with that purchase or sale, and (c) that the plaintiff was a purchaser or seller. The purchase or sale requirement derives from statutory language and is, generally speaking, broadly defined. The requirement that the plaintiff be a "purchaser or seller" is essentially a standing requirement. Unless a plaintiff bought or sold securities, he or she did not suffer the type of injury Section 10(b) and Rule 10b-5 are meant to remedy. For purposes of this article, these requirements simply mean that persons who bought, say, computers and software, because they were misled by statements regarding the characteristics of those products, can sue only on grounds of breach of warranty, common law fraud, consumer protection violations, and the like. Unless the persons were moved by the misrepresentations and omissions to buy the company's securities as well as its products, they would have no standing to bring a securities fraud suit under Section 10(b)/ Rule 10b-5.

The most important aspect of this area of Section 10(b)/Rule 10b-5 doctrine, insofar as this article is concerned, is the "in connection with" requirement. Proper analysis of this element requires that the topic be divided into cases primarily involving relatively private representations made by defendants to individual plaintiffs, and cases primarily involving public representations made by defendants to the market generally. Vaporware preannouncements and other forms of product marketing often involve both types of representations.

1. Private Representations

Courts traditionally construed the requirement that fraud be "in connection with" the purchase or sale of securities rather broadly in order to ease plaintiffs' pleading and proof burdens. The only Supreme Court case to address the matter, *Superintendent of Insurance of the State of New York v. Bankers Life and Casualty Co.*, [404 U.S. 6, 13 (1971),] announced that the requirement was satisfied by deceptive practices touching a purchase or sale of securities. A "touching" test ultimately proved too generous for the lower courts, which have searched for a more limiting principle.

Some courts have substantially equated the "in connection with" requirement to transaction causation. Other courts have examined the facts to determine whether a "nexus" existed between the defendant's fraud and plaintiff's investment decision, focusing on whether Section 10(b)'s purposes would be advanced by applying it to the particular transaction in question. The most restrictive view of the "in connection with" requirement demands that the fraudulent statement or omission complained of relate directly to the value of the security being sold or the consideration being offered therefor.

To illustrate the potential confusion caused by this array of approaches, consider the facts of *Brown v. Ivie.*, [661 F.2d 62 (5th Cir.), *cert. denied*, 455 U.S. 990 (1981)]. Plaintiff Brown and defendants Ivie and Lightsey were each officers, directors, and one-third shareholders of a small corporation. In 1979, defendants decided to oust plaintiff from the corporation and had a vehicle by which to do so—a 1976 shareholders' "buy-sell" agreement requiring any shareholder no longer employed by the corporation to sell his shares back to the corporation at book value. Unfortunately for defendants, the 1976 agreement was unenforceable because certain statutory formalities had not been observed in its drafting. Therefore, defendants used a pretense to induce plaintiff to sign a similar, enforceable agreement in 1979. As soon as plaintiff signed the agreement, defendants fired him from his position and invoked the buy-sell agreement to force plaintiff to sell his shares back to the corporation.

There is no doubt that defendants' fraud "touched" on the sale of plaintiffs' shares. Similarly, most courts would find transaction causation and a nexus between the defendants' fraud and plaintiff's sale. However, the defendants' lies (plaintiff was told that he had to sign the new agreement in order for the company to effectuate a change in insurance companies and to increase the amount of insurance held by the corporation on each shareholder) did not relate to either the value of the securities or the consideration given therefor. For that reason, courts taking the most limited view of the "in connection with" requirement would find that it was not met in this case, although the Fifth Circuit held that the "nexus" requirement applied and was met.

There will be some obvious cases where statements made to promote products will not under any approach be "in connection with" the purchase or sale of securities about which plaintiffs later complain. Consider *Jabend, Inc. v. Four-Phase Systems, Inc.*, [631 F. Supp. 1339 (W.D. Wash. 1986),] in which Grosenick had an idea to develop and market a computer hardware/software package for the insurance brokerage industry. Four-Phase assured Grosenick that its hardware was well-suited to Grosenick's purposes. Based on that assurance, Grosenick and Bender decided to pursue the venture. They chose the corporate form of business organization and formed Jabend, Inc. Naturally, they issued Jabend's stock to themselves in exchange for their capital investment. Four-Phase's product did not live up to representations, and Jabend ultimately went bankrupt. Grosenick sued Four-Phase under Section 10(b) and Rule 10b-5, claiming that he purchased Jabend stock in reliance on Four-Phase's representations about its computer hardware's abilities. The district court dismissed the suit for failing to meet the "in connection with" requirement because Four-Phase was trying to sell only computers and had nothing to gain by the sale of Jabend stock.

Under virtually all of the various approaches discussed above, the "in connection with" element would be missing in *Jabend*. The misrepresentations were not about the particular value of Jabend stock. Nor were the misrepresentations calculated to affect the price of Jabend stock, particularly since they were made before Jabend was ever formed. Because Four-Phase was seeking to sell computers rather than stock, there was no "nexus" between its representations and the subsequent sale of Jabend stock. Only an exceedingly liberal interpretation of the outdated "touching" test could provide even the slightest grounds for an argument that the "in connection with" test was met in *Jabend*.

2. Public Representations

The "in connection with" requirement is often at issue in class action securities fraud lawsuits under Section 10(b) and Rule 10b-5 that arise out of product representations, such as vaporware announcements, reaching the investing public in general. Fortunately for class action plaintiffs, in these situations courts generally find the "in connection with" requirement to be met where the misstatements or omissions are made in a setting reasonably calculated or reasonably expected to influence the investing public. If this is the test applied, most cases of misleading product marketing statements will satisfy the "in connection with" test.

For example, an optimistic vaporware announcement at a trade show or in the trade press will likely have a direct impact on the market price of the company's shares. As noted earlier in this article, such an announcement can be expected to, and is often calculated to, have a direct impact on the company's stock price. If the product representations made in the *Jabend* case, for example, had been communicated not to a single potential customer, but to the public at large, the "in connection with" requirement would no doubt have been met. The product press releases complained of in *Apple* clearly reached the investing public as could reasonably have been expected. Therefore, the "in connection with" requirement will not weed out too many plaintiffs' claims in the typical class action securities fraud suit.

G. Damages

Lastly, plaintiffs in a Section 10(b)/Rule 10b-5 suit must demonstrate that they were damaged as a result of the fraud alleged. Because remediation is a primary goal of federal securities laws, compensatory damages provide the appropriate remedy in most 10b-5 securities fraud cases. Section 28(a) of the 1934 Act limits recoveries to "actual damages," but it is not always clear how those damages are to be computed.

The courts have developed several approaches to calculating damages, but in the vast majority of the suits brought under Section 10(b) and Rule 10b-5, courts borrow from the common law of torts, applying an "out of pocket" measure. In such cases, plaintiffs are entitled to recover the difference between the price paid and the actual value at the date of the transaction, plus interest. An important indicator of the "actual value" at the date of purchase (or sale) is the amount the market price drops (or rises) upon the public correction of a previous misleading statement or omission.

Before the *Apple* verdict was overturned by the trial judge, the jury had found that the individual defendants, Markkula and Vennard, were responsible for $2.90 of the $8.00 stock drop because of the Twiggy vaporware announcement. Lawyers estimated that 33 million shares were traded during the class period, implying damages of at least $96 million, plus interest.

Occasionally courts have found that the investors sustained damage when the defendant withheld "good news," resulting in the plaintiffs selling shares at a lower price than they would have had the truth been disclosed. However, when it comes to the product marketing statements that are the focus of this article, understatement seldom occurs. Overstatement is typically the order of the day.

Courts do consider other causes that might affect a stock's price drop. For example, in the *Apple* case, disappointing quarterly earnings were announced at the same time as the decision to discontinue Twiggy and were apparently the cause of $5.10 of the $8.00 stock drop, at least in the jury's eyes. Such issues were discussed in the loss causation section above.

2. Examples of Fraudulent Representations Regarding Intellectual Property

Pommer v. Medtest Corporation

United States Court of Appeals for the Seventh Circuit

961 F.2d 620 (7th Cir. 1992)

EASTERBROOK, CIRCUIT JUDGE.

Medtest Corporation has a single asset: the intellectual property in a self-administered cervico-vaginal cytology testing process. Patrick Manning devised the process and together with Donald West, a lawyer, formed Medtest in December 1981 to obtain a patent and undertake development to make the process commercially attractive. Manning held 31% of the stock, West 26%, and the remainder was scattered among friends and relatives. In 1982 Manning sold some of his stock in Medtest to Robert and Anna Lisa Pommer: 250 shares in September for $25,000, and later another 2,750 shares for $175,000. The Pommers thus acquired 3% of Medtest's outstanding stock, which is valuable only to the extent the firm pays dividends, goes public, or is acquired by a third party.

None of these things has happened, and the Pommers believe that they are the victims of fraud. A jury agreed in this action under § 10(b) of the Securities Exchange Act of 1934, 15 U.S.C. § 78j(b), and the SEC's Rule 10b-5, 17 C.F.R. § 240.10b-5. It awarded the Pommers more than $300,000 in damages, representing the purchase price of the stock plus interest. A magistrate judge, presiding by consent under 28 U.S.C. § 636(c), set aside the verdict and entered judgment for the defendants. She concluded that none of the representations made to the Pommers was materially false.

I

Given the verdict, we must take all of the evidence in the light most favorable to the Pommers. A jury could have concluded that West told the Pommers, while they were negotiating to buy the stock, that Medtest had a U.S. patent on the process and that a sale of Medtest to Abbott Laboratories, at a price between $50 million and $100 million, was imminent ("almost a finished deal"). A 3% interest in Medtest would have been worth between $1.5 million and $3 million had such a sale been consummated. In fact Medtest did not have a patent at the time. Counsel informed West in December 1981 that the process was patentable; the firm filed an application on September 30, 1982, and the patent issued on August 14, 1984. Medtest was not in the last stage of negotiation with Abbott Laboratories; it raised the subject with Abbott, and Abbott's employees mentioned a price in the $50 to $100 million range, but no details had been discussed, no hands had been shaken — and on October 28, 1982, Abbott sent Medtest a letter stating that it was not interested in acquiring Medtest. Since then Medtest has been developing the process on its own.

The magistrate judge concluded that the representations about the existence of a patent were not material — and therefore did not support relief under the securities laws — because counsel had told West that the process was patentable, and Medtest obtained a patent in due course. The judge continued: "It is true that Pommer testified that he would not have purchased his shares had he known the patent had not actually issued, but he never explained this self-serving conclusion or suggested any reason why it would make a difference to him." As for the sale to Abbott, the judge wrote: "Pommer's own testimony demonstrated that he knew that the time of sale and its terms were indefinite. . . . . . . [A]ny person of Mr. Pommer's intelligence and sophistication [knows that nothing under negotiation is] absolutely certain. . . . Negotiations involving a price range of between 50 and 100 million dollars indisputably indicate that a lot remains to be negotiated and decided."

Considerations of this kind show that a verdict in defendants' favor could not be disturbed. They do not, however, show that no reasonable juror could think the statements material. A statement is material when there is "a substantial likelihood that the disclosure of the omitted fact would have been viewed by the reasonable investor as having significantly altered the 'total mix' of information made available." TSC Industries, Inc. v. Northway, Inc., 426 U.S. 438, 449, 96 S. Ct. 2126, 2132, 48 L. Ed. 2d 757 (1976), applied to § 10(b) actions by Basic Inc. v. Levinson, 485 U.S. 224, 231–32, 108 S. Ct. 978, 983, 99 L. Ed. 2d 194 (1988). West told the Pommers that Medtest had a patent, doubtless recognizing that in selling stock as in other endeavors a bird in the hand is worth two in the bush. Counsel's belief that the process is patentable is a fair distance from a patent. The examiner may disagree or insist that the applicant limit the claims in a way that affects the commercial value of the invention. If we take counsel's belief as signifying an 80% chance that Medtest will obtain a patent on the central claims, still the difference is material. Even a small probability of a bad event may be material, if that event is grave enough. And it does not matter that Medtest obtained the patent two years later. The securities laws approach matters from an ex ante perspective: just as a statement true when made does not become fraudulent because things unexpectedly go wrong, so a statement materially false when made does not become acceptable because it happens to come true. Good fortune may affect damages, but it does not make the falsehood any the less material.

So too with the negotiations to sell Medtest to Abbott Laboratories. Until the last minute a deal may collapse, but some deals are more likely to close than others. Probabilities determine the value of stock. At a 90% chance of a buyout for $50 million, the Pommers' stock was worth $1.35 million; at a 10% chance it was worth $150,000. A jury could determine that West conveyed to the Pommers a substantially higher probability than the facts supported—that although West represented that the parties were just about to sign on the dotted line, actually there had been no more than superficial discussions, and Abbott had no serious interest in acquiring Medtest. There is "a substantial likelihood" that the Pommers (and any other "reasonable investor") would have viewed the truth about the negotiations with Abbott as "significantly alter[ing] the 'total mix' of information made available."

Defendants insist that until the parties agree on the price and structure of a transaction, the issuer may say what it pleases. For this proposition they cite *Flamm v. Eberstadt,* 814 F.2d 1169 (7th Cir. 1987), overlooking three important ("material") facts about *Flamm.* First, we discussed whether an issuer has a duty to speak even though it would prefer silence; Medtest was not silent. Second, the Supreme Court disapproved the price-and-structure approach when issuers make false statements about ongoing negotiations. Third, contemporaneously with *Flamm* we decided [*Jordan v. Duff and Phelps, Inc.*, 815 F.2d 429 (7th Cir. 1987)], which holds that the price-and-structure rule does not apply to closely held corporations such as Medtest. *Jordan* observed that in aftermarket transactions duties to disclose come from state law, and states regularly apply a special rule requiring disclosure when a manager of a closely held firm sells stock to (or buys it from) an outsider in a face-to-face transaction. Defendants do not address the effect of *Jordan,* or for that matter *Basic;* they cite neither case.

One could recast the magistrate judge's conclusion about the sale to Abbott as a finding that the Pommers knew enough of the truth that West's lies did not significantly affect their appreciation of the situation. An issuer that utters a mixture of truth and falsehood may have furnished the information necessary for an accurate appreciation of the securities' value—especially when the truth is written and the lie is oral. "While a misleading statement will not always lose its deceptive edge simply by joinder with others that are true, the true statements may discredit the other one so obviously that the risk of real deception drops to nil." *Virginia Bankshares, Inc. v. Sandberg,* 501 U.S. 1083, 111 S. Ct. 2749, 2760, 115 L. Ed. 2d 929 (1991). Written disclosures of the truth are not only more compelling but also more verifiable. Memories may play tricks (or the parties may be less than candid about what they heard or said); writings are available for inspection. In shaping implied private rights of action, courts properly favor rules that simplify litigation, discourage unverifiable (and therefore irrefutable) claims, and reward issuers that commit their representations to writing.

The Pommers must have been aware that a deal with Abbott was not just around the corner. A substantial range of price implied that hard negotiations lay ahead. West told them that Medtest needed to secure foreign patents, and that with these in hand it would be an attractive acquisition candidate. As the magistrate judge remarked, foreign patents cannot be obtained in a flash. The Pommers waited more than a year before beefing; would they have sat quietly so long if they really thought they had been promised a bonanza in a few weeks? The price of the securities also implies that a sale was a long shot: Why would Manning sell 3% of Medtest to the Pommers for $200,000 if the stock soon would be worth $1.5 million and up? Even if Manning desperately needed to raise capital, better terms must have been available. Robert Pommer said at one point that he viewed the investment in Medtest as his chance to hit the Lotto—yet he persuaded the jury that the defendants sold him a sure thing.

Whether these things would be enough to neutralize the representations about Abbott we need not say. The falsehood about the patent remains. More, we have emphasized that an issuer needs to disclose the truth clearly before a lie becomes immaterial. It is not enough that the other party must have recognized a risk. Risks are ubiquitous. Disclosures assist investors in determining the magnitude of risks. Even savvy investors may recover when a bald lie understates the gravity of a known risk. A jury could find that defendants never told the truth. Although they direct us to an agreement between Manning and the Pommers, that two-page document contains no information beyond a boilerplate warning that Medtest's process "has only speculative value at the present time and may prove to be totally worthless, in which event the Shares purchased by Buyer pursuant hereto may also become worthless." Such generic warnings do not enlighten investors about the status of patent applications, negotiations to sell the business, and the like; they do nothing to disabuse an investor influenced by false oral statements purporting to describe the status of the firm's affairs. The truth, or an express disclaimer of reliance on oral representations protects a seller, but this record discloses neither.

II

Although defendants are not entitled to judgment notwithstanding the verdict, they sought a new trial in the alternative. The magistrate judge accepted their principal argument but did not formally grant the motion, deeming the subject moot. The Pommers ask us to disapprove the judge's conclusion, and thus avert any possibility of a new trial. Whether to grant a new trial is a question for the trial judge in the first instance, with deferential appellate review. The Pommers therefore must offer a compelling reason before we would forbid the magistrate judge from deciding on remand that a new trial would best serve the interests of justice.

The Pommers put before the jury Abbott's letter of October 28, 1982, disclaiming interest in Medtest. They contended that defendants' failure to show them this letter, while they were still paying for the stock, is an independent securities fraud. Defendants contended that the use of the letter should be restricted. The magistrate judge told the lawyers to argue their versions to the jury but after trial wrote that she should have kept the letter out of evidence, because the Pommers agreed to buy the stock before Abbott sent the letter. In contending that the judge's second thoughts are wrong, the Pommers again have an uphill contest, for our review of evidentiary matters is deferential.

The truth (or falsity) of defendants' statements, and their materiality, must be assessed at the time the statements are made, and not in the light of hindsight. We made exactly this point about the patent issued in 1984. The letter arrived after the Pommers agreed to purchase the stock. It was on this ground that the magistrate judge concluded that she should have restrained the Pommers' use of the document. Nonetheless, the Pommers contend, the judge was right the first time, because, if they had known that Abbott had broken off negotiations, they would have stopped paying.

If the Pommers were saying that they did not sign a contract to purchase the stock until after October 28, 1982, they would have a point. The statute of frauds is enforced rigorously in securities cases. If not bound by contract to pay for all 3,000 shares, the Pommers were making a fresh investment decision every time they sent a check. But the magistrate judge found that on October 19, 1982, they signed a note promising to pay $200,000 for the stock, and the Pommers do not rely on the statute of frauds.

Once they signed that note, the Pommers were committed under the law of contracts. There was no remaining investment decision. They might choose to balk and litigate, of course, but "[w]e have held repeatedly in recent years that the securities laws do not ensure that people will receive information sufficient to make correct decisions about filing or pursuing lawsuits.

According to the Pommers, *Goodman v. Epstein,* 582 F.2d 388, 409–14 (7th Cir. 1978), required defendants to show them the letter of October 28. *Goodman* held that a partnership making a call for further capital must reveal current, material information because each new contribution is a fresh investment decision. As the ninth circuit properly observed in *Roberts,* however, *Goodman* depends on the fact that the partnership agreement did not compel the investors to comply with each request for funds. They had to decide, and to decide needed accurate information. The Pommers were not deciding anew to buy Medtest stock every time they wrote a check. They were deciding, instead, whether to keep or break their promise. They may have reasons to do either, but the nature of the asset covered by the contract—3,000 shares of stock rather than, say, 3,000 crates of rutabagas—no longer matters. Once the written commitment is firm, we held in *LHLC,* the subject passes into the domain of contract law. The magistrate judge therefore acted within her discretion in concluding (on second thought) that the letter of October 28, reflecting an adverse turn of events after the sale of stock, should not have been used as substantive evidence. The judge may elect in her discretion to award the defendants a new trial on remand.

To say that withholding the letter from the Pommers is not an independent fraud is not (necessarily) to say that the letter is inadmissible. Although the parties stipulated that Medtest and Abbott conducted some negotiations, the letter may support an inference that these never became serious. Such an inference would assist the Pommers in demonstrating that the defendants acted with intent to defraud. Whether the letter may be used with appropriate cautions to the jury is a subject for the trial judge in the first instance.

. . . .

REVERSED AND REMANDED

Notes & Questions

1. Statements about diverse intellectual property features and related business activities have been claimed to be material misstatements in securities actions. Statements asserted to be material have included descriptions of the status of a patent application, the scope of a patent's claim coverage, the features of a company's intellectual property licensing activities, the expiration date of a patent, the nature of a patent attorney's opinion regarding the enforceability of a patent, and the status of patent litigation. *See* Robert S. Thomasa, *The Materiality Standard for Intellectual Property Disclosures,* 42 IDEA 205, 209–219 (2002).

2. To what extent does the materiality of a misstatement in conjunction with a stock sale turn on the particularity of the information that is misstated? Is a broadly

stated misrepresentation — e.g., a baseless assertion without having consulted counsel that "our company will gain patent protection for our new technology" — more likely to be seen as immaterial "puffing" than a more focused and precise misstatement of more particular information — e.g., where no patent was obtained, a statement like that in *Pommer* that "our company presently possesses patent protection for our key technology"?

3. Is the impact on potential investors of these two types of statements meaningfully different?

4. Should the liability of corporate insiders or their companies for these two types of misstatements vary?

Alna Capital Associates v. Wagner

United States District Court for the Southern District of Florida

532 F. Supp. 591 (S.D. Fla. 1982), *aff'd in relevant part,* 758 F.2d 562 (11th Cir. 1985)

Spellman, District Judge.

This securities fraud action is brought under § 10(b) of the Exchange Act of 1934, § 517.301 of the Florida Statutes, and Florida common law. Jurisdiction over the Rule 10b5 claim is based on Title 28 U.S.C. § 1331. The Court has heard the state claims on the basis of pendent jurisdiction. *United Mine Workers v. Gibbs*, 383 U.S. 715, 86 S. Ct. 1130, 16 L. Ed. 2d 218 (1966).

The Plaintiff, Alna Capital Associates, is a limited partnership of which Albert Nahmad is the general partner. The only asset of the partnership is its stock in Watsco, Inc. Alna Capital Associates succeeded Alna Capital, Inc., a closely held corporation composed of the same investors as in Alna Capital Associates. Albert Nahmad was the president of the corporation and its only asset was the stock owned later by Alna Capital Associates. Albert Nahmad spearheaded the organization of both Alna Capital Associates and Alna Capital, Inc. for the purpose of buying a 38% block of the outstanding shares of Watsco, Inc. on December 29, 1972 from the defendant, William Wagner. William Wagner was president and chairman of the board of directors of Watsco, Inc. at the time of the stock sale.

The Plaintiff alleges that the Defendant Wagner fraudulently misrepresented material information and withheld material information which he had an obligation to disclose in connection with the sale to Nahmad and his associates of 300,000 shares of Wagner's personally-held stock in Watsco.

The alleged misrepresentations and omissions can be grouped into three categories: (1) Financial reports — misstatements in the public financial reports of Watsco; (2) Winslow — misstatements and omissions with regard to contracts entered into by the Winslow division of Watsco; and (3) Chargefaster — misstatements and omissions concerning the operation and patent status of "Chargefaster", a refrigeration product manufactured by Watsco.

. . . .

Although the testimony was conflicting on many of the issues in this case, hereinafter set forth are the facts as the Court finds them in light of all the evidence submitted and considering the credibility of the witnesses.

The time frame of the allegedly actionable conduct was from August of 1972 until December 29, 1972. The events unfolded as follows. Albert Nahmad, a mechanical engineer with a Bachelor of Science degree from the University of New Mexico and a Master of Science degree in Industrial Administration from Purdue University, had been employed for several years by the accounting firm of Arthur Young and Company (hereafter "Arthur Young") in Indianapolis, Indiana. Subsequent to leaving Arthur Young, Nahmad went to New York City where he worked in the corporate acquisition department of W. R. Grace and Co. Nahmad left his job with W. R. Grace in 1971 and set about the task of finding a small manufacturing company to invest in and possibly manage. At the same time, William Wagner, the president of Watsco, was interested in selling his shares in the company and he hired brokers to effect a sale. One broker, Ted Murnick, contacted a Mr. Weiner, who in turn contacted his friend Albert Nahmad. Nahmad looked at Watsco financial reports and then decided to come to Hialeah, Florida to examine the Watsco business and speak to Wagner.

Nahmad spent three days with Wagner at the Watsco plant in August, 1972. Wagner asked $10.00 per share and Nahmad made a counteroffer of $8.50 per share. Wagner stated that he wanted a price of 15 times earnings while Nahmad suggested 12 times earnings. During the course of the meetings, Wagner had stated that Watsco's earnings for the year would be 70 cents per share.

Wagner also gave Nahmad a detailed description of Chargefaster, including the claim that the product transformed liquid refrigerant into saturated vapor, making it almost impossible for liquid to reach and damage the compressor of a cooling unit. Wagner explained that the marketing of Chargefaster had just begun and that a high profit margin would continue on the product because a patent would be obtained for Chargefaster.

Wagner described to Nahmad the marketing of the products manufactured by the Winslow division of Watsco, indicating that Winslow had oral wholesaling agreements.

After the meetings, Nahmad returned to New York. A few days later, a deal was agreed to by Nahmad and Wagner over the telephone whereby Nahmad and his associates would buy 300,000 shares from Wagner at $8.50 per share. Wagner's attorney, Carmen Accordino, prepared a draft agreement and sent it to Nahmad's attorney Michael Zuckerman in New York.

On September 26, 1972, an option agreement was signed by Nahmad and Wagner. Nahmad then hired Arthur Young & Co. in Miami, Florida to investigate and analyze the Watsco business as part of a pre-acquisition review, which that company undertook. Although the option agreement provided that Nahmad could request a physical inventory at his own expense, no such inventory was taken.

In October, Wagner and Nahmad discussed past litigation over Winslow distributorship agreements. Wagner did not mention the antitrust lawsuit filed by Clarence Firstenberg in Los Angeles or any other potential antitrust problems with Winslow's contracts.

Also in October, Wagner received a rejection from the United States Patent Office on his patent application for Chargefaster which was not communicated to Nahmad until long after the final closing.

As a result of the Arthur Young pre-acquisition review, Nahmad developed serious concerns about several matters, one of which was the inventory of Watsco, leading him to believe that the yearly profits of Watsco would be 64 cents instead of the projected 70 cents. Nahmad met with Wagner and informed him of his concerns about the inventory. Wagner reassured Nahmad that the inventory was fine, but Wagner did agree to lower the price per share to $8.00. As part of the renegotiation, Wagner's liability for a drop in shareholders' equity was reduced. Wagner also insisted that it was absolutely essential that the sale close by the end of the calendar year 1972.

Just prior to the signing of the November 27th agreement of sale, Watsco announced profits of 59 cents per share for the first three quarters of the fiscal year ending January 31, 1973. The November 27th agreement provided for Wagner to sell to Nahmad 300,000 shares of Watsco stock, which stock was registered and traded on the American Stock Exchange, for $8.00 per share. The contract provided for an initial cash payment of $700,000.00 plus 12 quarterly payments of approximately $141,666.00 plus 6% interest.

Section 3.16 of the contract provides that copies of all agreements to which Watsco was a party were attached to the contract of sale. Section 3.23 states that no amendments or terminations of agreements entered into by the company had occurred save those enumerated in Schedule E of the contract.

The sale closed on December 29, 1972. At the time of closing, Wagner was aware of Alna Capital, Inc., which was composed of Nahmad's associates.

Subsequent to closing, in early 1973, Arthur Young prepared the annual financial statement of Watsco. Arthur Young's initial version of the statement showed a 4th quarter loss of 9 cents per share, from 59 cents to 50 cents. The loss was occasioned by a combination of factors: a drop in the value of inventory due to obsolescence and shortages; a drop in the value of accounts receivable; and a recognition of a loss to Watsco in a "lease" transaction with Advanced Plastics Corporation. Arthur Young evaluated the striking change in the financial status of Watsco and determined that a restatement of the prior three quarterly reports was necessary to accurately reflect the financial condition of Watsco. Under the restatement, the quarterly earnings per share figures changed from

  1st Q — 17 cents to 1st Q — 13 cents

  2nd Q — 48 cents to 2nd Q — 37 cents

  3rd Q — 59 cents to 3rd Q — 45 cents

leaving the fourth quarter with 5 cents earnings per share.

Paul Manley of Arthur Young explained the restatement and its basis to the Defendant William Wagner at a meeting between the two. Wagner listened to the explanation by Manley and made no comment as to the significance or accuracy of the restatement.

The restatement was approved by the Watsco board of directors and was filed with the Securities Exchange Commission. With the public announcement of the restatement, the value of the market shares dropped from approximately $8.00 to approximately $4.00.

In the spring or summer of 1973, Nahmad became aware of written exclusive distributorship agreements between Watsco and the distributors of the Winslow hair spray products. Previously, Nahmad had been informed that Watsco merely had oral agreements with Winslow wholesalers. The undisclosed Winslow agreements had the effect of tying up the major national markets for distribution of Winslow products. In the summer of 1974, legal counsel to Watsco informed Nahmad that the Winslow distributorship agreements entailed serious antitrust problems.

Later in 1974, Nahmad became aware of certain problems relating to Chargefaster. Watsco had obtained a patent on Chargefaster in 1973 based on Wagner's renewed patent application, in which he claimed that the product converted all (100%) of liquid refrigerant into saturated vapor before it entered a cooling unit. Wagner had not yet informed Nahmad of the October, 1972 patent rejection or of its contents which stated that at least four other persons had previously produced devices capable of doing that which Chargefaster does.

When Wagner informed Nahmad that another manufacturer was infringing the Watsco Chargefaster patent, the company filed suit. The suit was subsequently dropped, partially on the basis of Wagner's advice. Subsequently, on advice of counsel and after the 1972 patent rejection became known to Nahmad, the Chargefaster patent was withdrawn by Watsco. Profits from Chargefaster had declined substantially since its first full year of sales.

In December of 1974, the present lawsuit was filed.

The complaint herein is founded on § 10(b) of the Exchange Act of 1934, 15 U.S.C. § 78j, on the Florida statutory version of Rule 10b5, F.S. § 517.301, and on Florida common law of fraud. 15 U.S.C. § 78j(b) reads as follows:

> It shall be unlawful for any person, directly or indirectly, by the use of any means or instrumentality of interstate commerce or of the mails, or of any facility of any national securities exchange-
>
> . . . .
>
> (b) To use or employ, in connection with the purchase or sale of any security registered on a national securities exchange or any security not so registered, any manipulative or deceptive device or contrivance in contravention

of such rules and regulations as the Commission may prescribe as necessary or appropriate in the public interest or for the protection of investors.

Rule 10b5 reads as follows:

EMPLOYMENT OF MANIPULATIVE AND DECEPTIVE DEVICES

It shall be unlawful for any person, directly or indirectly, by the use of any means or instrumentality of interstate commerce, or of the mails, or of any facility of any national securities exchange,

(1) to employ any device, scheme, or artifice to defraud,

(2) to make any untrue statement of a material fact or to omit to state a material fact necessary in order to make the statements made, in the light of the circumstances under which they were made, not misleading, or

(3) to engage in any act, practice or course of business which operates or would operate as a fraud or deceit upon any person, in connection with the purchase or sale of any security.

Florida Statute § 517.301, practically identical to the substantive prohibitions of Rule 10b5, differs only in reaching securities transactions which have no interstate connection.

Although the Florida Statute is basically identical to Rule 10b5, the courts have interpreted the two provisions differently in two important regards. Both Statutes require proof of (1) a misrepresentation or omission, (2) of information that is material to the sale transaction, and (3) where the purchaser relied on such misrepresentation or omission. However, Rule 10b5 requires proof of fraudulent intent, knowledge, or reckless disregard of the falsity of the misrepresentation. In addition, a 10b5 case must be proven by clear and convincing evidence. F.S. § 517.301 has a less stringent scienter requirement, making negligent misrepresentations actionable. Also, there is no burden under Florida law to prove the claim by clear and convincing evidence. Punitive damages, which are unavailable under 10b5, may be obtained under Florida law.

Under Florida common law fraud, mere negligence satisfies the scienter requirement and the requirements are otherwise identical to those for F.S. § 517.301.

. . . .

The third and final set of alleged misrepresentations concerns Chargefaster. Nahmad testified that Wagner never mentioned that Wagner's patent application for Chargefaster was initially rejected on the grounds that the product was not novel and that at least four different inventors had previously produced equivalent products. The Plaintiff also offered substantial evidence that Wagner falsely represented that Chargefaster converts into saturated vapor all of liquid refrigerant used to recharge cooling units. The evidence demonstrated that not all liquid refrigerant was converted by Chargefaster and that the product did not perform as advertised by Watsco under Wagner.

The Court finds that Wagner misrepresented the operation of Chargefaster to Nahmad. The sales history of Chargefaster subsequent to its first full year of sales confirms that it was not the revolutionary product Wagner claimed it to be. The tests conducted in the courtroom showed that the product did not convert all liquid refrigerant to saturated vapor but merely converted some of the liquid refrigerant into partially saturated vapor. Thus, Wagner misrepresented the performance of Chargefaster not only to the U.S. Patent Office, but also to Nahmad. Also, the evidence clearly shows that Wagner failed to state to Nahmad that the U.S. Patent Office had initially rejected his application for a Chargefaster patent in October, 1972.

MATERIALITY

The next pertinent inquiry with regard to the misrepresentations and omissions found by the Court is the question of materiality. The test of whether an omitted or misrepresented fact is material is whether a reasonable investor would have considered the fact important in deciding whether to invest. *S.E.C. v. Texas Gulf Sulphur Co.*, 401 F.2d 833 (2d Cir. 1968); *T.S.C. Industries, Inc. v. Northway, Inc.*, 426 U.S. 438, 96 S. Ct. 2126, 48 L. Ed. 2d 757 (1976); *Mills v. The Electric Auto-Lite Co.*, 396 U.S. 375, 90 S. Ct. 616, 24 L. Ed. 2d 593 (1969).

. . . .

The Chargefaster misrepresentations and omission were material. Chargefaster had become, almost overnight, a major contributor to the earnings of Watsco. It promised to continue to be profitable to the corporation if it could do what its inventor promised and could be patented. The non-disclosure of the patent rejection was thus highly material. Further, the misrepresentations as to the performance of the product were also material.

RELIANCE

After materiality, the next essential element of the Plaintiff's causes of action is reliance. With regard to omissions, the Supreme Court has stated that in a Rule 10b5 case, where there is an obligation to disclose and the Defendant fails to make disclosure, "positive proof of reliance is not a prerequisite to recovery. All that is necessary is that the facts withheld be material in the sense that a reasonable investor might have considered them important in the making of this decision." *Affiliated Ute Citizens v. United States*, 406 U.S. 128, 153–54, 92 S. Ct. 1456, 31 L. Ed. 2d 741 (1972). Under *T.S.C. Industries, Inc. v. Northway, Inc., supra*, the last part of that test would likely be altered to "... in the sense that a reasonable investor would have considered them important. ..."

Simon v. Merrill, Lynch, Pierce, Fenner and Smith, Inc., 482 F.2d 880 (1973), gives weight to the proposition that the Plaintiff's "general reliance" on the non-disclosure by the Defendant must be shown in a 10b5 case. However, unlike the facts in *Affiliated Ute*, the claim in *Simon* did not arise out of a face to face transaction.

If general reliance is required for omissions in this face to face transaction, under the common law fraud, the Florida Blue Sky Law, or the 10b5 standards, it has been clearly demonstrated in the present case. Wagner was the ultimate source of information about Watsco. Nahmad evaluated and hired others to evaluate the business condition of Watsco, but he relied on Wagner's representations and omissions concerning Watsco.

With regard to misrepresentations, the reliance issue is whether or not the purchaser actually relied on the misrepresentations in deciding to purchase. Basically, the test is one of subjective materiality. Did the misrepresentations play a significant part in the decision to purchase? The test can also be viewed as one of causation in fact. Did the Defendant's misrepresentations induce or cause the Plaintiff to make his investment decision?

In this part of the case, a critical question to be asked in relation to each misrepresentation is: What did Nahmad know of the true facts and when did he know it?

. . . .

Nahmad was aware prior to the November 27th agreement that there were serious problems with the quarterly financial statements of Watsco. The pre-acquisition review by Arthur Young alerted Nahmad to the faulty inventory control system of Watsco and the softness in accounts receivable, and gave him reason to question the validity of reported earnings and earnings projections. In fact, Nahmad renegotiated the contract of sale with Wagner due to his concern over the accuracy of the quarterly earnings statements. The pre-acquisition review led Nahmad to believe Watsco earnings for the year would be 6 cents less than projected by Wagner. Nahmad discussed with Wagner his concerns about inventory, but Wagner insisted that the earnings figures were correct and that Watsco would not have filed false public earnings statements since that would open them to a wide range of liability.

Nahmad was less than completely convinced by Wagner's protestations, and a renegotiation of the contract was worked out providing for a reduction in the purchase price of 50 cents per share and a substantial reduction in Wagner's potential liability for a drop in shareholders' equity.

The only fair conclusion to draw from the facts is that Nahmad relied substantially on the quarterly financial statements, even though he had real doubts that the company would live up to its earnings projection. The facts also indicate that Nahmad relied on the claims Wagner made regarding the performance of Chargefaster, which was, at that time, a major profits producer for Watsco.

SCIENTER

On the issue of scienter, the factual and legal questions become complex. Under the Florida common law claim, scienter may be satisfied by showing merely that the Defendant should have known that his misrepresentations were false. Otherwise stated, it is a mere negligence standard. That standard appears to be identical to the scienter requirement for violation of Florida Statute §517.301.

The scienter requirement for a violation of Rule 10b5 is much more stringent. In *Ernst & Ernst v. Hochfelder*, 425 U.S. 185, 214, 96 S. Ct. 1375, 47 L. Ed. 2d 668 (1976), the Supreme Court stated:

When a statute speaks so specifically in terms of manipulation and deception, and of implementing devices and contrivances — the commonly understood terminology of intentional wrongdoing — and when its history reflects no more expansive intent, we are quite unwilling to extend the scope of the statute to negligent conduct.

In *G. A. Thompson and Co., Inc. v. Partridge*, 636 F.2d 945, 961 (5th Cir. 1981), the Court held that proof of severe recklessness is sufficient to prove scienter in a 10b5 action.

The facts showed that Wagner had controlled Watsco (the Wagner Tool and Supply Company) since its origin in 1945. He operated the business in New York until 1956 when he moved the company to Hialeah. At all times through December 29, 1972, Wagner was the president and chairman of the board of directors of Watsco. In 1972, Wagner was making an active effort to sell Watsco. He had hired a broker to accomplish the sale.

Wagner's complete control of Watsco was emphasized by the fact that his son and his son-in-law occupied important, executive positions in the company. Wagner handled the daily business of the company. He examined all mail coming to or leaving Watsco. He used an intercom monitoring system at the plant to keep track of operations.

Wagner was actively involved in the many corporate acquisitions by Watsco over the eleven years preceding the sale to Nahmad. He reviewed all the raw financial figures and processed that information before sending it to his accountants, Bromberg & Aronow. In terms of financial decision-making, he had rejected a cost system for evaluating inventory and there was evidence that he was personally involved in the decision to treat the Advanced Plastics transaction as a lease. He was aware of major problems in the system of inventory control. He had a clear understanding of the positive effect overstating inventory value has on reported earnings. He also understood that the sale price of a corporation's stock by reference to a multiple of repeated earnings was a common practice.

When Paul Manley of Arthur Young & Co. confronted Wagner with the financial restatement and the reasons behind it, Wagner offered no explanation or contradiction. He merely acquiesced in the new figures.

Wagner admitted that he had direct knowledge of the Winslow contracts and the October, 1972 Chargefaster patent rejection. He knew of the Firstenberg antitrust litigation and of the Winslow contract cancellations. It must also be inferred from the facts that he understood that Chargefaster did not perform as promised.

Wagner was shown to have made several misstatements as a witness at the trial of this case. These include his denying recognition of his own handwriting on a memo concerning the deterioration of Winslow and on a paper where he had indicated the sale price of Watsco stock by reference to a multiple of earnings.

Under the standards enunciated in *G. A. Thompson and Co., Inc. v. Partridge, supra,* and *Huddleston v. Herman and MacLean*, 640 F.2d 534 (5th Cir. 1981), the Court finds that the scienter or fraud requirement has been satisfied by clear and convincing evidence. Conscious intent to defraud is obvious in the Winslow and Chargefaster misrepresentations. The accounting misrepresentations indicate that the Defendant must have known the true financial condition of the company. At a minimum, the monthly and quarterly financial statements were published with severe recklessness as to whether or not they were true.

The stringent 10b5 standard having been satisfied by the evidence in this case, the Court necessarily finds that the scienter requirements under the Florida Blue Sky Law and under common law fraud have been fully satisfied by the evidence.

. . . .

Notes & Questions

1. In order to form the basis for a securities fraud action under § 10(b) of the Exchange Act of 1934 and Rule 10b-5, a misrepresentation of material information must be made in connection with a purchase or sale of stock. However, federal courts have differed as to whether a purchase or sale of stock that for purpose other than making a traditional stock investment constitutes a purchase or sale of stock that is subject to federal anti-fraud provisions. For example, in *Alna Capital Associates v. Wagner*, 532 F. Supp. 591 (S.D. Fla. 1982), *aff'd in part*, 758 F.2d 562 (11th Cir. 1985), the purchase of stock was a means for acquiring ownership and control of the company involved rather than a means to gain a partial ownership interest and ongoing investment on the part of the stock purchaser. In these circumstances, some courts have held that a stock transaction aimed at carrying out a corporate acquisition is not a purchase or sale of stock covered by 10b-5. If a court reaches this conclusion, even a material misstatement of information in connection with an acquisition of a company through a stock sale will not trigger liability under federal securities fraud standards.

Does this distinction make sense? Is there any reason why federal securities laws should protect the interests of a small scale investor who acquires a few shares of stock in a company but not protect a party that buys a larger interest through a stock purchase that is sufficient to acquire complete ownership or practical control of the same company? How do the interests of a small scale investor in an intellectual property-based company differ from those of a party acquiring future control over the same company? Do those differences justify greater protections under securities laws for a small scale investor?

2. Should the nature of a company's business activities affect whether federal securities laws are deemed to apply to particular misstatements? Should federal securities laws be interpreted to be especially protective against misstatements about intellectual property considerations where a company's business operations rely heavily on the protections of intellectual property interests like patents that may be hard to assess from outside the corporation by a present or potential shareholder? Should federal securities laws provide more or less protection to a stock buyer where the object of a

stock purchase transaction is not a traditional investment goal but rather to take control over corporate assets like patents or other intellectual property interests held by the targeted company?

Even if federal securities laws do not apply because a stock sales transaction is not deemed to involve the type of investment-oriented transaction covered by federal anti-fraud standards, state securities laws or common law fraud standards may still provide relief. Thus, for example, in *Alna Capital,* the Court of Appeals for the Eleventh Circuit noted that, while it doubted that the contested stock transaction in that case was subject to 10b-5 due to the fact that the transaction was aimed at acquiring the company involved, the purchaser of stock had been given materially misleading information and this was sufficient to establish a claim for recovery under the state common law fraud theory raised by the purchaser. *See* 758 F.2d at 563 & n. 3.

Gompper v. VISX, Inc.

United States Court of Appeals for the Ninth Circuit

298 F.3d 893 (9th Cir. 2002)

BRUNETTI, CIRCUIT JUDGE.

The issue before us is whether the complaint in this securities fraud class action states a claim under the heightened pleading requirements of the Private Securities Litigation Reform Act of 1995 ("PSLRA"), 15 U.S.C. §78u-4(b)(1), (2). The district court held that it did not, and dismissed the complaint without leave to amend. The plaintiffs appeal, and we affirm.

I. BACKGROUND

This action is brought under §§ 10(b), 20(a) and 20A of the Securities Exchange Act of 1934, 15 U.S.C. §§78j(b), 78t(a), 78t-1. Plaintiffs are individuals who purchased VISX, Inc. ("VISX") stock during the class period. The defendants are VISX, and various individuals who are either officers, directors, or both. We summarize the facts from the complaint, and assume these facts to be true for the purpose of our decision.

VISX develops and sells laser vision-correction devices. Prior to February 22, 2000, VISX charged a $250 fee for each use of its patented excimer laser system (the "per procedure fee"). In early 1999, Nidek, a Japanese competitor, obtained FDA approval to sell its products in the United States. Nidek did not charge a per procedure fee and therefore presented a tremendous competitive threat to VISX. In response, VISX immediately filed a patent infringement suit in the U.S. District Court for the Northern District of California.

Within days of filing that suit, VISX brought a similar action against Nidek before the International Trade Commission ("ITC"). After a two-week trial in August 1999, an ITC administrative law judge ruled in Nidek's favor. In an order entered in December 1999, the administrative law judge determined that Nidek's products did not infringe on VISX's patents, and further concluded that one of VISX's core patents was invalid because the patent applicant, Dr. Trokel, had failed to name a co-inventor, Dr. Srinivasan.

A little over two months later, on February 22, 2000, VISX publicly announced, that as part of a new business strategy, it was reducing its per procedure fee to $100. VISX's stock plummeted, and plaintiffs brought this action. Plaintiffs allege each defendant is liable for making false statements or for failing to disclose adverse facts while selling VISX stock and participating in a fraudulent scheme.

The class period begins on March 1, 1999, the date VISX announced anticipated First Quarter Fiscal Year 1999 results, and ends February 22, 2000, the date VISX announced it was reducing its per procedure fee. Plaintiffs argue that during this period defendants made positive statements about VISX's business and its patent portfolio in order to artificially inflate the stock price. The thrust of the complaint is that these statements were false or misleading because defendants knew there was no basis for their core patent claims and thus, the revenue projections. Without a valid patent portfolio, plaintiffs argue, VISX could not possibly maintain its lucrative per procedure fee, and, thus could not deliver on the stated revenue projections. The complaint alleges that defendants had this knowledge during the class period, but engaged in false public rhetoric in order to inflate stock prices and benefit from their own massive insider trading before the truth was revealed.

II. DISCUSSION

A. Standard of Review

We review de novo the district court's dismissal of a complaint for failure to state a claim under Federal Rule of Civil Procedure 12(b)(6). *See In re Silicon Graphics Inc. Sec. Litig.*, 183 F.3d 970, 983 (9th Cir. 1999). On review, we accept the plaintiffs' allegations as true and construe them in the light most favorable to plaintiffs. Id.

B. Private Securities Litigation Reform Act of 1995

The PSLRA significantly altered pleading requirements in private securities fraud litigation by requiring that a complaint "plead with particularity both falsity and scienter." *Ronconi v. Larkin*, 253 F.3d 423, 429 (9th Cir. 2001). A securities fraud complaint must now "specify each statement alleged to have been misleading, the reason or reasons why the statement is misleading, and, if an allegation regarding the statement or omission is made on information and belief, the complaint shall state with particularity all facts on which that belief is formed." 15 U.S.C. 78u-4(b)(1). Further, the complaint must "state with particularity facts giving rise to a strong inference that the defendant acted with the required state of mind." 15 U.S.C. 78u-4(b)(2) (emphasis added); *see also Silicon Graphics*, 183 F.3d at 974 (facts must come closer to demonstrating intent, as opposed to mere motive and opportunity). Thus, the complaint must allege that the defendants made false or misleading statements either intentionally or with deliberate recklessness. *See Silicon Graphics*, 183 F.3d at 985.

C. Sufficiency of the Complaint under the PSLRA

As stated above, the gravamen of plaintiffs' cause is that defendants intentionally or recklessly misrepresented the truth when they made optimistic statements about VISX's future earnings and growth because they knew its patents were invalid, and, as a result, also knew that VISX could not possibly hope to maintain its current practice of charging $250 per procedure. Though the complaint adequately demonstrates the defendants were unquestionably aware of Dr. Srinivasan's claim against one of their core patents, in the end it fails to demonstrate the link between awareness of the claim and knowledge that the patents were therefore invalid. *See Ronconi*, 253 F.3d at 430 (no facts alleged that would support inference that corporation's optimistic predictions were known to be false or misleading at the time defendants made them); *accord City of Philadelphia v. Fleming Co.*, 264 F.3d 1245, 1265 (10th Cir. 2001) (evidence in complaint must lead to the conclusion that company and officers must have known that litigation against it would be meritorious in the end).

To the contrary, the facts alleged in the complaint indicate that VISX and its officers fervently believed in the viability of the patent portfolio, and litigated its defense with ferocity. Thus, we agree with the district court's thorough analysis and ultimate conclusion that the facts alleged by plaintiffs are not sufficient to satisfy the strong inference of defendants' knowledge, as required by the PSLRA. *See Ronconi*, 253 F.3d at 430 (facts must show insiders knew, at the time they made the statements, about the negative event the complaint claims would occur in the future).

. . . .

III. CONCLUSION

For the reasons given above, we AFFIRM the district court's dismissal of the securities fraud class action against VISX and the individual defendants.

Notes & Questions

1. As noted in *Gompper*, the Private Securities Litigation Reform Act of 1995 made a number of important changes in standards governing federal securities fraud claims by private parties. Some of these changes may impair plaintiffs' ability to raise claims based on misstatements of the future business significance of patents and other intellectual property interests.

Among other changes, the Act added several new pleading requirements for securities fraud claims. First, where a complaint alleges that a statement or omission is false or misleading, the complaint must specify which statement is misleading and the reasons why it is misleading. Second, when a complaint is submitted on information and belief, a plaintiff must state "with particularity all facts on which that belief is formed." Third, a plaintiff is required to "state with particularity facts giving rise to a strong inference that the defendant acted with the required state of mind." 15 U.S.C. § 78u-4(b)(1) & (2).

Since the passage of the Act, considerable confusion has arisen about the types of facts a plaintiff must plead to raise a "strong inference" that a defendant possessed the state of mind or "scienter" required for securities fraud liability. Some courts have asserted that the Act simply codifies standards applied in the Second Circuit before the passage of the Act. These standards required plaintiffs to meet the "burden of pleading circumstances that provide at least a minimal factual basis for their conclusory allegations of scienter." Such a burden could be met through allegations of a motive to deceive and access to accurate information. *See, e.g., Turkish v. Kasenetz*, 27 F.3d 23, 28–29 (2d Cir. 1994); *Connecticut National Bank v. Fluor Corp.*, 808 F.2d 957, 962 (2d Cir. 1987). At the opposite extreme, the Ninth Circuit has interpreted the Act to require more extensive allegations of scienter, obligating a plaintiff to plead strong circumstantial evidence of either "[an] intent to deceive, manipulate, or defraud [or] deliberate recklessness [involving] an extreme departure from the standards of ordinary care ... which presents a danger of misleading buyers or sellers that is either known to the defendant or is so obvious that the actor must have been aware of it." Schueneman v. Arena Pharm., Inc., 840 F.3d 698, 705 (9th Cir. 2016) (emphasis in the original; citations and internal quotation marks omitted). Most circuits have adopted intermediate approaches somewhere between the Second and Ninth Circuit approaches. *See* Michael A. Perino, *Did the Private Securities Litigation Reform Act Work?*, 2003 U. ILL. L. REV. 913, 925 (2003).

It is unclear how these changes may affect claims based on misrepresentations related to intellectual property interests. The complexity of insights held by corporate managers about the nature and business impacts of intellectual property interests may make it difficult or impossible for plaintiffs to detect and allege information needed to support securities fraud claims. Information about corporate executives' true insights about intellectual property interests and concerns affecting their businesses may not be shared beyond a few trusted corporate insiders, making it unlikely that this information will surface and be available to injured investors seeking to raise securities fraud claims. Absent this information, it may be very difficult for claimants to allege specific facts indicating that executives knew or were reckless about the inaccuracy of their representations concerning intellectual property interests. Even if fully disclosed and capable of proof, gaps between executives' personal understanding of intellectual property interests and their representations concerning those interests may seem so complex as to appear to be the product of mere negligence or over-confidence on the part of the executives involved. For these various reasons, the tightened pleading requirements applicable to federal fraud claims may prevent claimants from proceeding with some suits involving intellectual property misrepresentations that would have survived under prior pleading standards. However, even if this is the case, the same fraud actions may succeed under state securities laws or common law fraud theories where the special pleading requirements of the Act are not applicable.

2. The Private Securities Litigation Reform Act of 1995 also implemented important substantive changes by creating a "safe harbor" protecting corporations and their officials from liability for certain forward-looking statements about projected corporate performance. The forward-looking statements given special protection include financial projections, statements concerning managements' plans or objectives, statements of future economic performance, and statements of the assumptions underlying the foregoing. *See* 15 U.S.C. §§ 77z-2(c), 78u-5(c). Under the safe harbor provisions of the Act, a forward-looking statement, even if false, is not a basis for liability if it is

identified as a forward-looking statement and is "accompanied by meaningful cautionary statements identifying important factors that could cause actual results to differ materially from those in the forward-looking statement." 15 U.S.C. §§ 77z-2(c)(1)(A)(i), 78u-5(c)(1)(A)(i). In addition, a forward-looking statement that is not properly identified or is not accompanied by the appropriate cautionary language still falls within the safe harbor if the statement is immaterial or if the plaintiff fails to prove that the defendant had "actual knowledge" that the forward-looking statement was false or misleading. 15 U.S.C. §§ 77z-2(c)(1)(A)(ii) & (B), 78u-5(c)(1)(A)(ii) & (B).

While the safe harbor provisions of the Act may make it harder for plaintiffs to assert liability based on forward-looking statements about the anticipated impacts of patent interests on projected company performance, the safe harbor provisions of the Act will not protect defendants against claims based on representations of present conditions, such as a misrepresentation about the existence of a patent, the scope of an outstanding patent's claims, the nature of advice from patent counsel, and the status of patent enforcement litigation. Hence, while the safe harbor provisions may diminish claims that executives have overstated the future business significance of patents and other intellectual property protections, a broad range of misrepresentations regarding patents and patent rights will still form a substantial basis for private damage claims under federal securities laws. Furthermore, the Act has not limited state law claims based on materially misleading statements in stock sales transactions.

3. The cases in this set of readings all involve misstatements about patents or patent rights in the context of partially commercialized products and services covered by the patents at issue. To what extent is the materiality of misstatements about patents dependent on the existence of at least some accumulated track record of marketing and profits of products and services covered by the misrepresented patents? Does it matter that representations about the profitability of patented products or services are made concurrently with misrepresentations about the patents or patent rights involved? Must the products or services covered by patents constitute a large percentage of a company's business in order for misrepresentations about related patents to be material? Where a promising, patented product or service has not yet been commercialized, how should the financial implications of a misstatement of patent rights be projected? Should the materiality of a misstatement about patent rights turn solely on the scope of the adverse financial implications of the misrepresentation or are there other factors that would be sufficient to establish the materiality of such a misrepresentation even if its financial implications were uncertain? When should a patent be considered a valuable corporate asset *per se* (perhaps because of its licensing value) such that an inaccurate description of the patent is a material misrepresentation?

4. What types of misstatements about intellectual property interests by company executives should be considered to be immaterial because shareholders already have curative information correctly describing the interests? Are there certain inherent

risks associated with intellectual property interests and related business advantages that are so commonly understood that contrary information in a statement by company executives should not be considered to be a material misrepresentation? For example, consider a case where a company official knows that a competitor possesses a non-infringing product with similar functionality, but nonetheless makes an unqualified statement to the effect that the company's patent portfolio will ensure continuing profits in sales to customers in a particular market because other competitors will be excluded from similar sales. In this setting, is the chance that a competitor will develop a superior, non-infringing product that will make a company's patented product worthless such a commonly understood possibility that it constitutes a source of curative information rendering the unbalanced misstatement about company profits immaterial? What about misstatements by company managers despite their knowledge that the information they are representing is incorrect for unusual reasons falling outside the normal range of risks of inaccuracy affecting that type of information? For example, should it matter in determining the materiality of an inherently speculative statement like "we are confident of our ability to gain a patent for our key technology" that the company executive making the statement knows that there is a specific reason not normally associated with typical risks surrounding patent applications that makes it highly unlikely that the company will obtain a patent?

D. Fiduciary Duties of Corporate Leaders Regarding Intellectual Property Development and Management

State corporation laws impose duties on corporate directors, officers, and shareholders that govern how these corporate leaders should establish and develop the value of a company's intellectual property assets. Corporate leaders have two types of duties that bear upon the creation and management of intellectual property assets of their companies. The first is a duty of care obligating an individual to exercise reasonable care under the circumstances in managing corporate affairs. Typically this duty is seen to have been met if an individual engages in reasonable information gathering about company affairs and then makes an affirmative decision about the action (or lack of action) that will best serve corporate interests. This type of duty will obligate corporate leaders to be attentive to potential opportunities to develop, use, and dispose of valuable intellectual property assets. The second type of relevant duty is a duty of loyalty requiring a corporate leader to act as a fiduciary with respect to her corporation and to put the interests of the corporation ahead of her own where these interests conflict.

This last type of fiduciary obligation has figured in a number of disputes in which corporate leaders have acquired personal interests in intellectual property and then sought to manipulate the intellectual property in ways that are detrimental to their corporations. The following case describes some of the ways that these types of conflicts over intellectual property can arise, the fiduciary standards governing such conflicts, and the often sweeping relief that courts will grant in order to force an individual who has breached his fiduciary duties to his corporation to forfeit any resulting personal gains to the corporation involved.

Henderson v. Axiam, Incorporated

Superior Court of Massachusetts

1999 Mass. Super. LEXIS 580 (June 22, 1999)

FINDINGS OF FACT, RULINGS OF LAW AND ORDERS FOR JUDGMENT

JOSEPH A. GRASSO, JR., JUSTICE.

This case involves a bitterly fought battle for control of a closely held corporation. The action was commenced in December of 1996 with the filing of a Complaint in which a number of plaintiffs, individually and derivatively on behalf of the corporation, sought declaratory and injunctive relief, an accounting, and damages allegedly suffered as a result of various alleged breaches of contract, breaches of fiduciary duty, conversion of corporate assets and opportunities, and unfair and deceptive trade acts or practices by the individual defendants, Phillip E. Holt ("Holt") and Debbra Holt (or, alternatively, "Mrs. Holt") in both their individual and representative capacities. The [plaintiffs'] claims against Holt and Mrs. Holt assert that by violating their fiduciary and good faith duties to plaintiffs and by converting and misappropriating the assets, income, resources and properties of Axiam, Inc. ("Axiam") for their own personal accounts they have violated G.L.c. 93A, § 11. The Holts, as plaintiffs-in-counterclaim, contend that one of the plaintiffs, G.L. Cabot Henderson ("Cabot Henderson" or "Henderson"), during his tenure as a director of the corporation, violated his fiduciary duties to Axiam and its shareholders. The factual predicate for the claims and the counterclaims centers around the dealings and relationships of a number of individuals with the defendant Axiam during the period from 1992 to the present.

. . . .

An understanding of the matters in controversy requires a brief understanding of Axiam's genesis, its corporate history prior to the Holts' arrival at Axiam, and its products, including certain intellectual property which may or may not be patentable and which may or may not have significant value. Axiam is a closely held corporation, with fewer than thirty shareholders and approximately ten employees. Axiam was incorporated in Massachusetts on April 4, 1983. Axiam was founded by Clinton Rule ("Rule") and Robert M. Lee ("Lee"). Over the course of his involvement with Axiam, Rule invested almost $3,000,000 in the corporation. Rule's initial investment consisted of monies Rule had received upon the sale of his stock in Rule Industries, as well as a $900,000 loan secured by a mortgage on his personal residence in Gloucester.

Axiam is a high technology company, manufacturing and selling products that measure the roundness and geometry of parts of high-speed rotating devices. Axiam's products measure the roundness of objects in millionths of an inch. The precision with which Axiam's products can both measure the roundness of the parts and balance the assembled parts is of great value, especially in the manufacture of jet engines. Axiam's major business is assembly process control, including reduction and elimination of rotor vibration, for high-speed rotating devices, such as jet engines, wheels and shafts, as well as the space shuttle. Axiam's products consist of both hardware and the computer software which controls the hardware.

Axiam's first product was the RGS-640, which is used in the quality control process by manufacturers of jet engines and other high speed rotating devices subject to vibration to perform biplane deviation calculations, a significant measurement of vibration. The RGS-640 was conceived and developed by Rule and Lee as employees of Axiam. Following the RGS-640, Axiam's next generation product was the GMS 4000, which was (as the initials suggest) a geometric measuring system addressing issues of balance and vibration, as well as roundness. The GMS system was also developed and sold by Axiam prior to Holt's joining Axiam in 1992.

From its formation until 1992, Axiam was managed principally by its founders, Rule and Lee, each of whom served as president of the company at various times and each of whom served on the Board of Directors throughout that period. Prior to Holt's joining Axiam in 1992, and in response to a customer communication, Axiam had developed a product designed to eliminate vibration caused by the failure to align stacks of rotor disks vertically during assembly of high speed engines, such as jet engines. This product came to be known as Axiam's SmartStack system. This product was invented by employees of Axiam, with assistance from an M.I.T. professor, Dr. Kamal Yousef-Toumi ("Dr. Toumi"), who, under contract with Axiam, assisted in developing the mathematical algorithms for the computer software.

The Hiring of Holt and Mrs. Holt

Axiam hired Holt in January 1992 to provide day-to-day management and assist with the "turnaround" of Axiam. Holt served initially as general manager, becoming Senior Vice President and then, effective April 7, 1994, President of Axiam. His hiring was precipitated by Rule, who had met Holt a number of years earlier. Rule was impressed with Holt's computer expertise, and even more impressed with Holt's maverick style of cutting through bureaucracy. In hindsight, Holt's maverick style resulted in his taking control of Axiam in ways never envisioned at his hiring.

. . . .

The Newco Strategy and the Attempt to Strip Axiam of its Intellectual Property, including SuperStack

[Concomitant with his attempt to obtain control over other aspects of Axiam's corporate affairs through improper means,] Holt also had set about to obtain for himself the benefits of Axiam's intellectual property, including SuperStack, to the detriment of Axiam's shareholders and the convertible noteholders. To understand the perceived value of Axiam's intellectual property requires some background.

Development of SmartStack into SuperStack

In early 1994, Pratt & Whitney, Canada, an Axiam customer, had discussed with Lee the desirability of adding geometric balancing capabilities to the engine stacking technology of SmartStack. Beginning in January of 1995, Axiam employees, principally Ron Doss ("Doss"), Steve Kokkins ("Kokkins"), Fred Kastner ("Kastner") and Lee began developing this next generation of Axiam technology, known as the SuperStack system.

SuperStack is a technology that provides geometric balancing of rotors to permit an engine manufacturer to design the best overall assembly of the rotors in an engine to eliminate vibration. Geometric balancing involves assembly of rotor stacks to achieve the best possible stacking, with external weights to compensate for weight imbalances. SuperStack adds to Axiam's SmartStack technology the ability to determine where the weight distribution is on a rotor. As conceived, SuperStack would compensate for any weight imbalances, including banana shapes, which are a problem in rotors.

Upon becoming Director of Engineering in February 1995, Doss oversaw the entire SuperStack project. Under contract with Axiam, Dr. Toumi had developed mathematical algorithms to predict imbalances left by SmartStack and to decide where the counterbalances should go. Kastner then developed a software code, and wrapped it around the algorithms developed by Toumi. He took Toumi's developments (source code) and provided software interfaces, making them compatible with Axiam's products. Lee (and Kokkins after him) worked on defining inputs and outputs, or real life examples. By May 31, 1995, the SuperStack code had been completed.

Prior to his resignation from Axiam, Lee had also developed a master device to test it. The master device which Lee had designed to test SuperStack was essentially a dummy rotor with known imperfections for use in measurement. Prior to resigning from Axiam in April of 1995, Lee had sent his paper designs for the master device to a machine shop for fabrication, and had made arrangements for Axiam to rent time on a balancing machine for purposes of testing SuperStack. Once completed, the master device would permit testing of SuperStack. The master device itself had not yet been received from the machine shop by June 11, 1996, when Doss resigned from Axiam. However, by June 1996, the SuperStack software had undergone preliminary testing and was ready for second level testing.

The battle over SuperStack, its present and future state of development, is at the core of much of the dispute in this action. As he had done in connection with SmartStack, Dr. Toumi had developed the mathematical algorithms for SuperStack under contract with Axiam. Holt did not contribute at all in any of the development work on SuperStack. Only Kastner touched the source code as developed by Toumi. In July of 1995, Holt instructed Doss to cease work on SuperStack. Although Holt professed to Doss that expected funding from a Pratt & Whitney, Canada contract had not materialized, I infer that, at least in good part, the reason also related to Holt's desire to take all of the benefits of SuperStack for himself.

Holt was concerned that time was of the essence in developing SuperStack, which he called Axiam's "next generation product." In April 1995, he wrote a letter to Shea an investor that: "If we lose this window of opportunity, we shall have made a major mistake." In 1995, he told Pratt & Whitney, with whom Axiam was attempting to establish a strategic alliance for development of SuperStack: "If you loved SmartStack, you will be mad about SuperStack." However, not only did Holt not enter into agreement with Pratt & Whitney, he also instructed Doss to cease work on SuperStack.

In early 1996, Holt instructed Doss to recommence work on SuperStack, asserting that he had spoken with Pratt & Whitney, Canada and expected a contract to be forthcoming. However, Holt had also decided that SuperStack was too valuable to share with Lee and other of Axiam's initial developers. Holt wanted to establish a new and separate corporation, in which he had the majority interest, both to rid himself of Axiam's debt and its founders and to reap the benefits of its technology as a reward for his own hard work. As a result, Holt began to consider how he could siphon off Axiam's intellectual property so that he would profit, while others such as Rule, Lee, Eissner [Axiam's largest shareholders] would not. His answer was what came to be known as the Newco strategy. When the Newco strategy later foundered on the unwillingness of the other shareholders and of the convertible noteholders to convert their debt to equity, thus releasing the lien on Axiam's intellectual property, Holt resorted to a back-up plan, seizing control of Axiam by seizing control of the majority of Axiam's shares.

Holt's Attempt to Spin Off Axiam's Intellectual Property for His Own Benefit

Beginning in early 1996, Holt began to develop a strategy to spin off Axiam's intellectual property into a separate corporation for his own personal benefit. Recognizing that any such plan would be vulnerable to legal challenge, at the same time Holt planned to move Axiam to California, believing that through "time and distance" he could avoid legal challenge. To Holt, time and distance meant that with the passage of sufficient time to orchestrate his plan and with a base of Axiam's operations in California, a lawsuit by the minority shareholders or convertible noteholders would be more difficult and less likely.

By November of 1996, when it became apparent that he would not be able to get cooperation from the convertible noteholders or the Board, and fearing that he was going to be fired by Guild and Cabot Henderson (whose allegiance had clearly shifted), Holt seized control of Axiam through an illegal stock transaction and commenced implementation of his strategy without Board, noteholder or shareholder approval.

Newco

Beginning in the early spring of 1996, Holt commenced steps to establish a new corporation which he controlled as the vehicle for developing Axiam's next generation product (SuperStack). Believing correctly that Cabot Henderson was eager to profit as well from such a development, Holt initially charged Henderson with developing the strategy to accomplish his goal: to develop SuperStack in an entirely new corporation controlled by Holt. This became the "Newco strategy."

Holt intended to have at least a majority interest in the new company, and he intended to exclude Axiam's shareholders, especially Lee and Eissner, from the new company. Illustrative of his enmity was Holt's announcement at a May 1996 staff meeting discussing Newco that part of the reason for setting up Newco was to prevent the "assholes who were no longer around from reaping the benefits of our hard work."

On April 26, 1996, Holt wrote a memorandum to Cabot Henderson, which he copied to his other allies, George Moker and Debbra Holt, setting forth certain aspects of a potential Newco strategy. In his memorandum, Holt discussed forming Newco "ASAP," with the same officers and directors as Axiam, but with the ultimate ownership to be determined. Regarding ownership of Newco, Holt asked Cabot Henderson to develop by the next Board meeting an offer to Axiam's convertible noteholders, seeking to have them exercise their right to convert their debt in Axiam to equity in return for "suitable incentive," which Holt suggested might include "participation in Newco." Holt did so because he was fearful that the convertible noteholders, whose debt was secured by Axiam's intellectual property, could otherwise thwart his plans.

In an April 27, 1996 memorandum, Holt suggested that he meet with the convertible noteholders to tell them about Newco. He also stated that "Newco and its staff are now the owners of SuperStack — it's a product that I do not wish Oldco to develop." Oldco unmistakably refers to Axiam. In a handwritten note on the memorandum, referring to himself Holt added, "peh is the 'inventor' of SmartStack, it goes where I go." Holt later amended his handwritten note to read in pertinent part "peh is the inventor of SuperStack. It goes where I go."

In May 1996, mindful both that Cabot Henderson desired to share in the riches of Axiam's intellectual property and that the Henderson family owned considerable positions in convertible notes and bridge loans, Holt charged Henderson with helping develop the Newco strategy. He gave Cabot Henderson the title of Vice President for Finance and Special Projects. On May 8, 1996, Holt and Cabot Henderson met with two attorneys Penman and Baldiga of Brown, Rudnick, Freed & Gesmer concerning the Newco strategy. This meeting with counsel heightened Holt's and Cabot Henderson's concerns that the strategy was subject to legal challenge. In a follow-up memorandum regarding the meeting from Henderson to Holt dated May 10, 1996, Henderson identified several issues that needed to be resolved pertaining to a potential Newco strategy, including: "The key legal question . . . why license the technology to Newco and what benefits are there to Oldco?"; the need for Axiam shareholder and convertible noteholder approval; the need for establishing the fair market value of Axiam's intellectual property by independent appraisal; how to establish a "bright line" between Axiam's intellectual property and "software upgrades" that a Newco would perform; and how to transfer business of Axiam to Newco without leaving Axiam open to legal attack.

Wanting answers rather than questions, Holt responded angrily: He made a note at the top of the Henderson memorandum instructing Henderson to "read and return" the memorandum and not to make copies. He also wrote a note to his assistant, Ellen Fernandes ("Ms. Fernandes"), asking her to ensure that there were no copies of the memorandum. One of Holt's repeated criticisms of Henderson's May 10 memorandum was that it contained questions and "academic bullshit," not answers or strategies. Holt's handwritten comments questioned whether Axiam's shareholders should be allowed to vote on the transfer of Axiam's intellectual property to Newco. He dismissed Henderson's suggestion that the fair market value of Axiam's intellectual property should be established by independent appraisal, asking instead what would happen if the independent appraisal came back at $10,000,000. He obviously did not want to share such wealth with Axiam's shareholders or the convertible noteholders.

. . . .

Failure to Seek Patent Protection

As part of his scheme to spin off Axiam's valuable intellectual property into a separate corporation, Holt deliberately caused Axiam to delay pursuing the possibility of patent protection for its next generation product, SuperStack, and for enhancements of SmartStack. Whether SuperStack was patentable, or is patentable, has not been proven, and was not central to determination of the issues in this trial. Whether patentable or not, SuperStack was and is clearly an asset of *Axiam* not of Holt. Despite Holt's view, such as that contained in his April 27, 1996 memo to Henderson and George Moker in which he wrote "I want to be unequivocal here and to all concerned. PEH is the 'inventor' of SuperStack. It goes where I go." Holt is not the inventor of Axiam's SuperStack technology. This technology was developed by Lee, Doss, Kastner, and others at Axiam, using the algorithms devised by Toumi under contract to Axiam.

Holt also caused development of SuperStack within Axiam to be stopped, or delayed, for a variety of reasons, only some of which had to do with finances and the availability of finding a strategic partner with which to develop SuperStack. First and foremost, Holt wanted to complete the technology and market it through a new corporation which he controlled. Additionally, he wanted to make certain that lawyers' concerns about articulating a sound business reason for developing his Newco strategy did not interfere with his plans to pay as little as possible for Axiam's intellectual property should it be sold to Newco.

Axiam's intellectual property, including SmartStack and SuperStack, was believed by all of the so-called stakeholders in Axiam, both shareholders and convertible noteholders, to have very significant value. In the beginning of 1996, Holt directed Henderson, then Axiam's Vice President for Operations, to investigate obtaining patent protection for SuperStack and for enhancements to SmartStack. Henderson thereafter interviewed a number of patent law firms in order to select patent counsel. On February 21, 1996, Henderson reported in a memorandum to Holt that he had interviewed two law firms. On February 28, 1996, Henderson met with attorney Bruce Sunstein of the firm Bromberg & Sunstein, and provided him with product literature. On February 28, 1996, Henderson and Doss met with attorney Sunstein to discuss Axiam's intellectual property and the possibility of seeking patent protection for SuperStack. Attorney Sunstein subsequently visited Axiam, met with Axiam's engineers, and reviewed Axiam's technology.

On March 15, 1996, Henderson wrote a memo to Holt reporting on attorney Sunstein's visit to Axiam. Henderson stated that there were two main considerations in constructing Axiam's patent strategy: 1) patenting SuperStack to protect Axiam going forward and 2) patenting enhancements to SmartStack that had not been offered for sale within the past year. Henderson further reported that the goal was to file a provisional patent application for SuperStack as soon as possible. On March 15, 1996, attorney Sunstein sent a proposed engagement letter to Henderson. Sunstein estimated the cost of filing a provisional patent application for SuperStack to be approximately $10,000. Henderson told Holt of the engagement letter and asked for permission to engage Sunstein to begin the process of obtaining patent protection for Axiam's technology. Holt refused to permit Henderson to sign the engagement letter. Holt told Henderson that he could not sign the engagement letter because Holt did not want SuperStack to be patented in Axiam but in "Newco."

Although not a finished product at Axiam, clearly SuperStack exists in the development stage, and in fact was ready for testing at the second level when Doss left Axiam in June of 1996. All it needed was the master designed by Lee. Holt himself recognized this in his July 11, 1996 note to the SuperStack file that the "Software [was] ready to try."

Notwithstanding the importance to Axiam of completing SuperStack and protecting its intellectual property, to preserve his own opportunity to spin this intellectual property off into another corporation for his own personal benefit, Holt suspended Axiam's work on SuperStack during 1996 and refused to permit Axiam to engage the services of patent counsel to protect the intellectual property. This breach of fiduciary duty, however, is but a part of the larger breach of attempting to divert Axiam's corporate opportunities to himself.

. . . .

It is well settled in Massachusetts that the directors and officers of a corporation stand in a fiduciary relationship to the corporation. *Demoulas v. Demoulas Super Markets, Inc.*, 424 Mass. 501, 528 (1997); *Durfee v. Durfee & Canning, Inc.*, 323 Mass. 187, 196 (1948). They owe to the corporation and its shareholders a duty of care and a "paramount duty of loyalty." *Demoulas,* 424 Mass, at 528; *Spiegel v. Beacon Participations, Inc.*, 297 Mass. 398, 410–11 (1937) ("They are bound to act with absolute fidelity and must place their duties to the corporation above every other financial or business obligation . . . They cannot be permitted to serve two masters whose interests are antagonistic"). In the case of a close corporation, which resembles a partnership, duties of loyalty extend to shareholders, who owe one another substantially the same duty of utmost good faith and loyalty in the operation of the enterprise that partners owe to one another, a duty that is even stricter than that required of directors and shareholders in corporations generally. *Demoulas,* 424 Mass. at 529; *Donahue v. Rodd Electrotype Co. of New England, Inc.,* 367 Mass. 578, 592–94 (1975).

As Chairman of the Board, President, and significant shareholder of Axiam, a close corporation, Holt owes Axiam a duty of "utmost good faith and loyalty." *Demoulas,* 424 Mass. at 529. "Not honesty alone, but the punctilio of an honor the most sensitive, is then the standard of behavior." *Donahue,* 367 Mass, at 594. As a purported director, Treasurer and shareholder of Axiam, Mrs. Holt owes Axiam the same duty of utmost good faith and loyalty.

. . . .

The duty of loyalty requires that a director or officer of the corporation not take for personal benefit an opportunity or advantage that belongs to the corporation. *Demoulas,* 424 Mass. at 529. Under the corporate opportunity doctrine, an officer seeking to pursue a corporate opportunity must disclose material details and then either gain assent of disinterested directors or show the decision is fair to the corporation. *Hanover Ins. Co. v. Sutton,* 46 Mass. App. Ct. 153, 166 (1999).

Plaintiffs allege . . . that Holt engaged in a theft of corporate opportunity by making a presentation of the SuperStack technology for his own benefit in the name of his separate corporation. Holt failed to disclose the details of this presentation. It is incontrovertible that Holt's purpose in doing so was inappropriately to benefit himself rather than Axiam or its shareholders. To the contrary, Holt's goal was to siphon off to Newco Axiam's intellectual property. Such conduct constitutes a breach of his duty of loyalty.

. . . .

In claiming inventorship and ownership of SuperStack, failing to seek intellectual property protection for Axiam's intellectual property, and attempting to market SuperStack through his own separate corporation, ZeroVibe, Holt acted self-interestedly, wasted corporate assets, and breached his duty of loyalty. Holt's intentional failure to seek patent protection for SuperStack so that he could use that technology for his own benefit constitutes a breach of his fiduciary duty. The Zero-Vibe presentation furthered no valid *Axiam* corporate purpose and was unfair to Axiam and its shareholders. Accordingly, Holt breached his fiduciary duty in making a presentation of Axiam's technology on ZeroVibe's behalf to an Axiam customer. Holt's failure to disclose to the Board that he made a SuperStack presentation on behalf of ZeroVibe, a company he solely owned at the time, is evidence of his bad faith. His use of Axiam's resources, including its technology, to make the ZeroVibe presentation is evidence that the presentation was an Axiam corporate opportunity. See *Demoulas,* 424 Mass. 501, 536 (1997) (use of corporate resources to support other companies owned and controlled by defendant directors "indicates that they were wrongfully diverted corporate opportunities"), *citing* 1 J.D. Cox & T.L. Hazen, *Corporations* § 11.7, at 11.33, 11.39 (1995) (fiduciary's use of corporate assets or personnel to acquire or nurture opportunity indicates breach of duty of loyalty).

. . . .

As a consequence of the Holts' numerous violations of fiduciary duty, the shareholders are entitled to equitable relief designed to remove the Holts from the position of control they illegally obtained and to unwind the self-interested transactions in which they caused Axiam to engage while they were in control. It is well established that the courts of the Commonwealth have broad equitable powers to remedy breaches of fiduciary duty. *See Coggins,* 397 Mass. at 532 (awarding rescissory damages for directors' violations of fiduciary duty). This is especially true in cases involving bad faith of a director in a closely held corporation. *See Demoulas v. Demoulas,* 428 Mass. 555, 591 (1998) (affirming trial court's award of equitable relief for violations of fiduciary duty that "essentially restructured [the corporation's] corporate makeup"). "A court exercising its equitable power has no limit on its 'flexibility in devising a variety of remedies and shaping them to fit the circumstances of a particular case.' A lack of precedent, or mere novelty in incident should not be an obstacle." *Demoulas v. Demoulas,* 428 Mass. 543 (Mass. Super. 1996), *aff'd,* 428 Mass. 555 (1998), *quoting Brenner v. Berkowitz,* 617 A.2d 1225, 1233 (N.J. Super A.D. 1992).

. . . .

There is no adequate remedy at law to compensate the shareholders for the Holts' conduct. Under the Holts' control, Axiam has been looted of much value. Only an order restoring the balance between the shareholders, removing the Holts from their position of control, and securing the return of Axiam's intellectual property and its development can adequately remedy the wrongs committed by defendants.

. . . .

[P]laintiff shareholders seek a declaratory judgment that Axiam, not Holt, owns the SuperStack technology and any other technology related to Axiam's business developed by Holt while he was an officer or director of Axiam. Under G.L. c. 231, § 1, this Court is empowered to "make binding declarations of right, duty, status and other legal relations sought thereby, either before or after a breach or violation thereof has occurred in any case in which an actual controversy has arisen and is specifically set forth in the pleadings and whether any consequential judgment or relief is or could be claimed at law in equity or not . . ."

Declaratory relief is appropriate where: 1) an actual controversy has arisen in the case presented; 2) the plaintiffs have an interest therein; and 3) and the granting of declaratory relief will terminate the controversy. These three requirements are met here. There is an actual controversy between the shareholders, who assert that Axiam owns the SuperStack technology, and Holt, who asserts, somewhat inconsistently, that he owns it and that it does not exist. The shareholders have an obvious interest in confirming Axiam's ownership rights in its technology, since that technology constitutes Axiam's principal asset. Moreover, the shareholders are bringing this suit in a representative capacity to vindicate the interests of the corporation with respect to its technology. *Baker v. Allen,* 292 Mass. 169, 171 (1935) ("A suit in equity by minority stockholders in a representative capacity against directors for wrongs committed by them against the corporation is not in vindication of any personal rights . . . The interests of the corporation alone are immediately concerned"). Axiam clearly has an interest in protecting its own technology. Finally, granting this relief will terminate the controversy and remove the uncertainty as to the ownership rights of the SuperStack technology.

In the course of the trial, the defendants contended that SuperStack was a mere idea and, as such, Axiam is not entitled to any ownership rights in it.[39] Under Massachusetts law, an idea becomes an invention when it is put into practice or embodied in some tangible form. *Nat'l Development Co. v. Gray,* 316 Mass. 240, 249 (1944). From the facts found, it is clear that SuperStack fits that description. It is equally clear from the evidence that Holt did not invent SuperStack. He is neither the inventor nor the owner of it. Accordingly, the shareholders are entitled to a declaration that Axiam owns the SuperStack technology and any derivative of that technology. *See, e.g., Wireless Specialty Apparatus Co. v. Mica Condenser Co.,* 239 Mass. 158, 161 (1921) (former employee, who planned to take advantage of secret processes, machines, and other confidential information of plaintiff corporation, and who, in furtherance of the plan, formed a corporation whose officers and agents acted with notice, was enjoined from the use or disclosure of such processes and inventions).

The shareholders are also entitled to a declaration that Axiam owns all technology developed or under development at Axiam during the period of Holt's employment based on Holt's status as a fiduciary of Axiam. As found, Holt was not an inventor of Axiam's SmartStack or SuperStack technology. Even if he had been, where an inventor is more than a mere employee and occupies a special relationship of trust and confidence to the business, courts have consistently held that it is inequitable for the individual inventor to retain for himself a right which more properly belongs to the company. In such instances, the fiduciary is compelled to assign the technology rights to the corporation. *Kennedy v. Wright,* 676 F. Supp. 888, 891–92 (C.D. Ill. 1988); *cf. Wireless Specialty Apparatus Co.,* 239 Mass. at 163 (employee who had relation of trust and confidence with the corporation and who, in the course of his employment, received confidential information was estopped from claiming as his own property

---

39. Defendants also argue that this Court lacks the power to hear plaintiffs' claims with respect to SuperStack because it will require the Court to make "determinations as to the patentability of technology . . . [and] those matters are outside the subject matter jurisdiction of this Court." Def. Trial. Br. at 6. Defendants are wrong. Plaintiffs are not seeking a declaratory ruling that SuperStack is patentable. Plaintiffs are claiming that SuperStack is an invention and are seeking a declaratory judgment that Axiam, not Holt, owns this invention. Federal courts do not have exclusive jurisdiction over issues of ownership of, or rights of use in, inventions, confidential information or trade secrets. *Steranko v. Inforex, Inc.,* 5 Mass. App. Ct. 253, 269 (1977) (discussing Massachusetts common law principles relating to employer's entitlement to the inventions of employees).

inventions made in the course of his work even though there was no express agreement or understanding that inventions were to be the employer's property).

As a director, officer and significant stockholder of Axiam, Holt stands in a fiduciary relationship with the corporation. See *Demoulas*, 424 Mass. at 529; *Durfee*, 323 Mass. at 196; *Donahue*, 367 Mass. at 592–93. Accordingly, any rights he may claim to have in any inventions related to Axiam's business developed while he was an Axiam fiduciary belong to the corporation.

Notes & Questions

1. In what respects may the development or management of intellectual property be particularly susceptible to improper self-dealing by a corporate officer or shareholder who breaches his fiduciary duties by administering company activities to benefit himself at the expense of his company or fellow company owners? What aspects of intellectual property assets may make such misconduct unusually easy to accomplish or to conceal?

2. Why should corporate laws establish duties of corporate officers and shareholders leading to personal liability for breaches of fiduciary obligations rather than leaving the definition of such obligations and risks of liability to the contracting of a corporation with its officers or among the co-owners of a corporate enterprise? Should the irreducible duties of corporate officers specified by statute be weaker or stronger for executives in companies that rely heavily on the development or use of intellectual property than for executives in other types of companies?

3. Under what circumstances should a party who was a corporate officer in a company when that company developed new intellectual products be able to establish or work for a second concern that seeks to rely on the same intellectual products? Does the answer depend only on whether the second concern's use of the intellectual products is infringing under intellectual property law standards? Or should corporate fiduciary duties to the first concern impose more demanding requirements on the former corporate officer in these circumstances, obligating the former officer not to use the first company's intellectual products to the private advantage of the former officer and to the disadvantage of the individual's former company?

Chapter 3

Trade Secrets

Problem

Dr. See, the CEO of Digital Ignition Systems Corp., has come to you with a problem involving a leak of company trade secrets. The problem for Digital Ignition began when Jim Westphal, a disgruntled Digital Ignition marketing representative, emailed Edgar Sly, the CEO of Slick Auto, Inc., seeking employment with the company. Sly initially turned Westphal away, but Westphal begged him to reconsider and offered, "I will do *anything* to change your mind."

Sly, seeing a golden opportunity, replied to Westphal's email: "I will extend you an offer of employment if you demonstrate your true commitment to Slick Auto. My company has had trouble designing a digital ignition system. Any information about Digital Ignition's system would be of great interest to me. If you help us, we will help you."

Westphal replied, "As soon as I can get a hold of the information, I will mail it to you. As a bonus, I will also include a customer list in the package. The spy business is more stressful than I thought. I'm nervous about the confidentiality agreement I signed." Despite his reservations, two weeks after his last message, Westphal surreptitiously photocopied several files marked "confidential" and carried them home. He assembled a package for Slick Auto that contained, among other things, photocopies of information regarding the software that controls non-patented portions of Digital Ignition's systems, as well as a list of Digital Ignition's customers. After downing several beers to celebrate his first successful spy mission, Westphal scrawled an address on a mailing label, did a victory dance, slapped the label on the package, and took off for the post office.

Unfortunately for the hapless disgruntled marketing representative, the post office delivered the misaddressed package to the offices of Auto Dynamic. Westphal discovered his error only after he received a letter from Auto Dynamic stating, "Mr. Westphal, we believe we have received your package by mistake. We are holding onto the package until we are given further instruction from you as to how to proceed."

The mistake made Westphal increasingly nervous about his deal with Slick Auto. After several sleepless nights, he decided to back out of the deal, hoping that if he ignored it, the mess would go away on its own. Westphal never responded to Auto Dynamic's letter and never brought the letter to the attention of Digital Ignition management. He mentioned the errant package to no one. Hearing nothing back from Westphal, Auto Dynamic chose to hold on to Westphal's package. Auto Dynamic did not inquire further or attempt to contact anyone else at Digital Ignition.

A few months later, Auto Dynamic began selling plug-compatible ignition systems similar to Digital Ignition's system to Digital Ignition customers. Previously, Auto Dynamic had only sold automobile air fresheners and had shown no expertise or interest in ignition systems or the ignition system market. Concerned by the sudden development, Dr. See asked his engineers at Digital Ignition to purchase and analyze Auto Dynamic's ignition system. Their analysis revealed that portions of the software incorporated into the Auto Dynamic system were suspiciously similar to software that controls non-patented portions of Digital Ignition's systems, though the Auto Dynamic system did not incorporate Digital Ignition's patented hardware designs, nor did it use Digital Ignition's patented method of ignition control. The engineers suspected that Auto Dynamic might have copied portions of Digital Ignition's product, based on similarity of the software, coupled with the apparent lack of special expertise of Auto Dynamic concerning ignition systems.

Dr. See and Digital Ignition have asked for your advice on pursuing claims against Westphal, Slick Auto, and Auto Dynamic. Please help Digital Ignition make an informed decision on how to proceed by analyzing the possible theories that Digital Ignition might use in a lawsuit and the likelihood of success.

Focus of the Chapter

The readings in this chapter cover the intellectual property known as trade secrets. The first section of the chapter, Part A, defines the meaning of a trade secret under the Uniform Trade Secrets Act (UTSA), the Economic Espionage Act (EEA) as amended by the Defend Trade Secrets Act of 2016 (DTSA), and the Restatement of Torts.

The next section, Part B, discusses civil protection for trade secrets, specifically the federal protection afforded under the Defend Trade Secrets Act (DTSA), and state protection under the Uniform Trade Secrets Act (UTSA) and the Restatement of Torts. *Learning Curve Toys, Inc. v. Playwood Inc.* and *Mangren Research and Development Corp. v. National Chemical Co.* describe the application of the UTSA. *DeGiorgio v. Megabyte Int'l, Inc.* and *Fred's Stores, Inc. v. M & H Drugs, Inc.* examine the three elements necessary for information to qualify for trade secret protection. *Sylmark Holdings Ltd. v. Silicone Zone Intern. Ltd.* then provides an example of non-UTSA protection for trade secrets. Finally, defenses to misappropriation and rights against others are discussed, followed by comparisons of trade secret and patent law protections. This section ends with a brief discussion about the termination of trade secrets and exceptions to it.

The last section of the chapter, Part C, covers criminal protection for trade secrets. The section opens with a discussion of federal protection under the Economic Espionage Act (EEA) as amended by the Defend Trade Secrets Act of 2016 (DTSA). Continuing on, the section explores the liability arising from actual theft of trade secrets, as illustrated in *United States v. Lange.* Conspiracy to steal trade secrets is then covered in *United States v. Martin*, and disputes over jury instructions are illustrated by *United States v. Liew.* The section closes with an examination of state protection for trade secrets, as shown in *People v. Pribich,* and a comparison of state and federal trade secret protections.

Readings
A. Introduction — What Is a Trade Secret?

Trade secrets make up the bulk of intellectual property. Unlike patents, a trade secret does not need to possess novelty and non-obviousness to receive legal protection — though otherwise-patentable technology may be held as a trade secret. Unlike copyrights, the protection extended to trade secrets does not require originality and is not limited to the expression of an idea — although something held as a trade secret may be copyrightable as well. A trade secret may be just about anything, from the formula for a popular soft drink to the list of customers maintained by a small company.

There are a number of definitions available for what is a trade secret. The Uniform Trade Secret Act (UTSA), which governs civil litigation for trade secret misappropriation in most states, defines a trade secret as:

> information, including a formula, pattern, compilation, program, device, method, technique, or process, that: (i) derives independent economic value, actual or potential, from not being generally known to, and not being readily ascertainable by proper means by, other persons who can obtain economic value from its disclosure or use, and (ii) is the subject of efforts that are reasonable under the circumstances to maintain its secrecy.

Uniform Trade Secrets Act § 1(4).

The federal Economic Espionage Act (EEA) as amended by the Defend Trade Secrets Act (DTSA) has a slightly different definition of a trade secret:

> The term "trade secret" means all forms and types of financial, business, scientific, technical, economic, or engineering information, including patterns, plans, compilations, program devices, formulas, designs, prototypes, methods, techniques, processes, procedures, programs, or codes, whether tangible or intangible, and whether or how stored, compiled, or memorialized physically, electronically, graphically, photographically, or in writing if —
>
> > (A) the owner thereof has taken reasonable measures to keep such information secret; and
>
> > (B) the information derives independent economic value, actual or potential, from not being generally known to, and not being readily ascertainable through proper means by, another person who can obtain economic value from the disclosure or use of the information.

18 U.S.C. § 1839(3).

Both definitions feature common elements: trade secrets may be nearly any form of information, provided that: (1) reasonable measures are taken to keep the information secret; and (2) the information has some economic value through not being generally known by others.

Notes & Questions

1. "Not Being Generally Known To" Whom?

Prior to 2016, the EEA definition of a trade secret differed from the UTSA definition in how it defined the ability of a trade secret to derive economical value from not being generally known. The UTSA protects information that "derives independent economic value, actual or potential, from not being generally known to, and not being readily ascertainable by proper means by, *other persons who can obtain economic value from its disclosure or use*" (emphasis added). The original EEA definition, however, required the trade secret to "derive[] independent economic value, actual or potential, from not being generally known to, and not being readily ascertainable through proper means by, *the public.*" (emphasis added). This slight difference led to disputes about the scope of the protection awarded by different statutes as illustrated by several pages of the opinion in *United States v. Lange*, 312 F.3d 263 (7th Cir. 2002), appearing *infra*. In 2016, Congress passed the Defend Trade Secrets Act, which obviated the difference by replacing the word "public" in the EEA definition with the words "another person who can obtain economic value from the disclosure or use of the information." Pub. L. No. 114-153, § 2, 130 Stat. 376, 380 (2016). It remains to be seen if this change will improve uniformity in the application of federal and state trade secret statutes. *Cf.* Zach Wolfe, *One Year Later: A Review of the Defend Trade Secrets Act*, Hous. Law., July/August 2017, at 10, 13 (claiming that the DTSA "created more opportunities for conflict in trade secrets law").

2. The Restatements

Before the passage of the UTSA, the definition of trade secrets was drawn from the Restatement of Torts (1939) § 757:

> A trade secret may consist of any formula, pattern, device or compilation of information which is used in one's business, and which gives him an opportunity to obtain an advantage over competitors who do not know or use it. It may be a formula for a chemical compound, a process of manufacturing, treating or preserving material, a pattern for a machine or other device, or a list of customers.

Many state courts used the Restatement definition for years; several states still do. However, trade secrets as a subject was omitted from the Restatement (Second) of Torts (1978).

In 1995, the American Law Institute released the Restatement (Third) of Unfair Competition, which included trade secrets. This provided another definition of "trade secret":

> A trade secret is any information that can be used in the operation of a business or other enterprise and that is sufficiently valuable and secret to afford an actual or potential economic advantage over others.

Id. at § 39.

B. Civil Protection of Trade Secrets

Prior to the passage of the Defend Trade Secrets Act of 2016 (DTSA), the civil protection of trade secrets was almost entirely a state-level issue. The states may be divided into two categories: those that have adopted the Uniform Trade Secrets Act (UTSA), and those that have not. An overwhelming majority of jurisdictions have adopted the UTSA, either as written or slightly modified, but the jurisdictions that have not are significant. In 2016, the DTSA created a federal civil cause of action for misappropriation of trade secrets that are "related to a product or service used in, or intended for use in, interstate or foreign commerce." 18 U.S.C.A. § 1836.

1. Federal Protection

a. *Defend Trade Secrets Act*

Prior to 2016, civil enforcement of trade secret rights was exclusively a matter of state law. The Defend Trade Secrets Act of 2016 (DTSA) changed this by creating a federal private cause of action for trade secret misappropriation. However, unlike the federal copyright and patent statutes, the Act did not preempt state trade secret statutes, leaving trade secret owners with two independent levels of trade secret protection — state and federal.

The DTSA was adopted as an amendment to the Economic Espionage Act (EEA). In addition to modifying the EEA definition of a trade secret, as discussed above, *supra*, the DTSA amends 18 U.S.C.A. § 1836 to specifically provide federal courts with original jurisdiction over actions for misappropriation of trade secrets that relate "to a product or service used in, or intended for use in, interstate or foreign commerce."

Further, the Act provides a set of procedural tools to aid trade secret owners in preventing misappropriation and/or disclosure of their secret information. The new procedure that draws the most attention among commentators is civil seizure. According to the statute, in extraordinary circumstances a court, after an ex parte hearing, may issue an order providing for "the seizure of property necessary to prevent the propagation or dissemination of the trade secret that is the subject of the action." 18 U.S.C.A. § 1836(b)(2)(A)(i). The civil seizure provision is framed very narrowly. Before the court can order a seizure, the applicant must show that:

(1) no other statutory or equitable measure can adequately protect the trade secret;

(2) an immediate and irreparable injury will occur if seizure is not ordered;

(3) the harm to the applicant from denial of a seizure order: (a) outweighs the harm to the person against whom seizure would be ordered and (b) substantially outweighs the harm to any third parties who may be harmed by such seizure;

(4) the applicant is likely to succeed on the merits;

(5) the person against whom seizure would be ordered has actual possession of the trade secret and any property to be seized;

(6) the application describes with reasonable particularity the matter to be seized and, to the extent reasonable under the circumstances, identifies the location of the property to be seized;

(7) the person against whom seizure would be ordered, or persons acting in concert with such person, would destroy, move, hide, or otherwise make such matter inaccessible to the court, if the applicant were to proceed on notice to such person; and

(8) the applicant has not publicized the requested seizure.

18 U.S.C.A. § 1836(b)(2)(A)(ii).

The DTSA also makes clear that when an injunction preventing trade secret misappropriation is issued, such injunction may not "prevent a person from entering into an employment relationship." Any conditions placed on employment under an injunction "shall be based on evidence of threatened misappropriation and not merely on the information the person knows." 18 U.S.C.A. § 1836(b)(3)(A)(i). Finally, the Act provides whistleblowers with an immunity from liability under any federal or state trade secret law for the disclosure of a trade secret. An individual is immune so long as the disclosure is made in confidence to a federal, state, or local government official or an attorney "solely for the purpose of reporting or investigating a suspected violation of law," or made in a filing in a lawsuit "if such filing is made under seal."

Notes & Questions

1. Timing of Misappropriation Under the DTSA

The DTSA applies prospectively to trade secret misappropriations for which any act occurs on or after May 11, 2016. Pub. L. No. 114-153, 130 Stat. 376 (2016). Federal courts applying the DTSA allow claims that arise out of trade secret misappropriation that happened before the DTSA's enactment only if the misappropriated trade secret was *used* after May 11, 2016. *See, e.g., Adams Arms, LLC v. Unified Weapon Sys., Inc.*, No. 8:16-CV-1503-T-33AEP, 2016 WL 5391394, at *6 (M.D. Fla. Sept. 27, 2016). However, courts have dismissed cases where plaintiff failed to allege *specific instances of use* of misappropriated secret information after the DTSA enactment date. *See, e.g., Physician's Surrogacy, Inc. v. German*, No. 17CV0718-MMA (WVG), 2017 WL 3622329, at *9 (S.D. Cal. Aug. 23, 2017).

2. Ex Parte Seizure

The DTSA provides trade secret owners with an option to request civil seizure of any property to prevent potential misappropriation. Such a measure can be implemented by a federal court after an ex parte hearing, but "only in extraordinary circumstances." So far, courts have been reluctant to issue such ex parte seizure orders. Courts tend to look for other, less intrusive means to preserve trade secrets, such as temporary restraining orders, preliminary injunctions, or preservation orders. *See, e.g., OOO Brunswick Rail Mgmt. v. Sultanov*, No. 5:17-CV-00017-EJD, 2017 WL 67119, at *2 (N.D. Cal. Jan. 6, 2017). *See generally* Zach Wolfe, *One Year Later: A Review of the Defend Trade Secrets Act*, Hous. Law., July/August 2017.

3. Federalization of Trade Secret Law: Fears and Expectations

Although the DTSA enjoyed almost unanimous support in Congress, some opposed the statute, arguing that state law fulfills the mission of trade secret protection sufficiently well. Further, the opponents of the DTSA argued that its adoption would result in the creation of "trade secret trolls." *See* David S. Levine & Sharon K. Sandeen, *Here Come the Trade Secret Trolls*, 71 Wash. & Lee L. Rev. Online 230 (2015); Christopher B. Seaman, *The Case Against Federalizing Trade Secrecy*, 101 Va. L. Rev. 317 (2015). Others defended the idea of federal trade secret protection claiming that the fear of "trade secret trolls" is overstated. Instead, the DTSA proponents argued, the Act will create uniformity in the trade secret protection around the country. Further, the availability of nationwide protective measures, such as temporary restraining orders, injunctions, and civil seizures, will make preventive reactions to trade secret misappropriation quicker and more efficient. *See* James Pooley, *The Myth of the Trade Secret Troll: Why the Defend Trade Secrets Act Improves the Protection of Commercial Information*, 23 Geo. Mason L. Rev. 1045 (2016). Several years will need to pass before federal courts develop a body of case law that will determine if any of these fears and expectations come true.

2. State Protection

a. *Uniform Trade Secrets Act*

i. Introduction

According to the prefatory note to the amended Uniform Trade Secrets Act (1985), the need for a standardized approach to trade secrets grew out of Supreme Court rulings holding that trade secrets are not barred by federal patent or copyright law, continuing technological and economic pressures, and the confused and inconsistent statutes and common law across many jurisdictions. Additionally, the Restatement (Second) of Torts, published in 1978, eliminated the sections that addressed trade secrets, upon which many state courts had relied for consistency.

The National Conference of Commissioners on Uniform State Laws elected to address this need, and released the original version of the Uniform Trade Secrets Act in 1979. An amended version followed in 1985, and has been widely adopted throughout the states. According to the Uniform Law Commission's website, as of January 2015, 47 states, the District of Columbia, Puerto Rico, and the Virgin Islands have enacted the Uniform Trade Secrets Act, either in the original 1979 form or with the amendments made in 1985. Several prominent jurisdictions have not, including Massachusetts,[1] New York,[2] and North Carolina.[3]

ii. Application of the UTSA

Learning Curve Toys, Inc. v. Playwood Toys, Inc.

United States Court of Appeals for the Seventh Circuit

342 F.3d 714 (7th Cir. 2003)

RIPPLE, CIRCUIT JUDGE.

PlayWood Toys, Inc. ("PlayWood") obtained a jury verdict against Learning Curve Toys, Inc. and its representatives, Roy Wilson, Harry Abraham, and John Lee (collectively, "Learning Curve"), for misappropriation of a trade secret in a realistic looking and sounding toy railroad track under the Illinois Trade Secrets Act, 765 ILCS 1065/1 et seq. The jury awarded PlayWood a royalty of "8% for a license that would have been negotiated [absent the misappropriation] to last for the lifetime of the product." Although there was substantial evidence of misappropriation before the jury, the district court did not enter judgment on the jury's verdict. Instead, it granted judgment as a matter of law in favor of Learning Curve, holding that PlayWood did not have a protectable trade secret in the toy railroad track. PlayWood appealed. For the reasons set forth in the following opinion, we reverse the judgment of the district court and reinstate the jury's verdict.

Background

A. Facts

[In 1992, Robert Clausi and his brother-in-law Scott Moore began creating wooden toys under the name PlayWood Toys, Inc., a Canadian Corporation. Not having their own facilities, they contracted with Mario Borsato, who owned a wood-working facility, to manufacture toys based on PlayWood's specifications.

Clausi and Moore attended the New York Toy Fair in February 1993, where they were approached by Roy Wilson, Learning Curve's toy designer, who explained that

---

1. Most recently, a bill to adopt the UTSA in Massachusetts was introduced to both the Senate (Bill 1020) and the House (Bill 43) in 2017. As of December 28, 2017, the bill remains pending. Trade Secrets Act, Uniform Law Commission, *last accessed* December 28, 2017, http://www.uniformlaws.org/Act.aspx?title=Trade+Secrets+Act.

2. A bill to adopt the UTSA in New York was introduced to both the Senate (Bill 4688) and the Assembly (Bill 6419) in 2017. As of December 28, 2017, the bill remains pending. Trade Secrets Act, Uniform Law Commission, *last accessed* December 28, 2017, http://www.uniformlaws.org/Act.aspx?title=Trade+Secrets+Act.

3. Though North Carolina has not officially adopted the Uniform Trade Secrets Act, its state trade secret law contains many of the same key principles. N.C. Gen. Stat. §66-152 et seq.

Learning Curve had a license to manufacture Thomas the Tank Engine ("Thomas") toys. Wilson liked PlayWood's prototypes and raised the possibility of working together on the Thomas line. Harry Abraham, Learning Curve's vice president, and John Lee, Learning Curve's president, also stopped by and commented favorably on PlayWood's prototypes. The fair ended with the understanding that Abraham and Wilson would visit PlayWood in several days.]

On February 18, 1993, Abraham and Wilson visited PlayWood in Toronto as planned. The meeting began with a tour of Borsato's woodworking facility, where the prototypes on display at the Toy Fair had been made. After the tour, the parties went to the conference room at Borsato's facility. At this point, according to Clausi and Moore, the parties agreed to make their ensuing discussion confidential. Clausi testified:

> After we sat down in the board room, Harry [Abraham of Learning Curve] immediately said: "Look, we're going to disclose confidential information to you guys, and we're going to disclose some designs that Roy [Wilson of Learning Curve] has that are pretty confidential. If Brio were to get their hands on them, then we wouldn't like that. And we're going to do it under the basis of a confidential understanding."

> And I said: "I also have some things, some ideas on how to produce the track and produce the trains now that I've had a chance to look at them for the last couple of days, and I think they're confidential as well. So if we're both okay with that, we should continue." So we did.

The parties' discussion eventually moved away from train production and focused on track design. Wilson showed Clausi and Moore drawings of Learning Curve's track and provided samples of their current product. At this point, Abraham confided to Clausi and Moore that track had posed "a bit of a problem for Learning Curve." Abraham explained that sales were terrific for Learning Curve's Thomas trains, but that sales were abysmal for its track. Abraham attributed the lack of sales to the fact that Learning Curve's track was virtually identical to that of its competitor, Brio, which had the lion's share of the track market. Because there was "no differentiation" between the two brands of track, Learning Curve's track was not even displayed in many of the toy stores that carried Learning Curve's products. Learning Curve had worked unsuccessfully for several months attempting to differentiate its track from that of Brio.

After detailing the problems with Learning Curve's existing track, Abraham inquired of Clausi whether "there was a way to differentiate" its track from Brio's track. Clausi immediately responded that he "had had a chance to look at the track and get a feel for it [over] the last few days" and that his "thoughts were that if the track were more realistic and more functional, that kids would enjoy playing with it more and it would give the retailer a reason to carry the product, especially if it looked different than the Brio track." Clausi further explained that, if the track "made noise and looked like real train tracks, that the stores wouldn't have any problem, and the Thomas the Tank line, product line would have its own different track" and could "effectively compete with Brio." Abraham and Wilson indicated that they were "intrigued" by Clausi's idea and asked him what he meant by "making noise."

Clausi decided to show Abraham and Wilson exactly what he meant. Clausi took a piece of Learning Curve's existing track from the table, drew some lines across the track (about every three-quarters of an inch), and stated: "We can go ahead and machine grooves right across the upper section . . . , which would look like railway tracks, and down below machine little indentations as well so that it would look more like or sound more like real track. You would roll along and bumpity-bumpity as you go along." Clausi then called Borsato into the conference room and asked him to cut grooves into the wood . . . . Based on the sound produced by the track, Clausi told Abraham and Moore that if PlayWood procured a contract with Learning Curve to produce the track, they could call it "Clickety-Clack Track" . . . .

[When the meeting ended, Wilson took the piece of track with him. After several more meetings, PlayWood submitted a proposal, which Learning Curve rejected, saying their licensor wanted the Thomas products to be made in the United States.

In early 1994, PlayWood began to focus on the noise-producing track design. In December of 1994, Moore discovered that Learning Curve was marketing noise-producing track under the name "Clickety-Clack Track," very similar to the sample piece of track Wilson had taken from the meeting in February of 1993; Learning Curve was marketing its track as being the greatest recent innovation in wooden trains. Moore and Clausi were stunned.]

PlayWood promptly wrote a cease and desist letter to Learning Curve. The letter accused Learning Curve of stealing PlayWood's concept for the noise-producing track that it disclosed to Learning Curve "in confidence in the context of a manufacturing proposal." Learning Curve responded by seeking a declaratory judgment that it owned the concept.

Previously, on March 16, 1994, Learning Curve had applied for a patent on the noise-producing track. The patent, which was obtained on October 3, 1995, claims the addition of parallel impressions or grooves in the rails, which cause a "clacking" sound to be emitted as train wheels roll over them. The patent identifies Roy Wilson of Learning Curve as the inventor.

Clickety-Clack TrackTM provided an enormous boost to Learning Curve's sales. Learning Curve had $20 million in track sales by the first quarter of 2000, and $40 million for combined track and accessory sales.

B. District Court Proceedings

[The case went to trial on PlayWood's claim against Learning Curve, Wilson, Abraham, and Lee, where the jury found for PlayWood. The judge declined to enter judgment for PlayWood.]

The district court granted Learning Curve's motion and entered judgment in its favor on the ground that PlayWood presented insufficient evidence of a trade secret. Specifically, the court determined that PlayWood did not have a trade secret in its concept for noise-producing toy railroad track under Illinois law because: (1) PlayWood did not demonstrate that its concept was unknown in the industry; (2) PlayWood's concept could have been easily acquired or duplicated through proper means; (3) PlayWood failed to guard the secrecy of its concept; (4) Play-Wood's concept had no economic value; and (5) PlayWood expended no time, effort or money to develop the concept.

Discussion

A. Trade Secret Status

The parties agree that their dispute is governed by the Illinois Trade Secrets Act ("Act"), 765 ILCS 1065/1 et seq. To prevail on a claim for misappropriation of a trade secret under the Act, the plaintiff must demonstrate that the information at issue was a trade secret, that it was misappropriated and that it was used in the defendant's business. The issue currently before us is whether there was legally sufficient evidence for the jury to find that PlayWood had a trade secret in its concept for the noise-producing toy railroad track that it revealed to Learning Curve on February 18, 1993.

The Act defines a trade secret as:

[I]nformation, including but not limited to, technical or non-technical data, a formula, pattern, compilation, program, device, method, technique, drawing, process, financial data, or list of actual or potential customers or suppliers, that:

(1) is sufficiently secret to derive economic value, actual or potential, from not being generally known to other persons who can obtain economic value from its disclosure or use; and

(2) is the subject of efforts that are reasonable under the circumstances to maintain its secrecy or confidentiality.

765 ILCS 1065/2(d). Both of the Act's statutory requirements focus fundamentally on the secrecy of the information sought to be protected. However, the requirements emphasize different aspects of secrecy. The first requirement, that the information be sufficiently secret to impart economic value because of its relative secrecy, "precludes trade secret protection for information generally known or understood within an industry even if not to the public at large." The second requirement, that the plaintiff take reasonable efforts to maintain the secrecy of the information, prevents a plaintiff who takes no affirmative measures to prevent others from using its proprietary information from obtaining trade secret protection.

Although the Act explicitly defines a trade secret in terms of these two requirements, Illinois courts frequently refer to six common law factors (which are derived from §757 of the Restatement (First) of Torts) in determining whether a trade secret exists: (1) the extent to which the information is known outside of the plaintiff's business; (2) the extent to which the information is known by employees and others involved in the plaintiff's business; (3) the extent of measures taken by the plaintiff to guard the secrecy of the information; (4) the value of the information to the plaintiff's business and to its competitors; (5) the amount of time, effort and money expended by the plaintiff in developing the information; and (6) the ease or difficulty with which the information could be properly acquired or duplicated by others.

Contrary to Learning Curve's contention, we do not construe the foregoing factors as a six-part test, in which the absence of evidence on any single factor necessarily precludes a finding of trade secret protection. Instead, we interpret the common law factors as instructive guidelines for ascertaining whether a trade secret exists under the Act. The language of the Act itself makes no reference to these factors as independent requirements for trade secret status, and Illinois case law imposes no such requirement that each factor weigh in favor of the plaintiff. . . .

The existence of a trade secret ordinarily is a question of fact. As aptly observed by our colleagues on the Fifth Circuit, a trade secret "is one of the most elusive and difficult concepts in the law to define." In many cases, the existence of a trade secret is not obvious; it requires an ad hoc evaluation of all the surrounding circumstances. For this reason, the question of whether certain information constitutes a trade secret ordinarily is best "resolved by a fact finder after full presentation of evidence from each side." We do not believe that the district court was sufficiently mindful of these principles. The district court, in effect, treated the Restatement factors as requisite elements and substituted its judgment for that of the jury. PlayWood presented sufficient evidence for the jury reasonably to conclude that the Restatement factors weighed in PlayWood's favor.

1. Extent to which PlayWood's concept for noise-producing toy railroad track was known outside of PlayWood's business

PlayWood presented substantial evidence from which the jury could have determined that PlayWood's concept for noise-producing toy railroad track was not generally known outside of Playwood's business. It was undisputed at trial that no similar track was on the market until Learning Curve launched Clickety-Clack Track TM in late 1994, more than a year after PlayWood first conceived of the concept. Of course, as Learning Curve correctly points out, "[m]erely being the first or only one to use particular information does not in and of itself transform otherwise general knowledge into a trade secret." "If it did, the first person to use the information, no matter how ordinary or well known, would be able to appropriate it to his own use under the guise of a trade secret." However, in this case, there was additional evidence from which the jury could have determined that PlayWood's concept was not generally known within the industry.

First, there was substantial testimony that Learning Curve had attempted to differentiate its track from that of its competitors for several months, but that it had been unable to do so successfully.

[PlayWood's expert testified that PlayWood's concept was unique, and differentiated the design from the competition. Additionally, Learning Curve received a patent on the design, which required that it be novel. The court rejected Learning Curve's argument that PlayWood's design was not novel.]

2. Extent to which PlayWood's concept was known to employees and others involved in PlayWood's business

[The court held that this factor favored PlayWood.]

3. Measures taken by PlayWood to guard the secrecy of its concept

There also was sufficient evidence for the jury to determine that PlayWood took reasonable precautions to guard the secrecy of its concept. The Act requires the trade secret owner to take actions that are "reasonable under the circumstances to maintain [the] secrecy or confidentiality" of its trade secret; it does not require perfection. Whether the measures taken by a trade secret owner are sufficient to satisfy the Act's reasonableness standard ordinarily is a question of fact for the jury. Indeed, we previously have recognized that only in an extreme case can what is a 'reasonable' precaution be determined as a matter of law, because the answer depends on a balancing of costs and benefits that will vary from case to case.

Here, the jury was instructed that it must find "by a preponderance of the evidence that PlayWood's trade secrets were given to Learning Curve as a result of a confidential relationship between the parties." By returning a verdict in favor of PlayWood, the jury necessarily found that Learning Curve was bound to PlayWood by a pledge of confidentiality. The jury's determination is amply supported by the evidence. Both Clausi and Moore testified that they entered into an oral confidentiality agreement with Abraham and Wilson before beginning their discussion on February 18, 1993 . . . . In addition to this testimony, the jury heard that Learning Curve had disclosed substantial information to PlayWood during the February 18th meeting, including projected volumes, costs and profit margins for various products, as well as drawings for toys not yet released to the public. The jury could have inferred that Learning Curve would not have disclosed such information in the absence of a confidentiality agreement. Finally, the jury also heard (from several of Learning Curve's former business associates) that Learning Curve routinely entered into oral confidentiality agreements like the one with PlayWood.

PlayWood might have done more to protect its secret. As Learning Curve points out, PlayWood gave its only prototype of the noise-producing track to Wilson without first obtaining a receipt or written confidentiality agreement from Learning Curve — a decision that proved unwise in hindsight. Nevertheless, we believe that the jury was entitled to conclude that PlayWood's reliance on the oral confidentiality agreement was reasonable under the circumstances of this case. First, it is well established that "[t]he formation of a confidential relationship imposes upon the disclosee the duty to maintain the information received in the utmost secrecy" and that "the unprivileged use or disclosure of another's trade secret becomes the basis for an action in tort." Second, both Clausi and Moore testified that they believed PlayWood had a realistic chance to "get in the door" with Learning Curve and to produce the concept as part of Learning Curve's line of Thomas products. Clausi and Moore did not anticipate that Learning Curve would violate the oral confidentiality agreement and utilize PlayWood's concept without permission; rather, they believed in good faith that they "were going to do business one day again with Learning Curve with respect to the design concept." Finally, we believe that, as part of the reasonableness inquiry, the jury could have considered the size and sophistication of the parties, as well as the relevant industry. Both PlayWood and Learning Curve were small toy companies, and PlayWood was the smaller and less experienced of the two. Viewing the evidence in the light most favorable to PlayWood, as we must, we conclude that there was sufficient evidence for the jury to determine that PlayWood took reasonable measures to protect the secrecy of its concept.

4. Value of the concept to PlayWood and to its competitors

There was substantial evidence from which the jury could have determined that PlayWood's concept had value both to PlayWood and to its competitors. It was undisputed at trial that Learning Curve's sales skyrocketed after it began to sell Clickety-Clack TrackTM. In addition, PlayWood's expert witness, Michael Kennedy, testified that PlayWood's concept for noise-producing track had tremendous value. Kennedy testified that the "cross-cuts and changes in the [track's] surface" imparted value to its seller by causing the track to "look different, feel different and sound different than generic track." Kennedy further testified that, in his opinion, the track would have commanded a premium royalty under a negotiated license agreement because the "invention allows its seller to differentiate itself from a host of competitors who are making a generic product with whom it is competing in a way that is proprietary and exclusive, and it gives [the seller] a significant edge over [its] competition."

[The trial court concluded that PlayWood's prototype had no economic value, as it was imperfect: the grooves were too deep to allow the train to roll smoothly. The appellate court rejected that conclusion, as PlayWood's expert testified that contracts in the toy industry were often negotiated using such imperfect prototypes, and the value in PlayWood's prototype was from the idea; the product could be perfected later, as indeed it was.]

It is irrelevant under Illinois law that PlayWood did not actually use the concept in its business. "[T]he proper criterion is not 'actual use' but whether the trade secret is 'of value' to the company."[6] Kennedy's testimony was more than sufficient to permit the jury to conclude that the concept was "of value" to PlayWood. It is equally irrelevant that PlayWood did not seek to patent its concept. So long as the concept remains a secret, i.e., outside of the public domain, there is no need for patent

---

6. Both the Uniform Trade Secrets Act and the Restatement (Third) of Unfair Competition expressly reject prior use by the person asserting rights in the information as a prerequisite to trade secret protection. See Unif. Trade Secrets Act § 1 cmt. (1990) ("The broader definition in the proposed Act extends protection to a plaintiff who has not yet had an opportunity or acquired the means to put a trade secret to use."); Restatement (Third) of Unfair Competition § 39 cmt. e (1995) ("Use by the person asserting rights in the information is not a prerequisite to protection under the rule stated in this Section," in part, because such a "requirement can deny protection during periods of research and development and is particularly burdensome for innovators who do not possess the capability to exploit their innovations.").

protection. Professor Milgrim makes this point well: "Since every inventor has the right to keep his invention secret, one who has made a patentable invention has the option to maintain it in secrecy, relying upon protection accorded to a trade secret rather than upon the rights which accrue by a patent grant." 1 Roger M. Milgrim, MILGRIM ON TRADE SECRETS § 1.08[1], at 1-353 (2002). It was up to PlayWood, not the district court, to determine when and how the concept should have been disclosed to the public.

5. Amount of time, effort and money expended by PlayWood in developing its concept

PlayWood expended very little time and money developing its concept; by Clausi's own account, the cost to PlayWood was less than one dollar and the time spent was less than one-half hour. The district court determined that "[s]uch an insignificant investment is . . . insufficient as a matter of Illinois law to establish the status of a 'trade secret.'" We believe that the district court gave too much weight to the time, effort and expense of developing the track.

Although Illinois courts commonly look to the Restatement factors for guidance in determining whether a trade secret exists, as we have noted earlier, the requisite statutory inquiries under Illinois law are (1) whether the information "is sufficiently secret to derive economic value, actual or potential, from not being generally known to other persons who can obtain economic value from its disclosure or use;" and (2) whether the information "is the subject of efforts that are reasonable under the circumstances to maintain its secrecy or confidentiality." 765 ILCS 1065/2(d). A significant expenditure of time and/or money in the production of information may provide evidence of value, which is relevant to the first inquiry above. However, we do not understand Illinois law to require such an expenditure in all cases.

As pointed out by the district court, several Illinois cases have emphasized the importance of developmental costs. However, notably, none of those cases concerned the sort of innovative and creative concept that we have in this case. Indeed, several of the cases in Illinois that emphasize developmental costs concern compilations of data, such as customer lists. In that context, it makes sense to require the expenditure of significant time and money because there is nothing original or creative about the alleged trade secret. Given enough time and money, we presume that the plaintiff's competitors could compile a similar list.

Here, by contrast, we are dealing with a new toy design that has been promoted as "the first significant innovation in track design since the inception of wooden train systems." Toy designers, like many artistic individuals, have intuitive flashes of creativity. Often, that intuitive flash is, in reality, the product of earlier thought and practice in an artistic craft. We fail to see how the value of PlayWood's concept would differ in any respect had Clausi spent several months and several thousand dollars creating the noise-producing track. Accordingly, we conclude that PlayWood's lack of proof on this factor does not preclude the existence of a trade secret.

6. Ease or difficulty with which PlayWood's concept could have been properly acquired or duplicated by others

Finally, we also believe that there was sufficient evidence for the jury to determine that PlayWood's concept could not have been easily acquired or duplicated through proper means. PlayWood's expert witness, Michael Kennedy, testified: "This is a fairly simple product if you look at it. But the truth is that because it delivers feeling and sound as well as appearance, it isn't so simple as it first appears. It's a little more elegant, actually, than you might think." In addition to Kennedy's testimony, the jury heard that Learning Curve had spent months attempting to differentiate its track from Brio's before Clausi disclosed PlayWood's concept of noise-producing track. From this evidence, the jury could have inferred that, if PlayWood's concept really was obvious, Learning Curve would have thought of it earlier.

[The trial court concluded that PlayWood's design was not a trade secret, because as soon as it appeared on the market, it could have been easily reverse engineered and duplicated, destroying any trade secret protection. The appellate court agreed that it may be easy to reverse engineer, but at the time the track was disclosed confidentially to Learning Curve, it had not been disclosed to the public, and so was still secret.]

Conclusion

For the foregoing reasons, the judgment of the district court is reversed, and the jury's verdict is reinstated. The case is remanded to the district court for a jury trial on exemplary damages and for consideration of attorneys' fees by the court. Play-Wood may recover its costs in this court.

Mangren Research and Development Corp. v. National Chemical Company, Inc.

United States Court of Appeals for the Seventh Circuit

87 F.3d 937 (7th Cir. 1996)

Ilana Diamond Rovner, Circuit Judge.

[This case was a diversity action, brought under the Illinois Trade Secrets Act (ITSA). Mangren contended that the defendants misappropriated its trade secrets in the course of developing and marketing a competing mold release agent. At trial, the jury found for Mangren, awarding $252,684.69 in compensatory damages and $505,369.38 in exemplary damages, to which the court added Mangren's attorneys' fees and costs. Defendants contend that Mangren did not have any protectable trade secrets, or that defendants did not misappropriate any secrets.]

I.

A.

Mangren's story is one of a grass-roots operation that made good. The company was founded in 1974 by Ted Blackman and Peter Lagergren while they were chemistry students at the University of Texas. Mangren initially manufactured dog shampoo and industrial cleaners and solvents in a garage that belonged to Blackman's father-in-law. Eventually, however, the company began to produce mold release agents. Rubber and plastics manufacturers apply such agents to the molds and presses they use in the manufacturing process. Typically, the end-product is formed by filling a mold or press with a liquefied rubber or plastic and then heating, which causes the liquid to solidify and to take the shape of the vessel containing it. The mold release agent is designed to prevent the solidifying substance from sticking to the mold during this process.

[In the mid-1970's, at the request of Masonite, a major consumer of mold release agents, Mangren began development of a mold release agent; after eighteen months of study, they found a chemical that suited their needs in a particular type of polytetrafluoroethylene ("PTFE"). This type of PTFE had three essential characteristics: (1) it was highly degraded; (2) it had a low molecular weight; and (3) it had low tensile strength. At the time of this discovery, PTFE was never used as the primary component of a mold release agent. Mangren's first product made use of TL-102, a PTFE; Masonite approved the product after much testing. The agent was cheap to produce, but so valuable that Mangren was able to price it high and earn a considerable profit.]

Having had considerable success selling to Masonite, Mangren decided to market its product to others as well. It first compiled a list of companies that produced molded rubber and plastic products. Yet, because not all of those manufacturers would have the equipment necessary to use Mangren's mold release agent, the company contacted each one individually, explaining its product and the equipment needed to use it. In this way, Mangren developed a list of potential customers, but only after devoting a considerable amount of time and effort to the project.

Even as its sales grew, Mangren remained a small company, never having more than six employees at any one time. Because its success depended on the uniqueness of its mold release agent, Mangren took a number of steps to ensure that its formula remained secret. First, all employees were required to sign a confidentiality agreement, and non-employees were not permitted in the company's laboratory. Once chemical ingredients were delivered to the company's premises, moreover, the labels identifying those ingredients were removed and replaced with coded labels understood only by Mangren employees. The company's financial and other records also referred to ingredients only by their code names.

B.

The seeds of the present lawsuit were planted when Mangren made two ill-fated hiring decisions in the 1980s. First, it hired Rhonda Allen in 1986 to be its office manager. Eventually, however, Allen became Mangren's sales manager, a position that provided her access to Mangren's customers and its pricing policies. In 1988, Mangren hired Larry Venable, an organic chemist, to help Blackman develop a chromium-free mold release agent. Although Venable did not have prior experience with PTFE-based mold release agents, he and Blackman succeeded in developing a chromium-free product that also used a highly degraded PTFE with low molecular weight and low tensile strength.

For reasons not relevant here, Mangren terminated the employment of Allen and Venable in 1989. After holding two intervening jobs, Venable met William Lerch early in 1990. Lerch had recently incorporated defendant National Chemical Company, Inc. ("National Chemical"), which was but one of a number of companies he then owned. Venable told Lerch about his Mangren experience and about an idea he had for developing a mold release agent to be used in the rubber industry. Lerch was excited about the prospect and inquired about the market for such a product. Venable responded that Masonite was a large user and therefore a potential customer.

The two discussed the possibility that they might be sued by Mangren if they developed a competing mold release agent. Venable was especially concerned because he realized that any product he could develop would be similar to Mangren's mold release agent. He knew, for example, that a mold release agent using TL-102 — the PTFE that Mangren used—would be "potentially troublesome" and probably would prompt a lawsuit. Lerch told Venable not to worry about a misappropriation suit and explained that he had once been accused of trade secret infringement but had won the case by changing one ingredient or proportion of ingredients in creating his product. Lerch laughed and said the same thing would happen here. Shortly thereafter, Lerch and Venable incorporated defendant National Mold Release Company to manufacture the mold release agent that National Chemical would sell.

[Venable developed a mold release agent, mostly using a PTFE designated as TL-10, though he occasionally used TL-102 as well. Venable also recommended that Lerch hire Allen to market the product, and Allen was hired as a vice president and placed in charge of developing a customer base. Allen approached Mangren customers she was familiar with from her time there with news of the new product and a slightly lower price than Mangren's. Masonite in particular was interested and purchased the product after some testing.]

Venable and Allen left defendants in April 1991. Venable began to work as a consultant for Bash Corporation ("Bash"), a Chicago-based construction supply company. Venable provided Bash with a mold release agent formula that was substantially derived from defendants' formula. Allen, whom Bash had hired on Venable's recommendation, then presented Bash's product to Masonite as the same high quality product she had sold on behalf of National Chemical. Indeed, in a letter notifying Masonite of her association with Bash, Allen represented that:

> This change will not affect Masonite in any way, except for the better. You can still expect the same quality coatings and service I have provided you with in the past. . . . The only change will be in my company name and address. Even the names of the coatings will not change.

Because of its similarity to defendants' mold release agent, Bash was quickly able to qualify its product for use at Masonite and to begin selling to that company. Early in 1992, however, Bash went out of business, prompting Allen to incorporate Bash Chemical Corporation ("Bash Chemical") in Texas. That company then continued to manufacture and market the same mold release agent previously sold by the Illinois-based Bash.

. . . .

II.

. . . .

A.

Under the ITSA, the term "trade secret" means

> information, including but not limited to, technical or non-technical data, a formula, pattern, compilation, program, device, method, technique, drawing, process, financial data, or list of actual or potential customers or suppliers, that:

> (1) is sufficiently secret to derive economic value, actual or potential, from not being generally known to other persons who can obtain economic value from its disclosure; and

> (2) is the subject of efforts that are reasonable under the circumstances to maintain its secrecy or confidentiality.

This definition codifies two requirements for trade secret protection that had developed under the state's common law, both of which focus on the secrecy of the information sought to be protected. Defendants argue that Mangren failed to establish either element here.

Under the first statutory requirement, the information at issue "must be sufficiently secret to impart economic value to both its owner and its competitors because of its relative secrecy." This requirement precludes trade secret protection for information generally known within an industry even if not to the public at large. A plaintiff like Mangren must prove that the real value of the information "lies in the fact that it is not generally known to others who could benefit [from] using it." The evidence in this case presents a textbook example of information satisfying this requirement.

When Mangren first embarked on its mission to develop for Masonite a more effective mold release agent, Masonite was purchasing a product from DuPont that employed a flurotelemer as its primary ingredient. After eighteen months of intensive research and testing, Blackman and Lagergren found that a particular type of PTFE (one that was highly degraded and that had a low molecular weight and low tensile strength) would make their mold release agent more effective and less expensive than that of DuPont. When they made this discovery, the prevailing view was that such a PTFE was unsuited for the type of application that Blackman and Lagergren envisioned. Thus, Mangren was the first to successfully use this particular type of PTFE in a mold release agent. Although defendants are quick to point out that "[m]erely being the first or only one to use particular information does not in and of itself transform otherwise general knowledge into a trade secret", there was sufficient evidence for the jury to conclude that Mangren was not using general knowledge at all. A reasonable jury could find instead that Mangren had developed a distinctive formula based on information not generally known or accepted within the industry.

Mangren proved, moreover, that secrecy imparted considerable economic value to its new formula. Although its mold release agent was relatively inexpensive to produce, Mangren was able to exact a substantial price because of the product's value to the customers who used it. Masonite, in fact, attempted to find another supplier and even to develop its own mold release agent at one point, but was unable to find or to develop an equally effective product. Mangren, then, clearly satisfied the first of the statute's two requirements for a trade secret.

Defendants nonetheless contend that Mangren did not satisfy the second, as it did not make a reasonable effort to maintain the secrecy of its formula. They argue, for example, that all of Mangren's employees (of which there were never more than six at a time) knew Mangren's formula, that an observer of Mangren's premises could identify the formula's ingredients because Mangren did not replace existing labels with coded labels until ingredients had been delivered, and that Mangren could not produce signed agreements from Venable or Allen promising to maintain the confidentiality of its formula.

Arrayed against these purported deficiencies, however, is considerable evidence that the company made substantial efforts to protect the secrecy of its formula. Although Mangren was unable to produce confidentiality agreements for Venable and Allen, it presented to the jury signed agreements for other Mangren employees. Blackman testified, moreover, that each employee (including Venable and Allen) was required to sign a confidentiality agreement and that employees were further advised of the secret status of the company's mold release agent formula. Lagergren added that only Mangren employees were permitted in the company's laboratory. Mangren also demonstrated that it regularly replaced identifying labels with coded labels once ingredients were delivered to its premises. Those ingredients were then referred to in Mangren's financial and other records only by their code names. Even if Mangren could have taken further protective measures just in case, as defendants suggest, a devious potential competitor were to stake out its premises and attempt to identify the chemicals delivered there, whether or not the actions Mangren actually took were sufficient to satisfy the ITSA's reasonableness standard was a question for the jury. The evidence was certainly sufficient to enable reasonable jurors to conclude that Mangren made ample efforts to maintain the secrecy of its formula.

B.

Having determined that Mangren established a protectable trade secret in its mold release agent formula, we turn to the question of misappropriation. The ITSA defines a "misappropriation" in pertinent part as follows:

[D]isclosure or use of a trade secret of a person without express or implied consent by another person who:

> (B) at the time of disclosure or use, knew or had reason to know that knowledge of the trade secret was:
>
>> (I) derived from or through a person who utilized improper means to acquire it:
>>
>> (II) acquired under circumstances giving rise to a duty to maintain its secrecy or limit its use; or
>>
>> (III) derived from or through a person who owed a duty to the person seeking relief to maintain its secrecy or limit its use. . . .

Defendants argue that they did not "use" Mangren's trade secret under this definition because their mold release agent formula is not the same as Mangren's. Although they concede that the primary ingredient of their formula is also a highly degraded PTFE with a low molecular weight and low tensile strength, defendants emphasize that many of the other ingredients are different. Furthermore, the specific PTFE used in defendants' product is typically not the same as the one used by Mangren, although its essential characteristics are identical. Finally, defendants use a slightly smaller volume of PTFE in their mold release agent—twenty as opposed to twenty-three percent in Mangren's product. These differences, in defendants' view, should have precluded the jury from finding that they misappropriated Mangren's formula.

Defendants' argument, however, is inconsistent even with the jury instruction to which they agreed below. The jury was instructed that:

> In order for you to find that defendants misappropriated one of Mangren's trade secrets, you do not have to find that defendants copied or used each and every element of the trade secret. You may find that defendants misappropriated Mangren's trade secrets even if defendants created a new product if defendants could not have done so without use of Mangren's trade secret.

That instruction, as defendants apparently conceded below, is consistent with traditional trade secret law. We observed in *In re Innovative Constr. Sys.*, Inc., 793 F.2d 875, 887 (7th Cir. 1986), for example, that "the user of another's trade secret is liable even if he uses it with modifications or improvements upon it effected by his own efforts, so long as the substance of the process used by the actor is derived from the other's secret." Although that decision involved Wisconsin law, the law of Illinois is in accord. We have observed before, in fact, that if trade secret law were not flexible enough to encompass modified or even new products that are substantially derived from the trade secret of another, the protections that law provides would be hollow indeed.

Mangren emphasizes, moreover, that the trade secret misappropriated here was not necessarily its overall formula, but the essential secret ingredient—a highly degraded PTFE having a low molecular weight and low tensile strength, which had previously been considered unsuitable for such an application.[4] Defendants do not contest that they use a similar PTFE in their mold release agent and that it was Venable, the former Mangren employee, who revealed to them that such a PTFE could be used effectively. Once Venable let defendants in on the secret and defendants then used that secret to develop their own product, there plainly was a misappropriation even if defendants' product was not identical to Mangren's. In other words, reasonable jurors could conclude from the evidence in this case that defendants' mold release agent was substantially derived from Mangren's trade secret, for defendants could not have produced their product without using that secret. Defendants were not therefore entitled to judgment as a matter of law or to a new trial on the trade secret and misappropriation issues.

IV.

Because the trial evidence amply supports the jury's verdict, the district court properly denied defendants' renewed motion for judgment as a matter of law or for a new trial. The district court's judgment is therefore

AFFIRMED.

Notes & Questions

1. Application of the UTSA: Interpretive Force of the Restatement

Before the release of the UTSA, the definition of a trade secret in the RESTATEMENT OF TORTS § 757, comment b (1939), was the sole uniformly recognized definition of a

---

4. In their reply brief and again at oral argument, defendants stridently attacked this characterization of the trade secret:

> Mangren's argument seems to be that no one (at least not Venable, Allen or defendants) may ever use a PTFE similar to the one used by Mangren in its mold release formula. Mangren says this notwithstanding the fact that Blackman himself testified that Mangren used at least three different PTFEs which have the necessary characteristics for the mold release Mangren produced, and that there are dozens more of such PTFEs commercially available. If one is to take Mangren's argument literally, no one can ever use a highly degraded, low molecular weight, low tensile strength PTFE in a mold release agent without violating Mangren's alleged trade secret. Although such a conclusion makes bad law as well as bad sense, it is where Mangren's argument necessarily leads.

This hyperbolic argument misses the mark. Mangren has never suggested that because it was the first to develop a PTFE-based mold release agent, it has the exclusive right to produce and market such a product—as if it held a patent on the product, for example. Mangren would certainly have no claim for misappropriation if another company, after months of independent research and testing, developed a mold release agent using a similar PTFE. Under that scenario, of course, there would be no misappropriation at all because our hypothetical company would have developed its product in the same way that Mangren did—through its own ingenuity. But if, as Mangren proved to the jury's satisfaction in this case, the other company markets a PTFE-based mold release agent that it developed not through independent research and testing, but by using Mangren's trade secret, there was a misappropriation for which the law provides a remedy. That conclusion, which is actually where Mangren's argument leads, makes neither bad law nor bad sense.

trade secret. Today, the UTSA has received widespread adoption and all but a handful of states have adopted UTSA. Despite the UTSA's popular acceptance, the definition of the Restatement of Torts §757 still has application, even in UTSA states. Courts often give weight to the old Restatement definition and refer to it to when applying the UTSA.

2. Big Guys versus Little Guys

In *Learning Curve*, the court held that an oral confidentiality agreement was sufficient to establish reasonable efforts to keep information secret. When arriving at this conclusion, the court emphasized that Playwood was a small, unsophisticated party. The court recognized that "the expectations for ensuring secrecy are different for small companies than for large companies." *Learning Curve*, 342 F.3d at 724. Courts typically are not as lenient when it comes to larger, sophisticated businesses. For example, in *Fail-Safe, LLC v. A.O. Smith Corp.*, 674 F.3d 889 (7th Cir. 2012), the court denied trade secret protection to a sophisticated party who disclosed the information without obtaining a written confidentiality agreement. *Id.* at 894. There, the plaintiff, Fail-Safe, LLC (FS), claimed it reasonably believed it had entered into a joint venture with the defendant, AOS, and that AOS was under a duty of confidentiality. The court rejected this argument distinguishing the facts of the case from those in *Learning Curve*.

> Even assuming some sort of informal relationship existed that hinted at confidentiality, FS still failed to take any steps to maintain its secrecy, which was unreasonable under these circumstances. No information was ever marked confidential. Nor did FS take any steps to protect its claimed proprietary information, contractually or otherwise. FS volunteered its information to AOS. And, unlike in *Learning Curve*, the topic of confidentiality was never even broached by FS, a sophisticated party familiar with such agreements. AOS, with its one-way confidentiality agreement, was the only party that took any protective steps. Under these circumstances, FS's efforts (or lack thereof) to maintain secrecy of its claimed trade secrets were not reasonable.

Fail-Safe, 674 F.3d at 894. For a discussion of justifications for different standards of reasonable efforts depending on parties' sophistication, see Jermaine S. Grubbs, *Give the Little Guys Equal Opportunity at Trade Secret Protection: Why the "Reasonable Efforts" Taken by Small Businesses Should Be Analyzed Less Stringently*, 9 Lewis & Clark L. Rev. 421 (2005).

3. When Does a Claim Arise?

In *Cadence Design Systems, Inc. v. Avant! Corp.*, 253 F.3d 1147 (9th Cir. 2001), the Ninth Circuit certified the following question to be answered by the California Supreme Court:

> Under the California Uniform Trade Secrets Act ("UTSA"), when does a claim for trade secret infringement arise: only once, when the initial misappropriation occurs, or with each subsequent misuse of the trade secret?

At issue was an earlier settlement between Cadence and Avant!, wherein Avant! was released from all liability for any then-existing causes of action. Avant! continued to use Cadence's trade secret after this settlement, and Cadence argued that the continual use created new causes of action.

The California Supreme Court responded that continued use of misappropriated trade secrets was part of a single claim, arising at the time of initial misappropriation. *See Cadence Design Systems, Inc. v. Avant! Corp.*, 127 Cal. Rptr. 2d 169 (2002).

iii. Elements of Trade Secrets

Trade secrets, under most definitions, consist of (i) information (ii) that is valuable through not being generally known to others (iii) that the holder has tried to keep secret. In trade secrets cases, the issues of fact that usually present difficulties include: (i) whether the information claimed to be a trade secret was in fact a secret and (ii) whether the defendant obtained or used the information improperly. *See* Malla Pollack, *Litigating Misappropriation of Trade Secrets*, 127 Am. Jur. Trials 283 (originally published in 2012).

(1). Information

As noted by the UTSA definition, what "information" can make up a trade secret is an open-ended question: there is a wide range to be covered between designs for toys (*Learning Curve*) and chemical formulae (*Mangren*). One fairly common trade secret is customer list.

DeGiorgio v. Megabyte International, Inc.

Supreme Court of Georgia

468 S.E.2d 367 (Ga. 1996)

Carley, Justice.

[Megabyte is a distributor of computer hardware components. DeGiorgio was a salesman for Megabyte for several months before leaving to join American Megabyte Distributors, Inc. (AMDI), a newly formed competitor. At trial, Megabyte produced evidence that their customer and vendor lists, entrusted to DeGiorgio, had been faxed to AMDI's president by DeGiorgio. Megabyte was granted an interlocutory injunction by the trial court, and DeGiorgio and AMDI appealed.]

. . . .

2. Appellants further contend that the lists were not trade secrets which could support a grant of interlocutory injunctive relief under the Georgia Trade Secrets Act.

The lists at issue contained the identities of actual customers and vendors of Megabyte and specific information concerning them. Thus, the information on the lists was not readily ascertainable from any source other than Megabyte's business records. "Such a source would be improper if [Megabyte] had made a reasonable effort to maintain the secrecy of those customer [and vendor] lists." A review of the record reveals evidence from which the trial court could have found that Megabyte had made such a reasonable effort to maintain the secrecy of the customer and vendor lists which the trial court determined to be trade secrets. Accordingly, the trial court did not abuse its discretion in granting an interlocutory injunction under the Trade Secrets Act.

[The court then found that the injunction put in place by the trial court was overly broad, and reversed that portion of the lower court's holding, before remanding the case.]

Notes & Questions

1. Customer Lists: Tangible versus Memorized

In the end of its opinion in *DeGiorgio,* the Georgia Supreme Court emphasized that in Georgia "only tangible lists of customers and suppliers are the property of the employer and warrant protection as trade secrets." *DeGiorgio,* 468 S.E.2d at 369. Therefore, the appellants were free to utilize their "personal knowledge of customer and vendor information." *Id.* In other words, under *DeGiorgio,* if an employee, instead of copying the file containing the secret customer list, simply memorizes the entire list, the employee cannot be liable for trade secret misappropriation. Despite reaffirmation by the Georgia Supreme Court in *TMX Finance Holdings, Inc. v. Drummond Financial Services, LLC*, 797 S.E.2d 842, 845 (Ga. 2017), this rule is not the law in the majority of UTSA jurisdictions. The majority rule is that memorized information can be the basis for a trade secret violation. *Al Minor & Assoc., Inc. v. Martin*, 881 N.E.2d 850, 853–54 (Ohio 2008). In *Martin*, the Ohio Supreme Court held that a client list constituted a trade secret, and the fact that an employee stored it in his memory did not "remove it from the protection of the UTSA." *Id.* at 855.

Of course, even in minority view states like Georgia an employer is free to use a contract to explicitly prohibit utilizing memory or personal knowledge of customer and vendor information. If the use barred by contract is made, the employer's cause of action will be for breach of contract but not for trade secret misappropriation.

2. Recipe as a Trade Secret

In *Buffets, Inc. v. Klinke*, 73 F.3d 965 (9th Cir. 1996), the court denied trade secret protection to the recipes of basic American dishes such as BBQ chicken and macaroni and cheese, because they were widely known and used across the country. 73 F.3d at 968. Although *Buffets* created some uncertainty as to the availability of trade secret protection for the culinary industry, the subsequent case law corrected this misinterpretation. For example, in *Bimbo Bakeries USA, Inc. v. Sycamore*, No. 2:13-CV-00749 DN, 2017 WL 1405637 (D. Utah Apr. 12, 2017), the court held that the recipe for "Grandma Sycamore's" bread was protectable as a trade secret. There, the original owner of the recipe, Leland Sycamore, sold the recipe to a predecessor of the plaintiff,

Bimbo, in 1998. Despite the sale, Sycamore used the recipe in production of similar bread for Bimbo's competitor, US Bakery. The court denied defendant's motion for summary judgment, holding that the steps in the production of Grandma Sycamore's bread were specific and unique and, therefore, could qualify as a trade secret. The jury eventually found Sycamore and US Bakery liable and entered a $2.1 million verdict in favor of the recipe owner for the trade secret misappropriation.

In addition, the case that yielded the very first jury verdict under the DTSA involved a recipe for a popular jam. There the jury awarded a Florida-based jam company $500 million for misappropriation of its extensively safeguarded recipe and process of making of a gourmet fig spread. *See* Michael Songer & Ali Tehrani, *The First DTSA Verdict: $500,000 for Misappropriation of a Fig Spread Recipe*, LEX-OLOGY (Apr. 7, 2017), https://www.lexology.com/library/detail.aspx?g=e738bc35-4b41-4d46-a18f-93a1f40199a1.

3. Trade Secrets and High-Tech

Many trade secret misappropriation cases involve small amounts of information like a single customer list, a formula, or a manufacturing process. However, when it comes to high-tech industries, the amounts and sophistication of information at issue may complicate trade secret litigation. For example, in February 2017, one of the champions of the emerging self-driving car industry, Waymo, sued its competitor and another tech giant, Uber, for trade secret misappropriation. The information at issue in the case was contained in 14,000 secret files pertaining to autonomous driving technology referred to as LiDAR, which is a remote sensing system that allows self-driving vehicles to perceive objects around them. *See* Aarian Marshall, *The Uber-Waymo Lawsuit Gets a New Star—And Takes a Wild Turn*, WIRED (Nov. 30, 2017), https://www.wired.com/story/uber-waymo-richard-jacobs-lawsuit/. After nearly a year of litigation, the parties settled the dispute with Uber providing Waymo with 0.34 percent of its equity worth almost $245 million, according to the settlement agreement. Additionally, Uber promised that it would refrain from incorporating any of Waymo's confidential information in its autonomous driving technology. Daisuke Wakabayashi, *Uber and Waymo Settle Trade Secrets Suit Over Driverless Cars*, N.Y. TIMES, Feb. 9, 2018, https://www.nytimes.com/2018/02/09/technology/uber-waymo-lawsuit-driverless.html. Notably, the case involved claims under both the California Uniform Trade Secrets Act and the federal Defend Trade Secrets Act. The court observed that the relevant provisions of the two statutes were similar and applied the same analysis for both claims in ruling on Waymo's motion for provisional relief. *Waymo LLC v. Uber Techs., Inc.*, No. C 17-00939 WHA, 2017 WL 2123560, at *7 (N.D. Cal. May 15, 2017). The employment issues raised by the case are discussed in Chapter 4.

(2). **Value Through Secrecy**

To qualify as a trade secret information must have independent economic value, which must be derived from the secrecy of the information. Information that is widely known, or easily discoverable by proper means, is not protectable.

Fred's Stores of Mississippi, Inc. v. M & H Drugs, Inc. (Part One)

Supreme Court of Mississippi

725 So. 2d 902 (Miss. 1998)

PITTMAN, PRESIDING JUDGE:

[Plaintiff, M & H Drugs, Inc., the parent company of the Super D pharmacy store (Super D), employed Erik Broome (Broome) as the manager and a pharmacist. Part of Broome's job was to supervise the creation and maintenance of a master customer list (hereinafter "I.R.S. list") that Super D kept in case their customers would inquire as to their total expenditures on prescription medication for the year. In the summer of 1991, Broome left Super D to become the manager of a new pharmacy in the same town run by Fred's Stores of Mississippi, Inc. (hereinafter "Fred's"). When leaving Broome took the I.R.S. list with him. He subsequently gave the list to his supervisor at Fred's. Fred's used the list to send letters to at least 954 Super D's customers. When Super D became aware of the missing list, it filed a lawsuit against Fred's for trade secret misappropriation.]

. . .

The issue to be decided by this court is whether the I.R.S. list was a legally protectable trade secret as that term is defined by the Mississippi Uniform Trade Secrets Act. There is no Mississippi case law interpreting this statute, therefore it is a case of first impression for this Court. It is appropriate to look to the interpretations of other jurisdictions.

The I.R.S. list was quite obviously a compilation of information. The first question is whether the list "[d]erives independent economic value, actual or potential, from not being generally known to, and not being readily ascertainable by proper means by, other persons who can obtain economic value from its disclosure or use . . ." Miss. Code Ann. § 75-26-3(d)(i) (1991). The information contained on the I.R.S. list was partly information that was obtained by Super D when its customers filled out a patient history and insurance profile. However, all of the information obtained through the patient history was not reflected on the I.R.S. list. The list contained the patient's last name, first name, phone number, street address, city, state, zipcode, number of prescriptions filled in one year, and a dollar amount of the money spent on prescriptions at Super D for the year. Broome testified that as a pharmacist, he would consider the information on the I.R.S. list to be valuable information. Jerry Pardue, Vice President of loss prevention and human resources for Super D testified that the demographic information on the I.R.S. list had often been solicited by marketing companies. Casey, Senior Vice President of Fred's testified that Fred's would not release the amount of money an individual spent at Fred's in a given year to anyone other than that customer. Casey also testified that Fred's would not consider printing up a list of its customers and giving it to Super D. He testified that it would be a disadvantage to Fred's to do that.

Other jurisdictions have addressed the question of what evidence will support a finding that a customer list meets the first prong of the "trade secret" definition. In California, the first prong of the "trade secret" definition states:

> (1) Derives independent economic value, actual or potential, from not being generally known to the public or to other persons who can obtain economic value from its disclosure or use; . . .

Cal. Civil Code § 3426.1(d) (West 1997). Although this prong is defined slightly differently than in Mississippi, a look at its interpretation is helpful. The remainder of the "trade secret" definition is identical to Mississippi's. In *Courtesy Temporary Service, Inc. v. Camacho*, 222 Cal. App. 3d 1278, 272 Cal. Rptr. 352 (1990), the Court of Appeal found that a compilation of Courtesy's customers, who had demonstrated their willingness to use temporary employees, was the result of lengthy and expensive efforts, including advertising, promotional campaigns, canvassing, and client entertainment. The lower court had ruled that this "work effort" was not a secret entitled to protection. The Court of Appeal held that "it is this very 'work effort' or process of acquiring and retaining clientele, that constitutes a protectable trade secret."

In another California case, *Morlife, Inc. v. Perry*, 56 Cal. App. 4th 1514, 66 Cal. Rptr. 2d 731 (1997), the first prong of the "trade secret" definition was examined. In that case, Morlife was in the business of inspecting, maintaining, and repairing roofs primarily for commercial properties. Perry had been with the company since its formation as a sales representative. Perry and another employee discussed starting their own roofing business. When Perry left Morlife, he took his collection of customer business cards he had accumulated over his six years of employment. According to Perry's testimony at trial, the customer cards represented approximately 75 to 80 percent of Morlife's customer base. Morlife sued Perry for misappropriation of a trade secret. Judgment was awarded for Morlife in the trial court. The appellate court upheld the findings of the trial court which had held:

> "Morlife provides a relatively unusual roofing service, namely, commercial roof repair and maintenance, as distinguished from replacement roofing." Its customer list was "a compilation, developed over a period of years, of names, addresses, and contact persons, containing pricing information and knowledge about particular roofs and roofing needs of customers using its services: as such, it has independent economic value." The identity of those particular commercial buildings using such services is not generally known to the roofing industry."

Morlife, 66 Cal. Rptr. 2d at 735.

Under the Indiana Uniform Trade Secrets Act, the first prong of the "trade secret" definition is identical to that in Mississippi. In the case of *Kozuch v. CRA-MAR Video Center, Inc.*, 478 N.E.2d 110 (Ind. Ct. App. 1985), a video center sought to preliminarily enjoin a competitor from using its customer list. The trial court issued the injunction and the competitor appealed. The trial court's finding that the customer list met the first prong of the "trade secret" definition was upheld on appeal. The appellate court found that:

There was evidence presented at trial that CRA-MAR's customer list included only the names of owners of video hardware purchased at CRA-MAR and those who had purchased memberships in CRA-MAR's video rental club, and were therefore either customers or prospective customers for video movies. There was also evidence that the customer list could not have been created by any means other than through CRA-MAR's business operations. In addition, there was evidence that the list derived its independent economic value from not being generally known or ascertainable by CRA-MAR's competitors.

Kozuch, 478 N.E.2d at 113.

We conclude that the I.R.S. list did meet the first prong of the "trade secret" definition. The information on the list had independent economic value as evidenced by the fact that marketing companies are willing to pay money to obtain it. Further, the information on the list, especially the amounts of money spent by customers of Super D and the number of prescriptions filled, was not information that was known to Fred's or that was generally ascertainable to them by proper means. Finally, Fred's could obtain economic value from the disclosure of the list. This is evidenced by the fact that Fred's would not give this type of information to Super D. Also, there is value in knowing which customers are big spenders on prescription medication because there is an inference that the bigger spenders are those with more health problems, and therefore customers that Fred's would like to have.

Notes & Questions

1. Value through Secrecy: Factors to Consider

Courts look at variety of factors to determine whether information has independent economic value through not being generally known to those who can obtain economic value from its disclosure or use. Among the common factors are: (1) the amount of time, effort, and money spent in developing the trade secret; (2) market or competitive advantage that the information provides; and (3) other factors, such as importance to the business, and subjective opinion of the parties. *See* Alois Valerian Gross, *What Is "Trade Secret" so as to Render Actionable Under State Law Its Use or Disclosure by Former Employee*, 59 A.L.R. 4TH 641 (Originally published in 1988).

For example, in *Courtesy*, which was cited by the court in *Fred's Stores*, the customer list was protected because it was "the result of lengthy and expensive efforts, including advertising, promotional campaigns, canvassing, and client entertainment." *Courtesy*, 272 Cal. Rptr. at 354. In *Fred's Stores* itself, the court held that the IRS list had independent value because: (1) marketing companies were willing to pay for it; (2) the information was not known to Fred's Stores; (3) Fred's Stores would not give this type of information to Super D; and (4) there was value in knowing which customers had more health problems because Fred's Stores would like to have such customers. 725 So. 2d at 910. Finally, in *Buffets*, mentioned *supra*, the court held that the recipes for basic American dishes did not have an independent economic value because the plaintiff failed to demonstrate that its recipes played a role in limiting costs or that "its rivals [were] not succeeding because of inferior food quality" that access to the recipes would have helped the rivals to overcome. 73 F.3d at 968.

2. Combination Trade Secret

Typically, information that is commonly known cannot qualify for trade secret protection. But what if the subject matter of an asserted trade secret is a combination of otherwise well-known principles? What if the elements of the asserted trade secret are available in the technical literature? Do you believe trade secret protection can be extended to a combination of otherwise commonly known facts?

In *Heyden Chemical Corp. v. Burrell & Neidig, Inc.,* the plaintiff chemical manufacturer claimed its processes of manufacturing formaldehyde and pentaerythritol as trade secrets. The court agreed that the processes were trade secrets:

> Defendants say that the Heyden processes are not secret. The claim is that they have been known to the trade for years and are, in fact, in the public domain. In support of this assertion there were offered in evidence various essays, treatises and patents dealing with the manufacture of formaldehyde and pentaerythritol. In my opinion, these exhibits served to strengthen the plaintiff's claim. According to the testimony, there are to be found in the scientific literature some 800 to 1,000 references dealing with the production of formaldehyde and 500 to 600 references dealing with the production of pentaerythritol. Of the references on the subject of formaldehyde about 30 were offered in evidence. A like number dealing with pentaerythritol were introduced. In every one of the exhibits the systems discussed differed in major particulars from those used by Heyden. In some even the ingredients used were different. But regardless of how different the process described might be, if it contained a single element to be found in the Heyden system, the exhibit was offered to show a public disclosure of the Heyden process. Time and again while being examined on a particular exhibit, the witness would be asked to explain why an engineer, unfamiliar with the Heyden process, in setting up a formaldehyde or pentaerythritol plant, would select one element of the process described in the reference and discard the rest. A satisfactory answer to the question was never given.

> The truth is, of course, that only a person who knew the Heyden process could make the selection of literature references which were offered in evidence. Dr. Elderfield of Columbia University, who appeared as an expert for the plaintiff and who was referred to as one of the leading authorities on organic chemistry, testified flatly that an engineer unfamiliar with the Heyden system could not duplicate that system by using the information contained in the literature without long and expensive research and experimentation.

Heyden Chem. Corp. v. Burrell & Neidig, Inc., 64 A.2d 465, 467 (N.J. Supr. Ct. Ch. Div. 1949).

Combination theory, however, is not without its limits. For example, in *Strategic Directions Group, Inc. v. Bristol-Myers Squibb Co.,* 293 F.3d 1062 (8th Cir. 2002), the court held that the combination of nine questions selected from a longer list of questions, each of which had been previously disclosed in a book and a copyright filing, could not be protected as a trade secret. *Id.* at 1065. Even though someone was willing to pay money for the selection of questions, the court explained that "[t]he law of trade secrets will not protect talent or expertise, only secret information." *Id.* (citation omitted).

(3). Reasonable Efforts of Protection

Concurrent with the requirement of independent economic value derived from secrecy is the requirement that the user of a trade secret take reasonable efforts to maintain this secrecy. This can be accomplished through a combination of methods: in *Learning Curve*, PlayWood relied on confidentiality agreements with their outside contractor, as well as the small size of the company, to keep secret information secret; in *Mangren*, confidentiality agreements were paired with technological and physical protections, through the use of locked doors and coded ingredients. In both cases, the courts were satisfied by the efforts involved.

An additional portion of the court's opinion in the *Fred's Stores* case addresses this issue.

Fred's Stores of Mississippi, Inc. v. M & H Drugs, Inc. (Part Two)

Supreme Court of Mississippi

725 So. 2d 902 (Miss. 1998)

Pittman, Presiding Judge:

. . .

Fred's [] asserts that Super D's I.R.S. list was not the subject of reasonable efforts to maintain its secrecy, which is the second prong of the [Mississippi Uniform Trade Secrets Act trade secret] definition. Super D asserts that it took reasonable steps to maintain the secrecy of the I.R.S list.

Evidence at trial showed that the I.R.S. list was printed out once a year from the computer. The computer was accessed through a password. The list was kept in an accordion folder on the pharmacy counter during those months of the year when it was used frequently. It was kept in an unlocked filing cabinet when it was not being used frequently. The pharmacy platform was located in the back left corner of the building. There was a gate without a locking device at the entrance of the pharmacy platform. Access to the pharmacy was limited to pharmacists, pharmacy technicians, pharmacy students in internships, stock persons, and when absolutely necessary a counter person. People such as pest control servicemen were also allowed behind the counter, but were carefully monitored. Broome was not required to sign any sort of termination agreement ensuring confidentiality when he left Super D. However, a district manager who left Super D was. The list was not stamped with any sort of language identifying it as a secret or confidential. Broome testified he was never told the list was a trade secret. Broome said that he did not recall there ever being any trade secret policy. There were no instructions given to employees about what to do with the list after April 15th. Klepzig tossed it in the dumpster. Pardue testified that Super D would classify a customer list as a trade secret. Pardue testified that Super D had an employee handbook and an operations manual which both discussed confidential information. Neither the manual nor the handbook specifically mentioned trade secrets. Other than that, Pardue testified that Super D relies on the education of its pharmacists concerning ethics. Pardue testified that the patient history form, from which the I.R.S. list is compiled, tells the patient before he fills it out that all information is confidential.

Other jurisdictions have considered the question of what are "efforts that are reasonable under the circumstances to maintain secrecy." The Supreme Court of Alabama considered the question in *Allied Supply Co., Inc. v. Brown*, 585 So.2d 33 (Ala.1991). Allied contended that some former employees had misappropriated customer and vendor lists before they left Allied. The Supreme Court found that at least 10 Allied employees had access to the lists. The lists were not marked "confidential." The lists were taken home by employees. Multiple copies of each list existed, and the information on the lists was contained in the receptionist's Rolodex. The Court held that in light of the evidence, "Allied did not meet its burden of showing that it had taken reasonable steps to ensure that the lists remained a 'trade secret'."

In a Louisiana case, *Wyatt v. PO2, Inc.*, 651 So.2d 359 (La. Ct. App. 1995), where a former employee used the identities of PO2's clients in a new business, a Louisiana district court found that the client's identities were not a trade secret. Specifically, the court found that the PO2 computer had no access code to restrict entry and that there was no evidence of any contractual agreement regarding confidentiality of PO2 information or restricting competition.

In *Courtesy Temporary Service, Inc. v. Camacho, supra*, the California Court of Appeal found that Courtesy had taken reasonable steps to maintain the secrecy of its customer list where information on the list was not divulged to anyone outside of its business, employees were allowed access to the information on an "as needed basis" to perform their duties and access was limited to the branch in which they worked, and employees were told of the confidential and proprietary nature of the information.

In an Indiana case, *Ackerman v. Kimball International, Inc.*, 634 N.E.2d 778 (Ind. Ct. App. 1994), adopted in part by 652 N.E.2d 507 (Ind. 1995), the Court of Appeals held that customer and supplier lists and pricing information were trade secrets where the number of employees who had access to the information was limited, employees who did have access were instructed not to disclose it, the computer on which the information was stored was accessible only by password, and the computer displayed notice to the user indicating the proprietary nature of the information.

After a close examination of the facts in the case *sub judice*, we find that Super D's I.R.S. list was the "subject of efforts that are reasonable under the circumstances to maintain its secrecy." Access to the computer on which the list was stored was obtainable only through password. The list was printed out once a year, and was then maintained in the pharmacy platform area. We note specifically that we find it persuasive that the list was maintained in the same area as the prescription drugs to which any pharmacy should carefully monitor access. There was no evidence that Super D did not carefully monitor its drugs. The information on the I.R.S. list was also not divulged to anyone outside of the business save the customer who requested an accounting of his expenditures for the year. When a request was made by a customer, the pharmacist would look up the information and write it on a separate sheet of paper to give to the customer. This sheet of paper could be signed, as a pharmacist, only by Klepzig or Broome. The number of employees who had access to this list was limited and available only to those employees who needed to know the information. Although we do not find the steps taken by Super D to maintain secrecy to be elaborate steps, we do find them to be reasonable, and that will suffice. We find these steps to be particularly reasonable in this case because of the unique security necessary to protect prescription drugs in the pharmacy setting. If this list had been maintained behind the front counter of the Super D store as opposed to the pharmacy platform area, we may have decided this case differently. All that said, we conclude that the I.R.S. list was a trade secret as that term is defined by the Mississippi Uniform Trade Secrets Act, and this assignment of error is without merit.

[The court then discussed other issues, including causation and damages. It eventually reversed the award of compensatory damages in the amount of $56,100 because of failure to prove loss of net (as opposed to gross) profits, but affirmed the awards of $650 in compensatory damages and $300,000 in punitive damages.]

Notes & Questions

1. Protecting Confidential Information

In *Learning Curve*, PlayWood provided their "secret" design to Learning Curve, but under conditions that created a confidential relationship. In *Fred's Stores*, the court based its finding that Store D's efforts to maintain the customer list secret were reasonable substantially on the fact that the list was kept in the pharmacy platform area with restricted and monitored access. In *Buffets, Inc. v. Klinke*, however, the "secret" employee manuals were available to all employees and could be taken home if desired, a situation that the court held to be incompatible with any claim of secrecy. 73 F.3d at 969. *Buffets* also clarifies that if secrecy measures are weak, a trade secret owner cannot prevail even if a defendant's means of acquiring information is illegal.

> Finally, OCB argues that since the Klinkes illegally obtained the manuals, the question of whether the security measures taken to protect them were reasonable is irrelevant. This argument, however, misses the mark, as the issue of whether security measures were reasonable pertains to the preliminary question of whether the material is in fact a trade secret. If it is not,

then the Klinkes may be liable for stealing something, but they cannot be liable for misappropriation of trade secrets. . . . Thus, we affirm the court's finding that the manuals were not trade secrets.

Id.

2. How Much Effort?

Courts require trade secret owners to take "reasonable" efforts to protect the secrecy of a trade secret. In the determination, courts consider the entirety of circumstances surrounding the owner's use of the trade secret. Often, trade secret owners must show that protective measures were taken to the extent possible under the circumstances.

Interestingly, the greater the extent to which a trade secret owner uses measures to protect his information, the more likely a court will conclude that the information is a trade secret. Efforts to maintain the secrecy of information are probative of the trade secret status of the information itself. Of course, even an extreme amount of protection cannot transform information that is in the public domain into a trade secret.

b. Non-UTSA Jurisdictions

As noted previously, a number of prominent jurisdictions have not enacted the Uniform Trade Secrets Act. In those states, courts often rely on common law factors, such as those considered by the Seventh Circuit in *Learning Curve, supra*. Most of the common law developed, in turn, from the Restatement of Torts (1939) definition.

Sylmark Holdings Ltd. v. Silicone Zone Intern. Ltd.

Supreme Court, New York County, New York

783 N.Y.S.2d 758 (2004)

HERMAN CAHN, JUSTICE:

This is an action to enjoin and recover damages for defendants' alleged unlawful misappropriation of plaintiffs' confidential information and proprietary design for their "Hot Holder" silicone gloves, oven gloves which are heat resistant to 500 degrees Fahrenheit, and which have a left-hand and right-hand design.

Plaintiffs moved for a preliminary injunction, enjoining defendants from marketing or taking any action with respect to certain models, sample models and products for the Hot Holder oven mitts that were made in connection with certain agreements between the parties relating to the development of those oven mitts and for the Silicone Zone Two Hands left and right handed silicone oven mitts or any other products designs or ideas produced, developed, or derived from the trade secrets and/or confidential proprietary information that plaintiffs provided to defendants or which were developed by defendants for plaintiffs pursuant to the agreements between them . . . .

[Sylmark Holdings and Silicone Zone entered into several agreements under which Silicone Zone was to create models for plaintiffs Sylmark Holdings products. In the course of these agreements, the parties each agreed that all information exchanged was to be kept confidential. In the Confidentiality Agreement, Silicone Zone agreed that, "the Pot Holder and/or silicone mitt disclosed by Sylmark is an invention created solely by Sylmark, and the ownership of such an invention shall remain solely the exclusive property of Sylmark."]

[P]laintiff Sylmark alleges that it discovered an advertisement placed by Silicone Zone for a product, produced under the name of "Two Hands," which plaintiffs claim is virtually identical to its Hot Holder Gloves. The ad indicates that the gloves are silicone oven mitts, with a left and right-hand design, and are safe at 675 degrees Fahrenheit. Plaintiffs claim that the pictures in the ad show that these mitts are virtually identical to plaintiffs', that the ad wrongly states that Silicone Zone has a patent pending for them, and that it wrongly indicates that Silicone Zone owns the intellectual property for the gloves and may sell them. Plaintiffs also claim that they observed the "Two Hands" product at a trade show in March 2004, and that it was a near replica of the Sylmark "Hot Holder" gloves.

By letter dated November 19, 2003, Sylmark's counsel demanded that Silicone Zone cease and desist from manufacturing, advertising, and selling the "Two Hands" silicone gloves, which actions were in breach of the parties' agreements. Thereafter, Sylmark made several demands for the return of the Molds, Sample Molds, and Sample Products, which demands Silicone Zone ignored.

[Sylmark commenced proceedings in the High Court in Hong Kong seeking an order requiring return of the Molds. The Court granted the application and ordered Silicone Zone to return the Molds. Silicone Zone continued to market Two Hands gloves despite the order.]

The complaint alleges several causes of action [against Silicone Zone]. First . . . for breach of the Development, Confidentiality, and Mold Development agreements, based on defendants' failure, inter alia, to return plaintiffs' proprietary and confidential information and molds, and misappropriating and commercially exploiting such materials. The second and third . . . are for unjust enrichment and conversion. The [fourth] is for theft of trade secrets. The [fifth] is for violation of General Business Law §§ 349 and 350. The [sixth] seeks enforcement of the Hong Kong court's order. Finally, the [seventh] is for unfair competition and misappropriation.

. . . .

On their misappropriation of trade secrets claim, plaintiffs contend, again, that defendants acknowledge in the agreements that the information at issue is a trade secret, that plaintiffs invested time and effort to develop the information and maintain its secrecy, and that there are no other similar gloves on the market. They submit photos of both pairs of gloves as proof of the virtual identity of the defendants' gloves with Sylmark's "Hot Holder" gloves. Plaintiffs assert that the existence of

Silicone Zone's knock-off gloves is proof of the misappropriation of plaintiffs' trade secrets.

. . . .

Misappropriation of Trade Secrets

Plaintiffs have . . . demonstrated a likelihood of success on their claim for misappropriation of trade secrets. To establish a claim for misappropriation of trade secrets, plaintiff must show (1) that it possesses a trade secret, and (2) that defendant is using that trade secret in breach of an agreement, confidence, or duty, or as a result of discovery by improper means. *DoubleClick, Inc. v. Henderson*, 1997 N.Y. Misc. LEXIS 577 (Nov. 5, 1997). New York courts have adopted the trade secret definition set forth in the Restatement of Torts § 757, Comment B, as "any formula, pattern, device or compilation of information which is used in one's business, and which gives him an opportunity to obtain an advantage over competitors who do not know or use it." *Id.*; see *Ashland Mgt. Inc. v. Janien*, 82 N.Y.2d 395, 407, 604 N.Y.S.2d 912, 624 N.E.2d 1007 (1993); *U.S. Reinsurance Corp. v. Humphreys*, 205 A.D.2d 187, 191, 618 N.Y.S.2d 270 (1st Dept. 1994).

The factors considered in evaluating claims of trade secrecy include:

(1)   the extent to which the information is known outside of [the] business;

(2)   the extent to which it is known by employees and others involved in [the] business;

(3)   the extent of measures taken by [the business] to guard the secrecy of the information;

(4)   the value of the information to [the business] and [its] competitors;

(5)   the amount of effort or money expended by [the business] in developing the information;

(6)   the ease or difficulty with which the information could be properly acquired or duplicated by others.

Restatement of Torts § 757, Comment B.

In this case, it is important to note that Silicone Zone acknowledged in its agreements with Sylmark that the various confidential materials and information Sylmark was providing to it were secret, and that Silicone was obligated to maintain such confidentiality. Plaintiffs present proof that the design for Sylmark's "Hot Holder" gloves; the specifications and drawings; the information on how to best design the product, what size worked best, and how to ensure that the gloves were sufficiently heat resistant; and the design of the molds were not known outside a select few Sylmark employees.

Silicone Zone was obligated under the agreements to guard the secrecy of this information; Sylmark dealt with only a few of Silicone Zone's employees. Sylmark presents proof that it invested a great deal of time and effort to develop the information, including time spent analyzing how to design around a competitor's patent, developing marketing plans and sales projections. Sylmark sought and obtained a patent because the design was not generally known in the business. Defendants' assertions that the information was not secret because the patent was in the public domain, is not borne out by the record. The patent consists solely of six line drawings; it does not contain the precise dimensions, specifications, or other proprietary information with respect to the actual final design and manufacture of the gloves, as well as the marketing plans, sales projections, and legal analyses, that were specified in Sylmark's papers as trade secrets. Accordingly, Sylmark has demonstrated that it possessed trade secrets with respect to the "Hot Holder" gloves, which it shared with defendants in anticipation of defendants' role in manufacturing molds for the gloves, and which trade secrets defendants specifically acknowledged in their agreements with plaintiffs.

There is substantial evidence in the record that defendants misappropriated Sylmark's trade secret information, in violation of their agreements with Sylmark. As discussed above, the photos of Silicone Zone's "Two Hands" gloves show that they are nearly identical to the "Hot Holder" gloves, and may be held to be significant proof of misappropriation. Again, the development and sale of the "Two Hands" gloves before Sylmark's patent was issued, and while defendants were purportedly working on Sylmark's gloves, similarly points to defendants having likely misappropriated plaintiffs' trade secrets. Therefore, plaintiffs have shown a likelihood of prevailing on their claim of misappropriation of trade secrets.

[The court noted that, "[i]rreparable harm is presumed, where, as here, trade secrets have been misappropriated." *DoubleClick, Inc. v. Henderson*; *see Lumex Inc. v. Highsmith*, 919 F. Supp. 624, 628 (E.D.N.Y 1996). The court then concluded that, even without such presumption, plaintiffs sufficiently demonstrated that, without an injunction, they would continue to suffer irreparable harm. The court also concluded that plaintiffs sufficiently demonstrated that the balance of equities tips heavily in their favor. The court then noted that the injunction in effect would enforce the Hong Kong order and concluded that the pendency of the case in Hong Kong did not deprive this court of jurisdiction. Finally, the court denied plaintiffs request for attachment and granted plaintiffs' request for expedited discovery.]

ORDERED that defendants and all persons acting in concert with them, or subject to their supervision and control, are enjoined and restrained, during the pendency of this action from doing or suffering to be done, directly or through any attorney, agent, servant, employee or other persons under the supervision or control of the defendants any of the following acts:

> using, exploiting, transferring, marketing, manufacturing, selling, distributing, or taking any action with respect to certain molds, sample molds and products (a) for the "Hot Holder" oven mitts, and that were otherwise made in connection with certain agreements between the parties relating to the development of the oven mitts and (b) for the Silicone

Zone "Two Hands" left and right-handed silicone oven mitts, or any other product, designs or ideas produced, developed or derived from the trade secrets and/or confidential proprietary information that plaintiffs provided to defendants, or which were developed by defendants for plaintiffs pursuant to the agreements between the parties, including the molds, sample molds obtained from or produced for plaintiffs, sample products, information specifications, designs, drawings, models, research and development materials[.]

Notes & Questions

1. Process versus Product

Many business activities involve a secret process that creates an unprotected product. The protection for a secret process exists even where a product is unprotected, and may be reverse engineered. *See E.I. duPont deNemours & Co., Inc. v. Christopher*, 431 F.2d 1012 (5th Cir. 1970). Consider *Phillips v. Frey*, 20 F.3d 623 (5th Cir. 1994). Phillips owned a business that made collapsible single-pole deer stands. These stands supported elevated seats used by individuals in gun or bow hunting. Phillips' product was not protected by a patent and any purchaser could reverse engineer the product to determine how it was made. What Phillips relied on was his secret process, as any attempt to duplicate the stand, without knowledge of the process involved, would be cost-prohibitive. Frey asserted that their product was made by reverse engineering Phillips' work, but the court noted that while the *product* might have been obtained by reverse engineering, the *process* was not:

> Although it is likely appellants used reverse engineering for the design of [their competing stand], there was no evidence that the appellants used this method to acquire the manufacturing process employed by Ambusher. A process or device may be a trade secret even where others can gain knowledge of the process from studying the manufacturer's marketed product. Although trade secret law does not offer protection against discovery by fair and honest means such as independent invention, accidental disclosure, or "reverse engineering," protection will be awarded to a trade secret holder against the disclosure or unauthorized use by those to whom the secret has been confided under either express or implied restriction of nondisclosure or by one who has gained knowledge by improper means.

Id. at 629.

2. Restatement of Torts § 757

The definitional starting point of non-UTSA states, also known as Restatement states, are the definitions described in section 757 of the first Restatement of Torts. Comment b of the Restatement of Torts § 757 defines the meaning of a trade secret:

b. *Definition of trade secret.* A trade secret may consist of any formula, pattern, device or compilation of information which is used in one's business, and which gives him an opportunity to obtain an advantage over competitors who do not know or use it. It may be a formula for a chemical compound, a process of manufacturing, treating or preserving materials, a pattern for a machine or other device, or a list of customers. It differs from other secret information in a business (see § 759) in that it is not simply information as to single or ephemeral events in the conduct of the business, as, for example, the amount or other terms of a secret bid for a contract or the salary of certain employees, or the security investments made or contemplated, or the date fixed for the announcement of a new policy or for bringing out a new model or the like. A trade secret is a process or device for continuous use in the operation of the business. Generally it relates to the production of goods, as, for example, a machine or formula for the production of an article. It may, however, relate to the sale of goods or to other operations in the business, such as a code for determining discounts, rebates or other concessions in a price list or catalogue, or a list of specialized customers, or a method of bookkeeping or other office management.

Restatement of Torts § 757, cmt. b (1939).

The second edition of the Restatement of Torts intentionally omits the subject matter of § 757, reserving the topic instead for the Restatement of Unfair Competition §§ 38–49 (1995). Despite the widespread adoption of the Uniform Trade Secrets Act (UTSA), portions of § 757 of the Restatement (First) of Torts have been cited approvingly in virtually every state, even non-Restatement states. This is especially true of *comment b*, which defines the meaning of a trade secret.

c. *Defenses to Misappropriation and Rights against Others*

Now that your company has a trade secret, what happens when you discover that someone else is using it? The answer varies, depending on how your competitor came by the information. Unlike patent infringement, trade secret misappropriation is not a strict liability claim: the rights you have, and the liability your competitor may be subject to, are contingent upon the source of the competitor's knowledge.

i. The Honest Discoverer

Looking again to the Uniform Trade Secrets Act, we see that § 1(2) defines "Misappropriation":

(2) "Misappropriation" means: (i) acquisition of a trade secret of another by a person who knows or has reason to know that the trade secret was acquired by improper means; or (ii) disclosure or use of a trade secret of another without express or implied consent by a person who (A) used improper means to acquire knowledge of the trade secret; or (B) at the time of disclosure or

use knew or had reason to know that his knowledge of the trade secret was
(I) derived from or through a person who has utilized improper means to
acquire it; (II) acquired under circumstances giving rise to a duty to maintain its secrecy or limit its use; or (III) derived from or through a person
who owed a duty to the person seeking relief to maintain its secrecy or limit
its use; or (C) before a material change of his position, knew or had reason
to know that it was a trade secret and that knowledge of it had been acquired
by accident or mistake.

Inherent in this definition, and every other similar definition, is the requirement
that the secret information be obtained by "improper means." The United States
Supreme Court addressed the issue of trade secret laws in 1974, in *Kewanee Oil Co.
v. Bicron Corp.*, 416 U.S. 470. The Court held that federal patent laws did not preempt state trade secret laws on products that would otherwise be patentable subject
matter. With respect to "improper means," the court noted that:

> The protection accorded the trade secret holder is against the disclosure
> or unauthorized use of the trade secret by those to whom the secret has
> been confided under the express or implied restriction of nondisclosure
> or nonuse. The law also protects the holder of a trade secret against dis-
> closure or use when the knowledge is gained, not by the owner's volition,
> but by some 'improper means,' Restatement of Torts § 757(a), which may
> include theft, wiretapping, or even aerial reconnaissance. A trade secret
> law, however, does not offer protection against discovery by fair and hon-
> est means, such as by independent invention, accidental disclosure, or by
> so-called reverse engineering, that is by starting with the known product
> and working backward to divine the process which aided in its develop-
> ment or manufacture.

Id. at 475–76.

Honest discovery is a complete defense to a claim of misappropriation of trade
secrets. A competitor may develop the secret through their own inventive efforts, or
through reverse engineering of a released product. This concept of free discoverabil-
ity justifies trade secret protection: a competitor may pay you to license your secret,
or may expend the effort to discover the secret for itself; neither side gains an unde-
served edge in either case.

Theoretical independent development, that is, the idea that a competitor *could have*
independently developed the secret itself, is not a defense to misappropriation. That
a product *could have been* reverse engineered does not excuse improper means of
acquiring secret information. *See e.g. Boeing Co. v. Sierracin Corp.*, 108 Wash. 2d 38
(1987) (disallowing the use of evidence showing the hypothetical ease of reverse
engineering).

ii. The Innocent Wrongful User

Returning to the UTSA definition of misappropriation, we see that the UTSA bans the use of a trade secret when the user "at the time of disclosure or use knew or had reason to know that his knowledge of the trade secret was (I) derived from or through a person who has utilized improper means to acquire it; (II) acquired under circumstances giving rise to a duty to maintain its secrecy or limit its use; or (III) derived from or through a person who owed a duty to the person seeking relief to maintain its secrecy or limit its use." This is a gap in the protections provided by trade secret laws: a company may innocently hire a competitor's former employee, and gain benefits from that employee's knowledge of the competitor's trade secrets, without being subject to liability for misappropriation (though the former employee may be). The Court of Appeals of New York phrased it as "the discoverer of a new process or trade secret . . . has no exclusive right to it against . . . one who in good faith acquires knowledge of it without breach of contract or of a confidential relationship with the discoverer." *Speedry Chem. Products, Inc. v. Carter's Ink Co.*, 306 F.2d 328 (2d Cir. 1962).

The cure to this problem is notice. Upon learning of innocent wrongful use, the trade secret holder should immediately notify the user. The original Restatement of Torts (1939) addressed the issue of notice:

> One who learns another's trade secret from a third person without notice that it is secret and that the third person's disclosure is a breach of his duty to the other, or who learns the secret through a mistake without notice of the secrecy and the mistake,
>
> (a) is not liable to the other for a disclosure or use of the secret prior to receipt of such notice, and
>
> (b) is liable to the other for a disclosure or use of the secret after the receipt of such notice, unless prior thereto he has in good faith paid value for the secret or has so changed his position that to subject him to liability would be inequitable.

Restatement of Torts, § 758 (1939).

Practitioners should be aware of variations in the "Uniform" Trade Secrets Act throughout jurisdictions. Many states, in adopting the UTSA, made slight alterations to better conform with their own case law, or with their jurisdiction's view of trade secrets. In Virginia, for example, the language addressing this particular issue differs from the UTSA: the UTSA defines misappropriation, in part, to mean disclosure or use by a person who "before a material change of his position, knew or had reason to know that it was a trade secret and that knowledge of it had been acquired by accident or mistake"; the Virginia Act excludes the "material change" language. Uniform Trade Secrets Act § 1(2); Va. Code Ann. § 59.1-336 (West); *see* Milton E. Babirak, Jr., *The Virginia Uniform Trade Secret Act: A Critical Summary of the Act and Case Law*, 5 Va. J.L. & Tech. 15, ¶¶ 21–24 (2000).

d. Trade Secrets versus Patent

i. Scope of Protection

According to the first edition of the Restatement of Torts, trade secrets protection is distinguished from patent protection in that: (1) the former does not require novelty from an inventor, (2) it does not grant exclusive protection to an inventor, and rather allows a list of complete defenses to alleged competitors, and (3) once an invention is publicly disclosed to the public domain in a fair means, any relief under the former is irreversibly vanished. On the other hand, as long as the information remains secret, an owner of trade secrets would be protected indefinitely.

> *Novelty and prior art.* A trade secret may be a device or process which is patentable; but it need not be that. . . . Novelty and invention are not requisite for a trade secret as they are for patentability. These requirements are essential to patentability because a patent protects against unlicensed use of the patented device or process even by one who discovers it properly through independent research. The patent monopoly is a reward to the inventor. But such is not the case with a trade secret. Its protection is not based on a policy of rewarding or otherwise encouraging the development of secret processes or devices. The protection is merely against breach of faith and reprehensible means of learning another's secret. For this limited protection it is not appropriate to require also the kind of novelty and invention which is a requisite of patentability. . . .

Restatement of Torts § 757, cmt. b (1939).

ii. Choice: Trade Secrets versus Patent

In cases where newly discovered information describes patentable subject matter, an inventor with the information generally has two options: (1) protecting it under the patent laws by obtaining a patent or (2) relying on trade secrets protection. Since the inventor cannot rely on both forms of protection for the same subject matter, he or she should make a choice. Revelation of an invention design through publication of a patent or its underlying patent application will terminate any trade secret rights, while use of a trade secret for more than the permissible statutory period of one year prior to application for a patent will bar any right to a patent. *See* Michael J. Hutter, *Trade Secret Misappropriation*, 1 W. NEW ENG. L. REV. 1, 4–5 (1978).

There are several factors worth considering in making a decision: whether the newly discovered information can satisfy patentability requirements; whether an issued patent can be successfully defended in an infringement action; the likelihood of the information being independently developed and in what length of time; and whether the potential benefits from perpetual trade secret protection would outweigh the benefits of a 20-year term of patent protection granted on the conditions of full disclosure and free use after the patent term expires.

When trade secret protection is chosen, an inventor or the inventor's assignee will need to bear ongoing burdens to avoid information disclosures leading to loss of such protection. Potentially costly measures for preventing unwanted trade secret disclosures may include physical protections against disclosures, contractual protections and related enforcement lawsuits, and trade secret misappropriation actions.

e. Trade Secrets Termination

Knowing the rights granted to the trade secrets owner, one might naturally ask how and when trade secrets terminate. It is a general rule that trade secrets and a relevant claim to its protection are no longer legally recognized when the information is publicly disclosed. However, there are exceptions.

i. Public Disclosure

In general, disclosing trade secrets to others with no indication of it being confidential in the course of business terminates its trade secret status. However, many courts consider the "extent of public disclosure" in determining if a trade secret has been lost through limited disclosures, particularly those made inadvertently. Michelle L. Evans, *Abandonment of a Trade Secret*, 100 AM. JUR. *Proof of Facts* 3d 195 (originally published in 2008). For example, inadvertent disclosure can occur through an employee's email. *Id.* Disclosure can also occur through publication on the Internet or by placing information in the trash. *Id.* Whether actions such as these are sufficient to terminate a trade secret's legal protection depends on whether the disclosures involved are likely to bring the information involved into further public distribution and access.

ii. Exceptions

(1). Contract

Where a trade secret is disclosed to a person pursuant to a contract under which he is obligated to pay royalties for using the trade secret, he is still obligated to pay the royalties even after the trade secret has entered the public domain so long as he is still using it. *See Warner-Lambert Pharm. Co. v. John J. Reynolds, Inc.*, 178 F. Supp. 655 (S.D.N.Y. 1959) [For more detailed discussion, *see* Chapter 5, Section B(2)].

(2). Confidential Disclosure

Some courts have held that where there is disclosure of a trade secret within the bounds of a confidential relationship, the future public disclosure of the trade secret will not terminate its trade secret status in relation to the confidential disclosure. The disclosee then as an "absolute . . . duty not to use or disclose the secret." Hutter, *supra*, at 24.

On the other hand, some courts have held that once publicly disclosed, all trade secrets are terminated, unless the parties are under a contract that stipulates otherwise. In case the disclosee has gained a competitive advantage such as "accelerated market entry," some courts have ordered damages to run after the disclosure to compensate the trade secret owner for any unfair advantage obtained by the other party. *Id.*

C. Criminal Protection for Trade Secrets

In addition to civil enforcement of trade secret ownership, there are criminal sanctions in place to prevent the misappropriation of trade secrets. These sanctions are divided between federal and state legislation.

1. Federal Protection

The Economic Espionage Act (EEA), enacted in 1996, was the first federal statute that explicitly protected trade secrets, criminalizing the misappropriation, attempted misappropriation, or conspiracy to misappropriate trade secrets. In 2016, Congress enacted the Defend Trade Secret Act (DTSA), which amended the EEA. However, the DTSA did not materially alter the criminal protection system established by the EEA.

a. Economic Espionage Act

The Economic Espionage Act (EEA), as amended by the Defend Trade Secret Act of 2016 (DTSA), 18 USCA §§ 1831–1839, makes it a crime to steal, attempt to steal, or conspire to steal trade secrets.

18 USCA § 1831 Economic Espionage

(a) In general. — Whoever, intending or knowing that the offense will benefitanyforeigngovernment,foreigninstrumentality,orforeignagent,knowingly—

(1) steals, or without authorization appropriates, takes, carries away, or conceals, or by fraud, artifice, or deception obtains a trade secret;

(2) without authorization copies, duplicates, sketches, draws, photographs, downloads, uploads, alters, destroys, photocopies, replicates, transmits, delivers, sends, mails, communicates, or conveys a trade secret;

(3) receives, buys, or possesses a trade secret, knowing the same to have been stolen or appropriated, obtained, or converted without authorization;

(4) attempts to commit any offense described in any of paragraphs (1) through (3); or

(5) conspires with one or more other persons to commit any offense described in any of paragraphs (1) through (3), and one or more of such persons do any act to effect the object of the conspiracy,

shall, except as provided in subsection (b), be fined not more than $5,000,000 or imprisoned not more than 15 years, or both.

(b) Organizations. — Any organization that commits any offense described in subsection (a) shall be fined not more than the greater of $10,000,000 or 3 times the value of the stolen trade secret to the organization, including expenses for research and design and other costs of reproducing the trade secret that the organization has thereby avoided.

Section 1832 is nearly identical to Section 1831, with somewhat reduced penalties for parties who are not acting as foreign agents. Section 1833 creates exceptions for law enforcement officials and whistle-blowers. Section 1834 addresses the forfeiture of any property derived from the theft of trade secrets. Section 1835 empowers the court to issue orders to preserve the confidentiality of trade secrets during prosecution. Section 1836 allows for civil actions. Section 1837 extends the Act to violations committed outside the United States (1) by a citizen or permanent resident alien, or an organization organized under U.S. or state laws, or (2) if an act in furtherance of the offense was committed in the United States. Section 1838 indicates that EEA does not preempt state law. Section 1839, as was noted earlier, is the definition section, which includes, among others, the EEA's definitions of "trade secret" and "misappropriation."

Notes & Questions

1. Foreign Industrial Espionage

The background of the prosecution in *United States v. Hailong et al.*[4] illustrates the potential force of the Economic Espionage Act in policing trade secret misuse. In December 2013, Mo Hailong and several alleged co-conspirators were charged with stealing highly valuable genetically-modified corn seeds and attempting to ship the seeds back to China, where the seeds presumably would be duplicated. The defendants were all Chinese citizens, residing in the United States or Canada with visitor visas or as lawful permanent residents. They were all employees of Beijing Dabeinong Technology Group and/or its subsidiaries Beijing Kings Nower S&T Co., Ltd. and Kings Nower North America Company.

---

4. *See* United States of America v. Li Shaoming, Mo Hailong, Wang Lei, Wang Hongwei, Ye Jian & Lin Yong, Indictment, 4:13-cr-00147 (S.D. Iowa Dec. 17, 2013), http://www.prevendra.com/wp-content/uploads/bsk-pdf-manager/6_Mo-et-al-Indictment-12-17-2013.pdf (last visited 1/3/2018). For further details on this case, *see* John Eligon & Patrick Zuo, *Designer Seed Thought to be Latest Target by Chinese*, N.Y. Times (Feb. 4, 2017), http://www.nytimes.com/2014/02/05/us/chinese-implicated-in-agricultural-espionage-efforts.html?_r=0 (last visited 12/28/2017); David Martin, *Watch: Unraveling The Great Chinese Corn Seed Spy Ring*, Al Jazeera America (Oct. 6, 2014, 1:00 PM), http://america.aljazeera.com/watch/shows/america-tonight/articles/2014/10/6/unraveling-the-greatchinesecornseedspyring.html (last visited 12/28/2017); Grant Rodgers, *Chinese Businessman Gets Deal In Seed Theft Case*, Des Moines Register (Jan. 27, 2016, 5:44 PM), https://www.desmoinesregister.com/story/news/crime-and-courts/2016/01/27/chinese-businessman-pleads-seed-theft-case/79428650/ (last visited 12/28/2017).

Because the hybrid and modified seeds involved were so difficult and expensive to create, companies possessing them protected them as embodiments of trade secrets. If these secrets were disclosed, competitors would have a tremendous advantage in that they could reproduce the seeds without any of the initial research and development cost needed to develop the seeds. The identified "victim" seed companies— Pioneer Hi-Bred (a wholly-owned subsidiary of DuPont), Monsanto, and LG Seeds—employed numerous methods to ensure that their seeds could not be stolen in any of these manners. By employing several layers of confidentiality and extensive surveillance and control, the seed companies worked to ensure that their trade secrets were protected from disclosure and misappropriation.

Despite these efforts, the defendants were allegedly able to steal seeds from each of the victim seed companies. The arrest of Mo Hailong and his sister Mo Yun, in July came at the end of an extensive FBI investigation. Surveillance of these individuals included tapping cellphone calls, planting audio recording devices in rental cars, and setting up a video camera over a storage unit used by Mo and the alleged accomplices. The investigation was launched after a seed company security officer approached Mo Hailong digging in the company's field. When the officer approached Mo, he claimed to be a university researcher then sped away in a car idling nearby that was driven by an alleged conspirator. Several of the defendants were similarly observed near a field of inbred corn seed in Iowa several months later.

In September 2011, Mo shipped a package reported to be corn samples to his residence in Florida. In May 2012, several of the defendants attempted to ship approximately 250 pounds of corn seed via Federal Express to Hong Kong. In the following months, the defendants collected numerous samples from seed company fields. Recorded conversations revealed that the defendants knew their actions were illegal and that they faced potentially serious consequences if caught. The defendants also attempted to fly with seeds in their checked luggage from Chicago to Beijing.

In January 2016, Mo Hailong pled guilty to one count of conspiracy to steal trade secrets.[5] Charges against Mo Yun were dismissed earlier in July 2015 upon the government's request after the district court excluded from evidence excerpts of electronic-message conversations on which prosecutors relied in their case against Ms. Mo.

The federal government has also investigated a similar case involving Chinese citizens stealing agricultural trade secrets related to genetically modified rice in Kansas. In that case, a federal jury convicted Weiqiang Zhang, a Chinese national, of conspiring to steal samples of a variety of rice seeds from a Kansas biopharmaceutical research facility.[6] A doctoral graduate of Louisiana State University, Zhang worked

---

5. *See* Plea Agreement, United States v. Mo, Case No 4:13-cr-00147-SMR-CFB (filed Jan. 27, 2016), https://www.justice.gov/opa/file/816096/download.

6. *See* Press Release No 17-192, Department of Justice, Office of Public Affairs, Kansas Agricultural Scientist Convicted in Theft of Engineered Rice (Feb. 16, 2017), https://www.justice.gov/opa/pr/kansas-agricultural-scientist-convicted-theft-engineered-rice; *China scientist convicted in U.S.*

as a rice breeder for Ventria Bioscience Inc., which developed genetically programmed rice. According to trial evidence, he acquired without authorization hundreds of rice seeds produced by Ventria and stored them at his residence. Then, Zhang transferred the seeds to visiting personnel from a crop research institute in China who later attempted to transport them to China.

In yet another foreign espionage case, in May 2017, seven defendants were charged in the U.S. District Court for the District of Columbia with conspiracy to commit theft of trade secrets from an unnamed multinational company with a subsidiary in Houston on behalf of a Chinese manufacturer.[7] Among the defendants were four U.S. citizens, one Canadian citizen residing in Texas, one Chinese national residing in Texas as a permanent resident, and one Chinese citizen living in China. The technology alleged to have been stolen relates to a product called syntactic foam, "a strong, light material that can be tailored for commercial and military uses, such as oil exploration; aerospace; underwater vehicles, such as submarines; and stealth technology." According to the affidavit filed in support of the criminal complaint, the Chinese manufacturer intended to sell syntactic foam to both military and civilian, state-owned enterprises in China.

These high-profile cases lead scholars and law enforcement officials to believe there is a growing trend in foreign trade secret espionage.

2. Critical Commentary

The passage of the EEA drew a significant amount of controversy, both for potential vagaries in the language and to criticize the intent behind the Act. Some scholars had concerns with how various portions of the Act were going to be implemented by the Department of Justice, as well as with how various terms would be interpreted by courts. *See* John R. Bauer et al., *Criminalization of Trade Secret Theft: On the Second Anniversary of the Economic Espionage Act*, 8-SUM CURRENTS: INT'L TRADE L.J. 59 (1999).

Other scholars were less concerned with the wording than with the purpose of the Act. Professor Rochelle Dreyfuss criticized the Act by noting that "something seems to have gone awry in the intellectual property bargain," in that companies were gaining more tools for the acquisition of exclusive rights in information that is not new.

> One alternative available to Congress was to use its Commerce Clause author-
> ity to criminalize violations of state civil law: that is, to create criminal liability
> for committing the tort of misappropriation as defined by state law. Perhaps

---

of theft of engineered rice, REUTERS (Feb. 16, 2017, 4:19 PM), https://www.reuters.com/article/us -usa-justice-rice/china-scientist-convicted-in-u-s-of-theft-of-engineered-rice-idUSKBN15V2W0.

7. *See* Press Release No 17-116, Department of Justice, U.S. Attorney's Office for the District of Columbia, Seven People Charged With Conspiring to Steal Trade Secrets For Benefit of Chinese Manufacturing Company (May 24, 2017), https://www.justice.gov/usao-dc/pr/seven-people-charged -conspiring-steal-trade-secrets-benefit-chinese-manufacturing-company.

that is what the EEA was intended to do, but that conclusion is by no means clear. On the one hand, the EEA appears to track the subject matter definitions of state law, and to prohibit "unauthorized appropriation"—a term not too different from the familiar "misappropriation" of state law. At the same time, however, the statute departs from state trade secrecy law in several important respects. Its definition of unauthorized appropriation is different from that found in the states. The statute also includes state-of-mind elements, including the intent to benefit another entity and to deprive the "owner" of the secret's value, which are unknown to state causes of action—as, indeed, is the concept of owner, as opposed to rights holder. Finally, the statute creates rights against interceptions that occur outside the United States, which state laws could probably never reach, and—given its criminal nature—also departs from state legislation by substituting punishment for remedial action.

The result is something of a mongrel. The EEA's many novel provisions will provide courts with difficult questions to resolve, but since the Act is not based on federal intellectual property law, federal criminal law, or state intellectual property law, it is difficult to predict what case law and traditions courts will draw upon in resolving them.

Rochelle Cooper Dreyfuss, *Trade Secrets: How Well Should We Be Allowed to Hide Them? The Economic Espionage Act of 1996*, 9 Fordham Intell. Prop. Media & Ent. L.J. 1, 7–8 (1998). These debates persisted as Congress amended the EEA in 2016 to expand the scope of federal trade secret protection to civil actions.

b. Actual Theft of Trade Secrets

United States v. Lange

United States Court of Appeals for the Seventh Circuit

312 F.3d 263 (7th Cir. 2002)

Easterbrook, Circuit Judge.

[Matthew Lange was convicted of violating 18 USCA § 1832, for stealing trade secrets from his former employer, RAPCO, and attempting to sell them to a competitor. Lange denied the data met the statutory definition of a "trade secret."]

RAPCO is in the business of making aircraft parts for the aftermarket. It buys original equipment parts, then disassembles them to identify (and measure) each component. This initial step of reverse engineering, usually performed by a drafter such as Lange, produces a set of measurements and drawings. Because this case involves an effort to sell the intellectual property used to make a brake assembly, we use brakes as an illustration.

Knowing exactly what a brake assembly looks like does not enable RAPCO to make a copy. It must figure out how to make a substitute with the same (or better) technical specifications. Brakes rely on friction to slow the airplane's speed by converting kinetic energy to heat. Surfaces that do this job well are made by sintering—the forming of solid metal, usually from a powder, without melting. Aftermarket manufacturers must experiment with different alloys and compositions until they achieve a process and product that fulfills requirements set by the Federal Aviation Administration for each brake assembly. Completed assemblies must be exhaustively tested to demonstrate, to the FAA's satisfaction, that all requirements have been met; only then does the FAA certify the part for sale. For brakes this entails 100 destructive tests on prototypes, bringing a spinning 60-ton wheel to a halt at a specified deceleration measured by a dynamometer. Further testing of finished assemblies is required. It takes RAPCO a year or two to design, and obtain approval for, a complex part; the dynamometer testing alone can cost $75,000. But the process of experimenting and testing can be avoided if the manufacturer demonstrates that its parts are identical (in composition and manufacturing processes) to parts that have already been certified. What Lange, a disgruntled former employee, offered for sale was all the information required to obtain certification of several components as identical to parts for which RAPCO held certification. Lange included with the package—which he offered via the Internet to anyone willing to pay his price of $100,000—a pirated copy of AutoCAD®, the computer-assisted drawing software that RAPCO uses to maintain its drawings and specifications data. One person to whom Lange tried to peddle the data informed RAPCO, which turned to the FBI. Lange was arrested following taped negotiations that supply all the evidence necessary for conviction—if the data satisfy the statutory definition of trade secrets.

[The court considered Lange's argument that RAPCO did not take "reasonable measures to keep such information secret," and rejected it. RAPCO stored all of its drawings and data in a locked, alarmed room, and the number of copies was kept minimal. Some of the information was coded, with few people knowing the codes, and all documents carried warnings of RAPCO's intellectual property rights. RAPCO also split work among subcontractors, to ensure that no subcontractor could replicate their product.]

The second ingredient is that "the information derives independent economic value, actual or potential, from not being generally known to, and not being readily ascertainable through proper means by, the public[.]" According to Lange, all data obtained by reverse engineering some other product are "readily ascertainable . . . by the public" because everyone can do what RAPCO did: buy an original part, disassemble and measure it, and make a copy. The prosecutor responds to this contention by observing that "the public" is unable to reverse engineer an aircraft brake assembly.

[The court examined the usage of the word "public" in § 1839(3), as discussed earlier in the chapter. The discussion has less relevance after the Defend Trade Secret Act of 2016, which amended § 1839(3) replacing the word "public" with the words "another person who can obtain economic value from the disclosure or use of the information."]

Thus it is unnecessary here to decide whether "general" belongs in front of "public" — for even if it does, the economically valuable information is not "readily ascertainable" to the general public, the educated public, the economically relevant public, or any sensible proxy for these groups.

Another line of prosecutorial argument starts with the fact that § 1832(a)(4) makes it a crime to attempt to sell trade secrets without the owner's permission. Even if Lange did not have real trade secrets in his possession, the argument goes, he thought he did and therefore may be penalized for an attempted sale. The argument finds support in [*United States v. Hsu*, 155 F.3d 189 (3rd Cir. 1998)], which held that in order to avoid graymail — the threat that to obtain a conviction the prosecutor must disclose the secret by putting it in the trial record — a case may be based on § 1832(a)(4) without disclosing all details of the trade secret. We agree with the general approach of these decisions. *Hsu* analogized the attempted sale of information believed to be a trade secret to an attempt such as shooting a corpse, believing it to be alive, or selling sugar, believing it to be cocaine. Events of this sort underlie the maxim that factual impossibility is no defense to a prosecution for attempt. This does not mean, however, that the defendant's belief alone can support a conviction. All attempt prosecutions depend on demonstrating that the defendant took a substantial step toward completion of the offense, which could have been carried out unless thwarted. Although the American Law Institute recommends a definition of attempt linked closely to intent, the Supreme Court has not embraced this view and demands in cases under federal law that the prosecutor establish a probability of success. *See, e.g., Spectrum Sports, Inc. v. McQuillan*, 506 U.S. 447, 113 S. Ct. 884 (1993) ("dangerous probability" of success is an ingredient of attempted monopolization).

An attempted murder may be thwarted by substituting a sack of flour for the intended victim; a sale of drugs may be thwarted by substituting sugar for cocaine, or rock candy for crack. These situations present a good chance of success, but for the intervention. So does "the disgruntled former employee who walks out of his former company with a computer diskette full of engineering schematics" (*Hsu*, 155 F.3d at 201) — a fair description of Lange's conduct (though diskettes are obsolete). A sale of trade secrets may be thwarted by substituting a disk with the collected works of Shakespeare for the disk that the defendant believed contained the plans for brake assemblies, or by an inadvertent failure to download the proper file. The attempted sale of the disk is a culpable substantial step. But it is far less clear that sale of information already known to the public could be deemed a substantial step toward the offense, just because the defendant is deluded and does not understand what a trade secret is. Selling a copy of Zen and the Art of Motorcycle Maintenance is not attempted economic espionage, even if the defendant thinks that the tips in the book are trade secrets; nor is sticking pins in voodoo dolls attempted murder. Booksellers and practitioners of the occult pose no social dangers, certainly none of the magnitude of those who are tricked into shooting bags of sand that have been substituted for targets of assassination. Lange was more dangerous than our bookseller but much less dangerous than our hypothetical assassin. Perhaps data purloined from an ex-employer is sufficiently likely to contain trade secrets to justify calling the preparation for sale a substantial step toward completion of the offense, and thus a culpable attempt, even if the employee stole the wrong data file and did not get his hands on the commercially valuable information. We need not pursue the subject beyond noting the plausibility of the claim and its sensitivity to the facts—what kind of data did the employee think he stole, and so on. For it is not necessary to announce a definitive rule about how dangerous the completed acts must be in trade secret cases: the judge was entitled to (and did) find that Lange had real trade secrets in his possession.

Lange wants us to proceed as if all he tried to sell were measurements that anyone could have taken with calipers after disassembling an original-equipment part. Such measurements could not be called trade secrets if, as Lange asserts, the assemblies in question were easy to take apart and measure. But no one would have paid $100,000 for metes and bounds, while Lange told his customers that the data on offer were worth more than that asking price. Which they were. What Lange had, and tried to sell, were the completed specifications and engineering diagrams that reflected all the work completed after the measurements had been taken: the metallurgical data, details of the sintering, the results of the tests, the plans needed to produce the finished goods, everything required to get FAA certification of a part supposedly identical to one that had been approved. Those details "derive[d] independent economic value, actual or potential, from not being generally known to, and not being readily ascertainable through proper means by, the public[.]" Every firm other than the original equipment manufacturer and RAPCO had to pay dearly to devise, test, and win approval of similar parts; the details unknown to the rivals, and not discoverable with tape measures, had considerable "independent economic value . . . from not being generally known." A sensible trier of fact could determine that Lange tried to sell trade secrets. It was his customer's cooperation with the FBI, and not public access to the data, that prevented closing of the sale.

. . . .

Affirmed.

c. Conspiracy to Steal Trade Secrets

United States v. Martin

United States Court of Appeals for the First Circuit

228 F.3d 1 (1st Cir. 2000)

Torruella, Chief Judge.

[Dr. Stephen R. Martin and Caryn L. Camp were charged with ten counts of wire fraud, two counts of mail fraud, one count of conspiracy to steal trade secrets, one count of conspiracy to transport stolen goods, and one count of interstate transportation of stolen goods. Camp testified against Martin, and Martin was convicted on four counts of wire fraud, two counts of mail fraud, conspiracy to steal trade secrets, and conspiracy to transport stolen property in interstate commerce. The appeal challenged the sufficiency of the evidence.

Martin was a scientist. At the time he and Camp first came into contact, Martin was developing a company called "WDV." Sometime after they began conversing, Martin went to "Maverck." Camp was a chemist with IDEXX, which manufactured veterinary products. Martin had approached IDEXX previously with a proposal for research into HIV and feline immunodeficiency virus (FIV), which they rejected. As part of her employment, Camp had signed non-competition and non-disclosure agreements.

Camp found Martin in January, 1998, after becoming dissatisfied with her job. They began to correspond, first regarding the possibility of Camp working for WDV (and later Maverck), and then as pen-pals. During the course of this correspondence, Camp let slip minor confidential details of her work at IDEXX.]

. . . .

II. Events Between May 1, 1998 and July 18, 1998

The government's first six counts of wire fraud, on which Martin was acquitted, stem from correspondence occurring prior to July 18, 1998. One count of mail fraud, on which Martin was convicted, also stems from this period.

A. Martin's Initial Requests

On May 1, in response to Camp's lengthy e-mail detailing her trip, Martin made his first explicit request for information, asking for "any info . . . on the HOT topics in veterinary diagnostics." Martin renewed his request in a May 3 e-mail in which he asked a number of questions about IDEXX prices, test composition, and test use. In a subsequent message, Martin outlined his ability to avoid patent infringement with IDEXX and noted that "IDEXX is going to be in trouble very soon." On May 3, Camp responded with answers to most of Martin's questions. Attached was a letter detailing problems with a particular IDEXX product. In reference to a previous discussion about flying planes, Martin began to refer to Camp as "Ace," a moniker which would become "Agent Ace" as their "spy" business heated up.

B. Camp's Responses

On May 4, Camp wrote concerning IDEXX's legal problems. She also included "lots & lots of goodies for your next rainy day," including internal memoranda. Camp noted that the internal memoranda may have been confidential. "I feel like a spy," she commented. In a letter the next day, Camp regretted her actions, promising to "be good . . . and send no more dirty secrets from Idexx. . . ." Martin responded, claiming that he did "not want to know anything confidential about IDEXX," and asking only for "public information."

Despite Camp's repentance and Martin's denial of any desire for confidential or proprietary information, Camp continued to assemble and pass on information, an activity which she apparently viewed as ethically suspect.[2] Camp also relayed information on IDEXX's strategic plans, including a potential partnership with a company whose name, at least, was confidential. By late June, Camp appeared set on leaving IDEXX, as she commented that "I need to unload all of my stock options." Furthermore, Camp had received (and ignored) reminders of her non-compete and non-disclosure agreements; she forwarded these reminders to Martin, noting that "as a spy myself, I get a particular chuckle out of [them]," and that "my loyalty has ended." Camp and Martin began to formalize their plans for meeting at Lake Tahoe in early August, as well as for Camp's eventual move to Nevada.

. . . .

E. The First Package

On July 12, Camp sent Martin a large package of information via Priority Mail, including various devices, product inserts, USDA course materials, information on her own projects, miscellaneous IDEXX product information, and "Examples of My Work," labeled "Confidential." Camp also promised to send an actual test kit, if Martin wished. The mailing and receipt of this package formed the basis of a mail fraud charge, of which Martin was ultimately convicted. After receiving the package, Martin once more praised Camp's aggressiveness, encouraged her to "keep on charging," to "keep on thinking about the competition, and how we can beat them," and promised that "lips are sealed."

III. Events Between July 19, 1998 to August 16, 1998

Correspondence during the next several weeks provided the basis for Martin's conviction on four counts of wire fraud.

A. More Questions and Answers

In several e-mails between July 19 and July 21, Camp outlined a proposal for customer-friendly additions and modifications to current IDEXX technology. Martin explained how such a test might be constructed, telling Camp that if it could be marketed successfully, she would receive "enough bonus money to buy [a] house for cash." Camp clearly understood that the proposal was for technology competitive with that of IDEXX, as she suggested the possibility that "[she and Martin would] own the whole market."

Camp's proposal also prompted Martin to ask about the relevance and applicability of x-Chek or similar software. Camp offered to send Martin a copy of the

---

2. Camp's May 7 e-mail noted that "the fun part of my week has been putting together packages of information for you . . ." and celebrated "the intrigue of being Agent Ace." On June 22, she "couldn't resist playing Ace-the-Spy today . . . and so I am dropping a few more things in the mail." But her fun did not come without guilt: "I know I should be shot. But I just can't resist sending you this chain of internal Idexx e-mails regarding concern of a certain competitor;" "I am probably crossing the line with this [but] I've crossed lines worse than this one." However, Camp re-assured herself that she was doing nothing wrong, that she was forwarding "nothing proprietary" but simply the "dirty secrets of an IDEXX Livestock and Poultry weekly meeting."

software IDEXX had developed for poultry and livestock testing. Martin responded the same day, writing that "he would like to play with the software you mentioned." Camp immediately replied, promising "lots of cool goodies," including the x-Chek disks. Camp also indicated that she was on the verge of "cleaning out her office" and leaving IDEXX; however, she noted that she was speaking to headhunters in addition to Martin.

Martin's response to this last message re-affirmed his intention to compete with IDEXX. Moreover, Martin acknowledged Camp's potentially illicit activity, and exhorted her to continue in her final few days at work. "Before you bag IDEXX (I am embarrassed to ask this), absorb as much information, physically and intellectually, as you can. I never had a spy before." Camp's answer bemoaned the constraints on her information gathering (because co-workers knew she was preparing to leave), detailed her continued efforts to take home both information and property, and admitted the illegality (or at least inappropriateness) of her actions. However, Camp noted that she had as of yet been unwilling to copy "confidential" documents, although she admitted that she had copied "semi-confidential" internal e-mail. The next day, Camp promised to send Martin additional kits as her last "secret agent" act.

B. The Second Package

In Camp's last several days at IDEXX, she continued to collect products and information, which she forwarded to Martin on July 24. The package included operating manuals, IDEXX marketing materials, research and development data, a sales binder prepared by an independent contractor, as well as a binder labeled "Competition."

C. Found Out

Unfortunately for Camp and Martin, Camp inadvertently sent her July 25 e-mail (acknowledging that July 24 was her last day and detailing the contents of her second package) to John Lawrence, the global marketing manager for Poultry/Livestock at IDEXX. Camp informed Martin of what she had done, and continued on her vacation. According to Camp, Martin later recommended that she lie to IDEXX, i.e., that she tell them that he was interested only in limited information unrelated to IDEXX core businesses. Upon her return to Maine, Camp was intercepted and interviewed by an FBI agent at the Portland airport. An August 9, 1998 search of Martin's home found the contents of Camp's second package, including the x-Chek software.

Discussion

. . . .

II. Conspiracy to Steal Trade Secrets

The jury found Martin guilty of count 13, which charged him with conspiracy to steal trade secrets in violation of the Economic Espionage Act of 1996, specifically 18 U.S.C. § 1832(a)(5). In order to find a defendant guilty of conspiracy, the prosecution must prove (1) that an agreement existed, (2) that it had an unlawful purpose, and (3) that the defendant was a voluntary participant. The government must prove that the defendant possessed both the intent to agree and the intent to commit the substantive offense. In addition, the government must prove that at least one conspirator committed an "overt act," that is, took an affirmative step toward achieving the conspiracy's purpose.

The agreement need not be express, however, as long as its existence may be inferred from the defendants' words and actions and the interdependence of activities and persons involved. A so-called "tacit" agreement will suffice. Moreover, the conspirators need not succeed in completing the underlying act, nor need that underlying act even be factually possible.

As of yet, only the Third Circuit has had the opportunity to address § 1832(a), which specifically covers private corporate espionage. See *United States v. Hsu*, 155 F.3d 189 (3d Cir. 1998). The statute criminalizes the knowing theft of trade secrets, as well as attempts or conspiracies to steal trade secrets. The Act defines a "trade secret" broadly, to include both tangible property and intangible information, as long as the owner "has taken reasonable measures to keep such information secret" and the information "derives independent economic value . . . from not being generally known to . . . the public." 18 U.S.C. § 1839(3). This definition of trade secret "protects a wider variety" of information than most civil laws; however, "it is clear that Congress did not intend . . . to prohibit lawful competition such as the use of general skills or parallel development of a similar product," *Hsu*, 155 F.3d at 196–97, although it did mean to punish "the disgruntled former employee who walks out of his former company with a computer diskette full of engineering schematics," *id.* at 201. In other words, § 1832(a) was not designed to punish competition, even when such competition relies on the know-how of former employees of a direct competitor. It was, however, designed to prevent those employees (and their future employers) from taking advantage of confidential information gained, discovered, copied, or taken while employed elsewhere.

Martin contends that the evidence is factually insufficient to establish a "meeting of the minds" or agreement to violate § 1832(a), because (1) insufficient evidence exists to establish an agreement between Martin and Camp; (2) insufficient evidence exists to prove that Martin had the necessary intent to commit an act prohibited by § 1832(a), i.e., injure the owner of the trade secret (IDEXX); and (3) the information provided by Camp to Martin did not meet the statutory definition of a trade secret under § 1839(3). As we explain below, none of these arguments are persuasive.

First, the evidence is sufficient for a reasonable jury to conclude that Martin and Camp formed an agreement regarding the theft of trade secrets. Martin's argument against the existence of an agreement relies on the facts that (a) his early e-mails specifically requested that Camp not send him confidential information, and (b) Camp did not seem to know the distinction between confidential information, proprietary information, and office gossip. However, while Martin's disclaimer and Camp's confusion indicate the lack of an explicit agreement at that time, they do not necessarily negate the existence of an agreement. A rational jury could have plausibly concluded on the basis of the evidence presented at trial that an agreement existed. By July 21, Martin had received extensive correspondence from Camp that she had either marked "confidential" or "proprietary," or had expressed some hesitation in forwarding.[8] Despite his previous protestations that he wanted nothing to do with IDEXX or its confidential information, Martin asked Camp on July 21 to "absorb as much information, physically and intellectually, as you can," and included a set of questions to direct Camp's research. Throughout June and July, Martin referred to Camp as "Agent Ace," or as his "spy." Given the type of information that Martin had already received, a reasonable jury could have concluded that, whatever Martin's original intentions, as of July 21, Camp and Martin had reached a tacit agreement by which she would send him items and information that potentially fell under the trade secret definition of 18 U.S.C. § 1839(3). In other words, sufficient evidence exists to show an agreement between Camp and Martin to violate § 1832(a).

Second, the evidence is sufficient to show that Martin intended to injure IDEXX by obtaining IDEXX trade secrets and competing against IDEXX. Although Martin consistently claimed that he had no interest in developing products that competed with IDEXX, and hence had no intention of injuring IDEXX economically, his correspondence with Camp detailed a plan of competition. Martin had, among other things, considered the possibility of starting a competing veterinary lab, and had asked Camp to think, in particular, about ways to compete with tests that IDEXX manufactured. A reasonable jury could have found that Martin intended to use the information gained from Camp, particularly information on IDEXX's costs and customer dissatisfaction with IDEXX, to create a more successful competitor with greater capability to injure IDEXX.

Third, Martin's final argument—that he actually received no trade secrets—even if true, is irrelevant. Martin has only been found guilty of a conspiracy to steal trade secrets, rather than the underlying offense. The relevant question to determine whether a conspiracy existed was whether Martin intended to violate the statute. *See Hsu*, 155 F.3d at 198 ("[T]he crimes charged—attempt and conspiracy—do not require proof of the existence of an actual trade secret, but, rather, proof only of one's attempt or conspiracy with intent to steal a trade secret."). The key question is whether Martin intended to steal trade secrets. A rational jury, considering the information Camp had already sent Martin, could have concluded that his further queries indicated such an intention.

A reasonable jury could therefore have concluded that Martin and Camp formed an agreement by which Camp conveyed information and property to Martin that potentially fell under the definition of a trade secret in 18 U.S.C. § 1839. As a result, sufficient evidence existed to convict Martin of conspiracy to steal trade secrets.

---

8. Some of the information Martin received in their early correspondence clearly had the potential to fall within the § 1839 definition of trade secret: for example, cost information unavailable to the public included in Camp's message of May 2, a confidential IDEXX business plan included in Camp's June 8 message, and a customer list included in Camp's July 1 message.

Conclusion

A careful reading of the seven-month e-mail communication between Dr. Stephen Martin and Caryn Camp could lead to the conclusion Martin and his counsel urge— that this is simply a pen-pal relationship between a lonely Maine lab technician and a reclusive California scientist. However, the evidence could also lead a reader to the conclusion that something far more sinister was afoot: that an originally harmless communication mushroomed into a conspiracy to steal trade secrets and transport stolen property interstate, and that the electronic mail and U.S. mails were used to further a scheme to defraud IDEXX. Because we find there was sufficient evidence for a reasonable jury to conclude the latter beyond any reasonable doubt, we AFFIRM the defendant's conviction on all counts.

d. Disputes over Jury Instructions

United States v. Liew

United States Court of Appeals for the Ninth Circuit

228 F.3d 1 (9th Cir. 2017)

Owens, Circuit Judge:

Defendants Walter Liew and his company USA Performance Technology, Inc. ("USAPTI") appeal from their eight counts of conviction under the Economic Espionage Act of 1996 ("EEA") for conspiracy and attempt to commit economic espionage and theft of trade secrets, possession of misappropriated trade secrets, and conveying trade secrets related to E.I. du Pont de Nemours and Company ("DuPont") chloride-route technology for producing titanium dioxide ("TiO2")....

[In the early 1990s, Liew met with a high-ranking Chinese official who informed him that the development of chloride-route titanium dioxide (TiO2) technology was one of the priorities of the Chinese government. TiO2 is a commercially valuable white pigment with numerous uses, including coloring paint, plastics, and paper. Liew, aware that DuPont had owned a superior TiO2 production technology, solicited former DuPont employees, Robert Maegerle and Tim Spitler, to assist him in his efforts to convey DuPont's TiO2 technology to Chinese companies. Liew, Spitler, Maegerle, and USAPTI used DuPont's TiO2 trade secrets in building TiO2 chloride facilities for Pangang Group companies in China. Upon discovery of trade secret misappropriation, DuPont filed a civil suit against Liew and USAPTI. Meanwhile, the FBI began its investigation which became the ground for the final indictment in March 2013.

Liew, USAPTI, and Maegerle went to trial and were convicted. Spitler who was indicted separately was scheduled to enter a guilty plea to similar charges but committed suicide the week that he was scheduled to sign the plea agreement. Liew's convictions included tempering with a witness and evidence and obstructing justice, but they were reversed by the appellate court. Finally, in his appeal Liew accused FBI of not disclosing *Brady* materials, and the court of appeals remanded to the district court for in camera review of the material "to determine whether disclosure of the notes might have affected the outcome of the trial." This excerpt, however, focuses on the appellant's arguments concerning jury instructions.]

B. Jury Instructions

Defendants challenge (1) the district court's given instruction regarding compilations, and (2) its rejection of defendants' proposed instructions. For the first time on appeal, defendants argue that the compilation instruction was erroneous because it omitted reference to a "limiting principle" they take from a statement in *UniRAM Tech., Inc. v. Taiwan Semiconductor Mfg. Co.*, 617 F. Supp. 2d 938, 942–44 (N.D. Cal. 2007), that a compilation cannot constitute a trade secret if "one skilled in the art could view the nonsecret elements and replicate the combination without undue difficulty." This argument was never made to the district court; however, it essentially mirrors defendants' argument that the court improperly excluded their proposed instructions, as does defendants' contention that the error in giving the compilation instruction was compounded by the omission of the other instructions. Those contentions will be addressed below.

With respect to the given compilation instruction, defendants fail to show that the instruction was incorrect, misleading, or inadequate. Defendants' argument that the instruction would allow the jury to think "that nearly anything can be a trade secret," is defeated by the plain language of the instruction, which requires that any compilation meet the requirements of the trade secret definition to be deemed a trade secret. Defendants do not dispute this statement of law, and in fact suggested language that was used verbatim by the district court in this instruction. Accordingly, the district court did not err in giving the compilation instruction.

The real dispute is whether the district court erred in excluding defendants' proposed instructions, particularly the combination of the reverse engineering and general knowledge instructions. "A defendant is entitled to have the judge instruct the jury on his theory of defense, provided that it is supported by law and has some foundation in the evidence," but a defendant is "not entitled to the instructions of his choice." On appeal, the defendant must show: "(1) that his theory has some foundation in evidence; (2) that it is supported by law; and (3) that the given instructions did not adequately encompass his theory." Defendants challenge the rejection of three proposed instructions but treat them as two issues.

The first issue is the public disclosure instruction, the omission of which defendants argue could have led the jury to believe that information published in a patent or "obscure trade publication" would not qualify as being "generally known to the public." As the government argues, although defendants' proposed instruction was legally correct, it was superfluous, as the given instructions adequately covered this issue by informing the jury that generally known or readily ascertainable information could not qualify as trade secret material.

Moreover, it was undisputed at trial that disclosure in patents and textbooks would destroy trade secret protection, with the government acknowledging during closing arguments that both patents and textbooks are "publicly available." Instead, the dispute at trial was whether the material available in TiO2-related patents and textbooks was the same material DuPont claimed as its trade secrets and whether the information in those patents and textbooks would enable an individual to design a TiO2 chloride-route plant. For example, the government argued that "[t]he [necessary] information is not in textbooks" and that "textbooks and patents . . . don't help you design a titanium dioxide plant." Accordingly, the issue of whether patents and textbooks are generally known to the public was not contested and was adequately covered by the given instruction.

Defendants further argue, without citing any authority, that it was error not to instruct the jury that disclosure "to even a single recipient who is not legally bound to maintain [a trade secret's] secrecy" destroys trade secret protection because, absent such instruction, the government was able to argue that the Antioch/Ashtabula technology remained a trade secret. To the extent that defendants now argue that the district court should have given an additional disclosure instruction stating that disclosure to a single competitor destroys trade secret protection, this claim is subject to plain error review. This omission did not constitute plain error, because under the EEA's then-current definition of trade secrets, it was not "clear" or "obvious" that disclosure to a single competitor made information "generally known to" or "readily ascertainable" by "the public." *Chung*, 659 F.3d at 824–25 (quoting 18 U.S.C. § 1839(3) (2011)) (stating that "[t]here is some conflict between circuits as to whether [the EEA's definition] alters the 'readily ascertainable' analysis" as compared to the UTSA and declining to resolve the issue); see also *Walls*, 784 F.3d at 546 (under plain error standard of review, the error must be "clear or obvious, rather than subject to reasonable dispute").

Defendants' reliance on *Ruckelshaus v. Monsanto Co.*, 467 U.S. 986 (1984), does not change this result. Defendants contend that under *Monsanto*, DuPont's sale of the Ashtabula plant destroyed the trade secret status of its chloride-route technology, and the jury should have been instructed accordingly. *Monsanto* does not speak to when a trade secret becomes "generally known to" or "readily ascertainable" by "the public" according to the EEA. Instead, *Monsanto* establishes that trade secrets are property for the purposes of the Takings Clause of the Fifth Amendment but that a taking does not occur when a party discloses its trade secrets to the Environmental Protection Agency ("EPA") knowing that the EPA can use that information without permission after ten years, because such use does not interfere with the party's "reasonable investment-backed expectations." Monsanto therefore does not speak to the specific issue of whether disclosure to one competitor makes information generally known under the EEA, and defendants cite no authority suggesting otherwise. Without any clear or controlling authority addressing this question, the district court's omission of an additional disclosure instruction did not constitute plain error.

The second issue is the district court's rejection of the reverse engineering and general knowledge instructions, which defendants argue would have permitted the jury to find that Maegerle permissibly "work[ed] back" from non-secret Ashtabula technology and could have made fair use of the "general knowledge" he gained through his employment at DuPont to replicate the TiO2 technology, including "all the information and experience involved in building the Kuan Yin plant." The parties' arguments on this point are primarily ones regarding the sufficiency of the evidence supporting defendants' trade secret convictions and therefore overlook the only relevant question: whether the given instructions adequately covered the defense theory. They did. The instructions told the jury that individuals can independently develop technology through proper means and that someone like Maegerle is free to leave an employer and use non-trade secret information and skills gained through that employment. The given instructions as a whole were neither "misleading [n]or inadequate to guide the jury's deliberation."

Accordingly, the district court's rulings on these jury instructions are affirmed.

C. Conspiracy and Attempt Instructions

Defendants contend that the district court's given instructions regarding the conspiracy and attempt charges — Counts 1, 2, 3, and 5 — constructively amended the indictment and erroneously allowed the jury to convict on those charges without finding that the trade secrets involved were in fact trade secrets. Defendants waived their right to have this argument reviewed, as they were aware of the case law they now seek to distinguish or rely on, but they nonetheless agreed to the given instructions. Because defendants were "aware of the omitted element" in the instructions (the purported requirement that the trade secret status be proven), they "relinquished [their] right to have it submitted to the jury."

Even if this issue were reviewable, an intervening Ninth Circuit decision resolved it. While this appeal was being briefed, we issued our decision in *United States v. Nosal*, 844 F.3d 1024 (9th Cir. 2016). Defendants essentially concede that *Nosal* establishes that the attempt and conspiracy instructions were correct, and rightly so, because the decision speaks directly to the question raised here. In *Nosal*, the jury was instructed that for an EEA conspiracy charge "the government need not prove the existence of actual trade secrets and that Defendant knew that the information in question was a trade secret," but instead "must prove that Defendant firmly believed that certain information constituted trade secrets." The defendant argued that this instruction "constructively amended the indictment because the indictment allege[d] theft of actual trade secrets while the jury instruction did not require proof of actual trade secrets." We rejected this argument, finding that the instruction "reflects our circuit's precedent on conspiracy charges," under which "a conviction may be upheld even where the object of the crime was not a legal possibility."

We therefore "agree[d] with the other circuits that have applied this same principle to trade secrets," citing the circuit court decisions on which the district court and the government relied in the instant litigation. *Id.* (citing *United States v. Yang*,

281 F.3d 534, 544 (6th Cir. 2002); *United States v. Martin*, 228 F.3d 1, 13 (1st Cir. 2000); *Hsu*, 155 F.3d at 204). Finally, *Nosal* held that because the jury had found theft of actual trade secrets, any error was harmless.

Nosal establishes that the conspiracy and attempt instructions given here were legally correct and did not constructively amend the indictment. Moreover, Trade Secret 1, the main trade secret referenced in the conspiracy and attempt charges, included Trade Secrets 2 through 5, all of which the jury found to be actual trade secrets. Because we find the jury's convictions on the substantive trade secret charges to be supported by sufficient evidence, see *infra*, any error in the conspiracy and attempt instructions was harmless.

. . .

Notes & Questions

1. Legal Impossibility Is No Defense

Lange, *Martin*, and *Liew* all refer to *United States v. Hsu*, 155 F.3d 189 (3d Cir. 1998), the first appellate case to examine the provisions of the Economic Espionage Act. In *Hsu*, employees of Bristol-Meyer Squibb aided the FBI in conducting a "sting" operation against the defendants, who worked for a Taiwanese firm and were trying to procure secret procedures for the manufacture of a cancer drug. Because this was a sting operation, the actual trade secret was never in jeopardy. The defendants asserted, therefore, that there was no conspiracy to steal trade secrets. The court examined the argument within the scope of "legal impossibility":

> We hold that legal impossibility is not a defense to a charge of attempted misappropriation of trade secrets in violation of 18 U.S.C. § 1832(a)(4). We agree with the district court's conclusion that a charge of "attempt" under the EEA requires proof of the same elements used in other modern attempt statutes, including the Model Penal Code. A defendant is guilty of attempting to misappropriate trade secrets if, "acting with the kind of culpability otherwise required for commission of the crime, he . . . purposely does or omits to do anything that, under the circumstances as he believes them to be, is an act or omission constituting a substantial step in a course of conduct planned to culminate in his commission of the crime." Thus, the defendant must (1) have the intent needed to commit a crime defined by the EEA, and must (2) perform an act amounting to a "substantial step" toward the commission of that crime.

Id. at 202.

2. Companies as Criminals

The EEA includes provisions to charge organizations with the same crimes as individuals, and companies have been found guilty of attempted misappropriation of trade secrets. See *United States v. Yang*, 281 F.3d 534 (6th Cir. 2002), where the defendant and his corporation were charged with attempted theft of a trade secret and conspiracy to commit theft of a trade secret under § 1832. Both were convicted, and the company was originally sentenced to the statutory maximum fine of $5,000,000; the fine was vacated by the appellate court, as the trial judge did not provide his reasoning in imposing the maximum fine.

2. State Protection

Before the passage of the EEA and effective federal protection of trade secrets, a number of individual states passed specific statutes to criminalize the theft of trade secrets. California's penal code is representative of the various state statutes.

California Penal Code § 499c(b):

(b) Every person is guilty of theft who, with intent to deprive or withhold the control of a trade secret from its owner, or with an intent to appropriate a trade secret to his or her own use or to the use of another, does any of the following:

(1) Steals, takes, carries away, or uses without authorization, a trade secret.

(2) Fraudulently appropriates any article representing a trade secret entrusted to him or her.

(3) Having unlawfully obtained access to the article, without authority makes or causes to be made a copy of any article representing a trade secret.

(4) Having obtained access to the article through a relationship of trust and confidence, without authority and in breach of the obligations created by that relationship, makes or causes to be made, directly from and in the presence of the article, a copy of any article representing a trade secret.

(c) Every person who promises, offers or gives, or conspires to promise or offer to give, to any present or former agent, employee or servant of another, a benefit as an inducement, bribe or reward for conveying, delivering or otherwise making available an article representing a trade secret owned by his or her present or former principal, employer or master, to any person not authorized by the owner to receive or acquire the trade secret and every present or former agent, employee, or servant, who solicits, accepts, receives or takes a benefit as an inducement, bribe or reward for conveying, delivering or otherwise making available an article representing a trade secret owned by his or her present or former principal, employer or master, to any person not authorized by the owner to receive or acquire the trade secret, shall be punished by imprisonment in a county jail not exceeding one year, or by imprisonment pursuant to subdivision (h) of Section 1170 [of the California Penal Code (providing for imprisonment for 16 months or more)], or by a fine not exceeding five thousand dollars ($5,000), or by both that fine and imprisonment.

People v. Pribich

California Court of Appeal, Second District

27 Cal. Rptr. 2d 113 (Cal. App. 1994)

Boris Pribich appeals after a jury convicted him of one count of the theft of trade secrets (Pen. Code § 499c, subd. (b)(2)) and found the offense to be a misdemeanor petty theft. The court suspended imposition of sentence, placed appellant on summary probation for three years, ordered him to pay restitution of $400, and stayed payment of a $1,000 fine. Appellant contends that the evidence was insufficient to support his conviction and that there were various jury instruction errors. We find the evidence insufficient as to a requisite element of the offense and reverse.

Facts

[In April of 1990, Hancock, an officer of Aquatec, a water cooler company, hired Boris Pribich to work on a freonless cooler, using a thermal chip. Aquatec held patents on methods of using such a chip in water cooler. Pribich fell behind his anticipated schedule, which concerned Aquatec, as they wanted to display the cooler at an October trade show. Aquatec wanted to give Pribich the chance to succeed, and provided staff, workspace, and permission to work at home on his own computer.]

Hancock was familiar with some of the information in appellant's computer at work, such as graphs and equations on the performance of thermal electric chips. This information was necessary to Aquatec's objective of improving the performance of the thermal electric chip. Hancock thus considered the information in appellant's computer at work to constitute trade secrets belonging to Aquatec, since the information dealt with Aquatec's product and was not available to the general public.

To protect such trade secrets, Aquatec did not allow nonemployees to go into the building without being escorted and required employees to sign a confidentiality agreement. Even the sales people employed at Aquatec who had confidentiality agreements with the company were not permitted to view appellant's work product because, as Hancock stated, "We didn't want our competitors tipped off, we did not want the people to know what we were working on. And Aquatec is a start up company and could easily be outdone by someone with a large amount of cash and no one was going in our engineering department without a confidential[ity] agreement." According to Hancock, the information in appellant's work computer "would be of great interest . . . to our competitors."

Appellant was repeatedly absent from work, fell behind schedule, and Hancock became increasingly concerned that appellant could not finish his project to enable Aquatec to have an operating unit of its new product to demonstrate at the trade show in October of 1990. On September 17 and 19, 1990, Hancock asked appellant to have all the documents he had on his project available at the plant and to bring all the Aquatec documents and computer files or programs that he had at home to the plant. On September 20, Hancock asked appellant whether he brought all the information that had been requested and reminded appellant of the confidentiality agreement that he had signed. Appellant advised Hancock that the computer program was his property and stated, "You are a prick, I can be a prick, too." Hancock requested appellant to go to his work area and show another employee, Yongky Muljadi, what he was doing on the computer so that Muljadi could be brought up to date on appellant's project.

Hancock then called the company's patent counsel to alert him of the events. Appellant was very upset at that time. He showed Muljadi the files on the computer screen and claimed they belonged to him. However, based on the code letters of the files, Muljadi concluded that some of them were not appellant's files. Appellant proceeded to delete the files he claimed were his. After deleting the files, appellant left the building and never came back to work.

Hancock thereafter hired a computer consultant, Robert Torchon, to retrieve the data in appellant's work computer. Torchon and Muljadi were unable to retrieve the data. Hancock then contacted appellant and demanded that all the computer files and programs and other materials be returned to Aquatec. Appellant refused to do so, unless Aquatec paid a fair or reasonable price for them. Aquatec did not produce for the October trade show any prototype of a water cooler using a thermal electric chip.

On October 12, 1990, a Los Angeles police officer served a search warrant at appellant's residence. The police found two computers, computer discs, programs, and numerous papers. The police officer who served the warrant used a Turbo Basic program to obtain computer printouts generated from diskettes found in appellant's house. Most of the computer files found in appellant's house had "BAS" or "DWG" extension code letters, such as the code letters observed by Muljadi on the screen of appellant's work computer before appellant deleted the files.

According to Hancock, some of the documents obtained from appellant's home pertained to the work appellant was doing for Aquatec, constituted drawings of certain components that go into the coolers and certain information on the thermal electric cooler, and were deemed by Hancock to be proprietary documents or trade secrets of Aquatec. The documents included information about a heat exchanger, a heat problem in the thermal electric chip, and a bottle cap designed by Aquatec. A computer printout and computer programs, calculations, tests, and graphs regarding the performance of Aquatec's new cooler were also discovered pursuant to the search warrant. Appellant was not supposed to have retained those items seized and should have returned them to Aquatec as Hancock had requested.

In appellant's defense at trial, Dr. Martin Balaban, a mechanical engineer employed by Union Carbide to design heat exchangers and a consultant for the Rand Corp., testified that none of the prosecution's documentary evidence obtained from appellant's computer at home included any original concepts which could have given Aquatec an advantage over competitors who did not know of those documents. Moreover, the prosecution evidence included a document which showed appellant's coefficient of performance for a week when he was sick, another document constituting a milestone chart in which appellant outlined his project schedule, and other documents reflecting concepts which were in the public domain, though the exact numbers and dimensions set forth in the documents were not generally available to the public. According to Balaban, based upon his professional engineering expertise, it is not possible to make a thermal electric water cooler for the home or office which would be energy efficient and marketable.

Appellant claimed that he did not erase the files at work which belonged to Aquatec. As a part of his employment with Aquatec, he was required to use two computer programs, Auto Cad and Turbo Basic. Before he left Aquatec, appellant removed his Turbo Basic program, of which he was the registered owner, and a game-type program which he had in his work computer. He removed the programs in Muljadi's presence. When Hancock contacted appellant at home and demanded the program which he had taken, appellant claimed that he owned the programs and he never offered to sell them to Hancock. Appellant merely offered to convert his files into stand alone files, which could be used without the Turbo Basic program. Appellant admitted that most of the documents seized by the police at his home dealt with Aquatec's New Century water cooler project.

The jury found appellant not guilty of one of the two charged offenses, the unauthorized deletion of computer data. (Pen. Code, § 502, subd. (c)(4).) However, appellant was found guilty of the theft of trade secrets as a misdemeanor. (Pen. Code, § 499c, subd. (b)(2).)

DISCUSSION

To satisfy the elements of the crime with which appellant was charged, the fraudulent appropriation of an article representing a trade secret entrusted to him, the prosecution must, of course, establish that the article appropriated represented a trade secret. Penal Code section 499c, subdivision (a)(9) defines a trade secret, in pertinent part, as "any scientific or technical information, design, process, procedure, formula, computer program or information stored in a computer . . . which is secret and is not generally available to the public, and which gives one who uses it an advantage over competitors who do not know of or use the trade secret; and a trade secret shall be presumed to be secret when the owner thereof takes measures to prevent it from becoming available to persons other than those selected by the owner to have access thereto for limited purposes." One of the requisite elements of a trade secret is lacking in the present case. Specifically, there is no evidence that any of the items allegedly fraudulently appropriated by appellant and retrieved from his computer at home would give "one who uses [any of the items] an advantage over competitors who do not know of or use the trade secret."

In the present case, Hancock testified that he was familiar with some of the information in appellant's computer at work, which included graphs and mathematical models relating to the performance of thermal electric chips, that he considered the items observed on appellant's computer at work as trade secrets and that the items in appellant's computer at work would be of "great interest" to a competitor. However, Hancock described the information in appellant's computer at work and not in his computer at home. It was the information in appellant's computer at home which had been appropriated and which was alleged to constitute trade secrets. Although Hancock indicated that a computer printout reflecting information retrieved from appellant's computer at home contained a proprietary or trade secret of Aquatec, he stated only that "a lot of it is very familiar" and "looks like material that I saw on the screen that [appellant] was working on and certain other graphs I have certainly seen." However, Hancock could not indicate "the exact coding" for the printout. Such testimony by Hancock insufficiently addresses the items purportedly fraudulently appropriated by appellant, i.e., the numerous items generated from appellant's computer at home.

Most significantly, Hancock did not establish that the items seized from appellant's computer at home could give "one who uses it an advantage over competitors." Hancock did indicate that one of the items retrieved from appellant's computer was a milestone chart or work schedule which was not a technical document but which he considered proprietary to Aquatec. Hancock would not have wanted anyone to know appellant's work schedule because it would have revealed where Aquatec was at any point in time regarding its product development. However, Hancock did not specifically allege any advantage a competitor could obtain by theoretical access to such information. For example, there was no indication that any unspecified company could or would have worked any faster or differently if it had access to appellant's work schedule.

. . . .

Apart from whether a "substantial" competitive advantage is required for a violation of Penal Code section 499c, we find that the element of the offense that the prosecution establish the item appropriated give "one who uses it an advantage over competitors who do not know of or use the trade secret" requires more than merely conclusory and generalized allegations. Hancock asserted that the information in appellant's computer at work would be of "great interest" to a competitor and stated his desire not to have any competitors know appellant's work schedule, which was in appellant's computer at home. However, such statements do not reveal, except by an insufficient and generalized assumption, that any competitive advantage would specifically flow from the revelation of the information.

Indeed, it appears most unlikely that any competitive advantage could have been obtained by knowledge of appellant's work schedule or other information because, as indicated by the uncontradicted testimony of appellant's expert witness, it was impossible in light of known scientific principles to make a thermal electric water cooler for the home or office which would be energy efficient and marketable. Hancock himself acknowledged that one of the items retrieved from appellant's computer revealed appellant's opinion that the model under study was not suited for low-cost thermal electric modes and "was not working very well." Moreover, appellant's expert witness repeatedly stated during direct and cross-examination that none of the documents obtained from appellant's computer at home would give anyone who had them any advantage over competitors.

We note that in the prosecutor's argument to the jury, he belittled the defense expert's testimony regarding the lack of any advantage over competitors and urged that it was unrealistic to believe that no competitive advantage could ensue from the information, but the prosecutor pointed to no evidence at trial supporting this conclusion. Nor can we find in the record any substantial evidence as to this element of the offense.

Disposition

The judgment is reversed, and the trial court is directed to dismiss the information and to order any restitution and fine paid by appellant be remitted to him.

Notes & Questions

1. Differences in Federal and State Law

In *Pribich*, the conviction was reversed because the prosecution failed to prove that the information taken met the definition of a trade secret. In both *United States v. Martin* and *United States v. Hsu*, discussed *supra*, the federal appellate courts held that, for the charge of conspiracy to steal trade secrets, whether or not the information sought was actually a trade secret was irrelevant. Do you see any conflict between these holdings, and if so, does it trouble you?

2. Does Federal Patent Law Preempt State Trade Secret Law?

In *Kewanee Oil Co. v. Bicron Corp.*, 416 U.S. 470, 483 (1974), the United States Supreme Court faced the question of "whether those items which are proper subjects for consideration for a patent may also have available the alternative protection accorded by trade secret law." The Court recognized that the federal patent scheme and the state trade secret scheme could coexist:

> Certainly the patent policy of encouraging invention is not disturbed by the existence of another form of incentive to invention. In this respect the two systems are not and never would be in conflict. Similarly, the policy that matter once in the public domain must remain in the public domain is not incompatible with the existence of trade secret protection. By definition a trade secret has not been placed in the public domain.

Kewanee, 416 U.S. at 484. Consequently, the Court held that the federal patent law did not preempt Ohio trade secret law and that subject matter that otherwise qualifies for protection under the federal patent regime could also enjoy trade secret protection under state law.

In *Bonito Boats v. Thunder Craft Boats*, 489 U.S. 141 (1989), the Supreme Court determined the "limits the operation of the federal patent system places on the States' ability to offer substantial protection to utilitarian and design ideas which the patent laws leave otherwise unprotected." In *Bonito Boats*, a Florida statute offered patent-like protection for boat hulls. The Court held that federal patent law preempted the Florida law:

> States may not offer patent-like protection to intellectual creations which would otherwise remain unprotected as a matter of federal law. Both the novelty and the nonobviousness requirements of federal patent law are grounded in the notion that concepts within the public grasp, or those so obvious that they readily could be, are the tools of creation available to all. They provide the baseline of free competition upon which the patent system's incentive to creative effort depends. A state law that substantially interferes with the enjoyment of an unpatented utilitarian or design conception which has been freely disclosed by its author to the public at large impermissibly contravenes the ultimate goal of public disclosure and use which is the centerpiece of federal patent policy. Moreover, through the creation of patent-like rights, the States could essentially redirect inventive efforts away from the careful criteria of patentability developed by Congress over the last 200 years.

Bonito Boats, 489 U.S. at 156–57. Can the holding of *Bonito Boats* be reconciled with the holding of *Kewanee Oil*?

3. State versus Federal Protection

Professor Rochelle Dreyfuss has noted that while the EEA "appears to track the subject matter definitions of state law," the federal law "departs from state trade secrecy law in several important respects." The differences between the state and federal law include the divergent definitions of "unauthorized appropriation"; the inclusion in the EEA of "state-of-mind elements" absent from the state law; and the reach of the EEA to include "interceptions that occur outside the United States, which state laws could probably never reach . . . ." In addition, the EEA "—given its criminal nature—also departs from state legislation by substituting punishment for remedial action." Dreyfuss, *Trade Secrets: How Well Should We Be Allowed to Hide Them?*, *supra*. Professor Dreyfuss warns that as a result, "it is difficult to predict what case law and traditions courts will draw upon to resolve them." *Id.*

4. Use of State Courts by Foreign Corporations

Recently, state courts have seen trade secret cases brought by foreign corporations. For example, in 2003, semiconductor producer Taiwan Semiconductor Manufacturing

(TSMC) filed suit against Semiconductor Manufacturing International Corp (SMIC), a Chinese company, for patent infringement and misappropriation of trade secrets. This initial litigation was settled after a jury found SMIC liable. TSMC filed an amended complaint in 2006 alleging further patent infringement, trade secret misappropriation, and violation of the original settlement agreement. *Id.* Specifically, TSMC alleged that SMIC had hired a number of former TSMC employees and successfully requested that these new employees bring with them information about TSMC's processes. TSMC alleged 65 instances of trade secret theft; a jury found SMIC liable for the majority of those claims. The parties reached a settlement on damages. The settlement was reportedly valued at $200 million. Darin W. Snyder & David S. Almeling, Keeping Secrets: A Practical Introduction to Trade Secret Law and Strategy 35–36 (2012).

In addition to denying the intellectual property misuse claimed in the litigation, SMIC argued that the court involved—the California Superior Court in Oakland—lacked jurisdiction. After all, TSMC is a Taiwanese company, SMIC is a Chinese company, and the alleged thefts occurred in China. Presumably, TSMC brought its case through its North American affiliate to take advantage of the United States legal system, United States trade secret laws, and the potential in the United States for an award of substantial damages. The court found that it had jurisdiction, though it denied TSMC's motion for an injunction to stop SMIC from pursuing litigation between the parties in China. *TSMC North America v. Semiconductor Manufacturing Int'l Corp.*, 161 Cal. App. 4th 581 (2008).

Chapter 4

Employment Issues

Problem

Before founding Digital Ignition, Dr. See worked as an engineer at International Motors Corporation. International Motors is a multinational corporation engaged in the design, manufacturing, and marketing of automobiles and automotive equipment.

At International Motors, Dr. See worked with Dr. Paul Wilson, a fellow engineer in the electronic ignition systems design department. Dr. See and Dr. Wilson became good friends. Today, Dr. Wilson is the head of the department and is overseeing a project to improve the software incorporated in International Motors' ignition systems. The department conducts general research and development.

Dr. See wants to hire his friend, Dr. Wilson, to work for Digital Ignition. Dr. See has asked Dr. Wilson for the past six years to consider leaving International Motors. The prospect of working for a start-up appealed to the adventurous side of Dr. Wilson, but until this year he couldn't stomach the financial risk to his young family.

Yesterday, Dr. See met Dr. Wilson at a dinner at the house of a mutual acquaintance and jokingly suggested that Dr. Wilson join Digital Ignition. To his surprise, Dr. Wilson expressed interest in quitting International Motors for Digital Ignition. Dr. Wilson confided with Dr. See that two weeks ago, he had formulated an idea for an improved method for manufacturing digital ignition systems that he believes will drastically cut the cost of manufacturing digital ignitions—by 50 percent. Dr. Wilson came up with the idea over the course of a weekend while working in his garage but has not yet put his idea down in writing. Dr. Wilson believes that the idea could be worth millions and wants to develop the concept at Digital Ignition.

The following day, Dr. See comes to you with a copy of Dr. Wilson's employment contract with International Motors and explains that he would like to hire Dr. Wilson away from International Motors. A review of Dr. Wilson's employment contract reveals several of its provisions place restrictions on Dr. Wilson's subsequent employment. One provision recites that Dr. Wilson, by accepting employment with International Motors, recognizes that he will be in a position to receive confidential information and that he agrees not to use or disclose the information on behalf of anyone but International Motors. Another provision prohibits exiting employees from soliciting customers or other employees upon the termination of employment with International Motors. Yet another provision states that Dr. Wilson agrees to assign rights to all intellectual property he creates during the term of employment to International Motors. There is no trailer or holdover clause in Dr. Wilson's employment contract requiring him to assign rights in his post-employment inventions to International Motors.

Dr. See would like to offer Dr. Wilson a position with Digital Ignition and is excited about applying Dr. Wilson's idea to the manufacturing of Digital Ignition's product. He wishes to know whether any provisions in Dr. Wilson's employment contract with International Motors will pose a problem for Digital Ignition as the new employer. Please advise Dr. See of any risk to Digital Ignition in the event of a suit by International Motors. Dr. See also wishes to know whether the provisions will pose a problem for his friend Dr. Wilson. In formulating your response, consider what claims International Motors might level against Dr. Wilson should it sue to enforce the terms of the employment contract. In addition, evaluate whether Dr. Wilson will be able to take his idea with him to Digital Ignition.

Focus of the Chapter

The readings in this chapter focus on intellectual property issues that arise in the context of the employment relationship. Absent a private agreement to the contrary, statutory default rules dictate the assignment of ownership of employee-created intellectual property. In some circumstances, the default rules favor employee ownership of employee-created intellectual property. Employers consequently have opted to secure ownership in intellectual property created out of an employment relationship through the use of private contracts in the form of employment contract terms.

In Part A, the focus of the readings centers upon the ownership of intellectual property rights. The first subsection of Part A discusses the statutory default rules that govern the ownership rights of intellectual property created by employees. First, the readings examine the statutory rules that govern the assignment of patent rights in employee inventions, including the concepts of shop right and one hired to invent. Second, the readings discuss the ownership rights in trade secrets produced by employee inventors, including the implied duties owed by an employee to his employer. Next, the readings discuss ownership of employee-created works subject to copyrights. Finally, in the second subsection of Part A, the private adjustments to the default rules established by ownership assignment terms in an employment contract are considered.

After the termination of the employment relationship, issues can surface concerning the use or disclosure by an ex-employee of an employer's proprietary information. The readings in Part B of this chapter highlight the concerns that arise from transfers of intellectual property upon changes in employment. The first subsection discusses the enforceability of private agreements that place limits upon a former employee's ability to use and disclose the former employer's proprietary information. The readings illustrate the impact of measures such as nonuse and nondisclosure agreements, as well as covenants not to compete. The second subsection explores how employers may invoke the inevitable disclosure doctrine to restrict a former employee from using or disclosing information personal to the employee in subsequent employment. The last subsection then deals with the risks and liabilities a new employer may incur from hiring away inventive employees.

Readings

A. Ownership of Intellectual Property

1. Statutory Default Rules

a. *Patents*

Employee inventors develop the overwhelming majority of inventions patented today. Under the default rules, an employee owns the subject matter of his invention even if the invention was conceived during the course of employment. Absent an agreement to the contrary, the patent statute's default rule confers the rights of a patent to the employee inventor and not to the employer.

The default rule of patent ownership reflects the old notion of invention as the fruit of individual genius, rather than the product of corporate machinery. The requirements of the patent statute itself suggest that the old romantic image of the individual inventor remains. For example, patents issue in the name of individuals and not in the name of entities. Section 115 of the patent statute requires applicants to disclose the individual name of the true inventor. 35 U.S.C. §115. Under the default rule, each inventor must sign an oath or declaration in connection with the application. Even if, in exceptional circumstances, a person, other than the inventor, who has sufficient proprietary interest in the invention makes the application, the patent can only be granted to that person if sufficient notice to the true inventor is shown. 35 U.S.C. §118.

The Bayh-Dole Act (35 U.S.C. §§200–212), which regulates patent rights in inventions made with federal assistance, did not displace the norm that rights in an invention belonged to the inventor. *See Bd. of Trustees of Leland Stanford Junior Univ. v. Roche Molecular Sys., Inc.*, 563 U.S. 776 (2011). In 35 U.S.C. §202(a), the Act provides that federal contractors such as Stanford University could "elect to retain title to any subject invention," which indicates that the Act did not automatically extinguish the employee inventor's ownership rights or confer title to federally funded inventions on federal contractors. *Id.* at 789.

Even though an inventor generally owns the rights to an invention, the general rule is not without exception. An employee inventor's patent ownership rights may be subject to an obligation to assign the rights to his employer. Such is the case when an employee is "hired to invent." When an employee is hired for the purpose of employing his inventive abilities, the patent rights to his inventions belong entirely to the employer. Additionally, inventions may be subject to a "shop right," a compromise position that arises when the invention relates to employee duties or created with use of employer's time and resources. The shop right is a split entitlement that affords an employer a nonexclusive, nontransferable license to practice the invention, but retains the ownership of the patent in the employee inventor. Of course, independent inventions created by the employee without the use of employer time or resources and in a subject matter unrelated to the employee's duties belong solely to the employee.

i. Shop Right

McElmurry v. Arkansas Power & Light Co.

United States Court of Appeals for the Federal Circuit

995 F.2d 1576 (Fed. Cir. 1993)

RICH, CIRCUIT JUDGE.

. . . .

III. Shop Rights

A. Background

[Arkansas Power & Light Co. (AP&L)] hired Harold L. Bowman, the patentee, as a consultant on October 24, 1980, to assist in the installation, maintenance, and operation of electrostatic precipitators at AP&L's White Bluff Steam Electric Station (White Bluff) located near Redfield, Arkansas. An electronic precipitator is a device which removes granular ash particles (fly ash) from the gasses emitted by coal-fired boilers used to generate steam. As fly ash is removed, it is collected in hoppers referred to as precipitator hoppers. Prior to April of 1982, the precipitator hoppers at White Bluff employed a level detector system using a nuclear power source (K-ray system) to detect the level of fly ash in the hoppers.

AP&L was not satisfied with the K-ray system. As a result, in the early part of 1982, Bowman discussed with a Mr. Richard L. Roberts, an AP&L employee, replacing the K-ray system with a new level detector, an initial design of which they drew on a napkin. In the proposed level detector, a vacuum gauge was connected to a pipe inserted and welded into the wall of a precipitator hopper. If the level of the fly ash collected in the hopper extended above the point where the pipe was inserted into the hopper, the vacuum gauge would no longer indicate that a vacuum existed, as it would if the level of the fly ash were below that point. Thus, by monitoring the vacuum gauge, one could determine whether the fly ash exceeded a certain level in the hopper.

AP&L considered the proposed level detector and, during a power outage in March of 1982, ordered its installation on one hopper at White Bluff for testing purposes. When it proved successful, AP&L ordered that the level detector be installed on a total of sixteen (16) precipitator hoppers at White Bluff. In each case, level detectors were installed both near the bottom and top of the hopper, thus allowing for the detection of the fly ash at two different levels in the hopper. When this system proved successful, AP&L ordered that the level detectors be installed on the remaining one hundred and twelve (112) precipitator hoppers at White Bluff. All costs associated with the installation and testing of the level detector on the one hundred and twenty eight (128) hoppers at White Bluff, including materials and working drawings, were paid by AP&L.

On October 24, 1982, Bowman moved from White Bluff to AP&L's Independence Steam Electric Station (ISES) located near Newark, Arkansas, to assist in the start-up, maintenance, and operation of electronic precipitators at that facility. In November of 1982, Bowman formed White Rivers Technology, Inc. [WRT] with McElmurry and a Mr. Johnny Mitchum, to market certain inventions on which Bowman held patents or was planning to seek patent protection. Bowman filed a patent application on the level detector on February 18, 1983, and the patent-in-suit issued on July 9, 1985. At some point prior to its issuance, Bowman assigned his patent rights to WRT.

While at ISES, Bowman assisted another AP&L engineer, a Mr. Will Morgan, in installing the level detector on precipitator hoppers at that facility . . . . The level detectors had been installed and were in operation on all one hundred and twenty eight (128) precipitator hoppers by the end of 1984, prior to the issuance of the Bowman patent. Bowman's contract with ISES ended, however, in October of 1983 before completion of the project. All costs associated with the installation and testing of the level detectors at ISES, including materials and working drawings, were paid by AP&L even though some of the work was contracted out.

In 1985, based upon the success of the level detector on the precipitator hoppers at White Bluff and ISES, another AP&L engineer, a Mr. John Harvey, implemented a plan to install the level detector on fourteen (14) hydroveyer hoppers at ISES. Harvey informed Bowman of the plan to install the level detector on the hydroveyer hoppers, and Bowman indicated that he thought it was a good idea. Bowman also indicated that WRT would be interested in bidding on the project. AP&L ultimately awarded the contract, however, to another contractor because WRT was not the low bidder. In soliciting bids on the hydroveyer project, AP&L provided the contractors with specifications prepared by AP&L showing the work to be performed. The installation of the level detectors on the hydroveyor hoppers at ISES was completed in 1985, and all costs associated with their installation were paid by AP&L.

B. District Court Litigation

On April 25, 1990, WRT brought suit against AP&L for patent infringement based on AP&L's solicitation of and contracting with a party other than WRT to install Bowman's patented level detector on the hydroveyer hoppers at ISES. The district court granted summary judgment in favor of AP&L on the basis that AP&L had acquired a "shop right" in the level detector claimed in the Bowman patent. AP&L argued and the court agreed that, as a matter of law, Bowman's development of the patented level detector at AP&L's facilities at AP&L's expense entitled AP&L, under the "shop rights" rule, to reproduce and use the level detector in its business. WRT then appealed to this court.

C. Analysis

A "shop right" is generally accepted as being a right that is created at common law, when the circumstances demand it, under principles of equity and fairness, entitling an employer to use without charge an invention patented by one or more of its employees without liability for infringement. See generally D. Chisum, Patents,

§ 22.02[3] (1985 rev.); C.T. Dreschler, Annotation, Application and Effect of "Shop Right Rule" or License Giving Employer Limited Rights in Employee's Inventions and Discoveries, 61 A.L.R.2d 356 (1958); P. Rosenberg, Patent Law Fundamentals, § 11.04, 11-20 (1991). However, as recognized by several commentators, supra, the immense body of case law addressing the issue of "shop rights" suggests that not all courts agree as to the doctrinal basis for "shop rights," and, consequently, not all courts agree as to the particular set of circumstances necessary to create a "shop right."

For example, many courts characterize a "shop right" as being a type of implied license, and thus the focus is often on whether the employee engaged in any activities, e.g., developing the invention on the employer's time at the employer's expense, which demand a finding that he impliedly granted a license to his employer to use the invention. Other courts characterize a "shop right" as a form of equitable estoppel, and thus the focus is often on whether the employee's actions, e.g., consent or acquiescence to his employer's use of the invention, demand a finding that he is estopped from asserting a patent right against his employer. Neither characterization appears to be inherently better than the other, and the end result under either is often the same, given that the underlying analysis in each case is driven by principles of equity and fairness, and given that the courts often analyze a "shop right" as being a combination of the two even though they may characterize it in name as one or the other.

It is thus not surprising that many courts adopt neither characterization specifically, instead choosing to characterize a "shop right" more broadly as simply being a common law "right" that inures to an employer when the circumstances demand it under principles of equity and fairness. These courts often look to both the circumstances surrounding the development of the invention and the facts regarding the employee's activities respecting that invention, once developed, to determine whether it would be fair and equitable to allow an employee to preclude his employer from making use of that invention. This is essentially the analysis that most courts undertake regardless of how they characterize "shop rights."

In view of the foregoing, we believe that the proper methodology for determining whether an employer has acquired a "shop right" in a patented invention is to look to the totality of the circumstances on a case by case basis and determine whether the facts of a particular case demand, under principles of equity and fairness, a finding that a "shop right" exists. In such an analysis, one should look to such factors as the circumstances surrounding the development of the patented invention and the inventor's activities respecting that invention, once developed, to determine whether equity and fairness demand that the employer be allowed to use that invention in his business. A factually driven analysis such as this ensures that the principles of equity and fairness underlying the "shop rights" rule are considered. Because this is exactly the type of analysis that the district court used to reach its decision, we see no error in the district court's analysis justifying reversal.

To reach its decision, the district court looked to the discussion of "shop rights" set forth in the often-cited *Dubilier* case, in which the Court said:

where a servant, during his hours of employment, working with his master's materials and appliances, conceives and perfects an invention for which he obtains a patent, he must accord his master a nonexclusive right to practice the invention [citation omitted]. This is an application of equitable principles. Since the servant uses his master's time, facilities, and materials to attain a concrete result, the latter is in equity entitled to use that which embodies his own property and to duplicate it as often as he may find occasion to employ similar appliances in his business.

[*U.S. v. Dubilier Condenser Corporation*, 289 U.S. 178, 188–89 (1933)] . The district court also accepted a discussion of "shop rights" set forth in one of WRT's briefs filed in the district court action as correctly summarizing several factors that may be considered in analyzing a "shop rights" case. At pages 9–10 of its opinion, the district court included the following excerpt from pages 6–8 of WRT's Memorandum Brief in Support of Response to Motion for Summary Judgment:

> Because broad equitable principles are involved in determining whether shop rights in [an] invention arise, "the full nature of the parties' relationship must be examined to determine whether a shop right exists." Rosenberg, Patent Law Fundamentals, § 11.04, 11-20 (1991). The following factors have been considered: the contractual nature of the relationship between employer and employee, whether the employee consented to the employer's use of the invention, and whether the employee induced, acquiesced in, or assisted the employer in the use of the invention . . . . [footnote omitted]

> An employer will have shop rights in an invention in situations where the employer has financed an employee's invention by providing wages, materials, tools and a work place. Other factors creating shop rights include an employee's consent, acquiescence, inducement, or assistance to the employer in using the invention without demanding compensation or other notice of restriction. See Rosenberg, Patent Law Fundamentals § 11.04 (1991).

Applying *Dubilier* and the summary of the law set forth in WRT's own brief to the facts of this case, the district court properly found that AP&L had acquired a "shop right" in Bowman's patented level detector which entitled AP&L to duplicate the level detector for use in its business.

Bowman developed the patented level detector while working at AP&L and suggested it to AP&L as an alternative to the K-ray system. AP&L installed the level detector on one hundred and twenty eight (128) precipitator hoppers at White Bluff with Bowman's consent and participation. Bowman also consented to, and participated at least in part in, the installation of the level detector on one hundred and twenty eight (128) precipitator hoppers at ISES. In addition, the level detectors on half of the hoppers at ISES were installed by a contractor other than WRT, with Bowman's and WRT's knowledge and consent. All costs and expenses associated with the testing and implementation of the level detector on the hoppers at White Bluff and ISES were paid by AP&L.

Furthermore, Bowman never asserted that AP&L was precluded from using the level detector without his permission or that AP&L was required to compensate him for its use. Indeed, the record suggests that Bowman believed quite the opposite. As recognized by the district court at page 12 of its opinion,

> Bowman admitted in a deposition [footnote omitted] that he believed all along that AP&L would have shop rights. His patent attorney had informed him of that possibility and he subsequently shared the attorney's opinion with his partners in WRT. See Bowman deposition at 81–82.

WRT argues that Bowman's consent or acquiescence after he had assigned his rights in the Bowman application to WRT is irrelevant. Even if this were true, Bowman's actions at White Bluff prior to this assignment justify the district court's finding that a "shop right" was created. Nevertheless, WRT, of which Bowman was a part owner during the relevant time period, acquiesced both to AP&L's continued use of the level detector at White Bluff and ISES and to the installation of the level detector by outside contractors at ISES. This lends further support to the district court's decision.

WRT also argues that, even if AP&L had acquired a "shop right" to use the patented level detector, AP&L somehow exceeded the scope of that right when it allegedly "carelessly and casually disseminated the design and specifications of the patented device to private contractors." WRT argues that, by putting information of this nature on the open market, AP&L rendered the patent "worthless" and robbed Bowman of the "fruit of his labor." We find these arguments unpersuasive for two reasons.

First, WRT has failed to explain how AP&L's mere dissemination of specifications of the patented level detector constituted patent infringement. Clearly, it did not. The owner of a patent right may exclude others from making, using or selling the subject matter of a claimed invention. 35 U.S.C. §§ 154 and 271. AP&L's dissemination of information obviously does not fall into any of these categories. Even so, it is also unclear how disseminating specifications of the level detector after it was patented rendered the Bowman patent "worthless." The owner of the Bowman patent still retained the right to exclude all others than AP&L from practicing the claimed invention.

Second, we find no error in the district court's holding that AP&L's "shop right" entitled it to duplicate the level detector and to continue to use it in its business. Such a conclusion clearly finds support in the law. *H.F. Walliser & Co. v. F.W. Maurer & Sons Co.*, 17 F.2d 122, 124 (E.D. Pa. 1927); *see also Dubilier*, 289 U.S. at 188–89; *Thompson*, 174 F.2d at 778, 81 USPQ at 327–28; *Pure Oil Co. v. Hyman*, 95 F.2d 22, 25, 36 U.S.P.Q. (BNA) 306, 310 (7th Cir. 1938) ("shop right is co-extensive with the business requirements of the employer"). Furthermore, AP&L's "shop right" was not limited to AP&L's use of level detectors that AP&L itself had manufactured and installed. Quite to the contrary, we find that AP&L's "shop right" entitled it to procure the level detector from outside contractors. *Schmidt v. Central Foundry Co.*, 218 F. 466, 470 (D.N.J. 1914), *aff'd on other grounds*, 229 F. 157 (3d Cir. 1916).

Finally, WRT makes several arguments addressing the laws pertaining to the assignment of patent rights. However, AP&L has never asserted that it has any ownership rights in the Bowman patent. Rather, AP&L has merely claimed "shop rights" as a defense to WRT's patent infringement action. Accordingly, WRT's assignment arguments are considered irrelevant and thus unpersuasive.

AFFIRMED.

Notes & Questions

1. Shop Right

The "shop right" doctrine awards an employer a nontransferable, nonexclusive right to make use of an employee's invention without compensation. A court typically bases its award of a shop right on the doctrines of estoppel, license implied in fact, and equity and fairness. The limited right awarded under the doctrine is not an ownership interest, but rather a defense against claims of infringement on the patent. An employer obtains nothing more than a right to use the employee invention without apprehension of an infringement suit. The employee inventor retains full ownership rights and may assign or license the patent rights to others.

2. Use In-House versus Sale of an Invention

In 2013, the Court of Appeals for the Federal Circuit distinguished *McElmurray* from other shop right cases on the basis that AP&L hired a third party to use the invention in-house, rather than selling the invention to a third party. In *Beriont v. GTE Labs., Inc.*, 535 Fed. Appx. 919 (Fed. Cir. 2013), the court noted that "[t]he [shop right] doctrine has its limits . . . ; for example, it seems an employer can only use the invention internally in its own business." *Id.* at 923. Instead of hiring someone to install the patented invention in the plaintiff's own business, the defendant in *Beriont* "manufactured, sold, and continue[d] to sell or offer to sell the invention described in U.S. Patent # 05,920,802 for good and valuable consideration." *Id.* at 924.

ii. Hired to Invent

Standard Parts Co. v. Peck

Supreme Court of the United States

264 U.S. 52 (1924)

Mr. Justice McKenna delivered the opinion of the Court.

Suit for injunction, preliminary and perpetual, and accounting for profits and damages, upon the ground of infringement of Letters Patent No. 1,249,473, issued to William J. Peck, respondent.

The bill is the usual one in patent cases. For answer to it the Standard Parts Company admits the use of the devices of the patent and alleges they were constructed under the supervision of Peck and under the terms and provisions of a contract dated August 23, 1915, by and between him and the Hess-Pontiac Spring and Axle

Company, for and in behalf of the latter company and the Western Spring and Axle Company, and that it, the Standard Company, has succeeded to the entire assets, business and good will of those other companies, including all of their rights in said contract and devices. And the Standard Company avers that Peck was fully compensated for his connection with the devices.

. . . .

On the case as thus presented, Peck's testimony and some other testimony was taken, and certain exhibits introduced, and the judgment of the District Court was . . . "that the property in the invention belonged to the employer" (the Hess-Pontiac Spring and Axle Company), and that this property passed to the Standard Parts Company when it acquired the assets of the Axle Company, and that Peck holds the legal title in trust for the Standard Company. A decree was directed to be entered requiring an assignment of the legal title to the latter Company.

. . . .

The Circuit Court of Appeals reversed the decree of the District Court in so far as it decreed an assignment and transfer of the patent in suit and other patents and applications from Peck to the Standard Company.

. . . .

The courts reached different rulings because of different readings of the cases. That of the District Court was, that while the mere fact that one is employed by another does not preclude him from making improvements in the machines with which he is connected, and obtaining patents therefor, as his individual property, yet, if he "be employed to invent or devise such improvements his patents therefor belong to his employer, since in making such improvements he is merely doing what he was hired to do."

The Circuit Court of Appeals rejected this test. It conceded, however, that the deduction of the District Court was sustained by *Solomons v. United States*, 137 U.S. 342; *McAleer v. United States*, 150 U.S. 424, and *Gill v. United States*, 160 U.S. 426, and if correct, required the affirmance of the decree of the District Court. And the court admitted that there was no later declaration than that of those cases, nor any criticism of it. The court, nevertheless, dissented from it, subordinating it to other cases and reasoning, they establishing, it was considered, "that an invention does not belong to the employer, merely by virtue of an employment contract, as well when that employment is to devise or improve a specific thing as when the employment is to devise improvements generally in the line of the employer's business." And considering further that Peck's employment was to devise or improve a specific thing, decided that his contract did not "of its own force, convey to the employer the equitable title to the patentable inventions" which he "might make in the course of its execution" but gave "to the employer a license only."

It is going very far to say that the declaration of *Solomons v. United States*, repeated in subsequent cases, and apparently constituting their grounds of decision, may be put aside or underrated—assigned the inconsequence of dicta. It might be said that there is persuasion in the repetition. It cannot be contended that the invention of a specific thing cannot be made the subject of a bargain and pass in execution of it. And such, we think, was the object and effect of Peck's contract with the Hess-Pontiac Spring and Axle Company. That company had a want in its business, a "problem", is Peck's word, and he testified that "Mr. Hess thought probably" that he, Peck, "could be of some assistance to him [Hess] in working out" the "problem", and the "thought" was natural. Hess had previous acquaintance with Peck—his inventive and other ability, and approached him, the result being the contract of August 23, 1915, the material parts of which are as follows: "This Agreement Witnesseth, that second party is to devote his time to the development of a process and machinery for the production of the front spring now used on the product of the Ford Motor Company. First party is to pay second party for such services the sum of $300 per month. That should said process and machinery be finished at or before the expiration of four months from August 11, 1915, second party is to receive a bonus of $100 per month. That when finished, second party is to receive a bonus of $10 for each per cent of reduction from present direct labor, as disclosed by the books of first party."

By the contract Peck engaged to "devote his time to the development of a process and machinery" and was to receive therefore a stated compensation. Whose property was the "process and machinery" to be when developed? The answer would seem to be inevitable and resistless—of him who engaged the services and paid for them, they being his inducement and compensation, they being not for temporary use but perpetual use, a provision for a business, a facility in it and an asset of it, therefore, contributing to it whether retained or sold—the vendee (in this case the Standard Company) paying for it and getting the rights the vendor had (in this case, the Axle Company).

Other meaning to the contract would confuse the relation of the parties to it—take from the Axle Company the inducement the company had to make it—take from the company the advantage of its exclusive use and subject the company to the rivalry of competitors. And yet, such, we think, is the contention of Peck. He seems somewhat absorbing in his assertion of rights. He yields to the Axle Company a shop right only, free from the payment of royalty but personal and temporary—not one that could be assigned or transferred. Peck, therefore, virtually asserts, though stimulated to services by the Hess Company and paid for them—doing nothing more than he was engaged to do and paid for doing—that the product of the services was so entirely his property that he might give as great a right to any member of the mechanical world as to the one who engaged him and paid him—a right to be used in competition with the one who engaged him and paid him.

We cannot assent to this, nor even to the limitation the Court of Appeals put upon Peck's contention. We concur with the District Court, and therefore reverse the decree of the Circuit Court of Appeals.

Reversed.

Notes & Questions

1. A Beautiful Mind: An Employee Hired to Invent

Standard Parts Co. v. Peck marked the first time the United States Supreme Court held that an employee hired to apply his inventive ability owed a duty to assign patent rights to his or her employer. Notice that in *Standard Parts* the employee under scrutiny was directed to invent a specific improvement. Would the obligation to assign patent rights apply as well to an employee hired to conduct general research? What if the employer were the United States government? *See United States v. Dubilier Condenser Corp.*, 289 U.S. 178 (1933).

2. History of Default Patent Ownership

The default rule of patent ownership in the employment context has historically moved toward increasing protection for employer's rights. In *Removing the 'Fuel of Interest' from the 'Fire of Genius': Law and the Employee-Inventor*, 65 U. Chi. L. Rev. 1127 (1998), Catherine Fisk proposes that there are three overlapping periods in the development of employee inventor law. In the first period, during the early nineteenth century, the employee inventors exclusively owned the rights to their inventions. The ownership of inventions did not hinge upon the inventor's status as an employee. During this first period, "shop rights" were predicated on the doctrine of equitable estoppel rather than on the doctrine of employment law. The second period of the later nineteenth century saw a gradual shift toward awarding "shop rights" to employers on the basis of the employment relationship. In the third period, beginning at the turn of the twentieth century, the analysis of invention ownership was dominated by contract law, as employers increasingly relied upon employment contracts to protect valuable inventions developed within employment relationships.

3. How to Apportion the Fruits of Research

When a highly qualified researcher decides to quit a research institution to open a private business, complications may follow. This is well illustrated by litigation that revolved around UC Davis's celebrated strawberry breeding program. Starting in the early 1990s, professors Douglas Shaw and Kirk Larson successfully led the program for about 20 years. Reportedly, as of 2017, plants of types developed in their program were used to grow most of California's strawberries (which support a nearly $3 billion industry and account for 87 percent of the strawberries consumed in North America). *See* Michael Hiltzik, *Delicious and Litigious, UC's Strawberries Are in Court—Again*, L.A. Times, 8/19/2017, http://www.latimes.com/business/hiltzik/la-fi-hiltzik-strawberries-20170512-story.html (last visited 1/17/2019); *Strawberry Suit: UC Davis and Former Professors Clash over Who Owns the Fruits of Research*, L.A. Times, 8/19/2017, http://www.latimes.com/business/la-fi-strawberries-uc-davis-20170505-story.html (last visited 1/17/2019).

When both breeders decided to retire to open their own strawberry research company, they used some of the patented and unpatented plants that belonged to the university for the benefit of their private business without a license. A lawsuit followed. After a five-day trial, a federal jury found Shaw and Larson liable for patent infringement, breach of duties of loyalty and fiduciary duties, and conversion of plant materials. *The Regents of the University of California v. California Berry Cultivars, LLC*, 2017 WL 2842313 (N.D. Cal.).

The parties settled on the issue of damages after the judge in the case expressed disapproval of the behavior of both parties in the case. Notably, farmers all around California watched the dispute closely, because the outcome of the litigation could have had a substantial effect on the availability and affordability of high-quality strawberry plants. The case is an illustration of the disagreements about the ownership of the fruits of intellectual labor that may accompany a transition of key researchers from their research institution to private business.

b. Trade Secrets

i. Introduction

The employer-employee relationship gives rise to the majority of trade secret disputes. The law of trade secrets developed in response to the balancing of competing interests as between the employer and the employee. Employers often invest substantial resources toward the development and maintenance of trade secrets. If competitors were free to bypass the cost of independent development by obtaining trade secrets by means of hiring away a company's employees, then employers may be reluctant to risk the cost of developing trade secrets and entrusting the knowledge to employees. The law protects investment in trade secrets by imposing a duty upon employees to not use or disclose the employer's trade secrets. On the other hand, the law recognizes that employees have a right to use their skill, knowledge, and experience in pursuing their chosen career. The public policy interest of employee mobility may therefore impose a limit on employer trade secret protection. Problems may arise when an employee's knowledge and skill are inextricably intertwined with the employer's claimed trade secrets. The following case illustrates the tension between the interests of the employer and those of the departing employee.

Wexler v. Greenberg

Supreme Court of Pennsylvania

160 A.2d 430 (Pa. 1960)

COHEN, JUSTICE.

Appellees, trading as Buckingham Wax Company, filed a complaint in equity to enjoin Brite Products Co., Inc., and its officers, Greenberg, Dickler, and Ford, appellants, from disclosing and using certain formulas and processes pertaining to the manufacture of certain sanitation and maintenance chemicals, allegedly trade secrets. After holding lengthy hearings, the chancellor concluded that the four formulas involved are trade secrets which appellant Greenberg disclosed in contravention of his duty of nondisclosure arising from his confidential relationship with Buckingham. He decreed that appellants, jointly and severally, be enjoined permanently from disclosing the formulas or processes or any substantially similar formulas and from making or selling the resulting products. He also ordered an accounting for losses. After the dismissal by the court *en banc* of appellants' exceptions to the chancellor's findings of fact and conclusions of law, the chancellor's decree was made final and this appeal followed.

Buckingham Wax Company is engaged in the manufacture, compounding, and blending of sanitation and maintenance chemicals. In March, 1949, appellant Greenberg, a qualified chemist in the sanitation and maintenance field, entered the employ of Buckingham as its chief chemist and continued there until April 28, 1957. In the performance of his duties, Greenberg consumed half of his working time in Buckingham's laboratory where he would analyze and duplicate competitors' products and then use the resulting information to develop various new formulas. He would change or modify these formulas for color, odor or viscosity in order that greater commercial use could be made of Buckingham's products. The remainder of his time was spent in ordering necessary materials and interviewing chemical salesmen concerning new, better or cheaper ingredients for the multitude of products produced by Buckingham so that costs could be lowered and quality increased. As a result of his activities Greenberg was not only familiar with Buckingham's formulas, he was also fully conversant with the costs of the products and the most efficient method of producing them.

Appellant Brite Products Co., Inc., is a Pennsylvania corporation . . . . [F]rom August, 1956, until August 20, 1957, the date of Brite's last order, Brite exclusively purchased Buckingham's manufactured products. These products were in turn distributed by Brite to its customers, mostly industrial users, marked with labels which identified said products as products of Brite. Brite's purchases of sanitation and maintenance products from Buckingham amounted annually to approximately $35,000.

. . . .

In August, 1957, Greenberg left Buckingham and went to work for Brite. At no time during Greenberg's employment with Buckingham did there exist between them a written or oral contract of employment or any restrictive agreement.

Prior to Greenberg's association with Brite, the corporation's business consisted solely of selling a complete line of maintenance and sanitation chemicals, including liquid soap cleaners, wax base cleaners, disinfectants, and floor finishes. Upon Greenberg's arrival, however, the corporation purchased equipment and machinery and, under the guidance and supervision of Greenberg, embarked on a full-scale program for the manufacture of a cleaner, floor finish, and disinfectant, products previously purchased from Buckingham. The formulas in issue in this litigation are the formulas for each of these respective products. The appellants dispute the chancellor's findings as to the identity of their formulas with those of Buckingham, but there was evidence that a spectrophometer examination of the respective products of the parties revealed that the formulas used in making these products are substantially identical. Appellants cannot deny that they thought the products sufficiently similar as to continue delivery of their own products to their customers in the same cans and drums and with the same labels attached which they had previously used in distributing the products manufactured by Buckingham, and to continue using the identical promotional advertising material. Appellees' formulas had been developed during the tenure of Greenberg as chief chemist and are unquestionably known to him.

The chancellor found that Greenberg did not develop the formulas for Brite's products after he left Buckingham, but rather that he had appropriated them by carrying over the knowledge of them which he had acquired in Buckingham's employ. The chancellor went on to find that the formulas constituted trade secrets and that their appropriation was in violation of the duty that Greenberg owed to Buckingham by virtue of his employment and the trust reposed in him. Accordingly, the relief outlined above was ordered.

We are initially concerned with the fact that the final formulations claimed to be trade secrets were not *disclosed to* Greenberg by the appellees during his service or because of his position. Rather, the fact is that these formulas had been developed by Greenberg himself, while in the pursuit of his duties as Buckingham's chief chemist, or under Greenberg's direct supervision. We are thus faced with the problem of determining the extent to which a former employer, *without the aid of any express covenant,* can restrict his ex-employee, a highly skilled chemist, in the uses to which this employee can put his knowledge of formulas and methods he himself developed during the course of his former employment because this employer claims these same formulas, as against the rest of the world, as his trade secrets. This problem becomes particularly significant when one recognizes that Greenberg's situation is not uncommon. In this era of electronic, chemical, missile and atomic development, many skilled technicians and expert employees are currently in the process of developing potential trade secrets. Competition for personnel of this caliber is exceptionally keen, and the interchange of employment is commonplace. One has but to reach for his daily newspaper to appreciate the current market for such skilled employees. We must therefore be particularly mindful of any effect our decision in this case might have in disrupting this pattern of employee mobility, both in view of possible restraints upon an individual in the pursuit of his livelihood and the harm to the public in general in forestalling to any extent widespread technological advances.

The principles outlining this area of the law are clear. A court of equity will protect an employer from the unlicensed disclosure or use of his trade secrets by an ex-employee provided the employee entered into an enforceable covenant so restricting his use, *Fralich v. Despar,* 165 Pa. 24, 30 Atl. 521 (1894), or was bound to secrecy by virtue of a confidential relationship existing between the employer and employee, *Pittsburgh Cut Wire Co. v. Sufrin,* 350 Pa. 31, 38 A.2d 33 (1944). Where, however, an employer has no legally protectable trade secret, an employee's "aptitude, his skill, his dexterity, his manual and mental ability, and such other subjective knowledge as he obtains while in the course of his employment, are not the property of his employer and the right to use and expand these powers remains his property unless curtailed through some restrictive covenant entered into with the employer." *Id.* at 35. The employer thus has the burden of showing two things: (1) a legally protectable trade secret; and (2) a legal basis, either a covenant or a confidential relationship, upon which to predicate relief.

Since we are primarily concerned with the fact that Buckingham is seeking to enjoin Greenberg from using formulas he developed without the aid of an agreement, we shall assume for the purpose of this appeal that the appellees have met their burden of proving that the formulas in issue are trade secrets. The sole issue for us to decide, therefore, is whether or not a confidential relationship existed between Greenberg and Buckingham binding Greenberg to a duty of nondisclosure.

The usual situation involving misappropriation of trade secrets in violation of a confidential relationship is one in which an employer *discloses to his employee* a pre-existing trade secret (one already developed or formulated) so that the employee may duly perform his work. In such a case, the trust and confidence upon which legal relief is predicated stems from the instance of the employer's *turning over to the employee* the pre-existing trade secret. It is then that a pledge of secrecy is impliedly extracted from the employee, a pledge which he carries with him even beyond the ties of his employment relationship. Since it is conceptually impossible, however, to elicit an implied pledge of secrecy from the sole act of an employee turning over to his employer a trade secret which he, the employee, has developed, as occurred in the present case, the appellees must show a different manner in which the present circumstances support the permanent cloak of confidence cast upon Greenberg by the chancellor. The only avenue open to the appellees is to show that the nature of the employment relationship itself gave rise to a duty of nondisclosure.

The burden the appellees must thus meet brings to the fore a problem of accommodating competing policies in our law: the right of a businessman to be protected against unfair competition stemming from the usurpation of his trade secrets and the right of an individual to the unhampered pursuit of the occupations and livelihoods for which he is best suited. There are cogent socio-economic arguments in favor of either position. Society as a whole greatly benefits from technological improvements. Without some means of post-employment protection to assure that valuable developments or improvements are exclusively those of the employer, the businessman could not afford to subsidize research or improve current methods. In addition, it must be recognized that modern economic growth and development has pushed the business venture beyond the size of the one-man firm, forcing the businessman to a much greater degree to entrust confidential business information relating to technological development to appropriate employees. While recognizing the utility in the dispersion of responsibilities in larger firms, the optimum amount of "entrusting" will not occur unless the risk of loss to the businessman through a breach of trust can be held to a minimum.

On the other hand, any form of post-employment restraint reduces the economic mobility of employees and limits their personal freedom to pursue a preferred course of livelihood. The employee's bargaining position is weakened because he is potentially shackled by the acquisition of alleged trade secrets; and thus, paradoxically, he is restrained, because of his increased expertise, from advancing further in the industry in which he is most productive. Moreover, as previously mentioned, society suffers because competition is diminished by slackening the dissemination of ideas, processes and methods.

Were we to measure the sentiment of the law by the weight of both English and American decisions in order to determine whether it favors protecting a businessman from certain forms of competition or protecting an individual in his unrestricted pursuit of a livelihood, the balance would heavily favor the latter . . . . The chancellor's finding that Greenberg, while in the employ of Buckingham, never engaged in research nor conducted any experiments nor created or invented any formula was undisputed. There is nothing in the record to indicate that the formulas in issue were specific projects of great concern and concentration by Buckingham; instead it appears they were merely the result of Greenberg's routine work of changing and modifying formulas derived from competitors. Since there was no experimentation or research, the developments by change and modification were fruits of Greenberg's own skill as a chemist without any appreciable assistance by way of information or great expense or supervision by Buckingham, outside of the normal expenses of his job . . . . [W]e hold that this information forms part of the technical knowledge and skill [Greenberg] has acquired by virtue of his employment with Buckingham and which he has an unqualified privilege to use . . . .

Notes & Questions

1. Was Greenberg "Hired to Invent?"

Ownership of trade secrets in the employment setting depends upon three factors: (1) the nature of the work for which the employee was hired, (2) the degree to which the invention is related to the employer's business, and (3) the extent to which the employee used the employer's time and resources to develop the trade secret. When an employee is hired to invent, the product of his efforts belong to his employer. This is true even for a scientist hired to conduct general research and development, where the employer does not specify the thing or specific field in which the employee is to work. Nonetheless, *Wexler v. Greenberg* illustrates that under certain situations, the employee is free to use his unpatented discoveries. One explanation for the result in *Wexler* is that Greenberg was not engaged in research and development. Instead, Buckingham hired Greenberg for his general skill in chemistry, to duplicate the preexisting formulas of competitor's cleaning products. The formulas duplicated by Greenberg for his former employer resulted directly from his skill and experience rather than from company-sponsored independent research and development. Greenberg therefore was free to use his skill, knowledge, and experience, as embodied in the formulas, in the service of subsequent employers.

Factual analysis of the trade secret issue reveals another way to look at the result in *Wexler*. Notice that the *Wexler* court merely "assumed for the purposes of the appeal . . . that the formulas in issue are trade secrets." Greenberg's role at Buckingham was to reverse engineer cleaning products owned by third parties. If the formulas for the cleaning products are readily susceptible of copying, then anyone who purchases the cleaning products from the third parties may determine the underlying formulas. Where an employer cannot prove that a former employee took information that was a trade secret, then without an express restrictive covenant to the contrary, the employee is free to use his knowledge and skill to pursue his living wherever he so chooses.

2. Post-Employment Limits on Trade Secret Protection

After the termination of the employment relationship, an employee may use his skill, knowledge, and experience in subsequent employment so long as such use does not involve or threaten the disclosure of the former employer's trade secret or violate a restrictive covenant. An employer may not claim trade secret rights over the general knowledge of its employees. Such knowledge includes the employee's education, prior job experiences, and ability that he brings with him to the beginning of employment, as well as any job-enhanced skills he gains during the term of employment.

In addition, once the employment relationship terminates, the employee is no longer under an implied duty not to compete with his former employer. An employee is free to improve himself and leverage his superior abilities at the conclusion of the employment relationship into a better job, even one in competition with his former employer. The law generally favors employee mobility and competition. According to the federal Defend Trade Secrets Act, an injunction in a civil trade secret misappropriation case may not "prevent a person from entering into an employment relationship." Any conditions placed by the injunction on such employment "shall be based on evidence of threatened misappropriation and *not merely on the information the person knows*." 18 U.S.C. § 1836 (emphasis added). The balance between the employer's interest in secrecy and the employee's rights to mobility is drawn upon distinguishing between the employer's unique confidential knowledge that the law protects, and the employee's own general knowledge and experience, which the law allows the employee to take with him.

3. Social Media Features as Trade Secrets

Recently, judges have entertained arguments that social media accounts, or usernames and passwords for access thereto, constitute trade secrets. Under this view, when an employee who has access to an employer's social media account leaves his or her employment, the former employee's continued use of that social media account may constitute trade secret misappropriation. For example, in *Christou v. Beatport*, 849 F. Supp. 2d 1055 (D. Colo. 2012), the defendant was a former employee of the plaintiff. His job was to recruit DJs to play in nightclubs. *Id.* at 1062. Part of this job included access to the plaintiff's MySpace account and the "friends" list that account had accumulated. *Id.* When the defendant left the plaintiff's company and started his own competing business, he continued to use the MySpace account and friends list. *Id.* at 1074. The court refused to dismiss the plaintiff's argument that such continued use constituted trade secret misappropriation. The matter was later settled out of court. *Id.* at 1076.

Similarly, a federal district court in California considered a case in which a mobile news and reviews company sued a former employee for trade secret misappropriation based on the former employee's refusal to turn over a Twitter account. The account (@PhoneDog_Noah) was set up for the defendant when he started working for the company. Other employees of the company had similar accounts with user handles following the same naming convention (that is, @PhoneDog_USERNAME). When defendant left the company, he refused to turn over the account login information, changed the handle to @noahkravitz, and continued to use the account. The account had been used to tweet information on behalf of the company and had accumulated many followers. The plaintiff company, PhoneDog, alleged $340,000 in damages. The defendant filed a motion to dismiss for failure to state a claim, arguing that his failure to turn over the Twitter account did not amount to trade secret misappropriation. The court denied the motion to dismiss and the parties eventually settled out of court. *PhoneDog v. Kravitz*, 2011 U.S. Dist. LEXIS 129229 (N.D. Cal. Nov. 8, 2011).

4. *Waymo v. Uber*

As mentioned in Chapter 3, in February 2017, Waymo, Alphabet Inc.'s autonomous car company, sued Uber for trade-secret misappropriation. The suit involved employment issues as Waymo alleged that its former engineer and project leader, Anthony Levandowski, downloaded 14,000 secret documents from its system before leaving Waymo. He allegedly used the contents of the secret files to launch his own self-driving truck start-up, Otto, in January 2016. Uber acquired Otto later in 2016 and made Levandowski the head of Uber's driverless car operation. When Waymo discovered the theft and filed its suit, Levandowski exercised his Fifth Amendment rights to resist production of certain documents and was ordered to refrain from working on Uber's self-driving car project. He was later fired from Uber for failure to assist with its internal investigation. Joe Mullin, *Uber Engineer Levandowski, Accused of Massive Theft From Google, Has Been Fired*, ARSTECHNICA (May 30, 2017, 3:24 PM), https://arstechnica.com/tech-policy/2017/05/ubers-levandowski-gets-fired/. The discovery process in this case was complicated by the alleged use of disappearing messaging apps (like Wickr) by the employees of Uber in order to conceal the alleged trade secret misappropriation. Uber, at the time of the settlement the world's most valuable privately held start-up, eventually settled the case, transferring to Waymo a 0.34 percent stake in its equity, which was estimated to be worth close to a quarter billion dollars. Elizabeth Dwoskin & Peter Holley, *Uber CEO Plays It Safe in Risk-Loving Silicon Valley*, WASH. POST, Feb. 13, 2018, https://www.washingtonpost.com/news/the-switch/wp/2018/02/13/uber-ceo-plays-it-safe-in-risk-loving-silicon-valley/.

The employment issues raised by the *Waymo v. Uber* case drew significant attention from the legal community because of their potential impact on California's start-up culture. Generally, California's law favors employment mobility. For example, post-employment covenants not to compete are illegal in California. Some expressed concern that the *Uber* case could create a chilling effect on employment mobility.

Employers might be discouraged to hire highly qualified employees, like Levandowski, out of fear of multimillion-dollar suits similar to Waymo's. However, the evidence presented by Waymo at trial, as well as the media coverage, suggests that this case might be an outlier, because Uber's actions that prompted the lawsuit significantly departed from best practices of trade secret compliance. Particularly, Waymo claimed that Levandowski met with Uber's executives on the same day he downloaded confidential information from Waymo's server. Further, Waymo presented direct communications between Levandowski and Travis Kalanick, then Uber's CEO, where Levandowski suggested "I just see this as a race and we need to win, second place is first looser [sic]" and Kalanick used words such as "burn the village."

The fact that the case settled makes it harder to predict the effect of the dispute on Silicon Valley's start-up culture. On the one hand, the case may cause certain companies to abstain from hiring away highly qualified employees from their competitors out of fear of potential litigation. On the other hand, *Uber* might become a mere case study on what not to do in the employment context. Likely, even after *Uber*, as long as companies follow best practices in their hiring decisions and avoid mistakes that Uber made in this case, they will be safe in hiring even highly ranked employees of their competitors. *See* Daryl Lovell, *Waymo-Uber Case to Set New Implications for California's Start-Up Culture*, Syracuse Univ. News, Feb. 8, 2018, https://news .syr.edu/2018/02/waymo-uber-case-to-set-new-implications-for-californias-start -up-culture/.

5. Submission of Ideas by Employees

Every year, American employees submit ideas that save their employers millions of dollars. Submission of ideas by employees generally is governed by the common law of trade secrets, which gives an employer ownership rights to the trade secrets and ideas created by its employees. At minimum, if an idea is related to an employer's business and was developed by an employee on company time and using company resources, then the shop right doctrine generally entitles the employer to use the idea without compensating the employee.

ii. Implied Duties of Employees

When an employee accepts employment that places him in a position to gain knowledge of confidential information, he enters into a confidential relationship that implies a duty not to use or disclose the employer's trade secrets in competition with the employer. The law allows employers to divulge trade secrets to employees without jeopardizing trade secret protection. However, notice usually must be given prior to the disclosure of the confidential information to the employee. The form of the notice is unimportant so long as the notice ensures that the employee knows or has reason to know that the disclosure of information is made in confidence. It is with respect to the information that the employee knows or has reason to know is confidential that the implied duty of confidentiality arises.

Harry R. Defler Corporation v. Kleeman

Supreme Court of New York, Appellate Division, Fourth Department

19 A.D.2d 396 (N.Y.A.D. 1963)

Affirmed by 225 N.E.2d 569 (N.Y. 1967)

WILLIAMS, P. J.

. . . .

Since 1928, the plaintiff and its predecessor have engaged in the business of buying and selling industrial carbons, cokes, charcoal, graphite, and other related products. Over a period exceeding 25 years Harry R. Defler, the founder of plaintiff's predecessor, developed a large number of customers for these various products and compiled a comprehensive catalogue of information in the form of office records . . . . Plaintiff's compilation of information was not available to the general public and could not have been duplicated by one who had not had the actual experience of Harry R. Defler. The value of this information was confirmed by the fact that on the death of Harry R. Defler, the assets of the original corporation, consisting primarily of its goodwill, name, outstanding contracts, and business records, were sold to a purchaser who was himself familiar with the field, for $250,000. The physical assets of the corporation were of relatively slight value. The really substantial asset was Defler's property rights in the confidential information so transferred.

The purchaser organized the plaintiff corporation which continued doing business under the same name and in the same manner as in the past. On December 1, 1956 the plaintiff employed the defendant Francis S. Kleeman to serve as its general manager and elected him vice-president. As a necessary part of his employment as general manager, Kleeman, who had no previous experience in the type of business conducted by plaintiff, was furnished with free access to the business records containing all of such confidential information. There can be no question that this information was treated as confidential by the corporation and would not have been available to Kleeman if it were not essential for the performance of his duties as general manager. Kleeman was made aware of this when he entered plaintiff's employ.

Approximately one year after he became associated with the plaintiff, Kleeman hired the defendant Edward G. Schneider, Jr., to work for plaintiff as a salesman. Like Kleeman, Schneider had no previous experience in this particular type of business nor had he any knowledge of plaintiff's methods or of the information contained in its confidential records.

Sometime in the Spring of 1958 Kleeman and Schneider, although still in the plaintiff's employ and in violation of their duty of loyalty to the plaintiff's interests, embarked upon a course of action designed to divert to themselves the very business they had been employed to obtain and retain for the plaintiff. Mrs. Kleeman and Mrs. Schneider knowingly joined in the plan at a meeting in the Kleeman home, at which all four individual defendants were present, when it was agreed that the corporate defendant Carchem Products Corporation would be formed. The certificate of incorporation was executed on May 14, 1958. Thereupon Kleeman and Schneider ceased their efforts on behalf of their employer. Schneider, holding 50% of the stock of the new corporation, became its president, treasurer, chairman of the board, and sole salesman. Virginia Kleeman purchased the remaining 50% for $500 with a check drawn on her joint bank account with her husband. She also became comptroller and Patricia Schneider became secretary. Kleeman loaned the corporation $5,000 from his personal bank account, thus providing the working capital which enabled the corporation to commence doing business.

The new corporation proved to be an immediate success. Schneider, who had not been able up to that time to develop any business for the plaintiff suddenly became extremely productive. He guided the new corporation with such acumen that within two months the $5,000 loan from Kleeman had been repaid in full and the corporation was able to pay a total of $1,750 per month under the guise of salaries to Virginia Kleeman and the Schneiders. At that time Virginia Kleeman worked a total of 10 hours each week. The corporation also paid her a $50 monthly rental for a space in the Kleeman home where the corporation's books were kept.

Unfortunately for the plaintiff, the new corporation's business success was attributable to the fact that it dealt almost exclusively with customers and suppliers of plaintiff. Defendants, during their employment by plaintiff and while disloyal to it, continued to enjoy all of the benefits of their relationship with plaintiff. They freely exploited plaintiff's confidential information as to the identity and particular needs of customers, solicited customers, vouched for Carchem's credit in plaintiff's name, and even charged telephone and travel expenses to plaintiff although they were incurred in the interests of Carchem. Their audacity probably reached its peak when they paid, with plaintiff's funds, the legal fees incurred in connection with the incorporation of Carchem. Their conduct was not only reprehensible, but completely astounding.

The defendants' disloyalty continued apace after Schneider was discharged by the plaintiff on September 30, 1958. Kleeman not only acquiesced in Schneider's business transactions with plaintiff's customers and suppliers, in his wife's participation in the affairs of Carchem, and in the deposit of her salary in their joint bank account, but he withheld his knowledge of Schneider's activities from the other officers and directors of plaintiff. In some instances he actively diverted business to Carchem. Moreover, following his resignation from plaintiff's employment on February 25, 1960 he not only continued to divert business from plaintiff to Carchem but he procured business for himself in violation of a reasonable and valid noncompetition provision in his contract of employment.

The customers and suppliers of plaintiff, though perhaps well known in industrial fields, were not readily apparent as customers and suppliers for plaintiff's particular type of business. As we have observed, the information as to the availability of materials and the peculiar needs of plaintiff's customers was derived from the intimate knowledge acquired through years of experience by Defler. Therefore, the defendants by exploiting this information obtained an advantage not available to a stranger seeking to set himself up in fair competition with plaintiff. The actions of the defendants in this case amounted to a theft not only of customers which the plaintiff had discovered and developed but of the essential tools for serving such customers.

The conclusion is inescapable that the type of business piracy practiced by the defendants amounted to misconduct which the courts have not hesitated to restrain.

It has been well established that an employee, who has had entrusted to him confidential information pertaining to the conduct and clientele of his employer's business which he would not have obtained were it not for his status as a trusted employee and which affords him an advantage over other competitors to whom the information is not available, may not subsequently use that information to further his own ends . . . . This restriction arises because of the confidential nature of the employment relationship and is not dependent upon the presence in the employment agreement of a provision limiting activities after cessation of employment . . . . The courts have even extended this protective doctrine so that a former employee may not accomplish through indirect means, such as revealing the information to a third party, what he may not achieve directly. In such case the injunction may issue against the new employer attempting to use the information as well as against the former employee. There can be no question that the information which the defendants exploited falls well within the category of data to which protection has traditionally been accorded. "The principle of law, however, is not confined to secret processes of manufacture or methods of doing business, but has a much wider application . . . . The names of the customers of a business concern whose trade and patronage have been secured by years of business effort and advertising, and the expenditure of time and money, constituting a part of the good-will of a business which enterprise and foresight have built up, should be deemed just as sacred and entitled to the same protection as a secret of compounding some article of manufacture and commerce." (*Witkop & Holmes Co.* v. *Boyce, supra*, p. 131.) . . . . The question of the extent to which protection may be accorded customer lists was thoroughly reviewed in *Town & Country Serv.* v. *Newbery* (3 N.Y.2d 554). The criteria which the court relied upon in that case are equally applicable to the present case. It was stated (pp. 559, 560): "the plaintiff had obtained a customer list, the names of which 'could only be secured by the expenditure of a large amount of time, effort, and money in gathering together such a vast list of consumers who desired to do business in this peculiar way. These customers were not classified as likely customers in any public directory. They were not discoverable by any public display of their willingness to deal.' . . . It would be different if these customers had been equally available to appellants and respondent, but, as has been related, these customers had been screened by respondent as considerable effort and expense, without which their receptivity and willingness to do business with this kind of a service organization could not be known."

Plaintiff is, therefore, entitled to an injunction permanently restraining the defendants from continuing their illegal activities. In addition, plaintiff is entitled to be compensated for the damages which it has sustained as a consequence of the defendants' unlawful acts (*Town & Country Serv. v. Newbery, supra; Duane Jones Co. v. Burke*, 306 N.Y. 172, *supra; Electrolux Corp. v. Val-Worth, Inc.*, 6 N.Y.2d 556).

In cases of this nature an accounting for the profits realized by the defendants resulting from their illegal acts may furnish the most reliable method of computing the loss (see *Biltmore Pub. Co. v. Grayson Pub. Corp.*, 272 App. Div. 504; *Dad's Root Beer Co. v. Doc's Beverages*, 193 F.2d 77). However, in view of the substantial and unnecessary expenses incurred by the defendants in the form of excessive salaries and otherwise, a bare accounting for the defendants' profits may not make the plaintiff whole. The accounting Justice should determine what the plaintiff's margin of net profit would have been if it had retained the business which the defendants diverted (see *Westcott Chuck Co. v. Oneida Nat. Chuck Co.*, 199 N.Y. 247; *Santa's Workshop v. Sterling*, 2 A.D.2d 262). With respect to determining sales which the plaintiff could reasonably have expected to make but for defendants' disloyalties, there is in this case "a causal relation not wholly unsubstantial and imaginary, between the gains of the aggressor and those diverted from his victim." *Underhill v. Schenck*, 238 N.Y. 7, 17.

In view of the continuing nature of the damage sustained by the plaintiff and the fact that this proceeding is equitable in nature, the period of the accounting should extend to the date of the completion thereof, but without limiting plaintiff's right to future accountings. (Cf. *Duane Jones Co. v. Burke, supra.*)

An employee whose actions are disloyal to the interests of his employer forfeits his right to compensation for services rendered by him (*Lamdin v. Broadway Surface Adv. Corp.*, 272 N. Y. 133) and if he is paid without knowledge of his disloyalty he may be compelled to return what he has improperly received. . . . Therefore, the plaintiff may recover the amount of compensation paid to Kleeman and Schneider subsequent to May 14, 1958, the date on which the certificate of incorporation of Carchem was executed. . . . The defendants should also be required to account for any expenses of Carchem which were improperly charged to the plaintiff, and inasmuch as the defendant Francis S. Kleeman violated the provision in his employment agreement against competing with the plaintiff, directly or indirectly, for a period of three years following the termination of his employment, he should compensate the plaintiff for any damages sustained as the result.

Notes & Questions

1. Duration of an Employee's Duty to the Employer

The duty not to use or disclose an employer's trade secret exists during the term of the employment and may endure past the termination of the employment relationship. During employment, there exists an implied duty not to compete, though some jurisdictions allow an employee to engage in activities in anticipation of leaving his current employer, including efforts in furtherance of forming a competing business. However, an employee who begins working for a rival company before leaving the first goes too far and breaches his fiduciary duty to the first employer.

2. Employer's Efforts to Maintain Secrecy

While duty of confidentiality imposed upon employees exists even in the absence of an express confidentiality agreement, the extent to which the implied duties protect an employer's confidential information depend on the employer's efforts to keep the information secret. A lack of effort on the part of the employer to shield its information may jeopardize any implied protection for the information. In *Tyson Foods, Inc. v. Conagra, Inc.*, 79 S.W.3d 326 (Ark. 2002), the court held that Tyson's failure to guard the secrecy of the nutrient profile for its poultry feed defeated the company's attempt to invoke trade secret protection for the information.

> [I]t is the efforts taken by the *company* to safeguard the information that is critical, not the perception of individual officers. Absent clear corporate action to protect the nutrient profile as a trade secret, a subjective belief of an individual employee that the information is confidential or even had value seems largely irrelevant in our analysis.

Tyson, 79 S.W.3d at 483.

c. Copyrights

The copyright in a work initially vests in the author. 17 U.S.C. § 201(a). If more than one author prepares a work "with the intention that their contributions be merged into inseparable or interdependent parts of a unitary whole," then each of the authors owns an equal and undivided interest in the "joint work." 17 U.S.C. § 101.

In the employment context, an employer may commission and pay for a "work made for hire," defined in 17 U.S.C. § 101 as work "prepared by an employee within the scope of his or her employment." If an employee creates a work made for hire, then the employer is deemed the author and owns the copyright in the work. Unlike the laws governing patents and trade secrets, the legislative history of the Copyright Act reflects a rejection of the shop right doctrine. Instead of awarding the employer a mere shop right, a nonexclusive license to use the work, the Copyright Act awards outright ownership in the copyright to the employer. Not surprisingly, the determination of when a person qualifies as an employee has important consequences for proper assignment of the copyright in a work.

Community for Creative Non-Violence v. James Earl Reid

Supreme Court of the United States

490 U.S. 730 (1989)

MARSHALL, JUSTICE.

In this case, an artist and the organization that hired him to produce a sculpture contest the ownership of the copyright in that work. To resolve this dispute, we must construe the "work made for hire" provisions of the Copyright Act of 1976 (Act or 1976 Act), 17 U. S. C. §§ 101 and 201(b), and in particular, the provision in § 101, which defines as a "work made for hire" a "work prepared by an employee within the scope of his or her employment" (hereinafter § 101(1)).

I

Petitioners are the Community for Creative Non-Violence (CCNV), a nonprofit unincorporated association dedicated to eliminating homelessness in America, and Mitch Snyder, a member and trustee of CCNV. In the fall of 1985, CCNV decided to participate in the annual Christmastime Pageant of Peace in Washington, D. C., by sponsoring a display to dramatize the plight of the homeless. As the District Court recounted:

> "Snyder and fellow CCNV members conceived the idea for the nature of the display: a sculpture of a modern Nativity scene in which, in lieu of the traditional Holy Family, the two adult figures and the infant would appear as contemporary homeless people huddled on a streetside steam grate. The family was to be black (most of the homeless in Washington being black); the figures were to be life-sized, and the steam grate would be positioned atop a platform 'pedestal,' or base, within which special-effects equipment would be enclosed to emit simulated 'steam' through the grid to swirl about the figures. They also settled upon a title for the work—'Third World America'—and a legend for the pedestal: 'and still there is no room at the inn.'" 652 F. Supp. 1453, 1454 (DC 1987).

Snyder made inquiries to locate an artist to produce the sculpture. He was referred to respondent James Earl Reid, a Baltimore, Maryland sculptor. In the course of two telephone calls, Reid agreed to sculpt the three human figures. CCNV agreed to make the steam grate and pedestal for the statue. Reid proposed that the work be cast in bronze, at a total cost of approximately $100,000 and taking six to eight months to complete. Snyder rejected that proposal because CCNV did not have sufficient funds, and because the statue had to be completed by December 12 to be included in the pageant. Reid then suggested, and Snyder agreed, that the sculpture would be made of a material known as "Design Cast 62," a synthetic substance that could meet CCNV's monetary and time constraints, could be tinted to resemble bronze, and could withstand the elements. The parties agreed that the project would cost no more than $15,000, not including Reid's services, which he offered to donate. The parties did not sign a written agreement. Neither party mentioned copyright.

After Reid received an advance of $3,000, he made several sketches of figures in various poses. At Snyder's request, Reid sent CCNV a sketch of a proposed sculpture showing the family in a crèche like setting: the mother seated, cradling a baby in her lap; the father standing behind her, bending over her shoulder to touch the baby's foot. Reid testified that Snyder asked for the sketch to use in raising funds for the sculpture. Snyder testified that it was also for his approval. Reid sought a black family to serve as a model for the sculpture. Upon Snyder's suggestion, Reid visited a family living at CCNV's Washington shelter but decided that only their newly born child was a suitable model. While Reid was in Washington, Snyder took him to see homeless people living on the streets. Snyder pointed out that they tended to recline on steam grates, rather than sit or stand, in order to warm their bodies. From that time on, Reid's sketches contained only reclining figures.

Throughout November and the first two weeks of December 1985, Reid worked exclusively on the statue, assisted at various times by a dozen different people who were paid with funds provided in installments by CCNV. On a number of occasions, CCNV members visited Reid to check on his progress and to coordinate CCNV's construction of the base. CCNV rejected Reid's proposal to use suitcases or shopping bags to hold the family's personal belongings, insisting instead on a shopping cart. Reid and CCNV members did not discuss copyright ownership on any of these visits.

On December 24, 1985, 12 days after the agreed-upon date, Reid delivered the completed statue to Washington. There it was joined to the steam grate and pedestal prepared by CCNV and placed on display near the site of the pageant. Snyder paid Reid the final installment of the $15,000. The statue remained on display for a month. In late January 1986, CCNV members returned it to Reid's studio in Baltimore for minor repairs. Several weeks later, Snyder began making plans to take the statue on a tour of several cities to raise money for the homeless. Reid objected, contending that the Design Cast 62 material was not strong enough to withstand the ambitious itinerary. He urged CCNV to cast the statue in bronze at a cost of $35,000, or to create a master mold at a cost of $5,000. Snyder declined to spend more of CCNV's money on the project.

In March 1986, Snyder asked Reid to return the sculpture. Reid refused. He then filed a certificate of copyright registration for "Third World America" in his name and announced plans to take the sculpture on a more modest tour than the one CCNV had proposed. Snyder, acting in his capacity as CCNV's trustee, immediately filed a competing certificate of copyright registration.

Snyder and CCNV then commenced this action against Reid and his photographer, Ronald Purtee, seeking return of the sculpture and a determination of copyright ownership. The District Court granted a preliminary injunction, ordering the sculpture's return. After a 2-day bench trial, the District Court declared that "Third World America" was a "work made for hire" under § 101 of the Copyright Act and that Snyder, as trustee for CCNV, was the exclusive owner of the copyright in the sculpture. 652 F. Supp., at 1457. The court reasoned that Reid had been an "employee" of CCNV within the meaning of § 101(1) because CCNV was the motivating force in the statue's production. Snyder and other CCNV members, the court explained, "conceived the idea of a contemporary Nativity scene to contrast with the national celebration of the season," and "directed enough of [Reid's] effort to assure that, in the end, he had produced what they, not he, wanted." *Id.* at 1456.

. . . .

II

A

The Copyright Act of 1976 provides that copyright ownership "vests initially in the author or authors of the work." 17 U.S.C. § 201(a). As a general rule, the author is the party who actually creates the work, that is, the person who translates an idea into a fixed, tangible expression entitled to copyright protection. § 102. The Act carves out an important exception, however, for "works made for hire." If the work is for hire, "the employer or other person for whom the work was prepared is considered the author" and owns the copyright, unless there is a written agreement to the contrary. § 201(b). Classifying a work as "made for hire" determines not only the initial ownership of its copyright, but also the copyright's duration, § 302(c), and the owners' renewal rights, § 304(a), termination rights, § 203(a), and right to import certain goods bearing the copyright, § 601(b)(1). See 1 M. Nimmer & D. Nimmer, Nimmer on Copyright § 5.03 [A], pp. 5–10 (1988). The contours of the work for hire doctrine therefore carry profound significance for freelance creators—including artists, writers, photographers, designers, composers, and computer programmers—and for the publishing, advertising, music, and other industries which commission their works. Section 101 of the 1976 Act provides that a work is "for hire" under two sets of circumstances:

> (1) a work prepared by an employee within the scope of his or her employment; or

> (2) a work specially ordered or commissioned for use as a contribution to a collective work, as a part of a motion picture or other audiovisual work, as a translation, as a supplementary work, as a compilation, as an instructional text, as a test, as answer material for a test, or as an atlas, if the parties expressly agree in a written instrument signed by them that the work shall be considered a work made for hire.

Petitioners do not claim that the statue satisfies the terms of § 101(2). Quite clearly, it does not. Sculpture does not fit within any of the nine categories of "specially ordered or commissioned" works enumerated in that subsection, and no written agreement between the parties establishes "Third World America" as a work for hire.

The dispositive inquiry in this case therefore is whether "Third World America" is "a work prepared by an employee within the scope of his or her employment" under § 101(1). The Act does not define these terms. In the absence of such guidance, four interpretations have emerged. The first holds that a work is prepared by an employee whenever the hiring party retains the right to control the product. Petitioners take this view. A second, and closely related, view is that a work is prepared by an employee under § 101(1) when the hiring party has actually wielded control with respect to the creation of a particular work. This approach was formulated by the Court of Appeals for the Second Circuit, *Aldon Accessories Ltd. v. Spiegel, Inc.*, 738 F. 2d 548, cert. denied, 469 U.S. 982 (1984), and adopted by the Fourth Circuit, *Brunswick Beacon, Inc. v. Schock-Hopchas Publishing Co.*, 810 F. 2d 410 (1987), the Seventh Circuit, *Evans*

Newton, Inc. v. *Chicago Systems Software*, 793 F. 2d 889, cert. denied, 479 U.S. 949 (1986), and, at times, by petitioners, Brief for Petitioners 17. A third view is that the term "employee" within § 101(1) carries its common-law agency law meaning. This view was endorsed by the Fifth Circuit in *Easter Seal Society for Crippled Children & Adults of Louisiana, Inc.* v. *Playboy Enterprises*, 815 F. 2d 323 (1987), and by the Court of Appeals below. Finally, respondent and numerous *amici curiae* contend that the term "employee" only refers to "formal, salaried" employees.

The starting point for our interpretation of a statute is always its language. *Consumer Product Safety Comm'n* v. *GTE Sylvania, Inc.*, 447 U.S. 102, 108 (1980). The Act nowhere defines the terms "employee" or "scope of employment." It is, however, well established that "[w]here Congress uses terms that have accumulated settled meaning under . . . the common law, a court must infer, unless the statute otherwise dictates, that Congress means to incorporate the established meaning of these terms." *NLRB* v. *Amax Coal Co.*, 453 U.S. 322, 329 (1981); see also *Perrin* v. *United States*, 444 U.S. 37, 42 (1979). In the past, when Congress has used the term "employee" without defining it, we have concluded that Congress intended to describe the conventional master-servant relationship as understood by common-law agency doctrine. See, *e.g., Kelley* v. *Southern Pacific Co.*, 419 U.S. 318, 322–323 (1974); *Baker* v. *Texas & Pacific R. Co.*, 359 U.S. 227, 228 (1959) *(per curiam); Robinson* v. *Baltimore & Ohio R. Co.*, 237 U.S. 84, 94 (1915). Nothing in the text of the work for hire provisions indicates that Congress used the words "employee" and "employment" to describe anything other than "'the conventional relation of employer and employee.'" *Kelley, supra*, at 323, quoting *Robinson, supra*, at 94; cf. *NLRB* v. *Hearst Publications, Inc.*, 322 U.S. 111, 124–132 (1944) [(superseded on other grounds by statute as stated in *NLRB v. Town & Country Elec.*, 516 U.S. 85 (1995) & *NLRB v. United Ins. Co.*, 390 U.S. 254 (1968))] (rejecting agency law conception of employee for purposes of the National Labor Relations Act where structure and context of statute indicated broader definition). On the contrary, Congress' intent to incorporate the agency law definition is suggested by § 101(1)'s use of the term, "scope of employment," a widely used term of art in agency law. See Restatement (Second) of Agency § 228 (1958) (hereinafter Restatement).

. . . .

In contrast, neither test proposed by petitioners is consistent with the text of the Act. The exclusive focus of the right to control the product test on the relationship between the hiring party and the product clashes with the language of § 101(1), which focuses on the relationship between the hired and hiring parties. The right to control the product test also would distort the meaning of the ensuing subsection, § 101(2). Section 101 plainly creates two distinct ways in which a work can be deemed for hire: one for works prepared by employees, the other for those specially ordered or commissioned works which fall within one of the nine enumerated categories and are the subject of a written agreement. The right to control the product test ignores this dichotomy by transforming into a work for hire under § 101(1) any "specially ordered or commissioned" work that is subject to the supervision and control of the hiring party. Because a party who hires a "specially ordered or commissioned" work by definition has a right to specify the characteristics of the product desired, at the time the commission is accepted, and frequently until it is completed, the right to control the product test would mean that many works that could satisfy § 101(2) would already have been deemed works for hire under § 101(1). Petitioners' interpretation is particularly hard to square with § 101(2)'s enumeration of the nine specific categories of specially ordered or commissioned works eligible to be works for hire, e.g., "a contribution to a collective work," "a part of a motion picture," and "answer material for a test." The unifying feature of these works is that they are usually prepared at the instance, direction, and risk of a publisher or producer. By their very nature, therefore, these types of works would be works by an employee under petitioners' right to control the product test.

. . . .

We therefore conclude that the language and structure of § 101 of the Act do not support either the right to control the product or the actual control approaches. The structure of § 101 indicates that a work for hire can arise through one of two mutually exclusive means, one for employees and one for independent contractors, and ordinary canons of statutory interpretation indicate that the classification of a particular hired party should be made with reference to agency law.

This reading of the undefined statutory terms finds considerable support in the Act's legislative history. . . .

. . . .

In sum, we must reject petitioners' argument. Transforming a commissioned work into a work by an employee on the basis of the hiring party's right to control, or actual control of, the work is inconsistent with the language, structure, and legislative history of the work for hire provisions. To determine whether a work is for hire under the Act, a court first should ascertain, using principles of general common law of agency, whether the work was prepared by an employee or an independent contractor. After making this determination, the court can apply the appropriate subsection of § 101.

B

We turn, finally, to an application of § 101 to Reid's production of "Third World America." In determining whether a hired party is an employee under the general common law of agency, we consider the hiring party's right to control the manner and means by which the product is accomplished. Among the other factors relevant to this inquiry are the skill required; the source of the instrumentalities and tools; the location of the work; the duration of the relationship between the parties; whether the hiring party has the right to assign additional projects to the hired party; the extent of the hired party's discretion over when and how long to work; the method of payment; the hired party's role in hiring and paying assistants; whether the work is part of the regular business of the hiring party; whether the hiring party is in business; the provision of employee benefits; and the tax treatment of the hired party. See Restatement § 220(2) (setting forth a nonexhaustive list of factors relevant to determining whether a hired party is an employee). No one of these factors is determinative. See *Ward*, 362 U.S., at 400; *Hilton Int'l Co.* v. *NLRB*, 690 F. 2d 318, 321 (CA2 1982).

Examining the circumstances of this case in light of these factors, we agree with the Court of Appeals that Reid was not an employee of CCNV but an independent contractor. 270 U.S. App. D. C., at 35, n. 11, 846 F. 2d, at 1494, n. 11. True, CCNV members directed enough of Reid's work to ensure that he produced a sculpture that met their specifications. 652 F. Supp., at 1456. But the extent of control the hiring party exercises over the details of the product is not dispositive. Indeed, all the other circumstances weigh heavily against finding an employment relationship. Reid is a sculptor, a skilled occupation. Reid supplied his own tools. He worked in his own studio in Baltimore, making daily supervision of his activities from Washington practicably impossible. Reid was retained for less than two months, a relatively short period of time. During and after this time, CCNV had no right to assign additional projects to Reid. Apart from the deadline for completing the sculpture, Reid had absolute freedom to decide when and how long to work. CCNV paid Reid $15,000, a sum dependent on "completion of a specific job, a method by which independent contractors are often compensated." *Holt* v. *Winpisinger*, 811 F. 2d 1532, 1540, 258 U.S. App. D. C. 343, 351 (1987). Reid had total discretion in hiring and paying assistants. "Creating sculptures was hardly 'regular business' for CCNV." 270 U.S. App. D. C., at 35, n. 11, 846 F. 2d, at 1494, n. 11. Indeed, CCNV is not a business at all. Finally, CCNV did not pay payroll or Social Security taxes, provide any employee benefits, or contribute to unemployment insurance or workers' compensation funds.

Because Reid was an independent contractor, whether "Third World America" is a work for hire depends on whether it satisfies the terms of § 101(2). This petitioners concede it cannot do. Thus, CCNV is not the author of "Third World America" by virtue of the work for hire provisions of the Act. However, as the Court of Appeals made clear, CCNV nevertheless may be a joint author of the sculpture if, on remand, the District Court determines that CCNV and Reid prepared the work "with the intention that their contributions be merged into inseparable or interdependent parts of a unitary whole." 17 U.S.C. § 101. In that case, CCNV and Reid would be co-owners of the copyright in the work. See § 201(a).

For the aforestated reasons, we affirm the judgment of the Court of Appeals for the District of Columbia Circuit.

It is so ordered.

2. Private Adjustments Through Employment Contract Terms

a. Introduction

Statutory default rules that assign ownership in intellectual property as between employers and employees are gap-filling rules that come into play in the absence of an express agreement between the parties to the contrary. Parties may override the statutory default rules by entering into contractual agreements that expressly assign ownership in accordance with an agreement between the employer and employee. Because the default rules sometimes assign ownership in intellectual property to the employee, employers have increasingly turned to contracts to protect their proprietary information. Today, invention assignment provisions are commonplace in employment contracts for inventive employees.

Employers may use contracts not only to secure an invention assignment, but also to define other duties owed by an employee. Express agreements may expand the scope of the protection beyond those afforded by the duties implied by law. For example, a contract may impose restrictions on use and disclosure of information that does not qualify for trade secret protection, but that falls under the broader category of information that the employer deems confidential. The freedom to contract is not without limit. Covenants that restrict the use and disclosure of confidential information that is not a trade secret are strictly construed and covenants that restrain the communication of ideas in general are unreasonable and unenforceable.

Just as parties may agree to expand upon the employee's duties imposed by law, they may also covenant to relieve themselves of some of the duties. Parties may agree to expressly disclaim a confidential relationship. In *Anderson v. Century Prods. Co.*, 943 F. Supp. 137 (D.N.H. 1996), the defendant, Century, asserted that it had entered into an agreement with the plaintiff disclaiming a confidential relationship between the parties. The *Anderson* court stated:

> A confidential relationship may arise by operation of law from the affiliation of the parties and the context in which the disclosures are offered. But courts hold that an implied confidential relationship can be defeated if the parties, by agreement, expressly disclaim any such relationship. As one treatise on the subject has noted:
>
> "A disclosure expressly received in confidence may create a confidential relationship. Conversely, express disclaimer by the disclosee of a confidential relationship from the outset will dispel the existence of such a relationship."
>
> R. Milgrim, *Trade Secrets* §4.03 at 4-18 (1984). However, as it purports to waive tort liability, the language must clearly and explicitly indicate unwillingness to enter the relationship. This is the standard to which Century's waiver of confidential relationship must be held.

Anderson, 943 F. Supp. at 151. Express disclaimers negate the confidentiality obligations implied by law and permit the free use and disclosure of trade secrets acquired during the relationship. Since the law favors a strong policy of protecting trust, express disclaimers must use clear, unambiguous language. An agreement that ambiguously purports to disclaim a confidential relationship is considered ineffective.

b. Invention Assignments

In an invention assignment, an employee agrees to assign to the employer the rights to inventions created during the term of the employment relationship. Employers routinely use invention assignments to override the default rules that award owner-ship of inventions to employees. Courts enforce pre-invention assignment agree-ments according to their terms, subject to traditional contract doctrines. Valid invention assignments should be reasonable as to the scope of the matter assigned, should relate to the employer's business, and the time frame for assignment should be reasonable. An otherwise valid assignment agreement usually is enforceable despite a disparity in bargaining power as between the employer and the employee and despite being based on as little consideration as one dollar. Employers also often require a promise that an employee will assist in the prosecution of a patent applica-tion regarding the employee's invention and aid in perfecting the employer's title in the invention.

Freedom Wireless, Inc. v. Boston Communications Group, Inc.

United States District Court for the District of Massachusetts

220 F. Supp. 2d 16 (D. Mass. 2002)

Harrington, Senior District Judge.

This case involves a patent infringement suit by Freedom Wireless, Inc. ("Free-dom Wireless"). The two patents that are alleged to have been infringed in this case are U.S. Patent No. 5,722,067 (issued Feb. 24, 1998) and U.S. Patent No. 6,157,823 (issued Dec. 5, 2000), both of which were issued in the names of co-inventors Daniel Harned and Douglas Fougnies and assigned to Freedom Wireless by way of its pre-decessor company, Cellular Express, Inc. On June 3, 2002, Defendant Boston Com-munications Group, Inc., ("BCGI") filed a motion for summary judgment alleging that Freedom Wireless is not the owner of the two patents at issue and, therefore, lacks standing to sue for infringement. The Court heard argument on this issue on July 23, 2002.

It is a basic principle of patent law that a party who lacks legal ownership of a pat-ent is without standing to sue for infringement of that patent . . . .

It is undisputed that Mr. Harned and Mr. Fougnies conceived of the invention claimed in the two patents at issue sometime between late 1993 and early 1994, when Mr. Harned was working for Orbital Sciences Corporation/ Space Data Divi-sion ("Orbital"). As part of his employment contract with Orbital, Mr. Harned had agreed to the following covenant:

> The Employee agrees that all inventions, innovations or improvements in the Company's methods of conducting business (including new contributions, improvements, and discoveries) conceived or made by the Employee during his or her employment period belong to the Company. The Employee will promptly disclose such inventions, innovations or improvements to the Company and perform all actions reasonably requested by the Company to establish and confirm such ownership, including but not limited to coopera-tion in connection with the Company's obtaining patent and/or copyright protection.

BCGI argues that this agreement conveyed to Orbital an expectant interest in Mr. Harned's invention, which vested as a matter of law into full legal ownership at the moment Mr. Harned first conceived of his invention. Consequently, BCGI argues that Orbital is the owner of the patents at issue and that Mr. Harned's subsequent attempt to assign the invention to Freedom Wireless' predecessor company was a legal nullity.

The Court disagrees with BCGI's contention that the employment contract between Mr. Harned and Orbital created a valid assignment of Mr. Harned's invention. First, as a matter of contractual interpretation, this Court holds that under the terms of the contract Mr. Harned was only obligated to assign his rights to an invention if that invention was related to Orbital's methods of conducting business. This is because the agreement only applies to "inventions, innovations or improvements in the Company's methods of conducting business (including new contributions, improvements, and discoveries)." Under ordinary rules of English usage, the prepositional phrase "in the Company's methods of conducting business" modifies all three nouns in the preceding series. *See, e.g., Pandol Bros., Inc. v. Indemnity Marine Assur. Co.,* 1996 U.S. App. LEXIS 23378 (9th Cir. Aug. 30, 1996) (unpublished) ("Giving this paragraph its most natural meaning, the prepositional phrase . . . modifies all that comes before it . . . [particularly where] no commas set off this phrase from what precedes it."). Thus, under the agreement, Mr. Harned was only under an obligation to assign his ownership to any "invention . . . in the Company's methods of conducting business" that was conceived of by him during his period of employment with Orbital.

This interpretation of the contract as covering only inventions related to Orbital's methods of conducting business is particularly appropriate in light of the strong public policy discouraging contracts that create an unreasonable restraint on trade. For over one hundred years, courts have looked skeptically upon employment contracts that require an employee to assign his inventions to his employer. *See, e.g., Bates Mach. Co. v. Bates,* 192 Ill. 138, 145, 61 N.E. 518 (1901); *Guth v. Minn. Min. & Mfg. Co.,* 72 F.2d 385, 388 (7th Cir. 1934); *Ingersoll-Rand Co. v. Ciavatta,* 110 N.J. 609, 624, 542 A.2d 879–86 (1988). Where such contracts are open-ended with respect to time limit or subject matter, they may be considered unenforceable as against public policy. *See Ingersoll-Rand,* 110 N.J. at 624 ("Courts, however, will not enforce invention assignment contracts that unreasonably obligate an employee in each and every instance to transfer the ownership of the employee's invention to the employer."); *see also* Cal. Lab. Code § 2870 (2002) (providing that invention assignment contracts that are open-ended with respect to time and subject matter are against public policy and therefore unenforceable). Thus, public policy supports an interpretation of the invention assignment contract between Mr. Harned and Orbital that limits the agreement to inventions that are within the subject matter of the employment relationship.

Having first held that the contract between Orbital and Mr. Harned is limited to inventions relating to Orbital's methods of conducting business, this Court further holds that Mr. Harned was not required to assign the invention claimed in the patents at issue in this case because the invention did not relate to Orbital's methods of conducting business. The two patents at issue in this case are for prepaid wireless telephone billing, which is a form of wireless telephone communications that allows users to pay in advance for cellular telephone service. *See Freedom Wireless, Inc. v. Boston Communications Group, Inc.,* 198 F. Supp. 2d 11 (D. Mass. 2002) (describing the technology of prepaid wireless billing). In its most generic embodiment, prepaid wireless billing utilizes some form of electronic signaling in conjunction with a computer database to charge a customer's prepaid account every time a cellular call is made or received. On the other hand, Orbital is a space technology company that develops satellite-based and space-based services, including personal satellite navigation services and guidance systems for rockets. Prepaid wireless billing does not relate to the methods of conducting a business dedicated to developing satellite-based and rocket-based services. Thus, because the invention claimed in the patents at issue is not sufficiently related to Orbital's methods of conducting business, Mr. Harned was not obligated to assign his rights to Orbital.

Finally, in addition to the subject matter limitation contained in the invention assignment agreement between Orbital and Mr. Harned, there is another reason why Freedom Wireless does not lack standing to sue for patent infringement. Freedom Wireless does not lack standing to sue because the invention assignment contract in this case was merely an agreement by Mr. Harned to assign his invention to Orbital at some point in the future and not an actual present assignment. *Arachnid, Inc. v. Merit Indus., Inc.* 939 F.2d 1574, 1580–81 (Fed. Cir. 1991). In order for a pre-invention assignment contract to create a present assignment of an expectant interest in an invention that automatically vests by operation of law into an actual assignment upon conception, the contract must contain words of present conveyance and must require "no further act once an invention [comes] into being." . . . The agreement in this case, which states that "all inventions belong . . . to the Company," and which requires future acts by the inventor such as "disclosing" the invention and "performing" actions necessary to establish ownership, is not sufficient to convey legal title to the invention. *Arachnid,* 939 F.2d at 1581 ("The *legal* title to an invention can pass to another only by a conveyance.") (quoting G. Curtis, A Treatise on the Law of Patents § 170 (4th ed. 1873)). Thus, even if the contract between Mr. Harned and Orbital covered the invention claimed in the patents at issue, Freedom Wireless would still have legal title to the patent and standing to sue in this case because the employment contract did not contain terms sufficient to convey legal title to Orbital. *Arachnid,* 939 F.2d at 1581.

Because this Court rules that Freedom Wireless is the legal owner of the patents at issue in this case, BCGI's motion for summary judgment based on lack of standing is hereby denied.

Notes & Questions

1. "Freedom to Create" Statutes

Parties may override the common law default rules through use of contracts. Since the default rules assigning ownership rights favor employees, employers often seek to opt out of the rules by compelling assignment of inventions through contract. Nine states[1] have restricted the ability of employers to contract around common law rules. These states have enacted so-called "Freedom to Create" statutes that permit assignments of inventions only when the invention relates to the employer's business or results from work that the employee performed for the employer. An example of a typical "Freedom to Create" statute is section 2870 of the California Labor Code.

> § 2870. Application of provision that employee shall assign or offer to assign rights in invention to employer
>
> (a) Any provision in an employment agreement which provides that an employee shall assign, or offer to assign, any of his or her rights in an invention to his or her employer shall not apply to an invention that the employee developed entirely on his or her own time without using the employer's equipment, supplies, facilities, or trade secret information except for those inventions that either:
>
> > (1) Relate at the time of conception or reduction to practice of the invention to the employer's business, or actual or demonstrably anticipated research or development of the employer; or
> >
> > (2) Result from any work performed by the employee for the employer.
>
> (b) To the extent a provision in an employment agreement purports to require an employee to assign an invention otherwise excluded from being required to be assigned under subdivision (a), the provision is against the public policy of this state and is unenforceable.

Cal. Lab. Code § 2870 (West).

2. Federal or State Law?

Patents are creatures of federal law, but ownership rights in patented inventions may fall under the governance of state law. How can this be? When the parties opt to contract around the default rules governing ownership rights to an invention, state contract laws apply. State laws therefore dictate the ownership rights as between the employer and employee in the context of invention assignments. Only where state law creates a serious conflict with federal patent policy must state law yield to its federal counterpart.

3. Unambiguous Language

If the language in a contract is ambiguous, courts may interpret it in a way that thwarts the parties' original intentions. What is perceived as sufficient or clear language, however, may change with time. Justice Breyer notes that, prior to 1991, contract terms such as "agree to assign" and "do hereby assign" were indistinguishable because both conveyed equitable, but not legal, title. *Bd. of Trustees of Leland Stanford*

---

1. California, Delaware, Illinois, Kansas, Minnesota, Nevada, North Carolina, Utah, and Washington.

Junior Univ. v. Roche Molecular Sys., Inc., 563 U.S. 776, 800 (2011) (Breyer, J., dissenting). Neither operated upon the future invention automatically. *Id.* In 1991, however, the Federal Circuit adopted a new rule that in effect made the words "do hereby assign" trump "agree to assign." *FilmTec Corp. v. Allied-Signal, Inc.*, 939 F.2d 1568, 1572 (Fed. Cir. 1991). Stanford University, which contracted back in 1988 with the employee inventor under scrutiny in the *Stanford* case, probably thought it had secured a sufficient assignment by using the language "agree to assign." Unfortunately, the change in the Federal Circuit's reading of assignment contracts three years later rendered the University out of luck. The *Stanford* case is a good reminder that rather than being satisfied with an employee's mere promise to assign rights in the future, employers should use stronger and clearer language, perhaps requiring employees to assign all rights in their inventions to employers.

B. Transfers of Intellectual Property Upon Changes in Employment

1. Enforceability of Restrictions on Subsequent Employment for Parties Holding Trade Secrets

a. Nonuse and Nondisclosure Agreements

Express agreements defining a confidential relationship are called restrictive covenants or confidentiality agreements. Such nonuse and nondisclosure agreements recite that an employee will receive confidential information and the employee agrees not to use or disclose the information. Employers use contractual duties against use or disclosure to protect their secret information, which can include employee-created trade secrets. When employers use contract terms to protect trade secrets, the law usually construes such terms broadly. Because restrictions on use and disclosure are sometimes necessary to give meaningful protection to trade secrets, protection of trade secrets is per se justification for permitting the restrictions. The justification does not apply when employers use contract terms to protect information that is confidential but not a trade secret. The law therefore construes strictly contract terms that limit use and disclosure of confidential but non-trade secret information. In general, courts refuse to enforce agreements that unreasonably restrain competition or unduly hinder an employee from pursuing a livelihood.

Union Pacific Railroad Company v. Brent Mower

United States Court of Appeals for the Ninth Circuit

219 F.3d 1069 (9th Cir. 2000)

FISHER, CIRCUIT JUDGE.

Brent Mower is a former employee of Union Pacific Railroad Company ("UP"). UP obtained a broad injunction against Mower, prohibiting him from disclosing or revealing to third parties any confidential information he obtained while employed by UP. Mower appeals the issuance of that injunction . . . . We reverse and vacate the injunction.

FACTUAL AND PROCEDURAL BACKGROUND

A. *The Resignation Agreement*

UP employed Mower from 1979 to 1992. During that time, Mower rose from a low-level claims adjuster position to Director of Occupational and Environmental Issues. In his management position, Mower's primary responsibility was the investigation and resolution of thousands of occupational illness claims filed against UP. Mower worked closely with UP's legal department on certain issues and, for a portion of his career, was considered a member of the legal department.

In 1992, UP asked Mower to resign, and the parties entered into a resignation and consulting agreement on November 20, 1992 (the "Resignation Agreement"). The Resignation Agreement provided that Mower would serve as a consultant to UP for a period of three years. The Resignation Agreement also stipulated that, from November 1992 until December 31, 1995, Mower would not (1) reveal UP's confidential and privileged information or any other information "harmful" to UP's best interests, (2) "communicate with anyone with respect to the business or affairs of [UP]," or (3) consult with any person asserting claims against UP. It is undisputed on appeal that Mower complied with the terms of the Resignation Agreement through December 31, 1995.

B. *The Idaho Case*

In May 1997, Mariano Ybarra filed a complaint against UP in Idaho, alleging that he had sustained personal injuries while employed at UP and that such injuries were the result of UP's negligence. Ybarra moved to supplement his witness list during March 1998 to add Mower as a witness. In a sworn affidavit, Mower stated that he would testify about a particular study he conducted during 1989, relating generally to Ybarra's type of injury, and about a position paper he prepared in connection with the study and presented to senior management at UP. UP objected, claiming that Mower's proffered testimony related to privileged information. The Idaho trial court deferred ruling on the issue to afford UP's counsel the opportunity to depose Mower.

C. *The Injunction*

In April 1998, while the issue of Mower's testimony was still pending in the Idaho case, UP filed its complaint for an injunction against Mower in the federal district court in Oregon. In its complaint, UP argued that, if allowed to testify in the Idaho case or in any other case, Mower would reveal UP's confidential information and trade secrets and would violate . . . Mower's fiduciary duty to preserve confidential information. In particular, UP protested Mower's intention to testify regarding the particular study and position paper discussed in Mower's affidavit in the Idaho case. UP alleged that it would suffer irreparable damage from Mower's disclosure of the position paper or any other confidential information, because such information "may be used . . . in a number of lawsuits against [UP]." UP asked the district court to enjoin Mower from disclosing confidential information in any lawsuit, in order to "prevent a multiplicity of litigation."

Mower objected to UP's complaint on several grounds. Mower argued, among other things, that the information in question—in particular, the study and position paper discussed in his affidavit—was neither confidential nor privileged. He emphasized the publicly available resources he had consulted during the study, including on-line databases and various professionals and academics who were not associated with UP. Mower also contended that the Resignation Agreement's expiration at the end of 1995 left him free to disclose such information, even if confidential or privileged.

The district court granted UP's motion for a preliminary injunction against Mower, finding that the information obtained by Mower during his employment was highly confidential and that Mower owed UP an implied duty of confidentiality . . . .

Following the district court's grant of the preliminary injunction, UP and Mower stipulated to the issuance of a substantially similar permanent injunction; however, Mower reserved his rights to object to the form of the injunction and to appeal. The district court entered the permanent injunction against Mower on October 14, 1998, and this appeal followed.

DISCUSSION

. . . On appeal, Mower argues that the district court erred in concluding that he owes a continuing duty of confidentiality to UP and in issuing an injunction on that basis. Mower also suggests that the district court erred in concluding that the information held by Mower, particularly the study and position paper, was entirely confidential. As explained below, we conclude that the injunction is inappropriate.

A. *The Implied Duty of Confidentiality and the Resignation Agreement*

The district court issued the injunction against Mower based on its conclusion that, "after his employment and his services as a consultant terminated, defendant Mower remained under an implied duty not to disclose [UP's] confidential business information." The district court reasoned that Mower's duty of confidentiality "goes way beyond any express agreement that expired in 1995, but extends for his lifetime." The district court was correct only if Oregon law recognizes an implied duty of confidentiality and the Resignation Agreement either could not, as a matter of law, or did not, pursuant to its terms, serve to limit Mower's implied duty of confidentiality.[4]

Oregon law imposes on every employee a legal duty to protect an employer's trade secrets and other confidential information, an obligation that continues beyond the term of employment. In *McCombs v. McClelland*, 223 Ore. 475, 354 P.2d 311 (1960),

---

4. Because UP filed its complaint in Oregon district court and based its claim against Mower on that state's common law implied duty of confidentiality, we apply Oregon law to evaluate whether the district court's issuance of the injunction on that basis was appropriate. However, . . . Nebraska law governs our interpretation of the terms of the Resignation Agreement.

the Oregon Supreme Court held that ex-employees are under "an implied obligation . . . not to use [their former employers'] trade secrets or confidential information for [their] own benefit or that of third persons . . . ." *Id.* at 483, 354 P.2d at 315–16 (noting that "the law is well settled" on this issue (quoting Annotation, *Implied Obligation of Employee Not to Use Trade Secrets or Confidential Information for His Own Benefit or That of Third Persons After Leaving the Employment*, 165 A.L.R. 1453, 1454 (1946)) (internal quotation marks omitted)). Thus, the district court properly concluded that Oregon law recognizes an implied duty of confidentiality.

However, Oregon also generally permits parties to alter by negotiation duties that would otherwise be governed by state law. In *Owings v. Rose*, 262 Ore. 247, 497 P.2d 1183 (1972), for example, the Oregon Supreme Court held that, "where the parties have made an express contract of indemnity[,] its terms will control" despite Oregon's recognition of indemnity actions based on implied contract. *Id.* at 263, 497 P.2d at 1190; *see also Eggiman v. Mid-Century Ins. Co.*, 134 Ore. App. 381, 385–86, 895 P.2d 333, 335 (1995) (implied covenant of good faith and fair dealing applies unless altered by the express terms of an agreement); *White's Elecs., Inc. v. Teknetics, Inc.*, 67 Ore. App. 63, 67, 677 P.2d 68, 70–71 (1984) ("Absent an agreement to the contrary," an employee has a duty to assign patent rights to an employer.). Therefore, the general rule in Oregon appears to be that parties can "contract out" of implied duties.

Nor is there any indication that the outcome should be different with respect to the particular duty at issue in this case—the implied duty of confidentiality. In *McCombs*, the Oregon Supreme Court gave no indication that the duty of confidentiality should be regarded as inviolate. In fact, in recognizing the existence of this implied duty under Oregon law, the *McCombs* court relied on an American Law Reports annotation that suggests the contrary. *See McCombs*, 223 Ore. at 483, 354 P.2d at 315–16. The annotation notes that "the question as to the obligation of a former employee not to reveal . . . confidential information, *where there was an express contract in that regard*, is not within the scope of the annotation." Annotation, 165 A.L.R. at 1454 (emphasis added).

We conclude that, under Oregon law, parties have the power to alter the implied duty of confidentiality. The existence of an express agreement is relevant both in determining whether a particular employee is bound by a duty of confidentiality and in defining the scope of that duty. The remaining issue, therefore, is whether the Resignation Agreement affected Mower's implied duty of confidentiality. We believe it did.

The Resignation Agreement provided in relevant part:

4. *From now until December 31, 1995:*

(a) You will take no action, nor make any statement which, in the reasonable judgment of [UP's] management, would be harmful or otherwise detrimental to the best interests of [UP], any of its subsidiaries or its stockholders and, subject to your obligations to any future employer, you will use your best efforts to promote the business and affairs of [UP] and all of its subsidiaries in all reasonable ways at your disposal.

(b) You will make no statement or otherwise communicate with anyone with respect to the business or affairs of [UP] or any of its subsidiaries, except as may be (i) approved in writing by [UP] or (ii) required by any judicial or regulatory authority having jurisdiction over the subject matter. . . .

(c) You will remove no documents or other written materials, including copies of any kind, pertaining to the business or affairs of [UP] or any of its subsidiaries from the premises of [UP] and will promptly return to [UP] all such documents or materials now or hereafter in your possession.

5. *From now until December 31, 1995*, you agree that you will not . . . engage in any business of, . . . or consult with, directly or indirectly, any person, firm, corporation or other entity, which is engaged in the business or practice relating to the assertion of claims or lawsuits against [UP] . . . . You and [UP] agree and acknowledge that you have acquired special knowledge and expertise in the claims and litigation defense strategy used by [UP]. It is the purpose and intention of this agreement to protect [UP's] trade secrets and privileged communications and claims and litigation strategies which you have learned during the course of your employment. It is not the intention of this agreement to restrict your ability to work for a competing railroad or other transportation company, but to protect [UP's] privileged information and strategies from disclosure.

6. This agreement is not a "noncompetition" agreement and shall not prohibit an employment or consulting relationship between you and any railroad, firm or other entity engaged in the business of defending claims and suits, including investigation and negotiation.

(Emphases added).

Although the Resignation Agreement was drafted broadly to prevent Mower from revealing a wide range of information about UP—regardless of whether such information was properly considered "confidential"—it is clear that an intention to protect any confidential or privileged information held by Mower was at the core of the Resignation Agreement and its restrictions on Mower's activities. Surely, if the events spawning this litigation had occurred before the expiration of the Resignation Agreement, UP would have argued that Mower was prohibited (under both paragraphs 4 and 5 of the Resignation Agreement) from discussing the substance of his study and the resulting position paper or probably from even disclosing their existence.

Just as clearly, however, the Resignation Agreement limited its protection of such information to a distinct period of time, ending December 31, 1995. The unambiguous meaning of the Resignation Agreement was that, after that date, Mower's obligation to conduct his affairs in accordance with that agreement terminated and he would no longer be subject to its nondisclosure requirements.

UP does not suggest that the terms of the Resignation Agreement were ambiguous. Rather, UP argues that—even if, as we hold today, the implied duty of confidentiality can be altered by contract—the Resignation Agreement merely *supplemented* Mower's pre-existing duty without affecting the protections afforded UP by that duty. UP suggests that to find otherwise would be to add to the agreement rather than to construe it in accordance with its terms.

UP's argument is contrary to applicable principles of contract interpretation. We must give effect to the unambiguous time limitation established by the parties. Under Nebraska law, "a written contract which is expressed in clear and unambiguous language is not subject to interpretation or construction"; and "the meaning of an unambiguous contract presents a question of law." *Lueder Constr. Co. v. Lincoln Elec. Co.*, 228 Neb. 707, 710, 424 N.W.2d 126, 128–29 (1988) (citations omitted). Moreover, "[a] contract must be construed as a whole and, if possible, effect must be given to every part thereof." *Husen v. Husen*, 241 Neb. 10, 13, 487 N.W.2d 269, 272 (1992) (quoting *Crowley v. McCoy*, 234 Neb. 88, 91, 449 N.W.2d 221, 224 (1989)) (internal quotation marks omitted).

In effect, UP's contention is that the Resignation Agreement cannot be read to alter Mower's implied duty of confidentiality because the company would not have entered into the Resignation Agreement if it had known that, by doing so, it restricted what would otherwise have been a perpetual duty imposed by law. That may or may not be so, but UP's argument neither changes our interpretation of the unambiguous terms of the Resignation Agreement nor overcomes the inappropriateness of the injunction issued against Mower. UP apparently concluded that the value of the information in question would diminish after several years and opted for a blanket, extremely broad prohibition for a term of years as opposed to an indefinite protection against the dissemination of only that specific information properly deemed "confidential" under Oregon law. The fact that UP's choice may have proved unwise does not alter the legal effect of the bargain it made. *See Husen*, 241 Neb. at 14, 487 N.W.2d at 272 ("Although the respondent may be dissatisfied with the bargain [it] made, it is not for this court to rewrite the contract [it] executed.").

We hold, as a matter of law, that the Resignation Agreement supplanted—rather than supplemented—Mower's implied duty of confidentiality. By the terms of the Resignation Agreement, Mower's duty of confidentiality terminated as of December 31, 1995.

CONCLUSION

Mower's implied duty of confidentiality—whatever its original scope—was superseded by the unambiguous terms of the Resignation Agreement. The Resignation Agreement limited Mower's duty of confidentiality to a distinct time frame, which has since passed. Finding no alternative basis upon which to uphold the injunction, we conclude that the injunction must be REVERSED and VACATED.

Notes & Questions

1. Enforceability Requirements

A nonuse and nondisclosure agreement is enforceable if it: (1) exists at the time of the confidential disclosure, (2) is reasonable in scope, and (3) uses language that is clear and unambiguous. If an agreement places too onerous a burden on an employee, the agreement may be invalidated.

When determining whether the agreement imposes too great a burden on the employee, the court looks to whether the agreement creates a nondisclosure obligation, which is presumptively enforceable, or whether it compels restrictions on competition in general, which is disfavored. In addition, some jurisdictions place a limitation on duration, requiring that agreements be reasonable as to the duration of the agreement. Limitations may also be placed on the protected subject matter, requiring that the information underlying the covenant qualify as a trade secret. In general, the law disfavors agreements that tie the employee's hands too far into the future or too broadly limit the scope of useable information.

2. Maintaining a Trade Secret

To be a trade secret, information must be protected from uncontrolled disclosure. Failure to guard the secrecy of information underlying a trade secret can result loss of trade secret status. To protect the information underlying a trade secret, employers are allowed to limit the employee's ability to disclose the information to others. Use of nonuse and nondisclosure agreements may be necessary to give meaningful protection to trade secrets, especially when a knowledgeable employee exits the company. Not surprisingly, protection of a trade secret is per se justification for use of such restrictive agreements.

b. Covenant Not to Compete

i. Generally

Employers may also impose future restrictions that prevent departing employees from competing with the employer. Covenants not to compete protect the goodwill of the former employer's business. Courts enforce noncompete covenants so long as the scope, time, and territory covered are restricted to what is reasonably needed to protect the employer. Since courts regard covenants that impose restrictions on competition as restraints on trade, they are not as readily enforced as nonuse and nondisclosure agreements.

Nike, Inc. v. Eugene McCarthy

United States Court of Appeals for the Ninth Circuit

379 F.3d 576 (9th Cir. 2004)

FISHER, CIRCUIT JUDGE.

In this case we must determine the validity of a noncompete agreement under Oregon law. Eugene McCarthy left his position as director of sales for Nike's Brand Jordan division in June 2003 to become vice president of U.S. footwear sales and merchandising at Reebok, one of Nike's competitors. Nike sought a preliminary injunction to prevent McCarthy from working for Reebok for a year, invoking a noncompete agreement McCarthy had signed in 1997 when Nike had promoted him to his earlier position as a regional footwear sales manager. Under Oregon law, which governs here, a noncompete agreement generally is void and unenforceable unless agreed to "upon" either the employee's initial employment or—relevant here—the "subsequent bona fide advancement of the employee with the employer." Or. Rev. Stat. §653.295(1)(b) (2004). McCarthy's promotion to regional footwear sales manager was undisputedly an "advancement"; the critical issues are *when* the advancement occurred and whether Nike obtained McCarthy's agreement not to compete "*upon*" that advancement. Construing the Oregon statute and reviewing the circumstances surrounding McCarthy's promotion and the execution of the noncompete agreement, we hold that the agreement meets the statutory requirements to be enforceable. We also hold that Nike has a legitimate interest in enforcing the agreement, because there is a substantial risk that McCarthy—in shaping Reebok's product allocation, sales and pricing strategies—could enable Reebok to divert a significant amount of Nike's footwear sales given the highly confidential information McCarthy acquired at Nike. Thus, we affirm the district court's preliminary injunction enforcing the agreement.

I. FACTUAL AND PROCEDURAL BACKGROUND

McCarthy began working for Nike in 1993 and became a key account manager in 1995. During the spring of 1997, Nike undertook a major, national reorganization. Out of this came McCarthy's promotion to eastern regional footwear sales manager—and the present dispute as to when that promotion actually occurred. On February 28, John Petersen, McCarthy's supervisor, called McCarthy and asked, "How would you like to be the regional footwear sales manager for the eastern region?" McCarthy answered, "Absolutely, yes." Petersen mentioned there would be an increase in pay but did not say what the salary would be.

In the following weeks, McCarthy continued to perform some of his old duties while assuming some of the duties of his new position, including leading meetings and preparing a report. In order to perform these duties, McCarthy obtained confidential information he had not seen before that described the top-selling styles in the eastern region. During the week of March 10, Petersen announced to a group of employees that McCarthy was the new regional footwear sales manager. During the remainder of March, McCarthy took several business trips, which were expensed to the cost center for the regional footwear sales manager position.

On March 27, McCarthy received a letter from Petersen confirming the offer for the regional footwear sales manager position ("Offer Letter"). The letter indicated that the "start date" for the new position was April 1, 1997. According to several Nike executives, it is not unusual for an employee to begin to perform the duties of a new position prior to the start date, in order to ensure a smooth transition once he or she "officially" starts in the new position. The Offer Letter also specified that McCarthy's salary would be $110,000, which became effective April 1. Before that date, McCarthy's salary was charged to the cost center for the key account manager position.

In addition, the Offer Letter required McCarthy to sign an attached covenant not to compete and nondisclosure agreement as a condition of acceptance of the offer.

The covenant not to compete contained the "Competition Restriction" clause at issue here, stating in relevant part:

> During EMPLOYEE'S employment by NIKE . . . and for one (1) year thereafter, (the "Restriction Period"), EMPLOYEE will not directly or indirectly . . . be employed by, consult for, or be connected in any manner with, any business engaged anywhere in the world in the athletic footwear, athletic apparel or sports equipment and accessories business, or any other business which directly competes with NIKE or any of its subsidiaries or affiliated corporations.

McCarthy signed the agreement that day. It is this noncompete agreement that Nike now seeks to enforce.

Two years later, McCarthy was again promoted, this time to the position of director of sales for the Brand Jordan division, the position he held until he resigned from Nike in June 2003. He was not asked to sign a new noncompete agreement. During the spring of 2003, McCarthy accepted a position with Reebok as vice president of U.S. footwear sales and merchandising and tendered his resignation in June. McCarthy began working at Reebok on July 22, 2003.

On August 18, 2003, Nike filed suit in Oregon circuit court, claiming breach of contract and seeking a declaratory judgment that McCarthy's employment with Reebok violated the covenant not to compete . . . .

    . . . .

A. Oregon Revised Statute § 653.295(1)

We first address the merits of Nike's claims. McCarthy contends that the covenant not to compete is void under Oregon Revised Statute § 653.295(1) . . . . As applied to McCarthy's situation, the statute requires that (1) there was a "bona fide advancement" of McCarthy and (2) that the noncompete agreement was "entered into upon" that bona fide advancement. *Id.* Although the parties agree that McCarthy's promotion to regional footwear sales manager involved an advancement within Nike, they disagree as to *when* the advancement occurred. McCarthy contends Nike did not obtain his consent to the noncompete agreement "upon" his advancement but well after it had already been implemented, and thus the agreement came too late to be enforceable under the statute. Understanding what the statute contemplates by way of a bona fide advancement will help shed some light on how to determine when an employee's advancement has occurred so as to justify an employer securing a noncompete agreement.

1. Meaning of bona fide advancement

    . . . .

Although Oregon courts have interpreted section 653.295 before, they have not yet construed the meaning of "bona fide advancement." In the absence of a controlling interpretation by the Oregon Supreme Court, we must construe the term as we believe the Oregon Supreme Court would.

. . . .

The text and context of section 653.295(1)(b) do not clearly indicate what constitutes a bona fide advancement. The statute does not define the term, nor does it appear in other provisions of the same statute or other related statutes. Therefore, we look to the plain, natural, and ordinary meaning of the words. "Bona fide" is defined as "made or carried out in good faith; sincere." The American Heritage College Dictionary 158 (3d. ed. 2000). An "advancement" is "[a] forward step; an improvement," "[a] promotion, as in rank." *Id.* at 19.

Obviously, these definitions leave room for debate about what constitutes a bona fide advancement. In resolving this ambiguity, we find some helpful indicators of legislative intent in the statute's legislative history. In 1977, the Oregon legislature enacted section 653.295, which at that time provided that noncompete agreements were void unless entered into only at the time of initial hiring . . . .

Apparently responding to concerns that foreclosing non-compete agreements later in an employee's career created undesirable results for employers and employees, the Oregon legislature amended section 653.295 in 1983 to permit non-compete agreements to be entered "upon the subsequent bona fide advancement" of an employee within the company. Testimony before the Oregon Senate Committee on Business and Consumer Affairs explained that, under the proposed bill, "the employer still could not surprise the old employee with a new requirement, but the employer could impose the non-competition agreement as a condition of advancing to a higher position in which there is a real need and justification for a noncompete obligation." . . .

In light of this history, it is apparent that the legislature intended to permit employers to require existing employees to agree to a noncompete agreement, so long as the employee's job content and responsibilities materially increased and the employee's status within the company likewise improved. Otherwise, the employer would merely be imposing a new condition for the "same job." *Id.* Thus, an advancement would ordinarily include such elements as new, more responsible duties, different reporting relationships, a change in title and higher pay.

In McCarthy's case, his promotion included all of these elements. He received a new title of regional footwear sales manager and was presented to other employees as such. He undertook new duties associated with the new position, assumed a new supervisory role over other sales representatives, and received a higher salary of $110,000. The issue remains, however, as to when his "advancement" occurred for purposes of triggering Nike's limited opportunity to obtain a binding noncompete agreement "upon" McCarthy's advancement.

2. Meaning of "upon . . . the advancement"

McCarthy's advancement consisted of multiple elements that played out over several weeks, with his promotion not being formalized until he received his Offer Letter with the accompanying noncompete agreement on March 27, 1997, and his pay increase not effective until April 1. In such circumstances, the question arises as to when a noncompete agreement must be entered into relative to this process of advancement. All the statute tells us is that the agreement must be "entered into upon the . . . bona fide advancement of the employee with the employer." Or. Rev. Stat. § 653.295(1).

McCarthy argues that a noncompete agreement must be entered into as soon as the employee takes on any of the duties of the new position. Such an inflexible rule, however, would put employers at risk of losing their noncompete option during a period of "auditioning" an employee for possible promotion and thus could hinder the advancement of employees from within a company, a concern that prompted the state legislature to amend the statute in 1983.

On the other hand, the statute and its legislative history make clear the process is not open-ended. The legislative history suggests that the employer and employee would likely come to some agreement or understanding on the terms and conditions of the new job, in the process of which the employer would inform the employee of the need for a non-compete agreement as a condition of the advancement. This would be consistent with affording employees the intended protection against "surprise" and imposition of "new conditions." For similar reasons, the legislative history implies that an employer should not spring a noncompete agreement on an employee long after the commencement of the advancement process—for instance by unreasonably delaying a pay increase or title change, or deferring consummation of the employer's and employee's agreement on the terms and conditions of the new job. In short, although a non-compete agreement need not be entered into at the first instance that the employee assumes any elements of the new job, including new duties, neither does the window of opportunity to ask for a noncompete agreement remain open until the employer sees fit formally to finalize the advancement process.

. . . McCarthy's noncompete agreement would be enforceable under section 653.295. McCarthy signed the noncompete agreement on March 27 in conjunction with reaching a final agreement on the terms and conditions of his new job, and his pay increase did not take effect until April 1. Moreover, McCarthy's advancement evolved over a reasonably short period of time, with no unreasonable delays by Nike in finalizing the process. For these reasons, we conclude that the district court did not err in finding that McCarthy's noncompete agreement was "entered into upon" his bona fide advancement.

B. Protectable interest

Even if the covenant not to compete is not void under section 653.295, it is a contract in restraint of trade that must meet three requirements under Oregon common law to be enforceable:

> (1) it must be partial or restricted in its operation in respect either to time or place; (2) it must be on some good consideration; and (3) it must be reasonable, that is, it should afford only a fair protection to the interests of the party in whose favor it is made, and must not be so large in its operation as to interfere with the interests of the public.

Eldridge v. Johnston, 195 Ore. 379, 245 P.2d 239, 250 (Or. 1952). To satisfy the reasonableness requirement, the employer must show as a predicate "that [it] has a 'legitimate interest' entitled to protection." *North Pac. Lumber Co. v. Moore*, 275 Ore. 359, 551 P.2d 431, 434 (Or. 1976). McCarthy argues that Nike has failed to show such a legitimate interest in this case.

McCarthy's general skills in sales and product development as well as industry knowledge that he acquired while working for Nike is not a protectable interest of Nike's that would justify enforcement of a noncompete agreement. "It has been uniformly held that general knowledge, skill, or facility acquired through training or experience while working for an employer appertain exclusively to the employee. The fact that they were acquired or developed during the employment does not, by itself, give the employer a sufficient interest to support a restraining covenant, even though the on-the-job training has been extensive and costly." *Rem Metals Corp. v. Logan*, 278 Ore. 715, 565 P.2d 1080, 1083 (Or. 1977).

Nonetheless, an employer has a protectable interest in "information pertaining especially to the employer's business." *Id.*

Nike has shown that McCarthy acquired information pertaining especially to Nike's business during the course of his employment with Nike. As Brand Jordan's director of sales, McCarthy obtained knowledge of Nike's product launch dates, product allocation strategies, new product development, product orders six months in advance and strategic sales plans up to three years in the future. This information was not general knowledge in the industry. For instance, McCarthy was privy to information about launch dates—the date Nike plans to introduce a product in the marketplace—for Brand Jordan shoes up through the spring of 2004. According to the undisputed testimony of one of Nike's executives, if a company knew its competitor's launch dates, it could time the launch dates of its own products to disrupt the sales of its competitor.

Nevertheless, McCarthy argues that acquisition of confidential information alone is insufficient to justify enforcement of a noncompete agreement . . . .

. . . .

An employee's knowledge of confidential information is sufficient to justify enforcement of the noncompete if there is a "substantial risk" that the employee will be able to divert all or part of the employer's business given his knowledge. *See Volt Servs. Group v. Adecco Employment Servs., Inc.*, 178 Ore. App. 121, 35 P.3d 329, 334 (Or. Ct. App. 2001) (stating that customer contacts "can create a protectable interest when the nature of the contact is such that there is a substantial risk that the employee may be able to divert all or part of the customer's business"). Given the nature of the confidential information that McCarthy acquired at Nike and his new position with Reebok, there is a substantial risk that Reebok would be able to divert a significant part of Nike's business given McCarthy's knowledge. McCarthy had the highest access to confidential information concerning Nike's product allocation, product development, and sales strategies. As vice president of U.S. footwear sales and merchandising for Reebok, McCarthy would be responsible for developing strategic sales plans, providing overall direction for product allocation and shaping product lines, including how products are priced. Thus, McCarthy could help choose product allocation, sales, and pricing strategies for Reebok that could divert a substantial part of Nike's footwear sales to Reebok based on his knowledge of information confidential to Nike without explicitly disclosing this information to any of Reebok's employees. Accordingly, the potential use of confidential information by McCarthy in his new position with Reebok is sufficient to justify enforcing the noncompete agreement. We conclude that Nike has demonstrated a likelihood of success as to the enforceability of its noncompete agreement with McCarthy.

V. BALANCE OF HARDSHIPS

McCarthy contends that the district court erred in ruling that the balance of harm tipped in favor of Nike because the only harm that Nike would have suffered is "fair competition." Contrary to McCarthy's contention, Nike has shown potential harm from unfair competition due to McCarthy's knowledge of confidential information peculiar to Nike's products.

On the other side of the scale, a number of factors mitigate the potential harm to McCarthy from the preliminary injunction. First, Nike is obligated under the covenant not to compete to pay McCarthy his full salary during the restriction period. Second, Reebok has agreed to pay health and medical benefits for McCarthy and his family. Third, Reebok has agreed to keep the job offer to McCarthy open for a year. McCarthy, however, testified that the athletic footwear and apparel business is a fast-moving industry and that if he is forced to sit out for a year, he would have to do a lot of "catching up" after he returns to the industry. Nevertheless, the potential disruption to Nike's sales and products outweighs any harm that the injunction would cause McCarthy in the intermediate or long term. Thus, we conclude that the balance of harm tips in favor of Nike.

AFFIRMED.

Notes & Questions

1. Protecting an Employee's Interest in Pursuing a Living

Courts, sensitive to an employee's interest in moving freely from one job to another, refuse to enforce covenants that unduly hinder an employee from pursuing his chosen livelihood. One court, facing the dilemma of whether to enforce restrictions on a person's ability to pursue a career stated the issue so:

> [T]he right of an individual to follow and pursue the particular occupation for which he is best trained is a most fundamental right. Our society is extremely mobile and our free economy is based upon competition. One who has worked in a particular field cannot be compelled to erase from his mind all of the general skills, knowledge, and expertise acquired through his experience . . . . Restraints cannot be lightly placed upon his right to compete in the area of his greatest worth.

AMP, Inc. v. Fleischhacker, 823 F.2d 1199, 1202 (7th Cir. 1987) (quoting the Illinois Supreme Court in *ILG Industries v. Scott*, 273 N.E.2d 393, 396 (Ill. 1971)). The law favors mobility and disfavors covenants that place onerous burdens on an individual's ability to make a living.

2. Enforceability

Covenants not to compete are not enforceable unless their terms are reasonable. Courts look to several factors when determining whether a noncompete agreement is reasonable. First, the restrictions must further a legitimate business purpose or agreement. Second, the business must own a trade secret or other legally protectable interest. Third, the covenant must not be overly inclusive as to the subject matter encompassed, the duration of the protection, and the geographic territory affected. Finally, the employer must give adequate consideration in return for the employee's agreement not to compete. Even when a covenant meets the requirements for enforceability, courts often strictly construe the terms of the contract. Some states, most notably California, refuse to enforce post-employment covenants not to compete altogether.

3. "Blue Penciling" of Overbroad Covenants Not to Compete

Courts often refuse to enforce covenants not to compete where no legitimate business interest justifies an employer's use of the restrictions, where the covenant prevents competition for longer than necessary to protect a business interest, and where the territorial scope of the covenant encompasses an area broader than needed to protect the employer. Some jurisdictions allow a court to salvage an overbroad covenant not to compete by modifying the terms of the agreement and enforcing the covenant as modified, a practice known as blue penciling.

4. Noncompete Agreements Must be Supported by Consideration

When an employer requests that an employee promise to refrain from post-employment competition with the employer's business, the employer must give consideration in exchange for imposing a limit on the employee's employment opportunities. The Washington Supreme Court in *Labriola v. Pollard Group, Inc.*, 100 P.3d 791 (Wash. 2004), held that a noncompete agreement signed by an employee, five years after he was hired, was not supported by consideration when the employer offered no additional benefits or promises to the employee in exchange for his promise.

> Consideration is a bargained-for exchange of promises. A comparison of the status of the employer before and after the noncompete agreement confirms that the 2002 noncompete was entered into without consideration. Employer did not incur additional duties or obligations from the noncompete agreement. Prior to execution of the 2002 noncompete agreement, Employee was an "at will" Employee. After Employee executed the noncompete agreement, he still remained an "at will" employee terminable at Employer's pleasure. We hold that continued employment in this case did not serve as consideration by Employer in exchange for Employee's promise not to compete.

Labriola, 100 P.3d at 836. There was no independent consideration given by the employer at the time Labriola signed the noncompete agreement, and therefore no enforceable contract was formed between the parties.

ii. Hold-Over/Trailer Clauses

Milliken & Co. v. Morin
Supreme Court of South Carolina
731 S.E.2d 288 (S.C. 2012)

JUSTICE HEARN

Miliken & Company sued Brian Morin after he resigned from the company and started a new venture using Miliken's proprietary information. The crux of its suit was that Morin breached the confidentiality and invention assignment agreements he signed when he started working for Miliken. A jury found for Miliken, and the court of appeals affirmed. *Milliken & Co. v. Morin*, 386 S.C. 1, 11–12, 685 S.E.2d 828, 834–35 (Ct. App. 2009). We granted certiorari to review the narrow issue of whether these agreements are overbroad as a matter of law. We hold that they are not and affirm as modified.

FACTUAL/PROCEDURAL BACKGROUND

Morin began working for Miliken as a research physicist in 1995 in its Spartanburg, South Carolina facility. As a condition of his employment, Morin had to sign an "Associate Agreement" which contained provisions regarding confidentiality and the assignment of certain inventions.

. . . .

Morin's duty to assign his inventions to Miliken [reads, in part, as follows:]

> 4. INVENTIONS means discoveries, improvements, and ideas (whether or not shown or described in writing or reduced to practice), mask works, (topography or semiconductor chips) and works of authorship, whether or not patentable, copyrightable, or registerable, (1) which relate directly to the business of Miliken, or (2) which relate to Miliken's actual or demonstrably anticipated research or development, or (3) which result from any work performed by me for Miliken, or (4) for which any equipment, supplies, facility or Trade Secret or Confidential Information of Miliken is used, or (5) which is developed on any Miliken Time.

> . . . .

> A. With respect to Inventions made, authored, and conceived by me, either solely or jointly with others, (1) during my employment, whether or not during normal working hours or whether or not at Milliken's premises; or (2) within one year after termination of my employment, I will:

> a. Keep accurate, complete, and timely records of such Inventions, which records shall be Milliken property and retained on Milliken's premises.

b. Promptly and fully disclose and describe such Inventions in writing to Milliken.

c. Assign (and I do hereby assign) to Milliken all of my rights to such Inventions, and to applications for letters patent, copyright registrations and/or mask work registrations in all countries and to letters patent, copyright registrations and/or mask work registrations granted upon such Inventions in all countries.

d. Acknowledge and deliver promptly to Milliken (without charge to Milliken but at the expense of Milliken) such written instruments and to do such other acts as may be necessary in the opinion of Milliken to preserve property rights against forfeiture, abandonment or loss and to obtain, defend, and maintain letters patent, copyright registrations, and/or mask work registrations and to vest the entire right and title thereto in Milliken.

. . . .

Over the next nine years with Miliken, Morin was promoted twice, first to Senior Research Physicists then to Team Leader for the Advanced Yarns Team. During the time Morin was in charge of the Advanced Yarns Team, one of Miliken's goals was to investigate the use of additives and equipment modifications to create a new type of fiber. To seek out potential uses for such a product, Miliken sent Morin to a trade show in Anaheim, California, in the Fall of 2003. Shortly thereafter, he began drafting a business plan for his company, Innergrity, which could manufacture this new fiber. He then resigned from Miliken on May 19, 2004, and filed a patent for the fiber, which he labeled Innegra, the following November.

Milliken first caught wind of Morin's plans after he invited his former colleagues to attend a presentation he was giving at a gathering of venture capitalists in Greenville, South Carolina. After noting the similarities between Innegrity's business plan and certain projects being conducted at Milliken, Milliken raised concerns that Morin had violated the Associate Agreement. This suit soon followed.

Milliken brought several claims against Morin, but only its claims for breach of the confidentiality agreement, breach of invention assignment provisions, breach of the duty of loyalty, and violation of the South Carolina Trade Secrets Act were submitted to the jury. The jury found for Milliken on its breach of the confidentiality and invention assignment agreement claims, but it found for Morin on the remaining causes of action. In the end, the jury awarded Milliken $25,324 in damages. Morin appealed, arguing that these agreements are overbroad and therefore unenforceable, but the court of appeals disagreed and affirmed. *Milliken*, 386 S.C. at 11–12, 685 S.E.2d at 834–35. We granted certiorari.

. . . .

LAW/ANALYSIS

I. APPLICABLE STANDARD

We must first resolve a question left unanswered by the court of appeals, which is under what rubric we are to evaluate the enforceability of these agreements. Morin argues that we should analyze them as non-compete agreements and thus strictly construe them in favor of the employee. We disagree.

"According to the early common law of England, an agreement in restraint of a man's right to exercise his trade or calling was void as against public policy." *Standard Register Co. v. Kerrigan*, 238 S.C. 54, 59, 119 S.E.2d 533, 536 (1961). The rationale behind this categorical rule was that at the time a man had to be apprenticed in his trade and was bound by law to exercise it. *Id.* at 59–60, 119 S.E.2d at 536. "Hence, to enforce such an agreement was to deny such person the right to earn his living and to require him to violate an express provision of the law." *Id.* at 60, 119 S.E.2d at 536. As the law and realities of employment have progressed, however, there has been "'some amelioration of the ancient disfavor.'" *Id.* (quoting *Welcome Wagon, Inc. v. Morris*, 224 F.2d 693, 698 (4th Cir. 1955)).

> "Modern courts have usually, in passing on these contracts, employed three criteria: (1) Is the restraint, from the standpoint of the employer, reasonable in the sense that it is no greater than is necessary to protect the employer in some legitimate business interest? (2) From the standpoint of the employee, is the restraint reasonable in the sense that it is not unduly harsh and oppressive in curtailing his legitimate efforts to earn a livelihood? (3) Is the restraint reasonable from the standpoint of a sound public policy?"

Id. (quoting *Welcome Wagon*, 224 F.2d at 698). We reaffirmed and expounded upon these principles in *Rental Uniform Service of Florence, Inc. v. Dudley*, 278 S.C. 674, 301 S.E.2d 142 (1983). In doing so, we reiterated that "[r]estrictive covenants not to compete are generally disfavored and will be strictly construed against the employer" and added that they must also be reasonably limited "with respect to time and place." *Id.* at 675, 301 S.E.2d at 143. This is the framework Morin would have us apply here.

The agreements under review, however, are not in restraint of trade. *See* Louis Altman & Malla Pollack, *Callmann on Unfair Competition, Trademarks and Monopolies* § 14:6 (4th ed. 2009) ("An employee's express commitment not to disclose his employer's confidential information, whether or not it comprises trade secrets, 'unlike the covenant not to compete cannot be challenged as an unreasonable restraint of trade.'" (quoting *Lear Siegler, Inc. v. Ark-Ell Springs, Inc.*, 569 F.2d 286, 289 (5th Cir. 1978))); *id.* § 14:17 ("If the employee agrees that all inventions and improvements in the employer's field, patentable and unpatentable, which are developed by the employee during his employment shall be the employer's property, such a contract is not invalid or unenforceable as an unreasonable restraint. The contract may even expressly impose such a duty for a period of time after termination of the employment . . . .").

Holdover clauses do not fit this mold because they do "not limit the employee's post-employment activities except with respect to the affected inventions and improvements." *NovelAire Techs., L.L.C. v. Harrison*, 50 So. 3d 913, 919 (La. Ct. App. 2010) (quotations omitted). Furthermore, they "are simply a recognition of the fact of business life that employees sometimes carry with them to new employers inventions or ideas so related to work done for a former employer that in equity and good conscience the fruits of that work should belong to the former employer." *Dorr-Oliver, Inc. v. United States*, 432 F.2d 447, 452, 193 Ct. Cl. 187 (Cl. Ct. 1970). Thus, they do not operate in restraint of the employee's trade but merely vest ownership of an invention with the entity which ought to have it. Similarly, "noncompete agreements are viewed as restraints of trade which limit an employee's freedom of movement among employment opportunities, while nondisclosure agreements seek to restrict disclosure of information, not employment opportunities." *Revere Transducers, Inc. v. Deere & Co.*, 595 N.W.2d 751, 761 (Iowa 1999); *see also Hayes-Albion v. Kuberski*, 421 Mich. 170, 364 N.W.2d 609, 614 (Mich. 1984) (holding Michigan's non-compete statute "has no application where the plaintiff is not seeking to prevent the former employee from engaging in a similar business, but to prevent him from using the secret knowledge of his former employer").

Because these agreements are not in restraint of trade, we hold there is no "ancient disfavor" and thus they are not to be strictly construed in favor of the employee. *See Carolina Chemical Equip. Co. v. Muckenfuss*, 322 S.C. 289, 302, 471 S.E.2d 721, 728 (Ct. App. 1996) (Cureton, J., dissenting) ("'In this area, courts impose no presumptions against employers and do not subject the employee's promise or covenant not to disclose to a rigid test or analysis.'" (quoting Timothy D. Scranton & Cherie Lynne Wilson, *Postemployment Covenants Not to Compete in South Carolina: Wizards and Dragons in the Kingdom*, 42 S.C. L. Rev. 657, 682 (1991))). Accordingly, the scope of the restriction is determined using ordinary principles of contract law. *See Revere Transducers*, 595 N.W.2d at 761 ("Nondisclosure-confidentiality agreements enjoy more favorable treatment in the law than do noncompete agreements."); *NovelAire*, 50 So. 3d at 918 ("NovelAire contends that the Agreement is a standard contract to provide for the ownership, as between an employer and an employee, of discoveries the employee made while working for the employer, and to keep those discoveries as confidential. NovelAire contends that neither of these contractual requirements constitute non-compete contracts. We agree.").

Nevertheless, these agreements are still restrictive covenants and public policy demands their scope be subject to judicial review for reasonableness. When evaluating these provisions, courts should look to the more general standard enunciated in *Standard Register* namely whether the restriction is reasonable in that it is no greater than necessary to protect the employer's legitimate interests, and it is not unduly harsh in that it curtails the employee's ability to earn a living. 238 S.C. at 60, 119 S.E.2d at 536; *see also Revere Transducers*, 595 N.W.2d at 761–62 (noting that reasonableness elements of non-compete clause analysis still remain for confidentiality agreements and "[t]he determining factor of whether assignment-of-rights-agreements are enforceable seems to be one of reasonableness"); *Ingersoll-Rand Co. v. Ciavatta*, 216 N.J. Super. 667, 524 A.2d 866, 869 (N.J. 1987) (holding an invention assignment clause must "be reviewed as to its reasonableness, with an awareness of the practical realities of the business and employment world"); *Caldwell*, *supra*, at 292, 299 (stating the "subject matter is the only truly relevant factor" for holdover clauses, and it must be balanced by "'weigh[ing] the competing interest of employer and employee and giv[ing] full consideration to the public interest.'" (quoting *Universal Winding Co. v. Clarke*, 108 F. Supp. 329, 332 (D. Conn. 1952))).

II. ENFORCEABILITY OF AGREEMENTS

With this framework in mind, we turn next to the enforceability of the holdover and confidentiality agreements Morin signed. In our opinion, both of them are facially valid.

A. Holdover Clause

As has been eloquently stated, "A naked assignment or agreement to assign, in gross, a man's future labors as an author or inventor [—] in other words, a mortgage on a man's brain, to bind all its future products [—] does not address itself favorably to our consideration." *Aspinwall Mfg. Co. v. Gill*, 32 F. 697, 700, 1887 Dec. Comm'r Pat. 482 (C.C.D.N.J. 1887). However, where the agreement does not "implicate all of a researcher's future inventions 'in gross'" but rather applies to inventions derived from his work for the employer, it is enforceable. *St. John's Univ., N.Y. v. Bolton*, 757 F. Supp. 2d 144, 162 (E.D.N.Y. 2010). Morin himself even agrees that Milliken has no right to his "inventive ideas unless those ideas relate directly to his work for Milliken."

An employer therefore has a legitimate interest in protecting inventions that are the fruits of its employees' efforts while working for the company. Indeed, such provisions "are simply a recognition of the fact of business life that employees sometimes carry with them to new employers inventions or ideas so related to work done for a former employer that in equity and good conscience the fruits of that work should belong to the former employer." *Dorr-Oliver*, 432 F.2d at 452. Thus, we must first examine the scope of the invention assignment clause and determine whether it falls within these parameters.

The invention assignment agreement Morin signed is embodied in a complex set of paragraphs which by no means are an exercise in clarity. After sorting through the morass, however, the impact of the agreement is much narrower than it may appear initially. The agreement first applies to all inventions, a term which is defined quite broadly. It covers:

> discoveries, improvements, ideas (whether or not shown or described in writing or reduced to practice), mask works (topography or semiconductor chips), and works of authorship, whether or not patentable, copyrightable or registerable,
>
> (1) which relate directly to the business of Milliken, or
>
> (2) which relate to Milliken's actual or demonstrably anticipated research or development, or
>
> (3) which result from any work performed by me for Milliken, or
>
> (4) for which any equipment, supplies, facility or Trade Secret or Confidential Information of Milliken is used, or

(5) which is developed on any Milliken time.

Accordingly, any discovery, etc., which meets *any* of the five criteria contained in the agreement is an invention and is to be assigned.

However, the agreement also contains a rather broad exception to this inclusive definition. It excepts an invention, as defined above,

for which no equipment, supplies, facility, or proprietary information of Milliken was used *and*

which was developed entirely on your own time, *and*

(1) which does not relate

(a) directly to the business of Milliken or

(b) to Milliken's actual or demonstrably anticipated research or development, *or*

(2) which does not result from any work performed by you for Milliken.

(emphasis added).

Morin's contention is that the invention assignment clause is overbroad because it grants Milliken rights to one of Morin's inventions "irrespective of whether his invention is legitimately an extension of research he did for Milliken." This argument is based on a misreading of the agreement. Under general principles of contract law, we find first as a matter of law that this agreement is unambiguous. *See Miles v. Miles*, 393 S.C. 111, 117, 711 S.E.2d 880, 883 (2011) ("[W]hether a contract is ambiguous is a question of law."). We must therefore apply the contract's plain language. *Alexander's Land Co. v. M & M & K Corp.*, 390 S.C. 582, 598, 703 S.E.2d 207, 215 (2010). Under the terms of the agreement, if the invention *either* does not relate to Milliken's work or was not the result of work performed by the employee for Milliken, then it is not covered. Conversely, for the exception to *not* apply — and thus require assignment of the invention — it must *both* relate to Milliken's business/research and result from the employee's work at Milliken. Thus, so long as the invention does not relate to work performed by the employee, it is not to be assigned.

Accordingly, the agreement is not broader than necessary to protect Milliken's legitimate business interests. Moreover, the one-year holdover provision is eminently reasonable. *See Rental Uniform Serv.*, 278 S.C. at 676, 301 S.E.2d at 143 (finding a three-year restraint is not "obnoxious" even in the context of a non-compete agreement). It also is not unduly harsh or oppressive because Morin still is entitled to any invention that does not result from his work at Milliken; thus, he is still of great value to future employees. We therefore hold that Milliken's invention assignment and holdover clause is not so broad as to be unenforceable as a matter of law.

[The court then concluded that the confidentiality agreement was not unreasonable, and therefore that plaintiff had no viable claim.]

CONCLUSION

We therefore hold confidentiality and invention assignment clauses are not in restraint of trade and should not be strictly construed in favor of the employee.

Under a more general reasonableness standard of enforceability, Milliken's agreements here are reasonably tailored and therefore enforceable as a matter of law. We accordingly affirm the court of appeals, modifying its opinion only to the extent that we adopt the standard enunciated above.

Notes & Questions

1. Why Would an Employer Need a Hold-Over/Trailer Clause?

In a hold-over clause, also known as a trailer clause, an employee agrees to assign to the employer the rights to inventions created for a time following the termination of the employment relationship. Hold-over clauses developed in response to cases which held that, in the absence of an express contract to the contrary, a departing employee's invention did not belong to the employer unless the employee conceived of the idea during the term of employment. Employee inventors who did not wish to hand over an invention idea to the employer could postpone conception of the invention and depart the employment relationship with the inchoate idea of the invention. By holding off on refining the concept and writing it down in tangible form, the employee leaves no evidence of conception until after the termination of employment. Without objective evidence of conception, there is no proof of invention to trigger pre-invention assignment agreements, and the employee may take with him an invention that should rightfully have belonged to the employer.

Hold-over clauses allow employers to close the loophole by extending the period in which an employee is obligated to assign rights to an invention beyond the term of the employment relationship. The extended period serves to catch inventions in development during the time of the employee's departure and prevents exiting employees from violating their obligation to assign rights to the former employer.

2. Competing Policy Interests

For some employers, their business's most valuable assets reside in human capital, including the knowledge embodied in individual employees. Covenants not to compete allow employers to protect these assets by restricting employees' use of the employers' proprietary knowledge. In contrast to information recorded on paper or on a computer, protection for information inseparable from an individual's knowledge necessarily impinges upon an individual's freedom of mobility in employment. Without protection for their investments, employers may be reluctant to train employees for fear that employees privy to the employer's trade secret may one day turn and use the information against them. Courts recognize the interest of employers in protecting their investments and tolerate some degree of restraint on competition in permitting the use of covenants not to compete. Balanced against the employer's rights to secrecy are the rights of employees in mobility.

Some scholars have suggested that permitting employee mobility may enhance knowledge spillover and foster rapid progress in an industry. Specifically, when employees are free to move, they may serve as a conduit through which new ideas and developments may be disseminated to an entire industry. Scholars[2] have attributed the success of Silicon Valley as a high-technology industrial district and the decline of Boston's counterpart in Route 128 to California's refusal to recognize covenants not to compete[3] and Massachusetts's willingness to enforce noncompete agreements.

Recently, however, it has been discovered that many of the technology industry's biggest players agreed among themselves not to hire away ("poach") each other's employees. Employees of Apple, Adobe, Google, Intel, Pixar, Lucasfilm, and Intuit filed a class-action lawsuit in 2011 alleging that these companies made illegal hiring agreements that resulted in anticompetitive behavior and kept salaries artificially low. See *In re High-Tech Employee Antitrust Litigation*, 985 F. Supp. 2d 1167 (N.D. Cal. 2013). Pixar, Disney, and Intuit settled claims in this case for a total of $20 million. The remaining companies reached a settlement agreement for $325 million in April 2014, but the judge in the case rejected the agreement. The companies increased their settlement offer to $415 million in January 2015 and the judge approved it in September 2015. *In re High-Tech Employee Antitrust Litigation*, No. 11-CV-02509-LHK, 2015 WL 5159441 (N.D. Cal. Sept. 2, 2015). The Department of Justice has also investigated similar allegations of illegal conduct at these companies and at eBay. The antitrust implications of this behavior are discussed further in Chapter 11. For more information on this case and related litigation, *see* Joel Rosenblatt, *Evidence of Alleged Apple-Google No-Poaching Deal Triggers More Lawsuits*, BLOOMBERG (Nov. 19, 2014, 4:01 AM), http://www.bloomberg.com/news/2014-11-19/apple-google-no-poaching -evidence-triggers-more-lawsuits.html (last visited 12/19/17).

iii. Nonsolicitation Agreements

By securing a nonsolicitation agreement, an employer may restrict an exiting employee from enticing customers or employees away from the employer. Nonsolicitation agreements that prohibit solicitation of customers are enforceable if the employer can show that, if not for his association with the employer, the employee would not have come in contact with the customers. However, an employee is free to socially contact persons befriended before the commencement of the employment relationship.

Trujillo v. Great Southern Equipment Sales, LLC

Court of Appeals of Georgia

657 S.E.2d 581 (Ga. App. 2008)

BLACKBURN, PRESIDING JUDGE.

In this case regarding restrictive covenants in an employment agreement, Sarah Alexandra Trujillo ("Trujillo") appeals the trial court's interlocutory injunction in

---

2. ANNALEE SEXENIAN, REGIONAL ADVANTAGE: CULTURE AND COMPETITION IN SILICON VALLEY AND ROUTE 128 (1994). See also Ronald J. Gilson, *The Legal Infrastructure of High Technology Industrial Districts: Silicon Valley, Route 128, and Covenants Not to Compete*, 74 N.Y.U.L. Rev. 575 (1999).

3. California in effect bars most non-compete agreements: "every contract by which anyone is restrained from engaging in lawful profession . . . is to that extent void." Cal. Bus. & Prof. Code § 16600.

favor of her former employer, Great Southern Equipment Sales, LLC ("Great Southern"), contending that the court erred in finding that the restrictive covenants were enforceable. For the reasons set forth below, we reverse the part of the trial court's interlocutory injunction that found that the nonsolicitation and noncompetition covenants were enforceable, but we otherwise affirm.

The record shows that Great Southern is a company headquartered in Savannah and is engaged primarily in the business of selling transportation equipment such as containers, chassis, and trailers. In February 2005, Great Southern hired Trujillo to work as a salesperson. Over the next couple of months, Trujillo received on-the-job training from Great Southern's president. The president also provided Trujillo with lists of Great Southern's customers and introduced her to many of the company's customers and suppliers. In November 2005, Great Southern had Trujillo and another salesperson sign a "Confidentiality and Restrictive Covenant Agreement." In addition to a confidentiality provision, the agreement included separate nonsolicitation and noncompetition clauses.

In early May 2007, Trujillo resigned from her sales position with Great Southern. Within days of her resignation, Trujillo began engaging in the same type of business as Great Southern under the name "International Equipment Source of Savannah." Around this same time, Great Southern was notified by some of its customers that Trujillo had started competing with Great Southern and was soliciting its customers' business. Consequently, on May 7, 2007, attorneys for Great Southern demanded, via written correspondence, that Trujillo adhere to the terms of the "Confidentiality and Restrictive Covenant Agreement" and cease contacting Great Southern customers. In the same correspondence, the attorneys for Great Southern further demanded that Trujillo immediately return any Great Southern property in her possession.

Trujillo failed to comply with this demand. As a result, on May 29, 2007, Great Southern filed a lawsuit against her, seeking declaratory relief, injunctive relief, and damages for breach of contract; Great Southern also filed a motion for a temporary restraining order. The next day, the trial court granted Great Southern's motion for a temporary restraining order against Trujillo, enjoining her from competing with Great Southern and soliciting its customers. On July 3 and 5, 2007, the trial court held a hearing on Great Southern's motion for interlocutory injunction. After the hearing, the trial court ruled in favor of Great Southern. Subsequently, the court issued a written order, finding that the "Confidentiality and Restrictive Covenant Agreement" was enforceable, enjoining Trujillo from competing with Great Southern and soliciting its customers, and directing Trujillo to return any Great Southern property in her possession. This appeal followed.

. . . .

1. Trujillo initially contends that the trial court erred in granting the interlocutory injunction in favor of Great Southern, arguing that the "Confidentiality and Restrictive Covenant Agreement" was unenforceable as a matter of law. Following this general attack on the agreement's validity, she specifically argues that the court erred in finding that the agreement's nonsolicitation clause was enforceable despite the fact that the clause did not contain a geographic restriction. We agree.

"In considering whether a restrictive covenant is enforceable, a court must first determine the level of scrutiny to apply." *Dent Wizard Intl. Corp., supra* at 555(1). "Restrictive covenants that are ancillary to an employment contract are subject to strict scrutiny and will be voided by Georgia courts if they impose an unreasonable restraint on trade." *Stultz v. Safety & Compliance Mgmt. See Dent Wizard Intl. Corp., supra* at 555(1) . . . . Courts will enforce a restrictive covenant in an employment contract only if: "(1) the restraint is reasonable; (2) founded upon valuable consideration; (3) is reasonably necessary to protect the party in whose favor it is imposed; and (4) does not unduly prejudice the interests of the public." . . . "Moreover, such restrictions must be strictly limited as to time, territorial effect, capacity in which the employee is prohibited from competing, and as to overall reasonableness." *Id.* at 555–556(1). "Whether the restraint imposed by the employment contract is reasonable is a question of law for determination by the court." *W. R. Grace & Co. v. Mouyal.*

In this matter, the "Non-Solicitation of Customers Covenant" contained in the agreement signed by Trujillo provided:

> During Employee's employment with Employer and for a period of three (3) years following the Separation Date, Employee shall not solicit any person or entity to whom Employer has provided products or services during the three (3) years immediately preceding the Separation Date or to whom Employer is actively soliciting to provide products or services as of the Separation Date (collectively, "Customers") with the intent to sell or provide any product or service, competitive or potentially competitive, with any product or service sold or provided by Employer. The non-solicitation restriction set forth in this Section 2 is specifically limited to Customers of Employer with whom Employee had contact (whether personally, telephonically, or through written or electronic correspondence) during the three (3) year period immediately preceding the Separation Date *or about whom Employee had confidential or proprietary information because of his/her position with Employer.*

. . . .

The provision initially limited the nonsolicitation restriction to customers with whom Trujillo had contact while working for Great Southern. However, it significantly broadened that limitation in the very same sentence by also prohibiting Trujillo from contacting any customers about whom she at any point had confidential or proprietary information. Importantly, the prohibition contained no territorial restriction. "Georgia law is clear that unless the nonsolicit covenant pertains *only to those clients with whom the employee had a business relationship* during the term of the agreement, the nonsolicit covenant must contain a territorial restriction." *Advance Technology Consultants v. RoadTrac.* In *Mouyal, supra* at 467(2), n. 3, our Supreme Court explained that a restrictive covenant prohibiting a former employee from rendering services to *any* client of the employer must contain a territorial restriction expressed in geographic terms because that restriction, which does not take into account whether the employee had a business relationship with that client or whether it was the client who solicited the former employee, is otherwise unreasonable and overbroad in its attempt to protect the employer's legitimate interest in keeping the employee from taking advantage of the goodwill generated during his employment with the employer to lure employer customers away. "Thus, under *Mouyal,* a prohibition against doing business with *any* of an employer's customers, whether or not a relationship existed between the customer and the former employee, is overbroad in the absence of a reasonable territorial restriction." *Advance Technology Consultants, supra* at 322(3). Given that the nonsolicitation provision at issue here did not limit the prohibition to only customers with whom Trujillo had contact and did not contain a territorial restriction, the provision was overbroad and unenforceable. *See Mouyal, supra* at 467(2); *Advance Technology Consultants, supra* at 322(3).

We disagree with Great Southern's argument that the prohibition barring Trujillo from also contacting customers about whom she had confidential or proprietary information merely constituted a valid confidentiality provision and therefore did not render the nonsolicitation clause unenforceable. First, having had in her possession (not necessarily in her mind) at some point in her employment a comprehensive customer list that contained confidential information about each and every customer would preclude her from contacting any customers of Great Southern during the post-termination time period. Second, the employment agreement contained a separate confidentiality clause, which was found enforceable by the trial court. That finding has not been appealed. However, contrary to Great Southern's argument, the prohibition against contacting customers about whom Trujillo had confidential or proprietary information was not a reiteration of the confidentiality clause but rather was an effort to impermissibly broaden the class of customers whom Trujillo could not solicit.

2. Because the nonsolicitation clause was unenforceable, the noncompetition clause included in the agreement was likewise unenforceable. *See Riddle v. Geo-Hydro Engineers; Advance Technology Consultants, supra* at 320–321(2). "In restrictive covenant cases strictly scrutinized as employment contracts, Georgia does not employ the 'blue pencil' doctrine of severability." *Waldeck v. Curtis 1000, Inc.,* 583 S.E.2d 266 (2003). *See Advance Technology Consultants, supra* at 320(2). Thus, the trial court erred insofar as it enjoined Trujillo based on the unenforceable nonsolicitation and noncompetition clauses. Accordingly, we reverse that part of the court's injunction order supported by these erroneous legal conclusions, but we otherwise affirm the order.

Judgment affirmed in part and reversed in part.

Notes & Questions

1. Reasonableness of the Scope of Nonsolicitation Agreement

To determine whether a nonsolicitation restrictive covenant is enforceable, courts look at the totality of circumstances, including the nature and extent of the business involved and the situation of the parties. Further, when analyzing the language of a nonsolicitation restrictive covenant, courts look at three specific factors: duration, territorial coverage, and scope of prohibited activity. As illustrated by *Trujillo*, if the language of a nonsolicitation clause is broad and the clause does not contain a territorial restriction, a court typically will invalidate the clause.

In evaluating the reasonableness of the scope of a nonsolicitation clause, a court will generally consider the impacts of the clause on the legitimate interests of the benefited business and the restricted employee. These factors were at the heart of the court's analysis in *Murphree v. Yancey Bros. Co.*, 716 S.E.2d 824, 827 (Ga. App. 2011). There, an employee claimed that a nonsolicitation covenant was unreasonable in its scope because it failed to define clearly which activities would be prohibited. The agreement in *Murphree* provided that for two years after the termination of employment the employee could not "solicit, divert, or take away . . . any of the customers, clients, accounts or business of the Company serviced or procured by the Employee . . . at any time during the last 2 years of his/her employment" if such activities were engaged in "for the purpose of competing with the Company." The employee argued that the contract failed to make clear which actions would qualify as undertaken "for the purpose of competing," and, therefore, failed to "limit or define the scope of activity prohibited." The court was not persuaded by the argument:

> It is well established that an employer "has a protectable interest in the customer relationships its former employee established and/or nurtured while employed by the employer" and that an employer is thus "entitled to protect itself from the risk that a former employee might appropriate customers by taking unfair advantage of the contacts developed while working for the employer." Indeed, this is the very nature of the activities prohibited by a nonsolicitation clause, which differs from a noncompete clause.

> And here, this type of activity is exactly what Yancey sought to prohibit through the clause at issue—the solicitation, diversion, or taking away of customers served or procured by a former employee. And the use of "for the purposes of competing" served to qualify the type of solicitation that was prohibited. Thus, this covenant prohibited Murphree from initiating affirmative action to compete with Yancey by contacting former customers, but the clause would not have precluded him "from accepting unsolicited business from the forbidden clients." Accordingly, the trial court did not err in holding that the restrictive covenant was reasonable and, likewise, did not abuse its discretion by granting an interlocutory injunction to enforce same.

Murphree, 716 S.E.2d at 827–28.

2. Inevitable Disclosures of Trade Secrets as a Basis for Preemptive Employment Limitations

a. Generally

The doctrine of inevitability arises when an employee's knowledge and skills are inseparable from an employer's trade secrets such that the employee cannot avoid use of the trade secret during subsequent employment. A court may award an injunction restricting an employee's post-employment ability to use something that is conceptually a part of himself despite absence of a covenant not to compete.

Pepsico, Inc. v. Redmond

United States Court of Appeals for the Seventh Circuit

54 F.3d 1262 (7th Cir. 1995)

FLAUM, CIRCUIT JUDGE.

Plaintiff PepsiCo, Inc., sought a preliminary injunction against defendants William Redmond and the Quaker Oats Company to prevent Redmond, a former PepsiCo employee, from divulging PepsiCo trade secrets and confidential information in his new job with Quaker and from assuming any duties with Quaker relating to beverage pricing, marketing, and distribution. The district court agreed with PepsiCo and granted the injunction. We now affirm that decision.

I.

The facts of this case lay against a backdrop of fierce beverage-industry competition between Quaker and PepsiCo, especially in "sports drinks" and "new age drinks." Quaker's sports drink, "Gatorade," is the dominant brand in its market niche. PepsiCo introduced its Gatorade rival, "All Sport," in March and April of 1994, but sales of All Sport lag far behind those of Gatorade. Quaker also has the lead in the new-age-drink category. Although PepsiCo has entered the market through joint ventures with the Thomas J. Lipton Company and Ocean Spray Cranberries, Inc., Quaker purchased Snapple Beverage Corp., a large new-age-drink maker, in late 1994. PepsiCo's products have about half of Snapple's market share. Both companies see 1995 as an important year for their products: PepsiCo has developed extensive plans to increase its market presence, while Quaker is trying to solidify its lead by integrating Gatorade and Snapple distribution. Meanwhile, PepsiCo and Quaker each face strong competition from Coca Cola Co., which has its own sports drink, "PowerAde," and which introduced its own Snapple-rival, "Fruitopia," in 1994, as well as from independent beverage producers.

William Redmond, Jr., worked for PepsiCo in its PepsiCola North America division ("PCNA") from 1984 to 1994. Redmond became the General Manager of the Northern California Business Unit in June, 1993, and was promoted one year later to General Manager of the business unit covering all of California, a unit having annual revenues of more than 500 million dollars and representing twenty percent of PCNA's profit for all of the United States.

Redmond's relatively high-level position at PCNA gave him access to inside information and trade secrets. Redmond, like other PepsiCo management employees, had signed a confidentiality agreement with PepsiCo. That agreement stated in relevant part that he would not disclose at any time, to anyone other than officers or employees of [PepsiCo], or make use of, confidential information relating to the business of [PepsiCo] . . . obtained while in the employ of [PepsiCo], which shall not be generally known or available to the public or recognized as standard practices.

Donald Uzzi, who had left PepsiCo in the beginning of 1994 to become the head of Quaker's Gatorade division, began courting Redmond for Quaker in May, 1994. Redmond met in Chicago with Quaker officers in August, 1994, and on October 20, 1994, Quaker, through Uzzi, offered Redmond the position of Vice President — On Premise Sales for Gatorade. Redmond did not then accept the offer but continued to negotiate for more money. Throughout this time, Redmond kept his dealings with Quaker secret from his employers at PCNA.

On November 8, 1994, Uzzi extended Redmond a written offer for the position of Vice President — Field Operations for Gatorade and Redmond accepted. Later that same day, Redmond called William Bensyl, the Senior Vice President of Human Resources for PCNA, and told him that he had an offer from Quaker to become the Chief Operating Officer of the combined Gatorade and Snapple company but had not yet accepted it. Redmond also asked whether he should, in light of the offer, carry out his plans to make calls upon certain PCNA customers. Bensyl told Redmond to make the visits.

Redmond also misstated his situation to a number of his PCNA colleagues, including Craig Weatherup, PCNA's President and Chief Executive Officer, and Brenda Barnes, PCNA's Chief Operating Officer and Redmond's immediate superior. As with Bensyl, Redmond told them that he had been offered the position of Chief Operating Officer at Gatorade and that he was leaning "60/40" in favor of accepting the new position.

On November 10, 1994, Redmond met with Barnes and told her that he had decided to accept the Quaker offer and was resigning from PCNA. Barnes immediately took Redmond to Bensyl, who told Redmond that PepsiCo was considering legal action against him.

True to its word, PepsiCo filed this diversity suit on November 16, 1994, seeking a temporary restraining order to enjoin Redmond from assuming his duties at Quaker and to prevent him from disclosing trade secrets or confidential information to his new employer. The district court granted PepsiCo's request that same day but dissolved the order *sua sponte* two days later, after determining that PepsiCo had failed to meet its burden of establishing that it would suffer irreparable harm. The court found that PepsiCo's fears about Redmond were based upon a mistaken understanding of his new position at Quaker and that the likelihood that Redmond would improperly reveal any confidential information did not "rise above mere speculation."

From November 23, 1994, to December 1, 1994, the district court conducted a preliminary injunction hearing on the same matter. At the hearing, PepsiCo offered evidence of a number of trade secrets and confidential information it desired protected and to which Redmond was privy. First, it identified PCNA's "Strategic Plan," an annually revised document that contains PCNA's plans to compete, its financial goals, and its strategies for manufacturing, production, marketing, packaging, and distribution for the coming three years. Strategic Plans are developed by Weatherup and his staff with input from PCNA's general managers, including Redmond, and are considered highly confidential. The Strategic Plan derives much of its value from the fact that it is secret and competitors cannot anticipate PCNA's next moves. PCNA managers received the most recent Strategic Plan at a meeting in July, 1994, a meeting Redmond attended. PCNA also presented information at the meeting regarding its plans for Lipton ready-to-drink teas and for All Sport for 1995 and beyond, including new flavors and package sizes.

Second, PepsiCo pointed to PCNA's Annual Operating Plan ("AOP") as a trade secret. The AOP is a national plan for a given year and guides PCNA's financial goals, marketing plans, promotional event calendars, growth expectations, and operational changes in that year. The AOP, which is implemented by PCNA unit General Managers, including Redmond, contains specific information regarding all PCNA initiatives for the forthcoming year. The AOP bears a label that reads "Private and Confidential—Do Not Reproduce" and is considered highly confidential by PCNA managers.

In particular, the AOP contains important and sensitive information about "pricing architecture"—how PCNA prices its products in the marketplace. Pricing architecture covers both a national pricing approach and specific price points for given areas. Pricing architecture also encompasses PCNA's objectives for All Sport and its new age drinks with reference to trade channels, package sizes and other characteristics of both the products and the customers at which the products are aimed. Additionally, PCNA's pricing architecture outlines PCNA's customer development agreements. These agreements between PCNA and retailers provide for the retailer's participation in certain merchandising activities for PCNA products. As with other information contained in the AOP, pricing architecture is highly confidential and would be extremely valuable to a competitor. Knowing PCNA's pricing architecture would allow a competitor to anticipate PCNA's pricing moves and underbid PCNA strategically whenever and wherever the competitor so desired. PepsiCo introduced evidence that Redmond had detailed knowledge of PCNA's pricing architecture and that he was aware of and had been involved in preparing PCNA's customer development agreements with PCNA's California and California-based national customers. Indeed, PepsiCo showed that Redmond, as the General Manager for California, would have been responsible for implementing the pricing architecture guidelines for his business unit.

PepsiCo also showed that Redmond had intimate knowledge of PCNA "attack plans" for specific markets. Pursuant to these plans, PCNA dedicates extra funds to supporting its brands against other brands in selected markets. To use a hypothetical example, PCNA might budget an additional $500,000 to spend in Chicago at a particular time to help All Sport close its market gap with Gatorade. Testimony and documents demonstrated Redmond's awareness of these plans and his participation in drafting some of them.

Finally, PepsiCo offered evidence of PCNA trade secrets regarding innovations in its selling and delivery systems. Under this plan, PCNA is testing a new delivery system that could give PCNA an advantage over its competitors in negotiations with retailers over shelf space and merchandising. Redmond has knowledge of this secret because PCNA, which has invested over a million dollars in developing the system during the past two years, is testing the pilot program in California.

Having shown Redmond's intimate knowledge of PCNA's plans for 1995, PepsiCo argued that Redmond would inevitably disclose that information to Quaker in his new position, at which he would have substantial input as to Gatorade and Snapple pricing, costs, margins, distribution systems, products, packaging and marketing, and could give Quaker an unfair advantage in its upcoming skirmishes with PepsiCo. Redmond and Quaker countered that Redmond's primary initial duties at Quaker as Vice President — Field Operations would be to integrate Gatorade and Snapple distribution and then to manage that distribution as well as the promotion, marketing and sales of these products. Redmond asserted that the integration would be conducted according to a pre-existing plan and that his special knowledge of PCNA strategies would be irrelevant. This irrelevance would derive not only from the fact that Redmond would be implementing pre-existing plans but also from the fact that PCNA and Quaker distribute their products in entirely different ways: PCNA's distribution system is vertically integrated (i.e., PCNA owns the system) and delivers its product directly to retailers, while Quaker ships its product to wholesalers and customer warehouses and relies on independent distributors. The defendants also pointed out that Redmond had signed a confidentiality agreement with Quaker preventing him from disclosing "any confidential information belonging to others," as well as the Quaker Code of Ethics, which prohibits employees from engaging in "illegal or improper acts to acquire a competitor's trade secrets." Redmond additionally promised at the hearing that should he be faced with a situation at Quaker that might involve the use or disclosure of PCNA information, he would seek advice from Quaker's in-house counsel and would refrain from making the decision.

PepsiCo responded to the defendants' representations by pointing out that the evidence did not show that Redmond would simply be implementing a business plan already in place. On the contrary, as of November, 1994, the plan to integrate Gatorade and Snapple distribution consisted of a single distributorship agreement and a two-page "contract terms summary." Such a basic plan would not lend itself to widespread application among the over 300 independent Snapple distributors. Since the integration process would likely face resistance from Snapple distributors and Quaker had no scheme to deal with this probability, Redmond, as the person in charge of the integration, would likely have a great deal of influence on the process.

PepsiCo further argued that Snapple's 1995 marketing and promotion plans had not necessarily been completed prior to Redmond's joining Quaker, that Uzzi disagreed with portions of the Snapple plans, and that the plans were open to re-evaluation. Uzzi testified that the plan for integrating Gatorade and Snapple distribution is something that would happen in the future. Redmond would therefore likely have input in remaking these plans, and if he did, he would inevitably be making decisions with PCNA's strategic plans and 1995 AOP in mind. Moreover, PepsiCo continued, diverging testimony made it difficult to know exactly what Redmond would be doing at Quaker. Redmond described his job as "managing the entire sales effort of Gatorade at the field level, possibly including strategic planning," and at least at one point considered his job to be equivalent to that of a Chief Operating Officer. Uzzi, on the other hand, characterized Redmond's position as "primarily and initially to restructure and integrate our — the distribution systems for Snapple and for Gatorade, as per our distribution plan" and then to "execute marketing, promotion and sales plans in the marketplace." Uzzi also denied having given Redmond detailed information about any business plans, while Redmond described such a plan in depth in an affidavit and said that he received the information from Uzzi. Thus, PepsiCo asserted, Redmond would have a high position in the Gatorade hierarchy, and PCNA trade secrets and confidential information would necessarily influence his decisions. Even if Redmond could somehow refrain from relying on this information, as he promised he would, his actions in leaving PCNA, Uzzi's actions in hiring Redmond, and the varying testimony regarding Redmond's new responsibilities, made Redmond's assurances to PepsiCo less than comforting.

On December 15, 1994, the district court issued an order enjoining Redmond from assuming his position at Quaker through May, 1995, and permanently from using or disclosing any PCNA trade secrets or confidential information. The court entered its findings of fact and conclusions of law on January 26, 1995, *nunc pro tunc* December 15, 1994. The court, which completely adopted PepsiCo's position, found that Redmond's new job posed a clear threat of misappropriation of trade secrets and confidential information that could be enjoined under Illinois statutory and common law. The court also emphasized Redmond's lack of forthrightness both in his activities before accepting his job with Quaker and in his testimony as factors leading the court to believe the threat of misappropriation was real. This appeal followed.

II.

Both parties agree that the primary issue on appeal is whether the district court correctly concluded that PepsiCo had a reasonable likelihood of success on its various claims for trade secret misappropriation and breach of a confidentiality agreement. We review the district court's legal conclusions in issuing a preliminary injunction de novo and its factual determinations and balancing of the equities for abuse of discretion. *SEC v. Cherif,* 933 F.2d 403, 408 (7th Cir. 1991), *cert. denied,* 502 U.S. 1071, 112 S. Ct. 966, 117 L. Ed. 2d 131 (1992); *Somerset House, Inc. v. Turnock,* 900 F.2d 1012, 1014 (7th Cir. 1990).

A.

The Illinois Trade Secrets Act ("ITSA"), which governs the trade secret issues in this case, provides that a court may enjoin the "actual or threatened misappropriation" of a trade secret. 765 ILCS 1065/3(a). . . . A party seeking an injunction must therefore prove both the existence of a trade secret and the misappropriation. The defendants' appeal focuses solely on misappropriation; although the defendants only reluctantly refer to PepsiCo's marketing and distribution plans as trade secrets, they do not seriously contest that this information falls under the ITSA.

The question of threatened or inevitable misappropriation in this case lies at the heart of a basic tension in trade secret law. Trade secret law serves to protect "standards of commercial morality" and "encourage[] invention and innovation" while maintaining "the public interest in having free and open competition in the manufacture and sale of unpatented goods." [2 Melvin F. Jager, Trade Secrets Law § IL.03 at IL-12 (Clark Boardman Callaghan, rev. ed. 1994)]. Yet that same law should not prevent workers from pursuing their livelihoods when they leave their current positions. *American Can Co. v. Mansukhani*, 742 F.2d 314, 329 (7th Cir. 1984) . . . . This tension is particularly exacerbated when a plaintiff sues to prevent not the actual misappropriation of trade secrets but the mere threat that it will occur. While the ITSA plainly permits a court to enjoin the threat of misappropriation of trade secrets, there is little law in Illinois or in this circuit establishing what constitutes threatened or inevitable misappropriation. Indeed, there are only two cases in this circuit that address the issue: *Teradyne, Inc. v. Clear Communications Corp.*, 707 F. Supp. 353 (N.D. Ill. 1989), and *AMP Inc. v. Fleischhacker*, 823 F.2d 1199 (7th Cir. 1987).

In *Teradyne*, Teradyne alleged that a competitor, Clear Communications, had lured employees away from Teradyne and intended to employ them in the same field. In an insightful opinion, Judge Zagel observed that "threatened misappropriation can be enjoined under Illinois law" where there is a "high degree of probability of inevitable and immediate . . . use of . . . trade secrets." *Teradyne*, 707 F. Supp. at 356. . . .

In *AMP*, we affirmed the denial of a preliminary injunction on the grounds that the plaintiff AMP had failed to show either the existence of any trade secrets or the likelihood that defendant Fleischhacker, a former AMP employee, would compromise those secrets or any other confidential business information. AMP, which produced electrical and electronic connection devices, argued that Fleishhacker's new position at AMP's competitor would inevitably lead him to compromise AMP's trade secrets regarding the manufacture of connectors. *AMP*, 823 F.2d at 1207. In rejecting that argument, we emphasized that the mere fact that a person assumed a similar position at a competitor does not, without more, make it "inevitable that he will use or disclose . . . trade secret information" so as to "demonstrate irreparable injury." *Id*.

. . . .

The ITSA, *Teradyne*, and *AMP* lead to the same conclusion: a plaintiff may prove a claim of trade secret misappropriation by demonstrating that defendant's new employment will inevitably lead him to rely on the plaintiff's trade secrets. *See also* 1 Jager, *supra*, § 7.02[2][a] at 7-20 (noting claims where "the allegation is based on the fact that the disclosure of trade secrets in the new employment is inevitable, whether or not the former employee acts consciously or unconsciously"). The defendants are incorrect that Illinois law does not allow a court to enjoin the "inevitable" disclosure of trade secrets. Questions remain, however, as to what constitutes inevitable misappropriation and whether PepsiCo's submissions rise above those of the *Teradyne* and *AMP* plaintiffs and meet that standard. We hold that they do.

PepsiCo presented substantial evidence at the preliminary injunction hearing that Redmond possessed extensive and intimate knowledge about PCNA's strategic goals for 1995 in sports drinks and new age drinks. The district court concluded on the basis of that presentation that unless Redmond possessed an uncanny ability to compartmentalize information, he would necessarily be making decisions about Gatorade and Snapple by relying on his knowledge of PCNA trade secrets. It is not the "general skills and knowledge acquired during his tenure with" PepsiCo that PepsiCo seeks to keep from falling into Quaker's hands, but rather "the particularized plans or processes developed by [PCNA] and disclosed to him while the employer-employee relationship existed, which are unknown to others in the industry and which give the employer an advantage over his competitors." *AMP*, 823 F.2d at 1202. The *Teradyne* and *AMP* plaintiffs could do nothing more than assert that skilled employees were taking their skills elsewhere; PepsiCo has done much more.

Admittedly, PepsiCo has not brought a traditional trade secret case, in which a former employee has knowledge of a special manufacturing process or customer list and can give a competitor an unfair advantage by transferring the technology or customers to that competitor. . . . PepsiCo has not contended that Quaker has stolen the All Sport formula or its list of distributors. Rather PepsiCo has asserted that Redmond cannot help but rely on PCNA trade secrets as he help plots Gatorade and Snapple's new course, and that these secrets will enable Quaker to achieve a substantial advantage by knowing exactly how PCNA will price, distribute, and market its sports drinks and new age drinks and being able to respond strategically. . . . This type of trade secret problem may arise less often, but it nevertheless falls within the realm of trade secret protection under the present circumstances.

Quaker and Redmond assert that they have not and do not intend to use whatever confidential information Redmond has by virtue of his former employment. They point out that Redmond has already signed an agreement with Quaker not to disclose any trade secrets or confidential information gleaned from his earlier employment. They also note with regard to distribution systems that even if Quaker wanted to steal information about PCNA's distribution plans, they would be completely useless in attempting to integrate the Gatorade and Snapple beverage lines.

The defendants' arguments fall somewhat short of the mark. Again, the danger of misappropriation in the present case is not that Quaker threatens to use PCNA's secrets to create distribution systems or coopt PCNA's advertising and marketing ideas. Rather, PepsiCo believes that Quaker, unfairly armed with knowledge of

PCNA's plans, will be able to anticipate its distribution, packaging, pricing, and marketing moves. Redmond and Quaker even concede that Redmond might be faced with a decision that could be influenced by certain confidential information that he obtained while at PepsiCo. In other words, PepsiCo finds itself in the position of a coach, one of whose players has left, playbook in hand, to join the opposing team before the big game. Quaker and Redmond's protestations that their distribution systems and plans are entirely different from PCNA's are thus not really responsive.

The district court also concluded from the evidence that Uzzi's actions in hiring Redmond and Redmond's actions in pursuing and accepting his new job demonstrated a lack of candor on their part and proof of their willingness to misuse PCNA trade secrets, findings Quaker and Redmond vigorously challenge. The court expressly found that:

> Redmond's lack of forthrightness on some occasions, and out and out lies on others, in the period between the time he accepted the position with defendant Quaker and when he informed plaintiff that he had accepted that position leads the court to conclude that defendant Redmond could not be trusted to act with the necessary sensitivity and good faith under the circumstances in which the only practical verification that he was not using plaintiff's secrets would be defendant Redmond's word to that effect.

The facts of the case do not ineluctably dictate the district court's conclusion. Redmond's ambiguous behavior toward his PepsiCo superiors might have been nothing more than an attempt to gain leverage in employment negotiations. The discrepancy between Redmond's and Uzzi's comprehension of what Redmond's job would entail may well have been a simple misunderstanding. The court also pointed out that Quaker, through Uzzi, seemed to express an unnatural interest in hiring PCNA employees: all three of the people interviewed for the position Redmond ultimately accepted worked at PCNA. Uzzi may well have focused on recruiting PCNA employees because he knew they were good and not because of their confidential knowledge. Nonetheless, the district court, after listening to the witnesses, determined otherwise. That conclusion was not an abuse of discretion.

. . . .

Thus, when we couple the demonstrated inevitability that Redmond would rely on PCNA trade secrets in his new job at Quaker with the district court's reluctance to believe that Redmond would refrain from disclosing these secrets in his new position (or that Quaker would ensure Redmond did not disclose them), we conclude that the district court correctly decided that PepsiCo demonstrated a likelihood of success on its statutory claim of trade secret misappropriation.

. . . .

C.

For the same reasons we concluded that the district court did not abuse its discretion in granting the preliminary injunction on the issue of trade secret misappropriation, we also agree with its decision on the likelihood of Redmond's breach of his confidentiality agreement should he begin working at Quaker. Because Redmond's position at Quaker would initially cause him to disclose trade secrets, it would necessarily force him to breach his agreement not to disclose confidential information acquired while employed in PCNA . . . .

III.

Finally, Redmond and Quaker have contended in the alternative that the injunction issued against them is overbroad. They disagree in particular with the injunction's prohibition against Redmond's participation in the integration of the Snapple and Gatorade distribution systems. The defendants claim that whatever trade secret and confidential information Redmond has, that information is completely irrelevant to Quaker's integration task. They further argue that, because Redmond would only be implementing a plan already in place, the injunction is especially inappropriate.

While the defendants' arguments are not without some merit, the district court determined that the proposed integration would require Redmond to do more than execute a plan someone else had drafted. It also found that Redmond's knowledge of PCNA's trade secrets and confidential information would inevitably shape that integration and that Redmond could not be trusted to avoid that conflict of interest. If the injunction permanently enjoined Redmond from assuming these duties at Quaker, the defendants' argument would be stronger. However, the injunction against Redmond's immediate employment at Quaker extends no further than necessary and was well within the district court's discretion.

For the foregoing reasons, we affirm the district court's order enjoining Redmond from assuming his responsibilities at Quaker through May, 1995, and preventing him forever from disclosing PCNA trade secrets and confidential information.

AFFIRMED.

Notes & Questions

1. History of the Inevitable Disclosure Doctrine

Before the Seventh Circuit's decision in *PepsiCo, Inc. v. Redmond*, inevitable disclosure cases involved the situation where a plaintiff has a trade secret that the defendant competitor has tried but failed to independently develop. In an effort to obtain the trade secret, the defendant then hires away one of the plaintiff's employees who is privy to the trade secret. Typically, the plaintiff is the market leader in its field while the defendant is a competitor who has a smaller share of the market. Under these circumstances, the court assumes that the exiting employee cannot avoid using the knowledge of plaintiff's trade secret for his new employer, the defendant. *E.I. Du Pont de Nemours v. American Potash & Chemical Corp.*, 200 A.2d 428 (Del. Ch. 1964), is a good example of what commentators have called a "true" inevitable disclosure case. In the case, Du Pont brought an action to enjoin a former employee from disclosing Du Pont's secret process for manufacturing titanium dioxide pigments to American Potash. American Potash had tried unsuccessfully to obtain a license to use Du Pont's process and subsequently hired away one of Du Pont's managers who had knowledge of the process. The court denied American Potash's motion for summary judgment, holding that the record did not preclude a jury from finding that there was an imminent threat of a breach of the employee's fiduciary duty to Du Pont.

After *PepsiCo*, an employer may potentially obtain injunctive relief against an employee for "virtually *any* competitive employment taken by an individual who had held any kind of position . . . of responsibility with plaintiff but had not entered into a restrictive covenant and accordingly not been given any consideration for restricting his postemployment opportunities." MILGRIM ON TRADE SECRETS § 5.02[3][d]. Injunctive relief is no longer predicated on evidence of actual or threatened trade secret misappropriation.

2. Inevitable Disclosure and the Defend Trade Secrets Act

As discussed *supra*, the Defend Trade Secrets Act (DTSA) provides that an injunction to prevent trade secret misappropriation may not "prevent a person from entering into an employment relationship" and that any conditions placed on employment under an injunction "shall be based on evidence of threatened misappropriation and not merely on the information the person knows." 18 U.S.C.A. § 1836(b)(3)(A)(i). This language was interpreted by some to mean that the inevitable disclosure doctrine was overruled by the DTSA. So far there has been only one decision addressing the issue. In *Molon Motor & Coil Corp. v. Nidec Motor Corp.*, No. 16 C 03545, 2017 WL 1954531 (N.D. Ill. May 11, 2017), an opinion issued on the day of the first anniversary of the DTSA, a federal judge invoked the doctrine of inevitable disclosure to infer the probability of future harm to the plaintiff. Based on this finding, the judge denied a motion to dismiss the plaintiff's claims under the DTSA and Illinois trade secret law. In the motion to dismiss, the defendant argued that the DTSA did not apply to the case because the alleged acts at issue occurred before the DTSA was enacted in May 2016. The judge explained that, even if no acts occurred after the effective date of the Act, the inference of inevitable disclosure could reasonably extend to continued use of the information at issue beyond the Act's effective date. *Molon Motor*, 2017 WL 1954531, at *7. Although this decision indicates that inevitable disclosure might survive the DTSA, it is probably too early to make firm conclusions.

3. Framing the Dispute

Case law favors employee ownership in situations where an invention conception is completed after an employee's exit. Absent a hold-over or trailer clause, the exiting employee owns an invention conceived after the termination of the employment relationship. A dispute framed as an issue of ownership of an inchoate invention therefore favors the employee.

All disputes involving inchoate inventions may potentially be recast as trade secret misappropriation disputes, where the invention idea is the trade secret. By framing the issue as one of trade secret misappropriation, an employer can replace pro-employee case law governing ownership of inchoate inventions with more employer-friendly case law governing trade secret misappropriation. When the issue is reframed as a trade secret dispute, an employer may use the doctrine of inevitable disclosure to enforce what is in effect a covenant not to compete.

b. Hazards of Applying the "Inevitable Disclosure" Doctrine

The inevitable disclosure doctrine can impose the equivalent of an after-the-fact noncontractual covenant not to compete. Unlike a noncompete agreement, which must meet a contractual test for reasonableness, the doctrine of inevitability provides no frame of reference for courts aside from the uncertain standard of "inevitability." The doctrine in essence shifts the bargaining power to employers without giving employees the benefit of negotiations.

William Lejeune v. Coin Acceptors, Inc.

Court of Appeals of Maryland

849 A.2d 451 (Md. App. 2004)

BATTAGLIA, J.

This case of first impression involves the provisions of the Maryland Uniform Trade Secrets Act, codified under Maryland Code, Sections 11-1201 through 11-1209 of the Commercial Law Article (1975, 2000 Repl. Vol.). William LeJeune appeals from a preliminary injunction issued by the Circuit Court for Anne Arundel County, enjoining him from working for Mars Electronics, Inc. (hereinafter "Mars") in a number of specified industries. The Circuit Court found that, if LeJeune were permitted to work in those industries, his former employer and Mars' principal competitor, Coin Acceptors, Inc. (hereinafter "Coinco"), would suffer irreparable injury because LeJeune had misappropriated trade secrets that would give Mars an unfair competitive advantage. We conclude that the evidence supports a finding of trade secret misappropriation. We also conclude, however, that the Circuit Court erred in relying on the theory of "inevitable disclosure" when ruling on the preliminary injunction. Therefore, we vacate the injunction and remand this case to the Circuit Court for further proceedings consistent with this Opinion.

I. Background

A. Facts

Coinco is a Missouri corporation in the business of designing, manufacturing, and servicing coin acceptors, coin changers, bill validators, and similar machines. Coinco divides its efforts to market and sell these machines into three separate "channels": "Vending," which includes beverage bottlers such as Coke and Pepsi; "Amusement," which includes video game manufacturers and distributors; and "Specialty Markets," which includes transit or transportation companies or companies that offer "self-check-out" services.

LeJeune began his employment with Coinco in 1993 as a "Sales and Field Service Representative." While in this position, he sold currency equipment, performed field service on that equipment, and led seminars on the repair and maintenance of

Coinco's machines. In 1997, LeJeune was promoted to the position of Branch Manager and became responsible for managing every aspect of the Baltimore branch office, including the sales and field service of Coinco vending equipment in Maryland, Virginia, Delaware and West Virginia. LeJeune's job title changed again to Area Account Manager in 2002, when Coinco restructured its operations, eliminating the position of Branch Manager and creating three new positions: Area Account Manager (hereinafter "AAM"), Service Center Manager, and Customer Service Representative. As an AAM, LeJeune continued to be responsible for sales of Coinco's vending products but in an expanded region.

In January of 2003, Coinco introduced the MC2600 bill acceptor, a new product in the Amusement Market. Although LeJeune traditionally sold vending products, Coinco assigned him the responsibility of marketing and selling the MC2600 because many of the amusement customers were also Coinco's vending customers. LeJeune, however, never sold a single MC2600 in the Amusement Market and, actually, approached only one amusement industry customer to sell that product.

Coinco selected LeJeune in 2002 and 2003 to serve on a team of Coinco employees charged with investigating ways the company could cultivate clients in the Specialty Markets channel. LeJeune, the only AAM selected, attended the team's initial meeting, after which he was told by Coinco leadership to focus his work on the Vending Market and not to let his work on the Specialty Markets team interfere with that focus. LeJeune did not attend any subsequent meetings of the Specialty Markets team. Ultimately, the team generated a strategic plan, which analyzed the Specialty Markets and Coinco's opportunities in those markets. LeJeune received a copy of the plan, but he never reviewed it in detail.

While employed with Coinco, LeJeune never entered into a non-compete or confidentiality agreement with Coinco. He worked in sales and was not involved in manufacturing or research and development. He did, however, develop an extensive understanding of Coinco's products through his service and sales experience. He also learned of Coinco's pricing, pricing strategies, marketing and business initiatives, and selling strategies but was not privy to all information relating to Coinco's contracts with customers. LeJeune worked from his home in Annapolis, where he regularly received company documents.

Considering new employment in May and June of 2003, LeJeune had several interviews with Mars, Coinco's primary competitor in the currency acceptor industry. During an introductory telephone interview in May 2003, LeJeune described his work experience with Coinco and mentioned to the interviewer, Chris Mumford, that "Coinco recently added Money Controls products to [its] portfolio to call on retail/kiosk accounts east of the Mississippi." He also stated that Coinco was concerned that Conlux, a sister company of Mars, was cutting into Coinco's sales. LeJeune later traveled to Lancaster, Pennsylvania, where he interviewed with several other Mars personnel. LeJeune discussed his experience at Coinco and explained why he sought employment with Mars. One of the interviewers, Mary Rampe, twice explained to LeJeune that no confidential Coinco information should be discussed during the interview. On July 7, 2003, LeJeune signed a job-offer letter from Mars and accepted a position as an Amusement OEM (Original Equipment Manufacturer) Manager. The new position would require LeJeune to focus on selling to the amusement industry, although he would have some contact with "full line distributors" that serve both the amusement and vending markets.

On July 14, 2003, LeJeune informed his supervisor, William Morgan, that he was leaving Coinco to work for Mars. On July 16, 2003, Morgan and LeJeune met for several hours to review the status of LeJeune's accounts. Morgan asked LeJeune to continue to work for Coinco for two weeks so that LeJeune could introduce Coinco's clients to LeJeune's successor. During his conversations with Morgan, LeJeune stated that he would be in a "unique" position at Mars because of his experience at Coinco. Morgan understood this to mean that LeJeune intended to use his knowledge of Coinco's business strategies. LeJeune stated that the reference to his "unique" position described his situation as one with extensive experience in the vending industry entering a job with a focus on the amusement market. That same day, LeJeune returned his laptop computer to Morgan along with a box of Coinco documents and materials.

Prior to this meeting with Morgan, LeJeune, on three separate occasions, had transferred or "burned" digital copies of numerous documents from his Coinco laptop to a compact disc ("CD"). On July 8, LeJeune copied, among other documents, Coinco's Executable Budgeting Software, which includes Coinco's manufacturing costs and profit margins. LeJeune conducted a second "burn" on July 8, transferring numerous personal files that had been saved on the Coinco laptop. On July 16, LeJeune again copied various files from the laptop, one of which contained pricing information related to Coinco's Specialty Markets Strategic Plan. Sometime after copying all of the files onto the CD, LeJeune created a second copy of the disc.

LeJeune explained that he had done this because he wanted to retain personal files, such as wedding photographs, that had been saved under the "My Documents" file on the laptop. He stated that, for the sake of simplicity and because he did not know how to save individual files onto a CD, he had "burned" the entire "My Documents" folder and captured some of Coinco's business documents. LeJeune stated that he had not saved any Coinco documents with the intent to use those documents in his work with Mars. An expert in computer forensics testifying on behalf of Coinco, however, stated that, when LeJeune copied the Executable Budgeting Software, that file was not part of the "My Documents" folder. The expert also discovered that LeJeune had erased information from the Coinco laptop in an effort to hide the downloads. The erased information was recovered by computer forensic specialists.

In addition to the computer files, LeJeune also retained hard copies of a number of other Coinco documents. Included among those documents were Coinco's price and cost information, Coinco's service pricing, a list of Coinco's preferred distributors, and detailed technical specifications relating to a Coinco's amusement product, the MC2600, and a Coinco vending product, the Bill Pro Validator. The pricing and cost information is sensitive because Coinco uses a tiered-pricing system.

Coinco's efforts to maintain the confidentiality of company information included limiting access to company documents to only personnel who needed to know the information. To this end, Coinco guarded the computer files on its mainframe computer with a password system, which allowed Coinco to control the employees' access to company information. Coinco also negotiates "non-disclosure" agreements with many of its clients to ensure that those clients do not share pricing information with other Coinco customers or Coinco competitors. In addition, Coinco's "Employee Handbook" states that its business methods are "proprietary," and employees should protect such information as confidential. Many of Coinco's pricing documents and other strategic information, including information at issue in this case (i.e., the Specialty Markets Strategic Plan, pricing and cost documents, and Bill Pro Validator specifications), were marked "confidential."

LeJeune stated that he did not discuss proprietary Coinco information, such as Coinco's price list, customer list, or strategic plan, with anyone at Mars. According to LeJeune, he did not know that Coinco was concerned about his knowledge of confidential information until he learned of Coinco's suit against him, at which time he returned all of the alleged confidential Coinco documents and files.

. . . .

III. Discussion

A. Maryland Uniform Trade Secrets Act

. . . .

1. Coinco's Trade Secrets

[The court determined that the documents and information that LeJeune retained without Coinco's permission qualified as trade secrets under the Maryland Uniform Trade Secrets Act (MUTSA).]

2. Misappropriation

Coinco is not entitled to injunctive relief unless it has established that LeJeune misappropriated its trade secrets, including Coinco's Executable Budgeting Software, Specialty Markets Strategic Plan, hard-copy pricing and cost lists, and specifications of the MC2600 and Bill Pro Validator. LeJeune contends that the only basis for granting an injunction under MUTSA is a finding of "actual or threatened" misappropriation. The evidence admitted at the preliminary injunction hearing, LeJeune argues, does not establish any "actual or threatened" misappropriation of a trade secret. LeJeune maintains that he did not acquire any information improperly because Coinco voluntarily provided him with all retained documents and then did not ask for their return until the start of this litigation. Additionally, LeJeune argues that Coinco did not present any evidence that he had used or disclosed trade secrets or that he intended to do so.

In response, Coinco urges that the evidence does support a finding that LeJeune misappropriated trade secrets. Coinco also claims that the evidence demonstrates that LeJeune misappropriated this information by copying selected confidential files from the Coinco laptop onto a CD and by retaining hard-copy documents after allegedly telling Coinco that he had returned everything.

. . . .

Section 11-1201(c) of MUTSA defines "misappropriation" as follows:

"Misappropriation" means the:

(1) Acquisition of a trade secret of another by a person who knows or has reason to know that the trade secret was acquired by improper means; or

(2) Disclosure or use of a trade secret of another without express or implied consent by a person who:

   (i) Used improper means to acquire knowledge of the trade secret; or

   (ii) At the time of disclosure or use, knew or had reason to know that the person's knowledge of the trade secret was:

      1. Derived from or through a person who had utilized improper means to acquire it;

      2. Acquired under circumstances giving rise to a duty to maintain its secrecy or limit its use; or

      3. Derived from or through a person who owed a duty to the person seeking relief to maintain its secrecy or limit its use; or

   (iii) Before a material change of the person's position, knew or had reason to know that it was a trade secret and that knowledge of it had been acquired by accident or mistake.

Section 11-1201(c) of MUTSA. This section describes two general types of misappropriation: (1) acquisition of a trade secret by improper means or (2) disclosure of a trade secret. We must consider this definition in conjunction with the terms of Section 11- 1202(a) of MUTSA, which provides an injunction for "actual" or "threatened" misappropriation. A court, therefore, can issue an injunction to prevent either of the following: (1) the actual or threatened acquisition of a trade secret by improper means or (2) the actual or threatened disclosure of a trade secret.

a. Acquisition of a Trade Secret by Improper Means

The Circuit Court was persuaded that the evidence was sufficient that LeJeune had acquired trade secrets by improper means. Both parties agree that LeJeune possessed documents and files belonging to Coinco, and we determined that several of these documents (i.e., the budgeting software, Specialty Markets Strategic Plan, pricing and cost documents, and MC2600 and Bill Pro Validator specifications) qualified as trade secrets. MUTSA states that a trade secret is acquired by "improper means" when it has been acquired by "theft, bribery, misrepresentation, breach or inducement of a breach of duty to maintain secrecy, or espionage through electronic or other means." Section 11-1201(b) of MUTSA.

. . . .

Coinco did not give LeJeune permission to transfer trade secrets from the company laptop to a CD. In an attempt to justify his actions, LeJeune stated that he transferred the "My Documents" folder from the company laptop to retain personal files, such as wedding photographs, and in the process, captured numerous Coinco documents. Coinco's expert testified, however, that LeJeune did not download only the "My Documents" folder, but he also transferred selected, specific Coinco files containing trade secrets. Considering this evidence, the trial judge apparently did not believe LeJeune's version of the events, and we see no reason here to upset the fact-finder's credibility determination.

. . . .

[T]he trial court found and we agree that the information at issue is sensitive trade secret information. Moreover, . . . on the last day of his employment, LeJeune selected specific, confidential Coinco documents and actively transferred them from the Coinco laptop to a CD that he intended to keep for his personal use. After transferring the files, LeJeune then erased over four hundred files from the laptop. This suggests that LeJeune was attempting to hide his conduct and was aware that transferring the files was improper. LeJeune again demonstrated an intent to hide his possession of trade secrets when he told his supervisor that "everything" had been returned, although numerous hard-copy trade secrets remained in LeJeune's possession. The evidence in this case is sufficient to support the Circuit Court's finding that LeJeune acquired Coinco's trade secrets by improper means.

b. Inevitable Disclosure/Threatened Disclosure

Concluding that LeJeune misappropriated trade secrets by acquiring them improperly does not end our inquiry with respect to whether the Circuit Court's injunction was appropriate in this case. Injunctive relief, by its nature, addresses only what could happen in the future and cannot remedy misconduct, such as the improper acquisition of trade secrets, that occurred in the past. In fact, the injunctive remedies of Section 11-1202(a) of MUTSA provide no remedy at all for the past misappropriations. In other words, if LeJeune already had misappropriated the trade secrets and returned them, the court cannot craft an injunction to reverse time and erase whatever harm LeJeune caused by taking the trade secrets without consent.

Nevertheless, MUTSA's injunctive remedies could serve to protect Coinco if the evidence demonstrates a likelihood of some *future* misappropriation. As we stated previously, MUTSA permits a court to enjoin either (1) actual or threatened acquisition of a trade secret by improper means or (2) actual or threatened disclosure of trade secrets. With respect to the first category, the evidence clearly is insufficient to support a finding that LeJeune continues to acquire trade secrets improperly or that he has threatened other acquisition of Coinco's trade secrets by improper means. As to the second category, the record does not reveal any evidence that LeJeune actually had disclosed Coinco's trade secrets and that an injunction is necessary to stop that conduct. The sole question in the case at bar, therefore, is whether any threatened future disclosure or use of a trade secret justifies an injunction at this stage of the proceedings.[8]

The Circuit Court, however, did not make a finding of "threatened disclosure" of Coinco's trade secrets. Rather, it decided to issue the preliminary injunction based on a theory known as "inevitable disclosure." In making its ruling, the trial judge stated:

> I know I don't have to make a final ruling on whether the inevitable disclosure doctrine applies or not, but it is the court's position that with the knowledge that [LeJeune] has, it would be inconceivable to the court how he could do his job as the national accounts representative for the amusement industry without considering or weighing or taking into consideration the information that he acquired while he was employed with Coinco, and so for that reason, I do believe . . . that [Coinco] will suffer irreparable injury.

The theory of "inevitable disclosure" has been applied in courts outside of Maryland to enjoin a departing employee from working for a competitor when the court is persuaded that it is inevitable that the departed employee will use or disclose trade secrets in his or her work for the competitor. [Milton E. Babirak, Jr., *The Maryland Uniform Trade Secrets Act: A Critical Summary of the Act and Case Law*, 31 U. Balt. L. Rev. 181, 198 (2002)]. Put another way, "inevitable disclosure" cases are so named because they are based on the original employer's claim that a former employee who is permitted to work for a competitor will—even if acting in the utmost good faith— inevitably be required to use or disclose the former employer's trade secrets in order to perform the new job.

. . . .

Another commentator explained that the doctrine arises often when the former employee did not sign a non-compete agreement:

---

8. We have identified some evidence in the record suggesting that LeJeune has threatened disclosure of Coinco's trade secrets. When LeJeune met with his supervisor after announcing his resignation, he mentioned that he would be in a "unique" position at Mars, suggesting that he might use confidential Coinco information in his new employment. This comment raises suspicion particularly because, as we determined above, LeJeune had acquired trade secrets improperly by copying Coinco files onto his CD and by saving certain hard-copy trade secrets after he informed his supervisor "everything" had been returned. Further evidence of LeJeune's threatened disclosure comes from the discovery that not only did he burn one CD, but he also placed Coinco trade secrets on a second CD. If there is a second CD filled with trade secrets, it would come as no surprise that LeJeune had made a third or fourth CD to maintain for future reference. Even LeJeune's interview with Mars indicates his willingness to share trade secrets. When interviewing face-to-face with Mars personnel, he was reminded twice that confidential information should not be disclosed. One could infer from these reminders that LeJeune, in fact, had displayed some propensity to disclose trade secrets. Based on this evidence, we hold that Coinco will likely succeed on the merits of its claim of threatened misappropriation by disclosure of trade secrets.

> Significantly, the inevitable disclosure doctrine is utilized in cases where the employee has not signed, or has even refused to sign, a non-competition agreement or non-disclosure of proprietary information agreement with his prior employer, and where the employee has not threatened, directly or indirectly, to use or disclose the trade secrets of his former employer to his new employer.

Babirak at 198.

LeJeune claims that, because this Court has not recognized the theory of "inevitable disclosure," the Circuit Court erred in using it as a ground for issuing the preliminary injunction limiting his employment at Mars. LeJeune argues, however, that, even if this Court decides to adopt "inevitable disclosure," it should not be applied to his case. According to LeJeune, any trade secrets that LeJeune may have acquired while working in the Vending Channel at Coinco would not be useful to him while working in the Amusement Channel at Mars. Disclosure of the vending trade secrets, therefore, is not inevitable in LeJeune's opinion.

According to Coinco, however, "inevitable disclosure," although not expressly recognized in Maryland, was correctly applied in this case because it is a form of "threatened" misappropriation under MUTSA. Coinco claims that LeJeune inevitably would disclose his extensive knowledge about Coinco's business strategies while working for Mars, giving his new employer an unfair competitive advantage. This is so, in Coinco's view, because LeJeune has demonstrated a lack of candor and a willingness to use or disclose trade secrets. Coinco believes, therefore, that the theory of "inevitable disclosure" is appropriate in this case because LeJeune understands Coinco's strategic plan for the Amusement Channel, the market on which he would focus at Mars as a National Accounts Representative for the Amusement Industry. We disagree with Coinco and decline to adopt the theory of "inevitable disclosure" under the present circumstances.

Long before the adoption of the Uniform Act, the first reported cases applying "inevitable disclosure" involved extraordinary situations in which a company tried to guard the secrecy of some technology that had propelled the company into industry leadership. *See Allis-Chalmers Manufacturing Co. v. Continental Aviation & Engineering Corp.*, 255 F. Supp. 645 (E.D. Mich. 1966); *E.I. duPont de Nemours & Co. v. American Potash & Chemical Corp.*, 41 Del. Ch. 533, 200 A.2d 428 (Del. Ch. 1964); *B.F. Goodrich Co. v. Wohlgemuth*, 117 Ohio App. 493, 192 N.E.2d 99 (Ohio Ct. App. 1963).

Since the Uniform Act's adoption and widespread recognition by the states, the most notable case involving "inevitable disclosure" is *Pepsico, Inc. v. Redmond*, 54 F.3d 1262 (7th Cir. 1995). In that case, Pepsico sought to enjoin one of its former senior executives, Redmond, from working for Quaker Oats Company, Pepsico's rival in the sports beverage market. *Id.* at 1264. While at Pepsico, Redmond had access to confidential marketing strategies and "pricing architecture." *Id.* at 1265. Redmond continued to work for Pepsico while he secretly negotiated for employment with Quaker. Redmond accepted a senior sales position at Quaker and, when he informed Pepsico of that decision, misrepresented the nature of his new position. *Id.* Pepsico sued and obtained a preliminary injunction, barring Redmond from "assuming any duties with Quaker relating to beverage pricing, marketing, and distribution." *Id.* at 1263.

On appeal before the Seventh Circuit, Pepsico argued that Redmond would "inevitably disclose" trade secrets acquired at Pepsico because, at Quaker, he would be involved significantly in the marketing, pricing, and distribution of sports beverages. *Id.* at 1266. The court of appeals agreed, affirming the injunction and holding that "a plaintiff may prove a claim of trade secret misappropriation by demonstrating that defendant's new employment will inevitably lead him to rely on the plaintiff's trade secrets." *Id.* at 1269. The appellate court accepted the district court's reasoning that "unless Redmond possessed an uncanny ability to compartmentalize information, he would necessarily be making decisions about [Quaker's beverages] by relying on his knowledge of [Pepsico's] trade secrets." *Id.*

No court interpreting the provisions of MUTSA has applied the theory of "inevitable disclosure." Among other courts, including those interpreting other versions of the Uniform Act, the theory remains the subject of considerable disagreement. The court in *Whyte v. Schlage Lock Co.*, 101 Cal. App. 4th 1443, 125 Cal. Rptr. 2d 277 (Cal. Ct. App. 2002) recently presented a comprehensive discussion of the theory within the context of California law. Schlage Lock Company competed with Kwikset Corporation in the business of manufacturing and selling locks and related products to retailers. *Id.* at 1447. The Home Depot, one of the largest retailers of these products, accounted for a large percentage of Schlage's sales. As Schlage's vice-president of sales, Whyte was responsible for sales to several large retailers, including The Home Depot. *Id.* Although Whyte had signed a confidentiality agreement as to Schlage's proprietary information, he had not signed a covenant not to compete. Whyte was lured to join Kwikset, and Schlage sued, seeking an injunction based on the theory of inevitable disclosure. *Id.* at 1448. After surveying the cases that have considered the doctrine, the court opted to join those jurisdictions that have rejected it:

> The decisions rejecting the inevitable disclosure doctrine correctly balance competing public policies of employee mobility and protection of trade secrets. The inevitable disclosure doctrine permits an employer to enjoin the ormer employee without proof of the employee's actual or threatened use of trade secrets based upon an inference (based in turn upon circumstantial evidence) that the employee will use his or her knowledge of those trade secrets in the new employment. *The result is not merely an injunction against the use of trade secrets, but an injunction restricting employment.*

Id. at 1461–62 (emphasis added). The application of the doctrine, the court stated, "'creates a de facto covenant not to compete' and 'runs counter to the strong public policy in California favoring employee mobility.'" *Id.* at 1462 (quoting *Bayer Corp.*, 72 F. Supp. 2d at 1120). The court continued:

> The chief ill in the covenant not to compete imposed by the inevitable disclosure doctrine is in its after-the-fact nature: The covenant is imposed *after*

the employment contract is made and therefore alters the employment relationship without the employee's consent. When, as here, a confidentiality agreement is in place, the inevitable disclosure doctrine "in effect converts the confidentiality agreement into such a covenant [not to compete]. Or, as another federal court put it, "a court should not allow a plaintiff to use inevitable disclosure as an after-the-fact noncompete agreement to enjoin an employee from working for the employer of his or her choice."

Id. at 1462–63 (citations omitted); *see also EarthWeb*, 71 F. Supp. 2d at 311 ("Such retroactive alterations [as a result of applying inevitable disclosure] distort the terms of the employment relationship and upset the balance which courts have attempted to achieve in construing non-compete agreements."). The court was disturbed that the inevitable disclosure doctrine could "rewrite[] the employment agreement" by providing the employer with "the benefit of a contractual provision it did not pay for, while the employee is bound by a court-imposed contract provision with no opportunity to negotiate terms or consideration." *Id.* at 1463.

We find this reasoning persuasive, especially as applied to the circumstances in the case before us. Maryland has a policy in favor of employee mobility similar to that of California. Furthermore, Coinco decided not to enter into a confidentiality agreement or a covenant not to compete with LeJeune. To recognize "inevitable disclosure" in this case would allow Coinco the benefit of influencing LeJeune's employment relationship with Mars even though Coinco chose not to negotiate a restrictive covenant or confidentiality agreement with LeJeune. *See International Business Mach. Corp. v. Seagate Technology, Inc.*, 941 F. Supp. 98, 101 (D. Minn. 1992) ("A claim of trade secret misappropriation should not act as an ex post facto covenant not to compete."). Adopting the theory also would tend to permit a court to infer some inevitable disclosure of trade secrets merely from an individual's exposure to them. *See H & R Block Eastern Tax Servs. Inc. v. Enchura*, 122 F. Supp. 2d 1067, 1076 (W.D. Mo. 2000) (stating that no inference of inevitable disclosure can flow from exposure to trade secrets). For these reasons, we conclude that the theory of "inevitable disclosure" cannot serve as a basis for granting a plaintiff injunctive relief under MUTSA.

3. Risks to New Employers from Hiring Experienced High-Tech Employees

a. *Misappropriation: Wrongful Use or Disclosure*

i. Acts Giving Rise to Third Party Liability

Employers may hold third parties who are strangers to the employer-employee relationship liable for improperly acquiring, using, or disclosing a trade secret. Liability for improper means of acquiring another's trade secret can arise from causing an exiting employee to breach a duty to maintain secrecy. Section 1 of the Uniform Trade Secrets Act defines improper means to include a "breach or inducement of a breach of duty to maintain secrecy;" similarly, the definition of improper means in section 43 of the Restatement (Third) of Unfair Competition includes "inducement of or knowing participation in a breach of confidence." Third parties may also incur liability for using or disclosing information after receiving notice of its trade secret status. Actual notice of trade secret status is not necessary. It is enough that the third party knew or should have known that the party disclosing the information did not have authority to disclose it, or was breaching a contractual or fiduciary duty by disclosing, or that the information was disclosed by accident.

Colgate-Palmolive Co. v. Carter Products

United States Court of Appeals for the Fourth Circuit

230 F.2d 855 (4th Cir. 1956)

PARKER, CIRCUIT JUDGE.

This is an appeal in a case involving patent infringement and appropriation of trade secrets. The patent in suit is United States Patent No. 2,655,480 issued October 13, 1953 to one Spitzer and others relating to a pressurized shaving cream. The plaintiffs in the court below, appellees here, were Spitzer and his partner Small, holders by assignment from the other patentees, and Carter Products Inc., manufacturer of drugs and cosmetics and the holder of an exclusive license under the patent. The defendants below, appellants here, were the Colgate-Palmolive Company, the manufacturer of a pressurized shaving cream alleged to infringe, the Stalfort Pressure-Pak Corporation and John C. Stalfort & Sons, Inc., who packaged pressurized shaving cream alleged to infringe the patent for the Mennen Company, and the Read Drug & Chemical Company, Inc., which sold the pressurized shaving cream for Colgate and Mennen. Plaintiffs claimed infringement of only eight claims of the patent. Defendants admitted infringement if these claims were valid but denied their validity and asked judgment declaring them as well as all other claims of the patent invalid.

The trial court held the patent valid, and enjoined infringement thereof as well as the use of a trade secret held to have been wrongfully appropriated by Colgate. It also ordered Colgate to assign to plaintiffs rights under patent applications found to have been based upon the trade secret. The case was referred to a special master to determine and report as to damages resulting from infringement and also as to damages and profits for which Colgate should be required to account because of misappropriation of trade secrets and to make recommendations as to whether the damages on account of patent infringement should be increased as allowed by statute, reserving, however, for future determination the question as to whether increased damages should be awarded. Judgment was entered that plaintiffs recover their costs and taxable disbursements to date, including against Colgate reasonable attorneys' fees, and the special master was directed to include in his report a recommendation as to the amount of attorneys' fees to be allowed. Three principal questions are presented by the appeal: (1) Is the patent valid? (2) Should the findings of the trial court as to misappropriation of trade secrets be sustained? And (3) Is the decree proper?

1. The Validity of the Patent.

Spitzer, one of the patentees, in the year 1948 conceived the idea of developing a shaving lather which, like the lather produced by machines in barber shops, could be used as it came from the container without being worked up on the face. He employed Foster D. Snell, Inc., consulting chemists, to work out his idea for him in terms of a mixture that could be enclosed in a small container and, upon the opening of a valve, would emerge in the form of a durable lather, which, without whipping up or other agitation, could be used for shaving purposes. Snell put to work on the project two chemists, Reich and Fine, who after several months of work and experimentation developed an emulsion consisting of an aqueous soap solution mixed with certain gases liquefied by pressure, which they enclosed in a container. When the valve of the container was opened the pressure of the gases extruded the emulsion and, as it came from the can, the particles of gas expended into minute bubbles covered with soap which was the shaving lather desired. Patent, applied for November 2, 1949, was issued to Spitzer, Reich, and Fine October 13, 1953. In the meantime an exclusive license had been granted to Carter and the product was being marketed under the trade name of 'Rise'. It achieved at once outstanding commercial success. Sales of 'Rise' in 1950 amounted to $400,000, in 1951 to $800,000, in 1952 to $1,800,000 and in 1953 to $2,600,000. The sales of Colgate's infringing product in 1954 amounted to $5,000,000.

There was, of course, nothing novel in the use of soap to make lather, nor in the use of a can as a container, nor in the use of a gas liquefied by pressure and mixed with another liquid to spray the mixture from the can. What was novel was to get a mixture of the right gases, with the right soaps in the right proportions, confined in a container under the right pressure, so that a lather satisfactory for shaving purposes would be produced when the mixture was allowed to emerge. In producing such a mixture many problems were encountered and the record shows that their solution took many months. The first experiment consisted in mixing a liquid soap then on the market with nitrous oxide gas, the gas used with pressurized whipped cream. This was a failure because the gas was soluble in the aqueous soap solution and the product extruded from the container was not a lather useful for shaving but a mere soapy liquid. An emulsion consisting of the gas propellant Freon-12 (dichlordifluormethane) and the soap solution used in barber shop machines would not do because the pressure was too high. Reduction of the vapor pressure by mixing Freon-11 (monofluortrichlormethane) with Freon-12 produced a smarting, skin-irritating product not suitable for shaving. Reduction of vapor pressure with mineral oil solved the pressure problem but produced problems in connection with the soaps. Finally, after much experimentation, sodium soaps were eliminated and the soap solution adopted was a combination of 80 parts of TEA (triethanolamine) stearate and 20 parts of TEA cocoate, to prevent jelling. The proper propellant was found after much inquiry and experiment by mixing Freon-114 (1, 2 dichlor 1, 1, 2, 2 tetrafluorethane) with Freon-12 . . . .

        . . . .

The defendant Colgate-Palmolive became interested in a pressurized shaving cream when 'Rise' came on the market; but although it had 200 or more chemists in its service and although it purchased packages of 'Rise' and had them analyzed, the record shows that it was unable to develop a satisfactory product until it had employed Fine, who had been working for Snell in the development of 'Rise'. He gave Colgate the formula which brought success to its efforts and which embodied the formula of 'Rise' in combination with a formula which Colgate had theretofore not found successful. He gave Colgate, also, the benefit of knowledge obtained at Snell's with respect to improving the 'Rise' formula by superfatting so as to produce a smoother lather and one which gives the feeling on the skin produced by the so-called brushless shaving creams. Colgate had Fine to file applications for patents covering this improved lather. Notwithstanding this experience and attempts to obtain patents in its own behalf on the subject matter, Colgate argues that the patent here in suit is lacking in invention and is anticipated by both domestic and foreign patents and by prior use.

[The court determined that the 'Rise' patent was valid.]

. . . .

What we have here is a new and useful composition of matter produced after lengthy experimentation, in which the various elements combine to produce a new and useful result. To the presumption that the finding of the District Judge as to validity is correct, a finding based upon lengthy evidence and the testimony of experts must be added the presumptions of validity arising from the fact that the patent was issued by the Patent Office, from the fact that the patented product entered at once into wide public use and achieved outstanding commercial success, and from the fact that it was copied by an infringer who was one of the largest soap manufacturers of the country and who had been trying in vain to develop a similar product but had been unable to do so until the knowledge of one of the patentees was obtained.

2. The Trade Secrets.

. . . .

We agree with the District Judge that Colgate must be held to liability for the appropriation and use of the 'Rise' formula in developing its shaving cream. That formula had been developed in the confidential work of Snell for Spitzer. Fine as an employee of Snell was under contract with Snell not to disclose information obtained in the course of this work. Colgate knew of Fine's employment and of his work on the development of 'rise', which Colgate had been unable to produce even after purchasing it on the market and having it analyzed. Although Colgate had twice before this refused to employ Fine, and although it knew of the confidential nature of his employment with Snell, it proceeded to employ him while it was engaged in the effort to develop a pressurized shaving cream and, within a month of his employment, put him to work on the problem, which he solved immediately by using the 'Rise' formula in combination with a formula which Colgate had found unsuccessful.

With respect to the superfatting, it appears that this was worked out at Snell's to give the lather a 'brushless effect' after the patent in suit had been applied for. It also appears that Fine, who had developed the superfatting process in the course of his work at Snell's, suggested it to Colgate and that Colgate adopted the process and caused an application for a patent covering it to be filed by Fine.

On these facts, there can be no question but that Colgate used the knowledge of Fine in producing its pressurized shaving cream or that this knowledge related to matters which were trade secrets of Spitzer and his associates. That Colgate did not enter into an open bargain with Fine to disclose this confidential information is no defense. Nor is it a defense that Fine upon his employment was entitled to use his skill in Colgate's interest. He was not entitled to give to Colgate the benefit of business secrets which had been disclosed to him at Snell's; and Colgate could not close its eyes to facts which clearly indicated that this was what he was doing, even if he had not been employed for that express purpose. One may not escape liability for appropriating the business secrets of another by employing one who has been entrusted with the secrets and permitting him to make use of them. With respect to this the District Judge said:

> '... it is not necessary to, nor do we find that Colgate's employment of Fine was originally arranged for the specific purpose of having him divulge confidential information about the 'rise' patent that he had acquired at Snell's. The basis of our decision that Colgate's action was wrongful is that Colgate knew, or must have known by the exercise of fair business principles, that the precise character of Fine's work with Snell was, in all likelihood, covered by the agreement which Fine had with Snell not to divulge trade secrets, and that, therefore, Colgate was obligated to do more than it did towards ascertaining the extent to which Fine was, in fact, restricted in what he might disclose to Colgate. That it was wrong for Colgate not to go further than it did in this respect is confirmed by the very status of Fine when he came to Colgate. At that time Fine was a joint inventor and patentee of 'Rise.' In other words, Fine was willing to be, and was knowingly placed by Colgate in work that was in direct competition with the work in which Fine had shared at Snell's, resulting ultimately in his own patent. The very fact that Fine would do this should, per se, have raised in the minds of the representatives of Colgate, who arranged the employment of Fine, a feeling that he was entering upon a rather strange employment under the circumstances. It, therefore, was not enough for Colgate to say that they would see that Fine lived up to the limitations imposed by his contract with Snell. The weight of the credible evidence discloses that Colgate was far from being sufficiently avid to ascertain what those limitations really were, and to have Fine live up to them.'

The principles of law applicable are well settled and are well stated in section 757 of the A.L.I. Restatement of Torts as follows:

> 'One who discloses or uses another's trade secret, without a privilege to do so, is liable to the other if

(c) he learned the secret from a third person with notice of the facts that it was a secret and that the third person discovered it by improper means or that the third person's disclosure of it was otherwise a breach of his duty to the other, ...'

In [*Herold v. Herold China & Pottery Co.*, 6 Cir., 257 F. 911, 913 (6th Cir. 1919)], Judge Knappen, speaking for the Court of Appeals of the Sixth Circuit, stated the rule as follows:

> 'The rule is well settled that secret formulas and processes, such as are claimed to be involved here, are property rights which will be protected by injunction, not only as against those who attempt to disclose or use them in violation of confidential relations or contracts express or implied, but as against those who are participating in such attempt with knowledge of such confidential relations or contract, though they might in time have reached the same result by their own independent experiments or efforts.'

We do not think that the finding, 12(b), with respect to the annealing of the polyethylene tubes by dipping them in hot water can be sustained. While Fine learned of this at Snell's and communicated his knowledge to Colgate, the process was one which was well known and cannot be treated as a trade secret or a confidential disclosure. *American Potato Dryers v. Peters*, 4 Cir., 184 F.2d 165, 172; A.L.I. Restatement of Torts, sec. 757, Comment (b) pp. 5–6. This, however, is not material since no injunctive relief is granted with respect thereto and the damages, whether based on the use of the original 'Rise' formula or the superfatted formula, would not be affected thereby.

Notes & Questions

1. Notice as a Source of Fault for Trade Secret Misappropriation

Notice plays a role as a source of fault in trade secret misappropriation disputes. Without actual or constructive notice of the trade secret status of information, a third party to an employment relationship cannot be held liable for misappropriation of the trade secret. The privilege that shields a person who in good faith pays value for title in information is analogous to that found in patent, trademark, and copyright laws, and derives from the concept of voidable title. For example, in *Conmar Prods. Corp. v. Universal Slide Fastener Co.*, 172 F.2d 150 (2d Cir. 1949), the plaintiff brought an action that alleged that the defendants had induced plaintiff's employees to disclose a method for producing zippers. The defendant, ignorant of the fact that the employees were bound by a secrecy contract with plaintiff, had obtained the information innocently when it hired the employees. In an opinion by Judge Learned Hand, the court found that:

> the situation is proper for the application of the doctrine that a bona fide purchaser takes free from a trust. The act of inducing the breach is the wrong, and the inducer's ignorance is an excuse only because one is not ordinarily held liable for consequences which one could not have anticipated. Although it is proper to prevent any continued use of the secret after the inducer has

learned of the breach, the remedies must not invade the inducer's immunity over the period while he was ignorant.

Conmar, 172 F.2d at 156. The timing of the notice matters. A party does not incur liability for misappropriation of a trade secret if notice was given after they have already innocently used or disclosed the information. "Having acquired the secrets innocently, [the defendants] were entitled to exploit them till they learned that they had induced the breach of the contract." *Id.* at 157.

Where the third party has notice that information was acquired through misappropriation but disregards the notice, the third party may be held liable to the trade secret owner for misappropriation. Once a party is put on notice, they have a duty to inquire as to the authority of the transferor to disclose the information, as well as a duty not to further use or disclose the information.

2. Knowing Participation Is Why Uber Was in Trouble

As mentioned above, the *Waymo v. Uber* suit involved alleged misappropriation of large amounts of secret information by Waymo's former engineer, Anthony Levandowski, who used it to launch his own self-driving start-up, Otto. Why did Uber have anything to do with this lawsuit? The reason Uber was potentially on the hook was that Waymo claimed that Uber had been aware of the trade secret misappropriation. Waymo alleged that Uber had planned to acquire Otto even before Levandowski left Waymo and, despite being aware of Levandowski's misappropriation, Uber went ahead with the plan. In his opening statement to the jury, Waymo's attorney alleged that Levandowski met with Uber executives on the same day he downloaded the confidential information from Waymo's server. At trial, Waymo also presented communications between Levandowski and Uber's then-CEO Travis Kalanick, which indicated that both of them were highly interested in launching self-driving technology as quickly as possible. Waymo planned to use this evidence to support its allegation that Uber hired Levandowski to receive access to Waymo's trade secrets to get an advantage in its race into the market for the autonomous driving technology. Cara Bayles, *Google Co-Founder Mentor then Rival, Ex-Uber CEO Testifies*, Law360 (Feb. 7, 2018, 11:12 PM), https://www.law360.com/articles/1009958?scroll=1; Cara Bayles, *Uber Cheated in Self-Driving Car Race, Waymo Tells Jury*, Law360 (February 5, 2018, 9:47 PM), https://www.law360.com/articles/1008982?scroll=1. Therefore, if Waymo was to convince the federal jury that Uber was aware of the misappropriation, Uber would have been responsible for intentional inducement of a breach of Levandowski's employment contract with Waymo or knowing participation in trade secret misappropriation.

Ultimately, the case was settled before the jury was presented with all the evidence pertaining to the issue. After the case was dismissed pursuant to the settlement, Kalanick stated that "[N]o trade secrets ever came to Uber" and "had the case proceeded to trial, Uber would have won." Russ Mitchell & Tracey Lien, *Uber Reaches Settlement with Waymo in Dispute over Trade Secrets*, L.A. Times, Feb. 10, 2018, 12:45 PM, http://www.latimes.com/business/autos/la-fi-uber-waymo-settlement-20180209

-story.html. However, Uber's current CEO, Dara Khosrowshahi, was more conservative in his statement regarding the settlement. He expressed "regret for the actions that have caused [him] to write this letter" and acknowledged that "the prospect that a couple of Waymo employees may have inappropriately solicited others to join Otto, and that they may have potentially left with Google files in their possession, in retrospect, raised some hard questions." Dara Khosrowshahi, *Uber and Waymo Reach Settlement*, Uber Newsroom (Feb 9, 2018), https://www.uber.com/newsroom/uber-waymo-settlement/. Notwithstanding what actually occurred, pursuant to the settlement agreement, Uber paid Waymo almost $245 million in Uber's stock and promised not to use any of Waymo's confidential information in its self-driving technology development. Waymo in exchange abandoned any claims against Uber pertaining to any known violations. Elizabeth Dwoskin & Peter Holley, *Uber CEO Plays It Safe in Risk-Loving Silicon Valley*, Wash. Post, Feb. 13, 2018, https://www.washingtonpost.com/news/the-switch/wp/2018/02/13/uber-ceo-plays-it-safe-in-risk-loving-silicon-valley/. The settlement, however, does not relieve Levandowski himself from liability for his actions. In addition to potential civil liability to Waymo, he might be facing potential criminal investigation by the Department of Justice for trade secret theft.

3. Material Changes in Position and Detrimental Reliance

A third party who knew or should have known of the trade secret status of the information he received but nonetheless relied on it to materially change his position is liable for trade secret misappropriation. However, a third party is absolved of liability if he materially changed his position prior to discovering the nature of the information relied upon.

In *Vantage Point, Inc. v. Parker Bros.*, 529 F. Supp. 1204 (E.D.N.Y. 1981), the plaintiff, Vantage Point, sought damages from Milton Bradley for misappropriating its idea for a three-dimensional oil exploration game. The creator of the game had unsuccessfully shopped the idea around to several game companies, among them Parker Brothers. A game developer who had access to the plaintiff's game idea while at Parker Brothers quit his job and joined two other men to form a partnership that created and sold game and toy ideas. The group developed an oil exploration game, strikingly similar to Vantage Point's, and pitched it to Milton Bradley. Milton Bradley, unaware of any misconduct on the part of any member of the group, expressed an interest in the game, now named "King Oil." The record showed that Milton Bradley had no access to plaintiff's game idea prior to this time, and that by the time it received notice of possible misappropriation, it had materially changed its position.

> By May 1974 Milton Bradley had already changed its position by incurring costs in bringing King Oil to market. Harris testified that if Milton Bradley had pulled King Oil off the market immediately after [receiving notice], the company would have lost costs already incurred for tooling and other production components, for advertising and possibly some inventory. In these circumstances, "(t)he issue is whether the imposition of (a) duty" not to use

the idea after notice of its improper disclosure, "would be inequitable under the circumstances." Restatement, Torts, § 758, comment on clause (b), subsec. (e) at 22. The Court concludes that imposition of the duty plaintiff desires would be inequitable. It is plain that prior to receipt of notice, Milton Bradley "paid value for the secret or made other investments in connection with it." *Id.* at 21. Thus, imposition of the duty "would subject (it) to loss" for actions taken when there was no such duty. *See id.*

Vantage Point, 529 F. Supp. at 1215. Detrimental reliance may be an absolute bar to liability, or may be considered an "exceptional circumstance" for the purpose of determining injunctive relief. Courts award damages only if unauthorized use continues after the defendant receives notice of the trade secret status of the information; retrospective damages for use that occurred prior to notice are not allowed.

Sometimes third parties who have detrimentally relied upon information that is later revealed to be a trade secret wish to continue to use the information. Some courts refuse to impose a duty not to use the information where imposition of a duty would burden a defendant with a loss for action taken when he was subject to no duty. Other courts take a different approach and fashion a restitution-based remedy where the trade secret owner is awarded limited restitution based on the stranger's savings from not needing to independently develop the information, in exchange for allowing the third party to continue using the information. Courts may require the payment of reasonable royalties for future use of the trade secret.

4. Vicarious Liability

Under the doctrine of respondeat superior, a new employer may be held vicariously liable for misappropriation of a trade secret by a new employee. Some states, such as Washington and Virginia, have recognized the availability of vicarious liability under their versions of the UTSA. *See* Malla Pollack, *Litigating Misappropriation of Trade Secrets*, 127 Am. Jur. Trials 283 (originally published in 2012). However, the Indiana Supreme Court, based on the breadth of the preemption provision of the Indiana version of the UTSA, held that vicarious liability for trade secret misappropriation is not available in Indiana.

> Indiana's statute is based on the Uniform Trade Secrets Act and we are one of some forty states that have adopted it. The legislature announced its purpose in adopting the uniform act and provided some guidance on its general construction: "This chapter shall be applied and construed to effectuate its general purpose to make uniform the law with respect to the subject matter of this chapter among states enacting the provisions of this chapter." Ind. Code Ann. § 24-2-3-1(b) (West 1995). The General Assembly has also told us: "The chapter displaces all conflicting law of this state pertaining to the misappropriation of trade secrets, except contract and criminal law." Ind. Code Ann. § 24-2-3-1(c) . . . .
>
> As Infinity correctly points out, respondeat superior is a common law doctrine under which liability is imposed by law upon the master for acts done

by the servant, regardless of the master's complicity in the acts. Indeed, it may impose liability even when the master directed the servant to the contrary. Surely, this doctrine must be thought of as conflicting with the uniform act's requirements that a claimant demonstrate that the defendant "knows or has reason to know" that the trade secret at issue was acquired by improper means. It is thus displaced by the provisions of the uniform act.

Of course, the uniform act affords fulsome avenues of relief for persons who believe that secrets belonging to them have wrongly been misappropriated. It supplies a remedy for money damages under a standard of proof that is, at first blush, less onerous that the common law usually requires. It also authorizes injunctive relief both to shut down actual misappropriation and to thwart threatened misappropriation. Ind. Code Ann. § 24-2-3-3. And it authorizes the award of attorney's fees upon conditions more liberal than most parts of our code. Ind. Code Ann. § 24-2-3-5.

We conclude that the trial court correctly held that Fabri-Tech could not be held liable absent the proof of scienter required by the uniform act.

Infinity Prods. Inc. v. Quandt, 810 N.E.2d 1028, 1033–34 (Ind. 2004).

5. Liability of Corporate Shareholders and Directors

Shareholders and directors of a corporation who know of trade secret misappropriation by the corporation have an affirmative duty to take action to stop those activities. Shareholders and directors can be held personally liable if they fail to stop known acts of misappropriation.

b. *Intentional Interference with Contractual or Fiduciary Relationship*

i. Generally

When a third party induces a departed employee to breach a confidentiality agreement, the employer may be subject to liability for intentional interference with contractual or fiduciary relationship. The RESTATEMENT (SECOND) OF AGENCY, § 312, states, "A person who, without being privileged to do so, intentionally causes or assists an agent to violate a duty to his principal is subject to liability to the principal." Even when there is no express confidentiality agreement, a party who induces an agent to violate an implied duty to his former employer is liable to that former employer. Liability for intentional interference with contractual or fiduciary duties evinces an overlap between contractual obligations between parties and tort-based duties in conduct adversely affecting third parties. Inducement of a new employee to violate a special relationship not only serves as a form of improper means in trade secret cases, but is also a tort in and of itself.

The RESTATEMENT (SECOND) OF TORTS, §§ 766–767 list the elements of the tort of intentional interference with contractual relationship, which are: (a) intentional and (b) improper (c) interference with the (d) performance of a contract or other economic relations (e) causing pecuniary loss.

Robert L. Reeves v. Daniel P. Hanlon

Supreme Court of California

95 P.3d 513 (Cal. 2004)

BAXTER, J., expressing the unanimous view of the court.

. . . .

Plaintiffs Robert L. Reeves and Robert L. Reeves & Associates, A Professional Law Corporation, brought the instant lawsuit against defendants Daniel P. Hanlon, Colin T. Greene, and Hanlon & Greene, A Professional Corporation (H&G). The operative complaint included the following allegations: In 1995, Reeves's law firm, which emphasized immigration law and litigation, employed Hanlon as an attorney. In 1997, the firm employed Greene as an associate attorney. In 1998, Reeves entered into an agreement with Hanlon whereby Hanlon could earn an equity position in a law firm to be formed; thereafter, the firm's name was changed to "Reeves and Hanlon, Professional Law Corporation." On or about June 30, 1999, both Hanlon and Greene resigned from Reeves's firm without notice or warning. They improperly persuaded plaintiffs' employees to join H&G, personally solicited plaintiffs' clients to discharge plaintiffs and to instead obtain services from H&G, misappropriated plaintiffs' trade secrets, destroyed computer files and data, and withheld plaintiffs' property, including a corporate car . . . .

. . . .

Trial of the matter commenced in January 2001. Following the presentation of briefing, evidence, and arguments, the trial court issued a statement of decision concluding that Hanlon and Greene had assumed fiduciary duties to plaintiffs and that they had engaged in interference with contracts and prospective business opportunity, and misappropriation of trade secrets. The court determined that, for more than five months prior to their departure, Hanlon and Greene had accessed plaintiffs' password-protected computer database to print out confidential name, address, and phone number information on 2,200 clients and had fomented dissatisfaction among plaintiffs' personnel. Although Greene had been chair of plaintiffs' litigation department and Hanlon had been responsible for over 500 client matters when they abruptly resigned without notice, they left no status reports or lists of matters or deadlines on which they had been working. Nor did they attempt to cooperate with plaintiffs on a notice to clients. Shortly before resigning, Greene intentionally erased extensive computer files in plaintiffs' computer server containing client documents and form files used by plaintiffs. The evening of their resignations, defendants personally solicited plaintiffs' key employees. As a result, plaintiffs lost nine employees over the next 60 days, six of them joining defendants' new firm. Defendants also began a campaign to solicit plaintiffs' clients, contacting at least 40 clients by telephone without offering them a choice of counsel. All of this had been "intentionally done . . . to disrupt [plaintiffs'] ongoing business." Although historically, plaintiffs typically lost only one or two clients a month, plaintiffs lost 144 clients to defendants over the next 12 months.

. . . .

Discussion

A. *Intentional Interference with At-will Employment Relations*

What is disputed is the Court of Appeal's legal conclusion that "an employer may recover for interference with the employment contracts of its at-will employees by a third party when the third party does not show that its conduct in hiring the employees was justifiable or legitimate." Relying primarily on *GAB Business Services, Inc. v. Lindsey & Newsom Claim Services, Inc.* (2000) 83 Cal. App. 4th 409 [99 Cal. Rptr. 2d 665] (*GAB*), defendants argue California law does not and should not recognize a cause of action in favor of an employer against another employer for interference with contractual relations by virtue of an offer of employment to an at-will employee.

We start by observing that, in California, the law is settled that "a stranger to a contract may be liable in tort for intentionally interfering with the performance of the contract." To prevail on a cause of action for intentional interference with contractual relations, a plaintiff must plead and prove (1) the existence of a valid contract between the plaintiff and a third party; (2) the defendant's knowledge of that contract; (3) the defendant's intentional acts designed to induce a breach or disruption of the contractual relationship; (4) actual breach or disruption of the contractual relationship; and (5) resulting damage. To establish the claim, the plaintiff need not prove that a defendant acted with the primary purpose of disrupting the contract, but must show the defendant's knowledge that the interference was certain or substantially certain to occur as a result of his or her action.

May the tort of interference with contractual relations be predicated upon interference with an at-will contract? Historically, the answer is yes. A third party's "interference with an at-will contract is actionable interference with the contractual relationship" because the contractual relationship is at the will of the parties, not at the will of outsiders.

More specifically, may such tort be based on interference with an at-will employment relationship? Again, historically, the answer is yes.

As reflected in our decisional and statutory law, however, it has long been the public policy of our state that "[a] former employee has the right to engage in a competitive business for himself and to enter into competition with his former employer, even for the business of . . . his former employer, provided such competition is fairly and legally conducted." Consistent with this policy favoring competition, decisions involving parties in competition readily indicate that certain competitive conduct is nonactionable when it interferes with the at-will contract relations of another. *Buxbom v. Smith* (1944) 23 Cal.2d 535 [145 P.2d 305] (*Buxbom*), for example, explained that "where the means of interference involve no more than recognized trade practices such as advertising or price-cutting, the plaintiff's loss as a result of the competitive strife is deemed *damnum absque injuria*."

More to the point here, *Buxbom* observed that "it is not ordinarily a tort to hire the employees of another for use in the hirer's business." (*Buxbom, supra,* 23 Cal.2d at p. 547.) As *Buxbom* explained, however, this general rule is subject to one significant limitation: "This immunity against liability is not retained . . . if unfair methods are used in interfering in such advantageous relations." (*Ibid.*) In *Buxbom*, the record established that the defendant gained an unfair advantage over the plaintiff through "deceptive dealings" (*ibid.*) and "false promises" made in connection with a distribution contract between the parties that the defendant had no intention of performing (*id.* at p. 548). He "deliberately induced the plaintiff to build up his distributing organization" to perform the contract and in a matter of weeks became the plaintiff's sole customer. (*Id.* at p. 547.) Once the defendant acquired this strategic position, he breached the distribution contract "to cut off the work required to sustain plaintiff's organization" and "to prevent plaintiff from competing effectively for the retention of [his] employees." (*Id.* at p. 548.)

Buxbom first indicated that the defendant's breach of the distribution contract was "a wrong and in itself actionable," but then proceeded to find the breach also constituted "an unfair method of interference with advantageous relations." (*Buxbom, supra,* 23 Cal.2d at p. 548.) Its reasoning was this: "Although defendant's conduct may not have been tortious if he had merely broken the contract and subsequently decided to hire plaintiff's employees," he was "guilty of a tortious interference in the relationship between the plaintiff and his employees" because he "intentionally utilized" the breach of the distribution contract "as the means of depriving plaintiff of his employees." (*Ibid.*)

Subsequent to *Buxbom*, the court in *Diodes, Inc. v. Franzen* (1968) 260 Cal. App. 2d 244 [67 Cal. Rptr. 19] (*Diodes*) reiterated the so-called privilege of competition, as applied in the context of employment relations, as follows: "Even though the relationship between an employer and his employee is an advantageous one, no actionable wrong is committed by a competitor who solicits his competitor's employees or who hires away one or more of his competitor's employees who are not under contract, so long as the inducement to leave is not accompanied by unlawful action." (*Id.* at p. 255.) "However, if either the defecting employee or the competitor uses unfair or deceptive means to effectuate new employment, or either of them is guilty of some concomitant, unconscionable conduct, the injured former employer has a cause of action to recover for the detriment he has thereby suffered." (*Ibid.*; see also *Metro Traffic Control, Inc. v. Shadow Traffic Network* (1994) 22 Cal. App. 4th 853, 860 [27 Cal. Rptr. 2d 573] (*Metro*) ["[a]s a competitor of Metro, absent a showing of unlawful purpose or means, Shadow is privileged and not liable for inducing Metro's employees to leave and move to Shadow"].)

Strictly speaking, the foregoing authorities did not address the matter of competition in suits involving causes of action for intentional interference with at-will employment relations; rather, those cases involved breach of fiduciary duty claims (*Diodes*), claims for injunctive relief based on contractual noncompete clauses and trade secrets allegations (*Metro*), or claims for damages sustained in conjunction with a breach of contract (*Buxbom*).

Nonetheless, the same considerations support similar limitations for actions alleging interference with an at-will employment relation. Where no unlawful methods are used, public policy generally supports a competitor's right to offer more pay or better terms to another's employee, so long as the employee is free to leave. As Judge Learned Hand observed long ago, if the law were to the contrary, the result "would be intolerable, both to such employers as could use the employe[e] more effectively and to such employe[e]s as might receive added pay. It would put an end to any kind of competition." (*Triangle Film Corp. v. Artcraft Pictures Corp.* (2d Cir. 1918) 250 F. 981, 982.) Or as *Diodes* put it: "The interests of the employee in his own mobility and betterment are deemed paramount to the competitive business interests of the employers, where neither the employee nor his new employer has committed any illegal act accompanying the employment change." (*Diodes, supra,* 260 Cal. App. 2d at p. 255.)

Moreover, the economic relationship between parties to contracts that are terminable at will is distinguishable from the relationship between parties to other legally binding contracts. We have explained the policy generally protecting contracts this way: "The courts provide a damage remedy against third party conduct intended to disrupt an existing contract precisely because the exchange of promises resulting in such a formally cemented economic relationship is deemed worthy of protection from interference by a stranger to the agreement. Economic relationships short of contractual, however, should stand on a different legal footing as far as the potential for tort liability is reckoned." (*Della Penna v. Toyota Motor Sales, U.S.A., Inc.* (1995) 11 Cal. 4th 376, 392 [45 Cal. Rptr. 2d 436, 902 P.2d 740].)

But as the Restatement Second of Torts explains, if a party to a contract with the plaintiff is free to terminate the contractual relation when he chooses, "there is still a subsisting contract relation; but any interference with it that induces its termination is primarily an interference with the future relation between the parties, and the plaintiff has no legal assurance of them. As for the future hopes he has no legal right but only an expectancy; and when the contract is terminated by the choice of [a contracting party] there is no breach of it. The competitor is therefore free, for his own competitive advantage, to obtain the future benefits for himself by causing the termination. Thus, he may offer better contract terms, as by offering an employee of the plaintiff more money to work for him or by offering a seller higher prices for goods, and he may make use of persuasion or other suitable means, all without liability." (Rest.2d Torts, § 768, com. i.) Under this analysis, an interference with an at-will contract properly is viewed as an interference with a prospective economic advantage, a tort that similarly compensates for the loss of an advantageous economic relationship but does not require the existence of a legally binding contract.

We observe that in California, both of these torts protect the public interest in stable economic relationships and both share the same intent requirement. (*Korea Supply, supra,* 29 Cal. 4th at p. 1157 [defendant must know that interference was certain or substantially certain to occur as a result of its action].) But while many of the elements of the two torts are similar, a plaintiff seeking to recover for interference with prospective economic advantage must also plead and prove that the defendant engaged in an independently wrongful act in disrupting the relationship. (*Korea Supply, supra*, 29 Cal. 4th at p. 1158.) In this regard, "an act is independently wrongful if it is unlawful, that is, if it is proscribed by some constitutional, statutory, regulatory, common law, or other determinable legal standard." (*Ibid.*, fn. omitted.)

Consistent with the decisions recognizing that an intentional interference with an at-will contract may be actionable, but mindful that an interference as such is primarily an interference with the future relation between the contracting parties, we hold that a plaintiff may recover damages for intentional interference with an at-will employment relation under the same California standard applicable to claims for intentional interference with prospective economic advantage. That is, to recover for a defendant's interference with an at-will employment relation, a plaintiff must plead and prove that the defendant engaged in an independently wrongful act — i.e., an act "proscribed by some constitutional, statutory, regulatory, common law, or other determinable legal standard" (*Korea Supply, supra*, 29 Cal. 4th at p. 1159) — that induced an at-will employee to leave the plaintiff. Under this standard, a defendant is not subject to liability for intentional interference if the interference consists merely of extending a job offer that induces an employee to terminate his or her at-will employment.

. . . .

We now address whether application of the principles we announce today calls for affirmance of the $20,009.19 award against defendants. We conclude it does. Here, it is undisputed that Hanlon and Greene engaged in unlawful and unethical conduct in mounting a campaign to deliberately disrupt plaintiffs' business. Greene had been chair of plaintiffs' litigation department, and Hanlon had been responsible for over 500 client matters, and both had assumed fiduciary duties to plaintiffs. When the two abruptly resigned without notice, they left no status reports or lists of pending matters or deadlines on which they were working. Not only did they leave without providing such information, they acted unlawfully to delete and destroy plaintiffs' computer files containing client documents and forms. Additionally, Hanlon and Greene misappropriated confidential information, improperly solicited plaintiffs' clients, and cultivated employee discontent. While the computer files and the confidential information all appear to have pertained to plaintiffs' clients, not their employees, and while Hanlon and Greene waited until after their resignations to offer jobs to plaintiffs' employees, we cannot conclude the trial court abused its discretion in finding that defendants' unlawful and unethical actions were designed in part to interfere with and disrupt plaintiffs' relationships with their key at-will employees.

In short, defendants did not simply extend job offers to plaintiffs' at-will employees. Rather, defendants purposely engaged in unlawful acts that crippled plaintiffs' business operations and caused plaintiffs' personnel to terminate their at-will employment contracts. Accordingly, the Court of Appeal properly upheld the award of $20,009.19 for damages attributable to that wrongful conduct . . . .

ii. When Is Interference Considered Improper?

Interference by a third-party employer is generally improper if the third party does not act to protect its own financial interest or if it uses improper means. Courts look to the motive and means when determining whether interference is improper. For example, luring away an employee from a competitor is proper motive, even if it deprives the former employer of the employee's services; inducing an employee to violate duties to his former employer, on the other hand, is an example of improper motive. Even if the objectives are legitimate, liability can arise if the means used are improper, but courts disagree as to which means may be properly used.

Section 767 of the Restatement (Second) of Torts provides factors for determining whether interference is improper. These factors are as follows: (1) nature of defendant's conduct, (2) defendant's motive, (3) interests of the other with which the defendant's conduct interferes, (4) social and contractual interests, (5) interests pursued by the defendant, and (6) the relations between the parties.

Storage Technology Corp. v. Cisco Systems, Inc.

United States Court of Appeals for the Eighth Circuit

395 F.3d 921 (8th Cir. 2005)

Gibson, Circuit Judge.

Storage Technology Corporation appeals the district court's entry of summary judgment against it on its various claims against Cisco Systems, Inc. arising out of the hiring of a number of Storage Technology's employees by Cisco's predecessor, NuSpeed Internet Systems, Inc. The district court held that Storage Technology's claims for interference with contractual relations, inducing breach of contract, conversion, and breach of fiduciary duties failed because Storage Technology did not come forward with any evidence of recoverable damages. The district court held that Minnesota has not recognized a claim for "corporate raiding," or hiring away another firm's employees. The district court held that the remaining claim, for misappropriation of trade secrets, was not supported by evidence that satisfied the requirements of Fed. R. Civ. P. 56(e). We affirm the judgment of the district court.

In November 1999, Mark Cree and Clint Jurgens founded NuSpeed Internet Systems, Inc., a new computer technology company. Cree and Jurgens's plan was to develop a product to link computers at one location to data storage networks at other locations through the Internet or other Wide Area Network using Internet Protocols. On December 2, Cree and Jurgens offered employment to Mark Schrandt, an engineer at Storage Technology, which was developing data storage networking products. Schrandt accepted NuSpeed's offer and gave Storage Technology oral notice on or about December 3 that he was leaving. He later gave a written resignation effective at the end of December. Schrandt began work for NuSpeed in January 2000. In December, while Schrandt was still at Storage Technology, he told four other Storage Technology engineers, Mark Bakke, Ed Fiore, Tim Kuik, and Dave Thompson, that he was going to work for NuSpeed, and they expressed interest in following Schrandt. Schrandt met with them outside of work to discuss NuSpeed, and by mid-December, these four Storage Technology employees had signed on with NuSpeed. Through November 2000, NuSpeed hired twenty-two more engineers who were or had been employed at Storage Technology, as NuSpeed grew to employ seventy-eight people.

In February 2000, a new open Internet protocol was published, called iSCSI (for "Internet, Small Computer Systems Interface"). NuSpeed quickly began working on incorporating iSCSI in its product, the SN 5420, which linked storage area networks over the Internet. In April 2000, NuSpeed announced that it was developing a device to transmit data using the iSCSI protocol. NuSpeed aspired to be the first company to bring such a product to market. Cisco Systems, Inc. acquired NuSpeed in September 2000 in a stock-for-stock transaction in which NuSpeed's shareholders received $450 million in Cisco stock. Although the SN 5420 was indeed the first iSCSI device to market, Cisco never made a profit on NuSpeed, or the "Storage Router Business Unit," as it was called after the acquisition; as of January 2003, Cisco's operating losses for the unit stood at $50 million.

Storage Technology brought this suit against Cisco, alleging that NuSpeed had engaged in "corporate raiding" by hiring Schrandt, Bakke, Fiore, Kuik and Thompson, and the other former Storage Technology employees, alleging that the employees had gained knowledge at Storage Technology of a device for joining disparate and otherwise incompatible computer networks and NuSpeed had used that knowledge to develop a product based on Storage Technology's device. Storage Technology also alleged claims for interference with contractual relations for hiring away persons with whom Storage Technology had employment contracts; for inducing breach of contracts; for conversion of confidential information; for encouraging breach of fiduciary duties by former Storage Technology employees; and for misappropriation of trade secrets.

Cisco moved for summary judgment. Cisco denied that NuSpeed misappropriated any trade secret information or acted improperly in hiring Storage Technology engineers.

The district court granted summary judgment to Cisco . . . .

   . . . .

II.

Under Minnesota law, the elements of tortious interference with contract are (1) the existence of a contract, (2) the tortfeasor's knowledge of the contract, (3) the tortfeasor's intentional causation of a breach of the contract, (4) a lack of justification for the tortfeasor's action, and (5) damages resulting from the breach. *Bouten v. Richard Miller Homes, Inc.*, 321 N.W.2d 895, 900 (Minn. 1982). The tort of inducing a breach of contract, which Storage Technology pleads in a separate count, requires the same elements. *Aslakson v. Home Sav. Ass'n*, 416 N.W.2d 786, 788 (Minn. Ct. App. 1987).

We turn to the question of whether Storage Technology adduced any evidence to prove its damages for the alleged tortious interference with its employment contracts.

A.

The district court focused on the nature of damages in a tortious interference with contract case. Storage Technology has declined to prove damages to its own business and instead only attempted to establish a right to restitution in the amount of Cisco's alleged unjust enrichment. Cisco contends, and Storage Technology does not deny, that Cisco lost money on the NuSpeed product. At the deposition of Timothy Schulte, Storage Technology's counsel expressly denied that Storage Technology claims or has proven lost profits. Instead, Storage Technology contends it is entitled to $450 million, which was the price Cisco paid for NuSpeed. The district court held that "damages for interference with contract are limited to those that might have been recovered for a breach of the contract itself." The court held that because Storage Technology failed to prove what damages NuSpeed caused, Storage Technology had not made a showing sufficient to resist summary judgment.

The usual remedy provided by Minnesota law for interference with contract is to compensate the victim for the damages that resulted from the loss of the contract. The early case of *Swaney v. Crawley*, 133 Minn. 57, 157 N.W. 910, 911 (Minn. 1916), stated the principle that the "injured party is limited, as a general rule, to such damages as might have been recovered for a breach of the contract itself." *Potthoff v. Jefferson Lines, Inc.*, 363 N.W.2d 771, 777 (Minn. Ct. App. 1985), modified this statement by allowing the award of damages for emotional distress in an interference with contract suit, whereas such damages would not be available in a suit on the contract itself. *Potthoff* observed that the trial court had relied on the Restatement (Second) of Torts §774A (1979), which allows loss of the benefits of contract, consequential losses, and damages for emotional distress, all of which focus on loss to the aggrieved party. See also *Kallok v. Medtronic, Inc.*, 573 N.W.2d 356, 363–64 (Minn. 1998) (holding recovery for tortious interference can include costs of litigation to enforce contract).

However, breach of some covenants and duties attendant on the employment relation entitles the aggrieved employer to restitution. An employee who breaches a noncompetition or nondisclosure covenant can be required to account for his profits. *Cherne Indus., Inc. v. Grounds & Assoc., Inc.*, 278 N.W.2d 81, 94–95 (Minn. 1979). The remedy for breach of the fiduciary duty of loyalty is also restitutionary. *See Miller v. Miller*, 301 Minn. 207, 222 N.W.2d 71, 78 (Minn. 1974) (remedy for breach of fiduciary duty of loyalty is imposition of constructive trust).

Therefore, where the defendant has not merely enticed a competitor's employees to leave their employment, but also induced them to breach a fiduciary duty of loyalty or restrictive covenant, the remedy must reflect the underlying wrong. When the underlying wrong would have supported a claim of restitution, so should a claim for inducing that wrong. In *Cherne*, an employee of Cherne left and formed a corporation, Grounds & Associates, which hired away two other employees. 278 N.W.2d at 87. All three former employees had signed non-competition and non-disclosure-of-confidential-information covenants, *id.* at 86, which they breached in the service of the new corporation. *Id.* at 88–91. Grounds & Associates argued that the proper remedy was award of Cherne's lost profits, rather than a restitutionary award of Grounds's profits. The Minnesota Supreme Court held:

> Although damages for breach of contract are traditionally measured by the nonbreaching party's loss of expected benefits under the contract, where an employee wrongfully profits from the use of information obtained from his employer, the measure of damages may be the employee's gain. Also, this court has specifically found that the violator of a covenant not to compete may be required to account for his profits, and such illegal profits may properly measure the damages.

Id. at 94–95 (internal citations omitted). *Cherne* did not expressly discuss the fact that it was holding a third party liable for the employees' breach of the noncompetition covenants, but in a later case the Minnesota Supreme Court referred to *Cherne* as implicitly holding that "third-party interference with [a] noncompete agreement is a tort." *Kallok*, 573 N.W.2d at 361. Thus, where the interference alleged is inducement of breach of restrictive covenants or fiduciary duties, the remedy should mirror the restitutionary remedy available for the breach of the covenant or fiduciary duty.

Storage Technology's interference with contract theory is not clear from its complaint. The complaint's "interference with contractual relations" count only alleges that Storage Technology had employment contracts with its employees and that NuSpeed hired the employees without justification, knowing that they would then terminate their contracts with Storage Technology. It also alleges that NuSpeed accomplished the hiring by using knowledge about Storage Technology's pay structure, etc., but it does not pursue this theory before us. Thus, the count in the complaint appears to allege only hiring of plaintiff's at-will employees. However, Storage Technology pleads in separate counts that NuSpeed induced Schrandt, Fiore, Kuik, and Bakke to breach fiduciary duties to Storage Technology by disclosing confidential information and soliciting Storage Technology employees to leave Storage Technology. In its brief, it contends that Schrandt breached his duty of loyalty by recruiting Storage Technology employees for NuSpeed while still in Storage Technology's employ. In its reply brief, Storage Technology contends that it had a noncompetition agreement with Schrandt, which he violated. Storage Technology therefore appears to be pursuing a theory that NuSpeed induced Storage Technology's employees to breach noncompetition and nondisclosure covenants and to breach their fiduciary duty of loyalty to Storage Technology.

We conclude that Minnesota courts would allow a restitutionary remedy in a case in which the interference alleged was inducing an employee's breach of noncompetition and nondisclosure covenants and fiduciary duties. We further conclude that Storage Technology is alleging NuSpeed induced such breaches by Storage Technology's

employees. We therefore must ascertain whether Storage Technology has made a sufficient showing of unjust enrichment to survive summary judgment.

B.

Storage Technology's entire evidentiary basis for a restitutionary remedy consisted of
the report of its expert, George Norton, that "Cisco's valuation of NuSpeed (basically,
its key people and storage technology expertise) was $450 million and represents a
proper valuation of the damages to Storage Technology and due to it for the trade secret
appropriation, corporate raiding, and breach of contract and fiduciary responsibilities
promulgated." The district court rejected Norton's opinion as "rank speculation."

The first and most apparent problem with Norton's testimony is that he attributed the entire value of the NuSpeed acquisition to employees and trade secrets
wrongfully appropriated from Storage Technology, even though NuSpeed had other
assets and employees. Norton did not attempt to value the people or the technology
supposedly belonging to Storage Technology by any means other than by ascertaining what price Cisco paid for NuSpeed. The undisputed evidence shows that a crucial aspect of the acquisition was Cisco's desire to obtain NuSpeed's product
incorporating the iSCSI protocol, which had nothing to do with Storage Technology.

Norton opined, "The value inherent in the price Cisco paid for NuSpeed was in
the key employees of NuSpeed who embodied the storage expertise technology Cisco
sought." But Norton testified at his deposition that he did not know what the technology was. Norton later contended that the value of NuSpeed to Cisco was in the
fifteen key employees named in the acquisition documents. Of these, five are listed
as having come from firms other than Storage Technology. Norton did not know what
percentage of NuSpeed's total employees were from Storage Technology at the time
Cisco acquired the company. He did not know if the deal would have gone forward
if the people listed had not agreed to go to Cisco. Norton testified that he did not
take into account the terms of the employees' contracts with Storage Technology. See
Nordling v. N. State Power Co., 478 N.W.2d 498, 505 (Minn. 1991) ("The fact that the
contract is terminable at will . . . is to be taken into account in determining the damages that the plaintiff has suffered by reason of its breach.") (quoting Restatement
(Second) of Torts § 766, comment g (1979)).

Norton was unwilling or unable to answer questions exploring what proportion
of the acquisition price was attributable to what NuSpeed assets. His deposition was
singularly uninformative . . . . Moreover, there is crucial evidence, which Norton does
not take into account, that the reason Cisco was interested in NuSpeed was that
NuSpeed had begun work on using iSCSI to access stored data . . . . Nobody contends
that Storage Technology had anything to do with the idea of using software incorporating the iSCSI standard for storage networking. Storage Technology admitted that
no software was ever written for the "SAN Appliance"—which it contends was the
idea for a storage networking product that NuSpeed stole from Storage Technology.
In fact, iSCSI did not even exist until February 2000, after Schrandt, Bakke,
Thompson, Kuik and Fiore had already left Storage Technology. Norton did not take

into account any value that may have resulted from the incorporation of the iSCSI standard in the SN 5420 . . . .

. . . .

Storage Technology's failure to produce evidence substantiating any amount of damages or restitution is fatal to its claim for tortious interference with contractual relations, as well as to each of its other claims.

We affirm the judgment of the district court.

Notes & Questions

1. An Independent Tort

Under the tort of trade secret misappropriation, cases following the UTSA and RESTATEMENT consider inducement of a breach of a duty of confidentiality as one of the improper means of acquiring another's trade secrets (the other improper means being conversion, theft, misrepresentation, and industrial espionage). A finding of intentional interference with contractual or fiduciary duties therefore supports a finding of liability for the tort of misappropriation of a trade secret.

Notice, however, that the act of intentional interference with contractual or fiduciary duties is an independent tort in and of itself. RESTATEMENT (SECOND) OF TORTS § 766 (1979); RESTATEMENT (SECOND) OF AGENCY § 312. An aggrieved party need not rely solely on the tort of trade secret misappropriation to seek redress for a competitor's act of inducing a former employee to breach a duty of confidentiality.

2. What About Independent Contractors?

What results if a former employee bound by a confidentiality agreement is an independent contractor? Can a competitor hiring the former employee be liable for intentional interference with the confidentiality agreement when the former employee is an independent contractor? Does the status of a former employee as an independent contractor negate the possibility of liability for those that hire him? *See Curtis 1000, Inc. v. Pierce,* 905 F. Supp. 898 (D. Kan. 1995).

3. Former Employee as Plaintiff

The plaintiff in an intentional interference action is typically a former employer seeking to prevent a competitor from inducing the breach of a former employee's confidentiality agreement. Though this is the typical case, a former employee may very well be a plaintiff in an intentional interference action. Former employees accused of misappropriating trade secrets may claim that the former employer's actions to prevent use and disclosure of information interferes with a new contract of employment. Since the former employer is tying the employee's hands, the former employee may claim that the former employer is improperly interfering with his contract of employment for a new employer.

Chapter 5

Licensing in Business Organizations

Problem

Digital Ignition Systems Corporation (Digital Ignition) entered into a nonexclusive licensing agreement with Advanced Electronics, Inc. (AEI), a manufacturer of electrical devices. The license granted AEI, the licensee, permission to manufacture and sell products based on three patents owned by Digital Ignition. Digital Ignition offered the three patents as a package at a discount rate lower than what each patent would have cost if licensed individually. AEI accepted the patent package.

In addition to the three patents, the license included a transfer of trade secret know-how as well as trade secret information about an as-yet-unpatented improvement on the patented technology. Patent applications were pending for the licensed improvement, but a patent ultimately never issued. The trade secret know-how was transferred in the form of a printed manual. The royalty provisions in the licensing agreement separately allocated the royalties for the trade secrets and the patents. A confidentiality agreement was also included that barred the use and disclosure of any Digital Ignition trade secrets by AEI.

Because AEI believed that its company was relatively unknown in the automotive and racing markets, it also negotiated and received the right to sell the licensed product under the Digital Ignition trademark. A provision in the license agreement permits AEI to use the Digital Ignition trademark. The license sets standards for quality control over the product produced in association with the trademark and AEI agreed to allow Digital Ignition to supervise AEI's use of the mark.

For two years, AEI manufactured and sold digital ignition systems in accordance with its license with Digital Ignition without incident. Midway through the third year, AEI stopped paying royalties on the licensed patents and trade secrets. When contacted by Digital Ignition to provide an explanation for the delinquency, AEI claimed that it believed one of the patents in the package was invalid. Because of this, AEI assumed that it was no longer under an obligation to pay royalties on the patents or trade secrets.

At about the same time, Digital Ignition also became aware of AEI's use of Digital Ignition's trademark on a line of men's watches sold by AEI. The watches in question sported a racing car design with Digital Ignition's logo prominently displayed on the face of the watches. When questioned, AEI claimed that it has a license to use Digital Ignition's trademark.

The last problem arising out of the AEI licensing agreement was brought to the attention of Digital Ignition when it discovered that AEI was offering a how-to manual for sale to other manufacturers. The AEI manual excerpted whole sections of the Digital Ignition know-how manual. The AEI manual appeared to claim that the ideas described in the manual came from AEI.

Dr. See, the founder and CEO of Digital Ignition, has approached you for advice. He wants to know what action he should take against AEI in light of the alarming discoveries above. What advice would you give Dr. See? Would any additional information from Digital Ignition be helpful in making your recommendation? If so, what information?

Focus of the Chapter

This chapter focuses on the licensing of intellectual property and offers a survey of issues that arise concerning patent, trade secret, trademark, and copyright licensing. A license is a specialized type of contract. In return for payment or other appropriate consideration, the licensor grants some legal rights to the licensee. The first section of the chapter, Part A, considers licensing in the context of patents. This section covers the right of licensees to sue for infringement of licensed patents (*Morrow v. Microsoft Corp.*), challenges to patent validity by licensees and third parties as those challenges impact upon licensing agreements (*Blonder-Tongue Labs. v. Univ. of Ill. Found.*, *Lear Inc. v. Adkins*, and *MedImmune v. Genentech*), and the duration of licensees' obligations to pay royalties (*Kimble v. Marvel Entertainment, LLC* and *Aronson v. Quick Point Pencil Co.*). This section also discusses limits imposed by law on a patentee's rights to make, use, sell, and offer to sell a patented technology (*Quanta Computer Inc. v. LG Electronics Inc.*). The section then discusses patent cross licensing (*Texas Instruments, Inc. v. Hyundai Elec. Indus.*), patent pools (*Matsushita Elec. Indus. Co. v. Cinram Int'l, Inc.*), patent packages (*Wells Surveys, Inc. v. Perfo-Log, Inc.*), and licensing of university-created technologies.

The second section of this chapter, Part B, discusses licensing of trade secrets. The section provides an introduction to trade secret licensing and then explores the implications of the indefinite term of trade secret protections in defining a licensee's obligation to pay royalties on a licensed trade secret (*Warner-Lambert Pharm. Co. v. John J. Reynolds, Inc.*). Hybrid licensing of trade secrets in conjunction with patents is also discussed.

The next section, Part C, explores the issues that arise in trademark licensing. First, the section discusses the rule against "naked licensing" — the licensing of a trademark without a transfer of an already established product reputation or "good will" — and the nature of the required good will (*Int'l Cosmetics Exch. Inc. v. Gapardis Health & Beauty, Inc.*). Next, the section describes the type of control a licensor must maintain over the nature and quality of the goods or services offered in association with a licensed mark (*Dawn Donut Co. v. Hart's Food Stores, Inc.*). The section closes by considering antitrust concerns that arise from trademark licensing (*Principe v. McDonald's Corp.*).

Part D deals with copyright licensing. This section offers an introduction to the rights that may be transferred through copyright licensing (*Silvers v. Sony Pictures Entm't, Inc.*), including the scope of the use authorized under a license (*Harper-Collins Publishers LLC v. Open Road Integrated Media, LLP*). The section also touches upon the activities of performance rights organizations ASCAP and BMI in connection with copyright licensing.

The last section of the chapter, Part E, discusses the simultaneous licensing of multiple forms of intellectual property. Specifically, the section looks at problems that arise from hybrid licensing of patents with trade secrets and patents with trademarks.

Readings
A. Patent Licensing

A patent license is a contract whereby the owner of a patented invention authorizes the use of the invention without liability in exchange for payment or some other valuable consideration. In general, legal standards regulating the licensing of patents seek to protect, encourage, and reward inventors' creative efforts and to expand inventors' abilities to gain commercial returns from resultant end products, both tangible and intangible.

There are different kinds of patent licenses, such as a look-see agreement, an option agreement, a joint R&D agreement, a material transfer agreement, or a full-blown license. A patent license can also be granted as part of another type of agreement, such as a financing agreement, a security agreement, or a merger or acquisition agreement. Patents are frequently licensed in combination with licenses to use trade secrets associated with the patented inventions being licensed (hence this section will sometimes discuss trade secret licensing in association with patent licensing). The list below provides an overview of several key considerations related to defining and implementing patent licenses. Many of these considerations are discussed at later points in this chapter.

Key Patent License Terms & Considerations

1. Define the Property to be Licensed

   - Pending patent applications
   - Issued patents
   - Trade secrets, other know-how
   - Improvements

2. Define the Scope of the Licensed Grant

   - Exclusive versus non-exclusive
   - Make, use, sell, or lease
   - Right to sub-license
   - Technical field of use, geographic, time, and quantity limitations

3. Establish Payment/Compensation

   - Lump sum/up-front payment
   - Continuing royalties
   - Base for running royalties

- Flat-rate royalties versus royalties that vary with time versus royalty that varies with use or derivative use
- Non-monetary compensation
- Non-monetary compensation
  - Cross-licensing
  - Grant-back licensing
  - Access to know how
- Influence of scope of license rights
- Influence of industry norms
- Most favored licensee clauses
- Royalty procedures and auditing
  - Time/mode/place of payment
  - Record keeping

4. Apportion Risk
- Patent invalidity/unenforceability
- Indemnification for product injuries
- Obligation to take over patent prosecution
- Patent infringement concerns

5. Establish a Plan in the Event of Termination and/or Breach
- Early termination: specify the grounds and the ramifications
- Breach: specify what damages are available (ex. liquidated damages)

Keep in mind that not all of these considerations will need to be addressed in every license; a specific patent licensing agreement should be carefully tailored to the needs of the parties involved. Additionally, the parties may want to include a non-disclosure agreement, which can protect the confidentiality of the licensing agreement as well as of specific confidential information (such as trade secrets) licensed under the associated licensing agreement.

1. The Right to Sue for Infringement

Morrow v. Microsoft Corp.

United States Court of Appeals for the Federal Circuit

499 F.3d 1332 (Fed. Cir. 2007)

MOORE, CIRCUIT JUDGE.

I.

At Home Corp. (AGC) was a provider of internet services over the cable television infrastructure but filed a petition for bankruptcy under Chapter 11 on September 28, 2011. . . .

Under the liquidation plan, three trusts were created — the General Unsecured Creditors' Liquidating Trust (GUCLT), the At Home Liquidating Trust (AHLT), and the Bondholders Liquidating Trust (BHLT). . . . GUCLT received the rights to . . . causes of action (called "Estate Litigation"), including claims for misappropriation or infringement of AHC's intellectual property rights. AHLT (the "Plan Agent" in charge of conducting the administrative wind-down of the company's business) was given ownership rights in AHC's intellectual property, since all of the assets not distributed to BHLT or GUCLT were assigned to AHLT. Thus, AHLT received legal title to the '647 patent under the liquidation plan though it did not have the right to sue third parties for infringement of the patent. The liquidation plan and the associated agreements provided that AHLT's assets were to be managed for the benefit of the bondholders and the general creditors of BHLT and GUCLT.

II.

Spacone, as the trustee of GUCLT, filed suit against Microsoft on October 22, 2003 alleging infringement of the '647 patent. . . . On November 12, 2003, Microsoft answered and asserted counterclaims against Spacone and Crawford (trustee for AHLT), seeking a declaration of noninfringement, invalidity, and unenforceability of the '647 patent.

Microsoft filed a motion for summary judgment contending that GUCLT lacked standing. In response, Spacone filed a cross-motion for summary judgment that standing existed, asserting he had standing to pursue this action as trustee of GUCLT or alternatively on behalf of and in the name of AHLT. The district court denied Microsoft's standing motion and granted Spacone's cross-motion . . . .

ANALYSIS

I.

[The court first concluded that standing was to be determined under patent law, not under bankruptcy law.]

II.

B. Article III Standing Requirements

. . . .

A "patentee" is entitled to bring a "civil action for infringement of his patent." 35 U.S.C. § 281, and the "patentee" includes the patentee to whom the patent was issued and the "successors in title to the patentee," 35 U.S.C. § 100(d). The "successor[] in title" is the party holding *legal title* to the patent. *See Enzo Apa & Son, Inc. v. Geapag A.G.*, 134 F.3d 1090, 1093 (Fed. Cir. 1998); *Prima Tek II LLC v. A-Roo Co.*, 222 F.3d 1372, 1377 (Fed. Cir. 2000) (noting the assignee of all substantial rights under the patent becomes the effective patentee and can sue in its own name for infringement). A patent grant bestows the legal right to exclude others from making, using, selling, or offering to sell the patented invention in the United States, or importing the invention. *See* 35 U.S.C. § 154; 35 U.S.C. § 271 (describing permitted and prohibited actions with respect to the exclusionary rights). This right to exclude is the legal interest created by statute. [*Arachnid, Inc. v. Merit Indus., Inc.*, 939 F.2d 1574, 1577, 1578 (Fed. Cir. 1991).] Constitutional injury in fact occurs when a party performs at least one prohibited action with respect to the patented invention that violates these exclusionary rights. *See Lujan v. Defenders of Wildlife*, 504 U.S. 555, 560–61, 112 S. Ct. 2130, 119 L. Ed. 2d 351 (1992) (stating that constitutional injury arises from invasion of a legally protected interest which is concrete and particularized and actual or imminent rather than conjectural or hypothetical). The party holding the exclusionary rights to the patent suffers legal injury in fact under the statute.

There are three general categories of plaintiffs encountered when analyzing the constitutional standing issue in patent infringement suits: those that can sue in their own name alone; those that can sue as long as the patent owner is joined in the suit; and those that cannot even participate as a party to an infringement suit. The first category includes plaintiffs that hold all legal rights to the patent as the patentee or assignee of all patent rights—the entire bundle of sticks. Unquestionably, a patentee who holds all the exclusionary rights and suffers constitutional injury in fact from infringement is one entitled to sue for infringement in its own name. Additionally, if a patentee transfers "all substantial rights" to the patent, this amounts to an assignment or a transfer of title, which confers constitutional standing on the assignee to sue for infringement in its own name alone. [*Intellectual Prop. Dev. v. TCI Cablevision of Cal., Inc.*, 248 F.3d 1333, 1345 (2001).] When a party holds all rights or all substantial rights, it alone has standing to sue for infringement.

The second category of plaintiffs hold exclusionary rights and interests created by the patent statutes, but not all substantial rights to the patent. As the grantee of exclusionary rights, this plaintiff is injured by any party that makes, uses, sells, offers to sell, or imports the patented invention. [*Evident Corp. v. Church & Dwight Co.*, 399 F.3d 1310, 1313 (2005)]; *Intellectual Prop. Dev.*, 248 F.3d at 1346 ("A party such as IPD that has the right to exclude others from making, using, and selling an invention described in the claims of a patent is constitutionally injured by another entity that makes, uses, or sells the invention."). Parties that hold the exclusionary rights are often identified as exclusive licensees, because the grant of an exclusive license to make, use, or sell the patented invention carries with it the right to prevent others from practicing the invention.

However, these exclusionary rights "must be enforced through or in the name of the owner of the patent," and the patentee who transferred these exclusionary interests is usually joined to satisfy prudential standing concerns. *Indep. Wireless Tel. Co. v. Radio Corp. of Am.*, 269 U.S. 459, 467, 469, 46 S. Ct. 166, 70 L. Ed. 357, 1926 Dec. Comm'r Pat. 294 (1926). The patentee is joined for the purpose of avoiding the potential for multiple litigations and multiple liabilities and recoveries against the same alleged infringer. *Intellectual Prop. Dev.*, 248 F.3d at 1347 (indicating that joining the patentee satisfies a prudential not constitutional standing requirement); [*Propat Int'l Corp. v. RPost US, Inc.*, 473 F.3d 1187, 1193 (2007)]; *Indep. Wireless*, 269 U.S. at 469 (stating that where there is no express covenant by the patent owner to sue infringers it is an implied obligation to allow use of the licensor's name, which is indispensable to the enjoyment of the patent monopoly). When the patentee is the infringer, or the prudential concerns are not at play in a particular case, joinder of the patentee is not necessary. This joinder analysis has been incorporated in Federal Rule of Civil Procedure 19. *See* Fed. R. Civ. P. 19, Advisory Committee Note to Subdivision (a) (1937); *Prima Tek II*, 222 F.3d at 1377.

The third category of plaintiffs includes those that hold less than all substantial rights to the patent and lack exclusionary rights under the patent statutes to meet the injury in fact requirement. They are not injured by a party that makes, uses, or sells the patented invention because they do not hold the necessary exclusionary rights. Plaintiffs in this category lack constitutional standing. *See* [*Sicom Sys. v. Agilent Techs., Inc.*, 427 F.3d 971, 976 (2005)] ("A nonexclusive license confers no constitutional standing on the licensee to bring suit or even to join a suit with the patentee because a nonexclusive licensee suffers no legal injury from infringement." (internal citations omitted)). This standing deficiency cannot be cured by adding the patent title owner to the suit. *Propat*, 473 F.3d at 1189; *Intellectual Prop. Dev.*, 248 F.3d at 1348–49.

C. Injury in Fact

Here, we are faced with the question of whether GUCLT holds the exclusionary rights and suffers constitutional injury in fact. Microsoft asserts that GUCLT lacks sufficient rights to be a party to this case. Spacone argues that AHLT merely holds "bare" legal title to the '647 patent in trust for the benefit of GUCLT and that GUCLT had standing to sue because it possesses partial equitable title to the '647 patent. The question is whether GUCLT's interests in the patent include sufficient exclusionary rights such that GUCLT suffers an injury in fact from infringing activities. If GUCLT holds all substantial rights, it can sue in its name alone. If GUCLT holds less than all substantial rights but sufficient exclusionary rights that it suffers injury in fact, it can sue as a co-party with the legal title holder AHLT. If it lacks injury in fact, GUCLT lacks standing to be a party to this case.

GUCLT holds the right to sue parties (except for the controlling shareholders) for patent infringement. Its inability to sue controlling shareholders is a limitation on this right, as is the requirement that AHLT approve the settlement of any suits brought by GUCLT. Thus, GUCLT's right to sue comes with restrictions. In *Vaupel*, this court indicated that the right to sue is an important right, and like GUCLT Vaupel held the exclusive right to sue for infringement, subject only to the obligation to inform Markowsky of the suit. [*Vaupel Textilmaschinen KG v. Meccanica Euro Italia S.P.A.*, 944 F.2d 870 (1991).] But unlike GUCLT, Vaupel also held the exclusionary rights — an exclusive license (right to make, use, or sell the patented invention) along with the exclusive right license and the right to sublicense (subject to prior consent by Markowsky). The grant of this exclusive license and the right to sublicense constituted a transfer of the exclusionary rights to the patent to Vaupel. Within this context, Vaupel held all substantial rights as the "effective patentee" because it held the exclusionary rights and additional important patent rights including the right to bring a patent suit. *Vaupel*, 944 F.2d at 875. Vaupel could sue without joinder of Markowsky. In contrast, GUCLT lacks an exclusive license, the exclusive right to license, and the right to sublicense. These are important aspects of the exclusionary rights held by Vaupel.

Moreover, GUCLT's control with respect to infringement litigation does not lead to the conclusion that GUCLT suffers injury in fact from infringement. In *Sicom*, we held that Sicom lacked all substantial rights (it was not a category one plaintiff) because it did not have the right to settle litigation it initiated without prior written consent of the licensor, even though it had the right to sue *and* an exclusive license to the patent. *Sicom*, 427 F.3d at 979.

While GUCLT has been granted the right to sue infringers that are not controlling shareholders, AHLT is the patent title holder, holds the right to sell the patent, grant exclusive and nonexclusive licenses, grant the right to sublicense, or transfer any of the rights that AHLT holds to another party. The only limitations on AHLT's ability to control and transfer its patent rights is GUCLT's and BHLT's consent. In *Speedplay*, we noted that this type of consent requirement was not significantly restrictive of Speedplay's exclusionary patent rights, which included an exclusive license and the right to sublicense a potential infringer. [*Speedplay, Inc. v. Bebop*, 211 F.3d 1245, 1252 (2000).] In this case the requirement that GUCLT and BHLT consent to transfer of rights to the '647 patent is not significantly restrictive of AHLT's exclusionary rights. Nor does this consent requirement transfer to GUCLT any exclusionary rights to the patent. Moreover, there is no indication that AHLT is restricted as to the parties to whom it could transfer any of the exclusionary rights that it holds under the '647 patent. Thus, AHLT could grant an exclusive license to any party, which would transfer the right to exclude others from practicing the patented invention.

The problem for GUCLT and AHLT is that the exclusionary rights have been separated from the right to sue for infringement. The liquidation plan contractually separated the right to sue from the underlying legally protected interests created by the patent statutes — the right to exclude. For any suit that GUCLT brings, its grievance is that the exclusionary interests held by AHLT are being violated. GUCLT is not the party to which the statutes grant judicial relief. *See* [*Warth v. Seldin*, 422 U.S. 490, 500 (1975)]. GUCLT suffers no legal injury in fact to the patent's exclusionary rights. As the Supreme Court stated in *Independent Wireless*, the right to bring an infringement suit is "to obtain damages for the injury to his exclusive right by an infringer." *Independent Wireless Tel. Co*, 269 U.S. at 469; *see also Prima Tek II*, 222 F.3d at 1381 ("Standing to sue for infringement depends entirely on the putative plaintiff's proprietary interest in the patent, not on any contractual arrangements among the parties regarding who may sue"); [*Ortho Pharmaceutical Corp. v. Genetics Inst.*, 52 F.3d 1026, 1034 (1995)] ("[A] right to sue clause cannot negate the requirement that, for co-plaintiff standing, a licensee must have beneficial ownership of some of the patentee's proprietary rights.").

The importance of AHLT's right to license third parties to our constitutional standing analysis is underscored by *Textile Productions*. This court determined that the transfer of the right to sue in that case did not provide standing to even participate in the suit because the agreement did not clearly manifest that the owner would refrain from granting a license to anyone else in the particular area of exclusivity. [*Textile Prods. v. Mead Corp.*, 134 F.3d 1481, 1485 (1998).] We stated that the right to license third parties is an important patent right because implicit in the right to exclude is the right to waive that right; that is, to license activities that would otherwise be excluded. *See id.*; *Prima Tek II*, 222 F.3d at 1379. GUCLT does not have the right to license or sublicense or otherwise forgive activities that would normally be prohibited under the patent statutes. We "pay particular attention to whether the agreement conveys in full the right to exclude" in order to find standing. *Id.* at 1379–80.

Even in *Propat*, this court found that Propat had no standing to participate in an infringement suit though it enjoyed the exclusive right to sue third parties for patent infringement, the right to grant licenses to third parties, and the right to enforce license agreements. 473 F.3d at 1191. Propat's right to license and sue third parties was subject to prior approval by the legal title holder Authentix—approval that could not be unreasonably withheld. Propat was also required to receive the consent of Authentix before it assigned rights or obligations under the agreement to another party. This court held that Authentix did not assign all substantial rights to Propat and Propat could not even sue as a co-plaintiff with Authentix. *Propat*, 473 F.3d at 1189 (noting that even if Authentix was a party this would not ameliorate Propat's standing problem). Propat lacked sufficient exclusionary rights and therefore did not suffer statutory legal injury.

While GUCLT enjoys greater control over infringement litigation than did Propat, it lacks the important rights to grant and enforce licenses that Propat held. GUCLT lacks the right to waive the patent's exclusionary rights by waiving those rights in license or sublicense agreements.

Spacone asserts that this court's decision in *Evident* supports GUCLT's standing to bring suit now that AHLT is a party. We do not agree that GUCLT suffers the legal injury that entitles it to be a party to this infringement suit. In keeping with the decisions from this court, *Evident* stands for the proposition that a party with the rights of an exclusive licensee holds exclusionary rights and has standing to sue for infringement if the patentee joins the suit to satisfy any prudential concerns present in that case. *Evident*, 399 F.3d at 1314; *see also Propat*, 473 F.3d at 1193; *Intellectual Prop. Dev.*, 248 F.3d at 1345–46; *Textile Prods.*, 134 F.3d at 1484; *Abbott Labs.*, 47 F.3d at 1131. Unlike Evident, AHLT's participation as a third party defendant does not affect GUCLT's standing to bring this suit. To demonstrate entitlement to join as a *co-plaintiff* GUCLT must have the right to exclude others from making, using, or selling the invention in the United States. *See Ortho Pharms. Corp. v. Genetics Institute, Inc.*, 52 F.3d 1026, 1030–32 (Fed. Cir. 1995).

Contrary to the dissent's suggestion, GUCLT's beneficial ownership interest as the future beneficiary of 45% of whatever assets are still held by AHLT when it completes its wind-down of AHC's business does not affect the outcome of our standing analysis. Indeed, there is no indication as to what, if any, assets will flow to GUCLT after AHLT completes its work. Regardless, whatever interests in the '647 patent may flow to GUCLT in the future are insufficient to convert its equitable future interests in the patent into full legal exclusionary interests as of the time this suit was initiated. In *Arachnid, Inc. v. Merit Indus., Inc.*, 939 F.2d 1574, 1577, 1578 n.3 (Fed. Cir. 1991), the plaintiff also asserted that it had standing to sue for damages as the equitable title holder to the patent because in equity it was the real owner of the patent rights. It asserted that this equitable interest met the standing requirements because another party held legal title to the patent. This court rejected this equitable interest-based standing argument. We stated that equitable title to the patent is insufficient to confer standing to sue for legal relief from infringement. *Id.* at 1579–80 (noting that the owner of equitable title may seek redress in a court of equity such as rescission of title transfer but cannot bring an action at law for infringement damages). Similarly, GUCLT lacks the exclusionary rights under the '647 patent and relies on its equitable interests in AHLT's assets. But GUCLT lacks legal injury in fact, and its beneficial interest in assets held by AHLT or the fact that AHLT has been brought into this case as a third party defendant does not cure GUCLT's constitutional standing deficiencies.

Only when a party holds the exclusionary rights to the patent but lacks all substantial rights may the party join the legal title owner in a suit to enforce patent rights. Joining the legal title holder only satisfies prudential standing requirements. It cannot cure constitutional standing deficiencies. Since GUCLT fails to meet constitutional standing requirements, it cannot be a party to this suit for patent infringement.

CONCLUSION

Since GUCLT lacked standing to sue Microsoft for infringement of the '647 patent, the district court lacked jurisdiction. Thus, we will not consider the appealed infringement issues on the merits. We reverse as to standing and vacate the infringement rulings.

Notes & Questions

1. Who Brings the Infringement Suit?

Typically, the best interests of both the licensor and the licensee are served by halting the conduct of a party that infringes the subject matter of a patent license. The licensor has an interest in prohibiting unlicensed use of his patented subject matter because each infringing act by the accused party costs the licensor a royalty. The licensee has an interest in halting the infringing conduct since the accused party is a potential competitor. An infringing party is unburdened by the obligation to pay royalties and may therefore stand at a competitive advantage to undercut the sales of the licensee.

There is no definitive answer as to which party to a licensing agreement should bring suit. Arguably the larger entity, which has the benefit of deeper pockets and more experience in litigation, should decide whether to file an infringement action. A party's motivation to defend the validity of a licensed patent is another consideration. A licensor has more to lose if a patent underlying a licensing agreement is declared invalid and unenforceable. The interests of the licensor and licensee in protecting the validity of a licensed patent are divergent. For example, in *Abbott Laboratories v. Diamedix Corp.*, 47 F.3d 1128 (Fed. Cir. 1995), the licensor Diamedix feared that the licensee Abbott "ha[d] an incentive not to defend the validity of the patents with great vigor, since a decision invalidating the patents would free Abbott from its royalty obligations." *Id.* at 1130. A licensee may stand to benefit whether the patent is declared invalid and unenforceable, thus freeing him from the obligation to pay royalties, or whether the patent is enforced against the infringer. In addition to motivation, the licensor, as owner of the patent, may be in the best position to access and provide the information needed to defend the validity of a patent.

As *Abbott* illustrates, a party designated in an exclusive licensing agreement as having a right to bring suit for patent infringement is usually seen as having been given the right of first refusal, rather than an exclusive right to bring an infringement action. The other party to the agreement typically may step in, or initiate suit itself, if the designated party declines.

2. Who Controls the Litigation?

A licensor has the most to lose if a patent is declared invalid. Given that a licensee has incentives to not vigorously defend the validity of a patent, a licensor may be justified in doubting the commitment of the licensee as defender of the patent. A licensor should therefore reserve the right to intervene and defend the patent should the licensee fail to competently direct litigation.

Where a licensee controls litigation, a licensor may also wish to require a licensee to obtain its consent before entering into any settlement agreement. Additionally, a licensor who is named as a party to an infringement suit may be exposed to sanctions incurred during a botched litigation. For this reason, an agreement permitting a licensee to name the licensor as a party in an infringement suit may also include an indemnity clause to protect the licensor from the licensee's mishandling of litigation.

3. Suits Brought by Patent Assertion Entities

Recently, there has been much discussion regarding the role in patent litigation of patent assertion entities (PAEs) or non-practicing entities. These are companies that buy or license patents for the purpose of using the patents to illicit licensing fees from potential infringers. The PAEs do not themselves manufacture any products or practice the patents in any way. In *eBay, Inc. v. MercExchange, LLC.*, 547 U.S. 388 (2006), the Supreme Court considered whether such entities ought to be able to enjoin others from using their patents. Despite finding that the patents in question were valid and infringed, the district court in this case denied MercExchange's request for a permanent injunction on the basis that the "plaintiff's willingness to license its patents and its lack of commercial activity in practicing the patents would be sufficient to establish that the patent holder would not suffer irreparable harm if an injunction did not issue." *Id.* at 393. The appellate court reversed. The Supreme Court remanded the case to the district court with instructions to apply the traditional four-factor framework used to determine whether an injunction is appropriate. Under this framework, a plaintiff in a patent infringement action is only entitled to an injunction barring further infringement if the plaintiff can demonstrate "(1) that it has suffered an irreparable injury; (2) that remedies available at law, such as monetary damages, are inadequate to compensate for that injury; (3) that, considering the balance of hardships between the plaintiff and defendant, a remedy in equity is warranted; and (4) that the public interest would not be disserved by a permanent injunction." *Id.* at 391.

Policymakers and scholars have also engaged in lengthy debates about PAEs, with many alleging that these entities cost the economy vast amounts of money. President Obama issued an executive order, including legislative recommendations, to make litigation more difficult for patent holders. *See* Press Release, *White House Task Force on High-Tech Patent Issues: Legislative Priorities & Executive Actions* (June 4, 2013), http://www.whitehouse.gov/the-press-office/2013/06/04/fact-sheet-white-house -task-force-high-tech-patent-issues (last visited 12/29/2017). Careful studies of patent litigation, however, demonstrate that such concerns may have been overstated. *See* Christopher A. Cotropia, Jay P. Kesan & David L. Schwartz, *Unpacking Patent Assertion Entities (PAEs)*, 99 MINN. L. R. 649 (2014). Further, empirical studies show that different types of non-practicing entities behave differently in litigation, and therefore a generalized conclusion that all such entities ought to be restricted is not warranted. *See* Christopher A. Cotropia, Jay P. Kesan & David L. Schwartz, *Heterogeneity among Patent Plaintiffs: An Empirical Analysis of Patent Case Progression, Settlement, and Adjudication* (October 8, 2017), J. EMPIRICAL LEGAL STUD. (forthcoming 2018), available at: SSRN: https://ssrn.com/abstract=3049678. For example, universities, whose patents have been demonstrated to significantly benefit the economy as discussed at the end of this section, do not practice their inventions and monetize their inventions mainly through licensing and enforcement of their patent rights against infringers.

2. Challenges to Patent Validity

a. Res Judicata

Blonder-Tongue Laboratories, Inc. v. University of Illinois Foundation

Supreme Court of the United States

402 U.S. 313 (1971)

MR. JUSTICE WHITE DELIVERED THE OPINION OF THE COURT.

Respondent University of Illinois Foundation (hereafter Foundation) is the owner by assignment of U.S. Patent No. 3,210,767, issued to Dwight E. Isbell on October 5, 1965.

The patent has been much litigated since it was granted, primarily because it claims a high quality television antenna for color reception. One of the first infringement suits brought by the Foundation was filed in the Southern District of Iowa against the Winegard Co., an antenna manufacturer. Trial was to the court, and after pursuing the inquiry mandated by *Graham* v. *John Deere Co.*, 383 U.S. 1, 17–18 (1966), Chief Judge Stephenson held the patent invalid. . . . On appeal, the Court of Appeals for the Eighth Circuit unanimously affirmed Judge Stephenson. . . .

In March 1966, well before Judge Stephenson had ruled in the *Winegard* case, the Foundation also filed suit in the Northern District of Illinois charging a Chicago customer of petitioner, Blonder-Tongue Laboratories, Inc. (hereafter B-T), with infringing two patents it owned by assignment. . . .

Trial was again to the court, and on June 27, 1968, Judge Hoffman held that the Foundation's patents were valid and infringed. [The Seventh Circuit affirmed.]

B-T sought certiorari, assigning the conflict between the Courts of Appeals for the Seventh and Eighth Circuits as to the validity of the Isbell patent as a primary reason for granting the writ.

I

In *Triplett* v. *Lowell*, 297 U.S. 638 (1936), this Court held:

> "Neither reason nor authority supports the contention that an adjudication adverse to any or all the claims of a patent precludes another suit upon the same claims against a different defendant. While the earlier decision may be comity be given great weight in a later litigation and thus persuade the court to render a like decree, it is not *res adjudicata* and may not be pleaded as a defense."

297 U.S. at 642.

The holding in *Triplett* has been at least gently criticized by some judges.

. . . .

III

Some litigants—those who never appeared in a prior action—may not be collaterally estopped without litigating the issue. They have never had a chance to present their evidence and arguments on the claim. Due process prohibits estopping them despite one or more existing adjudications of the identical issue which stand squarely against their position. Also, the authorities have been more willing to permit a defendant in a second suit to invoke an estoppel against a plaintiff who lost on the same claim in an earlier suit than they have been to allow a plaintiff in the second suit to use offensively a judgment obtained by a different plaintiff in a prior suit against the same defendant. But the case before us involves neither due process nor "offensive use" questions. Rather, it depends on the considerations weighing for and against permitting a patent holder to sue on his patent after it has once been held invalid following opportunity for full and fair trial.

A.

Starting with the premise that the statutes creating the patent system, expressly sanctioned by the Constitution, represent an affirmative policy choice by Congress to reward inventors, respondents extrapolate a special public interest in sustaining "good" patents and characterize patent litigation as so technical and difficult as to present unusual potential for unsound adjudications. Although *Triplett* made no such argument in support of its holding, that rule, offering the unrestricted right to relitigate patent validity, is thus deemed an essential safeguard against improvident judgments of invalidity.

We fully accept congressional judgment to reward inventors through the patent system. We are also aware that some courts have frankly stated that patent litigation can present issues so complex that legal minds, without appropriate grounding in science and technology, may have difficulty in reaching decision. . . . But assuming a patent case so difficult as to provoke a frank admission of judicial uncertainty, one might ask what reason there is to expect that a second district judge or court of appeals would be able to decide the issue more accurately. Moreover, as *Graham* also indicates, Congress has from the outset chosen to impose broad criteria of patentability while lodging in the federal courts final authority to decide that question. In any event it cannot be sensibly contended that all issues concerning patent validity are so complex and unyielding. Nonobviousness itself is not always difficult to perceive and decide and other questions on which patentability depends are more often than not no more difficult than those encountered in the usual nonpatent case.

Even conceding the extreme intricacy of some patent cases, we should keep firmly in mind that we are considering the situation where the patentee was plaintiff in the prior suit and chose to litigate at that time and place. Presumably he was prepared to litigate and to litigate to the finish against the defendant there involved. Patent litigation characteristically proceeds with some deliberation and, with the avenues for discovery available under the present rules of procedure, there is no reason to suppose that plaintiff patentees would face either surprise or unusual difficulties in getting all relevant and probative evidence before the court in the first litigation.

Moreover, we do not suggest, without legislative guidance, that a plea of estoppel by an infringement or royalty suit defendant must automatically be accepted once the defendant in support of his plea identifies the issue in suit as the identical question finally decided against the patentee or one of his privies in previous litigation. Rather, the patentee-plaintiff must be permitted to demonstrate, if he can, that he did not have "a fair opportunity procedurally, substantively and evidentially to pursue his claim the first time." This element in the estoppel decision will comprehend, we believe, the important concerns about the complexity of patent litigation and the posited hazard that the prior proceedings were seriously defective.

Determining whether a patentee has had a full and fair chance to litigate the validity of his patent in an earlier case is of necessity not a simple matter. In addition to the considerations of choice of forum and incentive to litigate mentioned above, certain other factors immediately emerge. For example, if the issue is nonobviousness, appropriate inquiries would be whether the first validity determination purported to employ the standards announced in *Graham* v. *John Deere Co., supra*; whether the opinions filed by the District Court and the reviewing court, if any, indicate that the prior case was one of those relatively rare instances where the courts wholly failed to grasp the technical subject matter and issues in suit; and whether without fault of his own the patentee was deprived of crucial evidence or witnesses in the first litigation. But as so often is the case, no one set of facts, no one collection of words or phrases, will provide an automatic formula for proper rulings on estoppel pleas. In the end, decision will necessarily rest on the trial courts' sense of justice and equity.

We are not persuaded, therefore, that the *Triplett* rule, as it was formulated, is essential to effectuate the purposes of the patent system or is an indispensable or even an effective safeguard against faulty trials and judgments. Whatever legitimate concern there may be about the intricacies of some patent suits, it is insufficient in and of itself to justify patentees relitigating validity issues as long as new defendants are available. This is especially true if the court in the second litigation must decide in a principled way whether or not it is just and equitable to allow the plea of estoppel in the case before it.

B.

An examination of the economic consequences of continued adherence to *Triplett* has two branches. Both, however, begin with the acknowledged fact that patent litigation is a very costly process.

This statement . . . must be assessed in light of the fact that they are advanced by patentees contemplating action as plaintiffs, and patentees are heavily favored as a class of litigants by the patent statute. Section 282 of the Patent Code provides, in pertinent part:

> "A patent shall be presumed valid. The burden of establishing invalidity of a patent shall rest on a party asserting it."

If a patentee's expense is high though he enjoys the benefits of the presumption of validity, the defendant in an infringement suit will have even higher costs as he both introduces proof to overcome the presumption and attempts to rebut whatever proof the patentee offers to bolster the claims.

As stated at the outset of this section, the expense of patent litigation has two principal consequences if the *Triplett* rule is maintained. First, assuming that a perfectly sound judgment of invalidity has been rendered in an earlier suit involving the patentee, a second infringement action raising the same issue and involving much of the same proof has a high cost to the individual parties. The patentee is expending funds on litigation to protect a patent which is by hypothesis invalid. These moneys could be put to better use, such as further research and development. The alleged infringer—operating as he must against the presumption of validity—is forced to divert substantial funds to litigation that is wasteful.

The second major economic consideration is far more significant. Under *Triplett*, only the comity restraints flowing from an adverse prior judgment operate to limit the patentee's right to sue different defendants on the same patent. In each successive suit the patentee enjoys the statutory presumption of validity, and so may easily put the alleged infringer to his expensive proof. As a consequence, prospective defendants will often decide that paying royalties under a license or other settlement is preferable to the costly burden of challenging the patent.

The tendency of *Triplett* to multiply the opportunities for holders of invalid patents to exact licensing agreements or other settlements from alleged infringers must be considered in the context of other decisions of this Court. Although recognizing the patent system's desirable stimulus to invention, we have also viewed the patent as a monopoly which, although sanctioned by law, has the economic consequences attending other monopolies. A patent yielding returns for a device that fails to meet the congressionally imposed criteria of patentability is anomalous. . . .

One obvious manifestation of this principle has been the series of decisions in which the Court has condemned attempts to broaden the physical or temporal scope of the patent monopoly. . . .

A second group of authorities encourage authoritative testing of patent validity. In 1952, the Court indicated that a manufacturer of a device need not await the filing of an infringement action in order to test the validity of a competitor's patent, but may institute his own suit under the Declaratory Judgment Act. Other decisions of this type involved removal of restrictions on those who would challenge the validity of patents.

Two Terms ago in *Lear, Inc.* v. *Adkins*, 395 U.S. 653 (1969), we relied on both lines of authority to abrogate the doctrine that in a contract action for unpaid patent royalties the licensee of a patent is estopped from proving "that his licensor was demanding royalties for the use of an idea which was in reality a part of the public domain." The principle that "federal law requires that all ideas in general circulation be dedicated to the common good unless they are protected by a valid patent," found support in . . . the first line of cases discussed above. The holding that licensee estoppel was no longer tenable was rooted in the second line of cases eliminating obstacles to suit by those disposed to challenge the validity of a patent. Moreover, as indicated earlier, we relied on practical considerations that patent licensees "may often be the only individuals with enough economic incentive to challenge the patentability of an inventor's discovery."

To be sure, *Lear* obviates to some extent the concern that *Triplett* prompts alleged infringers to pay royalties on patents previously declared invalid rather than to engage in costly litigation when infringement suits are threatened. *Lear* permits an accused infringer to accept a license, pay royalties for a time, and cease paying when financially able to litigate validity, secure in the knowledge that invalidity may be urged when the patentee-licensor sues for unpaid royalties. Nevertheless, if the claims are in fact invalid and are identical to those invalidated in a previous suit against another party, any royalties actually paid are an unjust increment to the alleged infringer's costs. Those payments put him at a competitive disadvantage *vis-a-vis* other alleged infringers who can afford to litigate or have successfully litigated the patent's validity.

This has several economic consequences. First, the alleged infringer who cannot afford to defend may absorb the royalty costs in order to compete with other manufacturers who have secured holdings that the patent is invalid, cutting the profitability of his business and perhaps assuring that he will never be in a financial position to challenge the patent in court. On the other hand, the manufacturer who has secured a judicial holding that the patent is invalid may be able to increase his market share substantially, and he may do so without coming close to the price levels that would prevail in a competitive market. Because he is free of royalty payments, the manufacturer with a judgment against the patent may price his products higher than competitive levels absent the invalid patent, yet just below the levels set by those manufacturers who must pay royalties. Third, consumers will pay higher prices for goods covered by the invalid patent than would be true had the initial ruling of invalidity had at least the potential for broader effect. And even if the alleged infringer can escape royalty obligations under *Lear* when he is able to bear the cost of litigation, any royalty payments passed on to consumers are as a practical matter unrecoverable by those who in fact paid them. Beyond all of this, the rule of *Triplett* may permit invalid patents to serve almost as effectively as would valid patents as barriers to the entry of new firms—particularly small firms.

Economic consequences like these, to the extent that they can be avoided, weigh in favor of modification of the *Triplett* mutuality principle. Arguably, however, the availability of estoppel to one charged with infringement of a patent previously held invalid will merely shift the focus of litigation from the merits of the dispute to the question whether the party to be estopped had a full and fair opportunity to litigate his claim in the first action. It would seem sufficient answer to note that once it is determined that the issue in both actions was identical, it will be easier to decide whether there was a full opportunity to determine that issue in the first action than it would be to relitigate completely the question of validity. And, this does not in fact seem to have been a problem in other contexts, where strict mutuality of estoppel has been abandoned.

It has also been suggested that 35 U.S.C. § 285, which allows a court to award reasonable attorney's fees to a prevailing party "in exceptional cases," and 35 U.S.C. § 288, under which a patentee forfeits his right to recover costs even as to the valid claims of his patent if he does not disclaim invalid claims before bringing suit, work to inhibit repetitious suits on invalid patents. But neither of these provisions can operate until after litigation has occurred, and the outlay required to try a lawsuit presenting validity issues is the factor which undoubtedly forces many alleged infringers into accepting licenses rather than litigating. If concern about such license agreements is proper, as our cases indicate that it is, the accused infringer should have available an estoppel defense that can be pleaded affirmatively and determined on a pretrial motion for judgment on the pleadings or summary judgment. Fed. Rules Civ. Proc. 8 (c), 12 (c), and 56.

. . . .

D.

It is clear that judicial decisions have tended to depart from the rigid requirements of mutuality. In accordance with this trend, there has been a corresponding development of the lower courts' ability and facility in dealing with questions of when it is appropriate and fair to impose an estoppel against a party who has already litigated an issue once and lost. . . .

When these judicial developments are considered in the light of our consistent view—last presented in *Lear, Inc. v. Adkins*—that the holder of a patent should not be insulated from the assertion of defenses and thus allowed to exact royalties for the use of an idea that is not in fact patentable or that is beyond the scope of the patent monopoly granted, it is apparent that the uncritical acceptance of the principle of mutuality of estoppel expressed in *Triplett* v. *Lowell* is today out of place. Thus, we conclude that *Triplett* should be overruled to the extent it forecloses a plea of estoppel by one facing a charge of infringement of a patent that has once been declared invalid.

Notes & Questions

1. Patent Invalidity and Res Judicata: A One-Way Street

A final adjudication of *validity* of a patent is not binding on subsequent infringers who are not party to an action, even if a subsequent action relies upon identical grounds of attack. A patentee may therefore face several challenges to the validity of his patent, with no benefit of prior actions serving as precedent in subsequent litigation. Contrast this to the final adjudication of *invalidity* of a patent. A single final adjudication of invalidity is binding on the patent holder in other litigation and results in the termination of the patent.

2. Licensor's Reluctance to Sue?

While a licensee may not be the most committed to vigorously defend a licensed patent once an infringement suit is initiated, a licensor may have an incentive not to initiate a timely suit against an infringing party. A common defense raised when an action is brought against an accused infringer is an assertion that the patent at issue is invalid. Attacks on the validity of a patent can deter licensors from bringing suit against an infringer. This is because royalties stop once a patent is declared invalid. Since royalties paid prior to a judgment of invalidity are not subject to refund, a licensor may delay filing suit against an infringing party in order to push off the termination of licensees' royalty payment obligations. For this reason, a licensee may wish to include a provision in a licensing agreement that assures the timely filing of an infringement suit. In light of *res judicata* in the finding of invalidity of a patent, can you think of another reason that patentees shy away from bringing suit?

b. Estoppel

Lear, Inc. v. Adkins

Supreme Court of the United States

395 U.S. 653 (1969)

MR. JUSTICE HARLAN DELIVERED THE OPINION OF THE COURT.

In January of 1952, John Adkins, an inventor and mechanical engineer, was hired by Lear, Incorporated, for the purpose of solving a vexing problem the company had encountered in its efforts to develop a gyroscope which would meet the increasingly demanding requirements of the aviation industry. The gyroscope is an essential component of the navigational system in all aircraft, enabling the pilot to learn the direction and attitude of his airplane. With the development of the faster airplanes of the 1950's, more accurate gyroscopes were needed, and the gyro industry consequently was casting about for new techniques which would satisfy this need in an economical fashion. Shortly after Adkins was hired, he developed a method of construction at the company's California facilities which improved gyroscope accuracy at a low cost. Lear almost immediately incorporated Adkins' improvements into its production process to its substantial advantage.

The question that remains unsettled in this case, after eight years of litigation in the California courts, is whether Adkins will receive compensation for Lear's use of those improvements which the inventor has subsequently patented. At every stage of this lawsuit, Lear has sought to prove that, despite the grant of a patent by the Patent Office, none of Adkins' improvements were sufficiently novel to warrant the award of a monopoly under the standards delineated in the governing federal statutes. Moreover, the company has sought to prove that Adkins obtained his patent by means of a fraud on the Patent Office. In response, the inventor has argued that since Lear had entered into a licensing agreement with Adkins, it was obliged to pay the agreed royalties regardless of the validity of the underlying patent.

The Supreme Court of California unanimously vindicated the inventor's position. While the court recognized that generally a manufacturer is free to challenge the validity of an inventor's patent, it held that "one of the oldest doctrines in the field of patent law establishes that so long as a licensee is operating under a license agreement he is estopped to deny the validity of his licensor's patent in a suit for royalties under the agreement. The theory underlying this doctrine is that a licensee should not be permitted to enjoy the benefit afforded by the agreement while simultaneously urging that the patent which forms the basis of the agreement is void."

I.

At the very beginning of the parties' relationship, Lear and Adkins entered into a rudimentary one-page agreement which provided that although "all new ideas, discoveries, inventions, etc., related to . . . vertical gyros become the property of Mr. John S. Adkins," the inventor promised to grant Lear a license as to all ideas he might develop "on a mutually satisfactory royalty basis." As soon as Adkins' labors yielded tangible results, it quickly became apparent to the inventor that further steps should be taken to place his rights to his ideas on a firmer basis. On February 4, 1954, Adkins filed an application with the Patent Office in an effort to gain federal protection for his improvements. At about the same time, he entered into a lengthy period of negotiations with Lear in an effort to conclude a licensing agreement which would clearly establish the amount of royalties that would be paid.

These negotiations finally bore fruit on September 15, 1955, when the parties approved a complex 17-page contract which carefully delineated the conditions upon which Lear promised to pay royalties for Adkins' improvements. The parties agreed that if "the U.S. Patent Office refuses to issue a patent on the substantial claims [contained in Adkins' original patent application] or if such a patent so issued is subsequently held invalid, then in any of such events Lear at its option shall have the right forthwith to terminate the specific license so affected or to terminate this entire Agreement. . . ."

As the contractual language indicates, Adkins had not obtained a final Patent Office decision as to the patentability of his invention at the time the licensing agreement was concluded. Indeed, he was not to receive a patent until January 5, 1960. This long delay has its source in the special character of Patent Office procedures. [Review of the patent application by the Patent Office may include several rounds of rejection and amendments.] Thus, when Adkins made his original application in 1954, it took the average inventor more than three years before he obtained a final administrative decision on the patentability of his ideas, with the Patent Office acting on the average application from two to four times.

The progress of Adkins' effort to obtain a patent followed the typical pattern. In his initial application, the inventor made the ambitious claim that his entire method of constructing gyroscopes was sufficiently novel to merit protection. The Patent Office, however, rejected this initial claim, as well as two subsequent amendments, which progressively narrowed the scope of the invention sought to be protected. Finally, Adkins narrowed his claim drastically to assert only that the design of the apparatus used to achieve gyroscope accuracy was novel. In response, the Office issued its 1960 patent, granting a 17-year monopoly on this more modest claim.

During the long period in which Adkins was attempting to convince the Patent Office of the novelty of his ideas, however, Lear had become convinced that Adkins would never receive a patent on his invention and that it should not continue to pay substantial royalties on ideas which had not contributed substantially to the development of the art of gyroscopy. In 1957, after Adkins' patent application had been rejected twice, Lear announced that it had searched the Patent Office's files and had found a patent which it believed had fully anticipated Adkins' discovery. As a result, the company stated that it would no longer pay royalties on the large number of gyroscopes it was producing at its plant in Grand Rapids, Michigan (the Michigan gyros). Payments were continued on the smaller number of gyros produced at the company's California plant (the California gyros) for two more years until they too were terminated on April 8, 1959.

II.

Since the California Supreme Court's construction of the 1955 licensing agreement is solely a matter of state law, the only issue open to us is raised by the court's reliance upon the doctrine of estoppel to bar Lear from proving that Adkins' ideas were dedicated to the common welfare by federal law. In considering the propriety of the State Court's decision, we are well aware that we are not writing upon a clean slate. The doctrine of estoppel has been considered by this Court in a line of cases reaching back into the middle of the 19th century.

. . . .

III.

The uncertain status of licensee estoppel in the case law is a product of judicial efforts to accommodate the competing demands of the common law of contracts and the federal law of patents. On the one hand, the law of contracts forbids a purchaser to repudiate his promises simply because he later becomes dissatisfied with the bargain he has made. On the other hand, federal law requires that all ideas in general circulation be dedicated to the common good unless they are protected by a valid patent. *Sears, Roebuck* v. *Stiffel Co., supra; Compco Corp.* v. *Day-Brite Lighting, Inc., supra.* When faced with this basic conflict in policy, both this Court and courts throughout the land have naturally sought to develop an intermediate position which somehow would remain responsive to the radically different concerns of the two different worlds of contract and patent. The result has been a failure. Rather than creative compromise, there has been a chaos of conflicting case law, proceeding on inconsistent premises. Before renewing the search for an acceptable middle ground, we must reconsider on their own merits the arguments which may properly be advanced on both sides of the estoppel question.

A.

It will simplify matters greatly if we first consider the most typical situation in which patent licenses are negotiated. In contrast to the present case, most manufacturers obtain a license after a patent has issued. Since the Patent Office makes an inventor's ideas public when it issues its grant of a limited monopoly, a potential licensee has access to the inventor's ideas even if he does not enter into an agreement with the patent owner. Consequently, a manufacturer gains only two benefits if he chooses to enter a licensing agreement after the patent has issued. First, by accepting a license and paying royalties for a time, the licensee may have avoided the necessity of defending an expensive infringement action during the period when he may be least able to afford one. Second, the existence of an unchallenged patent may deter others from attempting to compete with the licensee.

Under ordinary contract principles the mere fact that some benefit is received is enough to require the enforcement of the contract, regardless of the validity of the underlying patent. Nevertheless, if one tests this result by the standard of good-faith commercial dealing, it seems far from satisfactory. For the simple contract approach entirely ignores the position of the licensor who is seeking to invoke the court's assistance on his behalf. Consider, for example, the equities of the licensor who has obtained his patent through a fraud on the Patent Office. It is difficult to perceive why good faith requires that courts should permit him to recover royalties despite his licensee's attempts to show that the patent is invalid.

Even in the more typical cases, not involving conscious wrongdoing, the licensor's equities are far from compelling. A patent, in the last analysis, simply represents a legal conclusion reached by the Patent Office. Moreover, the legal conclusion is predicated on factors as to which reasonable men can differ widely. Yet the Patent Office is often obliged to reach its decision in an *ex parte* proceeding, without the aid of the arguments which could be advanced by parties interested in proving patent invalidity. Consequently, it does not seem to us to be unfair to require a patentee to defend the Patent Office's judgment when his licensee places the question in issue, especially since the licensor's case is buttressed by the presumption of validity which attaches to his patent. Thus, although licensee estoppel may be consistent with the letter of contractual doctrine, we cannot say that it is compelled by the spirit of contract law, which seeks to balance the claims of promisor and promisee in accord with the requirements of good faith.

Surely the equities of the licensor do not weigh very heavily when they are balanced against the important public interest in permitting full and free competition in the use of ideas which are in reality a part of the public domain. Licensees may often be the only individuals with enough economic incentive to challenge the patentability of an inventor's discovery. If they are muzzled, the public may continually be required to pay tribute to would-be monopolists without need or justification. We think it plain that the technical requirements of contract doctrine must give way before the demands of the public interest in the typical situation involving the negotiation of a license after a patent has issued.

B.

The case before us, however, presents a far more complicated estoppel problem than the one which arises in the most common licensing context. The problem arises out of the fact that Lear obtained its license in 1955, more than four years before Adkins received his 1960 patent. Indeed, from the very outset of the relationship, Lear obtained special access to Adkins' ideas in return for its promise to pay satisfactory compensation.

Thus, during the lengthy period in which Adkins was attempting to obtain a patent, Lear gained an important benefit not generally obtained by the typical licensee. For until a patent issues, a potential licensee may not learn his licensor's ideas simply by requesting the information from the Patent Office. During the time the inventor is seeking patent protection, the governing federal statute requires the Patent Office to hold an inventor's patent application in confidence. If a potential licensee hopes to use the ideas contained in a secret patent application, he must deal with the inventor himself, unless the inventor chooses to publicize his ideas to the world at large. By promising to pay Adkins royalties from the very outset of their relationship, Lear gained immediate access to ideas which it may well not have learned until the Patent Office published the details of Adkins' invention in 1960. At the core of this case, then, is the difficult question whether federal patent policy bars a State from enforcing a contract regulating access to an unpatented secret idea.

Adkins takes an extreme position on this question. The inventor does not merely argue that since Lear obtained privileged access to his ideas *before 1960*, the company should be required to pay royalties accruing *before 1960* regardless of the validity of the patent which ultimately issued. He also argues that since Lear obtained special benefits before 1960, it should also pay royalties during the entire patent period (1960–1977), without regard to the validity of the Patent Office's grant. We cannot accept so broad an argument.

Adkins' position would permit inventors to negotiate all important licenses during the lengthy period while their applications were still pending at the Patent Office, thereby disabling entirely all those who have the strongest incentive to show that a patent is worthless. While the equities supporting Adkins' position are somewhat more appealing than those supporting the typical licensor, we cannot say that there is enough of a difference to justify such a substantial impairment of overriding federal policy.

Nor can we accept a second argument which may be advanced to support Adkins' claim to at least a portion of his post-patent royalties, regardless of the validity of the Patent Office grant. The terms of the 1955 agreement provide that royalties are to be paid until such time as the "patent . . . is held invalid," and the fact remains that the question of patent validity has not been finally determined in this case. Thus, it may be suggested that although Lear must be allowed to raise the question of patent validity in the present lawsuit, it must also be required to comply with its contract and continue to pay royalties until its claim is finally vindicated in the courts.

The parties' contract, however, is no more controlling on this issue than is the State's doctrine of estoppel, which is also rooted in contract principles. The decisive question is whether overriding federal policies would be significantly frustrated if licensees could be required to continue to pay royalties during the time they are challenging patent validity in the courts.

It seems to us that such a requirement would be inconsistent with the aims of federal patent policy. Enforcing this contractual provision would give the licensor an additional economic incentive to devise every conceivable dilatory tactic in an effort to postpone the day of final judicial reckoning. We can perceive no reason to encourage dilatory court tactics in this way. Moreover, the cost of prosecuting slow-moving trial proceedings and defending an inevitable appeal might well deter many licensees from attempting to prove patent invalidity in the courts. The deterrent effect would be particularly severe in the many scientific fields in which invention is proceeding at a rapid rate. In these areas, a patent may well become obsolete long before its 17-year term has expired. If a licensee has reason to believe that he will replace a patented idea with a new one in the near future, he will have little incentive to initiate lengthy court proceedings, unless he is freed from liability at least from the time he refuses to pay the contractual royalties. Lastly, enforcing this contractual provision would undermine the strong federal policy favoring the full and free use of ideas in the public domain. For all these reasons, we hold that Lear must be permitted to avoid the payment of all royalties accruing after Adkins' 1960 patent issued if Lear can prove patent invalidity.

C.

Adkins' claim to contractual royalties accruing before the 1960 patent issued is, however, a much more difficult one, since it squarely raises the question whether, and to what extent, the States may protect the owners of *unpatented* inventions who are willing to disclose their ideas to manufacturers only upon payment of royalties. The California Supreme Court did not address itself to this issue with precision, for it believed that the venerable doctrine of estoppel provided a sufficient answer to all of Lear's claims based upon federal patent law. . . . Consequently, we have concluded, after much consideration, that even though an important question of federal law underlies this phase of the controversy, we should not now attempt to define in even a limited way the extent, if any, to which the States may properly act to enforce the contractual rights of inventors of unpatented secret ideas. Given the difficulty and importance of this task, it should be undertaken only after the state courts have, after fully focused inquiry, determined the extent to which they will respect the contractual rights of such inventors in the future. Indeed, on remand, the California courts may well reconcile the competing demands of patent and contract law in a way which would not warrant further review in this Court.

Medimmune v. Genentech

Supreme Court of the United States

549 U.S. 118 (2007)

Justice Scalia delivered the opinion of the Court.

We must decide whether Article III's limitation of federal courts' jurisdiction to "Cases" and "Controversies," reflected in the "actual controversy" requirement of the Declaratory Judgment Act, 28 U.S.C. §2201(a), requires a patent licensee to terminate or be in breach of its license agreement before it can seek a declaratory judgment that the underlying patent is invalid, unenforceable, or not infringed.

I

Petitioner MedImmune, Inc., manufactures Synagis, a drug used to prevent respiratory tract disease in infants and young children. In 1997, petitioner entered into a patent license agreement with respondent Genentech, Inc. (which acted on behalf of itself as patent assignee and on behalf of the coassignee, respondent City of Hope). The license covered an existing patent relating to the production of "chimeric antibodies" and a then-pending patent application relating to "the coexpression of immunoglobulin chains in recombinant host cells." Petitioner agreed to pay royalties on sales of "Licensed Products," and respondents granted petitioner the right to make, use, and sell them. The agreement defined "Licensed Products" as a specified antibody, "the manufacture, use or sale of which . . . would, if not licensed under th[e] Agreement, infringe one or more claims of either or both of [the covered patents,] which have neither expired nor been held invalid by a court or other body of competent jurisdiction from which no appeal has been or may be taken." The license agreement gave petitioner the right to terminate upon six months' written notice.

In December 2001, the "coexpression" application covered by the 1997 license agreement matured into the "Cabilly II" patent. Soon thereafter, respondent Genentech delivered petitioner a letter expressing its belief that Synagis was covered by the Cabilly II patent and its expectation that petitioner would pay royalties beginning March 1, 2002. Petitioner did not think royalties were owing, believing that the Cabilly II patent was invalid and unenforceable, and that its claims were in any event not infringed by Synagis. Nevertheless, petitioner considered the letter to be a clear threat to enforce the Cabilly II patent, terminate the 1997 license agreement, and sue for patent infringement if petitioner did not make royalty payments as demanded. If respondents were to prevail in a patent infringement action, petitioner could be ordered to pay treble damages and attorney's fees, and could be enjoined from selling Synagis, a product that has accounted for more than 80 percent of its revenue from sales since 1999. Unwilling to risk such serious consequences, petitioner paid the demanded royalties "under protest and with reservation of all of [its] rights." This declaratory-judgment action followed.

Petitioner sought the declaratory relief discussed in detail in Part II below. The District Court granted respondents' motion to dismiss the declaratory-judgment claims for lack of subject-matter jurisdiction, relying on the decision of the United States Court of Appeals for the Federal Circuit in *Gen-Probe Inc. v. Vysis, Inc.*, 359 F.3d 1376 (2004). *Gen-Probe* had held that a patent licensee in good standing cannot establish an Article III case or controversy with regard to validity, enforceability, or scope of the patent because the license agreement "obliterate[s] any reasonable apprehension" that the licensee will be sued for infringement. The Federal Circuit affirmed the District Court, also relying on *Gen-Probe*. 427 F.3d 958 (2005).

. . . .

III

The Declaratory Judgment Act provides that, "[i]n a case of actual controversy within its jurisdiction . . . any court of the United States . . . may declare the rights and other legal relations of any interested party seeking such declaration, whether or not further relief is or could be sought." 28 U.S.C. § 2201(a).

There is no dispute that these standards would have been satisfied if petitioner had taken the final step of refusing to make royalty payments under the 1997 license agreement. Respondents claim a right to royalties under the licensing agreement. Petitioner asserts that no royalties are owing because the Cabilly II patent is invalid and not infringed; and alleges (without contradiction) a threat by respondents to enjoin sales if royalties are not forthcoming. The factual and legal dimensions of the dispute are well defined and, but for petitioner's continuing to make royalty payments, nothing about the dispute would render it unfit for judicial resolution. Assuming (without deciding) that respondents here could not claim an anticipatory breach and repudiate the license, the continuation of royalty payments makes what would otherwise be an imminent threat at least remote, if not nonexistent. As long as those payments are made, there is no risk that respondents will seek to enjoin petitioner's sales. Petitioner's own acts, in other words, eliminate the imminent threat of harm. The question before us is whether this causes the dispute no longer to be a case or controversy within the meaning of Article III.

Our analysis must begin with the recognition that, where threatened action by government is concerned, we do not require a plaintiff to expose himself to liability before bringing suit to challenge the basis for the threat—for example, the constitutionality of a law threatened to be enforced. The plaintiff's own action (or inaction) in failing to violate the law eliminates the imminent threat of prosecution, but nonetheless does not eliminate Article III jurisdiction. For example, in *Terrace v. Thompson*, 263 U.S. 197 (1923), the State threatened the plaintiff with forfeiture of his farm, fines, and penalties if he entered into a lease with an alien in violation of the State's anti-alien land law. Given this genuine threat of enforcement, we did not require, as a prerequisite to testing the validity of the law in a suit for injunction, that the plaintiff bet the farm, so to speak, by taking the violative action. Likewise, in *Steffel v. Thompson*, 415 U.S. 452 (1974), we did not require the plaintiff to proceed to distribute handbills and risk actual prosecution before he could seek a declaratory judgment regarding the constitutionality of a state statute prohibiting such distribution. As then-Justice Rehnquist put it in his concurrence, "the declaratory judgment procedure is an alternative to pursuit of the arguably illegal activity. In each of these cases, the plaintiff had eliminated the imminent threat of harm by simply not doing what he claimed the right to do (enter into a lease, or distribute handbills at the shopping center). That did not preclude subject-matter jurisdiction because the threat-eliminating behavior was effectively coerced. The dilemma posed by that coercion—putting the challenger to the choice between abandoning his rights or risking prosecution—is "a dilemma that it was the very purpose of the Declaratory Judgment Act to ameliorate."

Supreme Court jurisprudence is more rare regarding application of the Declaratory Judgment Act to situations in which the plaintiff's self-avoidance of imminent injury is coerced by threatened enforcement action of a private party rather than the government. Lower federal courts, however (and state courts interpreting declaratory-judgment acts requiring "actual controversy"), have long accepted jurisdiction in such cases.

The only Supreme Court decision in point is, fortuitously, close on its facts to the case before us. *Altvater v. Freeman*, 319 U.S. 359 (1943), held that a licensee's failure to cease its payment of royalties did not render nonjusticiable a dispute over the validity of the patent. In that litigation, several patentees had sued their licensees to enforce territorial restrictions in the license. The licensees filed a counterclaim for declaratory judgment that the underlying patents were invalid, in the meantime paying "under protest" royalties required by an injunction the patentees had obtained in an earlier case. The patentees argued that "so long as [licensees] continue to pay royalties, there is only an academic, not a real controversy, between the parties." We rejected that argument and held that the declaratory-judgment claim presented a justiciable case or controversy: "The fact that royalties were being paid did not make this a 'difference or dispute of a hypothetical or abstract character.' The royalties "were being paid under protest and under the compulsion of an injunction decree," and "[u]nless the injunction decree were modified, the only other course [of action] was to defy it, and to risk not only actual but treble damages in infringement suits." We concluded that "the requirements of [a] case or controversy are met where payment of a claim is demanded as of right and where payment is made, but where the involuntary or coercive nature of the exaction preserves the right to recover the sums paid or to challenge the legality of the claim."

The Federal Circuit's *Gen-Probe* decision distinguished *Altvater* on the ground that it involved the compulsion of an injunction. But *Altvater* cannot be so readily dismissed. More fundamentally, and contrary to the Federal Circuit's conclusion, *Altvater* did not say that the coercion dispositive of the case was governmental, but suggested just the opposite. The opinion acknowledged that the licensees had the option of stopping payments in defiance of the injunction, but explained that the consequence of doing so would be to risk "actual [and] treble damages in infringement suits" by the patentees. It significantly did not mention the threat of prosecution for contempt, or any other sort of governmental sanction. Moreover, it cited approvingly a treatise which said that an "actual or threatened serious injury to business or employment" by a private party can be as coercive as other forms of coercion supporting restitution actions at common law; and that "[t]o imperil a man's livelihood, his business enterprises, or his solvency, [was] ordinarily quite as coercive" as, for example, "detaining his property."

Respondents assert that the parties in effect settled this dispute when they entered into the 1997 license agreement. When a licensee enters such an agreement, they contend, it essentially purchases an insurance policy, immunizing it from suits for infringement so long as it continues to pay royalties and does not challenge the covered patents. Permitting it to challenge the validity of the patent without terminating or breaking the agreement alters the deal, allowing the licensee to continue enjoying its immunity while bringing a suit, the elimination of which was part of the patentee's quid pro quo. To begin with, it is not clear where the prohibition against challenging the validity of the patents is to be found. It can hardly be implied from the mere promise to pay royalties on patents "which have neither expired nor been held invalid by a court or other body of competent jurisdiction from which no appeal has been or may be taken[.]" Promising to pay royalties on patents that have not been held invalid does not amount to a promise not to seek a holding of their invalidity . . . .

We hold that petitioner was not required, insofar as Article III is concerned, to break or terminate its 1997 license agreement before seeking a declaratory judgment in federal court that the underlying patent is invalid, unenforceable, or not infringed. The Court of Appeals erred in affirming the dismissal of this action for lack of subject-matter jurisdiction.

The judgment of the Court of Appeals is reversed, and the cause is remanded for proceedings consistent with this opinion.

Notes & Questions

1. Licensee Estoppel and Royalty Payment Obligations

Courts do not enforce a promise not to challenge the validity of a licensed patent by a licensee if the licensor obtained the promise in order to shield the licensed patent from challenges to its validity. *Lear v. Adkins* and *MedImmune v. Genentech* made it clear that licensees have standing to challenge the validity of a patent. Moreover, a licensee may either stop paying royalties or pay royalties under protest during the time that the challenge is pending.

In *Studiengesellschaft Kohle, m.b.H. v. Shell Oil Co.*, 112 F.3d 1561 (Fed. Cir. 1997), the licensee, Shell Oil, sought to have the licensed patents declared invalid and unenforceable in response to an action brought by the licensor SGK, seeking relief for breach of contract and patent infringement. Shell alleged patent invalidity only after it was faced with a suit by SGK for failing to pay royalties as agreed to in its licensing agreement with the licensor. The court addressed the question of whether Shell was obligated to pay royalties on the challenged patent:

> [T]his court detects no significant frustration of federal patent policy by enforcing the 1987 license agreement between Shell and SGK, to the extent of allowing SGK to recover royalties until the date Shell first challenged the validity of the claims. First, ... Shell executed a contractual agreement which produced significant benefits for the corporation and attested to the worth of the patent. Under the agreement (with its provision for Shell to notify SGK of all polypropylene production), Shell had the benefits of producing polypropylene insulated from unlicensed competition, insulated from investigations of infringement, and even insulated from royalties (until SGK's discovery of the Seadrift Process). To these benefits, Shell now seeks to add the benefit of abrogating its agreement and avoiding its breach of the contract. . . . [T]his court must prevent the injustice of allowing Shell to exploit the protection of the contract and patent rights and then later to abandon conveniently its obligations under those same rights.

Just as important, however, Shell's apparent breach of its duty to notify under the agreement is itself more likely to frustrate federal patent policy than enforcement of the contract. As already noted, *Lear* focused on the "full and free use of ideas in the public domain." *Lear*, 395 U.S. at 674. By abrogating its notification duty, Shell delayed a timely challenge to the validity of the '698 patent and postponed the public's full and free use of the invention of the '698 patent. Shell enjoyed the protection of the license from 1987 until SGK became aware of the Seadrift Process. Upon SGK's discovery of its Seadrift process, Shell suddenly seeks the protection of the *Lear* policies it flaunted for many years. However, a licensee, such as Shell, cannot invoke the protection of the Lear doctrine until it (i) actually ceases payment of royalties, and (ii) provides notice to the licensor that the reason for ceasing payment of royalties is because it has deemed the relevant claims to be invalid. Other circuits addressing this issue have arrived at the same conclusion.

In this factual setting, therefore, enforcement of the license according to its terms, even if this entails a determination of whether the Seadrift process infringes a now-invalidated patent, does not frustrate federal patent policy. Accordingly, this court remands this case to the district court for enforcement of the license (prior to the date Shell first challenged the validity of the claims) and, if necessary, computation of back royalties.

Studiengesellschaft, 112 F.3d at 1568.

2. Assignor Estoppel

Related to the doctrine of licensee estoppel is the doctrine of assignor estoppel. Assignor estoppel prevents an inventor who has assigned her rights to a patent to subsequently challenge the validity of that assigned patent as a defense to infringement of the patent. The Federal Circuit addressed the issue for the first time in *Diamond Scientific Co. v. Ambico*, 848 F.2d 1220 (Fed. Cir. 1988), where the inventor-assignor left the employ of the assignee, Diamond, and started Ambico, a competing company:

Assignor estoppel is an equitable doctrine that prevents one who has assigned the rights to a patent (or patent application) from later contending that what was assigned is a nullity. . . .

The four most frequently mentioned justifications for applying assignor estoppel are the following: "(1) to prevent unfairness and injustice; (2) to prevent one [from] benefiting from his own wrong; (3) by analogy to estoppel by deed in real estate; and (4) by analogy to a landlord-tenant relationship." Although each rationale may have some utility depending on the facts presented by the particular case, our concern here is primarily with the first one.

Courts that have expressed the estoppel doctrine in terms of unfairness and injustice have reasoned that an assignor should not be permitted to sell

> something and later to assert that what was sold is worthless, all to the
> detriment of the assignee. Justice Frankfurter's dissent in *Scott Paper*
> explained that the doctrine was rooted in the notion of fair dealing. "The
> principle of fair dealing as between assignor and assignee of a patent
> whereby the assignor will not be allowed to say that what he has sold as a
> patent was not a patent has been part of the fabric of our law throughout
> the life of this nation." *Scott Paper Co. v. Marcalus Mfg. Co.*, 326 U.S. 249,
> 260, 66 S. Ct. 101, 90 L. Ed. 47 [(1945)] (Frankfurter, J., dissenting). "The
> essence of the principle of fair dealing which binds the assignor of a patent
> in a suit by the assignee, even though it turns out that the patent is invalid or
> lacks novelty, is that in this relation the assignor is not part of the general
> public but is apart from the general public." *Id.* at 261–62. In other words, it
> is the implicit representation by the assignor that the patent rights that he is
> assigning (presumably for value) are not worthless that sets the assignor
> apart from the rest of the world and can deprive him of the ability to chal-
> lenge later the validity of the patent. To allow the assignor to make that
> representation at the time of the assignment (to his advantage) and later to
> repudiate it (again to his advantage) could work an injustice against the
> assignee.

Diamond, 848 F.2d at 1224–25. A more recent case dealing with the issue of assignor estoppel is *Semiconductor Energy Lab. Co. v. Nagata*, 706 F.3d 1365 (Fed. Cir. 2013). Relying on *Diamond*, the Court of Appeals for the Federal Circuit once again reaffirmed that an assignee is estopped from challenging the validity of its patent as a defense to an infringement claim by the assignee. The court then clarified that assignor estoppel is an affirmative defense, not a cause of action:

> As the district court fittingly noted, "it simply makes no sense to use a doc-
> trine intended to estop a party from advancing a particular claim or defense in
> a legal case as a way to sue a non-party who has made no claim or defense in a
> legal case."

Semiconductor Energy Lab. Co., 703 F.3d at 1370. Further, in *MAG Aerospace Indus., Inc. v. B/E Aerospace, Inc.*, 816 F.3d 1374 (Fed. Cir. 2016), the court clarified that the doctrine of assignor estoppel extended to those in privity with the assignor. B/E, at the time of the suit, was the employer of Mark Pondelick, one of the inventors who originally assigned the patent at issue to MAG's predecessor. The court held that, as Pondelick's employer, B/E was in privity with one of the assignors of the patent and, therefore, was estopped from challenging the patent's validity when sued by MAG for patent infringement. *MAG Aerospace*, 816 F.3d at 1381.

The status of assignor estoppel in the U.S. Patent and Trademark Office's post-grant proceedings remains unclear, however. The Federal Circuit court declined to review a decision of the Patent Trial and Appeal Board instituting *inter partes* review and holding that assignor estoppel was inapplicable in the proceedings before the U.S. Patent and Trademark Office. *See Husky Injection Molding Sys. Ltd. v. Athena Automation Ltd.*, 838 F.3d 1236 (Fed. Cir. 2016).

3. Duration of Obligation to Pay Royalties

Generally, the obligation of a licensee to pay royalties for a patent license is limited in duration to the term of the patent. The expiration of a patent terminates the obligation to pay royalties on the patented invention. The patent policy in favor of free use and competition regarding a patented invention once the relevant patent expires weighs against licensors' use of licensing contracts and state contract law to extend the term of the patent protection beyond its statutory scope.

a. Post Patent Expiration Royalties

Kimble v. Marvel Entertainment, LLC

Supreme Court of the United States

135 S. Ct. 2401 (2015)

JUSTICE KAGAN DELIVERED THE OPINION OF THE COURT.

In *Brulotte v. Thys Co.*, 379 U.S. 29 (1964), this Court held that a patent holder cannot charge royalties for the use of his invention after its patent term has expired. The sole question presented here is whether we should overrule *Brulotte*. Adhering to principles of *stare decisis*, we decline to do so. Critics of the *Brulotte* rule must seek relief not from this Court but from Congress.

I

In 1990, petitioner Stephen Kimble obtained a patent on a toy that allows children (and young-at-heart adults) to role-play as "a spider person" by shooting webs — really, pressurized foam string — "from the palm of [the] hand." Respondent Marvel Entertainment, LLC (Marvel) makes and markets products featuring Spider-Man, among other comic-book characters. Seeking to sell or license his patent, Kimble met with the president of Marvel's corporate predecessor to discuss his idea for web-slinging fun. Soon afterward, but without remunerating Kimble, that company began marketing the "Web Blaster" — a toy that, like Kimble's patented invention, enables would-be action heroes to mimic Spider-Man through the use of a polyester glove and a canister of foam.

Kimble sued Marvel in 1997 alleging, among other things, patent infringement. The parties ultimately settled that litigation. Their agreement provided that Marvel would purchase Kimble's patent in exchange for a lump sum (of about a half-million dollars) and a 3% royalty on Marvel's future sales of the Web Blaster and similar products. The parties set no end date for royalties, apparently contemplating that they would continue for as long as kids want to imitate Spider–Man (by doing whatever a spider can).

And then Marvel stumbled across *Brulotte*, the case at the heart of this dispute. In negotiating the settlement, neither side was aware of *Brulotte*. But Marvel must have been pleased to learn of it. *Brulotte* had read the patent laws to prevent a patentee from receiving royalties for sales made after his patent's expiration. So the decision's effect was to sunset the settlement's royalty clause. On making that discovery, Marvel sought a declaratory judgment in federal district court confirming that the company could cease paying royalties come 2010 — the end of Kimble's patent term. The court approved that relief, holding that *Brulotte* made "the royalty provision . . . unenforceable after the expiration of the Kimble patent." The Court of Appeals for the Ninth Circuit affirmed, though making clear that it was none too happy about doing so. "[T]he *Brulotte* rule," the court complained, "is counter-intuitive and its rationale is arguably unconvincing."

We granted certiorari to decide whether, as some courts and commentators have suggested, we should overrule *Brulotte*. For reasons of *stare decisis*, we demur.

II

Patents endow their holders with certain superpowers, but only for a limited time. In crafting the patent laws, Congress struck a balance between fostering innovation and ensuring public access to discoveries. While a patent lasts, the patentee possesses exclusive rights to the patented article — rights he may sell or license for royalty payments if he so chooses. But a patent typically expires 20 years from the day the application for it was filed. And when the patent expires, the patentee's prerogatives expire too, and the right to make or use the article, free from all restriction, passes to the public.

This Court has carefully guarded that cut-off date, just as it has the patent laws' subject-matter limits: In case after case, the Court has construed those laws to preclude measures that restrict free access to formerly patented, as well as unpatentable, inventions. In one line of cases, we have struck down state statutes with that consequence. By virtue of federal law, we reasoned, "an article on which the patent has expired," like an unpatentable article, "is in the public domain and may be made and sold by whoever chooses to do so." In a related line of decisions, we have deemed unenforceable private contract provisions limiting free use of such inventions. In *Scott Paper Co. v. Marcalus Mfg. Co.*, 326 U.S. 249 (1945), for example, we determined that a manufacturer could not agree to refrain from challenging a patent's validity. Allowing even a single company to restrict its use of an expired or invalid patent, we explained, "would deprive . . . the consuming public of the advantage to be derived" from free exploitation of the discovery. And to permit such a result, whether or not authorized "by express contract," would impermissibly undermine the patent laws.

Brulotte was brewed in the same barrel. There, an inventor licensed his patented hop-picking machine to farmers in exchange for royalties from hop crops harvested both before and after his patents' expiration dates. The Court (by an 8–1 vote) held the agreement unenforceable — "unlawful *per se*" — to the extent it provided for the payment of royalties "accru[ing] after the last of the patents incorporated into the machines had expired." To arrive at that conclusion, the Court began with the statutory provision setting the length of a patent term. Emphasizing that a patented invention "become[s] public property once [that term] expires," the Court then quoted from *Scott Paper*: Any attempt to limit a licensee's post-expiration use of the invention, "whatever the legal device employed, runs counter to the policy and purpose of the patent laws." In the *Brulotte* Court's view, contracts to pay royalties for such use continue "the patent monopoly beyond the [patent] period," even though only as to the licensee affected. And in so doing, those agreements conflict with patent law's policy of establishing a "post-expiration . . . public domain" in which every person can make free use of a formerly patented product.

The *Brulotte* rule, like others making contract provisions unenforceable, prevents some parties from entering into deals they desire. As compared to lump-sum fees, royalty plans both draw out payments over time and tie those payments, in each month or year covered, to a product's commercial success. And sometimes, for some parties, the longer the arrangement lasts, the better—not just up to but beyond a patent term's end. A more extended payment period, coupled (as it presumably would be) with a lower rate, may bring the price the patent holder seeks within the range of a cash-strapped licensee. (Anyone who has bought a product on installment can relate.) Or such an extended term may better allocate the risks and rewards associated with commercializing inventions—most notably, when years of development work stand between licensing a patent and bringing a product to market. As to either goal, *Brulotte* may pose an obstacle.

Yet parties can often find ways around *Brulotte*, enabling them to achieve those same ends. To start, *Brulotte* allows a licensee to defer payments for pre-expiration use of a patent into the post-expiration period; all the decision bars are royalties for using an invention after it has moved into the public domain. A licensee could agree, for example, to pay the licensor a sum equal to 10% of sales during the 20–year patent term, but to amortize that amount over 40 years. That arrangement would at least bring down early outlays, even if it would not do everything the parties might want to allocate risk over a long timeframe. And parties have still more options when a licensing agreement covers either multiple patents or additional non-patent rights. Under *Brulotte*, royalties may run until the latest-running patent covered in the parties' agreement expires. Too, post-expiration royalties are allowable so long as tied to a non-patent right—even when closely related to a patent. That means, for example, that a license involving both a patent and a trade secret can set a 5% royalty during the patent period (as compensation for the two combined) and a 4% royalty afterward (as payment for the trade secret alone). Finally and most broadly, *Brulotte* poses no bar to business arrangements other than royalties—all kinds of joint ventures, for example—that enable parties to share the risks and rewards of commercializing an invention.

Contending that such alternatives are not enough, Kimble asks us to abandon *Brulotte* in favor of "flexible, case-by-case analysis" of post-expiration royalty clauses "under the rule of reason." Used in antitrust law, the rule of reason requires courts to evaluate a practice's effect on competition by "taking into account a variety of factors, including specific information about the relevant business, its condition before and after the [practice] was imposed, and the [practice's] history, nature, and effect." Of primary importance in this context, Kimble posits, is whether a patent holder has power in the relevant market and so might be able to curtail competition.

Resolving that issue, Kimble notes, entails "a full-fledged economic inquiry into the definition of the market, barriers to entry, and the like."

III

[The Court discusses the doctrine of *stare decisis* and applying it to the case finds no reason to overrule *Brulotte*.]

IV

Lacking recourse to those traditional justifications for overruling a prior decision, Kimble offers two different ones. He claims first that *Brulotte* rests on a mistaken view of the competitive effects of post-expiration royalties. He contends next that *Brulotte* suppresses technological innovation and so harms the nation's economy. . . .

[The Court considers the two claims, but finds that "Kimble's reasoning may give Congress cause to upset *Brulotte*, but does not warrant this Court's doing so."]

What we can decide, we can undecide. But *stare decisis* teaches that we should exercise that authority sparingly. Finding many reasons for staying the stare decisis course and no "special justification" for departing from it, we decline Kimble's invitation to overrule *Brulotte*.

For the reasons stated, the judgment of the Court of Appeals is affirmed.

It is so ordered.

JUSTICE ALITO, WITH WHOM THE CHIEF JUSTICE AND JUSTICE THOMAS JOIN, DISSENTING.

The Court employs *stare decisis*, normally a tool of restraint, to reaffirm a clear case of judicial overreach. Our decision in *Brulotte v. Thys Co.*, 379 U.S. 29 (1964), held that parties cannot enter into a patent licensing agreement that provides for royalty payments to continue after the term of the patent expires. That decision was not based on anything that can plausibly be regarded as an interpretation of the terms of the Patent Act. It was based instead on an economic theory—and one that has been debunked. The decision interferes with the ability of parties to negotiate licensing agreements that reflect the true value of a patent, and it disrupts contractual expectations. *Stare decisis* does not require us to retain this baseless and damaging precedent.

. . .

b. *License Royalties on Unpatented, Publicly Disclosed Products*

Aronson v. Quick Point Pencil Co.

Supreme Court of the United States

440 U.S. 257 (1979)

MR. CHIEF JUSTICE BURGER DELIVERED THE OPINION OF THE COURT.

We granted certiorari, 436 U.S. 943, to consider whether federal patent law preempts state contract law so as to preclude enforcement of a contract to pay royalties to a patent applicant, on sales of articles embodying the putative invention, for so long as the contracting party sells them, if a patent is not granted.

(1)

In October 1955 the petitioner, Mrs. Jane Aronson, filed an application, Serial No. 542677, for a patent on a new form of keyholder. Although ingenious, the design was so simple that it readily could be copied unless it was protected by patent. In June 1956, while the patent application was pending, Mrs. Aronson negotiated a contract with the respondent, Quick Point Pencil Co., for the manufacture and sale of the keyholder.

The contract was embodied in two documents. In the first, a letter from Quick Point to Mrs. Aronson, Quick Point agreed to pay Mrs. Aronson a royalty of 5% of the selling price in return for "the exclusive right to make and sell keyholders of the type shown in your application, Serial No. 542677." The letter further provided that the parties would consult one another concerning the steps to be taken "[in] the event of any infringement."

The contract did not require Quick Point to manufacture the keyholder. Mrs. Aronson received a $750 advance on royalties and was entitled to rescind the exclusive license if Quick Point did not sell a million keyholders by the end of 1957. Quick Point retained the right to cancel the agreement whenever "the volume of sales does not meet our expectations." The duration of the agreement was not otherwise prescribed.

A contemporaneous document provided that if Mrs. Aronson's patent application was "not allowed within five (5) years, Quick Point Pencil Co. [would] pay . . . two and one half percent (2 1/2%) of sales . . . so long as you [Quick Point] continue to sell same."**

In June 1961, when Mrs. Aronson had failed to obtain a patent on the keyholder within the five years specified in the agreement, Quick Point asserted its contractual right to reduce royalty payments to 2 1/2% of sales. In September of that year the Board of Patent Appeals issued a final rejection of the application on the ground that the keyholder was not patentable, and Mrs. Aronson did not appeal. Quick Point continued to pay reduced royalties to her for 14 years thereafter.

The market was more receptive to the keyholder's novelty and utility than the Patent Office. By September 1975 Quick Point had made sales in excess of $7 million

---

**In April 1961, while Mrs. Aronson's patent application was pending, her husband sought a patent on a different keyholder and made plans to license another company to manufacture it. Quick Point's attorney wrote to the couple that the proposed new license would violate the 1956 agreement. He observed that

> "your license agreement is in respect of the disclosure of said Jane [Aronson's] application (not merely in respect of its claims) and that even if no patent is ever granted on the Jane [Aronson] application, *Quick Point Pencil Company is obligated to pay royalties in respect of any keyholder manufactured by it in accordance with any disclosure of said application.*" (Emphasis added.)

and paid Mrs. Aronson royalties totaling $203,963.84; sales were continuing to rise. However, while Quick Point was able to pre-empt the market in the earlier years and was long the only manufacturer of the Aronson keyholder, copies began to appear in the late 1960's. Quick Point's competitors, of course, were not required to pay royalties for their use of the design. Quick Point's share of the Aronson keyholder market has declined during the past decade.

(2)

In November 1975 Quick Point commenced an action in the United States District Court for a declaratory judgment, pursuant to 28 U.S.C. § 2201, that the royalty agreement was unenforceable. Quick Point asserted that state law which might otherwise make the contract enforceable was pre-empted by federal patent law. This is the only issue presented to us for decision.

(3)

On this record it is clear that the parties contracted with full awareness of both the pendency of a patent application and the possibility that a patent might not issue. The clause de-escalating the royalty by half in the event no patent issued within five years makes that crystal clear. Quick Point apparently placed a significant value on exploiting the basic novelty of the device, even if no patent issued; its success demonstrates that this judgment was well founded. Assuming, *arguendo*, that the initial letter and the commitment to pay a 5% royalty was subject to federal patent law, the provision relating to the 2 1/2% royalty was explicitly independent of federal law. The cases and principles relied on by the Court of Appeals and Quick Point do not bear on a contract that does not rely on a patent, particularly where, as here, the contracting parties agreed expressly as to alternative obligations if no patent should issue.

Commercial agreements traditionally are the domain of state law. State law is not displaced merely because the contract relates to intellectual property which may or may not be patentable; the states are free to regulate the use of such intellectual property in any manner not inconsistent with federal law. *Kewanee Oil Co. v. Bicron Corp.*, 416 U.S. 470, 479 (1974); see *Goldstein v. California*, 412 U.S. 546 (1973). In this as in other fields, the question of whether federal law pre-empts state law "involves a consideration of whether that law 'stands as an obstacle to the accomplishment and execution of the full purposes and objectives of Congress.' . . . " If it does not, state law governs.

In *Kewanee Oil Co.*, we reviewed the purposes of the federal patent system. First, patent law seeks to foster and reward invention; second, it promotes disclosure of inventions to stimulate further innovation and to permit the public to practice the invention once the patent expires; third, the stringent requirements for patent protection seek to assure that ideas in the public domain remain there for the free use of the public.

Enforcement of Quick Point's agreement with Mrs. Aronson is not inconsistent with any of these aims. Permitting inventors to make enforceable agreements licensing the use of their inventions in return for royalties provides an additional incentive to invention. Similarly, encouraging Mrs. Aronson to make arrangements for the manufacture of her keyholder furthers the federal policy of disclosure of inventions; these simple devices display the novel idea which they embody wherever they are seen.

Quick Point argues that enforcement of such contracts conflicts with the federal policy against withdrawing ideas from the public domain and discourages recourse to the federal patent system by allowing states to extend "perpetual protection to articles too lacking in novelty to merit any patent at all under federal constitutional standards," *Sears, Roebuck & Co. v. Stiffel Co.*, 376 U.S. 225, 232 (1964).

We find no merit in this contention. Enforcement of the agreement does not withdraw any idea from the public domain. The design for the keyholder was not in the public domain before Quick Point obtained its license to manufacture it. In negotiating the agreement, Mrs. Aronson disclosed the design in confidence. Had Quick Point tried to exploit the design in breach of that confidence, it would have risked legal liability. It is equally clear that the design entered the public domain as a result of the manufacture and sale of the keyholders under the contract.

Requiring Quick Point to bear the burden of royalties for the use of the design is no more inconsistent with federal patent law than any of the other costs involved in being the first to introduce a new product to the market, such as outlays for research and development, and marketing and promotional expenses. For reasons which Quick Point's experience with the Aronson keyholder demonstrate, innovative entrepreneurs have usually found such costs to be well worth paying.

Finally, enforcement of this agreement does not discourage anyone from seeking a patent. Mrs. Aronson attempted to obtain a patent for over five years. It is quite true that had she succeeded, she would have received a 5% royalty only on keyholders sold during the 17-year life of the patent. Offsetting the limited terms of royalty payments, she would have received twice as much per dollar of Quick Point's sales, and both she and Quick Point could have licensed any others who produced the same keyholder. Which course would have produced the greater yield to the contracting parties is a matter of speculation; the parties resolved the uncertainties by their bargain.

(4)

No decision of this Court relating to patents justifies relieving Quick Point of its contract obligations. We have held that a state may not forbid the copying of an idea in the public domain which does not meet the requirements for federal patent protection. Enforcement of Quick Point's agreement, however, does not prevent anyone from copying the keyholder. It merely requires Quick Point to pay the consideration which it promised in return for the use of a novel device which enabled it to preempt the market.

In *Lear, Inc. v. Adkins*, 395 U.S. 653 (1969), we held that a person licensed to use a patent may challenge the validity of the patent, and that a licensee who establishes that the patent is invalid need not pay the royalties accrued under the licensing agreement subsequent to the issuance of the patent. Both holdings relied on the desirability of encouraging licensees to challenge the validity of patents, to further the strong federal policy that only inventions which meet the rigorous requirements of patentability shall be withdrawn from the public domain. Accordingly, neither the holding nor the rationale of *Lear* controls when no patent has issued, and no ideas have been withdrawn from public use.

Enforcement of the royalty agreement here is also consistent with the principles treated in *Brulotte v. Thys Co.*, 379 U.S. 29 (1964). There, we held that the obligation to pay royalties in return for the use of a patented device may not extend beyond the life of the patent. The principle underlying that holding was simply that the monopoly granted *under a patent* cannot lawfully be used to "negotiate with the leverage of that monopoly." The Court emphasized that to "use that leverage to project those royalty payments beyond the life of the patent is analogous to an effort to enlarge the monopoly of the patent . . . ." *Id.* at 33. Here the reduced royalty which is challenged, far from being negotiated "with the leverage" of a patent, rested on the contingency that no patent would issue within five years.

No doubt a pending patent application gives the applicant some additional bargaining power for purposes of negotiating a royalty agreement. The pending application allows the inventor to hold out the hope of an exclusive right to exploit the idea, as well as the threat that the other party will be prevented from using the idea for 17 years. However, the amount of leverage arising from a patent application depends on how likely the parties consider it to be that a valid patent will issue. Here, where no patent ever issued, the record is entirely clear that the parties assigned a substantial likelihood to that contingency, since they specifically provided for a reduced royalty in the event no patent issued within five years.

This case does not require us to draw the line between what constitutes abuse of a pending application and what does not. It is clear that whatever role the pending application played in the negotiation of the 5% royalty, it played no part in the contract to pay the 2 1/2% royalty indefinitely.

Our holding in *Kewanee Oil Co.* puts to rest the contention that federal law preempts and renders unenforceable the contract made by these parties. There we held that state law forbidding the misappropriation of trade secrets was not pre-empted by federal patent law. We observed:

> "Certainly the patent policy of encouraging invention is not disturbed by the existence of another form of incentive to invention. In this respect the two systems [patent and trade secret law] are not and never would be in conflict." 416 U.S. at 484.

Enforcement of this royalty agreement is even less offensive to federal patent policies than state law protecting trade secrets. The most commonly accepted definition of trade secrets is restricted to confidential information which is not disclosed in the normal process of exploitation. *See* Restatement of Torts § 757, Comment *b*, p. 5 (1939). Accordingly, the exploitation of trade secrets under state law may not satisfy the federal policy in favor of disclosure, whereas disclosure is inescapable in exploiting a device like the Aronson keyholder.

Enforcement of these contractual obligations, freely undertaken in arm's-length negotiation and with no fixed reliance on a patent or a probable patent grant, will

> "encourage invention in areas where patent law does not reach, and will prompt the independent innovator to proceed with the discovery and exploitation of his invention. Competition is fostered and the public is not deprived of the use of valuable, if not quite patentable, invention." 416 U.S. at 485 (Footnote omitted).

The device which is the subject of this contract ceased to have any secrecy as soon as it was first marketed, yet when the contract was negotiated the inventiveness and novelty were sufficiently apparent to induce an experienced novelty manufacturer to agree to pay for the opportunity to be first in the market. Federal patent law is not a barrier to such a contract.

Reversed.

Mr. Justice Blackmun, concurring in the result.

For me, the hard question is whether this case can meaningfully be distinguished from *Brulotte* v. *Thys Co.*, 379 U.S. 29 (1964). There the Court held that a patent licensor could not use the leverage of its patent to obtain a royalty contract that extended beyond the patent's 17-year term. Here Mrs. Aronson has used the leverage of her patent application to negotiate a royalty contract which continues to be binding even though the patent application was long ago denied.

The Court . . . asserts that her leverage played "no part" with respect to the contingent agreement to pay a reduced royalty if no patent issued within five years. Yet it may well be that Quick Point agreed to that contingency in order to obtain its other rights that depended on the success of the patent application. The parties did not apportion consideration in the neat fashion the Court adopts.

In my view, the holding in *Brulotte* reflects hostility toward extension of a patent monopoly whose term is fixed by statute, 35 U.S.C. § 154. Such hostility has no place here. A patent application which is later denied temporarily discourages unlicensed imitators. Its benefits and hazards are of a different magnitude from those of a granted patent that prohibits all competition for 17 years. Nothing justifies estopping a patent-application licensor from entering into a contract whose term does not end if the application fails. The Court points out, that enforcement of this contract does not conflict with the objectives of the patent laws. The United States, as *amicus curiae*, maintains that patent-application licensing of this sort is desirable because it encourages patent applications, promotes early disclosure, and allows parties to structure their bargains efficiently.

On this basis, I concur in the Court's holding that federal patent law does not preempt the enforcement of Mrs. Aronson's contract with Quick Point.

Notes & Questions

1. Royalties Prior to the Issuance of a Patent

Patent protection does not commence until the issuance of a patent. During the pendency of a patent application, the subject matter of the patent application may instead be protected under trade secret law. Any monetary consideration paid prior to the issuance of a patent therefore is not technically a patent royalty. Despite this fact, parties negotiating a licensing contract concerning a patent that is expected to result from a pending patent application may agree to the payment of a pre-issuance royalty.

Prior to the issuance of a patent, a licensor may characterize pre-issuance royalties as payment for the option to take a patent license once the patent issues, or as consideration in exchange for disclosure of the matter. By granting two separate contractual rights in the licensing contract, a licensor may avoid challenges by the licensee over the obligation to pay pre-issuance royalties.

2. Right to Elect Trade Secret Protection

So long as the subject matter of a patent application is maintained a secret, trade secret protection covers the period prior to patent issuance. Of course, inventors may choose to rely entirely on trade secret protection and elect not to patent their invention at all. Even if an inventor chooses to apply for a patent, certain aspects of the invention may be retained as a trade secret, so long as the best mode and written description requirements of patent law are met. Trade secret licensing is discussed later, in Section B of this chapter.

4. Limits on Patent Rights
a. Patent Exhaustion and the First Sale Doctrine

Quanta Computer, Inc. v. LG Electronics, Inc.
Supreme Court of the United States
553 U.S. 617 (2008)

JUSTICE THOMAS DELIVERED THE OPINION OF THE COURT.

For over 150 years this Court has applied the doctrine of patent exhaustion to limit the patent rights that survive the initial authorized sale of a patented item. In this case, we decide whether patent exhaustion applies to the sale of components of a patented system that must be combined with additional components in order to practice the patented methods. The Court of Appeals for the Federal Circuit held that the doctrine does not apply to method patents at all and, in the alternative, that it does not apply here because the sales were not authorized by the license agreement. We disagree on both scores. Because the exhaustion doctrine applies to method patents, and because the license authorizes the sale of components that substantially embody the patents in suit, the sale exhausted the patents.

I

Respondent LG Electronics, Inc. (LGE), purchased a portfolio of computer technology patents in 1999, including the three patents at issue here: U.S. Patent Nos. 4,939,641 ('641); 5,379,379 ('379); and 5,077,733 ('733) (collectively LGE Patents) . . . .

LGE licensed a patent portfolio, including the LGE Patents, to Intel Corporation (Intel). The cross-licensing agreement (License Agreement) permits Intel to manufacture and sell microprocessors and chipsets that use the LGE Patents (the Intel Products). The License Agreement authorizes Intel to "make, use, sell (directly or indirectly), offer to sell, import or otherwise dispose of" its own products practicing the LGE Patents. Notwithstanding this broad language, the License Agreement contains some limitations. Relevant here, it stipulates that no license "is granted by either party hereto . . . to any third party for the combination by a third party of Licensed Products of either party with items, components, or the like acquired . . . from sources other than a party hereto, or for the use, import, offer for sale or sale of such combination." The License Agreement purports not to alter the usual rules of patent exhaustion, however, providing that, "[n]otwithstanding anything to the contrary contained in this Agreement, the parties agree that nothing herein shall in any way limit or alter the effect of patent exhaustion that would otherwise apply when a party hereto sells any of its Licensed Products."

In a separate agreement (Master Agreement), Intel agreed to give written notice to its own customers informing them that, while it had obtained a broad license "ensur[ing] that any Intel product that you purchase is licensed by LGE and thus does not infringe any patent held by LGE," the license "does not extend, expressly or by implication, to any product that you make by combining an Intel product with any non-Intel product." The Master Agreement also provides that "a breach of this Agreement shall have no effect on and shall not be grounds for termination of the Patent License."

Petitioners, including Quanta Computer (collectively Quanta), are a group of computer manufacturers. Quanta purchased microprocessors and chipsets from Intel and received the notice required by the Master Agreement. Nonetheless, Quanta manufactured computers using Intel parts in combination with non-Intel memory and buses in ways that practice the LGE Patents. Quanta does not modify the Intel components and follows Intel's specifications to incorporate the parts into its own systems.

LGE filed a complaint against Quanta, asserting that the combination of the Intel Products with non-Intel memory and buses infringed the LGE Patents. The District Court granted summary judgment to Quanta, holding that, for purposes of the patent exhaustion doctrine, the license LGE granted to Intel resulted in forfeiture of any potential infringement actions against legitimate purchasers of the Intel Products. In a subsequent order limiting its summary judgment ruling, the court held that patent exhaustion applies only to apparatus or composition-of-matter claims that describe a physical object, and does not apply to process, or method claims that describe operations to make or use a product. Because each of the LGE Patents includes method claims, exhaustion did not apply.

The Court of Appeals for the Federal Circuit affirmed in part and reversed in part. It agreed that the doctrine of patent exhaustion does not apply to method claims. In the alternative, it concluded that exhaustion did not apply because LGE did not license

Intel to sell the Intel Products to Quanta for use in combination with non-Intel products.

II

The longstanding doctrine of patent exhaustion provides that the initial authorized sale of a patented item terminates all patent rights to that item.

. . . .

Although the Court permitted postsale restrictions on the use of a patented article in *Henry v. A.B. Dick Co.*, 224 U.S. 1 (1912), that decision was short lived. In 1913, the Court refused to apply *A.B. Dick* to uphold price-fixing provisions in a patent license. Shortly thereafter, in *Motion Picture Patents Co. v. Universal Film Mfg. Co.*, 243 U.S. 502 (1917), the Court explicitly overruled *A.B. Dick*. In that case, a patent holder attempted to limit purchasers' use of its film projectors to show only film made under a patent held by the same company. The Court noted the "increasing frequency" with which patent holders were using *A.B. Dick*-style licenses to limit the use of their products and thereby using the patents to secure market control of related, unpatented items. Observing that "the primary purpose of our patent laws is not the creation of private fortunes for the owners of patents but is 'to promote the progress of science and useful arts,'" (quoting U.S. Const., Art. I, § 8, cl. 8), the Court held that "the scope of the grant which may be made to an inventor in a patent, pursuant to the [patent] statute, must be limited to the invention described in the claims of his patent." Accordingly, it reiterated the rule that "the right to vend is exhausted by a single, unconditional sale, the article sold being thereby carried outside the monopoly of the patent law and rendered free of every restriction which the vendor may attempt to put upon it."

This Court most recently discussed patent exhaustion in *Univis*, 316 U.S. 241, on which the District Court relied. Univis Lens Company, the holder of patents on eyeglass lenses, licensed a purchaser to manufacture lens blanks by fusing together different lens segments to create bi- and tri-focal lenses and to sell them to other Univis licensees at agreed-upon rates. Wholesalers were licensed to grind the blanks into the patented finished lenses, which they would then sell to Univis-licensed prescription retailers for resale at a fixed rate. Finishing retailers, after grinding the blanks into patented lenses, would sell the finished lenses to consumers at the same fixed rate. The United States sued Univis under the Sherman Act, 15 U.S.C. §§ 1, 3, 15, alleging unlawful restraints on trade. Univis asserted its patent monopoly rights as a defense to the antitrust suit. The Court granted certiorari to determine whether Univis' patent monopoly survived the sale of the lens blanks by the licensed manufacturer and therefore shielded Univis' pricing scheme from the Sherman Act.

The Court assumed that the Univis patents containing claims for finished lenses were practiced in part by the wholesalers and finishing retailers who ground the blanks into lenses, and held that the sale of the lens blanks exhausted the patents on the finished lenses. The Court explained that the lens blanks "embodi[ed] essential features of the patented device and [were] without utility until . . . ground and polished as the finished lens of the patent. The Court noted that: "where one has sold an uncompleted article which, because it embodies essential features of his patented invention, is within the protection of his patent, and has destined the article to be finished by the purchaser in conformity to the patent, he has sold his invention so far as it is or may be embodied in that particular article."

In sum, the Court concluded that the traditional bar on patent restrictions following the sale of an item applies when the item sufficiently embodies the patent-even if it does not completely practice the patent-such that its only and intended use is to be finished under the terms of the patent.

With this history of the patent exhaustion doctrine in mind, we turn to the parties' arguments.

III

A.

LGE argues that the exhaustion doctrine is inapplicable here because it does not apply to method claims, which are contained in each of the LGE Patents. LGE reasons that, because method patents are linked not to a tangible article but to a process, they can never be exhausted through a sale. Rather, practicing the patent-which occurs upon each use of an article embodying a method patent-is permissible only to the extent rights are transferred in an assignment contract. Quanta, in turn, argues that there is no reason to preclude exhaustion of method claims, and points out that both this Court and the Federal Circuit have applied exhaustion to method claims. It argues that any other rule would allow patent holders to avoid exhaustion entirely by inserting method claims in their patent specifications.

Quanta has the better of this argument. Nothing in this Court's approach to patent exhaustion supports LGE's argument that method patents cannot be exhausted. It is true that a patented method may not be sold in the same way as an article or device, but methods nonetheless may be "embodied" in a product, the sale of which exhausts patent rights. Our precedents do not differentiate transactions involving embodiments of patented methods or processes from those involving patented apparatuses or materials. To the contrary, this Court has repeatedly held that method patents were exhausted by the sale of an item that embodied the method.

Eliminating exhaustion for method patents would seriously undermine the exhaustion doctrine. Apparatus and method claims "may approach each other so nearly that it will be difficult to distinguish the process from the function of the apparatus." By characterizing their claims as method instead of apparatus claims, or including a method claim for the machine's patented method of performing its task, a patent drafter could shield practically any patented item from exhaustion.

This case illustrates the danger of allowing such an end-run around exhaustion. On LGE's theory, although Intel is authorized to sell a completed computer system that practices the LGE Patents, any downstream purchasers of the system could nonetheless be liable for patent infringement. Such a result would violate the long-standing principle that, when a patented item is "once lawfully made and sold, there is no restriction on [its] use to be implied for the benefit of the patentee." We therefore reject LGE's argument that method claims, as a category, are never exhaustible.

B.

We next consider the extent to which a product must embody a patent in order to trigger exhaustion.

. . . .

We agree with Quanta that *Univis* governs this case. As the Court there explained, exhaustion was triggered by the sale of the lens blanks because their only reasonable and intended use was to practice the patent and because they "embodie[d] essential features of [the] patented invention." Each of those attributes is shared by the microprocessors and chipsets Intel sold to Quanta under the License Agreement.

First, *Univis* held that "the authorized sale of an article which is capable of use only in practicing the patent is a relinquishment of the patent monopoly with respect to the article sold." The lens blanks in *Univis* met this standard because they were "without utility until [they were] ground and polished as the finished lens of the patent." Accordingly, "the only object of the sale [was] to enable the [finishing retailer] to grind and polish it for use as a lens by the prospective wearer." Here, LGE has suggested no reasonable use for the Intel Products other than incorporating them into computer systems that practice the LGE Patents. Nor can we discern one: A microprocessor or chipset cannot function until it is connected to buses and memory. And here, as in *Univis*, the only apparent object of Intel's sales to Quanta was to permit Quanta to incorporate the Intel Products into computers that would practice the patents.

Second, the lens blanks in *Univis* "embodie[d] essential features of [the] patented invention." The essential, or inventive, feature of the Univis lens patents was the fusing together of different lens segments to create bi- and trifocal lenses. The finishing process performed by the finishing and prescription retailers after the fusing was not unique.

Like the Univis lens blanks, the Intel Products constitute a material part of the patented invention and all but completely practice the patent. Here, as in *Univis*, the incomplete article substantially embodies the patent because the only step necessary to practice the patent is the application of common processes or the addition of standard parts. Everything inventive about each patent is embodied in the Intel Products. . . . The Intel Products were specifically designed to function only when memory or buses are attached; Quanta was not required to make any creative or inventive decision when it added those parts. Indeed, Quanta had no alternative but to follow Intel's specifications in incorporating the Intel Products into its computers because it did not know their internal structure, which Intel guards as a trade secret. Intel all but practiced the patent itself by designing its products to practice the patents, lacking only the addition of standard parts.

With regard to LGE's argument that exhaustion does not apply across patents, we agree on the general principle: The sale of a device that practices patent A does not, by virtue of practicing patent A, exhaust patent B. But if the device practices patent A while substantially embodying patent B, its relationship to patent A does not prevent exhaustion of patent B. For example, if the Univis lens blanks had been composed of shatter-resistant glass under patent A, the blanks would nonetheless have substantially embodied, and therefore exhausted, patent B for the finished lenses. This case is no different. While each Intel microprocessor and chipset practices thousands of individual patents, including some LGE patents not at issue in this case, the exhaustion analysis is not altered by the fact that more than one patent is practiced by the same product. The relevant consideration is whether the Intel Products that partially practice a patent-by, for example, embodying its essential features-exhaust *that* patent.

C.

Having concluded that the Intel Products embodied the patents, we next consider whether their sale to Quanta exhausted LGE's patent rights. Exhaustion is triggered only by a sale authorized by the patent holder.

. . . .

LGE overlooks important aspects of the structure of the Intel-LGE transaction. Nothing in the License Agreement restricts Intel's right to sell its microprocessors and chipsets to purchasers who intend to combine them with non-Intel parts. It broadly permits Intel to "'make, use, [or] sell'" products free of LGE's patent claims. To be sure, LGE did require Intel to give notice to its customers, including Quanta, that LGE had not licensed those customers to practice its patents. But neither party contends that Intel breached the agreement in that respect. In any event, the provision requiring notice to Quanta appeared only in the Master Agreement, and LGE does not suggest that a breach of that agreement would constitute a breach of the License Agreement. Hence, Intel's authority to sell its products embodying the LGE Patents was not conditioned on the notice or on Quanta's decision to abide by LGE's directions in that notice.

LGE points out that the License Agreement specifically disclaimed any license to third parties to practice the patents by combining licensed products with other components. But the question whether third parties received implied licenses is irrelevant because Quanta asserts its right to practice the patents based not on implied license but on exhaustion. And exhaustion turns only on Intel's own license to sell products practicing the LGE Patents.

The License Agreement authorized Intel to sell products that practiced the LGE Patents. No conditions limited Intel's authority to sell products substantially embodying the patents. Because Intel was authorized to sell its products to Quanta, the doctrine of patent exhaustion prevents LGE from further asserting its patent rights with respect to the patents substantially embodied by those products.

Notes & Questions

1. Features of Patent Exhaustion and the First Sale Doctrine

Both patent exhaustion and the first sale doctrine are justified by the definition of a sale in commercial law. Under Article 2 of the Uniform Commercial Code, a sale of a good requires payment upon delivery in exchange for the full rights to use the item that is sold. *See* U.C.C. § 2-106(1) (Am. Law Inst. & Unif. Law Comm'n 2003) (defining a sale as a "the passing of title from the seller to the buyer for a price."). Because the passing of a title requires transferring full rights to use the item, all intellectual property rights in the item that is sold are exhausted. The Supreme Court clarified further features of patent exhaustion and the first sale doctrine in *Impression Products, Inc. v. Lexmark International, Inc.*, 137 S. Ct. 1523 (2017). *Impression Products* presented two questions about the scope of the patent exhaustion doctrine. The first question concerned whether a patentee that sells an item under an express restriction on the purchaser's right to reuse or resell the product may enforce that restriction through a patent infringement lawsuit. The second question concerned whether a patentee exhausts its patent rights by selling its product outside the United States, where American patent laws do not apply. The Supreme Court ruled that a patentee's decision to sell a product exhausts all of its patent rights in that item, regardless of any restrictions the patentee purports to impose or the location of the sale. Portions of the Court's opinion in *Impression Products* addressing the antitrust implications of the transactions at issue are reproduced in Section C(2) of Chapter 11.

2. License versus Sale

Under the first sale doctrine, the earliest sale of an article "exhausts" the owner's patent rights as to that article. To avoid triggering exhaustion under the first sale doctrine, transfers of rights may be couched in terms of a licensing agreement. As Justice Roberts explained in *Impression Products*, "a license does not implicate the same concerns about restraints on alienation as a sale." 137 S. Ct. at 1534. Expressing the transfer of rights in terms of a license rather than in terms of an outright sale might give the patent owner greater control over subsequent transfers. However, the opinion in *Impression Products* also makes it clear that "patentee's authority to limit *licensees* does not . . . mean that patentees can use licenses to impose post-sale restrictions on *purchasers* that are enforceable through the patent laws." *Id.* at 1534–35 (emphasis in original). If a licensee sells an item, such sale is considered authorized by the patent owner if the seller-licensee complies with the license. *Id.* at 1535. After such authorized sale, the only remedy against the purchaser that the patent owner might have is that provided by contract law.

Agricultural biotechnology is one field where use of such licensing is prevalent. Patented plants present the patent holder with the unique problem of being self-replicating inventions. "Plant innovation is borne in seeds, and at least in the case of self-pollinating plants (such as soybeans), seeds make hundreds of copies of themselves in the natural growth process. From the standpoint of a producer of innovation, the notion of a self-replicating invention presents as compelling a case for intellectual property intervention as can be imagined." Mark D. Janis & Jay P. Kesan, *U.S. Plant Variety Protection: Sound and Fury . . . ?*, 39 Hous. L. REV. 727, 730 (2002). Producers of patented seeds turn to "bag-tag" licenses to place restrictions on a grower's use of the seed, thus shielding the seed from being the "subject of any unconditional sale" and "allowing seed companies to assert that the patent law exhaustion doctrine should not be triggered." *Id.* at 771 n.156. In *Monsanto Co. v. McFarling*, 302 F.3d 1291 (Fed. Cir. 2002), *cert. denied*, 537 U.S. 1232 (2003), a farmer, McFarling, purchased patented genetically modified soybeans from Monsanto under a licensing agreement. He planted and harvested a crop and saved the seeds for planting in the next season. McFarling argued that, by purchasing the seed from Monsanto, he had acquired the right to produce additional seeds for planting under the doctrines of patent exhaustion and first sale. The Federal Circuit disagreed:

> The restrictions in the [parties' agreement] are within the scope of the patent grant, for the patents cover the seeds as well as the plants. The "first sale" doctrine of exhaustion of the patent right is not implicated, as the new seeds grown from the original batch had never been sold. The price paid by the purchaser "reflects only the value of the 'use' rights conferred by the patentee." (Citation omitted). The original sale of the seeds did not confer a license to construct new seeds, and since the new seeds were not sold by the patentee they entailed no principle of patent exhaustion.

Monsanto, 302 F.3d at 1298–99. "Bag-tag" licenses protect a patent owner by conferring less than all of the rights in a patented plant, and disclaiming an unconditioned sale of the entire material.

Software is another field where use of licensing agreements has attained widespread use. It is more common for software "sales" to be licenses rather than outright sales. Copyright law, like patent law, has a first sale doctrine. Form licenses for software were first developed to avoid the copyright first sale doctrine, which allowed an owner of a copy of a work to "sell or otherwise dispose of" the copy without the copyright holder's consent. *Step-Saver Data Systems, Inc. v. Wyse Technology*, 939 F.2d 91, 96 n.7 (3d Cir. 1991) (quoting *Bobbs-Merrill Co. v. Straus*, 210 U.S. 339 (1908)). Copying of the work was a great concern for software producers:

> Under [the first sale] doctrine, one could purchase a copy of a computer program, and then lease it or lend it to another without infringing the copyright on the program. Because of the ease of copying software, software producers were justifiably concerned that companies would spring up that would purchase copies of various programs and then lease those to consumers. Typically, the companies, like a videotape rental store, would purchase a number of copies of each program, and then make them available for over-night rental to consumers. Consumers, instead of purchasing their own copy of the program, would simply rent a copy of the program,

and duplicate it. This copying by the individual consumers would presumably infringe the copyright, but usually it would be far too expensive for the copyright holder to identify and sue each individual copier. Thus, software producers wanted to sue the companies that were renting the copies of the program to individual consumers, rather than the individual consumers. The first sale doctrine, though, stood as a substantial barrier to successful suit against these software rental companies, even under a theory of contributory infringement. By characterizing the original transaction between the software producer and the software rental company as a license, rather than a sale, and by making the license personal and non-transferable, software producers hoped to avoid the reach of the first sale doctrine and to establish a basis in state contract law for suing the software rental companies directly.

Step-Saver 939 F.2d at 96 n.7. The cost of software development, coupled with the ease of copying, encouraged software producers to protect their program by licensing their material, rather than subjecting it to an outright sale. With a license, the software producer may prohibit the consumer from making and selling unauthorized copies of the program.

3. Patent Exhaustion and Scope of an Implied License

Although most licenses are expressed as written agreements, a license may be implied from the circumstances of a sale. Two conditions are required to find an implied license: (1) the item sold must have no noninfringing uses, and (2) the circumstances of the sale must plainly indicate that the grant of a license should be inferred. In *Carborundum v. Molten Metal*, 72 F.3d 872 (Fed. Cir. 1995), Molten Metal Equipment Innovations, Inc. ("MMEI") sold unpatented pumps that allowed customers to practice the plaintiff's patented process for purifying metals. MMEI's patent infringement liability turned, in part, on sales activities of the plaintiff patent holder, doing business as Metaullics Systems Division and Metaullics Systems Co. L.P. (collectively "Metaullics"). The defendant's liability depended on the scope of the patent license that the plaintiff patent holder (acting through its Metaullics unit) impliedly gave to Metaullics' customers in connection with Metaullics' sales of unpatented equipment related to the patented process:

> MMEI argues that Metaullics' sale of the pumps, which had no other use than in the '584 gas injection apparatus, resulted in an unrestricted implied license to practice the invention for the entire term of the '584 patent. MMEI further asserts that restrictions on an implied license cannot be implied, but must be express. Because Metaullics placed no express restrictions on the use of the pumps, MMEI posits that Metaullics' customers obtained an unrestricted implied license to practice the invention. Thus, according to MMEI, customers who replaced a Metaullics pump with an MMEI pump could not be direct infringers under the unrestricted implied license. Absent

direct infringement, MMEI argues that it could not contribute to or induce infringement. Although we agree with MMEI that Metaullics' customers had an implied license to practice the invention claimed in the '584 patent, we disagree as to the scope and meaning of that license.

. . . .

Here, Metaullics sold an unpatented pump; the only use of the pump was in the metal purification apparatus of the '584 patent. Metaullics did not place any express restrictions on its customers as to the use of the pump. The circumstances of such a sale plainly indicate that a license should be implied under the apparatus patent. Metaullics and its customers are presumed to have intended that at the time the customer purchased the pump, the customer was free to use it for its intended purpose to practice the invention claimed in the '584 patent . . . . Otherwise, the pump was worthless because it had no other practical use. Moreover, once Metaullics sold the pump without restriction, the parties to the sale were presumed to have intended that the purchaser was free to repair it with parts obtained from any source. However, Metaullics and its customers cannot be presumed to have intended that under these circumstances the implied license extended beyond the life of the pump. Unless the circumstances indicate otherwise, an implied license arising from sale of a component to be used in a patented combination extends only for the life of the component whose sale and purchase created the license.

Carborundum, 72 F.3d at 878–79. Therefore, *Carborundum* is in accord with the notion that a license, whether express or implied, provides a licensee with only limited rights in the invention and, unlike a sale, does not exhaust the patentee's rights in the licensed technology.

b. Compulsory Licenses

A compulsory license is a license forced upon a patent holder or other intellectual property owner by statute or court order. In the United States compulsory licenses for patents are rarely awarded by courts or imposed by statutes. Even if a patentee refuses to license her patent to others, she usually may not be forced to do so against her will. The owner of a patent is not required to license the patent and is allowed to unilaterally refuse to grant a license.

Under limited circumstances, a court may award a mandatory license or dedicate the patent to the public. These circumstances include when a patentee is found to have engaged in illegal or injurious conduct beyond a mere refusal to grant a license; when the patentee is found to have violated antitrust laws; and when public health, public safety, or some other public interest is implicated. Compulsory licensing most commonly appears in fields that affect public health or safety, justified by "public necessity."

Besides judicially awarded compulsory licenses, Congress may enact statutes that permit use of a patented invention without the patent owner's consent. Congress has passed some mandatory licensing statutes that require patentees to license their inventions, for example, the Clean Air Act of 1970, 42 U.S.C. § 7608 [transferred: Air Pollution Prevention and Control Act]; the Plant Variety Protection Act, 7 U.S.C. § 2402; the Helium Act, 50 U.S.C. § 167. In addition, the United States government may take and use patented inventions. When the United States government uses a patented invention without the permission of the patent owner, Title 28 of the United States Code, Section 1498 restricts the remedy of the patent owner to "action against the United States in the United States Court of Federal Claims for the recovery of his reasonable and entire compensation for such use and manufacture." 28 U.S.C. § 1498.

The pharmaceutical industry is a favorite target of proposed mandatory licensing statutes. Congress has proposed bills that, for example, would have allowed the FTC to order the "unrestricted, unconditional compulsory licensing of patents and trademarks related to prescription pharmaceuticals." *See* H.R. 9276, 94th Cong., 1st Sess. ("Prescription Drug Patent Licensing Act"). Another bill would have imposed what would have amounted to a compulsory trademark and trade dress license by barring protection under the Lanham Act for distinctive colors and pharmaceutical product configurations. *See* H.R. 6840, 97th Cong., 2d Sess. None of these proposals have been enacted into law. In the aftermath of the tragedies of September 11, 2001, the United States faced a national crisis after 22 cases of anthrax were reported on the East Coast, resulting in five fatalities. Secretary of Health and Human Services, Tommy Thompson threatened to disregard the patent covering ciprofloxacin (Cipro), a drug approved to combat anthrax, if the drug manufacturer (Bayer) would not reduce its drug price. Bayer quickly complied.

Internationally, the World Trade Organization's agreement on Trade Related Intellectual Property Rights (TRIPS) established minimum standards of protection for intellectual property but also provided exceptions to override patent rights for public health reasons. Article 27(2) of the TRIPS agreement allows members to exclude patent protection to the extent "necessary to protect *ordre public* or morality, including to protect human, animal, or plant life or health or to avoid serious prejudice to the environment." Some have noted that the doctrine of *"ordre public"* may allow member countries to suspend patent protection for certain patents. In addition, article 31 of the TRIPS agreement expressly permits compulsory licensing. Member nations must first attempt unsuccessfully to obtain a voluntary license from the patent holder before compulsorily licensing the patent. However, the requirement for applying for a voluntary license is waived for "national emergency or other circumstances of extreme urgency or in cases of public noncommercial use." Further, for pharmaceuticals, Article 31(f) permits a country that lacks drug-manufacturing capabilities to import compulsorily licensed pharmaceuticals from another country.

5. Cross-Licensing

a. *Why Enter into a Cross-Licensing Agreement?*

Texas Instruments v. Hyundai Electronics Industries

United States District Court for the Eastern District of Texas

49 F. Supp. 2d 893 (E.D. Tex. 1999)

HEARTFIELD, DISTRICT JUDGE.

On May 1, 1998, Texas Instruments sued Hyundai for patent infringement in this Court and in several other courts across the nation and, eventually, around the world. Simultaneously, Hyundai sued Texas Instruments for declaratory judgment and, eventually, patent infringement.

Seven cases between Texas Instruments and Hyundai eventually ended up in this Court; this case (the "74 Case") was the first set for trial on Monday, March 8, 1999. . . . After approximately two days of deliberations, the jury returned a verdict of infringement against Hyundai and in favor of Texas Instruments assessing damages at twenty-five million, two-hundred thousand United States dollars ($25,200,000.00). The jury further found that Hyundai willfully infringed Texas Instruments' patents. After the jury returned a verdict of infringement against Hyundai and in favor of Texas Instruments, this Court tried the remaining defense of patent misuse. . . .

I. FINDINGS OF FACT

1. Article 5.2(A)(ii)—The Sales Cap Provision That Won't Go Away

So Article 5.2(A)(ii), we meet again. Article 5.2(A)(ii) is the "sale cap" termination provision that automatically terminates the parties' License Agreement when Hyundai's worldwide sales of royalty bearing products reaches three billion eight hundred ninety-five million United States dollars ($3,895,000,000.00). The parties fell into a dispute over the proper interpretation of this unique provision. Texas Instruments argued that "royalty bearing products" included *all* products sold by Hyundai regardless whether those particular products were "covered by" a valid Texas Instruments patent—products which practiced a Texas Instruments patent, in force at the time the product is sold, in the country in which the sale occurs (the "TI Countries"). Hyundai disagreed. Hyundai argued that "royalty bearing products" were limited to products "covered by" a valid Texas Instruments patent—that is, products which practiced a Texas Instruments patent, in force at the time the product is sold, in the country in which the sale occurs.

. . . .

3. A Primer on Patent Portfolio Cross-License Agreements

. . . Texas Instruments has over four thousand (4,000) patents and files between seven hundred (700) and eight hundred (800) patent applications each year. Just last year, Texas Instruments had six hundred and eleven (611) new patents issued.

Hyundai has over one thousand two hundred (1,200) patents in the United States with a large number of pending applications. Large companies like Texas Instruments and Hyundai literally have thousands of patents around the world. With so many patents worldwide, it is quite possible for Texas Instruments and Hyundai to have multiple patents maturing and expiring every day.

A party to a license agreement covering only a single patent would have to determine before selling its product in a different country whether its sales would infringe any patents of the other party. This patent-specific determination would have to be done continually since new patents are constantly being issued. Moreover, these searches would also have to be done every time a party made a change in an existing product or came up with a new product. This patent-specific endeavor is extremely expensive and time-consuming. The product in question would have to be examined in detail and compared to the elements of the claims of the patent in question. Depending on the type of product, this product examination could take several months and costs tens of thousands of dollars—all to evaluate a single product against a single patent.

For parties with large semiconductor patent portfolios like Texas Instruments and Hyundai, what is the solution? Enter the patent portfolio cross-license agreement. The portfolio license is widely used in the semiconductor industry because it is almost impossible on a patent-by-patent, country-by-country, product-by-product basis to determine whether someone is using a company's patents in a given country and provide protection for patents not yet issued. First, under a patent-specific license agreement, the parties have an extremely difficult time tracking the sales that should be included in the royalty base. This difficulty arises from the fact that the holder of a patent is entitled to receive royalties for items sold both directly and indirectly into the country where the patent exists. Parties to license agreements track indirect sales in order to receive full and fair value for their patents. If parties look only at direct sales, they are not receiving fair value for their patents. Tracking sales that come into a specific country is exceedingly difficult, for the party trying to track indirect sales has to know not only where the other party is selling its products, but also the identity of the purchasers in order to determine the likelihood that those products would come into a country where the other party has patents. Second, worldwide license rights are necessary in the semiconductor market because the semiconductor market is a worldwide market. Companies in the semiconductor market do not have the luxury of selling only in one country. Third, for parties with large patent portfolios like Texas Instruments and Hyundai, it is impossible to examine the entire portfolio on a patent-by-patent, country-by-country basis for all possible products. Finally, it is impossible to determine whether a specific product is "covered by" a patent without litigation. By using this expansive cross-license agreement mechanism—the portfolio license—mammoth companies in the semiconductor industry like Texas Instruments and Hyundai avoid the costly and inefficient endeavor of a patent-by-patent licensing scheme.

4. This License Agreement Was a Portfolio Cross-License Agreement

The 1993 License Agreement was a portfolio cross-license agreement because Hyundai wanted "as broad as possible [a] license under [Texas Instruments'] patents." Hyundai's Mr. M. B. Chung specifically asked for a ten-year license that included Texas Instruments' entire portfolio, worldwide in scope, including all of Hyundai's products. Having just completed a license agreement with Samsung, Texas Instruments offered Hyundai a license with the same terms. Hyundai refused and requested Texas Instruments first demonstrate its patents would be of value to Hyundai. This is not a cheap endeavor. Indeed, Texas Instruments spent tens of thousands of dollars and several months complying with Hyundai's request. Due to the expense and time involved in this endeavor, Texas Instruments used only a very few of its patents as a proxy for the value of its entire portfolio.

After Hyundai started to bite and the cork started to bob, Texas Instruments offered Hyundai the same terms previously accepted by Samsung—a "running royalty" of nine (9) percent on sales of DRAMs ("dynamic random access memory" products) in the United States, and three (3) percent on sales of DRAMs in Japan. Texas Instruments proposed the "running royalty" agreement because it is the easiest way to accurately measure royalties. With a "running royalty," if sales go up, so does the total royalty payment. Conversely, if sales go down, so does the total royalty payment. Simply put, a running royalty is self-correcting.

Hyundai absolutely refused to discuss any running royalty; instead, Hyundai insisted on a fixed (or lump-sum) approach. In April 1991, and again in June 1991, Texas Instruments offered Hyundai a running-royalty rate of nine (9) percent on United States DRAM sales, and three (3) percent on Japan DRAM sales. Why did Texas Instruments" running-royalty proposal focus on DRAM sales in the United States and Japan? At that time, Texas Instruments' negotiations with other semiconductor companies had established the reasonableness of Texas Instruments' proposed royalties, and because most DRAMs initially were sold into these two countries. Nonetheless, tracking sales into the United States and Japan remained an extremely difficult task because many companies were selling products into those countries F.O.B. ("free on board") at a foreign country. Further, tracking indirect sales requires pouring over licensee's books to see where and to whom products are being sold. There remains the task of contacting the licensee's customers to determine the quantity of DRAMs placed into a product delivered to the United States. All of this is virtually impossible; and the best a party can do is estimate the level of indirect sales.

Between April 1992 and September 1992, the parties underwent further negotiations. Not surprisingly, negotiations failed.

So, in September 1992, Texas Instruments filed a lawsuit against Hyundai in this very Court asserting Hyundai infringed a number of Texas Instruments' patents relating to the production of semiconductor memory chips. . . .

After the filing of the September 1992 lawsuit, Texas Instruments and Hyundai held two face-to-face meetings in October 1992—one in San Francisco and the other in Phoenix. Texas Instruments' initial objective during these and other negotiations was to obtain a running royalty from Hyundai's sale of semiconductor products. . . . At the other end of the spectrum, Hyundai's initial objective during these and other negotiations was to obtain a fixed (or lump-sum) royalty.

In October of 1992, Texas Instruments and Hyundai reached an agreement that Hyundai would pay one hundred and nine million, nine hundred ninety-two thousand United States dollars ($109,992,000.00) for a fixed ten (10) year license to Texas Instruments' patents to be paid over the life of the license. At Texas Instruments' request, these payments were structured as maximum annual royalties also known as "royalty caps." But a problem remained. This lump sum was not self-correcting like the running royalty often used by Texas Instruments. That is, if Hyundai experienced extraordinary growth during the term of the license, the fixed sum would not take that unexpected growth (and thus sales) into account. . . .

Enter the sales-cap termination clause. For the License Agreement, Texas Instruments would accept one hundred and ten million United States dollars ($110,000,000.00) for a certain *volume* of license rights. When Hyundai consumed those license rights, the License Agreement would automatically terminate. If Hyundai did not consume those license rights, the License Agreement would continue until December 31, 2000. In other words, this sales-cap termination clause is simply the converse of a running royalty. In a running royalty the term is fixed and the payment floats. Under this License Agreement and its sales-cap termination clause, the payment is fixed and the term floats. It was a rather clever solution.

Hyundai offered an additional five million United States dollars ($5,000,000.00) in royalties from 1997 through 2001 to address Texas Instruments' concerns about Hyundai's potential for extraordinary growth. This additional five million United States dollars ($5,000,000.00) in royalties would be forthcoming if Hyundai's growth rate from 1997 to 2001 exceeded a factor of 1.811.

But what if Hyundai's growth exceeded that? Well, under Hyundai's proposal, the risk of Hyundai's extraordinary growth fell on Texas Instruments since Texas Instruments would be limited to the five million United States dollars ($5,000,000.00) should that risk become a reality. By shoving the risk of its own growth onto Texas Instruments, Hyundai, through its own extraordinary growth, would profit from the License Agreement at the expense of Texas Instruments. If Hyundai experienced extraordinary growth, Texas Instruments would be denied a fair return on its intellectual property. Indeed, if Texas Instruments had agreed to Hyundai's proposal and Hyundai had indeed experienced extraordinary growth, Texas Instruments' ability to negotiate licenses with other companies would become much more difficult. Companies often discover what others pay for licenses, which in turn sets a ceiling on what these companies would be willing to pay in the next round of negotiations. The next company sitting across the table from Texas Instruments would want a similar deal *at Texas Instruments' expense*. Simply put, the next guy would want too sweet of a deal from Texas Instruments. The net result would be to deprive Texas Instruments of a fair return on its intellectual property and its investment in research and development. For these and various other reasons, Texas Instruments rejected Hyundai's proposal.

From November 1992 to March 1993 both Texas Instruments and Hyundai struggled to negotiate a compromise. . . . Texas Instruments would agree to a running royalty of eight and a half percent (8.5%) *after* the [sales cap] had been reached. . . . Hyundai responded to Texas Instruments' suggestion by proposing that the License Agreement terminate (instead of providing for a running royalty) [once the sales cap had been reached].

Article 5.2(A)(ii) contains the unique sales-cap termination clause. Hyundai argues that this unique sales-cap termination clause operates to "tie-out" Hyundai's sales, and, consequently, subject Texas Instruments to the defense of patent misuse. First, the sales-cap provision does not restrict Hyundai's sales. The obvious purpose of the provision was to satisfy Hyundai's desire for a definite and certain royalty obligation while also satisfying Texas Instruments' desire for protection from Hyundai's potential for extraordinary growth. Texas Instruments feared Hyundai's potential for extraordinary growth; running royalty was the common cure for such fear. Hyundai apparently had some aversion to the running royalty; instead, Hyundai desired a definite and more certain royalty obligation than the running royalty afforded. Thus, the parties worked together to create a unique solution; give Hyundai the lump sum it wanted but limit the life of the License Agreement to a certain amount of worldwide sales — Article 5.2(A)(ii). This provision picks up where the lack of a running royalty leaves off — it measures Hyundai's growth over the life of the agreement. If Hyundai indeed experiences extraordinary growth, Texas Instruments will not suffer under the License Agreement's fixed (lump) sum royalty since Article 5.2(A)(ii) will automatically terminate the License Agreement prior to Texas Instruments' failing to receive a fair return on its intellectual property.

Prior to the start of negotiations for a new license agreement, Hyundai never asserted any view of Article 5.2(A)(ii) that differed from Texas Instruments' view of this provision. Indeed, a March 25, 1993 Hyundai document reveals that Hyundai had exactly the same view as Texas Instruments. In that Hyundai memorandum from Mr. M.B. Chung to the Chairman of Hyundai, Mr. M.B. Chung told Hyundai's chairman that "our side" has proposed the termination cap and that Mr. M.B. Chung understood that, assuming sixteen percent (16%) growth by Hyundai, the License Agreement would expire in the first quarter of 1999. Indeed, in making that determination, Mr. M.B. Chung himself performed his calculation on Hyundai's worldwide sales of integrated circuits (IC).

Texas Instruments' fear of Hyundai's potential for "extraordinary growth" was soon realized. Since negotiating the License Agreement, Hyundai manufactured so many more DRAMs than originally expected that Hyundai moved from being in the top twenty-five (25) world DRAM manufacturers before the agreement to number two (2) in the world by 1998.

Article 5.2(A)(ii) — the unique sales-cap termination clause — does not penalize Hyundai. The cap merely reflects a compromise between the parties — a unique way to measure Hyundai's sales growth based on the administratively convenient measure of worldwide sales. Texas Instruments did not force or coerce Hyundai into entering into the License Agreement containing the termination cap.

Notes & Questions

1. Blocking Patents

Blocking patents are present where two or more parties hold patents that do not permit each party to practice its patent without obtaining permission from the other. This situation may arise, for example, when an inventor patents an improvement on a patented technology but does not hold the patent to the underlying technology. The holder of the improvement's patent cannot practice the improvement without permission from the patentee of the underlying technology. In this situation, the two patents block each other such that permission from both patent holders is required to practice the improvement. Facing such a conundrum, parties may enter into a cross-licensing agreement.

Cross-licensing eliminates an otherwise existing blockage by allowing parties to covenant not to sue for infringement on certain patents. Parties are then free to practice the patented technologies separately without fear of having to defend against an infringement suit. When cross-licenses are employed to eliminate blocking patents by allowing parties to use patented technology without being held up by other patent holders, the practice of using cross-licenses is considered productive, pro-competitive, and not in violation of antitrust laws. See Chapter 11 for a more detailed look at antitrust concerns in intellectual property licensing transactions. *See also* Dept. of Justice, *Antitrust Guidelines for the Licensing of Intellectual Property*, Jan. 2017, reprinted in relevant part in Chapter 11 and available in full at https://www.justice.gov/atr /IPguidelines/download (last visited 1/6/2018). These guidelines provide further discussions of antitrust principles governing patent licensing and examples of patent licensing arrangements violating antitrust standards.

2. Use of Cross-Licensing in Resolution of Patent Litigation

Notice that Texas Instruments and Hyundai entered into a cross-licensing agreement only after Texas Instruments had filed an action of infringement against Hyundai. Cross-licensing may be used to settle or avoid infringement actions. When a cross-licensing agreement is entered into as part of a settlement agreement to unblock conflicting patent claims, the use is not considered anticompetitive and does not run afoul of antitrust laws. In *Dunlap Corp. v. Deering Milliken, Inc.*, 540 F.2d 1215 (4th Cir. 1976), the court noted:

> [T]he settlement of patent litigation, in and of itself, does not violate the antitrust laws. It is well established that "where there are legitimately conflicting [patent] claims or threatened interferences, a settlement by agreement, rather than by litigation, is not precluded by the [Sherman] Act." . . . It

is only when settlement agreements are entered into in bad faith and are utilized as part of a scheme to restrain or monopolize trade that antitrust violations may occur.

Id. at 1220. Cross-licensing agreements run afoul of antitrust laws if they are means to carry out conduct that constitutes patent misuse, such as price fixing, tying, or market division.

3. Use in Joint R&D

In areas of developing technology, parties may enter into cross-licensing agreements in order to foster joint research and development (R&D) efforts. In 1984, Congress passed the National Cooperative Research Act (NCRA), 15 U.S.C. §4301 et seq. The NCRA eliminated the per se rule of illegality for joint R&D ventures under state or federal law. Instead, cross-licensing agreements are judged on the basis of the rule of reason, where the purpose of the agreement is unlawful only if the agreement is used to accomplish the following:

   (i) Preserve the parties' dominant or monopoly market share;

   (ii) Exclude competitors from the market;

   (iii) Block the issuance of further licenses without mutual consent from the parties;

   (iv) Fix prices;

   (v) Allocate customers or geographic markets—it is also unlawful for competitors limited to agree to cross licenses in a particular field of use, which has the effect of allocating customers or markets.

The NCRA also grants joint researchers immunity from treble damage liability for conduct in the course of the joint venture if the researchers notify the DOJ and Federal Trade Commission and publish a notice of the joint venture in the Federal Register. Additionally, the NCRA provides joint researchers additional protection by permitting recovery of attorneys' fees from claimants who unsuccessfully bring actions for damages against the joint venture's conduct. Recovery of the fees is limited to the extent that the claim was "frivolous, unreasonable, without foundation, or in bad faith." 15 U.S.C.A. §4304.

4. Unique Industry Practices

In some industries, the sheer number of patents and the difficulty of determining infringement among industry participants make cross-licensing an indispensable part of specialized industry practices. Without cross-licenses, threats of infringement suits impede the conduct of business by industry members. This problem gives rise to unique industry practices regarding cross-licensing. For example, cross-licensing has become a regular and highly important practice in the semiconductor device industry.

To resolve the patent blockage problem, dominant parties in an industry may create a form license agreement on behalf of the entire industry. The agreement often requires patent cross-licensing arrangements. Royalty arrangements in the form license may call for royalty-free licenses, or may alternatively require equal percentage royalties from all participants, with the party having the largest sales paying a "balancing" payment to the other participants for sales in excess of the other participant's sales. Industry licensing agreements usually cover patents that have issued, patents applied for up to the date of the agreement, and future patents that issue during a defined period, typically five years, after the date of the agreement.

A drafter of an industry form licensing agreement must take care to assure the clarity of the license, especially if they are the sole author of the agreement. Critically, in some jurisdictions, any ambiguity in an agreement is automatically resolved against its drafter. For example, in *Intel Corp. v. VIA Techs., Inc.*, 319 F.3d 1357 (Fed. Cir. 2003), an ambiguity in a cross-licensing agreement drafted solely by Intel was resolved against Intel without reference to extrinsic evidence.

5. Grant Back Provisions

Since the patentee has a strong interest in enjoying the supracompetitive rights under his patent, he would also have a parallel interest in maintaining control over improvements made to his patented technology. For this reason, grant-back provisions are often part of a patent license.

A grant-back provision is a condition in a licensing agreement that requires a licensee to grant to the licensor any improvements made upon the invention. A grant-back provision may require potential licensees to agree to grant back to the patentee their rights to improvement patents vis-à-vis the original patent. Likewise, a grant-back provision may require a patentee to grant potential licensees a license to use unpatented improvements on the patented invention.

> Since grant-backs are created by contract, they may vary both in the nature of the rights granted back and in the scope of future developments covered by the clause. When the original patentee acquires full patent rights to the improvement patents, the grant-back is termed an "assignment-back." When the licensee of the original patent retains the patent rights to the improvement patents and the original patentee is given only the right to use rather than to control the improvement patents, the grant-back is called a "license-back." Of course, a grant-back clause can contain characteristics common to both the assignment-back and license-back.

Richard Schmalbeck, *The Validity of Grant-Back Clauses in Patent Licensing Agreements*, 42 U. Chi. L. Rev. 733, 734 (1975).

Grant-back provisions are permitted so long as they are used to legitimately protect a licensor's position of competition in the market by allowing the licensor to keep current with improvements on his patented inventions. However, courts frown upon such provisions if they are used to extend the scope of the patentee's statutory monopoly for the purpose of creating a position of market control in violation of the Sherman Act.

b. Antitrust Considerations and Patent Misuse: The Texas Instruments Saga Continues

Texas Instruments v. Hyundai Electronics Industries

United States District Court for the Eastern District of Texas

49 F. Supp. 2d 893 (E.D. Tex. 1999)

HEARTFIELD, DISTRICT JUDGE.

. . . .

II. CONCLUSIONS OF LAW

1. The Life and Death of Per Se Patent Misuse Due to Tying

"Patent misuse is an affirmative defense to an accusation of patent infringement, the successful assertion of which 'requires that the alleged infringer show that the patentee has impermissibly broadened the "physical or temporal scope" of the patent grant with anticompetitive effect.'" All that a successful defense of patent misuse means is that a court of equity will not lend its support to enforcement of a misuser's patent. Patent misuse? Where did that come from? Apparently, it developed, in part, from salt tablets.

In 1942 the United States Supreme Court faced an attempt by G.S. Suppiger to make "use of its patent monopoly to restrain competition in the marketing of unpatented articles, salt tablets for use with the patented machines, and is aiding in the creation of a limited monopoly in the tablets not within that granted by the patent." *Morton Salt Co. v. G.S. Suppiger Co.*, 314 U.S. 488, 491 (1942). That is, the patentee G.S. Suppiger permitted the licensee to use with Suppiger's patented, salt-tablet-dispensing machines *only those salt tablets sold by the patentee*. Don't bother passing us the Suppiger salt, opined the Supreme Court as it affirmed the district court's dismissal of Suppiger's complaint "for want of equity[]." . . . That is, the Supreme Court would not maintain an infringement suit by Suppiger since it was engaged in patent misuse.

But what about *per se* patent misuse? Where did that come from? The rule was first enunciated in *International Salt Co. v. United States*, 332 U.S. 392, 396 (1947), and has been endorsed by this Court many times since. More important, does *per se* patent misuse still live? Texas Instruments says it is dead—laid to rest by Congress' passage of the 1988 Patent Misuse Act:

> (d) No patent owner otherwise entitled to relief for infringement of a patent shall be denied relief or deemed guilty of misuse or illegal extension of the patent right by reason of his having done one or more of the following:
>
> . . . .
>
> > (5) conditioned the license of any rights to the patent or the sale of the patented product on the acquisition of a license to rights in another patent or purchase of a separate product, unless, in view of the circumstances,

the patent owner has market power in the relevant market for the patent
or patented product on which the license or sale is conditioned.

35 U.S.C. § 271(d)(5).

First, this Court specifically notes that the Federal Circuit merely recognized that
the courts have *historically* identified tying practices as constituting *per se* patent misuse — something the Supreme Court itself has done before: "It is far too late in the
history of our antitrust jurisprudence to question the proposition that certain tying
arrangements pose an unacceptable risk of stifling competition and therefore are
unreasonable 'per se'" .... Moreover, § 271(d)(5) specifically notes that patent
misuse-tying analysis is to be considered "in view of the circumstances," strongly
suggesting that rule-of-reason analysis — not *per se* analysis — applies. According to
the Supreme Court, when conducting a rule-of-reason analysis, "the factfinder weighs
all of the circumstances of a case in deciding whether a restrictive practice should be
prohibited as imposing an unreasonable restraint on competition." Indeed, the legislative history of the 1988 Patent Misuse Reform Act supports the death of *per se*
patent misuse due to tying . . . .

In the House of Representatives, Rep. Kastenmeier discussed the intent to eliminate *per se* rules due to tying: "The underlying principle being advanced by this proposal is the elimination of any vestiges of a per se or automatic inference of patent
misuse from certain tying practices," Rep. Kastenmeier further remarked that Congress's decision to require a specific assessment of market power "in view of the circumstances" was "used in this context in order to permit the courts to reasonably
assess the potential for anticompetitive effect of a particular practice." Congress
intended for the courts to evaluate business justifications for certain licensing practices (like tying practices) under a rule-of-reason analysis. In words strikingly on
point for this case, Rep. Kastenmeier stated:

> It is also our intention to avoid the use of inflexible rules once a court has
> found that market power exists. There may be circumstances in which there
> is market power and a tie-in, but where a finding of misuse would be inap-
> propriate. One example would be where the patent owner has a business jus-
> tification for the licensing practice. In real world situations where the only
> practical way to meter output is to tie the sale of a patented product to the
> sale of another separate product, then such a practice would be legitimate,
> unless such a practice — on balance — has a generally anticompetitive effect.

In the Senate, Senators DeConcini and Leahy made clear that *per se* rules due to
tying were being abolished by Section 271(d)(5), and that showings of unreasonable-
ness and anticompetitive effect would be required before misuse based on tying
would be found. . . . No contrary statement appears in the legislative history of Section 271(d)(5). Although there may still be *per se* patent misuse lurking out there
somewhere, it does not exist for patent misuse due to tying. This Court holds that
the Patent Misuse Reform Act of 1988 removed the doctrine of *per se* patent misuse
due to tying.

Assuming *arguendo* that *per se* patent misuse somehow survived the 1988 Patent Misuse Reform Act (and it did not), it is of no consequence in this particular case. First, "it is only after considerable experience with certain business relationships that courts classify them as per se violations . . ." Both parties admit that the Article 5.2(a)(ii)—the "sales-cap" termination clause—is a unique provision. When queried by the Court whether either party knew of any misuse case that involved an arrangement identical or similar to the sales-cap provision at issue here, counsel for both Texas Instruments and Hyundai candidly admitted that they were aware of no such case. Moreover, the License Agreement and its unique sales-cap provision was the result of a settlement. Indeed, the parties entered into the April 26, 1993 License Agreement to settle litigation pending in this very court. In *Speed Shore Corp. v. Woudenberg Enterprises* the Ninth Circuit faced a similar situation. 605 F.2d 469 (9th Cir. 1979). There, defendants had previously admitted manufacturing shoring devices that infringed the plaintiff's patent. The parties negotiated a settlement and entered into a license agreement. Later, the defendants argued that the negotiated license agreement fostered patent misuse:

> It is well recognized that settlement agreements are judicially favored as a matter of sound public policy. Settlement agreements conserve judicial time and limit expensive litigation. The defendants seem to argue, however, that the equitable doctrine of patent misuse prevails over the policy of favoring the settlement or disputes. In this case we disagree . . . We feel that to allow a subversion of the deeply-instilled policy of settlement of disputes by applying the doctrine of inequitable conduct, in the manner contended for by the defendants, would have the effect of stripping good-faith settlements of any meaning. We do not believe that the doctrine of inequitable conduct was intended to extend so far.

Speed Shore, 605 F.2d at 473–74. Similarly, Texas Instruments and Hyundai negotiated a settlement and entered into the License Agreement—including the sales-cap provision that Hyundai now contends is an improper tie-out. Both parties literally invented the sales-cap provision as a compromise between Texas Instruments' desire for a running royalty and Hyundai's insistence on a lump sum. In this very Court Hyundai settled pending litigation by helping invent a unique sales-cap provision and entering the fifty-five (55) page License Agreement. Now, Hyundai wants to void that License Agreement with the very same provision—a provision Hyundai helped invent. That is, Hyundai wants this Court to exercise its *equitable* power to void a provision Hyundai helped create. Finally, and most important, this Court finds that even if *per se* patent misuse were still alive (and it is not), Hyundai has failed to establish facts necessary to support even that defunct doctrine.

2. Analysis

As Hyundai points out in its brief, "to establish [a now defunct] *per se* misuse through a tie-out, Hyundai must show that: (1) two separable items are involved in the tying arrangement; (2) the tied item is capable of substantial non-infringing use; and (3) the two items actually are tied. . . . Finally, Hyundai must show (4) that TI has market power in a relevant market encompassing the tying item."

A. Hyundai's "Separable Items" Should Be "Separate Products"—And There Are None

One of the fundamental requirements of a tying violation is that there be two *separate products* to tie together. Hyundai argues that the separate products (or "separable items" to borrow Hyundai's term) are: 1) "the right to make, use or sell products which are covered by TI's portfolio, patent portfolio"; and 2) "the unfettered right of Hyundai to make, use or sell those products which are entirely outside the scope of TI's patents." Hyundai does not contend that identifiably separate products are tied under the License Agreement. Hyundai admits that no customer ever walked into Hyundai's shop and asked to buy a "covered DRAM" as opposed to an "uncovered DRAM." DRAMs are DRAMs. Hyundai's theory of "separateness" or "separability" attempts to artificially separate *the same product* into two different "categories" based on legal status—specifically, whether a Texas Instruments patent "covers" the product in the place where the product is initially sold.

This Court holds that Hyundai has failed to show that separate products are tied by the License Agreement.... Hyundai's artificial division of products into "covered" and "uncovered" categories overlooks the critical fact that, in the real world, the "covered" or "uncovered" legal status of a Hyundai product is indeterminate absent patent-by-patent, product-by-product, country-by-country litigation. This is precisely why mammoth companies in the semiconductor industry, like Texas Instrument and Hyundai enter into portfolio cross-licenses like the License Agreement at issue here.

In truth, when Hyundai signed the License Agreement, it purchased one "product"— a unitary covenant that Texas Instruments would not sue Hyundai over any integrated circuit (IC), anywhere, during the term of the agreement. Under the License Agreement, Hyundai enjoyed complete freedom of operation. The License Agreement relieved Hyundai from the onerous burden of constantly monitoring whether Texas Instruments had obtained new patents (and in what countries), whether existing products infringed on existing patents or on those new patents, and whether newly developed products infringed any Texas Instruments patent. As this Court noted in its February 4, 1999 *Memorandum and Opinion Order* interpreting the License Agreement, this result could not have been reached through a patent-by-patent licensing scheme, even if the patent-by-patent license encompassed all of Texas Instruments' extant patents at the time the agreement was signed. Nor could it have been reached by limiting the license to products that were "covered" when sold, since that would have left unlicensed the many Hyundai products that, although "uncovered" by a Texas Instruments patent when sold, eventually made their way into a country where Texas Instruments had patents. The License Agreement provided a single protection to all Hyundai integrated circuits—it provided every integrated circuit manufactured by Hyundai with the freedom to be moved anywhere in the world with full protection from Texas Instruments claims of infringement....

B. Texas Instruments Does Not Have Market Power in a Relevant Market

Hyundai also fails to establish that Texas Instruments has market power in a relevant market. Market power requires that Hyundai show that Texas Instruments has the power "to force [Hyundai] to do something it would not do in a competitive market." . . . . Hyundai's allegation of market power is simply that the United States government has granted Texas Instruments the legitimate right to exclude others from Texas Instruments' patented technology. But antitrust law dictates this is not impermissible market power.

Hyundai relies heavily on the fact that Texas Instruments has licensed its portfolio of patents related to the manufacture of DRAMs . . . to most, if not all of the major manufacturers throughout the world, including Hyundai. Moreover, argues Hyundai, Texas Instruments considers the . . . patents "very important" to the "manufacturing of DRAMs in the United States." Indeed, Texas Instruments' own witnesses testified that the . . . patents are "key process patents" and "the lock to the door" with respect to the manufacturing of semiconductor DRAMs. So what? Once again, antitrust law holds this not impermissible market power.

Moreover, Hyundai's representative . . . and economic expert . . . urged that Texas Instruments' market power was measured by whether or not Texas Instruments has "blocking patents." Blocking patents? A blocking patent, in the case of a DRAM, would be a patent without which a DRAM could not be made. While Hyundai presented testimony that Texas Instruments believes [its] patents to be very important for the manufacture of DRAMs, Hyundai itself specifically testified it does not believe Texas Instruments has any blocking patents. . . .

Moreover, Hyundai has failed to show coercion. If, as Hyundai admitted, it did not believe Texas Instruments had blocking patents, how could it have been coerced?

C. Equity Does Not Lie with Hyundai

Patent misuse is an equitable defense. As such, Hyundai must be equitably entitled to invoke that defense. "'It is one of the fundamental principles upon which equity jurisprudence is founded, that before a complainant can have a standing in court he must first show that not only has he a good and meritorious cause of action, but he must come into court with clean hands.'"

Hyundai comes to this Court with unclean hands. Let's recap what Hyundai has done thus far. First, Hyundai approaches Texas Instruments in order to enter into a patent portfolio cross-license agreement. Texas Instruments, fearful of Hyundai's potential for extraordinary growth, suggests the self-correcting, oft-used "running royalty" which would accurately track Hyundai's sales and fairly compensate Texas Instruments for its intellectual property. Hyundai refuses to entertain the notion of a running royalty. Rather, Hyundai insists on paying a fixed (or lump) sum. If the parties use Texas Instruments' running royalty suggestion, the risk and expense of Hyundai's extraordinary growth falls on Hyundai, which must pay royalties on its unexpected, increased sales. Conversely, if the parties use Hyundai's fixed (or lump) sum suggestion, the risk and expense of Hyundai's extraordinary growth falls on Texas Instruments, which must sacrifice a fair return on its intellectual property as Hyundai's sales shoot through the roof and overshadows the fixed (or lump) sum.

So what did the parties do? What they should have done—they negotiated a compromise. Texas Instruments suggests a type of sales-cap termination clause that would measure the life of the License Agreement by the volume of Hyundai's sales. In response to this suggestion, Hyundai voluntarily helped create and refine a "sales-cap termination clause"—Article 5.2(A)(ii), the very sales-cap termination clause currently accused of generating patent misuse. This Court finds, as a matter of fact, that Hyundai *at the very least* helped draft and create the very sales-cap termination clause it now insists amounts to patent misuse. Hyundai signed the License Agreement with the sales-cap termination clause and Texas Instruments dismissed its pending lawsuit against Hyundai. All was well until. . . .

On January 20, 1998—roughly five years after the contract was signed—Hyundai injected a never before mentioned interpretation of Article 5.2(A)(ii) into the discussion—the "TI Country Concept." Why? Because Hyundai is trying to avoid the consequences of its own extraordinary growth. Rather than honor Article 5.2(A)(ii)—the sales-cap termination clause it helped create—Hyundai tries like the dickens to force the risk and expense of its own extraordinary growth onto Texas Instruments—*precisely what Article 5.2(A)(ii) was designed to avoid*. Much like its strained interpretation of the parties' License Agreement, it gets worse.

Hyundai carries its "TI Country Concept" into this Court and urges a strained interpretation of Article 5.2(A)(ii) contrary to what the extrinsic evidence now shows. Indeed, relying on New York law's inadmissibility of extrinsic evidence for the interpretation of unambiguous contracts, Hyundai actually urged an interpretation *opposite* to that of a patent portfolio cross-license. Despite being unable to consider the extrinsic evidence *which clearly shows this License Agreement to be a portfolio cross-license agreement*, this Court nonetheless rejected Hyundai's "TI Country Concept" and, for all practical purposes, held the License Agreement to be a portfolio cross-license agreement.

Then, six (6) days before the jury trial of this case, Hyundai amends its answer to include this defense of patent misuse. Despite a twenty-five million and two-hundred thousand United States dollar ($25,200,000.00) jury verdict in its favor, Texas Instruments must undergo further delay as it prepares for this subsequent bench trial. And prepare for what? The re-appearance of Hyundai's "TI Country Concept." Hyundai's defense of patent misuse relies upon the "TI Country Concept's" "covered" versus "uncovered" artificiality already rejected by this Court.

Ever since it introduced its "TI Country Concept" on January 20, 1998, Hyundai has consistently done one thing: try to avoid the risk and expense of its own extraordinary growth. Rather than honor Article 5.2(A)(ii)—the sales-cap provision designed to insure the risk of Hyundai's extraordinary growth would fall on

Hyundai *and not Texas Instruments*—Hyundai consistently tried to deflect the consequences of its extraordinary growth onto Texas Instruments.

Finally, it would be inequitable, and contrary to all notions of fairness, to allow Hyundai to claim that counting "uncovered" products toward the termination cap results in misuse, when Hyundai itself proposed a construction of the License Agreement that did the same thing.

Suffice it to say that Hyundai does not come to this Court with clean hands—just the opposite. Accordingly, equity does not lie with Hyundai.

D. The License Agreement Is Terminated—TERMINATED

It was with a tremendous amount of deja vu that this Court undertook this patent misuse defense discussion. In its February 4, 1999 *Memorandum and Opinion Order*, this Court ruled that the License Agreement terminated according to the automatic triggering of Article 5.2(A)(ii)—the sales-cap provision. In that opinion, this Court specifically rejected Hyundai's "covered" versus "uncovered" theory (the "TI Country Concept") with respect to the definition of "royalty bearing products" and, consequently, calculation of Hyundai's worldwide sales applicable to the sales-cap calculation. This Court thought it had laid to rest Hyundai's strained, artificial parsing of the License Agreement's language by rejecting Hyundai's "TI Country Concept" and finding that the contract had, in fact, terminated.

But nestled within that fifty-five (55) page, dead License Agreement (that Hyundai helped draft), Hyundai managed to discover (a mere six (6) days before trial) this defense of patent misuse. We've passed the point of beating a dead horse—now we're tenderizing it. It is time, once and for all, for Hyundai to come to grips with the death of the License Agreement—a death brought about by Hyundai's own extraordinary growth.

III. CONCLUSION

Hyundai's *per se* patent misuse defense fails for a variety of reasons. First, there is no such thing as *per se* patent misuse due to tying. Congress' passage of the Patent Misuse Reform Act of 1988 eliminated *per se* patent misuse due to tying. Hyundai's reading of the Federal Circuit's subsequent *Virginia Panel* case mirrors its strained interpretation of the parties' License Agreement. This Court does not read *Virginia Panel* for the proposition that Congress failed to eliminate *per se* patent misuse due to tying. Second, assuming *arguendo* that *per se* patent misuse still exists (and it does not), Hyundai fails as a matter of fact to establish there are separate products; Hyundai fails to show these "separable" products are tied; and Hyundai fails to establish that Texas Instruments has power in a relevant market. Finally, Hyundai comes to this Court with the same, tired "TI Country Concept" already rejected by this Court in its interpretation of the parties' License Agreement. Rather than honor Article 5.2(A)(ii)—the sales-cap termination clause—and assume the risk and expense of its own extraordinary growth, Hyundai resurrects its previously rejected "TI Country Concept" to bolster its patent misuse defense. Well, this Court puts it down again.

Hyundai does not [sic] come to this Court with unclean hands. Accordingly, even assuming Hyundai had established *per se* patent misuse or just plain patent misuse, this Court refuses to lend the support of equity to a party with such unclean hands.

In sum, Hyundai has significantly failed to make out the essential elements of its equitable patent-misuse defense. In light of this failure, and for the reasons set out above, this Court DISMISSES Hyundai's Sixth Affirmative Defense.

It is SO ORDERED.

6. Patent Pools

Matsushita Electrical Industrial Co., Ltd. v. Cinram International, Inc.

United States District Court for the District of Delaware

299 F. Supp. 2d 370 (Del. 2004)

Robinson, Chief Judge.

I. INTRODUCTION

Matsushita Electric Industrial Co., Ltd ("MEI") filed an action against Cinram International, Inc. ("Cinram") . . . for patent infringement . . . related to optical discs, including digital versatile discs ("DVDs"). Cinram filed . . . antitrust counterclaims against MEI. . . . Cinram specifically charges that MEI has conspired to restrain trade by participating in the non-exclusive DVD 6C Licensing Agency (the "6C Pool") in violation of Section 1 of the Sherman Act, 15 U.S.C. § 1. Cinram also alleges that MEI and other members of the 6C Pool have conspired, attempted, and committed the offense of monopolization in violation of Section 2 of the Sherman Act, 15 U.S.C. § 2. Cinram alleges that it has experienced harm to its business and properties and been forced to pay excessive patent royalties as a result of MEI's illegal actions. It also alleges that it is unable to license and exercise patents related to DVD technology on competitive terms. To redress these injuries, "Cinram seeks to have MEI license 6C Pool members and independent licensees, through the 6C Pool and individually, on non-discriminatory terms, so that pool members and independent licensees pay the same royalties (while each pool member receives a share of pool royalties collected based on its patent contribution). In short, Cinram . . . [seeks] to level the unlevel playing field."

II. BACKGROUND

. . . .

2. The 6C Pool

The DVD Forum [(a Standard Setting Organization or "SSO")] is an international association of companies that are engaged in the research, development, manufacture, and/or sales related to DVD technology. The DVD Forum was founded in 1995 by MEI under the name "DVD Consortium." Around 1995, the DVD Forum agreed on specifications for the recording, production, replication, and use of both DVDs and DVD equipment (the "DVD Standard Specification").

After establishing the DVD Standard Specification, six members of the DVD Forum, namely MEI, Hitachi, Mitsubishi, Toshiba, JVC, and AOL-Time Warner, organized the "6C Pool" and entered an agreement to manage the intellectual property rights around their DVD patented technology (the "6C Pool Formation Agreement").[2] Under the terms of the 6C Pool Formation Agreement, each member of the 6C Pool contributed one or more of its patents related to DVD technology to the pool to form a collection of patents "essential" to DVD production. Each pool member acquired a cross-license to the other members' "essential" patents in exchange for its contribution. The members agreed as part of formation to offer a non-exclusive, non-transferable license to these pooled patents to non-member companies interested in replicating DVDs in compliance with the DVD Standard Specification ("independent replicator"). To this end, the members drafted a standard license agreement to facilitate licensing the pooled patents (the "6C Pool License"). Section 2.1 of the 6C Pool License specifically recites:

> Licensor hereby grants to Licensee and its Affiliates a non-exclusive, non-transferable license to make, have made, use, sell, and otherwise dispose of DVD Products under the DVD Patents or any of their claims pursuant to the Conditions of Exhibit 3.

Also as part of formation, each member consented to offer individual licenses to its "essential" DVD patents on a non-exclusive basis to interested third party licensees as an alternative to the 6C Pool License. The members incorporated this option into the 6C Pool License to notify potential licensees of a separate means of acquiring licenses for "essential" patents. Section 2.3 of the 6C Pool License specifically recites:

> Instead of dealing with Licensor to obtain licenses for DVD patents of the members of the Group, Licensee shall have the option to negotiate and take a license under any DVD Patents and other related patents owned by each member of the Group pursuant to separate negotiations with each of the members on fair, reasonable, and non-discriminatory terms, whether or not Licensee intends to manufacture and/or sell DVD Products in conformity with the DVD Standard Specifications.

In view of Sections 2.1 and 2.3 of the 6C Pool License, an independent replicator who wishes to make DVDs without infringing any DVD patent, therefore, has the option of approaching either the 6C Pool for a 6C Pool License or each member of the 6C Pool for individual licenses.

---

2. [As of December 2014, the 6C Patent licensor group included: Hitachi Consumer Electronics Co., Ltd., JVC Kenwood Corp., Mitsubishi Electric Corp., Panasonic Corp., Samsung Electronics Co. Ltd., Sanyo Electric Co., Ltd., Sharp Corp., Toshiba Corp., and Warner Bros. Home Entertainment Inc.]

The 6C Pool initially charged independent replicators $0.075 per disc under the 6C Pool License. The members later lowered the price to $0.065 or $0.05 per disc, depending upon when the independent replicator negotiated its 6C Pool License. MEI serves as the licensing agent to the Americas on behalf of the 6C Pool.

In addition to owning patents relating to DVD technology, MEI, JVC, AOL-Time Warner, and Mitsubishi commercially replicate DVDs. These four pool members, consequently, are in competition with independent replicators who must take either a 6C Pool License or individual licenses to avoid patent infringement. Indeed, MEI is a direct competitor of Cinram in the market for wholesale production of DVDs in the DVD-Video and DVD-ROM formats. Moreover, MEI may practice DVD technology in compliance with the DVD Standard Specification without owing the same per disc license fees that Cinram must pay as a 6C Pool licensee; MEI only pays a $0.0015 per disc royalty whereas Cinram must pay a $0.05 per disc royalty.

3. Business Review Letter from the United States Department of Justice

In October 1998, the 6C Pool requested a Business Review Letter from the United States Department of Justice ("DOJ"). . . . The 6C Pool specifically asked for a statement of the DOJ's antitrust enforcement intentions with respect to the 6C Pool's plan to assemble and offer a package license to "essential" patents, to manufacture products in compliance with the DVD-ROM and DVD-Video formation, and to distribute royalty income to members of the 6C Pool. . . .

Based on [the representations offered by the 6C Pool], the DOJ issued a Business Review Letter on June 10, 1999 indicating that it would not initiate an enforcement action. The DOJ found that the 6C Pool was "likely to combine complementary patent rights, thereby lowering the costs of manufacturers that need access to them in order to produce discs, players and decoders in conformity with the DVD-Video and DVD-ROM formats." The DOJ concluded that the 6C Pool was not likely to violate antitrust laws.

IV. DISCUSSION

Under Section 1 of the Sherman Act, "every contract, combination . . . conspiracy, in restraint of trade or commerce . . . is hereby declared to be illegal." 15 U.S.C. § 1 (2003). Section 2 of the Sherman Act also makes it illegal for any person to "monopolize, or attempt to monopolize, or combine or conspire with any other person or persons, to monopolize any part of the trade or commerce." 15 U.S.C. § 2 (2003). The Supreme Court has advised that "the Sherman Act has always been discriminatingly applied in the light of economic realities." In addition, the Supreme Court has stated that "there are situations in which competitors have been permitted to form joint selling agencies or other pooled activities, subject to strict limitations under the antitrust laws to guarantee against abuse of the collective power thus created."

In determining whether a pooled activity violates antitrust laws, courts must consider whether to employ a per se or a rule of reason analysis. The per se approach treats certain practices as being so plainly anti-competitive and without redeeming virtue as to be per se unreasonable. The rule of reason approach, in contrast, broadly examines the business practices and related market factors to determine whether the questioned practice imposes an unreasonable restraint on competition. The Supreme Court has recognized that patent pools should be addressed under the rule of reason analysis, except for arrangements where the only apparent purpose is naked price fixing. In this context, the rule of reason analysis predominantly focuses on identifying pro-competitive benefits and balancing them against potential anti-competitive effects. Patent pooling arrangements may serve valid competitive objectives, especially in situations involving "blocking" and "complementary" patents. For example, where patents 'block' one another in the sense that neither can be used without infringing the other, pooling becomes necessary to remove the stalemate and facilitate exploitation of the patents. Similarly, if multiple patents complement each other to protect related but separate parts of a larger product or process, then pooling may be needed to produce a complete item. Pooling likewise may be justified as the best way of solving a patent interference or infringement dispute.

On the other hand, courts have recognized that certain types of pooling arrangements may significantly hurt competition. This is especially true when patents protect substitute goods that compete against each other in the marketplace. In these situations, patent pools should be scrutinized for naked price-fixing, output restraints, exclusionary practices, and foreclosure of competition in downstream or related markets. Trade is restrained, sometimes unreasonably, when the rights to use individual copyrights or patents may be obtained only by payment for a pool of such rights, but that the opportunity to acquire a pool of rights does not restrain trade if an alternative opportunity to acquire individual rights is realistically available. However, an antitrust plaintiff is not obliged to pursue any imaginable alternative, regardless of cost or efficiency, before it can complain that a practice has restrained competition. The true issue in situations involving a pool of rights is whether the antitrust plaintiff lacked a "realistic opportunity" as a "practical matter" to obtain individual licenses from individual owners as opposed to a single license from the pool. If the antitrust plaintiff has the opportunity to license independently, then the pool of rights does not restrain trade in violation of Section 1 of the Sherman Act. It likewise does not violate Section 2 of the Sherman Act because Section 2 requires proof of an anti-competitive act to acquire or maintain a monopoly.

MEI argues that the 6C Pool members each contractually agreed when they formed the 6C Pool to offer individual licenses for their "essential" patents to interested parties on fair, reasonable, and non-discriminatory terms as an alternative to the 6C Pool License. MEI points out that both the 6C Pool Formation Agreement and the actual 6C Pool License contain provisions reciting this obligation. In light of its contractual duties, MEI asserts that it is willing to grant an individual license to any company interested in its individual "essential" patents.

MEI maintains that it repeatedly notified prospective licensees of the availability of individual licenses. Specifically, MEI contends that it sent a letter, press release, application form for a 6C Pool License, and brochure of "essential" patents to

Cinram as early as July 1999. It also contends that it sent additional letters to Cinram on January 19, 2001, April 23, 2001, and April 30, 2001. MEI further avers that Mr. Lewis Ritchie, Chief Financial Officer, Executive Vice President of Finance and Administration, and Corporate Secretary of Cinram, attended a 6C Pool presentation on July 13, 2000 and was informed of the availability of individual licenses. Thereafter on July 14, 2002, MEI claims that it even provided Mr. Ritchie with a copy of the standard 6C Pool License which explains that individual licenses are available as an alternative to the 6C Pool License. MEI argues that Cinram did not respond to any of these notifications, nor did it seek to negotiate an individual license or ask for individual licensing rates, even though it met with 6C Pool representatives on seven occasions from August 2000 to February 2002. Moreover, MEI points out that Cinram did not approach other 6C Pool members to inquire about individual licenses. On this basis, MEI asserts that Cinram cannot meet its burden to establish that individual licenses are not a realistic alternative.

To counter MEI's argument, Cinram asserts that MEI's contractual obligation to offer individual licenses is illusory because, in reality, it does not offer such licenses on fair, reasonable, and non-discriminatory terms. To this end, Cinram maintains that the structure of the 6C Pool discourages individual licenses because such licenses would undercut the pool price. As well, Cinram charges that as its direct competitor in the DVD manufacturing area, MEI is less inclined to offer low individual licensing fees because it does not want to help the competition.

Cinram also argues that the terms for individual licenses are cost-prohibitive. Cinram explains that the cost for individual licenses from four of the six 6C Pool members totaled $0.11. Cinram points out that this total substantially exceeds the $0.05 per disc royalty that it currently pays for a 6C Pool License, thereby making individual licenses entirely impractical. Cinram substantiates its argument by noting that DOCdata, Quanta, Metatec, Asustek Computer Inc., Wistron Corp., CMC Magnetics Corp., Cyberlink, Richoh, and Nippon Columbia all explored the possibility of individual licenses with 6C Pool members, but abandoned efforts in favor of a 6C Pool License. Cinram further validates its position by noting that MEI told Mr. Ritchie on two separate occasions that individual licenses would be "more costly" than a 6C Pool License and not a realistic alternative.

Finally, Cinram maintains that MEI and other 6C Pool members purposefully delayed in responding to inquiries regarding individual licenses. Cinram points out that Metatac contacted MEI and the other 6C Pool members for individual licensing terms in August 1999, but only received feedback from JVC and Hitachi after several months of delay. Particularly, JVC waited until June 2000 to respond, but did not quote any terms. JVC then took an additional ten months until April 2001 to provide a rate quote. Hitachi delayed fourteen months to provide its quotation to Metatec. With regard to MEI, Metatec renewed its request several times in 2001 and finally received a term sheet from MEI two and one-half years after its initial request. Similarly, Cinram notes that DOCdata approached MEI and the other 6C Pool members regarding individual licenses in early November 2000. Hitachi provided a response on December 12, 2000; JVC provided a response on December 25, 2000; Mitsubishi provided a response on December 1, 2000, and Toshiba provided a response on March 16, 2001. Despite three written reminders, MEI did not acknowledge this inquiry until March 2001. At that time, MEI apologized for the delay and requested additional time to respond. MEI finally responded to DOCdata's request after a total lag of one year, but did not quote the price for an individual license to its essential patents. Likewise, AOL-Time Warner deferred responding for six months and then informed DOCdata that it had not yet formulated a specific policy for granting individual licenses, but that any individual offer would necessarily be at a rate greater than its share of the 6C Pool royalties.

Viewing the evidence of record and all reasonable inferences to be drawn therefrom in a light most favorable to Cinram as the non-moving party, the court finds that there are no genuine issues of material fact regarding whether individual licenses are a realistic alternative to the 6C Pool License. While this court previously recognized in *Broadcast Music, Inc., v. Moor Law, Inc.*, 484 F. Supp. 357, 367 (D. Del. 1980) (citations omitted) that a plaintiff is not required to attempt individual licensing negotiations before suing under antitrust law when it is clear that such gesture would be futile, the court concludes that Cinram realistically could avail itself of individual licenses to "essential" DVD patents. Cinram was presented with a plethora of information regarding individual licensing terms from MEI through letters, brochures, and a direct presentation; it simply chose to pursue a 6C Pool License instead. Additionally, the court concludes that MEI did not seek to entirely avoid discussions with independent replicators about individual licensing terms. Rather, the court finds that MEI showed a willingness to discuss such terms based upon its two conversations with Mr. Ritchie. While MEI's slowness could be construed as purposeful delay as suggested by Cinram, the court understands that communications often proceed very slowly and deliberately in the business world, particularly when such communications occur on a global scale as in the instant case.

Moreover, despite the fact that numerous independent replicators approached MEI for individual licenses but eventually settled on a 6C Pool License, the court is not persuaded that MEI merely gave lip service to the option of individual licenses. The 6C Pool License is the simplest way to acquire a license to all the "essential" DVD patents. It likewise is the most economical approach, given that (1) the cost of a 6C Pool License is less than the cost of obtaining multiple individual licenses and (2) the per disc royalty under the 6C Pool License is $0.05 whereas the per disc royalty under individual licenses exceeds $0.11. The Second Circuit has stated that the only valid test to prove that an alternative is too costly to be a realistic alternative is whether the price for such a license, in an objective sense, is higher than the value of the intellectual property rights being conveyed. In accord with this reasoning, the court concludes that the per disc royalty differential only causes the individual licensing option to be an unrealistic alternative if it is higher than the value of the DVD rights conveyed. The court finds that the facts at bar do not show this to be the case.

Furthermore, the court does not overlook the fact that the DOJ issued a Business Review Letter concluding that the 6C Pool was not likely to violate antitrust laws. The court appreciates the DOJ's familiarity and experience analyzing complex pooling arrangements and is strongly persuaded by the DOJ's conclusions. In light of these considerations, the court finds that there is enough evidence of record to enable a jury to reasonably decide that individual licenses present a realistic alternative to the 6C Pool License and that the 6C Pool, in turn, does not violate antitrust laws. Accordingly, the court concludes that summary judgment is appropriate and grants MEI's motion as to Cinram's antitrust claims.

V. CONCLUSION

For the reasons stated, MEI's motion for summary judgment as to Cinram's antitrust claims (D.I. 156) is granted.

Notes & Questions

1. Valid Objectives for Creation of Pooling Arrangements

Patent pools arise when two or more patent owners agree to exchange licenses in their patents. Participants in pools have access to each other's patents, freeing them to commercialize technology that might otherwise be blocked by a conflicting patent or that would raise an infringement claim. In some industries, overlapping patents controlled by competitors may cloud a field to an extent that a patentee in the industry finds it difficult in light of the existing patents held by others to discern his right to make, use, or sell his product. Not surprisingly, multiple infringement actions within an industry often are the impetus for creation of a patent pool.

Use of a pooling arrangement to avoid or resolve an infringement action among patent holders is recognized as a reasonable and pro-competitive practice. While pooling arrangements are especially common with patents, pools may also involve other forms of intellectual property.

2. Concerns Regarding Patent Pools

a. *Antitrust*—Pooling arrangements necessarily involve joint action, often between parties that are in competition. If parties to a pooling agreement consent to more than pure cross-licensing, antitrust risks arise. *See Hartford-Empire Co. v. United States,* 323 U.S. 386 (1945). For example, competitors that pool their patents together in order to facilitate price-fixing engage in an activity that is seen as exclusionary and anticompetitive. Another example of an anticompetitive arrangement is present when a patent pool collectively dominates a market and licensing arrangements are used to implement territorial or field of use allocations of business activities among the patent pool's members. Such a practice may be seen as achieving a horizontal allocation of markets in violation of antitrust laws.

b. *Invalid Patents*—Because a challenge to the validity of a patent pool fails if even one patent in the pool is valid, the cost and risks for a party wishing to mount a challenge to the validity of a patent increases when the patent is included in a pool. A patent pool may therefore shield an invalid patent from challenges of invalidity. The shielding effect of a pool may inhibit innovation in the field occupied by an invalid patent.

Challenges to a patent that is included in a patent pool should be limited to the patents owned by the licensor who is the addressee of the challenge, and not overreach to the patents owned by other licensors in the pool.

3. Standard Setting Organizations

In today's innovation market, there are often many companies working on developments that involve the same technology or set of technologies. It is typically more efficient for these companies to work together to create one standard for the technology that can be used in targeting subsequent innovation by all of the companies, rather than for each company to work on developing the technology for itself. Furthermore, once a standard for a technology is defined and any necessary licenses for use of the technology are implemented, the technology can be used across applications. *See* Mark A. Lemley, *Intellectual Property Rights & Standard Setting Organizations*, 90 CAL. L. REV. 1889, 1893 (2002) ("Telephones talk to each other, the Internet works, and hairdryers plug into electrical sockets because private groups have set 'interface' standards, allowing compatibility between products made by different manufacturers."). In order to collaborate in this fashion, companies employ standard setting organizations (SSOs).[1] Engineers then work together to establish standard specifications—lengthy, technical documents explaining in precise detail how the technologies covered by standards operate.

Once a standard specification is complete, the companies disclose which of their technical contributions, if any, are covered by patents. Patents associated with a standard are typically classified as: standard essential patents (SEPs), nonessential patents, or options. Most SSOs allow their members to own intellectual property rights, but require members to license their rights and forgo injunctive relief. Members are typically required to disclose any standard essential patents they hold and must commit to license these patents on fair, reasonable, and nondiscriminatory (FRAND) terms.[2]

---

1. Examples include: the European Telecommunications Standards Institute (ETSI), the Institute of Electrical and Electronics Engineers (IEEE), the Internet Engineering Task Force (IETF), and the World Wide Web Consortium (W3C). For a detailed examination of SSOs, *see* Mark A. Lemley, *Intellectual Property Rights and Standard—Setting Organizations*, 90 CAL. L. REV. 1889 (2002). *See also* Jonathan Barnett, *From Patent Thickets to Patent Networks: The Legal Infrastructure of the Digital Economy*, 55 JURIMETRICS J. 1–53 (2014), available at: SSRN: https://ssrn.com/abstract =2438364 (discussing the success of information and communication technology markets, which relied on patent pools, administered by organizations like MPEG LA, to both further technical progress and reduce final consumer prices).

2. These terms are also frequently referred to as simply as RAND (reasonable and nondiscriminatory). *See, e.g., Apple, Inc. v. Motorola, Inc.*, 869 F. Supp. 2d 901, 911–12 (N.D. Ill. 2012), in which Judge Posner notes that the term "fair" adds nothing to "reasonable" and "nondiscriminatory." An SSO may also require licensing on RAND-Z (RAND with zero royalty) or RAND-RF

Several legal questions regarding SSOs have yet to be settled. Are FRAND commitments enforceable when patents are transferred, and if so, under what circumstances? Typically, a commitment to FRAND licensing is viewed as stemming from a contract between the initial patent holder and the SSO. Under what circumstances should a successor in interest to the initial patent holder be bound by that contract? *See* Jay P. Kesan & Carol M. Hayes, *FRAND's Forever: Standards, Patent Transfers, and Licensing Commitments*, 89 INDIANA L. J. 231 (2014) (advocating that a FRAND commitment ought to be considered an encumbrance that runs with the patent). Can third parties (e.g. non-SSO members who wish to implement the standard) enforce the FRAND commitment? Is a SSO member bound to license on FRAND terms (or on any terms) standard-related patents the member acquires after a standard is established?

4. Determining What is Fair, Reasonable and Nondiscriminatory

Although SSOs involve cooperation between competitors, courts typically find that the procompetitive benefits of such organizations outweigh the anticompetitive concerns. Standards result in greater interoperability, which benefits both the technology producers and consumers. Such interoperability aids in the adoption of new technology by easing the transition from old to new technology. Additionally, widely adopted standards enable smaller companies to compete with large companies. *See* Kesan & Hayes, *FRAND's Forever, supra*. To avoid antitrust concerns, SSOs typically adopt vague language requiring fairness and reasonableness, leaving it to the courts to determine what license terms would be fair and reasonable.

In *Georgia-Pacific Corp. v. United States Plywood Corp.*, 318 F. Supp. 1116 (S.D.N.Y. 1970), the district court considered the amount of damages to be awarded to a patent holder under 35 USC § 284, which provides that "the court shall award the claimant damages adequate to compensate for the infringement, but in no event less than a reasonable royalty for the use made of the invention by the infringer . . . ." The court identified fifteen factors to consider in determining a reasonable royalty rate in such situations. *Id.* at 1120. In *Microsoft Corp. v. Motorola, Inc.*, 2013 U.S. Dist. LEXIS 60233 (W.D. Wash. Apr. 25, 2013), District Judge James L. Robart adjusted the *Georgia-Pacific* factors to establish criteria for determining fair and reasonable licensing terms in situations where parties cannot reach agreements about such terms on their own. According to Judge Robart, the relevant factors in determining fair and reasonable licensing terms complying with a RAND licensing commitment are as follows (with references to the factor numbers for the corresponding *Georgia-Pacific* factors):

> 100. Factor 1 examines the royalties received by the patentee for the licensing of the patent in suit, proving or tending to prove an established royalty. In the RAND context, such licensing royalties for a given patent(s) must be

---

(RAND Royalty Free) terms, meaning the licensor charges no royalty but the licensee must obtain permissible from the licensor before using the technology.

comparable to RAND licensing circumstances. In other words, to prove an established royalty rate for an SEP, the past royalty rates for a patent must be negotiated under the RAND obligation or comparable negotiation. Thus, license agreements where the parties clearly understood the RAND obligation, and as discussed below, patent pools, will be relevant to a hypothetical negotiation for SEPs.

101. Factor 4 considers the licensor's established policy and marketing program to maintain his patent monopoly by not licensing others to use the invention or by granting licenses under special conditions designed to preserve that monopoly. This factor is inapplicable in the RAND context because the licensor has made a commitment to license on RAND terms and may no longer maintain a patent monopoly by licensing to others. In fact, as the court has found in this case, the RAND commitment requires the SEP owner to grant licenses on RAND terms to all implementers of the standards.

102. Factor 5 examines the commercial relationship between the licensor and licensee, such as whether they are competitors in the same territory in the same line of business; or whether they are inventor and promoter. Similar to factor 4, this factor does not apply in the RAND context. This is because having committed to license on RAND terms, the patentee no longer may discriminate against its competitors in terms of licensing agreements. Instead, as explained, the patent owner is obligated to license all implementers on reasonable terms.

103. Factors 6 and 8 examine the importance of the patented invention to both the licensor and licensee's sales, as well as to derivative and convoyed sales to the licensee. Although both of these factors are relevant to a reasonable royalty in the RAND context, it is important to focus the analysis of both of these factors on the value of the patented technology apart from the value associated with incorporation of the patented technology into the standard.

104. With respect to Factors 6 and 8, a reasonable royalty would not take into account the value to the licensee created by the existence of the standard itself, but would instead consider the contribution of the patent to the technical capabilities of the standard and also the contribution of those relevant technological capabilities to the implementer and the implementer's products. This is because there is substantial value in the agreed standard itself apart from any contribution of the patented technology to the standard, and the RAND commitment exists so that SEP patent holders cannot demand more than they contribute.

105. Factor number 7 examines the duration of the patent and the term of the license. The analysis concerning Factor 7 is greatly simplified in the context of a dispute over a reasonable royalty for a RAND-committed patent because the term of the license would equate to the duration of the patent.

In many circumstances, this factor will have little influence on what constitutes a reasonable royalty under the RAND commitment.

106. Factor 9 considers the utility and advantages of the patent property over the old modes or devices, if any, that had been used for working out similar results. Through this factor, the parties to a hypothetical negotiation under a RAND commitment would consider alternatives that could have been written into the standard instead of the patented technology. The focus is on the period before the standard was adopted and implemented . . . .

107. Factor 10 generally relates to the character of the patented invention and the benefits to those who used the invention. Similarly, Factor 11 examines the extent to which the infringer has made use of the invention and value of that use to the infringer. In the RAND context, both of these factors focus the hypothetical negotiation on the contribution of the patent to the technical capabilities of the standard and also the contribution of those relevant technical capabilities to the implementer and the implementer's products. Again, in such an analysis, however, it is important to separate the patented technology from the value associated with incorporation of the patented technology into the standard. Nevertheless, evidence of the benefit and value of the patent to the owner and implementer is relevant to the contribution of the patent to the certain capabilities of the standard, as well as the contribution of the standard's capabilities to the implementer.

108. Factor 12 states, "the portion of the profit or of the selling price that may be customary in the particular business or in comparable businesses to allow for the use of the invention or analogous inventions." *Georgia-Pacific*, 318 F. Supp. at 1120. This factor must be viewed through the lens of business practices involving RAND commitments. In other words, licensing fees for non-RAND committed patents customary in a business industry cannot form the basis for comparison. Instead, Factor 12 must look to customary practices of businesses licensing RAND-committed patents.

109. Factor 13 looks at the portion of the realizable profit that should be credited to the invention as distinguished from non-patented elements, the manufacturing process, business risks, or significant features or improvements added by the infringer. As with many of the other factors, in the RAND context, it is critical to consider the contribution of the patented technology apart from the value of the patent as the result of its incorporation into the standard, the latter of which would improperly reward the SEP owner for the value of the standard itself. Rewarding the SEP owner with any of the value of the standard itself would constitute hold-up value and be contrary to the purpose behind the RAND commitment.

110. Factor 15 considers the amount that a licensor and a licensee would have agreed upon (at the time the infringement began) if both had been reasonably and voluntarily trying to reach an agreement. The SEP owner and the

implementer would consider the RAND commitment and its purposes in their efforts to reach a license agreement. In trying to reach an agreement, the SEP owner would have been obligated to license its SEPs on RAND terms which necessarily must abide by the purpose of the RAND commitment of widespread adoption of the standard through avoidance of holdup and stacking.

111. With respect to hold-up, the parties would examine a reasonable royalty rate under the RAND commitment based on the contribution of the patented technology to the capabilities of the standard, and in turn, the contribution of those capabilities of the standard to the implementer and the implementer's products. Thus, a patent that is extremely important and central to the standard would reasonably command a higher royalty rate than a less important patent. Importantly, however, because an "essential" patent is one that is necessary to implement either an optional or mandatory provision of a standard, a specific SEP may contribute greatly to an optional portion of a given standard, but if that portion is not used by the implementer, the specific SEP may have little value to the implementer.

112. With respect to stacking concerns, the parties attempting to reach an agreement would consider the overall licensing landscape in existence vis-a-vis the standard and the implementer's products. In other words, a RAND negotiation would not be conducted in a vacuum. The parties would instead consider other SEP holders and the royalty rate that each of these patent holders might seek from the implementer based the importance of these other patents to the standard and to the implementer's products.

113. Finally, reasonable parties in search of a reasonable royalty rate under the RAND commitment would consider the fact that, to induce the creation of valuable standards, the RAND commitment must guarantee that holders of valuable intellectual property will receive reasonable royalties on that property.

Microsoft Corp. v. Motorola, Inc., 2013 U.S. Dist. LEXIS 60233 at *57–*65.

Judge Robart's opinion in *Microsoft* immediately became the subject of much debate. Some applauded the decision as setting forth a thorough framework that can be applied in all similarly situated cases. *See* Jorge L. Contreras, *So That's What RAND Means?: A Brief Report on The Findings of Fact and Conclusions of Law in Microsoft v. Motorola*, PATENTLY O (Apr. 27, 2013), http://patentlyo.com/patent/2013/04/so-thats-what-rand-means-a-brief-report-on-the-findings-of-fact-and-conclusions-of-law-in-microsoft-v-motorola.html (last visited 1/19/2015); *see also Realtek Semiconductor Corp. v. LSI Corp.*, 2014 U.S. Dist. LEXIS 81673 (N.D. Cal. June 16, 2014) and *In re Innovatio IP Ventures, LLC*, 2013 U.S. Dist. LEXIS 144061 (N.D. Ill. Sept. 27, 2013) (both applying the test set forth in *Microsoft*; the court's opinion in *Innovatio* is reproduced in Section D of Chapter 11 of this casebook). However, many others criticize the *ex ante* incremental value approach as unworkable; fifteen factors without any assigned relative weight are difficult for a judge, let alone a jury, to decipher with consistency. The approach is also widely seen as contrary to the purpose of standard licensing. By severely limiting how much the SEP holder can recover from implementers, the approach may disincentivize patent holders from participating in standard setting. *See* Daryl Lim, *Standard Essential Patents, Trolls, and the Smartphone Wars: Triangulating the End Game*, 119 Penn S. L. Rev. 1 (2014); Richard A. Epstein & David J. Kappos, *Legal Remedies for Patent Infringement: From General Principles To FRAND Obligations For Standard Essential Patents*, 9 Competition Pol'y Int'l 69, 78 (2013); Damien Geradin, *The Meaning of 'Fair and Reasonable' in the Context of Third-Party Determination of FRAND Terms*, 21 Geo. Mason L. Rev. 919, 948 (2014).

Additionally, the hypothetical negotiation analysis fails to consider the fact that, in an actual negotiation, parties are unlikely to be certain that the patent which is the subject of licensing is valid and infringed. Professor Sidak argues that FRAND royalty disputes ought to be treated very differently than cases in which a court must determine an appropriate royalty rate as damages for infringement. FRAND royalty disputes are more analogous to contract disputes, in which the parties contest the meaning of a contract term, whereas infringement cases are more analogous to tort cases, in which the court is assessing liability damages. Rather than applying the same basic framework to these two contrasting sets of disputes, it may be more effective to think of standard setting participants as having specifically opted out of the common law framework for calculating royalties. J. Gregory Sidak, *The Meaning of FRAND, Part I: Royalties*, 9 J. Comp. L. & Econ 931 (2013).

7. Patent Packages

When a license includes several of the licensor's patents, the license is known as a patent package. It is not uncommon for an inventive company that is a pioneer in its field to obtain multiple related patents in that field. The scope of the inventive company's patent portfolio may be so broad as to dominate a field. A licensor interested in operating in the field consequently might be interested in obtaining a patent package in order to gain access to the full scope of the licensor's patents in the specific field.

Well Surveys, Inc. v. Perfo-Log, Inc.

United States Court of Appeals for the Tenth Circuit

396 F.2d 15 (10th Cir. 1968)

Breitenstein, Circuit Judge.

Appellant-plaintiff Well Surveys, Inc., sued appellee-defendant Perfo-Log, Inc., for infringement of the Swift Patent No. 2,554,844 and the Peterson Patent No. 2,967,994. Perfo-Log denies infringement and asserts patent misuse as a defense. The trial court granted summary judgment for Perfo-Log on the ground of misuse of the Swift patent.

. . .

The Swift patent covers a system of measuring radiation from the earth formations around a well casing and, at the same time, locating the collars of the casing as a positive indication of the depth at which particular radiation is measured. The expiration date of the Swift patent is May 29, 1968.

The Peterson patent relates to a type of collar locator which can be used with the Swift system. It expires January 10, 1978. Various other collar locators can be used for the same purpose as Peterson.

The district court found that licensees under the immunity agreements could not terminate until after the expiration of the Swift patent; and that there was no provision for change in royalty base or for diminution in royalty after the expiration of the Swift patent. On the basis of these findings the court held that WSI had misused the Swift patent and granted the Perfo-Log motion for summary judgment. The WSI motion for partial summary judgment was denied.

The courts withhold aid to a party who has used his patent right contrary to the public interest. A patentee is not entitled to continue to receive "the benefit of an expired monopoly." In our first *McCullough* decision we reviewed the principle of misuse and the package licensing of patents. We concluded that package licensing was not misuse in the absence of coercion and said: ". . . in order to constitute a misuse, there must be an element of coercion, such as where there has been a request by a prospective licensee for a license under less than all of the patents and a refusal by the licensor to grant such a license."

In the second *McCullough* decision we considered claims that WSI had misused its patents through monopolization of the well-logging industry, improper extension of its patent monopoly, and unfounded infringement threats and litigation. We held that the showing made was insufficient to establish a change in the licensing practices which we approved in the first *McCullough* decision and rejected the claims of misuse.

Perfo-Log says that the licenses which it submitted in support of a summary judgment motion establish per se a misuse of the Swift patent. Prime reliance is had on eight agreements which covered both the Swift and the Peterson patents. These agreements were not terminable at the will of the licensee until the lapse of varying periods after the expiration of the Swift patent. The uniform royalty rate of 5% was not diminished after the expiration of Swift. The royalty provision reads thus:

> "3.02 Company agrees to pay DII [WSI] as royalty on each Radioactivity Well Surveying operation conducted by Company, which, if unlicensed, would infringe the Patent Rights of DII [WSI] during the term of this agreement an amount equal to five per cent (5%) of the gross charge (exclusive of mileage) made for the survey so conducted or a sum of ten dollars ($10.00), whichever is greater."

The literal language does not exact a royalty on an expired patent because payment is required only for operations which infringe a patent right of WSI. There can be no infringement of an expired patent.

Although the royalty rate does not change, the base for that rate changes because after the expiration of Swift, no royalty is payable unless the Peterson patent is used in the logging operations. The lack of diminution in royalty rate for the use of Peterson without Swift and the provisions for termination do not of themselves establish coercion. The question is whether the licensee was forced to enter into a package arrangement. Perfo-Log offered nothing on this point but relied on the agreements. WSI submitted the affidavits of two officers to show a continuation of the license practices approved in our first McCullough decision. One of the affidavits stated:

> "Every prospective licensee was offered a license under any of the radioactivity well surveying patents of Dresser Industries, Inc. and/or Well Surveys, Inc. which it desired, individually or collectively, upon negotiated reasonable terms. No licensee or prospective licensee was ever coerced to pay royalty on or for any operations covered by any expired patent."

To support its argument that the licenses per se establish patent misuse, Perfo-Log relies on the decision in *Rocform Corp. v. Acitelli-Standard Concrete Wall, Inc.*, [367 F.2d 678 (6th Cir. 1966)]. That case concerned patents, one of which was of basic importance, for pouring concrete basement walls. The license agreement covered several patents and provided no royalty reduction after the expiration of the basic patent. The Sixth Circuit held that the lack of diminution in royalty and the absence of an appropriate termination clause established misuse. One judge dissented on the basis of our first *McCullough* decision. *Id.* at 682. In its statement of facts the Sixth Circuit said that Rocform offered to license only under its standard package agreement. In the case at bar, the affidavits submitted by WSI show willingness to license any or all patents under reasonable, negotiated terms. If the *Rocform* decision is taken as holding that a package license, including both important and unimportant patents, is misuse per se when there is no diminution in royalty, or provision for termination, after the expiration of an important patent, we respectfully disagree and adhere to our decision in the first *McCullough* case. The relative importance of patents has no significance if a licensee is given the choice to take a patent alone or in combination on reasonable terms. Freedom of choice is the controlling question.

Perfo-Log argues that the district judge drew a permissible inference of misuse from the licenses and that under *United States v. United States Gypsum Co.*, [333 U.S. 364 (1948)], this inference is binding on the appellate court unless clearly erroneous. The difficulty is that the inference was drawn on a motion for summary judgment. In such a situation "the inferences to be drawn from the underlying facts . . . must be viewed in the light most favorable to the party opposing the motion." Here the inference runs contrary to the uncontroverted showing by WSI that it offered to license any or all of its patents on reasonable, negotiated terms. In such circumstances the inference is not controlling. At the most it establishes a genuine issue as to a material fact and, under the provisions of Rule 56(c), F.R. Civ. P., precludes the grant of a summary judgment.

WSI urges that summary judgment on the misuse issue should have been given in its favor. Although we are convinced that the showing by WSI's affidavit of readiness to license any or all of its patents on reasonable terms is sufficient to defeat the Perfo-Log motion for summary judgment, we cannot say that such showing entitles WSI to the relief it seeks. The fact finder must weigh the provisions of the license agreements against the facts surrounding the grant of those licenses. In our opinion this is not a case for the use of the summary judgment procedure.

The judgment is reversed and the case is remanded for trial on the merits.

U.S. Philips Corporation v. International Trade Commission

United States Court of Appeals for the Federal Circuit

424 F.3d 1179 (Fed. Cir. 2005)

BRYSON, CIRCUIT JUDGE.

U.S. Philips Corporation appeals from a final order of the United States International Trade Commission, in which the Commission held six of Philips's patents for the manufacture of compact discs to be unenforceable because of patent misuse. The Commission ruled that Philips had employed an impermissible tying arrangement because it required prospective licensees to license packages of patents rather than allowing them to choose which individual patents they wished to license and making the licensing fee correspond to the particular patents designated by the licensees. . . . We reverse and remand.

I

Philips owns patents to technology for manufacturing recordable compact discs ("CD-Rs") and rewritable compact discs ("CD-RWs") in accordance with the technical standards set forth in a publication called the Recordable CD Standard (the "Orange Book"), jointly authored by Philips and Sony Corporation. Since the 1990s, Philips has been licensing those patents through package licenses. Philips specified that the same royalty was due for each disc manufactured by the licensee using patents included in the package, regardless of how many of the patents were used. Potential licensees who sought to license patents to the technology for manufacturing CD-Rs or CD-RWs were not allowed to license those patents individually and were not offered a lower royalty rate for licenses to fewer than all the patents in a package.

Initially, Philips offered four different pools of patents for licensing: (1) a joint CD-R patent pool that included patents owned by Philips and two other companies (Sony and Taiyo Yuden); (2) a joint CD-RW patent pool that included patents owned by Philips and two other companies (Sony and Ricoh); (3) a CD-R patent pool that included only patents owned by Philips; and (4) a CD-RW patent pool that included only patents owned by Philips. After 2001, Philips offered additional package options by grouping its patents into two categories, which Philips denominated "essential" and "nonessential" for producing compact discs compliant with the technical standards set forth in the Orange Book.

In the late 1990s, Philips entered into package licensing agreements with [Princo, GigaStorage, and Linberg]. Soon after entering into the agreements, however, Princo, GigaStorage, and Linberg stopped paying the licensing fees. Philips filed a complaint with the International Trade Commission that Princo, GigaStorage, and Linberg, among others, were violating section 337(a)(1)(B) of the Tariff Act of 1930, 19 U.S.C. § 1337(a)(1)(B), by importing into the United States certain CD-Rs and CD-RWs that infringed six of Philips's patents.

. . . .

II

Patent misuse is an equitable defense to patent infringement. It "arose to restrain practices that did not in themselves violate any law, but that drew anticompetitive strength from the patent right, and thus were deemed to be contrary to public policy." *Mallinckrodt, Inc. v. Medipart, Inc.*, 976 F.2d 700, 704 (Fed. Cir. 1992). The purpose of the patent misuse defense "was to prevent a patentee from using the patent to obtain market benefit beyond that which inheres in the statutory patent right." . . .

This court summarized the principles of patent misuse as applied to "tying" arrangements in *Virginia Panel Corp. v. MAC Panel Co.*, 133 F.3d 860, 868–69 (Fed. Cir. 1997). The court there explained that because of the importance of anticompetitive effects in shaping the defense of patent misuse, the analysis of tying arrangements in the context of patent misuse is closely related to the analysis of tying arrangements in antitrust law. The court further explained that, depending on the circumstances, tying arrangements can be viewed as per se patent misuse or can be analyzed under the rule of reason. Id. The court noted that certain specific practices have been identified as constituting per se patent misuse, "including so-called 'tying' arrangements in which a patentee conditions a license under the patent on the purchase of a separable, staple good, and arrangements in which a patentee effectively extends the term of its patent by requiring post-expiration royalties." Id. at 869 (citations omitted). If the particular licensing arrangement in question is not one of those specific practices that has been held to constitute per se misuse, it will be analyzed under the rule of reason. Id. We have held that under the rule of reason, a practice is impermissible only if its effect is to restrain competition in a relevant market. *Monsanto Co. v. McFarling*, 363 F.3d 1336, 1341 (Fed. Cir. 2004); [*Windsurfing Int'l, Inc. v. AMF, Inc.*, 782 F.2d 995, 1001–02 (Fed. Cir. 1986)].

The Supreme Court's decisions analyzing tying arrangements under antitrust law principles are to the same effect. The Court has made clear that tying arrangements are deemed to be per se unlawful only if they constitute a "naked restraint of trade with no purpose except stifling of competition" and "always or almost always tend to restrict competition and decrease output" in some substantial portion of a market. *Broad. Music, Inc. v. Columbia Broad. Sys., Inc.*, 441 U.S. 1, 19–20, 99 S. Ct. 1551, 60 L. Ed. 2d 1 (1979). The Supreme Court has applied the per se rule only when "experience with a particular kind of restraint enables the Court to predict with confidence that the rule of reason will condemn it. . . ." [citations omitted].

While the doctrine of patent misuse closely tracks antitrust law principles in many respects, Congress has declared certain practices not to be patent misuse even though those practices might otherwise be subject to scrutiny under antitrust law principles. In 35 U.S.C. § 271(d), Congress designated several specific practices as not constituting patent misuse. The designated practices include "conditioning the license of any rights to the patent or the sale of the patented product on the acquisition of a license to rights in another patent or purchase of a separate product," unless, in view of the circumstances, the patent owner "has market power for the patent or patented product on which the license or sale is conditioned." Id. § 271(d)(5). Because the statute is phrased in the negative, it does not require that patent misuse be found in the case of all such conditional licenses in which the patent owner has market power; instead, the statute simply excludes such conditional licenses in which the patent owner lacks market power from the category of arrangements that may be found to constitute patent misuse.

Although section 271(d)(5) does not define the scope of the defense of patent misuse, but merely provides a safe harbor against the charge of patent misuse for certain kinds of conduct by patentees, the statute makes clear that the defense of patent misuse differs from traditional antitrust law principles in an important respect, as applied to tying arrangements involving patent rights. In the case of an antitrust claim based on a tying arrangement involving patent rights, this court has held that ownership of a patent on the tying good is presumed to give the patentee monopoly power. Section 271(d)(5) makes clear, however, that such a presumption does not apply in the case of patent misuse. To establish the defense of patent misuse, the accused infringer must show that the patentee has power in the market for the tying product.

Philips argues briefly that it lacks market power and that it is thus shielded from liability by section 271(d)(5). Based on detailed analysis by the administrative law judge, however, the Commission found that Philips has market power in the relevant market and that section 271(d)(5) is therefore inapplicable to this case. We sustain that ruling.

Philips contends that at the time Philips and Sony first created their package license arrangements, CDs had significant competition among computer data storage devices and thus Philips lacked market power in the market for computer data storage discs. However, Philips first created the package licenses long before GigaStorage and Princo entered into their agreements. According to the administrative law judge, the patent package arrangements were instituted in the early 1990s. Yet Princo did not enter into its agreement until June of 1997, and GigaStorage did not enter into its licensing agreement until October of 1999. Thus, any lack of market power that Philips and its colicensors may have had in the early 1990s is irrelevant to the situation in the late 1990s, when the parties entered into the agreements at issue in this case. At that time, according to the administrative law judge's well-supported finding, compact discs had become "unique products [with] no close practice substitutes." Philips's argument about lack of market power is therefore unpersuasive, and for that reason section 271(d)(5) does not provide Philips a statutory safe haven from the judicially created defense of patent misuse.

Apart from its specific challenge to the Commission's ruling on the market power issue, Philips launches a more broad-based attack on the Commission's conclusion that Philips's patent licensing policies constitute per se patent misuse. . . .

A

In its brief, the Commission argues that it is "hornbook law" that mandatory package licensing has been held to be patent misuse. While that broad characterization can be found in some treatises, see 6 Donald S. Chisum, Chisum on Patents § 19.04[3] (2003), cited in *C.R. Bard, Inc.*, 157 F.3d at 1373; 8 Ernest B. Lipscomb III, Lipscomb's Walter on Patents § 27 28: (3d ed. 1989 & Supp. 2003), Philips invites us to consider whether that broad proposition is sound. Upon consideration, we conclude that the proposition as applied to the circumstances of this case is not supported by precedent or reason.

In its opinion, the Commission acknowledged that the *Virginia Panel* case and many other patent tying cases "involve a tying patent and a tied product, rather than a tying patent and a tied patent." (emphasis in original). The Commission nonetheless concluded that "finding patent misuse based on a tying arrangement between patents in a mandatory package license is a reasonable application of Supreme Court precedent." In so ruling, the Commission relied primarily on two Supreme Court cases: *United States v. Paramount Pictures, Inc.*, 334 U.S. 131, 156–59, 68 S. Ct. 915, 92 L. Ed. 1260 (1948), and *United States v. Loew's, Inc.*, 371 U.S. 38, 44–51, 83 S. Ct. 97, 9 L. Ed. 2d 11 (1962). Those cases condemned the practice of "block-booking" movies to theaters (in the *Paramount* case) and to television stations (in the *Loew's* case) as antitrust violations.

We do not agree with the Commission that the decisions in *Paramount* and *Loew's* govern this case. In *Paramount*, the district court held that the defendant movie distributor had engaged in unlawful conduct because it offered to permit exhibitors to show the films they wished to license only if they agreed to license and exhibit other films that they were not interested in licensing. The Supreme Court affirmed that ruling. The Court held that block-booking was illegal because it "prevents competitors from bidding for single features on their individual merits," and because it "adds to the monopoly of a single copyrighted picture that of another copyrighted picture which must be taken and exhibited in order to secure the first." 334 U.S. at 156–57. The result, the Court explained, "is to add to the monopoly of the copyright in violation of the principle of the patent cases involving tying clauses." Id. at 158.

Because the block-booking arrangement at issue in *Paramount* required the licensee to exhibit all of the films in the group for which a license was taken, the Paramount block-booking was more akin to a tying arrangement in which a patent license is tied to the purchase of a separate product, rather than to an arrangement in which a patent license is tied to another patent license. Indeed, all of the patent tying cases to which the Supreme Court referred in *Paramount* involved tying arrangements in which, as the Court described them, "the owner of a patent [conditioned] its use on the purchase or use of patented or unpatented materials." 334 U.S. at 157. Because the arrangement in the *Paramount* case was equivalent in substance to a patent-to-product tying arrangement, *Paramount* does not stand for the proposition that a pure patent-to-patent tying arrangement, such as Philips's package licensing agreement, is per se unlawful.

Philips gives its licensees the option of using any of the patents in the package, at the licensee's option. Philips charges a uniform licensing fee to manufacture discs covered by its patented technology, regardless of which, or how many, of the patents in the package the licensee chooses to use in its manufacturing process. In particular, Philips's package licenses do not require that licensees actually use the technology covered by any of the patents that the Commission characterized as nonessential. In that respect, Philips's licensing agreements are different from the agreements at issue in *Paramount*, which imposed an obligation on the purchasers of package licenses to exhibit films they did not wish to license. That obligation not only extended the exclusive right in one product to products in which the distributor did not have exclusive rights, but it also precluded exhibitors, as a practical matter, from exhibiting other films that they may have preferred over the tied films they were required to exhibit. Because Philips's package licensing agreements do not compel the licensees to use any particular technology covered by any of the licensed patents, the *Paramount* case is not a sound basis from which to conclude that the package licensing arrangements at issue in this case constitute patent misuse per se.

In the *Loew's* case, the district court determined that the licensee television stations were required to pay fees not only for the feature films they wanted, but also for additional, inferior films. As in *Paramount*, the fact that the package arrangement required the television stations to purchase exhibition rights for the package at a price that was greater than the price attributable to the desired films made the tying arrangement very much like a tying arrangement involving products. . . .

In this case, unlike in *Loew's*, there is no evidence that a portion of the royalty was attributable to the patents that the Commission characterized as nonessential. . . . There is therefore no basis for conjecture that a hypothetical licensing fee would have been lower if Philips had offered to license the patents on an individual basis or in smaller packages.

Aside from *Paramount* and *Loew's*, the Commission relies on cases involving tying arrangements in which the patent owner conditions the availability of a patent license on the patentee's agreement to purchase a staple item of commerce from the patentee. . . . Those cases, however, are readily distinguishable because of the fundamental difference between an obligation to purchase a product and the extension of a nonexclusive license to practice a patent.

A nonexclusive patent license is simply a promise not to sue for infringement. The conveyance of such a license does not obligate the licensee to do anything; it simply provides the licensee with a guarantee that it will not be sued for engaging in conduct that would infringe the patent in question.

In the case of patent-to-product tying, the patent owner uses the market power conferred by the patent to compel customers to purchase a product in a separate market that the customer might otherwise purchase from a competitor. The patent owner is thus able to use the market power conferred by the patent to foreclose competition in the market for the product.

By contrast, a package licensing agreement that includes both essential and nonessential patents does not impose any requirement on the licensee. It does not bar the licensee from using any alternative technology that may be offered by a competitor of the licensor. Nor does it foreclose the competitor from licensing his alternative technology; it merely puts the competitor in the same position he would be in if he were competing with unpatented technology.

A package license is in effect a promise by the patentee not to sue his customer for infringing any patents on whatever technology the customer employs in making commercial use of the licensed patent. That surrender of rights might mean that the customer will choose not to license the alternative technology offered by the patentee's competition, but it does not compel the customer to use the patentee's technology. The package license is thus not anticompetitive in the way that a compelled purchase of a tied product would be.

Contrary to the Commission's characterization, the intervenors were not "forced" to "take" anything from Philips that they did not want, nor were they restricted from obtaining licenses from other sources to produce the relevant technology. Philips simply provided that for a fixed licensing fee, it would not sue any licensee for engaging in any conduct covered by the entire group of patents in the package. By analogy, if Philips had decided to surrender its "nonessential" patents or had simply announced that it did not intend to enforce them, there would have been no way for the manufacturers to decline or reject Philips's decision. Yet the economic effect of the package licensing arrangement for Philips's patents is not fundamentally different from the effect that such decisions would have had on third parties seeking to compete with the technology covered by those "nonessential" patents. Thus, we conclude that the Commission erred when it characterized the package license agreements as a way of forcing the intervenors to license technology that they did not want in order to obtain patent rights that they did.

The Commission stated that it would not have found the package licenses to constitute improper tying if Philips had offered to license its patents on an individual basis, as an alternative to licensing them in packages. The Commission's position, however, must necessarily be based on an assumption that, if the patents were offered on an individual basis, individual patents would be offered for a lower price than the patent packages as a whole. If that assumption were not implicit in the Commission's conclusion, the Commission would be saying in effect that it would be unlawful for Philips to charge the same royalty for its essential patents that it charges for its patent packages and to offer the nonessential patents for free. Yet that sort of pricing policy plainly would not be unlawful. *See Directory Sales Mgmt. Corp. v. Ohio Bell Tel. Co.*, 833 F.2d 606, 609–10 (6th Cir. 1987).

To the extent that the Commission's decision is based on an assumption that individual licenses would necessarily be available for a lower price than package licenses, that assumption is directly contrary to the evidence and even to the administrative law judge's findings of fact. As noted above, the administrative law judge found that the royalty rate under Philips's package licenses depended on the number of discs the manufacturer produced under the authority of the license, not the number of individual patents the manufacturer used to produce those discs. That is, the royalty rate did not vary depending on whether the licensees used only the essential patents or used all of the patents in the package. Thus, it seems evident that if Philips were forced to offer licenses on an individual basis, it would continue to charge the same per unit royalty regardless of the number of patents the manufacturer chose to license. That alteration in Philips's practice would have absolutely no effect on the would-be competitors who wished to offer alternatives to the technology represented by Philips's so-called nonessential patents, since those patents would effectively be offered for free, and the competitors would therefore still have to face exactly the same barriers—the availability of a free alternative to the technology that they were trying to license for a fee.

More generally, the Commission's assumption that a license to fewer than all the patents in a package would presumably carry a lower fee than the package itself ignores the reality that the value of any patent package is largely, if not entirely, based on the patents that are essential to the technology in question. A patent that is nonessential because it covers technology that can be fully replaced by alternative technology that is available for free is essentially valueless. A patent that is nonessential because it covers technology that can be fully replaced by alternative technology that is available through a license from another patent owner has value, but its value is limited by the price of the alternative technology. Short of imposing an obligation on the licensor to make some sort of allocation of fees across a group of licenses, there is no basis for the Commission to conclude that a smaller group of the licenses—the so-called "essential" licenses—would have been available for a lower fee if they had not been "tied to" the so-called nonessential patents.

It is entirely rational for a patentee who has a patent that is essential to particular technology, as well as other patents that are not essential, to charge what the market will bear for the essential patent and to offer the others for free. Because a license to the essential patent is, by definition, a prerequisite to practice the technology in question, the patentee can charge whatever maximum amount a willing licensee is able to pay to practice the technology in question. If the patentee allocates royalty fees between its essential and nonessential patents, it runs the risk that licensees will take a license to the essential patent but not to the nonessential patents. The effect of that choice will be that the patentee will not be able to obtain the full royalty value of the essential patent. For the patentee in this situation to offer its nonessential patents as part of a package with the essential patent at no additional charge is no more anti-competitive than if it had surrendered the nonessential patents or had simply announced a policy that it would not enforce them against persons who licensed the essential patent. In either case, those offering technology that competed with the non-essential patents would be unhappy, because they would be competing against free technology. But the patentee would not be using his essential patent to obtain power in the market for the technology covered by the nonessential patents. This package licensing arrangement cannot fairly be characterized as an exploitation of power in one market to obtain a competitive advantage in another.

Aside from the absence of evidence that the package licensing arrangements in this case had the effect of impermissibly broadening the scope of the "essential" patents with anticompetitive effect, Philips argues that the Commission failed to acknowledge the unique procompetitive benefits associated with package licensing. Philips points to the federal government's guide lines for licensing intellectual property, which recognize that patent packages "may provide procompetitive benefits by integrating complementary technologies, reducing transaction costs, clearing block-ing positions, and avoiding costly infringement litigation. By promoting the dis-semination of technology, cross-licensing and pooling arrangements are often procompetitive." U.S. Department of Justice and Federal Trade Commission, Anti-trust Guidelines for the Licensing of Intellectual Property § 5.5 (1995); *see also* Her-bert Hovenkamp, IP and Antitrust § 34.2c, at 34-7 (2004).

Philips introduced evidence that package licensing reduces transaction costs by eliminating the need for multiple contracts and reducing licensors' administrative and monitoring costs. [citation omitted]. Package licensing can also obviate any potential patent disputes between a licensor and a licensee and thus reduce the like-lihood that a licensee will find itself involved in costly litigation over unlicensed pat-ents with potentially adverse consequences for both parties, such as a finding that the licensee infringed the unlicensed patents or that the unlicensed patents were invalid. *See* Steven C. Carlson, Patent Pools and the Antitrust Dilemma, 16 Yale J. on Reg. 359, 379–81 (1999). Thus, package licensing provides the parties a way of ensuring that a single licensing fee will cover all the patents needed to practice a par-ticular technology and protecting against the unpleasant surprise for a licensee who learns, after making a substantial investment, that he needed a license to more pat-ents than he originally obtained. Finally, grouping licenses in a package allows the parties to price the package based on their estimate of what it is worth to practice a particular technology, which is typically much easier to calculate than determining the marginal benefit provided by a license to each individual patent. In short, pack-age licensing has the procompetitive effect of reducing the degree of uncertainty asso-ciated with investment decisions.

The package licenses in this case have some of the same advantages as the pack-age licenses at issue in the *Broadcast Music* case. The Supreme Court determined in that case that the blanket copyright package licenses at issue had useful, pro-competitive purposes because they gave the licensees "unplanned, rapid, and indemnified access to any and all of the repertory of [musical] compositions, and [they gave the owners] a reliable method of collecting for the use of the their copyrights." [*Broadcast Music, Inc. v. Columbia Broadcasting System, Inc.*, 441 U.S. 1, 20 (1979)]. While "individual sales transactions [would be] quite expensive, as would be individual monitoring and enforcement," a package licensing agreement would ensure access and save costs. Id. Hence, the Supreme Court determined that such conduct should fall under "a more discriminating examination under the rule of reason." Id. at 24.

In light of the efficiencies of package patent licensing and the important differences between product-to-patent tying arrangements and arrangements involving group licensing of patents, we reject the Commission's conclusion that Philips's conduct shows a "lack of any redeeming virtue" and should be "conclusively presumed to be unreasonable and therefore illegal without elaborate inquiry as to the precise harm they have caused or the business excuse for their use." *N. Pac. Ry. Co. v. United States*, 356 U.S. 1, 5, 78 S. Ct. 514, 2 L. Ed. 2d 545 (1958). We therefore hold that the analysis that led the Commission to apply the rule of per se illegality to Philips's package licensing agreements was legally flawed.

B

In the alternative, Philips argues that the Commission's finding of per se patent misuse was not justified by the facts of this case. In particular, Philips contends that the evidence did not show that there were commercially viable alternatives to the technology covered by the so-called "nonessential" patents in the Philips licensing packages that any of its licensees would have preferred to use.

In order to show that a tying arrangement is per se unlawful, a complaining party must demonstrate that it links two separate products and has an anticompetitive effect in the market for the second product. The Supreme Court explained that the "essential characteristic" of an invalid tying arrangement

> lies in the seller's exploitation of its control over the tying product to force the buyer in to the purchase of a tied product that the buyer either did not want at all, or might have preferred to purchase elsewhere on different terms. When such "forcing" is present, competition on the merits in the market for the tied item is restrained . . . .

[*Jefferson Parish Hosp. Dist. No. 2 v. Hyde*, 466 U.S. 2, 12 (1984)]. . . . The Commission found that the "nonessential" patents . . . constituted separate products from the "essential" patents in the package and that the package licensing agreements adversely affected competition in the market for the nonessential technology. The Commission's analysis of that factual issue was flawed, however.

Patents within a patent package can be regarded as "nonessential" only if there are "commercially feasible" alternatives to those patents. *See Int'l Mfg. Co. v. Landon*, 336 F.2d 723, 729 (9th Cir. 1964). If there are no commercially practicable alternatives to the allegedly nonessential patents, packaging those patents together with so-called essential patents can have no anticompetitive effect in the marketplace, because no competition for a viable alternative product is foreclosed. In such a case, the only effect of finding per se patent misuse is to give licensees a way of avoiding their obligations under the licensing agreements, with no corresponding benefit to competition in any real-world market.

The Department of Justice has recognized that the availability of commercially viable alternative technology is relevant to the analysis of package licensing agreements. In particular, the Department has stated that patent packages do not have the undesirable effects of tying if they include patents to technology for which there is no practical or realistic alternative. *See, e.g.,* Business Review Letter, U.S. Department of Justice, Antitrust Division (Dec. 16, 1998). That principle is consistent with the main purpose of the separate-products inquiry in tying cases generally, which is to ensure that conduct is not condemned as anticompetitive "unless there is sufficient demand for the purchase of [the tied product] separate from the [tying product] to identify a distinct product market in which it is efficient to offer [the tied product]." *Jefferson Parish*, 466 U.S. at 21–22; *see* [*Mallinckrodt, Inc. v. Medipart, Inc.*, 976 F.2d 700, 704 (Fed. Cir. 1992)] (tying is misuse only when the patentee uses its patent to obtain "market benefit" beyond that conferred by the patent).

In this case, the evidence did not show that there were commercially viable substitutes for the ["nonessential"] patents that disc manufacturers wished to use in making compact discs compliant with the Orange Book standards. There was thus insufficient evidence that including the four "nonessential" patents in the Philips patent packages had an actual anticompetitive effect. That is, the evidence did not show that there were commercially viable substitutes for those four "nonessential" patents that disc manufacturers wished to use in making compact discs compliant with the Orange Book standards.

. . . .

Beyond the absence of factual support for the Commission's findings, the Commission's analysis of the four "nonessential" patents demonstrates a more fundamental problem with applying the per se rule of illegality to patent packages such as the ones at issue in this case. If a patentholder has a package of patents, all of which are necessary to enable a licensee to practice particular technology, it is well established that the patentee may lawfully insist on licensing the patents as a package and may refuse to license them individually, since the group of patents could not reasonably be viewed as distinct products. *See Landon*, 336 F.2d at 729. Yet over time, the development of alternative technology may raise questions whether some of the patents in the package are essential or whether, as in this case, there are alternatives available for the technology covered by some of the patents. Indeed, in a fast-developing field such as the one at issue in this case, it seems quite likely that questions will arise over time, such as what constitutes an "essential" patent for purposes of manufacturing compact discs compliant with the Orange Book standard. [citation omitted]. Under the Commission's approach, an agreement that was perfectly lawful when executed could be challenged as per se patent misuse due to developments in the technology of which the patentees are unaware, or which have just become commercially viable. Such a rule would make patents subject to being declared unenforceable due to developments that occurred after execution of the license or were unknown to the parties at the time of licensing. Not only would such a rule render licenses subject to invalidation on grounds unknown at the time of licensing, but it would also provide a strong incentive to litigation by any licensee, since the reward for showing that even a single license in a package was "nonessential" would be to render all the patents in the package unenforceable. For that reason as well, we reject the Commission's ruling that package agreements of the sort entered into by Philips and the intervenors must be invalidated on the ground that they constitute per se patent misuse.

III

In the alternative, the Commission held that Philips's package licensing agreements constituted patent misuse under the rule of reason. The Commission's analysis under the rule of reason largely tracked the analysis that led it to conclude that the package licensing agreements constituted per se patent misuse.

. . . .

Under the rule of reason, the finder of fact must determine if the practice at issue is "reasonably within the patent grant, i.e., that it relates to subject matter within the scope of the patent claims." . . .

The Commission's rule of reason analysis is flawed for two reasons. Most importantly, its conclusion was largely predicated on the anticompetitive effect on competitors offering alternatives to the four so-called nonessential patents in the Philips patent packages. Yet, as we have already held, the evidence did not show that including those patents in the patent packages had a negative effect on commercially available technology. The Commission assumed that there was a foreclosure of competition because compact disc manufacturers would be induced to accept licenses to the technology covered by [two of the "nonessential"] patents and therefore would be unwilling to consider alternatives. As noted, however, there was no evidence before the Commission that any manufacturer had actually refused to consider alternatives to the technology covered by those patents or for that matter that any commercially viable alternative actually existed.

In addition, as in its per se analysis, the Commission did not acknowledge the problems with licensing patents individually, such as the transaction costs associated with making individual patent-by-patent royalty determinations and monitoring possible infringement of patents that particular licensees chose not to license. The Commission also did not address the problem, noted above, that changes in the technology for manufacturing compact discs could render some patents that were indisputably essential at the time of licensing arguably nonessential at some later point in the life of the license. To hold that a licensing agreement that satisfied the rule of reason when executed became unreasonable at some later point because of technological development would introduce substantial uncertainty into the market and displace settled commercial arrangements in favor of uncertainty that could only be resolved through expensive litigation.

Finally, the Commission failed to consider the efficiencies that package licensing may produce because of the innovative character of the technology at hand. Given that the technology surrounding the Orange Book standard was still evolving, there were many uncertainties regarding what patents might be needed to produce the compact discs. As noted, package license agreements in which the royalty was based on the number of units produced, not the number of patents used to produce them, can resolve in advance all potential patent disputes between the licensor and the licensee, whereas licensing patent rights on a patent-by-patent basis can result in continuing disputes over whether the licensee's technology infringes certain ancillary patents owned by the licensor that are not part of the group elected by the licensee.

We therefore conclude that the line of analysis that the Commission employed in reaching its conclusion that Philips's package licensing agreements are more anticompetitive than procompetitive, and thus are unlawful under the rule of reason, was predicated on legal errors and on factual findings that were not supported by substantial evidence. For these reasons, we cannot uphold the Commission's decision that Philips's patents are unenforceable because of patent misuse under the rule of reason.

. . . .

REVERSED AND REMANDED.

Notes & Questions

1. Subsequent Results on Remand

After the Supreme Court refused to review the *Philips* decision, 547 U.S. 1207, on remand, the Commission rejected Princo's remaining theories of patent misuse. *In the Matter of Certain Recordable Compact Discs & Rewritable Compact Discs Comm'n Opinion*, USITC Inv. No. 337-TA-474 (Feb. 5, 2007). Princo again appealed. A divided panel of the Federal Circuit rejected most of Princo's arguments, but vacated the Commission's remedial orders and remanded the case for further proceedings on the issue of whether Philips and Sony had formed an agreement to suppress the technology embodied in Sony's Lagadec patent. *Princo Corp. v. Int'l Trade Comm'n*, 563 F.3d 1301 (Fed. Cir. 2009). However, the court agreed to review the latter issue *en banc* and eventually rejected the only remaining Princo arguments against Philips. *Princo Corp. v. Int'l Trade Comm'n*, 616 F.3d 1318, 1332 (Fed. Cir. 2010) (*en banc*). The Supreme Court denied certiorari in May 2011, ending the long-lasting dispute. 563 U.S. 987.

2. Concerns Relating to the Component Patents

A licensor of a patent package must be conscious of the fact that the individual patents in a package may expire on different dates, and some may become more valuable than others over time. One arrangement that addresses this problem is to offer a package of patents at a rate less than the cost of all of the patents individually. The license agreement should explicitly state the arrangement, or it should be reflected in the royalty allocation. In addition, a licensor can give the licensee the option to terminate the agreement when a patent expires and invite renegotiation or provide for renegotiation upon expiration of a patent, with an arbitration provision for dispute settlement.

3. Antitrust Concerns

A licensor may not condition a license for a patent that a licensee desires on the licensing of patents that the licensee does not want. A package license that forces licensees to pay for the licensing of unwanted patents runs afoul of antitrust laws. *See Zenith Radio Corp. v. Hazeltine Research Inc.*, 395 U.S. 100 (1969) (superseded on other grounds by statute as noted in *In re Recombinant DNA Technology Patent & Contract Litig.*, 850 F. Supp. 769 (S.D. Ind. 1994)). Packages for mutual convenience, however, are permissible. *See Valmont Indus., Inc. v. Yuma Mfg. Co.*, 296 F. Supp. 1291, 1299 (D. Colo. 1969). Parties are allowed to mutually agree to a license that includes multiple patents, provided that the arrangement achieves some administrative advantage or other convenient result for the parties.

8. University Licensing

Licensing patents resulting from university research and development has become big business at major universities. According to a recent study, during the period 1996–2015 academic patents and related licensing to industry increased U.S. industry gross output by up to $1.33 trillion, U.S. GDP by up to $591 billion, and supported up to 4,272,000 person years of employment. *See* Lori Pressman et al., *The Economic Contribution of University/Nonprofit Inventions in the United States: 1996–2015*, Biotechnology Innovation Organization & Association of University Technology Managers (Jun. 2017), https://www.bio.org/sites/default/files/June%20 2017%20Update%20of%20I-O%20%20Economic%20Impact%20Model.pdf. While most schools receive more modest royalty incomes, New York University took in $1.88 billion in gross licensing revenue from 2002 to 2011. Northwestern University, the University of California, Columbia University, and Emory University were also among the top five schools with the highest gross licensing revenue for this period. This section examines the unique concerns that apply to university licensing.

One concern a licensee must keep in mind when pursuing a license from a university is the role of government funding in creation of the invention. For some universities, up to 90 percent of research conducted by the university is funded by a government agency. As a consequence of accepting government funding, the Bayh Dole Act and related federal regulations restrict the university in transferring the rights to the fruits of the government-funded research. Typically, the government obtains a nonexclusive license to use the invention while the university maintains title to the inventions. A licensor should keep in mind the government's nonexclusive license in the patent when seeking a license and negotiating its terms.

Another concern that arises in university licensing involves the common university policy of encouraging the free dissemination of information. In *University of*

Colo. Found., Inc. v. Am. Cyanamid Co., 342 F.3d 1298 (Fed. Cir. 2003), two professors at the University of Colorado conducted a series of experiments as a favor to a colleague working for the pharmaceutical company Cyanamid. At the conclusion of the studies, the professors immediately wrote up their findings in an article titled "Inadequate Iron Absorption from Many Prenatal Multivitamin-Mineral Supplements," and submitted a manuscript for publication in the *New England Journal of Medicine*. Though the findings of the studies ultimately resulted in a patentable improvement to the formulation of a prenatal multivitamin/mineral supplement, the professors did not apply for a patent concerning their discoveries but rather intended that the discoveries be dedicated to the public. The court awarded damages to the professors and the university for Cyanamid's improper use of the journal manuscript to obtain a patent over their discovery. The court recognized that journal publication, in the academic realm, "provides another incentive separate and apart from the patent laws." In light of the academic policy that encourages free dissemination of information, a licensee must reconcile any confidentiality clause in the licensing agreement with the university's policy of information dissemination.

In *Stanford v. Roche*, 131 S. Ct. 2188 (2011), the Supreme Court ruled that The University and Small Business Patent Procedures Act of 1980 (Bayh-Dole Act) "does nothing more than clarify the order of priority of rights between the Federal Government and a federal contractor in a federally funded invention that already belongs to the contractor." *Id.* at 2195. Based on this construction of the Act, the Court "confirmed the general rule that rights in an invention belong to the inventor" and rejected Stanford's argument that "the Act automatically vests title to federally funded inventions in federal contractors." *Id.* at 2199. In effect, recognizing that "[a] patent is property and title to it can pass only by assignment," the Court made it clear that employee's invention does not automatically belong to employer absent an agreement between them. *Id.* at 2195. For more discussion on this and other related cases, see Chapter 12, Section A(3).

B. Trade Secret Licensing

1. Introduction

Trade secret protection requires only that an owner safeguard the information underlying a trade secret to prevent unauthorized use and disclosure. Unlike patent protection, the owner of the underlying subject matter need not meet high inventive standards or file disclosures to secure trade secret protection. The trade-off for lower requirements for obtaining protection is that trade secret protection only prevents the use or disclosure of the secret by those standing in a special relationship to the trade secret owner and those who utilized improper means to acquire the information. Trade secret protection does not protect the trade secret owner from independent discoverers.

A key right of a trade secret owner in the context of licensing is the right to control the disclosure of a trade secret. To maintain trade secret protection, however, a trade secret owner must show reasonable diligence in safeguarding the secrecy of the matter disclosed, even with disclosures to licensees. A licensor entering into negotiations involving the disclosure of trade secrets should ensure that the subject matter of the disclosure and the rights and duties of each party are clearly defined in a contractual agreement. Clearly defined duties are in the best interests of the licensee as well. Absent an express agreement, the confidential relationship arising as a consequence of the negotiations and disclosure between the licensor and licensee may subject the licensee to comparatively ill-defined duties that arise as a matter of law. Of course, the subject matter of a trade secret license must be a trade secret. The licensing agreement is revocable on the theory of mutual mistake of fact if the subject matter of a trade secret license is later determined to be otherwise.

The ability of a trade secret transferor to control the use, disclosure, and reverse engineering of the trade secret subject matter by a transferee depends on whether the negotiated transaction is a sale or a license. An outright sale of a trade secret limits a transferor's ability to enforce restrictions on the transferee as compared to a license. Since a transferor of a license has greater leeway to control the conduct of the transferee, many trade secret owners like software manufacturers turn to licensing to protect the trade secrets embodied in their programs. *See ProCD, Inc. v. Zeidenberg*, 86 F.3d 1447 (7th Cir. 1996); *Step-Saver Data Systems, Inc. v. Wyse Technology*, 939 F.2d 91 (3d Cir. 1991). To decide whether a transaction embodied in an agreement is a license or an outright sale, courts examine the substance of the contract. A contract may be characterized as providing for a sale if the terms exceed the transferred product's life, the agreement cannot be terminated except in the case of reverse engineering, there is no negotiated, signed licensing agreement, and the product is acquired from a retail sales outlet or by mail order.

Notes & Questions

1. Confidentiality & Post-Termination Clauses

A trade secret licensing agreement should include a confidentiality clause that clearly defines the steps the licensee must take to safeguard the secrecy of the trade secret. Specifically, an agreement should explicitly state the confidentiality requirements the licensee is expected to meet and make them binding. A licensor also needs to protect the secrecy of a trade secret after the termination of a licensing agreement. To accomplish this goal, an agreement may include a provision that requires the return of tangible embodiments of a trade secret at the end of a period of licensing and may extend the secrecy requirements binding upon the licensee beyond the end of the licensing period and beyond the entry of the trade secret into the public domain.

2. Multiple Trade Secrets

It is not uncommon for trade secret licenses to involve more than one trade secret. Licensing of multiple trade secrets, however, can give rise to Sherman § 2 monopolization and Clayton §7 asset acquisition issues under the antitrust laws. Licensors must pay careful attention to the concerns arising from the component trade secrets in a multiple trade secret license. Trade secret protection has the potential to endure indefinitely, so long as the information remains a secret. However, once information becomes generally known, the trade secret status of the information ends, and the value of that information decreases. Licensors should account for the uncertain duration of trade secret protection by either assigning separate royalty rates for each individual trade secret, or by including a means of adjusting the royalty rate when a trade secret enters the public domain.

2. Duration of Trade Secret Royalties

Warner-Lambert Pharmaceutical Company v. John J. Reynolds, Inc.

United States District Court for the Southern District of New York

178 F. Supp. 655 (S.D.N.Y. 1959)

(affirmed 280 F.2d 197 (2d Cir.1960) (per curiam))

BRYAN, J.

Plaintiff sues under the Federal Declaratory Judgment Act, 28 U.S.C. §§ 2201 and 2202, for a judgment declaring that it is no longer obligated to make periodic payments to defendants based on its manufacture or sale of the well known product 'Listerine', under agreements made between Dr. J. J. Lawrence and J. W. Lambert in 1881, and between Dr. Lawrence and Lambert Pharmacal Company in 1885. Plaintiff also seeks to recover the payments made to defendants pursuant to these agreements since the commencement of the action.

Plaintiff is a Delaware corporation which manufactures and sells Listerine, among other pharmaceutical products. It is the successor in interest to Lambert and Lambert Pharmacal Company which acquired the formula for Listerine from Dr. Lawrence under the agreements in question. Defendants are the successors in interest to Dr. Lawrence.

Jurisdiction is based on diversity of citizenship.

For some seventy-five years plaintiff and its predecessors have been making the periodic payments based on the quantity of Listerine manufactured or sold which are called for by the agreements in suit. The payments have totaled more than twenty-two million dollars and are presently in excess of one million five hundred thousand dollars yearly.

. . . .

In the early 1880's Dr. Lawrence, a physician and editor of a medical journal in St. Louis, Missouri, devised a formula for an antiseptic liquid compound which was given the name 'Listerine'. The agreement between Lawrence and J. W. Lambert made in 1881, and that between Lawrence and Lambert Pharmacal Company made in 1885, providing for the sale of the Lawrence formula, were entered into in that city. Lambert, and thereafter his corporation, originally engaged in the manufacture and sale of Listerine and other pharmaceutical preparations on a modest scale there. Through the years the business prospered and grew fantastically and Listerine became a widely sold and nationally known product. The Lambert Pharmacal Company . . . continued the manufacture and sale of Listerine and other preparations until March 31, 1955, when it was merged into Warner-Hudnut, Inc., . . . and the name of the merged corporation was changed to Warner-Lambert Pharmaceutical Company, Inc. The plaintiff in this action is the merged corporation which continues the manufacture and sale of Listerine.

Plaintiff's second amended complaint in substance alleges the following:

Prior to April 20, 1881 Dr. Lawrence furnished Lambert with an unnamed secret formula for the antiseptic compound which came to be known as "Listerine," and on or about that date Lambert executed the first of the documents with which we are concerned here. This document, in its entirety, reads as follows:

> "Know all men by these presents, that for and in consideration of the fact, that Dr. J. J. Lawrence of the city of St Louis Mo has furnished me with the formula of a medicine called Listerine to be manufactured by me, that I Jordan W Lambert, also of the city of St Louis Mo, hereby agree for myself, my heirs, executors and assigns to pay monthly to the said Dr. J. J. Lawrence his heirs, executors or assigns, the sum of twenty dollars for each and every gross of said Listerine hereafter sold by myself, my heirs, executors or assigns. . . ."

On or about May 2, 1881 Lambert began the manufacture of the formula and adopted the trademark "Listerine." The agreed payments under the 1881 agreement were reduced on October 21, 1881 . . . [and again on March 23, 1883 by letters addressed to Lambert by Lawrence to the amount of six dollars per gross amount of sales].

Thereafter Lambert assigned his rights to Listerine and other Lawrence compounds to the Lambert Pharmacal Company and this company on January 2, 1885 executed an instrument assuming Lambert's obligations under these agreements with Lawrence and other obligations on account of other formulas which Lawrence had furnished. . . .

The agreements between the parties contemplated, it is alleged, "the periodic payment of royalties to Lawrence for the use of a trade secret, to wit, the secret formula for" Listerine. After some modifications made with Lawrence's knowledge and approval, the formula was introduced on the market. The composition of the compound has remained the same since then and it is still being manufactured and sold by the plaintiff.

It is then alleged that the "trade secret" (the formula for Listerine) has gradually become a matter of public knowledge through the years following 1881 and prior to 1949, and has been published in the United States Pharmacopoia, the National

Formulary and the Journal of the American Medical Association, and also as a result of proceedings brought against plaintiff's predecessor by the Federal Trade Commission. Such publications were not the fault of plaintiff or its predecessors.

The complaint recites the chains of interest running respectively from Lambert to the present plaintiff and from Lawrence to the defendants, and concludes with a prayer for a declaration that plaintiff is "no longer liable to the defendants" for any further "royalties."

Despite the mass of material before me the basic issue between the parties is narrow. The plaintiff claims that its obligation to make payments to the defendants under the Lawrence-Lambert agreements was terminated by the public disclosure of the Listerine formula in various medical publications. The defendants assert that the obligation continued and has not been terminated.

(1).

The plaintiff seems to feel that the 1881 and 1885 agreements are indefinite and unclear, at least as to the length of time during which they would continue in effect. I do not find them to be so. These agreements seem to me to be plain and unambiguous.

In the 1881 agreement Lambert, for himself, his heirs, executors or assigns, agrees to pay Lawrence, his heirs, executors and assigns, "twenty dollars for each & every gross of said Listerine hereafter sold by myself my heirs executors or assigns." By the 1885 agreement the Lambert Pharmacal Company "agrees and contracts for itself & assigns to pay . . . J. J. Lawrence, his heirs executors & assigns, six dollars on each & every gross of Listerine . . . manufactured or sold by the said Lambert Pharmacal Co. or its assigns. . . ."

There is no ambiguity or uncertainty in this language. Nor can I ascertain any alternative or hidden meanings lurking within it.

The payments to Lawrence and his successors are conditioned upon the sale (in the 1881 agreement) and the manufacture or sale (in the 1885 agreement) of the medical preparation known as Listerine which Lawrence conveyed to Lambert. The obligation to pay on each and every gross of Listerine continues as long as this preparation is manufactured or sold by Lambert and his successors. It comes to an end when they cease to manufacture or sell the preparation. There is nothing which compels the plaintiff to continue such manufacture and sale. No doubt Lambert and his successors have been and still are free at any time, in good faith and in the exercise of sound business discretion, to stop manufacturing and selling Listerine. The plain meaning of the language used in these agreements is simply that Lambert's obligation to pay is co-extensive with manufacture or sale of Listerine by him and his successors.

(2).

The plaintiff, however, claims that despite the plain language of the agreement it may continue to manufacture and sell without making the payments required by the agreements because the formula which its predecessors acquired is no longer secret. To sustain this position plaintiff invokes the shade, if not the substance, of the traditional common law distaste for contractual rights and duties unbounded by definite limitations of time and argues that absent a construction that the obligation to pay is co-extensive only with the secrecy of the formula, it must be a forbidden "perpetuity" which the law will not enforce. I find no support for the plaintiff's theory either in the cases which it cites or elsewhere.

The word "perpetuity" is often applied very loosely to contractual obligations. Indiscriminate application of the term serves only to confuse. The mere fact that an obligation under a contract may continue for a very long time is no reason in itself for declaring the contract to exist in perpetuity or for giving it a construction which would do violence to the expressed intent of the parties.

. . . .

Contracts which provide no fixed date for the termination of the promisor's obligation but condition the obligation upon an event which would necessarily terminate the contract are in quite a different category and it is in this category that the 1881 and 1885 Lambert Lawrence agreements fall. On the face of the agreements the obligation of Lambert and its successors to pay is conditioned upon the continued manufacture or sale or Listerine. When they cease manufacturing or selling Listerine the condition for continued payment comes to an end and the obligation to pay terminates. This is the plain meaning of the language which the parties used.

Moreover, this is not a case in which the promisor's obligation will cease only on the occurrence of some fortuitous event unrelated to the subject matter of the contract. The obligation here is conditioned upon an event arising out of the very arrangement between the parties which is the subject matter of the contract.

. . . .

In the case at bar the obligation to continue payments as long as Lambert or his successors continue to manufacture or sell Listerine is plain from the language of the agreements and is implicit in their terms. There is no need to "construe" these contracts so as to import a condition or date of termination other than that expressed by the parties themselves in the agreements which they made. Courts must "concern (themselves) with what the parties intended, but only to the extent that they evidenced what they intended by what they wrote." An attempt to write new terms into this plain and simple agreement would be unwarranted and gratuitous. "We may not now imply a condition which the parties chose not to insert in their contract. . . ." Nor is there any need to resort to extrinsic evidence in order to ascertain what the intention of the parties was, or what the termination date of the obligation to pay would be, for the agreements themselves indicate the condition upon which the obligation terminates.

There is nothing unreasonable or irrational about imposing such an obligation. It is entirely rational and sensible that the obligation to make payments should be based upon the business which flows from the formula conveyed. Whether or not the obligation continues is in the control of the plaintiff itself. For the plaintiff has the right to terminate its obligation to pay whenever in good faith it desires to cease the manufacture or sale of Listerine. This would seem to end the matter.

(3).

However, plaintiff urges with vigor that the agreement must be differently construed because it involved the conveyance of a secret formula. The main thrust of its argument is that despite the language which the parties used the court must imply a limitation upon Lambert's obligation to pay measured by the length of time that the Listerine formula remained secret.

. . . .

In . . . patent and copyright cases the parties are dealing with a fixed statutory term and the monopoly granted by that term. This monopoly, created by Congress, is designed to preserve exclusivity in the grantee during the statutory term and to release the patented or copyrighted material to the general public for general use thereafter. This is the public policy of the statutes in reference to which such contracts are made and it is against this background that the parties to patent and copyright license agreements contract.

Here, however, there is no such public policy. The parties are free to contract with respect to a secret formula or trade secret in any manner which they determine for their own best interests. A secret formula or trade secret may remain secret indefinitely. It may be discovered by someone else almost immediately after the agreement is entered into. Whoever discovers it for himself by legitimate means is entitled to its use. But that does not mean that one who acquires a secret formula or a trade secret through a valid and binding contract is then enabled to escape from an obligation to which he bound himself simply because the secret is discovered by a third party or by the general public. I see no reason why the court should imply such a term or condition in a contract providing on its face that payment shall be co-extensive with use. To do so here would be to rewrite the contract for the parties without any indication that they intended such a result.

It may be noted that here the parties themselves made no reference to secrecy in either the 1881 or the 1885 agreements. The word "secret" is not used anywhere in either of them. It is true that I have assumed during this discussion that the plaintiff is correct in its contention that what Lambert bargained for was a "secret" formula. But that in no way justifies the further assumption that he also bargained for continuing secrecy or that there would be failure of consideration if secrecy did not continue.

The argument that there was failure of consideration in 1931 after the agreement had been in force for some forty-five years because of disclosure then, is wholly devoid of merit. The plaintiff does not question that the conveyance to it of the "secret formula" furnished consideration for the contract. Once a contract is supported by consideration its terms are up to the parties. Whether the consideration is adequate or not is no concern of the court. The parties are free to fix their own terms and they have done so here. Plaintiff's argument goes only to adequacy of consideration. There is no question of failure of consideration.

One who acquires a trade secret or secret formula takes it subject to the risk that there be a disclosure. The inventor makes no representation that the secret is non-discoverable. All the inventor does is to convey the knowledge of the formula or process which is unknown to the purchaser and which in so far as both parties then know is unknown to any one else. The terms upon which they contract with reference to this subject matter are purely up to them and are governed by what the contract they enter into provides.

If they desire the payments or royalties should continue only until the secret is disclosed to the public it is easy enough for them to say so. But there is no justification for implying such a provision if the parties do not include it in their contract, particularly where the language which they use by fair intendment provides otherwise.

The case at bar illustrates what may occur in such cases. As the undisputed facts show, the acquisition of the Lawrence formula was the base on which plaintiff's predecessors built up a very large and successful business in the antiseptic or germicide field. Even now, twenty-five or more years after it is claimed that the trade secret was disclosed to the public, plaintiff retains more than 50% of the national market in these products.

Plaintiff lays stress on the large sums which have been spent in advertising and promoting the product, and there is no doubt that this and the business acumen of plaintiff's predecessors have contributed greatly to the success of the business. But it may be noted that the advertising and promotional material is primarily based on what are claimed to be the extraordinary merits of the formula for Listerine which plaintiff's predecessors acquired from Dr. Lawrence. Plaintiff and its predecessors have proclaimed for many years through the widest variety of advertising and promotional media the unique, indeed, almost magical properties of the formula from which Listerine is still made which is the formula conveyed by Lawrence to Lambert.

At the very least plaintiff's predecessors, through the acquisition of the Lawrence formula under this contract, obtained a head start in the field of liquid antiseptics which has proved of incalculable value through the years. There is nothing novel about business being transacted only in a small way at the outset of a contract relationship and thereafter growing far beyond what was anticipated when the contract was made. Because the business has prospered far beyond anticipations affords no basis for changing the terms of the contract the parties agreed upon when the volume was small.

There is nothing in this contract to indicate that plaintiff's predecessors bargained for more than the disclosure of the Lawrence formula which was then unknown to it. Plaintiff has pointed to no principle of law or equity which would require or permit the court gratuitously to rewrite the contract which its predecessors made for these considerations.

If plaintiff wishes to avoid its obligations under the contract it is free to do so, and, indeed, the contract itself indicates how this may be done. The fact that neither the plaintiff nor its predecessors have done so, and that the plaintiff continues to manufacture and sell Listerine under the Lawrence formula with great success, indicates how valuable the rights under the contract are and how unjust it would be to permit it to have its cake and eat it too.

Thus, I hold that under the agreements in suit plaintiff is obligated to make the periodic payments called for by them as long as it continues to manufacture and sell the preparation described in them as Listerine.

Notes & Questions

1. Enforcement in Perpetuity

The holding of *Warner-Lambert* teaches that if parties to a trade secret license agree to royalty payments for use of the information, the royalties on the trade secret may be enforced in perpetuity. The result in *Warner-Lambert* is controversial. Some jurisdictions have followed the RESTATEMENT (THIRD) OF UNFAIR COMPETITION, which takes the position that an agreement is unenforceable as an unreasonable restraint of trade if it purports to protect information that is in the public domain. RESTATEMENT (THIRD) OF UNFAIR COMPETITION § 41 cmt. d.

2. Hybrid License

An inventor has the right to elect either patent or trade secret protection for subject matter that qualifies for protection under both regimes. The owner of the subject matter is also permitted to use both forms of protection simultaneously for different aspects of their invention. For instance, subject matter not described or disclosed in a patent may be retained as a trade secret, so long as the invention has been completely described and the best mode disclosed. Licenses that cover trade secrets and patents must clearly distinguish trade secret royalties from patent royalties, otherwise royalties for both become unenforceable once the patent term runs out. *See Brulotte v. Thys Co.*, 379 U.S. 29 (1964). The consideration for the trade secret should be stated separately from the consideration for the patent. Additionally, to avoid antitrust issues, the licensor should not require the licensee to take the trade secret as a condition for obtaining a license on the patent.

C. Trademark Licensing

Trademarks and service marks identify the source of goods or services. Marks help consumers distinguish the goods or services of one provider from the goods or services of another provider. When consumers associate a mark with high-quality, desirable goods or services, the mark may become a thing of value in and of itself. The licensing of trademarks allows owners of marks to benefit from the value accrued in their mark and also forms the backbone of the franchising industry.

1. Requirement of Good Will: Prohibition Against "Bare" or "Naked" License

International Cosmetics Exchange, Inc. v. Gapardis Health & Beauty, Inc.

United States Court of Appeals for the Eleventh Circuit

303 F.3d 1242 (11th Cir. 2002)

Birch, Circuit Judge.

I. BACKGROUND

CLM, a French corporation, manufactures and sells ethnic cosmetic products in France and Europe under its trademark "FAIR & WHITE." CLM's President, Xavier Tancogne, is a chemist with a doctorate in pharmacy and created the formula for the "FAIR & WHITE" products.

ICE, a United States company founded by Michael Aini, is engaged in the purchase, importation, sale and distribution of ethnic cosmetic products. Aini is also the owner of four "Home Boys" stores in Brooklyn, New York, which are discount stores selling health and beauty aids to the African-American community. While in France, Michael's brother Jacob ("Jack") became interested in "FAIR & WHITE." In 1998, Jack purchased small quantities of "FAIR & WHITE" products from CLM to test United States market acceptance. These products were sold in the "Home Boys" stores and were well received.

Thereafter, ICE and CLM entered into contract negotiations to continue "to develop, market and promote the "FAIR & WHITE" brand name in the United States." The Agreement stated that CLM was the owner of the "FAIR & WHITE" trademark in France and Europe, and that ICE was "the owner and holder of all rights, title and interest in the mark 'FAIR & WHITE' in the United States, Canada and Caribbean Islands." In return, the Agreement obligated ICE to sell $250,000 for the first year and use its best efforts to increase sales by 20 percent per year over the next five years. However, there were no provisions as to purchase or manufacture of the products. In the fall of 1999, ICE purchased approximately $125,000 of "FAIR & WHITE" product from CLM. ICE applied to register the mark with the United States Patent and Trademark Office in early 2000.

Meanwhile, . . . Gapardis, a distributor of ethnic products in Miami, became interested in "FAIR & WHITE" products and contacted Tancogne. On 13 April 2000, . . . Gapardis became the exclusive distributor in the United States for CLM's cosmetics bearing the "FAIR & WHITE" mark.

At some point, Tancogne became aware that counterfeit "FAIR & WHITE" goods were being sold in the United States. He believed that ICE was responsible and stopped providing ICE with product in April of 2000. ICE then took immediate steps to procure substitute "FAIR & WHITE" products from a Spanish manufacturer, Jabones Pardo. ICE provided Pardo with samples of "FAIR & WHITE" products and the formula of its active ingredients. Thereafter, ICE distributed non-CLM manufactured goods bearing the "FAIR & WHITE" mark and the associated trade names in the United States.

II. DISCUSSION

First, we affirm the ruling that the ICE/CLM Agreement was enforceable. CLM argues that the Agreement was an invalid "'assignment in gross,' which at minimum assigned the mark to ICE only in conjunction with the sale of genuine CLM-manufactured products." CLM maintains that ICE was only interested in owning the mark and did not purchase its formula or any assets. However, it is well-settled law that "the transfer of a trademark or trade name without the attendant good-will of the business which it represents is, in general, an invalid, 'in gross' transfer of rights." Although an assignment must be accompanied by the attendant good-will, there need not be any transfer of tangible assets. "An assignment of United States trademark rights by a foreign manufacturer to its United States distributor ordinarily will not be regarded as an assignment in gross, even if the transfer occurs after the designation has acquired trademark significance in this country." J. Thomas McCarthy, McCarthy on Trademarks and Unfair Competition § 29:8 (4th ed. 2002) (citation omitted).

As the district court correctly notes, the Agreement clearly recognizes the prior efforts of ICE with respect to "FAIR & WHITE" product:

> I.C.E. has developed, distributed and marketed the "FAIR & WHITE" brand name in connection with the Products in the United States . . . and as a result of I.C.E.'s efforts, the "FAIR & WHITE" brand name has achieved widespread popularity, recognition and awareness, and has become known to retailers and consumers in the United States . . . .

Thus, at the time the Agreement was created, the assignment was not in gross because it continued the association of the "FAIR & WHITE" trademark with the very goods which created its reputation. Thus, we agree with the district court that the Agreement was enforceable. Having established that the Agreement was enforceable, we analyze the appropriateness of injunctive relief.

"The grant or denial of a preliminary injunction is within the sound discretion of the district court and will not be disturbed absent a clear abuse of discretion." A party seeking a preliminary injunction for trademark infringement must establish four elements: "(1) a substantial likelihood of success on the merits; (2) a substantial threat of irreparable injury if the injunction were not granted; (3) that the threatened injury to plaintiffs outweighs the harm an injunction may cause the defendant; and (4) that granting the injunction would not disserve the public interest."

A. *ICE's Entitlement to Injunctive Relief*

The evidence supports the finding that there was an Agreement between CLM and ICE, and that ICE made an initial order for approximately $125,000 of product in August of 1999. CLM and ICE agreed that ICE would use its best efforts to sell $250,000 of "FAIR & WHITE" product within the first year of the Agreement and 20 percent more within the next five years. CLM failed to supply ICE with "FAIR & WHITE" product, and therefore, breached the Agreement. In addition, the district court concluded that CLM's contract with Gapardis further violated the Agreement, which granted ICE exclusive distribution rights in the United States as well as exclusive ownership of the "FAIR & WHITE" mark.

Since ICE had no right to continue using the "FAIR & WHITE" mark after losing access to the trademarked product, it also had no right to prevent CLM from using the trademark on the grounds that by doing so would confuse consumers. Any confusion is due to ICE's palming off another product as "FAIR & WHITE." Consequently, ownership rights to the "FAIR & WHITE" mark in the United States reverted back to CLM. Therefore, ICE is not entitled to injunctive relief because it has no longer has a property interest in the trademark.

B. *CLM's Entitlement to Injunctive Relief*

The district court found that when ICE began selling counterfeit product, it caused a likelihood of confusion regarding the "FAIR & WHITE" mark and that subsequent sales by [another party] added to the confusion. "While the trademark laws could not provide a basis for relief unless there was a breach of contract," CLM established that ICE breached the Agreement and thus trademark law is applicable to claims of unauthorized use of the mark. In order to succeed on the merits of a trademark infringement claim, CLM must show that the ICE used the mark in commerce without its consent and "that the unauthorized use was likely to deceive, cause confusion, or result in mistake." There can be no dispute that the parties' concurrent use of the "FAIR & WHITE" mark poses a substantial likelihood of confusion among consumers. The district court further decided that CLM demonstrated a substantial threat of irreparable injury if injunctive relief was not granted. It is clear from the evidence that ICE and [a third party] were selling counterfeit "FAIR & WHITE" product in the United States. Furthermore, as stated by the district court, "the threatened injury to CLM, by confusion in the market regarding the F&W Mark, outweighs any harm to ICE in preventing it from selling product supplied by third parties, particularly in light of the Court's finding that ICE is no longer the exclusive distributor."

AFFIRMED.

Notes & Questions

1. Why Require a Transfer of Good Will?

Prevention of consumer confusion and deception is the rationale behind the rule against assignments in gross. Over time, consumers associate particular goods or services with a mark. Through use in the market, a mark develops good will. The rule against a bare or naked license protects consumers' expectation by safeguarding the association between a mark and the underlying assets, or good will. Transfer of a trademark divorced from its good will is an assignment in gross and is an invalid transfer. A licensor who transfers a bare license without its good will may find that his mark is unenforceable against alleged infringers. Additionally, the licensor may face a charge of abandonment and lose ownership in the mark.

For a mark to have good will, the mark must be used in a market and not have been abandoned. The licensor of the mark must own the good will in the market. If the mark is not used in a market, then it has no good will in that market and cannot be transferred.

In order to avoid an assignment in gross, a trademark owner wishing to license his mark must transfer the good will associated with the mark along with the mark itself. Transfer of good will along with a mark is a requirement of 15 U.S.C. § 1060. Under the original strict interpretation of this rule, courts determined whether a trademark license transferred good will by looking for evidence that assets associated with the licensor's business were assigned along with the mark. *See Pepsico v. Grapette Co.*, 416 F.2d 285 (8th Cir. 1969). Today the requirement has relaxed and courts look for evidence that the license is used with a product or service that is sufficiently similar to that of the licensor's.

2. Good Will, Where Have You Gone?

More recently, courts have extended the scope of trademark protection to include a broadening array of uses. The extended scope of protection has spurred licensing activities. Some uses of a mark trigger non-source associations, such as the encouragement of team loyalty when a sports team licenses its name for use on apparel. Such uses of a mark for purposes other than source identification rarely impair the mark's potential for legal protection. A party who would otherwise be liable for infringement for selling apparel bearing the sports team's name will generally sign a licensing agreement with the owner for the use of the mark. Is this transfer not a form of naked licensing? How can this accepted practice be reconciled with the requirement that a licensor must transfer good will along with a mark?

3. Strategic or Defensive Transfer of Trademarks

Companies acquire trademarks for strategic or defensive purposes, as for example when a company launching a new product purchases another company's similar related mark in order to establish an earlier use date or to avoid conflicting marks. Even though such acquisitions may run counter to the prohibition against naked licensing, strategic acquisition of trademarks is an accepted and commonplace transaction. *See Money Store v. Harriscorp Finance Inc.*, 689 F.2d 666 (7th Cir. 1982); *Glamorene Products Corp. v. Procter & Gamble Co.*, 538 F.2d 894 (C.C.P.A. 1976).

2. Control Over the Mark

A licensor must maintain control over the quality of the goods or services offered under the licensed trademark. The validity of a trademark license depends on the control over the "nature" and "quality" of the goods or services offered by the licensee. A licensor's failure to exercise control has severe repercussions. Without control over the licensee's use, the mark may lose its significance and cease to function as a trademark. Once this occurs, the licensor loses his rights in the mark.

Dawn Donut Company v. Hart's Food Stores, Inc.

United States Court of Appeals for the Second Circuit

267 F.2d 358 (2d Cir. 1958)

Lumbard, Circuit Judge.

. . . .

Plaintiff, Dawn Donut Co., Inc., of Jackson, Michigan since June 1, 1922 has continuously used the trademark "Dawn" upon 25 to 100 pound bags of doughnut mix which it sells to bakers in various states, including New York, and since 1935 it has similarly marketed a line of sweet dough mixes for use in the baking of coffee cakes, cinnamon rolls and oven goods in general under that mark. In 1950 cake mixes were added to the company's line of products. Dawn's sales representatives call upon bakers to solicit orders for mixes and the orders obtained are filled by shipment to the purchaser either directly from plaintiff's Jackson, Michigan plant, where the mixes are manufactured, or from a local warehouse within the customer's state. For some years plaintiff maintained a warehouse in Jamestown, New York, from which shipments were made, but sometime prior to the commencement of this suit in 1954 it discontinued this warehouse and has since then shipped its mixes to its New York customers directly from Michigan.

Plaintiff furnishes certain buyers of its mixes, principally those who agree to become exclusive Dawn Donut Shops, with advertising and packaging material bearing the trademark "Dawn" and permits these bakers to sell goods made from the mixes to the consuming public under that trademark. These display materials are supplied either as a courtesy or at a moderate price apparently to stimulate and promote the sale of plaintiff's mixes.

The district court found that with the exception of one Dawn Donut Shop operated in the city of Rochester, New York during 1926–27, plaintiff's licensing of its mark in connection with the retail sale of doughnuts in the state of New York has been confined to areas not less than 60 miles from defendant's trading area. The court also found that for the past eighteen years plaintiff's present New York state representative has, without interruption, made regular calls upon bakers in the city of Rochester, N.Y., and in neighboring towns and cities, soliciting orders for plaintiff's mixes and that throughout this period orders have been filled and shipments made of plaintiff's mixes from Jackson, Michigan into the city of Rochester. But it does not appear that any of these purchasers of plaintiff's mixes employed the plaintiff's mark in connection with retail sales.

The defendant, Hart Food Stores, Inc., owns and operates a retail grocery chain within the New York counties of Monroe, Wayne, Livingston, Genesee, Ontario and Wyoming. The products of defendant's bakery, Starhart Bakeries, Inc., a New York corporation of which it is the sole stockholder, are distributed through these stores, thus confining the distribution of defendant's product to an area within a 45 mile radius of Rochester. Its advertising of doughnuts and other baked products over television and radio and in newspapers is also limited to this area. Defendant's bakery corporation was formed on April 13, 1951 and first used the imprint 'Dawn' in packaging its products on August 30, 1951. The district court found that the defendant adopted the mark 'Dawn' without any actual knowledge of plaintiff's use or federal registration of the mark, selecting it largely because of a slogan 'Baked at midnight, delivered at Dawn' which was originated by defendant's president and used by defendant in its bakery operations from 1929 to 1935. Defendant's president testified, however, that no investigation was made prior to the adoption of the mark to see if anyone else was employing it. Plaintiff's marks were registered federally in 1927, and their registration was renewed in 1947. Therefore by virtue of the Lanham Act, 15 U.S.C.A. § 1072, the defendant had constructive notice of plaintiff's marks as of July 5, 1947, the effective date of the Act.

. . . .

The final issue presented is raised by defendant's appeal from the dismissal of its counterclaim for cancellation of plaintiff's registration on the ground that the plaintiff failed to exercise the control required by the Lanham Act over the nature and quality of the goods sold by its licensees.

We are all agreed that the Lanham Act places an affirmative duty upon a licensor of a registered trademark to take reasonable measures to detect and prevent misleading uses of his mark by his licensees or suffer cancellation of his federal registration. The Act, 15 U.S.C.A. § 1064, provides that a trademark registration may be cancelled because the Trademark has been "abandoned." And "abandoned" is defined in 15 U.S.C.A. § 1127 to include any act or omission by the registrant which causes the trademark to lose its significance as an indication of origin.

Prior to the passage of the Lanham Act many courts took the position that the licensing of a trademark separately from the business in connection with which it had been used worked an abandonment. The theory of these cases was that:

> "A trade-mark is intended to identify the goods of the owner and to safeguard his good will. The designation if employed by a person other than the one whose business it serves to identify would be misleading. Consequently, 'a right to the use of a trade-mark or a trade-name cannot be transferred in gross.'"

Other courts were somewhat more liberal and held that a trademark could be licensed separately from the business in connection with which it had been used provided that the licensor retained control over the quality of the goods produced by the licensee. *E. I. DuPont de Nemours & Co. v. Celanese Corporation of America*, 1948, 167 F.2d 484, 35 CCPA 1061, 3 A.L.R.2d 1213; *see also* 3 A.L.R.2d 1226, 1277–1282 (1949) and cases there cited. But even in the *DuPont* case the court was careful to point out that naked licensing, viz. the grant of licenses without the retention of control, was invalid.

The Lanham Act clearly carries forward the view of these latter cases that controlled licensing does not work an abandonment of the licensor's registration, while a system of naked licensing does. 15 U.S.C.A. § 1055 provides:

> "Where a registered mark or a mark sought to be registered is or may be used legitimately by related companies, such use shall inure to the benefit of the registrant or applicant for registration, and such use shall not affect the validity of such mark or of its registration, provided such mark is not used in such manner as to deceive the public."

And 15 U.S.C.A. § 1127[3] defines "related company" to mean "any person who legitimately controls or is controlled by the registrant or applicant for registration in respect to the nature and quality of the goods or services in connection with which the mark is used."

Without the requirement of control, the right of a trademark owner to license his mark separately from the business in connection with which it has been used would create the danger that products bearing the same trademark might be of diverse qualities. If the licensor is not compelled to take some reasonable steps to prevent misuses of his trademark in the hands of others the public will be deprived of its most effective protection against misleading uses of a trademark. The public is hardly in a position to uncover deceptive uses of a trademark before they occur and will be at best slow to detect them after they happen. Thus, unless the licensor exercises supervision and control over the operations of its licensees the risk that the public will be unwittingly deceived will be increased and this is precisely what the Act is in part designed to prevent. Clearly the only effective way to protect the public where a trademark is used by licensees is to place on the licensor the affirmative duty of policing in a reasonable manner the activities of his licensees.

The critical question on these facts therefore is whether the plaintiff sufficiently policed and inspected its licensees' operations to guarantee the quality of the products they sold under its trademarks to the public. The trial court found that: "By reason of its contacts with its licensees, plaintiff exercised legitimate control over the

---

3. 15 U.S.C. § 1127 has been amended several times since 1958. The current version of this statutory provision defines "related company" as "any person whose use of a mark is controlled by the owner of the mark with respect to the nature and quality of the goods or services on or in connection with which the mark is used."

nature and quality of the food products on which plaintiff's licensees used the trademark 'Dawn.' Plaintiff and its licensees are related companies within the meaning of Section 45 of the Trademark Act of 1946." It is the position of the majority of this court that the trial judge has the same leeway in determining what constitutes a reasonable degree of supervision and control over licensees under the facts and circumstances of the particular case as he has on other questions of fact; and particularly because it is the defendant who has the burden of proof on this issue they hold the lower court's finding not clearly erroneous.

I dissent from the conclusion of the majority that the district court's findings are not clearly erroneous because while it is true that the trial judge must be given some discretion in determining what constitutes reasonable supervision of licensees under the Lanham Act, it is also true that an appellate court ought not to accept the conclusions of the district court unless they are supported by findings of sufficient facts. It seems to me that the only findings of the district judge regarding supervision are in such general and conclusory terms of to be meaningless. In the absence of supporting findings or of undisputed evidence in the record indicating the kind of supervision and inspection the plaintiff actually made of its licensees, it is impossible for us to pass upon whether there was such supervision as to satisfy the statute. There was evidence before the district court in the matter of supervision, and more detailed findings thereon should have been made.

Plaintiff's licensees fall into two classes: (1) those bakers with whom it made written contracts providing that the baker purchase exclusively plaintiff's mixes and requiring him to adhere to plaintiff's directions in using the mixes; and (2) those bakers whom plaintiff permitted to sell at retail under the "Dawn" label doughnuts and other baked goods made from its mixes although there was no written agreement governing the quality of the food sold under the Dawn mark. The contracts that plaintiff did conclude, although they provided that the purchaser use the mix as directed and without adulteration, failed to provide for any system of inspection and control. Without such a system plaintiff could not know whether these bakers were adhering to its standards in using the mix or indeed whether they were selling only products made from Dawn mixes under the trademark "Dawn."

The absence, however, of an express contract right to inspect and supervise a licensee's operations does not mean that the plaintiff's method of licensing failed to comply with the requirements of the Lanham Act. Plaintiff may in fact have exercised control in spite of the absence of any express grant by licensees of the right to inspect and supervise.

The question then, with respect to both plaintiff's contract and non-contract licensees, is whether the plaintiff in fact exercised sufficient control.

Here the only evidence in the record relating to the actual supervision of licensees by plaintiff consists of the testimony of two of plaintiff's local sales representatives that they regularly visited their particular customers and the further testimony of one of them, Jesse Cohn, the plaintiff's New York representative, that "in many cases" he did have an opportunity to inspect and observe the operations of his customers. The record does not indicate whether plaintiff's other sales representatives made any similar efforts to observe the operations of licensees.

Moreover, Cohn's testimony fails to make clear the nature of the inspection he made or how often he made one. His testimony indicates that his opportunity to observe a licensee's operations was limited to "those cases where I am able to get into the shop" and even casts some doubt on whether he actually had sufficient technical knowledge in the use of plaintiff's mix to make an adequate inspection of a licensee's operations.

The fact that it was Cohn who failed to report the defendant's use of the mark "Dawn" to the plaintiff casts still further doubt about the extent of the supervision Cohn exercised over the operations of plaintiff's New York licensees.

Thus I do not believe that we can fairly determine on this record whether plaintiff subjected its licensees to periodic and thorough inspections by trained personnel or whether its policing consisted only of chance, cursory examinations of licensees' operations by technically untrained salesmen. The latter system of inspection hardly constitutes a sufficient program of supervision to satisfy the requirements of the Act.

Therefore it is appropriate to remand the counterclaim for more extensive findings on the relevant issues rather than hazard a determination on this incomplete and uncertain record. I would direct the district court to order the cancellation of plaintiff's registrations if it should find that the plaintiff did not adequately police the operations of its licensees.

But unless the district court finds some evidence of misuse of the mark by plaintiff in its sales of mixes to bakers at the wholesale level, the cancellation of plaintiff's registration should be limited to the use of the mark in connection with sale of the finished food products to the consuming public. Such a limited cancellation is within the power of the court. Section 1119 of 15 U.S.C.A. specifically provides that "In any action involving a registered mark the court may ... order the cancellation of registrations, in whole or in part...." Moreover, partial cancellation is consistent with § 1051(a)(1) of 15 U.S.C.A.,[4] governing the initial registration of trademarks which requires the applicant to specify "the goods in connection with which the mark is used and the mode or manner in which the mark is used in connection with such goods...."

The district court's denial of an injunction restraining defendant's use of the mark "Dawn" on baked and fried goods and its dismissal of defendant's counterclaim are affirmed.

---

4. The requirement that an applicant describe "the goods in connection with which the mark is used" is specified under subsection (a)(2) in the current version of § 1051 of 15 U.S.C.A.

Notes & Questions

1. Quality Control

An owner of a trademark may transfer the rights to a mark, so long as the licensor maintains control over its use. One of the first cases to allow trademark licensing over the objection of abandonment was *E.I. du Pont de Nemours & Co. v. Celanese Corp. of America*, 167 F.2d 484 (C.C.P.A. 1948). In *Celanese*, the court refused to cancel Celanese's trademark even though the company licensed off its mark to another party. Cancellation was inappropriate because Celanese maintained control over the quality standards for the product produced under the licensed mark. In light of the rationale for the rule against assignments in gross, why would control over a mark be the key inquiry for cancellation of a mark?

Courts determine on a case-by-case basis whether a licensor has exerted sufficient control over the quality of the goods and services produced under a licensed trademark. The control exerted over the licensee must guarantee the quality of the goods and services produced. A licensor may rely on third parties to conduct product testing, but sole reliance on third parties to enforce quality control standards may not be sufficient.

In a trademark licensing agreement, a licensor is well advised to specify which products and services the licensor authorizes the licensee to use in connection with the mark and define the requirements governing the quality of the goods or services to be produced. A licensor who fails to supervise a licensee's use of a mark may face a charge of abandonment of the mark. Specifically, if a licensor acquiesces to the use of a mark by a licensee who is unwilling or unable to abide by the quality control requirements set forth in a licensing agreement, the licensor risks abandonment of his rights in the mark. The licensor has an affirmative duty to act when he discovers a licensee's deviations from the quality control standards specified in a licensing agreement.

2. Enforcement of the Quality Control Requirement

Courts do not always strictly enforce the quality control requirement over a licensed trademark. Under certain circumstances, sufficient control can be found even without actual control or express provisions of control in a licensing contract. *Taco Cabana v. Two Pesos*, 932 F.2d 1113 (5th Cir. 1991), provides an example of such a circumstance:

> The purpose of the quality-control requirement is to prevent the public deception that would ensue from variant quality standards under the same mark or dress. Where the particular circumstances of the licensing arrangement persuade us that the public will not be deceived, we need not elevate form over substance and require the same policing rigor appropriate to more formal licensing and franchising transactions. Where the license parties have engaged in a close working relationship, and may justifiably rely on each parties' intimacy with standards and procedures to ensure consistent

quality, and no actual decline in quality standards is demonstrated, we would depart from the purpose of the law to find an abandonment simply for want of all the inspection and control formalities.

The history of the Stehling brothers' relationship warrants this relaxation of formalities. Prior to the licensing agreement at issue, the Stehling brothers operated Taco Cabana together for approximately eight years. Taco Cabana and TaCasita do not use significantly different procedures or products, and the brothers may be expected to draw on their mutual experience to maintain the requisite quality consistency. They cannot protect their trade dress if they operate their separate restaurants in ignorance of each other's operations, but they need not maintain the careful policing appropriate to more formal license arrangements.

Taco Cabana, 932 F.2d at 1121–1122. Moreover, courts do not require bilateral quality monitoring on the part of licensors. In other words, there is no need for equivalent policing of the licensor's and licensee's operations; the law only requires consistent quality.

3. Licensor's Ownership Arising From Use by a Licensee

If a licensee makes first use of a mark, does the licensee's use create ownership rights in the licensor? Under the old view, trademarks had to be used in order to become subject to ownership rights. Until a licensor used a mark, he did not own the mark and therefore had no right to transfer it. More recent decisions do not require that a licensor make first use of the mark before he licenses it.

Use by a licensee may create or maintain ownership of the mark in the licensor. Section 5 of the Lanham Act provides that the use of a mark by a "related company" inures to the benefit of the licensor. A licensor may rely on a licensee's use of the mark for any purpose, including first use of a mark, so long as the licensor controls the nature and quality of the goods or services. Section 45 of the Lanham Act defines the term "related company" to mean any person whose use of a mark is supervised by the owner of the mark for the purpose of ensuring the nature and quality of the products. So long as a licensor retains control over the mark, use by the licensee will be considered a use by the licensor.

4. Degree of Control: Franchisee Distinguished from Licensee

The franchising system was made possible by controlled trademark licensing. A franchise relationship arises where a trademark owner exercises "significant control or assistance" over the activities of a franchisee related to the franchisee's entire method of operation. "Significant control or assistance" under § 5 of Federal Trade Commission Act is greater involvement than merely assisting a transferee in selling the trademarked product or service. Control necessary to protect a trademark owner's rights in a mark does not constitute "significant" control or assistance that gives rise to a franchise relationship. A licensor is permitted to exercise a degree of supervision and control over licensees in order to protect its trademark. Moreover, control for trademark protection purposes does not make the licensee the licensor's agent.

5. "Naked Licensing": What Are the Consequences?

If a trademark owner fails to exercise control over a mark, does this mean that the owner loses all rights in the mark? Not necessarily. In *Dawn Donut,* the court held that the cancellation of the plaintiff's registration should be limited to the retail market and should not affect trademark rights in the wholesale market. *Patsy's Italian Rest., Inc. v. Banas,* 658 F.3d 254 (2d Cir. 2011) explains the point:

> Appellants [. . .] argue that any finding of naked licensing necessarily acted as a total abandonment of all rights. We disagree. Although some forms of trademark abandonment may result in a loss of all rights in the mark, abandonment of a mark through naked licensing has different effects on the validity of the mark in different markets. For example, if a restaurant operates in both New York and California, but engages in naked licensing only in California, the restaurant's registered mark may lose its significance in California while retaining its significance in New York. Thus, naked licensing will lead to an abandonment of a mark only where the mark loses its significance. 15 U.S.C. § 1127.

Banas, 658 F.3d at 264–65.

3. Antitrust Concerns: Tying

Tying in the context of trademark licensing occurs when a trademark owner forces a licensee to purchase ingredients or other products from the licensor or restricts the licensee to purchase only from licensor-approved suppliers as a condition for obtaining the license. Another version of tying involves multiple trademarks, as when an owner conditions licensing of one mark on the licensing of another.

Trademark licensing practices that otherwise run afoul of antitrust laws prohibiting tying might be justified under certain circumstances. The first justification for tying involves the licensor's duty to police the quality and nature of the goods and services produced in association with the licensed mark. For unique products or those that embody secret formulas or trade secrets, a licensor is permitted to require licensees to purchase products or product components from the licensor or an approved source. On the other hand, for non-unique products for which the licensor can furnish product specifications or instructions, the licensor cannot require purchases by the licensee. A second circumstance in which otherwise illegal tying practices are tolerated is in infant industries. For a short time, a licensor may require the purchase of a product if the tied product is new and previously unknown. Another circumstance that justifies tying practices involves franchising agreements. The goal of franchising is to establish a standard identity of all franchisees in the public's mind. In a franchise relationship, the trademark of the franchisor serves as a unifying element that assures consumers that products or services offered under the mark meet a uniform standard of quality. Courts accept that in order to form a unitary identity in the minds of consumers, a franchisor may need to require a franchisee to license multiple related marks.

Principe v. McDonald's Corporation

United States Court of Appeals for the Fourth Circuit

631 F.2d 303 (4th Cir. 1980)

PHILLIPS, CIRCUIT JUDGE.

This appeal presents the question of whether a fast food franchisor that requires its licensees to operate their franchises in premises leased from the franchisor is guilty of an illegal tying arrangement in violation of § 1 of the Sherman Act, 15 U.S.C. § 1. On the facts of this case, we hold it does not and affirm the directed verdict for the defendants.

. . . .

II

. . . .

McDonald's is not primarily a fast food retailer. While it does operate over a thousand stores itself, the vast majority of the stores in its system are operated by franchisees. Nor does McDonald's sell equipment or supplies to its licensees. Instead its primary business is developing and collecting royalties from limited menu fast food restaurants operated by independent business people.

McDonald's develops new restaurants according to master plans that originate at the regional level and must be approved by upper management. Regional administrative staffs meet at least annually to consider new areas into which McDonald's can expand. Once the decision is made to expand into a particular geographic area, specialists begin to search for appropriate restaurant sites. . . .

As part of the planning process, McDonald's decides what type of store to build on each site and where to locate it on the land. Differences in lot size and shape necessitate adjustments in store and parking lot configurations. Projected market size dictates dining room size. Land elevation, sign restrictions, store visibility and local set back requirements control restaurant placement. . . .

As constructed, McDonald's restaurants are finished shells; they contain no kitchen or dining room equipment. Furnishing store equipment is the responsibility of the operator. . . . McDonald's does provide specifications such equipment must meet, but does not sell the equipment itself.

Having acquired the land, begun construction of the store and selected an operator, McDonald's enters into two contracts with the franchisee. Under the first, the franchise agreement, McDonald's grants the franchisee the rights to use McDonald's food preparation system and to sell food products under the McDonald's name. The franchise pays a $12,500 franchise fee and agrees to remit three per cent of his gross sales as a royalty in return. Under the second contract, the lease, McDonald's grants the franchisee the right to use the particular store premises to which his franchise pertains. In return, the franchisee pays a $15,000 refundable security deposit (as evidence of which he receives a twenty year non-negotiable non-interest bearing note) and agrees to pay eight and one half per cent of his gross sales as rent. These payments under the franchise and lease agreements are McDonald's only sources of income from its franchised restaurants. The franchisee also assumes responsibility under the lease for building maintenance, improvements, property taxes and other costs associated with the premises. Both the franchise agreement and the lease generally have twenty year durations, both provide that termination of one terminates the other, and neither is available separately.

III

The Principes argue McDonald's is selling not one but three distinct products, the franchise, the lease and the security deposit note. The alleged antitrust violation stems from the fact that a prospective franchisee must buy all three in order to obtain the franchise.

. . . .

IV

"There is, at the outset of every tie-in case, including the familiar cases involving physical goods, the problem of determining whether two separate products are in fact involved." *Fortner Enterprises, Inc. v. United States Steel Corp.*, 394 U.S. 495, 507, 89 S. Ct. 1252, 1260, 22 L. Ed. 2d 495 (1969) (Fortner I) [overruled on other grounds as stated in *SC Manufactured Homes, Inc. v. Liebert*, 162 Cal. App. 4th 68 (2008)]. Because we agree with McDonald's that the lease, note and license are not separate products but component parts of the overall franchise package, we hold on the facts of this case there was no illegal tie in. Accordingly, we affirm the summary judgment and directed verdict for McDonald's on the tying claims.

Given the realities of modern franchising, we think the proper inquiry is not whether the allegedly tied products are associated in the public mind with the franchisor's trademark, but whether they are integral components of the business method being franchised. Where the challenged aggregation is an essential ingredient of the franchised system's formula for success, there is but a single product and no tie in exists as a matter of law.

Applying this standard to the present case, we hold the lease is not separable from the McDonald's franchise to which it pertains. McDonald's practice of developing a system of company owned restaurants operated by franchisees has substantial advantages, both for the company and for franchisees. It is part of what makes a McDonald's franchise uniquely attractive to franchisees.

First, because it approaches the problem of restaurant site selection systematically, McDonald's is able to obtain better sites than franchisees could select. Armed with its demographic information, guided by its staff of experts and unencumbered by preferences of individual franchisees, McDonald's can wield its economic might to acquire sites where new restaurants will prosper without undercutting existing franchisees' business or limiting future expansion. Individual franchisees are unlikely to possess analytical expertise, undertake elaborate market research or approach the problem of site selection from an area wide point of view. Individual franchisees benefit from the McDonald's approach because their stores are located in areas McDonald's has determined will produce substantial fast food business and on sites where that business is most likely to be diverted to their stores. Because McDonald's purposefully locates new stores where they will not undercut existing franchisees' business, McDonald's franchisees do not have to compete with each other, a substantial advantage in the highly competitive fast food industry.

Second, McDonald's policy of owning all of its own restaurants assures that the stores remain part of the McDonald's system. McDonald's franchise arrangements are not static: franchisees retire or die; occasionally they do not live up to their franchise obligations and must be replaced; even if no such contingency intervenes, the agreements normally expire by their own terms after twenty years. If franchisees owned their own stores, any of these events could disrupt McDonald's business and have a negative effect on the system's goodwill. Buildings whose architecture identified them as former McDonald's stores would sit idle or be used for other purposes. Replacement franchisees would have to acquire new and perhaps less desirable sites, a much more difficult and expensive process after the surrounding business area has matured. By owning its own stores, McDonald's assures its continued presence on the site, maintains the store's patronage even during management changes and avoids the negative publicity of having former McDonald's stores used for other purposes. By preserving the goodwill of the system in established markets, company store ownership produces attendant benefits for franchisees.

Third, because McDonald's acquires the sites and builds the stores itself, it can select franchisees based on their management potential rather than their real estate expertise or wealth. Ability to emphasize management skills is important to McDonald's because it has built its reputation largely on the consistent quality of its operations rather than on the merits of its hamburgers. A store's quality is largely a function of its management. McDonald's policy of owning its own stores reduces a franchisee's initial investment, thereby broadening the applicant base and opening the door to persons who otherwise could not afford a McDonald's franchise. Accordingly, McDonald's is able to select franchisees primarily on the basis of their willingness to work for the success of their operations. Their ability to begin operating a McDonald's restaurant without having to search for a site, negotiate for the land, borrow hundreds of thousands of dollars and construct a store building is of substantial value to franchisees.

Finally, because both McDonald's and the franchisee have a substantial financial stake in the success of the restaurant, their relationship becomes a sort of partnership that might be impossible under other circumstances. McDonald's spends close to half a million dollars on each new store it establishes. Each franchisee invests over $100,000 to make the store operational. Neither can afford to ignore the other's problems, complaints or ideas. Because its investment is on the line, the Company cannot allow its franchisees to lose money. This being so, McDonald's works with its franchisees to build their business, occasionally financing improvements at favorable rates or even accepting reduced royalty payments in order to provide franchisees more working capital.

All of these factors contribute significantly to the overall success of the McDonald's system. The formula that produced systemwide success, the formula that promises to make each new McDonald's store successful, that formula is what McDonald's sells its franchisees. To characterize the franchise as an unnecessary aggregation of separate products tied to the McDonald's name is to miss the point entirely. Among would be franchisees, the McDonald's name has come to stand for the formula, including all that it entails. We decline to find that it is an illegal tie in.

Notes & Questions

1. The Single Product Defense

The practice of tying, disfavored by the courts as anticompetitive, is defined as the conditioning of the sale of one product upon the purchase of a different (tied) product. The single product defense is premised on the principle that there can be no unlawful tying where there is only one product. The court in *Principe v. McDonald's Corp.*, 631 F.2d 303 (4th Cir. 1980), relies on the single product defense in ruling in favor of McDonald's. The court states, "Where the challenged aggregation is an essential ingredient of the franchised system's formula for success, there is but a single product and no tie in exists as a matter of law." *Id.* at 309.

2. Territorial Limitations

The United States Supreme Court in *United States v. Topco Associates, Inc.*, 405 U.S. 596 (1972), held that horizontal territorial divisions used as schemes to suppress competition were illegal *per se* under the Sherman Act. In *Topco*, the government alleged that a cooperative supermarket association's horizontal territorial limitations over its members were illegal as anti-competitive horizontal territorial restraints. The Court agreed and struck down the scheme.

The result in *Topco* has been widely criticized because business practices like the one in *Topco* may be viewed as pro-competitive. The *Topco* cooperative allowed its members, independent small grocery stores, to pool their purchasing strength together and compete against much larger chain stores. The ruling in *Topco* effectively denied the independent grocery stores a workable scheme, without which they were at a competitive disadvantage compared to the larger grocery chain stores.

D. Copyright Licensing

1. Introduction

Historically, the doctrine of indivisibility under the Copyright Act of 1909 held that the bundle of exclusive rights associated with copyrights could not be assigned or transferred in parts. Today, owners of copyrights may divide up the rights in the copyright bundle and assign or license each separately. The current Copyright Act expressly recognizes the divisibility of a copyright: "Any of the exclusive rights comprised in a copyright, including any subdivision of any of the rights specified in section 106, may be transferred . . . and owned separately. The owner of any particular exclusive right is entitled, to the extent of the right, to all of the protection and remedies accorded to the copyright owner by this title." 17 U.S.C. § 201(d)(2).

Silvers v. Sony Pictures Entertainment, Inc.

United States Court of Appeals for the Ninth Circuit

402 F.3d 881 (9th Cir. 2005)

GRABER, CIRCUIT JUDGE.

May an assignee who holds an accrued claim for copyright infringement, but who has no legal or beneficial interest in the copyright itself, institute an action for infringement? After analyzing the 1976 Copyright Act and its history, as well as the scant, although persuasive, precedent that is available in analogous situations, we answer that question "no." Accordingly, we reverse the ruling of the district court, which allowed this action by the assignee to proceed.

FACTUAL AND PROCEDURAL BACKGROUND

[Nancey Silvers wrote the script of a made-for-television movie called "The Other Woman" as a work-for-hire. Her employer, Frank & Bob Films, owned the copyright. A few years later, Frank & Bob Films, while retaining copyright ownership, assigned to Silvers a right to sue Sony for a particular instance of infringement of "The Other Woman" by Sony's motion picture "Stepmom."]

Silvers then filed a complaint against Sony for copyright infringement, alleging that the movie "Stepmom" was substantially similar to the script for "The Other Woman." Sony moved to dismiss on the ground that Silvers lacked standing to bring an action for copyright infringement in the absence of some legal or beneficial ownership in the underlying copyright. The district court denied the motion and certified the issue for interlocutory appeal.

DISCUSSION

A. *The Statute*

. . .

Section 501(b) of the 1976 Copyright Act establishes who is legally authorized to sue for infringement of a copyright:

> The *legal or beneficial owner of an exclusive right under a copyright* is entitled, subject to the requirements of section 411, to institute an action for any infringement of that particular right committed while he or she is the owner of it.

17 U.S.C. § 501(b) (emphasis added). The meaning of that provision appears clear. To be entitled to sue for copyright infringement, the plaintiff must be the "legal or beneficial owner of an exclusive right under a copyright."

. . .

The statute does not say expressly that *only* a legal or beneficial owner of an exclusive right is entitled to sue. But, under traditional principles of statutory interpretation, Congress' explicit listing of who *may* sue for copyright infringement should be understood as an *exclusion of others* from suing for infringement. The doctrine of *expressio unius est exclusio alterius* "as applied to statutory interpretation creates a presumption that when a statute designates certain persons, things, or manners of operation, all omissions should be understood as exclusions."

. . .

We think the meaning of §501(b) is clear, but we recognize that its omission explicitly to address the present question may create an ambiguity. Therefore, we consult legislative history.

B. *Legislative History*

[The court concluded that legislative history of the Copyright Act indicated that Congress wanted to ensure that only owners of an exclusive right in the copyright could bring suit.]

C. *Patent Law*

[Recognizing that there is a "strong connection between copyright and patent law," the court concludes that the Supreme Court's interpretation of the patent statute, under which only a patent owner or an exclusive licensee have standing to sue, should also be applied in copyright context.]

CONCLUSION

The bare assignment of an accrued cause of action is impermissible under 17 U.S.C. §501(b). Because that is all Frank & Bob Films conveyed to Silvers, Silvers was not entitled to institute and may not maintain this action against Sony for alleged infringement of the copyright in "The Other Woman."

Reversed.

DRK Photo v. McGraw-Hill Global Education Holdings, LLC

United States Court of Appeals for the Ninth Circuit

870 F.3d 978 (9th Cir. 2017)

Hawkins, Circuit Judge:

This appeal raises the now often litigated issue of whether a stock photography agency — here, the Arizona-based agency DRK Photo ("DRK") — has standing under the Copyright Act of 1976 to pursue infringement claims involving photographs from its collection. Ultimately, there is no bright line answer to this question. Here, we affirm the grant of summary judgment in favor of defendants, McGraw-Hill Global Education Holdings, LLC and McGraw-Hill School Education Holdings, LLC (collectively, "McGraw-Hill"), because DRK is a nonexclusive licensing agent for the photographs at issue and has failed to demonstrate any adequate ownership interest in the copyrights to confer standing. . . .

BACKGROUND

DRK is a stock photography agency that markets and licenses images created by others to publishing entities, including defendants McGraw-Hill. . . .

With regard to its own licensing of the photographs, DRK historically has entered into "Representation Agreements" with the photographers of the images that make up its collection. These Representation Agreements have generally taken two forms: (1) agreements appointing DRK as the "sole and exclusive agent" to license and sell the covered photographs, and (2) agreements appointing DRK as a nonexclusive agent to license and sell the covered photographs. Only the latter are at issue in this appeal.

According to DRK's owner, the majority of its arrangements with photographers are nonexclusive. In relevant part, those Representation Agreements provide that DRK will act as the "agent with . . . respect to the sale or leasing of the photographs or transparencies" delivered to DRK. Many of the agreements further clarify:

> DRK PHOTO will not require, nor ask a photographer or agency for exclusivity of an image until such time that DRK PHOTO has made an exclusive sale of that image. . . . Without this condition of an exclusive license/sale being made, all parties are free to promote and/or market all images without restriction.

They also provide that DRK and the photographer will split evenly the proceeds from all sales made by DRK.

In 2008, DRK endeavored to register copyrights for the photographs in its collection. To that end, each of the photographers whose images are involved in this litigation executed identical agreements entitled "Copyright Assignment, Registration, and Accrued Causes of Action Agreement" (the "Assignment Agreements"). In relevant part, the agreements provide:

> The undersigned photographer . . . grants to DRK all copyrights and complete legal title in the Images. DRK agrees to reassign all copyrights and complete legal title back to the undersigned immediately upon completion of the registration of the Images . . . and resolution of infringement claims brought by DRK relating to the Images.

> The undersigned agrees and fully transfers all right, title and interest in any accrued or later accrued claims, causes of action, choses of action . . . or lawsuits, brought to enforce copyrights in the Images, appointing and permitting DRK to prosecute said accrued or later accrued claims, causes of action, choses in action or lawsuits, as if it were the undersigned.

The Assignment Agreements also provide that DRK and the photographers will share equally the proceeds of any litigation award or settlement.

According to DRK, "[t]he primary purpose of the assignments was to effect a transfer [of] copyright ownership to DRK that was sufficient to support its copyright enforcement efforts." [The court provides excerpts from DRK's email correspondence with different photographers which explain that the intention of the agreement is limited to copyright enforcement.]

Following execution of the Assignment Agreements, photographers who were parties to nonexclusive Representation Agreements with DRK continued to market and sell their photographs on their own and through other means according to the terms of the Representation Agreements. DRK admits that the photographers had no duty to account to DRK for their sales of the photographs following execution of the Assignment Agreements.

PROCEDURAL HISTORY

In May 2012, DRK sued McGraw-Hill, asserting claims for copyright infringement premised on allegations that McGraw-Hill exceeded the scope of its licenses with DRK by printing and distributing more textbooks containing licensed images than authorized. In full, DRK alleged that McGraw-Hill made 1,120 infringing uses of approximately 636 unique photographs.

The parties eventually cross-moved for summary judgment, and the district court granted partial summary judgment to McGraw-Hill on the basis that DRK lacked standing to pursue infringement claims for photographs taken by photographers for whom DRK was acting as a nonexclusive agent. . . .

DISCUSSION

Section 501(b) of the Copyright Act of 1976 establishes who has standing to sue for infringement: "The legal or beneficial owner of an exclusive right under a copyright is entitled, subject to the [registration] requirements of section 411, to institute an action for any infringement of that particular right committed while he or she is the owner of it." 17 U.S.C. § 501(b). Section 106 sets forth an exhaustive list of those exclusive rights. "They are the rights 'to do and to authorize' others to do six things with the copyrighted work: to reproduce the work, to prepare derivative works based upon the work, to distribute copies of the work, to perform the work publicly, to display the work publicly, and to record and perform the work by means of an audio transmission."

Here, DRK contends that it has standing as either a legal owner or as a beneficial owner of the copyrights. We evaluate each argument in turn.

I. Legal Ownership.

"Any of the exclusive rights comprised in a copyright, including any subdivision of any of the rights specified by section 106, may be transferred . . . and owned separately." 17 U.S.C. § 201(d)(2). "[E]ither an assignment (which transfers legal title to the transferee) or an exclusive license (which transfers an exclusive permission to use to the transferee) qualifies as a 'transfer' of a right in a copyright for the purposes of the Act." By contrast, a mere "nonexclusive license" does not constitute a "transfer of copyright ownership" and therefore cannot confer standing to assert an infringement claim.

To support its claim of legal ownership, DRK points to (1) the Representation Agreements, which grant DRK a license to authorize use of the photographs; and (2) the Assignment Agreements, which purport to transfer to DRK the legal title to and copyrights of the photographs along with accrued infringement claims.

A. The Representation Agreements.

We recently held in *Minden Pictures, Inc. v. John Wiley & Sons, Inc.* that a stock photography agency that served as the exclusive licensing agent for allegedly infringed photographs had standing to sue for infringement under the Copyright Act. DRK contends that *Minden* creates a bright line rule that stock photography agencies have standing to bring copyright infringement claims by virtue of their agency agreements with their contributing photographers. However, DRK reads *Minden* too broadly.

Minden indeed analyzed whether a stock photography agency, Minden Pictures, Inc. ("Minden"), had standing to sue a publisher for infringement after the publisher exceeded the scope of its licensing agreement with Minden. Like DRK, Minden also entered into agency agreements with its contributing photographers under which the photographers authorized Minden to license and sell certain photographs to third parties. Importantly, in those licensing agreements, the photographers agreed to appoint Minden "as sole and exclusive agent and representative with respect to the Licensing of any and all uses of [specified photographs]." Although the agreements "permit[ted] the photographers to issue some licenses themselves," the photographers were "prohibit[ed] . . . from hiring a licensing agent other than Minden." The publisher argued that Minden's agreements with the photographers did not "grant 'exclusive licenses' to Minden to grant licenses to third parties, because the photographers retain[ed] the right to issue licenses themselves."

Minden rejected that argument, and held that the agreements at issue granted exclusive licenses of the right to authorize, rendering Minden a "legal owner" with standing to sue. Relying on "the divisibility principle embodied by the 1976 [Copyright] Act," *Minden* explained that the fact that the photographers retained some ability to authorize use did not render Minden's license nonexclusive:

> [W]e agree with the Seventh Circuit that the essence of an "exclusive" license under the Act is that "the copyright holder permits the licensee to use the protected material for a specific use and further promises that the same permission will not be given to others." Minden has been given just such a promise. Under the Agency Agreements, Minden is the "sole and exclusive agent and representative with respect to the Licensing of any and all uses" of the photographs. That is, the photographers have promised that Minden, and only Minden, will have the power, as the photographers' licensing agent, to authorize third parties to reproduce, distribute, and display the photographs. That the photographers have retained some limited degree of authority to grant licenses themselves does not eliminate Minden's

interest in the copyright as the sole entity to act as the photographers' licensing agent. It merely means that both Minden and the photographers, under the terms of the Agreements, can prevent those third parties who have not received permission to use the photographs from using them.

As *Minden* explained, this concept of exclusivity as the right to exclude third parties, even when another entity can also exclude third parties, is consistent with patent law treatment of similar arrangements.

In so holding, *Minden* declined to apply a rigid test to determine exclusivity and adopted a more flexible approach that allows for a license to be exclusive even if the copyright owner retains some subset of the rights at issue. The key to determining whether Minden's agency agreements conferred a nonexclusive or exclusive license thus was not whether the photographers retained some fractional right but instead that the photographers promised "that Minden, and only Minden, will have the power, as the photographers' licensing agent, to authorize third parties to reproduce, distribute, and display the photographs."

DRK's Representation Agreements here at issue, on the other hand, are devoid of that key provision. They also lack any limitation whatsoever on the photographers' authority to contract with other licensing agents. In the absence of any such promise, DRK's Representation Agreements confer nonexclusive licenses and do not render DRK a legal owner for standing purposes.

DRK suggests that it nevertheless possesses an ownership interest merely because the Representation Agreements pertain to the right "to authorize" as opposed to one of the exclusive rights listed in section 106. Neither the statutory text nor the analysis in *Minden* suggests that, having been given the right "to authorize" others to exercise the rights of copyright holders, a nonexclusive licensee becomes a legal owner with standing to sue.

B. The Assignment Agreements.

DRK next contends that, even if it was not a legal owner originally by virtue of the Representation Agreements, it became the legal owner when the Assignment Agreements passed full legal title of each photograph and copyright along with all accrued claims to DRK. McGraw-Hill counters that the Assignment Agreements are nothing more than invalid attempts to transfer the bare right to sue.

In *Silvers v. Sony Pictures Entertainment*, 402 F.3d 881 (9th Cir. 2005) (*en banc*), we held that "an assignee who holds an accrued claim for copyright infringement, but who has no legal or beneficial interest in the copyright itself, [may not] institute an action for infringement." This conclusion naturally followed from the notable absence of the "right to sue" from the list of exclusive rights set forth in section 106 and was reinforced by the text and legislative history of the Copyright Act as a whole.

Later, we clarified that the purported transfer of legal title coupled with the transfer of accrued claims does not confer standing when the transaction, in substance and effect, merely transfers a bare right to sue. *Righthaven LLC v. Hoehn*, 716 F.3d 1166, 1169–70 (9th Cir. 2013). There, the plaintiff Righthaven LLC "was founded, according to its charter, to identify copyright infringements on behalf of third parties, receive 'limited, revocable assignment[s]' of those copyrights, and then sue the infringers." Righthaven asserted copyright infringement claims against two defendants for their allegedly unauthorized online posting of articles from the Las Vegas Review-Journal. Righthaven was not the owner of the copyrights of those articles at the time of the alleged infringement. Instead, the copyrights were owned by Stephens Media LLC, the company that owns the Las Vegas Review-Journal. After the alleged infringement, Stephens Media and Righthaven executed a copyright assignment agreement for each article. Those assignments provided that, "subject to [Stephens Media's] rights of reversion, Stephens Media granted to Righthaven all copyrights requisite to have Righthaven recognized as the copyright owner of the Work for purposes of Righthaven being able to claim ownership as well as the right to seek redress for past, present, and future infringements of the copyright . . . in and to the Work."

Prior to executing the assignments, Righthaven and Stephens Media executed a Strategic Alliance Agreement ("SAA"), which clarified that following an assignment of copyright Stephens Media would retain "an exclusive license to exploit the copyrights for any lawful purpose whatsoever" and upon thirty days prior notice could "revert the ownership of any assigned copyright back to itself." The SAA further provided that Righthaven had no right to exploit the copyrights or participate in any royalties.

Both defendants moved to dismiss for lack of standing. Righthaven and Stephens Media then executed a "Clarification and Amendment to Strategic Alliance Agreement" in which they "purported to clarify that the parties' intent in entering the SAA was to 'convey all ownership rights in and to any identified Work to Righthaven through a Copyright Assignment so that Righthaven would be the rightful owner of the identified Work.'" *Righthaven* held that, despite their language purporting to transfer title and ownership, the copyright assignments in their substance and effect did no more than transfer a right to sue. Looking to the combined effect of the assignment and the SAA, *Righthaven* recognized that Stephens Media retained all exclusive rights to the articles and Righthaven had little if any right to exploit the works absent Stephens Media's consent. Thus, for all practical purposes, the assignments did nothing more than transfer a right to sue.

Here, the parties similarly dispute whether the Assignment Agreements actually transferred ownership of the copyrights along with the accrued claims. . . .

Righthaven instructs that the assignment agreements' use of "language purporting to transfer ownership . . . is not conclusive . . . [and] [w]e must consider the substance of the transaction." Thus, as in *Righthaven*, we must consider the Assignment Agreements in conjunction with the Representation Agreements and the ongoing relationship between DRK and the individual photographers. The alleged acts of infringement occurred prior to the execution of the Assignment Agreements. DRK concedes that following the execution of the Assignment Agreements, photographers who were parties to nonexclusive Representation Agreements could continue to market and sell the covered photographs themselves and through other means under the terms of the Representation Agreements. The photographers did not pay royalties or fees of any kind to DRK following execution of the Assignment Agreements. DRK's admitted course of dealing with photographers following the execution of the Assignment Agreements demonstrates that each party retained the rights it had under the nonexclusive Representation Agreements—meaning the photographers retained the exclusive rights to the photographs and DRK retained a nonexclusive license to authorize their use. As the district court recognized, the email exchanges surrounding execution of the Assignment Agreements further underscore this reality.

DRK argues it was error to interpret the substance and effect of the Assignment Agreements contrary to DRK and the photographers' intent that DRK obtain the ownership interest necessary to register and pursue infringement claims on the copyrights at issue. DRK relies upon declarations submitted in opposition to McGraw-Hill's motion for summary judgment, which, like the clarification agreement in *Righthaven*, stated that the photographers "intended to transfer the copyrights to all . . . photographs" with the "intent that DRK should retain an ownership interest in the images until the full resolution of any infringement claims relating to those images" and so that DRK could "protect, by lawsuits if necessary, against unpermitted uses." As in *Righthaven*, however, "[t]he problem is not that the district court did not read the contract in accordance with the parties' intent; the problem is that what the parties intended was invalid under the Copyright Act." The undisputed evidence shows that for all practical purposes, the nonexclusive Representation Agreements continued to govern who controlled the exclusive rights associated with the photographs following execution of the purported copyright assignments; thus, the substance and effect of the Assignment Agreements was merely a transfer of the right to sue on accrued claims, which cannot confer standing. See *Silvers*, 402 F.3d at 890.

Finally, we reject DRK's contention that *Silvers* has been implicitly overruled by *Sprint Communications Co. v. APCC Services, Inc.*, 554 U.S. 269 (2008). A three-judge panel is bound by prior circuit authority unless the authority is "clearly irreconcilable" with intervening Supreme Court precedent. *Sprint* held that assignees of payphone operators' accrued claims under the Communications Act had Article III standing to bring the collection suit at issue. *Sprint* did not involve the Copyright Act, and its standing analysis was not predicated on any statutory provision analogous to section 501(b). Consequently, *Sprint* does not undercut the reasoning of *Silvers*, which was grounded on the specific statutory language and history of the Copyright Act's standing provision for infringement claims, and *Sprint* and *Silvers* are not "clearly irreconcilable." To be sure, *Righthaven*, which post-dates *Sprint*, also applied the rule of *Silvers*, and a three-judge panel of this court is bound by both *Silvers* and *Righthaven*.

Although we are certainly sympathetic to the practical challenges attendant to policing infringement of photographic art in the publishing industry, those practical considerations cannot override the Copyright Act's "carefully circumscribed" grant of the right to sue. *Silvers*, 402 F.3d at 885. The nonexclusive licenses and assignments of the bare right to sue present here do not render DRK a legal owner of the copyrights under controlling law and thus are insufficient to confer standing.

II. Beneficial Ownership.

In the alternative, DRK contends that it is the beneficial owner of the copyrights for the photographs at issue.

Although section 501(b) provides that a beneficial owner of a copyright is entitled to bring an infringement action, the Copyright Act does not define the term "beneficial owner." The classic example of a beneficial owner is "an author who ha[s] parted with legal title to the copyright in exchange for percentage royalties based on sales or license fees." By contrast, an author who receives royalties for a work created under a work-for-hire agreement, and thus who never had ownership of the work, is not a beneficial owner.

We have not previously explored the full extent of who may qualify as a beneficial owner of copyright, and we need not do so here. Indeed, to support its arguments that it is a beneficial owner, DRK once again points solely to the Representation Agreements and the Assignment Agreements. Yet, under those agreements, DRK is a nonexclusive licensing agent and an assignee of accrued causes of action. To hold that DRK is a beneficial owner simply on the very bases that it cannot be deemed the legal owner would effectively negate our holding in *Silvers* and render portions of section 501(b) superfluous. Thus, on the specific facts of this case, DRK has failed to demonstrate that it is a beneficial owner.

. . .

CONCLUSION

Ultimately, DRK failed to demonstrate or otherwise create a genuine dispute of material fact whether it is a legal or beneficial owner of any exclusive right under the copyrights at issue. Accordingly, DRK failed to meet the standing requirements of section 501(b), and summary judgment in favor of the defendants was warranted. . . .

Notes & Questions

1. Exclusive Versus Nonexclusive Licenses

The rights enjoyed by a copyright licensee are dictated in part by the exclusive or nonexclusive nature of a license. In general, an exclusive license must be conveyed in writing to be valid. Such a license is treated as a transfer of ownership because it conveys a part of a copyright holder's rights to the licensee. Consequently, an exclusive license grants the licensee standing to sue for infringement of the particular right covered by the license. A nonexclusive license, in contrast, allows a copyright holder to convey the same rights to more than one licensee and may be granted orally or implied from conduct. A licensee holding a nonexclusive license has no standing to sue and may be restricted in his ability to resell the licensed right. 1 Melville B. Nimmer & David Nimmer, Nimmer on Copyright § 10.02 [B][1], [4](a).

2. Implied Transfers

A license of a right to a copyrighted work may entail a concomitant transfer of collateral rights needed to permit the full enjoyment of the license. For example, a license to record a musical work implies a right to distribute and sell the musical work, and a license to make copies in a work implies that ownership of the copies produced shall be in the licensee.

In addition to the implied transfer of collateral rights, an owner of a copyright may be compelled by statute to grant a license in his work. Compulsory licensing includes licenses for secondary transmissions over cable television, for making ephemeral recordings, for playing of works in jukeboxes, for public broadcasting, for satellite retransmissions, for digital subscription transmissions of sound recordings, for making and distributing phonorecords, and for digital phonorecord deliveries.

3. Duration of the License

Generally, if a licensing contract does not expressly state the period or duration of the agreement, the license is assumed to be effective for the extent of the then-existing copyright term of the work. Once transferred, a license without an express term limit allows the licensee to enjoy the right transferred for the duration of the copyright.

One exception to this assumption is a license for publication. A license for publication of a work may automatically terminate before the end of the copyright term. For a publication license, termination of the license is triggered when the work ceases to be published. After termination, the licensee cannot thereafter use the work.

A licensee's duty to pay royalties does not end until either the copyright expires or the license expires, whichever occurs first.

4. Statutory Termination of Transfers and Nonexclusive Licenses

Copyright protection for a work of authorship lasts for the life of the author plus 70 years. An author of a copyrighted work initially owns the rights in the work but may transfer any or all of his rights to others through assignment or licensing. Typically, if the license does not explicitly state the period or duration of the licensing agreement, the license term is assumed to extend for the remaining duration of the copyright term.

Statutory termination permits authors to reclaim their rights in a work before the end of the copyright term. Under 17 U.S.C. § 203, an author may effect termination during a five-year period starting 35 years from the date of the grant. For a right of publication of a work, the period begins at 35 years from the date of publication, or 40 years from the date of the execution of the grant, whichever term ends earlier. To effect termination, written notice must be provided to the grantee and to the U.S. Copyright Office. Notice must be served "not less than two or more than ten years" before the effective date of the termination. 17 U.S.C. § 203(a)(4)(A). Works created before 1976 may be terminated pursuant to § 304.

Statutory termination allows a copyright grant to revert back to the author. Unless terminated, a grant continues unchanged. 17 U.S.C. § 203(b). Derivative works are an exception to the statutory termination of a grant. 17 U.S.C. § 304(c)(6)(A). Derivative works prepared under the authority of a grant may still be used after termination of the grant. Termination does, however, bar the creation of new derivative works. The derivative works exception is illustrated by *Mills Music, Inc. v. Snyder*, 469 U.S. 153 (1985). In *Mills Music*, the author's heirs terminated the author's grant of a copyright to a music publisher. Before the termination of the grant, the music publisher had awarded licenses to third parties to produce derivative works of the author's song pursuant to the author's grant. The publisher received royalties from the derivative works. The Court held that the derivative works exception permitted use of derivative works to continue under the terms of the grant after the grant's termination. The royalty-bearing licenses for the derivative works therefore remained in force even after the heir's termination of the author's grant.

2. Scope of the Use: Unforeseen Uses

HarperCollins Publishers LLC v. Open Road Integrated Media, LLP

United States District Court for the Southern District of New York

7 F. Supp. 3d 363 (S.D.N.Y. 2014)

NAOMI REICE BUCHWALD, DISTRICT JUDGE

BACKGROUND

I. Factual Allegations

The present dispute arises out of a publishing agreement (hereafter the "contract" or the "agreement") executed on April 13, 1971 by the author Jean George and the publishing house Harper & Row, plaintiff's predecessor in interest, which, broadly speaking, gave plaintiff the right to publish George's children's novel *Julie of the Wolves*. The novel was first published in hardcover format by Harper & Row in 1972. It won the Newbury Medal in 1973 for the most distinguished contribution to children's literature and was a finalist for the 1973 National Book Award. Between 1972 and December 2011, HarperCollins sold more than 3.8 million units of the novel in hardcover and paperback, among other formats. Then and in the years since, *Julie of the Wolves* has been considered a celebrated title in children's literature.

By the 1971 contract, Ms. George conveyed publishing rights to HarperCollins to publish *Julie of the Wolves* in exchange for a $2,000 advance and royalty payments of between ten and fifteen percent, depending on number of copies sold. The contract contemplated the sale of paperback editions ("cheap edition") but did not specify the royalty rate for paperbacks, instead indicating that the publisher would pay a paperback royalty "to be mutually agreed."

The contract contains several clauses critical to the outcome of this suit. Paragraph 1 of the agreement grants to HarperCollins "the exclusive right to publish" *Julie of the Wolves* "in book form" in the English language and within specified territory. In addition to this broad grant language, the contract provided in a paragraph entitled "Disposition of Subsidiary Rights" that "[i]t is understood and agreed that the Publisher shall have the exclusive right to sell, lease or make other disposition of the subsidiary rights in which he has an interest under the terms of clause (subject to the 'consultation' provision in 7f) 19 and 20."

Paragraph 20, in turn, makes the following provision:

> Anything to the contrary herein notwithstanding, the Publisher shall grant no license without the prior written consent of the Author with respect to the following rights in the work: *use thereof in storage and retrieval and information systems, and/or whether through computer, computer-stored, mechanical or other electronic means now known or hereafter invented* and ephemeral screen flashing or reproduction thereof, whether by print-out, phot[o] reproduction or photo copy, including punch cards, microfilm, magnetic tapes or like processes attaining similar results, and net proceeds thereof shall be divided 50% to the Author and 50% to the Publisher. However, such license shall not be deemed keeping the work in print once the work has gone out of print in all editions." (emphasis added)

This clause was inserted at the request of Ms. George's literary agency, Curtis Brown, which negotiated the contract on the author's behalf. The language of Paragraph 20 was drafted by Curtis Brown in 1967 and was apparently standard in contracts negotiated by Curtis Brown with American publishers. In fact, identical language was included in at least six contracts between Ms. George and Harper & Row that predate the operative contract in the instant matter. In eight subsequent contracts between Ms. George and HarperCollins, the words "and/or" were deleted, such that the relevant language read "use thereof in storage and retrieval systems, whether through computer, mechanical, or other electronic means now known or hereafter invented . . . ."

In addition to these critical clauses, the contract also contained other paragraphs pertinent to this action, including Paragraph 19, which gave the Publisher the right "to reprint the said Work in whole or in part in the form of excerpts, digests and selections in one or more issues of a newspaper, magazine, book or anthology," with revenues generally divided evenly between author and publisher. The contract also contained a "Reserved Rights" clause that reserved to the author "[a]ll rights in the Work now existing, or which may hereafter come into existence, not specifically herein granted," including motion picture rights. The contract provided for a New York choice of law.

In the decades that followed, the parties apparently coordinated with regard to the use of the work by third parties in electronic formats. Repeatedly in recent years,

HarperCollins forwarded requests to Ms. George "[p]er our agreement," to use text from *Julie of the Wolves* in CD-ROMs, online teaching materials, online examination materials and the like, including in August 1998 a request to include *Julie of the Wolves* in a test of an early e-book reading device. The record before us indicates that Ms. George generally agreed to these requests, sometimes after negotiating a more favorable royalty. The parties disagree, however, on the implication to be taken from these communications regarding third-party uses. HarperCollins asserts that this course of performance was undertaken pursuant to the requirements of Paragraph 20. Open Road contends that these uses fell under the "permissions" provision set forth in Paragraph 19; and further notes that Ms. George unilaterally granted electronic rights to the Work without HarperCollins's involvement (but apparently also without HarperCollins knowledge or consent).

The events immediately precipitating this lawsuit began in 2010, nearly forty years after the execution of the operative contract, at which point the publishing world featured an e-book market. E-book technology enables the full text of a book to be presented in digital form, to be read on a computer or portable electronic device, such as a dedicated e-book reader, a smart phone, or a pad/tablet. Defendant Open Road is an e-book publisher and multimedia content company established in 2009.

In 2010, Open Road approached Ms. George's literary agent Curtis Brown with a proposal to publish an e-book edition of *Julie of the Wolves* in exchange for a 50% royalty to Ms. George. Preferring initially to pursue an e-book publication with her longtime publisher HarperCollins, Ms. George authorized her agent to contact Harper-Collins and suggest the e-book publication, with the proviso that HarperCollins match Open Road's 50% royalty offer. HarperCollins expressed interest in electronic publication; however, they counter-offered only a 25% royalty. Dissatisfied with that offer and expressing her belief that she — not HarperCollins — owned the e-book rights, Ms. George instead contracted in April 2011 with Open Road to publish *Julie of the Wolves* as an e-book. Before doing so, Ms. George entered an agreement with Open Road, by which the electronic publisher agreed to indemnify Ms. George in the event HarperCollins asserted a claim against the author. Open Road subsequently distributed *Julie of the Wolves* as an e-book via a number of distribution channels; between October 2011 and March 2012, approximately 1,600 such e-book copies were sold.

Plaintiff HarperCollins filed suit against Open Road on December 23, 2011, alleging willful copyright infringement in violation of 17 U.S.C. § 106 and seeking injunctive relief, statutory or actual damages at its election, and the recovery of Open Road's profits and HarperCollins' costs. Defendant answered on February 16, 2012 and discovery followed. After briefing of the instant cross-motions was completed, oral argument was held on January 30, 2014.

DISCUSSION

. . . .

IV. New Use Precedent

In accord with these principles of contract construction, the Second Circuit's "new use" precedent sets forth a procedure for evaluating whether a contract covers later-developed technology. This Court is guided by several leading cases, including *Bartsch v. Metro-Goldwyn-Mayer, Inc.*, 391 F.2d 150 (2d Cir. 1968), *Bourne v. Walt Disney Co.*, 68 F.3d 621 (2d Cir. 1995), and *Boosey & Hawkes Music Publishers, Ltd. v. Walt Disney Co.*, 145 F.3d 481 (2d Cir. 1998), all of which arise in the context of the motion picture industry. *Bartsch* posed the question of whether an earlier grant of motion picture rights to a play also comprised the right to broadcast that movie on television 28 years later. *Bourne* and *Boosey* considered whether the holder of a license to use a piece of music in a motion picture also had the right to use the music in distribution of the movie via videocassette over forty years later. In these three cases, all of which evaluated contracts pursuant to New York law, the initial grant language was found to encompass the later-developed new use.

In a "new use" case, the Court must determine whether the new use "may reasonably be said to fall within the medium as described in the license." *Bartsch*, 391 F.2d at 155. The key interpretive principle to be applied is that the language of the contract itself governs. *Boosey*, 145 F.3d at 487.

In construing the scope of the contractual grant, the Court must apply "neutral principles of contract interpretation" and avoid any "default rule in favor of copyright licensees or any default rule whatsoever." *Id.* As the Second Circuit instructs, "[i]f the contract is more reasonably read to convey one meaning, the party benefitted by that reading should be able to rely on it; the party seeking exception or deviation from the meaning reasonably conveyed by the words of the contract should bear the burden of negotiating for language that would express the limitation or deviation." *Id.*

Indeed, in new use cases, the words of the contract may take on even greater significance than in a standard contract action in which the Court could review contemporaneous extrinsic evidence to elucidate the intent of the parties. Partly, this is because "many years after formation of the contract, it may well be impossible to consult the principals or retrieve documentary evidence to ascertain the parties' intent, if any, with respect to new uses." *Id.* at 488. *Bartsch* describes the problem more bluntly: "With Bartsch dead, his grantors apparently so, and the Warner Brothers lawyer understandably having no recollection of the negotiation, any effort to reconstruct what the parties actually intended nearly forty years ago is doomed to failure." 391 F.2d at 155.

Moreover, by their very nature, new use cases create a significant obstacle to the use of extrinsic evidence. An inquiry into the parties' intent "is not likely to be helpful when the subject of the inquiry is something the parties were not thinking about." *Boosey*, 145 F.3d at 487–88. Likewise, extrinsic evidence of the parties' course of dealing or industry practice is likely irrelevant, "because the use in question was, by hypothesis, new, and could not have been the subject of prior negotiations or established practice." *Id.* at 488.

Thus, the leading cases discussed here placed primary emphasis on the contractual language. They also considered the "foreseeability" of the new use at the time of contracting, and found, respectively, that "future possibilities of television were recognized by knowledgeable people in the entertainment and motion picture industries," *Bartsch*, 391 F.2d at 154; that "home viewing of motion pictures was within the contemplation of persons in the motion picture industry," *Bourne*, 68 F.3d at 630; and that "a nascent market for home viewing" existed at the time of contracting. *Boosey*, 145 F.3d at 486. Notably, however, and contrary to defendant's contention, the case law did not explicitly treat "foreseeability" of the new use at the time of contract as a *sine qua non*. Instead, whether foreseeability is required remains an open question. *See Boosey*, 145 F.3d at 486 (whether "a new-use license hinges on the foreseeability of the new channels of distribution at the time of contracting [was] a question left open in *Bartsch*").

V. Application

As an initial matter, we note that the parties have filed cross-motions for summary judgment. We agree with counsel's assessment that this action is well-suited to resolution upon summary judgment.

Based on a plain reading of the contractual language, we hold that the 1971 contract grants HarperCollins the exclusive right to license third parties to publish e-book versions of *Julie of the Wolves*. This determination follows from the contract as a whole, and chiefly from Paragraphs 1, 20 and 23.

A. Paragraph 1

Paragraph 1 conveyed to HarperCollins "the exclusive right to publish [*Julie of the Wolves*] . . . in book form." Relying heavily on prior precedent from this district, Open Road argues that this language cannot possibly extend to e-book publication rights. *See Random House, Inc. v. Rosetta Books LLC*, 150 F. Supp. 2d 613, 620 (S.D.N.Y. 2001). However, the operative contract here differs significantly from its counterpart in *Rosetta Books*, which was held to be limited to paper book publication. In the instant case, the governing grant conveys the right "to publish . . . in book form," whereas in *Rosetta Books*, the grant was one "to print, publish and sell." *Id.* As was explicitly argued in the earlier case, the inclusion of the word "print" has a limiting effect and a strong connotation of paper copy. *Id.* The word "print" is absent from the 1971 contract governing here, thereby distinguishing the case at bar from *Rosetta Books*.

Nonetheless, given that we must interpret the contract as a whole, we need not reach the issue of whether Paragraph 1 standing alone is sufficient to convey e-book publication rights. *See International Klafter Co. v. Continental Casualty Co.*, 869 F.2d 96, 99 (2d Cir. 1989). With that precept in mind, we turn next to evaluate Paragraph 20, which, by explicitly granting HarperCollins certain rights associated with use by "electronic means," created a critical distinction from *Rosetta Books*, whose contract made no mention of electronic exploitation at all.

B. Paragraph 20

Paragraph 20, supported by the grant provision in Paragraph 23, enables Harper-Collins to issue licenses, subject to the author's permission, to use the work in "in storage and retrieval and information systems, and/or whether through computer, computer-stored, mechanical or other electronic means now known or hereafter invented." This language, encompassing as it does the forward-looking reference to technologies "now known or hereafter invented," is sufficiently broad to draw within its ambit e-book publication. Although no commercial market for e-books existed at the time of its drafting, e-book technology comprises a later-invented version of the very "computer, computer-stored, mechanical or other electronic means" provided by Paragraph 20.

In light of precedent indicating that broad grant language will extend to later-invented uses, e-book publication "may reasonably be said to fall within the medium as described in the license." *Bartsch*, 391 F.2d at 155. Our conclusion that e-books constitute a permissible new use follows both from the expansive contractual language and from the lens through which the Second Circuit directs us to construe it. The applicable Second Circuit precedent cautions courts not to limit new uses to those that "fall within the unambiguous core meaning of the term" provided by the contract. *Id.* Rather, the e-book format constitutes a permissible extension of "book form" via "storage and retrieval and information systems, and/or whether through computer, computer-stored, mechanical or other electronic means" just as the television broadcast of a movie and the videocassette constituted a lawful extension of the motion picture form in *Bartsch* and *Boosey*, respectively.

When considered in comparison to contracts in similar cases, the contractual language here is as broad as that previously found to be sufficient to encompass a later-developed new use. The *Bourne* contract conveyed the "right to record such music mechanically in any and all other motion pictures to be produced . . . ." 68 F.3d at 624. In *Boosey*, the grant language provided rights "to record [the composition] in any manner, medium or form" for use "in [a] motion picture." 145 F.3d at 486. In *Bartsch*, the contract granted the right "to copyright, vend, license and exhibit such motion picture photoplays throughout the world; together with the further sole and exclusive rights by mechanical and/or electrical means to record, reproduce and transmit sound" — a conveyance that appears rather similar in scope to Ms. George's grant to HarperCollins of the "exclusive right to publish [*Julie of the Wolves*] in book form." 391 F.2d at 151. Notably, none of the contracts in *Bartsch*, *Bourne*, or *Boosey* included any reference to rights in future technologies that exists in the contract here.

By specifically providing for anticipated electronic means that might be "hereafter invented," the 1971 contract's grant language becomes greater in breadth, at least with respect to new uses, than the analogous contracts in Second Circuit new use precedent, which were themselves found sufficiently broad to encompass an electronic new use. Interpreting similar forward-looking contractual language in a new use context, another court in this district drew the same conclusion. *See Reinhardt v. Wal-Mart Stores, Inc.*, 547 F. Supp. 2d 346, 354–55 (S.D.N.Y. 2008). In *Reinhardt*, a 1984 recording agreement wherein "records" were defined as "all forms of reproduction including pre-recorded tapes and discs and electronic video recordings, *now or hereafter known*" was construed to authorize later-invented digital and internet-enabled uses. Id. (emphasis added). Relying, as we do here, on the Second Circuit standards set forth in *Boosey*, the district court in *Reinhardt* explained that "[t]he phrase 'now or hereafter known,' when referring to forms of reproduction, reveals that future technologies are covered by the agreement" and that the language "creates an expansive rather than a restrictive conveyance of rights." *Id.* at 354. The language of Paragraph 20 — "now known or hereafter invented" — tracks its analog in *Reinhardt* rather closely and results in a similarly expansive conveyance of rights with regard to future technologies.

Indeed, apparently recognizing the breadth of the language in Paragraph 20, Open Road's briefing largely ignored it. Instead, Open Road attempted to redirect the Court's attention to Paragraph 1 and to the *Rosetta Books* precedent, which, as discussed above, did not directly address the issues present here. To the extent that Open Road did grapple with the implications of Paragraph 20, its strategy has been to attempt to rewrite the provision. Specifically, Open Road entreats the Court to disregard the "and/or" language, thereby converting the latter clause from an independent to a dependent one as follows: "in storage and retrieval and information systems, [and/or] whether through computer, computer-stored, mechanical or other electronic means now known or hereafter invented." In support of this proposed *ex post* revision, Open Road argues that the "and/or" is "syntactically awkward," that it constitutes an "unnecessary insertion," that it would create meaningless surplusage, and that it would lead to an "absurd result." *Id.*

[The court rejected this argument on contract law grounds.]

C. Other Contract-Based Arguments

In addition to the arguments discussed *supra*, Open Road makes three other arguments involving interpretation of the contractual language, which the Court has considered and found unpersuasive. First, Open Road submits that Paragraph 20 grants HarperCollins no right to publish an e-book edition of *Julie of the Wolves* itself, which HarperCollins disputes. This argument is irrelevant to the inquiry at hand. The question before us is whether HarperCollins has exclusive rights to license the work's e-book publication, not whether HarperCollins may undertake such publication itself. Even were we to conclude that HarperCollins has no rights to the latter, it would not alter our decision regarding the former.

Secondly, Open Road argues that Paragraph 20 is missing an essential contractual term — to wit, a royalty rate — rendering it unenforceable for lack of the provision of the consideration to be paid under the contract. Once again, Open Road attempts to redirect attention to the question of whether HarperCollins has the right to publish an e-book version of the work, a question not before this Court and not germane to this litigation. Insofar as Paragraph 20 explicitly includes a royalty provision for third-party licenses by which HarperCollins and the author evenly divide the net proceeds, this argument is meritless.

Thirdly, Open Road presents the contract's reservation of rights clause in Paragraph 14, which reserves to the author "[a]ll rights in the Work now existing, or which may hereafter come into existence, not specifically herein granted," as evidence that Ms. George did not intend to convey e-book publication rights, arguing that to find otherwise would convert this provision to surplusage. As the Second Circuit observed in *Boosey,* the "reservation clause stands for no more than the truism that [the author] retained whatever [s]he had not granted . . . [i]t contributes nothing to the definition of the boundaries of the license." 145 F.3d at 488.

D. Foreseeability

Beyond the scope of the contractual language itself, Open Road's primary argument against HarperCollins' copyright claim involves the foreseeability inquiry that has arisen in the new use precedent. Open Road characterizes the new use standard as requiring "two analytical steps, both of which must be satisfied before the new use will be deemed conveyed:" first, a determination of the breadth of the grant language and second, a determination of the new use's foreseeability. The case law itself, however, contains no such explicit bifurcation. Further, the Second Circuit has left open the question of whether foreseeability is, in fact, required. *Boosey,* 145 F.3d at 486. Although *Bartsch, Bourne,* and *Boosey* all evaluate, to some extent, whether the new use was within contemplation at the time of the grant, plaintiff's presentation of Second Circuit law as requiring a separate and specific showing of foreseeability is, at best, an oversimplification and, at worst, a distortion of the explicit language of the relevant precedent.

To the extent that foreseeability at the time of the grant is required to extend a copyright to a new use, however, the language of the contract itself provided for foreseeable uses. The reference to electronic means "now known or hereafter invented" anticipated future technological uses for the work, which would one day include e-books. By this logic, the contract here may be said to fulfill the foreseeability standard, to the extent it exists, even without reference to the record evidence. *See, e.g., Reinhardt v. Wal-Mart Stores, Inc.,* 547 F. Supp. 2d 346, 354–55 (S.D.N.Y. 2008) ("The phrase 'now or hereafter known,' when referring to forms of reproduction, reveals that future technologies are covered by the agreement. . . . This unambiguous language [*inter alia*] forecloses other interpretations and the need to consider extrinsic evidence.").

Even if foreseeability were a requirement not satisfied by the contractual language, the record before us, particularly in the context of the new use precedent, would support our decision. Although no commercial e-book market existed at the time of the grant, knowledgeable industry members seem to have contemplated electronic or computer-assisted delivery of book text in much the same way that knowledgeable members of the motion picture industry could contemplate television broadcasts and videocassettes at the time of contracting in *Bartsch*, *Bourne*, and *Boosey*. Recall too that in those precedential cases, the Circuit did not require that industry participants foresee with specificity actual videocassette technology, for example. Rather, the Courts merely noted that, when the contracts at issue were drafted, industry participants recognized the possibility of a "home viewing" market. *Bourne*, 68 F.3d at 630; *Boosey*, 145 F.3d at 486. If videocassettes can be said to have been in contemplation of members of the motion picture industry in the 1930s, it follows *a fortiori* that the same can be said for e-books at the time of the 1971 contract. Open Road seemed almost to concede as much at oral argument, indicating that industry participants drafted Paragraph 20 and similar clauses elsewhere against the backdrop of contemporaneous university initiatives "digitizing the libraries, putting on electronic databases [of] books." Tr. at 22.

. . . .

CONCLUSION

For the foregoing reasons, plaintiff's motion for summary judgment is granted and defendant's cross-motion is denied.

3. Performance Rights Organizations: ASCAP & BMI

Collective rights organizations facilitate commerce in copyrighted content by allowing transactions to proceed without the roadblock of individual owners asserting their rights to their works. One area where collective rights organizations have developed is the area of performance rights in music. The owners of copyrights in musical works formed the performance rights organizations ASCAP (American Society of Composers, Authors, and Publishers) and BMI (Broadcast Music Inc.).

Both ASCAP and BMI act as centralized organizations for the management of copyrights in music. The origins of ASCAP and BMI are summarized by Justice White in *BMI v. CBS*, 441 U.S. 1 (1979):

> In 1914, Victor Herbert and a handful of other composers organized ASCAP because those who performed copyrighted music for profit were so numerous and widespread, and most performances so fleeting, that as a practical matter it was impossible for the many individual copyright owners to negotiate with and license the users and to detect unauthorized uses. 'ASCAP was organized as a "clearing-house" for copyright owners and users to solve these problems' associated with the licensing of music. 400 F. Supp. 737, 741 (S.D.N.Y. 1975). As ASCAP operates today, its . . . members grant it nonexclusive rights to license nondramatic performances of their works, and ASCAP issues licenses and distributes royalties to copyright owners in

accordance with a schedule reflecting the nature and amount of the use of their music and other factors.

BMI, a nonprofit corporation owned by members of the broadcasting industry, was organized in 1939, is affiliated with or represents ... publishing companies and ... authors and composers, and operates in much the same manner as ASCAP. Almost every domestic copyrighted composition is in the repertory either of ASCAP ... or of BMI. ...

Both organizations operate primarily through blanket licenses, which give the licensees the right to perform any and all of the compositions owned by the members or affiliates as often as the licensees desire for a stated term. Fees for blanket licenses are ordinarily a percentage of total revenues or a flat dollar amount, and do not directly depend on the amount or type of music used. Radio and television broadcasters are the largest users of music, and almost all of them hold blanket licenses from both ASCAP and BMI.

BMI, 441 U.S. at 4–5. Together, ASCAP and BMI account for 95% of the United States market for performance rights to musical compositions. The performance rights organizations issue licenses and collect and distribute royalty fees for members under an agreed formula. The organizations also play a copyright policing role by monitoring public performances and bringing actions against alleged infringers.

E. Licensing Multiple Types of Intellectual Property: Hybrid Licensing

Licenses involving more than one kind of intellectual property have become the norm. It is common for a license to include two patents rather than one and for a license covering a patent to also cover trade secrets or know-how. Special problems arise when a license transaction includes two or more kinds of intellectual property. Each form of intellectual property confers different rights, has a different duration of protection, and requires compliance with different procedures. Parties negotiating a license involving more than one kind of intellectual property must take great care to address the unique demands of each.

1. Patent and Trade Secret Licensing

The most common form of hybrid licensing involves patents and trade secrets. A licensor may be both a patentee and owner of trade secrets related to the patent. Moreover, patent license may include a provision whereby the licensor is obligated to convey to the licensee trade secret information about improvements to the patented invention.

A license involving both patents and trade secrets should specify royalties related to the patents separately from royalties related to the trade secrets. An obligation to pay royalties related to a patent terminates upon the expiration of the patent. In contrast, the obligation to pay royalties concerning a trade secret may last indefinitely since the term of trade secret protection lasts so long as the information is maintained as a trade secret. Since the term of protection for a patent usually ends before the term for a trade secret, a licensor risks losing royalties altogether when a patent expires if a license covering both the patent and related trade secrets does not separately define royalties for licensing the patent and for licensing the trade secrets. *See Bloggild v. Kenner Prods.,* 776 F.2d 1315 (6th Cir. 1985) (license that included both patent and trade secret was held invalid since the license was entered into before patents issued and required payment of royalties after the patents expired); *Pitney Bowes, Inc. v. Mestre,* 701 F.2d 1365 (11th Cir. 1983) (hybrid agreement licensing patent rights and trade secrets unenforceable beyond date of expiration of patent). Using an example from *Kimble, supra,* "a license involving both a patent and a trade secret can set a 5% royalty during the patent period (as compensation for the two combined) and a 4% royalty afterward (as payment for the trade secret alone)." *Kimble v. Marvel Entm't, LLC,* 135 S. Ct. 2401, 2408 (2015).

2. Patent and Trademark Licensing

Dual licenses involving patents and trademarks are common in industrial property licensing. Processes may be patented, with the resultant product being sold and marketed under a specific trademark. Licensing arrangements may be undertaken to transfer both rights to make and sell the patented invention and to use the related trademark. However, problems may arise from hybrid licenses of patents and trademarks.

One problem is the blurring of the licensor's permissible activities in controlling the activities of the licensee. A licensor of a trademark must control the quality and nature of the goods and services associated with the mark. To effectuate this type of control, a licensor is permitted to supervise a licensee's use of the mark. Such supervision may make the licensor privy to the licensee's improvements on the patented invention. The licensor may open himself to accusations of misappropriating the licensee's technology if he has no right to the improvements. To avoid unwitting misappropriations of information from the licensee, the parties need to develop a clear and workable confidentiality provision.

Another problem that may arise with a license involving a patented process and a trademark occurs when a licensee proposes to abandon the patented process in favor of another process while continuing to use the trademark. If the alternative process produces a product that meets trademark quality control standards under the license, the licensee may argue that the licensor is illegally attempting to condition the continued licensing of the mark on the use of the patented process.

Problems may also arise if a licensee, once having obtained a license to produce a patented product and to use a trademark, desires to discontinue using the licensor's mark and to manufacture the same product under licensee's own mark. Such an action on the part of the licensee may be viewed by the former licensor as a form of free riding, whereby the licensee trades off the good will established under the former licensor's mark. The licensor in such a situation may insist on a long-term license for the mark.

Chapter 6

Intellectual Property Assets and the Termination of a Business

Problem

Digital Ignition has licensed its patented plug-in technology to Colonel Motors, a mid-sized automotive company that specializes in the manufacture of elite, upscale automobiles. Digital Ignition also licenses some patented technology from Spintel, a microchip company. During a sharp downturn in the economy, both Colonel Motors and Spintel file for bankruptcy. Because of what is perceived to be the unfavorable terms of its license with Digital Ignition, Spintel seeks to reject the license in hopes of entering into a better deal with another automotive company. Colonel Motors also seeks to reject its license with Digital Ignition in hopes of finding a cheaper supplier of substitutes for the patented plug-in technology. Because of the downturn, Digital Ignition is also considering the termination and restructuring of one of its subsidiary companies, responsible for research and development in improving its plug-in technology. The subsidiary holds title jointly with Digital Ignition in many of its patents and trade secrets.

You are general counsel for Digital Ignition and are asked to assess the legal issues that these facts pose for your client. Specifically, you are asked for advice on how best to protect your client's business interests as Colonel Motors and Spintel undergo bankruptcy and as Digital Ignition's subsidiary is terminated.

Focus of the Chapter

An unfortunate truth of any business is the possibility that it might come to an end. The end may occur voluntarily as the owners decide to shift their capital investment into other ventures, or it may occur involuntarily as debts and economic downturns force the owners of the business to file for bankruptcy. As with any business contingency, many of the negative implications of business termination can be mitigated by foreseeing business issues and planning accordingly. This chapter focuses on the legal issues affecting intellectual property that arise when a business terminates, whether voluntarily or involuntarily.

Whether as a business attorney or an intellectual property attorney, you should pay special attention to the challenges for business termination planning posed by intellectual property. In the context of bankruptcy, you need to be aware of how intellectual property becomes a part of the bankruptcy estate, how bankruptcy proceedings can stay ongoing or pending intellectual property litigation, and, most important, how intellectual property licenses are treated in bankruptcy. Many of these problems raise questions of valuation and securitizing intellectual property that have been addressed in previous chapters. Terminating a business voluntarily can also raise questions of valuation and intellectual property ownership. Many of these questions can be addressed by careful drafting of business documents, such as the articles of incorporation, the partnership agreement, or contracts. Drafting these documents requires an understanding of the background legal principles presented in this chapter.

The materials in this chapter focus on what happens to the intellectual property assets of a business when it terminates. There are two ways in which a business can come to an end. The first is when a business entity becomes insolvent and goes through bankruptcy proceedings to obtain a fresh start. The second is through a decision by the pertinent members of a business entity to end the business as a going concern and liquidate the assets. Each of these situations raises unique intellectual property issues.

In intellectual property practice, you should be aware of the possibility of bankruptcy as you draft intellectual property licenses and structure assignments of intellectual property interests. Intellectual property is also an increasingly important asset for the purposes of finance. Patents, copyrights, and trademarks, as well as intellectual property-intensive goods like software and movies, serve as collateral for many businesses, both high and low tech. This sort of collateral is affected by bankruptcy law, which has special rules to deal with how to distribute assets among creditors and other parties who have a claim to the assets. These issues are discussed in the section titled "The Bankruptcy Estate." Furthermore, ongoing intellectual property litigation may be affected by bankruptcy law, particularly its automatic stay provisions, which are used to pause judicial proceedings. These issues are discussed in the section titled "The Automatic Stay." Finally, the Bankruptcy Code has special rules treating intellectual property licenses that allow the debtor to either assume or reject the obligations under these licenses. These special rules provide difficult traps for the unwary in both bankruptcy and intellectual property practice and are discussed in the section titled "The Intellectual Property License in Bankruptcy."

Termination outside of bankruptcy also raises special questions for intellectual property. For example, when a partnership terminates, decisions have to be made about how intellectual property assets and licenses will be divided among the former owners of the partnership. In general, whenever a business winds down, intellectual property assets are affected and questions have to be answered about the ownership and transfer of these assets. Many of these questions are answered by general contract and business law and are addressed in the section "Termination Outside of Bankruptcy."

Readings
A. Termination through Bankruptcy

Bankruptcy law allows insolvent debtors to obtain a fresh start either by allowing them to liquidate their assets and satisfy creditors under Chapter 7 of the Bankruptcy Code or by reorganizing their business structure in order to meet their obligations under Chapter 11 of the Bankruptcy Code. This section provides an overview of the bankruptcy processes that arise regardless of whether a debtor decides to liquidate or to reorganize. The focus will be on three issues: (1) the bankruptcy estate, (2) the automatic stay, and (3) the treatment of intellectual property licenses.

When a debtor enters bankruptcy, the court assigns a bankruptcy trustee to manage the debtor's estate. The role of the trustee is to put together the assets that comprise the estate in order to maximize its value. Assets can include property, contracts, and other obligations owed to the debtor, such as legal claims. The cases on the bankruptcy estate illustrate the types of intellectual property issues that arise in determining the bankruptcy estate.

Section 362 of the Bankruptcy Code states that the filing of a bankruptcy petition acts as a stay of various judicial, administrative, or other proceedings against the debtor. This automatic stay provision allows the debtor to pause ongoing or postpone prospective litigation. The cases on the automatic stay and intellectual property litigation illustrate the effect of Section 362 on pending or prospective infringement suits.

The most complicated and important provisions of the Bankruptcy Code deal with the treatment of intellectual property licenses and other so-called executory contracts. Often the debtor will be subject to continuing contractual obligations after filing for bankruptcy. For example, he may be leasing real or personal property or licensing a copyright or patent. These continuing contractual obligations are called executory contracts. Under Section 365, the bankruptcy trustee has the power to decide how to handle the obligations under executory contracts. The trustee has three options: to reject the contract, to assume the contract, or to assume and assign the contract. If the trustee rejects the contract, then the debtor is in breach and the other party has a claim for breach of contract against the bankruptcy estate. If the trustee assumes the contract, then the estate is under the continuing obligations of the contract. If the trustee assumes and assigns, then the continuing obligations and benefits of the contract are transferred to someone else.

Section 365 raises special concerns for debtors who are party to an intellectual property license. If the debtor is the licensor, then the licensee may be put in the position of not being able to use the intellectual property if the trustee chooses to reject the license. Section 365(n) was enacted in 1988 to protect the licensee by allowing the licensee to continue using the intellectual property in the situation where the debtor/licensor rejects the license. There are two important caveats to section 365(n). First, since the Bankruptcy Code does not include trademarks in the definition of intellectual property, section 365(n) does not protect licensees of trademarks when the debtor/trademark owner rejects trademark licenses. Second, section 365(n) does not apply to the situation where the licensee is the debtor and elects to reject the license. This latter scenario is particularly troubling when the debtor/licensee elects to assume the license and assign it to a competitor of the licensor. The cases on the intellectual property in bankruptcy illustrate this problem and other issues raised by section 365(n).

1. The Bankruptcy Estate

Patrick A. Casey, P.A. v. Joel S. Hochman, M.D.

Court of Appeals for the Tenth Circuit

963 F. 2d. 1347 (10th Cir. 1992)

WILLIAM J. HOLLOWAY, JR., CIRCUIT JUDGE.

On January 21, 1982, Dr. Joel Hochman, a psychiatrist, and his wife Darrellyn, a housewife, filed a Chapter 11 petition for bankruptcy . . . .

The Hochmans acted as debtors-in-possession under Chapter 11 from January 21, 1982, until May 3, 1984, when motions of creditors to convert the bankruptcy into a Chapter 7 liquidation were granted. In the interim, Dr. Hochman had created the device in question in early 1983. A specific finding to this effect was made by the bankruptcy judge, and this is not disputed. At the time of conversion of the bankruptcy case to a Chapter 7 proceeding, Dr. Hochman had unsuccessfully attempted to have the device patented.

The bankruptcy judge made extensive subsidiary historical findings of fact. These findings are not specifically attacked. As noted, this appeal challenges only the ruling of the bankruptcy judge determining that the device, the patent and income from the licensing agreement were part of the bankruptcy estate, which ruling was affirmed by the district judge on appeal. Further facts relating to the device will be detailed below.

The original Chapter 11 proceeding was commenced by the Hochmans on January 21, 1982. Well after the 1984 conversion of the proceeding into Chapter 7, three scheduled creditors filed a complaint in July 1988 under 11 U.S.C. § 727. They objected to a discharge in bankruptcy of the Hochmans, alleging acts calculated to defraud creditors by the concealment and misappropriation of assets of the bankruptcy estate. After a five-day trial the bankruptcy judge found that the Hochmans intentionally concealed rents from a ranch and other properties and proceeds and the patent and license fees paid on the Tamponator device. These actions were found to be in violation of § 727 and a discharge in bankruptcy was denied by the bankruptcy judge.

The Hochmans appealed to the district court, arguing that they had not had a fair trial and that the bankruptcy judge erred in his ruling that the Tamponator was part of the bankruptcy estate, inter alia. The district judge rejected an argument that the trial in the bankruptcy court was unfair. He also held that the determination that the device was part of the bankruptcy estate was "not clearly erroneous."

A notice of appeal to this court was timely filed. On this appeal the Hochmans raise only the issue concerning whether the Tamponator device, the patent, and income from the license agreement and other income related to the device are part of the Chapter 7 estate. This central argument is presented in two parts: (1) the Hochmans claim that the findings and consideration below as to whether the device was part of the bankruptcy estate were not adequate; and (2) the determination that the device, the patent, income from the license agreement and related income were part of the bankruptcy estate was error. . . .

We turn now to the merits of the rulings that the Tamponator device, the patent, and income from the licensing agreement and related efforts of the Hochmans were part of the bankruptcy estate. The findings of the bankruptcy judge were stated in his opinion in detail and we summarize them below.

The Hochmans commenced the bankruptcy case in Chapter 11 on January 21, 1982. The bankruptcy judge found that when the debtors filed a motion for reconsideration of conversion of their case to Chapter 7, they explained to the court and creditors that Dr. Hochman had obtained initial approval of a patent of a medical device "with an enormous income potential." The judge said that the transcript shows that Dr. Hochman knew and understood that the patentable medical device "was property of the estate." Significantly for our purposes, the judge found that "Dr. Hochman had created the device in early 1983." *Id.* Hochman filed a patent application, # 069740196, through a patent attorney on February 28, 1983. The patent office acted on the application on April 12, 1984, rejecting the sixteen claims and giving the debtors three months from April 12, 1984, to respond. The patent examiner noted that claims 11 through 15 were "free of the art of record." The bankruptcy judge found that the Hochmans did respond to the patent office just prior to expiration of their deadline and that on May 7, 1985, Patent No. 40515167 was issued for the invention.

The bankruptcy judge found that the "invention known as the tampenator [sic] was property acquired by the debtors during the Chapter 11 case and was property of the estate." The patent application made on February 28, 1983, and the rights thereunder "were property acquired by the debtors during the case and were property of the estate." The judge found that the debtors "knew that the invention and the patent were property of the estate" which they concealed.

It was found that on July 23, 1984, 81 days after conversion to Chapter 7, Dr. Hochman entered into two agreements with Hancock, Newton & Thomas concerning the invention. Dr. Hochman signed a licensing agreement giving this group the right to license, manufacture, use, sell and commercialize the invention for a license fee of $150,000 and royalties equivalent to six per cent of the selling price of each licensed product. $5,000 had already been paid to Dr. Hochman. Dr. Hochman represented that he was owner of the patent and had the right to grant an exclusive license. The agreement provided that Dr. Hochman would do all things necessary to obtain letters patent. The license agreement had been contingent upon Dr. Hochman securing the patent by December 12, 1984. . . .

The defendants-appellants, Dr. and Mrs. Hochman, challenge the rulings below that the Tamponator device, the patent thereof, and payments on the licensing agreement were within the Chapter 7 bankruptcy estate. They argue that 11 U.S.C. § 541(a) provides that commencement of a bankruptcy case creates the estate; the estate is comprised of all legal and equitable interests of the debtor in property as of the commencement of the case; and that when a Chapter 11 case is converted to a Chapter 7 case, the original filing date of the petition under Chapter 11 establishes the commencement of the case and the basis for determining the assets comprising the bankruptcy estate in accordance with 11 U.S.C. § 348(a). They say that § 348(a) makes it clear that the conversion to a Chapter 7 proceeding "does not effect a change in the date of the filing of the petition or the commencement of the case."

Further the defendants-appellants argue that the appellees fail to address the question whether an asset was acquired by the estate or by the debtors; that the appellees have blurred the distinction between property acquired by the estate and by the debtor. They conclude that since the device was invented in 1983, and the patent and payments in question followed, these were property acquired by the debtors.

We must agree. In these circumstances, upon conversion the assets which are the property of the Chapter 7 estate are determined with reference to the date of filing of the original Chapter 11 petition. . . . The bankruptcy judge found that the device was invented in early 1983 by Dr. Hochman. This finding is not questioned and there is no suggestion by the appellees that the device existed earlier. This was a year after the commencement of the first bankruptcy proceeding on January 21, 1982, with the filing of the Chapter 11 case. The basic rule is laid down by 11 U.S.C. § 541(a):

> (a) The commencement of a case under section 301, 302, or 303 [voluntary, involuntary, and joint cases] of this title creates an estate. Such estate is comprised of all the following property, wherever located:
>
> > (1) Except as provided in subsections (b) and (c)(2) of this section, all legal or equitable interests of the debtor in property as of the commencement of the case . . . .

The effect of § 541(a) is clearly stated in L. King, 4 Collier on Bankruptcy ¶ 541.05 at 541–24:

> As previously stated, under section 541(a) the estate is normally comprised only of property and interests therein belonging to the debtor at the time the petition is filed. In general, property not then owned but subsequently acquired by the debtor does not become property of the estate, but becomes the debtor's, clear of all claims that are discharged by the bankruptcy proceedings.

The basic principles stated in the treatise are clearly recognized in decisions under the Bankruptcy Act. In *Everett v. Judson*, 228 U.S. 474 (1913), the Supreme Court stated:

We think that the purpose of the law was to fix the line of cleavage with reference to the condition of the bankrupt estate as of the time at which the petition was filed and that the property which vests in the trustee at the time of adjudication is that which the bankrupt owned at the time of the filing of the petition. . . .

The appellants place their reliance on § 541(a)(6) and (7) as making the device, the patent and proceeds property of the Chapter 7 bankruptcy estate. Those subsections provide, inter alia, for inclusion in the estate of

(6) Proceeds, product, offspring, rents, and profits of or from property of the estate, except such as are earnings from services performed by an individual debtor after the commencement of the case.

(7) Any interest in property that the estate acquires after the commencement of the case.

The argument of the appellees confuses property acquired by the debtors and property acquired by the estate. In this connection we note that the bankruptcy judge made a finding that the "invention known as the Tamponator was property acquired by the debtors during the Chapter 11 case and was property of the estate." The judge further found, as noted, that Dr. Hochman developed the invention in 1983. We are persuaded that the facts found clearly establish that the device, the patent and proceeds from the licensing agreement were property acquired by the debtors, but we do not agree with the judge's conclusion that they were "property of the estate."

The appellees argue that property acquired post-petition is generally within the bankruptcy estate and that there are only two exceptions to this rule, those provided by § 541(a)(6) concerning proceeds, product, rents and profits from property of the estate. They also point to the 180-day limitation in § 541(a)(5) which places in the estate an interest in particular types of property (inheritances, property settlements, etc.) that would have been property of the estate if such interest had been an interest of the debtor on the date of filing of the petition, and if the debtor acquires or becomes entitled to it within 180 days after such date. The appellees simply have the general rule backwards; under § 541(a)(1) the general rule is that the estate includes interests of the debtor in property as of the commencement of the case. Both of these provisions relied on (§ 541(a)(5) and (6)) are actually exceptions from the general rule that post-petition acquisitions are property of the debtor—exceptions specially provided to include particular property within the bankruptcy estate.

Penick Pharmaceutical, Inc. & Unofficial Committee of Equity Holders of Penick Pharmaceutical, Inc. v. McManigle

United States Bankruptcy Court for the Southern District of New York

227 B.R. 229 (Bankr. S.D.N.Y.)

On June 9, 1994 (the "Petition Date"), the Debtors filed Chapter 11 petitions in this court. . . . Both pre- and post-petition, the Debtor has been engaged in the manufacture and sale of pharmaceutical products and in research and development with respect thereto.

On March 17, 1998, the Committee filed its complaint herein seeking a declaration that a certain new process relating to the manufacture of opium derivatives (the "Process") is not the property of the bankruptcy estate of the Debtor but is rather the property of the Debtor, free and clear of all claims of the Trustee, creditors and any other entity. . . .

The Process is the invention of Bao-Shan Huang ("Dr. Huang"), Yansong Lu ("Mr. Lu"), Ben-Yi Ji. ("Dr. Ji" and together with Dr. Huang and Mr. Lu, the "Employee Inventors") and Aris P. Christodoulou ("Dr. Christodoulou" and together with the Employee Inventors, the "Inventors"). Dr. Christodoulou was, at all relevant times until May 9, 1997, when he resigned, an officer and director of the Debtor. He is a shareholder of PPI and a member of the Committee. Dr. Huang was employed by the Debtor as a consultant to work in its research and development department (the "R & D Department") in 1994. In connection therewith, on May 10, 1994 he signed an Employee Confidentiality and Invention Assignment Agreement containing provisions in the following terms:

> 2. Employee shall disclose promptly to Employer any and all INVENTIONS conceived or made by him/her during his/her employment with Employer, whether or not made during his/her hours of employment or with the use of Employer facilities, materials, or personnel, and whether made solely or jointly with others, and hereby assigns all of his/her entire right, title and interest in any such INVENTIONS to Employer. As used herein, the term INVENTIONS means any and all developments, innovations, discoveries, improvements and ideas, whether patentable or not.

> 3. Employee shall, whenever requested to do so by Employer, execute any applications, confirmatory assignment documents, or other instruments which Employer shall consider necessary, to apply for and obtain Letters Patent in the United States, or any foreign country, and shall take such other action at Employer's expense as Employer deems necessary to protect Employer's interests in the INVENTIONS.

The agreement was signed by Dr. Christodoulou, as director, on behalf of the Debtor. In December of that year, Dr. Huang formulated certain synthetic routes for the Process. In June 1995, Dr. Huang was hired by the Debtor as an employee in the R & D Department and in that capacity, in January 1996, conducted the first laboratory test of the Process. In October 1996, Dr. Ji and Mr. Lu were hired by the Debtor, initially as consultants and then as employees in the R & D Department. Both signed Employee Confidentiality and Invention Assignment Agreements containing terms identical to those in Dr. Huang's Employee Confidentiality and Invention Assignment Agreement set forth above. Again, these agreements were signed by Dr. Christodoulou, as director, on behalf of the Debtor. Dr. Ji and Mr. Lu developed certain intermediate synthetic routes used in the Process. The respective fees and salaries of the Employee Inventors were paid by the Debtor's bankruptcy estate and laboratories, chemicals and equipment belonging to such estate were used in researching and developing the Process. Dr. Christodoulou's part in the invention of the Process was to conceptualize the use of morphine as a starting material for the preparation of certain opium derivatives.

The Debtor filed the first provisional application for the Process with the United States Patent & Trademark Office (the "PTO") on July 26, 1996, the second provisional patent application for the Process with the PTO on April 29, 1997 and the regular patent application for the Process with the PTO on July 11, 1997. The Debtor's basic patent application was allowed by the PTO and the Debtor is awaiting a response from the PTO with respect to six divisional patent applications arising from the regular patent application. The Debtor paid all costs and expenses in connection with such applications, including in respect of the hiring of special patent counsel, Burgess, Ryan & Wayne, whose appointment as special counsel to the Trustee was approved by this court on July 22, 1997.

Meanwhile, by an Assignment of Application for Patent (the "Assignment") dated July 8 and 9, 1997, "in consideration of . . . $1.00 . . . and other valuable consideration," the Inventors assigned to "Penick Corporation" their interest in the Process and the patent application and Letters Patent relating thereto, in the case of the Employee Inventors, in accordance with the terms of their respective Employee Confidentiality and Invention Assignment Agreements.

Discussion

When a debtor files for bankruptcy protection, a bankruptcy estate is created. Under section 541(a)(1) of the Bankruptcy Code, the estate includes "all legal or equitable interests of the debtor in property as of the commencement of the case." 11 U.S.C. § 541(a)(1)(1994). Property of the estate also includes "[p]roceeds, product, offspring, rents, or profits of or from property of the estate, except such as are earnings from services performed by an individual debtor after the commencement of the case," 11 U.S.C. § 541(a)(6) (1994), and "[a]ny interest in property that the estate acquires after commencement of the case." 11 U.S.C. § 541(a)(7) (1994). Thus, the estate does not remain static.

The Trustee, on the one hand, argues that the Process belongs to the bankruptcy estate of the Debtor pursuant to section 541(a)(6) or (7) of the Bankruptcy Code. The Committee, on the other hand, contends that the Process is not "property of the estate" under section 541(a)(6) because it is derived not from property of the estate but from "the minds and intellectual activity of [the Inventors]," nor under section 541(a)(7) because it was acquired not by the estate pursuant to the Assignment but by the "post-petition Debtor".

The parties have extensively briefed the question of whether a corporate debtor may hold property as non-estate property, the Trustee arguing, in essence, that postpetition property acquisitions necessarily constitute estate property under section 541(a)(6) or (7). For purposes of this motion, however, this court need not resolve the theoretical question because it is clear on the undisputed facts that the Process was derived from property of the estate so as to bring it within section 541(a)(6) and/or acquired by the estate so as to bring it within section 541(a)(7).

Upon the filing of a voluntary Chapter 11 petition, a debtor automatically becomes "debtor in possession." As such, it occupies the shoes of a bankruptcy trustee in every major way. As a de jure trustee, it holds its powers in trust for the benefit of creditors. Specifically, in the case of an inanimate debtor in possession such as a corporation, the fiduciary duties borne by a trustee for a debtor out of possession fall on the debtor's directors, officers and managing employees, who have a duty to maximize the value of the estate, and who are burdened to ensure that the resources that flow through the debtor in possession's hands are used to benefit the unsecured creditors and other parties in interest. Thus, upon filing its petition, the Debtor became debtor in possession and, through its management, including Dr. Christodoulou, was burdened with the duties and responsibilities of a bankruptcy trustee.

In addition, however, as debtor in possession and de jure trustee, the Debtor had certain statutory powers. Most importantly, it was authorized to operate its business pursuant to section 1108 of the Bankruptcy Code. Pursuant to section 363(c)(1) of the Bankruptcy Code, as debtor in possession, the Debtor was permitted to conduct its business in the ordinary course. As was the case outside of bankruptcy, the Debtor then acted through its directors and officers, including Dr. Christodoulou, who continued to operate its business.

Thus, in the course of the operation of the Debtor's business by the Debtor as debtor in possession, the Employee Inventors were employed by the Debtor on behalf of the Debtor's estate. When Dr. Christodoulou signed Dr. Ji and Mr. Lu's respective Employee Confidentiality and Invention Assignment Agreements on behalf of the Debtor, he did so as agent of the Debtor as debtor in possession and in furtherance of his aforementioned fiduciary duties. These Employee Confidentiality and Invention Assignment Agreements gave the Debtor, as debtor in possession, on behalf of the estate, certain rights in the inventions of the Employee Inventors. These rights became property of the estate pursuant to section 541(a)(7) of the Bankruptcy Code. The benefit of Dr. Huang's Employee Confidentiality and Invention Assignment Agreement, which predated the filing of the petition, was estate property pursuant to section 541(a)(1). The Employee Inventors' salaries were paid by the estate and when the Employee Inventors rendered their services, it was to the Debtor as debtor in possession. The laboratories, chemicals and equipment used by the Employee Inventors were property of the estate either because they were property of the Debtor at the Petition Date, see 11 U.S.C. § 541(a)(1) (1994), or were acquired by the estate using funds derived from the Debtor's continuing operation of its business and therefore property of the estate pursuant to section 541(a)(7). When the Employee Inventors entered into the Assignment, it was in furtherance of their respective obligations to the Debtor as debtor in possession under the Employee Confidentiality and Invention Assignment Agreements and in exchange for consideration provided by the estate. Similarly, Dr. Christodoulou assigned his interest in the Process in exchange for consideration provided by the estate. Finally, the application for patent protection of the Process was, until the appointment of the Trustee, prosecuted on behalf of the Debtor as debtor in possession, financed by estate funds. Upon the appointment of the Trustee, the Debtor's management was displaced and the Trustee assumed management of the operation of the Debtor's business for the estate. The patent application continued to be prosecuted on behalf of the estate.

Nobody would seriously doubt that the tangible product of a debtor manufactured by its employees' "hands" post-petition and pre-confirmation were property of the estate and the Process is no different merely by virtue of its being intangible and the product of an intellectual process. In fact, development of the Process was apparently not the product of a purely intellectual exercise as it required physical testing using estate property. While the Inventors' minds might not have been property of the estate, their work product indubitably was. To the extent that the Process does not constitute product of or from property of the estate within section 541(a)(6), it was acquired by the estate pursuant to the Assignment, and therefore property of the estate pursuant to section 541(a)(7) of the Bankruptcy Code.

[In *Casey v. Hochman*, 963 F.2d 1347 (10th Cir. 1992)], the court held that the patent on a device invented by a debtor after the filing of his Chapter 11 petition was not included in property of the estate. However, there the debtor was an individual who was not bound by any agreement or fiduciary duty to deliver up his invention to the estate. In contrast, here, the Employee Inventors were employed by the debtor in possession on behalf of the estate and bound by the terms of their employment to assign their inventions to their employer and, in fact, did so. Dr. Christodoulou was similarly bound by reason of his fiduciary obligations.

Simplified Information Systems, Inc. v. Cannon

United States District Court for the Western District of Pennsylvania

89 B.R. 538 (W.D. Pa. 1988)

GERALD J. WEBER, DISTRICT JUDGE.

Debtor has asserted that the computer software, created by Cannon, is property of the estate. Cannon argues that Debtor merely possesses an exclusive license to use the software for the life of the corporation, with reversion to Cannon upon corporate dissolution. Cannon bases this assertion upon his claim that Barthalow and he made an oral contract to that effect.

With the exception of certain factors not presently relevant, property of the estate includes ". . . all legal or equitable interests of the [D]ebtor in property as of the commencement of the case." 11 U.S.C. §541(a). This also includes both intangible and transitory property. Therefore, software ownership can be property of the estate. However, the parameters of Debtor's interest are determined by state and federal non-bankruptcy law. In the instant case we must turn to federal copyright law in order to determine ownership of the software design.

The right of copyright is statutorily created, and is based upon Article I, §8, cl. 8 of the U.S. Constitution. Section 102(a) of the Copyright Act states in pertinent part:

102(a). Copyright protection subsists in accordance with this title, in original works of authorship fixed in any tangible medium of expression, now known or later developed, from which they can be perceived, reproduced or otherwise communicated, either directly or with the aid of a machine or device. Works of authorship include the following categories:

(1) literary works; . . .

A computer program is a work of authorship and is classified as a literary work for the purpose of obtaining copyright protection.

Section 201(a) of the Copyright Act states that "[c]opyright in a work . . . vests initially in the author or authors," and, "[i]n the case of a work made for hire, the employer or other person for whom the work was prepared is considered the author . . . [and] owns all of the rights comprised in the copyright" unless otherwise expressly agreed in writing. Clearly then, the ownership of the copyright depends upon the identity of the statutory "author", which in turn depends upon whether the "work" is a "work made for hire".

A "work made for hire" is "a work prepared by an employee within the scope of his or her employment . . ." 17 U.S.C. § 101. Under the Copyright Act, one may be an employee without regard to the method of payment, i.e., salary, piecework, royalty, or gratis. The employer's president may also be considered an employee. Furthermore, the "work made for hire" doctrine is not avoidable merely by performing the work in a separate location, or on non-work time.

This doctrine does not prevent the employer and employee from forming an agreement to the contrary; the "work made for hire" doctrine creates a presumption in favor of its validity, which can be rebutted only by express written agreement of the parties.

In the case at bar, Cannon's claim to the software cannot be sustained. The whole purpose for the corporation's formation was the creation and marketing of a computer process which would assist doctors' staffs in their various clerical duties, such as scheduling, charting, and billing. The program written by Cannon was intended to perform these functions.

Cannon was the Debtor's President when he wrote the program; that he wrote it during "off" hours, or at his other business facility is not relevant. Cannon's employment contract required him to devote his time and attention, and his best effort ". . . to the discharge of his duties." His duty regarding the corporation was to create this software. From August 1981 to June 1982 Cannon received $400.00 per week, to sustain him and his family while he worked on the program. The Board of Directors even consented to his outside employment, so long as it did not interfere with the Debtor's business purpose—the development and marketing of the software for use in physicians' offices.

Cannon asserts that an oral agreement to the contrary was reached, creating authorship in Cannon, and an exclusive licensure with the Debtor; however, the Copyright Act requires a written agreement between the parties in order to rebut the "work for hire" presumption. There exists no such agreement in this case. To the contrary, the credible evidence presented leads to the conclusion that this software constitutes "work made for hire." As such, the statutory authorship of same goes to the Debtor corporation. Therefore, upon the filing of the bankruptcy petition, said software became and is property of the Debtor's estate.

C Tek Software, Inc. v. New York State Business Venture Partnership

United States Bankruptcy Court for the District of New Hampshire

127 B.R. 501 (Bankr. N.H. 1991)

JAMES E. YACOS, BANKRUPTCY JUDGE.

Debtor, C Tek Software, Inc., initiated an adversary proceeding against certain creditors to determine the validity, extent, or priority of certain liens. In an earlier opinion, I decided that New York State Business Venture Partnership ("NYSBVP") had a perfected security interest in the computer software ClienTrak. *See In re C Tek Software, Inc.*, 117 B.R. 762 (Bankr. D.N.H. 1990). However, I left for a further trial the question of "the extent of the security interest NYSBVP has in the source code in light of the enhancements made after the security interest was taken." *Id.* at 763 n.1. A trial was held on this matter on October 10, 1990, and I then took the matter under submission.

Findings of Fact

1. C Tek is the owner of a computer software known as "ClienTrak." This software is sold to companies in the financial services industry, principally banks and insurance companies. The software stores information and generates correspondence.

2. On October 26, 1987, NYSBVP took and perfected a security interest in some pieces of hardware owned by C Tek as well as "[t]he source code and all ownership rights to the computer software ClienTrak including copyrights 1983, 1984, 1985, 1986 and 1987."

3. On June 17, 1988, C Tek entered into a Master Distribution Agreement ("MDA") with Intelligent Investment Systems ("IIS"). The MDA is a ten year licensing agreement which gives IIS the exclusive worldwide right to sell and develop the software ClienTrak. Under the MDA, IIS promised to pay C Tek royalties, which would decrease in amount over time as IIS made changes to the software. Most importantly, paragraph 2.1(f) of the MDA gave IIS the right "to produce, copy, distribute and market derivative versions of the software and documentation without limitation."

4. At the time the MDA was executed, the software ClienTrak was at version 3.7.2B. It would have taken a group of programmers about five years to independently produce comparable software.

5. On April 6, 1989, C Tek filed a Chapter 11 petition in this court. On August 31, 1989, NYSBVP got a default order vacating the automatic stay but without prejudice to C Tek's rights to initiate this adversary proceeding.

6. IIS made revisions to thousands of lines of source code after receiving its licensing rights under the MDA. IIS employed several programmers to make the changes and assist users. The software is currently at version 4.1.8. The differences between this source code and the prior version delivered to IIS at the time the MDA was executed are of three types. First, the overwhelming majority of changes were the elimination of "bugs" i.e., minor defects in the source code so the software does not operate as intended. Second, some minor "cosmetic" changes were made to make the display and controls more user friendly. Third, three major changes were made to the import function, the report customizer, and the communications message exchange. This last group of changes are the only ones a programmer would call "enhancements." No new "modules" were added to the five modules existing in version 3.7.2B.

The Issue

IIS is not now contending that it has rights to market the software through version 3.7.2B after foreclosure. The dispute concerns who owns the changes made to the software after that point up to version 4.1.8. IIS recognizes that copyrights of a derivative work cover only the original matters added and not the underlying work.

There is little room to question IIS' right to attempt to copyright any derivative software it may develop under paragraph 2.1(f) of the MDA. NYSBVP argues that the MDA did not expressly say IIS had copyright rights in its derivative product only that IIS could produce derivative works. Yet, any other construction of this contractual provision would be contrary to the logical inference of this provision and the spirit and intent of the MDA. Also, it seems plain that if there was no agreement as to who owns copyrightable material it should be the author of such material.

NYSBVP also argues that paragraph 4.2(b) of the MDA provides that upon termination of the agreement C Tek will step into the shoes of IIS. However, this provision has nothing to do with copyrights in derivative works. Rather, it concerns sublicenses and subdistributorship agreements of the original software.

The only substantive question before me is whether some or all of the changes IIS made to the source code were significant enough to meet the "originality" requirement for copyright protection for a "derivative work".

Copyright Law

A derivative work is defined by statute as follows:

> A work based upon one or more preexisting works, [in] any . . . form in which a work may be recast, transformed, or adapted. A work consisting of editorial revisions, annotations, elaborations, or other modifications which as a whole represent an original work of authorship, is a "derivative work."

I start with the proposition established by the U.S. Supreme Court that:

> [t]he aspects of a derivative work added by the derivative author are that author's property, but the element drawn from the pre-existing work remains on grant from the owner of the pre-existing work.

In order to qualify as a derivative work, and thus qualify for copyright protection, the work must be "original." . . . "The test of originality is concededly one with a low threshold." All that is needed to satisfy both the Constitution and the statute is that the "author" contributed something more than a "merely trivial" variation, something recognizably "his own." Originality in this context "means little more than a prohibition of actual copying." No matter how poor artistically the "author's" addition, it is enough if it be his own.

Works substantially derived from prior works, whether the preexisting works are copyrighted or in the public domain, are also subject to copyright protection so long as the derivative work itself is original. The original aspects of the derivative work must themselves be nontrivial, and the copyright in the derivative work does not affect the copyright protection in the underlying work.

Unfortunately, that case involved a comparison of dolls which does not provide much guidance to this court. However, the language used did say originality is an easy concept to meet, and the court would not allow summary judgment against the derivative author even where it found the "[n]ontrivial differences between the . . . dolls are indeed difficult, if not impossible, to discern."

The [First Circuit has] stated:

> It is axiomatic that the designation "original" is not intended to be limited to works that are novel or unique. Rather, the word "original," which was "purposely left undefined" by Congress refers to works that have been "independently created by an author," regardless of their literary or aesthetic merit, or ingenuity, or qualitative value.

I find this point meaningful because NYSBVP has in part belittled the "bug" work as not being important enough to warrant protection. The law simply does not support this contention.

To answer completely the question of what is the test for originality in "knowledge" cases, I must look to a series of four Eighth Circuit cases.

The Eighth Circuit has issued a series of "knowledge" copyright cases that provide considerable guidance as to what constitutes originality in a "knowledge" case. The first case is *Hutchinson Tel. Co. v. Fronteer Directory Co. of Minnesota, Inc.*, 770 F.2d 128 (8th Cir. 1985). In this case, the Court held that the creation of a white pages telephone directory was an original work of authorship. The Court explained:

> "Originality" under the prior construction did not connote novelty or uniqueness but simply that the work be independently created. If a work is similar to preexisting works, it must show more than trivial variation from those works.

. . . .

Hutchinson's records are gathered and maintained for many purposes, including publication of a directory. The proper focus is not whether Hutchinson's sole motivation for maintaining the records is the publication of a directory, but whether the directory itself is derived from information compiled and generated by Hutchinson's efforts.

Thus, the court was focusing on the independent effort of the author in deeming the work original. The Court [in *The Toro Co. v. R & R Products Co.*, 787 F.2d 1208 (8th Cir. 1986)] held that a lawn care manufacturer's parts numbering system lacked even a low threshold of originality and commented:

Under originality case law a work need not be artistic or novel to achieve protection. *Mazer v. Stein*, 347 U.S. 201 [74 S. Ct. 460, 98 L. Ed. 630] (1954). Originality denotes only enough definite expression so that one may distinguish authorship.

. . . .

If the disputed work is similar to a pre-existing protected work or one in the public domain, the second work must contain some variation recognizable as that of the second author.

. . . .

The undisputed evidence below shows that appellant's "system" is composed of arbitrarily assigning to a particular replacement part a random number when appellant creates the part. Appellant's Vice President for Distribution testified that once a part is created "an arbitrary number is assigned" to the part to identify it. Appellant's counsel, when moving for a new trial, told the court that "it was undisputed at trial that Toro's parts numbering system was arbitrary and random." There was no evidence that a particular series or configuration of numbers denoted a certain type or category of parts or that the numbers used encoded any kind of information at all. In short, numbers were assigned to a part without rhyme or reason. This record establishes that appellant's parts numbering "system" falls short of even the low threshold of originality. The random and arbitrary use of numbers in the public domain does not evince enough originality to distinguish authorship. The expression itself is nothing more than the public domain numbers. There is no variation, other than the trivial hyphen, to establish authorship. Also, it is clear that no effort or judgment went into this selection or composition of the numbers, which distinguishes this case from the telephone directory cases. We are left, then, with the accidental marriage of a part and a number. We do not believe that such a marriage produces an original work of authorship. Appellant simply has not added enough to its parts numbers to make them original and remove them from the public domain. This is not to say that all parts numbering systems are not copyrightable. A system that uses symbols in some sort of meaningful pattern, something by which one could distinguish effort or content, would be an original work. Originality is a very low threshold, but still a threshold.

The next Eighth Circuit case on this issue is *West Publishing Co. v. Mead Data Central, Inc.*, 799 F.2d 1219, 1223 (8th Cir. 1986). In this case, the court held that the arrangement of page numbers by a legal publishing company was original. (The Court distinguished Toro on the grounds that the arrangement took some effort.) Thus, a competing computer legal research service could not appropriate the page numbering. This decision is obviously on the fringe end of originality requirements. Regardless, its definition of originality is highly instructive. The court stated:

> The standard for "originality" is minimal. It is not necessary that the work be novel or unique, but only that the work have its origin with the author — that it be independently created. Little more is involved in this requirement than "a prohibition of actual copying."

To be the original work of an author, a work must be the product of some "creative intellectual or aesthetic labor." However, "a very slight degree of such labor[,] ... almost any ingenuity in selection, combination or expression, no matter how crude, humble or obvious, will be sufficient" to make the work copyrightable.

Thus, the Court was once again looking at independent effort or judgment to deem something an original creation. In [*Applied Innovations, Inc. v. Regents of the University of Minnesota*, 876 F.2d 626 (8th Cir. 1989)], the court held that psychological test statements that were "independently created" are original and copyrightable. It also held that revisions to the questions "are recognizable as the work of the authors and thus are sufficiently original."

Applying these Eighth Circuit cases to my case I believe all of the efforts of IIS in revising the source code, when considered collectively, are original work entitled to copyright protection. The changes the IIS programmers made to the source code required independent effort and judgment. Even NYSBVP's own expert admitted that it is more difficult to modify another programmer's source code than to create one's own. IIS has created something that is recognizably its own in the source code. Admittedly, most of the changes are not important modifications to the functionality of the source code, but that is not the test under copyright law. IIS' changes are not "trivial" in the copyright sense; they required more than token independent effort or judgment. . . .

Finally, I find support in my decision if I look to the purpose of copyright law and the originality requirement. The purpose of copyright law is to encourage creative activity by granting a limited monopoly. What IIS did is socially useful work. NYSBVP's own expert said most of the work — the debugging work — was "warranty work." This is valuable work and should be encouraged.

Nor will the purpose of the originality requirement be thwarted. In a seminal opinion on originality, *L. Batlin & Son, Inc. v. Snyder*, 536 F.2d 486 (2d Cir. 1976), the court explained that the originality requirement is designed to prevent someone from making "minuscule variations", *id.* at 492, to monopolize preexisting work. One commentator has explained why courts should be particularly careful in assessing the originality requirement for derivative works:

> The requirement of originality is significant chiefly in connection with derivative works, where, if interpreted too liberally, it would paradoxically inhibit rather than promote the creation of such works by giving the first creator a considerable power to interfere with the creation of subsequent derivative works from the same underlying work.

IIS is not trying to monopolize preexisting work. It merely seeks copyright protection for its own derivative work, which is severable from the preexisting work.

Accession

Having determined that IIS has a copyright in changes from source code version 3.7.2B to 4.1.8, I am left with the question of how NYSBVP can foreclose on the source code. The testimony clearly established that IIS could return version 3.7.2B to the creditor. Therefore, under the law of accession this is all NYSBVP could get. A case illustrating this principle is *AMCA Int'l Finance Corp. v. Interstate Detroit Diesel Allison, Inc.*, 428 N.W.2d 128 (Minn. Ct. App. 1988). In this case the debtor replaced the engine of an excavator subject to a security interest, and was allowed to give the creditor the original engine when the creditor repossessed. The court explained:

> The only way, therefore, that [creditor] would have a security interest would be through the doctrine of accession. Accession is defined as follows:

> We think the general rule is quite well settled that, where the articles later attached to an automobile or other principal article of personal property became so closely incorporated with the principal article that they cannot be identified and detached therefrom without injury to the automobile or principal article, such articles become part of the machine or principal article to which they are so attached and will pass by accession to one having a chattel mortgage or other lien upon the principal article, if the lien is enforced. But when the articles added can be readily identified and detached without injury to the principal machine or article, they do not pass by accession to the one having a prior chattel mortgage or lien on the principal article.

Conclusion

IIS had a license from the debtor to copyright derivative software. The software IIS developed is copyrightable because it meets the originality requirements of copyright law. Thus, since the changes to the source code can be severed from the underlying work, IIS owns those changes free and clear of any lien of NYSBVP.

Notes & Questions

1. Bankruptcy law allows a financially distressed business (or person) to start over by liquidating all assets and satisfying creditors. The law also offers the alternative for a company to reorganize and restructure its debt. Under a liquidation, the business's assets are assembled to create the bankruptcy estate, which is managed by a

court-designated trustee whose decisions are reviewed by a bankruptcy judge. The assets are valued, and the estate is used to settle the business's debts, some of which are discharged as a result of the bankruptcy. Under a reorganization, the business changes its business form and the terms of its financial obligations are restructured.

2. Most companies and financial institutions treat patents as a valuable asset that can be bought and sold as well as licensed. Companies use patents as collateral securitizing debt obligations much like a company or an individual might mortgage land or a building. In addition, licensing revenues are not only an important part of a company's cash flow but also an alternative form of collateral for obtaining loans.

While collateralizing a patent and licensing revenues provides an important means to access credit, using either a patent or its licenses as collateral exposes the company to several risks. First, creditors can, in the event of default, foreclose on the patent much in the same way as it would foreclose on a house. Patent foreclosures have been rare, partly because the patent is often more valuable in the hands of the company, which has the know-how to effectively market and use the patent, than in the hands of the financial institution, which typically does not. Second, creditors often might have a say in the terms of how a patent is licensed in order to protect its financial interests. Often, the patent owner and creditor or a purchaser of a patent may create business entities whose sole function is to hold the patent as an asset.

3. Once patents are recognized as a business asset, patent owners, licensees, and creditors can adopt business strategies to protect their interests in bankruptcy. One tactic is to put the patent in a trust that is usually exempted from the bankruptcy estate under law. The Biopharma Royalty Trust, used by Bristol Meyers Squib for securitizing its license of the HIV/AIDS drug Zerit from Yale Medical Colleges, the patent owner, provides a model. While this trust has not been tested in bankruptcy, the use of a trust mechanism also permits the securitization of patents, or the selling of financial interests in the profit stream generated by a patent. The Biopharma Royalty Trust is the first pharmaceutical royalty rated by Standards & Poor's and consists of $57.15 million worth of royalty notes, maturing on June 6, 2006.

A trust is an example of a "bankruptcy remote entity" discussed above. Another example is the creation of a subsidiary corporation or some other separate business entity that would be the actual owner of the patent. This entity's sole purpose is to hold the patent and serve as the party through which royalties pass from the licensee to the original patent owner. In the event of bankruptcy, if the entity has been created correctly, the patent and the license will be sheltered from the estate.

4. Bankruptcy law allows the debtor business to manage its debts and effectively use its debts to satisfy the interests of the creditors and the business as a going concern. The bankruptcy court judge and the trustee play a crucial role in meeting these goals.

When a debtor enters into a business transaction while in bankruptcy, the trustee and bankruptcy judge oversee the negotiations to ensure that the debtor is obtaining maximum value. In the 1999 bankruptcy of National Health and Safety, Corp., the debtor entered into a sales transaction with Mednet Healthcare Network. The purpose of the sale was to transfer rights in National Health's intellectual property to Mednet, a company that could more effectively use and license the intellectual property within its network of healthcare providers. National Health's primary assets consisted of software copyrights, customer lists, and business methods associated with its network of uninsured customers that were sold access to health care services through National Health's plan.

This deal illustrates a common problem raised by intellectual property in bankruptcy: determining the value of the patents owned by the debtor. Sophisticated financial models are sometimes used to place a dollar value on these patents, but this approach is limited because of the uniqueness of each patent. Another way valuation issues are handled is by compensating the patent owner with a share of all future royalties earned by an assignee of the patent. The problem with this approach is that the assignee may not always effectively license the patent and may make a future transfer of the patent, potentially cutting off any rights of the original owner of the patent.

In the case of National Health, the debtor did retain the right to receive a share of the royalties. In addition, the debtor used an auction method to determine the value of the patents in this case, essentially transferring the patents to the highest bidder. The bankruptcy court approved the use of the auction method and also approved the royalty sharing agreement after imposing obligations on Mednet to report and account for all royalties earned by licensing the patents.

5. Domain Names. Courts are split on whether domain names are intellectual property that are part of the bankruptcy estate. In *Online Partners.Com Inc. v. Atlantic-Net Media Corp.*, 2000 U.S. Dist. LEXIS 783 (N.D. Cal. 2000), the court held that domain names are intellectual property and become part of the bankruptcy estate. However, in *Network Solutions, Inc., v. Umbro Int'l, Inc.*, 529 S.E. 2d 80 (Va. 2000), the Supreme Court of Virginia held that a domain name is not a property interest, but represents the contractual right to use the services of a domain name registrar.

6. Secured versus unsecured claims. Creditors can take security interests in intellectual property. Security interests in intellectual property have to be properly recorded and perfected. The steps needed to perfect security interests in intellectual property are discussed in detail in Chapter 2. If a security interest has not been properly recorded and perfected, the bankruptcy trustee has the right to set aside the security interest, rendering the creditor an unsecured creditor. An unsecured creditor is one who does not have a security interest in collateral backing the debt obligation.

In the distribution of assets among creditors, secured creditors have the right to receive the value of the collateral securing the debt before any unsecured creditors. Secured creditors can be forced to pay administrative expenses that the court deems to be "reasonable, necessary costs and expenses of preserving, or disposing of, such property to the extent of any benefit" to the secured creditor under section 506(c).

Unsecured creditors are paid out of any assets remaining from the collateral after the secured creditors have been compensated and from all assets that do not serve as collateral. There are, however, nine levels of priority that receive payment before unsecured creditors. The nine levels of priority, as described in Section 507, are, in order: (i) administrative expense claims; (ii) claims in the ordinary course of business; (iii) certain claims for wages, salaries, and commissions; (iv) certain claims for contributions to employee benefit plans; (v) certain special claims in the grain and fishing industries; (vi) certain individual claims for deposits for purchase, lease or rental of property or services; (vii) alimony and child support claims; (viii) tax claims of governmental units; and (ix) claims to government agencies to maintain capital of insured depository institutions.

2. The Automatic Stay and Intellectual Property Litigation

Checkers Drive-In Restaurants, Inc. v. Commissioner of Patents and Trademarks

Court of Appeals for the District of Columbia

51 F.3d 1078 (D.C. Cir. 1995)

HARRY T. EDWARDS, CHIEF JUDGE.

This appeal concerns the scope of the automatic stay provision under the Bankruptcy Code. This provision, which is found at 11 U.S.C. § 362(a) (1988), generally operates to block legal actions that could affect the property of a debtor in bankruptcy, and it serves both to shelter the debtor from harassment and to prevent creditors from engaging in a race to liquidate the estate's assets.

Appellant, Checkers Drive-In Restaurants, Inc., ("Checkers"), claims the automatic stay barred it from filing an affidavit as normally required to maintain its federal service mark registration pursuant to section 8 of the Lanham Trademark Act, 15 U.S.C. § 1058 (1988) ("Lanham Act"). Under section 8 of the Lanham Act, a service mark registration is canceled at the end of six years following the date of registration, unless the registrant files an affidavit (between the fifth and sixth years) setting forth his or her current use of the mark. Checkers's section 8 filing came due while it was pursuing a petition to cancel a competing service mark registration of a debtor in bankruptcy. Checkers failed to file the required affidavit during the statutory period, allegedly on the assumption that the Bankruptcy Code's automatic stay provision barred the required filing. The United States Patent and Trademark Office then canceled Checkers's service mark registration. Checkers appealed to the Commissioner of Patents and Trademarks ("Commissioner"), arguing that, because the automatic stay barred it from filing the affidavit, its failure to do so did not warrant the cancellation of its service mark registration under the Lanham Act. Rejecting this reasoning, the Commissioner denied Checkers's appeal. When Checkers challenged this decision in the District Court, the trial judge granted the Commissioner's motion for summary judgment. Checkers now appeals from that decision.

We affirm the judgment of the District Court. Although the Bankruptcy Code's automatic stay provision is broad in scope, it does not reach as far as Checkers would stretch it here. Checkers asserts that the section 8 filing requirement was stayed by operation of either of two subsections of the automatic stay provision. The first stays the continuation of any judicial, administrative, or other action against the debtor if the action was begun before the debtor filed its petition for bankruptcy. The second stays any act to take possession of, or exercise control over, property held by the bankrupt's estate. We find neither to apply. Checkers's filing of a section 8 affidavit was not part of its claim against the debtor, nor would it have affected the debtor's property. Rather, it would have merely maintained the status quo with respect to Checkers's own property. Accordingly, we hold that the Commissioner properly canceled Checkers's registration.

I. BACKGROUND

This case arises from a dispute between two owners of federally registered service marks, both of which employed the word "Checkers" in their design. Checkers owned, by assignment, a service mark for use in connection with its marketing of restaurant services. Checkers's mark was registered pursuant to the Lanham Act on October 23, 1984. By virtue of this registration, Checkers gained a number of benefits, for federal registration of a trademark or service mark constitutes "prima facie evidence of the validity of the registered mark and of the registration of the mark, of the registrant's ownership of the mark, and of the registrant's exclusive right to use the registered mark in commerce on or in connection with the goods or services specified in the [registration] certificate." Moreover, the Lanham Act provides registrants with the opportunity to recover treble damages for violations of their rights, and, after five years of continuous use, permits registrants to make their rights "incontestable" — i.e., to transform their registration into conclusive evidence of their rights — by filing an affidavit setting forth certain information.

However, section 8 of the Lanham Act provides that, to maintain these benefits, all registrants must file, between the fifth and sixth years after initial registration, an affidavit setting forth the continued use of the registered mark in commerce "on or in connection with" the goods or services listed in the registration statement for the mark, or providing an adequate explanation for nonuse of the mark. If a registrant fails to file the required affidavit, the Commissioner by law must cancel its registration at the end of the sixth year. Thus, Checkers was required to file its section 8 affidavit no later than October 23, 1990, to maintain the registration of its service mark.

On March 16, 1988, another service mark registrant, Checkers Restaurant Group, Inc., ("CRG"), petitioned the Trademark Trial and Appeal Board ("TTAB") to cancel Checkers's registration pursuant to 15 U.S.C. § 1064 (1988), which provides for the filing of such a cancellation petition "by any person who believes that he is or will be damaged by the registration of a mark on the principal register." In support of its petition, CRG argued, inter alia, that Checkers's registration interfered with CRG's federally guaranteed right to use its service mark "in other than its existing geographic area." Checkers answered this cancellation petition and counterclaimed, seeking to cancel CRG's own service mark on essentially the same grounds.

In August 1989, before these competing cancellation claims could be resolved, CRG filed a petition for relief under Chapter 11 of the federal Bankruptcy Code, in the United States Bankruptcy Court for the Eastern District of New York. In so doing, CRG triggered the application of the automatic stay provision, which provides that the filing of a bankruptcy petition "operates as a stay, applicable to all entities," of eight different categories of conduct encompassing a wide swath of legal actions, including litigation, lien enforcement, and administrative proceedings, that could affect or interfere with the property of the bankrupt's estate. Accordingly, on January 8, 1990, CRG petitioned the TTAB to stay all proceedings relating to the cross-cancellation petitions filed by itself and Checkers. The TTAB responded on February 16, 1990, with an order staying the cancellation proceeding "since petitioner's registration is the subject of a counterclaim."

Checkers and CRG then negotiated a settlement agreement by which CRG transferred all rights to its service mark to Checkers in exchange for $42,500, and Checkers granted CRG a license to use its service mark at CRG's two existing restaurants in New York City. On November 30, 1990, the Bankruptcy Court approved this settlement. Accordingly, on December 19, 1990, Checkers moved the TTAB to lift the stay it had imposed on the cancellation proceedings, dismiss those proceedings as moot, and accept a section 8 affidavit filed concurrently. In response, the TTAB dismissed the parties' cancellation petitions with prejudice, and forwarded Checkers's section 8 affidavit to the Post-Registration Section of the Patent and Trademark Office for consideration.

However, because Checkers filed the affidavit after October 23, 1990, that Office's Affidavit/Renewal Examiner rejected it as untimely and canceled Checkers's service mark registration. Checkers sought relief from the Commissioner, arguing that the automatic stay imposed by 11 U.S.C. § 362(a) prevented it from filing a section 8 affidavit during the pendency of the cancellation proceedings, and that, after the stay was lifted, its section 8 affidavit was timely filed pursuant to 11 U.S.C. § 108(c) (1988), which extends periods fixed by nonbankruptcy law "for commencing or continuing a civil action in a court other than a bankruptcy court on a claim against the debtor" until 30 days after a stay is terminated, if the period fixed by nonbankruptcy law already has run. The Commissioner rejected Checkers's argument, reasoning that

> this petitioner was not the party in bankruptcy and the filing of a Section 8 affidavit in relation to its [service mark registration] would not have been an exercise of control over a debtor in bankruptcy nor would it have furthered any claim against the debtor. The Section 8 filing would have spoken only to the petitioner's own continued use of its own registration.

Checkers sought judicial review of the Commissioner's decision by filing suit in the District Court. On January 7, 1994, the District Court granted summary judgment for the Commissioner, holding that the Bankruptcy Code did not stay Checkers's obligation to file a timely section 8 affidavit.

II. ANALYSIS

On appeal, Checkers claims the District Court erred in rejecting its argument that the automatic stay provision blocked the filing of a section 8 affidavit while Checkers was pursuing its cancellation petition against a debtor in bankruptcy. Specifically, Checkers claims that either of two subsections of the automatic stay provision operated to bar the required filing. The first stays "the commencement or continuation, including the issuance or employment of process, of a judicial, administrative, or other action or proceeding against the debtor that was or could have been commenced before the commencement of the" bankruptcy. The second stays "any act to obtain possession of property of the estate or of property from the estate or to exercise control over property of the estate." We review de novo the District Court's grant of summary judgment on this issue.

In the words of the Congress that enacted it, the automatic stay . . . "is one of the fundamental debtor protections provided by the bankruptcy laws." It gives the debtor a breathing spell from his creditors. It stops all collection efforts, all harassment, and all foreclosure actions. It permits the debtor to attempt a repayment or reorganization plan, or simply to be relieved of the financial pressures that drove him into bankruptcy.

The automatic stay also offers important protection for creditors. Without it, certain creditors would be able to pursue their own remedies against the debtor's property. Those who acted first would obtain payment of the claims in preference to and to the detriment of other creditors. Bankruptcy is designed to provide an orderly liquidation procedure under which all creditors are treated equally. A race of diligence by creditors for the debtor's assets prevents that.

To effectuate these congressional purposes, section 362(a) generally must be construed broadly. Its breadth is not unlimited, however. As the Ninth Circuit has stated, "while seemingly broad in scope, the automatic stay provisions should be construed no more expansively than is necessary to effectuate legislative purpose." Thus, we have held that, although the automatic stay blocks many legal actions against the debtor, it does not similarly bar claims brought by the debtor against other parties.

Checkers here asserts a construction of section 362(a) that would extend that provision "well beyond Congress's purpose." The policies underlying the automatic stay — those of sheltering the debtor from the demands of creditors and preserving the bankrupt's estate pending orderly distribution by a trustee — are not implicated by an act, such as Checkers's filing of a section 8 affidavit, that has no effect upon a claim against the debtor or the property of the estate, but rather maintains the status quo with respect to the property of an entity engaged in litigation with the debtor. We therefore reject Checkers's contention that the filing required by section 8 of the Lanham Act in this case would have constituted either the "continuation" of an "action or proceeding against the debtor" within the meaning of subsection 362(a)(1), or an act "to exercise control over property of the estate" within the meaning of subsection 362(a)(3).

A. Subsection 362(a)(1)

Checkers first claims that its filing of a section 8 affidavit was stayed by subsection 362(a)(1), which bars legal actions that continue a pre-petition claim against the debtor. Checkers rests its argument on that portion of its cancellation petition alleging that CRG's registration interfered with Checkers's right to use its service mark outside of its existing geographic area. Checkers contends that, because this claim alleged interference with a right guaranteed to Checkers by virtue of the federal registration of its service mark, its maintenance of federal registration was necessary to its ability to bring the claim. Thus, Checkers argues, any act to maintain its federal registration—such as the filing of a section 8 affidavit—constituted the "continuation" of its claim against the debtor within the meaning of subsection 362(a)(1). This is a specious claim.

Subsection 362(a)(1) stays the continuation of "a judicial, administrative, or other action or proceeding against the debtor." Checkers's interpretation of this provision would extend the automatic stay to encompass not only actions against the debtor, but also acts that maintain the status quo within which such actions exist. In this case, the action against the debtor was Checkers's cancellation claim against CRG. Checkers's filing of a section 8 affidavit constituted no part of that claim. Rather, the filing served merely to maintain the status quo with respect to Checkers's own pre-existing service mark registration. We discern nothing in the automatic stay provision nor in its underlying policy to suggest that Congress intended it to block actions that maintain the status quo between a debtor and its legal adversary. To the contrary, our review of the legislative history reveals precisely the opposite intent—for, as already mentioned, Congress included section 362(a) in the Bankruptcy Code to ensure the preservation of the status quo between a debtor and its creditors

The cases cited by Checkers are not to the contrary. Checkers relies on cases from the bankruptcy courts holding that the automatic stay barred filings required to revive a pre-petition judgment lien. While we express no view as to the merits of these decisions, we find each distinguishable from the present case for the simple reason that each involved a filing necessary to renew a legal action—be it a lien, an assignment of assets, or an attachment of property—operating directly against the debtor. Here, by contrast, Checkers's section 8 filing would have operated not to renew or sustain its cancellation petition against CRG—the action against the debtor—but, as we have said, merely to maintain the status of its own property.

We recognize that Checkers's filing of a section 8 affidavit could, in some attenuated sense, be deemed necessary to the maintenance of part of Checkers's cancellation petition against CRG. Without a valid federal registration, Checkers might not have had standing to pursue that portion of its cancellation petition claiming injury from CRG's alleged interference with rights guaranteed to Checkers by federal law. However, to acknowledge that the section 8 filing was tangentially related to Checkers's ability to litigate a portion of its claim against CRG is not to bring that filing within the scope of section 362(a). Any construction of section 362(a) that would reach the filing at issue here would extend the power of the bankruptcy courts into a whole host of activities far removed from the concerns addressed by the Bankruptcy Code. For example, under Checkers's construction of the provision, a homeowner involved in an action to quiet title against a debtor in bankruptcy could claim that section 362(a) stayed his payment of property taxes imposed by state law. Such payment certainly is in some sense necessary to the maintenance of good title in the property, and, therefore, could be described as the "continuation" of a claim against the debtor. However, not only does such a sweeping construction of section 362(a) have the potential to raise serious constitutional questions regarding the scope of the jurisdiction that may permissibly be exercised by non-Article III bankruptcy courts, but it is not even remotely necessary to the achievement of the provision's twin goals — namely, creating a "breathing spell" for the debtor and preventing a "race of diligence" by creditors. For these reasons, we reject it. . . .

B. Subsection 362(a)(3)

Checkers next argues that its filing of a section 8 affidavit was stayed by subsection 362(a)(3), which bars acts to exercise control over property of the bankrupt's estate. As Checkers sees it, by filing an affidavit necessary to maintain its own service mark registration, Checkers would have taken an act to exercise control over the right to use the "Checkers" service mark, in derogation of CRG's own claim to that right. Central to Checkers's theory is the notion that, by virtue of their cross-cancellation claims, Checkers and CRG each were vying for the single and exclusive federal right to use a service mark employing the word "Checkers" in interstate commerce. Thus, in Checkers's view, any act that served to maintain its own claim to that right was an act to "exercise control over" property of the bankrupt's estate within the meaning of subsection 362(a)(3).

Checkers misunderstands the nature of the right created by federal registration under the Lanham Act. We recognize that federal registration constitutes prima facie evidence of the registrant's "exclusive right to use the registered mark in commerce." However, we also note that each federal registration constitutes such evidence. In this case, therefore, the federal registrations of both Checkers and CRG constituted prima facie evidence that each enjoyed the exclusive right to utilize its respective service mark in commerce. While the cross-cancellation proceeding might ultimately have established that protection of the rights of one registrant required cancellation of the service mark of the other, each held an independent property right in its own service mark until that decision was made, if ever. Thus, contrary to Checkers's theory, its filing of a section 8 affidavit would have affected only its own property, not the property of CRG. Accordingly, the required filing was not stayed by subsection 362(a)(3).

C. Cancellation of a Registration Under Section 8 of the Lanham Act

Because we find that neither subsection 362(a)(1) nor subsection 362(a)(3) stayed Checkers's filing of a section 8 affidavit in this case, we hold that the Commissioner properly canceled Checkers's service mark. In so holding, we recognize that the circumstances of this case do not present the paradigmatic situation that prompted Congress to enact section 8 of the Lanham Act. Congress intended that section "to remove from the register automatically marks which are no longer in use. Failure of registrants to file affidavits results in removal of such deadwood." Nevertheless, in establishing cancellation as the penalty for failure to file the required affidavit, Congress made no exception for the innocent or the negligent. Thus, the Commissioner had no discretion to do other than cancel Checkers's service mark registration in this case.

Moreover, while the application of the section 8 filing requirement may appear harsh in this case, Checkers failed to avail itself of a simple means of avoiding this result. Checkers neglected to take the prudential step of seeking clarification from the bankruptcy court, or even from the Commissioner, as to whether its section 8 filing obligation was stayed. Checkers had ample time to make such an inquiry; CRG filed its petition for bankruptcy approximately two months before the first day of the year-long "window" during which Checkers was required to file its section 8 affidavit. By failing to inquire, Checkers assumed the risk that the required filing was not stayed. That gamble did not pay off, and accordingly, Checkers's service mark was canceled at the conclusion of the filing period.

In re: The Singer Company

United States Bankruptcy Court for the Southern District of New York

46 Collier Bankr. Cas. 2d. 962 (Bankr. S.D.N.Y. 2000)

Burton R. Lifland, Bankruptcy Judge.

The Singer Company B.V. (Singer B.V.) and Singer do Brasil Industria e Comercio Ltda ("Singer Brasil") (collectively "the Plaintiffs") commenced the instant adversary proceeding against Groz Beckert KG ("Groz") and Dyno Corporation ("Dyno") (collectively "the Defendants"), seeking a judgment . . . declaring that an action commenced by the Defendant Groz in the Southern District of Florida (the "Florida Action") prior to the effective date of the Debtor's plan of reorganization violates the automatic stay.

BACKGROUND

The Parties

On September 12 and 13, 1999, the Singer Company N.V. and certain of its affiliates (collectively the "Debtors"), filed voluntary petitions for relief under Chapter 11 of the Bankruptcy Code. On August 24, 2000, this Court entered an order confirming the Debtors' Joint Plan of Reorganization (the "Plan"). The Plan provided, among other things, that the automatic stay would remain in effect until the effective date of the Plan which occurred on September 14, 2000 (the "Effective Date"). Singer B.V. and Singer Brasil are Reorganized Debtors under the Plan.

Defendant Groz is a German corporation and is the plaintiff in the Florida action. Defendant Dyno is a Delaware corporation and is the defendant in the Florida Action. Dyno is the exclusive distributor in the United States of sewing machine needles manufactured by Singer Brasil.

Singer Spezialnadelfabric GmbH ("Singer Germany"), a former affiliated company, is a German corporation that was engaged in the business of manufacturing needles. Singer Germany is also subject to an insolvency proceeding in Germany (the "German Case") which is still pending.

The Dispute

The dispute between the parties centers around a U.S. patent for a sewing machine needle that was issued by Singer U.S. in 1985. In the Florida Action, Groz seeks to enjoin Dyno, Singer's distributor in the United States, from selling needles produced by Singer Brasil pursuant to the U.S. patent.

The Patent

In 1983, Singer Germany sold to Singer Brasil the specially designed equipment for manufacturing the then patent-pending needle (the "Equipment"). United States Patent and Trademark Office issued the '330 patent to Singer U.S. in May 1985. The '330 patent covers a certain needle for use in a sewing machine having a one-way needle clamp. Seven months after the patent application was granted, Singer U.S. assigned the '330 Patent to Singer Germany. Both prior to and after the assignment, Singer Germany provided Singer Brasil support for the installation, utilization and repair of the Equipment. Since 1983, Singer Brasil has openly manufactured the needles using the technology claimed in the '330 Patent. The Plaintiffs assert that, in light of the foregoing facts, Singer Brasil has an implied license to the '330 Patent which constitutes its estate property under section 541(a) of the Bankruptcy Code. There is substantial currency to the implied license argument from the facts presented.

Furthermore, since 1994, Dyno has exclusively distributed Singer Brasil's needles in the United States. Sales of the allegedly infringing needles represent almost 8.5% of Singer Brasil's aggregate sales.

The Florida Action

In November 1999, Groz purchased certain assets of Singer Germany in the course of the German case. Among those assets was the '330 Patent. On August 10, 2000, nearly nine months after purchasing the '330 Patent and two weeks before the scheduled hearing on confirmation of Singer's Plan, Groz commenced the Florida Action, alleging that Dyno's sale of needles manufactured abroad by Singer Brasil infringes the '330 Patent and seeking injunctive relief and damages to remedy the alleged infringement and stop the distribution of the needles. On September 11, 2000, Singer B.V. and Singer Brasil commenced the instant adversary proceeding against Groz and Dyno and filed a motion seeking to enjoin the Florida Action. On October 13, 2000, Groz filed a motion to dismiss the instant adversary proceeding.

DISCUSSION

As a threshold matter, Groz challenges the subject matter jurisdiction of this Court to enjoin its Florida Action against Dyno. However, one of the issues before this Court is an allegation that Groz violated the automatic stay when it commenced the Florida Action. Allegations concerning stay violations are claims arising under the Bankruptcy Code and give rise to core proceedings. Under this broad grant of subject matter jurisdiction, there can be no question that this Court now has jurisdiction to issue an injunction to stay Groz's action against Dyno. As discussed in more detail below, the Florida Action is inextricably related to the Singer bankruptcy proceedings and thus falls within the subject matter jurisdiction of this Court.

Groz violated Section 362(a)(1) of the Bankruptcy Code

Section 362(a)(1) of the Bankruptcy Code provides, in pertinent part that, when a bankruptcy petition is filed, "the commencement or continuation . . . of a judicial, administrative, or other action or proceeding against the debtor that was or could have been commenced before the commencement of the case under this title, or to recover a claim against the debtor that arose before the commencement of the case under this title" is stayed. 11 U.S.C. § 362(a)(1). Although the plain language of section 362 limits the extension of the automatic stay to a proceeding against the debtor, under specific circumstances non-debtors may be protected by the automatic stay. Several courts, for example, have held that actions are subject to the automatic stay even when the debtor is not a defendant, in situations where the debtor is the real party in interest and the action is merely a design to circumvent the automatic stay. The Plaintiffs contend that Groz's Florida Action, by not technically naming Singer Brasil a defendant, is not only an end run attempt to exercise control over Singer Brasil's implied license but is a violation of the automatic stay since Singer Brasil is the real party in interest. Groz argues that the Florida Action is merely a commercial lawsuit between two non-debtors seeking to prevent "allegedly unlawful conduct", specifically Dyno's sale of allegedly infringing needles manufactured by Singer Brasil. Groz also argues that even if Singer Brasil was the real party in interest and that the Florida Action was commenced while the automatic stay was still in effect, it is now moot because the Effective Date has now occurred and section 362 has ceased to have any application in this case.

With respect to the Effective Date argument, Groz seems to believe that, even if it did violate the automatic stay by commencing the Florida Action a few weeks before the Effective Date, it was only a "brief violation." Just like one cannot be slightly "enceinte", the same applies to a violation of the automatic stay. A violation of the automatic stay is just that, a violation of the automatic stay—there is no such thing as a slight violation. The occurrence of the Effective Date after such a violation has taken place does not somehow moot the violation.

Groz's assertion that the Florida Action is nothing more than a commercial dispute between two non-debtors is also without merit. It is painstakingly clear that Dyno's interests with respect to the Florida Action are so inextricably intertwined with the Debtors, that actions against them could be seen essentially as actions against the estate. The core of the Florida Action involves the '330 Patent. Dyno is merely Singer's distributor. Singer Brasil is the purported owner of the implied license to exploit the '330 Patent. It follows that Singer Brasil is the real party defendant for patent infringement. In effect, the Florida Action is nothing more than an effort to circumvent section 362 by suing Dyno when the real party in interest is Singer Brasil. Accordingly the commencement of Groz's action in the Southern District of Florida clearly violated the essence of section 362 of the Bankruptcy Code.

Groz violated section 362(a)(3) of the Bankruptcy Code

Section 362(a) of the Bankruptcy Code stays "any act to obtain possession of the property of the estate or of property from the estate or to exercise control over property of the estate." 11 U.S.C. § 362(a)(3). Courts have construed property of the estate so as to include all legal or equitable interests of the debtor in property, both tangible and intangible, including exempt property, as of the date the case is commenced. Singer Brasil asserts that it has an interest in the '330 Patent in the form of an implied license and that the Florida Action attempts to strip any value of Singer Brasil's license to the '330 Patent by, among other things, effectively preventing the distribution of Singer Brasil's needles in the United States. Whereas the applicable non-bankruptcy law determines the extent of an interest in property, absent an overriding federal policy, bankruptcy law determines whether that interest is "property of the estate."

In patent law, an implied license merely signifies a patentee's waiver of the statutory right to exclude others from making, using, or selling the patented invention. The burden of proving that an implied license exists is on the party asserting an implied license as a defense to infringement. The Supreme Court has held that:

> No formal granting of a license is necessary in order to give it effect. Any language used by the owner of the patent, or any conduct on his part exhibited to another from which that other may properly infer that the owner consents to his use of the patent in making or using it, or selling it, upon which the other acts, constitutes a license and a defense to an action for a tort.

The Federal Circuit has noted that the sale of unpatented equipment which is used to conduct a patented process may itself constitute the grant of an implied license to conduct such process. When a party argues that the sale of a device carries with it an implied license to use that device in practicing a patented invention, that party has the burden to show that, inter alia, the purchased device has no noninfringing uses and that the circumstances of the sale plainly indicated that the grant of a license should be inferred.

In order to imply that a license was given to Singer Brasil, Singer Brasil must demonstrate that the '330 Patent for which the implied license was sought was explicitly necessary to make use of an explicitly granted right. Singer argues that Singer Germany's sale of the specialized equipment, which had no other use than for the manufacturing of the needles utilizing the '330 Patent, resulted in an implied license for the '330 Patent. This argument is persuasive. Not only did Singer Germany sell Singer Brasil the specialized Equipment, but they both installed and, when necessary, repaired the Equipment for Singer Brasil. Furthermore, Singer Brasil has been openly manufacturing these needles for seventeen years. Based upon the facts at hand, it appears that the Plaintiffs have a substantial likelihood of success in proving that Singer Germany granted Singer Brasil an implied license for the '330 Patent. Consequently, Singer Brasil has an interest in the '330 Patent which constitutes property of the estate.

Furthermore, a purchaser of a patent takes it encumbered by prior licenses, including implied licenses. Groz allegedly purchased the '330 Patent in November 1999. It is the duty of the purchaser to inform himself of the nature of the licensee's ownership and the extent of his right. Since Singer Brasil has been openly manufacturing these needles for the past seventeen years and has been the sole manufacturer of these needles, it is highly unlikely that Groz did not know, or was unable to learn about the implied license given to Singer Brasil. Consequently, if it is found at a later date that Singer Brasil does indeed have an implied license, then Groz will be encumbered by it.

In light of the foregoing facts, I find that the Florida Action is a clear attempt to exercise control over property of Singer's Bankruptcy estate, specifically the interest Singer Brasil has in the '330 Patent, and that the commencement of that action prior to the Effective Date was a violation of the automatic stay.

Notes & Questions

1. Under section 362(a) of the Bankruptcy Code, the commencement of a bankruptcy case invokes the automatic stay, which stops virtually all collection efforts on account of pre-petition obligations of the debtor, including any foreclosure proceedings. The purpose of the automatic stay is to ensure that all disputes over the debtor's assets are adjudicated within the bankruptcy proceedings and to prevent a free-for-all as creditors attempt to assert their rights through individual lawsuits against the debtor. The stay gives the debtor a "breathing spell" as he attempts to reorganize his assets and satisfy all the creditors. Exceptions are available from the stay under section 362(b). Creditors can ask the court to lift the stay in two narrow situations: (i) when the creditor's interest in the property of the estate is not adequately protected by the bankruptcy proceeding or (ii) when the debtor has no equity in property that is not necessary for successful reorganization.

2. In light of the policies underlying the automatic stay, the decision in *Checkers* should not be surprising. The filing of the Section 8 affidavit by Checkers is not a claim against the debtor's estate that would affect the plan of reorganization. Put another way, the filing with the USPTO is not an end run around the bankruptcy court to liquidate assets of the bankruptcy estate. Checkers' failure to file the section 8 affidavit is an example of bad planning and confusion over the scope of the

stay. While it is true that the cancellation proceedings were stayed by the filing of the bankruptcy proceedings, Checkers was not stayed from filing the requisite affidavit in order to maintain its own service mark. Do you see why the cancellation proceeding was stayed by the filing of the bankruptcy proceeding? The outcome of the proceedings would have affected the debtor's estate and could have resulted in a creditor (namely Checkers) obtaining a benefit from the estate outside the formal bankruptcy proceedings.

3. Does the reasoning discussed in note 2 apply to the facts of *Singer*? The litigation was between Groz and a licensee of Singer, not Singer itself. Why should this litigation that does not include Singer be resolved in light of Singer's bankruptcy petition? The court describes Groz's lawsuit against Dyno as an end run to affect control over Singer's interest in the '330 patent. Make sure you understand the analysis. Is this an equitable argument or a legal argument based on the text of the Bankruptcy Code? Suppose the case involved a trademark and not a patent and that Dyno was a franchisee of Singer, the trademark owner. Would a lawsuit against the franchisee be stayed if the franchisor filed a bankruptcy petition?

4. Courts have held that the automatic stay provisions do not apply to a preliminary injunction against the debtor in a patent infringement suit. *See Seiko Epson Corp. v. Nu-Kote Int'l, Inc.*, 190 F. 3d 1360, 1364–65 (Fed. Cir. 1999) ("the statutory stay of proceedings . . . did not free [debtor] of the contempt orders and the injunctions upon which the contempt was based"). For a similar result in the context of trademark, see *In re Cinnabar 2000 Haircutters, Inc.*, 20 B.R. 575, 577 (Bankr. S.D.N.Y. 1982) (automatic stay not "a haven for contumacious conduct in violation of a party's judicially determined tradename rights").

3. The Intellectual Property License in Bankruptcy

a. *Statutory Background*

Bankruptcy Code

Section 365. Executory contracts and unexpired leases

> (a) . . . . the trustee, subject to the court's approval, may assume or reject any executory contract or unexpired lease of the debtor.
>
> . . . .
>
> (n)(1) If the trustee rejects an executory contract under which the debtor is a licensor of a right to intellectual property, the licensee under such contract may elect—
>
> > (A) to treat such contract as terminated by such rejection if such rejection by the trustee amounts to such a breach as would entitle the licensee to treat such contract as terminated by virtue of its own terms, applicable nonbankruptcy law, or an agreement made by the licensee with another entity; or

(B) to retain its rights (including a right to enforce any exclusivity provision of such contract, but excluding any other right under applicable nonbankruptcy law to specific performance of such contract) under such contract and under any agreement supplementary to such contract, to such intellectual property (including any embodiment of such intellectual property to the extent protected by applicable nonbankruptcy law), as such rights existed immediately before the case commenced, for—

    (i) the duration of such contract; and

    (ii) any period for which such contract may be extended by the licensee as of right under applicable nonbankruptcy law.

(2) If the licensee elects to retain its rights, as described in paragraph (1)(B) of this subsection, under such contract—

(A) the trustee shall allow the licensee to exercise such rights;

(B) the licensee shall make all royalty payments due under such contract for the duration of such contract and for any period described in paragraph (1)(B) of this subsection for which the licensee extends such contract; and

(C) the licensee shall be deemed to waive—

    (i) any right of setoff it may have with respect to such contract under this title or applicable nonbankruptcy law; and

    (ii) any claim allowable under section 503(b) of this title arising from the performance of such contract.

(3) If the licensee elects to retain its rights, as described in paragraph (1)(B) of this subsection, then on the written request of the licensee the trustee shall—

(A) to the extent provided in such contract, or any agreement supplementary to such contract, provide to the licensee any intellectual property (including such embodiment) held by the trustee; and

(B) not interfere with the rights of the licensee as provided in such contract, or any agreement supplementary to such contract, to such intellectual property (including such embodiment) including any right to obtain such intellectual property (or such embodiment) from another entity.

(4) Unless and until the trustee rejects such contract, on the written request of the licensee the trustee shall—

(A) to the extent provided in such contract or any agreement supplementary to such contract—

    (i) perform such contract; or

(ii) provide to the licensee such intellectual property (including any embodiment of such intellectual property to the extent protected by applicable nonbankruptcy law) held by the trustee; and

(B) not interfere with the rights of the licensee as provided in such contract, or any agreement supplementary to such contract, to such intellectual property (including such embodiment), including any right to obtain such intellectual property (or such embodiment) from another entity.

Section 101. Definitions

In this title —

. . . .

(35A) "intellectual property" means —

(A) trade secret;

(B) invention, process, design, or plant protected under title 35;

(C) patent application;

(D) plant variety;

(E) work of authorship protected under title 17; or

(F) mask work protected under chapter 9 of title 17;

to the extent protected by applicable nonbankruptcy law.

Notes & Questions

1. Section 365(a) applies to all executory contracts and unexpired leases in bankruptcy. Under 365(a), the trustee has the power, with the approval of the court, to assume or reject an executory contract or unexpired lease of the debtor. If the contract or lease is assumed, then it becomes part of the estate and both parties to the contract or lease are still subject to its terms. The trustee upon assumption must make adequate assurances to the other side of continuing performance and cure any defaults under the contract. If the trustee rejects, however, the rejection constitutes a breach of the contract or lease and the other party has a claim against the estate for contract breach. Except for non-residential real estate leases, the contract or lease must be assumed or rejected within 60 days after the order for relief in a Chapter 7 proceeding and anytime prior to the confirmation of a reorganization plan in a Chapter 11 proceeding. In addition, the non-debtor can file a motion with the court to compel the trustee to assume or reject in either type of proceeding.

2. What is an executory contract? Most courts have adopted the definition developed by Professor Vern Countryman in his article *Executory Contracts in Bankruptcy*, published at 57 MINN. L. REV. 439 (1973). According to Professor Countryman, an executory contract is "a contract in which the obligation of both the bankrupt and the other party to the contract are so far unperformed that the failure of either to complete performance would constitute a material breach excusing the performance

of the other." 57 MINN. L. REV. at 460. Some courts have adopted a definition that requires only one party to have unperformed obligations. *See, e.g., In re Tonry*, 724 F. 2d 467 (5th Cir. 1984). Yet other courts adopt a balancing of the equities approach that treats a contract as executory to the extent that such treatment is consistent with the policies of bankruptcy law. *See, e.g., In re Fox*, 83 B.R. 290 (Bankr. E.D. Pa. 1988).

3. Why does it matter if a contract is executory? The practical importance has to do with the trustee's ability to assume or reject the contract. As we will see in the discussion below, such a power can be very important in defining the scope of the bankruptcy estate and the ability of the debtor to operate the estate in bankruptcy.

4. Executory contracts involving intellectual property. In general, intellectual property licenses are deemed to be executory contracts as long as both licensor and licensee have ongoing obligations under the license. One court, however, denied executory contract treatment when a licensor of intellectual property had no obligations and only had the role of receiving royalty payments. *See In re Learning Publications, Inc.*, 94 B.R. 763 (Bankr. M.D. Fla. 1988). *See also Microsoft Corp. v. DAK Industries, Inc.*, 66 F.3d 1091 (9th Cir. 1995) (construing a software license as a sale since licensor Microsoft had no continuing obligations except the receipt of royalties); *In re Gencor*, 298 B.R. 902 (Bankr. M.D. Fla. 2003) (patent settlement agreement not executory). All courts recognize that the characterization of a contract as executory rests on the extent and type of remaining obligations and not on whether the licensor or the licensee is the debtor. Special issues arise, however, depending upon whether the debtor is the licensor or the licensee.

5. For an example of the treatment of a trademark license as an executory contract, see *In re Exide Technologies*, 607 F.3d 957 (3rd Cir. 2010). On appeal, the Third Circuit held that the trademark license was not executory because the trademark licensee, Enersys, had fulfilled its obligations under the license. A decade before filing for bankruptcy, Exide had licensed its trademark rights to Enersys for exclusive marketing of industrial batteries in North America. When Exide had sought to re-enter the North American market for industrial batteries, it sought to renegotiate the license with Enersys, who refused. Consequently, Exide was competing with Enersys' use of the trademark. When Exide entered bankruptcy, it sought to reject the license as an executory contract. The Third Circuit, overruling the bankruptcy court, found that the license was not executory since Enersys had fulfilled its performance obligations of payment through the lump sum paid at the initiation of the license. The Third Circuit rejected Exide's arguments that the license was executory because Enersys had substantial obligations to maintain quality assurance and use restrictions. The appellate court concluded that these obligations were not substantial ongoing obligations on the part of Enersys.

6. If the debtor is the licensor, section 365(n) places limitations on the trustee's ability to reject the license. Upon rejection by the trustee, the non-debtor licensee can elect to treat the rejection as a termination of the agreement or to retain its rights under the license. If the non-debtor licensee retains his rights under the license, the licensee has the right to use the intellectual property as it existed at the time of the

filing of the bankruptcy petition and must continue to make royalty payments. The trustee must provide the intellectual property to the licensee and must not interfere with the licensee's rights under the license.

7. Section 365(n) was enacted in 1988 and is known as the Intellectual Property Bankruptcy Protection Act. Congress enacted the provision in response to the court's decision in *Lubrizol Enters., Inc. v. Richmond Metal Finishers, Inc.*, 756 F.2d 1043 (4th Cir. 1985) (excerpted below). The *Lubrizol* decision was viewed as an inequitable to non-debtor licensees who, absent the protections of section 365(n), would be denied access to intellectual property when the licensor entered bankruptcy.

8. Notice that the definition of "intellectual property" in the Bankruptcy Code does not include "trademarks." The implication is that the protections of section 365(n) do not apply to trademark licensees. Congress deemed that trademarks should be excluded because the quality-control issues raised by trademark licensing could not be readily resolved by section 365(n). For a critical discussion of the exclusion of trademarks, see Xuan-Thao N. Nguyen, *Bankrupting Trademarks*, 37 U.C. Davis L. Rev. 1267 (2004) (arguing that the exclusion hurts business good will that trademark law is designed to protect). The one court to address the treatment of trademarks under section 365(n) extended the provisions to trademark licensees under equitable grounds. *See In re Matusalem*, 158 B.R. 514 (Bankr. S.D. Fla. 1993). In *Sunbeam Products, Inc. v. Chicago American Mg, LLC.*, 133 S. Ct. 790 (2012), the Seventh Circuit rejected the equitable application of section 365(n) to protect the rights of a trademark licensee. However, the appellate court affirmed the bankruptcy court's ruling in favor of the licensee under section 365(g), which classifies the rejection of an executory contract as a breach. The Seventh Circuit recognized the trademark licensee's rights to remedies for such a contract breach. Judge Easterbrook, who authored the unanimous opinion for the appellate court, pointed out that the *Lubrizol* decision (and hence the exclusion of trademarks from 365(n)) confused the rejection power with the power to avoid a contract. In addition, recording contracts between labels and artists are executory contracts but are, like trademarks, not covered by 365(n). See *Cloyd v. GRP Records*, 238 B.R. 328 (Bankr. E.D. Mich. 1999). Finally, note that Section 365(n) applies to intellectual property "in existence at the time of bankruptcy filing." See *In re Szombathy*, 1996 WL 417121 (Bankr. N.D. Ill. 1996), rev'd in part on other grounds, *Szombathy v. Controlled Shredders, Inc.*, 1997 WL 189314 (N.D. Ill. 1997).

9. If the debtor is the licensee, then section 365(n) does not apply. The debtor licensee has the right under 365(a) to either assume or reject the license. If the debtor licensee rejects, then the debtor loses all rights to use the intellectual property and the non-debtor licensor can sue for any contractual breach claims. The difficult question is the ability of the debtor licensee to assign the licensee upon assumption. Section 365(f)(1) permits such assignments subject to the limitations of section 365(c)(1). We will discuss the special problem of assignments by debtor licensees below. What is important to understand before reading the cases is the different treatment of exclusive versus non-exclusive licenses for the purposes of assignment.

In general, an assignment of a license by a debtor licensee is barred if the assignment is prohibited by applicable non-bankruptcy law and if the licensor does not consent to the assignment. If a license is non-exclusive, then the licensee in general does not have the ability to assign the license since a non-exclusive intellectual property license is viewed as personal to the licensee. If the license is exclusive, however, then the license might be assignable depending upon whether copyrights, patents, or trademarks are at issue. Under copyright law, for example, an exclusive license is viewed as a transfer of a property right and therefore the debtor licensee of a copyright can assign the copyright to someone else. Patent law and trademark law, however, do not treat exclusive licenses as transfers of property rights, and as a result the assignability of exclusive patent and trademark licenses is an open question. We will discuss these issues in greater detail below.

10. What happens if there is a conflict between United States bankruptcy law and the law of another jurisdiction? The district court for the Eastern District of Virginia confronted this issue in *In re Qimonda AG*, 433 B.R. 547 (E.D. Va. 2010), a proceeding involving a German company filing for bankruptcy in the United States after filing in Germany. The bankruptcy court in this case found that section 365(n) was in conflict with German bankruptcy law. It further found that principles of comity (or deference to the preexisting foreign bankruptcy proceeding) required the bankruptcy court to withhold enforcement of section 365(n). The district court rejected this application of the principle of comity and remanded the case to the bankruptcy court for more careful balancing of the interests and policies underlying section 365(n).

b. Licensor as Debtor

In re: Cellnet Data Systems, Inc.

United States Court of Appeals for the Third Circuit

327 F.3d 242 (3rd Cir. 2003)

Nygaard, Circuit Judge.

This appeal presents us with an issue of first impression involving elections under 11 U.S.C. § 365(n). CellNet Data Systems, Inc. sold its intellectual property to Schlumberger Resource Management Services, Inc., which specifically excluded the assets and liabilities of certain licensing agreements under the terms of the sale. After CellNet rejected those licensing agreements under 11 U.S.C. § 365(a) of the bankruptcy code, the licensee exercised its rights under § 365(n) to continue to use the intellectual property, subject to the royalty payments due under the original license. Both CellNet, as party to the contract, and Schlumberger, as holder of the intellectual property, claim the right to receive the royalty payments. The District Court determined that Schlumberger had expressly severed the royalties from the intellectual property by the terms of the purchase agreement and that the royalties remained in CellNet's estate. Although CellNet then rejected the license, the licensee, by operation of § 365(n), elected to enforce the license and thus the District Court concluded that the royalties due under the revived contract belonged to CellNet. We will affirm.

The essential facts are not in dispute, rather how those facts operate is at issue. In 1997, CellNet, a developer of a wireless data network for meter reading, now in bankruptcy, entered into a joint venture with Bechtel Enterprises, Inc., forming a company called BCN Data Systems LLC. As part of the joint venture, CellNet entered into several licensing agreements with BCN, that provided BCN with an exclusive license to use CellNet's intellectual property outside the United States. In return, CellNet received a royalty payment equal to three percent of BCN's gross revenues. The License Agreements also contained a covenant that CellNet would provide technological support to BCN during the lifetime of the Agreements.

Three years later, with CellNet on the verge of bankruptcy, Appellant, Schlumberger, proposed the sale of CellNet's assets. Schlumberger and CellNet entered into a Proposal Letter under which Schlumberger would purchase "all or substantially all of the assets and business operations of [CellNet] and its subsidiaries." The January 31, 2000 Proposal Letter also provided that Schlumberger "would acquire all assets of [CellNet] free and clear of all liens other than certain liens to be agreed (the 'Assets'), other than the Excluded Assets (as defined below), used in, held for use in, or related to the business and operations of [CellNet]." Thus, the proposal contemplated that certain assets of CellNet would not be subject to the ultimate purchase agreement. However, the term "Excluded Assets" was left open for future agreement by the parties.

CellNet filed for bankruptcy on February 4, 2000. On March 1, 2000, Schlumberger and CellNet entered into an Asset Purchase Agreement that mirrored the intent of the Proposal Letter, in that Schlumberger would purchase all of CellNet's assets, subject only to certain excluded assets. This time, however, the agreement included language that explained:

> At any time prior to March 25, 2000, [Schlumberger] shall be entitled unilaterally to amend this Agreement, including without limitation Schedules 1.01(a)(i) (Stock Acquired), 1.01(b) (Excluded Contracts) and 1.01(e) (Excluded Assets) attached hereto, solely for the purpose of excluding any or all of the stock, assets, liabilities and agreements of [CellNet] pertaining to [CellNet's] joint venture with Bechtel Enterprises, Inc., or its affiliates, (collectively, the "BCN Assets and Liabilities") from the stock, assets, liabilities and agreements being acquired or assumed by [Schlumberger] hereunder.

Thus, the Purchase Agreement provided that Schlumberger would purchase all of CellNet's intellectual property, etc., but would be able to specifically exclude all stocks, assets, liabilities, and agreements pertaining to CellNet's venture with BCN. Pursuant to a letter by counsel on March 24, 2000, Schlumberger elected to exercise its right to exclude the BCN assets and liabilities. The letter went on to specifically designate the License Agreements between CellNet and BCN as assets and liabilities excluded from the purchase under the heading "Excluded Contracts."

Despite excluding the License Agreements, Schlumberger asserted a right to the royalties under the Agreements prior to the approval of the Asset Purchase

Agreement by the bankruptcy court. This was based on the belief that CellNet would have to reject the Agreements under §365(a) as executory contracts that it could not fulfill and that Schlumberger would then be entitled to the royalties as owner of the underlying intellectual property. CellNet believed otherwise, but in an effort to complete the sale of its assets, agreed to reject the License Agreements and preserve the right of the parties to contest ownership of the royalties. The parties memorialized the decision to reject the License Agreements under §365(a) in an additional section of the Asset Purchase Agreement. The new section read:

> Schlumberger] has elected not to assume the License and Consulting Services Agreement between [CellNet] and BCN Data Systems, L.L.C. ("BCN"), dated January 1, 1997, the [OCDB License Agreement] between [CellNet] and BCN dated January 1, 1997 . . . (collectively, the "BCN License Agreements"). [CellNet] shall obtain an order from the Bankruptcy Court pursuant to Section 365(a) of the Bankruptcy Code rejecting the BCN License Agreements. The parties hereto acknowledge that if BCN elects to retain its rights under the BCN License Agreements in accordance with Section 365(n) (1)(B) of the Bankruptcy Code, then the rights and obligations of the parties with respect to the License Agreements, including without limitation any royalty rights thereunder, are disputed by the parties. Each party reserves all rights under this Agreement with respect to the BCN License Agreements, and neither this Amendment nor any action taken in connection herewith, including the filing of any modified Sale Order, shall be deemed to be a waiver or admission of any matter related to the dispute between [CellNet] and [Schlumberger] regarding the BCN License Agreements.

Under this agreement, CellNet agreed to reject the License Agreements pursuant to §365(a), but both parties acknowledged that a dispute over royalties would remain if BCN elected to retain its rights under §365(n). On May 4, 2001, the Bankruptcy Court approved the Asset Purchase Agreement with both the addition, as well as additional language that further expressed that the sale did not alter the rights of CellNet, Schlumberger, or BCN regarding the License Agreements and the royalties due thereunder.

Following approval of the sale, CellNet moved to reject the License Agreements under §365(a). Section 365(a) provides that "the trustee, subject to the court's approval, may assume or reject any executory contract or unexpired lease of the debtor." 11 U.S.C. §365(a). CellNet was permitted to act as the trustee because it was a debtor-in-possession pursuant to 11 U.S.C. §1107(a). The Bankruptcy Court approved the motion and CellNet informed BCN of its election. BCN, in turn, chose to retain its rights under §365(n). Section 365(n) provides that "[i]f a trustee rejects an executory contract under which the debtor is a licensor of a right to intellectual property, the licensee under such contract may elect" to either terminate the contract or retain certain rights under the license. Specifically, the licensee may elect:

> to retain its rights (including a right to enforce any exclusivity provision of such contract, but excluding any other right under applicable non-bankruptcy

law to specific performance of such contract) under such contract and under any agreement supplementary to such contract, to such intellectual property . . . as such rights existed immediately before the case commenced. . . .

If a licensee elects to retain its rights, section 365(n)(2)(B) of the Code requires it to "make all royalty payments due under such contract for the duration of such contract. . . ." By its election, and operation of § 365(n), BCN was permitted to continue to use the intellectual property originally licensed from CellNet, but was required to pay the royalties due under that license.

Rather than remain in a joint venture, CellNet and Bechtel agreed that Bechtel would acquire all of the assets and liabilities of BCN and make one lump sum payment to CellNet that would encompass the future royalty payments due under the License Agreements. The Bankruptcy Court approved the sale to Bechtel, and the negotiated amount of $2,250,000 for the future royalties was placed in escrow pending resolution of who was entitled to the royalties.

Both the Bankruptcy Court and the District Court found that CellNet was entitled to the royalties. In its opinion, the District Court addressed the same arguments now raised before us. Schlumberger argued that the Asset Purchase Agreement and its later rejection of the License Agreement did not operate to separate the right to the royalties from the underlying ownership of the intellectual property. Alternatively, Schlumberger asked the District Court to look past the original exclusion and find that because it owns the intellectual property and CellNet subsequently rejected the license under § 365(a), it has superior rights to the royalties.

In affirming the decision of the Bankruptcy Court in favor of CellNet, the District Court thoroughly analyzed the Asset Purchase Agreement and subsequent exclusion of License Agreements. After finding that the Purchase Agreement was not ambiguous, the District Court looked at the "express reservation" requirement necessary for the separation of royalties from intellectual property and decided that the Purchase Agreement could only be interpreted to separate the royalties due under the license from the intellectual property. The District Court also addressed Schlumberger's contention that it had superior rights under § 365 because it owned the intellectual property and CellNet had rejected the license pursuant to § 365(a). The District Court agreed with CellNet that the election of BCN pursuant to § 365(n) renewed certain obligations related to the license. The District Court found that under the License Agreements, the royalty payments were due to CellNet and that because Schlumberger had excluded those License Agreements from its purchase, CellNet "remains entitled to receive the BCN royalties pursuant to statutory authority even if it rejected the License Agreements and is not technically a party to them."

III. Discussion

A. The Effects of the Asset Purchase Agreement:

Schlumberger's first argument is that the Purchase Agreement and letter of March 2000 did not operate to sever the royalties from ownership of the intellectual property. Both the Bankruptcy Court and District Court disagreed and found that

Schlumberger had separated ownership from its rights by the plain language of the Purchase Agreement and March Letter Amendment. These findings are clearly correct.

On appeal, Schlumberger points to two cases from the bankruptcy court that would require an express reservation to separate the components. In *Chemical Foundation, Inc. v. E.I. du Pont De Nemours & Co.*, 29 F.2d 597 (D. Del. 1928) the court discussed the effects of assigning a patent on the right to receive royalties for that patent:

> Yet, as an assignment of a patent, without more, does not transfer to the assignee the right to recover damages or profits for prior infringements, although royalties to accrue and damages and profits for future infringements are incident to and accompany the patent unless separated by express reservation, and as a patentee may after assigning the patents sue and recover for past infringements, it would seem obvious that an assignor of a patent would have like rights with respect to royalties accrued at the time of the assignment. But the right to recover accrued royalties or damages and profits for past infringements may likewise be assigned.

Chemical espouses the proposition that royalties were inherent in ownership of a patent and flowed accordingly, although they could be divorced by an express reservation. This idea was expanded in *Crom v. Cement Gun Co.*, 46 F. Supp. 403 (D. Del. 1942), where the court discussed the ownership of a patent. After quoting much of the above language in *Chemical*, the court found that:

> Where an assignment conveys all the assignor's right, title and interest, if the right to receive royalties is to be severed from the beneficial ownership of the patent and remain in the assignor, there must be an express reservation or some agreement to that effect. I do not think that the mere retention of the 'license' . . . is sufficient to make the severance, particularly where, as in the present case, it is merely for the purpose of protecting a supposed but nonexistent shop right and is in contravention of the understanding of the parties.

Unlike the cases Schlumberger cites, the unambiguous Purchase Agreement and March Letter Amendment present here did expressly sever the royalties. This conclusion has support in a straightforward reading of the documents. The Purchase Agreement permitted Schlumberger "unilaterally to amend this Agreement . . . solely for the purpose of excluding any or all of the stock, assets, liabilities and agreements of [CellNet] pertaining to [CellNet's] joint venture with Bechtel Enterprises, Inc." Beyond this language, the Purchase Agreement also explained that "[n]otwithstanding anything herein to the contrary, the Purchaser shall not purchase or acquire, and shall have no rights or liabilities with respect to, any Excluded Asset." The Purchase Agreement further defined "Excluded Assets" to include "all rights of the Sellers under any Excluded Asset" and "all proceeds from any Excluded Asset."

These sections must be read in concert with the March 24, 2000 Letter, which sought to specify those items excluded from the Purchase Agreement. In that letter,

Schlumberger "elect[ed] to amend the Asset Purchase Agreement to exclude the BCN Assets and Liabilities from the stock, assets, liabilities and agreements of the Sellers being acquired or assumed under the Asset Purchase Agreement." The letter went on to specifically enumerate the various License Agreements between CellNet and BCN as excluded assets. Thus, Schlumberger expressly sought to exclude all rights and liabilities under the License Agreements, including its rights to all proceeds under those Agreements.

Schlumberger now attempts to argue that the Purchase Agreement and March Letter (both of which it drafted) are ambiguous and that extrinsic evidence is necessary to decide whether the Purchase Agreement contemplated severance of the royalties. This argument is unpersuasive. As the District Court correctly noted:

> The Asset Purchase Agreement and March 24 letter contain no ambiguities and, by those documents, Schlumberger excluded the License Agreements from the assets it was acquiring. While Schlumberger has argued that, under this pattern of events, it is entitled to receive the royalties from BCN, either as a matter of contract law or under the Bankruptcy Code, both parties agree the Asset Purchase Agreement and March 24 letter accurately represent the parties' intentions. Thus, it is only the legal effect of the transaction that Schlumberger challenges.

Under New York law, "ambiguity does not exist 'simply because the parties urge different interpretations.'" When Schlumberger elected to exclude "all the proceeds from [the BCN License Agreements]" it expressly excluded the royalties from these agreements from the intellectual property it was purchasing. The effect of this exclusion is that the License Agreements remain in CellNet's estate.

Schlumberger also finds fault with the District Court's holding that "[b]ecause the right to royalties arises only from the License Agreements, Schlumberger's exclusion of those agreements (and the royalties they set forth) was unambiguous and effective. Instead, Schlumberger argues that the right to the royalties derives from ownership of the intellectual property and not from the License Agreements. As a general proposition, Schlumberger is correct that it is the intellectual property that creates the right to royalties-as an owner may parcel out its "bundle of rights." However, this argument does not alter our analysis under these factual circumstances. At the time the License Agreements were created, CellNet owned the intellectual property and thus could license the right of exclusivity outside the United States to BCN in exchange for royalties. This separation of rights from the "bundle" was memorialized in the License Agreements. When Schlumberger purchased the intellectual property owned by CellNet, the license already existed and, pursuant to § 365(n), would likely continue to exist. Based on Schlumberger's acceptance that they would be purchasing CellNet's intellectual property subject to BCN's rights, and that BCN's rights existed solely from the excluded licenses, what Schlumberger bought was less than the full "bundle of rights" associated with ownership.

Thus, the initial right to royalties arose from the ownership of the intellectual property, but after Schlumberger elected to exclude the License Agreements, it severed those rights from the bundle it was purchasing. Once the royalties were divorced from the intellectual property, the only authority for their existence was the License Agreement. Because Schlumberger had excluded the Agreements, CellNet remained a party to those Agreements and would be entitled to the royalties thereunder.

Finding that CellNet would be otherwise rightfully entitled to the royalties once Schlumberger separated the royalties from the intellectual property that it purchased, we now turn to the question of how CellNet's rejection of the License Agreements under 11 U.S.C. § 365(a) and BCN's subsequent revival under § 365(n) affects the rights of the parties.

B. After the 11 U.S.C. § 365(n) Election, Who Is Entitled to the Royalties?

Under the Bankruptcy Code, a trustee may elect to reject or assume its obligations under an executory contract. This election is an all-or-nothing proposition — either the whole contract is assumed or the entire contract is rejected. Pursuant to its Purchase Agreement with Schlumberger, CellNet, as trustee, rejected the License Agreements under 365(a). Normally in bankruptcy, this would end the obligations between the contracting parties and relegate the non-breaching party to an unsecured creditor. . . . Congress, however, altered this system by passing an amendment that added § 365(n). Section 365(n) only applies to intellectual property and grants the licensee of intellectual property certain rights not enjoyed by other contracting parties. Specifically, if a trustee rejects an executory contract under § 365(a), the licensee of intellectual property may elect either:

(A) to treat such contract as terminated by such rejection if such rejection by the trustee amounts to such a breach as would entitle the licensee to treat such contract as terminated by virtue of its own terms, applicable nonbankruptcy law, or an agreement made by the licensee with another entity; or

(B) to retain its rights (including a right to enforce any exclusivity provision of such contract, but excluding any other right under applicable nonbankruptcy law to specific performance of such contract) under such contract and under any agreement supplementary to such contract, to such intellectual property (including any embodiment of such intellectual property to the extent protected by applicable nonbankruptcy law), as such rights existed immediately before the case commenced, for —

(i) the duration of such contract; and

(ii) any period for which such contract may be extended by the licensee as of right under applicable nonbankruptcy law.

Looking to the facts before us, Schlumberger excluded the License Agreements from its purchase, and then CellNet rejected the Agreements under § 365(a). In turn, BCN elected to retain its rights and was thus obligated to "make all royalty payments due under such contract for the duration of such contract." Schlumberger argues that because CellNet rejected the contract, it has not assumed the benefits of the contract and thus has no rights under the contract. Schlumberger then posits that because it owns the underlying intellectual property, it has superior rights to the royalties— despite not purchasing the License Agreements. We disagree.

The District Court found that CellNet was entitled to the royalties because "§ 365(n) of the Bankruptcy Code renews certain obligations related to the license." Despite Schlumberger's argument that because "§ 365(n)(2) does not designate that the payment of royalties must be made to any particular party," it should be entitled to the royalties, the District Court focused instead on the language stating that the "licensee shall make all royalty payments due under such contract." The District Court concluded "that Congress intended the language 'due under the contract' to provide both the quantity of the royalty payments and the designation of the party intended to receive those payments, whether the debtor or its contractual assignee." Because Schlumberger excluded the contract from its purchase, "CellNet remains entitled to receive the BCN royalties pursuant to statutory authority even if it rejected the License Agreements and is not technically a party to them." The District Court concluded that "royalty payments made pursuant to § 365(n)(2)(B) of the Bankruptcy Code are the property of the licensor, even though the licensor may have transferred its intellectual property assets during the bankruptcy."

Schlumberger makes essentially three arguments related to the effects of § 365(n). First, Schlumberger claims that CellNet has no rights because it rejected the contract under § 365(a). To support this conclusion, Schlumberger cites our opinion in *In Re Bildisco*, 682 F.2d 72, 82 (3d Cir. 1982), where we held that "as a matter of law, a debtor-in-possession is '[a] new entity . . . created with its own rights and duties, subject to the supervision of the bankruptcy court.'" Schlumberger claims that this demonstrates that the License Agreements were not part of the estate because they were never assumed by CellNet as debtor-in-possession. Schlumberger is incorrect. In *NLRB v. Bildisco*, 465 U.S. 513, 104 S. Ct. 1188, 79 L. Ed. 2d 482 (1984), the Supreme Court affirmed our previously cited opinion. The Court, however, stated that:

> Obviously if the [debtor-in-possession] were a wholly 'new entity,' it would be unnecessary for the Bankruptcy Code to allow it to reject executory contracts, since it would not be bound by such contracts in the first place. For our purposes, it is sensible to view the debtor-in-possession as the same 'entity' which existed before the filing of the bankruptcy petition, but empowered by virtue of the Bankruptcy Code to deal with its contracts and property in a manner it could not have done absent the bankruptcy filing.

This implies that the License Agreements were property of the bankruptcy estate after Schlumberger excluded them and before CellNet rejected them. Schlumberger contends that the act of rejection serves to remove the contract from the bankruptcy estate and points to *In Re Access Beyond Technologies, Inc.*, 237 B.R. 32, 47 (D. Del. 1999), for the proposition that "[a]n executory contract does not become an asset of the estate until it is assumed pursuant to § 365(a) of the Code." That case however, is factually distinguishable from ours. In *Access*, the debtor attempted to assign its rights under a patent cross-license agreement. The debtor characterized the transaction as a sale under 11 U.S.C. §363, but the court held that the debtor must first assume the agreement in order to transfer it. The court noted that otherwise, "[i]f the debtor does not assume an executory contract, it is deemed rejected. Thus, if a debtor does not assume an executory contract before he sells it . . . , the buyer may be purchasing an illusion: the executory contract will disappear on conclusion of the bankruptcy case." *Access* did not deal with our situation, which involves an executory contract after an election by a licensee under §365(n). We need not specify the exact status of the contract. For our purposes it is suffice to say that after a licensee has resorted to §365(n), the rights of the contract as they existed pre-petition and pre-rejection are in force.

The plain language of §365(n)(2)(B) indicates that the renewed royalties are directly linked to the rejected contract, not the intellectual property. The section specifically provides that the "licensee shall make all royalty payments due under such contract for the duration of such contract." Thus, the contract is the primary mechanism for determining where the royalties flow. Although Schlumberger is correct that §365(n)(2)(B) does not specify that the royalties must be paid to the trustee, the immediately preceding section says that "trustee shall allow the licensee to exercise such rights," and the next section deals with the rights of the licensee against the trustee. The several sections of §365(n)(2) make sense only in contemplation of an ongoing relationship between the licensee and the licensor/trustee.

Schlumberger next argues that the legislative history of §365(n) favors awarding it the royalties. It notes that the legislative history of §365(n) explains that the subsection parallels §365(h), which deals with real estate and allows a similar retention of rights by holders of real estate leases. With this link in place, Schlumberger analogizes that its position in this case would be the equivalent of where a purchaser bought a shopping center, but did not assume the lease of an occupying tenant. Under §365(h), the tenant could choose to remain in possession and pay rent, but the rent would belong to the new owner. According to Schlumberger, the position taken by CellNet and the District Court would alter the above situation and provide that the tenant could still remain in possession, but would pay rent to the former owner of the shopping center.

Although this analogy is powerful, and the logic deceptively simple, Schlumberger's reasoning is specious because it rests on a flawed comparison of the parties. Although both sections of the Bankruptcy Code discuss their respective elections as being limited by non-bankruptcy law, the concept of tenants remaining in possession when a new landlord gains control is fraught with state law property principles not applicable in the intellectual property context. We find that there is no relationship between Schlumberger and the License Agreements-which it specifically did not purchase-that can be equated with the relationship of possessory control by a new landlord over a tenant remaining in possession.

Schlumberger's final argument is that the long-standing principle that the benefits of a contract should accompany the burden dictates that they should retain the royalties. Its argument, however, is trumped by the facts. It is true that the burden of the License Agreements falls on Schlumberger, who cannot use the intellectual property outside the United States and that the benefit to that burden is the royalty payments. However, state law allows the severance of the benefit from the burden and Schlumberger has done just that by excluding the License Agreement from its purchase and not contracting with CellNet for the royalties.

Lubrizol Enterprises, Inc. v. Richmond Metal Finishers, Inc.

United States Court of Appeals for the Fourth Circuit

756 F.2d 1043 (4th Cir. 1985)

JAMES DICKSON PHILLIPS, CIRCUIT JUDGE.

The question is whether Richmond Metal Finishers (RMF), a bankrupt debtor in possession, should have been allowed to reject as executory a technology licensing agreement with Lubrizol Enterprises (Lubrizol) as licensee. The bankruptcy court approved rejection pursuant to 11 U.S.C. § 365(a), but the district court reversed on the basis that within contemplation of § 365(a), the contract was not executory and, alternatively, that rejection could not reasonably be expected substantially to benefit the bankrupt debtor. We reverse and remand for entry of judgment in conformity with that entered by the bankruptcy court.

I

In July of 1982, RMF entered into the contract with Lubrizol that granted Lubrizol a nonexclusive license to utilize a metal coating process technology owned by RMF. RMF owed the following duties to Lubrizol under the agreement: (1) to notify Lubrizol of any patent infringement suit and to defend in such suit; (2) to notify Lubrizol of any other use or licensing of the process, and to reduce royalty payments if a lower royalty rate agreement was reached with another licensee; and (3) to indemnify Lubrizol for losses arising out of any misrepresentation or breach of warranty by RMF. Lubrizol owed RMF reciprocal duties of accounting for and paying royalties for use of the process and of cancelling certain existing indebtedness. The contract provided that Lubrizol would defer use of the process until May 1, 1983, and in fact, Lubrizol has never used the RMF technology.

RMF filed a petition for bankruptcy pursuant to Chapter 11 of the Bankruptcy Code on August 16, 1983. As part of its plan to emerge from bankruptcy, RMF sought, pursuant to § 365(a), to reject the contract with Lubrizol in order to facilitate sale or licensing of the technology unhindered by restrictive provisions in the Lubrizol agreement. On RMF's motion for approval of the rejection, the bankruptcy court properly interpreted § 365 as requiring it to undertake a two-step inquiry to determine the propriety of rejection: first, whether the contract is executory; next, if so, whether its rejection would be advantageous to the bankrupt.

Making that inquiry, the bankruptcy court determined that both tests were satisfied and approved the rejection. But, as indicated, the district court then reversed that determination on the basis that neither test was satisfied and disallowed the rejection. This appeal followed.

II

We conclude initially that, as the bankruptcy court ruled, the technology licensing agreement in this case was an executory contract, within contemplation of 11 U.S.C. § 365(a). Under that provision a contract is executory if performance is due to some extent on both sides. This court has recently adopted Professor Countryman's more specific test for determining whether a contract is "executory" in the required sense. By that test, a contract is executory if the "'obligations of both the bankrupt and the other party to the contract are so far unperformed that the failure of either to complete the performance would constitute a material breach excusing the performance of the other.'" This issue is one of law that may be freely reviewed by successive courts.

Applying that test here, we conclude that the licensing agreement was at the critical time executory. RMF owed Lubrizol the continuing duties of notifying Lubrizol of further licensing of the process and of reducing Lubrizol's royalty rate to meet any more favorable rates granted to subsequent licensees. By their terms, RMF's obligations to give notice and to restrict its right to license its process at royalty rates it desired without lowering Lubrizol's royalty rate extended over the life of the agreement, and remained unperformed. Moreover, RMF owed Lubrizol additional contingent duties of notifying it of suits, defending suits and indemnifying it for certain losses.

The unperformed, continuing core obligations of notice and forbearance in licensing made the contract executory as to RMF. In *Fenix Cattle Co. v. Silver* (*In re Select-A-Seat Corp.*), 625 F.2d 290, 292 (9th Cir. 1980), the court found that an obligation of a debtor to refrain from selling software packages under an exclusive licensing agreement made a contract executory as to the debtor notwithstanding the continuing obligation was only one of forbearance. Although the license to Lubrizol was not exclusive, RMF owed the same type of unperformed continuing duty of forbearance arising out of the most favored licensee clause running in favor of Lubrizol. Breach of that duty would clearly constitute a material breach of the agreement.

Moreover, the contract was further executory as to RMF because of the contingent duties that RMF owed of giving notice of and defending infringement suits and of indemnifying Lubrizol for certain losses arising out of the use of the technology. Contingency of an obligation does not prevent its being executory under § 365. Until the time has expired during which an event triggering a contingent duty may occur, the contingent obligation represents a continuing duty to stand ready to perform if the contingency occurs. A breach of that duty once it was triggered by the contingency (or presumably, by anticipatory repudiation) would have been material.

Because a contract is not executory within the meaning of § 365(a) unless it is executory as to both parties, it is also necessary to determine whether the licensing agreement was executory as to Lubrizol. We conclude that it was.

Lubrizol owed RMF the unperformed and continuing duty of accounting for and paying royalties for the life of the agreement. It is true that a contract is not executory as to a party simply because the party is obligated to make payments of money to the other party. Therefore, if Lubrizol had owed RMF nothing more than a duty to make fixed payments or cancel specified indebtedness under the agreement, the agreement would not be executory as to Lubrizol. However, the promise to account for and pay royalties required that Lubrizol deliver written quarterly sales reports and keep books of account subject to inspection by an independent Certified Public Accountant. This promise goes beyond a mere debt, or promise to pay money, and was at the critical time executory. Additionally, subject to certain exceptions, Lubrizol was obligated to keep all license technology in confidence for a number of years.

Since the licensing agreement is executory as to each party, it is executory within the meaning of § 365(a), and the district court erred as a matter of law in reaching a contrary conclusion.

III

There remains the question whether rejection of the executory contract would be advantageous to the bankrupt. Courts addressing that question must start with the proposition that the bankrupt's decision upon it is to be accorded the deference mandated by the sound business judgment rule as generally applied by courts to discretionary actions or decisions of corporate directors.

As generally formulated and applied in corporate litigation the rule is that courts should defer to—should not interfere with—decisions of corporate directors upon matters entrusted to their business judgment except upon a finding of bad faith or gross abuse of their "business discretion." Transposed to the bankruptcy context, the rule as applied to a bankrupt's decision to reject an executory contract because of perceived business advantage requires that the decision be accepted by courts unless it is shown that the bankrupt's decision was one taken in bad faith or in gross abuse of the bankrupt's retained business discretion.

In bankruptcy litigation the issue is of course first presented for judicial determination when a debtor, having decided that rejection will be beneficial within contemplation of § 365(a), moves for approval of the rejection. The issue thereby presented for first instance judicial determination by the bankruptcy court is whether the decision of the debtor that rejection will be advantageous is so manifestly unreasonable that it could not be based on sound business judgment, but only on bad faith, or whim or caprice. That issue is one of fact to be decided as such by the bankruptcy court by the normal processes of fact adjudication. And the resulting fact determination by the bankruptcy court is perforce then reviewable up the line under the clearly erroneous standard.

Here, the bankruptcy judge had before him evidence not rebutted by Lubrizol that the metal coating process subject to the licensing agreement is RMF's principal asset and that sale or licensing of the technology represented the primary potential source of funds by which RMF might emerge from bankruptcy. The testimony of RMF's president, also factually uncontested by Lubrizol, indicated that sale or further licensing of the technology would be facilitated by stripping Lubrizol of its rights in the process and that, correspondingly, continued obligation to Lubrizol under the agreement would hinder RMF's capability to sell or license the technology on more advantageous terms to other potential licensees. On the basis of this evidence the bankruptcy court determined that the debtor's decision to reject was based upon sound business judgment and approved it.

On appeal the district court simply found to the contrary that the debtor's decision to reject did not represent a sound business judgment. The district court's determination rested essentially on two grounds: that RMF's purely contingent obligations under the agreement were not sufficiently onerous that relief from them would constitute a substantial benefit to RMF; and that because rejection could not deprive Lubrizol of all its rights to the technology, rejection could not reasonably be found beneficial. We conclude that in both of these respects the district court's factual findings, at odds with those of the bankruptcy court, were clearly erroneous and cannot stand.

A

In finding that the debtor's contingent obligations were not sufficiently onerous that relief from them would be beneficial, the district court could only have been substituting its business judgment for that of the debtor. There is nothing in the record from which it could be concluded that the debtor's decision on that point could not have been reached by the exercise of sound (though possibly faulty) business judgment in the normal process of evaluating alternative courses of action. If that could not be concluded, then the business judgment rule required that the debtor's factual evaluation be accepted by the court, as it had been by the bankruptcy court.

B

On the second point, we can only conclude that the district court was under a misapprehension of controlling law in thinking that by rejecting the agreement the debtor could not deprive Lubrizol of all rights to the process. Under 11 U.S.C. § 365(g), Lubrizol would be entitled to treat rejection as a breach and seek a money damages remedy; however, it could not seek to retain its contract rights in the technology by specific performance even if that remedy would ordinarily be available upon breach of this type of contract.

Even though § 365(g) treats rejection as a breach, the legislative history of § 365(g) makes clear that the purpose of the provision is to provide only a damages remedy for the non-bankrupt party. For the same reason, Lubrizol cannot rely on provisions within its agreement with RMF for continued use of the technology by Lubrizol upon breach by RMF. Here again, the statutory "breach" contemplated by § 365(g) controls, and provides only a money damages remedy for the non-bankrupt party. Allowing specific performance would obviously undercut the core purpose of rejection under § 365(a), and that consequence cannot therefore be read into congressional intent.

IV

Lubrizol strongly urges upon us policy concerns in support of the district court's refusal to defer to the debtor's decision to reject or, preliminarily, to treat the contract as executory for § 365(a) purposes. We understand the concerns, but think they cannot control decision here.

It cannot be gainsaid that allowing rejection of such contracts as executory imposes serious burdens upon contracting parties such as Lubrizol. Nor can it be doubted that allowing rejection in this and comparable cases could have a general chilling effect upon the willingness of such parties to contract at all with businesses in possible financial difficulty. But under bankruptcy law such equitable considerations may not be indulged by courts in respect of the type of contract here in issue. Congress has plainly provided for the rejection of executory contracts, notwithstanding the obvious adverse consequences for contracting parties thereby made inevitable. Awareness by Congress of those consequences is indeed specifically reflected in the special treatment accorded to union members under collective bargaining contracts, and to lessees of real property. But no comparable special treatment is provided for technology licensees such as Lubrizol. They share the general hazards created by § 365 for all business entities dealing with potential bankrupts in the respects at issue here.

The judgment of the district court is reversed and the case is remanded for entry of judgment in conformity with that entered by the bankruptcy court.

Notes & Questions

1. The *Cellnet* and *Lubrizol* cases illustrate the treatment of intellectual property and technology licenses by debtor licensors when section 365(n) applies and when it does not. Work through the details of *Cellnet* to obtain a sense of the logic of sections 365(a) and 365(n). Schlumberger's argument is that as a purchaser of Cellnet's intellectual property, it has the rights to the royalties once the licensee decides to retain its rights under the license and pay royalties. Cellnet's argument is that Schlumberger's rights are limited to what it acquired via contract, which severed the royalty rights. The court agreed with Cellnet. In your opinion, who has the better argument? Is this a case about poor contract drafting or about bankruptcy policy favoring the debtor licensor? Note that courts tend to adopt a broad reading of royalty payments to include licensing fees and other payments. *See Encino Bus. Mgmt., Inc. v. Prize Frize, Inc.*, 32 F.3d 426 (9th Cir. 1994).

2. The *Lubrizol* case was the impetus for Congress to enact section 365(n) as a protection for non-debtor licensees. Absent section 365(n), how could the licensee have protected itself in *Lubrizol*? One option would have been language in the license that

limited the licensor's ability to reject in the event of bankruptcy. Another option would have been to purchase the intellectual property outright rather than to license it. Are these feasible options for licensees? Would they have been feasible under the facts of *Lubrizol*? Is a statutory solution such as section 365(n) a better option?

3. Notice that the holding of the *Lubrizol* case will apply whenever section 365(n) does not. Specifically, section 365(n) does not apply to trademarks or trade names. Therefore, drafters of license agreements in these contexts need to be especially wary of the possibility of bankruptcy by the licensor. There is one other situation where section 365(n) protections would not apply, and the *Lubrizol* trap may arise: foreign copyrights. The definition of intellectual property includes "works of authorship protected under Title 17," a reference to copyright law. If the work of authorship, such as software, was created outside of the United States or a country with which the United States has a treaty agreement, then the work may not be "protected under Title 17." This situation is unusual and would apply, for example, to a foreign company that is licensing its copyright to a United States licensee. If the foreign company files for bankruptcy in the United States, the company as debtor may be able to reject the license like the debtor in *Lubrizol*.

4. One contingency that the non-debtor licensee needs to be aware of is a sale of intellectual property by the debtor licensor free and clear of any interest to a third party. If the sale goes through, then the third party purchaser would obtain the intellectual property free of any licenses. The debtor licensor has the right to initiate such a transaction under section 365(f), but the court must approve it. In such an eventuality, the debtor has the right to object to the sale before the bankruptcy court. Notice that section 365(n) protections do not apply to the debtor licensor's decision to sell the intellectual property, but only to the decision to reject the license. Therefore, it is up to the non-debtor licensee to convince the court not to approve the proposed sale given the equities of the situation or at the least to obtain adequate protection for its interests if the sale is approved. Although there is no precedent involving intellectual property transferred under these circumstances, there is some precedent involving the sale of real estate free and clear of existing leases. See the discussion in *Precisions Industries, Inc. v. Qualitech Steel SBQ*, 327 F. 3d 537 (7th Cir. 2003) (allowing the sale of real estate free and clear of existing leases). With this problem in mind, reconsider Schlumberger's argument about real property transfers in the *Cellnet* case. Do you think the court's distinction between real property and intellectual property for the purposes of section 365(a) and non-debtor licensee protection makes sense?

5. One lesson to draw from this material is the importance of good drafting in protecting one's interests in intellectual property and licenses, particularly in the shadow of bankruptcy. One example of creative lawyering to deal with these problems is provided by the "source code escrow," a common tool to protect a software licensee's rights in the event of a licensor's bankruptcy. A source code escrow is an agreement among a licensor, a licensee and a third party escrow agent. Under the terms of the agreement, the agent secretly retains the source code, which may be

released to the licensee in the event of certain contingencies such as the licensor's failure to perform maintenance obligations under the terms of the license. For a discussion, see N. Neville Reid & Sajida Mahdi, *Intellectual Property and Bankruptcy— Salient Issues*, 862 PLI/COMM 313 (April–May, 2004).

c. Licensee as Debtor

Institut Pasteur v. Cambridge Biotech Corporation

United States Court of Appeals for the First Circuit

104 F.3d 489 (1st Cir. 1997)

CYR, CIRCUIT JUDGE.

Unsuccessful in their intermediate appeal to the district court, Institut Pasteur and Pasteur Sanofi Diagnostics [collectively: "Pasteur"] again appeal from the bankruptcy court order which confirmed the Chapter 11 reorganization plan ("Plan") proposed by debtor-in-possession Cambridge Biotech Corporation ("CBC"), the holder of two licenses to utilize Pasteur patents. The Plan provision central to the present dispute calls for the sale of all CBC stock to a subsidiary of bioMerieux Vitek, Inc. ("bio-Merieux"), a major competitor of appellant Pasteur. Finding no error, we affirm.

I

BACKGROUND

CBC manufactures and sells retroviral diagnostic tests for detecting the human immunodeficiency virus (HIV) associated with AIDS. Its HIV diagnostics division annually generates approximately $14 million in revenues. Institut Pasteur, a nonprofit French foundation engaged in AIDS-related research and development, owns various patented procedures for diagnosing HIV Virus Type 2 ("HIV2 procedures"). Pasteur Sanofi Diagnostics holds the exclusive right to use and sublicense Institut Pasteur's patents.

In October 1989, CBC and Pasteur entered into mutual cross-license agreements, whereby each acquired a nonexclusive perpetual license to use some of the technology patented or licensed by the other. Specifically, CBC acquired the right to incorporate Pasteur's HIV2 procedures into any diagnostic kits sold by CBC in the United States, Canada, Mexico, Australia, New Zealand and elsewhere.

Each cross-license broadly prohibits the licensee from assigning or sublicensing to others. ("[N]o other person shall acquire or have any right under or by virtue of this Agreement."). Nevertheless, either Pasteur or CBC was authorized to "extend to its Affiliated Companies the benefits of this Agreement so that such party shall remain responsible with regard [to] all [license] obligations." "Affiliated Company" is defined as "an organization which controls or is controlled by a party or an organization which is under common control with a party."

CBC filed its Chapter 11 petition on July 7, 1994, and thereafter continued to operate its retroviral diagnostic testing business as debtor-in-possession. Its reorganization plan proposed that CBC assume both cross-licenses, continue to operate its retroviral diagnostics division utilizing Pasteur's patented HIV2 procedures, and sell all CBC stock to a subsidiary of bioMerieux, a giant French biotechnology corporation and Pasteur's direct competitor in international biotechnology sales. Pasteur previously had licensed bioMerieux to use its HIV2 procedures, but the earlier license related to a single product manufactured by bioMerieux (i.e., bioMerieux's VIDAS automated immunoassay test system), and applied only to VIDAS sales in markets other than the United States, Canada, Mexico, Australia, and New Zealand, markets expressly encompassed within the CBC cross-licenses.

Not surprisingly, in due course Pasteur objected to the Plan. Citing Bankruptcy Code § 365(c), 11 U.S.C. § 365(c), it contended that the proposed sale of CBC's stock to bioMerieux amounted to CBC's assumption of the patent cross-licenses and their de facto "assignment" to a third party in contravention of the presumption of non-assignability ordained by the federal common law of patents, as well as the explicit nonassignability provision contained in the cross-licenses. Isabelle Bressac, Pasteur's licensing director, attested that Pasteur would not have granted its competitor, bioMerieux, or a subsidiary, a patent license under the terms allowed CBC.

The bankruptcy court authorized CBC to assume the cross-licenses over Pasteur's objection. It ruled that the proposed sale of CBC stock to bioMerieux did not constitute a de facto "assignment" of the cross-licenses to bioMerieux, but merely an assumption of the cross-licenses by the reorganized debtor under new ownership, and that Bankruptcy Code § 365(c) enabled CBC to assume the cross-licenses as debtor-in-possession because the prepetition licensing relationship between Pasteur and CBC was neither "unique" nor "something in the category of a personal services contract." The district court upheld the bankruptcy court ruling on intermediate appeal.

II

DISCUSSION

. . . .

Pasteur argues that the CBC Plan effects a de facto assignment of its two cross-licenses to bioMerieux, contrary to Bankruptcy Code § 365(c)(1) which provides as follows:

> The trustee [viz., CBC] may not assume or assign any executory contract . . . , whether or not such contract . . . prohibits or restricts assignment of rights or delegation of duties, if—
>
> (1)(A) applicable law excuses a party[] other than the debtor[] [viz., Pasteur] to such contract . . . from accepting performance from or rendering performance to an entity other than the debtor or the debtor in possession, whether or not such contract . . . prohibits or restricts assumption or assignment; and
>
> (B) such party [viz., Pasteur] does not consent to such assumption or assignment . . . .

11 U.S.C. § 365(c)(1).

Pasteur argues that in order to encourage optimum product innovation the federal common law of patents presumes that patent licensees, such as CBC, may not sublicense to third parties absent the patent holder's consent. This federal common law rule of presumptive nonassignability thus qualifies as an "applicable law," within the meaning of Bankruptcy Code § 365(c)(1)(A), which precludes Pasteur from being compelled to accept performance from any entity other than CBC—e.g., bioMerieux's subsidiary—and therefore prevents CBC from either assuming or assigning these cross-licenses. Further, says Pasteur, even assuming that section 365(c) might allow a debtor simply to assume the cross-licenses without a subsequent assignment to a third party, CBC formally structured this Plan transaction as an assumption by the debtor-in-possession, whereas in substance it was an assignment of the cross-licenses to bioMerieux, a complete stranger to the original cross-licensing agreements.

These contentions are foreclosed by our decision in *Summit Inv. & Dev. Corp. v. Leroux (In re Leroux)*, 69 F.3d 608 (1st Cir. 1995), which analyzed and interpreted companion Bankruptcy Code subsections 365(c) and (e) and their relevant legislative history. As in the present case, in *Leroux* we were urged to interpret subsections 365(c) and (e) as mandating a "hypothetical test." Under such an approach, the Chapter 11 debtor would lose its option to assume the contract, even though it never intended to assign the contract to another entity, if either the particular executory contract or the applicable nonbankruptcy law purported to terminate the contract automatically upon the filing of the Chapter 11 petition or to preclude its assignment to an entity not a party to the contract.

We rejected the proposed hypothetical test in *Leroux*, holding instead that subsections 365(c) and (e) contemplate a case-by-case inquiry into whether the nondebtor party (viz., Pasteur) actually was being "forced to accept performance under its executory contract from someone other than the debtor party with whom it originally contracted." *Id.* Where the particular transaction envisions that the debtor-in-possession would assume and continue to perform under an executory contract, the bankruptcy court cannot simply presume as a matter of law that the debtor-in-possession is a legal entity materially distinct from the prepetition debtor with whom the nondebtor party (viz., Pasteur) contracted. Rather, "sensitive to the rights of the nondebtor party (viz., Pasteur)," the bankruptcy court must focus on the performance actually to be rendered by the debtor-in-possession with a view to ensuring that the nondebtor party (viz., Pasteur) will receive "the full benefit of [its] bargain."

Given the pragmatic "actual performance" test adopted in Leroux, the ultimate findings of fact and conclusions of law made by the bankruptcy court below did not constitute error. CBC simply does not occupy the same position as the debtor in *CFLC, Inc.*, 89 F.3d 673 (9th Cir. 1996), upon which Pasteur relies most heavily. The Plan in *CFLC, Inc.* unmistakably provided for an outright assignment of the debtor's patent license to an entirely different corporation with which the patent holder Cadtrak Corporation had never contracted. By contrast, CBC all along has conducted, and proposes to continue, its retroviral diagnostic enterprise as the same corporate entity which functioned prepetition, while utilizing Pasteur's HIV2 procedures in that same prepetition endeavor.

Pasteur nonetheless insists that the reorganized CBC is different than the prepetition entity, not due merely to its Chapter 11 filing but because it is now owned by a different legal entity than before—namely, bioMerieux's subsidiary qua CBC shareholder. Pasteur's contention finds no support, however, either in Massachusetts law, see supra note 1, or in the cross-license provisions it negotiated.

Stock sales are not mergers whereby outright title and ownership of the licensee-corporation's assets (including its patent licenses) pass to the acquiring corporation. Rather, as a corporation, CBC "is a legal entity distinct from its shareholders." Absent compelling grounds for disregarding its corporate form, therefore, CBC's separate legal identity, and its ownership of the patent cross-licenses, survive without interruption notwithstanding repeated and even drastic changes in its ownership. Pasteur cites no apposite authority to the contrary.

Furthermore, Pasteur's position finds no support in the negotiated terms of its cross-licenses. As the patent holder—and given CBC's corporate form and the governing Massachusetts law, supra—Pasteur was free to negotiate restrictions on CBC's continuing rights under the cross-licenses based on changes in its stock ownership or corporate control. Nevertheless, these cross-licenses contain no provision either limiting or terminating CBC's rights in the event its stock ownership were to change hands. The generic nonassignability provisions found in these cross-licenses ("This Agreement . . . has been made solely for the benefit of the parties hereto" and "no other person shall acquire or have any right under or by virtue of this Agreement.") plainly do not address the circumstance presented here. Rather, these nonassignability provisions simply beg the essential question, which is whether bioMerieux's subsidiary, by virtue of its acquisition of CBC stock, terminated CBC 's rights under the cross-licenses. Interpreted as Pasteur proposes, CBC's own rights under the cross-licenses would terminate with any change in the identity of any CBC stockholder.

Other cross-license provisions directly undercut Pasteur's interpretation as well. These cross-licenses explicitly authorize CBC to share its license rights with any "affiliated company," which on its face presumably encompasses a parent corporation such as bioMerieux's subsidiary (defining "Affiliated Company" as "an organization which controls . . . a party or an organization which is under common control with a party"). Yet more importantly, CBC insisted upon a provision which would afford it the unilateral right to terminate any sublicense Pasteur might extend to a company called Genetic Systems "if control of Genetic Systems shall . . . be acquired, directly or indirectly, by any person or group of connected persons or company not having such control at the date hereof, by reconstruction, amalgamation, acquisition of shares or assets or otherwise." Taken together, these provisions persuade us that Pasteur foresaw, or reasonably should have foreseen, that CBC might undergo changes of stock ownership which would not alter its corporate legal identity, but nonetheless chose not to condition the continued viability of its cross-licenses accordingly.

III

CONCLUSION

As CBC remains in all material respects the legal entity with which Pasteur freely contracted, Pasteur has not made the required individualized showing that it is or will be deprived of "the full benefit of [its] bargain," under the ruling challenged on appeal. Accordingly, the district court judgment is affirmed and costs are awarded to appellee.

In re Catapult Entertainment, Inc.

United States Court of Appeals for the Ninth Circuit

165 F.3d 747 (9th Cir. 1999)

FLETCHER, CIRCUIT JUDGE.

Appellant Stephen Perlman ("Perlman") licensed certain patents to appellee Catapult Entertainment, Inc. ("Catapult"). He now seeks to bar Catapult, which has since become a Chapter 11 debtor in possession, from assuming the patent licenses as part of its reorganization plan. Notwithstanding Perlman's objections, the bankruptcy court approved the assumption of the licenses and confirmed the reorganization plan. The district court affirmed the bankruptcy court on intermediate appeal. Perlman appeals that decision. We are called upon to determine whether, in light of § 365(c)(1) of the Bankruptcy Code, a Chapter 11 debtor in possession may assume certain nonexclusive patent licenses over a licensor's objection. We conclude that the bankruptcy court erred in permitting the debtor in possession to assume the patent licenses in question.

I.

Catapult, a California corporation, was formed in 1994 to create an online gaming network for 16-bit console videogames. That same year, Catapult entered into two license agreements with Perlman, wherein Perlman granted to Catapult the right to exploit certain relevant technologies, including patents and patent applications.

In October 1996, Catapult filed for reorganization under Chapter 11 of the Bankruptcy Code. Shortly before the filing of the bankruptcy petition, Catapult entered into a merger agreement with Mpath Interactive, Inc. ("Mpath"). This agreement contemplated the filing of the bankruptcy petition, followed by a reorganization via a "reverse triangular merger" involving Mpath, MPCAT Acquisition Corporation ("MPCAT"), and Catapult. Under the terms of the merger agreement, MPCAT (a wholly-owned subsidiary of Mpath created for this transaction) would merge into Catapult, leaving Catapult as the surviving entity. When the dust cleared, Catapult's creditors and equity holders would have received approximately $14 million in cash, notes, and securities; Catapult, in turn, would have become a wholly-owned subsidiary of Mpath. The relevant third party creditors and equity holders accepted Catapult's reorganization plan by the majorities required by the Bankruptcy Code.

On October 24, 1996, as part of the reorganization plan, Catapult filed a motion with the bankruptcy court seeking to assume some 140 executory contracts and leases, including the Perlman licenses. Over Perlman's objection, the bankruptcy court granted Catapult's motion and approved the reorganization plan. The district court subsequently affirmed the bankruptcy court. This appeal followed.

II.

Section 365 of the Bankruptcy Code gives a trustee in bankruptcy (or, in a Chapter 11 case, the debtor in possession) the authority to assume, assign, or reject the executory contracts and unexpired leases of the debtor, notwithstanding any contrary provisions appearing in such contracts or leases. See 11 U.S.C. § 365(a) & (f). This extraordinary authority, however, is not absolute. Section 365(c)(1) provides that, notwithstanding the general policy set out in § 365(a):

> (c) The trustee may not assume or assign any executory contract or unexpired lease of the debtor, whether or not such contract or lease prohibits or restricts assignment of rights or delegation of duties, if
>
> (1)(A) applicable law excuses a party, other than the debtor, to such contract or lease from accepting performance from or rendering performance to an entity other than the debtor or the debtor in possession, whether or not such contract or lease prohibits or restricts assignment of rights or delegation of duties; and (B) such party does not consent to such assumption or assignment. . . .

Our task, simply put, is to apply this statutory language to the facts at hand and determine whether it prohibits Catapult, as the debtor in possession, from assuming the Perlman licenses without Perlman's consent.

While simply put, our task is not so easily resolved; the proper interpretation of § 365(c)(1) has been the subject of considerable disagreement among courts and commentators. On one side are those who adhere to the plain statutory language, which establishes a so-called "hypothetical test" to govern the assumption of executory contracts. On the other side are those that forsake the statutory language in favor of an "actual test" that, in their view, better accomplishes the intent of Congress. [T]oday we hold that we are bound by the plain terms of the statute and join the Third and Eleventh Circuits in adopting the "hypothetical test."

III.

We begin, as we must, with the statutory language. The plain language of § 365(c)(1) "link[s] nonassignability under 'applicable law' together with a prohibition on assumption in bankruptcy." In other words, the statute by its terms bars a debtor in possession from assuming an executory contract without the nondebtor's consent where applicable law precludes assignment of the contract to a third party. The literal language of § 365(c)(1) is thus said to establish a "hypothetical test": a debtor in possession may not assume an executory contract over the nondebtor's objection if applicable law would bar assignment to a hypothetical third party, even where the debtor in possession has no intention of assigning the contract in question to any such third party.

Before applying the statutory language to the case at hand, we first resolve a number of preliminary issues that are either not disputed by the parties, or are so clearly established as to deserve no more than passing reference. First, we follow the lead of the parties in assuming that the Perlman licenses are executory agreements within the meaning of § 365. Second, it is well-established that § 365(c)'s use of the term "trustee" includes Chapter 11 debtors in possession. Third, our precedents make it clear that federal patent law constitutes "applicable law" within the meaning of § 365(c), and that nonexclusive patent licenses are "personal and assignable only with the consent of the licensor."

When we have cleared away these preliminary matters, application of the statute to the facts of this case becomes relatively straightforward:

(c) Catapult may not assume . . . the Perlman licenses, . . . if

(1)(A) federal patent law excuses Perlman from accepting performance from or rendering performance to an entity other than Catapult . . . ; and (B) Perlman does not consent to such assumption. . . .

Since federal patent law makes nonexclusive patent licenses personal and nondelegable, § 365(c)(1)(A) is satisfied. Perlman has withheld his consent, thus satisfying § 365(c)(1)(B). Accordingly, the plain language of § 365(c)(1) bars Catapult from assuming the Perlman licenses.

IV.

Catapult urges us to abandon the literal language of § 365(c)(1) in favor of an alternative approach, reasoning that Congress did not intend to bar debtors in possession from assuming their own contracts where no assignment is contemplated. In Catapult's view, § 365(c)(1) should be interpreted as embodying an "actual test": the statute bars assumption by the debtor in possession only where the reorganization in question results in the nondebtor actually having to accept performance from a third party. Under this reading of § 365(c), the debtor in possession would be permitted to assume any executory contract, so long as no assignment was contemplated. Put another way, Catapult suggests that, as to a debtor in possession, § 365(c)(1) should be read to prohibit assumption and assignment, rather than assumption or assignment.

Catapult has marshalled considerable authority to support this reading. The arguments supporting Catapult's position can be divided into three categories: (1) the literal reading creates inconsistencies within § 365; (2) the literal reading is incompatible with the legislative history; and (3) the literal reading flies in the face of sound bankruptcy policy. Nonetheless, we find that none of these considerations justifies departing from the plain language of § 365(c)(1).

A.

Catapult first argues that a literal reading of § 365(c)(1) sets the statute at war with itself and its neighboring provisions. Deviation from the plain language, contends Catapult, is necessary if internal consistency is to be achieved. We agree with Catapult that a court should interpret a statute, if possible, so as to minimize discord among related provisions. However, the dire inconsistencies cited by Catapult turn out, on closer analysis, to be no such thing.

Catapult, for example, singles out the interaction between § 365(c)(1) and § 365(f)(1) as a statutory trouble spot. Subsection (f)(1) provides that executory contracts, once assumed, may be assigned notwithstanding any contrary provisions contained in the contract or applicable law:

(f)(1) Except as provided in subsection (c) of this section, notwithstanding a provision in an executory contract or unexpired lease of the debtor, or in applicable law, that prohibits, restricts, or conditions the assignment of such contract or lease, the trustee may assign such contract or lease under paragraph (2) of this subsection. . . .

The potential conflict between subsections (c)(1) and (f)(1) arises from their respective treatments of "applicable law." The plain language of subsection (c)(1) bars assumption (absent consent) whenever "applicable law" would bar assignment. Subsection (f)(1) states that, contrary provisions in applicable law notwithstanding, executory contracts may be assigned. Since assumption is a necessary prerequisite to assignment under § 365, a literal reading of subsection (c)(1) appears to render subsection (f)(1) superfluous. In the words of the Sixth Circuit, "[S]ection 365(c), the recognized exception to 365(f), appears at first to resuscitate in full the very anti-assignment 'applicable law' which 365(f) nullifies." Faced with this dilemma, one district court reluctantly concluded that the "[c]onflict between subsections (c) and (f) of § 365 is inescapable."

Subsequent authority, however, suggests that this conclusion may have been unduly pessimistic. The Sixth Circuit has credibly reconciled the warring provisions by noting that "each subsection recognizes an 'applicable law' of markedly different scope." Subsection (f)(1) states the broad rule—a law that, as a general matter, "prohibits, restricts, or conditions the assignment" of executory contracts is trumped by the provisions of subsection (f)(1). Subsection (c)(1), however, states a carefully crafted exception to the broad rule—where applicable law does not merely recite a general ban on assignment, but instead more specifically "excuses a party . . . from accepting performance from or rendering performance to an entity" different from the one with which the party originally contracted, the applicable law prevails over subsection (f)(1). In other words, in determining whether an "applicable law" stands or falls under § 365(f)(1), a court must ask why the "applicable law" prohibits assignment. Only if the law prohibits assignment on the rationale that the identity of the contracting party is material to the agreement will subsection (c)(1) rescue it. We agree with the Sixth and Eleventh Circuits that a literal reading of subsection (c)(1) does not inevitably set it at odds with subsection (f)(1).

Catapult next focuses on the internal structure of § 365(c)(1) itself. According to Catapult, the literal approach to subsection (c)(1) renders the phrase "or the debtor in possession" contained in § 365(c)(1)(A) superfluous. In the words of one bankruptcy court, "[i]f the directive of Section 365(c)(1) is to prohibit assumption whenever applicable law excuses performance relative to any entity other than the debtor, why add the words 'or debtor in possession?' The [hypothetical] test renders this phrase surplusage."

A close reading of § 365(c)(1), however, dispels this notion. By its terms, subsection (c)(1) addresses two conceptually distinct events: assumption and assignment. The plain language of the provision makes it clear that each of these events is contingent on the nondebtor's separate consent. Consequently, where a nondebtor consents to the assumption of an executory contract, subsection (c)(1) will have to be applied a second time if the debtor in possession wishes to assign the contract in question. On that second application, the relevant question would be whether "applicable law excuses a party from accepting performance from or rendering performance to an entity other than . . . the debtor in possession." Consequently, the phrase "debtor in possession," far from being rendered superfluous by a literal reading of subsection (c)(1), dovetails neatly with the disjunctive language that opens subsection (c)(1): "The trustee may not assume or assign. . . ."

A third potential inconsistency identified by Catapult relates to § 365(c)(2). According to Catapult, a literal reading of subsection (c)(1) renders subsection (c)(2) a dead letter. Subsection (c)(2) provides:

> (c) The trustee may not assume or assign any executory contract or unexpired lease of the debtor, whether or not such contract or lease prohibits or restricts assignment of rights or delegation of duties, if
>
> . . . .
>
> (2) such contract is a contract to make a loan, or extend other debt financing or financial accommodations, to or for the benefit of the debtor, or to issue a security of the debtor. . . .

According to Catapult, the contracts encompassed by subsection (c)(2) are all non-assignable as a matter of applicable state law. As a result, a literal reading of subsection (c)(1) would seem to snare and dispose of every executory contract within subsection (c)(2)'s scope. Perlman, however, persuasively rebuts this argument, noting that even if the state law governing the assignability of loan agreements and financing contracts is relatively uniform today, Congress by enacting subsection (c)(2) cemented nationwide uniformity in the bankruptcy context, effectively ensuring creditors that these particular contracts would not be assumable in bankruptcy. Put another way, it is the national uniformity of applicable state law that has rendered subsection (c)(2) superfluous, not the terms of subsection (c)(1).

In any event, subsection (c)(1) does not completely swallow up subsection (c)(2). Subsection (c)(1) by its terms permits assumption and assignment of executory loan agreements so long as the nondebtor consents. Subsection (c)(2), in contrast, bans assumption and assignment of such agreements, consent of the nondebtor notwithstanding. Accordingly, contrary to Catapult's assertion, subsection (c)(1) does not necessarily catch upriver all the fish that would otherwise be netted by subsection (c)(2). Once again, the "inconsistency" identified by Catapult proves evanescent under close scrutiny. We see no reason why these two provisions cannot happily coexist.

We conclude that the claimed inconsistencies are not actual and that the plain language of § 365(c)(1) compels the result Perlman urges: Catapult may not assume the Perlman licenses over Perlman's objection. Catapult has not demonstrated that, in according the words of subsection (c)(1) their plain meaning, we do violence to subsection (c)(1) or the provisions that accompany it.

B.

Catapult next urges that legislative history requires disregard of the plain language of § 365(c)(1). First off, because we discern no ambiguity in the plain statutory language, we need not resort to legislative history.

We will depart from this rule, if at all, only where the legislative history clearly indicates that Congress meant something other than what it said. Here, the legislative history unearthed by Catapult falls far short of this mark. [T]here exists no contemporaneous legislative history regarding the current formulation of subsection (c)(1). Catapult, however, argues that the language as ultimately enacted in 1984 had its genesis in a 1980 House amendment to an earlier Senate technical corrections bill. The amendment was accompanied by "a relatively obscure committee report." In explaining the amendment, the report stated:

> This amendment makes it clear that the prohibition against a trustee's power to assume an executory contract does not apply where it is the debtor that is in possession and the performance to be given or received under a personal service contract will be the same as if no petition had been filed because of the personal service nature of the contract.

However, since the report relates to a different proposed bill, predates enactment of § 365(c)(1) by several years, and expresses at most the thoughts of only one committee in the House, we are not inclined to view it as the sort of clear indication of contrary intent that would overcome the unambiguous language of subsection (c)(1).

C.

Catapult makes the appealing argument that, as a leading bankruptcy commentator has pointed out, there are policy reasons to prefer the "actual test." That may be so, but Congress is the policy maker, not the courts.

Policy arguments cannot displace the plain language of the statute; that the plain language of § 365(c)(1) may be bad policy does not justify a judicial rewrite. And a rewrite is precisely what the actual test requires. The statute expressly provides that a debtor in possession "may not assume or assign" an executory contract where applicable law bars assignment and the nondebtor objects. The actual test effectively engrafts a narrow exception onto § 365(c)(1) for debtors in possession, providing that, as to them, the statute only prohibits assumption and assignment, as opposed to assumption or assignment.

V.

Because the statute speaks clearly, and plain language does not produce a patently absurd result or contravene any clear legislative history, we must "hold Congress to its words." Accordingly, we hold that, where applicable nonbankruptcy law makes an executory contract nonassignable because the identity of the nondebtor party is material, a debtor in possession may not assume the contract absent consent of the nondebtor party. A straightforward application of § 365(c)(1) to the circumstances of this case precludes Catapult from assuming the Perlman licenses over Perlman's objection. Consequently, the bankruptcy court erred when it approved Catapult's motion to assume the Perlman licenses, and the district court erred in affirming the bankruptcy court.

Notes & Questions

1. A great deal hinges on whether a specific intellectual property license is characterized as exclusive or nonexclusive. In general, nonexclusive licenses are deemed to be personal to the licensee and thus nonassignable. If they are non-assignable, then they will be nonassumable under section 365(a) when the licensee files for bankruptcy. *See In re CFLC, Inc.*, 89 F.3d 673 (9th Cir. 1996). The treatment of exclusive licenses is a little bit more uncertain. Exclusive copyright licenses are viewed as transfers of property rights and therefore are more likely to be assignable and thus assumable. *See In re Golden Books Family Entertainment, Inc.*, 269 B.R. 311 (Bankr. D. Del. 2001). But despite the statutory characterization of exclusive copyright licenses as transfers of property rights, one court has found that a specific exclusive license was not assignable. *See Gardner v. Nike*, 279 F.3d 774 (9th Cir. 2002). Exclusive patent and trademark licenses have in general been found to be non-assignable. *See In re Hernandez*, 285 B.R. 435 (Bankr. D. Ariz. 2002) (patent license); *Tap Publ'n, Inc. v. Chinese Yellow Pages (New York), Inc.*, 925 F. Supp. 212 (S.D.N.Y. 1996) (trademark license).

2. Much also rests on the drafting of the license. If the licensor is concerned about the assumption and assignment of the license by a debtor licensee, he can protect his interests through creative drafting. The licensor should make sure that the license will not be construed as a sale by avoiding conveyance and granting language as well as by imposing some continuing obligations upon himself. The licensor can also incorporate section 365(n)-like language into the license to protect himself in the event of the licensee's bankruptcy.

3. Can you think of one simple drafting trick that could have avoided the problem in *Institut Pasteur*? Note that the problem is that under the terms of the reorganization the debtor is owned by the licensor's competitor who owns a controlling

share of the debtor licensee. By assuming the license, the debtor licensee would be shifting effective control over the intellectual property to the licensor's competitor. Hence, the uproar. Of course, a similar problem could have occurred outside of bankruptcy if the competitor had acquired the licensee. In either case, the licensor could have protected himself by including a clause in the license that terminated the license in the event of a change in corporate control of the licensee.

4. There is currently a circuit split over the correct standard for determining when a nonexclusive licensee of intellectual property can assume a license in bankruptcy. The First Circuit adopts an "actual test," which looks to see if the debtor licensee will assign the assumed license in derogation of applicable law against assignments. The Third, Ninth, and Eleventh Circuits adopt a "hypothetical test," which looks to see if the debtor licensee could, upon assumption, assign the license in derogation of applicable law against assignments. How would *Catapult,* the Ninth Circuit case, have come out under the actual test? How would *Institut Pasteur*, the First Circuit case, have come out under the hypothetical test? Is there a substantive difference between the two tests?

5. One difference between these tests is that the hypothetical test tends toward a categorical rule that bases assumability on the nature of the license. In *Catapult*, the court denies assumption largely on the fact that the license was nonexclusive. The actual test tends to be more case-by-case and contextual and less rule-like. In *Institut Pasteur*, the court allows assumption of a nonexclusive license because there is no evidence that it would be assigned improperly. Despite its reliance on a test based on actual assignment, does the First Circuit ignore the business realities of allowing the assumption of an intellectual property license by an entity whose controlling shareholder is the licensor's competitor? The First Circuit's decision arguably rests on a formalistic notion of an assignment. On the other hand, a corporation is a distinct entity from its shareholders, and there is no actual assignment from CBC to bioMerieux. Do you think the hypothetical test would have treated the assumption by CBC when it was controlled by bioMerieux the same as an outright assignment from CBC to bioMerieux?

B. Termination Outside of Bankruptcy: Business Dissolutions and Joint Ventures

Hapgood v. Hewitt

Supreme Court of United States

119 U.S. 226 (1886)

BLATCHFORD, J.

[Hapgood & Co., a Missouri corporation,] was in existence from before August 1, 1873, to January 1, 1880, when it was dissolved. At the latter date the three trustees constituted its board of directors, and [Charles H.] Hapgood was president. By virtue of the laws of Missouri, Hapgood and the other two persons became trustees of the corporation, with power to settle its affairs, and recover the debts and property belonging to it. Hapgood was the president of the corporation during its entire existence, and had the control and management of its business. All the officers and employees were under his direction. He had power to hire and discharge all agents and employees of every grade, to determine the classes and kinds of goods that should be manufactured, and the general way in which the business should be conducted. The corporation employed a large number of manual laborers, and various employees of higher grades, among them a superintendent, a secretary, a foreman, and a traveling salesman, all of whom had charge of different departments, but were under the control and direction of the president, as chief executive officer. The duties of the superintendent were to having general charge of the manufacturing department, subject to the discretion of the president, and to devise and get up such new devices, arrangements, and improvements in the plows manufactured as should adapt them to the market, and as should be needed, from time to time, to suit the wants of customers.

Shortly before August 1, 1873, Hewitt represented to the corporation that he was a man of large experience in mechanical pursuits; that he had been for several years immediately preceding engaged with Avery & Sons, plow manufacturers in Louisville, and had been since 1868 familiar with the manufacturing of plows and agricultural implements; that he had been instrumental in devising and getting up the best plows manufactured by Avery & Sons; that the most valuable improvements in the plows manufactured by them had been devised by him, and adopted at his suggestion and instigation; that since 1869 he had given his undivided attention to the manufacture of plows, and understood thoroughly the different kinds of plows in the market, and the classes of plows needed for the trade; and that he could and would give to any manufacturer who should secure his services the benefit of his experience in devising and making improvements in the plows manufactured. In consequence of these representations, and relying upon them, the corporation employed Hewitt to devote his time and services to getting up, improving, and perfecting plows and other goods, and to introducing the same; and, that he might be more fully identified with the corporation, he purchased one share of its stock, and was elected vice-president. At some time in 1874, Hewitt increased his interest in the company by purchasing one-half of the shares owned by the president. As a part of the same transaction, it was agreed between Hewitt and the corporation that from that date Hewitt should fill the position of superintendent of the manufacturing department, and, as such, not only exercise a general supervision over that department, subject to the president, but also devote his time and services to devising improvements in, and getting up and perfecting, plows adapted to the general trade of the corporation. He accepted the position, and held it until the fall of 1877, when his connection with the corporation ceased.

He agreed, in such new position, to use his best efforts, and devote his knowledge and skill, in devising and making improvements in the plows manufactured by the corporation, and in getting up and perfecting plows and other agricultural imple-ments adapted to its trade. In view of the expected value of his services in this latter direction, the corporation was induced to pay him, and did pay him, a salary of $3,000 a year. It was manufacturing a plow known as a sulky or riding plow, so arranged that the plow was carried on a frame supported by wheels, and that the driver of the horses rode on the frame. Down to the year 1876 this sulky plow had a wooden frame. During that year it was thought desirable by the officers of the corporation that a change should be made by the substitution of an iron frame for the wooden one. The officers, including Hewitt, had frequent conversations during the winter of 1875–76 with reference to such change. In those conversations, and in personal conversa-tions with Hewitt, the president stated that he was anxious to retain in the iron sulky all the essential features of the wooden sulky, so far as was consistent with the use of an iron frame, and suggested other features which he thought it important to adopt in the new plow, and Black, a salesman, urged the importance of having an iron axle of an arched form.

As the result of these conversations and deliberations, Hewitt was, early in the summer of 1876, directed by the president to proceed at once to devise and build an iron sulky plow according to the suggestions so made; that is, that he should retain in the new plough all the valuable features of the wooden sulky which the corpora-tion had been manufacturing, should construct the plow of wrought and malleable iron, should adopt the other features suggested by the president and the arch sug-gested by Black, and should add such additional features as might seem advanta-geous to him (Hewitt). He was directed to proceed with the work without delay, so that the corporation might be ready to manufacture the new plow for the season of 1877. In accordance with those directions, Hewitt devised and constructed a sulky plow, in wrought and malleable iron, and, after some delays, about the first of April, 1877, produced a plow satisfactory to the president. During all the time that he was engaged in devising and constructing the new plow he was in the employ of the cor-poration, and drawing a salary of $3,000 a year. The time during which he was so engaged was the regular working hours in the factory. The men who did the manual labor on the new plow were all employees of and paid by the corporation, and all the materials used in its construction were bought and paid for by the corporation. The work, as it progressed, was under the general superintendence of Hewitt, but the work in the respective departments was also under the special superintendence of the respective foremen of those departments, who were also paid by the corpora-tion. During the whole time of the construction of the plow it was understood by all the parties engaged therein, and by those at whose instance its construction was commenced, that it was being devised and constructed for the use and benefit of the corporation, and as a model for the future construction of sulky plows by it.

After the plow was completed, and been accepted by the president as satisfactory, the latter directed Hewitt to go to Chicago and have the necessary malleable cast-ings made for the construction of plows after the model. Hewitt did so, obtaining at Chicago castings, moulds, and other things necessary for the future building of plows after the model. During the time so spent he was drawing his regular salary; and all his expenses, as well as the price of the models, castings, and other things obtained by him, were paid by the corporation During the time Hewitt remained in its employ he never made any claim of property in any of the devices and improvements made or suggested by him in the new plow, and never stated or claimed that he was entitled to a patent on any of said improvements, or that he had any rights adverse to the corporation in any of said improvements or devices; and never, during the term of his employment, asserted any right to a patent in his own name for such improvements or devices, or any of them. After his connection with the corporation had ceased, and after he had made an arrangement with the president, whereby the latter bought back all his (Hewitt's) stock in the corporation, and after the corporation had been for many months, with the knowledge of Hewitt, engaged in the manufacture of such plows, Hewitt, on January 14, 1878, applied for a patent on the improvements in the plow, and on the twenty-sixth of March, 1878, a patent was granted to him, covering certain parts of the plow; being devices which had been theretofore used by the corporation, with his knowledge and consent. After this patent was issued he, for the first time, claimed, as he has since claimed, that he had and has an exclusive right to manufacture such parts of the plow as are covered by the patent, and has threatened to enforce his rights under the patent, as against the corporation, its representatives, successors, and assigns, and to hold them liable in damages for any infringement of the same.

The bill also alleges that, in devising and constructing the plow, Hewitt was only performing his duty as an employee of the corporation, and carrying out his contract with it; that he was doing only what he was hired and paid to do; that the result of his labors belonged to the corporation; that it became, in equity and good conscience, the true and rightful owner of the right to manufacture the plow; that, if there is any part thereof which is patentable, the patent belonged to the corporation as equitable assignee of Hewitt and that he was and is bound, in equity and good conscience, to make an assignment of the patent to the corporation, or to its trustees.

The bill also alleges that, upon the dissolution of the corporation of Hapgood & Company, the stockholders thereof organized another corporation, under the laws of Illinois, under the name of the Hapgood Plow Company, one of the plaintiffs; that the Hapgood Plow Company succeeded to the business of the prior corporation, and became, by assignment from it, the owner of all the latter's assets, whether legal or equitable, including the rights in the patent, issued to Hewitt, which such prior corporation had, or was entitled to, whether legal or equitable, and its right to manufacture a sulky plow in accordance with the model plow made by Hewitt, including all the devices covered, or claimed to be covered, by the patent; and that all the rights in the premises which the prior corporation had, have been fully transferred to and vested in the new corporation. The bill then alleges a refusal by Hewitt to assign the patent to the plaintiffs, and that he claims to hold it adversely to them.

The prayer of the bill is for a decree directing the defendant to make an assignment of the patent, or of such interest as he may have therein, and of all his rights thereunder, to the Hapgood Plow Company, assignee of Hapgood & Company, or to the trustees of Hapgood & Company, in trust for the Hapgood Plow Company, vesting the title to the patent, or to the defendant's rights thereunder, in the Hapgood Plow Company, or in said trustees in trust for that corporation, and that he be enjoined and restrained from maintaining any action at law or in equity for any infringement of the patent by Hapgood & Company, or for the use by that corporation of any of the devices or improvements covered by the patent.

The decision of the circuit court was placed on the ground (1) that Hewitt was not expressly required, by his contract, to exercise his inventive faculties for the benefit of his employer, and there was nothing in the bill from which it could be fairly inferred that he was required or expected to do so; (2) that whatever right the employer had to the invention by the terms of Hewitt's contract of employment was a naked license to make and sell the patented improvement as a part of its business, which right, if it existed, was a mere personal one, and not transferable, and was extinguished with the dissolution of the corporation.

We are of opinion that the views taken of the case by the circuit court were correct. There is nothing set forth in the bill as to any agreement between the corporation and Hewitt that the former was to have the title to his inventions, or to any patent that he might obtain for them. The utmost that can be made out of the allegations is that the corporation was to have a license or right to use the inventions in making plows. It is not averred that anything passed between the parties as to a patent. We are not referred to any case which sustains the view that, on such facts as are alleged in the bill, the title to the invention, or to a patent for it, passed. . . .

Whatever license resulted to the Missouri corporation, from the facts of the case, to use the invention, was one confined to that corporation, and not assignable by it. . . . The Missouri corporation was dissolved. Its stockholders organized a new corporation under the laws of Illinois, which may naturally have succeeded to the business of the prior corporation; but the express averment of the bill is that it took, by assignment, the rights it claims in this suit. Those rights, so far as any title to the invention or patent is concerned, never existed in the assignor. As to any implied license to the assignor, it could not pass to the assignee.

As to so much of the prayer of the bill as asks that Hewitt be enjoined from maintaining any action at law or in equity for any alleged infringement of the patent by the prior corporation, or for its use of any of the devices or improvements covered by the patent, which is all there is left of the prayer of the bill, any suit to be brought would not be a suit against the corporation, for it is dissolved; and could not be a suit in equity against its trustees, for they are not alleged to be using the invention. It could only be a suit at law against the trustees or the stockholders of the old corporation for infringement by it while it existed. The theory of the bill is that there is a perfect defense to such a suit. In such a case a court of equity, certainly a circuit court of the United States, will not interfere to enjoin even a pending suit at law, much less the bringing of one in the future.

Decree affirmed.

Pav-Savr Corp. v. Vasso Corp.

Appellate Court of Illinois for the Third District

493 N.E. 2d 423 (Ill. App. Ct. 1986)

JUSTICE BARRY DELIVERED THE OPINION OF THE COURT.

The matter before us arises out of the dissolution of the parties' partnership, the Pav-Saver Manufacturing Company. The facts are not in dispute, and only those needed to explain our disposition on the issues on appeal will be stated.

Plaintiff, Pav-Saver Corporation ("PSC") is the owner of the Pav-Saver trademark and certain patents for the design and marketing of concrete paving machines. Harry Dale is the inventor of the Pav-Saver "slip-form" paver and the majority shareholder of PSC, located in Moline, Illinois. H. Moss Meersman is an attorney who is also the owner and sole shareholder of Vasso Corporation. In 1974 Dale, individually, together with PSC and Meersman formed Pav-Saver Manufacturing Company for the manufacture and sale of Pav-Saver machines. Dale agreed to contribute his services, PSC contributed the patents and trademark necessary to the proposed operation, and Meersman agreed to obtain financing for it. The partnership agreement was drafted by Meersman and approved by Attorney Charles Peart, president of PSC. The agreement contained two paragraphs which lie at the heart of the appeal and cross-appeal before us:

"3. The duties, obligations and functions of the respective partners shall be:

A. Meersman shall provide whatever financing is necessary for the joint venture, as required.

B. (1) PAV-SAVER shall grant to the partnership without charge the exclusive right to use on all machines manufactured and sold, its trade mark 'PAV-SAVER' during the term of this Agreement. In order to preserve and maintain the good will and other values of the trademark PAV-SAVER, it is agreed between the parties that PAV-SAVER Corporation shall have the right to inspect from time to time the quality of machines upon which the licensed trademark PAV-SAVER is used or applied on machines for laying concrete pavement where such machines are manufactured and/or sold. Any significant changes in structure, materials or components shall be disclosed in writing or by drawings to PAV-SAVER Corporation.

(2) PAV-SAVER grants to the partnership exclusive license without charge for its patent rights in and to its Patent # 3,377,933 for the term of this agreement and exclusive license to use its specifications and drawings for the Slip-form paving machine known as Model MX 6-33, plus any specifications and drawings for any extensions, additions and attachments for said machine

for said term. It being understood and agreed that same shall remain the property of PAV-SAVER and all copies shall be returned to PAV-SAVER at the expiration of this partnership. Further, PAV-SAVER, so long as this agreement is honored and is in force, grants a license under any patents of PAV-SAVER granted in the United States and/or other countries applicable to the Slip-Form paving machine.

. . . .

11. It is contemplated that this joint venture partnership shall be permanent, and same shall not be terminated or dissolved by either party except upon mutual approval of both parties. If, however, either party shall terminate or dissolve said relationship, the terminating party shall pay to the other party, as liquidated damages, a sum equal to four (4) times the gross royalties received by PAV-SAVER Corporation in the fiscal year ending July 31, 1973, as shown by their corporate financial statement. Said liquidated damages to be paid over a ten (10) year period next immediately following the termination, payable in equal installments."

In 1976, upon mutual consent, the PSC/Dale/Meersman partnership was dissolved and replaced with an identical one between PSC and Vasso, so as to eliminate the individual partners.

It appears that the Pav-Saver Manufacturing Company operated and thrived according to the parties' expectations until around 1981, when the economy slumped, sales of the heavy machines dropped off significantly, and the principals could not agree on the direction that the partnership should take to survive. On March 17, 1983, Attorney Charles Peart, on behalf of PSC, wrote a letter to Meersman terminating the partnership and invoking the provisions of paragraph 11 of the parties' agreement.

In response, Meersman moved into an office on the business premises of the Pav-Saver Manufacturing Company, physically ousted Dale, and assumed a position as the day-to-day manager of the business. PSC then sued in the circuit court of Rock Island County for a court-ordered dissolution of the partnership, return of its patents and trademark, and an accounting. Vasso counterclaimed for declaratory judgment that PSC had wrongfully terminated the partnership and that Vasso was entitled to continue the partnership business, and other relief pursuant to the Illinois Uniform Partnership Act. Other related suits were filed, but need not be described as they are not relevant to the matters before us. After protracted litigation, the trial court ruled that PSC had wrongfully terminated the partnership; that Vasso was entitled to continue the partnership business and to possess the partnership assets, including PSC's trademark and patents; that PSC's interest in the partnership was $165,000, based on a $330,000 valuation for the business; and that Vasso was entitled to liquidated damages in the amount of $384,612, payable pursuant to paragraph 11 of the partnership agreement. Judgment was entered accordingly.

Both parties appealed. PSC takes issue with the trial court's failure to order the return of its patents and trademark or, in the alternative, to assign a value to them in determining the value of the partnership assets. Further, neither party agrees with the trial court's enforcement of their agreement for liquidated damages. In its cross-appeal, PSC argues that the amount determined by the formula in paragraph 11 is a penalty. Vasso, on the other hand, contends in its appeal that the amount is unobjectionable, but the installment method of pay-out should not be enforced.

In addition to the afore-cited paragraphs of the parties' partnership agreement, the resolution of this case is controlled by the dissolution provision of the Uniform Partnership Act. The Act provides:

"(2). When dissolution is caused in contravention of the partnership agreement the rights of the partners shall be as follows:

(a) Each partner who has not caused dissolution wrongfully shall have

. . . .

II. The right, as against each partner who has caused the dissolution wrongfully, to damage for breach of the agreement.

(b) The partners who have not caused the dissolution wrongfully, if they all desire to continue the business in the same name, either by themselves or jointly with others, may do so, during the agreed term for the partnership and for that purpose may possess the partnership property, provided they secure the payment by bond approved by the court, or pay to any partner who has caused the dissolution wrongfully, the value of his interest in the partnership at the dissolution, less any damages recoverable under clause (2a II) of this section, and in like manner indemnify him against all present or future partnership liabilities.

(c) A partner who has caused the dissolution wrongfully shall have:

. . . .

II. If the business is continued under paragraph (2b) of this section the right as against his co-partners and all claiming through them in respect of their interests in the partnership, to have the value of his interest in the partnership, less any damages caused to his co-partners by the dissolution, ascertained and paid to him in cash, or the payment secured by bond approved by the court and to be released from all existing liabilities of the partnership; but in ascertaining the value of the partner's interest the value of the good will of the business shall not be considered."

Initially we must reject PSC's argument that the trial court erred in refusing to return Pav-Saver's patents and trademark pursuant to paragraph 3 of the partnership agreement, or in the alternative that the court erred in refusing to assign a value to PSC's property in valuing the partnership assets. The partnership agreement on its face contemplated a "permanent" partnership, terminable only upon mutual approval of the parties. It is undisputed that PSC's unilateral termination was in contravention of the agreement. The wrongful termination necessarily invokes the provisions of the Uniform Partnership Act so far as they concern the rights of the partners. Upon PSC's notice terminating the partnership, Vasso elected to continue the business pursuant to section 38(2)(b) of the Uniform Partnership Act. As correctly noted by Vasso, the statute was enacted "to cover comprehensively the problem of dissolution . . . [and] to stabilize business." Ergo, despite the parties contractual direction that PSC's patents would be returned to it upon the mutually approved expiration of the partnership, the right to possess the partnership property and continue in business upon a wrongful termination must be derived from and is controlled by the statute. Evidence at trial clearly established that the Pav-Saver machines being manufactured by the partnership could not be produced or marketed without PSC's patents and trademark. Thus, to continue in business pursuant to the statutorily-granted right of the party not causing the wrongful dissolution, it is essential that paragraph 3 of the parties' agreement—the return to PSC of its patents—not be honored.

Similarly, we find no merit in PSC's argument that the trial court erred in not assigning a value to the patents and trademark. The only evidence adduced at trial to show value of this property was testimony relating to good will. It was unrefuted that the name Pav-Saver enjoys a good reputation for a good product and reliable service. However, inasmuch as the Uniform Partnership Act specifically states that "the value of the good will of the business shall not be considered," we find that the trial court properly rejected PSC's good will evidence of the value of its patents and trademark in valuing its interest in the partnership business.

Next, we find no support for PSC's argument that the amount of liquidated damages awarded to Vasso pursuant to the formula contained in paragraph 11 of the parties' agreement is a "penalty." The test for determining whether a liquidated damages clause is valid as such or void as a penalty is stated in Section 356 of the Restatement (Second) of Contracts:

> "(1) Damages for breach by either party may be liquidated in the agreement but only at an amount that is reasonable in the light of the anticipated or actual loss caused by the breach and the difficulties of proof of loss. A term fixing unreasonably large liquidated damages is unenforceable on grounds of public policy as a penalty."

The burden of proving that a liquidated damages clause is void as a penalty rests with the party resisting its enforcement.

PSC has not and does not argue that the amount of liquidated damages was unreasonable. (Significantly, neither party purported to establish that actual damages suffered by Vasso were either more or less than $384,612.) PSC now urges, however, that "[t]he ascertainment of the value of the Pav Saver partnership for purposes of an accounting are [sic] easily ascertained. The accountants maintain detailed records of accounts payable and receivable and all equipment." In advancing this argument, PSC misconstrues the two-part test of a penalty: 1) whether the amount fixed is reasonable in light of the anticipated or actual loss caused by the breach; and 2) the difficulty of proving a loss has occurred, or establishing its amount with reasonable certainty. The difficulty or ease of proof of loss is a matter to be determined at the time of contracting—not, as PSC suggests, at the time of the breach.

It appears clear from the record that Meersman, with some insecurity about his partner's long-term loyalty to the newly-formed partnership, insisted on a liquidated damages provision to protect his financial interests. Nonetheless the record discloses that the agreement was reviewed by Peart and not signed until it was acceptable to both parties. As of December 31, 1982, the date of its last financial statement prior to trial, Pav-Saver Manufacturing Company carried liability on notes owed to various banks amounting to $269,060. As of December 31, 1981, the loans outstanding amounted to $347,487. These loans, the record shows, were obtained primarily on the basis of Meersman's financial ability to repay and over his signature individually. The amount of liquidated damages computed according to the formula in the parties agreement—$384,612—does not appear to be greatly disproportionate to the amount of Meersman's personal financial liability. As earlier stated, the slip-form Pav-Saver machines could not be manufactured and marketed as such without the patents and trademark contributed by Pav-Saver Corporation. Likewise, the services of Dale were of considerable value to the business.

In sum, we find there is no evidence tending to prove that the amount of liquidated damages as determined by the formula was unreasonable. Nor can we say based on the evidence of record that actual damages (as distinguished from a mere accounting) were readily susceptible to proof at the time the parties entered into their agreement. Suffice it to say, the liquidated damages clause in the parties' agreement appears to have been a legitimate matter bargained for between parties on equal footing and enforceable upon an unilateral termination of the partnership. We will not disturb the trial court's award of damages to Vasso pursuant to the liquidated damages formula.

We turn next to Vasso's arguments urging reversal of the trial court's decision to enforce paragraph 11 of the parties' agreement with respect to the manner of paying out the amount of damages determined by the formula. The paragraph provides for the liquidated sum to be paid out in equal installments over a 10-year period. The trial court held that the $384,612 owed by PSC should be paid in 120 monthly installments of $3205.10 each commencing with March 17, 1983. In support of its argument that it was entitled to a set-off of the full amount of liquidated damages, including the unaccrued balance, Vasso argues that the doctrine of equitable set-off should apply on these facts and further urges that such set-off is required by statute.

In considering whether the liquidated damages formula contained in paragraph 11 of the partnership agreement was enforceable, we necessarily scrutinized the totality of the agreement—not merely the dollar figure so determined. Certainly at first blush the formula appears to yield a suspiciously high amount that is not directly related to any anticipated damages that either party might incur upon a wrongful termination of the agreement by the other. The manner of pay-out however—equal installments over a 10-year period—appears to temper the effect that the amount of liquidated damages so determined would have on the party who breached the agreement. In our opinion, the validity of the clause is greatly influenced by the pay-out provision. What might have been a penalty appears to be a fairly bargained-for, judicially enforceable liquidated damages provision. While, in hindsight, Vasso may sense the same insecurity in enforcement of the paragraph in toto that Meersman had hoped to avoid by insisting on the provision in 1974 and 1976, Vasso's concerns of PSC's potential insolvency are neither concrete nor sufficiently persuasive to entitle it to a right of set-off.

The primary authority cited in support of Vasso's equitable set-off argument (*North Chicago Rolling Mill Co. v. St. Louis Ore & Steel Co.*, 152 U.S. 596, 14 S. Ct. 710, 38 L. Ed. 565 (1894)) is inapposite. There, the debtor was insolvent. In this case, PSC has been shown to have relatively little in operating finances, but has not been proved incapable of paying its creditors. Were PSC obliged to pay out the full amount of liquidated damages at this point, PSC's insolvency would be a certainty. However, PSC's assets and financial condition were known to Vasso at the time the parties agreed to become partners. Vasso cannot contend that its partner's potential insolvency in the event of a wrongful termination by it was unforeseeable at the time of contracting. We do not find that the equities so clearly favor Vasso as to require application of the doctrine of equitable set-off in disregard of the parties' agreement for installment payments.

Further, our reading of section 38(2) of the Uniform Partnership Act fails to persuade us that the statute requires a set-off of the liquidated damages. That section permits the partner causing the dissolution (PSC) to have the value of its interest in the partnership, less "any damages recoverable [by Vasso]" (sub-paragraph (b)) or "any damages caused [by PSC]" (sub-paragraph (c)), paid in cash. It does not require a cash set-off, however, in the unusual event (this case) wherein damages exceed the value of the terminating partner's interest.

Where, as here, a valid liquidated damages clause is enforceable, that clause may be implied into the statute to the extent that it does not violate the legislative intent of the Act. We do not believe that the legislative purpose of stabilizing business (Kurtzon) is frustrated by limiting Vasso's statutory set-off to past accrued damages and enforcing the pay-out terms of the parties' agreement. Under the circumstances, we perceive of no compelling grounds, legal or equitable, for ignoring or rewriting paragraph 11 of the parties' agreement. Therefore, all statutory references to "damages" recoverable by Vasso are supplanted by the parties' agreement for liquidated damages. As the trial court properly ruled, enforcement of the agreement results in a judgment for PSC in the amount of its share of the value of the partnership assets ($165,000) set off by past due installments of liquidated damages accrued from the date of the partnership's termination (March 17, 1983), and an ongoing obligation to pay out the balance monthly during the 10- year period which would end in March of 1993.

For the foregoing reasons, we affirm the judgment of the circuit court of Rock Island County.

Affirmed.

Justice STOUDER concurring in part—dissenting in part.

I generally agree with the result of the majority. I cannot, however, accept the majority's conclusion the defendant is entitled to retention of the patents.

The Uniform Partnership Act is the result of an attempt to codify and make uniform the common law. Partners must act pursuant to the provisions of the Act which apply when partners have not agreed how they will organize and govern their ventures. These UPA provisions are best viewed as "default" standards because they apply in the absence of contrary agreements. The scope of the Act is to be determined by its provisions and is not to be construed to extend beyond its own proper boundaries. When the partnership contract contains provisions, imposing on one or more of the partners obligations differing from those which the law ordinarily infers from the partnership relation, the courts should strive to construe these provisions so as to give effect to the honest intentions of the partners as shown by the language of the contract and their conduct under it.

The plaintiff (PSC) brought this action at law seeking dissolution of the partnership before expiration of the agreed term of its existence. Under the Uniform Partnership Act where dissolution is caused by an act in violation of the partnership agreement, the other partner(s) are accorded certain rights. The partnership agreement is a contract, and even though a partner may have the power to dissolve, he does not necessarily have the right to do so. Therefore, if the dissolution he causes is a violation of the agreement, he is liable for any damages sustained by the innocent partner(s) as a result thereof. The innocent partner(s) also have the option to continue the business in the firm name provided they pay the partner causing the dissolution the value of his interest in the partnership.

The duties and obligations of partners arising from a partnership relation are regulated by the express contract as far as they are covered thereby. A written agreement is not necessary but where it does exist it constitutes the measure of the partners' rights and obligations. While the rights and duties of the partners in relation to the partnership are governed by the Uniform Partnership Act, the uniform act also provides that such rules are subject to any agreement between the parties. It is where the express contract does not cover the situation or question which arises that they are determined under the applicable law, The Uniform Partnership Act.

The partnership agreement entered into by PSC and Vasso in pertinent part provides:

> "3.B.(2) [PSC] grants to the partnership exclusive license without charge for its patent rights . . . for the term of this agreement. . . . [I]t being understood and agreed that same shall remain the property of [PSC] . . . and shall be returned to [PSC] at the expiration of this partnership. . . ."

The majority holds this provision in the contract is unenforceable. The only apparent reason for such holding is that its enforcement would affect defendant's option to continue the business. No authority is cited to support such a rule.

The partnership agreement further provides:

"11. . . . If either party shall terminate or dissolve said [partnership], the terminating party shall pay to the other party as liquidated damages . . . [$384,612]."

This provision becomes operative at the same time as the provision relating to the return of the patents.

Partnership agreements are governed by the same general rules of construction as are other written agreements. If their provisions are explicit and unambiguous and do not violate the duty of good faith which each partner owed his co-partners, the courts should carry out the intention of the parties. The Uniform Partnership Act should not be construed to invalidate an otherwise enforceable partnership agreement entered into for a legitimate purpose.

Here, express terms of the partnership agreement deal with the status of the patents and measure of damages, the question is settled thereby. I think it clear the parties agreed the partnership only be allowed the use of the patents during the term of the agreement. The agreement having been terminated, the right to use the patents is terminated. The provisions in the contract do not conflict with the statutory option to continue the business and even if there were a conflict the provisions of the contract should prevail. The option to continue the business does not carry with it any guarantee or assurance of success and it may often well be that liquidation rather than continuation would be the better option for a partner not at fault.

As additional support for my conclusion, it appears the liquidated damages clause was insisted upon by the defendant because of earlier conduct of the plaintiff withdrawing from a former partnership. Thus, the existence of the liquidated damages clause recognizes the right of plaintiff to withdraw the use of his patents in accordance with the specific terms of the partnership agreement. Since liquidated damages depends on return of the patents, I would vacate that part of the judgment providing defendant is entitled to continue use of the patents and provide that use shall remain with plaintiff.

Southwest Whey Inc. v. Nutrition 101, Inc.

United States District Court for the Central District of Illinois

117 F. Supp. 2d 770 (C.D. Ill. 2000)

RICHARD MILLS, DISTRICT JUDGE.

If you do not want another to tell your secrets, you must not tell them yourself.

Seneca: Phaedra

I. BACKGROUND

On May 10, 1989, Plaintiff Southwest Whey, Inc., ("Southwest Whey") and Defendant Nutrition 101, Inc., ("Nutrition 101") entered into a written agreement to operate a joint venture. Southwest Whey agreed to obtain whey from dairies and Nutrition

101 agreed to market whey to hog farmers in the region east of the Mississippi River and in other areas by mutual agreement. The joint venture was dissolved by Southwest Whey on September 16, 1993.

For most of the 1980's, Southwest Whey's business largely consisted of obtaining and selling whey west of the Mississippi River. Jack Muse ("Muse"), Southwest Whey's president, wanted to expand the business geographically. However, his efforts to obtain contracts with dairies or pork producers east of the Mississippi prior to the commencement of the joint venture produced little, if any, success.

Nutrition 101 was owned and operated by Ross Peter ("Peter"). Nutrition 101 primarily sold feed to pork producers. Peter was experienced in marketing feed to farmers and had an extensive customer base of pork producers. Peter and Muse began discussions which led to the formation of the joint venture on May 13, 1989. A written agreement was included "to guide the joint venture." Southwest Whey "agreed to procure whey from dairies and Nutrition 101 agreed to market whey to hog farmers in the region east of the Mississippi River." The agreement did not specifically include a non-compete restrictive covenant to govern the parties' actions or competition following dissolution.

Neither Southwest Whey nor Nutrition 101 had a written compilation of claimed trade secrets prior to or during the joint venture. The farmer and dairy contracts used by the parties did not contain any confidentiality or non-disclosure provisions. Moreover, Southwest Whey did not impose any confidentiality restrictions upon the dairies to prevent the disclosure of information learned by them from the joint venture regarding the sale, storage, transfer, or delivery of whey. Similarly, no confidentiality restrictions were imposed upon the truck drivers who transported the whey regarding any knowledge they had or may acquire because of their dealings with the joint venture.

By late 1992, a conflict had arisen between the partners to the joint venture. Southwest Whey suggested to Nutrition 101 that the parties consider shutting down the business. In January 1993, the parties met to discuss a proposed buy-sell agreement to wind up the joint venture. Nutrition 101's proposal was not acceptable to Southwest Whey. Southwest Whey's proposal included a restrictive covenant preventing Nutrition 101 from competing with them for ten years. This proposal was rejected by Nutrition 101. The parties were unable to agree to any of the proposals.

By the summer of 1993, Muse began to inform dairies of his plan to end Nutrition 101's interest in the joint venture. Muse visited farmers who purchased whey from the joint venture in St. Louis, Missouri, during the first week of September of 1993. He inquired as to whether farmers would continue to purchase whey at the same terms and prices if the joint venture ended and Southwest Whey ended up with the business. Muse indicated that each farmer agreed that they would continue to purchase from Southwest Whey.

On September 16, 1993, Southwest Whey informed Nutrition 101 that it had decided to cease operations as a joint venture, and that Nutrition 101 would no longer have access to whey from dairies under contract with the joint venture. One month later, Southwest Whey notified the customers of the dispute and solicited their continued business. Southwest Whey had no written contracts with pork producers who had no obligation to continue to take whey and could at any time "come and go."

This case was originally filed on September 11, 1998. On March 31, 2000, Southwest Whey filed its eight-count amended complaint against Nutrition 101, alleging (I) Breach of Contract; (II) Interference with Prospective Advantage; (III) Violation of Illinois Trade Secrets Act ("ITSA"); (IV) Violation of Illinois Trade Secrets Act—Exemplary Damages; (V) Conversion; (VI) Breach of Fiduciary Duty; (VII) Breach of Fiduciary Duty—Exemplary Damages; and (VIII) Breach of Good Faith and Fair Dealing.

Nutrition 101 has moved for summary judgment on [Counts II, III, IV, and VIII].

IV. Trade Secrets (Counts III and IV)

Southwest Whey alleges that it has developed and used certain trade secrets in connection with the marketing and distribution of whey as a hog feed element. Following the dissolution of the joint venture, Southwest Whey alleges that Nutrition 101's efforts in connection with the marketing and distribution of whey as a hog feed element constitute the misappropriation of trade secrets of Southwest Whey in violation of ITSA. Nutrition 101 moves for summary judgment on Counts III and IV.

In Illinois, a trade secret is defined as:

> information, included but not limited to, technical or non-technical data, a formula, pattern, compilation, program, device, method, technique, drawing, process, financial data, or list of actual or potential customers or suppliers, that:
>
> (1) is sufficiently secret to derive economic value, actual or potential, from not being generally known to other persons who can obtain economic value from its disclosure or use; and
>
> (2) is the subject of efforts that are reasonable under the circumstances to maintain its secrecy or confidentiality.

In order to establish improper use of trade secrets, there must be a showing that the information at issue was (1) secret (not generally known in the industry); (2) misappropriated; and (3) used in the appropriator's business.

Southwest Whey essentially alleges that it brought several methods, techniques, and practices into the joint venture which are the basis of its trade secrets claim. Specifically, in an answer to an interrogatory, Southwest Whey identified the following thirty-one methods, techniques, and practices which constitute trade secrets in connection with the marketing and distribution of whey as a hog feed element: (1) Contract language with farmers; (2) Contract language with dairies; (3) Allowable distance for hauling whey from dairy to farmer for freshness; (4) Allowable distance for hauling whey from dairy to farmer for profit; (5) Techniques for hook ups at dairies; (6) Tank cleaning techniques; (7) Tank configurations, including the pumping equipment and appurtenances; (8) Pricing strategies; (9) How to prevent the whey from destroying concrete; (10) Knowledge of feed characteristics of whey; (11) Knowledge of whey sources generally; (12) Knowledge that farmers would pay for whey; (13) Routes from dairies to the farmers; (14) Customer lists; (15) Vendor lists; (16) Techniques for identifying suppliers and customers; (17) Marketing methods for farmers; (18) Marketing methods for dairies; (19) How to mix and/or dilute whey to make it an effective supplemental feed source; (20) Studies on the nutritional value of whey; (21) Handling plants and managers to minimize inconvenience with truckers; (22) Siting of loading operations; (23) Use tracking at farms to maximize sales and ensure continued customer care; (24) Confinement and location techniques and procedures for use at farms; (25) Development of on-farm delivery system; (26) Use of cone bottom tanks; (27) Recirculation techniques and the need for them; (28) Tank agitation techniques; (29) Screening techniques; (30) Gauge for tank management; and (31) Use of elevator buckets and other products for delivery of whey at farms.

Southwest Whey asserts that it attempted to protect the thirty-one "trade secrets" by not giving them to anyone in their entirety other than Nutrition 101. Thus, they contend that even if some or most of the thirty-one enumerated elements do not constitute trade secrets, "the whole package put together" is a trade secret. Specifically, the various elements combine to form the "overall trade secret" which Southwest Whey has acquired after years of trial and error that has come at great expense.

The Court first notes that a "trade secret" "may include a compilation of confidential business and financial information." The key inquiry in ascertaining whether information is a trade secret under the ITSA is on the secrecy of the information sought to be protected. Specifically, courts look at how easily information can be duplicated without involving substantial time, effort, or expense. Factors in determining whether information constitutes a trade secret include the following: (1) The extent to which the information is known outside the business; (2) The extent to which it is known by others involved in the business; (3) The extent that measures have been taken to guard the secrecy of the information; (4) The value of the information to the party and his competitors; (5) The amount of money or effort expended by the party in developing the information; and (6) The ease or difficulty with which the information at question could be obtained or duplicated by others.

The Court notes that the statutory protection afforded trade secrets reflects the balancing of social and economic interests. An individual who has put forth the time, money, and effort to obtain a secret advantage should be protected from a party who obtains the secret through improper means. Nevertheless, in a competitive market, a party is entitled to utilize the general knowledge and skills acquired through experience in pursuing his chosen occupation.

Moreover, merely being the first or only one to use certain information does not alone turn what is otherwise general knowledge into a trade secret. Otherwise, no matter how ordinary or well known the information, the first person to use it would be able to obtain the protection of the statute. Additionally, "generalized confidential business information" does not constitute a protectable trade secret. Specifically, the mere legwork in acquiring this information cannot be the basis for a claim. Any other result would mean that a party who learns the basics of an industry from an individual would be precluded from entering the business at all in a competitive relationship. Such a result is contrary to a free market economy.

Southwest Whey basically asserts that it is the total process gained over the years that is the trade secret at issue in this case. Southwest Whey has alone on a large scale been able to transform this process into a workable, profitable enterprise. Southwest Whey contends that it has taken sufficient measures to protect its trade secrets. Specifically, although certain aspects of the process were revealed to the dairies, truckers, farmers or supply vendors, only that which was necessary for the process to function was revealed at any time. Muse indicated that only Southwest Whey and Nutrition 101 knew the entire process of marketing and delivering whey. Therefore, the trade secret in the "whole package" was protected.

Moreover, the record reveals that Nutrition 101 is Southwest Whey's only competitor on a major scale in the procurement and selling of whey. There have been, however, a few individual truckers or farmers in the same geographical area engaging in this process on a much smaller scale. These instances are basically limited to the occasional farmer or trucker who hauls whey for the price of freight alone on nothing more than an individual dairy basis. No other entity in the area has engaged in the procurement and selling of whey on such a large scale.

One of the factors in determining whether information constitutes a trade secret involves an analysis of the measures taken to protect the secrecy of the information. Southwest Whey asserts that it never revealed the entire process to any individual or group. Rather, the dairies, farmers, truckers, and supply vendors would learn only that which was needed to fulfill their duties. Thus, although the different segments would learn parts of the overall process, only Nutrition 101 was told everything regarding Southwest Whey's enterprise. However, none of the contracts with the other segments contained confidentiality or non-disclosure clauses.

The parties in the instant action dispute whether there was a non-compete clause between them. Paragraph (13) of the Joint Venture agreement reads "101 personnel to sign agreement not to pass information or data to noninvolved parties or be involved in any aspect of whey marketing other than as representatives of 101." Southwest Whey contends that this language constitutes a non-compete clause. Nutrition 101 alleges that this language merely means that if an employee were to leave Nutrition 101, he could not use this information further. This provision only involved Nutrition 101 because only they had employees. Moreover, Nutrition 101 contends that the fact that the parties discussed a possible restrictive covenant when they discussed the buy/sell arrangement of the joint venture is evidence that there was not a non-compete clause in the original agreement.

Southwest Whey also alleges that when the agreement was made, the parties contemplated that no termination would occur. "It's either for life or we won't do it." Therefore, the agreement contains no provision detailing what Nutrition 101 could do following a termination. Nutrition 101 contends that because the agreement does not provide for a dissolution date or event, it could be terminated by either party at any date. Moreover, it was Southwest Whey who eventually terminated the agreement.

The Court will now address whether each of the statutory prongs is met.

(A) Sufficiently Secret to Derive Economic Value

Pursuant to the statute, the Court must determine first whether the information sought to be protected as a trade secret is sufficiently secret to derive economic value from not being generally known. Certainly, the affidavit and deposition testimony of Jack Muse is important to this inquiry. Muse indicated that Southwest Whey alone was engaged in the business on a major scale. Moreover, they were the first to engage in the process of successfully marketing and delivering whey on such a scale. These facts indicate that Southwest Whey was engaged in a profitable enterprise. However, the fact that a party was the first or only entity to utilize certain information does not turn what is otherwise general information into a trade secret. As Nutrition 101 contends, some of the individual "secrets" that make up the whole package do seem to constitute general information that can be readily ascertained. For example, the individual secrets that relate to Southwest Whey's knowledge of whey characteristics could be construed as general knowledge that has long been available to the public.

Moreover, Southwest Whey alleges that its process of hauling whey from a dairy to a farmer while maintaining the freshness and making a profit is also a trade secret. However, as Nutrition 101 notes, farmers had been doing this since before the joint venture began, albeit on a smaller scale. Southwest Whey contends that because this has only been done on a smaller scale, issues of freshness and profits are more applicable to their transportation of whey. The fact that these farmers did this on a smaller scale does not mean that issues of profits and freshness were not important. The farmers were no less trying to maintain the freshness and make a profit.

Moreover, some of what are alleged to constitute a portion of the trade secret appear to amount to nothing more than Muse's legwork in establishing his business. Mere legwork in identifying the basics of the industry cannot serve as the basis for a claim under the Act. Muse contends that one component of the overall trade secret is his pricing strategy. His basic strategy has been to charge $4 a ton margin over the cost of freight. This appears to be the result of Muse's legwork in identifying how much he could charge while still making a good profit within the industry. As Nutrition 101 contends, it cannot be true that anyone who employs a similar pricing strategy in seeking to make a profit on whey is violating a trade secret.

Nonetheless, Southwest Whey maintains that it is the "whole package" which constitutes a trade secret. The first prong of the statute requires the Court to assess whether the relevant information was sufficiently secret to derive economic value. At this stage, the Court must view the evidence in the light most favorable to Southwest Whey. It is undisputed that Southwest Whey's only competitor on a major scale is Nutrition 101. Although there may have been individual truckers or farmers engaged in the business on a much smaller scale, there were no other participants in the industry of the same magnitude as Southwest Whey. This is instructive in determining whether Southwest Whey's collection of information acquired over the years is sufficiently secret to derive economic value. It is true that some of the items that constitute a portion of the trade secret are not trade secrets. However, the fact that only Southwest Whey has engaged in the business at this level at least raises a material fact as to the first prong of the statute. Specifically, there is a material issue as to whether the entire package is sufficiently secret to derive economic value.

(B) Reasonable Efforts to Maintain Secrecy

The second prong involves the efforts of the owner to maintain the secrecy of the alleged trade secret. Nutrition 101 alleges that Southwest Whey has failed to take any affirmative measures to protect its trade secret.

The record reveals that no restrictive covenant was signed between the parties to the action. However, it is important to note that a restrictive covenant or confidentiality agreement is not a prerequisite to recovery under the ITSA. Nonetheless, some affirmative step must be taken to maintain the trade secret. Southwest Whey contends that the language in Paragraph 13 of the written agreement constitutes a restrictive covenant: "101 personnel to sign agreement not to pass information or data to noninvolved parties or to be involved in any aspect of whey marketing other than as representatives of 101." However, the Court finds that this language was included in the agreement to prevent employees of Nutrition 101 from entering the market on their own. The Court notes that the parties discussed the possibility of entering into a restrictive covenant when they discussed terminating the joint venture. This indicates that there was no restrictive covenant from the outset. Thus, the language in the agreement does not constitute a restrictive covenant.

Southwest Whey attempts to get around this by arguing that their agreement with Nutrition 101 was an agreement to do business forever. Muse indicated that he would not have entered into the agreement if it had an end to it. However, the written agreement between the parties does not specify a definite term or a particular undertaking. According to Illinois partnership law, "dissolution is caused . . . by the expressed will of any partner when no definite term or particular undertaking is specified." Therefore, Southwest Whey's argument that the partnership was an agreement to do business forever is without merit.

The record is clear that there was no written record of trade secrets at any time prior to or during the joint venture. Nonetheless, Southwest Whey alleges that Nutrition 101 would not have been exposed to their trade secrets and allowed into the partnership unless it was for life. However, because the partnership agreement did not specify a particular amount of time, it was subject to dissolution at any time. Therefore, the Court rejects Southwest Whey's contention that their means of protecting their trade secrets was to form a partnership for life.

Moreover, neither the farmer nor the dairy contracts used by the joint venture contained any confidentiality or non-disclosure provisions. Southwest Whey imposed no restrictions upon the dairies in their negotiation of contracts regarding the disclosure of information about the joint venture regarding the sale, storage, transfer, or delivery of whey. Similarly, no restrictions were placed on the truck drivers who hauled the whey regarding any knowledge they had or might acquire because of their relationship with the joint venture. In short, Southwest Whey did not insist on any non-disclosure clauses. This is true despite the fact that such clauses were not uncommon in the industry.

Southwest Whey responds by noting that Nutrition 101 was the only other entity which knew everything about the process of successfully marketing and delivering whey. Muse's approach was to keep the different segments of his business separate. Moreover, he did not tell his clients about his business or reveal its contract terms with the farmers to the dairies. Thus, although the various entities could learn bits and pieces, only Nutrition 101 was exposed to the whole process.

The Court is not persuaded that Southwest Whey used reasonable efforts to maintain the secrecy of its trade secrets. The record does not reveal any affirmative steps taken by Southwest Whey to protect its trade secrets.

Southwest Whey did not insist upon Nutrition 101 signing a restrictive covenant at any time before, during, or after the joint venture. Moreover, they did not require any of the truckers, farmers, dairies, or other parties to sign non-disclosure clauses. The argument that no specific entity other than Nutrition 101 was exposed to the entire process does not constitute a reasonable effort to maintain the secrecy. This merely means that Southwest Whey did not reveal all of the thirty-one enumerated secrets that make up the entire package except to Nutrition 101. However, some of the trade secrets deal specifically with a particular industry. The Court notes that it would only make sense that the secrets related to the dairy industry would only be revealed to those in the dairy industry, not in the farming industry. Thus, the twelve secrets that may be classified as involving the dairy industry were revealed only to those in the dairy industry. Nothing prevented those in the dairy industry from sharing these secrets. The fact that these dairy secrets may not have been revealed to those in the transportation industry is not a reasonable effort to maintain the secrecy. Similarly, Southwest Whey took no reasonable steps to prevent the truckers from revealing the secrets that pertain to the transportation industry. Nothing prevented these truckers from sharing the secrets. The fact that these secrets may not have been revealed to those in the dairy industry does not constitute a reasonable effort to maintain the secret.

Accordingly, even when viewing the evidence in the light most favorable to Southwest Whey, there is no genuine issue of material fact that they failed to take any reasonable efforts to maintain the secrecy of the trade secrets. This is a prerequisite under the Trade Secrets Act. Therefore, summary judgment is allowed as to Counts III and IV.

Because Southwest Whey has failed to establish the existence of a trade secret pursuant to the statute, the Court need not address whether any trade secret was misappropriated by Nutrition 101.

Ronald S. Laurie, Inflexion Point Strategy, LLC, Intellectual Property Allocation Strategies in Joint Ventures

Practising Law Institute PATENTS, COPYRIGHTS, TRADEMARKS, AND LITERARY PROPERTY COURSE HANDBOOK SERIES

PLI Order Number 5923, March, 2005*

I. INTRODUCTION

The term "joint venture" is commonly used to mean "an association of economically independent business entities . . . for a common commercial purpose of defined scope and duration, by contract or in the form of a new business entity, and by means of which the [v]enturers pool resources and share risks, rewards and control." Typically, each joint venturer contributes a unique attribute (e.g., technology, capital, management expertise, or product distribution and marketing) toward a shared common objective and acceptance of risk. Other terms that are commonly used to describe joint ventures include "strategic alliance," and "partnership."

. . . .

III. IP ALLOCATION GENERALLY

In order to operate the joint venture—whether under the contractual, entity-based or two-stage models—the joint venturers and/or the JV entity will need to either own, or be licensed under, IP rights related to their business to operate. The choice of ownership versus licensing depends on a variety of factors. One factor is whether the IP arose independently of the JV (e.g., pre-existing or created by one of the joint venturers outside of the JV) or arose from operation of the JV. The former is often referred to as "Background IP," whereas the latter is often referred to as "Foreground IP."

Another factor is whether the JV is contractual, entity-based or established pursuant to the two-stage model. If the JV is entity-based or follows from the two-stage model, the relevant IP either can be owned by the JV, owned by one or both of the joint venturers and licensed to the JV, or some combination of the foregoing. For example, background IP might be owned by its creator (one of the joint venturers) and licensed to the JV entity, or even assigned to the JV entity. Similarly, foreground IP (which in this instance would have been created by the JV entity) could be owned by the JV entity, or allocated to the joint venturers individually, who would then grant appropriate licenses to the JV entity. If the JV is contractually based, both the foreground and background IP must be owned by one (or both) of the joint venturers and licensed to the other. Nevertheless, many other variations are also possible.

A. Default Allocation Paradigm: Joint Ownership

In situations where IP is to be owned by the joint venturers themselves (under either the contractual, entity or two-stage models), the most common form of IP allocation is some form of "joint ownership." For example, foreground IP is often allocated as follows: IP developed solely by one joint venturer is solely owned by that joint venturer, while IP developed jointly by the joint venturers is owned jointly by those joint venturers. Indeed, even if the joint venturers fail to expressly allocate IP ownership under the contractual JV model, this type of IP allocation will arise under default law, because (at least in the United States) ownership initially vests with the creators of the subject matter in question.

1. Conflicting Rights Under Default Laws

The default rights of joint owners (to exploit and/or to enforce) are governed by respective national laws applicable to the type of IP asset in question.

a) Right to Exploit

For example, consider U.S. patent rights. Absent an agreement to the contrary, the default rule is that each joint owner can exploit the patent without the permission of the other and without any duty to share royalties. Further, the joint owner's right to exploit includes the right to license third parties. The freedom to license without accounting enables a savvy prospective patent licensee to play the joint owners against one another other to maximize favorable deal terms for the licensee.

The situation becomes even more complicated when dealing with multiple IP types. For example, while U.S. patent law imposes no duty of accounting among exploiting joint owners, U.S. copyright law does impose such a duty.

b) Right to Enforce

The counterpart of exploitation is enforcement and, here as well, joint ownership presents pitfalls for the unwary. Again taking U.S. patent law as an example, normally, each joint owner must join in a suit to enforce the patent against a third party. This requirement protects a defendant from defending against multiple suits on the same patent and an absent joint owner from a finding of invalidity or unenforceability negatively affecting his rights. Consequently, any joint owner can hinder an offensive patent infringement action by refusing to join as a plaintiff.

Thus, joint owners of a U.S. patent find themselves in a situation where each joint owner can freely license without obligation to the other, but where each joint owner can prevent the other from suing by refusing to join the suit. In such a case, the rewards of licensing go to the joint owner who either grants a license first, or undercuts another joint owner's offer with a more favorable deal. It is no wonder that courts have characterized patent joint owners as being "at the mercy of each other."

A non-litigant joint owner can grant the defendant a license—even after initiation of the action—which will cut off part or all of the relief the litigant joint owner may obtain by exercising its unilateral right to sue. Specifically, a nonexclusive license (even post-suit) will prevent the litigant joint owner from obtaining injunctive relief, and will also protect the defendant from liability for post-grant (but not pre-grant) damages. But if the non-litigant joint owner grants the defendant an exclusive license (even post-suit), the non-litigant joint owner no longer can consent to join the suit as a joint owner of the patent, and the suit must be dismissed.

c) International Considerations

Further complexity as to joint owners' rights ensues because different countries have different default laws. For example, consider the copyright joint ownership laws of three major industrialized countries: the United States, the United Kingdom, and Japan. Under U.S. law, joint owners of a copyright can freely exploit for themselves. Under U.K. law, the joint owners cannot exploit for themselves without consent of the other joint owners. Under Japanese law, the joint owners cannot exploit without consent, but such consent cannot be unreasonably withheld.

Indeed, parties in different countries—looking at joint ownership through the prism of their individual national laws—may have entirely different expectations of what it means to be a joint owner. Based on the example above, American and British joint owners of a copyright might have had entirely different expectations regarding their individual rights to exploit. Some lawyers have been called to renegotiate joint ownership agreements when it became apparent, years after execution, that the joint owners had no meeting of the minds on their respective rights to exploit and enforce jointly developed subject matter.

2. Enforceability of Contractual Provisions

a) Against Third Parties

The previous two sections demonstrate the considerable variation in the default rules for the different types of intellectual property, as well as under the different national laws. An astute joint owner therefore will negotiate provisions in the JV agreement setting forth, in detail, the joint owners' respective rights and obligations. For example, such provisions might include covenants regarding unilateral exploitation, licensing of competitors, sharing of royalties, joining suits, and sharing of enforcement costs and proceeds. However, the effectiveness of these covenants remains uncertain as they may not always be enforceable.

Consider, for example, that the joint owners have agreed not to unilaterally exploit a jointly owned IP asset for the benefit of third parties. Such a covenant may be unenforceable against a third party who is held by a court to be a bona fide purchaser for value ("BFP") from one of the joint owners.

b) Against Joint Owners Themselves

Unlike the uncertainty surrounding contractual covenants with respect to third parties, such agreements should be enforceable against the joint owners themselves. For example, breach of a joint owner's covenant not to use for itself should be enforceable against that joint owner. However, this may prove untrue in some situations.

For example, where a joint owner goes bankrupt, the bankruptcy court (or trustee) generally has the power either to assume or reject a contract held by the bankrupt party. If the court rejects the JV agreement, the non-bankrupt joint owner may lose the benefit of the contractual provisions restricting the activity of the bankrupt joint owner. Conversely, the court might assume the JV agreement, but assign it to a third party (typically in connection with a sale of the joint ownership interest). In this scenario, the court would effectively divest the bankrupt joint owner of its joint ownership rights and vest those rights in a new joint owner (i.e., the third party) — perhaps even a competitor.

3. Recommendations

Joint ownership is fraught with pitfalls and should be avoided wherever possible. However, joint ownership may sometimes be unavoidable. For example, one joint venturer may oppose the formation of the joint venture on any other terms. In such a situation, the joint venturers must think through all issues and carefully plan for all contingencies. The joint owners cannot simply rely on default rules because, as discussed above, the rights to exploit and enforce vary with the type of intellectual property and applicable national laws. Such variation makes it impossible for the joint owners to effect an integrated and consistent plan for development, use and distribution of the subject matter covered by the jointly owned IP. Instead, the joint venturers should use the contractual or JV agreement to override the hodgepodge of inconsistent default laws by clearly allocating all the rights and responsibilities of the joint owners.

There are many possible alternatives to joint ownership, all of which involve some form of allocating IP ownership to individual parties (whether the joint venturers or the JV entity), who would then grant appropriate licenses to other parties as needed. In the next section, we explore some of these IP allocation possibilities.

B. Preferred IP Allocation Strategies

1. IP Ownership: Background, Non-Derivative Foreground and Derivative Foreground IP

In order to properly allocate ownership of IP under the preferred approach, the first step is to classify the IP based on the nature of the IP. Indeed, the election of a JV structural model and an associated IP allocation strategy are interdependent and, in turn, the IP allocation strategy is contingent on whether the IP asset represents Background, Non-Derivative Foreground or Derivative Foreground technology.

Background IP includes both IP in technology developed by the joint venturers prior to the formation of the JV ("Pre-existing Background IP") and in technology developed during the existence of the JV, but not pursuant to it ("New Background IP"). Specifically, Pre-existing Background IP comprises IP in technology created by each joint venturer prior to JV formation, that is necessary or useful in conducting the business of the contemplated joint venture, or required to commercially exploit the Foreground IP (as defined below). New Background IP also constitutes IP in technology necessary or useful in conducting the business of the joint venture, or required to commercially exploit the Foreground IP; but the difference lies in its development taking place during the JV and yet not pursuant to the JV development activity. The concept of New Background IP becomes more relevant in the case where one or more joint venturers is a large enterprise having multiple groups doing similar developments.

In contrast, Foreground IP describes IP associated with technology developed pursuant to the JV by the joint venturers, either individually or jointly, and in furtherance of the JV. Derivative Foreground IP is a subset of Foreground IP comprising IP developed pursuant to the JV that extends the core technology of one (and only one) joint venturer.

2. Optimizing Rights to Use of the Non-IP Owning Joint Venturers

a) Licenses: Exclusivity, Field of Use and Royalties

Once IP ownership is allocated, the rights of the other (non-owning) joint venturers to use such IP are defined under appropriate license provisions. These licenses include licenses among joint venturers, from a joint venturer to the new JV entity ("NewCo") if applicable, or from NewCo to the joint venturers. In this respect, many combinations of licensing parameters are possible and the joint venturers should decide at the outset which is suitable to their relationship. These licensing parameters include, e.g., whether the license is exclusive or non-exclusive, whether it is limited to a specific field of use, and whether it is royalty-bearing or royalty-free. The parameters are used in various combinations to prescribe (i.e., enable and/or restrict) permissible competitive use of the Background and Foreground IP by the joint venturers and NewCo with respect to one another.

b) Non-Competition Covenants

Non-competition covenants are a useful adjunct to IP licenses in terms of restricting competitive activity among the joint venturers on the one hand, and between the joint venturers and NewCo on the other. Non-competition covenants can be both more restrictive and less restrictive than IP licenses. They are less restrictive because they typically have a shorter term. Thus, while the IP licenses may extend during the existence of the JV (and possibly beyond), non-competition covenants are typically for a much shorter term, e.g., several years. They are more restrictive because they extend beyond use of the licensed IP by proscribing all competitive activity within a defined field. The scope of the non-compete is usually co-extensive with the area outside of any field-limited licenses.

. . . .

V. EXIT STRATEGIES

This section examines the disposition of the IP assets under different exit strategies available for the unwinding of the joint venture business. Possible exit strategies include merger or acquisition, dissolution, and bankruptcy. The IP assets of concern include owned IP (e.g., patents, trademarks and copyrights for which the JV itself is the registered owner, and trade secrets), and licensed-in IP (e.g., inbound IP licenses from the joint venturers and from third parties).

For convenience, the disposition of IP assets will be discussed in the context of a separate JV entity, although many of the concepts will be equally applicable to rights held by an individual joint venturer for the benefit of itself and its partners in the joint venture.

A. Merger or Acquisition of the JV Entity

If the joint venturers wish to allow for the possibility of merger or acquisition of the independent JV entity, they should negotiate appropriate provisions at the time of forming the JV entity. For example, all inbound licenses should be negotiated and drafted to facilitate their transfer to a potential acquirer of the JV business.

Also, a joint venturer might wish to be protected in the event the JV is acquired by a competitor, for example, by a provision automatically terminating any inbound license from such joint venturer upon a change of control of the JV to a competitor of the minority joint venturer. These competitors may be expressly identified or not. Or, if the license is not terminated, its scope can be "frozen," limiting it to the portion of the acquirer's business represented by the JV before the acquisition. These provisions ensure that, after the acquisition of the JV entity by a competitor of a joint venturer, any inbound licenses from such joint venturer to the JV entity do not accrue (or only accrue in a limited way) to the benefit of the competitor.

B. Dissolution of the JV Entity

Dissolution of the JV entity as an exit strategy must be analyzed in terms of three distinct considerations: IP owned by the JV entity, IP licensed from third parties, and IP licensed from the joint venturers.

1. IP Owned by the JV Entity

The analysis of the disposition of the owned IP further must be divided into two competing objectives: protecting the joint venturers' right to use and preventing the joint venturers' continued right to use such IP.

Where the joint venturers wish to continue to make use of the IP owned by the JV following its dissolution, assignment of the IP to the joint venturers as joint owners should be avoided because doing so raises the problems of joint ownership already discussed in III A above. Instead, ownership of the IP assets should vest in one joint venturer with grantback licenses flowing to the other former joint venturers. Alternatively, the joint venturers can choose to maintain the JV solely as an IP holding company (i.e. a shell company) where the joint venturers in turn have a license under the IP. The latter alternative of establishing an IP holding company is especially advantageous for enforcing the joint venture's IP rights against third parties and for the further licensing of the IP to third parties if so desired by the joint venturers. In either case, the scope of any licenses to the former joint venturers (e.g., term of the license grant, exclusivity provision, right to sublicense, field of use, royalty payment, etc.) should be negotiated at the time of forming the JV entity.

Another option is to structure the JV agreement to prohibit grantback licenses. This has the benefit of discouraging dissolution of the JV in the first instance.

However, the IP assets risk being wasted unless a third party buyer can be found. Alternatively, the JV agreement could provide that a specified joint venturer has the right to buy out the other joint venturers upon dissolution of the JV, and thus to gain sole ownership of the owned IP. The proceeds from the owned IP will be distributed to the joint venturers in accordance with their original equity stakes in the JV.

2. Inbound Licenses from Third Parties

Inbound licenses from third parties represent an asset of the JV just like the owned IP and thus will be treated in a similar manner. Issues relating to the inbound licenses, such as their transferability, divisibility and sublicensing, should be specified at the time these licenses are negotiated.

3. Inbound Licenses from Joint Venturers

Joint venturers inbound licenses typically cover background IP of the joint venturers closely related to their individual fields of business. Thus, upon dissolution, these licenses usually revert back to the granting joint venturer. However, in some instances, the licensor subsequently may grant equivalent field of use licenses to the other former joint venturers under separate license agreements. Again, these options should be contemplated at the time of JV formation.

4. Outbound Licenses from JV entity

The JV also may have granted licenses to third parties (i.e., outbound licenses). Upon dissolution, such licenses can either be: (i) left with the JV to be disposed of as part of the corporate unwinding process; or (ii) transferred to an entity that obtains ownership of the underlying (IP, technological and/or human) assets related to the subject matter of the license. If the license is a "naked" license that includes no obligations on the part of the licensor (i.e., the JV), option (i) is acceptable. But if the license imposes any such obligations (e.g., support, updates, maintenance, further development, etc.), then choice (ii) is appropriate (and the licensee will so insist).

VI. CONCLUSION

IP allocation represents one of the most important strategic assessments when considering a joint venture and should be addressed in the JV agreement itself at the time of formation. Preferably, the joint venturers are advised to avoid joint ownership of the developed IP in favor of one of the alternate IP allocation models presented in this paper or otherwise. In these alternative models, ownership of each distinct IP asset is granted to an individual party (e.g., joint venturer or the JV entity), with appropriate licenses to other parties as needed. It is also important to plan in advance for possible dissolution of the JV, so that ownership and rights to use the JV's IP assets are appropriately distributed among the former joint venturers.

Notes & Questions

1. Many of the issues raised by these materials will be explored again in the context of mergers and acquisitions, which often involve the termination of some business enterprise. Especially keep in mind the drafting and other contractual issues

raised by these cases. Business strategies as well as careful contract drafting are frequently important in resolving these issues. A successful termination of a business enterprise often rests on developing meaningful exit strategies.

2. The *Hapgood* case provides a colorful illustration of employment issues that affect the ownership of intellectual property. The Court may have been motivated by a desire to protect the employee inventor against the corporation in this case. Note the discussion of assignments and compare it with the discussions in the bankruptcy cases. Contractually the problem posed by the case could be addressed by including a term in the initial license or assignment that would make the patent fully assignable or transferable upon a change in corporate structuring, especially upon as simple an event as a corporate name change.

3. The *Pav-Saver* and *Southwest Whey* cases illustrate the problems of intellectual property ownership and allocation in joint ventures. The decisions in *Pav-Saver* demonstrate the importance of partnership agreement drafting in resolving disputes over intellectual property ownership in partnerships. Did the majority interpret the partnership agreement correctly? How could *Pav-Saver* have retained more effective control over its patents in the event of partnership termination? Note that the dissent bases its analysis on the provisions in the Uniform Partnership Act regarding the termination of partnerships. To what extent does the Uniform Partnership Act deal with the special ownership issues raised by intellectual property?

4. The *Southwest Whey* decision provides a review of trade secret law and may appear to say little about the law of business enterprises. Note that the court avoids the business questions by finding that there was no trade secret here. Is the court's analysis convincing? If there was a trade secret, how would you envision that the business issues would have been resolved in light of *Pav-Saver* and the discussion in the Laurie reading?

5. The Laurie reading provides an overview of intellectual property issues in the context of joint ventures. Many of the issues addressed in this reading also arise in connection with transfers of intellectual property in mergers and acquisitions. These transfers are discussed in detail in Chapter 7.

Chapter 7

Intellectual Property Issues in Mergers and Acquisitions

Problem

Dr. Y.L. See, Chief Executive Officer (CEO) of Digital Ignition Systems Corporation, has been approached by the CEO of Automated Rotary Systems, Incorporated, (ARS) to discuss the possibility of a transaction to pool the two companies' efforts in developing and marketing engine parts for automobiles, motorboats, and small jets. Dr. See is interested in working with ARS because of the possibilities of expanding the market for Digital Ignition's products and obtaining access to proprietary software and customer lists owned by ARS. Dr. See is considering several possible arrangements. One is to organize a joint venture between the two companies for product development. Since this type of project raises significant antitrust concerns, Dr. See has deferred consideration of this arrangement until later (see Chapter 11). The second possibility is a merger of the two businesses to produce a bigger entity, perhaps still called Digital Ignition Systems Corporation, with the combined management and assets of the two businesses. The third possibility is a straight purchase by Digital Ignition Systems of the principal assets of ARS. Dr. See has asked you, his general counsel, to assess the relative merits of the last two possibilities. Specifically, he would like an analysis of the potential liabilities associated with each type of transaction and the benefits and costs of these alternative transactional structures.

Focus of the Chapter

A desire to capture intellectual property value often motivates executives to consider the merger of two companies or the acquisition of one company by another. If two companies utilize the same technology or engage in similar research and development projects, executives of the two companies may find it desirable to pool their assets in order to take advantage of synergies that may arise from complementary intellectual property. Alternatively, one company may acquire the intellectual property and operational capabilities of the other by buying all of its assets. Mergers or acquisitions undertaken to pool or transfer assets in these ways often raise complex corporate and securities law issues. When intellectual property is involved in such transactions, special attention must be paid to how intellectual property ownership and infringement liability questions will be resolved for the surviving entities.

In order to assist clients with these sorts of arrangements, transactional and intellectual property attorneys must understand not only the law of mergers and acquisitions, but also the way in which the arrangements should be structured. Attorneys' efforts in these contexts often focus on the drafting of key transactional documents, such as the merger agreement specifying the terms on which two companies will be combined. Successful drafting of these sorts of documents typically requires a deep understanding of the details of a business combination transaction, including the impact of the transaction on assets and rights associated with the affected companies' intellectual property portfolios. As with any complex legal transaction, due diligence is of central importance, and the well-trained attorney needs to be attentive to the details of what a company purports to own and how assets will be transferred. The final case in this chapter involving a multi-million dollar judgment against the Weyerhaeuser Company provides a harsh lesson about what can happen when attorneys fail to investigate or fail to disclose the details of an intellectual property portfolio.

The questions discussed in this chapter are fundamental. They pertain to issues of property ownership, liability risks, and contract rights, the basic building blocks of many legal transactions. While the factual contexts addressed in some of the materials are quite complex, by focusing your attention on these three types of issues you will be able to interpret and understand the complicated fact patterns. Pay special attention to how descriptions of the intellectual property and transactions at stake affect the results.

The materials in this chapter are divided into five parts. Part A provides a general overview of basic concepts and legal standards pertaining to mergers and the sale of corporate assets. This part focuses on the corporate law of Delaware (the most important state for business incorporations) as the source of examples of relevant legal standards. With this background, we turn to four types of issues that are frequently raised by intellectual property in mergers and acquisitions: (1) ownership; (2) liability; (3) transfer; and (4) due diligence.

Part B addresses issues of intellectual property ownership in mergers and acquisitions. The article by David Kennedy provides a helpful overview of the reallocation of intellectual property rights resulting from a merger or sale of assets. Kennedy also discusses the transfer of licensing rights in the context of a merger. The Kennedy reading is followed by three cases that illustrate the types of intellectual property ownership issues that can arise when a company transfers its assets to or merges with another company. The cases emphasize the importance of contract drafting in securing and clarifying the allocation of rights.

Part C addresses the following question: Once corporate property and activities are reallocated through a merger or other acquisition, does pre-existing liability for intellectual property infringement follow? The first case in this part discusses the concept of successor liability, a central doctrine for determining liability in the context of a merger or acquisition. The second case presents an application of the doctrine of successor liability in the context of a dispute involving trade secrets and other confidential data.

Part D presents a case that demonstrates the problems that can arise in drafting transfer documents in a merger or acquisition. The case illustrates the role of contractual remedies, particularly remedies for breaches of warranties.

Part E continues this discussion through a major decision involving the Weyerhaeuser Company's liability for breaches of warranties made in the transfer of intellectual property rights to its subsidiary. This final case offers a fairly deep discussion of the important intellectual property considerations surrounding a particular corporate acquisition transaction and a review of concepts from the discussions in other chapters on bankruptcy (see Chapter 6) and due diligence in securities transactions (see Chapter 8).

Readings
A. Some Basic Terminology

This section provides some general background on the two types of corporate transactions that are the subject of this chapter: mergers and acquisitions. Courses in mergers and acquisitions or advanced corporate law will provide greater depth on these topics. Our goal here is to familiarize you with the basic concepts so that you can understand the cases in this chapter and the intellectual property issues that arise in mergers and acquisitions.

A merger is a legal transaction joining together two corporate entities. The resulting combined entity bears the name of one of the original companies and is treated as a legal continuation of that company. In a second, related type of transaction called a consolidation, the combined entity is a new corporation, with a new name but many of the characteristics of the original corporations. Because there are frequently benefits from continuing the name and reputation of one of the combined entities, mergers are far more common than consolidations and the remainder of our discussions here will address mergers rather than consolidations. In general, the legal standards governing mergers and consolidations are the same, although you should note that the Delaware Corporations Code, as excerpted below, refers to mergers and consolidations separately.

In a merger, the corporation that continues to exist is called the acquiring or surviving company. The other concern is called the target or disappearing company.

For tax or regulatory reasons, a merger may take a more complicated form called a triangular merger. A triangular merger is so named because it involves three entities: an acquiring company, its subsidiary, and a target. The subsidiary is a company whose stock is owned at the outset of the merger by the acquiring company. One type of triangular merger is called a forward triangular merger. This type of merger involves the merger of the subsidiary into the target so that the subsidiary is the surviving company. You can envision the situation as follows:

The other type of triangular merger is called a reverse triangular merger. This type of merger involves the target merging into the subsidiary so the target is the surviving company. You can envision the situation as follows:

An acquiring company may adopt a triangular merger form in order to keep some distance between itself and the target company for tax or regulatory purposes. The choice between a reverse and forward triangular merger will depend in part on the characteristics of the subsidiary and target companies and whether it is legally advantageous to have one or the other be the surviving entity (for example, because one of the companies has already qualified for business licenses, but the licenses will only continue in force if that entity survives the merger and continues in existence). The choice between a reverse and forward triangular merger will also sometimes depend on tax considerations (such as different taxation standards applicable to the subsidiary and target companies in their respective states of incorporation) or corporate law considerations (such as differences in the state laws applicable to the subsidiary and target companies regarding how to properly structure shareholder voting and managerial decision making needed to approve a merger). Notice that in both a reverse and forward triangular merger the acquiring company stays the same except that as the result of the merger it owns stock in an entity that is a combination of the subsidiary and the target with the name of either the subsidiary or target depending upon whether the merger is undertaken in the reverse or forward format.

Procedures for mergers are governed primarily by state laws although, as you will see in the materials below, federal law—particularly federal securities law—can come into play. Delaware Corporations Code § 251, the major sections of which are reprinted below, provides an overview of the major steps that must be followed in completing a merger involving a Delaware corporation:

§ 251. Merger or consolidation of domestic corporations and limited liability company.

 (a) Any 2 or more corporations existing under the laws of this State may merge into a single corporation, which may be any 1 of the constituent corporations or may consolidate into a new corporation formed by the consolidation, pursuant to an agreement of merger or consolidation, as the case may be, complying and approved in accordance with this section.

 (b) The board of directors of each corporation which desires to merge or consolidate shall adopt a resolution approving an agreement of merger or consolidation and declaring its advisability. The agreement shall state: (1) The terms and conditions of the merger or consolidation; (2) the mode of carrying the same into effect; (3) in the case of a merger, such amendments or changes in the certificate of incorporation of the surviving corporation as are desired to be effected by the merger, or, if no such amendments or changes are desired, a statement that the certificate of incorporation of the surviving corporation shall be its certificate of incorporation; (4) in the case of a consolidation, that the certificate of incorporation of the resulting corporation shall be as is set forth in an attachment to the agreement; (5) the manner, if any, of converting the shares of each of the constituent corporations into shares or other securities of the corporation surviving or resulting from the merger or consolidation, or of cancelling some or all of such shares, and, if any shares of any of the constituent corporations are not to remain outstanding, to be converted solely into shares or other securities of the surviving or resulting corporation or to be cancelled, the cash, property, rights or securities of any other corporation or entity which the holders of such shares are to receive in exchange for, or upon conversion of such shares and the surrender of any certificates evidencing them, which cash, property, rights or securities of any other corporation or entity may be in addition to or in lieu of shares or other securities of the surviving or resulting corporation; and (6) such other details or provisions as are deemed desirable, including, without limiting the generality of the foregoing, a provision for the payment of cash in lieu of the issuance or recognition of fractional shares, interests or rights, or for any other arrangement with respect thereto, ... Any of the terms of the agreement of merger or consolidation may be made dependent upon facts ascertainable outside of such agreement, provided that the manner in which such facts shall operate upon the terms of the agreement is clearly and expressly set forth in the agreement of merger or consolidation. The term "facts," as used in the preceding sentence, includes, but is not limited to, the occurrence of any event, including a determination or action by any person or body, including the corporation.

 (c) The agreement required by subsection (b) of this section shall be submitted to the stockholders of each constituent corporation at an annual or special meeting for the purpose of acting on the agreement. Due notice of the time, place and purpose of the meeting shall be mailed to each holder of stock, whether voting or nonvoting, of the corporation at the stockholder's address as it appears on the records of the corporation, at least 20 days prior to the date of the meeting. The notice shall contain a copy of the agreement or a brief summary thereof, as the directors shall deem advisable. At the meeting, the agreement shall be considered and a vote taken for its adoption or rejection. If a majority of the outstanding stock of the corporation entitled to vote thereon shall be voted for the adoption of the agreement, that fact shall be certified on the agreement by the secretary or assistant secretary of the corporation. If the agreement shall be so adopted and certified by each constituent corporation, it shall then be filed and shall become effective, . . . In lieu of filing the agreement of merger or consolidation required by this section, the surviving or resulting corporation may file a certificate of merger or consolidation, . . . which states:

(1) The name and state of incorporation of each of the constituent corporations;

(2) That an agreement of merger or consolidation has been approved, adopted, certified, executed and acknowledged by each of the constituent corporations in accordance with this section;

(3) The name of the surviving or resulting corporation;

(4) In the case of a merger, such amendments or changes in the certificate of incorporation of the surviving corporation as are desired to be effected by the merger, or, if no such amendments or changes are desired, a statement that the certificate of incorporation of the surviving corporation shall be its certificate of incorporation;

(5) In the case of a consolidation, that the certificate of incorporation of the resulting corporation shall be as set forth in an attachment to the certificate;

(6) That the executed agreement of consolidation or merger is on file at an office of the surviving corporation, stating the address thereof; and

(7) That a copy of the agreement of consolidation or merger will be furnished by the surviving corporation, on request and without cost, to any stockholder of any constituent corporation.

Many of the rights and responsibilities of the companies involved in a merger will be determined by the merger agreement between the companies. This agreement will often address the ownership of intellectual property and other assets, as well as liabilities of the companies with respect to intellectual property and other property rights.

The second type of corporate transaction we will focus on in this section is the acquisition of all or substantially all of the assets of a corporation. In many ways, this should be a more familiar transaction. An acquisition of this type involves one company, the acquirer, purchasing a substantial share of the assets of another company, the target. The acquisition is structured through an asset purchase contract, but is also subject to corporate law limitations. The Delaware Corporations Code contains the following provision regarding these sorts of corporate asset acquisitions:

§ 271. Sale, lease or exchange of assets; consideration; procedure.

(a) Every corporation may at any meeting of its board of directors or governing body sell, lease or exchange all or substantially all of its property and assets, including its goodwill and its corporate franchises, upon such terms and conditions and for such consideration, which may consist in whole or in part of money or other property, including shares of stock in, and/or other securities of, any other corporation or corporations, as its board of directors or governing body deems expedient and for the best interests of the corporation, when and as authorized by a resolution adopted by the holders of a majority of the outstanding stock of the corporation entitled to vote thereon or, if the corporation is a nonstock corporation, by a majority of the members having the right to vote for the election of the members of the governing body, at a meeting duly called upon at least 20 days' notice. The notice of the meeting shall state that such a resolution will be considered.

(b) Notwithstanding authorization or consent to a proposed sale, lease or exchange of a corporation's property and assets by the stockholders or members, the board of directors or governing body may abandon such proposed sale, lease or exchange without further action by the stockholders or members, subject to the rights, if any, of third parties under any contract relating thereto.

Sometimes a target company may dissolve after selling substantially all of its assets to an acquirer. In such a situation, the result may look much like a merger since the target company is gone and the acquirer has assumed the assets of the target. Because of the similarity between the two transactions, the acquisition of the target followed by its dissolution is sometimes referred to as a de facto merger and subjected to the requirements applicable to a merger. Although the doctrine is somewhat out of favor, particularly in Delaware, the concept is important to be aware of and arises in some of the materials below.

Intellectual property poses several special problems for both mergers and acquisitions. We will focus on four questions:

(1) Who owns intellectual property after a merger or acquisition?

(2) Who is liable for intellectual property infringement after a merger or acquisition?

(3) How is intellectual property transferred in a merger or acquisition?

(4) How is the transfer of intellectual property made effective through due diligence in a merger or acquisition?

We will consider materials addressing each of these questions.

B. Ownership Issues

David H. Kennedy, Intellectual Property Issues Arising Out of Acquisitions

Practicing Law Institute, PATENTS, COPYRIGHTS, TRADEMARKS, AND LITERARY PROPERTY COURSE HANDBOOK SERIES

PLI Order Number 6056 March–May 2005*

I. ALLOCATION OF IP RIGHTS IN CONNECTION WITH SALE OF BUSINESS UNIT

A. Summary Comparison of Ownership vs. License Rights

1. Sole Ownership

Sole ownership of IP has the following elements:

- Unfettered discretion to use, distribute to third parties and commercially exploit the IP in any manner (including through sublicensing and assignment);

- Permanent, non-terminable rights; and

- Ability to solely control the enforcement of rights against infringing or mis-appropriating third parties.

2. Joint Ownership

Subject to any applicable agreement of the joint owners, a party that jointly owns IP rights generally will have the same rights as apply in the context of sole owner-ship, except as follows:

- A single joint owner will not have the power to grant exclusive licenses to third parties without the agreement of the other joint owner (nor will a joint owner be able to assign outright the entirety of the IP rights in question);

- The joint owners usually will agree as to whether and to what extent each has any obligation to account to the other for profits realized from the exploitation of the jointly-owned IP (depending on the nature of the IP, joint owners may or may not have an obligation to account to each other);

- The ability of a joint owner to enforce the IP rights against infringing third par-ties may be constrained depending on the applicable arrangements agreed to by the joint owners (problems may arise if the joint owners disagree regarding the manner in which an action is prosecuted against a third party infringer or whether an action should be brought against a given suspected infringer); and

- The protection and maintenance of jointly-owned IP is more complex because arrangements must be agreed by the joint owners with respect to (i) whether a patent should be sought for a particular invention (or whether trade secret pro-tection should be relied on instead), and (ii) allocation of responsibility for

---

prosecution of patent applications and for payment of fees and the other administrative activities required to maintain in effect patents and other "registered" intellectual property.

3. Exclusive License

An exclusive license to IP rights includes the following elements (in contrast to ownership rights):

- Rights that are exercisable are only those specifically granted (which may be limited in nature);

- In the case of an exclusive license within a defined field of use of the IP rights in question, an exclusive license would be tantamount to sole ownership in the field of use as to which the exclusivity is applicable, except to the extent that the license would be terminable or there would be limitations imposed on sublicensing or assignment;

- Exclusive licensees can be given the right to enforce the licensed IP rights against third party infringers in the field of use to which the exclusivity applies (although for standing reasons, the exclusive licensee may be required to join the IP owner as a party to any enforcement action);

- In contrast to ownership, an exclusive (or non-exclusive) license usually is terminable (for breach or other specified reasons) or expires at the end of a specified license term;

- An exclusive license (again, in contrast to the rights inherent in ownership) may not be freely assignable or sublicensable; and

- Exclusive licensees usually have no role in determining how to protect IP (patent vs. trade secret), in prosecuting patent applications that are included in the licensed IP and in many cases the licensor will not be willing to covenant to maintain in effect licensed patents or other "registered" IP, although it would not be unusual in this context for an exclusive licensee to be given the right, at its option and expense, to maintain in force patents or to continue the prosecution of patent applications that the licensor determines to abandon.

4. Non-Exclusive License

A non-exclusive license generally has the same elements as an exclusive license (other than the licensed rights are not exclusively licensed) subject to the following:

- A non-exclusive licensee has no right to enforce the licensed rights against suspected third party infringers;

- A licensor generally will have no obligation to enforce the licensed IP against third parties (in some cases, however, a non-exclusive licensee is entitled to an adjustment in the royalty rate if the licensor fails to bring, at the licensee's request, an enforcement action against unlicensed competitor of the licensee);

- A non-exclusive licensee generally has no role in the prosecution of pending patent applications or the maintenance in force of licensed patents; and

- A non-exclusive patent and copyright licensee that enters bankruptcy proceedings may not be able to retain its rights (without the agreement of the licensor) even in the context of a successful reorganization.

B. Allocation of Ownership of Seller IP in a Sale of a Business Unit

The allocation rule that applies to the Seller's intellectual property to be transferred to the Buyer will be the same rule that applies to the other assets to be transferred in the transaction.

The most often applied rule for determining what assets are to be included in the sale of a division or other business unit of a Seller is one based on whether the intellectual property or other asset of the Seller "primarily relates to the Business" or is "used primarily in connection with the Business", with the term "Business" being defined to consist of the business unit of Seller that is being purchased by the Buyer (oftentimes with express reference to the principal products of the business unit in question).

Infrequently, the ownership allocation test may be based on whether an asset is "used exclusively in connection with the Business" or is "used in connection with Business" (in each case, subject to specific exceptions).

Regardless of the ownership allocation rule that is utilized, patents and patent applications are usually reviewed on a patent-by-patent basis with a view to the Seller and Buyer agreeing on a specific list of which patents are to be transferred to the Buyer (which the parties may or may not agree is exhaustive).

It usually will not be practicable to specifically identify the trade secrets and copyrights to be transferred and, therefore, the general allocation rules are used to specify what trade secrets and copyrights are to be transferred, although the parties may seek to describe the trade secrets and copyrights through high level descriptions (difficulties in identifying and segregating trade secrets and copyrights may make the parties more inclined to agree to joint ownership or for one side or the other to settle for broad license rights instead of ownership).

Third party license agreements generally need to be reviewed on a case-by-case basis to determine whether the licensed third party technology is used principally in the Business purchased by the Buyer or the businesses retained by the Seller.

- Generally there will be no ability to transfer third party technology by sublicense to the Buyer (with the Seller retaining rights as a licensee) or for the underlying agreement to be assigned subject to the Seller retaining rights in the third party technology on a sublicensing basis (thus, in the case of third party technology that is used by both the transferred Business and the retained businesses, one side or the other will need to assume the cost of obtaining replacement licenses from the respective third party licensors).

- Consent to assign to the Buyer any third party license agreements usually will be required.

[T]he "Business" [for purposes of these provisions] is usually defined to be the business in question, as conducted by the Seller as of the Closing Date.

- The definition may or may not expressly refer to predecessor operations and discontinued operations of such businesses and operations.

- The definition may also expressly refer to products in development to make explicit that the concept of taking a "snapshot" of the business at the Closing does not operate to limit the business to the shipping products to the exclusion of products in development.

The concept of primarily relating to the Business usually is not fleshed out with further definition or otherwise given further content. Application of this test to a particular intellectual property asset could be considered to include the following factors:

- Does the intellectual property asset in question cover or protect any products of the Business (and, conversely, does it cover or protect any products of the businesses being retained by the Seller) or is it otherwise actively used in connection with the Business as well as the businesses being retained by the Seller?

- What are the respective revenues of the Business and of the Seller's retained businesses from products that are covered or protected by the intellectual property asset and how significant are these revenues in relation to the Seller's and Buyer's respective total revenues?

- Was the inventor or developer of the intellectual property asset employed by the Business at the time the intellectual property asset was created or developed (or, if multiple inventors or developers were involved, which side of the business employed a majority of the inventors/developers)?

- Which business unit actually funded the development of the intellectual property asset in question?

- What is the overall size of the market for products sold by the retained business of the Seller that are covered or protected by the intellectual property asset relative to the overall size of the market for products sold by the Business that are covered or protected by the intellectual property asset?

C. Selected Discussion Issues for License Agreements Relating to Sale of Business Unit

Scope of Licenses. The initial issue to be addressed is the scope of the license rights to be granted by the Seller to the Buyer and from the Buyer to the Seller.

- Internal Use Rights. As to some technology, the rights licensed by one side or the other may be limited to a license for internal use purposes only.

- Distribution Rights. Usually the licenses that are negotiated in this context include distribution or other commercial exploitation rights.

- If distribution rights are granted and the products in question are software, the respective agreements should specify whether the licensee party is authorized to provide only object code to its customers.

- If software products are involved, it may be necessary for the licensee party to be granted the right to establish customary source code escrows and to license

API's in connection with licensing software that will be integrated in an OEM's product (and, depending on the licensee party's business model, broader source code licensing rights may be required).

- Sublicenses. The extent of each party's sublicensing rights should be clearly specified.

- If software is involved, the licensee party will require sublicensing rights to the extent necessary to distribute its products to its customers.

- It would not be unusual for consultants and other independent contractors who are working on development with the licensee party to be permitted to have access to and use the licensed IP and for the licensee party to be permitted to sublicense wholly owned subsidiaries (and sometimes majority-owned subsidiaries).

- The licensee party also might require broad sublicensing rights in connection with technology partnering arrangements and joint ventures or in connection with the co-development of a joint or bundled product.

- Sublicensing rights are more problematic in the case of patent licenses: "naked" patent sublicensing often is not permitted.

- In the case of patent rights, the licensor party often will desire to include "anti-foundry" or "anti-patent laundering" provisions in an non-exclusive license to prevent an infringer of the licensor party's patents from seeking to avoid infringement by having the licensee party make or sublicense products for or to the infringing third party.

Extent of Exclusive Rights. Will the license under the retained IP granted by Seller to Buyer (the "Seller License") or the license granted back by Buyer to Seller under the purchased IP (the "Buyer License") be exclusive (in a specified field) or non-exclusive?

- It is not unusual for the seller of a division or other business unit who is retaining IP that is used in the retained businesses to grant an exclusive license within the field of use applicable to the transferred business, which may be supplemented with a general non-compete covenant by the Seller for a duration that typically runs between three and five years.

- If the Seller License is non-exclusive in all respects, the Seller would be permitted to exercise or authorize others to exercise the right to utilize the retained IP to make, sell, etc., products that are the same or similar to the products sold by the transferred business.

- Sometimes, given the similarity of the Seller's retained business and the Business being sold to the Buyer and/or the overlapping of target markets of the Seller and Buyer, it is very difficult to define a field in which the Seller is willing to give exclusive rights to the Buyer under the Seller's retained IP.

- If the Seller License is to be exclusive, it would not be unusual for the Buyer License to be exclusive as well in the field(s) of the Seller's retained businesses.

Improvements: New Developments.

- Ownership. Usually agreements in this context provide that the Buyer will own any improvements it makes to the technology licensed to it under the Seller License and Seller will own any improvements made by Seller with regard to the technology licensed to it under the Buyer License (and of course the developing party would own any new developments it might create).

- Sometimes agreements in this context provide that the owner of the underlying technology on which the improvement is based will own all improvements to such technology, whether made by the Buyer or the Seller (note that such provisions may raise concerns under antitrust laws).

- Inclusion in License Grant. The transaction could provide either for (i) no disclosure to the other party of improvements by the party making the improvement or (ii) disclosure to the other party of material improvements at reasonable periodic intervals by the party making the improvement.

- The rule could be different depending on whether the improvement is made by a licensor or a licensee (e.g., a license agreement could provide for disclosure to the licensor of improvements made by the licensee but not any disclosure by the licensor of improvements made by it).

- The license agreement could provide for no obligation to disclose any improvements, but still provide for a license of improvements so that: (i) if there is any voluntary disclosure by one side to the other, the other automatically is licensed to use the disclosed improvement within its field to use or (ii), in the case of patentable improvements, one side would not be able fence in the other with new patents that block off independent developments by the other side.

- In some contexts, a Buyer and a Seller may negotiate broad patent cross licenses or covenants not to sue that apply to all new developments (and not just improvements) to ensure that neither side is in a position to acquire and enforce patents against the other.

- Sometimes this license or covenant not to sue is limited to patents that would be infringed by the existing products or services of the other party that are shipping or being provided at the time of closing; in other cases, the license or covenant not to sue may be extended to cover enhancements, new versions or successor products or services developed after the sale closing date sometimes being (this is intended to give comfort to each side that it would be free of interference from the other side with respect to its existing products, as enhanced, for a specified "breathing period").

- Such licenses or covenants not to sue may be further limited by excluding any new products or services with substantial additional functionality or features (this is intended to ensure that potentially valuable new developments covered by a Seller's retained IP that have application to existing products and services of the business being sold are not incorporated into the products or services by the Buyer after the Closing without appropriate compensation being given to the Seller).

Termination; Irrevocability. Should the Seller License and Buyer License be terminable for breach or upon the occurrence of specified events?

- Where there are no ongoing payment obligations, the parties may prefer to provide for perpetual and irrevocable licenses (if the Buyer is a new company that is obtaining funding in connection with the purchase of the business from the Seller, any right of the Seller to terminate the license granted to Buyer may be problematic).

- Where one side or the other is very concerned about the possibility of the other party exercising rights beyond the scope of the license grant, a termination for breach may be desired (with a covenant included to the effect that the licensee party will not exercise rights outside the scope of the license).

- Some licensors insist on retaining the right to terminate by reason of a breach of a confidentiality covenant or the transfer of the license agreement by the licensee in violation of any applicable limitations on transfer such as an attempt to transfer the license to a competitor of the licensing party.

  Assignability. Generally licenses will be non-transferable without the prior written consent of the licensing party. In some cases, a significant amount of negotiations take place as to whether the licensee party is permitted to transfer the license in connection with the sale of all or substantially all of its business, whether by stock purchase, merger or asset purchase.

- The licensor party may be concerned about a competitor acquiring the other party and thereby gaining access to the license granted by the licensor and also may be concerned about a party with whom it is engaged, or is about to be engaged, in IP or other litigation acquiring the licensee party to gain the benefit of the license.

- The licensor party might agree to allow the transfer of the license in connection with the sale of the licensee party's business subject to the prior written consent of the licensor party, which the licensor party might agree not to unreasonably delay or withhold (and the licensee party perhaps acknowledging that the withholding of consent by the licensor party shall be deemed to be reasonable if the proposed assignee is a competitor of the licensor party).

- Alternatively, the agreement might prohibit assignment in connection with the sale of the business if the proposed assignee is a competitor of the licensor party. The definition of competitor of the licensor party could be based on a list of competitors attached at the time of signing, together with any successor or affiliate thereof. The licensor party will desire to have future competitors included as well, either automatically (with the licensing party having a duty to check with licensor to find out who the then relevant competitors are for this purpose or the licensor party instead having the right to update the list of competitors from time to time in its reasonable discretion).

- The licensor party also may be troubled with the notion of a broad field of use patent license being transferable to a large company that acquires the licensee party without any additional consideration being payable to the licensor party.

- The acquiror could, e.g., be a company with products that infringe the licensor party's patents and that is engaged in cross-licensing negotiations or litigation with the licensor party; in this case, the ability of the infringing third party to acquire the licensee party and thereby acquire the shelter of the licensee party's license could dramatically affect the "balance of power" between the licensor party and the infringing third party.

- In order to limit the value available to an infringing third party that seeks to acquire a broad field of use license from the licensee party, in some contexts the license granted to the licensee party is "frozen" in connection with the sale of the licensee party's business (including in connection with a change of control by stock purchase or merger) so that the licensed rights thereafter can only be utilized with respect to any then commercially launched products but not for any new or significantly improved products.

Enforcement of IP. If an exclusive license is provided for, it would not be unusual for the exclusive licensee to be granted the right to enforce the licensed IP against infringers in the field of use of the exclusive license, with any recoveries in such field of use being retained by the exclusive licensee.

- The licensee party may not have standing to sue third party infringers of the licensed IP and it would be customary to include provisions obligating the licensor party, at the licensee party's request and expense, to become a named party in any enforcement action and otherwise to cooperate with licensee party in taking enforcement action against infringers that licensee party requests.

- In a purely non-exclusive license context, it generally is not workable for there to be any arrangements by which the licensed IP can be enforced against the licensee party's competitors for the benefit of the licensee party (this whole notion is contrary to the concept of a non-exclusive license).

- In unusual cases (such as a spinoff of a subsidiary), the licensor may agree to "rent" a patent to the licensee party for use as a defensive weapon in infringement litigation commenced against the licensee party by one of its competitors.

- In some cases, a non-exclusive licensee may be given the right to request the licensor party to bring infringement actions against non-licensed competitors, but licensors generally insist in the context of a non-exclusive license that they be given absolute discretion with regard to the conduct of enforcement actions.

Maintenance of Patents/Assignment of Rights upon Abandonment. Agreements in this context sometimes may provide for any obligation on the part of the respective licensor either to continue to prosecute diligently any patent applications included in the licensed IP or to maintain in force any licensed patents, but in many cases licensors retain absolute discretion in this regard.

- Where there is no covenant on the part of the licensor party to continue to prosecute diligently any patent applications included in the licensed IP or to maintain in force any licensed patents, the licensee party may desire to include an obligation on the part of the licensor party to notify the licensee party if maintenance fees are not going to be paid and a patent is going to be abandoned or if prosecution of a pending patent application is going to be abandoned.

- Where the licensor party has the obligation to give notice to the licensee of any such abandonment, the licensee party, at its election and at its cost, may be given the rights to step in and continue the prosecution process or to pay any maintenance fees owing, in either case with the licensing party assigning ownership to the other party subject to an irrevocable non-exclusive license in favor of the abandoning party in the relevant field of use.

II. LICENSES AND MERGERS

As the creation and commercialization of intellectual property has come to play an increasingly important role in the modern economy, intellectual property considerations have moved from peripheral to central in determining the structures of business transactions. Multi-billion dollar companies more and more frequently have their origins in a set of ideas, and the entire life cycles of world-leading enterprises are governed by the legal relationships created between inventors, investors, producers and consumers of intellectual property.

Lawyers who assume the responsibility for advising participants in an economy driven by advances in the creation of intellectual property need to have a broad perspective on how the structure of transactions entered into at various stages of the capitalization and commercialization of intellectual property will impact the future value of the property. For example, the form of a security interest granted to an early-stage lender may have important ramifications in an emerging company's ability to secure future financing or to be sold. The failure to make provision for the occurrence of certain future events, such as a merger or bankruptcy by or of one of the parties, may result in lost opportunities or crippling litigation. Similarly, decisions made in structuring merger or workout transactions will impact the ability of companies acquiring intellectual property assets to exploit those assets through future financing or licensing transactions.

The following contains a discussion of structural issues arising at the confluence of the laws governing licensing and merger transactions and bankruptcy.

Although mergers and bankruptcies are often considered by creators and licensors of intellectual property as eventualities so remote that they needn't be given serious consideration during the negotiation of license agreements or other intellectual property transactions, attorneys advising such clients should give full consideration to merger and bankruptcy issues and not merely adopt boilerplate contractual provisions that may or may not protect their clients' interests. While there continues to be some uncertainty in the governing law, the structure of a license agreement may determine whether or not the license will survive a merger or bankruptcy event.

As the Ninth Circuit Court of Appeals recognized in *Linney v. Cellular Alaska Partnership*, 151 F.3d 1234, 1241 (9th Cir. 1998), "the legal status of a merger under an anti-assignment clause is 'less than clear.'" (citing *Star Cellular Telephone Company, Inc. v. Baton Rouge CGSA, Inc.*, 1993 Del. Ch. LEXIS 158 (July 30, 1993), aff'd, 1994 Del. LEXIS 190 (1994). Because of this uncertainty in the underlying law, the parties to a license agreement are well advised to include provisions specifically addressing the issue of future mergers, in addition to general provisions prohibiting or permitting assignment of the license.

Merger transactions are generally governed by state corporate law. The assignment of copyright licenses and transfer of copyright ownership, however, is governed by federal law, which preempts conflicting state law. See *Everex Sys., Inc. v. Cadtrak Corp. (In re CFLC, Inc.)*, 89 F.3d 673, 677–680 (9th Cir. 1996); *Mai Systems Corp. v. Peak Computer, Inc.*, 991 F.2d 511, 518–519 (9th Cir. 1993); *DSC Communications Corp. v. Pulse Communications, Inc.*, 170 F.3d 1354, 1360–1362 (Fed. Cir. 1999). "The enforcement of a copyright license raises issues that lie at the intersection of copyright and contract law, an area of law that is not yet well developed." *Sun Microsystems, Inc. v. Microsoft Corp.*, 188 F.3d 1115, 1122 (9th Cir. 1999). The rules of contract construction embodied in state law control the interpretation of license agreements, "provided that such rules do not interfere with federal copyright law and policy." (quoting *S.O.S., Inc. v. Payday, Inc.*, 886 F.2d 1081, 1088 (9th Cir. 1989).

Although the Ninth Circuit has recognized the uncertainty in the law in its *Linney* decision, 151 F.3d at 1241, and has also noted the conflicting policy goals of state laws and policies favoring the transferability of property and federal patent and copyright laws and policies favoring retention of control over their intellectual property by inventors and authors, *see, e.g.*, *Everex*, 89 F.3d at 677–80; *Cohen*, 845 F.2d at 853, there is at present no clearly controlling authority which establishes whether a merger transaction, and in particular the widely used reverse triangular merger structure, results in a transfer by the acquired company of its rights under license agreements. Although the U.S. District Court for the Northern District of California, in the case of *SQL Solutions, Inc. v. Oracle Corp.*, 1991 U.S. Dist. LEXIS 21097 (N.D. Cal. Dec. 18, 1991), expressly held that under California law a transfer of rights occurred as a result of a reverse triangular merger through which SQL became a wholly owned subsidiary of Sybase, the opinion is of questionable precedential value. It may have been reversible error for the court to fail to expressly consider the relevant merger statute, and other aspects of the court's analysis may fairly be criticized as lacking a sound basis.

The *SQL Solutions* opinion has not been affirmed or cited by any appellate court, and has only been cited (in passing and not for its primary holding) by two lower courts during the twelve years since its issuance. Moreover, in a comprehensive and persuasive opinion that was affirmed by the Delaware Supreme Court and cited by the Ninth Circuit in *Linney*, the Delaware Court of Chancery in *Star Cellular Telephone Company, Inc. v. Baton Rouge CGSA, Inc.*, 1993 Del. Ch. LEXIS 158 (July 30, 1993), aff'd 1994 Del. LEXIS 190 (1994), concluded that a change of control in a merger transaction would not be deemed to result in a transfer of a federally-issued cellular telephone license. Other courts have also reached or suggested the conclusion that no legally significant transfer of property rights occurs as a result of a reverse triangular merger. *See, e.g., TXO Production Co. and Marathon Oil Co. v. M.D. Mark, Inc.*, 999 S.W. 2d 137 (Tex. App. 14th Dist., 1999) (in merger of a subsidiary into a parent, Texas Court of Appeals found that no prohibited transfer occurred under Texas merger statute); *International Paper Company v. Ernest Broadhead*, 662 So. 2d 277 (Ala. Civ. App. 1995) (finding that a merger did not constitute a transfer or assignment).

Delaware Corporations Code Section 259 provides that all property rights of constituent corporations "shall be vested" in the corporate entity surviving or resulting from the merger, and there is ample case law establishing that in general, the property rights of the constituent corporations continue to reside in the surviving corporation after a merger. *See, e.g., Texaco Ref. & Mktg., Inc. v. Delaware River Basin Comm'n*, 824 F. Supp. 500 (D. Del. 1993), aff'd 30 F.3d 1488 (3d Cir. 1994). Similarly, California Corporations Code Section 1107 provides that "[u]pon merger pursuant to this chapter, the separate existence of the disappearing corporations ceases and the surviving corporation shall succeed, without other transfer, to all the rights and property of each of the disappearing corporations and shall be subject to all the debts and liabilities of each in the same manner as if the surviving corporation had itself incurred them." Courts applying Section 1107 and its predecessors have found that property rights arising under state law, e.g., rights pertaining to real property, are generally not affected by merger transactions and continue to reside with the corporate entity surviving the transaction. *See, e.g., Treadaway v. Camellia Convalescent Hospitals, Inc.*, 43 Cal. App. 3d 189 (1974).

A licensee, however, cannot assign a non-exclusive copyright license without the express authorization of the licensor. *Everex*, 89 F.3d at 677–80; *Harris v. Emus Records Corp.*, 734 F.2d 1329, 1333–1335 (9th Cir. 1984). See also *S.O.S.*, 886 F.2d at 1088 (under federal copyright policy, "copyright licenses are assumed to prohibit any use not authorized"); *Cohen v. Paramount Pictures Corp.*, 845 F.2d 851, 853 (9th Cir. 1988) (licenses must be analyzed to determine what use they affirmatively permit); 17 U.S.C. § 204(a) (transfer of copyright ownership must be in writing). Although the "first sale doctrine" permits the owner of a copy of a copyrighted computer program to sell or otherwise transfer ownership of that copy without the authority of the copyright owner, the conditions under which a possessor of a copy of a copyrighted program will be deemed an "owner" for purposes of the first sale doctrine are strictly limited. See *Adobe Systems, Inc. v. One Stop Micro, Inc.*, 84 F. Supp. 2d 1086, 1089–1092 (N.D. Cal. 2000); *DSC Communications*, 170 F.3d at 1360–1362; *Mai Systems*, 991 F.2d at 518–519.

Other than *SQL Solutions*, there does not appear to be any case which squarely addresses the issue of whether an expressly non-assignable copyright license will survive a reverse triangular merger transaction. The *SQL Solutions* opinion cites two principal cases as the grounds for its conclusion that "[m]ore fully reasoned cases have held that a transfer of rights is no less a transfer because it occurs by operation of law in a merger." 1991 U.S. Dist. LEXIS 21097. The court characterized the two cases as follows:

> *Koppers Coal & Transportation Co. v. U.S.*, 107 F.2d 706, 708 (3d Cir. 1939) (interpreting the Delaware merger statute and criticizing as "metaphysical" the notion, based on the theory of corporate continuity, that no transfer occurs); *PPG Industries, Inc. v. Guardian Industries Corp.*, 597 F.2d 1090, 1096 (6th Cir. 1979), *cert. denied*, 444 U.S. 930 (1979) (interpreting the Ohio merger statute).

There are a number of reasons why the *SQL Solutions* court's conclusion regarding transfers by operation of law is questionable.

First, the court may have erred by failing to expressly take into consideration the provisions of California Corporations Code Section 1107. See *U.S. v. Oil Resources, Inc.*, 817 F.2d 1429, 1432 (9th Cir. 1987) (remanding for further proceedings because district court erred by failing to consider applicable statutes in finding shareholders personally liable for corporate taxes under "trust fund" theory articulated in *Trubowitch*, 182 P.2d at 188). Second, the 1939 *Koppers Coal & Transportation* decision (which is also the primary authority relied upon by the 6th Circuit in its 1979 *PPG Industries* decision) does not appear to be a reliable source for ascertaining the present state of Delaware law regarding the issue of whether a transfer occurring by operation of law in a merger is distinguishable from a sale, gift or other active transfer of property.

In *Star Cellular Telephone Company*, it was held that a contractual prohibition against assignments did not prohibit a transfer of a federally-issued cellular telephone license which occurred by operation of law in a merger. Although a complete discussion of the basis for the *Star Cellular* holding is beyond the scope of this discussion, the court attempted to ascertain the intent of the parties at the time they entered into the agreement as to whether the licensed rights would be prohibited from surviving a merger transaction. The court first examined the provisions of the contract addressing transferability, then the other recitals and provisions of the contract, then extrinsic evidence. Finding it impossible to determine the parties' actual intent, the Court attempted to determine the parties' likely intent by lastly resorting to an interpretation of the transferability provisions "grounded on principles fundamental to the law of assignments."

PPG Industries, Inc. v. Guardian Industries Corp.

Court of Appeals for the Sixth Circuit
597 F.2d 1090 (6th Cir. 1979)

LIVELY, CIRCUIT JUDGE.

The question in this case is whether the surviving or resultant corporation in a statutory merger acquires patent license rights of the constituent corporations. The plaintiff, PPG Industries, Inc. (PPG), appeals from a judgment of the district court dismissing its patent infringement action on the ground that the defendant, Guardian Industries, Corp. (Guardian), as licensee of the patents in suit, was not an infringer. Guardian cross-appeals from a holding by the district court that its alternate defense based on an equipment license agreement was ineffective.

I

Prior to 1964 both PPG and Permaglass, Inc., were engaged in fabrication of glass products which required that sheets of glass be shaped for particular uses. Independently of each other the two fabricators developed similar processes which involved "floating glass on a bed of gas, while it was being heated and bent." This process is known in the industry as "gas hearth technology" and "air float technology"; the two terms are interchangeable. After a period of negotiations PPG and Permaglass entered into an agreement on January 1, 1964 whereby each granted rights to the other under "gas hearth system" patents already issued and in the process of prosecution. The purpose of the agreement was set forth in the preamble as follows:

> WHEREAS, PPG is desirous of acquiring from PERMAGLASS a world-wide exclusive license with right to sublicense others under PERMAGLASS Technical Data and PERMAGLASS Patent Rights, subject only to reservation by PERMAGLASS of non-exclusive rights thereunder; and

> WHEREAS, PERMAGLASS is desirous of obtaining a nonexclusive license to use Gas Hearth Systems under PPG Patent Rights, excepting in the Dominion of Canada.

This purpose was accomplished in the two sections of the agreement quoted below:

> SECTION 3. GRANT FROM PERMAGLASS TO PPG

> 3.1 Subject to the reservation set forth in Subsection 3.3 below, PERMAGLASS hereby grants to PPG an exclusive license, with right of sublicense, to use PERMAGLASS Technical Data in Gas Hearth Systems throughout the United States of America, its territories and possessions, and all countries of the world foreign thereto.

> 3.2 Subject to the reservation set forth in Subsection 3.3 below, PERMAGLASS hereby grants to PPG an unlimited exclusive license, with right of sublicense, under PERMAGLASS Patent Rights.

> 3.3 The licenses granted to PPG under Subsections 3.1 and 3.2 above shall be subject to the reservation of a non-exclusive, non-transferable, royalty-free, world-wide right and license for the benefit and use of PERMAGLASS.

> SECTION 4. GRANT FROM PPG TO PERMAGLASS

> 4.1 PPG hereby grants to PERMAGLASS a non-exclusive, non-transferable, royalty-free right and license to heat, bend, thermally temper and/or anneal glass using Gas Hearth Systems under PPG Patent Rights, excepting in the Dominion of Canada, and to use or sell glass articles produced thereby, but no license, express or implied, is hereby granted to PERMAGLASS under any

claim of any PPG patent expressly covering any coating method, coating composition, or coated article.

Assignability of the agreement and of the license granted to Permaglass and termination of the license granted to Permaglass were covered in the following language:

SECTION 9. ASSIGNABILITY

9.1 This Agreement shall be assignable by PPG to any successor of the entire flat glass business of PPG but shall otherwise be non-assignable except with the consent of PERMAGLASS first obtained in writing.

9.2 This Agreement and the license granted by PPG to PERMAGLASS hereunder shall be personal to PERMAGLASS and non-assignable except with the consent of PPG first obtained in writing.

SECTION 11. TERMINATION

11.2 In the event that a majority of the voting stock of PERMAGLASS shall at any time become owned or controlled directly or indirectly by a manufacturer of automobiles or a manufacturer or fabricator of glass other than the present owners, the license granted to PERMAGLASS under Subsection 4.1 shall terminate forthwith.

Eleven patents are involved in this suit. Nine of them originated with Permaglass and were licensed to PPG as exclusive licensee under Section 3.2, Supra, subject to the non-exclusive, non-transferable reservation to Permaglass set forth in Section 3.3. Two of the patents originated with PPG. Section 4.1 granted a non-exclusive, non-transferable license to Permaglass with respect to the two PPG patents. In Section 9.1 and 9.2 assignability was treated somewhat differently as between the parties, and the Section 11.2 provisions with regard to termination apply only to the license granted to Permaglass.

As of December 1969 Permaglass was merged into Guardian pursuant to applicable statutes of Ohio and Delaware. Guardian was engaged primarily in the business of fabricating and distributing windshields for automobiles and trucks. It had decided to construct a facility to manufacture raw glass and the capacity of that facility would be greater than its own requirements. Permaglass had no glass manufacturing capability and it was contemplated that its operations would utilize a large part of the excess output of the proposed Guardian facility.

The "Agreement of Merger" between Permaglass and Guardian did not refer specifically to the 1964 agreement between PPG and Permaglass. However, among Permaglass' representations in the agreement was the following:

(g) Permaglass is the owner, assignee or licensee of such patents, trademarks, trade names and copyrights as are listed and described in Exhibit "C" attached hereto. None of such patents, trademarks, trade names or copyrights is in litigation and Permaglass has not received any notice of conflict with the asserted rights of third parties relative to the use thereof.

Listed on Exhibit "C" to the merger agreement are the nine patents originally developed by Permaglass and licensed to PPG under the 1964 agreement which are involved in this infringement action.

Shortly after the merger was consummated PPG filed the present action, claiming infringement by Guardian in the use of apparatus and processes described and claimed in eleven patents which were identified by number and origin. The eleven patents were covered by the terms of the 1964 agreement. PPG asserted that it became the exclusive licensee of the nine patents which originated with Permaglass under the 1964 agreement and that the rights reserved by Permaglass were personal to it and non-transferable and non-assignable. PPG also claimed that Guardian had no rights with respect to the two patents which had originated with PPG because the license under these patents was personal to Permaglass and non-transferable and non-assignable except with the permission of PPG. In addition it claimed that the license with respect to these two patents had terminated under the provisions of Section 11.2, Supra, by reason of the merger.

One of the defenses pled by Guardian in its answer was that it was a licensee of the patents in suit. It described the merger with Permaglass and claimed it "had succeeded to all rights, powers, ownerships, etc., of Permaglass, and as Permaglass' successor, defendant is legally entitled to operate in place of Permaglass under the January 1, 1964 agreement between Permaglass and plaintiff, free of any claim of infringement of the patents. . . ."

After holding an evidentiary hearing the district court concluded that the parties to the 1964 agreement did not intend that the rights reserved by Permaglass in its nine patents or the rights assigned to Permaglass in the two PPG patents would not pass to a successor corporation by way of merger. The court held that there had been no assignment or transfer of the rights by Permaglass, but rather that Guardian acquired these rights by operation of law under the merger statutes of Ohio and Delaware. The provisions of the 1964 agreement making the license rights of Permaglass non-assignable and non-transferable were held not to apply because of the "continuity of interest inherent in a statutory merger that distinguishes it from the ordinary assignment or transfer case."

With respect to the termination provision in Section 11.2 of the 1964 agreement, the district court again relied on "the nature of a statutory merger in contrast to an outright sale or acquisition of stock" in holding that a majority of the voting stock of Permaglass did not become owned or controlled by Guardian.

II

Questions with respect to the assignability of a patent license are controlled by federal law. It has long been held by federal courts that agreements granting patent licenses are personal and not assignable unless expressly made so. This has been the rule at least since 1852 when the Supreme Court decided *Troy Iron & Nail v. Corning*, 55 U.S. (14 How.) 193, 14 L. Ed. 383 (1853). The district court recognized this rule in the present case, but concluded that where patent licenses are claimed to pass by operation of law to the resultant or surviving corporation in a statutory merger there has been no assignment or transfer.

There appear to be no reported cases where the precise issue in this case has been decided. At least two treatises contain the statement that rights under a patent license owned by a constituent corporation pass to the consolidated corporation in the case of a consolidation, W. Fletcher, Cyclopedia of the Law of Corporations s 7089 (revised ed. 1973); and to the new or resultant corporation in the case of a merger, A. Deller, Walker on Patents § 409 (2d ed. 1965). However, the cases cited in support of these statements by the commentators do not actually provide such support because their facts take them outside the general rule of non-assignability. Both texts rely on the decision in *Hartford-Empire Co. v. Demuth Glass Works, Inc.*, 19 F. Supp. 626 (E.D.N.Y. 1937). The agreement involved in that case specified that the patent license was assignable and its assignability was not an issue. Clearly the statement in the Hartford-Empire opinion that the merger conveyed to the new corporation the patent licenses owned by the old corporation results from the fact that the licenses in question were expressly made assignable, not from any general principle that such licenses pass to the resultant corporation where there is a merger. It is also noteworthy that the surviving corporation following the merger in Hartford-Empire was the original licensee, whereas in the present case the original licensee was merged into Guardian, which was the survivor. Fletcher also cites *Lightner v. Boston & A. R. Co.*, 1 Low Dec. 338, 15 Fed. Cas. No. 8,343, p. 514 (C.C. Mass. 1869). In that case both of the constituent corporations had been licensed by the patent holder. Thus, the reason for the rule against assignability was not present; the patent holder had selected both as licensees. There was also language in one of the licensing agreements involved in Lightner which indicated to the court that a consolidation was anticipated and that use of the patented mechanism by the consolidated corporation was authorized. Again, this decision does not indicate that the general rule of non-assignability of patent licenses does not apply in merger situations.

Guardian relies on two classes of cases where rights of a constituent corporation have been held to pass by merger to the resultant corporation even though such rights are not otherwise assignable or transferable. It points out that the courts have consistently held that "shop rights" do pass in a statutory merger. A shop right is an implied license which accrues to an employer in cases where an employee has perfected a patentable device while working for the employer. Though the employee is the owner of the patent he is estopped from claiming infringement by the employer. This estoppel arises from the fact that the patent work has been done on the employer's time and that the employer has furnished materials for the experiments and financial backing to the employee.

The rule that prevents an employee-inventor from claiming infringement against a successor to the entire business and good will of his employer is but one feature of the broad doctrine of estoppel which underlies the shop right cases. No element of estoppel exists in the present case. The license rights of Permaglass did not arise by implication. They were bargained for at arm's length and the agreement which defines the rights of the parties provides that Permaglass received non-transferable, non-assignable personal licenses. We do not believe that the express prohibition against assignment and transfer in a written instrument may be held ineffective by analogy to a rule based on estoppel in situations where there is no written contract and the rights of the parties have arisen by implication because of their past relationship.

The other group of cases which the district court and Guardian found to be analogous hold that the resultant corporation in a merger succeeds to the rights of the constituent corporations under real estate leases. The most obvious difficulty in drawing an analogy between the lease cases and those concerning patent licenses is that a lease is an interest in real property. As such, it is subject to the deep-rooted policy against restraints on alienation. Applying this policy, courts have construed provisions against assignability in leases strictly and have concluded that they do not prevent the passage of interests by operation of law. There is no similar policy which is offended by the decision of a patent owner to make a license under his patent personal to the licensee, and non-assignable and non-transferable. In fact the law treats a license as if it contained these restrictions in the absence of express provisions to the contrary.

We conclude that the district court misconceived the intent of the parties to the 1964 agreement. We believe the district court put the burden on the wrong party in stating:

> Because the parties failed to provide that Permaglass' rights under the 1964 license agreement would not pass to the corporation surviving a merger, the Court finds that Guardian succeeded to Permaglass' license pursuant to 8 Del. C. § 259, and Ohio Revised Code §§ 1701.81 and 1701.83.

The agreement provides with respect to the license which Permaglass granted to PPG that Permaglass reserved "a non-exclusive, non-transferable, royalty-free, worldwide right and license for the benefit and use of Permaglass." (emphasis added). Similarly, with respect to its own two patents, PPG granted to Permaglass "a non-exclusive, non-transferable, royalty-free right and license. . . ." Further, the agreement provides that both it and the license granted to Permaglass "shall be personal to PERMAGLASS and non-assignable except with the consent of PPG first obtained in writing."

The quoted language from Sections 3, 4 and 9 of the 1964 agreement evinces an intent that only Permaglass was to enjoy the privileges of licensee. If the parties had intended an exception in the event of a merger, it would have been a simple matter to have so provided in the agreement. Guardian contends such an exception is not necessary since it is universally recognized that patent licenses pass from a licensee to the resultant corporation in case of a merger. This does not appear to be the case. . . . We conclude that if the parties had intended an exception in case of a merger to the provisions against assignment and transfer they would have included it in the agreement. It should be noted also that the district court in *Packard*, supra, held that an assignment had taken place when the licensee was merged into another corporation.

The district court also held that the patent licenses in the present case were not transferred because they passed by operation of law from Permaglass to Guardian. This conclusion is based on the theory of continuity which underlies a true merger. However, the theory of continuity relates to the fact that there is no dissolution of the constituent corporations and, even though they cease to exist, their essential corporate attributes are vested by operation of law in the surviving or resultant corporation. It does not mean that there is no transfer of particular assets from a constituent corporation to the surviving or resultant one.

The Ohio merger statute provides that following a merger all property of a constituent corporation shall be "deemed to be Transferred to and vested in the surviving or new corporation without further act or deed. . . ." (emphasis added). Ohio Revised Code, (former) § 1701.81(A)(4). This indicates that the transfer is by operation of law, not that there is no transfer of assets in a merger situation. The Delaware statute, which was also involved in the Permaglass-Guardian merger, provides that the property of the constituent corporations "shall be vested in the corporation surviving or resulting from such merger or consolidation. . . ." 8 Del. C. § 259(a). The Third Circuit has construed the "shall be vested" language of the Delaware statute as follows:

> In short, the underlying property of the constituent corporations is Transferred to the resultant corporation upon the carrying out of the consolidation or merger. . . . *Koppers Coal & Transportation Co. v. United States*, 107 F.2d 706, 708 (3d Cir. 1939).

In his opinion in *Koppers*, Judge Biggs disposed of arguments very similar to those of Guardian in the present case, based on the theory of continuity. Terming such arguments "metaphysical" he found them completely at odds with the language of the Delaware statute. Finally, on this point, the parties themselves provided in the merger agreement that all property of Permaglass "shall be deemed transferred to and shall vest in Guardian without further act or deed. . . ." A transfer is no less a transfer because it takes place by operation of law rather than by a particular act of the parties. The merger was effected by the parties and the transfer was a result of their act of merging.

Thus, Sections 3, 4 and 9 of the 1964 agreement between PPG and Permaglass show an intent that the licenses held by Permaglass in the eleven patents in suit not be transferable. While this conclusion disposes of the license defense as to all eleven patents, it should be noted that Guardian's claim to licenses under the two patents which originated with PPG is also defeated by Section 11.2 of the 1964 agreement. This section addresses a different concern from that addressed in Sections 3, 4 and 9. The restrictions on transferability and assignability in those sections prevent the patent licenses from becoming the property of third parties. The termination clause, however, provides that Permaglass' license with respect to the two PPG patents will terminate if the ownership of a majority of the voting stock of Permaglass passes from the 1964 stockholders to designated classes of persons, even though the licenses themselves might never have changed hands.

Apparently PPG was willing for Permaglass to continue as licensee under the nine patents even though ownership of its stock might change. These patents originated with Permaglass and so long as Permaglass continued to use the licenses for its own benefit a mere change in ownership of Permaglass stock would not nullify the licenses. Only a transfer or assignment would cause a termination. However, the agreement provides for termination with respect to the two original PPG patents in the event of an indirect takeover of Permaglass by a change in the ownership of a majority of its stock. The fact that PPG sought and obtained a stricter provision with respect to the two patents which it originally owned in no way indicates an intention to permit transfer of licenses under the other nine in case of a merger. None of the eleven licenses was transferable; but two of them, those involving PPG's own development in the field of gas hearth technology, were not to continue even for the benefit of the licensee if it came under the control of a manufacturer of automobiles or a competitor of PPG in the glass industry "other than the present owners" of Permaglass. A consistency among the provisions of the agreement is discernible when the different origins of the various patents are considered.

III

The second issue in the case does not require detailed consideration. Guardian maintains that it was licensed to use four furnace units which are alleged to infringe the eleven patents in suit. This argument is based on an "Exclusive License Agreement" of February 24, 1969 between PPG and Permaglass which Guardian contends was an "equipment license" rather than a license for processes covered by the various patents. It argues that it was free to operate the four furnace units under either the 1964 or the 1969 agreement. PPG agrees that Guardian succeeded to whatever rights Permaglass had under the 1969 agreement, but maintains that this agreement merely licensed a different group of patents relative to the "air form development," an improved method which had recently been perfected. PPG states that it is not claiming infringement of any of the "air form" patents referred to in the 1969 agreement and that rights which Permaglass acquired under that agreement afford no defense to the present infringement action.

The district court attempted to determine whether the four units operated by Guardian are "licensed furnace units" under the agreement. This involved, among other things, the necessity of trying to decipher the meaning of "and/or" as used by the parties always a nettlesome task. However, if PPG's claim that none of the eleven patents in suit is covered by the 1969 agreement is correct, for purposes of this appeal the definition of "licensed furnace units" is immaterial. The district court did hold that the 1969 agreement was not intended to modify the 1964 agreement. This finding is fully supported by the evidence. It was the 1964 agreement which defined the rights of Permaglass with respect to the eleven patents in suit. We have held that the rights of Permaglass under the 1964 agreement terminated upon its merger into Guardian. Since the 1969 agreement was not intended to modify the 1964 agreement in any way, it cannot afford a defense as a matter of law to the claim of infringement. Though facts may be developed at trial which will require further consideration of this particular defense, the district court was correct in denying dismissal on the basis of the 1969 agreement.

The judgment of the district court is reversed on appeal and affirmed on cross-appeal, and the cause is remanded for further proceedings.

Verson Corporation v. Verson International Group, PLC

District Court for the Northern District of Illinois

899 F. Supp. 358 (N.D. Ill. 1995)

Moran, Senior District Judge.

Plaintiff Verson Corporation brought this lawsuit alleging that defendants Verson International Group, Verson Wilkins Limited, and Verson International Limited violated a license agreement for intellectual property. Before us now is defendants' motion to dismiss plaintiff's amended complaint. For the reasons set forth below, the motion is denied.

BACKGROUND

Verson Corporation (Verson), the successor to Verson Allsteel Press Company (VASP) and the wholly-owned subsidiary of Allied Products Corporation, manufactures presses for the metal-forming industry. In the early 1980s VASP began experiencing financial difficulties. In order to ease through its financial downturn VASP and a group of its international managers entered into an agreement wherein the managers would buy out VASP's international operations with a newly formed independent company, Verson International Limited (collectively referred to herein, along with Verson Wilkins Limited and Verson International Limited, as "VIL"). VIL and VASP entered into a series of agreements to facilitate the management buyout (MBO), the most important for our purposes being the VASP/VIL License Agreement (license agreement). In that agreement VASP agreed to turn over to VIL its patents and non-patented trade secrets, and allowed VIL to use this know-how. The license agreement called for both parties to turn over all newly developed know-how to the other for a period of five years. The parties also agreed to a series of restrictive covenants that gave VASP the exclusive right to market its products in the United States and Canada and gave VIL the exclusive right to market its products in the rest of the world. Both territorial restrictions were to last five years.

In the first lawsuit between the parties VIL sued VASP alleging that VASP had violated the license agreement's restrictive covenants and seeking an injunction requiring Verson to turn over certain know-how. VASP argued that the territorial and durational restrictions violated state and federal antitrust laws. We enforced the restrictions only in part, finding that VIL was barred only from the use of VASP know-how in the United States and Canada, and that VASP was barred only from marketing its products in Europe. Verson Wilkins Ltd. v. Allied Products Corp., 723 F. Supp. 1, 20 (N.D. Ill. 1989). We also required VASP to turn over the know-how covered under the license agreement. In 1990 the parties executed a settlement agreement disposing of the remaining disputes regarding exchange of the know-how.

Soon thereafter VIL entered into an agreement with Enprotech Mechanical Services, Inc. (Enprotech), a direct competitor of Verson in the North American market. In this agreement VIL turned over know-how it received from VASP in the 1985 license agreement and granted Enprotech the exclusive right to use this know-how to manufacture replacement parts for Verson presses. This arrangement spawned the present lawsuit. In its complaint Verson alleged that VIL violated Article 16 of the 1985 license agreement which required VIL to obtain VASP's approval before licensing the know-how to another party, by turning over VASP know-how to Enprotech. Defendants moved to dismiss the complaint, claiming that Article 16 did not survive the termination of the agreement. We granted that motion on December 30, 1994. Verson moved for reconsideration of our order and for leave to amend its complaint, arguing that the Enprotech agreement, which Verson claims is an assignment, violated the license agreement's restriction on VIL's right to assign the know-how. Although this constituted a new line of attack for Verson, we allowed it to amend its complaint to more fully make out this claim. Verson has since amended its complaint to incorporate the assignment argument. Before us now is VIL's motion to dismiss the amended complaint. VIL argues that the 1990 settlement agreement prevents Verson from maintaining this action; that it is the co-owner of the know-how, not a licensee, and thus had the right to assign it to Enprotech; that the right to assign the know-how was implicit in the 1985 licensing agreement; that a perpetual ban on assignability would be an unreasonable restraint of trade; and that its transaction with Enprotech is a sublease rather than an assignment. We will examine each of these arguments in turn.

DISCUSSION

A. The 1990 Settlement Agreement

VIL argues that a settlement agreement executed in connection with the earlier case involving these parties bars Verson's action here. In the first lawsuit VIL obtained an injunction requiring Verson to turn over various types of know-how related to the licensing agreement. The case was still pending, however, because the parties disputed what documents needed to be produced and who was to pay for the copying. The parties entered into a settlement in which VIL accepted some of the disputed know-how in complete satisfaction of any claim for know-how it might have had under the licensing agreement, and Verson agreed not to challenge VIL's right to use this know-how. VIL argues that this action challenging VIL's assignment (or sublease) of the know-how to Enprotech is a restriction on the use of the know-how and thus violates the settlement agreement. Verson responds that VIL's right to assign or transfer the know-how remained as it was under the licensing agreement.

We agree with Verson that the 1990 settlement agreement does not prevent it from attempting to restrict VIL's right to assign the know-how. In settlements, as in all contracts, every effort should be made to give force to the words employed by the parties and to not imply words that the parties could have used but did not. Through the settlement Verson agreed only not to restrict VIL's use of the know-how. The word "use" does not ordinarily also include sale, transfer, or assignment. This is especially so when dealing with the right to use intellectual property. One can use know-how, trade secrets, or patents freely, but still not transfer or assign that information. The right to the know-how at issue here could easily be separated into the right to use the know-how and the right to sell, transfer, or assign the know-how, and the parties' selection of the word "use" provides support for the view that they did not intend for the settlement agreement to grant VIL a right to assign the know-how that was not already granted under the terms of the license agreement. The parties could have added "transfer or assign" to "use," and the fact that they did not is probative of the issue.

Other sections of the settlement also provide some support for that view. Under a section entitled "Reservation of Rights," both parties reserved the right to sue each other for any breach of the licensing agreement. The fact that both parties sought to preserve their rights under the licensing agreement arguably indicates that the settlement was intended only to resolve the dispute as to what know-how Verson was required to turn over and who was to pay for the copying costs. VIL's reading of the reservation-of-rights clause, that the parties intended only to prevent public disclosure of the know-how, is strained, given that the parties could have easily drafted the clause to reflect that intent but did not. Therefore, we hold that the 1990 settlement agreement was not an unambiguous waiver of Verson's right to challenge VIL's assignment of the know-how.

B. Is VIL a Co-Owner of the Know-How or Only a Licensee?

The premise behind Verson's complaint is that VIL is a non-exclusive licensee of the know-how. In earlier orders we expressed some doubt regarding this proposition and left open the question whether VIL is a co-owner of the know-how. VIL seizes upon this language and presses the argument here.

The starting place for determining whether VIL is a co-owner of the know-how is the 1985 license agreement. The agreement states that "[u]pon expiration of the term of this Agreement, subject to [confidentiality provisions], Licensee shall have the non-exclusive perpetual royalty free right to continue to exercise, use or practice the rights granted Licensee under Section 2.01 without limitation as to Territory. . . ." As we indicated above, the use of know-how can be readily distinguished from the ownership of the know-how. Thus, one meaning of the license agreement grants VIL only the right to use the know-how to compete with Verson worldwide. The language of this provision, or the other provisions in the agreement, do not necessarily indicate the parties intended for VIL to become co-owner of the know-how at the termination of the five-year period.

Despite the lack of any express provision in the license agreement granting it co-ownership of the know-how, VIL presents four arguments to support its claim: first, that the amount it paid in connection with the MBO indicates that VIL would become co-owner of the know-how; second, that it developed some of the know-how itself; third, that the clear intent of the MBO and license agreement was to make VIL and Verson head-to-head competitors after five years; and, fourth, that VIL acquired property rights to the know-how when it acquired VASP's international operations.

We find that none of these four arguments helps VIL's cause here, even if we can entertain them in support of a motion to dismiss. First, the amount VIL paid in connection with the MBO does not by itself demonstrate anything about the parties' intent. The license agreement was just one part of a series of agreements executed in connection with the MBO. It is impossible to say as a matter of law that the consideration paid by VIL was to acquire ownership rights to the know-how after five years. VIL may be able to present evidence that the true value of what it received in the MBO could not come near the $8 million it actually paid if ownership of the know-how were not included, and in such a situation we could find the consideration paid to be probative of the parties' intent. However, we cannot make that determination on a motion to dismiss.

Second, Verson disputes VIL's claim that it developed part of the know-how at issue here. It is clear that whether or not VIL did develop this know-how is a disputed question of fact that cannot be resolved on a motion to dismiss. Such a determination must await further development by the parties.

Third, we have repeatedly recognized that the goal of the MBO in general, and the license agreement in particular, was to place VIL and Verson as head-to-head competitors at the end of five years, as VIL argues. That proposition does not, however, establish VIL's ownership of the know-how. At the end of the agreement, VIL had every right to compete with Verson in any market in the world. In that respect the two firms were head-to-head competitors. Limiting VIL to the right to use, instead of assign, the know-how does not appear to frustrate this goal. All VIL is prevented from doing is assigning or selling the know-how to a competitor. This limitation has no effect on VIL's ability to compete with Verson in the manufacture, sale, or repair of presses.

Finally, it is not clear at this point what rights VIL acquired in the MBO when it took over VASP's international operations. Until now we have never been faced with determining exactly what rights VIL acquired in the MBO. Verson has submitted a number of the agreements involving VASP and its many subsidiaries, that purportedly demonstrate that VIL acquired only licensing rights, not ownership rights, to the know-how. VIL has not contradicted Verson's recitation of the corporate history. Accepting Verson's allegation that no ownership rights were transferred in the MBO—an allegation supported by the submitted documents—we hold that Verson has properly alleged that VIL was a mere licensee, not a co-owner, of the know-how.

C. Implied Right of Assignability

VIL does not dispute that there is no provision in the license agreement granting it an explicit post-termination right to assign the know-how. Yet it argues that despite this lack of express authority, authority to assign its rights under the agreement must be inferred from the circumstances and the parties' conduct.

Under well-established law the holder of a nonexclusive patent license may not assign its license unless the right to assign is expressly provided for in the license agreement. Under . . . longstanding federal case law, patent licenses are treated as personal to the licenseholder and therefore are presumed to be not assignable. *Id.*

VIL argues that his presumption against assignability may be overcome by the circumstances and the conduct of the parties. We seriously doubt whether [the cases cited] survive the later developed line of cases refusing to imply a right of assignability of patent licenses. Even if some vestige of Farmland and Bowers remains, we cannot overlook decades of precedent to the contrary. Therefore, we feel bound to require compelling evidence of the parties' intent before implying a right to assign. Such evidence is not presented here, nor may it be considered to resolve a motion to dismiss.

VIL points to two aspects of the parties' conduct to support its claim that a right of assignment should be inferred. First, it argues that the fact that the license agreement gave it broad authority to sublicense its rights without Verson's approval establishes conclusively that the parties did not believe that the patented rights were highly personable and therefore could be assigned. We disagree. VIL seeks to bootstrap its negotiated right to sublicense into a right to assign. Were VIL correct, every license granting a right to sublicense would also implicitly contain a right of assignment. That is clearly not the case. On the contrary, under the axiom of expressio unius, the presence of the provision on sublicensing indicates that the parties did not intend to allow assignments. Further, VIL cannot seriously maintain that Verson did not consider the know-how to be highly personable. The license agreement contained a strict confidentiality clause and every indication from the parties' conduct since the MBO is that the know-how is vital to successful competition in the industry. Therefore, it is clear that VIL's right to sublicense does not establish as a matter of law an intent to also allow it to assign its rights.

VIL also claims that Article 16 of the licensing agreement, which required VIL to first obtain Verson's approval before assigning its rights to a competitor, demonstrates that when the parties sought to restrict the right to assign they did so expressly, and the fact that there is no provision limiting VIL's right to assign post-termination establishes that no such limitations were intended by the parties. In addition, VIL argues that because our order of December 30, 1993, ruled that Article 16 did not survive the termination of the licensing agreement, preventing VIL from assigning its rights post-termination would mean that it had greater leeway to assign before the termination than after, which it asserts is an absurd result.

We are not persuaded that the presence of Article 16 overcomes the strong presumption against implying a right to assign licenses for intellectual property. Article 16 and a post-termination restriction on assignment are not, as VIL suggests, in hopeless conflict. It is reasonable for Verson to have allowed VIL greater leeway to assign its rights during the five-year period of the licensing agreement because VIL was prohibited by the agreement from competing with Verson in North America. After the termination of the agreement, however, VIL could compete directly with Verson in North America, which may have prompted Verson to restrict VIL's right to assign. In any event, we need not rule that this is what the parties intended. Rather, we conclude that the license agreement does not conclusively refute Verson's claim that the know-how cannot be assigned. . . .

[The court's discussion of VIL's restraint of trade is omitted here.]

E. Assignment or Sublicense

VIL's final argument is that its agreement with Enprotech is not an assignment at all, but rather is a sublicense, and since the license agreement granted VIL the authority to sublicense its rights, Verson's suit must fail.

Verson argues that intellectual property rights can be severed and assigned separately. That is, a patentee may assign the right to use a patent for sale of a product but retain the right to use the patent for other purposes. Support for this proposition can be found in tax cases, and in some of the cases dealing with who has standing to sue for patent infringement. Under this view the answer depends on whether the patentee has transferred all its rights in a particular market (an assignment) or has transferred only some of those rights, retaining others for itself (a license). During the course of this litigation VIL has retreated from its earlier opposition to this principle and now seems content to argue that, even if that were the law, the Enprotech agreement still cannot be considered an assignment.

Verson claims that the Enprotech agreement is an assignment rather than a sublicense because VIL transferred all the rights associated with the after-market for Verson presses. Specifically, the Enprotech agreement states:

> [VIL] (i) grants and assigns to [Enprotech] (1) the exclusive (as between Licensor and Licensee), royalty free right and license to utilize the Proprietary Rights in the Territory for the manufacture and sale of Verson Parts and for the rebuilding and modernization of Verson Presses and subject to the reserved rights of [VIL], the maintenance and repair of Verson Presses, and (2) the right and license to use the Trademark in connection with the manufacture and sale of Verson Parts and, subject to the review and consent of [VIL], which consent will not be unreasonably withheld, the maintenance, repair, rebuilding and modernization of Verson Presses and (ii) sells to Enprotech the Technical Information and Other Information subject to the terms and conditions of this Agreement.

The "territory" is defined to include certain countries in North America and Central America. "Proprietary rights" and "technical information" basically entail the Verson technology that VIL received under the licensing agreement.

VIL counters that it has retained sufficient rights to the after-market to render the Enprotech agreement a sublicense rather than an assignment. It identifies five such rights: (1) the right to make replacement parts in connection with the sale of new presses; (2) the exclusive right to provide service for the enhancement retrofit of Verson presses; (3) the exclusive right to provide service work for the maintenance and repair of Verson presses; (4) a fifty-year period for the agreement; and (5) a parts supply agreement requiring Enprotech to purchase spare parts from a corporation affiliated with VIL.

We can quickly dispense with VIL's argument that rights two and three render the agreement a sublicense. Those rights do not limit the agreement's grant to Enprotech of an exclusive right to manufacture replacement parts; the issue of repair service does not limit Enprotech's ability to use the know-how in the replacement parts market.

Similarly, the fifty-year period does not, as a matter of law, render the agreement a sublicense. Verson has alleged that the fifty-year period far exceeds the useful life of any of the know-how, given the normal rate of change in technology in the industry, and thus the fifty-year period does not serve as any practical restraint on Enprotech's rights under the agreement. Since VIL has not demonstrated that this well-pleaded allegation is incorrect as a matter of law, we must accept it as being true for the purposes of this motion to dismiss.

Nor does the parts supply agreement, as a matter of law, render the Enprotech agreement a sublicense. Although Enprotech is required to purchase certain products from a VIL-affiliated corporation, the agreement states that Enprotech's failure to abide by the parts supply agreement does not affect its exclusive rights granted elsewhere in the agreement. Therefore, the parts supply agreement need not be read to limit Enprotech's right to the use the know-how in the parts market.

That leaves the Enprotech agreement's provision granting VIL the right to manufacture replacement parts in connection with the sale of new presses. It is too early at this juncture to determine as a matter of law that VIL's retention of this right limits Enprotech's interest to a mere sublicense rather than an assignment. VIL may be able to demonstrate that its retained right to provide replacement parts as part of contracts for the sale of new presses represents a sufficiently large portion of the replacement part market to make the Enprotech agreement a sublicense, but we are not in a position to make that determination here. Since VIL has failed to demonstrate that the Enprotech agreement is a license as a matter of law, we must deny its motion to dismiss. VIL is free to renew this argument at a later stage if it can present extrinsic evidence clarifying the ambiguity in the Enprotech agreement.

[MOTION DENIED]

Motorola, Inc. v. Amkor Technology, Inc.

Supreme Court of Delaware

849 A.2d 931 (Del. 2004)

HOLLAND, JUSTICE:

The dispute involves third-party Citizen Watch Co., Ltd.'s ("Citizen") assignment of its Patent License Agreement ("PLA") with Motorola to Amkor.

Motorola contends that Motorola's and Citizen's intent in entering into the Agreement, as expressed in the plain terms of the PLA, precludes the assignment. Amkor claims that the assignment is valid. We conclude that, in the context of the PLA, the terms "license" and "assignment" are ambiguous and a material issue of fact exists, precluding summary judgment. Therefore, the judgment of the Superior Court must be reversed.

Facts

Amkor and Motorola are currently in the business of, among other things, developing and providing semiconductor assembly test services and products, commonly referred to as ball grid array packages ("BGA Packages"). BGA Packages are a housing apparatus for integrated circuit structures that are used to make semiconductor products. Both Motorola and Amkor hold patents relating to BGA Packages. Prior to selling its BGA Assembly Business Unit to Amkor on March 28, 2002, Citizen was also in this business and also held certain patents relating to BGA Packages.

On June 30, 1993, Motorola and Amkor entered into an Immunity Agreement, pursuant to which Motorola and Amkor provided each other with cross-releases and cross-licenses for their BGA Package patents. In consideration of Motorola's grant of a license to Amkor, the Immunity Agreement required Amkor to pay royalties to Motorola on a quarterly basis for use of Motorola's BGA Package patents. The royalty payments were based on Amkor's quarterly use of the technology covered by the patents. Amkor paid Motorola approximately $36.8 million under the Immunity Agreement for use of Motorola's technology. The Immunity Agreement expired by its own terms on December 31, 2002.

On January 25, 1996, Motorola entered into the PLA with Citizen. The PLA grants Citizen the right to use the same Motorola BGA Package patents that are the subject of the Immunity Agreement between Motorola and Amkor. The PLA grants at least two specific rights to Citizen that were not granted to Amkor. First, Motorola and Citizen cross-license their respective patents governing BGA packaging technology on a royalty-free basis. Second, the PLA with Citizen includes an assignment from Motorola to Citizen of an undivided one-half interest in two of Motorola's U.S. patents: Patent No. 5,241,133 (the "Mullin Patent"); and Patent No. 5,216,278 (the "Lin Patent"). Amkor was required to pay Motorola for use of these two patents under the Immunity Agreement, and was granted no ownership interest in them.

The PLA also contains restrictions on Citizen's ability to transfer its royalty-free rights to third parties. These restrictions are set forth in Sections 4.1 and 5.1 of the PLA. Section 4.1 of the PLA expressly prohibits Citizen from entering into contracts with a set list of companies to license its royalty-free rights to the Mullin and Lin patents:

> CITIZEN agrees not to offer to enter into or to enter into a contract with current BGA licensees of MOTOROLA, including those listed in Appendix A [inter alia, Amkor], for a license to make, have made, or sell BGAs under U.S. Patent Nos. 5,241,133 [Mullin] and/or 5,216,278 [Lin].

Section 5.5 of the PLA limits Citizen's ability to transfer or assign its rights under the agreement, as follows:

> The rights or privileges provided for in this Agreement may be assigned or transferred by either party only with the prior written consent of the other

party and with the authorization or approval of any governmental authority as then may be required, except to a successor in ownership of all or substantially all of the assets of the assigning party relating to the business unit employing the patents licensed hereunder but such successor, before such assignment or transfer is effective, shall expressly assume in writing to the other party the performance of all the terms and conditions of this Agreement to be performed by the assigning party.

On March 28, 2002, Amkor purchased substantially all of the assets of Citizen's BGA Assembly Business Unit. Concurrently with the sale of Citizen's business, Citizen and Amkor entered into an Intellectual Property Assignment Agreement ("IPAA") that "assigns" to Amkor Citizen's PLA with Motorola as well as Citizen's one-half interest in the Mullin and Lin Patents. The IPAA requires Citizen to gain the necessary consents for the alleged assignments from all relevant entities but "exclud[es] any consent that may be required from Motorola."

After the IPAA was executed, Amkor advised Motorola that Amkor had taken over Citizen's ownership rights in the Mullin and Lin Patents, and acquired a royalty-free license to the Motorola BGA patent portfolio under the PLA. Motorola informed both Citizen and Amkor that they were in material breach of their respective agreements with Motorola, and that the alleged transfers were invalid under Section 4.1. Amkor stopped paying royalties to Motorola for the second and third quarters of 2002, and stated that it would not pay royalties for the fourth quarter of 2002....

The Superior Court noted that the PLA contained no definitions of the terms "license" or "assignment." Therefore, it looked to the "commonly accepted meanings" from Black's Law Dictionary, which defined an assignment as the "act of transferring to another all or part of one's property, interest, or rights." Black's defined a license as "a personal privilege to do some particular act or series of acts . . . ." Based on these definitions, the Superior Court rejected Motorola's claim that a license is subsumed in the definition of an assignment.

Instead, the Superior Court concluded that the terms license and assignment "are distinct and separate, as used in Section 4.1 and Section 5.5, involving different obligations and responsibilities." Consequently, the Superior Court held that "[a]lthough Motorola may not have intended to allow Citizen and Amkor to circumvent [Section] 4.1 by assigning the patents to Amkor via [Section] 5.5, that is what is permitted by the clear meaning of the language of the . . . PLA." Accordingly, the Superior Court granted Amkor's motion for summary judgment and denied Motorola's cross-motion. . . .

Illinois Contract Law

The PLA contract at issue in this case expressly provides that it is governed by the law of Illinois, under which "the primary goal in construing a contract is to give effect to the intent of the parties." In determining the parties' intent, the contract must be read as a whole. When the language of the contract is clear and unambiguous, the parties' intent must be determined solely from the plain language of the contract. If the contract language creates an ambiguity, however, extrinsic evidence is permissible and the interpretation of the language becomes a question of fact.

Illinois follows the general rule that a contract is not ambiguous merely because the parties disagree as to its meaning. Rather, "[a] contract is properly found ambiguous when the language used is susceptible to more than one meaning or is obscure in meaning through indefiniteness of expression." Therefore, if reasonable people may draw different inferences from the undisputed facts, an ambiguity exists and summary judgment is inappropriate.

Parties' Intent

In construing a contract, the primary objective for any court is to give effect to the parties' intent. Accordingly, in deciding on the interpretation of the PLA, the Superior Court's principal goal under Illinois law was to ascertain Citizen's and Motorola's intent in entering into the contract. Thus, the dispositive question in this litigation is what was the parties' intention?

In determining the parties' intent with regard to Section 4.1 and 5.5, Illinois law required the Superior Court to consider the contract as a whole and not focus on the sections as isolated provisions. Section 4.1 of the PLA explicitly precludes Citizen from "licensing" its rights to the Mullin and Lin Patents to Amkor. If an "assignment" to Amkor is allowed by Section 5.5, however, Motorola argues that such an assignment will render the restrictions of Section 4.1 meaningless.

Motorola argues that it intended to preclude current BGA licensees, such as Amkor, from obtaining royalty-free use of the BGA Package patents from Citizen. Section 4.1 of the PLA expressly prohibits Citizen from contracting for a license with "current BGA licensees" of Motorola. It is undisputed that Amkor was a current BGA licensee. Amkor concedes that Section 4.1 creates a bar to its agreement with Citizen.

Nevertheless, Amkor argues that Section 5.5 of the PLA creates a specific exception to the prohibition in Section 4.1. In support of this argument, Amkor points to the language of Section 5.5, which allows assignment of the BGA Package patents without the express written consent of Motorola if the acquiring party succeeds in ownership in "all or substantially all of the assets of the assigning party relating to the business unit employing the patents licensed hereunder. . . ." Accordingly, Amkor contends that the PLA restricts Citizen from sublicensing the technology for profit, but allows assignment of all of Citizen's rights that would be occasioned by a sale of all or substantially all of its relevant business unit assets.

Contract Ambiguous

Whether Motorola's or Amkor's interpretation of the parties' intent is correct is dependent on the meaning of the terms "license" and "assignment." Amkor argues that the plain meaning of those terms show that they are separate and distinct. Conversely, Motorola argues that a "license" is subsumed within an "assignment." Thus, under Amkor's reading of the contract, the PLA precludes a "license" but allows "assignment." Under Motorola's reading, by prohibiting Citizen from "licensing" the BGA Package Patents to current licensees such as Amkor, the PLA necessarily precludes an "assignment" as well.

Both Motorola's and Amkor's interpretations of the PLA contract language may be reasonable. Where more than one plausible construction of a contract exists or the contract is ambiguous because two or more key provisions conflict, an issue of material fact arises and summary judgment must be denied. A provision is "key" or "material" if a reasonable person would "attach importance to [it] . . . in determining his choice of action in the transaction in question. . . ."

The Superior Court held that the specific licensing restrictions of Section 4.1 do not modify the general assignment provisions of Section 5.5, with the result that as long as the requirements of Section 5.5 are met, the assignment is valid. To reach that conclusion, the Superior Court relied upon Black's Law Dictionary's definitions of the terms "license" and "assignment." The Superior Court held that, as long as the assignment provisions of Section 5.5 are met, the licensing prohibitions of Section 4.1 are irrelevant.

The Superior Court concluded that although "Motorola may not have intended to allow Citizen and Amkor to circumvent [Section] 4.1 by assigning the patents to Amkor via [Section] 5.5, that is what is permitted by the clear meaning of the Motorola/Citizen PLA." As a general rule, whenever it is possible, a court must preserve the reasonable expectations that form the basis of the parties' contractual relationship. In this case, contrary to that legal principle, the Superior Court held that the language in Section 5.5 bound Motorola to what may have been the unintended consequences that Section 4.1 prohibited. The Superior Court's construction of Section 5.5, in apparent isolation from Section 4.1, was contrary to the law of Illinois.

Contract terms are controlling when they establish the parties' common meaning so that a reasonable person in the position of either party would have no expectations inconsistent with the contract language. When the provisions in controversy are fairly susceptible of different interpretations or may have two or more different meanings, there is ambiguity. In those circumstances, the interpreting court must look beyond the language of the contract to ascertain the parties' intentions. In this case, the Superior Court should have, but did not, look to parol evidence to interpret the PLA.

To the extent that the parties' intent cannot be determined from the plain terms of the PLA or the parties' intent is open to more than one interpretation, the Superior Court should have considered parol evidence to resolve the ambiguity. The ambiguity in the meaning and the application of the contract language in the PLA created material issues of fact that required the Superior Court to admit and consider parol evidence. Those material issues of fact must be resolved by the trier of fact, and cannot be resolved by a summary judgment procedure.

[REVERSED]

Notes & Questions

1. The Kennedy reading points out that both mergers and bankruptcies raise questions about the treatment of third-party licenses with respect to assignments and sublicensing. We discussed the bankruptcy treatment of third-party licenses in Chapter 6. As we noted there, bankruptcy resolves the status of these licenses in accordance with section 365 of the Bankruptcy Code, which provides for the assumption and assignment of executory contracts by a bankrupt debtor. As the Kennedy reading states, however, the solution in the merger context is far from clear. Because of this lack of clarity in statutory and case law, the resolution of questions about the treatment of third-party licenses in a merger often rests with contract law and the ability of the parties to a merger or acquisition to clearly state their intentions with respect to the transferability of licenses. What this means is that care must be taken in drafting both intellectual property license agreements to clearly state the parties' rights with respect to transfers and assignments and merger or corporate asset sales agreements to clearly describe what rights are transferred or assigned. The scope of potential liability if a party breaches should also be clearly stated in the respective documents.

2. The treatment of assignments of intellectual property licenses in mergers and acquisitions reflects a tension between state law, in favor of alienability, and federal intellectual property law, in favor of retaining control by the intellectual property owner. The California court's resolution of this tension in *SQL Solutions*, cited in the Kennedy reading, reflects a minority, and perhaps erroneous, viewpoint. Think about how bankruptcy law deals with this tension in Section 365. How is this tension different in the bankruptcy context than in the mergers and acquisitions context? Does the fact that rights stemming from bankruptcies, like many intellectual property rights, are matters of federal law remove the tension? Should there be a federal statute that addresses this ambiguity in the law? If so, which side should the statute favor—alienability or control?

3. The ambiguity highlighted by Kennedy concerning the treatment of assignments is illustrated by the three cases in this section. Each offers a different perspective on how courts can address the problem. In *PPG*, a case about which Kennedy expresses some skepticism, the court holds that intellectual property licenses are not transferred as part of a merger. Its reasoning rests on the reading of state corporate law, which characterizes a merger as a transfer by operation of law. Since the license at issue prohibited all transfers of intellectual property rights, the new entity after the merger could not obtain any rights under the license. Does the court in *PPG* miss something? Should intellectual property be treated in the same way as other types of assets? The courts in *Verson* and *Motorola* take an approach that looks more closely at the underlying contracts. Do the courts interpret the relevant contracts correctly? Is there one contract that clearly memorializes the agreement? If not, how does each court construct the intention of the parties? What lessons are to be drawn for the transactional or intellectual property attorney from these cases? Notice the distinction the court draws in *Motorola* between an assignment and a license. Why is that distinction relevant? Does the court get it right? For recent treatments of this issue, see *Cincom*

Systems, Inc. v. Novelis, Corp., 581 F.3d 431 (6th Cir. 2009) (following *PPG Industries* to conclude that software license was not assignable in a merger). But see *In re XMH Corp.*, 647 F.3d 690 (7th Cir. 2011) (ruling that software license was an assignable service contract and rejecting argument that agreement was a trademark license unassignable in gross).

4. Can a successor corporation enforce a covenant not to compete entered into by component companies in a merger where the employees involved continue to work for the new entity? The answer depends on state law, which can introduce some idiosyncrasies.

The majority rule is that the successor corporation can enforce the covenant not to compete. *See, e.g., Peters v. Davidson*, Inc., 359 N.E.2d 556 (Ind. App. 1977) (holding that the date of termination for purposes of measuring the two-year restricted period in a covenant not to compete was when the restricted employee later resigned from his position with a successor corporation). A majority of courts reject the argument that covenants not to compete are unassignable personal service contracts.

It is good practice to have a "successors or assigns" clause in the original covenant to provide support for enforcement by any future successors. But courts have allowed successors to enforce covenants not to compete even in the absence of such language. *See, e.g., Special Prod. Mfg., Inc. v. Douglass*, 553 N.Y.S.2d 506 (N.Y. App. Div. 1990). Some courts have seen additional complexity in these situations, interpreting questions of successors' rights to enforce covenants not to compete as dependent on third party beneficiary considerations. These courts treat a covenant after a merger as the equivalent of a third-party beneficiary contract with the successor the beneficiary of the agreement between the predecessor and the employee. Factors such as assent by the employee and continued receipt of benefits from a successor can support enforcement of the covenant by the successor. For a good overview of these issues, see Paul E. Starkman, *Mergers & Acquisitions: A Checklist of Employment Issues*, 13 DEPAUL BUS. L.J. 47, 98 (2001).

C. Liability Issues

Ed Peters Jewelry Co., Inc. v. C & J Jewelry Co., Inc.
United States Court of Appeals for the First Circuit
124 F.3d 252 (1st Cir. 1997)

CYR, CIRCUIT JUDGE.

[BACKGROUND: Peters was a sales agent for Anson, a financially strapped jewelry manufacturer in Rhode Island. Because of financial difficulties, Fleet, Anson's creditor, foreclosed on Anson's assets, selling them to C & J Jewelry, a corporation owned equally by Considine Family Trust and Jacobsen. Peters brought an action against Anson, Fleet, and C & J Jewelry to recover unpaid commissions. The excerpt from the opinion below addresses Peters' case against C & J.]

. . . .

Peters invokes the "successor liability" doctrine, by contending that C & J is simply Anson reorganized in another guise, and therefore answerable in equity for Anson's outstanding liabilities, including the $859,068 debt due Peters in sales commissions. *See H.J. Baker & Bro. v. Orgonics, Inc.*, 554 A.2d 196 (R.I. 1989).

Under the common law, of course, a corporation normally may acquire another corporation's assets without becoming liable for the divesting corporation's debts. But since a rigid nonassumption rule can be bent to evade valid claims, the successor liability doctrine was devised to safeguard disadvantaged creditors of a divesting corporation in four circumstances. An acquiring corporation may become liable under the successor liability doctrine for the divesting corporation's outstanding liabilities if: (1) it expressly or impliedly assumed the divesting entity's debts; (2) the parties structured the asset divestiture to effect a de facto merger of the two corporations; (3) the divesting corporation transferred its assets with actual fraudulent intent to avoid, hinder, or delay its creditors; or (4) the acquiring corporation is a "mere continuation" of the divesting corporation.

The district court dismissed the instant successor liability claim on the ground that Peters could not have been prejudiced, because Fleet had a legitimate right to foreclose and Peters did not prove the Anson assets were worth more than the total Anson indebtedness to Fleet. On appeal, C & J takes essentially the same position, but with the flourish that the successor liability doctrine is inapplicable per se where the divesting corporation's assets were acquired pursuant to an intervening foreclosure, rather than a direct purchase. We do not agree.

First and foremost, existing case law overwhelmingly confirms that an intervening foreclosure sale affords an acquiring corporation no automatic exemption from successor liability.

Second, by its very nature the foreclosure process cannot preempt the successor liability inquiry. Whereas liens relate to assets (viz., collateral), the indebtedness underlying the lien appertains to a person or legal entity (viz., the debtor). Thus, although foreclosure by a senior lienor often wipes out junior-lien interests in the same collateral. As one might expect, therefore, UCC § 9-504 focuses exclusively on the effect a foreclosure sale has upon subordinate liens, see R.I. Gen. Laws § 6A-9-504(4), supra, rather than any extinguishment of the underlying indebtedness. Whereas the successor liability doctrine focuses exclusively on debt extinguishment, be the debt secured or unsecured.

Following the October 1993 foreclosure sale by Fleet, the then-defunct Anson unquestionably remained legally obligated to Peters for its sales commissions, even if the lack of corporate wherewithal rendered the obligation unenforceable as a practical matter. True, Fleet might have sold the Anson assets to an entity with no ties to Anson, but that is beside the point, since the Peters successor liability claim alleges that C & J is Anson in disguise. As Peters simply seeks an equitable determination that C & J, as Anson's successor, is liable for the sales commissions

Peters earned from Anson, its claim in no sense implicates any lien interest in any former Anson asset. Third, successor liability is an equitable doctrine, both in origin and nature. Moreover, the UCC, as adopted in Rhode Island, provides that generally applicable principles of equity, unless expressly preempted, are to supplement its provisions. Moreover, R.I. Gen. Laws §6A-9-504 neither explicitly nor impliedly preempts the successor liability doctrine.

Finally, the fact that C & J acquired the Anson assets indirectly through Fleet, rather than in a direct sale from Anson, does not trump the successor liability doctrine as a matter of law, since equity is loath to elevate the form of the transfer over its substance, and deigns to inquire into its true nature. Thus, were C & J otherwise qualified as Anson's "successor" under Rhode Island law, because its principals acted with intent to evade the Peters claim, see infra, there would be no equitable basis for treating the asset transfer by foreclosure differently than a direct transfer from Anson to C & J. Consequently, we reject the contention that C & J's acquisition of Anson's assets through the Fleet foreclosure pursuant to R.I. Gen. Laws §6A-9-504, warranted dismissal of the successor liability claim as a matter of law.

Thus, Peters was entitled to attempt to prove that C & J, as Anson's "successor," became liable for the Anson debt to Peters because C & J is a "mere continuation" of the divesting corporate entity. The "mere continuation" determination turns upon factfinding inquiries into five emblematic circumstances: (1) a corporation transfers its assets; (2) the acquiring corporation pays "less than adequate consideration" for the assets; (3) the acquiring corporation "continues the [divesting corporation's] business"; (4) both corporations share "at least one common officer who [was] instrumental in the transfer"; and (5) the divesting corporation is left "incapable of paying its creditors."

(i) "Transfer" of Assets

Anson transferred all its operating assets, thereby enabling C & J to continue the identical product line without interruption. C & J nonetheless contends that a cognizable "transfer" could not have occurred, because Anson did not convey all its assets to C & J; that is, it conveyed its real property to Little Bay Realty. We disagree.

[Under the first criterion], the plaintiff need only demonstrate "a transfer of corporate assets." That is, it is not necessary, as a matter of law, that a single corporation acquire all the divesting corporation's assets, though the relative inclusiveness of any such asset transfer may prove to be a very pertinent factual consideration which the factfinder would take into account in the overall mix.

Yet more importantly, however, this is not an instance in which the divesting corporation transferred its real estate to a third corporation which was beyond the de facto control of the principals of the corporation which acquired the operating assets. Considine and Jacobsen deliberately structured the overall transaction so as to keep the Anson operating assets and real property under the ownership of two separate entities, C & J and Little Bay Realty respectively, concurrently established and controlled by them. Once again, therefore, since the successor liability doctrine is equitable in nature, it is the substance of the overall transaction which controls, rather than its form. Thus, the fact that C & J leased the real property from Little Bay is not controlling, since C & J (through Considine and Jacobsen) retained de facto control of the former Anson real estate following its transfer to Little Bay. Accordingly, viewing the evidence in the light most favorable to Peters, we cannot conclude, as a matter of law, that no cognizable "transfer" occurred.

(ii) "Inadequate Consideration"

Peters likewise adduced sufficient evidence from which a rational jury could conclude that the operating assets were transferred to C & J for "inadequate consideration." The second . . . factor rests on the theory that inadequate consideration is competent circumstantial evidence from which the factfinder reasonably may infer that the transferor harbored a fraudulent intent to evade its obligations to creditors. On the other hand, a valuable consideration negotiated at arm's-length between two distinct corporate entities normally is presumed "adequate," particularly if the divesting corporation's creditors can continue to look to the divesting corporation and/or the sales proceeds for satisfaction of their claims.

The total consideration for all Anson assets in this case was less than $500,000. Fleet effectively wrote off its outstanding balances ($10,628,000) on the Anson loan in 1993, and provided C & J and Little Bay Realty "new" financing totaling approximately $2.9 million. Thus, though normally loans obtained by buyers to finance asset acquisitions would be considered in calculating the total consideration paid, here the two newly-formed acquiring companies actually incurred no "new" indebtedness to Fleet. In fact, if the two companies were determined to be Anson's "successors," the asset sale would have gained them loan forgiveness approximating $7.728 million (i.e., $10,628,000, less new indebtedness of only $2.9 million), given their total exoneration from Anson's preexisting indebtedness to Fleet. Since the "new" Fleet loans cannot count as "consideration," at least as a matter of law, C & J and Little Bay paid a combined total of only $1 million in additional cash consideration for the Anson operating assets and real estate, of which $550,000 was immediately reinjected into the two acquiring companies for capital improvements and debt service. As a practical matter, therefore, C & J and Little Bay acquired all the Anson assets for only $450,000. Finally, the remaining $550,000 in new capital was directed back into the C & J and Little Bay coffers, where it served as an immediate benefit to Considine and Jacobsen, not a detriment.

Although Peters utterly failed to demonstrate that the Anson assets were worth as much as $12,738,000, it nevertheless adduced competent evidence as to their minimum value. Thus, the trial record would support a rational inference that the assets transferred by Anson had a fair value of just under $4 million. Fleet documents indicate that the book value of the operating assets approximated $5.2 million; Fleet's conservative estimate of their value approximated $2.11 million; and its conservative valuation of the real property was $1.78 million. Therefore, with a total minimum asset value just under $4 million, and a de facto purchase price below

$500,000, a rational jury could conclude that C & J and Little Bay acquired the Anson assets at 12.5 cents on the dollar.

At these minimal levels, adequacy of consideration presents an issue for the factfinder. On the present record, therefore, it was error to determine as a matter of law that no rational factfinder could conclude that 12.5% of fair value was "inadequate" consideration for the Anson assets.

Moreover, even assuming arguendo that the circumstantial evidence of fraudulent intent presented by Peters, in the way of demonstrating "inadequate consideration," could not have survived the Rule 50(a) motion for judgment as a matter of law, Peters adduced competent direct evidence of actual fraudulent intent as well. Actual fraud is a successor liability test entirely independent of the circumstantial "mere continuation" test.

Peters adduced direct evidence that Considine and Jacobsen entered into the asset transfer with the specific intent to rid the business of all indebtedness due entities not essential to its future viability, including in particular the Peters sales commissions. Peters notified Anson in March 1993 that it intended to pursue Anson vigorously for payment of its sales commissions. The intention to evade the Peters debt is explicitly memorialized in Jacobsen's notes, and yet more explicitly in the May 5, 1993 memo from Considine to Fleet ("If Fleet can find a way to foreclose the company [viz., on its security interests in Anson's real estate and operating assets] and sell certain assets to our company that would eliminate most of the liabilities discussed above, then we would offer Fleet . . . $3,250,000."). Thereafter, Fleet presciently forewarned Considine that its counsel was "not convinced that you will be able to do this [i.e., shed the Peters debt] without inviting litigation," and then insisted on an indemnification clause from C & J should any such litigation eventuate. Moreover, it is immaterial whether Considine believed that this evasive maneuver was essential to ensure the solvency and success of the Anson business; fraudulent intent need not be malicious.

(iii) "Continuation of Business"

Furthermore, Peters proffered ample evidence on the third factor in the Baker test, by demonstrating that C & J did "continue [Anson's] business." Among the considerations pertinent to the business continuity inquiry are: (1) whether the divesting and acquiring corporations handled identical products; (2) whether their operations were conducted at the same physical premises; and (3) whether the acquiring corporation retained employees of the divesting corporation.

C & J was incorporated in October 1993 for the specific purpose of acquiring the assets of the then-defunct Anson. Peters adduced evidence that C & J not only continued manufacturing the same jewelry products as Anson, but conducted its manufacturing at the same physical premises and continued servicing Anson's principal customer, Tiffany's. Moreover, its uninterrupted continuation of the Anson manufacturing business was prominently announced to Anson's customers in an October 1993 letter from C & J. In its October 1993 letter, C & J stated that it had "acquired all of the assets of Anson," that it was its "intention to build on [Anson's '55-year heritage of quality'] to reestablish the Anson brand as the pre-eminent one [in the jewelry market]," and that C & J had therefore "retained all of the former Anson employees [including Anson's 'current retail sales representation'] — the core of any business." Finally, in order to facilitate the product-line continuation, C & J specifically assumed responsibility for, and paid off, all indebtedness due Anson's "essential" trade creditors. Thus, the Peters proffer handily addressed the third factor in the Baker inquiry.

(iv) Commonality of Corporate Officers

Fourth, Peters adduced sufficient evidence at trial that C & J and Anson had "at least one common officer [viz., Considine or Jacobsen] who [was] instrumental in the [asset] transfer." C & J responds, inappositely, that the respective ownership interests held by the principals in the divesting and acquiring corporations were not identical, as Considine owned 52% of the Anson stock, whereas Jacobsen and the Considine Family Trust were equal shareholders in C & J.

The present inquiry does not turn on a complete identity of ownership (i.e., shareholders), however, but on a partial identity in the corporate managements (i.e., "officers"). Thus, the fact that Jacobsen not only held a corporate office in both Anson and C & J but was instrumental in negotiating the asset transfer to C & J was sufficient in itself to preclude a Rule 50 dismissal under the fourth prong, even if he were not an Anson shareholder.

Further, the same result obtains even if we were to assume that the "one common officer" — referred to in Baker — must be a shareholder as well. Prior to Baker, the Rhode Island Supreme Court did not require complete identity between those who "controlled" the two corporations or the asset transfer, whether their "control" derived from stock ownership or from their management positions. For example, the court had upheld a judgment for plaintiff, following trial, even though the officers and incorporators of the divesting and acquiring corporations were not the same, on the ground that the principals involved in the sale "all had a[] [common] interest in the transaction." Considine easily fits the bill here. After all, "C & J" stands for something and Jacobsen conceded at trial that Considine "participates in the management of C & J Jewelry." Moreover, Considine admitted that no C & J decision could be taken without Considine's prior approval.

C & J heavily relies as well on the fact that Considine, individually, held no direct ownership interest in C & J, but instead had conveyed his interest to the Considine Family Trust. Once again, however, as equity looks to substance not form, the fact that Considine established a family trust to receive his ownership interest in C & J did not warrant a Rule 50 dismissal, especially in light of his concession that he actively participates in the management of C & J. See Fleet Credit Memo (10/14/93), at 1 ("[T]hese transactions will be considered a Troubled Debt Restructure ('TDR') because of Considine's effective control of the assets both before and after the contemplated transaction."); (noting that Considine would be a "Principal" of C & J, although his "involvement in day-to-day operations will be limited"). Moreover, such intra-family transfers may be nominal only, and thus may constitute circumstantial evidence of a fraudulent, manipulative intent to mask the continuity in corporate control. Focusing on the transactional substance, rather than its form, therefore, we cannot conclude that a rational factfinder could not decide that Considine used the family trust to camouflage his ultimate retention of control over the Anson jewelry manufacturing business which C & J continued to conduct, without interruption, after Anson's demise.

(v) Insolvency of Divesting Corporation

Finally, C & J does not dispute that Anson is a defunct corporation, consequently unable to pay its debt to Peters. . . .

Accordingly, since the Peters proffer, at the very least, generated a trialworthy dispute under each of the five Baker factors, the motion [for judgment as a matter of law] was improvidently granted.

TXO Production Co. & Marathon Oil Co. v. M.D. Mark, Inc.

Court of Appeals of Texas

999 S.W. 2d 137 (Tex. App. 1999)

TXO was an oil and gas exploration company and a wholly-owned subsidiary of Marathon. PGI was a geophysical consulting firm which conducted seismic surveys. PGI and TXO entered into a series of contracts between 1979 and 1989 that allowed TXO to use certain seismic data. The contracts changed over the years, but each contained a confidentiality provision that the data "shall not be sold, traded, disposed of, or otherwise made available to third parties." Marathon eventually merged with TXO, and when TXO informed PGI of the merger and that the data would be automatically transferred to Marathon pursuant to the applicable merger statutes, PGI sought a $200 per mile transfer fee to allow Marathon to use the data. Marathon never paid the fee.

Mark subsequently acquired the rights to PGI's data and, based on Marathon's refusal to pay the transfer fee, sued appellants for breach of contract, conversion, and misappropriation of trade secrets. Appellants filed a motion for summary judgment, asserting the statute of limitations barred Mark's conversion and misappropriation claims. Mark filed a response to appellants' motion and its own motion for summary judgment on the breach of contract claim. The trial court found that (1) the merger was a transfer of the seismic data constituting a breach of the parties' agreements; (2) the conversion and misappropriation claims were barred by limitations; (3) Mark's damages were limited to the $200 per mile transfer fee.

Whether the Merger Violated the Non-Disclosure Agreements

In their first and second points of error, appellants contend the trial court erred in holding, as a matter of law, that their merger violated the non-disclosure agreements. They argue the court's construction of the contract conflicts with the majority of jurisdictions which have considered the issue.

We begin by noting that no case in Texas and or in any other jurisdiction has addressed this specific issue. However, courts in other jurisdictions have addressed the effect of a merger on other restrictive provisions. For example, courts have addressed the effect of a merger on a non-assignment clause in an insurance policy which called for termination of the contract in the event of an assignment to which the insurer did not consent. . . . Numerous courts also have addressed the effect of a merger on a non-assignment clause in a real estate lease. . . . An obvious basis for the outcome in the above cases is that courts disfavor forfeiture in insurance policies and leases. Courts, however, have been equally unwilling to find that merger breaches a non-assignment provision in other circumstances.

Mark cites to cases that have found a corporate merger violates an anti-assignment provision. Mark relies primarily on [*PPG Indus., Inc. v. Guardian Indus. Corp.*, 597 F.2d 1090, 1095 (6th Cir. 1979)]. In that case, PPG and Permaglass each independently developed a process to fabricate glass, and they agreed to grant each other rights to their patents. The agreement granting the rights contained a non-assignability provision, which PPG claimed Permaglass breached when it later merged with an unrelated third party. The court agreed, noting that if the parties desired an exception to their non-assignability provision in case of merger, they could have so provided. Since they did not, the provision of non-assignability prevailed.

We disagree with the reasoning and outcome of *PPG* and [*Nicolas M. Salgo Assocs. v. Continental Ill. Properties*, 532 F. Supp. 279 (D.D.C. 1981)]. Furthermore, those cases are distinguishable because there, the corporations merged into unrelated entities. In . . . the present case, a subsidiary merged into a parent corporation. Because the change was merely one of corporate form, . . . the merger did not involve an increased risk to [a] non-merging party. By contrast, the non-merging parties in *PPG* and *Salgo* were obviously prejudiced as a result of the merger: in *PPG*, the third party into which Permaglass merged gained access to a patent right it would not otherwise have had absent the merger, and in *Salgo*, the non-merging party was forced to accept a partner with whom it did not agree to form a partnership. Finally, the holdings of both cases are contrary to the merger statutes, as addressed more fully below.

Appellants contend the court's order conflicts with the applicable merger statutes, i.e., the Delaware Code, the Ohio Code, and the Texas Business Corporation Act. In general, these statutes provide that all rights, privileges, and obligations belonging to the merging corporation vest in the surviving corporation upon merger. All of these merger statutes are based upon the Model Business Code, the comments to which explicitly state that a merger is not a conveyance or transfer and that the surviving corporation automatically becomes the owner of all real and personal property in the event of a merger.

According to appellants, the court's interpretation prevents the flow of TXO's contractual rights to Marathon, in violation of the statutes. We agree. Under the merger statutes it is clear that all of TXO's interests vested in Marathon immediately upon the merger. Further, under these provisions there is no transfer of the rights of the merging corporation; rather, the rights vest automatically and without further action. Accordingly, a requirement that the surviving corporation pay a fee in the event of a merger unnecessarily hinders the free flow of those rights to the surviving corporation.

The merger statutes also refute Mark's claim of harm resulting from the disclosure. Mark contends that the merger allowed Marathon to have access to seismic data that it would otherwise not have had. Furthermore, Mark notes that both Marathon and TXO were its customers prior to the merger, but the merger allowed two entities to have access to data for which only one paid a fee. To the contrary, the merger statutes make clear that, after a merger, there remains only one entity, and the separate existences of the merging corporations cease. Because Marathon did not have access to the seismic data until after the merger, and because after the merger only one entity existed, Mark cannot claim it was entitled to a fee from both entities and thus sustained a monetary loss.

We next look to the contracts themselves for guidance as to the effect of the merger on the non-disclosure provisions. A number of courts that have found mergers do not violate anti-assignment provisions have considered the parties' failure to expressly state that the provision is triggered by a merger. We also reiterate that the Texas Legislature intended by its amendments to the Business Corporations Act that a prohibited transfer would not be implied by merger but would only occur in the event the parties agreed that merger specifically violated an anti-assignment provision.

Here, the contracts provided that the data "shall not be sold, traded, disposed of, or otherwise made available to third parties." Arguably, the agreements' prohibitions on making the seismic data "available" could encompass statutory merger, which by operation of law makes all property of the merging corporation the property of the survivor, thereby making that property available to the survivor. However, the possibility of merger was certainly foreseeable under the circumstances. The parties could have easily specified that the non-disclosure provision was implicated by a statutory merger, but they chose not to do so. In accordance with the holdings of the cases cited above and the policy enunciated by the drafters of the Texas Corporations Business Act, we will not imply a violation of the non-disclosure agreement in light of the parties' failure to address this situation.

Conclusion

The trial court held that as a matter of law, the merger of Marathon and TXO constituted a transfer of the seismic data to a third party. This holding conflicts with the applicable merger statutes and the majority of cases which have considered similar issues. As such, we find Mark was not entitled to judgment as a matter of law, and the trial court erred in granting summary judgment in its favor. We further hold that, as a matter of law, the merger did not constitute a prohibited transfer or disclosure, and appellants were entitled to summary judgment.

Notes & Questions

1. Look back at the provisions of Delaware Corporations Code Section 251 dealing with mergers. The surviving entity in a merger assumes the assets and liabilities of the merging companies, subject to any limitations in the merger agreement. This means that a merger will result in the surviving company being burdened by the liabilities of the merging companies, both contractual and tort, even if executives of the companies were not aware of the liabilities at the time of the merger.

2. The treatment of liabilities in acquisitions of corporate assets is different from the treatment in mergers. In general, a company that buys the assets of another company does not usually assume the selling corporation's liabilities. However, the doctrine of successor liability explained in *Peters* does transfer liabilities along with assets in some situations. These situations include (summarizing the standards mentioned in the *Peters* decision) acquisitions of corporate assets involving: (1) an express or implied assumption of liability; (2) a de facto merger; (3) the use of an acquisition to perpetrate fraud; and (4) a transaction producing an acquiring company that is a mere continuation of the asset seller's business. The *Peters* court also identifies five factors that are considered in determining if one business is a mere continuation of another: (1) the transfer of operating assets; (2) inadequate consideration paid for assets transferred; (3) the continuation of business activities; (4) a commonality of officers; and (5) the incapability of the selling company to pay ongoing obligations. The *Peters* case offers a good example of how these factors can be applied.

3. Think about how the doctrine of successor liability would apply when a company buys the intellectual property assets of another company, such as in the *Weyerhaeuser* case discussed below in Section E. Warranties in an asset sales agreement may also establish liability of a seller of intellectual property, allowing a buyer to recover amounts that will offset successor liability. As we will see in the *Weyerhaeuser* case, if Company A buys the intellectual property of Company B, that property is warranted to be free of related infringement liability, and the use of that intellectual property in turn is infringing, then Company A may be liable for the infringement and have a cause of action for breach of warranty against Company B.

4. The *TXO* case is another example of how ownership of intellectual property is treated in the case of a merger. Note that the court takes an approach that is very different from the *PPG* court. While both courts appeal to state corporate law, the *TXO* court holds that the merger statute considered there did not provide for a transfer of assets but a transfer of corporate identity. Note that the *TXO* court also states that if the parties wanted to limit transferability of intellectual property through a merger, they could have expressed that intention in their merger contract. Therefore, the decision rests in part on the interpretation of the statute and in part on contract law. Is the fact that PGI was aware that TXO was a subsidiary of Marathon at the time of the license relevant to the court's decision? Is that fact what distinguishes *TXO* from *PPG*?

D. Transfer Issues

Biolife Solutions, Inc. v. Endocare, Inc.

Court of Chancery of Delaware

838 A.2d 268 (Del. Chan. 2003)

Lamb, Vice Chancellor.

I.

The plaintiff sold assets to a competitor in return for a mixture of cash and shares of the competitor's publicly traded common stock. The purchaser later refused to perform its obligation under a related registration rights agreement to file a registration statement covering the shares so that they could be sold in compliance with the federal securities laws. Shortly afterwards, the market price of the shares plummeted, and, eventually, the shares were delisted after the seller's public accountants withdrew their report on its prior period financial statements.

The seller sought a variety of remedies for this breach of contract, including specific performance and, alternatively, money damages. The claim for money damages was tried beginning on March 31, 2003. In this post-trial opinion, the court concludes that the seller is entitled to damages measured by reference to the market price of the shares over a period of five consecutive trading days beginning when the seller could first have sold them had the necessary registration statement been filed in a timely manner.

II.

A. The Parties

Plaintiff BioLife Solutions, Inc., which was formally named Cryomedical Sciences, Inc. ("CMS"), is a Delaware corporation with its principal place of business in Binghamton, New York. BioLife's current business is the development, manufacture and marketing of solutions for the preservation of cells, tissues and organs at low temperatures (the "Solutions Business"). Before June 24, 2002, BioLife also was engaged in developing, manufacturing and marketing minimally invasive cryosurgical devices for the ablation of tissues (the "Cryosurgical Business").

CMS was one of the first companies to perfect the use of cryosurgical devices for the treatment of prostate diseases. During the early 1990s, it had essentially 100% of the worldwide market for this application. CMS began to struggle thereafter, and was quickly passed in marketplace acceptance by Endocare, Inc. (and a competitor, Galil Medical Systems, Inc.), whose cryosurgical equipment was viewed as superior for the treatment of prostate cancer. By the spring of 2002, CMS was facing severe financial difficulties.

Defendant Endocare, is a Delaware corporation with its principal place of business in Irvine, California. Endocare is engaged primarily in the development, manufacture, and marketing of temperature-based, minimally invasive surgical devices and technologies designed to treat certain cancers. Endocare was a direct competitor of CMS. By the spring of 2002, Endocare had approximately 80% of the market share for cryosurgical equipment used for prostate cancer.

B. The Transaction

In early 2002, BioLife and Endocare entered into negotiations regarding the acquisition of the Cryosurgical Business by Endocare. On May 28, 2002, BioLife and Endocare entered into an Asset Purchase Agreement (the "Agreement"). Closing on the Agreement occurred on June 24, 2002 (the "Closing"). Pursuant to the Agreement, Endocare acquired all of the tangible and intangible assets relating to BioLife's Cryosurgical Business. At the Closing, Endocare paid to BioLife $2,200,000 in cash, and provided BioLife with a stock certificate representing 120,022 shares of Endocare's common stock.

Included among the financial information provided in the Agreement was the Statement of Operations for the CMS business. This Statement showed that CMS's revenue for calendar year 2001 was approximately $954,000 (or an average of approximately $240,000 per quarter), while its revenue for the first three months of 2002 (the only quarter available as of either the signing of the Agreement or the Closing) had declined to $82,893.

At Closing, the parties also entered into a Registration Rights Agreement. Pursuant to Section 1.2 of the Registration Rights Agreement, Endocare agreed, "as soon as reasonably practicable after the [June 24, 2002] Closing Date . . . but in no event more than 90 days thereafter" to file a registration statement on SEC Form S-3 and "as soon as reasonably practicable thereafter, effect all such qualifications and compliances as may be reasonably necessary and as would permit or facilitate the sale and distribution of" the stock transferred pursuant to the Agreement. Because the closing occurred on June 24, 2002, this 90-day period expired on September 22, 2002.

Section 1.2(a) of the Registration Rights Agreement also gave Endocare the right to delay filing the Form S-3, but only under the following limited circumstances:

1. where the "Form S-3 is not available for such offering;" or

2. until Endocare received "the consents and the financial statements and other financial information required by the [Securities] Act [of 1933] and the SEC to be included in such registration statement from the independent certified public accountants of both [Endocare] and [BioLife];"

3. "if [Endocare] shall furnish to [BioLife] a certificate signed by [Endocare's] Chief Executive Officer stating that in the good faith judgment of the Board, it would be seriously detrimental to [Endocare] and its stockholders for such Form S-3 Registration to be effected at such time, in which event [Endocare] shall have the right to defer the filing of the Form S-3 registration for a period of not more than 90 days after receipt of the request of [BioLife] under this Section 1.2;" or

4. where the filing of the registration statement or effecting qualification or compliance "in any particular jurisdiction" that would require Endocare "to

qualify to do business or to execute a general consent to service of process in effecting such registration, qualification or compliance."

C. Delivery Of The Assets

Pursuant to Section 2.1 of the Agreement, the assets sold to Endocare consisted for the most part of intellectual property, 47 pieces of tangible assets (primarily equipment), inventory and accounts receivable. According to Endocare, "[t]he primary assets sought . . . were the intangible assets held by BioLife — its patents, trademarks, and customer lists."

1. The "Primary Assets"

The intellectual property (the patents, trademarks, and copyrights) were delivered at Closing in the form of an Assignment of Patents, an Assignment of Servicemarks and Trademarks, and an Assignment of Copyrights. The customer lists were provided to Endocare on May 27, 2002, the day before the Agreement was signed.

In addition to the actual assignment of the patents, there were also patent files that BioLife was required to deliver to Endocare. These files, which were maintained by BioLife's patent attorneys, contained the material that had been collected in connection with the various patent applications-correspondence to the patent office and the client, and notes and memoranda to the file by the patent attorneys. There is no doubt that Endocare was entitled to receive those documents, and there is also no doubt that delivery of those documents occurred slowly.

On August 9, 2002, Lawrence Ginsberg, Endocare's intellectual property counsel, contacted the law firm of Pillsbury Winthrop, LLP, which had represented BioLife in connection with the Agreement. The purpose of this call was to ascertain why the patent files had not been transferred and when they would be transferred. Following that initial conversation, Ginsberg again made contact with Pillsbury, and was told by Glenn Perry, a Pillsbury attorney, that he would "set the wheels in motion." BioLife, through Pillsbury, forwarded what it believed were the correct patent files to Endocare on September 3, 2002. In fact, some of the files sent were not related to patents that had been assigned under the Agreement, and certain patent files that were assigned were not actually sent. On October 14, after recognizing this error, Ginsberg e-mailed Anthony Miele, BioLife's new patent attorney at the law firm of Palmer & Dodge, LLP, to inquire about transferring the proper patent files. Miele responded later that day, stating that the patent file transfers "were in the works" and that he would "push these along." On October 21, Ginsberg again e-mailed Miele to inquire about the status of the patent file transfers. Finally, on November 4, 2002, Ginsberg e-mailed Miele, reiterating Endocare's need to obtain the patent files.

On November 11, 2002, BioLife transferred what Endocare initially thought were the complete patent files. However, not all the patent files had in fact been transferred to Endocare. Several patent files were not turned over to Endocare until March 13, 2003.

John Baust, CMS's president and CEO at the time of the Agreement, testified at trial that the late delivery of these patent files was due to the actions of one of CMS's former patent firms. He stated:

> [t]here was an earlier firm we dealt with in the early nineties, Sherman & Shalloway, in Alexandria, who were retaining patent files that, frankly, neither of the other patent firms [that CMS utilized], to my knowledge knew about. Nor did I.

> And when we found out about that, we then asked Sherman & Shalloway to transfer those files to Mr. Miele, at Palmer Dodge, so that he could determine what was appropriate to forward to Endocare, because I had no idea what was in those files.

> That took some time. Sherman & Shalloway was reluctant to transfer. They felt there was an outstanding bill from the mid-nineties, and they were holding those files until that bill was satisfied. And so it took some months for them to be convinced to transfer the files.

Although Endocare argues that BioLife's failure to provide all the patent files constitutes a material breach of the Agreement, it is clear that Endocare was primarily concerned with one particular patent file. By the time of trial, Endocare focused its argument in this regard almost exclusively on the patent file for the urethral warmer (Patent No. 5,437,673; the "673 Patent"). In particular, Paul Mikus, Endocare's former CEO and current chairman of its board, claimed at trial that Endocare's patent counsel needed the file related to the 673 Patent in order to perform proper due diligence on its contents before determining whether to commence an infringement action against one of Endocare's competitors (Galil). . . .

IV

. . . .

B. Endocare Has Not Shown That Failure To Deliver Certain Assets Was Material To The Transaction

A party is excused from performance under a contract if the other party is in material breach thereof. "The converse of this principal is that a slight breach by one party, while giving rise to an action for damages, will not necessarily terminate the obligations of the injured party to perform under the contract." Non-performance by an injured party under such a circumstance operates as a breach of contract. "The question whether the breach is of sufficient importance to justify non-performance by the non-breaching party is one of degree and is determined by 'weighing the consequences in the light of the actual custom of men in the performance of contracts similar to the one that is involved in the specific case.'"

Section 241 of the Restatement (Second) of Contracts sets forth several factors to consider when determining whether "a failure to render . . . performance is material" (thus justifying repudiation of a contract). These factors include: (a) the extent to which the injured party will be deprived of the benefit which he reasonably expected; (b) the extent to which the injured party can be adequately compensated for the part of that benefit of which he will be deprived; (c) the extent to which the party failing to perform or to offer to perform will suffer forfeiture; (d) the likelihood that the party failing to perform or to offer to perform will cure his failure, taking account of all the circumstances including any reasonable assurances; and (e) the extent to which the behavior of the party failing to perform or to offer to perform comports with standards of good faith and fair dealing.

Endocare argues that even if it breached the Registration Rights Agreement, it was justified in doing so because BioLife had already materially breached its obligations under the Agreement. The first document that formally set forth Endocare's position regarding its refusal to file a registration statement was a letter dated September 12, 2002 from Endocare's outside attorneys to BioLife's Chief Executive Officer. That letter states that "[a]s of the date hereof, Endocare has not received any material portion of the Assets from Cryomedical." In its letter, Endocare did not mention any specific assets that had not been delivered. By trial, however, Endocare's claim regarding BioLife's failure to deliver assets had been essentially reduced to two categories: documents necessary for FDA compliance and the patent files.

1. Documents Required To Be Maintained By The FDA

Endocare claims that it never received either (a) the FDA-required documents with respect to how to build the cryosurgical equipment it was acquiring from BioLife or (b) the service records with respect to that equipment. As discussed below, the failure to timely deliver these assets was not a material breach, and materially all of the assets were in fact delivered before Endocare was obligated to file a registration statement.

a. Endocare Had No Real Interest In Acquiring An Ongoing Business

Evidence adduced at trial demonstrated that Endocare never intended to build new CMS cryosurgical equipment. Instead, its focus was on CMS's existing customer base transfer to Endocare's equipment.

The cryosurgical equipment acquired from CMS was a very different technology than Endocare's own. CMS's equipment "was a liquid nitrogen system." "Endocare took a different approach to their fundamental design, and they used what is called a Joule Thompson effect. They used a pressurized gas." Although CMS had been "the company that originally founded the commercial application for cryosurgery, . . . Endocare had come along with the next generation technology and . . . taken most of the market share away." Because of these radically different designs, the manufacturing process of these two systems was not similar. As a result, the two companies' cryosurgical equipment was not interchangeable. Thus, probes from one system could not be used with consoles from another.

It would be unreasonable to believe that Endocare meant to acquire CMS—in its view a second-rate system incompatible with its own—and then try to sell it to customers. Mikus's testimony supports the conclusion that Endocare's purchase of the Cryosurgical Business was done only to eliminate competition. For example,

Endocare did little due diligence with respect to the Cryosurgical Business, as Mikus did not know if anyone had toured CMS's facilities before the Closing. Moreover, Endocare had no plans to hire any former CMS employees (with the possible exception of the former Chief Executive Officer). In addition, Mikus did not know how many active accounts CMS had as of the Closing.

Another example of Endocare's lack of interest in the continuation of the Cryosurgical Business relates to CMS's inventory of cryosurgical consoles. Although CMS had an inventory of cryosurgical consoles as of the Closing, Mikus did not know if CMS was still manufacturing consoles or when the last console had been made. Moreover, Mikus admitted that Endocare never intended to manufacture new CMS consoles. Cannon, who had been hired to continue a mobile services division, only used CMS's equipment for about six weeks after Closing, when he switched to Endocare's equipment.

With respect to cryosurgical probes, Mikus did not know if CMS was still manufacturing them as of the Closing, did not know how many probes were in CMS's inventory, and did not know, post-Closing, if all probes had been used. Moreover, Endocare had no intention of manufacturing new CMS probes. According to Cannon, much of the equipment was "junked" because Endocare was not going to use it.

Endocare argues it entered into the Agreement "with the expectation that it would receive substantial revenue from BioLife's existing cryosurgical business." Endocare alleges "[t]he revenue from the cryosurgical business had been represented as approximately $1 million in 2001, and Endocare expected to realize revenues in that range going forward." The documentary evidence in the case suggests otherwise-specifically, one of the attachments to the Agreement was Part 3.3, which sets forth certain financial information of CMS (without its BioLife component). Included in this information was the Statement of Operations from the CMS business alone. This statement showed that CMS's revenue for calendar year 2001 was approximately $954,0000 (or an average of approximately $240,000 per quarter), while its revenue for the first three months of 2002 (the only quarter available as of the Closing) had declined to $82,923. Such a decline in revenue is startling, and it is simply not credible for Endocare to argue that it continues to expect $1 million in revenue per year based on these most recent results.

b. All Necessary Documents Were Delivered

Although Endocare originally claimed, on September 12, 2002, that it had "not received any material portion of the Assets from Cryomedical," it has since conceded that most of the FDA-required documents "were ultimately collected through Charlie Cannon's efforts prior to September 20, 2002." The only specific FDA-required documents that Endocare claims were not produced are "the service records related to its mobile services business" citing to the deposition of Cannon at various places.

Cannon actually testified in a manner contrary to what Endocare implies. In particular, Cannon explained that he maintained his own equipment for the mobile services, and kept the service records for that equipment at his office in Jersey Shore, Pennsylvania. Moreover, Cannon testified that Dave Rust, an Endocare regional manager, "came down [to Jersey Shore] and collected copies of the shipping and mobile service records." Thus, the record evidence implies that Endocare actually does have these records in its possession. Finally, Cannon testified that Endocare never intended to continue the mobile services using CMS's equipment. Thus, Endocare would have had no use for service documents for equipment it had no intention of using, manufacturing, or supporting.

For all of these reasons, the court finds that to the extent certain physical assets (or documents related to those assets) were not delivered or were delivered late, such non-delivery or late delivery might have given rise to a damages claim by Endocare, but it did not give rise to a material breach of the Agreement thereby excusing Endocare from filing a registration statement pursuant to the Registration Rights Agreement.

2. The Patent Files

BioLife does not dispute, because it cannot, that it failed to transfer certain patent files to Endocare by September 20, 2002, the last business day during the 90-day period under the Registration Rights Agreement. The undisputed evidence in the case demonstrates that BioLife transferred additional patent files on November 11, 2002, but that it was not until March 13, 2003 that it transferred what it now contends are all the remaining patent files. This late transfer of patent files, however, did not amount to a material breach of the Agreement sufficient to justify Endocare's refusal to file a registration statement.

First, the Agreement itself places no heightened emphasis on the patent files themselves. This is so despite the fact that Endocare now claims that the patent files, and particularly the patent file associated with the 673 Patent, were the cornerstone of its acquisition of CMS. Second, had those patent files been material to the Agreement, one would expect Endocare to have made arrangements to receive them at Closing or at least to specifically mention them by name in its September 12 letter when it relied on the alleged failure to deliver assets to justify its decision to refuse to file a registration statement. Instead, the September 12 letter merely stated, in a substantial overstatement, that "Endocare has not received any material portion of the Assets from [CMS]. . . ."

Finally, Endocare now has the patent files it complains it never received. Although Endocare may have suffered some damage as a result of the late delivery, such damage cannot be so material as to justify its refusal to file a registration statement. Endocare primarily sought the 673 Patent file to determine if another competitor (Galil) could be subject to a patent infringement lawsuit. Now that Endocare has the patent files associated with the 673 Patent, it can presumably reach a decision whether to pursue its lawsuit against Galil.

Endocare also complains about having never received a so-called "lab notebook" for the 673 Patent. Responding to questions regarding whether there were "any notebooks in existence at CMS that showed an early date of invention for the ure-thral warming system [the system covered by the 673 Patent]," Baust stated that this system was developed at Allegheny General Hospital between 1991 and 1993. He further testified that "[t]he development notebooks would have been maintained by either Doctor Onik, Doctor Reyes or Allegheny General. . . . We focused on the patent-related information and secured the patent, but those files, to my knowledge, were not with CMS."

For all these reasons, the court concludes that the failure to timely deliver patent files was not a material breach of the Agreement by BioLife, and that Endocare was not justified in refusing to satisfy its filing obligation under the Registration Rights Agreement.

[JUDGMENT FOR BIOLIFE]

Notes & Questions

1. The *Biolife Solutions* case illustrates some of the mechanics of acquisition trans-actions involving intellectual property. In analyzing the case, you should focus on the elements of the deal. What did each side want? What did each side have to do? Pay special attention to the asset transfer. How is intellectual property transferred from one party to another? Features of due diligence reviews of intellectual prop-erty interests and infringement risks are discussed in more detail in Chapter 8. In the context of mergers and acquisitions, these reviews typically focus on the validity and scope of intellectual property interests and the likely effectiveness of merger and acquisition agreements in transferring those interests.

2. The court at one point states that Endocare had no interest in acquiring an ongoing business. Why is this finding relevant? What does it say about the expecta-tions of the parties and performance obligations under the contract? Why would Endocare have entered into this deal if it did not want to acquire an ongoing busi-ness? The court suggests that Endocare was primarily interested in the acquisition of the targeted company's customer lists. Is a corporate acquisition an expensive means to that end?

3. The case also discusses requirements for filing stock registration documents with the Securities and Exchange Commission. Note that part of the consideration to be received by BioLife in the disputed acquisition was stock. Whenever a company issues stock over a particular value, it must register the stock with the Securities and Exchange Commission before it can make the issuance. Since Endocare seemed to be delaying the registration process, BioLife had special reasons to be concerned about whether it would receive the consideration it expected from the transaction. Endo-care, of course, was arguing that its performance obligation was excused because Bio-Life was in breach by not turning over its patent files and other assets.

4. Notice that the transfer of intellectual property assets occurs through assign-ments. The transfer of the patent files is incidental to the assignments, but part of the transaction. Why would Endocare want the patent files? The contents of these

files describe the prosecution history of each of the patents and therefore are important for litigation as well as for other purposes. Do you think that a serious acquirer would have asked to see the files before the transaction was completed? Do you think Endocare had looked at the files beforehand? Why would it be a good idea to look at the files? One answer is provided by the case discussed in Section E, which deals with due diligence.

E. Impacts of Ineffective Transfers and Inadequate Diligence

Paragon Trade Brands, Inc. v. Weyerhaeuser Company

United States Bankruptcy Court for the Northern District of Georgia

324 B.R. 829 (Bankr. N.D. Ga. 2005)

MURPHY, BANKRUPTCY J.

. . . .

II. FINDINGS OF FACT

A. Background of the Private-Label Baby Diaper Business Weyerhaeuser Transferred to Paragon in the IPO

. . . .

5. Weyerhaeuser commenced a baby diaper business in 1972. This business consisted largely of selling a private-label diaper to large retail establishments that placed their store names on the package and sold the diaper on their shelves at lower prices than the branded diapers sold by [Procter & Gamble (PG)], which sold the "Pampers" and "Luvs" brands, and [Kimberly-Clark Corporation (KC)], which sold the "Huggies" brand. The diaper was the primary product in Weyerhaeuser's Personal Care Products ("PCP") Division.

6. In the late 1980s, Weyerhaeuser embarked on a plan to refocus on its core businesses. Because the baby diaper business was not considered one of its core businesses, the diaper business was targeted for divestment. Weyerhaeuser informed the investment community about its refocusing and proceeded to move as quickly as possible to dispose of its baby diaper business (the "Business").

7. The Business had performed well in the early 1980s, earning pre-tax profits for Weyerhaeuser in 1983 and 1984 of $31 to $39 million. A key to Weyerhaeuser's success during these years was a "brand matching" practice, which included utilizing an elastic leg gather feature patented under PG's Buell '003 patent. This strategy gave Weyerhaeuser's private-label diaper an advantage over its competitors' private-label diapers.

8. In 1981, PG sued Weyerhaeuser for infringing the Buell patent, seeking an injunction against use of the patented feature, damages for a reasonable royalty, and

enhanced damages for willful infringement. Weyerhaeuser asserted various invalidity defenses to PG's Buell patent, and elected to take the case to trial instead of removing the feature or re-designing its diaper to avoid the infringement claim. The jury found that Weyerhaeuser willfully infringed PG's Buell patent, and that a reasonable royalty would have been 1% of sales. The trial court rejected Weyerhaeuser's invalidity defenses. On July 2, 1985, the trial court entered judgment against Weyerhaeuser, permanently enjoining it from making its private-label diaper as it was then designed, and awarding PG reasonable royalty damages of $2.3 million, plus prejudgment interest and attorneys' fees.

. . . .

12. [Weyerhaeuser sought to improve its diaper business.] The primary means for improvement was the addition of a newer feature known as the inner leg gather, or "ILG." An ILG, in layman's terms, is a second elasticized inner barrier cuff in the diaper that contains or channels effluent, and thus reduces leakage. Because leakage prevention is the primary purpose of a diaper, the ILG was the most important new feature for diapers ever incorporated in disposable diapers. Weyerhaeuser internally concluded that failure to add the ILG would negatively impact its sales volume by one million cases (1% of market share, or 1/12 its sales) in the first year and another 500,000 cases in the second through fourth years. Weyerhaeuser personnel believed that having the ILG on its Ultra diaper was essential for it to compete in the private-label diaper market. KC's ILG was marketed nationally in early 1990, and PG was expected to do so in September, 1990.

. . . .

14. PG and KC, however, each had patent claims encompassing the ILG feature, under PG's "Lawson" patent and KC's "Enloe" patent. PG's Lawson patent described an ILG that was fluid impermeable or hydrophobic, and KC's Enloe patent described an ILG that was fluid pervious. For each day after March 1991 that Weyerhaeuser earned sales and profits using the ILG technology, its potential liability for patent infringement grew.

. . . .

16. . . . Weyerhaeuser obtained patent opinions from outside counsel that the Lawson, Dragoo and Enloe patents were invalid based on certain cited prior art. Weyerhaeuser had received a similar invalidity opinion regarding Buell that was proven wrong at trial. These opinions did not guarantee success in litigation, but would help protect Weyerhaeuser against a willful infringement finding, which carried the threat of enhanced or treble damages. Weyerhaeuser knew that issued patents, such as Lawson, Dragoo and Enloe, are presumed valid, and that a party attacking validity has the burden of overcoming this presumption by clear and convincing evidence. The patent opinions Weyerhaeuser obtained did not assess the probability or likelihood that a court would find invalid the presumptively valid ILG patents of PG and KC, and Pat Coogan, Weyerhaeuser's in-house patent counsel with oversight responsibilities for the PCP Division, testified he did not request such an assessment from

outside counsel. In what appears to have been a lengthy meeting held September 5, 1991, Mr. Coogan advised Weyerhaeuser's General Counsel, Bob Lane, that Weyerhaeuser's chance to succeed on an invalidity defense to PG's Lawson or KC's Enloe patent infringement claims was no better than "50/50."

17. In the year before launching its ILG diaper in March, 1991, Weyerhaeuser negotiated with PG to obtain a license to use its ILG feature, offering on many occasions to pay royalties or to trade licenses to various Weyerhaeuser patents for the right to use the ILG feature. These negotiations failed in May 1991 because PG demanded a 3% royalty to license the ILG feature, an amount Weyerhaeuser stated it could not afford to pay and remain competitive in the diaper market.

18. Also in 1991, PG and KC were litigating with each other in federal district court in Seattle, Washington (the "Seattle litigation" or "Seattle trial") over whose ILG invention was reduced to practice first and which had priority of invention. As issued on September 22, 1987, PG's Lawson patent made claims to both the generic ILG invention and ILGs made of impermeable materials. KC's Enloe patent, issued November 3, 1987, made claims to ILGs made of "fluid pervious" materials (referred to later as "Enloe I"). KC sought to establish Enloe's priority of invention to invalidate Lawson's claims and to establish a right to have Lawson's ILG claims transferred to an amended Enloe application filed with the Patent And Trademark Office ("PTO").

19. Weyerhaeuser expected that the Seattle litigation was of sufficient scope for the winner between PG and KC to be found to have a "likelihood of success" in a later action to enjoin Weyerhaeuser from making and selling its private-label ILG Ultra diaper, and from using the ILG on any other product. In June 1991, trial of the Seattle litigation was conducted. Weyerhaeuser's in-house patent counsel Pat Coogan attended most of the trial.

20. In March 1991, a few months before the Seattle trial started, Weyerhaeuser's Investment Evaluation Department ("IED") commenced efforts to value the Business and determine how to sell it to obtain the best value. Weyerhaeuser also hired the investment banking firm of Morgan Stanley to advise on the Business's likely market value and likely buyers. In a report issued August 28, 1991, Weyerhaeuser's IED concluded that the Business's value was $90 million. Morgan Stanley's base case valuation of the Business was between $75 and $95 million. Neither the valuation of Morgan Stanley nor Weyerhaeuser's IED, however, assumed any royalty payable to KC or PG for the ILG technology, or payment of damages for past infringement. Morgan Stanley also reported to Weyerhaeuser an "unusually limited universe of buyers" for the Business and a significant risk that no transaction would result from a sale process.

21. In its valuation study, the IED reported that (i) each percentage point change in the Business's market share would change the Business's value by about $30 million; and (ii) a $1 change in the gross profit margin per standard case sold would change the Business value by $80 million. Assuming, however, a combined 5.5%

royalty payable by the Business (which equaled PG's and KC's last demands before Weyerhaeuser closed the IPO, as discussed beginning at page 13, ¶ 29), Weyerhaeuser's gross profit margin per case would drop by $1.49, from $5.62 to $4.13. According to Weyerhaeuser's valuation analysis before the 1992–93 IPO, if paying these royalties, the Business would have zero or negative value. Notes prepared by a Weyerhaeuser IED officer of a meeting with Mr. Coogan, Mr. Robert Dowdy, and others August 20, 1991, reflect discussions over possibly putting the diaper division in a separate subsidiary to protect Weyerhaeuser from what was then stated to be a substantial and growing infringement liability. In November 1991, Chemical Bank, a bank with whom Weyerhaeuser had a relationship through its investment banking arm, advised Weyerhaeuser that the Business might not be saleable at anything better than a "fire sale" price. In early 1992, Weyerhaeuser also investigated disposing of the Business through a leveraged management buyout.

22. On September 10, 1991, while Weyerhaeuser was reviewing disposition of the Business, the decision in the Seattle litigation awarded priority of invention to KC's Enloe patent. As a result, Lawson's claims to generic ILGs were held invalid as obvious or anticipated in light of Enloe. The district court, however, held that Lawson's claims to impermeable, or hydrophobic, ILGs remained valid despite Enloe, given that Enloe's "fluid pervious" ILG patent taught away from Lawson's impermeable ILG design. The consequence of this decision was that Weyerhaeuser's largely impermeable ILG diaper stood squarely within Lawson patent claims of PG that did survive the Seattle trial, and Weyerhaeuser knew it. Weyerhaeuser had no solid non-infringement position against the surviving Lawson impermeable ILG patent claims. Mr. Coogan also realized that the Seattle court's decision meant Lawson's generic claims to all ILGs (regardless of permeability) would, in due course, be transferred to Enloe and issue in an amended Enloe patent that would encompass all ILGs, including ILGs used on Weyerhaeuser's Ultra diaper. Mr. Coogan reported this expectation to nine different Weyerhaeuser officers and lawyers, including its CFO and CEO, in his September 13, 1991 memorandum sent three days after the Seattle decision issued.

23. The Seattle trial result put Weyerhaeuser in the predicament of having to license the technology to make and sell its impermeable ILG diaper from not just one, but two competitors: PG, holding Lawson's surviving impermeable ILG patent claims; and KC, which would be granted an amended Enloe patent claiming all ILGs, regardless of hydrophobicity. Weyerhaeuser expected the prevailing party in the Seattle litigation, which was on appeal, would demand royalties from Weyerhaeuser for use of the ILG feature, and if a license and royalty agreement could not be resolved, that one or the other—PG or KC—would sue to enjoin Weyerhaeuser from using the ILG and for damages, including lost profits and/or reasonable royalties. Weyerhaeuser representatives were aware during this period that its potential liability for infringing PG's ILG patents included damages for lost profits on sales Weyerhaeuser was taking from PG, and that such damages could be "enormous" because PG's profit margin on the Weyerhaeuser ILG diaper sales approached 30%.

24. In December 1991, PG formally notified Weyerhaeuser that its Ultra diaper infringed PG's Lawson and Dragoo patents. In a December 1991 meeting, Weyerhaeuser's General Counsel, Bob Lane advised Weyerhaeuser's auditor, Arthur Andersen, that the damages arising from such a PG claim could be "enormous" for Weyerhaeuser. On February 10, 1992, Mr. Lane reported to Weyerhaeuser's auditor, Arthur Andersen, that the PG claim could result in a 3% royalty payable and an injunction.

25. By early 1992, Weyerhaeuser had been unable to sell the Business through traditional means. In March 1992, Weyerhaeuser launched a plan to dispose of the Business through an initial public offering of 100% of stock of a newly-formed Weyerhaeuser subsidiary into which it would transfer the Business. Weyerhaeuser retained Merrill Lynch to be the lead underwriter for this offering. Merrill Lynch retained the Skadden Arps law firm as its counsel. Weyerhaeuser retained the Paul Weiss law firm to be its counsel. The newly-formed company, which became Paragon, had no separate counsel. Weyerhaeuser employees responsible for the Business were expected to become the managers of the newly-formed public company after the IPO. The Business had a successful year (on paper) in 1991, earning over $33 million in operating profit on net sales over $396 million. Its performance was up significantly from its $2 million operating profit in 1990 on net sales of about $286 million, and significantly better than the Business's performance the prior four years, 1986–89. The Business's successful results in 1991 and 1992 positioned Weyerhaeuser to pursue the IPO.

26. Weyerhaeuser incorporated Paragon Trade Brands, Inc. in June 1992 as its wholly-owned subsidiary, to own the business Weyerhaeuser planned to take public. Initially, the IPO was planned to close in late August or September 1992, but it was tabled in early September due to concerns over the effect a PG diaper price reduction would have on the Business's narrow profit margin.

27. In August 1992, two separate events occurred that confirmed the problematic ILG patent predicament facing the Business. First, on August 14, 1992, the PTO decided in Enloe's (KC's) favor the pending interference action fought between PG and KC over ILG patent priority. Weyerhaeuser's in-house patent counsel, Mr. Coogan, knew that as a result, KC's Enloe patent would be amended to include the generic ILG claims originally granted to Lawson. This new patent, which would not be limited to "impermeable" or "fluid pervious" iterations, would squarely encompass Weyerhaeuser's Ultra ILG diaper.

28. The second event with impact on the ILG patent predicament facing Weyerhaeuser occurred August 26, 1992, when the Federal Circuit Court of Appeals affirmed the Seattle trial court's decision as to priority of invention in the Seattle litigation, again leaving PG's Lawson patent with valid claims to ILGs made of impermeable materials. Based on this ruling, Weyerhaeuser's ILG diaper remained squarely within the claims of what was now a litigation-tested Lawson patent of impermeable diaper ILGs. It was foreseeable by Weyerhaeuser and known within the patent law practice at the time of the IPO that a license can be required from two different parties in order to sell a particular product.

29. Weyerhaeuser expected that both PG and KC would seek royalties from Weyerhaeuser for use of the ILG or, failing an agreed payment, would sue for an injunction against use of the feature and damages. In fact, Weyerhaeuser conducted dual license negotiations with PG and KC in the months before closing the IPO transaction to obtain freedom to use the ILG feature. No license agreement with PG or KC was concluded before closing. PG's last demand before the IPO closed was for a 3% royalty on net sales of all ILG products in return for a license under Lawson and the companion ILG patent, Dragoo. No evidence shows that PG offered, before the IPO closed, to forgive past infringement as part of a license agreement. KC's last demand before the IPO closed was a 2.5% royalty on net sales of ILG products for seven and a half years in return for a license under Enloe I and the to-be-issued generic ILG patent (which later issued as Enloe III), which would be deemed fully paid after the 7.5 years. The proposed KC license did not contemplate a separate payment for past infringement. Both PG and KC rejected Weyerhaeuser's various counteroffers, which consisted of cross-licenses of various Weyerhaeuser diaper patents, or a royalty as low as 0.2%.

30. Weyerhaeuser could not have proceeded with the IPO had the Business been paying royalties in the range demanded by PG and KC. In the IPO Prospectus, which Weyerhaeuser and its attorneys drafted, Weyerhaeuser disclosed the existence of PG's and KC's ILG patent claims, but Weyerhaeuser did not disclose the level of royalties demanded or the severe impact the royalties would have on the Business if forced to pay them. Weyerhaeuser did not disclose that past attempts to license the feature from PG had failed; it downplayed the negotiations as "discussions"; and, the IPO Prospectus represented to the new public shareholders in at least three places that "the Company believes that any outcome with respect to these [ILG patent] matters will have no material adverse effect on its financial position or its results of operations." A 5.5% royalty (the aggregate amount PG and KC were demanding) would have eliminated virtually all of the Business's 6% profit margin. A 4% royalty (approximately the amount the Business eventually agreed to pay in 1999 in the settlement agreements with PG and KC) would have eliminated approximately two-thirds of the Business's profit margin.

31. Weyerhaeuser had withheld needed capital from the Business in the years before the IPO. The plan was for Paragon, after the IPO, to use its profits to finance its four-year capital improvement program, which was designed to (i) make its operations more cost-efficient so it could survive anticipated pricing actions of the brands and its private-label competitors, (ii) add and improve product features to keep pace with expected continuing diaper improvements in the industry, and (iii) expand production capacity. Being forced to pay royalties in the range of 5% would have severely undermined, if not destroyed, the Business's ability to make the capital investments necessary to survive the pending and anticipated future diaper price wars. In fact, PG and KC did continue their price wars after the IPO, and diaper prices sharply declined by 15 to 22% within three years. Had the Business been forced to pay substantially all its profits to PG and KC in royalties to use the ILG feature, the

Business would not have been a viable, on-going business after the IPO, and the IPO likely would not have occurred.

32. The evidence showed that the Business could not, and its managers did not expect it could, independently raise its diaper prices to recoup the extra costs of ILG royalties. As a private-label manufacturer, the Business was a known price follower of the branded manufacturers' (PG and KC) prices. No evidence was presented to show that any of its managers expected they could rely on PG and KC to raise their prices if the Business paid them royalties, thus allowing price increases to recoup the royalty costs. PG and KC, with aggregate market share of 70%, had been chronically engaged in "fierce battles" inter se over market share, and were lowering prices. In addition to the pressures from PG and KC, Paragon faced, as Weyerhaeuser had, vigorous competition from its private-label competitors that further constrained its ability to raise prices.

33. At the time of the IPO, the Business had no alternative, market-tested design that could be used to replace the ILG feature for the Ultra diaper. Dropping the ILG feature from the Ultra diaper would have been disastrous to the Business, returning it to the "sick" condition from which the ILG feature had rescued it. The Ultra diaper, which was the Business's premium quality private-label diaper, represented approximately 84% of its net sales. The Business also produced and sold a line of economy diapers (the "Economy diaper") that had fewer features than the Ultra diaper. The Economy diaper, which represented about 14% of net sales in 1993 (15% in 1992), did not utilize an ILG feature when the IPO closed. At the time of the IPO, the Business had just introduced a training pant, which is a form of diaper used by older toddlers. The training pant did not then utilize an ILG and represented about 1% of the net sales of the Business at that time. Accordingly, as sold to the public through the IPO, the Business had essentially been built as, and was, a company with a single product—the Ultra ILG diaper—but with good potential for growth and expansion.

34. The consequences of not having the right to use the key ILG feature had been discussed within Weyerhaeuser as similar to the consequences it suffered from the 1985 Buell injunction. These consequences included an injunction requiring the Business to pull the Ultra diaper from retailer shelves, costs to develop a new diaper design, lost sales and profits from being forced to sell an inferior, non-ILG product, payment of the substantial royalties PG and KC were demanding for a license to continue using the ILG feature, and liability to PG and KC for their lost profits, which Weyerhaeuser knew could be substantial.

B. The IPO

36. At [the closing of the IPO of Paragon stock in 1993], Weyerhaeuser transferred the Business to Paragon by executing an Asset Transfer Agreement (ATA) and Intellectual Property Agreement (IPA) (together, the ATA and IPA are the "Transfer Agreements"). The ATA and IPA, as finally executed at the IPO closing, contained assumption of liabilities clauses, whereby Paragon assumed virtually all liabilities of

Weyerhaeuser relating to operation of the Business, past and prospective (defined as the "Assumed Liabilities"), including patent liabilities. The Transfer Agreements, at ATA Section 11.02(a) and IPA Section 4.01, also contained certain provisions providing that Paragon would indemnify and defend Weyerhaeuser from the Assumed Liabilities, including any third party claims against Weyerhaeuser for patent infringement relating to operation of the Business. As discussed at length in the Summary Judgment Order entered October 30, 2002, assumption of liability and indemnity clauses existed in early drafts of these contracts, prepared months earlier than the February 2, 1993 actual closing. Later, however, numerous warranties were added to the contracts. Plaintiff sued on four of the warranties. Two are found in the ATA, and were made with no limitation as to Weyerhaeuser's knowledge. In the final, signed ATA, these two warranties provide, in relevant part:

> 3.01(c): [Weyerhaeuser] has, and will transfer to [Paragon] at the Closing, good title to all of the other Assets [all assets other than Real Property] . . . free and clear of any and all mortgages, security interests, liens, claims, charges, options and encumbrances of any nature whatsoever, except for minor defects and irregularities in title or encumbrances that do not materially impair the use of any such Assets for the purposes for which they are held.

> 3.01(d): The Transferred Assets and the services and materials to be provided pursuant to the Related Agreements are sufficient to conduct the Business as now being conducted.

The other two warranties, in the IPA, provide that, "to the best of [Weyerhaeuser's] knowledge":

> 3.11(ii): "Schedules 3.01(a) and 3.01(b) are accurate and complete lists of all Patent Rights and Trademarks, as used in connection with the Business or the Products."

> 3.11(vii): "[T]he Primary Intellectual Property plus Trademarks and Secondary Intellectual Property are adequate for the continuation of the Business as currently conducted."

At closing of the IPO, Weyerhaeuser certified the warranties were true and correct. In Section 3.01(a) of the ATA, Weyerhaeuser represented and warranted to Paragon that the ATA warranties were enforceable on their terms. The IPA and ATA were each fully integrated contracts, which, pursuant to merger clauses in each, superseded all prior discussions between the parties over the subject matter of the agreements. The IPA and ATA were required to be, and were, filed with the SEC as "material contracts" and made a part of the Registration Statement for Paragon's newly issued common stock. Weyerhaeuser, in Section 11.02(b) of the ATA, agreed to indemnify Paragon for all losses, costs, expenses and damages arising from a breach of any of the four warranties at issue.

C. Paragon After The IPO

37. After the IPO, the Business now known as Paragon continued to make and sell the Ultra diaper with the same ILG feature Weyerhaeuser had used before the

IPO. For infringement purposes, Paragon's ILG feature did not change from the feature on which Weyerhaeuser had built the Business. Paragon also continued to sell the Economy diaper and training pant. After the IPO, in the mid to late 1990s, Paragon added the ILG feature to the Economy diaper and to the training pant. Also after the IPO, Paragon began to sell a "Supreme" diaper. No credible evidence was introduced to show that this product ever had an ILG.

38. After the IPO, Paragon continued to employ the same outside patent counsel that Weyerhaeuser had used on diaper patent issues before the IPO. After the IPO and through at least 1996, Paragon's attorneys continued to consult Weyerhaeuser's in-house patent attorney, Pat Coogan, regarding the ILG patent matters. For the first two years after the IPO, PG and KC lowered their diaper prices by more than 20%, and Paragon was forced to respond by lowering its diaper prices accordingly.

39. After the IPO, the representations in the IPO Prospectus that "the Company believes any outcome of [the ILG patent] matters will have no material adverse effect" on the Business restrained Paragon from agreeing to licenses with PG and KC at royalty rates that would have so eroded Paragon's profits as to be a material adverse effect on Paragon's financial position. On January 20, 1994, PG sued Paragon in federal district court in Delaware for infringing PG's Lawson and Dragoo patents (the "Delaware Litigation"). In return for dismissal of the lawsuit, PG demanded that Paragon pay a 2.5% royalty. Paragon sought an alternative resolution by tendering several alternative diaper designs to PG, and asked PG to agree that the designs would not infringe its patents. On February 28, 1994, PG responded to Paragon's request, agreeing that two of the samples would not infringe Lawson or Dragoo. PG asserted, however, that even if Paragon elected to switch to one of these designs. Paragon would still be required to pay a 2.5% royalty on all past infringement of Lawson and Dragoo, back to 1991 (approximately $30 million), plus a 1% royalty on future net sales of the sample diaper for licenses under PG's Aziz and Buell patents, because PG claimed the sample diaper infringed Aziz and Buell.

40. Paragon rejected PG's offer. Paragon had not commercially tested the samples it had delivered to PG, and believed them to be inferior designs, which were not a commercially viable option. Paragon countered PG's offer by offering to pay a 0.1% royalty for licenses of Lawson and Dragoo for three years, after which no further royalties would be due. Paragon's offer and position was consistent with the IPO Prospectus immateriality disclosure, and with the pre-IPO advice of Mr. Coogan as to what would be a "reasonable royalty" for PG's ILG patents. PG rejected Paragon's counteroffer, telling Paragon it believed the parties were at an impasse. Consequently, pretrial discovery proceeded.

41. During 1995, KC filed a lawsuit against Paragon in Dallas, Texas for infringing its Enloe and Enloe II ILG patents. By July 1996, after settlement discussions with PG had resumed, PG had lowered its royalty demand for Lawson and Dragoo licenses to 2%, but still demanded Paragon pay $30 million for past infringement back to 1991, when Weyerhaeuser had begun selling the ILG diaper. Even though this was PG's lowest settlement offer, Paragon believed it could not afford to pay PG a 2%

royalty, given its competitive situation and the likelihood that this rate would become precedent for a royalty payable to KC for licensing KC's Enloe patents, which Paragon considered stronger, more defensible patents than Lawson. The pendency of the KC claims under Enloe, which would (soon) include a generic claim for all ILGs, materially limited Paragon's options in reaching a settlement with PG. From the time of the IPO through the February 1997 PG trial in Delaware, Paragon continued to study alternative designs to avoid paying any royalty, but found no viable alternative to the ILG design on its diaper. Removing the ILG altogether was not a viable option for Paragon.

42. Before the trial in Delaware and thereafter, Stephen Judlowe, Paragon's trial counsel who had originally been selected by Mr. Coogan, Weyerhaeuser's in-house patent counsel, was advising Paragon that the likelihood of Paragon's success at trial against PG's claims was very high, and as high as 80%, and that even if Paragon lost on PG's claims it would win on its counterclaim for PG's alleged infringement of Paragon's Pieniak patent and would, "at the end of the day walk away making money" on the litigation. Paragon relied on Mr. Judlowe's advice and rejected PG's settlement offer. PG and Paragon proceeded to trial.

. . . .

44. When the patent infringement lawsuits were filed against Paragon, Paragon did not send Weyerhaeuser a formal written notice demanding that Weyerhaeuser defend it or indemnify it for liability. Weyerhaeuser had actual notice, however, that Paragon had been sued by PG for infringing Lawson and Dragoo: Mr. Coogan was consulted after the IPO by Paragon in-house counsel, and was deposed in the PG case. Mr. Abraham testified he instructed each of Paragon's general counsels to consult with Mr. Coogan on ILG claims and strategy. Susan Barley, Paragon's General Counsel from at least January 1994 through the summer of 1995, provided credible testimony that she kept Mr. Coogan up to date on the progress of the negotiations with PG while she was at Paragon, and that Mr. Coogan attended meetings with her and lawyers from Mr. Milnamow's firm to strategize about PG and KC ILG patent issues. Cathy Hasbrouck, who was hired as its General Counsel when Paragon moved from Seattle to Georgia in 1996 and remained in that position through conclusion of Paragon's bankruptcy case, provided credible testimony that she also discussed these patent issues with Mr. Coogan during the period leading to trial, and received advice from him on the defense of the case that was consistent with the bullish advice received from Paragon's outside counsel. Mr. Coogan, while admitting receiving a call from a "woman in Georgia," claimed not to remember such a discussion. His denial was not credible.

D. Paragon Is Driven To Bankruptcy By Intellectual Property Inadequacies

45. The Delaware Court's December 30, 1997 judgment, entered January 6, 1998, against Paragon, held that its ILG feature infringed PG's Lawson and Dragoo patents and permanently enjoined Paragon from selling its primary product, the private-label "Ultra" diaper. The judgment also required Paragon to pay PG lost

profits damages, royalty damages equal to 2% of past infringing sales, and enhanced damages for what had been Weyerhaeuser's willful infringement of Dragoo equal to 100% of the damages award attributable to the March through December 1991 period. By order dated May 28, 1998, the damages portion of the judgment against Paragon was found to be $178,429,536.00.

46. The Delaware Court's judgment precipitated the filing of Paragon's Chapter 11 bankruptcy petition January 6, 1998. Ten days later the United States Trustee appointed an Official Committee of Unsecured Creditors ("Creditors' Committee"). Weyerhaeuser was appointed as one of nine creditors to serve on the Creditors' Committee. Weyerhaeuser served as a Creditors' Committee member throughout the duration of Paragon's case in this court. On November 2, 1998, the United States Trustee also appointed an Official Committee of Equity Security Holders (the "Equity Committee").

E. Paragon's Losses For Which Plaintiff Seeks Damages

[Paragon sought recovery from Weyerhaeuser for breach of warranties resulting in the following damages: 1) bankruptcy-related costs; 2) product re-design costs; 3) lost profits; 4) obligations incurred to PG and KC from the litigation; and 5) Paragon's losses from its inability to exercise options with a Mexican company because of the bankruptcy.]

F. Plan Confirmation and Proceedings in This Adversary Proceeding

71. Over Weyerhaeuser's opposition, the Equity Committee in Paragon's bankruptcy, on behalf of the Paragon Estate, commenced this breach of warranty adversary proceeding against Weyerhaeuser October 4, 1999, contending Weyerhaeuser breached the four ATA and IPA warranties (quoted above at page 17, ¶ 36). Following hearings on confirmation thereof, Paragon's Modified Second Amended Plan Of Reorganization (the "Plan") was confirmed by order entered January 13, 2000 (the "Confirmation Order"), and the effective date of the Plan was January 28, 2000. The Plan and Confirmation Order reaffirmed the reasonableness of and necessity for Paragon to settle with PG and KC. Pursuant to the Plan and Confirmation Order, Mr. Randall Lambert was appointed the Paragon Estate's Litigation Claims Representative to pursue this and other claims of the Estate. Accordingly, Mr. Lambert was substituted for the Equity Committee as Plaintiff in this action. Following the close of discovery, Plaintiff moved for partial summary judgment holding Weyerhaeuser liable for breaching the four warranties at issue. Weyerhaeuser cross-moved for complete summary judgment or dismissal. In support of the summary judgment motions, the parties jointly submitted an extensive record of more than nine volumes of joint exhibit appendices and twenty-five deposition transcripts. Oral argument on the motions was heard June 24, 2002.

72. The Summary Judgment Order entered October 30, 2002, found Weyerhaeuser breached all four warranties as a matter of law on the grounds that Paragon's intellectual property was not adequate or sufficient at the IPO closing, so that Weyerhaeuser's warranties were not true. Because Paragon lacked the licenses then

necessary to operate its business, the Delaware Judgment, the risks of continued litigation, the disruption to Paragon's business from its inability to sell the ILG diaper, and the allowed claims of and license fees to PG and KC—which were necessary for Paragon to incur to obtain rights to use the ILG technology it did not have at closing of the IPO—constituted a stark gap in Paragon's intellectual property, known to Weyerhaeuser and undisclosed in the IPO. As a result, Plaintiff is entitled to damages for the breaches. For the reasons set forth in the Summary Judgment Order, Weyerhaeuser's arguments—that Paragon's indemnity of Weyerhaeuser against intellectual property claims in IPA Section 4.01, and other assumption of liability promises in the ATA and IPA precluded Plaintiff's breach of warranty claims and entitlement to damages—were rejected.

73. Weyerhaeuser filed a motion for reconsideration of the Summary Judgment Order November 12, 2002. In its Reply to Plaintiff's response to its motion for reconsideration, Weyerhaeuser raised for the first time a new document and argument it had failed to raise either in the original proceedings or in its motion to reconsider: a U.S. Assignment And Assumption Agreement signed by Paragon at the IPO closing. Weyerhaeuser also raised for the first time the Tyco decision's issues discussed above, despite having notice of the trial and appellate court decisions at or near the time they issued, and despite entry of the Federal Circuit's Tyco decision over a year before oral argument on the summary judgment motions. Following oral argument on the motion for reconsideration, Weyerhaeuser's motion was denied. This matter was then set for trial only on damages.

74. During a fourteen-day damages trial conducted October 30 to November 6, November 24 and 25, and December 3 to 10, 2003, Plaintiff presented evidence and argument on the issue of damages for Weyerhaeuser's breach of warranties. Plaintiff argued three alternative common law measures of damages: a "cost to cure" measure, a "difference in value" measure, and a "destruction of business" measure, plus consequential damages under the first two measures. Alternatively, Plaintiff argued for damages pursuant to the indemnity provision in ATA Section 11.02(b), in which Weyerhaeuser promised to pay Paragon for all "Losses" arising from or relating to a breach of warranty. Plaintiff also seeks prejudgment interest and attorneys' fees under each remedy as well.

75. Weyerhaeuser contends Plaintiff is limited to the ATA Section 11.02(b) indemnity remedy for its breach of warranties, to the exclusion of a common law remedy customarily available for breach of warranty. Weyerhaeuser contends Plaintiff is entitled to no damages under the purportedly exclusive ATA Section 11.02(b) remedy because (i) given that Paragon settled, Plaintiff did not establish Paragon was actually liable to PG or KC for patent infringement, and (ii) Paragon and Plaintiff did not provide Weyerhaeuser sufficient notice of the PG and KC actions to be entitled to indemnity, and Weyerhaeuser was actually prejudiced from the lack of notice. Weyerhaeuser also argues that Paragon's agreements to indemnify and defend Weyerhaeuser from certain intellectual property liabilities under ATA Section 11.02(a) and

IPA Section 4.01 require Paragon to repay to Weyerhaeuser any liability Weyerhaeuser owes Paragon for breach of Weyerhaeuser's warranties.

76. Finally, Weyerhaeuser contends that under Washington law, the only proper common law measure of damages is difference in value at the time of sale. Weyerhaeuser argues that under that measure, Plaintiff's damages are limited to what the missing PG and KC licenses hypothetically would have cost Paragon, both reduced to after-tax dollars and discounted to present value as of February 2, 1993, and then further reduced by Weyerhaeuser's assumption that Paragon would have raised prices and recouped much of the increased royalty costs to acquire the licenses. Plaintiff responds that it is not limited to a difference in value measure, and may recover all damages and losses necessary to put Paragon in the position it would have occupied if it had received Weyerhaeuser's baby diaper business in its as-warranted condition — that is, with sufficient intellectual property to conduct the ILG diaper business. Plaintiff submits the measure that best accomplishes that goal is an equivalent to a "cost to cure" measure.

77. Among other contentions, Weyerhaeuser contends that the consequential damages Plaintiff seeks are not recoverable under Washington law, that Plaintiff's damages should be limited for Paragon's alleged failure to mitigate damages, and that no damages should be allowed for KC-related losses because of the Tyco decision. Weyerhaeuser also asserts Plaintiff is not entitled to pre-judgment interest on any damage element. The parties have stipulated, however, to Plaintiff's entitlement to recover a certain amount of Plaintiff's attorneys fees and costs upon being awarded damages.

[Judge Murphy levied a judgment of $458 million against Weyerhaeuser. Paragon had been seeking $700 million in damages. Judge Murphy stated: "The gravamen of Weyerhaeuser's liability, is that, in addition to the funds that Weyerhaeuser received in connection with the IPO, the primary benefit of the bargain to Weyerhaeuser was divorcing itself from what it knew to be an enormous potential patent infringement liability that was substantially certain to occur. Additionally, Weyerhaeuser was able to reap the benefit of an unpredictably successful IPO. To reward Weyerhaeuser's strategic divestment by limiting damages . . . would encourage other large corporations to evade liabilities by transferring assets to a subsidiary and divesting themselves of their liability-laden subsidiaries."

Notes & Questions

1. In 2007, the District Court for the Northern District of Georgia reversed the Bankruptcy Court's ruling on breach of warranty. The heart of the District Court's reasoning was as follows:

> Considering the adequacy and sufficiency warranties in isolation, Paragon and Weyerhaeuser's interpretations are both reasonable. Focusing on the "continuation" language, the warranties can be read as a guarantee that after

the closing, Paragon would be able to continue producing the Ultra ILG diaper, Weyerhaeuser's primary product prior to the closing. Focusing instead on the "as now being conducted" and "as currently conducted" language, the warranties can be read to guarantee only that Paragon would receive all of the assets and intellectual property that Weyerhaeuser was using in the business prior to the closing, including any faults or defects.

Reading the warranties in the context of the entire agreement and applying basic rules of contract interpretation, however, Weyerhaeuser's reading of the warranties is the only reasonable interpretation.

Weyerhaeuser Co. v. Lambert, 2007 U.S. Dist. LEXIS 71550 (N.D. Ga. 2007), affirmed by *In re Paragon Trade Brands, Inc.*, 278 Fed. Appx. 1000 (11th Cir. 2008). The District Court considered both the language of the agreement and extrinsic evidence. Although the principal ground for liability was reversed in the District Court's opinion based on a fact-specific reinterpretation of the warranty terms at issue, we include the *Weyerhaeuser* case and notes below to illustrate the treatment of intellectual property in a corporate acquisition, the potential risks in an acquisition transaction of inadequate due diligence inquiries regarding intellectual property, and the calculation of damages potentially arising from an intellectual property warranty breach in an acquisition context.

2. Review Paragraph 16 of the preceding reading, which describes Weyerhaeuser's use of opinion letters from outside counsel. In 2004, the Federal Circuit ruled that no adverse inference for willfulness could be made from a litigant's failure to obtain an opinion letter or from the refusal to turn over such a letter protected by attorney-client privilege. *See Knorr-Bremse v. Dana Corp.*, 383 F.3d 1337 (Fed. Cir. 2004). The facts of the *Weyerhaeuser* case predated this important decision. Does the decision in *Knorr-Bremse*, as summarized here, seem sensible in light of cases like *Weyerhaeuser*? If the company could have claimed attorney-client privilege, should it have? Would refusal to turn over the opinion letter or the decision not to get one have been sensible under the facts of *Weyerhaeuser*? Notice that the *Knorr-Bremse* decision deals specifically with the question of willfulness in a patent infringement suit. A breach of warranty case might raise different concerns regarding the use of opinion letters.

3. Look at the discussion of valuation in Paragraph 20 of the preceding opinion. What method of valuation did Weyerhaeuser use here? Review the section on valuation in Chapter 1. For thorough discussions of valuation methods for intellectual property, see Richard Razgaitis, VALUATION AND PRICING OF TECHNOLOGY-BASED INTELLECTUAL PROPERTY (John Wiley & Sons, Inc. 2003); Gordon V. Smith & Russell L. Parr, VALUATION OF INTELLECTUAL PROPERTY AND INTANGIBLE ASSETS (John Wiley & Sons, Inc. 2000). Accounting issues are also critical to the careful consideration of intellectual property in mergers and acquisitions. *See* Andrew W. Carter, *Accounting for Intellectual Property During Mergers and Acquisitions* in Lanning Bryer & Melvin Simensky, eds., INTELLECTUAL PROPERTY ASSETS IN MERGERS AND ACQUISITIONS 5.1–5.11 (John Wiley & Sons, Inc. 2002). An important question to think

about is the need for better financial accounting standards for intellectual property. In reading the facts of *Weyerhaeuser*, would better, less manipulatable accounting standards have helped?

4. Consider the discussion of the P&G and Kimberly Clark patent litigation in paragraphs 22 and 23 of the preceding opinion as well as the discussion of the subsequent licensing negotiations in paragraph 29. To what extent did Weyerhaeuser's problems stem from an uncertain and unpredictable patent system? How would you, in advising companies like Weyerhaeuser, counsel a client about the risks of patent infringement litigation? Should Weyerhaeuser have intervened in the lawsuit? Should Weyerhaeuser have worked more to invent around the existing patents on the assumption that the patents were valid, even if ownership of the patents was uncertain?

5. Paragraphs 30 and 31 discuss disclosures made by Weyerhaeuser as part of the IPO of Paragon stock. Do these disclosures seem adequate? How would you have advised Weyerhaeuser both prospectively (before the case was decided) and retrospectively (after the case was decided)?

6. Look at the Asset Transfer Agreements and the Intellectual Property Agreements discussed in paragraph 36. These are standard agreements with standard terms. What does each agreement cover? What do each of the excerpted terms mean? Do the terms provide any basis for Weyerhaeuser to escape liability?

7. Paragraphs 38, 42, and 44 provide insights into what Weyerhaeuser's and Paragon's attorneys were doing in negotiating the IPO. The materials in Chapter 8 provide more information about due diligence reviews of intellectual property and potential infringement liability. How could due diligence reviews have been better conducted here? Could purchasers of stock in the IPO have been more diligent in scrutinizing the transaction, perhaps insisting that Paragon have independent counsel? Can the uncertainties of the patent system discussed above in note 3 explain some of the behavior here?

8. Paragraph 71 offers a glimpse of the bankruptcy procedures that formed the background to the *Weyerhaeuser* case. Review the introductory materials to Chapter 6, which discuss bankruptcy proceedings. Could Paragon have impleaded Weyerhaeuser in the intellectual property litigation because Weyerhaeuser was obligated to indemnify Paragon regarding its liabilities determined in the litigation? Was there an advantage to litigating and settling and then suing Weyerhaeuser for breach of warranty?

9. The judge adopted the cost to cure measure of damages, advocated by Paragon, over the difference in value measure, advocated by Weyerhaeuser. The difference in value measure was based on the difference between the value of the business as actually delivered to Paragon and the value of the business as warranted. The cost to cure measure, on the other hand, included the costs to Paragon of the infringement lawsuit, the costs of bankruptcy, and consequential damages such as business operating losses and costs of product redesigns. Attorney's fees and costs would be in

addition to these damages. The following is a breakdown of the damages awarded to Paragon by the court:

Element of Damage	Dollar Amount
Damages related to infringement of P&G patent (consisting of settlement payments and litigation expenses)	$219,100,000
Damages related to infringement of KC patent (consisting of settlement payments and litigation expenses)	$158,300,000
Product redesign costs (consequential damages including prejudgment interest)	$14,982,556
Bankruptcy retention bonuses (consequential damages including prejudgment interest)	$7,002,301
Bankruptcy fees and costs (consequential damages including prejudgment interest)	$40,773,293
Lost profits (consequential damages)	$17,700,000

The damages totaled $457,858,150, to which the court added attorney's fees and costs of $3,017,210. By way of comparison, the court calculated damages under a difference in value measure of $284,625,000.

Chapter 8

Intellectual Property Due Diligence and Disclosures in Public Sales of Stock

Problem

Digital Ignition is preparing for an initial public offering (IPO) of its stock. The company has developed a group of popular consumer products in its plug-compatible ignition systems, but is unable to meet consumer demand for these products through its present manufacturing and distribution channels. Digital Ignition's executives believe that a public offering of Digital Ignition stock will aid the company in expanding its manufacturing and product distribution operations concerning its consumer products.

As part of its preparation for this IPO, Digital Ignition has engaged your law firm to address a number of intellectual property issues related to the proposed offering. The attorneys at your firm working on this matter are Todd Alvarez, a partner with extensive experience concerning securities law and intellectual property issues in IPOs of high tech companies, and you, Sue Kim, a third-year associate working under Alvarez's direction.

You and Alvarez have met with Digital Ignition's general counsel and senior executives and have a general idea of the type of offering that the company is planning. The tentative plan is to offer 4,000,000 shares of company stock at an initial price of approximately $10.00 per share to generate approximately $40 million dollars in new financing. Further financial details regarding the proposed stock offering are being developed by the financial executives at Digital Ignition, with assistance from the investment bankers who are aiding the company in defining the features of the offering and the underwriters who will handle the offering. These financial details are not the concern of your firm; rather, you have been engaged to ensure that Digital Ignition properly identifies and discloses its operating risks as required by securities laws governing offerings of stock in public markets.

The legal team at your firm has started to develop some of the disclosure documents that will need to be filed with the federal Securities and Exchange Commission (SEC) at the outset of the IPO and that will ultimately become part of the publicly available prospectus describing Digital Ignition and its IPO. As part of the disclosures in these documents, company officials will need to describe the company's present and planned business activities and the impact of intellectual property interests in aiding or limiting these business activities.

Due Diligence

In order to properly identify and disclose these intellectual property impacts, your law firm will conduct a "due diligence" review of Digital Research's intellectual property interests and the intellectual property interests held by other parties that may limit Digital Research's planned activities. This review should involve reasonable fact finding and analysis to support the representations that Digital Research will ultimately make in its disclosure documents about the company's future business plans and prospects and the projected impact of intellectual property interests on these aspects of business performance.

Alvarez has asked you to develop a plan for collecting information about Digital Research's intellectual property interests and associated operating risks as part of the due diligence review of the company preceding its IPO. Based on initial discussions with Digital Ignition's executives and counsel, Alvarez wrote a memorandum (reproduced below) summarizing several intellectual property features of Digital Ignition's operations, which should be scrutinized in the due diligence review. Alvarez would like you to address the following three questions:

1. Are there any other types of intellectual property interests or risks beyond those mentioned in the memorandum that are likely to enhance or impede Digital Ignition's operations and that should be considered in the due diligence review?

2. Regarding the intellectual property interests mentioned in Alvarez's memorandum or others you may identify as relevant, what types of practical business risks or advantages may these interests create for Digital Ignition?

3. Given these potential risks and advantages, what types of factual inquiries and sources of information at Digital Ignition should be pursued in the due diligence review of the company to reasonably clarify the impact of intellectual property interests on the company's operations and to form the basis for disclosure statements to be filed in connection with the company's IPO?

In addressing these questions, you are not expected to provide a detailed description of the intellectual property-based risks and advantages associated with the IPO. Rather, the goal of your answers should be to define an initial plan for gathering information on the intellectual property aspects of the company's business activities, specifying the types of information to be obtained and the evaluations to be conducted. You should consider the materials and cases in the readings describing the features of reasonable due diligence reviews under federal securities laws and the defenses to liability that such reviews may support.

Alvarez's memorandum to you reads as follows:

TO: Sue Kim
FROM: Todd Alvarez
SUBJECT: Initial IP Considerations in Due Diligence Review of Digital Ignition

Based on our initial consultations with Digital Ignition's management, I want to start planning for the due diligence review of the company's intellectual property interests in connection with its proposed IPO. The company's business is strongly influenced by its own intellectual property interests and may be constrained by the interests of other companies. The relevant intellectual property interest will generally fall into one of the following four categories:

1. Intellectual property created by Digital Ignition that may provide the company with a competitive advantage by establishing domains of exclusive business activity;

2. Intellectual property acquired by Digital Ignition that may provide the company with a competitive advantage by establishing domains of exclusive business activity;

3. Intellectual property that Digital Ignition may license to others to create sources of income; and

4. Intellectual property of other parties that may conflict with the planned business activities of Digital Ignition.

While there may be other important sources of concern, based on the description of the company's business we were given, the due diligence review of Digital Ignition should consider at least the following:

1. Patents and related trade secret know-how concerning the company's core digital ignition technology developed by Dr. See in the early 1980s;

2. Further patents on improvements to that technology developed and patented in the 1990s;

3. Trademarks under which the company has initiated marketing of its consumer products;

4. Trade secrets that Dr. See or other employees of Digital Ignition may have brought to the company, intentionally or inadvertently, from their prior employers in the automobile ignition field or allied engineering areas;

5. Patents held by other concerns in the ignition equipment field that may limit Digital Ignition's ability to manufacture and sell its devices;

6. Copyrights on software from other companies that was used to create Digital Ignition's products, portions of which copyrighted software may have been included in the software controls embedded in Digital Ignition's products;

7. Patents held by Ignition Horizons, Inc., another innovative concern that has developed advances that complement the advances covered by Digital Ignition's patents. Digital Ignition has licensed the exclusive rights under Ignition Horizons' patents to make plug-compatible replacement ignition systems containing the features covered by Ignition Horizons' designs. These components significantly enhance the performance of the ignition systems and Digital

Ignition's executives believe that their company's exclusive ability to offer ignition systems with these licensed features will be an important marketing advantage for the company.

Disclosure Completeness

In discussions with Digital Ignition executives, Alvarez has identified a trademark enforcement issue related to the company's plans for international marketing of its products. The issue appears to involve material risks for the company and will therefore probably need to be described in the company's prospectus filed with the federal Securities and Exchange Commission (SEC) and released to the public in connection with Digital Ignition's IPO. Alvarez is asking for your assistance in developing the language to be included in the portion of the prospectus that will address this risk.

The risk at issue involves planned efforts of Digital Ignition to expand its marketing of consumer-oriented ignition systems in the United States and abroad. One of the company's business strategies is to market its ignition products for consumers under a brand name that consumers already recognize and respect. Accordingly, the company has concluded a licensing agreement with Hollywood Auto Parts, Inc., allowing Digital Ignition to market ignition products in this country and abroad under the "Hollywood Auto" trademark. Hollywood Auto has been a successful retailer of a broad range of consumer-oriented auto products for some years and has a generally favorable reputation for product quality among consumers. Hollywood Auto has used the "Hollywood Auto" trademark extensively both here and abroad, having regularly and systematically registered the mark for some years. The company's marketing efforts and trademark registrations have included the use of the "Hollywood Auto" trademark for various car ignition products.

An early draft of Digital Ignition's prospectus described the company's licensing arrangement with Hollywood Auto and Digital Ignition's plans for expanded marketing under the Hollywood Auto trademark as follows:

> Digital Ignition intends to utilize rights to market goods under the "Hollywood Auto" trademark to expand the global market penetration of all of its products, particularly in Latin America. As an established and well respected retailer of automobile products in this country and abroad, Hollywood Auto, Inc., has developed considerable consumer recognition for its brand name and achieved extensive marketing success. Hollywood Auto's products are well known by consumers in the United States, Latin America, and other parts of the world. Products manufactured by Digital Ignition and sold under the "Hollywood Auto" trademark are expected to be marketed through a wide variety of distributors and retail stores. Digital Ignition believes that consumers' existing positive impressions of Hollywood Auto's products will carry over to Digital Ignition's newly introduced ignition systems for consumers. Digital Ignition's marketing of consumer-oriented ignition systems under the "Hollywood Auto" trademark should be of

particular significance in aiding Digital Ignition's ability to target sales by sellers of auto supplies in Latin America, including mass merchandisers, wholesalers, warehouse clubs and online marketers. Overall, the company believes that the marketing of its goods under the "Hollywood Auto" brand name will be an important new source of sales revenues.

Todd Alvarez has asked you to review this language and revise it as necessary. He has raised several concerns about the present prospectus language quoted above and has stated that a revised section on Digital Ignition's plans for marketing under the "Hollywood Auto" trademark will probably need to be drafted. The specific concerns he sees with the present language include the failure to adequately describe business and legal risks associated with:

1. Hollywood Auto's possible failure to properly secure the trademark rights on which Digital Ignition plans to rely;

2. The possibility that Digital Ignition has not concluded agreements with Hollywood Auto that are sufficient to secure rights to market products in the full range of countries, business settings, and product domains where Digital Ignition hopes to market consumer-oriented ignition systems;

3. The scope of product quality requirements and associated policing arrangements that will be part of the trademark licensing relationship between Hollywood Auto and Digital Ignition and that may impose significant obligations and costs on Digital Ignition and reduce its freedom to control the nature and marketing of its products;

4. Grounds for breach of the licensing agreement between the firms and the associated possibility that Hollywood Auto will withdraw the right to use its mark if the terms of the licensing agreement are not met;

5. The possibility that, even if Digital Ignition successfully secures rights to use the "Hollywood Auto" trademark in the countries of interest, the laws of some of these countries or the weak enforcement of trademark rights in these countries may provide such poor protection to Digital Ignition that it may not achieve the exclusive marketing opportunities and related profits it indicates that it expects; and

6. The risk that, even if Digital Ignition successfully secures exclusive rights to the "Hollywood Auto" trademark in a particular jurisdiction, additional business activity limitations under the laws of that jurisdiction—for example, the requirement in some countries that Digital Ignition or an applicable subsidiary must register and qualify to do business in those countries to sell its products even if Hollywood Auto has previously qualified—may preclude Digital Ignition making effective business use of its licensed trademark rights.

You have been asked to consider whether these and other trademark-related risks associated with Digital Ignition's proposed marketing under the "Hollywood Auto" trademark are adequately described in the prospectus language above. In particular, you should address three matters:

1. Are there any trademark-related risks other than those mentioned above that are raised by Digital Ignition's proposed marketing under the "Hollywood Auto" trademark?

2. Regarding the risks described above and any further ones that you have identified, are there any changes in Digital Ignition's licensing arrangements or proposed marketing practices that would significantly reduce the business risks associated with the company's use of the "Hollywood Auto" trademark and thereby avoid the need for disclosure of some of the material risks presently embodied in the proposed practices?

3. As to any remaining or unavoidable risks, what changes in the portions of Digital Ignition's prospectus quoted above should be made to adequately disclose the material trademark-related risks and heighten the likelihood that the company will be immune from securities fraud claims should Digital Ignition's efforts to market products under the "Hollywood Auto" trademark produce unfavorable corporate results?

Focus of the Chapter

Subsections A and B of this chapter address the legal significance of due diligence reviews of intellectual property interests and liability risks in connection with initial public offerings (IPOs) of stock, along with the proper scope of these due diligence reviews. Subsection A summarizes the circumstances in which due diligence reviews can provide defenses to civil liability that would otherwise result when a party makes inaccurate statements about intellectual property interests in public disclosure statements filed with the federal Securities and Exchange Commission (SEC) and disclosed to the investing public in advance of an IPO. Since this type of liability can be enormous, the value of a due diligence review that can avoid this liability is similarly large.

Subsection B discusses the features of reasonable due diligence reviews addressing intellectual property interests and related liabilities. The readings in this section discuss the types of information to target in these reviews and how experts conducting the reviews should interpret and respond to the information that is gathered.

Subsection C moves on to address how intellectual property risks should be disclosed in connection with an IPO. SEC standards specify several types of business risks and features that must be disclosed before an IPO can be completed. Failures to make these minimum disclosures will violate federal securities laws even if no affirmatively misleading information is disclosed. The readings in Subsection C address how to determine if IP risks and features fall within the range of the SEC's required disclosures and how to adequately describe IP characteristics or related business features once it is determined that these must be disclosed under SEC standards.

Readings

A. Legal Significance of Due Diligence Reviews of Intellectual Property Prior to an IPO

1. Basic Features of Due Diligence Reviews of Intellectual Property

Due diligence reviews of intellectual property interests are conducted in a variety of business settings in which a party needs to assess the future business prospects of a concern and to take intellectual property impacts into account in making these assessments. The nature of the intellectual property assessments that are needed will depend somewhat on the nature of the business setting involved and the type of decision making the due diligence inquiries will support. Settings in which businesses commonly conduct due diligence reviews of intellectual property include merger transactions (in which the focus of a due diligence review is typically the intellectual property of the target company being acquired), transactions involving the sale of a corporate subsidiary or other business unit (in which the focus of a due diligence review is the value of the business unit being sold off and the impact of intellectual property interests on that value), and initial public stock offerings (in which the focus of a due diligence review is the impact of intellectual property interests on the future business prospects of the company that is making the offering). The common feature of due diligence reviews of intellectual property in these settings is the need to project how intellectual property interests held by the company under scrutiny may enhance the business potential of that company and how the intellectual property interests of other parties may limit the company's actions or create expensive infringement liability.

Careful due diligence studies can contribute to positive business actions in preparation for an IPO. Steps taken by an IPO candidate to identify and resolve potential business problems prior to initiating an IPO are forms of "corporate housekeeping." Detecting key intellectual property assets and removing weaknesses in those assets are important parts of this housekeeping:

> Nearly every IPO company has intellectual property assets. For companies in technology or life sciences fields, intellectual property is often their lifeblood—central to their business models, competitive positions, and valuations. Other companies may not think of themselves as IP-reliant, but they almost certainly rely on trade secrets, trademarks, copyrights, domain names, and other intellectual property in their businesses. Every company going public should pay attention to its intellectual property assets. An excellent means for a company to take stock of its intellectual property assets is a so-called intellectual property audit, and an opportune time to conduct one is during corporate housekeeping in connection with an IPO.

David A. Westenberg, *Corporate Housekeeping*, Initial Public Offerings: A Practical Guide to Going Public ch. 3 (Practising Law Institute 2nd Ed. 2012 & October 2017 Supp.) (available from PLI-Plus research service).

A due diligence review of intellectual property in connection with an IPO is aimed at identifying aspects of intellectual property that will materially affect a company's future prospects for success after the IPO is completed. A reasonable due diligence inquiry is one that seeks to identify these material aspects of intellectual property without wasteful fact finding of no additional value. The scope of a reasonable inquiry will depend on a balance between the costs of additional fact finding and the probable importance of the information that additional fact finding might reveal:

> It is imperative that the metes and bounds of intellectual property due diligence be carefully defined in advance. When establishing such parameters, one must strike a commercially reasonable balance between assuring that the investigation is broad enough in scope to identify that which is material to the transaction, but not so extensive as to be wasteful of time and resources. Moreover, the results of the defining process provide a guide for the intellectual property due diligence team and a checklist to assure thoroughness. The due diligence team must have a basic understanding of the target company's primary product lines, business environment, and future plans so that it can focus on the intellectual property assets that are relevant to the business. It is also important to remember that because the intellectual property due diligence is normally conducted as part of a total transactional investigation, the objectives of the intellectual property investigation must be consistent with the overall objectives (and, of course, budget) of the total due diligence activity, and coordinated with the responsible attorney and the project's diligence attorney.

Gary M. Lawrence, Due Diligence in Business Transactions § 13.03 (2005).

At least four types of intellectual property interests may affect the future prospects of an IPO candidate and will consequently be targets of fact finding and analyses in due diligence reviews preceding an IPO. First, a company's own intellectual property interests may define attractive manufacturing and marketing opportunities for products or services that can only be pursued by the intellectual property holder. Second, intellectual property interests held by competitors or other parties may limit a company's potential business activities and constrain its profit making opportunities. Third, intellectual property interests of suppliers may affect the availability and price of key components incorporated in company products. Fourth, a company's intellectual property may provide profitable opportunities for licensing, either as a means to expand the scale of the licensor's business activities (by sharing similar activities with one or more licensees) or as a means to transfer intellectual property into new business domains not addressed by the licensor.

Due diligence inquiries into intellectual property features and other business characteristics of IPO candidates are wise business steps in managerial terms beyond their advantages in potentially reducing liability for inaccurate disclosures. Reviews that identify intellectual property problems in advance of an IPO may convince company managers that the IPO should not go forward. Some problems identified in this fashion may also be alleviated before an IPO proceeds, thereby avoiding liability problems or adverse public perceptions that might have interfered with the success of the IPO. Careful due diligence assessments may identify previously unappreciated intellectual property risks that must be disclosed in filings with the SEC, thereby shaping the drafting of disclosure documents of the sort addressed further in Subsection C of this chapter.

2. Potential Impacts of Due Diligence Reviews on Liability for Inaccurate or Incomplete Disclosures in an IPO

An additional advantage of conducting a reasonable due diligence review of intellectual property interests in the preparations for an IPO is that certain parties who rely on the results of such a review will gain a defense to later civil liability should the statements that these parties make or oversee about the IPO candidate turn out to be inaccurate. In essence, reviews of intellectual property and other business features can provide some parties making or reviewing disclosures in an IPO with a due diligence defense to liability for misstatements under federal securities laws.

a. Liability for Misstatements and Omissions in an IPO

In connection with making an IPO, the company whose stock will be sold to the public must file a disclosure document commonly referred to as a "registration statement" with the SEC. Misstatements of material facts or omissions of required contents in a registration statement can produce civil damage liability for the parties who have prepared the disclosure statement. As described by one leading court, this type of liability arises under the following standards:

> Section 11(a) of the Securities Act of 1933 provides for civil liability for misstatements and omissions in a registration statement. 15 U.S.C. § 77k(a). It reads:
>
>> (a) In case any part of the registration statement, when such part became effective, contained an untrue statement of a material fact or omitted to state a material fact required to be stated therein or necessary to make the statements therein not misleading, any person acquiring such security (unless it is proved that at the time of such acquisition he knew of such untruth or omission) may, either at law or in equity, in any court of competent jurisdiction, sue [to recover damages or obtain equitable relief].
>
> . . . .
>
> In nonquantitative terms a fact is "material" in a registration statement whenever a rational connection exists between its disclosure and a viable

alternative course of action by any appreciable number of investors. Materiality is then a question of fact to be determined in the context of a particular case.

Feit v. Leasco Data Processing Equipment Corporation, 332 F. Supp. 544, 568, 571 (E.D.N.Y. 1971). This type of liability will generally apply to an issuer of stock in an IPO that has included materially misleading information in its registration statement—that is, to a company that sells its stock to the public despite having made a materially misleading or incomplete statement in its registration statement. Similar liability will also apply to individuals such as company directors, officers, accountants, and lawyers who prepare or approve of the inclusion of inaccurate statements in registration statements. Such liability will also extend to underwriters, who are securities specialists that help companies prepare for IPOs and then aid in the initial sales of stock to the public.

b. Due Diligence Defense

For the individuals involved in this liability scheme, due diligence reviews offer a possible defense to liability. As noted by the court in *Feit*:

Section 11[b] (3) (A) [of the Securities Act of 1933] provides a "due diligence" in investigation defense to all defendants but the issuer.

"(b) Notwithstanding the provisions of subsection (a) of this section no person, other than the issuer, shall be liable as provided therein who shall sustain the burden of proof

. . . .

(3) that (A) as regards as part of the registration statement not purporting to be made on the authority of an expert, and not purporting to be a copy of or extract from a report or valuation of an expert, and not purporting to be made on the authority of a public official document or statement, he had, after reasonable investigation, reasonable ground to believe and did believe, at the time such part of the registration statement became effective, that the statements therein were true and that there was no omission to state a material fact required to be stated therein or necessary to make the statements therein not misleading;"

15 U.S.C. §77k(b) (3) (A).

The defendant must establish: (1) that he conducted a reasonable investigation and (2) that after such investigation he had reasonable ground to believe and did believe the accuracy of the registration statement. Thus, a defendant may fulfill his burden of investigation and still not have reasonable cause to believe in the completeness of the prospectus or he may simply fail in his duty to investigate. Liability will lie in either case.

The standard of reasonableness that applies is that of a reasonably prudent man managing his own property. As stated in Section 11(c):

"In determining, for the purpose of paragraph (3) of subsection (b) of this section, what constitutes reasonable investigation and reasonable ground for belief, the standard of reasonableness shall be that required of a prudent man in the management of his own property."

15 U.S.C. §77k(c)

There is little judicial gloss on this defense. In fact, Judge McLean's opinion in [*Escott v. BarChris Construction Corp.*, 283 F. Supp. 643 (S.D.N.Y. 1968)] is the only one [the court in *Feit*] found that treats the subject at any length. The key to reasonable investigation as expressed in that opinion is independent verification of the registration statement by reference to original written records. The facts in *BarChris* revealed a consistent pattern of directors and underwriters who relied on the oral word of management regarding the accuracy of the registration statement. They made little, if any, effort to verify management's representations by reference to materials readily available such as corporate minutes, books, loan agreements, and various other corporate agreements.

Judge McLean makes it plain that a completely independent and duplicative investigation is not required but, rather, that the defendants were expected to examine the documents that were readily available. Speaking of the attorney-director's contentions, he noted:

"It is claimed that a lawyer is entitled to rely on the statements of his client and that to require him to verify their accuracy would set an unreasonably high standard. This is too broad a generalization. It is all a matter of degree. To require an audit would obviously be unreasonable. On the other hand, to require a check of matters easily verifiable is not unreasonable. Even honest clients can make mistakes. The statute imposes liability for untrue statements regardless of whether they are intentionally untrue. The way to prevent mistakes is to test oral information by examining the original written record.

There were things which Grant could readily have checked which he did not check. For example, he was unaware of the provisions of the agreements between BarChris and Talcott [(one of BarChris' key business contacts and a large source of BarChris' revenues)]. He never read them."

BarChris, supra, 283 F. Supp. at 690.

This theme of an obligation of reasonable verification is also reflected in the commentators' analysis of the *BarChris* case. The reasonable investigation-verification-requirement is simply one means of promoting the full disclosure policy of Section 11.

"The purpose of the civil liability imposed by section 11 is to protect the investor through full disclosure, and the standards of reasonable investigation must be framed in light of this goal. They should also reflect the two criteria set forth in the legislative history: (1) the importance of the role played by each participant in the scheme of distribution and (2) the reliance that the investor is justified in placing upon each participant. These criteria seem to be satisfied by a requirement that some of the parties to the registration process play a more adverse role vis-a-vis management than they may have in the past. The less a participant relies on management, the more the investor may rely on the involvement of the participant in the registration process."

Comment, *BarChris: Due Diligence Refined*, 68 Colum. L. Rev. 1411, 1419 (1968).

Feit v. Leasco Data Processing Equipment Corporation, 332 F. Supp. 544, 575–577 (E.D.N.Y. 1971).

c. *Minimum Features of a Reasonable Investigation Supporting the Defense*

An officer or director will only be able to raise a defense to liability for an inaccurate registration statement where the individual relied on an investigation that was reasonable in scope. The legal requirements for a reasonable investigation were also addressed in *Feit:*

What constitutes "reasonable investigation" and a "reasonable ground to believe" will vary with the degree of involvement of the individual, his expertise, and his access to the pertinent information and data. What is reasonable for one director may not be reasonable for another by virtue of their differing positions.

"It was clear from the outset, however, that the duty of each potentially liable group was not the same. The House report on the bill that became the original Securities Act stated that the duty of care to discover varied in its demands upon the participants with the importance of their place in the scheme of distribution and the degree of protection that the public had a right to expect from them. It has been suggested that although inside directors might be better able to show that they undertook some investigation, the outside director could more easily demonstrate that the investigation he actually undertook was sufficient to sustain his defense."

Comment, *BarChris: Due Diligence Refined*, 68 Colum. L. Rev. 1411, 1416 (1968).

Inside directors [who are also corporate officers] with intimate knowledge of corporate affairs and of the particular transactions will be expected to make a more complete investigation and have more extensive knowledge of facts supporting or contradicting inclusions in the registration statements than outside directors [who are not also corporate officers]. Similarly, accountants and underwriters are expected to investigate to various degrees. Each must undertake that investigation which a reasonably prudent man in that position would conduct.

Feit v. Leasco Data Processing Equipment Corporation 332 F. Supp. 544, 577–578 (E.D.N.Y. 1971).

Notes & Questions

1. In addition to establishing possible defenses to liability for misstatements, due diligence reviews of intellectual property interests and risks prior to public stock offerings serve significant business interests in structuring the terms of the offerings and in encouraging investors to participate in the offerings. Due diligence reviews help potential purchasers of stock ensure that they are "getting what they pay for." The results of these reviews can affect not only key offering terms—such as the size of an offering and initial price of the securities involved—but also whether the prospects of the companies involved seem sound enough to support the type of investor trust and interest needed to complete a successful public stock offering.

In private placements of stock where new stock offerings are sold directly to purchasers, a buyer may either conduct his own due diligence review of a company's intellectual property interests or be given access to the results of the company's own review. In a public stock offering, underwriters, who set the price at which new stock will initially trade, often play important roles in due diligence reviews. The underwriters serve as representatives for stock purchasers in assessing the strength of an issuer's intellectual property position and in appropriately valuing the company involved:

> In the context of a public offering, where the underwriters serve as the surrogates of the ultimate investors with respect to conducting due diligence; the underwriters are putting their name and reputation on the line when they market an issuer to prospective purchasers, and it is crucial that they have conducted sufficient diligence to support their "promotion" of the issuer's business and prospects. For example, few underwriters will allow a public offering to go effective until they have evaluated the issuer's business by speaking directly with some of the issuer's principal customers. Similarly, in the case of a biotechnology company issuer, the underwriters and their counsel will want to verify that the issuer has sufficient patent protection for its new drug developments and is taking appropriate steps to obtain the requisite regulatory approvals, because failure in either case could have significant adverse consequences on the issuer's business.

Mitchell S. Bloom & Lawrence A. Gold, PUBLIC OFFERINGS AND PRIVATE PLACEMENTS § 1.1.2 (2000).

2. Systematic due diligence reviews of a company's intellectual property interests and risks are often critically important features of private sales transactions in which a company sells off a subsidiary or division to a particular buyer or group of buyers. The sales agreement covering such a transaction will typically involve provisions in which the seller warrants the transferred company's ownership of key intellectual property interests and the lack of known infringement of intellectual property rights of others. In addition, the seller may warrant that the intellectual property rights being transferred to the buyer or group of buyers are sufficient to support the business activities of the company being transferred. Reasonable due diligence reviews are important means to confirm the accuracy of the warranties being made in these contexts and the scope of contractual liability the seller may risk by agreeing to these sorts of warranty terms.

The following contract terms are excerpted from an agreement governing the sale of all of the stock of a subsidiary of gambling giant Harrah's Entertainment Corporation. These terms illustrate the scope of intellectual property warranties that may be incorporated in a corporate sales agreement and, by implication, the types of due diligence reviews that should precede a seller's agreement to such terms:

> Section 3.10 Intellectual Property. The Company [for which ownership is transferred under the stock sales agreement] owns or has the defensible right to use, whether through ownership, licensing or otherwise, all material Intellectual Property used in the businesses of the Company and each Subsidiary of the Company in substantially the same manner as such businesses are conducted on the date hereof ("Material Intellectual Property"). Except as set forth in Section 3.10 of the Company Disclosure Letter and except as would not, individually or in the aggregate, reasonably be expected to have a material adverse impact on the validity or value of any Material Intellectual Property, (A) no written claim of invalidity or conflicting ownership rights with respect to any Material Intellectual Property has been made by a third party and no such Material Intellectual Property is the subject of any pending or, to the Company's knowledge, threatened action, suit, claim, investigation, arbitration or other proceeding, (B) no individual, corporation, limited liability company, partnership, association, trust, unincorporated organization, other entity or "group" (as defined in Rule 13d-5(b)(1) under the Exchange Act) (each, a "Person") has given written notice to the Company or any Subsidiary of the Company that the use of any Material Intellectual Property by the Company, any Subsidiary of the Company or any licensee is infringing or has infringed any domestic or foreign patent, trademark, service mark, trade name, or copyright or design right, or that the Company, any Subsidiary of the Company or any licensee has misappropriated or improperly used or disclosed any trade secret, confidential information or know-how, (C) the making, using, selling, manufacturing, marketing,

licensing, reproduction, distribution, or publishing of any process, machine, manufacture or product related to any Material Intellectual Property, does not and will not infringe any domestic or foreign patent, trademark, service mark, trade name, copyright or other intellectual property right of any third party, and does not and will not involve the misappropriation or improper use or disclosure of any trade secrets, confidential information or know-how of any third party of which the Company has knowledge, (D) (i) neither the Company nor any Subsidiary of the Company has performed prior acts or is engaged in current conduct or use, or (ii) to the knowledge of the Company, there exists no prior act or current use by any third party, that would void or invalidate any Material Intellectual Property, and (E) the execution, delivery and performance of this Agreement and the Ancillary Agreement by the Company and the consummation of the transactions contemplated hereby and thereby will not breach, violate or conflict with any instrument or agreement that the Company is party to and that concerns any Material Intellectual Property, will not cause the forfeiture or termination or give rise to a right of forfeiture or termination of any of the Material Intellectual Property or impair the right of P[the acquiring company] to make, use, sell, license or dispose of, or to bring any action for the infringement of, any Material Intellectual Property. Pursuant to that certain Exclusive License Agreement dated as of July 2, 1998, by and between Horseshoe Gaming, L.L.C. and Horseshoe License (the "Intellectual Property License Agreement"), the Company has an exclusive, irrevocable, fully paid license to use the Property (as defined in the Intellectual Property License Agreement) in perpetuity anywhere in the world, except for the State of Nevada.

Richard A. Goldberg & Monique K. Moore, *Negotiating the Purchase Agreement* in A GUIDE TO MERGERS & ACQUISITIONS 2005 425, 692 (PLI 2005).

3. Beyond the role of due diligence reviews in preparing for public offerings of stock and other transfers of corporate ownership, systematic reviews of intellectual property interests can serve important management functions and avoid certain types of liability for management errors. For example, responsible monitoring of intellectual property interests and liabilities through due diligence reviews can aid corporate directors in meeting their corporate law duties and avoiding personal liability to their companies for corporate losses. In general, corporate board members must exercise due care in making decisions about corporate actions. As intellectual property interests have become more and more important to the success of various types of businesses, the significance of efforts by corporate directors to learn about and make informed decisions concerning their companies' intellectual property interests has grown as well.

Where corporate directors know (or should have known through reasonable information gathering) about intellectual property risks that are likely to adversely affect planned corporate actions, yet the directors disregard these risks to the detriment of their corporations, the directors may face personal liability to their companies for the resulting corporate losses. *See generally* In re *Caremark International Inc. Derivative Litigation*, 698 A.2d 959, 1996 Del. Ch. LEXIS 125 (1996). Due diligence in monitoring intellectual property interests and risks has major importance in companies that base their business strategies on the strength of their intellectual property and on the lack of business barriers due to the intellectual property interests of others. *See* Steven E. Bochner & Susan P. Krause, *Intellectual Property Management and Board Liability* in Practising Law Institute, CORPORATE LAW AND PRACTICE COURSE HANDBOOK SERIES No. B0-004Y at p. 457–58 (August 1998). These issues are addressed further in Chapter 2.

4. Companies sometimes make public statements expressing a positive belief that they are not infringing the intellectual property rights of others. For example, investor information filed with the SEC by Agilent Technologies (a maker of a wide variety of communications, electronics, life sciences and chemical analysis products) contains the following representations about the company's activities and possible infringement of intellectual property rights of other concerns:

> While we do not believe that any of our products infringe the valid intellectual property rights of third parties, we may be unaware of intellectual property rights of others that may cover some of our technology, products or services. Any litigation regarding patents or other intellectual property could be costly and time-consuming and could divert our management and key personnel from our business operations. The complexity of the technology involved and the uncertainty of intellectual property litigation increase these risks. Claims of intellectual property infringement might also require us to enter into costly license agreements. However, we may not be able to obtain license agreements on terms acceptable to us, or at all. We also may be subject to significant damages or injunctions against development and sale of certain of our products.

Agilent Technologies, Inc., Form 10-K at p. 67–68 (12/21/2004).

What type of self-scrutiny of claims or assertions of intellectual property infringement should a company make before representing that "we do not believe that any of our products infringe the valid intellectual property rights of third parties"? Is it sufficient that additional portions of the company's web site indicate that there may be intellectual property interests and acts of infringement that the company has not detected yet? Does the statement that "we do not believe" that there is infringement imply that this belief is based on a reasonable inquiry or is it enough if the executives making the statement were personally unaware of infringement? What should be the impact on corporate liability if persons at a middle management or operating employee level of the corporation had knowledge of the probable infringement of another party's intellectual property interest, but this knowledge had not risen upward in the corporation's hierarchy so as to reach the executives who made the representation about the company's lack of infringement?

B. Conducting a Reasonable Due Diligence Review

Diane J. Kasselman, Intellectual Property Due Diligence in Business Transactions

Practising Law Institute

Patents, Copyrights, Trademarks, and Literary Property Course

Handbook Series No. G0-011U (October, 2002)*

I. Introduction

Conducting intellectual property due diligence is like participating in an archeological dig. You must sift through many layers of information to discover accurate details relating to a company's intellectual property assets. This article discusses: (i) why we conduct intellectual property due diligence; (ii) the components of intellectual property due diligence; and (iii) the issues that may arise based on the findings of intellectual property due diligence.[1]

II. Intellectual Property Due Diligence

Black's Law Dictionary defines "due diligence" as

[s]uch a measure of prudence, activity or assiduity as is properly to be expected from and ordinarily exercised by a reasonable and prudent man under the particular circumstances; not measured by any absolute standard but depending upon the relative facts of the special case.

In the context of mergers, acquisitions, joint ventures or public or private offerings, "due diligence" involves an evaluation of a company's assets as they relate to the operation of the business, or businesses, contemplated in the proposed transaction.

A. What is Intellectual Property Due Diligence?

Just as corporate due diligence identifies the corporate assets implicated in a proposed business transaction (e.g., receivables, real estate, inventory, etc.), intellectual property due diligence ("IP Due Diligence") focuses specifically on the intellectual property assets. These include: trademarks, service marks, patents, copyrights, Internet domain names, software, trade secrets and any agreements granting or obtaining rights in intellectual property.

Many believe that IP Due Diligence is necessary only in connection with "high-tech" industries. This could not be further from the truth. Virtually all companies, in every industry, own and/or use intellectual property in the operation of their

---

1. This article generally addresses due diligence concerns from the buyer's perspective. However, sellers apply the same diligence methods to ensure that representations and warranties are true. Independent of proposed business transactions, periodic IP Due Diligence is a useful tool to keep a company's intellectual property assets "in order."

businesses. IP Due Diligence is required in order to identify and assess the company's intellectual property in light of the proposed transaction.

B. Why Perform Due Diligence?

Would you buy a house without knowing whether there is clear title to the property; whether there is a Certificate of Occupancy for the addition the seller put on last year; or whether the neighbor has an easement on the property? Of course not! Similarly, no business transaction should be completed without determining what is being sold (all corporate assets and goodwill) and whether is it worth the price. Intellectual property assets are identified and scrutinized to determine:

- the importance of intellectual property within the framework of the deal;
- the commercial advantage of the company's intellectual property portfolio; and
- the potential liabilities associated with the company's intellectual property portfolio or in the use of intellectual property in the operation of the business.

IP Due Diligence will reveal whether those assets can pass to the buyer "free and clear," or whether there are problems that must be corrected before the completion of the transaction. It is always good business practice to perform adequate due diligence for proposed transactions. In the context of acquisitions, the diligence effort is ultimately a business decision. Conversely, public offerings subject issuers to strict liability under securities law for material nondisclosure or misrepresentations in the offering. However, a "due diligence defense" is available to experts (including attorneys and accountants), underwriters, etc. if they exercised the appropriate level of due diligence.[2]

C. What is the Scope of Due Diligence?

The scope and level of scrutiny of the IP Due Diligence depends on the structure of the business transaction. There are different considerations for an asset deal, a merger, a stock purchase and public or private offering. For example, in an asset purchase, diligence should determine transferability of the intellectual property owned and licensed by the company from third parties, and in a stock sale, diligence may uncover issues related to restrictive change-of-control provisions.

III. Components of Intellectual Property Due Diligence

IP Due Diligence consists of the following steps:

- Understand the business
- Review documents
- Conduct searches
- Conduct interviews
- Identify issues
- Report findings

---

2. See sections 11 and 12 of the Securities Act of 1933.

Each step is an important part of the overall due diligence process. The information gathered and analyzed during IP Due Diligence joins with the results of corporate's, and other specialty areas', diligence efforts to determine the continued viability of the proposed transaction.

A. Understand the Business

The first step in IP Due Diligence is to understand the nature and operation of the business under scrutiny. Although virtually every business has intellectual property to evaluate (e.g. trademarks, copyrights, patents, licenses), the particular industry may generate a more detailed level of scrutiny. For example, aerospace companies may have used government funding that requires a license back to the government of the developed intellectual property; a pharmaceutical company considers patents in light of abbreviated new drug applications to the United States Food and Drug Administration; the film industry usually implicates issues with respect to rights of publicity and software providers may raise issues with respect to open source code and export restrictions.

Once there is a clear understanding of: (i) the nature of the business (with any industry-specific nuances), (ii) the structure of the deal and (iii) the value of the intellectual property in relation to the deal, the researcher can develop an IP Due Diligence plan to find the answers.

B. Review Documents

Documents and information about the company (including intellectual property-related documents and information) are usually provided in response to the potential buyer's document request list. All transactions are not alike, and, because there are so many distinct factors that make deals different, a due diligence request list should be tailored to reflect the proposed transaction. Generally, in performing IP Due Diligence, the diligence team will want to ask for and review the following genre of documents, including:

- Schedules of registered, applied-for and material unregistered intellectual property (including Internet domain name registrations), along with underlying documentation (e.g. certificates of registration, copies of applications, etc.)

- Licenses or other agreements granting or obtaining rights in intellectual property (ask for descriptions of any oral agreements)

- Assignment of intellectual property by or to the company

- Other agreements affecting the company's use of intellectual property including, consulting, research and development, joint venture, prior acquisitions, consent to use, covenants not to sue, etc.

- Confidentiality, non-disclosure, non-compete and employee/consulting agreements covering rights in intellectual property (e.g., assignment of inventions, discoveries, improvements, works of authorship, etc.)

- List of software (proprietary and third party)

- Summary description of subject matter held as trade secrets
- Opposition, reexamination, interferences or other adversarial proceedings before any intellectual property registry
- Intellectual property-related claims and correspondence, including pending and threatened claims, cease-and-desist letters and contacts. . . .

A sample Intellectual Property Due Diligence Request List is attached [at the end of this article].

In reviewing the documents, identify the extent of the company's rights in existing intellectual property and in intellectual property not yet developed. For example:

- whether a license grants exclusive or non-exclusive rights?
- what is the field of use?
- what is the territory?
- what is the duration of the license?

In addition, in determining the extent, if any, of a company's copyright protection in an original work of authorship created for the company by an independent consultant, IP Due Diligence will reveal whether it qualifies as a "work-for-hire" under U.S. copyright law.

C. Conduct Searches

One of the most critical aspects of IP Due Diligence is to determine what intellectual property the company owns. Even if the company provides detailed schedules in response to the diligence request, it is important to conduct independent searches.

On-line Searches. Online searches[3] are simple and relatively inexpensive methods to verify, and possibly augment, a company's disclosed schedule. You can search: (i) by scheduled intellectual property; and (ii) by company name.

- *By Scheduled Intellectual Property.* Generally, searches using the number listed on the schedule will locate record(s) in the database. However, information with respect to U.S. patent applications is not available to the public [in the early stages of the application],[4] and trademark information is not available for every country where trademark protection exists.[5]

---

3. [These online searches can be conducted through] Dialog's databases, e.g., Inpadoc, Derwent, Trademarkscan, Patfull, US Copyrights and LitAlert, and Thomson & Thomson's Saegis database.

4. Patents filed exclusively in the United States were generally held confidential until the patent issued [prior to 2000]. Effective in November 2000, patent applications are held in confidence for 18 months and then disclosed, unless the application qualifies for an exception to maintain secrecy.

5. These databases contain information with respect to trademarks registered or applied for in the United States (federal and state), Canada, Austria, Benelux (Belgium, Netherlands and Luxembourg), Denmark, Finland, France, Germany, Italy, Liechtenstein, Monaco, Norway, Spain, Sweden, Switzerland and the United Kingdom. Information is also available for Japan and Community

- *By Company.* A search in the name of the company and any subsidiaries and/or affiliates included in the transaction may reveal additional intellectual property that should be included in the disclosure schedules.

On-line searches can provide the following information:

- the "record owner" — the person who, in the records of that registry, is the current owner;
- the current status — whether the property is active, abandoned or expired;
- encumbrances — whether there are security interests granted in the property;
- oppositions, reexaminations and other adversarial proceedings; and
- litigation.

Information contained on-line is not always accurate and may not reflect the most current information. This may be due to backlogs in the registries, failure of the new owner of the intellectual property to record new information in the registries or typographical errors in recordation. For example, on-line records may not reflect that an issued patent is the subject of a reexamination, or that a bank's security interest in a trademark has been released. In addition, a slip of the finger during the recordation process at an intellectual property registry may result in the erroneous allocation of one company's intellectual property to another company![6]

Searches in the Registries. Because on-line searches do not always reflect the most current information and because there are frequently typographical errors in on-line records, it may be advisable to review the actual documents filed in the intellectual property registries. Even if the company has provided the "prosecution history" or "file wrapper" for the particular item of intellectual property, there is no way to ascertain its completeness without requesting the records from the applicable registries.

In the United States, records for applications for trademark registration, registered trademarks, and copyrights and issued patents may be ordered from the U.S. Patent and Trademark Office ("PTO") and United States Copyright Office without the consent of the owner. Files pertaining to patent applications may be obtained with the patent applicant's consent. Similarly, public records relating to state registrations of trademarks and perfected security interests in the intellectual property being reviewed can be obtained from the applicable Secretary of state. However, the fees associated with ordering information from intellectual property registries and Secretaries of state (and foreign registries, if applicable,[7] and the time spent reviewing such folders may translate into a sizeable expense.

Trademark applications consisting of 15 countries (Austria, Belgium, Germany, Denmark, Spain, Finland, France, U.K., Greece, Ireland, Italy, Luxembourg, Netherland, Portugal and Sweden).

6. To avoid this, carefully review the Notice of Recordation from all applicable intellectual property registries. In the U.S. Patent and Trademark Office and United States Copyright Office, errors made by those offices may be corrected without additional fees.

7. It may be advisable to retain local counsel when evaluating the company's rights in any foreign intellectual property.

Ultimately, the extent of the searches should be commensurate with the relative value of the company's intellectual property to the proposed transaction.

D. Conduct Interviews

Interviews with the people familiar with the business put the proposed transaction into focus. Interviews can provide answers to questions that only an "insider" knows and will fill in the "missing pieces" from your review of the materials provided by the company or obtained independently. For example, the seemingly impressive portfolio of the company's patents, trademarks and copyrights may be given "short shrift" by key company business people who intend to abandon certain trademarks and to cease paying maintenance fees for certain patents. In most cases, there will be a "contact" person with whom you can speak. However, when secrecy cloaks the proposed transaction, the person who has the knowledge you seek may be unaware of the deal, and therefore, unavailable to you.

Whom Do You Interview? — Ideally, you want to speak with people familiar with the business and the intellectual property used in connection with the business. This could be any one, or combination of the following:

- the company's in-house counsel
- outside firm(s) — one or more firms that handle intellectual property prosecution and litigation (e.g. one firm for patent prosecution, another for trademark and copyrights, and yet another to handle intellectual property-related litigation)
- people in the company familiar with particular aspects of the business (e.g., research & development, information technology, marketing)

What Do You Ask? — The interview(s) should provide you with information regarding the company's:

- intellectual property portfolio (including how it was acquired)
- licensing of its own, and third party intellectual property (including inter-company licensing)
- use of intellectual property in the business
- information technology operations (including websites)
- marketing strategies
- research and development
- policies with respect to obtaining, maintaining and protecting intellectual property
- pending and threatened litigation or adversarial proceedings before intellectual property registries
- restrictions on intellectual property due to settlements, covenants not to sue, consents to use, cross licenses, licenses to the U.S. government or restrictive covenants in other agreements

E. Identify the Issues

Throughout IP Due Diligence, the researcher must be alert to spot issues that could affect the transaction. For example, a diminished intellectual property portfolio (in material areas of the business) may lead to negotiations to adjust the purchase price. Similarly, flaws in title, shared intellectual property, ongoing litigation and unreleased liens may result in modifications to the representations, warranties, covenants and/or indemnification sections of the deal documents. These issues are addressed in Section IV, "Issues Arising from Intellectual Property Due Diligence".

F. Report Your Findings

At the conclusion of IP Due Diligence the researcher should be able to identify:

- material intellectual property
  - who owns it
  - whether it is active
  - how it is used in the business (and in the company's other businesses)
- material third party agreements
- existing and potential liabilities
  - relating to owned or licensed intellectual property
  - with respect to the operation of the business

With this information at hand, the researcher will be able to produce a report that can be used to determine the benefits and risks associated with the proposed transaction.

Diligence reports can be narrow or comprehensive. This is generally dictated by the importance of intellectual property to the deal and the structure of the deal. Diligence reports can be presented in many formats, including:

- oral report
- e-mail report
- detailed written memorandum (with schedules)
- summary written reports featuring (i) material intellectual property assets (including agreements) and (ii) identifying key business points and potential problem areas

IV. Issues Arising from Intellectual Property Due Diligence

A. Status of Intellectual Property

In response to the IP diligence request, many companies list all intellectual property, regardless of its status. Therefore, IP Due Diligence may reveal that large portions of the company's IP assets are no longer active. Initially, this may cause concern until the reason for the early cancellation or abandonment is explained.

Often, a product that was marketed under a now abandoned brand name is no longer being manufactured and/or sold by the company. There would be no reason to continue to pay maintenance fees on trademarks that the company ceased using in commerce and intends not to use in the future.

Similarly, there would be no need to maintain a patent in a technology that is no longer "state-of-the-art" and that is no longer practiced.

However, to the extent that any material registered or issued intellectual property has expired, been abandoned or cancelled, the prospective buyer will need to determine a course of action. Abandoned or cancelled applications for trademarks and patents that have been identified as material to the business also need to be scrutinized to determine the reason the application was not pursued. Obtaining the prosecution history enables the researcher to review what objections the PTO raised against the trademark or patent and the company's responses.

In assessing a diminished intellectual property portfolio with respect to material items, the buyer may consider:

- whether the business remains viable without the intellectual property
- whether there are alternatives to the intellectual property
- if the intellectual property was issued or registered, whether it can be reinstated
- whether continued use of the intellectual property poses risks of litigation
- whether entry of the intellectual property into the public domain reduces the company's competitive edge

B. Ownership

Two ownership issues frequently occur as a result of IP Due Diligence: (i) the company is not listed in the applicable intellectual property's records as the "owner;" and (ii) there is a gap in the chain of title.

The Company is Not the Record Owner. The entity identified as the "owner" of the intellectual property listed on the schedule provided by the company is not the "current owner" according to the records of the applicable intellectual property registry. Common reasons include:

- the company's name change was never recorded
- intellectual property is in the name of an affiliated entity (parent, subsidiary or affiliate)
- the acquisition pursuant to which the company obtained rights in intellectual property was never recorded
- the inventor/author never assigned his/her rights in the intellectual property to the company
- the company no longer owns the intellectual property

Ideally, the researcher has a corporate structure chart and will be able to determine, based on the structure of the deal, whether the error is problematic. For example, if buyer will obtain the stock of the company and its subsidiaries (including the subsidiary that is the "record owner" of the intellectual property at issue), then ownership is not a problem. Conversely, if buyer is purchasing the assets of the company related to a particular business, then, if certain intellectual property necessary for the operation of the business is not in the company's name, the manner in which title will pass to the buyer may become a "deal issue."

If the discrepancy is not easily discerned from documents provided by the company, the researcher should request explanations from the company. In all cases, the researcher should request the copies of any underlying documents that demonstrate "beneficial" ownership in the company (e.g., certificate of name change, assignments, mergers, etc.).

Gap in the Chain of Title. Although the company can be traced as the most recent, and therefore is the "record owner," of the intellectual property, there are gaps in the chain of title. In other words, there is not a traceable path leading from the first registered owner to the company. For example:

- A patent issued to Company A in 1990.
- In 1993, Company A assigned all its right, title and interest in and to that patent to Company B.
- Company B never recorded the assignment in the PTO.
- In 1995, Company B assigned the patent to Company C.
- Company C recorded the assignment.
- In 2002, your client wants to acquire the assets of Company C, including this patent.

In this example, the records in the PTO indicate that Company C is the "record owner." However, the records reflect that a company without recorded ownership (Company B) assigned its rights in this patent to Company C. There is a gap in the chain linking Company A's interest in that patent to Company C.

The resolution of these discrepancies (e.g., whether to record the evidence closing the gap, whether to assign the intellectual property to a different entity, whether to obtain royalty-free licenses or whether to do nothing) and the obligation and expense of recordation to correct incomplete or incorrect records becomes a business point.

C. Encumbrances

Companies seeking financing for acquisitions or other business loans routinely use intellectual property as collateral. Typically, the company seeking financing will grant to the financial institution a continuing security interest (until the loan is paid) in all existing and after-acquired intellectual property.

Financial institutions are usually diligent in recording liens on the individual intellectual property in intellectual property registries and in the states (through UCC filings). However, once the loan is paid off, evidence that the loan has been satisfied, usually a Release Letter from the bank, is often not recorded in the applicable intellectual property registry. Accordingly, IP Due diligence may reveal one or more unreleased lien in favor of different financial institutions. Inquiry into this matter often reveals that the loan has been paid off. In this case, the researcher should request written evidence of the pay-off. If no release was executed, it may be necessary to obtain releases from the financial institutions and record the releases in the applicable registries.

Another form of "encumbrance" is a limitation on, or an impediment to, one's ability to exploit its own intellectual property. For example:

- Licenses to the U.S. government due to government funds received by the company
- Exclusive licenses to third parties, precluding the company's use (even internal use) of the intellectual property
- Covenants not to sue.

D. Assignability/Change of Control

Anti-assignment clauses or change of control provisions that are triggered by the structure of the proposed transaction may become deal issues. This is most critical in asset deals where consents must be obtained and transfer fees paid. In connection with the proposed structure, there should be a clear understanding of:

- whether consents will be obtained
- who will obtain the consents
- who will bear the expenses related to consents
- when consents should be obtained
- the effect on the business if consent is denied
- the potential liabilities if consent is required but the company transferred the assets without requesting consent

E. Litigation

IP Due Diligence focuses on any active or threatened litigation relating to the company's material intellectual property. Usually, the company provides a brief summary of the claims and does not provide detailed documentation with respect to that claim. The researcher must speak with the person familiar with the litigation (this may be outside counsel) to determine the company's position on the merits. Depending on the materiality of the intellectual property, the researcher may want to review the intellectual property's underlying documents as well as the litigation file.

F. Shared Intellectual Property

IP Due Diligence may reveal that not all intellectual property is used exclusively in the business being acquired. In other words, after divesting itself of the business, seller will still require the use of certain intellectual property in its other businesses. Depending on who owns the intellectual property, the nature of the intellectual property and how it is to be used by both businesses, there are many choices, including:

- assignment of intellectual property to buyer with a license back to the seller
- buyer retains ownership of the intellectual property and licenses it to buyer
- seller retains ownership of intellectual property in all other fields of use, other than the fields of use used in the business[8]
- other creative solutions to be determined by the parties (e.g. joint ownership, assignment to a licensing entity that licenses the intellectual property to both buyer and seller, etc.)
- in the case of third party licensed intellectual property:
  - buyer retains the license and sublicenses to seller
  - buyer assigns the license to seller and becomes a sublicensee of seller
  - buyer covenants to assist seller in obtaining licenses from third party licensor on terms as favorable as seller's license

Naturally, the decision on how to handle shared intellectual property is a business point that will be a bargaining and/or negotiating tool in the deal.

V. Summary

A carefully planned and executed IP Due Diligence plan, that includes understanding the nature and operation of a company's business, and using that understanding as a filter during the actual diligence process (e.g. searches, document review, interviews, issue spotting and diligence report) is a key element in the successful conclusion of a proposed business transaction.

<u>Intellectual Property Due Diligence Request</u>

A. SCHEDULES of all United States and foreign intellectual property owned by the Company [and its subsidiaries/affiliates], including:

1. <u>Patents and Patent Applications</u> (includes invention disclosures), identifying

- Title
- Patent number and/or application number
- Issue date and/or application date
- Country
- Record owner
- For invention disclosures, identify:
  - Title
  - Identification number
  - Subject matter

---

8. This solution may pose a risk of impermissible trademark splitting which could result in the abandonment of the trademark(s) at issue.

2. <u>Trademarks and Trademark Applications</u> (includes trademarks, service marks, collective marks, certification marks, material unregistered marks and trade names or other fictitious business names), identifying:

- Mark
- Registration number and/or application number
- Registration date and/or application date
- Country
- Record owner
- For material unregistered marks, identify:
  - Date of first use
  - Nature of goods and/or services

3. <u>Copyrights and Copyright Applications</u> (includes material unregistered copyrights), identifying:

- Title
- Nature of the work
- Registration number
- Registration date or date application sent
- Effective date of the registration
- Country
- Record owner
- Author(s)
- Type of ownership (e.g., single, joint, work for hire)

4. <u>Domain Names</u>, identifying:

- Domain name
- Registrant
- Registry
- Date of Registration
- Date of Expiration
- Contact information (technical and administrative)

5. <u>Material Software and Databases</u> (includes algorithms, toolkits, methodologies or code, whether independent or embodied in the company's products), identifying:

- Title (e.g. name, description, etc.)
- Owner (if the company is not the owner, list the agreement in Section B, below)
- If the company is owner, indicate method of creation (e.g. authorship, work for hire (employee or consultant))
- Function/application

6. <u>Trade Secrets</u>, identifying:

Summary description of the subject matter held as a trade secret

B. AGREEMENTS RELATING TO INTELLECTUAL PROPERTY, including:

1. <u>Licenses and Other Agreements</u> (including assignments, settlement agreements, consents-to-use, inter-company (affiliate) agreements, joint venture, etc.) granting or obtaining rights in, or involving the ownership or use of, intellectual property (including patents, trademark, copyright, software, trade secret, rights of publicity, know-how, technology, database, etc.), identifying:

- Title
- Parties
- Who is Licensor
- Who is Licensee
- Date of execution
- Subject matter

2. <u>Consulting or Development Agreements</u> related to the development of intellectual property by independent consultants, identifying:

- Title
- Parties
- Date of execution
- Subject matter

3. <u>Confidentiality Agreements</u> relating to the disclosure of confidential information, trade secrets, know-how, inventions and other proprietary information, identifying:

- Title
- Parties
- Date of execution
- Subject matter

4. <u>Employee Agreements</u> relating to the development and assignment of intellectual property to the company.

5. <u>Escrow Agreements</u> (including software and technology), identifying:

- Title
- Parties (include Escrow Agent)
- Date of execution
- Subject matter

6. <u>Web Site Agreements</u> (including, linking, hosting, connectivity, development, advertising and content provider agreements) <u>and Service Agreements</u> (including software service, outsourcing, maintenance, on-line service etc.), and E-Commerce Agreements (including electronic data exchange, electronic mail, etc.), identifying:

- Title

- Parties

- Date of execution

- Subject matter

- Web site involved

7. <u>Web Site Policies</u> (including, terms and conditions of use, privacy policies, etc.).

8. Provide copies of the agreements listed in Section B, 1 through 7, above.

C. CLAIMS, THREATENED CLAIMS AND RELATED MATTERS relating to intellectual property, including:

1. <u>Adversarial Proceedings</u> (includes litigation, interference, cancellation, opposition, reexamination or other adversarial proceedings pending before any court or intellectual property registry), provide:

- A schedule of all pending proceedings, identifying:
  - Caption, title or description of action
  - Forum
  - Nature of action (infringement, opposition, etc.)
  - Parties
  - Date commenced
  - Current status of action
  - Copies of papers related to the scheduled pending proceedings (e.g. complaints, answers, correspondence, etc.)

2. <u>Threatened Actions</u> (includes cease-and-desist letters, oral communications) by or against the company, provide:

- A schedule of all Threatened Actions, identifying:
  - Party threatening action
  - Subject matter
  - Date of threatened action
  - Copies of papers related to the scheduled threatened action

3. <u>Audit Requests</u> (from government agencies and intellectual property rights protection groups such as Business Software Alliance, ASCAP, BMI, etc.), provide:

- A schedule of all Audit Requests, identifying:
  - Requestor
  - Subject matter
  - Date of Request

- Copies of papers related to the scheduled Audit Request, including the Company's response.

4. <u>Legal Opinions</u>. Provide copies of all legal opinions provided to the Company within [] years.

5. <u>Agreements</u>. Provide copies of all judgments, consent decrees, orders, settlement agreements, covenants not to sue or other agreements that grant or prohibit the company's use of intellectual property

D. MISCELLANEOUS, including:

1. <u>"Form-Of" Agreements</u> (including employee invention assignment and non-disclosure agreements, consultant agreements, confidentiality agreements).

2. <u>Intellectual Property Policies</u> related to the use, protection and maintenance of the company's intellectual property, provide:

- Copies of all written policies, or
- Description of such policies and practices

3. <u>Encumbrances</u>. For all company intellectual property in which there exists an unreleased security interest, lien or other encumbrance, provide documents granting encumbrance.

4. <u>Other Materials.</u> Copies of written materials describing the company, including its intellectual property (e.g., 10K, public or private offerings, sales materials, etc.)

E. CONTACTS. Provide the name and contact information for the following people, as applicable:

1. In-house counsel

2. Outside intellectual property counsel(s):

- Litigation
- Prosecution

3. Business contact(s):

- Marketing
- Research & development
- Information Systems

Mary J. Hildebrand & Jacqueline Klosek, Intellectual Property Due Diligence: A Critical Prerequisite to Capital Investment

http://library.findlaw.com/2003/Dec/1/133278.html
(Accessed June 5, 2018)*

Tips in Conducting Intellectual Property Due Diligence:

---

1. *Include intellectual property experts in the due diligence team.* Prior to commencing any intellectual property due diligence, effort should be directed to ensure that the proper team is in place. As a threshold matter, the legal team that undertakes to conduct intellectual property due diligence must have a basic understanding of the primary product lines, business environment and future plans of the target to ensure that the team remains focused primarily on the intellectual property assets that are relevant to the business. Since the intellectual property due diligence team will participate in the investor's evaluation of a proposed transaction, it is also essential that the team understand the relative importance of the proposed investment to the client. Early familiarity with these issues should enable the legal team to contribute to the entire process in a meaningful way.

2. *Ensure that the intellectual property due diligence plan reflects the importance of the deal.* Once the proper team has been assembled, a necessary step is to develop a well-drafted intellectual property due diligence request that will use questions that are designed to assist in identifying areas that merit further inquiry as evidenced by a positive response. By the same token, a negative response to certain questions permits the legal team to move on to areas of genuine concern that are relevant to the business and/or the specific transaction at issue.

3. *Take nothing on faith.* Our firm recently dealt with a matter in which a client was attempting to acquire a target whose main asset was a business method for processing insurance claims over the Internet. As part of our efforts, patent counsel did a search on the target's business method. Not only did we find that the target's invention might be infringing another patent, we also found that there was active litigation between an entity that was holding a patent on a similar method and another company using a method similar to the one used by the target. The target later admitted that they had discussed this issue with other attorneys. They did not, however, disclose it in response to the intellectual property due diligence request.

Depending on the nature of the responses, the deal and the business, further investigative activities may include (a) conducting searches in appropriate databases in all relevant jurisdictions to identify patent rights including pending and/or provisional patent applications, registered patents, registered copyrights and registered trademarks, (b) examination, analysis and verification of the results of such searches, (c) verification of claimed but unregistered intellectual property rights, (d) review and analysis of relevant provisions of executed agreements that could include licenses, consulting and confidentiality agreements, assignments and other documents, (e) interviews with key business and technology development staff at the target and, where the situation warrants, with previous employees and consultants, (f) examination and analysis of potentially infringing registrations and third-party intellectual property rights, and (g) other efforts appropriate to the situation.

4. *Confirm everything.* In another matter, our client was making a $50 million investment into a target company holding numerous patents that were of interest to our client. As part of our intellectual property due diligence, patent attorneys conducted a

computerized search of the relevant patents. This search revealed that the ownership interests were not what we expected them to be. As is our custom, this initial computerized search was followed with a manual search. The manual search of the actual documentation revealed that the ownership interests were indeed as they were expected to be and that the computerized search was erroneous. In this case, the inaccuracy in the computerized search was the result of a secretarial error in preparing the filing documents. Consider, however, the results if the opposite had occurred, that is to say, that the computerized search appeared to be accurate but was not and no further manual search was performed. This highlights the importance of verifying information that is presented through more than one source.

5. *Understand the dynamic relationship between the documents and the core business.* While it is extremely important to examine all agreements, registrations, filings and other documents to ensure that they are valid, the legal team must clearly establish a relationship between such documentation and the relevant intellectual property assets. We recently represented a client that was interesting in acquiring a division of a target that held a large collection of patents. Prior to the investment, the target provided us with voluminous documentation purportedly pertaining to its patents. However, an inspection of the documentation revealed that the information provided concerned patents that had nothing to do with the target's core business.

6. *Foreign laws may impact the deal.* In recent years, the number of cross-border mergers and acquisitions has increased dramatically. This fact, combined with the reality that many individuals developing intellectual property assets for American companies are from outside of the United States, increases the likelihood that intellectual property due diligence will involve review and analysis of non-US intellectual property assets. When analyzing such assets, it must be recalled that few countries treat intellectual property in the exact same way and rights often depend on complex treaties and conventions executed by and among many different nations. Accordingly, it will be important to avoid making assumptions about such foreign assets based upon an understanding of US laws and procedures pertaining to intellectual property.

C. Making Sufficient Disclosures

1. Drafting a Prospectus for a Public Offering

In order to proceed with an initial public offering (IPO) of stock, a description of the company conducting the IPO (the "offeror" or "issuer" of new stock) and the offering transaction must be filed with the federal Securities and Exchange Commission (SEC). The primary disclosure document is a "prospectus" that is initially reviewed by the SEC for informational sufficiency and then released to the public, at which point it becomes the main vehicle for investors to learn about the offeror and to consider whether to purchase stock in the IPO. In addition to specific information about the nature of the new stock interests the company conducting the IPO will issue, a prospectus must contain a broad range of background information on the financial and business condition of the company. This information must address both the present condition of the firm at the time of its public offering and the major considerations likely to affect the future of the company and its merit as a target of investment.

Drafting a prospectus is a collaborative process involving significant contributions from professionals such as legal counsel and underwriters and from company managers. Professionals ensure that disclosures in a prospectus are framed with the proper scope and form to gain SEC approval and to provide investors with an adequate basis to make investment decisions. Company managers provide much of the raw information about company characteristics and plans that is reshaped to comprise the descriptive contents of the prospectus. Considerable give and take between professionals drafting or reviewing portions of a prospectus and company officials supplying necessary information is typically needed before an adequate document is produced.

a. Goals in Drafting a Prospectus

Overall, a prospectus is both a disclosure and a marketing tool. As noted by one commentator:

> the extensive disclosure requirements in [federal securities laws] are designed to ensure that the issuer prepares and organizes a wide range of historical and prospective information regarding its business and operations. However, . . . the prospectus is also a "marketing tool," usually the issuer's first opportunity to describe and position itself and its business to the broader business and investment community. . . . Moreover, the type and format of disclosure in the IPO prospectus will become the basis for preparing future disclosure documents under [federal securities laws] and the issuer's widely disseminated annual report. Accordingly, it is quite important that the initial analysis of the issuer's strategic advantages at the time of the IPO be broad and thorough, and completed in a fashion which enables the issuer and its counsel to quickly identify areas of possible change during the period beyond the filing and effectiveness of the registration statement.

Alan S. Gutterman, *Strategic Business Planning Analysis and Marketing the High Technology Initial Public Offering Candidate*, 6 Santa Clara Computer & High Tech L.J. 197, 208 (1991).

b. Typical Contents of a Prospectus

A typical prospectus will include the following major sections and topics:

1. *Basic Offering Information*—A prospectus must contain a variety of descriptive information about the company involved and its proposed offering of new stock to the public. Topics that must be addressed include the

company's business and risk factors, the anticipated use of the proceeds of the stock sale, the dilution (that is, percentage decrease) in present stock ownership interests that will result if the sale is completed, the securities to be offered and the rights to be acquired by buyers, the plan for initial sales and distribution of the new stock, information about present securities holders, if any, who will participate in the offering by selling securities, and descriptions of experts and counsel who are aiding in the completion of the offering and the interests of these parties in the offeror.

2. *Description of Business, Products, and Legal Proceedings* — The prospectus must include a description of the offeror's recent business activities and results in order to provide a "baseline" for later disclosures about developments in the offeror's business. Topics that should be addressed include the offeror's primary products and services, customer base, research and development activities, and competitive environment. The disclosed information should also include a description of key corporate properties that are material to the company's business activities. While this portion of the prospectus may emphasize the "strategic advantages" that distinguish the offeror from its competitors, the analysis of the offeror's business strengths must not be one-sided, but must instead also describe the legal or business factors that will constrain the future success of the company.

3. *Securities* — The prospectus must also address additional information about the characteristics of both the new securities to be offered and the company's existing securities. The description must include information on the market for the common stock of the issuer, as well as the past dividends for that stock and expected future policies regarding dividends.

4. *Financial Information* — The prospectus must describe a range of basic financial information about the issuer, as well as disclosing any disagreements with the company's accountants regarding the presentation of its accounting information or other matters.

5. *Management and Key Security Holders* — A prospectus must describe an offeror's directors and officers, the compensation of key executives, securities or other interests in the company held by key executives, and the scope of securities holdings by other parties who own a significant percentage of shares. The company must also disclose significant transactions and relationships between it and other parties who manage or otherwise control the company.

6. *Exhibits* — The prospectus must also include a summary of the contents of material contracts affecting the company's business or the terms of the offering. These contracts must be included with the prospectus as exhibits unless special "confidential treatment" is requested.

See SEC Rule S-K; Robert G. Heim, GOING PUBLIC IN GOOD TIMES AND BAD 224–25 (2002).

c. Disclosures in Prospectuses Regarding Intellectual Property

Discussions of intellectual property interests and their present or potential business impacts may appear in portions of a prospectus describing an IPO company's business, its assets, significant risks affecting future operations, legal proceedings related to enforcement of intellectual property interests, or material contracts for licensing intellectual property. Discussions of intellectual property in these portions of a prospectus may include the following:

1. *Description of the Offeror's Business:* Where a company is relying heavily on intellectual property interests in order to secure an exclusive business opportunity for the concern, the description of its business in its prospectus will need to address the nature of its intellectual property interests and their expected impact on company operations and competitive threats. While intellectual property interests are often important means to protect valuable business opportunities and can properly be identified as such in prospectus disclosures, descriptions of intellectual property protections and their beneficial impact on company operations must be carefully tailored so as to be balanced presentations, not just optimistic descriptions of hoped-for results.

2. *Profile of the Offeror's Assets:* A company that has developed a new technology or business method will view intellectual property interests protecting the new technology or business method as highly important assets. In many instances, the future attractiveness of the company as a potential target for takeover and buyout will depend on whether such an acquisition will include the transfer of valuable intellectual property asserts. Furthermore, in the absence of such a buyout, the company's enforceable intellectual property rights may provide the means for the company to reserve certain business opportunities to itself. To the extent that a company expects to rely on intellectual property interests in these ways, these interests will generally be material assets of the company that should be addressed in the corresponding portions of the company's prospectus.

3. *Risks Associated with the Offeror's Operations:* Intellectual property interests may raise two types of risks in connection with an offeror's business activities: risks associated with the unexpected unenforceability or diminished commercial impact of the company's own intellectual property interests and further risks from infringement claims based on the intellectual property rights of others. Particularly where a company is relying on the exclusivity of certain manufacturing or marketing opportunities as protected by intellectual property rights, the unenforceability of those rights after significant resources have been committed to pursuing related business opportunities may be very harmful to the company. Similarly, even if intellectual property rights remain enforceable, but competitors adopt means to supply consumers with products or services without infringing the relevant intellectual property rights, the commercial impact of those rights may be drastically reduced, leading to associated corporate losses. Finally, the intellectual property rights of

others may raise additional risks. If the company devotes significant resources to activities that are unexpectedly found to infringe the intellectual property rights of another party, the company may be forced to pay significant damages for past infringement and to cease the affected operations or to obtain a license to use the related intellectual property at highly unfavorable royalty rates. These types of risks arising out of the company's ownership or use of intellectual property and leading to material threats to company success should be addressed in the discussions of business operation risks in the company's prospectus.

4. *Legal Proceedings Affecting the Offeror:* Where a company has already been subjected to or meaningfully threatened with legal proceedings that, if successful, will materially affect the ways that the company uses intellectual property and achieves value and profits from such property, the existence and status of these legal proceedings must be disclosed in the company's prospectus. For example, where a key patent that the company is relying on to establish a future business opportunity is slated by the United States Patent and Trademark Office for reexamination—meaning that the patent may be rendered invalid or diminished in scope—the existence of this pending proceeding must be disclosed. Similarly, where the company has been threatened with or subjected to infringement litigation under the patents of another party and the litigation will have a material impact on the company's business activities if successful, this litigation, its expected merit, and its potential impact on company operations if successful should be disclosed.

5. *Material Contracts:* A company's material contracts may include at least two types of intellectual property licensing agreements that should be disclosed in a prospectus. First, inbound licensing contracts through which the company acquires the rights to use certain technologies or other intellectual property may be material where the company is relying on using the intellectual property of another party in significant corporate activities. The absence of an enforceable licensing contract—or the company's failure to comply with the terms of that contract and loss of rights to use the corresponding intellectual property—may cause severe disruptions in company operations and significant company losses as needed intellectual property becomes unavailable. Second, outbound licensing contracts may also be material where the company plans to license its own intellectual property to others and to generate significant licensing revenues. Descriptions of the corresponding licensing agreements, as well as the means that the company will use to monitor licensees' adherence to the agreements and to bring enforcement actions against licensees who do not comply with licensing terms, should be part of the company's discussions of material contracts in its prospectus.

These types of discussions of intellectual property interests in prospectuses will be subject to the "bespeaks caution" doctrine. This doctrine limits the personal liability of persons making or verifying misleading statements in prospectuses and other public disclosures. The doctrine applies where misleading statements are surrounded by qualifying or cautionary language that would indicate to the reasonable investor that the accuracy and implications of the statements should be taken with caution. In general,

> "[t]he bespeaks caution doctrine provides a mechanism by which a court can rule as a matter of law (typically in a motion to dismiss for failure to state a cause of action or a motion for summary judgment) that defendants' forward-looking representations contained enough cautionary language or risk disclosure to protect the defendant against claims of securities fraud."

Donald C. Langevoort, *Disclosures that "Bespeak Caution,"* 49 Bus. Law. 481, 482–83 (1994). The doctrine reflects a pragmatic interpretation of two of the requirements for liability under federal securities laws governing public disclosures of information about companies: the requirement that misstated information be material to a reasonable investor and the need for some form of reliance of an investor on a misstatement or omission before a civil damage claim will lie. As noted by one court:

> The "bespeaks caution" doctrine ... reflects a relatively recent, ongoing, and somewhat uncertain evolution in securities law, an evolution driven by the increase in and the unique nature of fraud actions based on predictive statements. In essence, predictive statements are just what the name implies: predictions. As such, any optimistic projections contained in such statements are necessarily contingent. Thus, the "bespeaks caution" doctrine has developed to address situations in which optimistic projections are coupled with cautionary language — in particular, relevant specific facts or assumptions — affecting the reasonableness of reliance on and the materiality of those projections. To put it another way, the 'bespeaks caution' doctrine reflects the unremarkable proposition that statements must be analyzed in context.

Rubinstein v. Collins, 20 F.3d 160, 167 (5th Cir. 1994).

Courts need to be careful not to apply the bespeaks caution doctrine too broadly, as this would undercut the deterrents created by federal securities laws regarding misleading statements. The concern is that:

> an overbroad application of the doctrine would encourage management to conceal deliberate misrepresentations beneath the mantle of broad cautionary language. To prevent this from occurring, the bespeaks caution doctrine applies only to precise cautionary language which directly addresses itself to future projections, estimates or forecasts in a prospectus. By contrast, blanket warnings that securities involve a high degree of risk [are] insufficient to ward against a federal securities fraud claim.

In re Worlds of Wonder Securities Litigation, 35 F.3d 1407, 1414 (9th Cir. 1994) (quoting with approval *In re Worlds of Wonder Securities Litigation*, 814 F. Supp. 850, 858 (N.D. Cal. 1993)).

2. Regulatory Standards

SEC Standards for Prospectus Contents: Regulation S-K (Excerpts)

United States Securities and Exchange Commission

17 C.F.R Part 229

[The following are selected portions of the SEC's standards governing the types of disclosures that a company must make in a prospectus in order to register newly issued securities and to engage in a public offering of those securities. The company making the disclosures is referred to here as the "registrant." The portions of the standards presented here are those most likely to require disclosures about intellectual property interests and related business risks.]

§ 229.101 (Item 101) Description of business.

(a) General development of business. Describe the general development of the business of the registrant, its subsidiaries and any predecessor(s) during the past five years, or such shorter period as the registrant may have been engaged in business. Information shall be disclosed for earlier periods if material to an understanding of the general development of the business.

. . . .

(c) Narrative description of business.

(1) Describe the business done and intended to be done by the registrant and its subsidiaries, focusing upon the registrant's dominant segment or each reportable segment about which financial information is presented in the financial statements. To the extent material to an understanding of the registrant's business taken as a whole, the description of each such segment shall include the information specified in paragraphs (c)(1)(i) through (x) of this section. The matters specified in paragraphs (c)(1)(xi) through (xiii) of this section shall be discussed with respect to the registrant's business in general; where material, the segments to which these matters are significant shall be identified.

(i) The principal products produced and services rendered by the registrant in the segment and the principal markets for, and methods of distribution of, the segment's principal products and services. In addition, state for each of the last three fiscal years the amount or percentage of total revenue contributed by any class of similar products or services which accounted for 10 percent or more of consolidated revenue in any of the last three fiscal years or 15 percent or more of consolidated revenue, if total revenue did not exceed $50,000,000 during any of such fiscal years.

(ii) A description of the status of a product or segment (e.g. whether in the planning stage, whether prototypes exist, the degree to which product design has progressed or whether further engineering is necessary), if there has been a public announcement of, or if the registrant otherwise has made public information about, a new product or segment that would require the investment of a material amount of the assets of the registrant or that otherwise is material. This paragraph is not intended to require disclosure of otherwise nonpublic corporate information the disclosure of which would affect adversely the registrant's competitive position.

. . . .

(iv) The importance to the segment and the duration and effect of all patents, trademarks, licenses, franchises and concessions held.

. . . .

(x) Competitive conditions in the business involved including, where material, the identity of the particular markets in which the registrant competes, an estimate of the number of competitors and the registrant's competitive position, if known or reasonably available to the registrant. Separate consideration shall be given to the principal products or services or classes of products or services of the segment, if any. Generally, the names of competitors need not be disclosed. . . . The principal methods of competition (e.g., price, service, warranty or product performance) shall be identified, and positive and negative factors pertaining to the competitive position of the registrant, to the extent that they exist, shall be explained if known or reasonably available to the registrant.

. . . .

Instructions to Item 101:

1. In determining what information about the segments is material to an understanding of the registrant's business taken as a whole and therefore required to be disclosed, pursuant to paragraph (c) of this Item, the registrant should take into account both quantitative and qualitative factors such as the significance of the matter to the registrant (e.g., whether a matter with a relatively minor impact on the registrant's business is represented by management to be important to its future profitability), the pervasiveness of the matter (e.g., whether it affects or may affect numerous items in the segment information), and the impact of the matter (e.g., whether it distorts the trends reflected in the segment information). Situations may arise when information should be disclosed about a segment, although the information in quantitative terms may not appear significant to the registrant's business taken as a whole.

. . . .

§ 229.103 (Item 103) Legal proceedings.

Describe briefly any material pending legal proceedings, other than ordinary routine litigation incidental to the business, to which the registrant or any of its subsidiaries is a party or of which any of their property is the subject. Include the name of the court or agency in which the proceedings are pending, the date instituted, the principal parties thereto, a description of the factual basis alleged to underlie the proceeding and the relief sought. Include similar information as to any such proceedings known to be contemplated by governmental authorities.

Instructions to Item 103:

. . . .

2. No information need be given with respect to any proceeding that involves primarily a claim for damages if the amount involved, exclusive of interest and costs, does not exceed 10 percent of the current assets of the registrant and its subsidiaries on a consolidated basis. However, if any proceeding presents in large degree the same legal and factual issues as other proceedings pending or known to be contemplated, the amount involved in such other proceedings shall be included in computing such percentage.

. . . .

§ 229.503 (Item 503) Prospectus Summary, Risk Factors, and Ratio of Earnings to Fixed Charges.

The registrant must furnish this information in plain English.

. . . .

(c) Risk factors. Where appropriate, provide under the caption "Risk Factors" a discussion of the most significant factors that make the offering speculative or risky. This discussion must be concise and organized logically. Do not present risks that could apply to any issuer or any offering. Explain how the risk affects the issuer or the securities being offered. Set forth each risk factor under a subcaption that adequately describes the risk.

. . . .

§ 229.601 (Item 601) Exhibits.

. . . .

(b) Description of exhibits. Set forth below is a description of each document listed in the exhibit tables.

. . . .

(10) Material contracts—

(i) Every contract not made in the ordinary course of business which is material to the registrant and is to be performed in whole or in part at or after the filing of the registration statement or report or was entered into not more than two years before such filing.

. . . .

(ii) If the contract is such as ordinarily accompanies the kind of business conducted by the registrant and its subsidiaries, it will be deemed to have been made in the ordinary course of business and need not be filed unless it falls within one or more of the following categories, in which case it shall be filed except where immaterial in amount or significance:

. . . .

(B) Any contract upon which the registrant's business is substantially dependent, as in the case of continuing contracts to sell the major part of registrant's products or services or to purchase the major part of registrant's requirements of goods, services or raw materials or any franchise or license or other agreement to use a patent, formula, trade secret, process or trade name upon which registrant's business depends to a material extent;

3. Examples of Intellectual Property Disclosures

S.E.C. Form S-1 Santarus, Inc (Excerpts)

Filed: March 31, 2004

PROSPECTUS SUMMARY

The following summary is qualified in its entirety by, and should be read together with, the more detailed information and financial statements and related notes appearing elsewhere in this prospectus. Before you decide to invest in our common stock, you should read the entire prospectus carefully, including the risk factors and the financial statements and related notes included in this prospectus.

Santarus, Inc.

We are a specialty pharmaceutical company focused on acquiring, developing and commercializing proprietary products for the prevention and treatment of gastrointestinal diseases and disorders. The primary focus of our current efforts is the development and commercialization of next generation proton pump inhibitor, or PPI, products—the most frequently prescribed drugs for the treatment of many upper gastrointestinal, or GI, diseases and disorders. The PPI market, including five delayed-release PPI brands, had U.S. sales of $12.9 billion in 2003, according to IMS Health, an independent pharmaceutical market research firm. Also, according to IMS Health, total U.S. prescriptions for PPIs grew from 86.3 million in 2002 to 95.2 million in 2003—a 10% increase.

We submitted our first new drug application, or NDA, in August 2003 for RapinexTM powder-for-suspension 20mg and our second NDA in February 2004 for Rapinex powder-for-suspension 40mg, which are immediate-release formulations of omeprazole, a widely prescribed PPI currently available for oral use only in delayed-release formulations.

. . . .

RISK FACTORS

. . . .

All of our product development and clinical research activities are currently dedicated to developing our Rapinex product candidates. Because each of the three Rapinex product candidates [Rapinex powder-for-suspension, Rapinex capsule and Rapinex chewable tablet], is derived from the same intellectual property rights licensed from the University of Missouri, each product candidate is vulnerable to substantially the same risks stemming from potential patent invalidity, misappropriation of intellectual property by third parties, reliance upon a third party for patent prosecution and maintenance and unexpected early termination of our license agreement.

. . . .

The pharmaceutical industry is intensely competitive, particularly in the GI field, where currently marketed products are well-established and successful. Competition in our industry occurs on a variety of fronts, including developing and bringing new products to market before others, developing new technologies to improve existing products, developing new products to provide the same benefits as existing products at lower cost and developing new products to provide benefits superior to those of existing products. In addition, our ability and that of our competitors to compete in our industry will depend upon our and their relative abilities to obtain and maintain intellectual property protection for products and product candidates.

. . . .

Risks Related to Our Intellectual Property and Potential Litigation

The protection of our intellectual property rights is critical to our success and any failure on our part to adequately secure such rights would materially affect our business.

Patents. Our commercial success will depend in part on the patent rights we have licensed or will license and on patent protection for our own inventions related to the product candidates that we intend to market. Our success also depends on maintaining these patent rights against third-party challenges to their validity, scope or enforceability. Our patent position is subject to the same uncertainty as other biotechnology and pharmaceutical companies. For example, the U.S. Patent and Trademark Office, or PTO, or the courts may deny, narrow or invalidate patent claims, particularly those that concern biotechnology and pharmaceutical inventions.

We may not be successful in securing or maintaining proprietary or patent protection for our product candidates, and protection that we do secure may be challenged and possibly lost. Our competitors may develop products similar to ours using methods and technologies that are beyond the scope of our intellectual property rights. Other drug companies may be able to develop generic versions of our products if we are unable to maintain our proprietary rights. For example, although we believe that we have valid patent protection in the U.S. for our product candidates until at least 2016, it is possible that generic drug makers will attempt to introduce generic immediate-release omeprazole products similar to ours prior to the expiration of our patents. Any patents related to our Rapinex product candidates will be method and/or formulation patents and will not protect the use of the active pharmaceutical ingredient outside of the formulations described in the patents and patent applications licensed to us. In addition, our competitors or other third parties, including generic drug companies, may challenge the scope, validity or enforceability of our patent claims. As a result, these patents may be narrowed in scope or invalidated and may fail to provide us with any market exclusivity or competitive advantage even after our investment of significant amounts of money. We also may not be able to protect our intellectual property rights against third-party infringement, which may be difficult to detect. If we become involved in any dispute regarding our intellectual property rights, regardless of whether we prevail, we could be required to engage in costly, distracting and time-consuming litigation that could harm our business.

To date, four U.S. patents have been issued relating to technology we license from the University of Missouri and several U.S. and international or foreign counterpart patent applications are pending. The initial U.S. patent from the University of Missouri does not have corresponding international or foreign counterpart applications and there can be no assurance that we will be able to obtain foreign patent rights to protect our products. We consult with the University of Missouri in its pursuit of the patent applications that we have licensed, but the University of Missouri remains primarily responsible for prosecution of the applications. We cannot control the amount or timing of resources that the University of Missouri devotes on our behalf. It may not assign as great a priority to prosecution of patent applications relating to technology we license as we would if we were undertaking such prosecution ourselves. As a result of this lack of control and general uncertainties in the patent prosecution process, we cannot be sure that any additional patents will ever be issued.

Trade Secrets and Proprietary Know-how. We also rely upon unpatented proprietary know-how and continuing technological innovation in developing our product candidates. Although we require our employees, consultants, advisors and current and prospective business partners to enter into confidentiality agreements prohibiting them from disclosing or taking our proprietary information and technology, these agreements may not provide meaningful protection for our trade secrets and proprietary know-how. Further, people who are not parties to confidentiality agreements may obtain access to our trade secrets or know-how. Others may independently develop similar or equivalent trade secrets or know-how. If our confidential, proprietary information is divulged to third parties, including our competitors, our competitive position in the marketplace will be harmed and our ability to successfully penetrate our target markets could be severely compromised.

Trademarks. Our trademarks will be important to our success and competitive position. We have received U.S. and EU trademark registration for our corporate name, Santarus®, and we have applied for U.S. and EU trademark registration for

Rapinex, and for various other names. However, there is no guarantee we will be able to secure any of our trademark registrations with the PTO or comparable foreign authorities. For example, our application for the trademark Rapinex has been opposed in the EU, and we have opposed a biotechnology company's applications for the marks 'Santaris' and 'Santaris Pharma' in the EU.

If we do not adequately protect our rights in our various trademarks from infringement, any goodwill that has been developed in those marks would be lost or impaired. We could also be forced to cease using any of our trademarks that are found to infringe upon the trademark or service mark of another company, and, as a result, we could lose all the goodwill which has been developed in those marks and could be liable for damages caused by any such infringement.

Our Rapinex product candidates depend on technology licensed from the University of Missouri and any loss of our license rights would harm our business and seriously affect our ability to market our products.

Each of our Rapinex product candidates is based on patented technology and technology for which patent applications are pending that we have exclusively licensed from the University of Missouri. A loss or adverse modification of our technology license from the University of Missouri would materially harm our ability to develop and commercialize our current product candidates, Rapinex powder-for-suspension, Rapinex capsule and Rapinex chewable tablet, and other product candidates based on that licensed technology that we may attempt to develop or commercialize in the future.

The licenses from the University of Missouri expire in each country when the last patent for licensed technology expires in that country and the last patent application for licensed technology in that country is abandoned. In addition, our rights under the University of Missouri license are subject to early termination under specified circumstances, including our material and uncured breach of the license agreement or our bankruptcy or insolvency.

Further, we are required to use commercially reasonable efforts to develop and sell products based on the technology we licensed from the University of Missouri to meet market demand. If we fail to meet these obligations in specified countries, after giving us an opportunity to cure the failure, the University of Missouri can terminate our license or render it nonexclusive with respect to those countries. To date, we believe we have met all of our obligations under the University of Missouri agreement. However, in the event that the University of Missouri is able to terminate the license agreement for one of the reasons specified in the license agreement, we would lose our rights to develop, market and sell our current Rapinex product candidates and we would not be able to develop, market and sell future product candidates based on those licensed technologies. We would also lose the right to receive potential milestone and royalty payments from [TAP Pharmaceutical Products Inc. (TAP)] based on its development of products under our sublicense to TAP of the University of Missouri technology. Our ability to market our products is subject to the intellectual property rights of third parties.

The product candidates we currently intend to market, and those we may market in the future, may infringe patent and other rights of third parties. In addition, our competitors, many of which have substantially greater resources than us and have made significant investments in competing technologies or products, may seek to apply for and obtain patents that will prevent, limit or interfere with our ability to make, use and sell products either in the U.S. or international markets. Intellectual property litigation in the pharmaceutical industry is common, and we expect this to continue. In particular, intellectual property litigation among companies targeting the treatment of upper GI diseases and disorders is particularly common and may increase due to the large market for these products.

. . . .

If we or our third-party manufacturers are unsuccessful in any challenge to our rights to market and sell our products, we may be required to license the disputed rights, if the holder of those rights is willing, or to cease marketing the challenged products, or, if possible, to modify our products to avoid infringing upon those rights. If we or our third-party manufacturers are unsuccessful in defending our rights, we could be liable for royalties on past sales or more significant damages, and we could be required to obtain and pay for licenses if we are to continue to manufacture and sell our products. These licenses may not be available and, if available, could require us to pay substantial upfront fees and future royalty payments. Any patent owner may seek preliminary injunctive relief in connection with an infringement claim, as well as a permanent injunction, and, if successful in the claim, may be entitled to lost profits from infringing sales, attorneys' fees and interest and other amounts. Any damages could be increased if there is a finding of willful infringement.

Even if we and our third-party manufacturers are successful in defending an infringement claim, the expense, time delay and burden on management of litigation could have a material adverse effect on our business. We may be subject to damages resulting from claims that we or our employees have wrongfully used or disclosed alleged trade secrets of their former employers.

Many of our employees were previously employed at universities or other biotechnology or pharmaceutical companies, including our competitors or potential competitors. In addition, certain of our employees are parties to non-compete and non-disclosure agreements with their prior employers. Although no claims against us are currently pending, we may be subject to claims that these employees or we have inadvertently or otherwise breached these non-compete agreements or used or disclosed trade secrets or other proprietary information of their former employers. Litigation may be necessary to defend against these claims. Even if we are successful in defending against these claims, litigation could result in substantial costs and be a distraction to management. If we fail in defending such claims, in addition to paying money claims, we may lose valuable intellectual property rights or personnel. A loss of key research personnel or their work product could hamper or prevent our ability to commercialize product candidates, which could severely harm our business.

. . . .

<u>BUSINESS</u>

. . . .

<u>Intellectual Property</u>

Our goal is to obtain, maintain and enforce patent protection for our products and product candidates, compounds, formulations, processes, methods and other proprietary technologies invented, developed, licensed or acquired by us, preserve our trade secrets, and operate without infringing on the proprietary rights of other parties, both in the U.S. and in other countries. Our policy is to actively seek to obtain, where appropriate, intellectual property protection for our product candidates, proprietary information and proprietary technology through a combination of contractual arrangements and laws, including patents, both in the U.S. and elsewhere in the world. We regard the protection of patents, trademarks and other proprietary rights that we own or license as critical to our success and competitive position. Laws and contractual restrictions, however, may not be sufficient to prevent unauthorized use or misappropriation of our technology or deter others from independently developing products that are substantially equivalent or superior to our products.

Due to the length of time and expense associated with bringing new pharmaceutical products to market, we recognize that there are considerable benefits associated with developing, licensing or acquiring products that are protected by existing patents or for which patent protection can be obtained. Although we do not currently own any issued patents, all of the product candidates we currently intend to market will incorporate patented technology owned by others that we have licensed. In addition, we have applied and intend to continue to apply for patent protection for new technology we develop whenever we determine that the benefit of patent protection outweighs the cost of obtaining patent protection.

Our ability to assert our patents against a potential infringer depends on our ability to detect the infringement in the first instance. Many countries, including certain European countries, have compulsory licensing laws under which a patent owner may be compelled to grant licenses to third parties in some circumstances (for example, the patent owner has failed to 'work' the invention in that country, or the third party has patented improvements). In addition, most countries limit the enforceability of patents against government agencies or government contractors. In these countries, the patent owner may be limited to monetary relief and may be unable to enjoin infringement, which could materially diminish the value of the patent. Compulsory licensing of life saving drugs is also becoming increasingly popular in developing countries either through direct legislation or international initiatives. Such compulsory licenses could be extended to include some of our product candidates, which could limit our potential revenue opportunities. Moreover, the legal systems of certain countries, particularly certain developing countries, do not favor the aggressive enforcement of patents and other intellectual property protections, which makes it difficult to stop infringement.

Our success will also depend in part on our not infringing patents issued to others, including our competitors and potential competitors. If our product candidates are found to infringe the patents of others, our development, manufacture and sale of such potential products could be severely restricted or prohibited. For example, Astra-Zeneca may sue us for patent infringement in connection with the commercialization of our Rapinex product candidates. . . . Although we believe that we have meritorious defenses to any claims related to AstraZeneca's patents, AstraZeneca may nevertheless pursue litigation against us. The outcome of any such litigation is uncertain and defending such litigation would be expensive, time-consuming and distracting to management. It is likely that in the future we will encounter other similar situations which will require us to determine whether we need to license a technology or face the risk of defending an infringement claim.

Patent litigation can involve complex factual and legal questions and its outcome is uncertain. Any claim relating to infringement of patents that is successfully asserted against us may require us to pay substantial damages. Even if we were to prevail, any litigation could be costly and time-consuming and would divert the attention of our management and key personnel from our business operations. Furthermore, a patent infringement suit brought against us or any strategic partners or licensees may force us or any strategic partners or licensees to stop or delay developing, manufacturing or selling potential products that are claimed to infringe a third party's intellectual property, unless that party grants us or any strategic partners or licensees rights to use its intellectual property. In such cases, we may be required to obtain licenses to patents or proprietary rights of others in order to continue to commercialize our products. However, we may not be able to obtain any licenses required under any patents or proprietary rights of third parties on acceptable terms, or at all. Even if any strategic partners, licensees or we were able to obtain rights to the third party's intellectual property, these rights may be non-exclusive, thereby giving our competitors access to the same intellectual property. Ultimately, we may be unable to commercialize some of our potential products or may have to cease some of our business operations as a result of patent infringement claims, which could severely harm our business.

We also depend upon the skills, knowledge and experience of our scientific and technical personnel, as well as that of our advisors, consultants and other contractors. To help protect our proprietary know-how that is not patentable, and for inventions for which patents may be difficult to enforce, we rely on trade secret protection and confidentiality agreements to protect our interests. To this end, we require our employees, consultants, advisors and certain other contractors to enter into confidentiality agreements which prohibit the disclosure of confidential information and, where applicable, require disclosure and assignment to us of the ideas, developments, discoveries and inventions important to our business. Additionally, these confidentiality agreements require that our employees, consultants and advisors do not bring to us, or use without proper authorization, any third party's proprietary technology.

While we intend to take the actions that we believe are necessary to protect our proprietary rights, we may not always be successful in doing so. We may be dependent on the owners of the proprietary rights we license to protect those rights. Our current licensor remains, and any future licensors may remain, responsible for the prosecution of patent applications relating to the technology licensed from them. These licensors are not our employees and we cannot control the amount or timing of resources they devote on our behalf or the priority they place on prosecuting these patent applications. In addition, we and our licensors may face challenges to the validity and enforceability of proprietary rights and may not prevail in any litigation regarding those rights. As a result, these patents may be narrowed in scope, deemed unenforceable or invalidated and may fail to provide us with any market exclusivity or competitive advantage even after our investment of significant amounts of money.

We have received U.S. and EU trademark registration for our corporate name, Santarus, and have opposed a third-party biotechnology company's applications for the marks 'Santaris' and 'Santaris Pharma' in the EU. We have applied for U.S. and EU trademark registration for the name Rapinex and for various other names. Our application for the trademark Rapinex has been opposed in the EU. In addition, in connection with our initial NDA submission for Rapinex powder-for-suspension 20mg, the FDA indicated to us that it objects to our use of the Rapinex name for our product candidates. The FDA may object to a product name if it believes there is potential for confusion with other product names or if it believes the name implies medical claims. We have responded to the objection in an effort to preserve the name and the resources we have already devoted to the Rapinex trademark registration. However, we may not prevail or we may determine to adopt an alternative name for our initial product candidates in the interest of time or for other reasons. If we adopt an alternative name, we would lose the benefit of our existing trademark applications for Rapinex and may be required to expend significant additional resources in an effort to identify a suitable product name that would qualify under applicable U.S. and EU trademark laws, not infringe the existing rights of third parties and be acceptable to the FDA. Over time, we intend to introduce new trademarks, service marks and brand names and maintain registrations on trademarks that remain valuable to our business.

License Rights from the University of Missouri

In January 2001, we entered into an exclusive, worldwide license agreement with the University of Missouri for all of its patents and pending patent applications relating to specific formulations of PPIs with antacids and other buffering agents. Currently, four U.S. patents have been issued and several U.S. patent applications and international or foreign counterpart applications are pending and are subject to this license. The four issued patents, U.S. Patent Nos. 5,840,737, 6,489,346, 6,645,988 and 6,699,885, together generally cover pharmaceutical compositions combining PPIs with buffering agents, such as antacids, and methods of treating GI disorders by administering solid or liquid forms of such compositions. U.S. Patent Nos. 5,840,737, 6,489,346 and 6,645,988 expire in July 2016. We expect that U.S. Patent No. 6,699,885 and any patents that may be issued on pending patent applications will expire no earlier than July 2016.

Pursuant to the terms of the license agreement, we paid the University of Missouri a one-time licensing fee of $1.0 million in 2001 and a one-time $1.0 million milestone payment upon the filing of our first NDA in 2003. We are required to make additional milestone payments to the University of Missouri upon the achievement of certain regulatory events, and we are required to bear the costs of prosecuting and maintaining the licensed patents but our licensor remains responsible for prosecution of any applications. These future success-based development milestone payments may total up to $8.5 million in the aggregate, including $5.0 million upon approval in the U.S. of our first product based on the licensed technology. We are also required to make milestone payments based on first-time achievement of significant sales thresholds, up to a maximum of $86.3 million, and to pay royalties on net sales of our products. In addition, we issued to the University of Missouri 164,284 shares of our common stock in connection with the license agreement. Under the license agreement, we are permitted to sublicense our rights to third parties. We are obligated to pay to the University of Missouri a portion of any sublicense fees, milestone payments or royalties that we receive from any sublicense, including our sublicense to TAP. Under the license agreement, we are required to carry occurrence-based liability insurance with policy limits of at least $5.0 million per occurrence and a $10.0 million annual aggregate.

The license from the University of Missouri expires in each country when the last patent for licensed technology expires in that country and the last patent application for licensed technology in that country is abandoned, provided that our obligation to pay certain minimum royalties in countries in which there are no pending patent applications or existing patents terminates on a country-by-country basis on the 15th anniversary of our first commercial sale in such country. If we fail to meet diligence obligations in specified countries, the University of Missouri can terminate our license or render it non-exclusive with respect to those countries. Our rights under this license are also generally subject to early termination under specified circumstances, including our material and uncured breach or our bankruptcy or insolvency. We can terminate this agreement at any time, in whole or in part, with 60 days written notice.

Notes & Questions

1. Santarus' disclosure statement filed with the SEC in conjunction with the company's IPO pointed out that its business model depended heavily on the strength of the patents that it licensed from the University of Missouri. Santarus' exclusive license to produce drugs incorporating the advances covered by these patents defined its major commercial advantage over other potential producers of the same drugs. The importance of these patents and their significance for Santarus' business success was clearly demonstrated in the ups and downs Santarus experienced during later litigation involving its licensed patents.

In 2007, Par Pharmaceutical Companies, Inc. (Par) filed an application for FDA approval of marketing by Par of drugs covered by the patents licensed by Santarus.

Santarus and The Curators of the University of Missouri (University of Missouri) filed a lawsuit against Par claiming infringement of several of the licensed patents. Unfortunately for Santarus, on April 14, 2010, the district court in this case ruled in Par's favor, finding that the plaintiffs' patents were invalid as being obvious and without adequate written description. *See Santarus, Inc. v. Par Pharmaceutical, Inc.*, 720 F. Supp. 2d 427, 437–459 (D. Del. 2010). On July 1, 2010, Par launched its sales of drugs covered by the disputed patents. *See* Par Pharmaceutical Companies, Inc. Form 8-K (9/22/2014).

Meanwhile, the price of Santarus' stock plummeted in the wake of the invalidation of the licensed patents. The price of the company's shares went down nearly 40 percent following announcement of the adverse ruling regarding its licensed patents. *See* Thomas Kupper, *Santarus Stock Hit After Patent Invalidations*, U-T SAN DIEGO (April 15, 2010). Investors had previously counted on the exclusivity protected by the invalidated patents as a driver of Santarus' growth. *See, e.g.,* Zacks Equity Research, *Neutral on Santarus* (January 6, 2010) (downgrading its previous recommendation of Santarus' stock, noting that Par's then-pending patent challenge raised concerns and that an adverse patent ruling would be "devastating" to Santarus' future growth).

Were this the end of the Santarus story, it would be a cautionary tale about building a company on the projected strength of a few patents and, additionally, an illustration of the risks involved in seeking to commercialize products derived from university research. However, the story did not end there. Following the initial adverse ruling on Santarus' licensed patents, Par vigorously marketed its generic versions of the patented drugs. Unfortunately, it apparently acted too soon. On September 4, 2012, following an appeal by Santarus and the University of Missouri, the Court of Appeals for the Federal Circuit reversed the district court's finding of invalidity and remanded the case to the district court for further proceedings. *See Santarus, Inc. v. Par Pharmaceutical, Inc.*, 694 F.3d 1344, 1350–1359 (Fed. Cir. 2012). Par found this reversal sufficiently intimidating that it immediately ceased sales of its generic versions of the contested drugs. Santarus was acquired by Salix Pharmaceuticals, Inc. (Salix), on January 2, 2014. Later in 2014, Par agreed to pay Salix and the University of Missouri $100 million to settle this case. *See* Par Pharmaceutical Companies, Inc. Form 8-K (9/22/2014). Thus, ultimately, Santarus' patent-based business strategy prevailed, producing large payments for both Salix (as Santarus' successor) and the University of Missouri.

2. Intellectual property features of IPO candidates are often key company characteristics, making accurate and complete disclosures about these key features particularly important. The same is true for possible weaknesses in intellectual property, such as pending litigation that may invalidate important interests. Enforceable intellectual property interests supporting market differentiation of company products or services are core features of most successful IPO candidates:

> *Market Differentiation:* IPO candidates need a superior technology, product, or service in a large and growing market. Ideally, they are viewed as market

leaders. Appropriate intellectual property protection is expected of technology companies, and in some sectors patents are de rigueur.

David A. Westenberg, *An Introduction to the IPO Market*, INITIAL PUBLIC OFFERINGS: A PRACTICAL GUIDE TO GOING PUBLIC ch. 1 (Practising Law Institute 2nd Ed. 2012 & October 2017 Supp.) (available from PLI-Plus research service).

3. Disclosures about intellectual property in conjunction with an IPO may reveal a wide variety of previously confidential business plans and weaknesses. Company leaders may choose to reveal their future business plans to explain and clarify the projected value of their company's intellectual property assets. At the same time, securities laws may compel company leaders to disclosure intellectual property weaknesses that the company had previously kept confidential.

Where a company possesses a significant intellectual property portfolio, the company may choose to describe previously confidential business plans and anticipated features of future products that are projected to link the company's intellectual property interests to business opportunities and enhanced company value. Absent disclosures about these otherwise confidential business features, the company involved may be undervalued by potential investors despite its substantial intellectual property holdings. Investor understanding of the company's full intellectual property strengths may best be achieved by revealing future business plans that indicate how the company's intellectual property will be used to corporate advantage, despite the fact that the same plans might normally be kept confidential to avoiding signaling competitors about future company actions. *See* Ceyda A. Maisami & Leslie A. McDonell, *IPOs and Patents: Friends, Enemies, or Strangers?*, LANDSLIDE, May/June, 2012, at 54, 56–57.

Required disclosures in connection with IPOs may also reveal present or potential intellectual property problems. Previously confidential infringement claims and litigation expenses may first come to light in this way. For example, in disclosure statements filed with the SEC in connection with the company's 2011 IPO, Zillow, Inc., revealed that it was the target of five patent infringement claims asserted since 2009 and that its legal expenses increased by $400,000 between 2009 and 2010 due to the company's heightened litigation activity. *See id.*

4. Judicial Evaluations of Asserted Misstatements

In re Stac Electronics Securities Litigation

United States Court of Appeals for the Ninth Circuit

89 F.3d 1399 (9th Cir. 1996)

T.G. NELSON, CIRCUIT JUDGE.

OVERVIEW

Timothy J. Anderson and other class representatives (collectively "Anderson") who purchased stock in Stac Electronics ("Stac") between May 7 and July 20, 1992, appeal the district court's dismissal of their class action under Sections 11 and 15 of the

Securities Act of 1933, 15 U.S.C. §§ 77k, 77o, and Sections 10(b) and 20 of the Securities Exchange Act of 1934, 15 U.S.C. §§ 78j(b) and 78t. Anderson alleges that Stac, certain of its officers and directors, and its lead underwriters, Alex. Brown & Sons, Inc., and Montgomery Securities ("Alex. Brown" and "Montgomery," respectively; collectively, "Underwriters"), made material misrepresentations or omissions regarding Stac's initial public offering ("IPO") of May 7, 1992. We have jurisdiction under 28 U.S.C. § 1291, and we affirm.

FACTS AND PROCEDURAL HISTORY

This case arises from Stac's May 7, 1992, IPO of stock in its computer products company. Stac's most prominent product was the "Stacker," a data-compressing device which doubles storage capacity of disk drives in computers using Microsoft's MS-DOS and compatible systems.

The district court related the following facts, which are not disputed by the parties:

> Before it went public, Stac's performance was mixed: it reported net losses per share in 1988, 1989, and 1990, and a net income per share of $.01 in 1991. It also reported revenues hovering around three quarters of a million dollars for 1988 and 1989, with increased revenues in 1990 (to $1.7 million) and 1991 (to $8.3 million).

> There was a pronounced move upward—in both revenues and earnings per share—immediately prior to the initial public offering of Stac stock. While Stac reported revenues of $2.3 million and a loss of $.04 per share in the six months prior to March 31, 1991, it reported revenues of $17 million and earnings of $.21 per share in the six months prior to March 31, 1992. The increased revenues and earnings for the 1992 six month period derived from sales of Stacker.

> On May 7, 1992, Stac went public, with an initial offering of 3,000,000 shares of common stock. The stock was sold to the public at $12.00 a share, with the individual named Defendants—except for Hoff, Finch and Robelen—selling some 508,000 shares. Neither Hoff, Finch, Robelen nor any of the venture capital Defendants is alleged to have sold any Stac stock during the class period [May 7 to July 20, 1992]. Defendants Alex. Brown & Sons, Inc. and Montgomery Securities acted as co-lead underwriters for the offering; they received substantial fees—some $2.5 million—for their services.

In connection with the IPO, Stac issued a Registration Statement and Prospectus ("Prospectus"), dated May 7, 1992, which included a four-page section on risk factors warning investors, inter alia, of Stac's competition, its dependence on Stacker, its reliance on distributors, its limited source of supply, and the potential volatility of its stock price. The Prospectus specifically discussed Microsoft's competitive threat, Stac's return policy and return allowances, and the possible effects on revenues of "channel fill," or heavy purchasing by distributors immediately following the introduction of a new product.

Apart from the Prospectus, information about Stac was disseminated to the public through "roadshow" presentations preceding the IPO and through analysts' reports and press statements by Stac officers and Underwriters following the IPO. All of these portrayed Stac as a good investment.

While these portrayals at first seemed accurate—Stac rose to $15 after the IPO—success was short-lived. Stac's stock price fell on July 2, 1992, on the heels of another computer software company's announcement of poor third quarter results.

Stac Director Gary Clow ("Clow") and both Underwriters made statements to Dow Jones News Wire distinguishing Stac from the faltering software company. While Alex. Brown continued to rate Stac highly, Montgomery reduced its rating and earnings estimate for Stac on July 6, 1992. On July 20, 1992, Stac disclosed a disappointing third quarter performance, and on July 21, 1992, Stac stock declined to $5.50 per share. Within two days, plaintiffs filed suit. This initial suit was consolidated in the First Amended Class Action Complaint ("the FAC"), filed December 4, 1992.

. . . .

The complaint basically alleged that Stac went public knowing, but without disclosing, that Microsoft was about to come out with a competitive product (a new version of DOS incorporating Stacker-like data compression capabilities) that would take away Stac's market; that Stac engaged in sham licensing negotiations with Microsoft in order to stall introduction of its new product until Stac could make an IPO and unload stock; and that Stac insiders artificially inflated Stac's stock price prior to the IPO through channel "stuffing" and other fraudulent practices.

The district court dismissed the FAC with leave to amend in a detailed order dated September 17, 1993. *Anderson v. Clow*, Fed. Sec. L. Rep. (CCH) ¶ 97,807 at 97,994–95 (S.D. Cal. 1993). The district court held that plaintiffs had failed to state a claim against Stac, the Underwriters, or any other named defendant, primarily on the basis of its finding that, to the extent it was required to do so, Stac had adequately disclosed all purported omissions in its Prospectus in a way that rendered the Prospectus not misleading. The order also stayed discovery.

On November 18, 1993, the plaintiffs filed a Second Amended Complaint ("the SAC"), asserting the same claims as the FAC and adding nine new individual defendants. The district court dismissed the SAC with prejudice for failure to state a claim under Fed. R. Civ. P. 12(b)(6) and for failure to meet the particularity requirements of Fed. R. Civ. P. 9(b). Like the first order, the order appealed from is extremely thorough. Anderson's appeal was timely.

DISCUSSION

. . . .

I

Primary Liability.

Anderson argues that by "falsifying" its financial statements and failing to disclose pertinent information in its possession regarding Microsoft's plans to include data compression in its newest version of DOS, Stac misled investors and violated Section 11 of the Securities Act of 1933, 15 U.S.C. § 77k(a), Section 10(b) of the Exchange Act of 1934, 15 U.S.C. § 78j(b), and Rule 10b-5 of the Securities and Exchange Commission ("SEC"), 17 C.F.R. § 240.10b-5. The district court held that the SAC failed to state a claim under Section 11, Section 10(b), or Rule 10b-5. It further held that the SAC failed to plead with sufficient particularity its Section 10(b) and Rule 10b-5 claims, as required by Fed. R. Civ. P. 9(b). We address the adequacy of Anderson's claims de novo.

On appeal, Anderson stresses the following: Stac and its officers: 1) failed to disclose imminent competition from Microsoft and deliberately stalled licensing negotiations with Microsoft in order to delay Microsoft's market entry; and 2) falsified its financial statements by artificially inflating reported results through channel "stuffing," accomplished by offering customers "special terms," including discounts and exceptional rights of return; understating its existing reserves; and failing to disclose Stac's "inevitable" impending decline.

Both Section 11 of the Securities Act and Section 10(b) of the Exchange Act require a plaintiff "adequately [to] allege a material misrepresentation or omission." Section 11 creates a private remedy for any purchaser of a security if any part of the registration statement,

> when such part became effective, contained an untrue statement of a material fact or omitted to state a material fact required to be stated therein or necessary to make the statements therein not misleading. . . .

15 U.S.C. § 77k(a). "The plaintiff in a § 11 claim must demonstrate (1) that the registration statement contained an omission or misrepresentation, and (2) that the omission or misrepresentation was material, that is, it would have misled a reasonable investor about the nature of his or her investment." "No scienter is required for liability under § 11; defendants will be liable for innocent or negligent material misstatements or omissions."

. . . .

A. Stac's Prospectus.

The district court found that all of the omissions alleged by Anderson were either actually disclosed, or need not have been disclosed, in Stac's prospectus. The "materiality" of an omission is a fact-specific determination that should ordinarily be assessed by a jury. "[O]nly if the adequacy of the disclosure or the materiality of the statement is so obvious that reasonable minds could not differ are these issues appropriately resolved as a matter of law."

1. Microsoft's plans to include data compression.

The gravamen of Anderson's complaint concerns Stac's alleged failure to disclose its knowledge of Microsoft's plans to introduce data compression in its upcoming version of DOS. According to Anderson, Stac entered into "sham" licensing negotiations with Microsoft merely to stall Microsoft's introduction of its new product. In the SAC, Anderson also alleged that Stac's patents were inadequate to prevent others from using its technology to create competitive products. Prior to the district court's ruling, however, Stac won a $120 million judgment against Microsoft for patent infringement relating to Stacker. The district court properly took judicial notice of this judgment in determining that the proprietary and patent information provided in the Prospectus was not misleading. Anderson does not raise the patent issue on appeal.

Regarding the threat of Microsoft "looming," the district court correctly observed that the Prospectus makes detailed disclosures concerning the risk of competition. For instance, the Prospectus states that "[a] number of competitors offer products that currently compete with [Stac's] products" and that these companies "could seek to expand their product offerings by designing and selling products using data compression or other technology that could render obsolete or adversely affect sales of [Stac's] products." After noting Stac's dependence on sales of DOS-compatible products, the Prospectus observes that:

> One developer of a compatible operating system has licensed a competitive data compression product for incorporation into the latest version of the operating system. There can be no assurance that Microsoft . . . will not incorporate a competitive data compression technology in their products or that such a technology will not emerge as an industry standard.

Further, the Prospectus reveals that "[Stac] has licensed and intends to license portions of its core technology to others," a practice which it cautions could result in more competition and price reductions.

Anderson alleges that the "no assurance" language is inadequate and that Stac committed fraud because it knew that Microsoft was going to come out with a competitive product, but masked this knowledge as a contingency. Anderson quotes repeatedly the following statement: "To warn that the untoward may occur when the event is contingent is prudent; to caution that it is only possible for the unfavorable events to happen when they have already occurred is deceit."

We have rephrased this principle as follows: "There is a difference between knowing that any product-in-development may run into a few snags, and knowing that a particular product has already developed problems so significant as to require months of delay.'" [*In re Convergent Technologies Sec. Litig.*, 948 F.2d 507, 515 (9th Cir. 1991) (quoting *In re Apple Computer Sec. Litig.*, 886 F.2d 1109, 1115 (9th Cir. 1989), *cert. denied*, 496 U.S. 943 (1990))]. The latter scenario characterizes the situation we encountered in *Warshaw v. Xoma Corp.*, 74 F.3d 955 (9th Cir. 1996). Corporate officers of Xoma, a biotech company which had yet to make a profit on its research, assured stockholders that FDA approval of its new drug was imminent, in spite of knowledge that the drug might not work and was unlikely to receive such approval. Anderson has not alleged any such contradictory statements here. In [*In re Convergent Technologies Sec. Litig.*, 948 F.2d 507, 515 (9th Cir. 1991)], we proceeded to distinguish the case before us from the Fifth Circuit case quoted, noting that Convergent's prospectus "virtually overflow[ed]" with risk factors, and to hold that the defendant company was not obliged to disclose its internal projections because such projections are tentative. We cited as adequate multiple warnings in the Convergent prospectus stating that "there is no assurance" of financial success given a variety of named obstacles to production. We therefore cannot agree with Anderson's characterization of Stac's "no assurance" language as "misleading" or inadequate.

Anderson argues that Stac should have explicitly disclosed its ongoing negotiations with Microsoft and its knowledge that Microsoft intended to introduce data compression technology in its new version of DOS. In short, Anderson suggests that Stac was obliged not only to report on its own product line and marketing plans, but to report on and make predictions regarding Microsoft's intentions.

Stac counters, and we have held, that a company is not required to forecast future events or to caution "that future prospects [may not be] as bright as past performance." In *re Worlds of Wonder Sec. Litig.*, 35 F.3d 1407, 1420 (9th Cir. 1994) ("WOW") ("'Absent allegations that [the issuer] withheld financial data or other existing facts from which forecasts are typically derived, the alleged omissions are not of material, actual facts. Therefore, the forecasts need not have been disclosed, and the failure to make the omitted forecasts did not render the other statements that were made misleading.'").

We agree with Stac that another company's plans cannot be known to a certainty. Even assuming, as we must, that Microsoft had informed Stac that it planned to introduce data compression, Stac could not have known whether or not Microsoft would truly do so. As Stac points out, the contingency of the event is underscored by the fact that a competitive product was liable to violate Stacker's patent, as borne out by the state judgment against Microsoft. Also, the market already knew of the potential for Microsoft's inclusion of data compression technology, as Anderson alleged in the FAC.

. . . .

For the reasons stated above, the district court's opinion is affirmed.

Sherleigh Associates, LLC v. Windmere-Durable Holdings, Inc.

United States District Court for the Southern District of Florida

178 F. Supp. 2d 1255 (S.D. Fla. 2000)

LENARD, DISTRICT JUDGE.

I. Factual Background

This is a securities class action on behalf of all persons who purchased the publicly traded securities of Defendant Windmere-Durable Holdings, Inc. ("Windmere") between May 12, 1998 and September 22, 1998, including those who acquired Windmere common stock and 10% Senior Subordinated Notes in Windmere's July 22, 1998 public offering. This action alleges violations of the Securities Act of 1933 (the "'33 Act") and the Securities Exchange Act of 1934 (the "'34 Act").

As alleged in the Consolidated Amended Class Action Complaint (hereinafter "Amended Complaint"), Windmere is a diversified international manufacturer and distributor of small electrical kitchen appliances and other household items. On May 11, 1998, Windmere issued a press release, filed with the Securities and Exchange Commission ("SEC") in a Form 8-K and signed by Defendant Harry D. Schulman ("Schulman"), the Chief Operating and Financial Officer, announcing Windmere's acquisition of the Home Products Group ("HPG") of the Black & Decker Corporation ("Black & Decker"). According to the press release, the HPG purchase would give Windmere a license to use the valuable Black & Decker brand name in North and Latin American markets, and would increase Windmere's manufacturing and distribution capacity.

Windmere acquired HPG on June 26, 1998 for $315 million in cash. Windmere financed its purchase of HPG with a "bridge loan" from NationsBank. To repay the NationsBank bridge loan, Windmere, along with the lead underwriter, Defendant Montgomery, offered its debt and equity securities to investors in a public offering on July 22, 1998 (the "July Offering"). The July Offering commenced pursuant to a registration statement, which included the Prospectus and two Prospectus supplements (collectively, the "Registration Statement"), that the SEC declared effective on June 4, 1998. In the July Offering, Windmere offered $103 million of common stock, approximately three million shares at $34 per share, and $130 million of 10% Senior Subordinated Notes.

The Registration Statement stated that the proceeds of the offering would be used to pay, in part, the NationsBank bridge loan. The Registration Statement further explained that Windmere "intended to utilize the marketing and distribution channels acquired through HPG to expand global market penetration of its products, particularly in Latin America." The acquisition, the Registration Statement explained, offered "immediate growth opportunities" and "uniquely positioned [Windmere] to capitalize on growth opportunities" in the household appliance and personal care markets. The Registration Statement went on to describe Windmere's 50% ownership of NewTech Electronics Industries ("NewTech"), and that Windmere would recognize 50% of the net earnings and losses of NewTech.

As alleged in the Amended Complaint, Windmere, Montgomery, Schulman and Defendant David M. Friedson ("Friedson"), Windmere's Chairman and Chief Executive Officer, promoted and sold the Windmere securities by issuing positive statements in pre-offering road show presentations to investors between July 6, 1998 and July 21, 1998. During these road show presentations, Plaintiffs allege, Defendants represented that Windmere was enjoying substantial benefits from the "complimentary strengths" between Windmere's existing operations and those of the recently acquired HPG. Windmere further represented that it "continued to enjoy strong revenue growth with a decreasing cost structure."

During this period, several adverse material facts were allegedly concealed or not disclosed by Defendants. . . . Windmere did not have the requisite licenses required to operate HPG and to sell HPG products in various Latin American countries and thus could not sell HPG products in these Latin American countries or even call on HPG's then-existing customer base, until such time as the licenses were obtained. Windmere allegedly knew as early as March, 1998 that, after the acquisition but prior to the July Offering, it was obligated by local law in each Latin American country to create a new company for HPG, and to register those entities with the authorities in each country. Windmere had not yet begun this complicated and time-consuming process, however. At the time of the July Offering and during the Class Period, Plaintiffs allege Windmere's failure to obtain such licenses was causing Windmere to experience declining international sales and undermining the business objectives that the HPG acquisition was intended to serve.

. . . .

On September 23, 1998, eight weeks after the July Offering, Windmere issued a press release stating that it was experiencing weak international sales, particularly in Latin America, and that NewTech was experiencing lower than expected earnings. That day, Windmere's stock price dropped to $7.1875 per share, down $27 per share from the $34 July Offering price. Between September 23, 1998 and February 23, 1999, the price further declined from $7 per share to below $4 per share. Although Windmere had previously expected 1998 earnings per share to be $1.50, Windmere in actuality realized earnings of only $0.57 per share for 1998.

A. Specific Allegations of False and Misleading Statements

1. Statements Prior to the July Offering

Plaintiffs allege Windmere issued a series of false and misleading statements in connection with the July Offering. On May 11, 1998, Windmere issued a press release announcing the acquisition of HPG (the "May 11 Press Release").[1] This release stated, in part, "Windmere and Black & Decker have established a long-term licensing

---

1. This press release and others referred to in the Amended Complaint are referenced or reproduced in part within the pleading, but not attached thereto. The entire press release documents are provided by the Windmere Defendants, however. The following excerpts of the May 11 Press Release appear at pages 13–14 of the Amended Complaint:

> Windmere-Durable Holdings, Inc., a diversified manufacturer and distributor of a broad range of consumer products, including personal care products for the home and professional salons, kitchen electric appliances and consumer electronics, today announced that it has signed a definitive agreement to acquire The Black & Decker Corporation's Household Products Group, which will include the Cooking, Garment Care, Food Preparation and Beverage categories.
> Pursuant to the terms of the acquisition agreement, Windmere will purchase the assets of The Black & Decker Corporation's Household Products Group for $315 million in cash. In connection with the transaction, Windmere and Black & Decker have established a long-term licensing arrangement which will allow Windmere to continue to market products under the Black & Decker brand name in the Cooking, Garment Care, Food Preparation and Beverage categories in North and Latin America, excluding Brazil, for a minimum of six and one-half years on a royalty-free basis, with potential renewal periods upon mutual agreement.
> . . . .

arrangement which will allow Windmere to continue to market products under the Black & Decker brand name in . . . North and Latin America . . . for a minimum of six and one-half years on a royalty-free basis[.] . . . The combined company will be uniquely positioned to capitalize on growth opportunities[.] Immediate growth opportunities will result from . . . [these] marketing capabilities[.]"

Plaintiffs further allege that on May 12, 1998, Defendants Schulman and Friedson convened a nationwide conference call for large Windmere shareholders and potential shareholders, including hedge funds, stock traders, brokers and securities analysts ("the May 12 Conference Call"). During the May 12 Conference Call, Defendants allegedly stated: (1) the acquisition would "more than triple" Windmere's 1998 revenues; (2) the acquisition would be "accretive," allow Windmere to obtain substantial cost synergies, and allow Windmere to market its products using HPG's well-recognized brand name; and (3) that Windmere was on target to post revenue of $750 million and earnings per share of $1.50 for 1998.

Plaintiffs allege these statements were materially false and misleading. At the time of the May 11 Press Release and the May 12 Conference Call, Windmere allegedly did not have the licenses needed to conduct business in the Latin American countries in which it proposed to sell and market HPG products. The Latin American market was a linchpin, Plaintiffs allege, of Windmere's expected "immediate growth opportunities" that would result from the acquisition.

On May 15, 1998 Windmere filed a Form 10-Q for the first quarter of 1998, the period ending March 31, 1998, reporting sales of $55.3 million and net earnings of $1.136 million for the quarter. This Form 10-Q also reported Windmere's decision to purchase HPG and thereby obtain the purported ability to market products in North and Latin America. On June 10, 1998, Windmere issued a press release to announce management changes "that will successfully integrate the recent acquisition of [HPG]." (the "June 10 Press Release") The June 10 Press Release reported "Windmere-Durable's revenues for 1997 were $261.9 million, and with the pending acquisition of Black & Decker Corporation's Household Products Group, Windmere's annualized revenue rate will be approximately $750 million."

On June 23, 1998, Plaintiffs allege Windmere issued a press release (the "June 23 Press Release") relating to its acquisition, stating in pertinent part:

> We look for the integration of The Black & Decker Household Products Group to begin as soon as the transaction is completed," added Mr. Friedson. "We expect to benefit from the significant business growth and operating synergies created by this acquisition beginning in the first six months of the acquisition and continuing through the next several years.

The combined company will be uniquely positioned to capitalize on growth opportunities within the personal care and kitchen appliance categories. Immediate growth opportunities will result from the combination of innovative product development, marketing capabilities and manufacturing infrastructure.

After the May 12 Conference Call, analyst reaction was allegedly favorable, with one industry analyst, CIBC Oppenheimer, issuing a favorable rating based in part on "sales synergies" such as expanding into new categories and selling products in Latin America.

2. The Road Show

During the pre-offering road show, from July 6, 1998 to July 21, 1998, Plaintiffs allege Defendants Montgomery, Schulman and Friedson "participated in oral presentations, including demonstrative presentations with graphs and diagrams, stressing the success that Windmere was having and would continue to have after the acquisition[.]" Plaintiffs state that "Defendants were under intense pressure to complete the offering as soon as possible, as the proceeds were needed to repay Nations-Bank for the bridge loan used to pay for the HPG acquisition."

3. The Registration Statement

Plaintiffs assert the Registration Statement, effective June 4, 1998, materially misstated the nature of the acquisition, in that it did not adequately describe the requirements of Windmere's integration with HPG, and the specific financial, legal and logistical risks that were ongoing or were foreseeable at the time. The Registration Statement stated, "[t]he Company has combined top brand names and a reputation for quality and innovation with its efficient, low-cost, vertically integrated manufacturing capabilities. The Company expects to continue to achieve growth and increased profitability by pursing the following strategies[.]" Plaintiffs then highlight two strategic categories, "Leverage Manufacturing Capabilities," and "Expansion of the Company's International Presence." [Regarding international sales,] the Registration Statement states:

> The Company intends to utilize the marketing and distribution channels acquired through the HPG Acquisition to expand the global market penetration of all of its products, particularly in Latin America. As a result of the HPG Acquisition, the Company has acquired the leading market share in irons, and a smaller market presence in the blender category, in Argentina, Colombia, Ecuador, Puerto Rico, Venezuela, Chile, Mexico and the Caribbean. In addition to targeting mass merchandisers, wholesalers, warehouse clubs and government institutions in Latin America, the Company intends to pursue alternative channels of distribution in Latin America which it believes will continue to be important sources of sales. On a pro forma basis, after giving effect to the HPG Acquisition, the Company's international sales would have been $218.9 million in 1997, as compared to $82.1 million in international sales for Windmere-Durable alone in 1997.

Plaintiffs contend these facts were materially false and misleading, and that the true facts were:

a) On or prior to the effective date of the Prospectus, July 22, 1998, Windmere could not use Black & Decker's existing licenses to operate its business in Latin America. PG Latin America was not previously run as a separate entity by Black & Decker, but functioned as part of Black & Decker's Power Tools Division. When Windmere acquired HPG, it was required to undergo the complicated and time-consuming process of creating a new company for HPG in each Latin American country in which HPG operated and was required to register those entities to do business. Thus, Windmere could not even call on HPG's existing customers in Latin America for continued business because it lacked the proper licenses to sell HPG's produces in those foreign countries. Windmere had internally projected that these corporate entities would be organized between March and June 1998. Nevertheless, the corporate requirements had not been met prior to the Class Period or the July Offering. Thus, at the time the Company issued the above statements, it was unable to "utilize the marketing and distribution channels" of HPG to expand market penetration in Latin America until it had obtained the requisite licenses. In July 1998, a former HPG employee visited the Company's manufacturing plant in Queretaro, Mexico, and learned that Windmere could still not call on HPG's existing customers and was losing business as a result. Indeed, Windmere had not obtained the necessary licenses throughout the Class Period. In late July and August, Windmere's General Counsel sought to move the licensing process forward, but without success. As a result, throughout the Class Period, Windmere failed to meet the necessary corporate requirements and obtain the needed licenses to do business in Latin America. The Company would not be able to realize significant profits in Latin America until the legal requirements of doing business there had been met. The Company's lack of the necessary licenses prior to Windmere's takeover of the HPG business in Latin America constituted a principal cause for the Company's later revealed poor performance during the Class Period.

b) Moreover, in a summer 1998 senior-staff meeting, significant problems with the integration of HPG's Latin American Division were discussed. Soon after it acquired HPG on June 26, 1998, Windmere discovered that Latin American retailers' warehouses were overstocked with HPG products. As a result, Windmere could not sell product in Latin America competitively because retailers were saturated resulting from prior sales of HPG products to them at discounted prices or on other favorable terms. Windmere was fully aware of the excessive inventory build-up problem in Latin America at least as early as when the Company acquired HPG. By the time Windmere acquired HPG on June 26, 1998 and for almost a full month thereafter before the July 22, 1998 effective date of the Registration Statement, the inventories of Latin American retailers were bloated with HPG products and additional sales of HPG products to them at least throughout the remainder of 1998 would [be] very difficult to achieve until those inventories had been substantially sold off. Defendants . . . had begun operating HPG by June 26, 1998, when HPG was acquired. Indeed, Defendants themselves told the marketplace and investors during road show presentations that Windmere was already in the process of integrating the operations of HPG. There was thus a large build-up of HPG products on the shelves of HPG's Latin American retailers before the July Offering[.] Despite the severity of the sales problem for Windmere, the Company failed to disclose it to the investing public in the Registration Statement and instead emphasized the dramatic increase in sales which would purportedly result from the HPG acquisition.

Plaintiffs further allege Defendants made material misstatements in the section entitled, "Risks of International Operations and Expansion," describing certain international economic and political variables that could affect the company's business, including "the burdens and costs of compliance with a variety of foreign laws and, in certain parts of the world, political instability[.]" Plaintiffs claim this description was materially false and misleading because, at the time the statement was made, Windmere "was already materially reducing sales in Latin America because the Company could not do business with HPG's existing customers. In considering the HPG acquisition, the Company had internally projected that it would obtain the required licenses between March and June 1998, a period well before the issuance of the above statements." Thus, Plaintiffs allege, the discussion of risk in the Registration Statement was "but a generic warning containing no meaningful factual disclosure of the adverse facts which were then actually negatively impacting Windmere's business by at least July 22, 1998."

In addition, Plaintiffs contend, the "High Volume, Low-Cost Manufacturing Capabilities" section contained material misstatements. There, the Registration Statement states, "[t]he Company believes that its high volume, vertically integrated manufacturing capabilities provide the Company flexibility and cost advantages[.] The Company intends to take advantage of its capabilities as a multinational manufacturer to reduce operating costs and increase productivity." Plaintiffs allege these statements were false because certain manufacturing integration within the combined company "would take a significant amount of time, and Windmere would have to find its own companies to create HPG products. Windmere nevertheless told the public in its June 23, 1998 release . . . that it expected to enjoy the benefits and synergies from the HPG acquisition 'beginning in the first six months of the acquisition.'"

 . . . .

III. Discussion and Analysis

First analyzing the appropriate pleading standards for securities fraud claims under the '33 Act and the '34 Act, the Court analyzes the allegations in the Amended Complaint under the appropriate standard of review. Finding Plaintiffs have stated actionable securities fraud claims on all counts, except for Count IV as to Defendant Montgomery only, the Court determines that the Motion of the Windmere Defendants shall be denied in its entirety, and the Motion of Defendant Montgomery shall be granted as to Count IV only and denied in all other respects.

A. Sections 11 and 12(a)(2) of the Securities Act of 1933

The allegations in Counts I and II claim all Defendants violated sections 11 and 12(a)(2) of the '33 Act by making material omissions or misstatements in connection with the July Offering. Section 11 allows any purchaser of a security to bring a cause of action based on material misstatements, if any part of the registration statement,

> when such part became effective, contained an untrue statement of a material fact or omitted to state a material fact required to be stated therein or necessary to make the statements therein not misleading. . . .

15 U.S.C. § 77k(a). A plaintiff may bring a section 11 claim against any person who signed the prospectus, the officers and board of directors of the issuing corporation, the underwriters of the securities offering, or any expert whose profession gives authority to that part of the registration statement he or she prepared.

In order to state a section 11 claim, the plaintiff "must demonstrate (1) that the registration statement contained an omission or misrepresentation, and (2) that the omission or misrepresentation was material, that is, it would have misled a reasonable investor about the nature of his or her investment." As the Supreme Court explained:

> Section 11 was designed to assure compliance with the disclosure provisions of the ['33] Act by imposing a stringent standard of liability on the parties who play a direct role in a registered offering. If a plaintiff purchased a security issued pursuant to a registration statement, he need only show a material misstatement or omission to establish his prima facie case. Liability against the issuer of the security is virtually absolute, even for innocent misstatements. Other defendants bear the burden of demonstrating due diligence.

Herman & MacLean, [459 U.S. 375, 381–82 (1983)].

Under section 12(a)(2), on the other hand, any person who "offers or sells a security . . . by means of a prospectus or oral communication" that "includes an untrue statement of a material fact or omits to state a material fact necessary in order to make the statements, in the light of the circumstances under which they were made, not misleading," shall be liable to any "person purchasing such security from him." 15 U.S.C. § 77l(a)(2). Thus, section 12(a)(2) liability may be based on oral as well as written communications.

Where a section 11 claim "sounds in fraud," the particularity requirements of Federal Rule of Civil Procedure 9(b) may apply. In such a case, Plaintiffs must allege: (1) the precise statements, documents, or misrepresentations made; (2) the time, place, and person responsible for the statement; (3) the content and manner in which these statements misled the plaintiffs; and (4) what the defendants gained by the alleged fraud. Yet, where particularity requirements are applied to such claims, "[a] balance must be struck between allowing bald allegations of material misstatements or omissions with little factual basis, on the one hand, and so tightening the requirements of pleading that Plaintiffs must plead evidence, on the other."

1. Plaintiffs Have Adequately Pled Section 11 and 12(a)(2) Claims for Material Omissions in the Registration Statement Against All Defendants.

The most significant of Plaintiffs' allegations are the assertions that at the time of the July Offering, "Windmere did not have the requisite licenses in place required to operate HPG and to sell HPG produces in Latin America and thus could not, until such time as the licenses were obtained, sell HPG products in Latin America or even call on HPG's then-existing customer base." Plaintiffs contend that the disclosures regarding the HPG acquisition triggered a duty to disclose, among other things, the risk that, after the acquisition, months could pass during which Windmere would be unable to move or sell products in Latin America until these license issues were resolved.

The Eleventh Circuit has stated that "[a] duty to disclose may . . . be created by a defendant's previous decision to speak voluntarily. Where a defendant's failure to speak would render the defendant's own prior speech misleading or deceptive, a duty to disclose arises." Similarly, the First Circuit has explained that "the obligations that attend the preparation of a registration statement and prospectus filed in connection with a public stock offering . . . embody nothing if not an affirmative duty to disclose a broad range of material information." Consequently, in connection with a public stock offering, "there is a strong affirmative duty of disclosure."

Here, the Registration Statement made a number of affirmative statements regarding Windmere's acquisition of HPG and the HPG's operations at that time. For example, the Registration Statement discussed HPG's "marketing and distribution channels" and "leading market share" in Latin America as well as the expectation of Windmere's international sales on a pro forma basis, including HPG's 1997 results. Additional facts relevant to this risk, but not disclosed by Defendants are: (1) alleged "stuffed channels" within the HPG's chain of distribution, such that prior to the acquisition Windmere should have disclosed these particular market conditions; (2) that certain specific difficulties with integrating HPG manufacturing facilities in Mexico with the remainder of Windmere's operations, amounted to a material risk that Windmere would not be able to sell products in Latin America until these obstacles were cleared; and (3) the "pro-forma" comparison of a combined Windmere-HPG organization was misleading given that at the time of the Registration Statement Windmere was not in a position to operate HPG in its Latin American markets.

The Windmere Defendants spoke voluntarily in the Registration Statement and the press releases about Windmere's intention to use the distribution channels acquired by purchasing HPG to expand the sales of its products, "particularly in Latin America." Further, the Company proclaimed that it intended "to pursue alternative channels of distribution in Latin America which it believes will continue to be important sources of sales."

2. The Registration Statement Does Not Disclose The Risk of Latin American Licensing or Distribution Problems.

In the section entitled "Risk Factors" at pages S-14 to S-24, the Registration Statement provides detailed information on certain risk factors accompanying any investment in Windmere securities and associated with the acquisition of HPG. Upon review of the numerous risk subsections, the Court finds four categories relate to national licensing agreements and distribution within Latin American markets:

"Risks of International Operations and Expansion," "Dependence on International Trademarks," "Risks Associated with Integration of Black & Decker Household Products Group," and "Government Regulation."

After carefully reviewing the entire Registration Statement and these risk sections in particular, and comparing these with the factual allegations which the Court must take as true, the Court finds none of these risk sections or additional cautionary language in the Registration Statement adequately address the issue of renewed licenses in Latin American markets—the allegedly undisclosed material risk here—under the "meaningful cautionary language" standard discussed below. As related to certain, specifically alleged integration difficulties, the Registration Statement's risk discussion does not adequately cover the real or foreseeable risk that ongoing international sales of Windmere's products would or could be foreseeably jeopardized by the need to obtain such licenses. Further, as discussed below, the "cautionary language" attached to various press release statements also fails to meet the "meaningful cautionary language" standard that would allow a reasonable investor to understand these alleged material risks. The section entitled, "Risk of International Operations," for example, addresses issues relating to international sales and marketing in foreign jurisdictions, including Latin America. The section does state that, "[b]ecause the Company manufactures its products and conducts business in several foreign countries, the Company is affected by economic and political conditions in those countries, including ... the burdens and costs of compliance with a variety of foreign laws and, in certain parts of the world, political instability." No mention is made, however, of the risk of licensing Windmere's operations subsequent to the HPG acquisition, or the specific requirement to seek licenses in various Latin American markets. Rather, the section focuses on currency, economic, and political considerations, particularly as they relate to the People's Republic of China.

The "Dependence on Trademarks" section, on the other hand, touts the fact that "[a]s part of the JPG Acquisition, the Company licensed the *Black & Decker* brand for use in marketing HPG products in North America, Central America, South America (excluding Brazil) and the Caribbean under a licensing arrangement with a minimum term of six and one-half years." This section describes the licensing arrangement between Windmere and Black & Decker, and goes on to describe risks relating to trademark exploitation, but does not substantively address Windmere's need to get approval of domestic governments or licenses to sell Black & Decker products after the acquisition was consummated.

Similarly, the "Patents and Protection of Proprietary Technology" section addresses "patent and design registration," and discusses the risks of creating new proprietary technology and patent registration once new technology is created. Again absent, however, is any mention of the need to get approval of domestic governments or licenses to sell Black & Decker products after the sale was consummated.

After reviewing the entire Registration Statement, the Court finds notably absent any section that addresses what would allegedly cause the significant gap in sales volume: risks relating to international intellectual property generally, risks relating to international licensing requirements specifically, or related risks due to uncertainty of various national licensing requirements.

. . . .

4. Safe Harbor and Bespeaks Caution Doctrine Are Not Applicable.

Defendants argue the challenged statements are forward looking in nature, are subject to the statutory safe harbor, and thus not actionable. The Private Securities Litigation Reform Act of 1995, Pub. L. No. 194-67 (hereinafter "Reform Act"), "provides a safe harbor from liability for certain 'forward-looking' statements." Pursuant to the safe harbor, "corporations and individual defendants may avoid liability for forward-looking statements that prove false if the statement is 'accompanied by meaningful cautionary statements identifying important factors that could cause actual results to differ materially from those in the forward-looking statement.'" Thus, the Court must discern whether any such statement is accompanied by "meaningful cautionary language." Yet the harbor has limits, for "a defendant can fully benefit from the safe harbor's shelter only when it has disclosed risk factors in a warning accompanying the forward-looking statement." The cautionary language must therefore meet a threshold of specificity. *See* [*Harris v. Ivax*, 182 F.3d 799, 807 (11th Cir. 1999)] (holding that "when an investor has been warned of risks of a significance similar to that actually realized, she is sufficiently on notice of the danger of the investment").

Moreover, where plaintiffs allege a "material omission," the cautionary language must be sufficiently "meaningful," such that it discloses "important factors that could cause actual results to differ materially from those in the forward-looking statement." The *Harris* court found general disclosures relating to a goodwill writedown, and consequential one-time charge to earnings, adequate for a reasonable investor to assess the risk associated with certain forward-looking statements, and thus an accompanying warning was "of a significance similar to that [risk] actually realized." The court concluded, "[i]n short, where an investor has been warned of risks of a significance similar to that actually realized, she is sufficiently on notice of the danger of the investment to make an intelligent decision about it according to her own preferences for risk and reward."

Here, the Court has analyzed the Registration Statement and additional documents for both general "boilerplate" cautionary language, and for specific cautionary language of risks relating to international licensing issues. Plaintiffs allege Defendants failed to reveal either known, present facts, or facts that should have been known through due diligence, regarding Windmere's lack of licenses to operate HPG. Plaintiffs further allege certain risk factors and cautionary statements were, themselves, materially misleading or devoid of material risk disclosures, and that therefore the statements cannot be within the safe harbor because the disclosures were inadequate. Plaintiffs argue that "to caution that it is only possible for the unfavorable events to happen when they have already occurred is deceit."

After comparing the Amended Complaint's factual allegations and the various cautionary statements within the ambit of the Reform Act's safe harbor provision, the Court finds the cautionary language, both in the aggregate and when analyzed for specifics, when cast against the alleged omissions and misstatements here, did not fairly and adequately warn potential investors of the alleged risks associated with investing in Windmere securities. Thus, the Court finds the Reform Act's safe harbor provision does not apply to the allegations in the Amended Complaint.[5]

5. Material Omissions or Misstatements Amount to Actionable Claim

Taken together, the allegations of material misstatements and omissions in the Amended Complaint adequately state claims against all Defendants for violations of sections 11 and 12(a)(2) of the '33 Act. Plaintiffs have alleged through specific factual allegations: (1) that the registration statement contained omissions or misrepresentations; and (2) that the omissions or misrepresentations were material, that is, would have misled a reasonable investor about the nature of his or her investment. As such, the Court denies the motions to dismiss Counts I and II as to all Defendants.

Notes & Questions

1. Disclosures in a prospectus or other company documents regarding intellectual property strengths or weaknesses may figure in claims against parties other than the company making the disclosures. For example, where a customer sued a brokerage firm asserting that she was improperly induced to hold previously purchased stock by a constant flow of favorable but untrue and misleading information from brokers at the firm, the contents of a prospectus provided to the shareholder by the brokers was deemed sufficient to put the shareholder on notice of certain patent infringement risks facing the company in which the customer held stock. *See Parsons v. Hornblower & Weeks-Hemphill*, 447 F. Supp. 482 (M.D.N.C. 1977). The district court in this case found that the following discussion in the company's prospectus adequately addressed the uncertain patent position of the corporation involved:

> RISK FACTORS
>
> 10. Although the Company has filed a number of patent applications pertaining to various aspects of the CARTRIVISION system, it does not expect to obtain fundamental patent protection for the basic concept or design of its system. No assurance can be given that patent infringement claims will not be asserted which may adversely affect the Company or that any valid patent protection will be obtained by the Company. The Company may be

---

5. Defendants further argue the "bespeaks caution doctrine" applies to the challenged statements, and that certain cautionary language associated with the disclosures was "sufficient to render the alleged omissions or misrepresentations immaterial as a matter of law." *Saltzberg v. TM Sterling/Austin Assocs., Ltd.*, 45 F.3d 399, 400 (11th Cir. 1995). Here, the Defendants allegedly made present, known misrepresentations or omissions, as the Defendants knew or should have known the licensing requirement was not met but nonetheless failed to disclose the requirement, or failed to disclose the lack of licenses could result in drastically decreased revenue. *See, e.g., Stac Elecs.*, 89 F.3d at 1408 ("By definition, the bespeaks caution doctrine applies only to affirmative, forward-looking statements"). The Court will reserve final ruling on this issue pending fact discovery.

required to obtain patent licenses in order to produce and market the CAR-TRIVISION system, but no assurance can be given that such licenses can be obtained.

HISTORY AND BUSINESS

Patents and Trademarks

There can, however, be no assurance that patents will issue on the Company's patent applications or on any application it files in the future or that patents issued to the Company will be enforceable, if litigated, nor does the Company believe that it has established a unique proprietary position.

Messrs. Townsend and Townsend do not know of any clearly valid adversary United States patents which can successfully be asserted against the Company's presently proposed recorder-playback unit and cartridge, although the prior art in the field discloses a number of patents which relate in varying degrees to the CARTRIVISION system and adversary claims could be made at any time by competitors of the Company.

A United States patent relating to a type of frequency modulation recording has been called to the Company's attention by a substantial United States patent owner in view of the proposed use of frequency modulation recording in the CARTRIVISION system. The validity of this patent has never been adjudicated.

Id. at 492.

2. Fast-moving technological or business developments may rapidly reveal that earlier disclosures in a prospectus of a high-tech company, which were thought to be accurate when made, were actually inaccurate. For example, newly discovered prior art may call into question the validity of patents that were emphasized in prior disclosures as a basis for a key business initiative. Or product announcements of a competitor (based on patented product features that will not be available for general adoption in the same industry) may undercut earlier projections in a prospectus describing the likely value of a new line of business in glowing terms. When should disclosures that were apparently accurate when made be required to be revised based on new information that indicates that the original disclosures may be materially misleading? Should the nature of the duty to update and correct prior disclosures depend on the scope of the positive statements made in the original disclosures? For example, should parties who made broad statements in a prospectus to promote their company's efforts to raise funds have equally broad obligations to monitor the accuracy of their statements and to correct those statements found to be inaccurate upon receipt of further information?

3. When are "boilerplate" provisions describing a company's potential intellectual property problems in general terms adequate to inform shareholders about the business risks associated with the problems and to preclude successful claims by the shareholders that they were misled about the absence of such problems? For

example, assume that a publishing company includes in its prospectus a general statement that its published works may inadvertently incorporate works that are copyrighted by other parties, thereby raising a risk of copyright infringement liability for the publishing company. Once the management of the company realizes that a particular book that it has published includes work plagiarized from another work and that the author of the other work is threatening to institute a major copyright infringement action, will the earlier notice to shareholders of the possibility of this type of suit and liability be a sufficient disclosure? Should it matter whether the author with the possible claim has already filed suit or whether management feels that the copyright claims are likely to result in liability for the publisher if the claims are pursued in litigation? What probability or amount of copyright infringement liability should raise a need for further disclosures to shareholders?

Chapter 9

Advanced Techniques for Maximizing Intellectual Property Value in Mature Companies

Problem

Digital Ignition has successfully developed and marketed automobile ignition products for 20 years. Company engineers have pursued an effective research program, with the result that the company has obtained a regular stream of new patents on advances in computer-controlled automobile ignition systems. Many of these patents protect commercially significant features of the company's products. However, some of the patents address technologies that have not proven useful in the company's products so far, but may still be the basis for marketable products manufactured by Digital Ignition or other companies.

Recognizing that a balance among innovation, manufacturing, and marketing activities, as well as the full commercial use of the company's intellectual property, is important to Digital Ignition's continued success, the company has hired Duane Sawyer, an experienced computer industry executive, to serve as Digital Ignition's new Vice President of Technology Development. As one of his first tasks, Sawyer has been asked by Digital Ignition's Chief Executive Officer to undertake a broadly focused review of how the company is developing new technologies and utilizing those technologies to the company's commercial advantage.

This study will address not only the means whereby Digital Ignition allocates resources to the development and acquisition of new technologies (including how it obtains the rights to use such technologies), but also the steps the company takes to commercialize intellectual property and related rights that are generated in Digital Ignition's research programs. The aim of this review will be to suggest new ways the company can maximize the value of its investments in technology development and the value of intellectual property resulting from these development efforts.

Broad ranges of potential business strategies are to be considered in the upcoming study, including Digital Ignition's decision-making processes for allocating resources between innovative (e.g., technology development) and non-innovative (e.g., product marketing) expenditures, the company's means for identifying new technologies that will be developed internally rather than being acquired from other sources, strategies for realizing the value of intellectual property rights beyond the simple marketing of related products and the licensing of others to do the same, and the circumstances, if any, in which the low-cost licensing or relinquishment of the company's intellectual property rights to further research by others will aid Digital Ignition's ultimate commercial interests.

Questions about the best ways to protect Digital Ignition's intellectual property rights as research goes forward and about how to use those rights in marketing the company's existing products (including the types of issues addressed in Chapter 1), are not the focus of the new study. Digital Ignition's senior executives are convinced that careful attention to these matters over the years has produced generally effective intellectual property protection and product marketing practices for the company. Rather, top management is looking for new ideas about means that a well-established, well-organized, and well-funded technology innovator such as Digital Ignition can use to focus its resources effectively on technology development and then use the resulting new technologies and intellectual property rights to the best advantage of the corporation.

Duane Sawyer is embarking on the first stages of this study. He has contacted your law firm—an experienced intellectual property firm that Sawyer worked with repeatedly in his former capacity as a computer industry executive—for ideas about the types of intellectual property development and administration strategies that he should consider and analyze in the course of his study. Sawyer wants your firm to develop a listing of new business management strategies that a company like Digital Ignition might use to improve its technology development and intellectual property administration. The listing should include brief descriptions of the benefits that are likely to be achieved through each of the new strategies, the risks or other detrimental features associated with each strategy, and the basic changes in business practices needed to implement each strategy.

Using this information, Sawyer will work with the company's executives and managers to determine which of the potential strategies will be beneficial to Digital Ignition as well as how to best implement those strategies within the company's existing operations. Because the implementation advantages and methods will be worked out later by corporate insiders having the relevant operating information, your firm need not worry about the detailed features of Digital Ignition's operations, but should rather focus on techniques and strategies that have a significant potential for success in firms like Digital Ignition.

Please provide Sawyer with an overview of advanced organizational management strategies that may aid Digital Ignition in making effective decisions about developing new intellectual property and maximizing the value of rights associated with that property.

Focus of the Chapter

The readings in this chapter describe a number of corporate management strategies that can aid an organization in improving technology development decisions and the organization's use of related intellectual property.

The first several readings address ways in which corporations and other organizations can structure operations and related decision-making processes to improve their development and use of intellectual property. The initial reading by Professor George G. Triantis describes how operating a corporation in a multi-divisional structure or other similar arrangement can be used to clarify resource allocation decisions and improve the effectiveness of resource allocations to technology development.

The second reading by Professor Dan Burk explains how choices by corporate managers about whether to "make or buy" corporate resources (such as decisions about whether to develop a new technology internally or to acquire such a technology from outside sources) define the scope of internal corporate activities and are influenced by the nature of intellectual property rights. The third reading by Professor David McGowan describes how a combination of intellectual property rights and carefully crafted contractual licenses can be used to promote a multi-party, highly distributed effort to develop a new technology — in this case, the open source movement advancing the development of certain computer software systems.

Additional readings describe several recently-developed techniques for generating revenues from intellectual property (sometimes referred to as techniques for "monetizing" intellectual property). The readings analyze these monetizing techniques and provide further insights into the types of entities that have been specially created to advance intellectual property monetizing efforts.

The next several readings focus on tactical measures that an organization can use to increase the value of its intellectual property interests. The first of these readings describes a particular financing technique — intellectual property securitization — in which royalties from intellectual property licenses are used to pay interest on related bonds, which are sold based on the income strength or "securitization" of the intellectual property interests. This technique has been used in a number of fields to realize immediate financial returns from intellectual property interests having proven value and royalty potential.

The next set of readings analyzes the use of insurance to benefit intellectual property owners and to enhance the commercialization of intellectual property. These readings briefly describe the use of intellectual property enforcement insurance as a means to bolster the enforcement of intellectual property rights and to ensure that owners gain the full value of these interests. The benefits of this and other forms of insurance in spreading costs and reducing the potential business effects of intellectual property risks are summarized in this section.

Further readings in this chapter focus on potentially valuable dispositions of intellectual property. The dispositions explored here include auctions of intellectual property interests (either by intellectual property owners who are voluntarily shedding interests that they do not expect to use in their future business activities or by bankruptcy trustees who are seeking to realize the maximum sales price for intellectual property assets of bankrupt companies), privately negotiated sales of intellectual property (often by intellectual property brokers), contributions of intellectual property interests to charitable organizations to gain tax deductions, and commitments by intellectual property owners to non-enforcement of their rights in order to spur technology development by other parties (such as open source software developers) whose efforts are expected to benefit the intellectual property owners at a later point.

The next readings in this chapter focus on intellectual property portfolios and the ways that the coordinated acquisition and management of groups of related intellectual property interests can benefit companies. By treating the validity and enforcement of a portfolio of intellectual property interests as sources of corresponding business risks and opportunities, techniques used for financial portfolio management can be translated into corresponding strategies for intellectual property portfolio acquisitions and enforcement.

The last set of readings discusses joint ventures as means to increase the value of intellectual property. Joint ventures can produce new intellectual property and expand on the commercial use of existing intellectual property. Such ventures can also be sources of new intellectual property ownership issues and enforcement problems. The readings explore the purposes and planning considerations underlying joint ventures to develop new intellectual property or to use existing intellectual property in new ways. The intellectual property challenges involved in setting up, conducting, and terminating joint ventures are also addressed.

Readings

A. Sources of Innovation and New Intellectual Property

1. Allocating Resources to Innovation within Companies: Multi-Divisional Corporations as Internal Capital Markets

One potentially important source of new intellectual property in a well-established company is the carefully targeted use of corporate resources to support internal innovation efforts and the creation of new intellectual property within the company. However, corporate resources to support new activities are often highly limited. Additional funding and support for internal corporate innovation will come at the cost of reductions in support for other corporate activities. These types of funding are therefore in competition with each other. Whether or not additional support for innovation and the creation of new intellectual property is the best way for a company to use its resources and maximize its likelihood of future corporate profits or other desirable corporate results will depend on careful analyses of the profit potential of alternative uses of available corporate resources.

To make these comparisons in careful, thorough ways, some companies use multi-divisional management and budgeting techniques to structure their resource allocation decisions and to increase the likelihood of efficient use of corporate resources. Corporations adopting multi-divisional organizational structures or other arrangements facilitating shifts in resources to back various types of profit-making activities can implement the equivalent of capital markets regarding the use of corporate resources. Allocations of limited operating resources to activities within portions of such companies are counterparts within the companies to external capital investments by shareholders in smaller companies. By establishing competition among corporate subunits for additional corporate funds, these arrangements tend to allocate corporate resources to future projects—such as additional innovation efforts or expansion of non-innovative efforts such as additional marketing efforts for existing products—that promise the greatest returns on investments.

Because corporate managers have private information about the capabilities of corporate operating subunits and the probable value of particular new activities undertaken in the context of other corporate business operations, managers allocating resources within internal corporate capital allocation processes can often achieve greater returns on investments than their external counterparts making investments as less well informed shareholders in small companies. In the particular context of decisions about whether to back the development of new intellectual property, firms that use internal information about existing corporate products, operating strengths, and technical expertise to tailor the scope and timing of backing for innovative activities can maximize the future value of their intellectual property in several ways. They can target the development of new intellectual property in ways that enhance the value of existing products, better utilize the present strengths of business operations, and emphasize innovation projects that utilize the body of shared and distinctive technological knowledge and skills of company employees. They can also match work on new intellectual property to other corporate activities and thereby reduce costs of producing intellectual property and increase the range of commercial applications for such property.

Internal capital markets—that is, internal management practices that simulate or substitute for external capital markets supporting shareholder investments—can promote efficient corporate choices between innovative and non-innovative activities, based on the projected profit-making potential associated with the available alternatives. For example, a corporation may choose to allocate $1,000,000 to the development of new products or to the enhancement of marketing efforts for existing products, whichever is predicted to be likely to produce the most additional corporate profits per dollar spent. Similarly, within a range of available innovation efforts, corporate decision processes implementing internal capital markets can help companies to allocate their resources to their most promising innovation projects. In these capital markets and associated evaluations, intellectual property protections and related projections of exclusive commercial opportunities often play key parts in clarifying the probable value of potential courses of action.

The following reading describes how large corporate organizations implement internal capital markets and the reasons why resulting investments of resources can be more profitable than equivalent investments made by persons outside of corporate organizations. The focus of this reading is on investments in corporate activities generally, rather than on allocations of corporate resources to innovative activities in particular. However, the principles discussed here apply to decisions about investments in innovative activities, explaining why large organizations such as major corporations and the management processes they conduct can sometimes be especially efficient in allocating investments of resources in the development of new intellectual property.

George G. Triantis, Organizations as Internal Capital Markets: The Legal Boundaries of Firms, Collateral, and Trusts in Commercial and Charitable Enterprises
117 HARV. L. REV. 1102, 1105, 1109–15 (2004)*

. . . .

[T]his Article presents a distinct . . . explanation of the legal boundaries of organizations. These boundaries define internal capital markets within which resources may be readily redeployed, but across which redeployment may occur only at some cost. Internal capital markets permit capital to move between projects; in the language of real options, they enhance the value of "switching options," or the ability to delay a capital allocation decision until more information becomes available. The distinction between external and internal capital markets is that capital moves between projects by contract in the former case and by authority or fiat in the latter. A corporate manager might finance a new venture by contracting with outside investors (external) or by shifting resources from an existing project within the firm (internal). For example, capital is redeployed through external markets when one firm distributes some of its assets to investors and another firm sells securities to those investors, or when two separate firms contract with each other to move capital between projects managed by each firm. If instead the two projects were contained in an internal capital market, the new project might be financed by diverting cash flow from the existing project, by liquidating some of that project's assets, or by borrowing against those assets.

Internal capital enables a firm to avoid the information asymmetry between a firm's managers and outside investors, or between two firms, that may impede or may raise the cost of external finance. Internal capital thereby reduces the cost of switching capital allocations and increases investment flexibility. There is a tradeoff, however, between this gain and the agency costs of having this flexibility managed by an agent who can exploit her private information for her own benefit. A manager may reallocate capital within internal markets to maximize her private benefits rather than firm value, and she may use her informational advantage to conceal from investors the shift in resources or its impact on firm value.

. . . .

An internal capital market permits the reallocation of capital between projects at a lower cost than through external capital markets because project managers possess expertise and private information that cannot be efficiently communicated to outside investors. Managers of internal capital markets are informed but self-interested agents. The internal capital markets thesis of organizational boundaries may be framed as addressing a balance between the benefits and the costs of leaving investment switching options in the hands of agents. Therefore, three factors define the optimal size (or boundaries) of an internal capital market: the value of the flexibility to adjust over time the allocation of capital among available projects, the value added by a competent and informed agent who manages that flexibility, and the incentive conflicts resulting from the agent's control over that flexibility.

Investment flexibility can be framed in terms of real options. In this context, a real option is the ability to adjust an investment decision when better information is obtained. In the realm of capital budgeting, real options include the ability to defer, abandon, accelerate, or decelerate projects. The ability to reallocate capital between projects may be viewed as a switching option—that is, the abandonment or deceleration of one project and the initiation, continuation, or acceleration of another project. For example, suppose an investor initially funds two ventures, V1 and V2, based on incomplete information. When new information is subsequently revealed, the investment mix may be changed, albeit at some cost. This switching option—the ability to adjust the investment mix with the benefit of new information—is valuable because the option will be exercised only if the reallocation of capital between the two projects increases the aggregate return. One might similarly view the ability to divert cash flow from one project to another as a switching option by presuming that the cash flow is reinvested in the source project unless the option to switch is exercised.

Real options analysis offers several important insights. First, the value of the switching option is a function of the correlation between the payoff distributions of the two projects. The less positively correlated and the more negatively correlated the distributions, the more valuable the option to switch between projects.

Second, a switching option is valuable and often worth incurring some cost to create and preserve. Suppose that the return from V1 is initially expected to exceed the return from V2. It may nevertheless be advisable to invest enough in V2 to keep alive the option of later engaging more fully in V2 by moving capital from V1, especially if the distributions of returns from the two projects are negatively correlated. The more valuable the option, the greater the return from investments to create and preserve it. Therefore, to the degree that internal capital markets increase the value of switching options, they also encourage the creation of such options.

Third, the value of an option depends on the proper timing of its exercise. Switching between projects is costly. Therefore, even when new information about the relative returns on the two projects justifies the partial liquidation of the first and the shifting of capital to the second, switching should be deferred until further information confirms the superior returns of the second project. As a general proposition, the costly exercise of an option should be deferred until the option matures;

accordingly, the value of an option typically depends on the time until maturity. Several factors, however, may accelerate the optimal timing of the decision to switch: in particular, the costs of switching may increase over time if the salvage values of assets in the source project deteriorate, and the value of switching to the second project may be compromised by delay if competitors can enter the product market in the meantime.

If reallocation occurs through external capital markets, an organization must distribute capital from one project (perhaps from cash flow or partial liquidation of the project) to investors, who must then finance a second project in another organization. Alternatively, capital may move directly between firms without passing through the hands of investors, such as through interfirm loans.

Reallocation through internal capital markets may occur by any of the following means. First, the cash flow from one project may be diverted to fund another. Second, assets of one project may be sold and the proceeds transferred to another project. Third, the firm may implicitly borrow against the assets of one project to finance another venture whenever liability is incurred by the organization as a whole, because all of its assets are available to satisfy the creditor. Indeed, the firm may enhance its cross-financing option by giving the new creditor a security interest—and therefore priority—in the assets of the first project, even though the loan proceeds fund the second project. Fourth, two projects may share common expenses, such as administrative overhead, and an organization can shift capital between projects by changing the portion of organizational overhead allocated to each project. Fifth, the projects may trade goods or services with each other at internally determined rates. As explained later in this Article, organizations are not required by law to use market or arm's-length prices for such transfers, and managers can reallocate capital between projects by selecting exchange terms in favor of one or the other project.

The advantage of an internal capital market is that it facilitates the delegation of control over switching options from investors to managers, who have superior expertise and access to information regarding available projects. The value of a switching option depends on the competence of decisionmaking with respect to the creation, preservation, and exercise of the option. The competence of such decisionmaking in turn relies on the quality of information about factors that affect the distribution of the projects' future payoffs—factors such as projected costs, revenues, technology, and competitors. A significant portion of this information may be unobservable or "soft," in the sense of being difficult to communicate to investors. The decisions of investors initially to determine the distribution of capital and subsequently to reinvest it are impaired by their inferior information about the expected returns from each project and the obstacles to effective disclosure by project managers (for example, the cost of revealing information to competitors or even government regulators). The greater the asymmetry of information and expertise between managers and investors, the greater the potential contribution by managers and the more significant the potential gain from an internal capital market. A similar information asymmetry also impedes the direct movement of capital from one firm to another (without passing through the hands of investors). Indeed, such obstacles to contracting between firms are compounded by the agency problems existing between each firm and its investors. Options that are effectively managed in this respect are more valuable, and accordingly, investors are more willing to invest ex ante to create and preserve such options. Specifically, investors are more likely to create an option to switch from V1 to V2 by investing a small amount in V2 if the option will be exercised subsequently by a competent manager.

. . . .

The value of a switching option in the hands of an agent is impaired by incentive conflicts. In particular, an agent may switch (or abstain from switching) capital allocations in order to maximize her private benefits rather than the aggregate return to the enterprise. Managers enjoy private benefits that are not shared by other investors because of their control over decisionmaking. These benefits typically include opportunities to self-deal, build empires, entrench positions, enhance professional reputations, and consume perquisites. Whether managerial pursuit of private benefits conflicts with the interests of investors in the exercise of shifting options depends on the type of private benefit in question. Compare the following three examples. First, empire building is unlikely to skew switching incentives because, for any given firm size, a manager wants to maximize profitability. Second, private benefits from entrenchment or shirking may lead to suboptimal switching activity; some studies, for instance, find that managers are reluctant to abandon losing projects. Third, private benefits from social prestige or investment in portable human capital may respond to social fads and thereby induce excessive switching and overinvestment in the creation of options.

There is a range of well-known mechanisms that restrain the extraction of private benefits to some degree. If investors receive low payoffs at the end of one period, they will be reluctant to make new investments with the same manager in future periods. Therefore, managers may forego private benefits in the current period to raise the likelihood that the enterprise will continue. Tax authorities might also provide some discipline. Stockholders have legal rights to enforce the duties of loyalty owed by managers to the corporation. Shareholders can also vote to replace directors and thereby remove misbehaving managers, and in many cases, they can veto extraordinary decisions. Debtholders (and less frequently, stockholders) can seek to control by contract the appropriation of private benefits.

The ability of shareholders and debtholders to monitor managerial misbehavior is impaired by the fact that the information necessary to detect opportunistic switching is frequently not verifiable, even if observable. The suspect reallocation itself may be subtle and not apparent to the investor. For example, there may be little evidence that cash is commingled, that administrative burdens are shifted between projects, or that transfers occur between ventures at prices at odds with arm's-length terms. Indeed, the very expertise and informational advantage that investors wish to exploit in assigning to their managers the task of reallocating capital over time also undermine the ability of investors to monitor and discipline their managers' self-interested exercise of discretion. Incentive-based compensation such as stock ownership may align managerial incentives with those of their principals, but only at the cost of imposing risk on the managers and inducing risk-averse decisionmaking. Thus, even in the aggregate, these various constraints on the extraction of private benefits are not completely effective and leave residual agency conflicts. As such, internal capital markets may yield inefficient reallocation of capital and a consequent reduction in the value of investor interests. In these cases, investors may seek to control the switching authority of their managers.

Investors are unlikely to be able to specify ex ante optimal switching strategies because information asymmetries prevent investors from observing or verifying the efficiency of reallocations. Therefore, investors may instead seek to control ex ante the ability of their managers to move capital among projects, whether or not switching would be efficient. If managerial bias is against switching, investors may wish to compel periodic review of the allocation of capital, and . . . they may delegate the review to intermediaries. For example, investors may fund projects in stages or through short-term debt contracts that must be refinanced periodically. Conversely, if managers are prone to make inefficient reallocations, investors may seek to encumber their managers' discretion to switch by constraining the internal capital market.

    . . . .

2. Developing Intellectual Property Inside or Outside Companies: Decisions to "Make or Buy" New Intellectual Property

Where a company is interested in offering new products or entering into new types of business activities, new intellectual property (in various forms from new patented technologies, to new brands and marketing strategies, to new business practices protected by trade secrets) may be needed. Sometimes, the needed intellectual property will be available from either internal or external sources—that is, a company will have a choice to develop the intellectual property internally (the equivalent of making a new product component within the company) or to acquire the new intellectual property from an outside source (the equivalent of buying a product component from an outside source). This sort of "make or buy" decision regarding acquisitions of additional intellectual property turns on a variety of factors related to the relative abilities of parties inside and outside the company to produce the needed intellectual property and the costs involved.

These sorts of considerations have been studied for many years in the context of decisions about whether to "make or buy" physical corporate resources and product components. Much of the learning that has been built up regarding "make or buy" decisions in the context of physical product production can be usefully translated into guidance for equivalent decisions about the production of new intellectual property inside and outside of corporations. These sorts of decisions not only affect whether a company obtains the intellectual property that it needs in an efficient way, these decisions influence the content and scope of company activities. Items sought to be produced internally (including new intellectual property) imply a related range of corporate activities to produce the items, while items sought to be acquired from outside imply only sets of acquisition transactions in a variety of relevant markets. Thus, a corporate strategy to make new intellectual property will imply that a firm should have an extensive research staff and associated allocations of resources; by contrast, a decision to buy new intellectual property means that the equivalent research staff will not be found in-house, but that the firm involved will wish to emphasize business practices and a staff that looks to outside sources for the development of new intellectual property and that obtains appropriate licenses or assignments for the company to acquire rights to use that intellectual property.

A branch of economic analyses revolving around Ronald Coase's "Theory of the Firm" holds that these "make or buy" decisions about the proper scope of corporate internal activities will evolve toward efficient equilibriums and will therefore tend to be made so as to minimize the transaction costs associated with accomplishing organizational tasks. Coase's approach suggests that corporate boundaries (that is, the limits on the activities undertaken internally by corporations) are set based on the following principles:

> (1) the choice between firm and market organization is neither given, nor largely determined, by technology, but mainly reflects efforts to economize on transaction costs; (2) the study of transaction costs is preeminently a comparative institutional undertaking; and (3) this very same comparative approach in which microanalytic features are brought under scrutiny applies not merely to firm and market organization but also generalizes to the study of externalities, regulation, and other forms of complex economic organization.

Oliver E. Williamson, *Book Review*, 77 Cal. L. Rev. 223, 223–24 (1989) (reviewing R. H. Coase, The Firm, the Market, and the Law (1988)).

The theory of the firm explored by Coase has been seen by some analysts as a useful tool for assessing the scope of innovative activities maintained internally by large corporations that have sufficient resources to be able to choose whether to produce or acquire new technologies. These analysts use the theory of the firm to interpret how intellectual property protections influence corporate decision making and choices between internal technology development and external technology acquisitions. As noted by one observer:

> Intellectual property law is [a] field where the theory of the firm is beginning to make inroads. One important observation is that intellectual property is sometimes a substitute for vertical integration. In other words, a stronger intellectual property regime makes it profitable to move transactions to the market rather than keep them within the firm. Outsourcing research has been made easier by stronger patent rights. Research and invention make

difficult subject matter for contract because unforeseen research developments are common, and the output of a research project is difficult to describe. Patents give rights to the patent owner that act as a substitute for usage terms that otherwise would have to be specified in a contract.

Michael J. Meurer, *Law, Economics, and the Theory of the Firm*, 52 BUFF. L. REV. 727, 746–47 (2004).

In the following reading, Professor Dan L. Burk extends this analysis further, contending that the theory of the firm should be a fundamental starting point for interpreting the proper scope of intellectual property rights so as to minimize transaction costs and facilitate efficient decisions by organizational personnel about means to develop and acquire innovative technologies.

Dan L. Burk, Intellectual Property and the Firm
71 U. CHI. L. REV. 3 (2004)*

Since its articulation by Ronald Coase, the economic theory of the firm has generated an enormous body of literature in corporate law and related fields. That literature has become increasingly dominated by property-based theories of the firm that consider the allocation and disposition of institutional assets. Given this influence and direction, it is curious that the theory of the firm has received relatively little attention in intellectual property scholarship. In a so-called information age, where the most important assets of firms increasingly are intangible assets, one might expect that property-based theories of the firm would be readily applied to intellectual property.

While the dearth of such analysis might suggest that theories of the firm have little to tell us regarding intellectual property, this supposition is not only counterintuitive, but belied by scholarship employing these theories in the intellectual property context, which is now beginning to emerge. Some work in this regard has already been done by Robert Merges, considering the law of ownership applicable to inventions created by employees. Although Merges does not explicitly invoke the theory of the firm, his analysis has elements common to such theories. Merges has also explicitly applied the theory of the firm to consider the control of innovators over inputs into their production.

More recently, David McGowan has considered theories of the firm in relation to the licensing of copyrighted "open-source" software. He suggests that the purportedly decentralized open-source programming community operates more as an economic firm than romanticized visions of this community might suggest. McGowan's work in this context implies, though does not explicitly state, that intellectual property licensing may be a coordinating factor in the production function of economic firms. Likewise, D. Gordon Smith has considered fiduciary duties in light

---

of property-based theories of the firm. Smith does not explicitly consider intellectual property, but his analysis clearly maps onto the law of trade secrecy.

This scholarship suggests that there are insights to be gained by considering intellectual property in light of theories of the firm. However, as indicated, much of the work to date only hints at the fruits that such an exercise might bear. Even where the conjunction of the two is explicit, the commentators tend to take the state of intellectual property doctrine as given. Both Merges and McGowan are interested in the theory of the firm primarily as a vehicle to evaluate the innovative practices of certain industries, rather than as a tool to assess the state of intellectual property law itself.

In this Essay I wish to employ the theory of the firm in this latter fashion. I offer a preliminary examination of the relationship between intellectual property and theories of the firm, considering whether intellectual property law has progressed in the way we might have predicted in light of the theory of the firm, and to the extent that it has not, asking whether the theory of the firm has any recommendation to make for its improvement. In particular, I examine whether existing intellectual property law provides for efficient allocation of intellectual property rights within firms in a manner that comports with property-based theories of the firm. I begin with a short overview of property-based theories of the firm, and then suggest how such theories might fit one conception of intellectual property law. Finally, I focus briefly on doctrines in several major areas of intellectual property that suggest themselves for consideration in light of theories of the firm.

I. Theories of the Firm

Modern theories of the firm, particularly the property-based theories considered here, have evolved in order to explain and justify the presence of organizational hierarchies within free market systems. But, paradoxically, the economic theory of the firm has yet to include any commonly accepted definition of the organization contemplated, that is, the concept of the "firm." Certainly the term as used in this context is not synonymous with its meaning in everyday conversation or even in legal parlance; the economic firm is not necessarily a legally recognized organization, although some legally recognized firms are also economic firms. The economic literature on the firm generally uses the term to denote an area of economic activity characterized by hierarchical organization and command production, rather than by market negotiation. The production center thus denoted is generally conceived to encompass an entrepreneur controlling a variety of inputs, including employees, via a complex of relationships, usually contractual in nature.

This conception of the firm, derived from the early work of Coase and of F.H. Knight, exists to explain the presence of hierarchical organizations within free markets. Coase, in particular, developed his early theory of the firm to explain why firms should exist even though markets are considered an efficient mechanism to coordinate productive activity. As in much of Coase's other influential work, the answer depends largely upon an inefficiency of markets, transaction costs that attend negotiated bargains. Firms, Coase postulated, exist in order to lower such transaction costs. Under this model, the productive activities of the firm are directed by an entrepreneurial fiat, rather than being realized via negotiated market transactions. In some cases, hierarchical production may prove less costly than market production due to the transaction costs of the market. In such cases, competitive pressures will tend to compel the formation of firms, as market participants organize themselves to minimize inefficiencies or face displacement by competitors that have already done so.

This model predicts the emergence of firm organizations where the transaction costs of the market become too high. Commentators expanding upon Coase's insight have identified opportunism as one of the key transaction costs associated with bargaining in the marketplace and have introduced theories of incomplete contracting into the analysis. Parties to a transaction cannot anticipate all future contingencies and, as a consequence, any contract they negotiate will be incomplete. Thus, contracts will necessarily present opportunities for one or the other party to take advantage of unforeseen developments. In particular, a party to a contract may attempt to "hold up" the other party, extorting additional concessions once resources have been committed to a project and cannot be easily recommitted to another venture. Such relationship-specific resources, by virtue of their tailoring to a particular project, increase the efficiency of projects but also create this potential for opportunism. Generalized resources may be more easily recommitted to new uses but are less well suited to any given project. Thus, in the face of possible hold-ups, parties may face an undesirable incentive to avoid asset specificity.

The development of a firm, which organizes production by command rather than by negotiation, may be explained as an attempt to deter such hold-up problems by eliminating repeated negotiations. If production is organized by executive fiat rather than by negotiation, there may be fewer opportunities for hold-ups to occur. However, by integrating production into a hierarchical structure, hold-up problems may simply be moved within the firm. Employment relationships are themselves contractual, and the boundary between internal and external contracts may be difficult or impossible to define. Some commentators have suggested that the relationships that comprise the firm are subject to much the same incentives and characteristics as those between firms; other commentators have extended this concept, modeling the firm as a nexus of contractual relationships, where team production is organized through a web of contractual arrangements. At some point, these employment contracts spill over into arms-length relationships with independent contractors outside the firm. The resulting model portrays the firm in many ways as a microcosm of market relationships, reflecting in miniature the same contractual structures within and without the firm's boundary.

This suggests that the major transaction costs delineating the boundaries of the firm may be coordination and agency costs: the interests of employees may not be perfectly aligned with that of the entrepreneur directing firm activity, prompting opportunistic behavior. Employees may see opportunities to exploit situations not foreseen in their employment agreements, and, once assets have been devoted to a project, they may hold up the firm for additional concessions. Commentators ana-lyzing this scenario have argued that opportunism can be deterred only by some form of "gap-filling" provision allocating control of resources in situations not contem-plated by contract. The analysis suggested by these commentators places property rights into this role, effectively to serve as the default for incomplete contracts. Allo-cation of ownership rights to the firm is thus advanced to ameliorate the problem of opportunism within the firm; proprietary control of relationship-specific assets pre-vents employees from using them to hold up the firm. Thus, under a property-based model, the right to exclude, and the concomitant right to grant access to the assets of the firm, ultimately define the boundary of the firm.

The types of assets contemplated by developers of this property-based model appear to have been the largely traditional physical assets of production: buildings, machinery, furnishings, paper clips. Less tangible assets, such as specialized finan-cial instruments, may also have been contemplated, and specific human capital has surely been a key consideration in the model's approach to hold-ups. But the assets of the modern firm are at least equally likely to accrue as intangible resources: ideas, know-how, information, inventions, goodwill, and the like. Thus, consonant with the transactional and property-based models reviewed here, the firm might be mod-eled as a nexus of intellectual property rights vested in entrepreneurs, together with actual or implied licenses based on those rights, permitting employees to use and modify the firm's intellectual property.

II. Proprietary Knowledge

In the United States, intellectual property systems have most often been charac-terized as instruments to induce investment in creative products that, in the absence of a proprietary right, might be under-produced. Creative products frequently dis-play characteristics similar to those of "public goods," that is, goods that can be enjoyed by more than one individual simultaneously, and from which it is difficult to exclude consumers. Since consumers cannot easily be excluded from enjoying the good, they would be unlikely to pay for it, and creators, knowing this, will be unlikely to invest in producing it in the first place. Proprietary rights give the creator a legal right to exclude, which allows the creator to derive an income stream from selling access to the work, either by selling the work directly or by collecting royalties from others who sell the work.

Typically, then, intellectual property rights have been viewed as the basis for mar-ket negotiation; by assigning exclusive interests in creative works, intellectual prop-erty facilitates bargaining. In other words, intellectual property rights are conceived of primarily as mechanisms for coordinating activities between firms. However, as detailed above, the boundary of the firm is often indeterminate, and the distinction separating contractual relationships within the firm from contractual relationships between firms may be ambiguous. Property-based theories of the firm suggest that the right to access and use dedicated resources must be allocated within the firm as well as beyond the firm. This means that, in addition to their recognized inter-firm functions, proprietary rights may also serve to coordinate resources within a firm.

This function of proprietary rights in the firm has not been the focus of the standard explanations for intellectual property. However, at least one theory of intellectual property has focused on the assignment of proprietary rights as a mechanism to coordinate development of the creative product. This "prospect theory" of intellectual property is most closely associated with the work of Edmund Kitch, who argued that the assignment of intellectual property places development of valuable innovation in the hands of an entrepreneur who can then coordinate development of that resource. Following this rationale, one may argue that by vesting firms with control of such intangible assets, the exclusive intellectual property rights found in patent, copyright, and trade secrecy may serve to prevent opportunism and promote coordination of intangible resources. Employees or potential licensees who wish to develop proprietary information must seek the permission of the rights-holding entrepreneur. This view of the "prospect" coordination rationale is also consonant with models of the firm as a nexus of contractual production. Employees routinely make, use, sell, offer for sale, reproduce, distribute, adapt, and otherwise make use of the firm's intellectual property in ways that would constitute infringement if the uses were unauthorized. We typically presume that such uses are authorized but may have given little thought to the source of the authorization—the license that allows employees to make use of the firm's intangible assets in the course of their employment.

On this model, firms may be reluctant to develop project-specific intellectual property if control is incompletely allocated, as this sets the stage for potential hold-up by employees. Allocation of rights may be relatively obvious where tangible property or monetary assets are concerned; the employee who converts or appropriates such assets to his own use is guilty of theft, embezzlement, or waste. But misappropriation of intangible assets such as know-how, concepts, inventions, or designs is more problematic because the nonrivalrous nature of the resource leaves the appearance that nothing has been "taken." Indeed, if rights to intangible assets are left inchoate, employees may be unable to distinguish their personal knowledge and creative resources from those developed under the auspices of the firm.

The point is perhaps most clear in the case of trade secrecy, which arises out of a complex pedigree of tort, contract, and equitable legal claims. Although trade secrecy disputes occasionally involve blatant industrial espionage, more typically they arise in cases of employee mobility, where a departing employee is purported to have taken proprietary information. Other typical cases involve instances of corporate divorce, where a former corporate ally is purported to have misused proprietary information after a joint venture or licensing relationship had gone sour. Resolving trade secrecy disputes is especially problematic in the case of employee departure, as courts are reluctant to curtail the mobility of labor. Society typically will benefit if workers are encouraged to acquire employable skills. But such general ability may be difficult to separate from the specific human capital in which an employer has invested for a particular project. Thus both employee and venture situations are characterized by the need to identify and allocate assets that were specifically dedicated to the particular relationship.

As such, much of trade secrecy law is concerned with demarcation of firm assets, designating incentives and methods for giving proper notice to employees, partners, or licensees of the business information considered to be proprietary and confidential. The substantive law reflects such attempts at demarcation. Trade secrecy is typified by a duty of confidentiality arising in a business relationship. Confidence cannot be imposed upon another party without that party's implied or express consent, so the circumstances giving rise to trade secrecy must be such that a party knew or should have known of the confidentiality obligation. Such obligations may arise from the formal statement of a written contract, or from a contract implied in fact based upon the behavior of the parties, or even from a contract implied in law based upon the general expectations of society. Firms are also expected to take "reasonable measures" to ensure secrecy of their proprietary information—for example, marking confidential information as confidential, password protecting or physically securing such information, and logging or monitoring use of the information.

Such measures signal to employees which assets are considered valuable and project-specific by the employer. Moreover, the additional investment in confidentiality measures is unlikely to be made in generalized assets that pose no danger of hold-up. Consonant with this principle, the law of trade secrecy excludes from protection information that is either generally known or readily ascertainable from information that is generally known. Neither does trade secrecy law protect against reverse engineering or independent discovery of the secret. Generally ascertainable knowledge, or knowledge that can be independently discovered at a low enough cost to make such re-creation feasible, is unlikely to be information that is project-specific, nor is such knowledge likely to represent enough of a project-specific investment to make hold-up likely.

Indeed, the remedies available for misappropriation of trade secrets might be characterized as designed to negate the benefits of hold-up, placing the opportunist monetarily or injunctively where he would have been without the benefit of the proprietary information. Courts may delay use of the misappropriated information for the period of time that it would have taken to reverse engineer or independently develop the secret, or deprive the wrongdoer of the profits gained by not having to expend resources on reverse engineering or independent development. Such head-start damages or head-start injunctions effectively place the opportunist where he would have been had he been operating wholly outside the boundaries of the firm. This characterization additionally implies that joint ventures or licenses that convey project-specific assets fall within the boundaries of the firm for purposes of the property-based theory, even though the entities involved may be separate actors for legal purposes.

Yet, paradoxically, trade secrecy does not confer a property right, or at best it confers an incomplete property right. Trade secrecy does not confer a right as against the world, but only as against a limited number of individuals that stand in a confidential relationship with the proprietor. Courts have displayed some confusion as to this quasi-property right, sometimes treating it as property and other times repudiating that label. But under a firm-based analysis, this incomplete propertization is not a problem; confidential information does not confer a right as against the world, but it need not, and public welfare dictates that it probably should not. A full discussion of the economic and constitutional limits of trade secrecy lies beyond the scope of this Essay, but for this discussion, it is enough to recognize that trade secrecy need only confer an allocative property right against opportunism as between the parties to the secret.

III. Copyright

The discussion to this point suggests that many aspects of trade secrecy are consonant with the need to distinguish project-specific from general assets and to allocate specific assets so as to avoid opportunism—thus trade secrecy law aligns fairly well with the property-based theory of the firm. At the same time, trade secrecy is costly, requiring cumbersome secrecy measures and detailed confidentiality agreements—in other words, requiring parties to an employment contract to largely foresee the conditions of possible opportunism. Allocation of more complete rights via patent or copyright avoids the need for cumbersome secrecy or for ex ante contractual obligations to establish proprietary rights in information insofar as these systems enable the firm to establish an exclusive right in intangible relationship-specific assets.

In the case of copyright, this outcome has been statutorily formalized under United States law via the work made for hire doctrine. Under this doctrine, individual employees who create copyrightable works while operating within the scope of their employment are not considered to be the authors of those works. Rather, the institution employing the creator becomes the legally recognized author. Thus, the key considerations determining whether a work is made for hire are the statutory criteria of "employee" and "scope of employment."

The Supreme Court has interpreted the statute to require that "employees" be distinguished from independent contractors on the basis of agency principles. The factors used to assess an individual's employment status may include the ability of the worker to accept or decline assignments, the provision of materials by the employer, the duration of the relationship, tax treatment of the worker, and provision of benefits. The test is flexible, with no particular factor designated as dispositive, although some lower courts have given greater weight to certain ubiquitous factors. The scope of employment criterion is similarly judged under agency principles. Relying upon the Restatement of Agency, courts have defined the scope of employment in terms of the type of work the individual was hired to perform, the temporal and locational boundaries of the employment, and the motivation for creating the copyrightable work. Under the third factor, the creative activity must have been motivated at least in part to serve the interests of the employer.

The work is considered by statutory default to be made for hire whenever these criteria obtain. This has several legal consequences, but for the present discussion, the most relevant consequence of work made for hire status is the default ownership of the work. Designating the employer as author means that ownership rests with the firm, subject to contractual transfer, rather than initial employee ownership subject to contractual transfer.

The copyright statute also allows designation of authorship for certain commissioned works. In certain statutorily defined situations, the employee and employer may designate by contract whether the work will be considered a work made for hire. Thus, both ownership and authorship are open to negotiation in these situations. There is a good deal of historical path dependence to the statutory list of commissioned works. Industry organizations must have sufficient political capital to have a type of commissioned work added to the list, or, as in the case of sound recordings' brief appearance on the list, sufficient political capital to effect removal.

But in general, the list contemplates subject matter that is highly collaborative or requires multi-party coordination: motion pictures, compilations, atlases. Such works are among the most likely to be subject to hold-up problems if property rights are fragmented. Such works are also most likely to involve negotiations on the border of the firm, where firms are engaged in recruiting contractors who may sometimes fall inside the firm's transactional boundaries and sometimes outside. In the latter case, market negotiations will be more efficient than entrepreneurial fiat. Some flexibility in adopting or eschewing the property default rule makes sense in these instances, as the parties will know best on which side of the firm boundary a contractor's activity falls.

Of course, copyrightable works created outside an agency relationship may always be assigned to an employer by means of an employment contract. This is the common practice in U.S. patent law, which lacks a work made for hire provision. But reliance on contractual assignment re-introduces the problem of indefiniteness. Copyright, in particular, may foster ambiguities, as the statute requires a signed writing to transfer exclusive rights in a work, purportedly in order to create certainty in transfers. Blanket assignment of works in advance of an individual's general employment may not satisfy this statutory requirement, as the contract would not contemplate the transfer of any specific work. Pre-assignment might be more viable where an individual is engaged to create a specifically contemplated work, and this is indeed the situation under the "commissioned works" categories. One can imagine that a duty to transfer or a nonexclusive license might also be implied from the employment relationship, as has commonly been the case in patent law. Indeed, an implied non-exclusive license would look like patent law's shop right. But all of these permutations create ambiguities that might prove opportune for hold-up.

Work made for hire sidesteps this possibility by creating an allocative default rule. In several dimensions, the conceptual structure of copyright's work made for hire doctrine appears a natural extension from the fiduciary-based principles of trade secrecy reviewed above. The doctrine has developed via application of agency principles, which, like fiduciary principles, have been identified as consonant with property-based theories of the firm. Tellingly, in the work made for hire situation, courts are not typically concerned with the classic agency situations—claims of third parties against a principal for actions of the purported agent or claims by principals against an agent for breach of a fiduciary duty. Rather, agency principles are used to allocate control of what Gordon Smith has called a "critical resource" in which the firm has invested, and in which we would wish to encourage specific investment.

This division appears roughly consonant with the criterion of "asset specificity" under a property-based theory of the firm. The factors and categories defining employee works made for hire, or commissioned works, will tend to define situations where we would want to encourage development of project-specific resources. However, the doctrine as currently constituted may also allocate some nonspecific assets to the control of the firm. This occurs when authorship, and not simply ownership, is allocated to the firm. By erasing the identity of the natural creator, work made for hire removes from the natural author a reputational interest that is otherwise specific to the natural person, and not the firm. This interest is recognized most strongly in nations with strong moral rights regimes and less so in U.S. copyright. But work made for hire denies the natural author even the limited U.S. moral rights regime of the Visual Artists Rights Act. Thus, an "asset specificity" approach suggests that authorship and ownership should perhaps be bifurcated under work made for hire, allocating the reputational interest to the natural author even while assigning default ownership of the work to the firm.

IV. Patent Law

Unlike copyright law, U.S. patent law lacks a work made for hire provision. Although corporations or institutions can be authors, they cannot be inventors; only natural persons can be so designated. This is something of a puzzle, as the need for a default rule of institutional ownership might seem more pronounced in patent law than in copyright. With a few exceptions, such as large motion picture projects, creativity within the traditional subject matter of copyright tends to be relatively low-cost; a modest investment in pencil and paper may suffice. Patent development may sometimes be similarly inexpensive. But corporate research and development is typically expensive, nearly always collaborative, and frequently critical to a firm's survival. These factors should militate toward developing the sort of clear ownership rule that has emerged in copyright, but oddly has not in patent.

Of course, one might argue that patent law has no need for institutional inventors because a patent law work made for hire doctrine is rendered unnecessary by liberal application of contract law. As a matter of employment practice, sophisticated research operations routinely require employees, as part of their employment agreements, to assign patents or other invention rights to the employer. In theory, such "pre-assignment" contracts will create a duty for an employee to assign the rights to whatever may be discovered. But, as a practical matter, in a significant number of situations the contracts either are never executed or fail to anticipate the circumstances of invention, lending support to the concern regarding incomplete contracts. And, unlike copyright, the default rule for patent allocates property rights to the employee rather than to the firm.

In the absence of explicit contractual terms requiring an assignment, an implied duty to assign may be found. Courts have tended to recognize such an implied duty to assign patent rights in situations where an employee hired to solve a problem engages in research, and the invention relates to that effort. Initially, courts recognized this duty only where employees were hired to solve a specific problem, but the rule has evolved to apply to employees engaged to perform general research and development, as well as those engaged for specific research. In each case, invention was part of the employment duties undertaken, so a duty to assign the invention to the employer should come as no surprise to the employee.

In situations where an employee was not hired to engage in research, but developed an invention in which the employer has an interest, courts have assigned to the employer a nonexclusive license known as the "shop right." The shop right, in some cases, is characterized as a contract implied in fact, inferred to exist in situations where the inventor appeared to acquiesce to the employer's use of the invention. In other cases, it appears as a license implied in law, arising from an equitable sense that the employer is entitled to use an invention developed on the employer's time by means of the employer's materials. This implied license evolved into an independent right of the employer, although a limited one: the right is personal and nonexclusive and does not pass by license or assignment.

Although the shop right arises in situations involving non-research employees, inventions subject to the shop right must still relate to the employment. In determining the existence of the shop right, courts have taken into account whether the invention relates to the duties of the employee, whether the invention falls within the scope of the employer's business, and whether the invention was created with materials supplied by the employer or was developed during working hours. When the invention falls within these criteria, the employer enjoys the shop right. The employee need not convey the full interest in the invention, however, due to what the courts perceive as the "peculiar nature of the act of invention," which courts characterize as springing from the employee's own inventive genius, and not from the material contributions of the employer.

This characterization of the inventive process appears out of step with the reality of industrial research and development, but it does suggest a possible reason for the absence of a work made for hire doctrine in patent law: a romantic notion of the inventor inventing in an individual flash of genius may be exerting an even greater influence upon patent doctrine than that of the romantic author upon copyright law. The result of imposing the shop right is to effectively grant the employer a compulsory license at a zero royalty. The lack of exclusivity, however, leaves the employer at the mercy of the employee's residual control of the invention.

Professor Merges has suggested that these employee contract rules might be explained under contractual theories of "penalty defaults." These theories share with property-based theories of the firm a pedigree rooted in concepts of incomplete contract. The general argument suggests that in the face of incompleteness, contractual defaults can play an information-forcing role. Thus, the terms of the contract should be calibrated to penalize the party with the greatest informational advantage if that party is not forthcoming in the contracting process. In the specific case of employee inventions, the implication is that the employer, being the more sophisticated party to the contract, will be more forthcoming in negotiating invention assignments under the threat of a default rule that strips the employer of invention ownership.

But the information-forcing story is a largely unsatisfying explanation for the rules that have developed, supplying at best an incomplete justification of the employee ownership doctrine. There would seem to be relatively little information to force. The employment contract is signed at the beginning of the relationship between employer and employee, when the employer has relatively little information about the employee's abilities, creativity, or work habits. To be sure, the employer will have scrutinized the employee's references, resume, transcripts, and interview responses, but these are likely to provide little indication of the types of inventions the employee may develop, or the circumstances under which she may develop them. For that matter, invention is frequently serendipitous, defying premeditation and fostering the image of the romantic inventor. But we nonetheless would wish to encourage investment in the environment that fosters such serendipity, even if the employer has no advance information about the precise outcome.

The theory of the firm may supply a more complete explanation of employee ownership rules, setting default rules to ensure residual control rather than to force information disclosure. In developing employee ownership rules, courts have essentially dragooned doctrines of implied contract or fiduciary duty into bridging the gaps left by incomplete contracts. The doctrines play precisely the role contemplated by property rights under property-based theories of the firm. The criteria chosen for these employee rules suggest that courts are groping toward the demarcation line of asset specificity. Inventions created by employees specifically employed to do research are perhaps most likely to be those in which the firm has become irrevocably invested. Inventions created by non-research employees, even those using the firm's resources, may be those on which the firm is less likely to be dependent. As such, the latter inventions are less likely candidates for opportunism. As with copyright's work made for hire doctrine, an employee's activity within the "scope of employment" and use of firm resources are indicators of relationships lying within the boundaries of the firm, rather than out in the market.

At the same time, such judicial gap-filling is just that—attempts to fill gaps in incomplete contracts by inferring the existence of unarticulated agreements from the parties' actions, or creating obligations in law that appear to result in more-just outcomes. The solution itself is piecemeal, developed ad hoc, and riddled with discontinuity. While the case law tends toward stable designation of residual rights, it lacks the certainty of an actual property allocation.

This same uncertainty appears in the employment-related aspects of substantive patent law itself, especially in the concept of the "inventive entity." Inventive entities may be composed of a single individual inventor or a group of inventors. Inventive groups composed of different individuals constitute different inventive entities even if their memberships partially overlap. In other words, an inventive entity composed of Alice, Bob, and Carol is not the same inventive entity as that composed of Alice and Carol, or of Ted, Carol, and Bob. Because patent law recognizes natural individuals, and not juridical individuals, as inventors, firms are not typically considered inventive entities. Instead, research groups within a firm are considered inventive entities.

Inventions must be novel and nonobvious to qualify for patent protection. The novelty requirement is typically operationalized under the statute by requiring that the invention cannot have been known or used by "others" in the United States. But different inventive entities, even when including some of the same individuals, might constitute "others" for purposes of the statute. Thus, one research group could generate prior art that might interfere with the patentability of related inventions created by another research group composed of some of the same personnel. The inventive entity comprising Alice, Bob, and Carol might generate prior art against a related invention created by Bob, Carol, and Ted, or even by Bob and Carol. The common knowledge carried by natural persons into each of these inventive entities almost ensures overlapping discoveries, but any difference in membership causes that knowledge to be imputed to a different "inventor." Prior art generated by another overlapping entity could also be used to deny patents on grounds of obviousness, as prior art that qualifies for section 102 novelty purposes may also be used to measure obviousness.

Courts recognizing this problem began by carving out exceptions where the outcome of this rule seemed unduly harsh. Congress has addressed other parts of the problem through piecemeal legislation. For example, Congress has twice amended section 103 of the patent statute in order to exclude categories of subject matter from consideration as prior art if the subject matter and claimed invention were either commonly owned or subject to a common assignment. The statutory amendments track the general rule against an inventor defeating his own novelty. Public knowledge will generally be held as prior art against the inventor, but the rule excludes privately held, proprietary knowledge from the prior art category. This arrangement, as Professor Merges observes, will encourage the inventor to invest in such knowledge prior to the beginning of an inventive project. Such preliminary investigation may be useful in focusing or directing the actual project, making the conduct of the research proper more efficient. Translated into the nomenclature of theories of the firm, such knowledge constitutes a project-specific asset, a type of investment that should be encouraged.

But project-specific knowledge may also provide an opportunity for hold-up if the residual rights in the knowledge are not specifically allocated. The statutory amendments condition prior art consideration of commonly developed subject matter upon whether the invention is "owned by the same person or subject to an obligation of assignment to the same person." Thus the statute itself relies to some extent upon the nature of the employment agreement, and to the extent that such agreements may be incomplete, upon the courts' willingness to plug gaps in the agreement. Under the conditions of employee mobility most likely to lead to hold-up, the inventions of inventive entities with overlapping memberships may frequently not be subject to assignment to the same "person." This suggests a need to fully vest firms with resid-ual inventive rights under a doctrine of "invention made for hire."

Conclusion

I have suggested in this Essay that certain intellectual property doctrines may be better understood when viewed through the lens of property-based theories of the firm, and that certain doctrines, such as work made for hire, might be adjusted in light of such theories. In doing so, I have focused primarily on doctrines of owner-ship allocating residual rights between employees and employers. Other relevant rela-tionships in the intellectual property context, such as partnerships or joint ventures, may also be amenable to such analysis. Similarly, we might profit by analyzing other intellectual property doctrines, such as joint authorship in copyright or double pat-enting, in light of property-based theories of the firm. Additionally, because different forms of intellectual property likely entail different degrees of asset specificity, firm-based comparisons between different regimes of intellectual property may be fruit-ful for understanding the role of intellectual property in the firm. These possibilities suggest that the theory of the firm should be a useful tool in further examination of intellectual property law.

Notes & Questions

1. A number of additional analysts have evaluated the impacts of IP rights on the form and quantity of organizational transactions. As summarized by Mark A. Lemley,

> [n]ew institutional economics theory suggests that patents may affect trans-actions, causing individuals to organize either within or outside firms depending on the scope of ownership rights. *See, e.g.,* Robert P. Merges, *A Transactional View of Property Rights*, 20 Berkeley Tech. L.J. 1477, 1479–89 (2005) (arguing that the "transactional role" of property rights deserves increasing attention); Robert P. Merges, *Intellectual Property Rights and the New Institutional Economics*, 53 Vand. L. Rev. 1857, 1863–64 (2000) (apply-ing a transaction cost theory to show that patents can have an effect on the way firms structure transactions); *see also* Johnathan M. Barnett, *Intellectual Property as a Law of Organization*, 84 S. Cal. L. Rev. 785, 824 (2011) (argu-ing that patents expand an innovator's transactional opportunities); Dan L. Burk, *Intellectual Property and the Firm*, 71 U. Chi. L. Rev. 3, 9 (2004) (argu-ing that the exclusive property rights in patents might prevent opportunism and promote coordination of intangible resources in transactions). *Cf.* Jona-than S. Masur, *Patent Liability Rules as Search Rules*, 78 U. Chi. L. Rev. 187, 187 (2011) ("The infringement doctrines . . . allocate search responsibilities (and search costs) among the same parties. The rules governing patent lia-bility are also rules that govern patent search. The explanation lies with the incentives that these rules create for parties to learn of patents (and infring-ing goods) earlier or later in time."). Whether increasing the number of

transactions is itself desirable is a contested proposition, however. *See* Michael J. Burstein, *Patent Markets: A Framework for Evaluation*, 47 Ariz. St. L.J. 507, 512 (2015) ("[T]ransactional efficiency in itself is neither the goal of the patent system nor of financial markets."); Robert P. Merges, *The Trouble with Trolls: Innovation, Rent-Seeking, and Patent Law Reform*, 24 Berkeley L.J. 1583, 1603 (2009) ("[I]t is quite apparent that we should not be blinded by fears of shutting down or regulating an existing market. The market for patents unrelated to innovation adds nothing to overall social welfare. Rent seekers who employ patents are often said to engage in a form of extortion. When a charge like this is true, conventional wisdom suggests only one efficient (and proper) course of action: shutting the socially wasteful market down." (footnote omitted)).

Mark A. Lemley, *The Surprising Resilience of the Patent System*, 95 Tex. L. Rev. 1, 53 n.247 (2016).

2. Deciding whether a company should "make or buy" new intellectual property (IP) is but one means of advancing company interests through careful IP management. Melvin C. Garner describes the following general framework for evaluating the business advantages of different methods of IP management:

A "value chain" is a high-level model developed and explained by Michael Porter in his 1980 book "Competitive Advantage." The value chain model is used to describe the process by which businesses receive raw materials, add value to the raw materials through various processes to create a finished product, and then sell that end product to customers. Companies conduct value-chain analysis by looking at every production step required to create a product and identifying ways to increase the efficiency of the chain.

The overall goal is to deliver maximum value for the least possible total cost and create a competitive advantage. The value chain concept separates useful activities (which allow the company as a whole to gain competitive advantage) from the wasteful activities (which hinder the company from getting a lead in the market).

Intellectual property ("IP"), including patents, trademarks, copyrights, and trade secrets, can have significant value for a company. Just as the value of IP has been recognized and has been seen as growing in value, companies have also come to realize that the management of IP assets cannot be left to chance, and require close attention by a part of the management of the company. This part of the company's management can be most effective when IP is not considered in isolation, but as an integral part of an overall business strategy. In particular, IP can be considered as part of the company's value chain, and the study of the creation and effective use of IP can be analyzed as a value chain.

Thus, IP is most effective when it is acquired and managed so as to support the business objectives of the company. Companies can use intellectual

property assets to protect market position, gain income or obtain the freedom to operate because its use can be divided according to the relationship
the IP has to the company's key products, geographic locations and objectives. However, the use of IP in business transactions to support a company's
business objectives can also be achieved in a more efficient way by creating
a portfolio of the proper IP assets and then managing those assets in a strategic way to support various business objectives.

Melvin C. Garner, *Designing, Creating and Managing an IP Portfolio* in Practising Law
Institute, IP ISSUES IN BUSINESS TRANSACTIONS 2017 ch. 7 (2017)(available from PLI-
Plus research service).

3. Developing Intellectual Property Through Communities: Open Source Processes as Complements to Corporate Activities

David McGowan, Legal Implications of Open-Source Software

2001 U. ILL. L. REV. 241, 242–45, 285–87 (2001)*

. . . .

The production and distribution of open-source or "free" software presents an
interesting case study of the relationships among the theory of the firm, intellectual
property rights, and contract law. Firms such as Red Hat, Inc. have built businesses
successful enough to win the approval of financial markets and maintain large market capitalizations even though they did not develop the software on which their work
is based, do not employ the programmers who created and maintain it, do not control its future development, and cannot control any improvements they themselves
make to it. One might explain all of this with a standard model in which firms make
money on service, or by arguing that the capital markets for Internet firms have been
irrational. But even if such explanations are true they tell only a part of the story.
They do not explain how the operating system was produced in the first place.

The open-source program behind Red Hat's business model is an operating system that is a variant of Unix. The program consists of a kernel of Linux code and a
shell of code developed by the GNU Project, which together I will refer to as the GNU/
Linux operating system (OS). This operating system is not "owned" by anyone if we
use that term in its conventional sense—to refer to the exclusion of consumers from
using the owner's code as a means of inducing payment for use. The components of
the GNU/Linux OS are copyrighted, and the rights are held by identifiable persons
and firms. Under the open-source model of software production, however, these
rights are used to enforce norms of the open-source community: Code may be freely
copied, modified, and distributed, but only if the modifications (derivative works)
are distributed on these terms as well.

These restrictions are imposed in form agreements such as the GNU General Public License (GNU GPL). The licenses, and the GNU GPL in particular, represent an elegant use of contractual terms and property rights to create social conditions in which software is produced on a model of openness rather than exclusion. The licenses have not been tested in court, and some analysts question whether they create legally binding rights and obligations. It is therefore all the more remarkable that the social structure these licenses support has produced valuable software that is important to the operation of the Internet and, in the case of the GNU/Linux OS, presents a credible source of future competition for Microsoft's operating systems.

The development of the GNU/Linux OS presents an interesting case for exploring the theory of the firm. Following Coase, we often think of firms as institutions in which activity is arranged by authoritative command rather than negotiation. On this view, the firm consists of various inputs controlled by an entrepreneur; the scope of the firm is determined by the cost of in-house production compared to the cost of a market transaction with another firm. Viewing firms as areas of market-like activity organized hierarchically to minimize costs allows us to focus on persons within firms as individual economic agents. A rational actor assumption leads to the fear that these agents will try to do what is best for themselves rather than the firm — shirking work, appropriating opportunities, and the like.

Following Jensen and Meckling, we have given the name "agency costs" to the sum of the costs of agent misbehavior plus costs incurred to discover and stop such misbehavior. One implication of seeing the world in agency-cost terms is that we should expect firms to use various devices to align the interests of agents and firms, and such devices are in fact common. Monitoring agents is expensive for firms; that they are willing to incur such costs suggests that agent opportunism is a real and significant concern. Yet large numbers of programmers have spent time working to develop the GNU/Linux OS, and they generally have not been paid for this work. If conventional technology firms find it necessary to pay salaries and grant options to hire bright programmers who will work long hours designing and coding software, how is it that the GNU/Linux OS has become a commercially viable product that can sustain firms such as Red Hat?

These questions bring us quickly to property rights. The standard explanation for copyright is that it is a reward system in which creators are given a right to exclude others from their work, which allows them to earn returns by charging a fee for access. The reward model sees the revenue creators earn as necessary to induce them to create the work in the first place. The cost of excluding the public from use is tolerated on the assumption that it succeeds in inducing creation that would not otherwise occur. The optimal copyright system is therefore one in which the marginal gain in creativity induced by the rights exceeds the marginal cost of exclusion plus the cost of administering the system. The production of commercially viable software under a regime of free copying, modification, and distribution therefore deserves attention. We should study the case of open-source software production to see whether our existing legal rules could produce socially desirable results at a lower cost.

This case study seeks to answer these questions: How is it that the GNU/Linux OS was produced in the first place? Is the model in which this operating system was produced sustainable? Is it generalizable? What role, if any, does the law play in making such production possible? My answers, in brief, are as follows.

Open-source software production is not about the absence or irrelevance of intellectual property rights. Open-source production instead rests on the elegant use of contractual terms to deploy those rights in a way that creates a social space devoted to producing freely available and modifiable code. In open-source production, property rights are held in reserve to discipline possible violations of community norms. Open-source production therefore does not take place in a true commons, though the low cost of copying and using code combined with the broad grants of the relevant licenses creates a situation that resembles a commons in some respects.

Though individuals or firms may charge for open-source code, the ability of community members to copy and distribute the code severely constrains pricing for the code itself. In many cases, persons who wish to obtain the code without charge may do so. The right to exclude is not actively employed to secure payment for code. Open-source works may therefore be more widely and cheaply available than code produced in a conventional, exclusion-based model.

If other variables—such as the rate of innovation and production—can be held equal, then the social cost associated with open-source production will be lower than the cost associated with conventional production. Whether the rate of innovation and production in general can be held equal is an open question. In some cases open-source production might be slower than conventional production, while in others it might be faster. Rates of development might also vary within projects, with core technical problems being solved faster than problems related to making a program easier for non-expert consumers to use.

The licenses that enforce the property rights on which this structure rests are important to its success. The licenses provide a mechanism for enforcing norms, for distinguishing the open-source community from conventional software production and, in some cases, for providing incentives to programmers who require them. Although the agreements that define open-source code are sometimes said to create de facto property rights or "covenants running with the code," these agreements in fact create a nonexclusive permission to use the code subject to certain conditions. The relevant property right is copyright, which does run with the code, which is why the permissions granted by the licenses must run with the code as well.

"Open-source" or "free" software refers to a type of license and not to the economic characteristics of particular projects. These terms encompass projects involving a million lines of code and projects involving only a thousand lines of code. The Linux kernel and a network printer patch might both be "open-source" software, but that fact shows only that such labels do little analytical work on their own.

The social structures necessary to support production of large, complex projects are different from the structures, if any, necessary to support small projects. It is a mistake to speak generally of the incentives or motivations behind "open-source" or "free" software production. The costs of coordination and working on particular projects must be taken into account. Large, complex projects have to provide some form of reward to induce programmers to contribute their work while accepting the hierarchy necessary to coordinate production. Smaller, less complex projects need not incur coordination costs, and therefore have no need for such payoffs. Programmers may receive reputational payoffs from working on such projects, but they also may work on such projects for personal reasons, such as the sheer enjoyment of programming.

The importance of intellectual property rights and open-source licenses increases as the complexity of projects and the cost of coordinating them increases. Where significant costs have to be sunk to ensure success, more robust legal and social structures are required. Where no such costs are needed, production may succeed in more anarchic structures.

. . . .

[T]he Internet made the open-source production model viable by lowering the costs of coordination. These costs include identifying a problem to be tackled, recruiting programmers, receiving and incorporating their input, and giving reputational or other forms of social returns to programmers who require them. Open-source production may therefore be seen as an example in which high coordination costs led to the creation of firms devoted to conventional production models—the expected Coasean result—but in which a reduction in those costs allowed the formation of less centralized, unconventional "firms" devoted to particular projects. Though hierarchy persists in these firms, the hierarchies appear to be very narrow bands sitting atop a relatively decentralized set of producing agents, a similarly expected Coasean result.

By making widespread distribution of code possible, technology also allows programmers who maximize reputation to reap greater returns from their work. Though programmers on these projects are not subject to fiat control by project maintainers, projects may command a degree of loyalty by providing a forum for programmers to develop their reputational capital or to satisfy an urge to create in a social context supporting that creation. The social structure of the projects themselves is therefore a large part of the point of open-source production. To some and perhaps many programmers, the community of a given project—including its hierarchy—may be as relevant a product of their work as the code itself. For open-source production, therefore, the social consequences of cost-reducing technology are as significant as the ability of such technology to lower the cost of production.

With respect to small projects that do not require extensive coordination, logic and experience to date suggest that the open-source model is sustainable. For interesting problems encountered by a large number of programmers—such as fixes to popular hardware or software—the model is likely to be quite robust. We cannot in the abstract say how sustainable or robust the model is for complex projects that require coordination and, therefore, some form of hierarchy. Complex projects are costlier to produce than simple ones and therefore require stronger supporting structures if production is to go forward. We may say that projects that are important to the community as a whole are more likely to succeed than niche projects; projects that compete with a dominant and aggressive firm are more likely to succeed than those that do not; projects that present interesting technical questions are more likely to succeed than projects that do not; and projects that attract large numbers of developers and provide them with reliable feedback and reputational payoffs are more likely to succeed than projects that do not. In each case, these variables relate to the conditions necessary for the formation of norms that support hierarchical production models outside the traditional firm context.

We may also say that the payoffs these variables provide will have to track, in at least a rough way, the complexity and cost of the project. Greater project complexity implies a more complex hierarchy, which is costlier to administer and carriers a greater risk of error. These factors may reduce some payoffs to programmers. The success of such projects will, in any event, depend on whether their maintainers can minimize coordination costs—importantly including the cost of processing and evaluating information—relative to conventional production. To the degree that software production becomes componentized, for example, coordination costs will decrease and open-source production of components will become more robust. Coordination and assembly of components will still be costly, of course. But Red Hat's viability to date is some evidence that even now firms can provide such services without the active use of exclusion to facilitate conventional software production.

Notes & Questions

1. What are the features of complex software programs that make them suitable for development through open source processes? Are there technologies other than software that can be developed through similar open source communities linked in part by copyright interests and conditional licensing arrangements?

2. Can intellectual property interests other than copyrights—such as patents, trademarks, or trade secrets—be used with selective licensing arrangements to establish and administer open source technology development projects?

B. Intellectual Property Monetization

This subsection describes several steps that holders of valuable IP interests have taken to extract present revenues from their IP and thereby "monetize" the interests. Techniques for IP monetization have been the objects of significant innovation and expanded use in recent years, resulting in not only a number of new methods for extracting value from IP, but also in new techniques for raising and deploying capital in connection with these new IP monetization methods. The following reading describes several of the most common business models for IP monetization.

Federal Trade Commission

Evolving Patent Assertion Business Models

The Evolving IP Marketplace: Aligning Patent Notice and Remedies
with Competition 62–67 (2011)

The . . . secondary market for patents [supporting the monetization of those interests] includes many types of actors. New business models, some of which are increasingly sophisticated and complex, have emerged over the past ten years to capitalize on that market. One panelist [at hearings conducted by the Federal Trade Commission] described 17 business models designed to promote the sale and/or licensing of patent assets. These business models fall into several broad categories, described below, although an individual firm's activities may place it in more than one category. . . .

Patent enforcement and licensing companies. These firms acquire an interest in patents and assert them against operating companies that they claim are infringing. When operating companies refuse to license, the patent enforcement firms assemble the legal and financial resources required to pursue patent litigation. Patent enforcement firms may also file an infringement lawsuit before opening licensing negotiations. Typically, their primary activities are buying, selling, licensing and litigating patents. They do not conduct research, development, technology transfer or commercialization activities. Some patent enforcement firms have been formed by patent litigation attorneys.

One panelist described his firm, Acacia, as an intermediary between small patent holders, who otherwise would lack the resources to enforce their patents, and large alleged infringers. He explained that Acacia facilitates licensing by screening out many patents and "giving inventors realistic expectations" regarding the value of their inventions. While initially, failed start-ups and independent inventors supplied many of the patents purchased by [patent assertion entities (PAEs)], a large portion now originate with practicing entities, including large corporations. As one panelist explained, companies that had been accumulating patents for defensive purposes have recently decided that "they have adequate defenses" and now want "to start generating some return on [their portfolios], either through licensing or through sales."

Litigation finance firms. Litigation finance firms raise money from institutional investors and others to provide capital and other resources to support the patent enforcement efforts of small companies and independent inventors. In exchange, they take a financial interest in patent portfolios. For example, Altitude Capital Partners makes strategic investments in patent owners who are seeking to enforce patents. It also evaluates patent portfolios and designs enforcement approaches. One panelist reported that contingent fee arrangements are becoming less common for small companies, but that institutional investment funds will now partner with small companies and independent inventors to support patent enforcement.

Patent aggregators. Patent aggregators build very large portfolios of purchased patents and implement a licensing strategy to earn returns for investors. The most prominent aggregator is Intellectual Ventures (IV), which was founded in 2000 and began operations in 2003. IV has reportedly amassed more than 30,000 patents. One panelist estimated that IV accounted for half of all patent purchases over the past few years, and that its recent reduction in purchases had significantly diminished demand in the market for patents.

Intellectual Ventures makes patent acquisitions through funds, which have reportedly raised $5 billion, and returned $1 billion to investors to date. The main revenue stream for the funds reportedly comes from partnership or licensing fees paid by large IT companies. While not ruling out legal actions, IV emphasized through much of its history that it always reached voluntary licensing agreements. However, in 2009, it began transferring patents to third parties to bring litigation. And at the end of 2010, IV began enforcing patents directly, bringing several high-profile actions against major segments of the high tech industry.

Some industry participants have expressed concerns that IV's ability to assert a virtual armada of patents gives it an unusually strong bargaining position. One panelist described IV as betting on a "volume strategy," based on approaching potential licensees with a large portfolio and asking them "how much do you want to bet that at least one of them is really good." Panelists suggested that it would not be pragmatic to refuse to license similar offers.

Defensive buying funds. Responding to the rise of IV and other PAEs, "defensive aggregators" acquire patents on behalf of a group of potential PAE targets. Participating firms pay a fee to support patent purchases and the fund licenses back the patents to them. The purchases take patents "off the street" by preventing a PAE from acquiring and asserting the patents against members. The defensive buying funds generally resell the patents into the marketplace, subject to the licenses, to reduce members' costs and prevent non-members from free-riding on their activities. One panelist explained that this business model can help IT firms manage their potential liability and take advantage of arbitrage opportunities in the market for patents. Such defensive buying funds include Allied Security Trust, and RPX (Rational Patent Exchange). One panelist reports that Allied Security Trust has been "successful" in helping to address the volume of patents on the market. RPX reported in 2010 that it had 35 members and had spent "$200 million to acquire more than 1,300 patents and patent rights" covering IT technology.

Intermediaries. Licensing agents, brokers and other consultants have emerged to help clients navigate the complex patent landscape and make deals. They help patent owners find licensees and buyers. Other mechanisms, such as patent auction houses and online technology exchanges, also attempt to connect patent owners and potential customers with varying levels of success.

Notes & Questions

1. Risk asymmetries between IP holders and infringers explain many of the IP monetization strategies and associated IP transfers undertaken in recent years. The

implications of such asymmetries in the context of patent enforcement include the following:

> [A]symmetrical risks drive patent transactions. That is to say, that a major force (if not "the" major force) behind patent licensing and assignment transactions is the existence of patent rights imbalances as measured in terms of economic value. [T]here are at least two types of asymmetry: exposure asymmetry (as in the case of [non-practicing entities that hold patents but do not make related goods]) and portfolio asymmetry (as illustrated by the case of Google's experience with Android). Exposure asymmetry occurs when a party who does not have an exposed business (i.e. one that could theoretically infringe a patent) holds patents that are potentially infringed by another. Portfolio asymmetry occurs when both parties to a potential patent infringement action have exposed businesses, but one party effectively "outguns" the other owing to an imbalance in the size of relevant patent they hold compared to the other party. Each of these asymmetry types have had their own market reaction and call for their own strategies (which in some cases overlap and in others do not).

> One effective reaction to exposure asymmetry is to use the market to deprive the other side of unencumbered patents that are useful against you. . . . More recently this strategy plays itself out through defensive patent aggregators that use economies of scale to purchase patents that could otherwise be asserted against their members. . . .

> Portfolio asymmetry is a bit more straightforward. In the past portfolio asymmetry was commonly handled through cross licensing, often including some number of years of future patent filings, with any actual and expected differences in exposure being compensated for by a balancing payment to the party perceived to have the stronger relevant portfolio. . . . More recent additions to the available mechanisms for handling portfolio asymmetry include going to the market itself in a "just in time" manner to purchase relevant patents. In an even pseudo-open open patent market portfolio asymmetry has the interesting effect of creating increasing demand for patents that read against an entity as a function of that entities aggressiveness in attempting to exploit the asymmetry.

Marc A. Ehrlich & Richard M. Ludwin, *Caveat Inventor: How Patent Monetization Is Evolving and Why You Should Care* in Practising Law Institute, IP MONETIZATION 2014: MAXIMIZE THE VALUE OF YOUR IP ASSETS 261, 275–276 (2014)(available from PLI-Plus research service).

2. Companies interested in monetizing their IP interests are sometimes aided by businesses that provide related financing. For example, private equity firms have supplied financing for litigation needed to support IP enforcement efforts and related IP licensing programs:

> [C]ompanies (whether operating or non-operating) sometimes do not have, or are unwilling to make, the resources available to pursue a licensing and/

or an enforcement program that will yield a sufficient financial gain to justify the investment. This is particularly true where business distraction costs combined with outside counsel's legal fees could potentially dwarf the revenues generated. A number of [private equity firms (PEFs)] have responded to this issue by offering funds to companies and law firms to help pay for the investment needed (e.g., expertise of outside counsel) to pursue these IP monetization efforts.

One of the most recent trends involves a PEF establishing a fund for the law firm to pay for a certain percentage of legal fees and disbursements associated with IP monetization efforts in exchange for a pre-negotiated return based on the amount of funds used by the firm. This allows the firm to offer companies substantial discounts on their fees in exchange for the company giving up some of the upside in the event of a financial recovery. For example, a monetary recovery would be split among the PEF, client and law firm based on their respective pre-set negotiated percentages. The PEF gets paid a pre-set amount out of the law firm's percentage. This arrangement is ultimately a win-win-win for all parties who took an interest and risk in the IP monetization opportunity.

. . . .

The elegance of this model, from the perspective of the PEF, is that the risk, similar to other investments, is diversified and not tied to a single company, licensing effort or litigation, as was the case in past models. Instead, the risk is spread across several matters and IP monetization efforts such that a single monetization effort within the portfolio could by itself pay for the investment. For example, if there are three monetization efforts underway, two of those efforts could yield no revenues, but one could be large enough to cover the costs of the other two. Under this scenario, the PEF would obtain its expected return.

Mark Baghdassarian, *The Latest Trend in Private Equity Funding of IP Monetization*, LEXOLOGY, October 14, 2013.

3. IP sales marketplaces to support IP ownership transfers have been created through online sales platforms. For example, the Ocean Tomo Bid-Ask™ Market (OTBA) was built to further enhance Intellectual Property (IP) liquidity and transaction transparency. OTBA provides a platform to purchase or sell patents and patent applications globally. This market is supported by Ocean Tomo Transactions and affiliate international brokers. Ocean Tomo, LLC, Ocean Tomo Bid-Ask Market, http://www.oceantomobidask.com/bid-ask_about.html (last visited 11/14 /2017).

4. The popularity of the secondary market for patent transfers has tracked the perceived liquidity of patents. As analyzed by Chris Donegan and Matthew Vella of Invention Capital Associates, this has driven significant swings in patent marketplace popularity:

Liquidity for infringed patents emerges as the driver for growth

The most attractive patents for the secondary market were those with the most predictable licensing value. These were patents where infringement, damages and invalidity risks could be managed. In an adaptation of modern portfolio theory, the creation of resilient multi-patent portfolios emerged as a primary risk management strategy for licensors to hedge against potential failures of individual patents. However, adding resilience to portfolios was costly.

Smaller companies or individual inventors could not afford the legal costs of monetization and lacked the appropriate risk management skills that fuelled this market. For these patent owners, secondary market liquidity was the only way to generate value from their IP rights. But the 'little guy' was by no means the only provider of inventory, and multinational companies seeking to maximize shareholder returns also sought to monetize both core and non-core patents. Licensing revenue was pure bottom line for patent owners large and small.

When Google, Apple, Samsung and others gate-crashed the smartphone market between 2007 and 2010, even more liquidity was injected into the secondary market. The smartphone wars violently disrupted what Sanford Bernstein called the "oligopolistic Gentleman's Club" of telecommunications companies. In a technology built on a high density of innovations, progenitor patents held great value and portfolios traded at unprecedented prices as speculators followed the money to help smartphone vendors shape their defensive strategies.

Chris Donegan & Matthew Vella, *The Secondary Market in Patents: What Went Right, What Went Wrong and How to Fix It*, Intellectual Asset Management (10/12/2017), https://www.lexology.com/library/detail.aspx?g=eb9a1c79-3da0-4371 -9171-ded3d3a62141 (last visited 11/16/2017).

However, by 2017, patent liquidity had diminished for a variety of reasons affecting the popularity of patent marketplaces:

The reduction in market liquidity arose from three changes that collectively offset the all-important opportunity scale developed by [non-practicing entities (NPEs)] over the past decade. These are well known, but perhaps not previously expressed in this manner:

Net present value discounting — the realizable financial (non-operating) value for patents was reduced:

> damages were reduced;
> the credible threat of injunctions was removed;
> subject-matter restrictions were imposed (software);
> inter partes reviews increased time-to-money by 12 to 18 months;

district court judgments were reversed by the Federal Circuit; and antitrust scrutiny for NPEs was increased.

Increase in weighted average cost of capital—the cost of realizing value was increased in terms of time, money and risk as the number of patents that could trade decreased:

reduction in portfolio scale and size increased concentration risk; more binary portfolio outcomes made returns more volatile; increase in unit valuation and realization costs per patent drove up [capital expenditures needed to acquire patents]; and fee shifting for bringing and maintaining weak cases removed the valuation floor.

Change in market dynamics—the fundamental nature of the market had changed with reference to what was traded, why and how:

reduction of asymmetric threat to incumbents reduced demand for patent rights; market migration towards technology away from patents reduced supply; consolidation of intermediaries and reduction in market capacity also reduced supply; focus was placed back on strategic versus non-core assets; and [reductions in activity by Intellectual Ventures] and many vendors for strategic and operational reasons wounded the market.

Id.

These changes resulted in reductions in the numbers of patents seen as good candidates for monetization and associated transfers in patent marketplaces, as well as a sense that larger amounts of capital were needed to participate in those marketplaces. In response to these changes, the secondary market's largest participants gradually scaled down their operations and the secondary market itself saw reduced activity. *See id.*

What characteristics and capabilities of online marketplaces are likely to aid in IP transfers and asset liquidity? What features of these marketplaces are ill-suited to IP transfers?

C. Intellectual Property Securitization

Intellectual property securitization involves the use of a stream of royalty payments generated by the licensing of intellectual property to pay interest amounts due on bonds. By selling bonds specifying that future interest payments will be made in this way, an intellectual property holder can realize the value of an intellectual property interest at the time of the bond sales rather than waiting for later royalty payments. The following reading describes the use of this technique in the music industry, as well as some of the complex business relationships and potential pitfalls involved.

Hewson Chen, Don't Sell Out, Sell Bonds: The Pullman Group's Securitization of the Music Industry

2 Vand. J. Ent. L. & Prac. 161 (2000)*

If opposites attract, then perhaps there is an explanation for the unlikely marriage between rock 'n roll and the bond market. One can only wonder what strange magnetism is powerful enough to wed the "youthful, wild and unpredictable" rock culture with the world of "dry, cautious, and mind-numbingly technical" investment finance. Indeed, some strange voodoo magic has luminaries like David Bowie, James Brown, and Holland-Dozier-Holland all singing the same tune, and "securitization" is its name.

Securitization is the selling of debt to investors. In general, securitization converts future income streams like credit card receivables or auto loan payments to present in-pocket cash. Notably, this transformation from future income to current wealth gives the issuer of the security immediate access to cash at less cost than other financing methods such as bank loans. In the 1970s, this technique was applied to the housing industry, and since then, securitization has evolved into greater varieties of income streams, including medical insurance, typhoon insurance, and unused airline tickets. The application of securitization in the entertainment industry, however, remains largely untested.

Is securitization a viable model for financing intellectual properties in the music industry? David Pullman, Founder, Chairman, and CEO of The Pullman Group, LLC, thinks so. In 1997, Pullman, as managing director of Fahnestock & Company's Structured Asset Sales Group, successfully orchestrated the issuance of $55 million in bonds backed by singer David Bowie's royalty and publishing income. To date, Pullman has proven the viability of this concept by issuing similar bonds for legendary artists like James Brown, Holland-Dozier-Holland, and Ashford & Simpson. These music legends are interested in securitizing because these deals promise several benefits to the established artist. The securitization deal is more attractive than a traditional royalty/advance agreement because the artist retains 100 percent of the copyright, generates an immediate monetary windfall, and saves money on taxes because the sale of the bonds is not treated as a taxable event. Securitization deals are more attractive than bank loans. Unlike bank loans, which are short-term in nature and involve a floating rate, Pullman's securities are fixed rate, non-recourse, and long-term in nature, translating into less risk for the artist. Also, bank loans typically only yield about one-tenth what the artist can get through securitization.

According to the Pullman Group, the benefits of securitization translate into at least 20 percent extra income for the artist.

This increased amount of money up-front can result in additional indirect advantages. "By gaining control of the net sum of future royalties today, the artist can reinvest and diversify," making the artist's wealth less dependent on the success or failure of any specific market. Moreover, the ability to control the net value of future royalties today facilitates estate planning, so the artist's heirs will have money available to pay taxes without being forced to sell off the artist's catalog.

As the innovator who first married securitization to star power, David Pullman is one of few financiers who can successfully structure such deals, and, in fact, such bonds bear his name in industry vernacular. The overall idea behind a "Pullman Bond" is that the artist makes money up front by selling bonds to investors. The interest on these bonds is then paid with the income stream resulting from certain assets, typically a catalog of songs.

A number of steps ensure that risks to the investor are minimized. The income producing assets are insulated from possible bankruptcy proceedings by transferring the assets temporarily from the artist to a special purpose vehicle ("SPV"). Credit enhancements such as cash reserve accounts, financial guarantees, letters of credit, or default insurance may be used to reduce the risk of default of payment on the bonds. Finally, an artist's works may be pooled with the works of other artists to diversify "the risk that a particular artist's popularity may decrease and affect future royalty payments negatively."

However, there are many critics who remain skeptical of entertainment securitization. Some of the banks that have tried to enter the entertainment securitization market now dismiss the deals to be "more about hype than value." Pullman regards these criticisms as grumblings from disgruntled competitors. "When I did the Bowie deal people thought I was crazy," he notes. "Three months after I started it, other people tried to copy me. Six months later, it was everyone else's idea. We keep going at it. Other people have tried and failed."

. . . .

The main reason behind Pullman's heavy market share of the music bonds industry is that "the assets are complex." As he observes, it is a "world-wide industry" with "world-wide cash flows." For example, the Bowie deal took months to devise, cost over a million dollars, and resulted in a thousand pages of documentation. But even with the experience of numerous music securitization deals, Pullman notes that these transactions are still difficult to orchestrate: "I thought that after doing a series of these deals, things would get easier, and they haven't. So that's what's amazing about it all—that they don't become cookie cutter."

Indeed, the difficulty of creating deals and the few successes of music securitization may well limit music bonds to the fringes of the industry. Some commentators have said that music securities are "lousy investments," where "the seller is smarter than the buyer." This potential information asymmetry also raises policy concerns. Securitization shifts the risk of success or failure from the record company and publisher onto the investor, who is in arguably the worst position to assess the odds. Instead, the risk of a particular catalog is perhaps most efficiently allocated to record companies and publishers, who have ready access to income stream histories and industry tracking data. Pullman counters this criticism by pointing out that his focus is different from that of the average record company. "[We deal with] people who are already successful and are legends with a steady income stream, and, in general, the majority of artists in a record company's roster don't fit that example. We're dealing with a select few, the cream of the crop, in terms of artists that have longevity."

This focus on artists of legendary stature also allows Pullman to avoid the uncertainty of predicting the popularity of entertainers in a fickle market. With regard to songs that have achieved "classic" status, income streams are relatively stable. For example, "with Ziggy Stardust it's nearly 30 years later and we know if it's still producing income 30 years later—remember with artists, 90 percent of the income comes in the first 6 months after release—so if this song's producing this 30 years out, that's what it should do going forward."

But with business limited to artists of legendary status, some think that the real money to be made from intellectual property securitization lies outside of the music industry. In 1997, an attorney who worked with Pullman on the Bowie Bond deal observed that "the music business is a limited market. . . . But if you can get to the software companies, then this could be a huge business." However, Pullman remains optimistic about the future of music bonds. Despite the music industry's focus on short-term artists with one- to three-record careers and the implication that the pool of viable securitization candidates is dwindling, Pullman maintains:

> We're just at the beginning of [music securitization]. What [the increasing focus on short-term artists] is really doing is making catalogs like James Brown, David Bowie, Ashford and Simpson, or Holland-Dozier-Holland . . . more valuable, because there are fewer people creating catalogs that have standards, or that have long careers or that have created a new sound. So we think that's better, that we have these gems that don't really have to compete with a lot of the different artists that are out there. . . . James Brown doesn't compete against a new artist. In fact, James Brown, the Isley Brothers, these guys are sampled over and over again by [new artists]. So [are] Ashford and Simpson.

Furthermore, the slow adoption of music securitization should be no surprise. Pullman points out that traditional securities markets also encountered hesitation and skepticism in their infancy:

> I started when there was not one auto loan or credit card security. Asset-backed securities were brand new, [but] it kept evolving. Newer and newer

asset classes. . . . Around 1990, not all banks did securitization, and a lot of banks questioned it. In the year 2000, there's not one bank that doesn't securitize its assets. They were all naysayers about securitization, the banks, just the way that they are about entertainment royalty securitization.

Over time, Pullman predicts, music securitization will become more commonplace, and there is some indication that Pullman has successfully raised awareness and acceptance about these more progressive bonds. Though the Bowie deal was partially guaranteed by EMI Records, the later Holland-Dozier-Holland deal was struck without any similar guarantee.

> I think that each year we move further and further down the line. So in terms of the first deal with Bowie, people said that we couldn't repeat it . . . that it was a one-time event, and that it was unique, that he had his record masters and publishing and the writer's share. And now we're able to obtain ratings on deals that are just based on the writer's share, probably something that most artists still retain. . . . So, therefore, I think that each year we'll go further and further out on the curve. And then at some point in time meet with what the record companies and publishers have traditionally done as a business. Right now I think [record companies and entertainment bond firms] complement each other more. But the future is that, what I hear in terms of feed-back, is that artists would much rather do this deal than sell [their works]. And with the consolidation of the industry, artists want the flexibility to go where they can.

One of the reasons why securitization will likely be viewed with greater acceptance is that securitization provides a potential win-win opportunity for record companies as well. Specifically, as a result of securitization,

> [record companies] have more money in their coffers to offer other artists, as opposed to all of their money going out to one artist . . . So if we're talking about a $30 million James Brown deal or a $55 million David Bowie deal, [obtaining that money from the sale of bonds instead of from record company advances] gives these companies more money to put out for new artists. Think of it this way: 55 million is the equivalent of 55 one million dollar advances, 550 hundred thousand dollar advances, and 5500 ten thousand dollar advances. So you can sign on more new artists. . . .

At least for now, the proponents of music securitization are in a dilemma. Securitization promises to revolutionize the music industry, yet it is still so obscure that only one firm, the Pullman Group, has been able to make it work. Even so, the pro-artist values advanced by music securitization should be encouraged in an industry where record companies of increasing size flex overwhelming bargaining power over artists. Securitization remains intensely specialized and somewhat untested in the music business. But does it also promote democracy and diversity in the recording industry? "Definitely," says David Pullman, the only man who, so far, seems to be able to make the bonds sing.

Notes & Questions

1. Assuming that a securitization arrangement calls for payment of bond interest at a fixed rate (say 5%) out of an artist's song publishing royalties, what is the resulting allocation of risks and opportunities between the artist and the bond holders? Why do artists tend to prefer this type of arrangement over payments of cash for outright assignments of their royalty interests in particular works?

2. What features of an intellectual property interest make it a good candidate for securitization? Will securitization — which has thus far been used mostly for royalties from copyright licensing — work equally well with royalties from licensing other types of intellectual property interests?

3. Securitization efforts involving IP royalty streams have emerged regarding remarkably diverse types of IP. One of the most unusual such efforts has securitized the income potential (including IP royalty income) of professional athletes. In 2014, Fantex, a San Francisco start-up company, began selling stock linked to the future income of several professional football players. The first offering involved stock linked to the income of Vernon Davis, then a 30-year old tight end playing for the San Francisco 49ers. Fantex paid Davis $4 million upfront, with the amount later recouped by the company via sales of shares of stock to the public. Davis agreed to give Fantex 10 percent of his future income from playing contracts, corporate endorsements, and any related post-playing-career activities such as broadcasting jobs or book deals. Fantex is entitled to keep 5 percent of the income it receives from Davis and the rest is allocated to the shareholders to be paid as possible dividends. In its dependency in part on IP related to endorsements and book revenues, this is a hybrid form of IP and other income securitization. The primary advantage of these arrangements for players is the opportunity to gain substantial upfront payments while the scope of their future careers and associated payments are in doubt because of uncertainty regarding their professional success and continued good health. Payments such as those made by Fantex provide short-term certainty to the players that the players' team contracts do not because these contracts are generally not guaranteed. Of course, the associated risks of early contract termination or production of low income levels for other reasons are partially transferred to shareholders who acquire interests tied to the players' future income. Fantex completed a second offering of stock linked to a professional football player in mid-2014 and had another such deal in the works at that time. *See* William Alden, *Initial Pigskin Offering*, New York Times, August 31, 2014, at 12–13.

4. A number of very large intellectual property (IP) securitization transactions have been completed with a variety of types of IP and in a diverse range of industries. Some of the largest transactions include the following:

> Domino's Pizza, Dunkin Brands (Dunkin' Donuts and Baskin Robbins brands), Sears Holdings Corp. (Kenmore, Craftsman and Diehard brands), IHOP and Applebee's each closed securitizations based on their brands in transactions worth $1.85 billion, $1.7 billion, $1.8 billion, $200 million and $1.79 billion respectively, during 2006 and 2007.

. . .

DRI Capital closed (i) a $220 million securitization of eighteen bundled pharmaceutical royalty interests based on eleven pharmaceutical products in December 2012 and (ii) a $450 million securitization in June 2014. In the latter case, the collateral is royalty revenue from 31 royalty streams on 14 patent-protected drugs and technologies.

. . .

In August 2014, Miramax secured a $25 million credit facility and $250 million securitization, which it plan[ed] to use to pay down debt and to support its television and film ventures. The company used its 700-film library to secure the notes.

Jose A. Esteves, *Overview of IP Monetization Techniques* in Practising Law Institute, IP MONETIZATION AND INVESTMENT 2017: MAXIMIZE YOUR FINANCIAL AND STRATEGIC OPTIONS ch. 1 (2017)(available from PLI-Plus research service; footnotes omitted).

D. Insurance Aiding Intellectual Property Owners

1. Intellectual Property Enforcement Insurance

Insurance payouts aiding intellectual property owners in pressing infringement claims can be important business tools in realizing the value of intellectual property interests. Intellectual property enforcement insurance (most commonly issued in the form of patent enforcement insurance) compensates insured parties for the costs of litigation needed to enforce infringement claims. Insurance policies covering risks of incurring litigation expenses to enforce the policyholder's own interests are sometimes referred to as legal expenses, offensive, abatement, or enforcement policies. *See* Leib Dodell and Kimberly Cauthorn, *Using Insurance to Manage Patent Risks,* INTELLECTUAL ASSET MANAGEMENT, March/April 2011, at 37, 40. A more limited form of litigation-related insurance (providing partial protection against the deterrent threats of potential litigation expenses) protects patent holders against losses due to fee-shifting awards in patent lawsuits. *See, e.g.,* Athena FSP, *Patent Fee Shifting Protection to Protect Patent Owners under Section 285 and Proposed Congressional Reforms* (2017), http://www.athenafsp.com/ (last visited 11/14/2017).

Insurance compensation for litigation expenses can ensure that the sometimes extreme burdens of rights enforcement litigation will not cause intellectual property owners to hesitate in asserting infringement claims. Rather, with the support provided by intellectual property enforcement insurance, intellectual property owners can realize the full value of their interests by compelling parties to stop infringing activities that compete with and undercut the commercial activities of the intellectual property owners. In a similar fashion, enforcement insurance can help rights holders to realize the full value of their interests by assisting (through actual or viably threatened litigation) in efforts to force infringers to pay licensing fees for their infringing activities. Intellectual property enforcement insurance can also spread the costs of rights enforcement over extended periods during which insurance premiums are paid rather than having the full costs of litigation fall on an intellectual property owner in the particular period when litigation occurs.

Additional considerations affecting the desirability of intellectual property enforcement insurance include the following:

Advantages

1. Insurance will deter infringement because the owner of an intellectual property interest will be perceived as having the financial power to protect the interest;

2. Insurance reduces pressure on the interest owner to settle infringement suits to minimize litigation expenses;

3. Insurance may encourage investment in companies holding intellectual property interests by reducing shareholders' apparent risks; and

4. Insured interests may be easier to license because licensees will perceive that the interest holders will be likely to pursue infringers and that licensees are therefore obtaining opportunities to use the licensed intellectual property that will not be available to others absent similar licenses and associated royalty payments.

Disadvantages

1. Insurance premiums are often based on the number of intellectual property interests held rather than the likelihood of enforcement litigation;

2. Policyholders must periodically update their list of covered intellectual property interests or risk having uncovered litigation expenses related to uncovered interests;

3. Disputes may arise between policyholders and their insurers about the scope of coverage, leading to further litigation costs;

4. Insurance may encourage policy holders to litigate weak infringement claims; and

5. Money spent on premiums might better be spent on new product development and marketing.

See generally Bruce E. Burdick, *Patent Insurance, Is It Worth It?* (2002), https://web
.archive.org/web/20040810175028/http://burdicklawfirm.tripod.com/insurart.htm
(last visited 11/14/2017).

2. Other Insurance Benefiting Intellectual Property Owners

Intellectual property owners may also wish to use other types of insurance to protect aspects of the value of their interests or to address risks of loss in commonly encountered intellectual property transactions. Two types of insurance benefiting these rights holders address risks associated with findings that intellectual property interests are invalid or otherwise unenforceable and risks arising out of merger and acquisition transactions. In the context of protecting the value of patent interests, these sorts of insurance policies can cover the following risks:

> **Patent asset value and revenue protection**
>
> Insurance policies can . . . be obtained to protect against the first-party financial loss of the insured caused by a legal finding of invalidity, successful title challenges or unenforceability of the covered patent(s). Variations of this coverage have been offered as a way to protect third parties' financial interests in the patent, such as those of investors and lenders. . . .
>
> **Representations and warranties, and other M&A-related coverage**
>
> In certain merger and acquisition (M&A) transactions where representations and warranties insurance is required in order for the transaction to be completed, carriers will sometimes cover the IP-related representations and warranties, including representations and warranties regarding no knowledge of infringement, validity/enforceability and title. Alternatively, a separate IP representations and warranties policy may be purchased. Such insurance covers legal expenses and damages/settlement associated with the breach of IP-related representations and warranties made in the context of the sale of a business, products, technology or intellectual property.

Leib Dodell and Kimberly Cauthorn, *Using Insurance to Manage Patent Risks*, Intellectual Asset Management, March/April 2011, at 37, 40.

E. Valuable Transfers of Intellectual Property

1. Intellectual Property Auctions

Where an intellectual property owner cannot commercialize an interest through the production of related products — either because the interest falls outside of the owner's main line of business or because the owner has gone bankrupt and has terminated normal business operations — the owner (or a successor such as a bankruptcy trustee) may seek to dispose of the intellectual property interest through an auction aimed at obtaining the maximum price for an assignment of the interest. Auctions of intellectual property interests initiated by interest owners are now conducted through a number of Internet sites. *See, e.g.,* Idea Buyer, http://www.idea buyer.com/ (last visited 11/14/2017); IP Offerings, https://www.ipofferings.com /patent-auction.html (last visited 11/14/2017); Ocean Tomo, LLC, http://www .oceantomo.com/auctions/ (last visited 11/14/2017); Patent Auction.com, http:// www.patentauction.com/ (last visited 11/14/2017).

The ICAP Patent Brokerage and Ocean Tomo, LLC, a merchant banking firm focusing on intellectual property assets, have conducted a number of live auctions of intellectual property interests. The results have varied. In the most successful of these auctions conducted in 2008, 85 intellectual property lots were offered, 53 sold, and intellectual property sellers realized $19,629,500. In another auction conducted in 2006, sales of 26 lots netted intellectual property sellers $23,903,000. However, not all of the live auctions have achieved such high sales volumes and substantial revenues. *See* B. Collins, *Going. Going. Gone?*, Inventors Digest (October 21, 2009), https://www.inventorsdigest.com/articles/going-going-gone/ (last visited 11/14/2017).

Government agencies have used auctions as means to convert corporate intellectual property into cash, with the goal of using the resulting cash to satisfy corporate obligations to the government. For example, the Internal Revenue Service (IRS) conducted a live auction of the domain name DoctorTalk.com due to nonpayment of taxes. United States Department of the Treasury, Internal Revenue Service, *Notice of Public Auction Sale: Domain Name and Website Known as DoctorTalk.com on November 11, 2008*, https://web.archive.org/web/20081210090555/http://www.treasury .gov/auctions/irs/ocok_inte_3148.htm (last visited 11/14/2017). The auction was conducted with the assistance of appraisal and marketing experts from IPAuctions, Inc. *See DoctorTalk.com Website to Be Sold by IRS and IPAuctions* (9/15/2008), http://www .domaininformer.com/news/press/080915DoctorTalkcomWebsite.html (last visited 11/14/2017); Marie Price, *The DoctorTalk.com Web Site and Domain Name to be Auctioned Off by the IRS*, Okla. City Journal Record, 9/17/2008, 2008 WLNR 25761311.

Bankruptcy trustees and courts have also shown interest in intellectual property auctions as means to maximize the sale value of a bankrupt firm's assets and thereby increase the amount of funds available to bankruptcy claimants. In one case where this technique was used, the patents and other business assets of e-business applications developer Commerce One, Inc., were separately sold at auction in late 2004. The patents realized $15.5 million, while the non-patent assets, sold to a different party, only realized $4.1 million. These results provide concrete evidence of the degree to which the value of intellectual property held by a bankrupt high-tech company can far exceed the value of the company's other business assets. *See generally* Renee Boucher Ferguson, *Commerce One Patents Auctioned Off* (Dec. 8, 2004), http://www .eweek.com/c/a/Web-Services-Web-20-and-SOA/Commerce-One-Patents-Auctioned -Off/ (last visited 11/14/2017). However, at least one commentator has criticized this result as reflecting an improper trend toward viewing patents as weapons with disruptive value independent of associated product production capabilities. *See* Jason Schultz, *When Dot-Com Patents Go Bad: The Auction of Commerce One's Intellectual Property Demonstrates that Patents are Worth More Today as Weapons Than Anything Else. That's Wrong*," https://www.salon.com/2004/12/13/patent_reform/ (Dec. 13, 2004) (last visited 11/14/2017).

Following a particularly large-scale patent auction conducted in 2011, bankruptcy courts in the United States and Canada approved a sale of a portfolio of more than 6,000 patents held by Nortel Networks Corporation (Nortel). This sale was part of more than two years of bankruptcy proceedings winding up and liquidating

Nortel's operations due to the company's insolvency. The auction of Nortel's patents proceeded in two phases.

In the first phase, an initial or "stalking horse" bid was selected through competitive bidding. Google, Inc., was the prevailing party in this first phase, offering to pay approximately $900 million for Nortel's patents. Google agreed that this amount would serve as the opening bid in the second phase of the auction. If no higher bid was obtained in this second phase, Google was obligated to purchase the patents at the opening bid price. However, the terms of the first phase of the auction provided that, if Google's bid was bested in the second phase of the auction, Google would receive $29 million as a consolation payment for being the winning bidder in the first phase and serving as a "stalking horse" attracting additional bidders by identifying the potential value of the Nortel patents. *See* Peg Brickley, *Nortel Gets Court Nod for Auction of Patents*, WALL STREET JOURNAL, May 3, 2011, at B5.

In the second phase of the auction, Google was not the prevailing party. A consortium of high tech companies including Apple, Microsoft, Research in Motion, Sony, Ericsson, and EMC outbid Google and Intel and acquired the Nortel patents. The winning bid by the consortium was $4.5 billion in cash. The sale of Nortel's patents via this auction raised more money for the benefit of Nortel's creditors than the sales in the company's bankruptcy proceedings of all of the rest of Nortel's assets combined. *See* Chris V. Nicholson, *Nortel Sells Last Patent Assets for $4.5 Billion to Alliance Including Apple and Microsoft*, N.Y. TIMES, at B3 (July 2, 2011).

Procedures for auctioning IP interests must address difficult problems, including providing information to potential bidders on auctioned interests, determining whether potential bidders have the resources needed to follow through on their bids, specifying effective means for considering competing bids, and establishing steps through which successful bidders will receive title to auctioned interests. The reading below describes the procedures used in one court-supervised auction of a bankrupt company's intellectual property assets.

In re: Commerce One, Inc.

United States Bankruptcy Court for the Northern District of California

Case No. 04-32820 DM

DENNIS MONTALI, BANKRUPTCY JUDGE

ORDER APPROVIING OVERBID PROCEDURES AND RELATED MATTERS RE SALE OF CERTAIN ASSETS OF THE DEBTORS

. . . .

EXHIBIT B: BIDDING PROCEDURES RE WEB SERVICES PATENTS

The following constitute the bidding procedures ("Bidding Procedures") established by the Court for persons wishing to present an offer with respect to the Purchased Assets comprised of the Debtors' Web Services Patents:

i. On or before November 12, 2004, by 5:00 p.m. prevailing Pacific time (the "Bid Deadline"), any bidder ("Bidder") must submit its bid ("Bid") providing an aggregate purchase price consisting of cash in an amount not less than $1,000,000. Bids may not be subject to any contingency for financing, due diligence or otherwise and must provide for a closing no later than the fifth (5th) business day following the date on which any agreed closing conditions have been satisfied or are waived (the "Closing Date").

ii. The Bid must be in writing setting forth all material terms and conditions of the Bid, and be addressed to [several specified attorneys] (the "Bid Notification Parties")[.]

Upon receipt of any Bid, Debtors' counsel shall also provide a copy of the Bid to any other bidders, to counsel for the creditors' committee ("Committee") formed in the cases, and if requested, to the Office of the United States Trustee.

iii. A Bid must be accompanied by a good faith cash deposit in the form of a cashier's check made payable to "Commerce One, Inc." in an amount not less than $100,000 which will be credited towards the Purchase Price if the sale is completed with the Bidder making the deposit.

iv. In the event of the approval of the Bid, such Bidder's deposit shall become non-refundable if (i) the Bid is accepted, (ii) the Bidder fails to close if and as required by the terms of such Bid, and (iii) the Debtors are otherwise ready, willing and able to close under the Bid and are not in default under the Bid. If the Debtors close a sale of the Purchased Assets to another Bidder, the deposit will be refunded within three (3) business days of such closing. In the event a dispute arises over whether a deposit is refundable or non-refundable, the Debtors shall hold the deposit pending a determination of the issue by the Court or written agreement of the Debtors and the Bidder who made the deposit.

v. Simultaneous with submission of the Bid, the Bidder must provide to the Debtors reasonably satisfactory evidence of its financial ability to fully and timely consummate the sale on the terms of the Bid.

vi. If the Bidder is an entity formed for the purpose of acquiring the Purchased Assets, the Bidder shall also provide to the Debtors current audited financial statements or other evidence satisfactory to the Debtors and the Committee and their respective advisors of the equity holder(s) of the Bidder who shall guarantee the obligation of the Bidder or such other form of financial disclosure and credit-quality support or enhancement acceptable to the Debtors.

vii. The Bidder must agree to keep its final and highest bid open pending a closing of a sale to an entity other than the Bidder. In the event a Bid is approved but not consummated by the Closing Date (or such later time as the Debtors and the Bidder shall mutually agree in writing), the next highest bid shall be approved without the necessity of further Court order.

viii. A bid from a bidder that delivers items i–vii above, whose financial information and credit quality support or enhancement demonstrate the financial capability of the bidder to consummate the sale, and that Debtors, in consultation with the Committee, determine is reasonably likely (based on availability of financing, experience and other considerations) to be able to consummate the sale if selected as the Successful Bidder (defined below), will be deemed to be a "Qualifying Bid."

ix. Debtors shall notify each bidder whether the bidder's bid is a Qualifying Bid by no later than November 15, 2004. Debtors will reserve the right under the Bidding Procedures to reject any Bidder's offer which, in its judgment after consultation with the Committee, is inadequate or insufficient or which is contrary to the best interests of the Debtors' bankruptcy estates. Debtors, in consultation with the Committee, will also notify all bidders submitting a Qualifying Bid of Debtors' determination of the highest and best offer. Each Qualifying Bidder must inform the Debtors whether it intends to participate in the auction (see section "x" immediately below) (the "Auction"). Only Qualifying Bidders who appear in person (through an authorized representative) will be eligible to participate in the Auction.

x. If Debtors receive Qualifying Bids, Debtors will conduct the Auction at the Sale Hearing. At the Auction, if Buyer or a bidder that submitted a Qualifying Bid elects to submit a subsequent competing bid after a Qualifying Bid has been accepted (a "Subsequent Competing Bid"), such Subsequent Competing Bid must be in an amount that exceeds the Initial Bid by not less than $25,000, and each bid made after a Subsequent Competing Bid, and each bid thereafter, must be in an amount that exceeds the previous high bid by not less than $25,000.

xi. Bidders will be required to execute appropriate nondisclosure or confidentiality agreements as may be reasonably required by the Company. However, in order to obtain due diligence access or additional information from the Debtors, a prospective bidder must first advise the Debtors in writing of its preliminary (non-binding) proposal regarding (i) the assets sought to be acquired, (ii) the price proposed to be paid, (iii) the structure and financing of the transaction, (iv) any additional conditions to closing that it may wish to impose, and (v) the nature and extent of additional due diligence it may wish to conduct. If based on the preliminary proposal and such additional factors as Debtors determine are relevant, Debtors, in their business judgment, determine that the preliminary proposal is reasonably likely to result in a bona fide and serious higher and better offer for the Purchased Assets, Debtors shall afford the bidder due diligence access to the Company, provided, however, that any such bidder that is a competitor of the Company will be provided with certain customer and supplier information initially on an anonymous basis to maintain the confidential and proprietary customer and supplier information, pricing information, and marketing, sales and other business strategies, dissemination of which could compromise the value of the Purchased Assets. Such bidders will be provided full disclosure of customer and supplier identities only upon a determination of Debtors, after consultation with the Committee and advance notice to Buyer, that such bidder is a serious, bona-fide bidder prepared to submit a Qualifying Bid. Debtors will coordinate all reasonable requests for additional information and due diligence from such bidders. Any additional due diligence shall not continue after the Bid Deadline.

xii. The Debtors reserve the right, in consultation with the Committee, to adopt additional rules for bidding at the Auction that, in their business judgment, and subject to approval of the Court, will better promote the goals of the bidding process and that are not inconsistent with any of the provisions of the sale procedures, the Bankruptcy Code or any order of the Bankruptcy Court entered in connection therewith.

xiii. Immediately prior to the conclusion of the Auction, Debtors will, in consultation with the Committee, (i) review each Qualifying Bid on the basis of financial and contractual terms and the factors relevant to the sale process, including those factors affecting the speed and certainty of consummating the sale and (ii) identify the highest and best offer for the Purchased Assets of the Debtors at the Auction (the "Successful Bid") and notify all bidders at the Auction prior to its adjournment of the name or names of the maker of the Successful Bid, and the amount and other terms of the Successful Bid. The Successful Bidder will be required to complete and execute all agreements or other documents with the Debtors evidencing and containing the terms and conditions upon which the Successful Bid was made.

. . . .

Notes & Questions

1. In what ways are intellectual property auctions in bankruptcy different from auctions in such proceedings of debtors' real or personal property? When will the auctioning of a company's patents make sense as a means to maximize the value of a bankruptcy estate and to serve the interests of claimants in a related bankruptcy proceeding?

2. What types of inquiries might potential bidders wish to make before submitting a bid in a patent auction like the one conducted in the Commerce One bankruptcy proceeding? If the bidders are potential competitors of each other, will disclosures of information about the possible weaknesses of intellectual property interests or the ways those interests might be used in business activities raise confidentiality problems or reduce subsequent competition in undesirable ways?

In connection with their live auctions of intellectual property interests, the ICAP Patent Brokerage firm provides for the following due diligence inquiries by potential auction bidders:

> ICAP Patent Brokerage oversees the due diligence process on every portfolio for sale. Our team acts as liaison between sellers and potential bidders to ensure all necessary documents and contracts are submitted.
>
> **Online Secure Data Room.** Qualified Bidders will have access to a password-protected online data room that will contain detailed information regarding the intellectual property and related items for sale. The IPB Parties make no representation or warranty that any documentation provided in any data

room is either complete or accurate, and the IPB Parties shall have no liability in connection therewith.

One-to-One Meetings. Potential Bidders will have the option of arranging private due diligence meetings or conference calls with the Seller prior to the event and during the event. Prior to the event, potential Bidders interested in contacting a seller should arrange such conference calls through ICAP Patent Brokerage to protect anonymity. At a Live Auction event, please check the registration desk for a representative who will arrange the meeting if not already scheduled. These meetings will provide the potential Bidder with the opportunity to interact with the Seller and/or corporate representative and conclude any remaining due diligence.

Seller Agreements. Consignment agreements are signed by every seller. As a condition of participation, each seller and bidder agrees not to use the participation of any registered seller or bidder as evidence in any action seeking to enforce a patent, copyright, or trademark for any purpose.

ICAP Patent Brokerage, *Due Diligence,* http://icappatentbrokerage.com/auction /duediligence (last visited 11/14/2017).

3. How might a bankruptcy trustee disposing of an intellectual property interest in an auction (or a private intellectual property owner auctioning off an interest outside of a bankruptcy proceeding) take steps prior to the bidding to maximize the amounts obtained for the interest in the auction? Would disclosures of the bankrupt company's prior efforts in commercializing the interest at issue be enough to attract potential bidders? What other steps to clarify the enforceability and commercial significance of an intellectual property interest being sold at auction might increase the apparent value of the interest?

2. Transfers Through Intermediaries

Intellectual property owners have increasingly used a number of processes in addition to auctions to facilitate transfers of ownership of intellectual property interests and thereby obtain immediate payment for the value of those interests.

Activities of non-practicing entities that acquire patents and then seek licensing revenues from the enforcement of the patents have created active markets for transfers of ownership of patents. These entities are sometimes pejoratively described as "patent trolls" because of their perceived tendency to leap out of nowhere to threaten asserted infringers with patent enforcement litigation and to charge for continued use of patented technologies, much as a troll in a fairy tale might unexpectedly leap out from under a bridge and charge a toll to cross the bridge. For some patent holders, such as independent inventors or companies with patents in areas that they do not plan to commercialize, offers of patent acquisitions by non-practicing entities provide means to gain immediate compensation for the value of patents that the patent holders would otherwise find difficult to commercialize. In this sense, non-practicing entities serve as "market makers" for patent transfers and increase the value and rewards that inventors and small companies can realize from patents. At the same time, patent enforcement by non-practicing entities (undertaken without themselves producing products covered by the patents) places a drag on the production of patented items by the targets of enforcement and increases the costs of the items to consumers. Whether the market-making benefits of non-practicing entities outweigh the cost-enhancing detriments of their activities is the subject of intense debate in patent circles. *See generally* Robert P. Merges, *The Trouble With Trolls: Innovation, Rent-Seeking, and Patent Law Reform*, 24 Berkeley Tech. L.J. 1583 (2009).

Some intellectual property owners have relied on the efforts of intellectual property brokers to pursue carefully marketed transfers of intellectual property interests. These brokers serve functions in intellectual property transfers that are similar to the functions served by real estate brokers in real estate sales. Intellectual property brokers can not only aid intellectual property holders in finding buyers for their interests, they can enhance competition between buyers by describing the advantages of acquiring interests to keep the interests out of the hands of other prospective buyers. One leading patent brokerage firm describes the scope and advantages of its brokerage services as follows:

> Our private-sale approach allows all potential bidders every opportunity to evaluate the IP and get involved. The phases we typically work through include:
>
>> Creating an Opportunity Summary to characterize the IP and the markets it relates to.
>>
>> Developing a ranked list of ten to forty prospective bidders in each market segment based on our network of industry relationships and our connection within the IP brokerage community.
>>
>> Establishing a time-line and alerting prospective bidders to the launch of the private sale process.
>>
>> Working with bidders on a one-to-one basis to facilitate their diligence.
>>
>> Contacting all bidders prior to critical dates in the time-line.
>>
>> Engaging with finalists and working toward a final transaction to sell the patents being offered.

Inflexion Point, *Service Profile/Patent Sale and EFOU Licensing*, http://www.ip-strategy.com/Patent_Sale.html (last visited 11/14/2017).

Patent brokers can also work with firms that are seeking to acquire patents to fend off potential litigation by other parties with large patent portfolios. In these situations, the services of the patent broker may initially focus on the types of patent interests the buying party will need to achieve its defensive purpose. Then the broker will seek out parties who are trying to sell patents of the needed character. One leading firm describes its services for "buy-side" clients as follows:

> Identifying the potential adverse parties and/or industry standards that may be involved.

Analyzing both the patent holdings and product lines of the target companies or standards and determining the key associated technologies.

Characterizing these technologies in terms of potential "pain points" within specific potential aggressors so that technology areas can be prioritized for maximum economic impact.

Working through our extensive network of contacts both in industry and within the patent broker community to determine the availability of patents that relate to the technologies of interest.

Establishing discussions with patent owners regarding a potential patent acquisition or an exclusive field-of-use license for those patents.

Working with our client and the patent owner to consummate a transaction.

Providing anonymity to our client at every stage, as may be appropriate.

Inflexion Point, *Service Profile/Strategic Patent Acquisition,* http://www.ip-strategy .com/Strategic_Patent_Acquisition.html (last visited 11/14/2017).

Several large-volume patent sales — some accomplished through auctions and others completed through privately negotiated sales — have transferred patents worth enormous amounts. In addition to the bankruptcy-driven auction sale of Nortel's 6,000-patent portfolio for $4.5 billion, large-volume patent transfers have included Kodak's sale of a portfolio of patents for $525 million to help the company emerge from bankruptcy, Google's acquisition of Motorola Mobility and its more than 20,000 patents for $12.5 billion, AOL's sale of a portion of its patent portfolio (and granting of licenses under the remainder of its patents) to Microsoft for $1.1 billion, Microsoft's later sale to Facebook of a large portion of the patent portfolio Microsoft acquired from AOL, and patent sales by IBM to Google and Facebook. *See* Jose A. Esteves, *Overview of IP Monetization Techniques,* in Practising Law Institute, IP Monetization 2014: Maximize the Value of Your IP Assets 43, 82–83 (2014). These sorts of patent transfers "have significantly raised the profile of patents as high-value corporate assets, and are fundamentally changing the way that companies view and exploit their patent assets." *Id.* at 83.

F. Other Valuable Dispositions of Intellectual Property

1. Donations to Charitable Organizations

Donations of intellectual property interests to charitable organizations can produce valuable tax deductions in a manner similar to donations of other types of property. However, several special issues surround charitable donations of intellectual property, including questions about the types of donations of partial interests in intellectual property that warrant deductions, the proper valuation of intellectual property interests for purposes of determining the amounts of deductions, and the potential of donated interests to produce future income for the recipient charities that may influence the proper size of charitable deductions. For thorough discussions of these and other tax law issues surrounding intellectual property, see generally Jeffrey A. Maine & Xuan-Thao N. Nguyen, INTELLECTUAL PROPERTY TAXATION: TRANSACTION AND LITIGATION ISSUES (2004).

Because the value of an intellectual property interest may be unclear at the time of a donation, the amount of the tax deduction allowed for this type of donation has been the focus of numerous disputes. In most situations, the amount of a deduction for a charitable donation of property equals the fair market value of the property transferred, less any reciprocal benefits given back to the donor. However, in the context of intellectual property donations, determining the fair market value of donations has proven problematic. The suspicion of the Internal Revenue Service has been that intellectual property donors may tend to overstate the value of donated interests in order to qualify for large tax deductions and that donees may cooperate with these overstatements because they want to encourage donations by aiding donors and have few if any reasons to seek lower valuations. In addition, at the time an intellectual property donation is made, there is often no active market for transfer of the interest or other neutral source of valuation information regarding the value of the donated intellectual property that might be used in challenging the donor's asserted valuation of the interest. While valuation estimates based on the potential of a donated intellectual property interest to produce future income might ideally be used to ascertain the value of the interest, these estimates are often inaccurate since they are based on highly speculative interpretations of future business opportunities and income streams. For evaluations of the valuation issues and other problems surrounding charitable donations of intellectual property, see Don Macbean, *Better to Give Than to Receive: Evaluating Recent IP Donation Tax Policy Changes*, 2005 DUKE L. & TECH. REV. 19 (2005).

In 2004, Congress addressed these problems with legislation that specified special rules for the treatment of intellectual property donations under federal tax laws. These rules significantly changed the treatment of these donations. The standards specified in this legislation govern intellectual property donations made on or after 6/3/2004. In general, these standards limit a deduction for a charitable donation of intellectual property to the amount of the donor's tax basis in the intellectual property, plus possible additional amounts determined from the income realized from the intellectual property by the donee. *See* 26 U.S.C. § 170(e)(1)(B)(iii) & (m).

These standards raise additional problems in part because they focus deduction determinations on an intellectual property owner's tax basis in a donated interest. The initial tax basis amount for an intellectual property interest that is acquired from another party will typically be the acquisition price paid for the interest. However, if intellectual property is created by a corporation or other business, the initial basis will typically be the cost of producing the intellectual property, less the portions of that cost that have already been deducted as business expenses. Determining this type of production cost may involve complicated allocations to intellectual property interests of research and development expenses and other corporate expenses.

Depreciation considerations (reflecting the presumed reduction in intellectual property value over time) may add to the complexity of determining the relevant basis figure for a donation of intellectual property. *See* generally Mary LaFrance, *Days of Our Lives: The Impact of Section 197 on the Depreciation of Copyrights, Patents, and Related Property*, 24 HOFSTRA L. REV. 317 (1995).

2. Commitments to Non-Enforcement of Intellectual Property Rights to Enhance Open Source Product Development

Steve Seidenberg, Big Blue Discovers New Way to Leverage Patents: Open-Source Revolution Keeps IBM in the Black

CORPORATE LEGAL TIMES, p. 24 (April 2005)*

What do you call a company that spends vast sums on R&D to obtain new patents; then suddenly makes 500 of its patented inventions available to everyone else, including its competitors . . . for free? Do you call it misguided? Altruistic? Insane? Stupid?

No, you call it IBM.

On Jan. 11, the world's biggest patent owner made 500 of its patents available to the public for free. Valued at more than $10 million, these patents cover a broad spectrum of software technology, including dynamic link libraries, interfaces, multiprocessing and databases.

But there is a catch. The patented technology is freely available only to those who want to use it in open-source software (which is software that lets users see, copy and modify the code). Developers can't use it in proprietary software, such as Microsoft Windows.

Many experts are impressed by IBM's latest step in exploiting its intellectual property.

"They are right for business reasons, but I don't think it was an easy decision to make," says Jeffrey Matsuura, an expert in high-tech law and business at the Alliance Law Group, a Virginia-based law firm. "I think other companies should—and will—consider doing the same thing."

Open-Source Movement

Most companies use patents in three ways: to exclusively exploit their inventions in the marketplace, license patents to other companies for big bucks, and protect themselves against infringement claims. IBM definitely isn't turning its back on those strategies. But the company also is exploring a fourth way to leverage patents.

"We are trying to use patents in a way that companies haven't done before," says Manny Schecter, IBM's associate general counsel for IP law. "We are trying to foster more collaborative innovation and create a patent commons in the open-source software space."

The company's action was spurred, in part, by a December 2004 report issued by The Council on Competitiveness, "The National Innovation Initiative." The report's authors argued that traditional methods for exploiting IP are no longer enough to promote innovation.

"No single organization has the scale to build today's complicated [IT] systems," the report stated. The authors of the study believe companies need to move away from proprietary software regimes and embrace open standards to ensure compatibility between IT products.

Some experts say that open-source development helps large and small developers avoid a growing threat to innovation: the proliferation of exclusive patent rights. Eben Moglen, an expert in intellectual property law who teaches at Columbia Law School, describes this as the anti-commons problem: "When there are too many exclusive rights in an area, you have to negotiate with an unmanageable number of people to do research, and the transaction costs become too high," he argues. "This happened in the biotech area during the 1990s. It was hard to do research because one had to buy rights from 20 to 30 different inventors."

This same problem now may be interfering with software development. "Patent lawyers are telling me software patents are more trouble than they are worth," he says. "They create a whole series of problems with companies taking in each others' laundry."

Big companies can leverage their patent portfolios to negotiate necessary cross-licenses. However, small- and medium-sized software businesses usually don't own enough patents to press for similar deals. They must either pay hard-earned cash for patent licenses, spend time and money trying to design around patents, or simply give up on innovating in patent-infested areas.

Because of this, many smaller tech companies look askance on software patents. It also is the reason many companies in Europe have actively opposed a proposal to legalize software patents in the European Union. Open source advocates also have joined the chorus against the proposed EU software patents, claiming that such patents would hinder innovation and thus harm society.

Big Blue Consultant

Protecting innovation is an admirable goal. But what does IBM get out of it? How does the company benefit by promoting new open-source technologies it can't own?

First, IBM obtains a defensive benefit. When developers create open-source technologies, IBM's rivals can't exclusively exploit these technologies.

Second, new open-source technologies can help IBM sell its other services. As customers flock to open-source IT products, they will hire companies such as IBM to install, maintain and customize these products. For instance, Deutsche Bahn, which runs Germany's railway system, hired IBM to advise it on how best to switch from the proprietary Unix operating system, to Linux, an open-source alternative. And Deutsche Bahn is running its new Linux system on new IBM servers—which means more profit for Big Blue.

"What IBM understands is that its success in the 21st Century isn't in making low-end hardware; it isn't in its interest to make propriety products that have interoperability problems; and it isn't in its interest to license Microsoft products," Moglen says. Instead, he says, "IBM is turning itself into the most important information consultancy in the world."

IBM isn't unique. Many other companies can benefit by making some of their patents available to the open-source community.

"One class of companies want open source to flourish because their business model includes use of open-source code, and they sell services and hardware around it. For these companies, [IBM's] type of donation makes a lot of sense," says Kevin Rivette, an IP management consultant with The Boston Consulting Group and author of the popular IP management book, Rembrandts in the Attic.

And there are plenty of such companies. For instance, just days after IBM announced it was donating 500 patents to open source, Sun Microsystems followed suit by making available 1,600 of its patents. This donation was aimed at strengthening Sun's OpenSolaris open-source operating system.

Buzz Kill

Many other companies are firmly opposed to open-source. Microsoft, for example, has been waging a PR campaign to convince businesses that open-source software is not as safe, less powerful and more expensive than products such as Windows.

Yet experts argue even companies that are committed to selling proprietary software eventually will embrace open source.

"Slowly and quietly people will change their business models to adopt open source," Rivette says. "Open source is creeping into so many things. How can you avoid putting open source into your business model?"

Rivette sees only one thing that can stop the eventual success of open-source software: companies that make their living not by selling products, but enforcing their software patents against others. These companies may have key patents essential to open-source software, and no financial incentive to make their patents available to the open-source community.

Acacia Research, for example, produces no IT goods or services, but makes lots of money from its patents on methods for sending compressed audio and video over the Internet. Acacia has sued many companies for allegedly violating these patents, and the patent owner has reached remunerative settlements with more than 227 firms.

Yet even companies such as Acacia may wind up accepting open source. "They will come around because they are business people," Rivette says. "If they figure out how to make money off it, they will use it."

Matsuura also predicts a rosy future for open-source software, expecting more companies to use it and in more contexts. This will benefit software users, who will get high quality, customizable software at lower prices. It also will help IT companies that want to use open source to enhance the sales of their own products and services.

As for companies that stubbornly fight against open source, they could wind up in trouble. "Customers want products that are secure, interoperable, innovative — all features that are associated with open source," Schecter says. "If other companies don't participate in the open-source movement, they might get left behind."

Notes & Questions

1. IBM's published statement about the non-enforcement of its patents against open source software developers was as follows:

IBM Statement of Non-Assertion of Named Patents Against OSS

IBM is committed to promoting innovation for the benefit of our customers and for the overall growth and advancement of the information technology field. IBM takes many actions to promote innovation. Today, we are announcing a new innovation initiative. We are pledging the free use of 500 of our U.S. patents, as well as all counterparts of these patents issued in other countries, in the development, distribution, and use of open source software. We believe that the open source community has been at the forefront of innovation and we are taking this action to encourage additional innovation for open platforms.

The following is the text of our pledge. It is our intent that this pledge be legally binding and enforceable by any open source software developer, distributor, or user who uses one or more of the 500 listed U.S. patents and/or the counterparts of these patents issued in other countries.

IBM's Legally Binding Commitment Not To Assert the 500 Named Patents Against OSS

The pledge will benefit any Open Source Software. Open Source Software is any computer software program whose source code is published and available for inspection and use by anyone, and is made available under a license agreement that permits recipients to copy, modify and distribute the program's source code without payment of fees or royalties. All licenses certified by opensource.org and listed on their website as of 01/11/2005 are Open Source Software licenses for the purpose of this pledge.

IBM hereby commits not to assert any of the 500 U.S. patents [listed in this notice], as well as all counterparts of these patents issued in other countries, against the development, use or distribution of Open Source Software.

In order to foster innovation and avoid the possibility that a party will take advantage of this pledge and then assert patents or other intellectual property rights of its own against Open Source Software, thereby limiting the freedom of IBM or any other Open Source Software developer to create innovative software programs, the commitment not to assert any of these 500 U.S. patents and all counterparts of these patents issued in other countries is irrevocable except that IBM reserves the right to terminate this patent pledge and commitment only with regard to any party who files a lawsuit asserting patents or other intellectual property rights against Open Source Software.

IBM Statement of Non-Assertion of Named Patents Against OSS, http://www.ibm.com /ibm/licensing/patents/pledgedpatents.pdf (last visited 11/14/2017).

2. IBM's commitment not to enforce certain of its patents against open source developers was part of a broader reassessment of patent enforcement strategy within the company. IBM executives apparently concluded that the company's patent enforcement strategy warranted a number of changes aimed at enhancing collaborative software development. This change of strategy was seen as a means to encourage new modes and quantities of software development:

> I.B.M. executives say the company's new approach to intellectual property represents more than a rethinking of where the company's self-interest lies. In recent speeches, for example, Samuel J. Palmisano, I.B.M.'s chief executive, has emphasized the need for more open technology standards and collaboration as a way to stimulate economic growth and job creation.

> On this issue, I.B.M. appears to be siding with a growing number of academics and industry analysts who regard open-source software projects as early evidence of the wide collaboration and innovation made possible by the Internet, providing opportunities for economies, companies and individuals who can exploit the new model.

> "This is exciting," said Lawrence Lessig, a professor at Stanford Law School and founder of the school's Center for Internet and Society. "It is I.B.M. making good on its commitment to encourage a different kind of software development and recognizing the burden that patents can impose."

Steve Lohr, *IBM to Give Free Access to 500 Patents*, NEW YORK TIMES, January 11, 2005, at C1.

3. Some advocates of open source software development have argued that the commitment of IBM and others not to enforce their patents concerning open source software development projects is not enough to spur open source software development since the companies involved were already supporters of open source software development and were unlikely to have enforced these patents even absent their commitments. The real source of threats to open source development, these critics argue, are companies like Microsoft that have strong business reasons to oppose certain open source projects (such as the development of open source operating system software products like Linux, which compete with Microsoft's Windows products)

and have large patent arsenals to use against open source developers. The critics suggest that contributions of patents from IBM and others to create an opposing body of patents that are enforceable against Microsoft and others would be more useful in staving off patent enforcement threats and in reassuring open source developers. They see open source development as the equivalent of a Cold War battlefield where the only real protection lies in building up opposing patent positions that establish a state of "mutually assured destruction" in which large companies are deterred from asserting their patent rights and open source developers are correspondingly reassured in their efforts to produce new software that may infringe the patents of these companies. *See* Matthew Broersma, *Open Source Patent Pool Mooted and Booted* (8/15/2005), http://news.techworld.com/applications/4209/open-source-patent-pool -mooted-and-booted/ (last visited 11/14/2017).

4. Tesla, Inc., has made a particularly broad commitment to refrain from enforcing its patent rights. "In perhaps the boldest form of a patent pledge to date, the carmaker Tesla announced that it was giving up its rights to all of its patents and stated to the world that 'all our patents belong to you.' Although not all of Tesla's patents will become public, at least hundreds and likely thousands will become public.... Some media outlets have speculated that Tesla's unique nature in the electric car industry allowed it to make such a bold pledge." Victoria F. Maroulis & Patrick Burns, *Emerging Trends in Managing Risk of Patent Litigation* in Practising Law Institute, IP MONETIZATION 2015: MAXIMIZE THE VALUE OF YOUR IP ASSETS ch. 2 (2015) (available from PLI-Plus research service). Tesla's Chief Executive Officer Elon Musk explained Tesla's action as follows:

> At Tesla . . . we felt compelled to create patents out of concern that the big car companies would copy our technology and then use their massive manufacturing, sales and marketing power to overwhelm Tesla. We couldn't have been more wrong. The unfortunate reality is the opposite: electric car programs (or programs for any vehicle that doesn't burn hydrocarbons) at the major manufacturers are small to non-existent, constituting an average of far less than 1% of their total vehicle sales.
>
> At best, the large automakers are producing electric cars with limited range in limited volume. Some produce no zero emission cars at all.
>
> Given that annual new vehicle production is approaching 100 million per year and the global fleet is approximately 2 billion cars, it is impossible for Tesla to build electric cars fast enough to address the carbon crisis. By the same token, it means the market is enormous. Our true competition is not the small trickle of non-Tesla electric cars being produced, but rather the enormous flood of gasoline cars pouring out of the world's factories every day.
>
> We believe that Tesla, other companies making electric cars, and the world would all benefit from a common, rapidly-evolving technology platform.
>
> Technology leadership is not defined by patents, which history has repeatedly shown to be small protection indeed against a determined competitor,

but rather by the ability of a company to attract and motivate the world's most talented engineers. We believe that applying the open source philosophy to our patents will strengthen rather than diminish Tesla's position in this regard.

Elon Musk blog, All Our Patents Belong To You, teslamotors.com (June 12, 2014), available at: http://www.teslamotors.com/blog/all-our-patent-are-belong-you (last visited 11/14/2017).

At least one industry analyst saw Tesla's move as an indication that the company thought it would benefit from more emphasis on electric vehicle technology development and that releasing its patents would create valuable technology development competition. According to Clem Chambers:

> In effect Musk is saying the car companies are not his competition. They aren't. Ford, GM, Fiat and even hybrid savvy Toyota are not competition.
>
> It's not the companies that are the competition, it's the internal combustion engine itself that is Tesla Motors' competition and he is not beating it, yet.
>
> OK, saying Tesla is not winning the battle with old technology is a little harsh but as Musk's says, his sales are only a splash in the ocean in comparison to the vast fleets of gas fueled cars being shelled out of giant factories around the globe by the millions. It is Musk's vision that if Tesla had some competition it would actually be good for Tesla and would help grow his business.

Clem Chambers, *Tesla Giving Away Its Patents Makes Sense* (June 13, 2014), http://www.forbes.com/sites/investor/2014/06/13/tesla-giving-away-its-patents-makes-sense/ (last visited 11/14/2017).

3. Open Source Releases of IP to Promote Indirect Monetization

Open source releases of otherwise proprietary software have helped a number of companies to generate revenues through "indirect monetization" of the value of the released software. Companies employing this technique use the released software to promote commercial transactions and generate company profits in other contexts:

> Companies that market software, hardware, and services may open source some of their software as a "loss leader" to drive sales of other products. Google, for example, uses an indirect monetization strategy in the mobile phone space through its Android operating system, which is available without charge under a combination of open source and proprietary licenses, to encourage development of Android devices and applications. The resulting Android smart phones, manufactured by companies such as Samsung, Motorola, LG, and HTC, drive advertising revenue back to Google, along with a percentage of the fees paid for Android apps and other Google Play store purchases (music, movies, etc.) made on the phone. Apple's Safari

browser is another example: the core WebKit browser software is available under the [Lesser General Public License (LGPL) and Berkeley Software Distribution (BSD) open source licenses], but when embedded in the iPhone iOS, it is part of a proprietary software stack.

A. Clifford Allen, Jason S. Buttura & Alan Stern, *Open Source Licensing* (August 2016) in Practising Law Institute, Understanding the Intellectual Property License 2016 ch. 15 (2016) (available from the PLI-Plus research service).

4. Defensive Use of IP on Behalf of Customers

Firms have used IP interests to promote product sales by offering the interests for defensive use by customers of the firms, thereby making the firms' product offerings more attractive. Confronted with extensive IP litigation risks, many businesses have sought protections that reduce the likelihood of infringement liability (and, ideally, reduce the likelihood of infringement litigation itself). Some vendors with large IP holdings have offered such protections to their customers by providing access to IP interests that set up counterclaims deterring IP infringement suits against the customers.

One broadly applicable example of such protections is offered by Microsoft Corporation (Microsoft) in connection with its Azure cloud computing services. Azure is a cloud computing platform that subscribers can use as a basis for many software and business services offerings. *See generally* Microsoft Corporation, Azure Products, https://azure.microsoft.com/en-us/services/. Microsoft offers three types of intellectual property litigation protections to Azure subscribers: (1) indemnification and defense cost coverage by Microsoft for any litigation costs and liability due to IP infringement claims arising from customers' use of Microsoft cloud platform technologies and included open source components; (2) a "springing license" upon subscription allowing subscribers to use any technology covered by patents that Microsoft has previously transferred to non-practicing entities (NPEs), which aim to enforce the patents against other, non-licensed parties; and (3) rights to use additional Microsoft-owned patents to mount counterclaims against parties suing the subscribers for intellectual property infringement. These last protections are achieved via tactical transfers of ownership of the Microsoft patents to the subscribers as needed to oppose and deter intellectual property litigation. *See generally* Microsoft Corporation, Azure IP Advantage, https://azure.microsoft.com/en-us/overview/azure-ip -advantage/.

Tactical transfers from a list of Microsoft patents posted on the internet ("the Patent List") are provided to Azure subscribers ("Qualified Customers") under the following terms:

4. PATENT PICK PROCESS

4.1 Submission of Patent Request Form. During the [term of an agreement for Azure services], if a Qualified Customer or its Affiliates are sued by a

Commercial Entity (such Entity including its current Affiliates, "Plaintiff") for utility patent infringement with respect to software or services deployed by a Qualified Customer or its Affiliates on Azure ("Plaintiff Lawsuit"), then a Qualified Customer may, within six (6) months of the filing of such Plaintiff Lawsuit, submit a request to [Microsoft Technology Licensing, LLC. (MTL)] to purchase a single Patent from the then-current Patent List by fully completing and sending to MTL a Patent Request Form; provided, however, only one Patent may be purchased per Plaintiff Lawsuit, and only one Patent may be purchased during any given one year period. If all of the Conditions have been met, MTL will sell the requested Patent to a Qualified Customer by executing the Patent Sales Agreement. Any Patent Request Forms submitted by a Qualified Customer shall be deemed incorporated into these Terms and are subject to all of these Terms.

4.2 Conditions. The following conditions ("Conditions") must be met prior to MTL executing any Patent Sales Agreement:

(a) Qualified Customer was a Qualified Customer on the date of the filing of the Plaintiff Lawsuit and on the date of submitting the Patent Request Form, and Qualified Customer has not (and its Affiliates have not) maintained a lawsuit Initiated by Qualified Customer (or its Affiliates) against Microsoft, its Affiliates or their customers for patent infringement with regard to Azure or software or services running on Azure within two years prior to the date of the Patent Request Form.

(b) The patent infringement claim in the Plaintiff Lawsuit is not subject to an indemnification obligation by Microsoft, a supplier of Qualified Customer or any other Entity.

(c) Qualified Customer reasonably believes that Plaintiff is infringing the Patent identified in the Patent Request Form and intends in good faith to assert such patents against Plaintiff in the Plaintiff Lawsuit with respect to the specific software, products or services of Plaintiff identified in the Patent Request Form ("Identified Products").

(d) Plaintiff does not have a license or similar rights to the Patent with respect to the Identified Products and Microsoft or any of its Affiliates are not obligated to provide such license or similar rights to Plaintiff upon the sale or assignment of such patents.

(e) Qualified Customer submits the Patent Request Form to MTL within six (6) months of the filing of the Plaintiff Lawsuit, and the Patent Request Form is fully and accurately completed, including attaching a properly and fully executed Patent Sales Agreement.

(f) MTL reasonably believes that all of the above conditions in this Section 4.2 have been met, the Qualified Customer is a bona fide user of Azure, and all of the conditions and representations in the Patent Request Form, are true.

4.3 MTL Response to Submission. Within thirty (30) days of receipt of the Patent Request Form, MTL will reject or accept the submission. If MTL rejects the submission, MTL will state the reason(s) for the rejection in its response. If MTL accepts the submission, MTL will execute the Patent Sales Agreement attached to the Patent Request Form and the parties will perform under the terms and conditions of such Patent Sales Agreement.

4.4 No Assistance. Qualified Customer understands and acknowledges that Microsoft and MTL will provide no guidance, diligence or other assistance to Qualified Customer regarding which patents, if any, Qualified Customer will identify in any submission.

Microsoft Corporation, Microsoft Azure IP Advantage Benefit Terms and Conditions, https://cloud-platform-assets.azurewebsites.net/azure-ip-advantage/ (last visited 11/14/2017). These terms are clearly intended to reassure potential Azure users, encouraging them to become and stay Azure subscribers. Microsoft asserts that these terms will help Azure subscribers to "[d]efend against patent lawsuits targeting [the subscribers'] innovation with access to a large patent portfolio. [Subscribers] become eligible for this benefit simply by using Azure on a regular basis. If sued, eligible Azure customers can acquire one of 10,000 patents that Microsoft makes available to help counter assert against an aggressor." Microsoft Corporation, Azure IP Advantage, https://azure.microsoft.com/en-us/overview/azure-ip-advantage/ (last visited 11/14/2017).

However, critics have pointed out that tactical transfers of patents under the Patent Pick Process may provide little or no protection against patent suits by patent trolls that are non-practicing entities (NPEs). These entities are not producing or selling products or services and are, therefore, unlikely to infringe any of the patents available from Microsoft for transfers under the Patent Pick Process. Absent such infringement, the threat of a countersuit protecting Azure users may be nonexistent and offer no deterrent to litigation by NPEs. *See, e.g.,* Barry Sookman, *Feeling Safer under Microsoft's Cloud Patent Shield? Don't,* The Register, 10/13/2017, https://www.theregister.co.uk/2017/03/03/feeling_safer_under_microsofts_cloud_patent_shield_dont/ (last visited 11/14/2017).

G. Creation and Management of Intellectual Property Portfolios

Once a company has developed some critical technologies from which it has derived intellectual property assets, it may wish to extend and use those assets by approaching this process as a form of portfolio management. You can imagine a company's technologies and intellectual property assets as a portfolio, similar to its financial assets. While managing a financial portfolio most often involves understanding market trends and following fluctuations in returns, managing an intellectual property portfolio involves combining business activity strategies with complementary acquisitions of legal rights and choices about how to enforce those rights. The readings in this subsection describe some of the most important business and legal issues that arise as companies pursue intellectual property portfolio management.

The excerpt from the article by Polk and Parchomovsky that follows introduces the concept of the patent portfolio and illustrates several methods of patent portfolio management with case studies. Polk and Parchomovsky argue that companies seek to maximize the value of a set of critical technologies rather than focusing on rights to one key invention or a series of unrelated patents. According to their interpretation, patenting strategies should be seen as attempts by companies to create optimal patent portfolio designs. This excerpt raises provocative questions of how to determine what constitutes an optimal patent portfolio and how to design a patenting strategy to obtain the optimal portfolio.

R. Polk Wagner & Gideon Parchomovsky, Patent Portfolios

154 U. PENN. L. REV. 1 (2005)*

[W]e will present three case studies that illustrate how companies employ the portfolio theory to gain and preserve a dominant position in their respective industries. It bears emphasis that the examples we use here are highly representative. There is ample evidence that the desire to achieve a strong patent portfolio shapes the patenting activities of virtually all innovating firms.

A. Dominating a Technology via a Patent Portfolio: The Case of Qualcomm

Qualcomm rose to prominence in the mid-90s as part of the wave of technology firms that capitalized on the value of their patent portfolios by aggressively pursuing licensing agreements. The leap to superstardom, however, didn't occur until 1999, when the company began spinning off divisions in order to focus squarely on its intellectual property portfolio, and saw its stock soar over 2,000% (noteworthy even amidst the flurry of speculation driving the dot-com bubble). Despite suffering through the subsequent market downturn, the company has experienced significant growth over the past three years, including a $200 million increase in revenue from its licensing division.

This meteoric success can be traced back to 1989, when the four-year-old start-up introduced "code division multiple access" (CDMA) wireless technology as a better alternative to the "time division multiple access" (TDMA) digital system which had just been endorsed by the Cellular Telecommunications Industry Association (CTIA) after a two-year dispute over the industry standards. Despite the network externalities which created a substantial barrier to entry into the wireless market at that time, CDMA eventually supplanted TDMA, largely by virtue of being a superior technology.

Qualcomm's insight was not simply in championing CDMA, but in anticipating future developments and aggressively pursuing an array of patents covering diverse applications of the standard. The benefits to Qualcomm of this approach are two-fold: the company generates a dual revenue stream and prevents competitors from entering any aspect of the CDMA market.

Qualcomm's official statements (in annual reports, press releases, and presentations to both investors and the media) make it clear that the company views the portfolio, rather than the individual patent, as the relevant level of abstraction for managing intellectual property assets. Filings with the SEC further reflect a recognition of the portfolio as a distinct commodity. Finally, the company consistently emphasizes the growing number of patents which it applies for and receives each year, as well as the broad applicability of the portfolio as a whole to a wide range of wireless technologies.

B. Building Scale and Diversity: The Case of IBM

When it comes to numbers, nobody beats Big Blue. Since 1994, IBM has amassed a total of 24,665 US patents, far more than any other company, each year ranking first on the USPTO's list of top patent earners. Its closest competitor in that regard, Canon Kabushiki Kaisha, received only 16,570 patents during the same period. Moreover, the number of ideas being patented each year is on the rise—several times in the past decade, IBM set new records for the most US patents received by an organization in a single year.

In the 1980s, IBM struggled as the national consciousness came to associate excellence in technology with foreign-produced goods. Moreover, the once-progressive company grew stagnant, falling from its perch as the leader in innovation. But even then, IBM recognized the bargaining value of a robust portfolio, as well as the leverage such a portfolio could provide when seeking to compel licensing agreements from potential infringers (perhaps unscrupulously). Still, after a decade of very public management snafus, analysts and economists were writing the company's obituary.

The turn-around began with the arrival of Lou Gerstner as CEO in 1993, appointed to replace John Akers after the company suffered its worst year ever. Among the changes instituted under Gerstner's watch: substantially increasing efforts to exploit the company's intellectual property assets, mandating a narrower focus on less theoretical and more product-oriented research, and slashing the R&D budget while simultaneously initiating a campaign to increase the number of patents the company received. This led to the remarkable growth of the company's patent portfolio, but also to the significantly reduced ratio of research dollars spent to patents earned. Even taking into account the approximately 28-months required for the average patent prosecution, patent intensity—patents obtained per R&D dollar—at IBM has exploded.

By some measures, IBM's portfolio-building success has come at the price of its patent quality: although the undisputed leader based on sheer numbers, the company lags behind peers such as Microsoft, Cisco and Sun Microsystems on indexes which measure how often a company's patents are cited as prior art and how close its portfolio is to the cutting edge of research. Nevertheless, IBM's dramatic overhaul paid off: the portfolio provides the company's engineers with the freedom to experiment unhindered by concerns of infringing on other's patents, and IBM has turned intellectual property licensing into a "fine art" which division has become so profitable and efficient that IBM now provides the service of counseling other firms on how to maximize income from their own patent portfolios.

C. Assembling a Patent Portfolio from Alternative Sources: The Case of Gemstar

Henry Yuen launched Gemstar in 1989 with a simple dream: to help the nation program its VCRs. He (along with partner David Kwoh) developed an algorithm for converting information about a TV show into a short string of numbers, convinced newspapers and TV Guide to carry the codes in their listings, and designed a set-top box to convert those codes back into instructions telling the device the date, time, and channel of the program the end-user wanted to record. The VCR Plus+ was an immediate success, and Yuen raked in millions.

As the company grew, it sought to apply its patented technology to related emerging fields. Yuen's vision was for Gemstar to assemble a portfolio of patents which could be used to claim coverage over all aspects of on-screen guides and interactive program listings. Although the company conducted some research in-house, Gemstar's primary method of expansion was to acquire smaller companies with potentially valuable patents, and to use the threat of expensive infringement litigation to force competitors either into licensing deals or out of the field.

Gemstar soared through the 1990s with a string of high-profile successes, most notably the acquisition of TV Guide (which resolved a long-standing patent dispute). But Yuen's aggressive strategy prompted an industry backlash, and a series of courtroom defeats led competitors and licensees to question the strength of Gemstar's patent portfolio. Yuen was finally ousted in 2002 following revelations that the company was overstating revenue.

Today, Gemstar still maintains a portfolio of over 260 patents on listing and interactive technologies, and numerous analysts believe the size of this portfolio, combined with a less-combative attitude towards licensees, leaves the company poised for a long-term dominant role in the industry.

Notes & Questions

1. What lessons can be learned from these three case studies regarding patent strategy? Does the pursuit of a patent portfolio resolve some of the antitrust issues raised by patent pooling that are discussed in Chapter 11? To what extent are the benefits of lowered antitrust scrutiny offset by the loss in specialization that results from focusing on a few core patents?

2. The Wagner and Parchomovsky reading discusses Lou Gerstner, chief executive officer of IBM, who cut the company's research and development budget while expanding the company's patent portfolio. How are these strategies consistent? Is

there a trade-off between basic research and commercial research? Between improving existing products and developing breakthrough innovations?

3. Clayton M. Christensen, a professor at Harvard Business School, has pointed out that disruptive technologies can cause even well-managed companies to fail because of the inability to recognize changes in the marketplace that result from the technologies. He calls this problem "the innovator's dilemma." Does the focus on patent portfolios exacerbate or ameliorate the innovator's dilemma? How would a company design a patent portfolio in order to avoid the dilemma: create a seminal product and then work on improvements or strive to develop a series of breakthrough products?

4. The potential benefits of patent portfolios have counterparts with respect to copyright and trademark interests. Under copyright law, a copyright owner has the ability to control derivative works and the range of rights in derivative works developed either in-house or through licensing can be understood as defining a copyright portfolio. A copyright portfolio can allow a company to segment a market and serve a wider customer base at a higher return through price discrimination. A copyright strategy emphasizing a portfolio approach should not focus solely on the creation of a single copyrighted work, but rather on the creation of an initial work and a series of derivative works that allow the company involved to pursue a more expansive business strategy. Similarly with trademarks, a company might attempt to use a familiar mark to branch out into different marks. The use of a family of marks, such as the different uses of Coca-Cola (Coca-Cola light, Cherry Coke, etc.) or of McDonald's (Big Mac, McGriddle), allows a company to expand the reach of consumer recognition developed for the company's primary mark. For an excellent discussion of trademark management practices and branding, see Nancy F. Koehn, Brand New: How Entrepreneurs Earned Customers' Trust from Wedgewood to Dell (2001).

5. Josh Lerner, a professor at Harvard University and a frequently-cited scholar in the area of patent policy, found the following patterns of patenting in a study of 419 biotechnology firms:

> First, firms with high litigation costs are less likely to patent in subclasses with many previous awards by rival biotechnology firms. Firms with the highest litigation costs are twice as likely as others to patent in subclasses with no rival awards. When high-litigation-cost firms do patent in subclasses in which rival biotechnology firms have already patented, they tend to choose less crowded subclasses. In the case of firms with high litigation costs, the preceding award to a rival was 303 days earlier. In the case of other firms' patents, an interval of 208 days separated the last prior rival award.

> Second, firms with high litigation costs are less likely to patent in subclasses where firms with low litigation costs have previously patented. A patent awarded to a firm with low litigation costs is followed by an award to a firm with high litigation costs 11 percent of the time; awards to other firms are

followed by a patent to a firm with high litigation costs 21 percent of the time. The results are robust to controls for a variety of sample selection biases, such as the changing mixture of firms over time and the different technological focuses of various vintages of firms.

Josh Lerner, *Patenting in the Shadow of Competitors*, 38 J. L. & Econ. 463, 463 (1995). Professor Lerner concludes that his findings are relevant to the criticism that "the 1982 reform of the patent system [with the creation of the Federal Circuit] has led to aggressive efforts by large firms to extract favorable settlements from smaller concerns and consequent distortions in the innovative activity of smaller concerns." *Id.* at 464.

6. Michael Melton, former general counsel for Pitney-Bowes, makes an important distinction between "intellectual capital" (IC) and "intellectual property" (IP). Intellectual capital is defined by the knowledge base of a company, embodied in its technologies and human know-how. Mr. Melton reasons:

> The first element of any IP strategy must be to protect technology important to the corporation. A corporation must develop the appropriate IP infrastructure as a first step in securing protection for all strategically significant technology with particular emphasis on its implementation in the products and services the corporation delivers. The transformation of IC into IP through contracts, patents, copyrights and other IP protection must have a special focus in this plan. Tools must be woven into this fabric to enhance the creation of the most effective barriers to product or service substitution or emulation by our competitors, to safeguard a corporations global market positions and to provide freedom of action for the introduction of new products. This protection should include a focus on technology that if known by competitors would be immediately embraced. In order to identify a competitor's interest, a corporation must deploy appropriate tools for understanding and exploiting the strengths and weaknesses of their competitors. These tools are commonly referred to as corporate intelligence tools.

See Michael Melton, *Transforming Intellectual Capital Into Strategic Corporate Assets* in Practising Law Institute, Patents, Copyrights, Trademarks, and Literary Property Course Handbook Series PLI Order No. G0-00JN (February 2001).

7. Are Professor Lerner's findings consistent with Mr. Melton's discussion of the importance of "intellectual capital"? To what extent should the ability to restrain competition shape intellectual property strategies? Needless to say, a company cannot be open about any anti-competitive purpose. At the same time, the exclusivity provided by intellectual property will have some effect on the competitive process. Review the materials in Chapter 11 on antitrust concerns to think about how companies can best pursue an aggressive intellectual property position without crossing the limits imposed by antitrust law.

H. Intellectual Property Goals and Challenges of Joint Ventures

Kurt M. Saunders, The Role of Intellectual Property Rights in Negotiating and Planning a Research Joint Venture

7 Marq. Intell. Prop. L. Rev. 75 (2003)*

. . . .

Research has been the wellspring for all of the advanced technological innovations that have appeared in the last twenty years. Indeed, many of the most successful and globally competitive industries in the United States, including computers, semiconductors, pharmaceuticals, aeronautics, and biotechnologies, are the products of basic and applied research. Basic and applied research is usually considered to be the point of departure for dynamic models of technology transfer, leading eventually to product development and diffusion. However, a single firm may not have sufficient resources to undertake a project of research and development alone. In such instances, the firm may consider entering into a research and development collaboration with another firm as a means of pursuing innovation. These types of cooperative efforts have become increasingly prevalent in many industries, benefiting not only the firms involved, but also enhancing overall U.S. economic competitiveness.

As a business endeavor, a joint venture "represents a collaborative effort between [two] companies—[which] may or may not be competitors—to achieve a particular end. . . ." This form of business association combines certain attributes of one firm with complementary features of another firm to engage in a specific project. The enterprise involves special contributions by each partner, rather than the mere pooling of funds by investors to fund a project that is too costly for either to fund alone. Two or more firms form a joint venture to pursue a program of research activities. The partners jointly engage in these activities for the benefit of the joint venture and each of the partners. The partners share risks and investment costs and pool technologies and know-how, to expand the capabilities of each partner. Likewise, the partners may conduct research to develop a product that will be marketed later by the joint venture, or the research joint venture may subsequently license or assign the intellectual property rights to each of the partners for further exploitation. Thus, the primary motives for forming a research joint venture are likely to be the desire to establish a vertical relationship in the market, to achieve an expansion of a geographic market for a product, or to achieve an expansion into related product areas.

The role of intellectual property rights in forming and conducting the research and development effort may be significant; however, intellectual property rights may

---

also be of central concern to the partners and to antitrust regulators even after the project is completed and the research joint venture is dissolved. This Article explores the importance of intellectual property rights in the formation of a research joint venture between two firms. The Article first considers the structural advantages afforded by the joint venture arrangement as to basic and applied research. Next, it identifies the intellectual property rights that the joint venture partners may bring into or develop during the term of their collaboration. This Article then considers the relevant antitrust implications of shared development of intellectual property rights. Finally, it assesses the intellectual property rights concerns that may arise at each stage of the research joint venture life cycle and offers strategies for addressing these concerns during the negotiation and planning stages of the collaboration.

. . . .

V. Intellectual Property Rights and their Part in Planning the Research Joint Venture

Intellectual property rights may be the strategic objective of an inter-firm research collaboration. At the same time, they are a source of risk and uncertainty that impact the planning and organization of the joint venture. There are a multitude of contingencies and considerations that the parties to a research joint venture should address in negotiating and constructing the endeavor. We have already considered a number of such issues so far in this discussion. The threshold issues in all joint ventures concern the compatibility of each firm's expectations and objectives, as well as ongoing administrative matters. For instance: what are the reasons of each partner for forming the joint venture? Will one or more partners be limited in its future actions because of the venture? How will disputes as to purposes of venture be settled? Will such disputes be decided jointly, or does one partner have a controlling vote? Who will manage and direct the venture? How will they be chosen and what is their authority? On the other hand, intellectual property rights raise unique concerns at each stage of the joint venture life cycle. Here, we examine these concerns as they may arise in each phase of this process.

A. Conveying Pre-Existing Intellectual Property Rights

Intellectual property rights may be conveyed to the research joint venture in the joint venture agreement, a separate license agreement, a separate assignment, or all three. Conveyance of intellectual property rights should be discussed in a joint venture agreement or separate agreement, which references back and between both agreements, and which describes the intellectual property rights and subject matter with specificity, specifying the consideration and defining any license or assignment as exclusive or nonexclusive. As mentioned above, the decision as to whether to assign or license intellectual property rights depends on many factors, including the specifics of the transaction and the nature of the assets.

Other considerations include: the contributing partners' plans as to continued use and exploitation of the intellectual property rights in geographic and product markets, other than those acquired by the joint venture; tax and accounting issues;

allocation of rights and responsibilities with respect to prosecution, enforcement, and defense of intellectual property rights infringement claims; the types of intellectual property rights to be granted; and any other legal constraints, such as antitrust, filing, registration requirements, or limitations. The partners should also determine ownership and licensing rights in improvements to, and derivative works of, pre-existing intellectual property rights; intellectual property rights developed by one of the partners after the joint venture is created that would be used by the research joint venture; and intellectual property rights developed by the joint venture. Finally, the partners should decide whether the joint-venture entity will have the right to assign or sublicense rights licensed or granted to it by the partners. If sublicensing rights are granted, the joint venture must ensure that the sublicenses adequately protect the intellectual property rights, including all confidential information and trade secrets, and provide adequate contract defenses, including intended third-party beneficiary status for partners.

B. Rights and Duties During the Research Joint Venture

The joint venture agreement must also address the respective rights and obligations of the joint venture and the partners with respect to protecting, prosecuting, and obtaining intellectual property rights; pursuing claims of infringement and misappropriation against third parties; and defending such actions brought by third parties. When the joint venture is permitted to use technologies of one partner that are protected by patent or trademark, the partner will want assurances that the joint venture and other partner's use will not damage partner's reputation or decrease the value of its brand name.

Additionally, the joint venture agreement should address responsibility and control issues with respect to litigation against third parties based on the intellectual property. It should also set forth which parties will bear the costs associated with such litigation and how they will share in any recovery. Research partners must agree to maintain records in sufficient detail and in a good scientific manner so as to: permit partners to pursue patent protection for any new invention that results; maintain confidentiality to prevent disclosure of trade secrets or proprietary information; cooperate in perfecting and maintaining intellectual property rights; and implement procedures to protect trade secrets and other confidential information developed during the course of the research joint venture.

C. Termination of the Research Joint Venture

Negotiation of termination provisions, especially those that govern the disposition of intellectual property acquired during the collaboration, are crucial. Termination provisions related to intellectual property rights should provide for an orderly disposition of the intellectual property rights both contributed by the partners and created by the research joint venture. Termination provisions should state: which of any original technologies and pre-existing intellectual property rights should be assigned back to the original owner; which of any original technologies and intellectual property rights should be cross-licensed between the partners or sublicensed to the research joint venture (if it is to continue); which jointly developed technologies and intellectual property rights should be licensed or sublicensed to each partner by the research joint venture; which partner is entitled to improvements made to the technology by the research joint venture; and what types of ancillary agreements, such as noncompetition or nondisclosure covenants, are reasonably necessary to protect the respective legitimate business interests of the partners.

VI. Conclusion

Individual firms may lack the resources and incentives to invest at a socially optimal level in uncertain research and innovation. Research collaboration among firms can correct such market failures and increase the rate of technology creation and diffusion in an industry. As Congress has recognized, "technological innovation and its profitable commercialization are critical components of the ability of the United States to raise the living standards of Americans and to compete in world markets. . . . [C]ooperative arrangements among nonaffiliated businesses . . . are often essential for successful technological innovation. . . ."

The research joint venture arrangement offers numerous advantages for collaborative basic and applied research and innovation. Intellectual property rights, whether brought into the venture by one or more of the partners or generated during the term of the venture, raise critical concerns about disclosure, ownership, use, and management that should be addressed in the negotiation and planning phase of the collaboration. Antitrust considerations that relate to the cooperative disclosure, ownership, use, and management of intellectual property rights are also relevant. If the partners to a research joint venture are pro-active in addressing these issues, they can anticipate and mange many of the legal risks involved and maximize the many benefits and efficiencies that result from collaboration.

David J. Teece, Profiting from Technological Innovation: Implications for Integration, Collaboration, Licensing and Public Policy

Practising Law Institute PATENTS, COPYRIGHTS, TRADEMARKS, AND LITERARY PROPERTY COURSE

No. G0-007N (October 7–8, 1999)*

EMI's failure to reap significant returns from the CAT scanner can be explained in large measure by [failures in appropriate intellectual property management]. The scanner which EMI developed was of a technical sophistication much higher than would normally be found in a hospital, requiring a high level of training, support, and servicing. EMI had none of these capabilities, could not easily contract for them, and was slow to realize their importance. It most probably could have formed

---

a partnership with a company like Siemens to access the requisite capabilities. Its failure to do so was a strategic error compounded by the very limited intellectual property protection which the law afforded the scanner. Although subsequent court decisions have upheld some of EMI's patent claims, once the product was in the market it could be reverse engineered and its essential features copied. Two competitors, GE and Technicare, already possessed the complementary capabilities that the scanner required, and they were also technologically capable. In addition, both were experienced marketers of medical equipment, and had reputations for quality, reliability and service. GE and Technicare were thus able to commit their R&D resources to developing a competitive scanner, borrowing ideas from EMI's scanner, which they undoubtedly had access to through cooperative hospitals, and improving on it where they could while they rushed to market. GE began taking orders in 1976 and soon after made inroads on EMI. In 1977 concern for rising health care costs caused the Carter Administration to introduce "certificate of need" regulation, which required HEW's approval on expenditures on big ticket items like CAT scanners. This severely cut the size of the available market.

By 1978 EMI had lost market share leadership to Technicare, which was in turn quickly overtaken by GE. In October 1979, Godfrey Houndsfield of EMI shared the Nobel prize for invention of the CT scanner. Despite this honor, and the public recognition of its role in bringing this medical breakthrough to the world, the collapse of its scanner business forced EMI in the same year into the arms of a rescuer, Thorn Electrical Industries, Ltd. GE subsequently acquired what was EMI's scanner business from Thorn for what amounted to a pittance. Though royalties continued to flow to EMI, the company had failed to capture the lion's share of the profits generated by the innovation it had pioneered and successfully commercialized.

If EMI illustrates how a company with outstanding technology and an excellent product can fail to profit from innovation while the imitators succeeded, the story of the IBM PC indicates how a new product representing a very modest technological advance can yield remarkable returns to the developer.

The IBM PC, introduced in 1981, was a success despite the fact that the architecture was ordinary and the components standard. Philip Estridge's design team in Boca Raton, Florida, decided to use existing technology to produce a solid, reliable micro rather than state of the art. With a one-year mandate to develop a PC, Estridge's team could do little else.

However, the IBM PC did use what at the time was a new 16-bit microprocessor (the Intel 8088) and a new disk operating system (DOS) adapted for IBM by Microsoft. Other than the microprocessor and the operating system, the IBM PC incorporated existing micro "standards" and used off-the-shelf parts from outside vendors. IBM did write its own BIOS (Basic Input/Output System) which is embedded in ROM, but this was a relatively straightforward programming exercise.

The key to the PC's success was not the technology. It was the set of complementary assets which IBM either had or quickly assembled around the PC. In order to expand the market for PCs, there was a clear need for an expandable, flexible microcomputer system with extensive applications software. IBM could have based its PC system on its own patented hardware and copyrighted software. Such an approach would cause complementary products to be cospecialized, forcing IBM to develop peripherals and a comprehensive library of software in a very short time. Instead, IBM adopted what might be called an "induced contractual" approach. By adopting an open system architecture, as Apple had done, and by making the operating system information publicly available, a spectacular output of third party software was induced. IBM estimated that by mid-1983, at least 3000 hardware and software products were available for the PC. Put differently, IBM pulled together the complementary assets, particularly software, which success required, without even using contracts, let alone integration. This was despite the fact that the software developers were creating assets that were in part cospecialized with the IBM PC, at least in the first instance.

A number of special factors made this seem a reasonable risk to the software writers. A critical one was IBM's name and commitment to the project. The reputation behind the letters I.B.M. is perhaps the greatest cospecialized asset the company possesses. The name implied that the product would be marketed and serviced in the IBM tradition. It guaranteed that PC-DOS would become an industry standard, so that the software business would not be solely dependent on IBM, because emulators were sure to enter. It guaranteed access to retail distribution outlets on competitive terms. The consequence was that IBM was able to take a product which represented at best a modest technological accomplishment, and turn it into a fabulous commercial success. The case demonstrates the role that complementary assets play in determining outcomes.

The spectacular success and profitability of G.D. Searle's NutraSweet is an uncommon story which is also consistent with the above framework. In 1982, Searle reported combined sales of $74 million for NutraSweet and its table top version, Equal. In 1983, this surged to $336 million. In 1985, NutraSweet sales exceeded $700 million and Equal had captured 50 percent of the U.S. sugar substitute market and was number one in five other countries.

NutraSweet, which is Searle's tradename for aspartame, has achieved rapid acceptance in each of its FDA approved categories because of its good taste and ability to substitute directly for sugar in many applications. However, Searle's earnings from NutraSweet and the absence of a strategic challenge can be traced in part to Searle's clever strategy.

It appears that Searle has managed to establish an exceptionally tight appropriability regime around NutraSweet — one that may well continue for some time after the patent has expired. No competitor appears to have successfully "invented around" the Searle patent and commercialized an alternative, no doubt in part because the

FDA approval process would have to begin anew for an imitator who was not violating Searle's patents. A competitor who tried to replicate the aspartame molecule with minor modification to circumvent the patent would probably be forced to replicate the hundreds of tests and experiments which proved aspartame's safety. Without patent protection, FDA approval would provide no shield against imitators coming to market with an identical chemical and who could establish to the FDA that it is the same compound that had already been approved. Without FDA approval on the other hand, the patent protection would be worthless for the product would not be sold for human consumption.

Searle has aggressively pushed to strengthen its patent protection. The company was granted U.S. patent protection in 1970. It has also obtained patent protection in Japan, Canada, Australia, U.K., France, Germany, and a number of other countries. However, most of these patents carry a 17-year life. Since the product was only approved for human consumption in 1982, the 17-year patent life was effectively reduced to five. Recognizing the obvious importance of its patent, Searle pressed for and obtained special legislation in November 1984 extending the patent protection on aspartame for another 5 years. The U.K. provided a similar extension. In almost every other nation, however, 1987 will mark the expiration of the patent.

When the patent expires, however, Searle will still have several valuable assets to help keep imitators at bay. Searle has gone to great lengths to create and promulgate the use of its NutraSweet name and a distinctive "Swirl" logo on all goods licensed to use the ingredient. The company has also developed the "Equal" tradename for a table top version of the sweetener. Trademark law in the U.S. provides protection against "unfair" competition in branded products for as long as the owner of the mark continues to use it. Both the NutraSweet and Equal trademarks will become essential assets when the patents on aspartame expire. Searle may well have convinced consumers that the only real form of sweetener is NutraSweet/Equal. Consumers know most other artificial sweeteners by their generic names—saccharin and cyclamates.

Clearly, Searle is trying to build a position in complementary assets to prepare for the competition which will surely arise. Searle's joint venture with Ajinomoto ensures them access to that company's many years of experience in the production of biochemical agents. Much of this knowledge is associated with techniques for distillation and synthesis of the delicate hydrocarbon compounds that are the ingredients of NutraSweet, and is therefore more tacit than codified. Searle has begun to put these techniques to use in its own $160 million Georgia production facility. It can be expected that Searle will use trade secrets to the maximum to keep this know-how proprietary.

By the time its patent expires, Searle's extensive research into production techniques for L-phenylalanine, and its 8 years of experience in the Georgia plant, should give it a significant cost advantage over potential aspartame competitors.

Trade secret protection, unlike patents, has no fixed lifetime and may well sustain Searle's position for years to come.

Moreover, Searle has wisely avoided renewing contracts with suppliers when they have expired. Had Searle subcontracted manufacturing for NutraSweet, it would have created a manufacturer who would then be in a position to enter the aspartame market itself, or to team up with a marketer of artificial sweeteners. But keeping manufacturing in-house, and by developing a valuable tradename, Searle has a good chance of protecting its market position from dramatic inroads once patents expire. Clearly, Searle seems to be astutely aware of the importance of maintaining a "tight appropriability regime" and using cospecialized assets strategically.

Notes & Questions

1. The Saunders reading raises many of the issues discussed elsewhere in this text in the chapters on start-up companies (Chapter 2), mergers and acquisitions (Chapter 7), and antitrust concerns (Chapter 11). His discussion is worth comparing with Michael Melton's views on internal corporate development of intellectual property. When should a company decide to enter into a joint venture rather than develop a new technology in-house? Consider the reading on patent portfolios above. How is the decision to enter into a joint venture affected by a company's patent portfolio strategy? The presence of blocking patents held by the company and another party and the corresponding need for cross-licensing are certainly important concerns that may motivate a company to pursue a joint venture rather than just relying on developing a technology within the protections of the company's own patent portfolio. A company should consider the implications of joint research and development regarding the joint ownership of resulting patents. Finally, many of the intellectual property transfer issues described in the materials on employment law and mergers and acquisitions may also arise in connection with the types of joint venture activities described in the Saunders reading.

2. The Teece reading provides several useful case studies regarding joint venturing and associated intellectual property strategies. Compare the EMI case study with the IBM case study. What explains one company's failure and the other's success? Does the difference stem from different laws, different business strategies, or different technologies and market structure? What could EMI have done differently? Could EMI, for example, have emulated some of IBM's choices?

3. The Teece reading provides an interesting comparison with the earlier discussions of patent portfolios in this chapter. Consider the Searle case study discussed in the Teece article. It could be argued that Searle's success rested not on determining the best mix of patents, but on leveraging its patents to create a market position that was sustainable even after the patents expired. Does this interpretation contradict points made in the patent portfolio article? Teece describes the strategy as one of creating complementary assets that support and sustain new technology. What role does intellectual property play in creating these complementary assets and using

them to generate economic and business value? In thinking about this question, keep in mind that some of the value may be appropriated through service contracts and commercialization of specialized know-how that may not always be protected as property.

4. After reading these materials, you should have a sense of the business and legal decisions that are involved in the management of intellectual property. These decisions relate to not only the determination of patenting strategies, but also the coordination of intellectual property acquisition with technological and market realities. In reviewing these materials, try to identify as many different legal and business strategies as possible and see how each strategy or set of strategies takes advantage of the law, the underlying technology, and the related markets.

Chapter 10

Advanced Techniques for Minimizing Risks of Intellectual Property Infringement in Mature Companies

Problem

Digital Ignition's engineers have recommended a change in one of the company's computer-controlled ignition products that may raise new risks of copyright infringement liability for the company. For some time, Digital Ignition has successfully marketed a computer-based system for controlling ignition processes in consumer automobiles. The computer programming involved in the original version of this product was all produced by Digital Ignition's employees and the company holds the copyrights regarding the resulting software.

The proposed engineering change is to include "Linux," an open source software program, in Digital Ignition's product for consumer automobile ignition systems. Linux is a well-known software program developed through the open source process in which various programmers contribute components or improvements of a particular software program with the expectation that their work will be incorporated in the whole and distributed as part of subsequent versions of the software program. The change to a Linux-based system will allow Digital Ignition's product to be built with computer hardware commonly used in personal computer systems and will allow Digital Ignition's programmers to develop and test new software for the product using the wide array of software programming and testing tools already available for Linux-based systems.

The proposed redesign of Digital Ignition's product appears to have substantial engineering merit, but has raised some questions about new intellectual property infringement risks that the company may face if it markets products incorporating Linux. In particular, Dr. Y.L. See (Digital Ignition's chief executive officer) and several of the company's other senior officers are aware that a number of companies—including the International Business Machines Corporation (IBM)—have been sued based on claims of copyright infringement in connection with the use or marketing of Linux-based software products. These suits have been brought by parties claiming to have a copyright interest in portions of Linux and asserting that they have never granted a license allowing the use and distribution of their copyrighted material as part of Linux. Digital Ignition's executives are concerned that they will be opening their company up to similar claims by marketing the proposed new ignition system. Such claims might be based on direct infringement of copyrights in Linux as Digital Ignition produces copies of Linux for inclusion in its products or as Digital Ignition produces further derivative works based on Linux for use in its products. Further infringement claims might also be based on the advertising and sales of Linux-based systems to consumers on the theory that such sales entail the illegal and infringing distribution of unlicensed copies of copyrighted Linux components.

Assuming that there is some likelihood (albeit small) of copyright infringement liability on one of these grounds, uncertainty about the identify and location of the programmers who have contributed to Linux and the corresponding difficulty of obtaining licenses from all of the relevant parties suggest that reducing the company's infringement risks through a systematic effort to gain copyright licenses is not a realistic option. Dr. See is seeking advice on further means (such as insurance or careful management responses to infringement claims) that will reduce the company's financial risks from infringement liability should the company go forward with marketing the proposed new ignition system based on Linux. Dr. See, Digital Ignition's Vice-President of Engineering, and the company's Vice-President of Marketing—all three of whom are both officers of Digital Ignition and members of the company's board of directors—also wish to know if they will face any risks of personal liability as company officers or directors if they authorize the production and marketing of the Linux-based product. They are concerned that this may be seen as improper management of the company in a later legal action given that they know Digital Ignition's production and sale of the Linux-based product may involve copyright infringement and lead to losses to the company from infringement liability. Please provide the requested advice to Dr. See and the other Digital Ignition executives.

Focus of the Chapter

The readings in this chapter describe a particular intellectual property infringement threat facing many large, mature firms—the possibility that their use or incorporation in products of open source software may raise uncertain copyright infringement claims. The chapter also describes insurance and corporate management tools that companies can use to reduce corporate threats from these sorts of uncertain infringement risks.

The development processes for open source software were previously considered in Chapter 9. This chapter examines the intellectual property risks to users of open source software, including companies that wish to remarket open source software components within broader products.

The initial reading on open source software and related intellectual property issues specifies how intellectual property interests may constrain the distribution of products incorporating open source software components and how unexpected copyright infringement claims may arise where the interests of an author of a component of an open source work have not been properly taken into account in the software licensing and distribution process.

The next group of readings addresses insurance coverage for intellectual property infringement risks. These readings begin with an article providing an overview of the types of insurance policies that can help companies reduce the financial risks of unknown intellectual property infringement threats. This article is followed by several cases involving disputes concerning the scope of insurance protections for losses from intellectual property infringement. These cases describe the range of insurance protections against intellectual property infringement or misappropriation liability that are available under a variety of types of policies, including policies covering commercial general liability, losses of physical property, and losses stemming from management errors and omissions. These cases also illustrate, through the situations giving rise to the insurance claims in the cases, a number of types of corporate practices that can produce unexpected intellectual property infringement liability.

The last reading in this chapter describes how systematic management attention to intellectual property infringement risks and claims can aid companies in avoiding infringement liability and in preventing personal liability for corporate officers and directors where corporate actions they have authorized produce unexpected infringement liability for their companies.

Readings

A. Responding to Partially Understood Threats: The Example of Intellectual Property Risks Associated with Open Source Products

Open source software is increasingly used in corporate business environments, but its use raises some unusual intellectual property infringement risks. As noted by one observer:

> "Open source" software is not new, but it has recently attracted much more attention from in-house counsel and private practitioners. As more companies incorporate open source software into their internal systems and commercial products, lawyers need to ensure that underlying licenses are not violated and that proprietary improvements are not compromised. Not all open source licenses are equally "open," and such software has already prompted multi-billion-dollar litigation. The advantages of open source products far outweigh the risks, so long as users are adequately informed of pertinent issues.

Lori E. Lesser, *Open Source Software: Risks, Benefits, and Practical Realities in the Corporate Environment*, *in* Practising Law Institute, Open Source Software: Risks, Benefits, and Practical Realities in the Corporate Environment, 808 PLI/Pat. 29, 29 (2004).

The following reading describes the licensing terms under which most open source software is distributed and some of the risks that can arise when open source software is incorporated in broader commercial products.

Lori E. Lesser, Simpson Thacher & Bartlett, LLP, A Hard Look at the Tough Issues in Open Source Licenses

Practising Law Institute

OPEN SOURCE SOFTWARE 2005:

CRITICAL ISSUES IN TODAY's CORPORATE ENVIRONMENT (2005)*

Introduction

An examination of the predominant "open source" software licenses prompts a multitude of legal questions, many of which the courts have not yet answered. These licenses are designed to be binding contracts just like any other privately-negotiated agreement. Yet, the courts have not yet provided guidance on critical issues, such as the meaning of license terms, their validity and enforceability, the proper parties in any related litigation, and the reasonable penalties for breach. Until such specific guidance is obtained, in-house counsel and private practitioners are examining long-standing general principles of licensing law to advise clients accordingly.

I. Background on Open Source Software

A. Creation of Open Source

1. In the early 1980s, Richard Stallman of MIT began creating his own operating system, named GNU (for "GNU's Not Unix"). Stallman and his colleagues had been writing software for the mainframe computer of MIT's Artificial Intelligence Laboratory, but a newly installed mainframe—with proprietary source code—rendered their work moot and obsolete. Stallman founded the Free Software Foundation, and in 1985, Stallman published the "GNU Manifesto," stating his mission to develop a Unix-compatible software system that was and would remain free for users. GNU had many higher-level functions.

2. In 1987, Professor Andrew Tanenbaum developed an open source Unix clone named Minix.

3. In 1991, Linus Torvalds of Finland began creating his own operating system "kernel," which contained "lower level" functionality governing basic interactions with the computer's hardware. The system used inexpensive PC hardware, but had the functionality of a more expensive Unix system. Torvalds posted his source code on the Internet and incorporated many programmers' suggestions and improvements into his system.

4. The combination of Stallman and Torvalds' work became GNU/Linux, and is now known as Linux. The Linux kernel is still licensed under the [General Public License (GPL) discussed below].

B. Open Source Principles

1. The open source movement believes that software users should have the right to access and modify source code (the part of the code that is readable by human software programmers), which requires legal permission from the copyright owner and physical possession of the code. . . . Source code access is critical to allow the necessary "tinkering" that produces innovation—just like a student annotates a textbook or a mechanic "soups up" an exhaust system. The theory is that, if thousands of programmers have access to source code and exchange their improvements, and innovation will occur more quickly and efficiently.

2. Open source licenses are not uniform in their provisions as to how programmers must share derivative works created from the open source base. Indeed, several popular open source licenses differ in this regard. The GPL license (discussed below) requires users who distribute integrated derivative works to do so without charge.

3. The Open Source Initiative (www.opensource.org) lists 10 principles to qualify a software license as an "open source" license. Dozens of licenses currently comply.

a. Free distribution

b. Availability of source code

c. Permission to make derivative works

d. Integrity of the author's source code

e. No discrimination against users/groups

f. No discrimination against fields of use

g. Distribution of original license with product

h. License is not product specific

i. No restriction of accompanying software

j. License is technology neutral

C. Open Source Myths

1. *Open source software is new.* As noted above, the first open source software has its origins in the early 1980s.

2. *Open source software is "free."* The word "free" is frequently used in connection with "open source" software, but it does not mean that the software is dedicated to the public, *Planetary Motion, Inc. v. Techsplosion, Inc.*, 261 F.3d 1188, 1198 (11th Cir. 2001) (noting that software distributed pursuant to GPL license "is not necessarily ceded to the public domain" and the licensor purports to retain ownership rights). Nor does it mean that open source software will always be available without monetary cost. Open source developers may charge for their specific products; however, users can copy and modify the open source code incorporated therein without paying further royalties. Further, certain open source licenses allow derivative works to remain proprietary, and those owners may extract fees for copying and redistribution of such works. Open source users may need to pay for top-line user support, bug

fixing, patches or proprietary applications running on an open source operating system. Stallman has said, "Think free speech, not free beer." Similarly, think "free puppy," due to later accompanying costs.

3. *A prudent company would not give away open source products for free.* Such a strategy may be profitable in the long run, if a vendor sells accompanying hardware, support or training services or compatible applications. Certain Internet companies have profited by offering free content or services, and thereby attracting users and driving them to for-profit services or supporting an advertising base.

4. *There is a standard open source license.* The Open Source Initiative website (www .opensource.org/licenses) lists dozens of open source licenses, including samples from Apache, Apple, BSD, Eclipse, Entessa, GNU, IBM, Intel, Lucent, MIT, Mozilla, Nokia, Python, RealNetworks, Sun, Sybase and Vovida. The GPL and BSD licenses are the more commonly-used and discussed agreements.

5. *Open source products are not mainstream.* Open source products are found at many large U.S. companies and institutions and include: Red Hat Linux (operating system), Apache (webpage server), Tomcat (Java servlet engine), Sendmail (mail server), MySQL (relational database system), Emacs (development tool), Snort (intrusion detection tool), Sun Microsystems' StarOffice (office suite), and Solaris 10 (operating system), BIND (Internet domain name service) and OpenSSL (security protocols).

6. *Open source products are niche products and do not support most user needs.* Personal computers are now being sold with complete open source "office suite programs" (word processor, spreadsheet program, presentation builder, image editor). For home users or corporate staff needing minimal computer access for Internet browsing and e-mail (e.g., complaint departments or sales support), open source products may be sufficient for all daily needs.

I. Types of Open Source Software Licenses (www.opensource.org)

A. GNU Model (Free Software Foundation)

1. [The] GNU General Public License, GNU Lesser General Public License, [and] GNU Free Documentation License [cover software and documentation related to the] initial kernel of Linux. *See* www.gnu.org/licenses.

2. These licenses are the most protective, in license terms of preserving the "openness" of open source. The GPL license requires that all modified software be redistributed under the same license. The licenses are several pages long.

3. Provisions of GPL — Summary:

a. Users may copy and distribute verbatim copies of the program's source code, if they publish copyright notice and warranty disclaimers on every copy, and provide the GPL license to every recipient of the program. Users may charge a fee for the physical transfer of a copy of the program or may offer warranty protection for a fee.

b. If users distribute any modifications to the program (which is at the users' discretion), it must be under the above terms, and users must: (i) have the modified files prominently note such modifications and the dates thereof; (ii) distribute or publish any derivative works under the terms of this license and not charge for a license to such works as a whole; and (iii) cause the modified program to print a copyright notice and warranty disclaimer when starting to run.

c. The forced re-licensing of a derivative work does not apply to "identifiable sections of that work that are not derived from the Program, and can be reasonably considered independent and separate works in themselves" that are distributed as "separate works." If such sections are distributed as part of a whole that is a derivative work of the program, such distribution is subject to the GPL.

. . . .

B. BSD (Berkeley Software Distribution) Model

1. OpenBSD, FreeBSD, Apache, [and MIT Licenses are based on this model].

2. The University of California at Berkeley developed the BSD model in the 1970s. To distribute an open source program or derivative work under BSD, in either source code or object code form, one must affix a copyright notice, the license's brief conditions, a disclaimer of warranties and limitation of liability, and a prohibition against using contributors' names to promote products created with the program. BSD users are not, however, required to distribute any derivative work free of charge. These licenses are the least protective of the "openness" of open source works.

3. These licenses are generally short. The license template requires publication of standard copyright notice (e.g., © name and year), publication of a damages and warranty disclaimer and little else. The license provides that redistribution and use of the program are permitted, in source or object code form, with or without modification.

C. Corporate Authors/Miscellaneous

1. Dozens of open source licenses are offered by corporations and private organizations, including Mozilla, Sun, Nokia, Apple and IBM.

2. The Mozilla public license is a basis for many future ones. In 1998, Netscape released its browser software under an open source license through Mozilla.

3. The licenses written by corporations are drafted by attorneys and have more substance than the BSD models. In style and structure (but not substantive terms), many resemble mass-market object code licenses.

III. Risks of Open Source Software

A. Mandatory Licensing

1. In theory, if an in-house programmer incorporates a small portion of GPL-licensed code into an integrated proprietary product and the integrated product is distributed, the source code to the entire derivative work becomes subject to the GPL

license. This specific issue has never been litigated. It is unclear how the "derivative work" subject to the GPL license would be defined—a single module or an entire program. It is also unclear when GPL-protected code is deemed integrated into the derivative work, or when it is sufficiently "independent or separate" so as not to trigger the mandatory licensing obligation.

2. In *Progress Software Corp. v. MySQL AB*, 195 F. Supp. 2d 328 (D. Mass. 2002), MySQL moved for a preliminary injunction regarding Progress' distribution of its Gemini program based upon MySQL, pursuant to an end-user license that was not GPL compliant. The court denied the injunction. It noted that a factual dispute remained whether Progress' program was a derivative work governed by the GPL or a separate and independent work not subject to the GPL, but noted that Progress had released Gemini's source code, thereby arguably curing any breach of the GPL. The court further noted that MySQL had not demonstrated irreparable harm, given that the Gemini source code had been released and that Progress planned to withdraw its end use license for commercial users. Meanwhile, given that Progress' product line using MySQL was significant to one of its subsidiaries, Progress had demonstrated that the balance of harm tipped in its favor, regarding its use of MySQL pursuant to the GPL license.

3. [In 2005, a] Munich court . . . enjoined a British software company from selling or distributing software incorporating GPL-licensed code that did not comply with the GPL's terms. *Welte v. Fortinet UK Ltd.*, Landgericht Muenchen 1, No. 21 0 7240105. The firm settled quickly and modified its end-user licenses to comply with the GPL. *See* BNA ELECTRONIC COMMERCE AND LAW REPORT, Vol. 10, No. 18, May 4, 2005.

4. Recent commentators have noted that the GPL "derivative works" issue is still unresolved, citing *Progress Software v. MySQL*. *See* Lerner, J., *The Scope of Open Source Licensing*, J. LAW, ECONOMICS & ORGANIZATION (April 2005); Carver, B., *Share and Share Alike: Understanding and Enforcing Open Source and Free Software Licenses*, 20 BERK. TECH. L.J. 443, 460 (2005) (referring to *MySQL* case; "Ultimately, the issue of what constitutes a derivative software work must be addressed by statute or the courts. There was some hope that the issue would be decided in a case from 2002, but the court did not reach this issue.").

B. Validity and Enforcement

1. Open source licenses are not signed. Therefore, it is unclear if all open source users or contributors have "accepted" the terms of their open source licenses and formed a valid contract, particularly if the license's terms are embedded in the program code. Absent a signature (or clicking "I agree"), such licenses arguably function as "browsewrap" agreements that are accepted when the user avails him/herself of the program governed by the license. Browsewrap agreements have had mixed results in the courts in terms of their validity and enforceability.

. . . .

2. It is unlikely that a user who has modified open source software will claim he/she did not have a valid license that was properly accepted, because absent such a license, such modifications would amount to copyright infringement.

3. Given that an open source program may have multiple authors worldwide who create overlapping or duplicate improvements of varying sizes and importance, it is unclear who will have standing (or the desire) to bring litigation against a particular user. As with proprietary licenses, an unrelated third party may claim a certain version of open source software infringes its copyrights or patents. Unlike proprietary software, however, there are no warranties (or generally, indemnities) supporting the end user's right to use an open source product against any third-party claims.

4. If software that was previously proprietary and licensed to end users is released as open source, such release may affect the rights and obligations of previous licensees.

C. Litigation

1. Stallman worked vigorously to acquire ownership of the intellectual property rights to GNU, so the license's forced re-licensing of derivative works could not be challenged by third parties claiming to own the copyright in some portion of the program and not to be bound by the GPL license.

2. Torvalds did not engage in similar activities, and the authorship of various portions of Linux is disputed.

3. SCO v. IBM

a. *The SCO Group, Inc. v. International Business Machines Corp.*, Case No. 03-CV-0294 OAK (D. Utah). SCO initially sued IBM in March 2003, alleging that IBM improperly used SCO's "trade secrets" in the Linux operating system, despite the fact that the source code of Linux is publicly available. SCO later amended its complaint to allege that SCO's copyrightable Unix code, and not trade secrets, are improperly incorporated into Linux. IBM has counterclaimed for patent and copyright infringement.

b. In 2001, SCO bought Unix, the AT&T operating system for mainframe and minicomputers, which had been licensed to thousands of users. SCO alleges that fragments of Unix are incorporated into the foundation "kernel" of Linux.

c. In late May 2003, Novell claimed that it owned the Unix rights that SCO claimed as its own. *See SCO Group Inc. v. Novell Inc.*, 377 F. Supp. 2d 1145 (D. Utah June 27, 2005) (denying Novell's motion to dismiss SCO's slander of title claim).

d. SCO has also sued end-user Linux customers—AutoZone and Daimler-Chrysler—and sent 1,500 letters to other Linux end-user customers.

e. Red Hat claims in the suit below that SCO has never identified a specific piece of Unix code that was unlawfully copied into Linux.

f. In February 2005, the court denied IBM's motion for summary judgment, but chided SCO for not providing "any competent evidence" that would raise a genuine issue of material fact as to whether IBM committed copyright infringement. Judge

Kimball noted that the discovery process was not yet complete and that IBM had yet to hand over certain documents, but invited IBM to refile the motion for summary judgment at the end of discovery. *See The SCO Group, Inc. v. International Business Machines Corp.*, 2005 U.S. Dist. LEXIS 21408, 2005 Corp. L. Dec. ¶ 28,957 (D. Utah, Feb. 9, 2005).

g. [On September 21, 2007, Judge Kimball administratively closed the case of SCO v. IBM on the basis of SCO's filing for bankruptcy. The result was that all actions in SCO v. IBM were stayed until SCO emerges from bankruptcy proceedings, if and when it does. *See IBM Case Administratively Closed; Will be Reopened When Stay Lifted*, Groklaw (September 21, 2007), http://groklaw.net/article.php?story =2007092110013091 (last visited 6/1/2011).]

4. *Red Hat, Inc. v. The SCO Group, Inc.*, No. Civ. 03-772-SLR, 2004 U.S. Dist. LEXIS 7077 (D. Del. Apr. 6, 2004). Red Hat sued for a declaratory judgment regarding the potential copyright and patent infringement by Linux of SCO's Unix OS software, citing SCO's public statements that it intended to sue Red Hat after IBM. The court stayed the action pending the resolution of the SCO/IBM litigation in Utah. Red Hat's complaint alleges that SCO's statements "are solely designed to create an atmosphere of fear, uncertainty and doubt about Linux." Comp., ¶ 2.

5. Other cases make passing reference to "open source" software. *See Computer Associates Int'l v. Quest Software, Inc.*, 333 F. Supp. 2d 688, 698 (N.D. Ill. 2004) (noting that GPL license restricts modification and subsequent distributions of freeware programs, but finding that program output at issue was not subject to GPL license); *Massachusetts v. Microsoft Corp.*, 373 F.3d 1199, 1228–32 (D.C. Cir. 2004) (addressing open source provision of remedial antitrust consent decree).

D. Remedies

1. Non-compliance with an open source license may amount to a material breach of its terms. As with other intellectual property licenses, every material breach may not rise to the level of copyright infringement. Exceeding the scope of a license (e.g., publishing in an unauthorized country, medium or distribution channel) generally constitutes copyright infringement, while breach of a covenant separate from the license grant (e.g., failure to make timely royalty payments) is only breach of contract. *See Allman v. Capricorn Records*, 2002 U.S. App. LEXIS 14615, 2002 Copr. L. Dec. ¶ 28,467 (9th Cir. July 16, 2002); *Sun Microsystems, Inc. v. Microsoft Corp.*, 188 F.3d 1115, 1121 (9th Cir. 1999) (licensor can sue for copyright infringement if licensee acts outside scope of limited license; otherwise, claim is only for breach of contract); *Graham v. James*, 144 F.3d 229, 237 (2d Cir. 1998) (if licensee's breach of license is failure to satisfy condition on license, conduct may rise to infringement).

2. From a plaintiff's point of view, alleging copyright infringement is better, because it allows the plaintiff to seek an injunction, statutory damages and attorney's fees. Further, the plaintiff can bring its case in Federal court. Breach of contract claims, which are litigated in state court absent diversity jurisdiction, generally do not allow such enhanced remedies.

E. Copyright Misuse

1. The issue of copyright misuse is mentioned in connection with open source software. Copyright misuse is use of a copyright in a manner contrary to public policy, such as requiring a copyright licensee to refrain from competitive activities that are *not* related to the license. It is an affirmative defense to a copyright infringement claim, and to the extent the defense succeeds, the plaintiff's copyright is unenforceable in such instance. *See Video Pipeline, Inc. v. Buena Vista Home Entm't, Inc.*, 342 F.3d 191, 204 (3d Cir. 2003); *Practice Mgmt. Info. Corp. v. American Medical Assoc.*, 121 F.3d 516, 520–21 (9th Cir. 1997); *Lasercomb America, Inc. v. Reynolds*, 911 F.2d 970, 973 (4th Cir. 1990).

2. A defendant in a copyright infringement case could raise a copyright misuse defense concerning the GPL or similar open source licenses. Yet, this argument seems unlikely to prevail, because the restrictions in the GPL license relate to use of the licensed code itself (or modifications thereto), which the code's creators are under no obligation to license at all. The GPL license also specifically provides that it does not attempt to regulate sections of the user's derivative works that are *not* derived from the licensed code.

3. A party demanding a license fee for use of patent or copyright dedicated to the public may be liable for patent or copyright misuse, rendering such license unenforceable. *See Assessment Technologies of WI, LLC v. Wiredata, Inc.*, 361 F.3d 434, 437 (7th Cir. 2004) (noting that claim of copyright in public domain data "came close" to copyright misuse). Yet open source software is *not* public domain, but is licensed with written conditions.

F. Support

1. There is no free lunch. While open source software is initially available for free, not all programs have high-quality vendors offering support, bug fixes and training. User groups, websites and listservs abound of uneven quality.

2. Open source licenses disclaim all warranties and most disclaim indemnification, as well.

Notes & Questions

1. What are the sources of operational and infringement risks to product users in adopting an open source software product (such as Linux or the Linux-based product described in the Problem above) versus the risks of adopting an equivalent software product (such as Microsoft Windows) produced and sold by a single software developer?

2. Should a commercial party be able to profit by building a broader, copyrighted product around a core of open source software or is this type of commercial reuse and extension of open source components inconsistent with either the spirit of open source software development or the legally authorized scope of open source software use? What would be the implications for the subsequent use of open source software of simply precluding its incorporation in any commercial product?

B. Infringement Insurance

Steven E. Tiller & Briggs Bedigian, Intellectual Property and Technological Insurance Coverage

MARYLAND BAR JOURNAL, Nov./Dec. 2001, p. 35*

. . . .

In light of the emphasis on [intellectual property (IP)] and technical know-how in today's marketplace, insurance coverage for possible infringement and other related claims can be critical to the continued success of any company. Insurance coverage can provide the funds to defend a claim; pay a judgment in the event of an adverse ruling; and even, in the appropriate situation, provide an IP owner with the resources to bring suit against an infringer. Such coverage is often the difference between life and death for a company facing an infringement claim as such claims are quite expensive to defend. For example, the average patent infringement suit costs between $775,000 and $2.5 million. [*See*] *Finding Intellectual Property Liability Coverage In The New Business Era — Part I*, THE METROPOLITAN CORPORATE COUNSEL, July 2000.

Traditionally, the only potential coverage available for such claims could be found under the advertising injury provision of a business' commercial general liability (CGL) policy. These policies, however, were drafted long before the garage doors began opening in the new technical revolution, and were not designed to cover most of these emerging forms of litigation. The absence of coverage for most infringement claims has led to the development of new types of policies that provide coverage, at a cost, for many types of infringement claims.

1. IP Coverage Under Traditional CGL Policies

An insurer's duty to defend and/or indemnify generally depends on the allegations comprising the claim against its insured, and the language of the policy. Traditionally, coverage for IP claims has only been found in the advertising injury provisions of CGL policies. These provisions typically provide coverage for damages arising from:

1) Publication of material that slanders or libels a person or organization, or disparages a person's or organization's goods, products or services;

2) Publication of material that violates a person's right to privacy;

3) Misappropriation of advertising ideas or style of doing business; or

4) Infringement of copyright, title or slogan.

Two criteria must be met before coverage for advertising injuries will be extended. First, the alleged conduct must fall within the scope of one of the enumerated offenses described as an advertising injury. The alleged conduct must also not otherwise fall within the scope of one of the policy's exclusions. Second, the offense must have been

---

committed in the course of advertising the insured's goods, products or services—commonly referred to as the "nexus requirement." If one of these two elements is absent, no coverage will extend.

The majority of courts find a nexus if the following requirements are met:

1) the complaint filed against the injured alleges an offense covered by the advertising injury provision;

2) the alleged offense occurred during the term of the policy;

3) the claim arose out of the insured's advertising activities; and

4) the offense occurred in the course of the insured's advertising activities.

So where does coverage stand today? The answer to that question can differ depending on what type of intellectual property dispute is in question.

A. Advertising Injury Coverage For Patent Infringement

. . . .

Computer technology coupled with the patentability of biotechnology has led to a sharp increase in the number of patent disputes. Attempts to obtain coverage under CGL policies, however, are difficult because it is hard to show that the infringement occurred during the course of the insured's advertising. If the insured is unable to establish a nexus between the allegedly infringing conduct and its advertising efforts, the nexus requirement is not met, and coverage will not extend. Moreover, many CGL policies contain specific exclusions for patent infringement, thereby negating any argument that coverage should apply.

B. Advertising Injury Coverage For Trademark Infringement

It is typically argued that coverage for trademark infringement claims is provided under the provisions for "misappropriation of advertising ideas or style of doing business" and "infringement of title or slogan." Although courts are split on the issue, a majority have found that the language of those two clauses generally grants coverage for trademark infringement claims. *See, e.g., Bay Elec. Supply, Inc.,* 61 F. Supp. 2d at 617 (holding that misappropriation of advertising ideas or style of doing business encompasses claims for trademark and trade dress infringement); *Lebas Fashion Imports of USA, Inc. v. ITT Hartford Insurance Group,* 50 Cal. App. 4th 548, 565–66 (Cal. App. 1996) (finding the enumeration of "misappropriation of advertising ideas or style" ambiguous and, therefore, holding in favor of the insured).

Other courts, however, have found that there is no duty to cover trademark or trade dress infringement claims. *See, e.g., Callas Enters. Inc. v. Travelers Indem. Co. of America,* 193 F.3d 952, 956 (8th Cir. 1999), following *Advance Watch Co. v. Kemper Nat'l. Ins. Co.,* 99 F.3d 795, 801–802 (6th Cir. 1996) (holding that the "misappropriation of advertising ideas or style of doing business" provisions could not be so broadly construed as to include trademark or trade dress infringement). The Sixth Circuit in *Advance Watch* reasoned that "if the insurer had intended to provide coverage for such liability, they would have referred to it by name in the policy, as they did in the case of infringement of copyright, title or slogan." *Advance Watch,* 99 F.3d at 803.

C. Advertising Injury Coverage For Copyright Infringement

With the advent of the Internet, copyright infringement is as easy as down-loading a copyrighted document or computer program onto a hard drive, or forwarding protected material via e-mail. As copyright infringement is specifically mentioned in typical CGL policies, most assume that coverage is a given. However, this may not always be the case. Not every case of copyright infringement is related to the insured's advertising efforts, and therefore coverage may not be provided.

With the uncertainty of coverage for most IP claims, including a complete lack of coverage for any claim not arising out of one's advertising efforts, companies have desperately been looking for alternatives. Insurance companies are finally obliging.

2. Intellectual Property Insurance

Separate IP insurance may benefit both large and small companies. IP can be a business' primary asset and at the very least a valued commodity. In fact, it was estimated in 1999, that of Microsoft's $300 billion market capitalization, $284 billion of that was made up of IP. Kevin M. Quinley, DEFENDING AND HANDLING INTELLECTUAL PROPERTY CLAIMS, Insurance Information Institute, Inc., 1999.

A. Who and What Are Typically Covered By Intellectual Property Insurance?

Prior to the 1980's, IP was generally not considered insurable. IP assets were considered difficult to quantify, and infringement claims were even harder to underwrite. New IP insurance policies, however, have transformed the intangible into the tangible. IP insurance keeps a business' bottom line intact by controlling unexpected costs of litigation, and reducing the pressure a business may feel to settle because of the mountain of legal fees that can accumulate during the course of IP litigation. There are currently two prominent forms of IP coverage: 1) enforcement policies, also known as pursuit, abatement or offensive coverage; and 2) defense (liability) policies.

B. Enforcement Policies

The most common type of IP enforcement policy available today is for patent infringement. This type of policy applies to situations where an insured's patent is allegedly infringed by another, and the insured wishes to bring an infringement claim. These policies typically cover: 1) the cost of bringing suit against an alleged infringer; 2) the cost to defend against counterclaims alleging invalidity of the insured's patent; 3) the cost of reexamination of the insured's patent in the Patent and Trademark Office; and 4) the cost to reissue the patent. Betterley, INTELLECTUAL PROPERTY INSURANCE MARKET SURVEY 2000, Betterley Risk Consultants, Inc. at p. 8.

These policies come at a cost. Premiums can be expensive, and many companies require validity opinions to be prepared by qualified patent counsel at the cost of the insured.[1]

---

1. Intellectual property enforcement policies and their use to protect intellectual property owners are described more fully in Chapter 9.

C. Defense Policies

Defense coverage is more traditional, and generally protects an insured against allegations that it has infringed upon the IP of another. A company's IP needs are often very specialized, and policies designed to cover the unique needs of each area of IP are now available. Moreover, insurers' premiums and coverages are as varying as the products they insure.

The types of policies offered vary with the type of protection sought. Policies are not limited to patent, trademark and copyright infringement policies, or strictly third party liability coverage. In fact, many insurance companies are now offering both first and third party coverage for emerging liabilities.

. . . .

The following is a general synopsis . . . of the various types of coverage that are available in today's market:

1) Intellectual property liability insurance: These policies are being offered by a number of carriers who offer blanket coverage for all forms of IP infringement litigation. Such policies generally provide coverage for most IP claims or suits brought against the insured.

2) Patent infringement liability insurance: This type of coverage generally provides coverage for any patent infringement related to the manufacture, use, distribution, or sale of an allegedly infringing product.

3) Warranty and representation insurance: This type of policy generally covers costs associated with the breach of IP warranties and/or representations made in IP transactions, and also provides first party coverage for damages and losses.

4) Technology liability insurance: These policies generally cover damages that the insured is obligated to pay resulting from its wrongful acts in connection with the provision of technological services or products. Technological services include such things as systems analysis, programming, data processing, repair and maintenance of computer products, and design of networks and systems.

5) Intellectual property agreement insurance: These policies generally provide coverage for disputes arising from agreements including licenses, confidentiality, nondisclosure, and other technology or IP related agreements.

6) Media liability insurance: These policies are specially tailored for technology and Internet companies. They generally cover liabilities including Internet advertising and webcasting, as well as material published, transmitted, disseminated, distributed, created, originated, exhibited or displayed on the Internet in the course of business. These policies often cover allegations of defamation, product disparagement, trade libel, infringement of copyright, title or slogan, trademark, trade name, trade dress or service name, plagiarism, piracy, misappropriation of ideas under implied contracts, invasion or infringement of privacy and public disclosure of private facts.

7) <u>Internet professional liability insurance</u>: This type of coverage is also geared to the technology sector, and combines media liability coverage with professional services liabilities, such as Internet technology services (consulting, systems analysis, systems programming, data processing, system integration, development, repair or maintenance of computer products) and Internet professional services (design, construction or maintenance of internet site, providing electronic mail services, maintaining chat rooms, etc.).

8) <u>Internet and computer network security insurance</u>: This type of policy combines media liability coverage with security liability coverage which covers the failure of hardware, software, or firmware whose function or purpose is to protect a computer from attack, unauthorized access, unauthorized use, disclosure of confidential or private information or transmission of malicious code. Some of these policies also add cyber-extortion coverage, a criminal reward fund and crisis management coverage. Another similar policy provides for asset and income protection coverage that will cover losses attributed to a company's information assets, as well as any lost profits that may occur if such information is lost.

9) <u>Errors and omission insurance</u>: These policies are relatively new and are generally designed to cover damages arising from the insured's negligence arising out of the provision of technology services.

Notes & Questions

1. The threat of patent infringement liability—particularly as a result of suits by non-practicing entities that do not make or sell patented items but rather specialize in patent enforcement—has led to organized efforts to bolster the defensive capabilities of infringement litigation targets. A number of the resulting defensive arrangements extend beyond simple insurance. For example,

> "[d]efensive patent aggregators" are third party organizations that act like insurance companies by using the pooled resources of [their] member companies to purchase patents that might otherwise be purchased by non-practicing entities (NPEs) or other repeat plaintiffs and asserted against those members. Members usually pay an annual fee to participate and receive license agreements indefinitely when the aggregator purchases the patent. Thus, even if an NPE later buys the patent, it cannot assert it against the member companies who have been granted licenses through the aggregators. The most well-known defensive patent aggregators include RPX corporation ("RPX"), Unified Patents, and Allied Security Trust ("AST").

> All three of these companies have different structures in terms of how they purchase patents and protect their members. However, the goal for all of them is the same: to provide an actuarial model that allows its members to pay insurance costs for the purchases of patents that might otherwise be asserted against the members by NPEs. The arrangements theoretically allow the members of the companies to avoid costly litigation fees either by avoiding litigation completely or settling with NPEs soon after litigation is initiated.

Victoria F. Maroulis & Patrick Burns, *Emerging Trends in Managing Risk of Patent Litigation* in Practising Law Institute, IP Monetization 2015: Maximize the Value of Your IP Assets ch. 2 (2015) (available from PLI-Plus research service).

2. In what types of cases would payments to patent aggregators (or aggregators of other IP interests) be effective in limiting infringement liability risks? In what circumstances would these arrangements be ineffective and traditional liability insurance more useful in limiting infringement liability risks?

Mez Industries, Inc. v. Pacific National Insurance Company

California Court of Appeals

90 Cal. Rptr. 2d 721 (1999)

Croskey, J.

This case presents the question of whether a liability insurer providing coverage for "advertising injury" is required to defend its insured in an action charging the insured with *inducement* of patent infringement. When the respondent, Pacific National Insurance Company ("Pacific") refused to provide such a defense to the appellant, Mez Industries, Inc. ("Mez"), Mez filed this action for declaratory relief and breach of contract. The trial court sustained Pacific's demurrer without leave to amend and thereafter entered a judgment of dismissal.

Because we conclude that the advertising injury provisions of Pacific's policy did not provide coverage to Mez for inducement of patent infringement and, in any event, such coverage would have been precluded by Insurance Code section 533, we conclude that no potential for coverage existed as a matter of law and thus no duty to defend ever arose. The trial court ruled correctly and we therefore affirm.

FACTUAL AND PROCEDURAL BACKGROUND

Mez is engaged in the business of manufacturing, distributing and selling components used for the connection of joints in airflow conduction systems (such as central heating and air conditioning systems). It manufactures these components and advertises them for sale through wholesalers to mechanical and sheet metal construction contractors who use the components to create duct systems in various building projects throughout the United States.

On April 10, 1995, Ductmate Industries, Inc. ("Ductmate") filed a complaint against Mez in the United States District Court for the Northern District of Ohio in an action styled as "Ductmate Industries, Inc. v. Mez Industries, Inc.," U.S.D.C. N.D. Ohio Case No. 4:95CV00815 (hereinafter, the "Ductmate action"). Stripped to its relevant essentials, the complaint in that action alleged that Mez had induced its customers to infringe at least four of Ductmate's patents for certain "flange-type duct joint assembl[ies] and seal arrangement[s] [therefor]."[4]

---

4. Ductmate also alleged other misconduct by Mez including active direct infringement of Ductmate's patents. However, on appeal, the only alleged conduct which Mez claims justifies a

Ductmate's alleged claims of inducement of patent infringement pursuant to 35 U.S.C. § 271(b) were not based upon Mez's manufacture of the individual component parts for a duct system joint assembly, but rather upon those activities of Mez that caused or encouraged *others* to take those component parts and put them together in a way which infringed Ductmate's patents. Those activities by Mez necessarily involved its *advertising* activities, which encouraged and solicited others to buy Mez's products and assemble them in a particular manner. For example, Ductmate featured in its own advertising its "Slide-On Connectors" for use in putting together a conduction system and provided step-by-step instructions for assembly and installation. Mez has distributed a variety of advertising brochures, mailers, and promotional booklets depicting HVAC duct joint assemblies which graphically illustrated how Mez's corners, flanges and seals could work as substitutes for Ductmate's Slide-On Connectors corner units and related products. In addition, Mez's assembly and installation instructions produced the same HVAC ducts as depicted in Ductmate's advertising materials.

At least for our purposes, there is no contention that Mez's products themselves infringed upon any of Ductmate's patents. Rather, the relevant essence of the Ductmate action is that Mez's advertising, marketing and sales promotion activities solicited, encouraged and induced engineers, contractors, distributors and builders to purchase Mez's products and to combine and assemble them in a manner which did infringe Ductmate's patents.

Mez tendered defense of the Ductmate action to Pacific on or about July 6, 1995. Mez asserted that it was entitled to coverage and a defense of the action under the "Advertising Injury" section of Pacific's liability policy. As relevant to the issues before us, that policy promised both indemnity and a defense for an injury caused by one or both of the following two "offenses" committed *in the course of advertising* goods, products or services in the coverage territory during the policy period:

(1) "Misappropriation of advertising ideas or style of doing business," and

(2) "Infringement of copyright, title or slogan."[5]

---

defense of the Ductmate action by Pacific are the allegations that Mez induced others to infringe Ductmate's patents. Mez made this clear in the initial paragraph of its Opening Brief: "Mez seeks a determination that Pacific owes it a duty of defense for claims of *inducing patent infringement* under its 'advertising injury' coverage for [1] 'misappropriation of advertising ideas or style of doing business' or [2] 'infringement of title.'" (Italics added.) As will become apparent, such a limitation on its scope of coverage argument was necessary to satisfy the requirement that the alleged misconduct for which a defense was sought had an advertising nexus.

5. The specific provisions of Pacific's policy here at issue are as follows: "Coverage B—Personal and Advertising Injury Liability1. Insuring Agreement

a. We will pay those sums that the insured becomes legally obligated to pay as damages because of . . . 'advertising injury' to which this coverage part applies. We will have the right and duty to defend any 'suit' seeking those damages.

b. This insurance applies to:

(1) . . .

On or about November 22, 1995, after a review of the matter, Pacific denied coverage and refused to provide a defense. On June 4, 1997, Mez filed this action alleging essentially the forgoing facts and asserting that Pacific had wrongfully denied coverage. Mez alleged that it was entitled to a defense and sought a declaratory judgment for Pacific's breach of its contractual obligations under the policy.

Pacific attacked this complaint by demurrer, asserting that, as a matter of law, there could be no potential for coverage and thus no duty to defend. Pacific argued that the claim of inducing patent infringement is simply not a covered offense under the advertising provisions of the policy and, in any event, coverage for such an act would be precluded under section 533. The trial court agreed and, on January 9, 1998, sustained Pacific's demurrer without leave to amend. A judgment of dismissal was thereafter entered on January 27, 1998. Mez has filed this timely appeal.

CONTENTIONS OF THE PARTIES

Mez contends that there is at least a potential for coverage under the Pacific policy. It argues that the offenses of (1) "misappropriation of advertising ideas or style of doing business" and (2) "infringement of copyright, title or slogan" are both ambiguous and each could reasonably include the alleged inducement of patent infringement. Therefore, Mez concludes, Pacific had a duty to provide Mez with a defense to the Ductmate action and the trial court erred when it sustained Pacific's demurrer and entered a judgment of dismissal.

Pacific rejects these contentions and reasserts the same basic arguments which the trial court accepted and upon which it based its ruling.

DISCUSSION

. . . .

2. *Advertising Injury Coverage Cannot Be Established In This Case*

Advertising injury liability has become part of the coverage offered in Commercial General Liability ("CGL") policies only recently. Prior to 1986, this coverage was offered by a separate broad form endorsement for which an additional premium was charged. It is important to understand that this coverage is entirely distinct from the bodily injury and property damage coverage which has long been the standard fare of CGL policies.

---

(2) 'Advertising injury' caused by an offense *committed in the course of advertising* your goods, products, or services; but only if the offense was committed in the 'coverage territory' during the policy period."
Section 5 of the Primary Policy provides in pertinent part:"1. 'Advertising Injury' means injury arising out of one or more of the following offenses:
(a) Oral or written publication of material that slanders or libels the person or organization or disparages a person's or organization's goods, products, or services;
(b) Oral or written publication of material that violates a person's right of privacy;
(c) Misappropriation of advertising ideas or style of doing business; or
(d) *Infringement of copyright, title* or slogan." (Italics added.)

Bodily injury and property damage coverage is dependent upon an "accident" or "occurrence" and coverage is not triggered until an injury or damage results. Advertising injury, on the other hand, applies to injury resulting from the commission of certain specified offenses. It does *not* depend upon an accident, but may be based (and often is) on the *intentional* acts of the insured. Thus, even certain intentional torts may be covered (subject, of course, to the statutory exclusion under section 533, which we discuss below). The event triggering coverage is the commission of the specified offense during the policy period, provided that it is committed in the course of advertising goods, products or services.

a. *There Is No Coverage For a Patent Infringement Claim*

The specified "offenses" with which we are concerned here are the (1) "misappropriation of an advertising idea or style of doing business" and (2) "infringement of copyright, title or slogan." If Mez's alleged inducement of the infringement of Ductmate's patents fits either of these two offenses, and was committed in the course of Mez's advertisement of its own products, then coverage would be available. It is doubtless because of this latter requirement that Mez does not argue on appeal that coverage is provided for the direct patent infringement which is also alleged in the Ductmate action. Under *relevant* applicable federal law (i.e., prior to the 1996 effective date of the 1994 amendment), patent infringement occurs when a party makes, uses or sells a product incorporating a patented invention. (35 U.S.C. § 271(a).)[8] Where the claim in the underlying action is that an insured directly infringed the patents of another by the *sale* of its products, rather than by the form of the insured's advertisements, then the patent infringing act did not occur in the course of the insured's advertising activities within the meaning of the relevant policy language. (*Bank of the West v. Superior Court* (1992) 2 Cal. 4th 1254, 1275, 10 Cal. Rptr. 2d 538, 833 P.2d 545.) An advertising injury must have a causal connection with the insured's advertising activities before there can be coverage. (*Id.* at p. 1277, 10 Cal. Rptr. 2d 538, 833 P.2d 545.) As there is no contention here that Mez directly violated any of Ductmate's patents by its advertising activities, Mez cannot claim coverage for the allegations of

---

8. We note that in 1994, Congress amended the Patent Act to include "offers to sell" (e.g., advertising) as conduct which could constitute patent infringement, and this amendment became effective in 1996. (35 U.S.C. § 271(a); see also Historical and Statutory Notes re 1994 Amendments and Effective Date of 1994 Amendments.) At least one court has concluded that this amendment "indicates that the insured could have an objectively reasonable expectation that it could be prosecuted for -advertising injury in a claim for patent infringement." (See *Everett Associates, Inc. v. Transcontinental Ins. Co.* (N.D. Cal. 1999) 57 F. Supp. 2d 874, 882.) Assuming arguendo that the Everett court reached a proper result, a matter on which we express no opinion, this statutory change would appear to have nullified the argument that direct patent infringement could not arise out of an insured's advertising activities. However, the amendment has no impact on the issue before us because the alleged misconduct of Mez occurred prior to 1996 and Mez makes no claim for coverage based upon Ductmate's allegations of patent infringement. Moreover, even though a direct patent infringement might now be committed during the course of an advertising activity, such circumstance does not help us to resolve the question as to whether patent infringement itself will fall within one of the covered "offenses."

direct patent infringement. Thus, Mez has limited its coverage argument to the allegations that *inducement* of infringement is alleged by Ductmate and that such allegation is enough to justify coverage.

b. *There Is No Coverage For an Inducement of Patent Infringement Claim*

Federal law also proscribes *inducing* patent infringement. (35 U.S.C. 271(b).) This section provides that "[w]hoever actively induces infringement of a patent shall be liable as an infringer." However, the alleged infringer must be shown to have *knowingly* induced infringement. "It must be established that the defendant possessed specific intent to encourage another's infringement and not merely that the defendant had knowledge of the acts alleged to constitute inducement. The plaintiff has the burden of showing that the alleged infringer's actions induced infringing acts and that he knew or should have known his actions would induce actual infringements."

Unlike direct infringement, it is possible for inducement to infringe to occur during the course of advertising activities; indeed, advertising has been found to be a sufficient basis for a claim of inducement.[9] (*U.S. Fidelity & Guar. Co. v. Star Technologies* (1996) 935 F. Supp. 1110, 1116; *New Hampshire Ins. v. R.L. Chaides Const.* (N.D. Cal. 1994) 847 F. Supp. 1452, 1458.) However, liability can only be found if the inducement is "active"; that is, a party must "purposefully cause, urge or encourage another to infringe." Something *more* is required than simply the advertising of a product for sale. "In addition, the advertisement must instruct or explain to the purchaser exactly how to recreate or reassemble the product into one that infringes a patent." (*U.S. Fidelity & Guar. Co. v. Star Technologies, supra*, 935 F. Supp. at p. 1116; see also *Fromberg, Inc. v. Thornhill* (5th Cir. 1963) 315 F.2d 407, 412 [defendant advertised and personally demonstrated to purchasers how his device could be inserted into another object to recreate a patented product].)

Having in mind these general principles, we address the two questions which are raised by the parties' briefs as to whether coverage was provided for such conduct under Pacific's policy: (1) is the inducement of patent infringement an advertising offense within the meaning of the policy and, in any event, (2) is coverage under the policy for such an act barred by section 533?

(1) *Inducing Patent Infringement Does Not Constitute An Advertising Injury Offense*

Pacific argues that neither direct patent infringement nor the inducement thereof is included within either the (1) "misappropriation of an advertising idea or style of doing business" or (2) "infringement of copyright, title or slogan." Mez responds that those terms are ambiguous, as they are subject to at least one reasonable interpretation which would include patent infringement or at least its inducement.

---

9. As it seems clear, at least from Mez's complaint, that the alleged acts of inducement were committed in the course of Mez's advertising and marketing of its products, we assume, *for purposes of our decision*, that Mez has satisfied the "in the course of advertising" element required under Pacific's policy.

It is now settled that the interpretation of an insurance policy is no different than the interpretation of contracts generally. The mutual intention of the parties at the time the contract is formed governs interpretation. Such intent is to be inferred, if possible, solely from the written provisions of the contract. The "clear and explicit" meaning of these provisions, interpreted in their "ordinary and popular sense," unless "used by the parties in a technical sense" or "a special meaning is given to them by usage," will control judicial interpretation.

On the other hand, "'[i]f the terms of a promise are in any respect ambiguous or uncertain, it must be interpreted in the sense in which the promisor believed, at the time of making it, that the promisee understood it.' This rule, as applied to a promise of coverage in an insurance policy, protects not the subjective beliefs of the insurer but, rather, 'the objectively reasonable expectations of the insured.' Only if this rule does not resolve the ambiguity do we then resolve it against the insurer. [¶] In summary, a court that is faced with an argument for coverage based on assertedly ambiguous policy language must first attempt to determine whether coverage is consistent with the insured's objectively reasonable expectations. In so doing, the court must interpret the language in context, with regard to its intended function in the policy. This is because '*language in a contract* must be construed in the context of that instrument as a whole, and in the circumstances of that case, and *cannot be found to be ambiguous in the abstract.*'" (*Bank of the West v. Superior Court, supra*, 2 Cal. 4th at pp. 1264–1265, 10 Cal. Rptr. 2d 538, 833 P.2d 545; italics in original, citations omitted.)

The *Bank of the West* court made it clear that it was no longer enough to find an abstract ambiguity or a meaning for a disputed word or phrase which was simply "semantically permissible." In order to conclude that an ambiguity exists which will be construed against an insurer, it is necessary first to determine whether the coverage under the policy, which would result from such a construction, is consistent with the insured's *objectively reasonable expectations*. In order to do this, the disputed policy language must be examined *in context* with regard to its intended function in the policy. This requires a consideration of the policy as a whole, the circumstances of the case in which the claim arises, and "common sense." Such an evaluation of an insured's *objectively* reasonable expectations under that criteria may result in a restriction of coverage rather than an expansion. An insured will not be able successfully to claim coverage where a reasonable person would not expect it.

We recently had occasion to apply these principles in the context of a *trademark* infringement dispute. In *Lebas Fashion Imports of USA, Inc. v. ITT Hartford Ins. Group* (1996) 50 Cal. App. 4th 548, 59 Cal. Rptr. 2d 36 (*Lebas*), we concluded that the advertising offense "misappropriation of an advertising idea or style of doing business" was indeed ambiguous and, *in the context of the facts of that case*, the insured could have objectively reasonable expectations of coverage. However, the scope of our conclusion was necessarily confined by the specific circumstances in which it was reached. In *Lebas*, we were dealing with an insured that allegedly had appropriated the proprietary mark and name of an international distributor of high fashion perfume and cosmetics, and that was utilizing such mark and name in the labeling, marketing and advertising of its own line of clothing. We noted that, contrary to the fundamental purposes of a *patent*, one of the three fundamental purposes of a *trademark* was to advertise the products of the trademark holder and that an infringement of the trademark frequently occurred in the course of advertising. Moreover, a trademark often represented the manner and means of such advertising, or at the least was an integral part thereof, and as such could easily and reasonably be considered to fall within the definition of an "advertising idea" and be considered a part of the trademark holder's "style of doing business." Thus, an insurer's promise to provide coverage for the insured's misappropriation of either an "advertising idea" or a "style of doing business" could reasonably be construed by a layperson insured to include a trademark infringement. This was particularly true in light of the fact that, in *Lebas*, the record reflected that these new policy definitions of advertising injury offenses (which had replaced prior offenses described as "piracy" and "unfair competition") were accompanied by the *deletion* of an exclusion for trademark infringement that had been a part of the prior policy.

Understandably, Mez asks us to apply the same reasoning in this case and to find the policy's misappropriation offense ambiguous. However, we cannot go that far. In *Lebas*, we did not find that clause to be ambiguous in the abstract. We only reached the conclusion we did in the *context* of (1) the language of the policy, (2) the general circumstances of that particular case and (3) "common sense." We examined the policy language in that context with regard to its intended function in the policy and attempted to evaluate the insured's *objectively* reasonable expectations under that criteria. We have examined this same language in Pacific's policy and use the same criteria as we did in *Lebas*, but in the context of the facts in this case, we reach an entirely different result. We do not see how Mez's inducement of the infringement of Ductmate's particular patents reasonably could be considered to be the misappropriation of an "advertising idea" or "style of doing business." Similarly, as we discuss below, we see no reasonable basis for characterizing such inducement as constituting the infringement of a "copyright, title or slogan." As the federal cases we discuss below have said, such a construction would be offensive to both commonly understood meaning as well as common sense.

While we are aware of at least two cases which have concluded that the language in pre-1986 policies which described the offense of "piracy" was ambiguous enough to embrace patent infringement (see *New Hampshire Ins. v. R.L. Chaides Const., supra*, 847 F. Supp. at p. 1456; *National Union Fire Ins. Co. v. Siliconix, Inc.* (N.D. Cal. 1989) 729 F. Supp. 77, 79),[14] we are aware of no California or federal case which has reached a similar result with respect to the *post*-1986 policy language before us.

---

14. Mez also cites us to the decision of the Nebraska Supreme Court (*Union Insurance Co. v. Land and Sky, Inc.* (Neb. 1995) 247 Neb. 696, 529 N.W.2d 773) which held that an insured, under a policy defining one of the advertising injury offenses as "piracy," was entitled to a defense in a patent infringement action. Not only did that case involve a pre-1986 policy, and is thus not very

On the other hand, there are a number of cases which have concluded that the new language is not ambiguous, *at least in the context of a coverage claim for patent infringement*, and that no coverage is provided. Obviously, if patent infringement cannot properly be characterized as an advertising injury offense, then neither could its inducement. In *Owens-Brockway Glass v. International Ins. Co.* (E.D. Cal. 1995) 884 F. Supp. 363, the court rejected the coverage claim of an insured who had suffered a judgment for non-willful patent infringement in the sum of $36,485,400.

When the insured sued its insurer to recover the judgment, the court concluded that patent infringement simply was not covered. The *Owens-Brockway* court applied the same principles of policy construction discussed above and then stated:

> "Plaintiff argues that patent infringement is included within the policy language insuring advertising injury as 'infringement of title' or 'misappropriation of style of doing business.' Plaintiff consults the dictionary to find that the word 'title' can refer to ownership of property such as a patent. Under this argument, the phrase 'infringement of . . . title' could refer to infringement of a patent. Similarly, plaintiff argues that 'misappropriation of style of doing business' could refer to patent infringement. Neither claim is reasonable, however, when the words 'title' and 'style of doing business' are examined in the context of their use and in the light of common sense. [¶] First, and perhaps most significantly, there is the glaring absence of the word 'patent' anywhere in the policy language defining advertising injury. The language defining 'advertising injury' includes 'slander[,]' 'libel,' 'right of privacy,' 'advertising ideas,' 'style of doing business,' and 'copyright.' These are specific terms connected to well known legal categories, just as a claim of patent infringement is a distinct legal claim. But there is not a mention of 'patent' anywhere in the definition or elsewhere in the policy. Surely if coverage for patent infringement were anticipated there would be some mention of the term itself just as 'copyright' is explicitly listed. Several courts have commented vigorously on the significance of the omission of any reference to patent in the definition of advertising injury: [¶] [I]t is nonsense to suppose that if the parties had intended the insurance policy in question to cover patent infringement claims, the policy would explicitly cover infringements of 'copyright, title or slogan,' but then include patent infringement, sub silentio, in a different provision, by reference to 'unauthorized taking of . . . [the] style of doing business.' [Citation.] . . . 'It is even more absurd to suggest that the phrase "infringement of . . . title," as used in the clause "infringement of copyright, title or slogan", encompasses patent infringement or inducement to infringe. Basic common sense dictates that if these policies covered any form of patent infringement, the word "patent" would

---

helpful to us, but also the same insurer had issued the insured an excess policy which had expressly excluded coverage for patent infringement. The *Land and Sky* court found the term "piracy" to be ambiguous primarily because of this inconsistency between these two policies.

appear in the quoted "infringement" clauses.' [Citation.] Moreover, as noted above, the policy language at issue here does not include the terms 'piracy' or 'unfair competition'; it lists well recognized and narrow categories of legal claims among which patent infringement is notably absent. [¶] Second, neither the term 'infringement of title' nor 'misappropriation of style of doing business' suggests coverage of patent claims when these terms are viewed in the context of their use. One of the most significant parts of that context is that both terms are part of the definition of 'advertising injury.' There is nothing about the term 'advertising injury' itself that remotely suggests coverage of patent infringement." (884 F. Supp. at p. 367, fns. omitted.)

In *Gencor Industries v. Wausau Underwriters Ins. Co.* (M.D. Fla. 1994) 857 F. Supp. 1560, the court concluded that neither patent infringement nor inducement of infringement were covered offenses under this same policy language. Its reasoning was identical to that expressed by the *Owens-Brockway* court. (857 F. Supp. at p. 1564.) Finally, in *St. Paul Fire & Marine v. Advanced Interventional* (E.D. Va. 1993) 824 F. Supp. 583, 584–587, the court, applying California law, reached that same conclusion.

We think the analysis of these federal decisions is persuasive and we adopt their reasoning here. In the *context of the facts and circumstances of this case*, the policy terms "misappropriation of an advertising idea or style of doing business" and "infringement of copyright, title or slogan" simply could not be reasonably read by a layperson to include either patent infringement or the inducement thereof. This conclusion is consistent with the principles of contextual reasonableness which we have already summarized. Clearly, the Ductmate patents did not involve any process or invention which could reasonably be considered an "advertising idea" or a "style of doing business."

With respect to Mez's argument that there is coverage under the "infringement of . . . title . . ." provision in the policy, we reach the same conclusion. Our construction of that phrase is informed by the doctrine of *ejusdem generis* under which a term is interpreted by reference to the surrounding language. (*See, e.g., American Motorists Ins. Co. v. Allied-Sysco Food Services, Inc.* (1993) 19 Cal. App. 4th 1342, 1349, 24 Cal. Rptr. 2d 106, disapproved of on another ground in *Buss v. Superior Court* (1997) 16 Cal. 4th 35, 50, fn. 12, 65 Cal. Rptr. 2d 366, 939 P.2d 766 [policy covering "humiliation" was "limited to those cases in which humiliation damages arise out of the types of torts in which it is grouped—i.e., libel, slander, defamation of character, and invasion of the right to privacy"]; *Waranch v. Gulf Insurance Co.* (1990) 218 Cal. App. 3d 356, 360–361, 266 Cal. Rptr. 827 ["private occupancy," when grouped with "wrongful entry" and "wrongful eviction," could only mean occupancy of *real property*, not a motor vehicle]; *Martin Marietta Corp. v. Insurance Co. of North America* (1995) 40 Cal. App. 4th 1113, 1133, 47 Cal. Rptr. 2d 670 [the policy term "other invasion of the right of private occupancy" must be read as similar to terms "eviction" and "trespass" appearing in same coverage phrase]; *Truck Ins. Exchange v. Bennett* (1997) 53 Cal. App. 4th 75, 86, 61 Cal. Rptr. 2d 497 [coverage for "disparagement" tort "cannot reasonably be read to include any more than those causes of action customarily grouped together into the legal category of defamation"]. Applying this principle here, Mez's contention that a claim of patent infringement falls within the "infringement of ... title ..." must be rejected. The advertising offense, "infringement of copyright, title or slogan" must be read as a whole and interpreted by reference to all of the words used, and in full recognition that the words "patent infringement" are *not* included. In our view, reading the phrase as a whole compels the reasonable conclusion that coverage is *at most* provided for claims involving (1) those matters which are protected by copyright statutes and decisions, and (2) those literary, musical, artistic or commercial titles, marks or slogans which are protected by common law principles of unfair competition.[17] The phrase simply cannot reasonably be interpreted to encompass claims involving patent infringement.

A number of courts agree with this conclusion. (*Owens-Brockway Glass v. International Ins. Co., supra*, 884 F. Supp. at p. 368 ["The term 'infringement of title' is part of a list that includes copyright and slogan. In company with these terms, 'title' apparently refers to a name, such as a name of a literary or artistic work, rather than to ownership of an invention or other thing"]; *ShoLodge, Inc. v. Travelers Indem. Co. of Illinois* (6th Cir. 1999) 168 F.3d 256, 259–260 [in a service mark infringement case, the court held the term "title" was *unambiguous* and was defined as the "non-copyrightable title of a book, film, or other literary or artistic work"]; *Atlantic Mut. Ins. Co. v. Brotech Corp.* (E.D. Pa. 1994) 857 F. Supp. 423, 429 [the court declined to hold infringement of title encompassed patent infringement on the ground that the term "title" referred to a distinctive name or designation, rather than to the legal concept of ownership of property].)

Recently, another court had occasion to construe this same policy language in a case where coverage was sought for a claim of patent infringement asserted in the underlying lawsuit. That court, as do we, placed emphasis on the absence of any reference to "patent infringement" in the policy language. The court then stated, "The drafters of this policy placed 'title' between 'copyright' and 'slogan.' A slogan is a brief, attention-getting phrase used in advertising or promotion. A copyright is the exclusive right, granted by statute to an author or original creator to reproduce, publish and sell the matter and form of a literary, musical or artistic work or production. Neither of these terms has any apparent connection to the concept of ownership interests in

---

17. This conclusion is consistent with our Supreme Court's recent decision in *Palmer v. Truck Insurance Exchange* (1999) 21 Cal. 4th 1109, 90 Cal. Rptr. 2d 647, 988 P.2d 568, where the court considered the scope of the coverage provided under this same clause (1) in the context of a claim for infringement of a registered business mark, (2) where the insured's policy contained an exclusion for claims based on "infringement of registered trade mark service mark or trade name," except for those relating to "titles or slogans." In the presence of such policy language, the work "title" could not subsume "trade mark," "service mark" or "trade name." Therefore, the court concluded, "[o]nly one definition fits: the name of a literary or artistic work. Because these names can be trademarked, adopting this definition of 'title' carves out a limited exception and gives effect to every part of the policy's trademark exclusion clause." (*Id.* at p. 1117, 90 Cal. Rptr. 2d 647, 988 P.2d 568.)

property, let alone the legal right to make use, sell or offer to sell a patented invention. Hence, while dictionaries attribute several meanings to the word *title*, including the legal ownership of property (Black's Law Dict. (5th ed. 1979) p. 1331, col. 1), when read in the context of the CGL policy, 'title' can only mean a distinctive name, designation or other appellation." (*Maxconn Inc. v. Truck Ins. Exchange* (1999) 74 Cal. App. 4th 1267, 1276–1277, 88 Cal. Rptr. 2d 750, fn. omitted.)

Thus, when read in the context of the entire policy, the general circumstances of this case and simple common sense, the advertising injury provisions simply do not extend to patent infringement. Moreover, even if the policy language is not totally free from some ambiguity, Mez could not, in light of such contextual considerations, have had an *objectively reasonable* expectation of coverage for a claim of *inducing* willful patent infringement. Therefore, such a claim would not be covered as an advertising injury offense.

(2) Coverage For Inducement of Patent Infringement Is Barred By Section 533

As our brief initial discussion of inducing patent infringement demonstrated, in order to be found liable, a party must have the specific intent to induce another to infringe the patent holder's prior right. (*Manville Sales Corp. v. Paramount Systems, Inc., supra*, 917 F.2d at p. 553.) Accordingly it must be shown that "the defendant possessed *specific intent* to encourage another's infringement and *not merely that the defendant had knowledge* of the acts alleged to constitute inducement." (*Id.* at p. 553; italics added; see also *National Presto Industries, Inc. v. West Bend Co.* (Fed. Cir. 1996) 76 F.3d 1185, 1194, italics added [the "statutory liability for inducement of [patent] infringement derives from the common law, wherein acts that *the actor* knows will lead to the commission of a wrong by another, place shared liability for the wrong on the actor"].)

In *Dynamis, Inc. v. Leepoxy Plastics, Inc.* (N.D. Ind. 1993) 831 F. Supp. 651, the court stated: "'[A] person infringes by actively and *knowingly* aiding and abetting another's direct infringement. Although section 271(b) does not use the word "knowing," the case law and legislative history uniformly assert such a requirement.'" (*Id.* at p. 656, italics in the original, citing *Water Technologies Corp. v. Calco, Ltd., supra*, 850 F.2d at p. 668.) Thus, "it is clear that under § 271(b) an accused infringer must be shown to have actual knowledge of the patent and the infringement *and have the actual intent to induce the infringement*." (*Id.* at p. 657; italics added.) Absent proof that the defendant "had an actual intent to induce infringement," there is no liability and summary judgment in favor of the judgment must be granted. (*Id.* at p. 657; see also *Hewlett-Packard Co. v. Bausch & Lomb, Inc.* (Fed. Cir. 1990) 909 F.2d 1464, 1469, fn. omitted ["we are of the opinion that proof of actual intent to cause the acts which constitute the infringement is a necessary prerequisite to finding active inducement. And it is proof of that intent which is missing in the present case"]; *R2 Medical Systems, Inc. v. Katecho, Inc.* (E.D. Ill. 1996) 931 F. Supp. 1397, 1440–1441 [liability for inducing infringement under section 271(b) requires proof that defendant knew that the combination for which its component was especially designed was both patented and infringed and that the defendant "specifically intended that its sale or other challenged acts induce its customers to engage in the conduct that allegedly directly infringes"].)

A "willful act" under section 533 will include either "an act deliberately done for the *express purpose* of causing damage or intentionally performed *with knowledge* that damage is highly probable or *substantially certain* to result." (*Shell Oil Co. v. Winterthur Swiss Ins. Co.* (1993) 12 Cal. App. 4th 715, 742, 15 Cal. Rptr. 2d 815; italics added.) It also appears that a willful act includes an intentional and wrongful act in which "the harm is inherent in the act itself." (*J.C. Penney Casualty Ins. Co. v. M.K.* (1991) 52 Cal. 3d 1009, 1025, 278 Cal. Rptr. 64, 804 P.2d 689.) In an earlier case, the Supreme Court had said that "even an act which is 'intentional' or 'willful' within the meaning of traditional tort principles will not exonerate the insurer from liability . . . unless it is done with a 'preconceived design to inflict injury.' [Citations.]" (*Clemmer v. Hartford Insurance Co.* (1978) 22 Cal.3d 865, 887, 151 Cal. Rptr. 285, 587 P.2d 1098.) However, the issue to which the *Clemmer* court spoke involved a question of the insured's mental capacity. Subsequent decisions have made clear that the "preconceived design to injure" standard is relevant only when the insured's "mental capacity is an issue or the insured's intent or motive might justify an otherwise wrongful act." (*Shell Oil Co. v. Winterthur Swiss Ins. Co., supra*, 12 Cal. App. 4th at p. 740, 15 Cal. Rptr. 2d 815; *J.C. Penney Casualty Ins. Co. v. M. K., supra*, 52 Cal.3d at p. 1023, 278 Cal. Rptr. 64, 804 P.2d 689.) Citing *J.C. Penney*, the *Shell Oil* court emphasized that "section 533 precludes *indemnification, whether or not the insured subjectively intended harm*, if the insured seeks coverage for an intentional, wrongful act that is inherently and necessarily harmful." (*Shell Oil Co. v. Winterthur Swiss Ins. Co., supra*, 12 Cal. App. 4th at pp. 740–741, 15 Cal. Rptr. 2d 815; italics added.)

Although it was speaking in the context of an environmental pollution case, the *Shell Oil* court properly summarized the rule which governs the scope and application of section 533: "We conclude that section 533 prohibits indemnification of more than just intentional acts that are subjectively desired to cause harm and acts that are intentional, wrongful, and necessarily harmful regardless of subjective intent. *A 'willful act' under section 533 must also include a deliberate, liability-producing act that the individual, before acting, expected to cause harm. Conduct for which the law imposes liability, and which is expected or intended to result in damage, must be considered wrongful and willful. Therefore, section 533 precludes indemnification for liability arising from deliberate conduct that the insured expected or intended to cause damage.*" (*Id.* at pp. 742–743, 15 Cal. Rptr. 2d 815, italics added.)

We believe that the circumstances presented here clearly come within this analysis of the proper application of section 533. An inducement to patent infringement under 35 U.S.C. § 271(b), as alleged in the underlying *Ductmate* action, could not be committed except as a knowing, intentional and purposeful act that is clearly wrongful and necessarily harmful. A defendant would have to intend the act, that is, to intend that the induced party infringe the patent. Such an impermissible motivation is necessary to liability for the act of inducement and it thus involves willful and intentional misconduct. Obviously, damage would flow in the form of a loss to

Ductmate and a gain to Mez through the sale of *its* products. Plainly, such a result would necessarily have to be within Mez's knowledge. Indeed, it would be Mez's presumed purpose. This is enough to satisfy the requirements of section 533.

Thus, even if the post-1986 policy language embraced patent infringement, its inducement would be excluded under section 533. Two recent cases which have directly considered this question have expressly so held. (*Aetna Casualty & Surety Co. v. Superior Court (Watercloud Bed Co.)* (1993) 19 Cal. App. 4th 320, 330–333, 23 Cal. Rptr. 2d 442; *Intex Plastics Sales Co. v. United Nat. Ins.* (9th Cir. 1994) 23 F.3d 254, 256–257.) Mez argues that we should reject those cases as wrongly decided. We decline to do so. Our discussion and analysis, which is based in part on prior decisions of this court examining the scope and breadth of section 533 (see *Downey Venture v. LMI Ins. Co.* (1998) 66 Cal. App. 4th 478, 500–502, 78 Cal. Rptr. 2d 142 and *B & E Convalescent Center v. State Compensation Ins. Fund* (1992) 8 Cal. App. 4th 78, 94, 97–99, 9 Cal. Rptr. 2d 894), has caused us to reach the same conclusion as did the *Aetna* and *Intex* courts. We believe they were correctly decided. There is no potential coverage for Mez under the Pacific policy.

3. *Pacific Had No Duty To Defend Mez in the Ductmate Action*

What Mez seeks to accomplish in this action is the vindication of its contention that Pacific owed it a duty to defend it in the Ductmate action. It is well settled that where there is no potential for coverage under a liability policy, the insurer owes no duty to defend. It is the potential for coverage under a particular policy, and in light of the specific pleadings and known facts of the third party claim, which establishes the insurer's obligation to defend.

However, where a denial of indemnification is based on the application of section 533, it does not necessarily follow that no duty to defend exists. As we stated in *B & E Convalescent Center*, . . . "'[S]ection 533 precludes only *indemnification* of willful conduct and not the *defense* of an action in which such conduct is alleged. [Citation.] . . . [¶] . . . [E]ven though public policy or section 533 precludes an insurer from indemnifying an insured in an underlying action the duty to defend still exists so long as the "insured reasonably expect[s] the policy to cover the types of acts involved in the underlying suit[.]" [Citation.]' [Citation]. Put another way, 'if the reasonable expectations of an insured are that a defense will be provided for a claim, then the insurer cannot escape that obligation merely because public policy precludes it from indemnifying that claim.' [Citation.]" (*B&E Convalescent Center v. State Compensation Insurance Fund, supra*, 8 Cal. App. 4th at p. 93, 9 Cal. Rptr. 2d 894, italics in original.)

As we have explained, however, no potential for coverage exists in this case and Mez could not have had *any* objectively reasonable expectation of such coverage. Similarly, to the extent that section 533 alone is relied upon to preclude coverage, we see nothing in this record or in the arguments of Mez which would prompt us to conclude that Mez had any reasonable expectation of a defense even though indemnification was excluded. Therefore, for the reasons discussed above, Pacific owed no duty to defend Mez in the Ductmate action and the trial court correctly sustained Pacific's demurrer to Mez's complaint.

DISPOSITION

The judgment is affirmed. Pacific shall recover its costs on appeal.

Notes & Questions

1. Assuming that infringement claims would otherwise be covered by a policy, what types of intellectual property infringement would be excluded from insurance coverage under a provision like that of California Insurance Code § 533 barring insurance for "a loss caused by the willful act of the insured"? What aspect of an infringer's conduct must be willful before insurance is precluded? Why should the limits of coverage be restricted by statute if an insurance company is willing to provide insurance protection against a wider range of infringement-related losses?

2. Should insurance policies covering losses from "misappropriation of style of doing business" be construed broadly to provide recoveries for patent infringement losses incurred by businesses that inadvertently adopt patented business methods for Internet transactions or other business activities?

Zurich Insurance Co. v. Killer Music, Inc.

United States Court of Appeals for the Ninth Circuit

998 F.2d 674 (1993)

BEEZER, CIRCUIT JUDGE:

Killer Music, Inc., doing business as HLC Partnership; TTBB, Inc., doing business as Killer Tracks; and Ron Hicklin (collectively, "Killer Music") appeal the district court's grant of Zurich Insurance Co.'s ("Zurich") motion for summary judgment on Zurich's declaratory judgment action and the dismissal of Killer Music's counterclaims on a motion for summary judgment. The issues are whether Zurich had a duty to defend and indemnify Killer Music in a suit brought by a third party (Pfeifer) and whether Zurich's denial of coverage was in bad faith. We reverse and remand because we hold that Zurich wrongfully refused to defend Killer Music. We affirm the summary judgment on the bad faith issue.

I

Killer Music contracted with Pfeifer to sell jingles which Pfeifer produced to radio and television stations and movie studios. Killer Music agreed to pay Pfeifer for each jingle sold. The contract also provided that Pfeifer would perform on certain songs, and that he would be paid for these performances when the songs were sold. That contract expired in 1988.

After that date, Killer Music compiled and sold a music library which included Pfeifer songs which had not been sold during the contract period. The songs were not attributed to Pfeifer and no compensation was paid. In April 1990, Pfeifer filed a complaint in which he alleged copyright infringement, false designation of origin,

unfair competition, palming off, conversion, and unjust enrichment. He sought punitive and compensatory damages, an accounting, the establishment of a constructive trust, and attorneys' fees.

Killer Music was insured under a Comprehensive General Liability Policy written by Zurich. The policy was sold by DeWitt Stern, an insurance broker. The policy covers "advertising injury," which includes "those sums that the insured becomes legally obligated to pay as damages because of 'personal injury' or 'advertising injury' to which this insurance applies." "Advertising injury" is defined to include injury from infringement of copyright. The policy excludes coverage, however, for advertising injury "arising out of breach of contract."

Killer Music first learned of the Pfeifer litigation when they were notified that Pfeifer had obtained a temporary injunction against them. At this point, Killer Music contacted DeWitt Stern, advised a clerk there that the Pfeifer suit was going to be filed against them, and asked her to check into the matter. Killer Music did not ask that the insurer defend them. The clerk may or may not have contacted persons at Zurich to confer about the policy coverage; at any rate, she advised Killer Music that they were not covered. Another telephone call was made to another clerk that same week, who also reported that there was no coverage. Killer Music never followed up with any written notice of claim either to Zurich or DeWitt, nor did Killer Music transmit any of the court documents to either company.[1]

Killer Music settled with Pfeifer soon after the suit was filed. Under the settlement agreement, Pfeifer transferred his rights to the songs which had been used in the music library, and agreed to drop his suit, in exchange for a $175,000 settlement.

At this point, Killer Music, through counsel, began corresponding with Zurich over the issue of coverage, seeking recovery of defense costs in the suit and indemnification. Zurich responded by filing an action for a declaratory judgment that it had no duty to defend or indemnify. Killer Music counterclaimed and asserted that Zurich breached its duty of good faith. The district court granted Zurich's motions for summary judgment on both its claim and the counterclaim.

. . . .

III

Under the contract with Killer Music, Zurich had "the right and duty to defend any 'suit' seeking [damages for 'advertising injury']." "Advertising injury" was defined to include infringement of copyright. Pfeifer alleged copyright infringement, among other causes of action, in his complaint against Killer Music. The policy excludes coverage, however, for advertising injury "arising out of breach of contract." Zurich,

---

1. The policy provides in relevant part:
   b. If a claim is made or 'suit' is brought against any insured, you [the insured] must see to it that we receive prompt written notice of the claim or 'suit.'
   c. You and any other involved insured must . . . [i]mmediately send us copies of any demands, notices, summonses or legal papers received in connection with the claim or 'suit.'

based on a reasonable reading of case law, including *Home Indem. Co. v. Avol*, 706 F. Supp. 728 (C.D. Cal. 1989) (applying California law), *aff'd without opinion*, 912 F.2d 469 (9th Cir. 1990), and *Allstate Ins. Co. v. Hansten*, 765 F. Supp. 614 (N.D. Cal. 1991) (applying California law), determined that Pfeifer's copyright infringement claim arose out of a breach of contract and was therefore not covered. Other cases suggest, however, that the Pfeifer action should be characterized as sounding in tort. *See Fragomeno v. Insurance Co. of the West*, 207 Cal. App. 3d 822, 255 Cal. Rptr. 111 (1989); *Fireman's Fund Ins. Co. v. City of Turlock*, 170 Cal. App. 3d 988, 216 Cal. Rptr. 796 (1985). Under California law, "the duty to defend is so broad that as long as the complaint contains language creating the potential of liability under an insurance policy, the insurer must defend an action against its insured." *CNA Casualty of California v. Seaboard Sur. Co.*, 176 Cal. App. 3d 598, 606, 222 Cal. Rptr. 276 (1986); *Republic Indem. Co. v. Superior Court*, 224 Cal. App. 3d 492, 500, 273 Cal. Rptr. 331 (1990). Based on our reading of the California cases, we conclude that there was at least a "potential of liability" so Zurich had a duty to defend Killer Music in that action.

IV

Zurich contends that the claim was not potentially covered because coverage was excluded by operation of California Insurance Code § 533. Section 533 provides that "[a]n insurer is not liable for a loss caused by the willful act of the insured . . . ." According to Zurich, Pfeifer's suit against Killer Music was based on intentional misconduct, a "willful act" by Killer Music. Killer Music argues that the use of Pfeifer's music in the music library was inadvertent and certainly not "willful" as defined in the statute.

A "clear line of authority" in California directs that "even an act which is 'intentional' or 'willful' within the meaning of traditional tort principles will not exonerate the insurer from liability under [§] 533 unless it is done with a 'preconceived design to inflict injury.'" The term "willful" is used to describe "an act done with malevolence." A "'willful act' within the meaning of section 533 means 'something more than the mere intentional doing of an act constituting [ordinary] negligence', and appears to be something more than the intentional violation of a statute."

Killer Music's actions were not proven to be "willful" as a matter of law. While Zurich characterizes Killer Music's infringement as "knowing," Killer Music's president Hicklin, by sworn affidavit, indicated that he did not know that any of Pfeifer's work was being used in the music library and that he "never intended to engage in any unauthorized use of any work owned in whole or in part by Pfeifer." He also disavowed any intent to injure or harm Pfeifer.

Zurich points out that California courts have been willing to find some activities "willful" as a matter of law "if the harm is inherent in the act itself." *B & E Convalescent Center*, 8 Cal. App. 4th at 97, 9 Cal. Rptr. 2d 894 (citation omitted). It is true that a subjective desire to injure or harm need not always be proven and can be assumed by the nature of the act. However, copyright infringement is not one of those activities that is "willful" per se. Zurich admits in its brief that "[c]opyright infringement can be innocent or intentional . . . . Innocent infringement may be covered."

The possibility that §533 might operate to exclude coverage does not excuse Zurich's initial decision to deny coverage. "[I]n order to rely upon Section 533 to justify its refusal to defend, [Zurich] must show that information available to it at that time demonstrated that [Pfeifer] was required to establish that [Killer Music] intended him harm, not merely that it intended to act." Zurich did not demonstrate that Pfeifer was required to prove Killer Music's intent to harm him to succeed on his claim for copyright infringement; indeed, Zurich itself noted that "[c]opyright infringement can be innocent or intentional." We hold that the district court erred in granting Zurich's motion for summary judgment on the basis of §533.

V

Zurich argues that it had no duty to cover Killer Music's claim since no written notice was given, as required by the policy, and Zurich had no actual or constructive notice of the claim. Although the parties dispute whether Zurich ever received actual notice of the claim from an employee of DeWitt Stern, this question is immaterial since under California Civil Code §2332 notice to an agent is equivalent to notice to the principal. It is clear that DeWitt Stern must be considered Zurich's agent. The only address on the policy for the insured to contact was DeWitt Stern's. *See* California Civil Code §§2300, 2317 (1992). The lack of written notice alone does not excuse Zurich's refusal to defend. Here Zurich's agent had actual notice and, without requesting a copy of the complaint, the agent decided not to defend on the basis of lack of coverage, not inadequate notice. *See, e.g., Clemmer v. Hartford Ins. Co.*, 22 Cal. 3d 865, 151 Cal. Rptr. 285, 587 P.2d 1098 (1978) (insurer made no showing that it would have defended if it had had timely tender of defense).

VI

We now address the consequences of Zurich's breach. As to the settlement, the mere fact that Zurich failed to defend does not mean that Zurich is liable for the amount of the settlement. Zurich is liable only for the amount of a "reasonable settlement of the claim in good faith." "A reasonable settlement made by the insured to terminate the underlying claim against him may be used as presumptive evidence of the insured's liability on the underlying claim, and the amount of such liability." This presumption "may be overcome by proof" that the settlement agreement is unreasonable in amount.

We recognize that the settlement agreement represents, in part, an exchange of cash consideration for the rights to Pfeifer's songs, not simply compensation for damages from copyright infringement. We also note that Zurich had no control over the terms of the settlement agreement, which was structured so that Killer Music received the rights to the songs. When the issue of the amount of a reasonable settlement in good faith is addressed on remand, Zurich will have the opportunity to demonstrate that some portion, if not all, of the settlement amount is allocable to the value of the songs which Killer received in the settlement agreement.

By breaching its duty to defend, Zurich is also liable for attorneys' fees as provided in the policy or as "incurred in good faith, and in the exercise of a reasonable discretion" in defending the action. California Civil Code § 2778. Zurich's liability extends to fees arguably allocable to defense of noncovered claims. Zurich is not liable for fees incurred by Killer Music in bringing this action in the district court, since Killer Music "is not entitled to an award of attorney's fees incurred in a separate action in which [it] seeks to enforce [its] right to be defended or to be reimbursed for attorney's fees previously incurred in an action which should have been defended by the insurer."

VII

As to Killer Music's counterclaim alleging bad faith on Zurich's part, there is no evidence of bad faith in this record. Although Zurich breached its duty to defend, "breach of the implied covenant of good faith and fair dealing involves something beyond breach of the contractual duty itself." Zurich did not reasonably investigate the claim to determine coverage, but "without actual presentation of a claim by the insured in compliance with claims procedures contained in the policy, there is no duty imposed on the insurer to investigate the claim." Here it is undisputed that Killer Music failed to follow explicit policy conditions requiring written notice, conditions that were incorporated into the contract to avoid just the sort of out-of-channel coverage decision that took place in this case. The fact that Zurich brought a declaratory judgment action to determine its liability for coverage is not bad faith. The district court did not err in granting Zurich's motion for summary judgment on the bad faith counterclaim.

VIII

We reverse the summary judgment on Zurich's claim and remand for a determination of the damages attributable to a reasonable settlement in good faith and for a determination of attorneys' fees incurred in the defense of the Pfeifer suit. We affirm the grant of Zurich's motion for summary judgment on the bad faith counterclaim. Neither party shall recover costs on appeal.

Notes & Questions

1. Why is the duty to defend an insured under a General Liability Policy applicable in a wider range of circumstances than the obligation to compensate the insured's losses? What type of evidence of potentially covered intellectual property infringement liability should be present before the duty to defend is triggered?

2. Why was the type of copyright infringement at issue in the *Killer Music* case sufficiently related to advertising activities to at least arguably involve an "advertising injury" within the coverage of the General Liability Policy present in that case? Did the company infringe any copyrights in its advertising? At what point and in what way were the company's advertising activities related to its infringement liability?

3. Why should General Liability Policies exclude coverage of losses related to breaches of contracts like the copyright royalty agreement present in *Killer Music*? How might claims under such a contract differ from claims of copyright

infringement brought for unauthorized use of the same intellectual property if no licensing and royalty agreement were present?

State Farm Fire and Casualty Insurance Company v. White

United States District Court for the Northern District of Georgia

777 F. Supp. 952 (1991)

HAROLD L. MURPHY, DISTRICT JUDGE.

This case is before the Court on seven motions for summary judgment filed by the Plaintiff in this action for declaratory judgment. The motions, however, rely on substantially similar legal positions and will therefore be consolidated for the purpose of this Court's discussion.

This action arises out of a companion case pending in this Court and styled *Greg Simms and North Georgia Partnership v. Edward White, et al.*, Civil Action File No. 4:89-cv-306-HLM. In the underlying action Greg Simms and North Georgia Partnership allege that Edward White, Howard Rozell, and Neal Davis, and their various development associations built apartment complexes relying on plans that were written and owned by themselves. Plaintiffs in the underlying action allege that "Defendants are guilty of predicate acts of theft, conversion and/or unjust enrichment from theft and conversion and/or conspiracy to convert to their own use certain architectural and business plans and other intellectual property of the Plaintiff's in that said Defendants jointly and severally have taken and used certain architectural plans, designs, trade dress, and specifications which were and are the property of the Plaintiff and for which the Defendants are liable to the Plaintiffs in conversion, quantum meruit, assumpsit, violation of common law copyright, copyright infringement, and unfair business practices all in violation of State and Federal Law . . . ." Plaintiff in the instant action, through its Motions for summary judgment, seeks a judicial determination that its insurance policies do not provide coverage to the Defendants in the above referenced action.

Plaintiff's argument, presented in basically the same format given that certain of the insurance policies vary in detail, is that the underlying action against the insured sounds in copyright. The insurance policies involved, however, insure only the loss of use of "tangible" property.[1] Plaintiff argues that the architectural plans allegedly

---

1. The potentially relevant third party liability coverage, common to all of the subject insurance policies, is as follows:

> "*Coverage L — Business Liability*, the company will pay on behalf of the insured all sums which the insured shall become legally obligated to pay as damages because of bodily injury, property damage or personal injury caused by an occurrence to which this insurance policy applies."
>
> "*Property damage* means (a) physical injury to or destruction of tangible property which occurs during the policy period including the loss of use thereof at any time resulting therefrom; or (b) loss of use of tangible property which has not been physically injured or destroyed provided such loss of use is caused by an occurrence during the policy period."

converted by the Defendants can only be considered intangible intellectual property and, therefore, the potential loss of use of these plans is not insured.

Plaintiff thus emphasizes the term "tangible" as it modifies the property loss coverage of the relevant insurance policies to conclude that theft or conversion of intellectual property is not within the coverage definitions. By the same token, claims for copyright violations, and unfair business practices are similarly not covered by the relevant insurance policies. Plaintiff contends that it is entitled to a Court order ratifying this position.

Defendants, generally, disagree. None of these Defendants contend that the policy coverage should extend to claims for copyright infringement; however all oppose the grant of summary judgment as to other claims. Defendants argue that the claims for copyright violation are only a portion of the underlying Plaintiff's complaint. Laying aside the issue of copyright violation, Defendants argue that the claims for conversion, assumpsit, and quantum meruit, punitive damages, attorney's fees, and costs are covered by the relevant insurance policies.

Defendants argue that the architectural plans are "tangible" property. Once the "idea" which is validly considered intangible intellectual property has been reduced to physical plans and drawings, Defendants contend, they have assumed a tangible form. Consequently the "loss of use" of these plans is a loss of use of tangible property and, therefore, within the policy definition of "property loss."

The resolution of this dispute revolves around the legal definition of "tangible property," the Georgia common law rules of contract construction, and, ultimately, the role of this Court on summary judgment. According to O.C.G.A. 48-8-2(11), tangible property is "property which may be weighed, measured, felt or touched, or is in any manner perceptible to the senses." Likewise, Black's Law Dictionary defines tangible property as "that which may be felt or touched, and is necessarily corporeal, although it may either be real or personal." Under these definitions an architectural plan, in its physical form, is obviously tangible, its finite mass lending weight and sensory perception.

Plaintiff argues, nonetheless, that the aspects of the architectural plan which lends its tangible qualities are simply the paper and ink. The value of such a plan, Plaintiff contends, is in the intellectual property which is represented on the paper. Plaintiff points out that under Georgia law, "where the language of a contract is clear and unambiguous, and capable of only one *reasonable* interpretation, no construction is necessary or even permissible." *Stern's Gallery, Inc. v. Corporate Property Investors, Inc.*, 176 Ga. App. 586, 337 S.E.2d 29 (1985) (emphasis supplied). According to the

---

In the policies which define the term "occurrence" it is defined as:

"*Occurrence* means an accident, including continuous or repeated exposure to conditions, which result in bodily injury, or property damage, neither expected nor intended from the standpoint of the insured . . . ."

Plaintiff, the term "tangible property," applied to the facts of this case, can only reasonably be interpreted as excluding coverage for the loss of use of architectural plans.[3]

Another relevant principle of contract construction, however, is that "a contract of insurance is construed most strongly against the insurer, particularly where the insurer denies coverage based upon a policy exclusion."

Nonetheless in the view of this Court, the conclusive consideration is this Court's role in deciding the instant motions for summary judgment. Plaintiff's motion for summary judgment seeks to absolve itself of any liability for the loss of use the architectural plans in question on the ground that they are not "tangible" property. Both parties agree, however, that the architectural plans, in the sense of their being printed on paper, meet the legal definition of tangible property. Therefore while the parties may argue about the value of the paper printed plan vis a vis the concept reproduced on the paper, it seems that at least whatever value is assigned to the paper would fall within insurance policy definition of property loss. Accordingly, what remains is a question of fact regarding the relative valuation of the components of a printed architectural plan. Given that this Court is precluded, on a motion for summary judgment, from resolving genuine issues of material fact, Plaintiff's argument on this point must fail.

. . . .

Notes & Questions

Under what circumstances should a physical item containing intellectual property (such as a book, movie, or computer software diskette) be deemed tangible property for purposes of an insurance policy covering losses to tangible property? Where an item of this sort is stolen or destroyed, when will its status as a covered item of tangible property be sufficiently possible to trigger the duty to defend the insured under a policy covering tangible property losses?

American Century Services Corp. v. American International Specialty Lines Insurance Co.

United States District Court for the Southern District of New York

U.S. Dist. LEXIS 15016 (Aug. 14, 2002)

LYNCH, J.

On December 20, 1998, defendant American International Specialty Lines Insurance Company ("AISLIC") issued a two-year investment management insurance policy (the "Policy") to plaintiff American Century Services Corporation ("American Century"). For a premium of $414,800, AISLIC offered up to $10,000,000 liability

---

3. Plaintiff points out that no recovery is sought for the loss of the paper on which the plans were printed, rather it is the loss of the "idea" contained on that paper which the Defendants would be seeking under the policies.

coverage, less a $350,000 retention, for various enumerated risks. In this action, American Century seeks a declaratory judgment, pursuant to 28 U.S.C. § 2201, that the Policy requires AISLIC to pay the costs and settlement amounts of certain patent infringement claims raised by third parties against American Century during the policy period. The plaintiff now moves for summary judgment. After full briefing, and oral argument before this Court on February 8, 2002, the motion will be denied, for the reasons that follow.

BACKGROUND

This dispute concerns coverage for patent infringement claims raised by non-party patent owners Leon Stambler ("Stambler"), whose patents relate to internet security technology, and Ronald A. Katz ("Katz"), whose patents relate to automated telephone technology. American Century, a Missouri corporation with its principal place of business in Kansas City, Missouri, used allegedly infringing internet and telephone technology in providing investment management and related services to a group of mutual funds (the "Funds"). These internet and telephone systems allow American Century customers to obtain account and market information, make transfers between the Funds, and contact American Century representatives. American Century has since settled with Katz. Stambler is not actively pursuing his claim. Plaintiff seeks a declaratory judgment as to coverage for both alleged infringements under its Policy with AISLIC, an Alaskan corporation with its principal place of business in New York.

The first patent infringement claim arrived on March 27, 2000, when Stambler notified American Century that its use of certain secure internet services software infringed his patents. Plaintiff relayed this information to AISLIC on July 3, 2000. (*Id.* Ex. 5.) In a letter dated September 1, 2000, AISLIC responded that "It appears that coverage, *if any*, would fall under Coverage B as the allegation is based upon the insured's use of secure internet services software in the operation of their mutual fund business," Coverage B reaches "all sums which the Insured shall become legally obligated to pay as damages resulting from any claim or claims first made against the Insured . . . for any Wrongful Act of the Insured . . . but only if the Wrongful Act occurs prior to the end of the Policy Period and solely in the course of the management and/or operations of the Fund(s)." AISLIC also concluded that, "[i]f, in fact, [Stambler] has a patent . . . which the insured has used in the management of their mutual fund business without payment of royalties due, then this would be a gaining of profit or advantage to which they are not legally entitled." Defendant concluded that such "royalties owed" fall under Exclusion 4(I)(2), which denies coverage for "any actual or alleged gaining of any profit or advantage to which the Insured is not legally entitled." AISLIC later agreed to advance reasonable defense costs once the $350,000 retention had been exhausted. No settlement has been reached with Stambler, who apparently has not pursued his claim since a letter to plaintiff dated September 29, 2000.

On September 26, 2000, American Century received notice of the second patent infringement claim. This claim came from Katz, who informed American Century that he believed its interactive automated telephone system infringed one or more of his patents. American Century notified AISLIC of Katz's claim on October 17, 2000. AISLIC again denied coverage. This time, however, AISLIC concluded that on the facts presented neither Coverage A, B, C, D, nor the Policy's amendment for Employment Practices Liability Insurance applied to Katz's claim, and accordingly, did not consider the applicability of any of the Policy's exclusions. American Century settled with Katz for $3,403,321 on February 28, 2001.

In addition to seeking a declaration that the Policy covers Stambler's and Katz's claims, plaintiff demands damages for breach of contract and wrongful denials of coverage, including the costs of bringing this action, compensatory damages for $3,053,321 (the settlement with Katz less the retention), and pre- and post-judgment interest.

DISCUSSION

. . . .

III. *Interpretation of the Policy*

Whether an investment management insurance policy of the type issued by AISLIC to American Century covers patent infringement claims is a novel question. Neither plaintiff nor defendant has produced cases on this issue, and the Court's own research suggests that none exist.

Insurance coverage for patent infringement claims, however, is not a new issue and has been frequently debated. The majority of the cases, as well as the academic scholarship on the topic, focus on whether insurers have a duty to defend insureds against infringement claims under the advertising injury provisions of commercial general liability insurance policies. Such policies generally include provisions providing coverage for injuries such as libel, infringement of copyright, or unfair competition, caused in the course of the insured's advertising activities. The New Jersey courts have refused coverage of patent infringement under such policies, concluding that the claims are not within the commonly understood meanings of the covered terms and that to extend the policies to include patent claims, when they are silent on such coverage, would be "nonsense." Such denials of coverage accord with the general trend in other courts throughout the United States, which have usually ruled against insureds seeking to recover from their insurers for patent infringement. *See, e.g.*, Gauntless, *Patents and Insurance*, 4 B.U. J. Sci. & Tech. L. at 6.

Moreover, separate insurance for patent infringement claims is available in the market. "[I]nsisting that the comprehensive policies weren't designed for patent disputes," insurers like American International Group Inc. ("AIG"), which processes claims for AISLIC, and AISLIC itself, have introduced patent-specific plans with higher deductibles and premiums to reflect the greater risks in assessing possible liability. Introduction of such policies "reflects the growing importance of patent protection." Without coverage, insureds face potentially large judgments on their own. On the other hand, "some patent specialists worry that the availability of insurance" will generate more litigation and make insured companies potential targets.

But while this context may highlight the issues at stake in this case, its resolution depends not upon broad issues of patent policy or trends in the insurance business, but upon the meaning of the particular Policy at issue here (specifically, the scope of Coverage B and of the Policy's exclusion for illegally obtained gains). In interpreting the Policy under New Jersey law, we "'are bound to protect the insured to the full extent that any fair interpretation will allow.'" If the language supports two meanings, the one resulting in coverage must be applied.

A. *Waiver and Estoppel*

American Century argues that AISLIC's defenses should be limited to those cited in its denial letters. In advocating such a limitation, the plaintiff seems to rely on theories of waiver and/or estoppel. Neither prevents the defendant from asserting the defenses raised in its brief.

. . . .

Accordingly, AISLIC can argue as to both claims that Coverage B does not include patent infringement and, even if it did, liability is excluded under Exclusion 4(I)(2).

B. *Coverage B*

Under Coverage B, the defendant must pay on behalf of the plaintiff "all sums which the Insured shall become legally obligated to pay as damages resulting from any claim" for a "Wrongful Act" occurring during the Policy period and "solely in the course of the *management and/or operation* of the Fund(s)." As amended, "'Wrongful Act' means any breach of duty, neglect, error, misstatement, misleading statement, omission or other act wrongfully done or attempted by the Insured or *so alleged* by any claimant."

Katz and Stambler charged that American Century infringed their patents. Since allegations of wrongdoing are sufficient to trigger coverage under the Policy, it is clear that American Century's use of the allegedly infringing telephone and internet systems was a Wrongful Act for the purpose of coverage. The parties, however, disagree about whether the patented technologies were used in the "management and/or operation" of the Funds. "Under New Jersey law, the words of an insurance contract should be given their everyday and common meaning." The defendant argues that the common meanings of "management" and "operation" do not cover the plaintiff's use of the disputed systems. Specifically, AISLIC claims that "management" and "operation" requires the "application of judgment, skill or education . . . as opposed to a mere technical operation," and that the systems were used merely in the "process of managing the funds."

AISLIC's argument is unpersuasive. Defendant attempts to limit "management" and "operation" to a class of activities far narrower than those understood by those terms. Under New Jersey law, we must "construe words granting coverage liberally." But even without this encouragement to liberal construction, it is difficult to conceive of language broader, in relation to the activities of a business, than the "management and/or operation" of the business. The first listed definition of "management" in Webster's New Collegiate Dictionary (9th ed. 1985) ("Webster's") is "the act or art of managing: the conducting or supervising of something (as a business)." The more elaborate definition in the current online Oxford English Dictionary ("OED") begins with "the action or manner of managing, in senses of the v[er]b," and the leading definitions of "manage" thus incorporated (following a specialized meaning in the equestrian world) are at least as general: "2. . . . To handle, wield, make use of; . . . 3. a. To conduct or carry on (a war, a business, an undertaking, an operation." "Operation" is equally general in meaning: Webster's first definition is "performance of a practical work or of something involving the practical application of principles or processes." The OED's first non-obsolete meaning is "Working; exertion of force, energy, or influence; actions, activity, agency; manner of working, the way in which anything works."

Black's Law Dictionary (6th ed. 1990) ("Black's"), the only source relied on by AISLIC, is not to the contrary. Far from limiting the definition of "management" to exclude technical processes or apply only to the application of investment skills, Black's defines "management" as "[g]overnment, control, superintendence, physical or manual handling or guidance; act of managing by direction or regulation, or administration, as management of family, or of household . . . or of great enterprises." AISLIC attempts to import the concept of "skill and judgment" into this definition from Black's definition of "manage" as "[t]o control and direct, to administer, to take charge of. To conduct; to carry on the concerns of a business or establishment. Generally applied to affairs that are somewhat complicated and that involve skill and judgment." Even if this highly selective reading is accepted, it does not disqualify plaintiff's claim. Selecting and installing high technology equipment is surely a part of the "somewhat complicated" business of "conduct[ing]" or "carry[ing] on the concerns of" any modern "business or establishment," and is surely one that involves "skill and judgment."[6]

These definitions would certainly cover anything done in connection with carrying on a business. Surely, the installation of telephone or internet technology by an investment fund to enable its customers to contact the fund, review accounts, and engage in transactions with the fund is an act undertaken in the "conduct" of the fund's business — indeed, in the modern world, the use of such systems in a normal and nearly indispensable aspect of the operation of such a business. It is difficult to imagine what the installation and use of such technology could be called other than a part of the "management and/or operation" of the fund.

---

6. Black's definition of "operation" as "[e]xertion of power; the process of operating or mode of action; an effect brought about in accordance with a definite plan; action; activity," is at least as broad as Webster's or the OED's. Even if we allow AISLIC's arbitrary decision to ignore the breadth of the definition and to focus solely on the phrase "in accordance with a definite plan," there is no reason to adopt its peculiar conclusion that the adoption of modern communications technology was not part of American Century's "plan . . . to achieve gains for its customers through application of the skill of its employees."

Moreover, AISLIC has not offered a reasonable alternative reading of the contract raising a question of fact whose meaning can only be resolved at trial. Whether a contract is ambiguous is a question of law. In determining whether a contract is ambiguous, we look to "'words of the agreement, alternative meanings suggested by counsel, and extrinsic evidence offered in support of those meanings." The contract language is not ambiguous. As noted by the plaintiff in oral argument, the Policy was designed "to cover the broad range of risks that mutual fund companies are subject to" and "involves very hefty premiums and also involves a high deductible . . . [T]his is big problem insurance." Coverage B sweeps exceedingly broadly, to cover any allegedly wrongful act undertaken in connection with the conduct of the Funds managed by American Century. Patent infringement is a wrongful act, and the infringements alleged by Katz and Stambler were committed (if they occurred at all) in the ordinary course of conducting—that is, managing and operating—American Century's investment funds.

C. *Exclusion 4(I)(2)*

Finding that the claims fall into Coverage B, however, does not end the inquiry. The Policy includes an exclusion for illegal profit and advantage, which AISLIC claims applies to patent infringement damages. This exclusion, in keeping with favoring the insured in construction of policies, must be strictly interpreted.

The Policy does not cover "any actual or alleged gaining of profit or advantage to which any Insured is not legally entitled." In a patent infringement action, the patent owner can recover damages for reasonable royalties, lost profits, and other compensatory damages. AISLIC argues that the exclusion precludes coverage of the patent infringement claims here, since those claims seek damages not for actual harms done to Katz and Stambler by American Century, but rather for royalties and profits that they would have received had American Century properly negotiated for licensing the use of their allegedly patented technology. In other words, the infringer must compensate the patentee for the gains and advantages it had while using the patented inventions illegally.

Citing cases from jurisdictions other than New Jersey, American Century argues that the illegal profit or advantage exclusion applies only to claims seeking the disgorgement of gains, and not to the type of claims advanced here. Even interpreting the exclusion strictly, nothing in its language suggests such a limitation. Katz and Stambler alleged that American Century enjoyed the use of their telephone and internet systems without payment. If American Century had identified Katz as the holder of a valid patent before using the telephone system and had agreed to purchase a license to use it, American Century would have paid Katz for the privilege of using the phone system. It would not have been entitled to coverage under the Policy for that license fee, as the Policy only covers Wrongful Acts and not the ordinary costs of doing business, such as payments for the use of desired technologies. If an employee of American Century had stolen tangible goods to be used in the course of its business, and the company then settled a lawsuit by agreeing to pay for the stolen materials, AISLIC would not be required to fund that settlement, because the settlement would simply require American Century to pay for an "actual or alleged gaining of profit or advantage to which the Insured is not legally entitled." To the extent that American Century has agreed with Katz to pay license fees for past and future use of Katz's intellectual property in connection with its business, the same rule applies. Such license fees are simply normal expenses of doing business, against which AIS-LIC has not contracted to insure the plaintiff, whether they are agreed to and paid with or without a threatened lawsuit.

For these reasons, American Century has not established that it is entitled to a judgment of coverage. AISLIC, on the other hand, has not moved for summary judgment, and may not be entitled to it. Material issues of fact may still exist as to the precise nature of the settlement with Katz or of the claims that Stambler has asserted against American Century.

To the extent that the settlement reflects expenses that plaintiff was required to pay for the past or future use of a valuable technology in the course of its business, such royalties or fees are within the exclusion and are not covered by the Policy. American Century cannot shift to its insurer the cost of patented technology it would like to use by failing to license the technology and waiting to be sued for damages for infringement by the patent holder. American Century has argued, however, that some portion of the settlement extends beyond simple royalties or fees, and represents some additional component of damages beyond what is necessary for Katz to recoup the royalties he would have received if plaintiff had simply negotiated up front for the use of his technology. The Court expresses no opinion, based on the limited record before it, as to whether any portion of the Katz settlement, or any aspect of potential further claims by Stambler, might go beyond recovery of the fair market value of intellectual property American Century used without payment in the course of its business, which it should have to disgorge as an illegal benefit or advantage it gained by appropriation. To the extent, however, that at least some portions of those claims sought restitution for precisely such misappropriation, the claims are to that degree within the exclusion from coverage cited by AISLIC.

Accordingly, plaintiff's motion for summary judgment must be denied.

CONCLUSION

For the reasons stated above, plaintiff's motion for summary judgment is denied.

SO ORDERED.

Notes & Questions

If an insurance policy is interpreted like that in *American Century* to exclude recoveries for royalties that the insured should have paid for infringing conduct, what types of patent infringement on the part of an insured will ever produce recoverable losses? Should it matter that the royalties, if paid, would have gained the company access to intellectual property that aided profit-making activities of the insured? Would the same insurance policy exclusion properly apply if payment of the royalties would have added sufficient costs to the insured's related business activities to make those activities unprofitable and unlikely to have been pursued?

C. Monitoring of IP Risks by Corporate Officers and Directors

Steven E. Bochner & Susan P. Krause,[1] Intellectual Property Management and Board Liability

PRACTISING LAW INSTITUTE, ADVANCED SECURITIES LAW INSTITUTE

1065 PLI/Corp 453 (1998)*

A Case for Increased Board Scrutiny of Intellectual Property Management

The need for a well thought out strategy, both offensive and defensive, for the management of intellectual property rights, is becomingly increasingly crucial as the pace of patent filings and issuances, infringement claims, and licensing royalties continues to escalate. Moreover, intellectual property is increasingly recognized as a business asset that should produce not only strategic advantages, but a suitable return on research and development investments as well. The cumulative effect of these developments is likely to be that intellectual property will play an increasingly important role in the enterprise value and, as a result, in corporate transactions such as acquisitions, corporate partnering arrangements and public offerings. As further discussed below, these trends create potentially greater liability implications for Boards of Directors under corporate . . . laws in connection with allegations of mismanagement, inattention and/or inadequate disclosure with respect to intellectual property issues. These factors are also likely to lead to increasing Board of Director scrutiny of the management of intellectual property assets.

. . . .

Board of Directors' Fiduciary Duties and Intellectual Property

[D]irectors may find themselves subject to potential liability for alleged [breaches of fiduciary duties] arising out of inadequate intellectual property management. A director's fiduciary duty is a creation of state corporate law. A director's fiduciary duties typically fall into two categories, a duty of care and a duty of loyalty.

The duty of care has two facets. First, directors have a duty to carefully consider the implications of corporate actions before permitting the corporation to take them. Second, the Board may be liable for a loss which arises from an unconsidered failure

---

1. Mr. Bochner practices corporate and securities law at Wilson Sonsini Goodrich & Rosati, Palo Alto, California. Ms. Krause is the former Vice President, General Counsel, and Secretary of Sirenza Microdevices, Inc. The views expressed are those of the authors only, and do not necessarily represent those of their firm or former corporate employer.

*Copyright © 1998 Steven E. Bochner and Susan P. Krause. All rights reserved. Reprinted by permission.

of the Board to act in circumstances in which due attention would, arguably, have prevented the loss. In *In re Caremark*,[6] the Delaware Chancery Court . . . addressed the legal standard governing a Board's obligation to supervise or monitor corporate performance. In *Caremark*, the corporation had been indicted for breaking a federal law governing payments to participants in drug studies. The plaintiffs in *Caremark* alleged that the Caremark Board breached its duty of care by failing adequately to supervise the conduct of Caremark employees, or institute corrective measures, thereby exposing Caremark to legal liability. In evaluating the plaintiffs' claims, the court in *Caremark* reasoned that a director's obligation includes a duty to "attempt in good faith to assure" the implementation of information and reporting systems in the corporation reasonably designed, in the view of the Board, to provide senior management and the Board with timely, accurate information sufficient to allow each to reach informed judgments concerning compliance with law and business performance. However, the standard set by the *Caremark* court to establish lack of good faith requires a "sustained or systematic failure of the Board to exercise oversight."

Accordingly, as intellectual property management becomes more critical from a strategic, financial and competitive point of view, directors may face similar potential liability based on claims of a breach of fiduciary duty in situations where a company faces a material loss in value due to insufficient attention given to the management of intellectual property assets.

Under most formulations of the duty of care, directors are entitled to the protection of the business judgment rule. The business judgment rule under both Delaware and California law essentially provides that a director shall not be held liable, even for bad business decisions, provided the director acts in good faith and in a manner the director believes to be in the best interests of the corporation and the shareholders, and with such care, including reasonable inquiry, as an ordinarily prudent person in a like position would use under similar circumstances. The purpose of the business judgment rule is to encourage qualified individuals to serve on corporate Boards with the assurance that they will not be second-guessed, and held liable, if they act in good faith following a reasonable investigation. Fiduciary duty cases often turn on whether a reasonable investigation has been performed. In the case of the management of intellectual property assets, the question becomes what amount of oversight and investigation with respect to such assets is sufficient to avoid claims of director inattention or failure to perform a reasonable investigation. While the outcome of such claims is highly fact-specific, prudent Boards will ensure that they are sufficiently briefed on a company's intellectual property management strategy, as well as any attendant risks and uncertainties.

"Red Flags" in Corporate Transactions

Corporate and securities lawyers conducting due diligence in financings and acquisition transactions, as well as management and intellectual property counsel

---

6. In re Caremark International Inc. Derivative Litigation, 698 A.2d 959, 1996 Del. Ch. LEXIS 125 (1996).

performing similar due diligence investigations, need to be sensitive to potential red flags signaling inadequate attention to intellectual property management. For example, the inability of senior management to articulate the Company's IP strategy may be a sign of trouble. Can senior management describe the Company's intellectual property assets (patents, copyrights, trade secrets, trademarks and domain names), and tie these to core products and features? Also, is there a process for determining when key patents expire and evaluating the potential impact on the company? Another problem area would be a lack of knowledge regarding competition and industry patents, particularly those in the field engaged in aggressive patent licensing activities. Finally, senior management should help implement, and be aware of, a company policy to ensure that newly hired employees, especially those hired from competitors, do not inadvertently or otherwise bring with them or use proprietary information belonging to their employers.

A thorough understanding should be obtained in how intellectual property is used, including use as a competitive barrier to entry, defensively in licensing negotiations and/or to achieve a financial return on research and development investments.

Insufficient involvement of intellectual property counsel is also a potential sign of trouble, as is the absence of a trade secrets policy or appropriate inventions assignment clauses in agreements with employees and consultants.

<u>Recommendations</u>

For many companies, strategic intellectual property management is a new concept. A company's first step in developing a strategy for the management of intellectual property issues is understanding what assets are in its portfolio and how the intellectual property is connected with the company's products and key product features, as well as those of its competitors. A good intellectual property strategy should be able to address the company's needs from an offensive viewpoint (what intellectual property protection is needed for the company's own work) and from a defensive viewpoint (what risks exist for the portion of the company's business which is dependent on intellectual property). A coherent offensive intellectual property strategy should seek to fully utilize the assets owned by the company and extract the maximum value from such assets. Such strategy should determine which patents, copyrights and trade secrets cover which products, establish criteria for which inventions should be patented based on the company's business goals, establish criteria for seeking foreign patents based on the company's business goals and on a realistic assessment of the value of foreign patents, and provide a mechanism to periodically prune out U.S. and foreign patents (as well as pending applications) that no longer provide meaningful coverage. A defensive strategy includes routine monitoring of competitors' issued patents and published patent applications and a system of product clearances (patent and trademark) on all new products.[8]

---

8. These points are taken from a list of questions that an attorney can pose to his client listed in Gregory A. Stobbs' article *Evolution or Extinction — Your Intellectual Property Strategy*, published in IPWW OUTLOOK.

To minimize the potential liability of corporate officers and directors, management should routinely make presentations to the Board of Directors regarding the company's intellectual property management strategy, including key patents, copyrights and trade secrets, potential infringement issues and other developments which could impact shareholder value. The goal of these sessions is to make sure the Board is performing reasonable oversight regarding key intellectual property issues, and has the protection of the business judgment rule with respect to decisions made. For public companies, particularly during financing activities, part of a Board's due diligence procedures should include an inquiry into material intellectual property matters. Consideration should also be given as to the level of risk disclosure required in public filings and offering documents concerning intellectual property issues. In particular, a public company's obligations in its quarterly and annual reports concerning disclosure of known events, trends, and uncertainties which could likely result in a material impact on the company should be assessed in the context of any intellectual property developments in the company or in the industry generally.

<u>Summary</u>

Intellectual property management, or the lack thereof, is likely to play an increasing role in securities and fiduciary duty litigation as the need to manage intellectual property assets becomes more critical. The rapidly increasing number of patents applied for and issued, patent litigation and licensing activities will have the effect of accelerating these trends. Corporate and intellectual property counsel need to work more closely together in advising Boards of Directors concerning the increasing role of intellectual property on the enterprise value, and the resulting potential for these issues to arise in lawsuits directed against corporations and their directors and officers.

Notes & Questions

1. What types of monitoring of intellectual property risks or developments will help to protect corporate directors and officers from personal liability once they have notice of a possible infringement problem associated with their company's practices—for example, if they learn about infringement claims against other companies undertaking similar practices?

2. What are a company's options regarding changes in business practices once company officials learn that the company's present or contemplated actions involve some probability of intellectual property infringement claims?

Chapter 11

The Antitrust Perils of a Dominant Intellectual Property Position

Problem

Digital Ignition, in order to allay concerns about the service and repair of the company's ignition systems, requires all replacement parts for the systems to be purchased by automobile manufacturers from Digital Ignition. This requirement is imposed under the contracts for the sale of the ignition systems to automobile manufacturers who are incorporating the systems in newly manufactured cars. The provision imposing the requirement is written to apply to manufacturer-owned car dealers that engage in automobile service and repair. The sale of replacement parts is further conditioned on the purchase and use of a special lubrication fluid that Digital Ignition manufactures. While Digital Ignition does not monitor the actual use of the fluid, purchasers of the replacement parts must buy the fluid. Over time, specialized companies have started to repair and maintain the ignition systems of automobiles. These companies work on all brands of ignition systems, including those manufactured by Digital Ignition. Some of these companies have designed their own replacement parts for different brands of ignition systems. Digital Ignition has aggressively pursued patent infringement suits against these companies regarding replacement parts that are asserted to have incorporated Digital Ignition's patented designs. Some of the suits have forced the companies out of the marketplace; others have resulted in licensing arrangements with Digital Ignition for the making of the replacement parts.

Dr. See, the chief executive officer of Digital Ignition, has been very active in the Automobile Manufacturers Association of America (AMAA). The AMAA is an industry organization that engages in a variety of activities, including the setting of manufacturing and performance standards for automobiles. The Electric Automobile Standards Organization (EASO) is a body within the AMAA that proposes standards to the federal government concerning the design and performance of hybrid and electric cars. One standard that EASO has been working on is for the fuel systems of the next generation of hybrid cars that include both gas engines and electric motors in order to optimize fuel efficiency and engine performance. The proposed standard for the fuel systems of hybrid cars incorporates of some of Digital Ignition's proprietary technology. Under the policies and procedures of EASO, any member of the AMAA whose proprietary technology is incorporated in an EASO-proposed standard that is adopted by a federal or state agency must disclose the information needed to use the technology effectively and forebear from enforcing restrictive intellectual property rights in the technology against other members of the AMAA and the government.

When the EASO developed its standard in 2010, Dr. See owned two patents related to the standard. One patent (referred to here as the '051 patent) covered a novel fuel additive that, when combined with gasoline, served to lubricate engines in hybrid automobiles thereby causing the engines to run more efficiently and to make the transition from gas to electric power more smoothly. The second patent (referred to here as the '062 patent) covered the functionality of a component in a hybrid car transmission that switched the energy source for an automobile from gas to electric (and back) based on the driving conditions for the automobile (such as outside temperature, terrain, and speed) and their effects on fuel efficiency. Both of these inventions were incorporated into the standard adopted by EASO, and the organization's statement of policies and procedures included references to each of these patents. Dr. See, speaking on behalf of his company Digital Ignition which was the initial assignees of the patents, made an oral pledge at the EASO annual meeting where the standard was adopted to license the two patents on fair, reasonable, and nondiscriminatory terms to any competing company making items conforming to the standard. A few days after that meeting, Dr. See memorialized the pledge in writing and the written pledge was included as an appendix to the published policies and procedures of the EASO. Other than the document in the appendix, there is no other recordation, such as the filing of a notice of assignment, of the pledge or other transfers of Dr. See's patent rights.

In 2014, Dr. See obtained two additional patents relating to the hybrid engine. One (referred to here as the '951 patent) is for the novel fuel additive for use in a hybrid motorcycle engine. The other (referred to as the '962 patent) is for the transmission component as used in a motorcycle engine. Late in 2014, Dr. See discovered that a new entrant in the market, Nikolai Motors, has been using all four patented technologies in its line of hybrid cars and hybrid motorcycles without obtaining a license from Dr. See or from Digital Ignition. Nikolai Motors joined the AMAA in 2013 when it began production of its line of vehicles. In light of the facts presented above and the materials that are presented in this Chapter, advise Dr. See and Digital Ignition on potential antitrust liability for the actions against competing replacement parts manufacturers discussed in the first paragraph. In addition, Dr. See and Digital Ignition seek to bring a lawsuit against Nikolai Motors for patent infringement on all four patents. Advise Dr. See and Digital Ignition about the role of FRAND licensing in this potential lawsuit.

Focus of the Chapter

Intellectual property laws give an owner the right to exclude others, including competitors, from the use of proprietary technology. At the same time, antitrust laws disfavor business conduct that excludes parties from markets or other competitive situations. Ever since the enactment of statutory antitrust laws in the United States in 1890, jurists and practitioners have attempted to reconcile the right to exclude under intellectual property laws with the prohibitions of exclusionary conduct under antitrust laws. In the early twentieth century, the view that the two were irreconcilable prevailed, with antitrust trumping intellectual property rights. After World War II, an increased recognition of the importance of intellectual property for stimulating innovation led to a waning of the hostility to intellectual property rights under antitrust law. But it is not necessarily the case that clarity has resulted. Instead, as the material below shows, there is still much disagreement on when the right to exclude needs to be limited by the prohibition on exclusionary conduct.

As a practitioner, you will come across these issues in many ways. First, as an antitrust practitioner, it is very likely that you will have to deal with intellectual property issues, whether in a challenge by the government or in private litigation. Furthermore, to the extent that you represent an intellectual property owner engaged in licensing and contracting, you will need to consider the antitrust implications of your client's business practices. Finally, in negotiating licensing terms for a licensee, you should keep in mind the possible antitrust limitations on what a licensor proposes to include in a licensing arrangement.

The readings in this section are divided into five parts. Section A presents the principal statutes that constitute antitrust law: the Sherman Act, the Clayton Act, and the Federal Trade Commission Act. Together, these three statutes define the powers of the United States Department of Justice and the Federal Trade Commission to police anticompetitive behavior. In addition, the National Cooperative Research Act of 1984 and federal antitrust enforcement agencies' 1995 Guidelines on the Licensing of Intellectual Property are discussed. These last two standards respond directly to the problem of applying antitrust principles to limit the right to exclude under intellectual property law. Section B presents the Supreme Court's 2013 decision in *FTC v. Actavis*, a case dealing on the surface with "reverse payment settlements" by pharmaceutical patent owners paying generic companies to delay entering markets with sales of generic drugs. Beyond resolving the issues raised by the facts of the case, the opinion suggests a change in how the Court views the relationship between intellectual property and antitrust laws. Section C presents excerpts from the Court of Appeals opinion reviewing the federal government's antitrust case against the Microsoft Corporation based on challenges to the company's software licensing practices. Section D presents an important court decision on the enforcement of FRAND (aka RAND) licensing terms. The *Innovatio* case and the materials discussed in the notes that follow illustrate the contemporary problems raised by intellectual property in standard setting processes. Finally, Section E presents a memo drafted by the European Competition Commission on barriers to entry for generic pharmaceuticals. The memo provided the basis for a large fine levied by the European Commission against the patent owner Lundbeck and generic drug companies shortly after the *Actavis* decision in the United States. The materials in Section E illustrate the international issues raised by the interplay between intellectual property and antitrust laws.

Readings

A. Statutory Overview

Sherman Act

15 USC §§ 1, 2 (2003)

Section 1. Trusts, etc., in restraint of trade illegal; penalty

"Every contract, combination in the form of trust or otherwise, or conspiracy, in restraint of trade or commerce among the several States, or with foreign nations, is declared to be illegal. Every person who shall make any contract or engage in any combination or conspiracy hereby declared to be illegal shall be deemed guilty of a felony, and, on conviction thereof, shall be punished by fine not exceeding $10,000,000 if a corporation, or, if any other person, $350,000, or by imprisonment not exceeding three years, or by both said punishments, in the discretion of the court."

Section 2. Monopolizing trade a felony; penalty

"Every person who shall monopolize, or attempt to monopolize, or combine or conspire with any other person or persons, to monopolize any part of the trade or commerce among the several States, or with foreign nations, shall be deemed guilty of a felony, and, on conviction thereof, shall be punished by fine not exceeding $10,000,000 if a corporation, or, if any other person, $350,000, or by imprisonment not exceeding three years, or by both said punishments, in the discretion of the court."

Clayton Act

15 USC §§ 14, 18 (2003)

Section 14. Sale, etc., on agreement not to use goods of competitor

"It shall be unlawful for any person engaged in commerce, in the course of such commerce, to lease or make a sale or contract for sale of goods, wares, merchandise, machinery, supplies, or other commodities, whether patented or unpatented, for use, consumption, or resale within the United States or any Territory thereof or the District of Columbia or any insular possession or other place under the jurisdiction of the United States, or fix a price charged therefor, or discount from, or rebate upon, such price, on the condition, agreement, or understanding that the lessee or purchaser thereof shall not use or deal in the goods, wares, merchandise, machinery, supplies, or other commodities of a competitor or competitors of the lessor or seller, where the effect of such lease, sale, or contract for sale or such condition, agreement, or understanding may be to substantially lessen competition or tend to create a monopoly in any line of commerce."

Section 18. Acquisition by one corporation of stock of another

"No person engaged in commerce or in any activity affecting commerce shall acquire, directly or indirectly, the whole or any part of the stock or other share capital and no person subject to the jurisdiction of the Federal Trade Commission shall acquire the whole or any part of the assets of another person engaged also in commerce or in any activity affecting commerce, where in any line of commerce or in any activity affecting commerce in any section of the country, the effect of such acquisition may be substantially to lessen competition, or to tend to create a monopoly.

No person shall acquire, directly or indirectly, the whole or any part of the stock or other share capital and no person subject to the jurisdiction of the Federal Trade Commission shall acquire the whole or any part of the assets of one or more persons engaged in commerce or in any activity affecting commerce, where in any line of commerce or in any activity affecting commerce in any section of the country, the effect of such acquisition, of such stocks or assets, or of the use of such stock by the voting or granting of proxies or otherwise, may be substantially to lessen competition, or to tend to create a monopoly."

Federal Trade Commission Act
15 USC § 45 (2003)

Section 45. Unfair methods of competition unlawful; prevention by Commission

(a) Declaration of unlawfulness; power to prohibit unfair practices

(1) Unfair methods of competition in or affecting commerce, and unfair or deceptive acts or practices in or affecting commerce, are hereby declared unlawful.

National Cooperative Research Act
15 USC §§ 4301, 4302 (2003)

Section 4301. Definitions

. . . .

(6) The term "joint venture" means any group of activities, including attempting to make, making, or performing a contract, by two or more persons for the purpose of—

(A) theoretical analysis, experimentation, or systematic study of phenomena or observable facts,

(B) the development or testing of basic engineering techniques,

(C) the extension of investigative findings or theory of a scientific or technical nature into practical application for experimental and demonstration purposes, including the experimental production and testing of models, prototypes, equipment, materials, and processes,

(D) the production of a product, process, or service,

(E) the testing in connection with the production of a product, process, or service by such venture,

(F) the collection, exchange, and analysis of research or production information, or

(G) any combination of the purposes specified in subparagraphs (A), (B), (C), (D), (E), and (F), and may include the establishment and operation of facilities for the conducting of such venture, the conducting of such venture on a protected and proprietary basis, and the prosecuting of applications for patents and the granting of licenses for the results of such venture, but does not include any activity specified in subsection (b) of this section.

(b) The term "joint venture" excludes the following activities involving two or more persons:

(1) exchanging information among competitors relating to costs, sales, profitability, prices, marketing, or distribution of any product, process, or service if such information is not reasonably required to carry out the purpose of such venture,

(2) entering into any agreement or engaging in any other conduct restricting, requiring, or otherwise involving the marketing, distribution, or provision by any person who is a party to such venture of any product, process, or service, other than—

(A) the distribution among the parties to such venture, in accordance with such venture, of a product, process, or service produced by such venture,

(B) the marketing of proprietary information, such as patents and trade secrets, developed through such venture formed under a written agreement entered into before June 10, 1993, or

(C) the licensing, conveying, or transferring of intellectual property, such as patents and trade secrets, developed through such venture formed under a written agreement entered into on or after June 10, 1993,

(3) entering into any agreement or engaging in any other conduct—

(A) to restrict or require the sale, licensing, or sharing of inventions, developments, products, processes, or services not developed through, or produced by, such venture, or

(B) to restrict or require participation by any person who is a party to such venture in other research and development activities, that is not reasonably required to prevent misappropriation of proprietary information contributed by any person who is a party to such venture or of the results of such venture,

(4) entering into any agreement or engaging in any other conduct allocating a market with a competitor,

(5) exchanging information among competitors relating to production (other than production by such venture) of a product, process, or service if such information is not reasonably required to carry out the purpose of such venture,

(6) entering into any agreement or engaging in any other conduct restricting, requiring, or otherwise involving the production (other than the production by such venture) of a product, process, or service,

(7) using existing facilities for the production of a product, process, or service by such venture unless such use involves the production of a new product or technology, and

(8) except as provided in paragraphs (2), (3), and (6), entering into any agreement or engaging in any other conduct to restrict or require participation by any person who is a party to such venture, in any unilateral or joint activity that is not reasonably required to carry out the purpose of such venture.

Section 4302. Rule of reason standard

In any action under the antitrust laws, or under any State law similar to the antitrust laws, the conduct of any person in making or performing a contract to carry out a joint venture shall not be deemed illegal per se; such conduct shall be judged on the basis of its reasonableness, taking into account all relevant factors affecting competition, including, but not limited to, effects on competition in properly defined, relevant research, development, product, process, and service markets. For the purpose of determining a properly defined, relevant market, worldwide capacity shall be considered to the extent that it may be appropriate in the circumstances.

Antitrust Guidelines for the Licensing of Intellectual Property

Issued by the U.S. Department of Justice and The Federal Trade Commission

APRIL 6, 1995

1. Intellectual property protection and the antitrust laws

1.0 These Guidelines state the antitrust enforcement policy of the U.S. Department of Justice and the Federal Trade Commission (individually, "the Agency," and collectively, "the Agencies") with respect to the licensing of intellectual property protected by patent, copyright, and trade secret law, and of know-how. By stating their general policy, the Agencies hope to assist those who need to predict whether the Agencies will challenge a practice as anticompetitive. However, these Guidelines cannot remove judgment and discretion in antitrust law enforcement. Moreover, the standards set forth in these Guidelines must be applied in unforeseeable circumstances. Each case will be evaluated in light of its own facts, and these Guidelines will be applied reasonably and flexibly.

In the United States, patents confer rights to exclude others from making, using, or selling in the United States the invention claimed by the patent for a period of seventeen years from the date of issue. To gain patent protection, an invention (which may be a product, process, machine, or composition of matter) must be novel, nonobvious, and useful. Copyright protection applies to original works of authorship embodied in a tangible medium of expression. A copyright protects only the expression, not the underlying ideas. Unlike a patent, which protects an invention not only from copying but also from independent creation, a copyright does not preclude others from independently creating similar expression. Trade secret protection applies to information whose economic value depends on its not being generally known. Trade secret protection is conditioned upon efforts to maintain secrecy and has no fixed term. As with copyright protection, trade secret protection does not preclude independent creation by others.

The intellectual property laws and the antitrust laws share the common purpose of promoting innovation and enhancing consumer welfare. The intellectual property laws provide incentives for innovation and its dissemination and commercialization by establishing enforceable property rights for the creators of new and useful products, more efficient processes, and original works of expression. In the absence of intellectual property rights, imitators could more rapidly exploit the efforts of innovators and investors without compensation. Rapid imitation would reduce the commercial value of innovation and erode incentives to invest, ultimately to the detriment of consumers. The antitrust laws promote innovation and consumer welfare by prohibiting certain actions that may harm competition with respect to either existing or new ways of serving consumers.

2. General principles

2.0 These Guidelines embody three general principles: (a) for the purpose of antitrust analysis, the Agencies regard intellectual property as being essentially comparable to any other form of property; (b) the Agencies do not presume that intellectual property creates market power in the antitrust context; and (c) the Agencies recognize that intellectual property licensing allows firms to combine complementary factors of production and is generally procompetitive.

2.1 Standard antitrust analysis applies to intellectual property

The Agencies apply the same general antitrust principles to conduct involving intellectual property that they apply to conduct involving any other form of tangible or intangible property. That is not to say that intellectual property is in all respects the same as any other form of property. Intellectual property has important characteristics, such as ease of misappropriation, that distinguish it from many other forms of property. These characteristics can be taken into account by standard antitrust analysis, however, and do not require the application of fundamentally different principles.

Although there are clear and important differences in the purpose, extent, and duration of protection provided under the intellectual property regimes of patent, copyright, and trade secret, the governing antitrust principles are the same. Antitrust analysis takes differences among these forms of intellectual property into account in evaluating the specific market circumstances in which transactions occur, just as it does with other particular market circumstances.

Intellectual property law bestows on the owners of intellectual property certain rights to exclude others. These rights help the owners to profit from the use of their property. An intellectual property owner's rights to exclude are similar to the rights enjoyed by owners of other forms of private property. As with other forms of private property, certain types of conduct with respect to intellectual property may have anticompetitive effects against which the antitrust laws can and do protect. Intellectual property is thus neither particularly free from scrutiny under the antitrust laws, nor particularly suspect under them.

The Agencies recognize that the licensing of intellectual property is often international. The principles of antitrust analysis described in these Guidelines apply equally to domestic and international licensing arrangements. However, as described in the 1995 Department of Justice and Federal Trade Commission Antitrust Enforcement Guidelines for International Operations, considerations particular to international operations, such as jurisdiction and comity, may affect enforcement decisions when the arrangement is in an international context.

2.2 Intellectual property and market power

Market power is the ability profitably to maintain prices above, or output below, competitive levels for a significant period of time. The Agencies will not presume that a patent, copyright, or trade secret necessarily confers market power upon its owner. Although the intellectual property right confers the power to exclude with respect to the specific product, process, or work in question, there will often be sufficient actual or potential close substitutes for such product, process, or work to prevent the exercise of market power. If a patent or other form of intellectual property does confer market power, that market power does not by itself offend the antitrust laws. As with any other tangible or intangible asset that enables its owner to obtain significant supracompetitive profits, market power (or even a monopoly) that is solely "a consequence of a superior product, business acumen, or historic accident" does not violate the antitrust laws. Nor does such market power impose on the intellectual property owner an obligation to license the use of that property to others. As in other antitrust contexts, however, market power could be illegally acquired or maintained, or, even if lawfully acquired and maintained, would be relevant to the ability of an intellectual property owner to harm competition through unreasonable conduct in connection with such property.

2.3 Procompetitive benefits of licensing

Intellectual property typically is one component among many in a production process and derives value from its combination with complementary factors. Complementary factors of production include manufacturing and distribution facilities, workforces, and other items of intellectual property. The owner of intellectual property has to arrange for its combination with other necessary factors to realize its commercial value. Often, the owner finds it most efficient to contract with others for these factors, to sell rights to the intellectual property, or to enter into a joint venture arrangement for its development, rather than supplying these complementary factors itself.

Licensing, cross-licensing, or otherwise transferring intellectual property (hereinafter "licensing") can facilitate integration of the licensed property with complementary factors of production. This integration can lead to more efficient exploitation of the intellectual property, benefiting consumers through the reduction of costs and the introduction of new products. Such arrangements increase the value of intellectual property to consumers and to the developers of the technology. By potentially increasing the expected returns from intellectual property, licensing also can increase the incentive for its creation and thus promote greater investment in research and development.

Sometimes the use of one item of intellectual property requires access to another. An item of intellectual property "blocks" another when the second cannot be practiced without using the first. For example, an improvement on a patented machine can be blocked by the patent on the machine. Licensing may promote the coordinated development of technologies that are in a blocking relationship.

Field-of-use, territorial, and other limitations on intellectual property licenses may serve procompetitive ends by allowing the licensor to exploit its property as efficiently and effectively as possible. These various forms of exclusivity can be used to give a licensee an incentive to invest in the commercialization and distribution of products embodying the licensed intellectual property and to develop additional applications for the licensed property. The restrictions may do so, for example, by protecting the licensee against free-riding on the licensee's investments by other licensees or by the licensor. They may also increase the licensor's incentive to license, for example, by protecting the licensor from competition in the licensor's own technology in a market niche that it prefers to keep to itself. These benefits of licensing restrictions apply to patent, copyright, and trade secret licenses, and to know-how agreements.

. . . .

5. Application of general principles

5.0 This section illustrates the application of the general principles discussed above to particular licensing restraints and to arrangements that involve the cross-licensing, pooling, or acquisition of intellectual property. The restraints and arrangements identified are typical of those that are likely to receive antitrust scrutiny; however, they are not intended as an exhaustive list of practices that could raise competitive concerns.

5.1 Horizontal restraints

The existence of a restraint in a licensing arrangement that affects parties in a horizontal relationship (a "horizontal restraint") does not necessarily cause the arrangement to be anticompetitive. As in the case of joint ventures among horizontal competitors, licensing arrangements among such competitors may promote rather than hinder competition if they result in integrative efficiencies. Such efficiencies may arise, for example, from the realization of economies of scale and the integration of complementary research and development, production, and marketing capabilities.

[H]orizontal restraints often will be evaluated under the rule of reason. In some circumstances, however, that analysis may be truncated; additionally, some restraints may merit per se treatment, including price fixing, allocation of markets or customers, agreements to reduce output, and certain group boycotts.

Example 9

Situation: Two of the leading manufacturers of a consumer electronic product hold patents that cover alternative circuit designs for the product. The manufacturers assign their patents to a separate corporation wholly owned by the two firms. That corporation licenses the right to use the circuit designs to other consumer product manufacturers and establishes the license royalties. None of the patents is blocking; that is, each of the patents can be used without infringing a patent owned by the other firm. The different circuit designs are substitutable in that each permits the manufacture at comparable cost to consumers of products that consumers consider to be interchangeable. One of the Agencies is analyzing the licensing arrangement.

Discussion: In this example, the manufacturers are horizontal competitors in the goods market for the consumer product and in the related technology markets. The competitive issue with regard to a joint assignment of patent rights is whether the assignment has an adverse impact on competition in technology and goods markets that is not outweighed by procompetitive efficiencies, such as benefits in the use or dissemination of the technology. Each of the patent owners has a right to exclude others from using its patent. That right does not extend, however, to the agreement to assign rights jointly. To the extent that the patent rights cover technologies that are close substitutes, the joint determination of royalties likely would result in higher royalties and higher goods prices than would result if the owners licensed or used their technologies independently. In the absence of evidence establishing efficiency-enhancing integration from the joint assignment of patent rights, the Agency may conclude that the joint marketing of competing patent rights constitutes horizontal price fixing and could be challenged as a per se unlawful horizontal restraint of trade. If the joint marketing arrangement results in an efficiency-enhancing integration, the Agency would evaluate the arrangement under the rule of reason. However, the Agency may conclude that the anticompetitive effects are sufficiently apparent, and the claimed integrative efficiencies are sufficiently weak or not reasonably related to the restraints, to warrant challenge of the arrangement without an elaborate analysis of particular industry circumstances.

5.2 Resale price maintenance

Resale price maintenance is illegal when "commodities have passed into the channels of trade and are owned by dealers." *Dr. Miles Medical Co. v. John D. Park & Sons Co.*, 220 U.S. 373, 408 (1911). It has been held per se illegal for a licensor of an intellectual property right in a product to fix a licensee's resale price of that product. *United States v. Univis Lens Co.*, 316 U.S. 241 (1942); *Ethyl Gasoline Corp. v. United States*, 309 U.S. 436 (1940). [T]he Agencies will enforce the per se rule against resale price maintenance in the intellectual property context.

5.3 Tying arrangements

A "tying" or "tie-in" or "tied sale" arrangement has been defined as "an agreement by a party to sell one product . . . on the condition that the buyer also purchases a different (or tied) product, or at least agrees that he will not purchase that [tied] product from any other supplier." *Eastman Kodak Co. v. Image Technical Services, Inc.*, 112 S. Ct. 2072, 2079 (1992). Conditioning the ability of a licensee to license one or more items of intellectual property on the licensee's purchase of another item of intellectual property or a good or a service has been held in some cases to constitute illegal tying. Although tying arrangements may result in anticompetitive effects, such arrangements can also result in significant efficiencies and procompetitive benefits. In the exercise of their prosecutorial discretion, the Agencies will consider both the anticompetitive effects and the efficiencies attributable to a tie-in. The Agencies would be likely to challenge a tying arrangement if: (1) the seller has market power in the tying product, (2) the arrangement has an adverse effect on competition in the relevant market for the tied product, and (3) efficiency justifications for the arrangement do not outweigh the anticompetitive effects. The Agencies will not presume that a patent, copyright, or trade secret necessarily confers market power upon its owner.

Package licensing—the licensing of multiple items of intellectual property in a single license or in a group of related licenses—may be a form of tying arrangement if the licensing of one product is conditioned upon the acceptance of a license of another, separate product. Package licensing can be efficiency enhancing under some circumstances. When multiple licenses are needed to use any single item of intellectual property, for example, a package license may promote such efficiencies. If a package license constitutes a tying arrangement, the Agencies will evaluate its competitive effects under the same principles they apply to other tying arrangements.

5.4 Exclusive dealing

In the intellectual property context, exclusive dealing occurs when a license prevents the licensee from licensing, selling, distributing, or using competing technologies. Exclusive dealing arrangements are evaluated under the rule of reason. See *Tampa Electric Co. v. Nashville Coal Co.*, 365 U.S. 320 (1961) (evaluating legality of exclusive dealing under section 1 of the Sherman Act and section 3 of the Clayton Act); *Beltone Electronics Corp.*, 100 F.T.C. 68 (1982) (evaluating legality of exclusive dealing under section 5 of the Federal Trade Commission Act). In determining whether an exclusive dealing arrangement is likely to reduce competition in a relevant market, the Agencies will take into account the extent to which the arrangement (1) promotes the exploitation and development of the licensor's technology and (2) anticompetitively forecloses the exploitation and development of, or otherwise constrains competition among, competing technologies.

The likelihood that exclusive dealing may have anticompetitive effects is related, inter alia, to the degree of foreclosure in the relevant market, the duration of the exclusive dealing arrangement, and other characteristics of the input and output markets, such as concentration, difficulty of entry, and the responsiveness of supply and demand to changes in price in the relevant markets. If the Agencies determine that a particular exclusive dealing arrangement may have an anticompetitive effect, they will evaluate the extent to which the restraint encourages licensees to develop and market the licensed technology (or specialized applications of that technology), increases licensors' incentives to develop or refine the licensed technology, or otherwise increases competition and enhances output in a relevant market.

5.5 Cross-licensing and pooling arrangements

Cross-licensing and pooling arrangements are agreements of two or more owners of different items of intellectual property to license one another or third parties. These arrangements may provide procompetitive benefits by integrating complementary technologies, reducing transaction costs, clearing blocking positions, and avoiding costly infringement litigation. By promoting the dissemination of technology, cross-licensing and pooling arrangements are often procompetitive.

Cross-licensing and pooling arrangements can have anticompetitive effects in certain circumstances. For example, collective price or output restraints in pooling arrangements, such as the joint marketing of pooled intellectual property rights with collective price setting or coordinated output restrictions, may be deemed unlawful if they do not contribute to an efficiency-enhancing integration of economic activity among the participants. Compare *NCAA* 468 U.S. at 114 (output restriction on college football broadcasting held unlawful because it was not reasonably related to any purported justification) with *Broadcast Music*, 441 U.S. at 23 (blanket license for music copyrights found not per se illegal because the cooperative price was necessary to the creation of a new product). When cross-licensing or pooling arrangements are mechanisms to accomplish naked price fixing or market division, they are subject to challenge under the per se rule. See *United States v. New Wrinkle, Inc.*, 342 U.S. 371 (1952) (price fixing).

Settlements involving the cross-licensing of intellectual property rights can be an efficient means to avoid litigation and, in general, courts favor such settlements. When such cross-licensing involves horizontal competitors, however, the Agencies will consider whether the effect of the settlement is to diminish competition among entities that would have been actual or likely potential competitors in a relevant market in the absence of the cross-license. In the absence of offsetting efficiencies, such settlements may be challenged as unlawful restraints of trade. Cf. *United States v. Singer Manufacturing Co.*, 374 U.S. 174 (1963) (cross-license agreement was part of broader combination to exclude competitors).

Pooling arrangements generally need not be open to all who would like to join. However, exclusion from cross-licensing and pooling arrangements among parties that collectively possess market power may, under some circumstances, harm competition. Cf. *Northwest Wholesale Stationers, Inc. v. Pacific Stationery & Printing Co.*, 472 U.S. 284 (1985) (exclusion of a competitor from a purchasing cooperative not per se unlawful absent a showing of market power). In general, exclusion from a pooling or cross-licensing arrangement among competing technologies is unlikely to have anticompetitive effects unless (1) excluded firms cannot effectively compete in the relevant market for the good incorporating the licensed technologies and (2) the pool participants collectively possess market power in the relevant market. If these circumstances exist, the Agencies will evaluate whether the arrangement's limitations on participation are reasonably related to the efficient development and exploitation of the pooled technologies and will assess the net effect of those limitations in the relevant market.

Another possible anticompetitive effect of pooling arrangements may occur if the arrangement deters or discourages participants from engaging in research and development, thus retarding innovation. For example, a pooling arrangement that requires members to grant licenses to each other for current and future technology at minimal cost may reduce the incentives of its members to engage in research and development because members of the pool have to share their successful research and development and each of the members can free ride on the accomplishments of other pool members. However, such an arrangement can have procompetitive benefits, for example, by exploiting economies of scale and integrating complementary capabilities of the pool members, (including the clearing of blocking positions), and is likely to cause competitive problems only when the arrangement includes a large fraction of the potential research and development in an innovation market.

Example 10

Situation: As in Example 9, two of the leading manufacturers of a consumer electronic product hold patents that cover alternative circuit designs for the product. The manufacturers assign several of their patents to a separate corporation wholly owned by the two firms. That corporation licenses the right to use the circuit designs to other consumer product manufacturers and establishes the license royalties. In this example, however, the manufacturers assign to the separate corporation only patents that are blocking. None of the patents assigned to the corporation can be used without infringing a patent owned by the other firm.

Discussion: Unlike the previous example, the joint assignment of patent rights to the wholly owned corporation in this example does not adversely affect competition in the licensed technology among entities that would have been actual or likely potential competitors in the absence of the licensing arrangement. Moreover, the licensing arrangement is likely to have procompetitive benefits in the use of the technology. Because the manufacturers' patents are blocking, the manufacturers are not in a horizontal relationship with respect to those patents. None of the patents can be used without the right to a patent owned by the other firm, so the patents are not substitutable. As in Example 9, the firms are horizontal competitors in the relevant goods market. In the absence of collateral restraints that would likely raise price or reduce output in the relevant goods market or in any other relevant antitrust market and that are not reasonably related to an efficiency-enhancing integration of economic activity, the evaluating Agency would be unlikely to challenge this arrangement.

5.6 Grantbacks

A grantback is an arrangement under which a licensee agrees to extend to the licensor of intellectual property the right to use the licensee's improvements to the licensed technology. Grantbacks can have procompetitive effects, especially if they are nonexclusive. Such arrangements provide a means for the licensee and the licensor to share risks and reward the licensor for making possible further innovation based on or informed by the licensed technology, and both promote innovation in the first place and promote the subsequent licensing of the results of the innovation. Grantbacks may adversely affect competition, however, if they substantially reduce the licensee's incentives to engage in research and development and thereby limit rivalry in innovation markets.

A non-exclusive grantback allows the licensee to practice its technology and license it to others. Such a grantback provision may be necessary to ensure that the licensor is not prevented from effectively competing because it is denied access to improvements developed with the aid of its own technology. Compared with an exclusive grantback, a non-exclusive grantback, which leaves the licensee free to license improvements technology to others, is less likely to have anticompetitive effects.

The Agencies will evaluate a grantback provision under the rule of reason, see generally *Transparent-Wrap Machine Corp. v. Stokes & Smith Co.*, 329 U.S. 637, 645–48 (1947) (grantback provision in technology license is not per se unlawful), considering its likely effects in light of the overall structure of the licensing arrangement and conditions in the relevant markets. An important factor in the Agencies' analysis of a grantback will be whether the licensor has market power in a relevant technology or innovation market. If the Agencies determine that a particular grantback provision is likely to reduce significantly licensees' incentives to invest in improving the licensed technology, the Agencies will consider the extent to which the grantback provision has offsetting procompetitive effects, such as (1) promoting dissemination of licensees' improvements to the licensed technology, (2) increasing the licensors' incentives to disseminate the licensed technology, or (3) otherwise increasing competition and output in a relevant technology or innovation market. See section 4.2. In addition, the Agencies will consider the extent to which grantback provisions in the relevant markets generally increase licensors' incentives to innovate in the first place.

5.7 Acquisition of intellectual property rights

Certain transfers of intellectual property rights are most appropriately analyzed by applying the principles and standards used to analyze mergers, particularly those in the 1992 Horizontal Merger Guidelines. The Agencies will apply a merger analysis to an outright sale by an intellectual property owner of all of its rights to that intellectual property and to a transaction in which a person obtains through grant, sale, or other transfer an exclusive license for intellectual property (i.e., a license that precludes all other persons, including the licensor, from using the licensed intellectual property). Such transactions may be assessed under section 7 of the Clayton Act, sections 1 and 2 of the Sherman Act, and section 5 of the Federal Trade Commission Act.

Example 11

Situation: Omega develops a new, patented pharmaceutical for the treatment of a particular disease. The only drug on the market approved for the treatment of this disease is sold by Delta. Omega's patented drug has almost completed regulatory approval by the Food and Drug Administration. Omega has invested considerable sums in product development and market testing, and initial results show that Omega's drug would be a significant competitor to Delta's. However, rather than enter the market as a direct competitor of Delta, Omega licenses to Delta the right to manufacture and sell Omega's patented drug. The license agreement with Delta is nominally nonexclusive. However, Omega has rejected all requests by other firms to obtain a license to manufacture and sell Omega's patented drug, despite offers by those firms of terms that are reasonable in relation to those in Delta's license.

Discussion: Although Omega's license to Delta is nominally nonexclusive, the circumstances indicate that it is exclusive in fact because Omega has rejected all reasonable offers by other firms for licenses to manufacture and sell Omega's patented drug. The facts of this example indicate that Omega would be a likely potential competitor of Delta in the absence of the licensing arrangement, and thus they are in a horizontal relationship in the relevant goods market that includes drugs for the treatment of this particular disease. The evaluating Agency would apply a merger analysis to this transaction, since it involves an acquisition of a likely potential competitor.

6. Enforcement of invalid intellectual property rights

The Agencies may challenge the enforcement of invalid intellectual property rights as antitrust violations. Enforcement or attempted enforcement of a patent obtained by fraud on the Patent and Trademark Office or the Copyright Office may violate section 2 of the Sherman Act, if all the elements otherwise necessary to establish a section 2 charge are proved, or section 5 of the Federal Trade Commission Act. . . . Inequitable conduct before the Patent and Trademark Office will not be the basis of a section 2 claim unless the conduct also involves knowing and willful fraud and the other elements of a section 2 claim are present. . . . Actual or attempted enforcement of patents obtained by inequitable conduct that falls short of fraud under some circumstances may violate section 5 of the Federal Trade Commission Act. Objectively baseless litigation to enforce invalid intellectual property rights may also constitute an element of a violation of the Sherman Act.

Notes & Questions

1. Although common law antitrust law can be dated back to England and continued in the United in the eighteenth and nineteenth centuries as the restraint of trade doctrine, antitrust law had its statutory origins with the enactment of the Sherman

Act in 1890. Judicial glosses on the Sherman Act that in many ways weakened its application were addressed through the enactment of the Clayton Act and the Federal Trade Commission Act in 1914. Prior to 1914, antitrust enforcement involved private causes of action and cases brought by the Department of Justice. In 1914, the Federal Trade Commission was created to deal with the policing of harms to competition, particularly those arising from deceptive and unfair trade practices. These three statutes are the foundation of antitrust law in the United States. Occasionally, Congress has enacted new statutes to address cutting edge issues in antitrust law. One example of such intervention is the National Cooperative Research Act, passed in 1984, to exempt certain joint research ventures from the antitrust laws. For more complex areas of the law, the Department of Justice and the Federal Trade Commission sometimes jointly release guidelines to aid in the application of antitrust law. An example of such guidelines is the 1995 Joint Guidelines on the Licensing of Intellectual Property. The legal documents presented here provide the backbone for understanding the relationship between intellectual property and antitrust, the subject of this chapter. For an excellent history of the origins of U.S. antitrust law, see Hans B. Thorelli, THE FEDERAL ANTITRUST POLICY: ORIGINATION OF AN AMERICAN TRADITION 9-53 (1954).

2. The first two sections of the Sherman Act are the substance of antitrust law. Together they cover the range of anticompetitive activities that antitrust law regulates. Section One of the Sherman Act criminalizes and establishes civil liability for restraints of trade. Incorporating common law doctrine, Section One addresses agreements among two or more firms in an industry to control the competitive process. The underlying principle is that firms in an industry should be competing with each other in order to ensure the best products at the lowest prices to consumers. Cooperation among firms, according to this principle, is a basis for suspicion since such cooperation may serve as a way to raise prices or restrain the quality and quantity of products in the marketplace.

Section Two of the Sherman Act criminalizes and establishes civil liability for anticompetitive conduct by one firm in an industry. Section Two does not make it illegal to be a monopolist, but it is illegal to monopolize or attempt to monopolize. Monopolization occurs when a firm that has a dominant presence in a market engages in conduct that hurts the competitive process. As with Section One, the underlying principle is that competition is the source of strength in an economy. Monopolistic acts that limit the entry of new firms or new products or new ideas into a marketplace are contrary to the principle of competition. Notice an important tension in Section Two: simply being a monopolist is not enough to violate the antitrust laws. Being a monopolist, in other words, is not inconsistent with the principle of competition since one would expect that competition would lead to strong and sometimes large firms surviving through skill and superior ability.

3. The Sherman Act was a controversial piece of legislation when enacted, and some courts attempted to narrow its scope through interpretation. One distinction that arose in the law of Section One was that between per se violations of the Sherman

Act and violations under the rule of reason. Per se violations were just that: violations establishing strict liability for certain acts deemed to be anticompetitive independent of any showing of harm. Rule of reason violations, on the other hand, rested on a consideration of competitive harms and benefits that might result from a particular business arrangement. The distinction between per se and rule of reason violations continues today. Two categories of behavior that are considered per se violations are agreements among competitors to set prices (price fixing agreements) and agreements among competitors to divide up markets geographically (horizontal territorial agreements). In general, agreements that do not fall into one of these categories are analyzed under the rule of reason, which requires a court to consider the economic benefits and harms of an agreement to determine a Section One violation.

4. Congress remedied the confusion created by judicial interpretations of the Sherman Act with the passage of the Clayton Act in 1914. The Clayton Act was more detailed than the Sherman Act, with specific provisions designed to limit judicial discretion in applying the law. Two provisions of the Clayton Act are excerpted here. Section 14 deals with restraints placed on purchasers by sellers of products or services; section 18 deals with mergers and acquisitions. The key thing to notice about these provisions is the legal standard for liability that Congress adopted. Under both provisions, liability is imposed if a business activity "substantially lessens competition" or tends to "create a monopoly." These standards were meant to move away from the confusion over per se versus rule of reason violations under Section One of the Sherman Act and confusion about business justifications under Section Two of the Sherman Act to impose antitrust liability upon a finding of harm to competition.

The Clayton Act did not overrule the Sherman Act. Antitrust claims can be based on the Clayton Act, the Sherman Act, or both. For example, a merger or acquisition is actionable under the Clayton Act Section 18 and under the Sherman Act, as either a restraint on trade or monopolization. Over time, the standards for analysis of mergers and acquisitions under the two Acts have converged. For a discussion of the application of antitrust law to a merger that involved the acquisition of patent rights, see *SCM Corporation v. Xerox Corporation*, 645 F.2d 1195 (2d Cir. 1981) ("analyzing the lawfulness of the acquisition of a patent necessitates that we primarily focus upon the circumstances of the acquiring party and the status of the relevant product and geographic markets at the time of acquisition").

Notice also that Clayton Act is more specific than the Sherman Act, meaning that some business conduct may not be actionable under the Clayton Act, but would be actionable under the Sherman Act. For example, if a purchaser places a restraint on the seller of a product (for example, a retailer tells a manufacturer not to sell to any other retailer), the conduct would be actionable under the Sherman Act, but not the Clayton Act (which covers only restraints placed on purchasers by sellers). These idiosyncrasies reflect legislative compromises regarding particular types of antitrust abuses that were viewed with concern at the time each of the Acts was passed. For example, the asymmetry between restraints on purchasers and restraints on sellers under the Clayton Act reflects Congress's belief in 1914 that the practices of manufacturers, which tended to be large entities, were potentially more harmful to competition than the practices of retailers, which were relatively small at the time. Of course, nowadays with the growth of retailers throughout the twentieth century, some retailers are larger than many manufacturers. The Sherman Act with its broad provisions, however, reaches the full gamut of business conduct while the Clayton Act remains more narrowly focused.

5. The Federal Trade Commission Act was another innovation in 1914. The Act created the Federal Trade Commission (FTC) as a government agency for policing markets regarding unfair and deceptive trade practices. While the Sherman and Clayton Acts were enacted to prevent harms to the marketplace as a whole, the Federal Trade Commission Act was aimed at preventing harms to consumers resulting from such activities as false advertising or deceptive contract terms. The Federal Trade Commission, however, also deals with mergers and activities and has concurrent jurisdiction with the Department of Justice in reviewing and challenging mergers under the Clayton Act.

6. The National Cooperative Research Act of 1984 was enacted to allow some amount of cooperation among competitors for the purposes of technological innovation and research and development. Prior to the enactment of the NCRA, cooperative ventures would run the risk of being found to be a restraint of trade under the Sherman Act or the Clayton Act. The NCRA exempts "joint ventures" from per se treatment and imposes liability based on the reasonableness of the joint ventures' activities. In addition, if a joint venture files a notification with the Department of Justice, any antitrust damages would be limited to actual damages without the possibility of treble damages. Notice the definition of a joint venture, particularly the exclusions. The exclusions were meant to ensure that anticompetitive agreements among competitors, such as agreements to fix prices, divide territories, or share manufacturing information, were not protected from antitrust scrutiny by being implemented through a joint venture.

7. The 1995 Antitrust Guidelines on the Licensing of Intellectual Property reflect a more flexible treatment of intellectual property licensing under the antitrust laws. The case law in the early to mid-twentieth century demonstrated a hostility to intellectual property under the antitrust laws. Courts would often find that the exclusivity provided by intellectual property, particularly patents, translated into potentially illegal market power under the antitrust laws. In the 1970s, the Department of Justice (DOJ) identified nine specific licensing activities that were clearly forbidden by the antitrust laws:

- Mandatory package licensing, also known as patent pools;

- Tying of unpatented supplies;

- Compulsory payments of royalties in amounts not reasonably related to sales of patented products;

- Mandatory grantbacks;
- Licensee veto power over the licensor's grant of further licenses;
- Restrictions on sales of unpatented products made by patented processes;
- Post-sale restrictions on resale by purchasers of patented products;
- Specifying price licensee can charge on resale of licensed products;
- Tie-outs, which are restrictions on a licensee's ability to sell products that compete with licensor's patented products.

These nine prohibited practices reflected a hostility to the exclusivity of intellectual property law. The 1995 Guidelines clearly show a mellowing by both the DOJ and the FTC, particularly in identifying the pro-competitive benefits of intellectual property licensing. One very important change in the case law since the enactment of the Guidelines is the reversal of the *Dr. Miles* precedent mentioned in Section 5.2 of the Guidelines. In *Leegin Creative Leather Products, Inc. v. PSKS, Inc.*, 551 U.S. 877 (2007), the Supreme Court overruled the per se rule against minimum resale price maintenance from *Dr. Miles* and held that contractual limitations setting a minimum price for resale was subject to the rule of reason.

8. Pay particular attention to the discussion of specific licensing practices in section five of the Guidelines. The discussion of tying is important and should be kept in mind when reading the *Microsoft* case below. The one area where scrutiny of business practices by federal antitrust officials remains close is the enforcement of invalid patents as discussed in section six of the Guidelines. Keep the Guidelines in mind when reading the rest of this Chapter.

B. The Interface of Antitrust & Intellectual Property

Federal Trade Commission v. Actavis, Inc.

United States Supreme Court

133 S. Ct. 2223 (2013)

JUSTICE BREYER DELIVERED THE OPINION OF THE COURT.

Company A sues Company B for patent infringement. The two companies settle under terms that require (1) Company B, the claimed infringer, not to produce the patented product until the patent's term expires, and (2) Company A, the patentee, to pay B many millions of dollars. Because the settlement requires the patentee to pay the alleged infringer, rather than the other way around, this kind of settlement agreement is often called a "reverse payment" settlement agreement. And the basic question here is whether such an agreement can sometimes unreasonably diminish competition in violation of the antitrust laws. See, e.g., 15 U.S.C. § 1 (Sherman Act prohibition of "restraint[s] of trade or commerce"). *Cf. Palmer v. BRG of Ga., Inc.*, 498 U.S. 46, 111 S. Ct. 401, 112 L. Ed. 2d 349 (1990) (per curiam) (invalidating agreement not to compete).

In this case, the Eleventh Circuit dismissed a Federal Trade Commission (FTC) complaint claiming that a particular reverse payment settlement agreement violated the antitrust laws. In doing so, the Circuit stated that a reverse payment settlement agreement generally is "immune from antitrust attack so long as its anticompetitive effects fall within the scope of the exclusionary potential of the patent." *FTC v. Watson Pharmaceuticals, Inc.*, 677 F.3d 1298, 1312 (11th Cir. 2012). And since the alleged infringer's promise not to enter the patentee's market expired before the patent's term ended, the Circuit found the agreement legal and dismissed the FTC complaint. *Id.* at 1315. In our view, however, reverse payment settlements such as the agreement alleged in the complaint before us can sometimes violate the antitrust laws. We consequently hold that the Eleventh Circuit should have allowed the FTC's lawsuit to proceed . . . .

Solvay's patent, if valid and infringed, might have permitted it to charge drug prices sufficient to recoup the reverse settlement payments it agreed to make to its potential generic competitors. And we are willing to take this fact as evidence that the agreement's "anticompetitive effects fall within the scope of the exclusionary potential of the patent." 677 F.3d, at 1312. But we do not agree that that fact, or characterization, can immunize the agreement from antitrust attack.

For one thing, to refer, as the Circuit referred, simply to what the holder of a valid patent could do does not by itself answer the antitrust question. The patent here may or may not be valid, and may or may not be infringed. "[A] valid patent excludes all except its owner from the use of the protected process or product," *United States v. Line Material Co.*, 333 U.S. 287, 308, 68 S. Ct. 550, 92 L. Ed. 701 (1948) (emphasis added). And that exclusion may permit the patent owner to charge a higher-than-competitive price for the patented product. But an *invalidated* patent carries with it no such right. And even a valid patent confers no right to exclude products or processes that do not actually infringe. . . .

Given these factors, it would be incongruous to determine antitrust legality by measuring the settlement's anticompetitive effects solely against patent law policy, rather than by measuring them against procompetitive antitrust policies as well. And indeed, contrary to the Circuit's view that the only pertinent question is whether "the settlement agreement . . . fall[s] within" the legitimate "scope" of the patent's "exclusionary potential," 677 F.3d, at 1309, 1312, this Court has indicated that patent and antitrust policies are both relevant in determining the "scope of the patent monopoly"—and consequently antitrust law immunity—that is conferred by a patent.

Thus, the Court in *Line Material* explained that "the improper use of [a patent] monopoly," is "invalid" under the antitrust laws and resolved the antitrust question in that case by seeking an accommodation "between the lawful restraint on trade of the patent monopoly and the illegal restraint prohibited broadly by the Sherman Act." 333 U.S., at 310, 68 S. Ct. 550. To strike that balance, the Court asked questions such as whether "the patent statute specifically gives a right" to restrain competition in the manner challenged; and whether "competition is impeded to a greater degree" by the restraint at issue than other restraints previously approved as reasonable. *Id.* at

311, 68 S. Ct. 550. See also *United States v. United States Gypsum Co.*, 333 U.S. 364, 390–391, 68 S. Ct. 525, 92 L. Ed. 746 (1948) (courts must "balance the privileges of [the patent holder] and its licensees under the patent grants with the prohibitions of the Sherman Act against combinations and attempts to monopolize"); *Walker Process Equipment, Inc. v. Food Machinery & Chemical Corp.*, 382 U.S. 172, 174, 86 S. Ct. 347, 15 L. Ed. 2d 247 (1965) ("[E]nforcement of a patent procured by fraud" may violate the Sherman Act). In short, rather than measure the length or amount of a restriction solely against the length of the patent's term or its earning potential, as the Court of Appeals apparently did here, this Court answered the antitrust question by considering traditional antitrust factors such as likely anticompetitive effects, redeeming virtues, market power, and potentially offsetting legal considerations present in the circumstances, such as here those related to patents. Whether a particular restraint lies "beyond the limits of the patent monopoly" is a conclusion that flows from that analysis and not, as the Chief Justice suggests, its starting point. *Post*, at 2239, 2241–2242 (dissenting opinion).

For another thing, this Court's precedents make clear that patent-related settlement agreements can sometimes violate the antitrust laws. In *United States v. Singer Mfg. Co.*, 374 U.S. 174, 83 S. Ct. 1773, 10 L. Ed. 2d 823 (1963), for example, two sewing machine companies possessed competing patent claims; a third company sought a patent under circumstances where doing so might lead to the disclosure of information that would invalidate the other two firms' patents. All three firms settled their patent-related disagreements while assigning the broadest claims to the firm best able to enforce the patent against yet other potential competitors. *Id.* at 190–192, 83 S. Ct. 1773. The Court did not examine whether, on the assumption that all three patents were valid, patent law would have allowed the patents' holders to do the same. Rather, emphasizing that the Sherman Act "imposes strict limitations on the concerted activities in which patent owners may lawfully engage," *id.* at 197, 83 S. Ct. 1773, it held that the agreements, although settling patent disputes, violated the antitrust laws. *Id.* at 195, 197, 83 S. Ct. 1773. And that, in important part, was because "the public interest in granting patent monopolies" exists only to the extent that "the public is given a novel and useful invention" in "consideration for its grant." *Id.* at 199, 83 S. Ct. 1773 (White, J., concurring). See also *United States v. New Wrinkle, Inc.*, 342 U.S. 371, 378, 72 S. Ct. 350, 96 L. Ed. 417 (1952) (applying antitrust scrutiny to patent settlement); *Standard Oil Co. (Indiana) v. United States*, 283 U.S. 163, 51 S. Ct. 421, 75 L. Ed. 926 (1931) (same).

Similarly, both within the settlement context and without, the Court has struck down overly restrictive patent licensing agreements—irrespective of whether those agreements produced supra-patent-permitted revenues. We concede that in *United States v. General Elec. Co.*, 272 U.S. 476, 489, 47 S. Ct. 192, 71 L. Ed. 362 (1926), the Court permitted a single patentee to grant to a single licensee a license containing a minimum resale price requirement. But in *Line Material, supra*, at 308, 310–311, 68 S. Ct. 550, the Court held that the antitrust laws forbid a group of patentees, each owning one or more patents, to cross-license each other, and, in doing so, to insist that each licensee maintain retail prices set collectively by the patent holders. The Court was willing to presume that the single-patentee practice approved in *General Electric* was a "reasonable restraint" that "accords with the patent monopoly granted by the patent law," 333 U.S., at 312, 68 S. Ct. 550, but declined to extend that conclusion to multiple-patentee agreements: "As the Sherman Act prohibits agreements to fix prices, any arrangement between patentees runs afoul of that prohibition and is outside the patent monopoly." *Ibid*. In *New Wrinkle*, 342 U.S., at 378, 72 S. Ct. 350, the Court held roughly the same, this time in respect to a similar arrangement in settlement of a litigation between two patentees, each of which contended that its own patent gave it the exclusive right to control production. That one or the other company (we may presume) was right about its patent did not lead the Court to confer antitrust immunity. Far from it, the agreement was found to violate the Sherman Act. *Id*. at 380, 72 S. Ct. 350.

Finally in *Standard Oil Co. (Indiana)*, the Court upheld cross-licensing agreements among patentees that settled actual and impending patent litigation, 283 U.S., at 168, 51 S. Ct. 421, which agreements set royalty rates to be charged third parties for a license to practice all the patents at issue (and which divided resulting revenues). But, in doing so, Justice Brandeis, writing for the Court, warned that such an arrangement would have violated the Sherman Act had the patent holders thereby "dominate[d]" the industry and "curtail[ed] the manufacture and supply of an unpatented product." *Id*. at 174, 51 S. Ct. 421. These cases do not simply ask whether a hypothetically valid patent's holder would be able to charge, e.g., the high prices that the challenged patent-related term allowed. Rather, they seek to accommodate patent and antitrust policies, finding challenged terms and conditions unlawful unless patent law policy offsets the antitrust law policy strongly favoring competition.

Thus, contrary to the dissent's suggestion, *post*, at 2239–2241, there is nothing novel about our approach. What does appear novel are the dissent's suggestions that a patent holder may simply "pa[y] a competitor to respect its patent" and quit its patent invalidity or noninfringement claim without any antitrust scrutiny whatever, *post*, at 2239, and that "such settlements . . . are a well-known feature of intellectual property litigation," *post*, at 2243. Closer examination casts doubt on these claims. The dissent does not identify any patent statute that it understands to grant such a right to a patentee, whether expressly or by fair implication. It would be difficult to reconcile the proposed right with the patent-related policy of eliminating unwarranted patent grants so the public will not "continually be required to pay tribute to would-be monopolists without need or justification." *Lear, Inc. v. Adkins*, 395 U.S. 653, 670, 89 S. Ct. 1902, 23 L. Ed. 2d 610 (1969). And the authorities cited for this proposition (none from this Court, and none an antitrust case) are not on point. Some of them say that when Company A sues Company B for patent infringement and demands, say, $100 million in damages, it is not uncommon for B (the defendant) to pay A (the plaintiff) some amount less than the full demand as part of the settlement—$40 million, for example. See Schildkraut, *Patent-Splitting Settlements and the Reverse Payment Fallacy*, 71 Antitrust L.J. 1033, 1046 (2004) (suggesting that this hypothetical settlement includes "an implicit net payment" from A to B of $60 million—i.e., the amount of the settlement discount). The cited authorities also indicate that if B has a counterclaim for damages against A, the original infringement plaintiff, A might end up paying B to settle B's counterclaim. Cf. *Metro-Goldwyn Mayer, Inc. v. 007 Safety Prods., Inc.,* 183 F.3d 10, 13 (C.A.1 1999) (describing trademark dispute and settlement). Insofar as the dissent urges that settlements taking these commonplace forms have not been thought for that reason alone subject to antitrust liability, we agree, and do not intend to alter that understanding. . . .

We recognize the value of settlements and the patent litigation problem. But we nonetheless conclude that this patent-related factor should not determine the result here. Rather, five sets of considerations lead us to conclude that the FTC should have been given the opportunity to prove its antitrust claim.

First, the specific restraint at issue has the "potential for genuine adverse effects on competition." *Indiana Federation of Dentists,* [476 U.S. 447, 460–461 (1986)], 106 S. Ct. 2009 (citing 7 Areeda ¶ 1511, at 429 (1986)). The payment in effect amounts to a purchase by the patentee of the exclusive right to sell its product, a right it already claims but would lose if the patent litigation were to continue and the patent were held invalid or not infringed by the generic product. Suppose, for example, that the exclusive right to sell produces $50 million in supracompetitive profits per year for the patentee. And suppose further that the patent has 10 more years to run. Continued litigation, if it results in patent invalidation or a finding of noninfringement, could cost the patentee $500 million in lost revenues, a sum that then would flow in large part to consumers in the form of lower prices.

We concede that settlement on terms permitting the patent challenger to enter the market before the patent expires would also bring about competition, again to the consumer's benefit. But settlement on the terms said by the FTC to be at issue here—payment in return for staying out of the market—simply keeps prices at patentee-set levels, potentially producing the full patent-related $500 million monopoly return while dividing that return between the challenged patentee and the patent challenger. The patentee and the challenger gain; the consumer loses. Indeed, there are indications that patentees sometimes pay a generic challenger a sum even larger than what the generic would gain in profits if it won the paragraph IV litigation [—involving litigation like that in the present case provoked by action of the generic challenger under 35 U.S.C. § 355(j)(2)(A)(vii)(IV) —] and entered the market. See Hemphill, [*Paying for Delay: Pharmaceutical Patent Settlement as a Regulatory Design Problem,* 81 N.Y.U. L. Rev. 1553, 1581 (2006)]. See also Brief for 118 Law, Economics, and Business Professors et al. as Amici Curiae 25 (estimating that this is true of the settlement challenged here). The rationale behind a payment of this size cannot in every case be supported by traditional settlement considerations. The payment may instead provide strong evidence that the patentee seeks to induce the generic challenger to abandon its claim with a share of its monopoly profits that would otherwise be lost in the competitive market.

But, one might ask, as a practical matter would the parties be able to enter into such an anticompetitive agreement? Would not a high reverse payment signal to other potential challengers that the patentee lacks confidence in its patent, thereby provoking additional challenges, perhaps too many for the patentee to "buy off?" Two special features of Hatch-Waxman mean that the answer to this question is "not necessarily so." First, under Hatch-Waxman only the first challenger gains the special advantage of 180 days of an exclusive right to sell a generic version of the brand-name product. And as noted, that right has proved valuable—indeed, it can be worth several hundred million dollars. See Hemphill, *supra*, at 1579; Brief for Petitioner 6. Subsequent challengers cannot secure that exclusivity period, and thus stand to win significantly less than the first if they bring a successful paragraph IV challenge. That is, if subsequent litigation results in invalidation of the patent, or a ruling that the patent is not infringed, that litigation victory will free not just the challenger to compete, but all other potential competitors too (once they obtain FDA approval). The potential reward available to a subsequent challenger being significantly less, the patentee's payment to the initial challenger (in return for not pressing the patent challenge) will not necessarily provoke subsequent challenges. Second, a generic that files a paragraph IV after learning that the first filer has settled will (if sued by the brand-name) have to wait out a stay period of (roughly) 30 months before the FDA may approve its application, just as the first filer did. See 21 U.S.C. § 355(j)(5)(B)(iii). These features together mean that a reverse payment settlement with the first filer (or, as in this case, all of the initial filers) "removes from consideration the most motivated challenger, and the one closest to introducing competition." Hemphill, *supra*, at 1586. The dissent may doubt these provisions matter, *post*, at 2234–2236, but scholars in the field tell us that "where only one party owns a patent, it is virtually unheard of outside of pharmaceuticals for that party to pay an accused infringer to settle the lawsuit." 1 H. Hovenkamp, M. Janis, M. Lemley, & C. Leslie, IP and Antitrust § 15.3, p. 15–45, n. 161 (2d ed. Supp. 2011). It may well be that Hatch-Waxman's unique regulatory framework, including the special advantage that the 180-day exclusivity period gives to first filers, does much to explain why in this context, but not others, the patentee's ordinary incentives to resist paying off challengers (i.e., the fear of provoking myriad other challengers) appear to be more frequently overcome. See 12 Areeda ¶ 2046, at 341 (3d ed. 2010) (noting that these provisions, no doubt unintentionally, have created special incentives for collusion).

Second, these anticompetitive consequences will at least sometimes prove unjustified. See 7 id., ¶ 1504, at 410–415 (3d ed. 2010); *California Dental Assn. v. FTC*, 526 U.S. 756, 786–787, 119 S. Ct. 1604, 143 L. Ed. 2d 935 (1999) (Breyer, J., concurring in part and dissenting in part). As the FTC admits, offsetting or redeeming virtues are sometimes present. Brief for Petitioner 37–39. The reverse payment, for example, may amount to no more than a rough approximation of the litigation expenses saved through the settlement. That payment may reflect compensation for other services that the generic has promised to perform—such as distributing the patented item or helping to develop a market for that item. There may be other justifications. Where a reverse payment reflects traditional settlement considerations, such as avoided litigation costs or fair value for services, there is not the same concern that a patentee is using its monopoly profits to avoid the risk of patent invalidation or a finding of non-infringement. In such cases, the parties may have provided for a reverse payment without having sought or brought about the anticompetitive consequences we mentioned above. But that possibility does not justify dismissing the FTC's complaint. An antitrust defendant may show in the antitrust proceeding that legitimate justifications are present, thereby explaining the presence of the challenged term and showing the lawfulness of that term under the rule of reason. See, e.g., *Indiana Federation of Dentists*, *supra*, at 459, 106 S. Ct. 2009; 7 Areeda ¶¶ 1504a–1504b, at 401–404 (3d ed. 2010).

Third, where a reverse payment threatens to work unjustified anticompetitive harm, the patentee likely possesses the power to bring that harm about in practice. See *id.* ¶ 1503, at 392–393. At least, the "size of the payment from a branded drug manufacturer to a prospective generic is itself a strong indicator of power" — namely, the power to charge prices higher than the competitive level. 12 *id.* ¶ 2046, at 351. An important patent itself helps to assure such power. Neither is a firm without that power likely to pay "large sums" to induce "others to stay out of its market." *Ibid*. In any event, the Commission has referred to studies showing that reverse payment agreements are associated with the presence of higher-than-competitive profits — a strong indication of market power. See Brief for Petitioner 45.

Fourth, an antitrust action is likely to prove more feasible administratively than the Eleventh Circuit believed. The Circuit's holding does avoid the need to litigate the patent's validity (and also, any question of infringement). But to do so, it throws the baby out with the bath water, and there is no need to take that drastic step. That is because it is normally not necessary to litigate patent validity to answer the antitrust question (unless, perhaps, to determine whether the patent litigation is a sham, see 677 F.3d, at 1312). An unexplained large reverse payment itself would normally suggest that the patentee has serious doubts about the patent's survival. And that fact, in turn, suggests that the payment's objective is to maintain supracompetitive prices to be shared among the patentee and the challenger rather than face what might have been a competitive market — the very anticompetitive consequence that underlies the claim of antitrust unlawfulness. The owner of a particularly valuable patent might contend, of course, that even a small risk of invalidity justifies a large payment. But, be that as it may, the payment (if otherwise unexplained) likely seeks to prevent the risk of competition. And, as we have said, that consequence constitutes the relevant anticompetitive harm. In a word, the size of the unexplained reverse payment can provide a workable surrogate for a patent's weakness, all without forcing a court to conduct a detailed exploration of the validity of the patent itself. 12 Areeda ¶ 2046, at 350–352.

Fifth, the fact that a large, unjustified reverse payment risks antitrust liability does not prevent litigating parties from settling their lawsuit. They may, as in other industries, settle in other ways, for example, by allowing the generic manufacturer to enter the patentee's market prior to the patent's expiration, without the patentee paying the challenger to stay out prior to that point. Although the parties may have reasons to prefer settlements that include reverse payments, the relevant antitrust question is: What are those reasons? If the basic reason is a desire to maintain and to share patent-generated monopoly profits, then, in the absence of some other justification, the antitrust laws are likely to forbid the arrangement.

In sum, a reverse payment, where large and unjustified, can bring with it the risk of significant anticompetitive effects; one who makes such a payment may be unable to explain and to justify it; such a firm or individual may well possess market power derived from the patent; a court, by examining the size of the payment, may well be able to assess its likely anticompetitive effects along with its potential justifications without litigating the validity of the patent; and parties may well find ways to settle patent disputes without the use of reverse payments. In our view, these considerations, taken together, outweigh the single strong consideration—the desirability of settlements—that led the Eleventh Circuit to provide near-automatic antitrust immunity to reverse payment settlements.

. . . .

CHIEF JUSTICE ROBERTS, with whom JUSTICE SCALIA and JUSTICE THOMAS join, DISSENTING.

Solvay Pharmaceuticals holds a patent. It sued two generic drug manufacturers that it alleged were infringing that patent. Those companies counterclaimed, contending the patent was invalid and that, in any event, their products did not infringe. The parties litigated for three years before settling on these terms: Solvay agreed to pay the generics millions of dollars and to allow them into the market five years before the patent was set to expire; in exchange, the generics agreed to provide certain services (help with marketing and manufacturing) and to honor Solvay's patent. The Federal Trade Commission alleges that such a settlement violates the antitrust laws. The question is how to assess that claim.

A patent carves out an exception to the applicability of antitrust laws. The correct approach should therefore be to ask whether the settlement gives Solvay monopoly power beyond what the patent already gave it. The Court, however, departs from this approach, and would instead use antitrust law's amorphous rule of reason to inquire into the anticompetitive effects of such settlements. This novel approach is without support in any statute, and will discourage the settlement of patent litigation. I respectfully dissent.

. . . .

The point of antitrust law is to encourage competitive markets to promote consumer welfare. The point of patent law is to grant limited monopolies as a way of encouraging innovation. Thus, a patent grants "the right to exclude others from profiting by the patented invention." *Dawson Chemical Co. v. Rohm & Haas Co.*, 448 U.S. 176, 215, 100 S. Ct. 2601, 65 L. Ed. 2d 696 (1980). In doing so it provides an exception to antitrust law, and the scope of the patent—i.e., the rights conferred by the patent—forms the zone within which the patent holder may operate without facing antitrust liability.

This should go without saying, in part because we've said it so many times. *Walker Process Equipment, Inc. v. Food Machinery & Chemical Corp.*, 382 U.S. 172, 177, 86 S. Ct. 347, 15 L. Ed. 2d 247 (1965) ("'A patent . . . is an exception to the general rule against monopolies'"); *United States v. Line Material Co.*, 333 U.S. 287, 300, 68 S. Ct. 550, 92 L. Ed. 701 (1948) ("[T]he precise terms of the grant define the limits of a patentee's monopoly and the area in which the patentee is freed from competition"); *United States v. General Elec. Co.*, 272 U.S. 476, 485, 47 S. Ct. 192, 71 L. Ed. 362 (1926) ("It is only when . . . [the patentee] steps out of the scope of his patent rights" that he comes within the operation of the Sherman Act); *Simpson v. Union Oil Co. of Cal.*, 377 U.S. 13, 24, 84 S. Ct. 1051, 12 L. Ed. 2d 98 (1964) (similar). Thus, although it is per se unlawful to fix prices under antitrust law, we have long recognized that a patent holder is entitled to license a competitor to sell its product on the condition that the competitor charge a certain, fixed price. See, e.g., *General Elec. Co., supra*, at 488–490, 47 S. Ct. 192.

We have never held that it violates antitrust law for a competitor to refrain from challenging a patent. And by extension, we have long recognized that the settlement of patent litigation does not by itself violate the antitrust laws. *Standard Oil Co. (Indiana) v. United States*, 283 U.S. 163, 171, 51 S. Ct. 421, 75 L. Ed. 926 (1931) ("Where there are legitimately conflicting claims or threatened interferences, a settlement by agreement, rather than litigation, is not precluded by the [Sherman] Act"). Like most litigation, patent litigation is settled all the time, and such settlements—which can include agreements that clearly violate antitrust law, such as licenses that fix prices, or agreements among competitors to divide territory—do not ordinarily subject the litigants to antitrust liability. See 1 H. Hovenkamp, M. Janis, M. Lemley, & C. Leslie, IP and Antitrust § 7.3, pp. 7-13 to 7-15 (2d ed. 2003) (hereinafter Hovenkamp).

The key, of course, is that the patent holder—when doing anything, including settling—must act within the scope of the patent. If its actions go beyond the monopoly powers conferred by the patent, we have held that such actions are subject to antitrust scrutiny. See, e.g., *United States v. Singer Mfg. Co.*, 374 U.S. 174, 196–197, 83 S. Ct. 1773, 10 L. Ed. 2d 823 (1963). If its actions are within the scope of the patent, they are not subject to antitrust scrutiny, with two exceptions concededly not applicable here: (1) when the parties settle sham litigation, cf. *Professional Real Estate Investors, Inc. v. Columbia Pictures Industries, Inc.*, 508 U.S. 49, 60–61, 113 S. Ct. 1920, 123 L. Ed. 2d 611 (1993); and (2) when the litigation involves a patent obtained through fraud on the Patent and Trademark Office. *Walker Process Equipment, supra*, at 177, 86 S. Ct. 347.

Thus, under our precedent, this is a fairly straight-forward case. Solvay paid a competitor to respect its patent—conduct which did not exceed the scope of its patent. No one alleges that there was sham litigation, or that Solvay's patent was obtained through fraud on the PTO. As in any settlement, Solvay gave its competitors something of value (money) and, in exchange, its competitors gave it something of value (dropping their legal claims). In doing so, they put an end to litigation that had been dragging on for three years. Ordinarily, we would think this a good thing.

. . . .

Today, however, the Court announces a new rule. It is willing to accept that Solvay's actions did not exceed the scope of its patent. *Ante*, at 2230–2231. But it does not agree that this is enough to "immunize the agreement from antitrust attack." *Ibid.* According to the majority, if a patent holder settles litigation by paying an alleged infringer a "large and unjustified" payment, in exchange for having the alleged infringer honor the patent, a court should employ the antitrust rule of reason to determine whether the settlement violates antitrust law. *Ante*, at 2236–2237.

The Court's justifications for this holding are unpersuasive. [T]he majority explains that "the patent here may or may not be valid, and may or may not be infringed." *Ante*, at 2231. Because there is "uncertainty" about whether the patent is actually valid, the Court says that any questions regarding the legality of the settlement should be "measur[ed]" by "procompetitive antitrust policies," rather than "patent law policy." *Ante*, at 2231. This simply states the conclusion. The difficulty with such an approach is that a patent holder acting within the scope of its patent has an obvious defense to any antitrust suit: that its patent allows it to engage in conduct that would otherwise violate the antitrust laws. But again, that's the whole point of a patent: to confer a limited monopoly. The problem, as the Court correctly recognizes, is that we're not quite certain if the patent is actually valid, or if the competitor is infringing it. But that is always the case, and is plainly a question of patent law.

The majority, however, would assess those patent law issues according to "antitrust policies." According to the majority, this is what the Court did in *Line Material*—i.e., it "accommodat[ed]" antitrust principles and struck a "balance" between patent and antitrust law. *Ante*, at 2231. But the Court in Line Material did no such thing. Rather, it explained that it is "well settled that the possession of a valid patent or patents does not give the patentee any exemption from the provisions of the Sherman Act beyond the limits of the patent monopoly." 333 U.S., at 308, 68 S. Ct. 550 (emphasis added). It then, in the very next sentence, stated that "[b]y aggregating patents in one control, the holder of the patents cannot escape the prohibitions of the Sherman Act." *Ibid.* That second sentence follows only if such conduct—the aggregation of multiple patents—goes "beyond the limits of the patent monopoly," which is precisely what the Court concluded. See *id.* at 312, 68 S. Ct. 550 ("There is *no suggestion in the patent statutes* of authority to combine with other patent owners to fix prices on articles covered by the respective patents" (emphasis added)). The Court stressed, over and over, that a patent holder does not violate the antitrust laws when it acts within the scope of its patent. See *id.* at 305, 68 S. Ct. 550 ("Within the limits of the patentee's rights under his patent, monopoly of the process or product by him is authorized by the patent statutes"); *id.* at 310, 68 S. Ct. 550 ("price limitations on patented devices *beyond the limits of a patent monopoly* violate the Sherman Act" (emphasis added)).

The majority suggests that "[w]hether a particular restraint lies 'beyond the limits of the patent monopoly' is a conclusion that flows from" applying traditional antitrust principles. *Ante*, at 2231. It seems to have in mind a regime where courts ignore the patent, and simply conduct an antitrust analysis of the settlement without regard to the validity of the patent. But a patent holder acting within the scope of its patent does not engage in any unlawful anticompetitive behavior; it is simply exercising the monopoly rights granted to it by the Government. Its behavior would be unlawful only if its patent were invalid or not infringed. And the scope of the patent—i.e., what rights are conferred by the patent—should be determined by reference to patent law. While it is conceivable to set up a legal system where you assess the validity of patents or questions of infringement by bringing an antitrust suit, neither the majority nor the Government suggests that Congress has done so.

. . . .

Notes & Questions

1. In an important speech addressing the relationship between intellectual property licensing and antitrust laws, former Assistant Attorney General for Antitrust, Hewitt Pate, stated: "A unilateral, unconditional refusal to license a valid patent cannot, by itself, result in antitrust liability under U.S. law. It is instructive that the very notion of such liability was not even discussed in the 1995 Guidelines. Instead, the Guidelines unequivocally state that, even in the case of IP that conveys market or monopoly power, that power does not 'impose on the intellectual property owner an obligation to license the use of that property to others.'" See R. Hewitt Pate, *Competition and Intellectual Property in the U.S.: Licensing Freedom and the Limits of Antitrust*, 2005 EU Competition Workshop, Florence, Italy (June 3, 2005). Is the Court's decision in *Actavis* consistent with this view? If a patent owner can decline to license, why cannot a patent owner license, as part of a settlement or other agreement, the patent subject to certain conditions? The dissenters adopt the view that licensing should be relatively liberally allowed and that antitrust scrutiny should apply only in two narrow instances—that is, in cases of fraud and sham litigation. The *Actavis* decision may mark a radical shift in the application of antitrust laws to patents. At the same time, the 1995 Guidelines point to the rule of reason analysis as the proper means for assessing the antitrust impacts of licensing agreements. The *Actavis* decision is consistent with this standard as it adopts the rule of reason approach. One way to reconcile the Guidelines with *Actavis* is to interpret *Actavis* as rejecting both per se legal and per se illegal approaches to reverse payment settlements. Instead the Court splits the difference by allowing antitrust scrutiny based on a reasonableness standard.

2. At the heart of the disagreement between the majority and the dissent in *Actavis* is the meaning of exclusivity under patent law. Exclusivity provided by intellectual property interests may be sufficiently limited to allow wide room for antitrust enforcement that will curtail business activities involving intellectual property. If an

intellectual property owner has only a right to exclude parties from infringing conduct, then the right to commercialize protected intellectual property can still be broadly limited under antitrust laws. Note the citation to and discussion of the *Trinko* decision, a telecommunications case in which Justice Scalia stated that the Sherman Act "does not give judges carte blanche to insist that a monopolist alter its way of doing business whenever some other approach might yield greater competition." 540 U.S. at 416. What this statement means is not completely clear, but the *Trinko* decision suggests that there may be broad limits to antitrust law when Congress has created exclusive property rights in a particular area to further a regulatory purpose as Congress did with rights created in schemes for telecommunications regulation. Justice Breyer cites *Trinko* for the proposition that collusion among competitors is an antitrust wrong. By contrast, the dissent seems to view Hatch-Waxman as creating a regulatory regime that is largely exempt from antitrust scrutiny. The problem with the dissent's view is that Hatch-Waxman was implemented to facilitate generic competition with patented pharmaceuticals within the parameters of food and drug laws. Arguably, allowing reverse payment settlements would be inconsistent with that goal of the Hatch-Waxman Act. At the same time, treating reverse payment settlements as per se illegal would not be consistent with the protections for patent owners under the Act. Hence, the rule of reason approach provides a compromise position.

3. The First Circuit held in *In re Loestrin 24 Fe Antitrust Litig.*, 814 F.3d 538 (1st Cir. 2016), that the standards of *Actavis* apply when the consideration exchanged for delay is non-monetary. In that case, the patent owner agreed not to market its own generic version of the patented drug in exchange for delay by the generic entrant.

4. In 2003 and 2004, the patent system was under intense scrutiny by the FTC and the National Academy of Sciences, each of which released detailed reports identifying potentially anticompetitive effects of the patent system. See Fed. Trade Comm'n, To Promote Innovation: The Proper Balance of Competition and Patent Law and Policy (2003); National Academy of Sciences, A Patent System for the 21st Century (2004). The FTC revisited certain features of the patent system and made additional proposals for reforms in 2011. *See* Fed. Trade Comm'n, The Evolving IP Marketplace: Aligning Patent Notice and Remedies With Competition (2011).

5. In 2011, employees in Silicon Valley brought a class action law suit against several high-profile tech companies alleging a conspiracy among the companies not to poach each other's employees. With the granting of class certification in 2013 and the rejection of a settlement in 2014, several subsequent complaints were filed. The cases include In re High-Tech Employee Antitrust Litigation, 11-cv-02509; Nitsch v. DreamWorks Animation SKG Inc., 14-cv-04062; Garrison v. Oracle Corp., 14-cv-04592; and Ryan v. Microsoft Corp., 14-cv-04634, U.S. District Court, Northern District of California (San Jose). Recall the California statutory bar against covenants not to compete imposed on employees. The antitrust lawsuits allege that companies have agreed not to compete among themselves for employees (and, by implication, not to look to the creativity of the other companies' employees as sources

of new intellectual property). Such an agreement would be a per se violation of the antitrust laws as a horizontal collusive agreement to split the market, in this case the market for high tech employees.

6. The behavior of nonpracticing entities (or NPEs) has recently caught the attention of policymakers and practitioners. While the definition of a NPE is controversial, the basic idea is that a NPE is a patent owner which has obtained patent rights (most often through acquisition) for the sole purpose of enforcing the rights through litigation rather than commercializing the technology. The following is a good description of the possible harms from NPEs:

> While increased invention and patenting activity will lead to increased innovation in many contexts, it can decrease innovation in others. The risk that patentees that have made no technical contribution to a product can extract hold-up value from manufacturers increases uncertainty and costs, and discourages innovation by those manufacturers.

See Fed. Trade Comm'n, The Evolving IP Marketplace: Aligning Patent Notice and Remedies With Competition 227 (2011). The concept of "hold-up" will appear again below in Section D, which focuses on standard setting organizations and FRAND. Does antitrust law play a role in controlling NPE's? Can bringing a lawsuit solely to obtain economic returns from a patent be anticompetitive? The answer to this question reflects many of the issues confronting the Supreme Court in *Actavis*. On the one hand, the legitimate owner of a valid patent has the right to enforce it. On the other hand, the patent system was designed to promote innovation and any use of the patent right that harms innovation would be inconsistent with that policy. If the second point trumps the first, the hard question is how to put limits on the rights of the patent owner. Antitrust may not be the most appropriate way to deal with NPE's since by definition the patent owner is not competing with the alleged infringer. Unlike the facts of the *Actavis* case, a suit by a NPE does not divide a market. Furthermore, while a lawsuit does impose costs on the actual commercializer of the invention and thereby harms consumers, these costs are no different from any legitimate patent lawsuit. For further discussion of these issues, *see* Colleen Chien & Edward Reines, *Why Technology Customers Are Being Sued En Masse for Patent Infringement and What Can Be Done*, 49 Wake Forest L. Rev. 235, 239 (2014); David L. Schwartz & Jay P. Kesan, *Analyzing the Role of Non-Practicing Entities in the Patent System*, 99 Cornell L. Rev. 425 (2014); Christopher A. Cotropia et. al., *Unpacking Patent Assertion Entities (PAEs)*, 99 Minn. L. Rev. 649 (2014); Mark A. Lemley & A. Douglas Melamed, *Missing the Forest for the Trolls*, 113 Colum. L. Rev. 2117 (2013); Colleen V. Chien, *Of Trolls, Davids, Goliaths, and Kings: Narratives and Evidence in the Litigation of High-Tech Patents*, 87 N.C. L. Rev. 1571 (2009). The activities of NPEs—including the potentially procompetitive impacts of NPEs in enhancing patent values and the commercial opportunities of innovators—are addressed further in sections 9(B) & 9(E) of this casebook.

C. Improper Conduct

1. Restricting Competitors

United States v. Microsoft

United States Court of Appeals for the District of Columbia

253 F.3d 34 (D.C. Cir. 2001)

[PER CURIAM]

I. Introduction

  A. Background

In July 1994, officials at the Department of Justice ("DOJ"), on behalf of the United States, filed suit against Microsoft, charging the company with, among other things, unlawfully maintaining a monopoly in the operating system market through anti-competitive terms in its licensing and software developer agreements. The parties subsequently entered into a consent decree, thus avoiding a trial on the merits. *See United States v. Microsoft Corp.*, 56 F.3d 1448 (D.C. Cir. 1995) ("Microsoft I"). Three years later, the Justice Department filed a civil contempt action against Microsoft for allegedly violating one of the decree's provisions. On appeal from a grant of a preliminary injunction, this court held that Microsoft's technological bundling of IE 3.0 and 4.0 with Windows 95 did not violate the relevant provision of the consent decree. *United States v. Microsoft Corp.*, 147 F.3d 935 (D.C. Cir. 1998) ("Microsoft II"). We expressly reserved the question whether such bundling might independently violate §§ 1 or 2 of the Sherman Act.

On May 18, 1998, shortly before issuance of the Microsoft II decision, the United States and a group of State plaintiffs filed separate (and soon thereafter consolidated) complaints, asserting antitrust violations by Microsoft and seeking preliminary and permanent injunctions against the company's allegedly unlawful conduct. The complaints also sought any "other preliminary and permanent relief as is necessary and appropriate to restore competitive conditions in the markets affected by Microsoft's unlawful conduct." Relying almost exclusively on Microsoft's varied efforts to unseat Netscape Navigator as the preeminent internet browser, plaintiffs charged four distinct violations of the Sherman Act: (1) unlawful exclusive dealing arrangements in violation of § 1; (2) unlawful tying of IE to Windows 95 and Windows 98 in violation of § 1; (3) unlawful maintenance of a monopoly in the PC operating system market in violation of § 2; and (4) unlawful attempted monopolization of the internet browser market in violation of § 2. The States also brought pendent claims charging Microsoft with violations of various State antitrust laws.

The District Court scheduled the case on a "fast track." The hearing on the preliminary injunction and the trial on the merits were consolidated pursuant to Fed. R. Civ. P. 65(a)(2). The trial was then scheduled to commence on September 8, 1998, less than four months after the complaints had been filed. In a series of pretrial orders, the

District Court limited each side to a maximum of 12 trial witnesses plus two rebuttal witnesses. It required that all trial witnesses' direct testimony be submitted to the court in the form of written declarations. The District Court also made allowances for the use of deposition testimony at trial to prove subordinate or predicate issues. Following the grant of three brief continuances, the trial started on October 19, 1998.

After a 76-day bench trial, the District Court issued its Findings of Fact. *United States v. Microsoft Corp.*, 84 F. Supp. 2d 9 (D.D.C. 1999) ("Findings of Fact"). This triggered two independent courses of action. First, the District Court established a schedule for briefing on possible legal conclusions, inviting Professor Lawrence Lessig to participate as amicus curiae. Second, the District Court referred the case to mediation to afford the parties an opportunity to settle their differences. The Honorable Richard A. Posner, Chief Judge of the United States Court of Appeals for the Seventh Circuit, was appointed to serve as mediator. The parties concurred in the referral to mediation and in the choice of mediator.

Mediation failed after nearly four months of settlement talks between the parties. On April 3, 2000, with the parties' briefs having been submitted and considered, the District Court issued its conclusions of law. The District Court found Microsoft liable on the § 1 tying and § 2 monopoly maintenance and attempted monopolization claims, Conclusions of Law, at 35-51, while ruling that there was insufficient evidence to support a § 1 exclusive dealing violation. As to the pendent State actions, the District Court found the State antitrust laws conterminous with §§ 1 and 2 of the Sherman Act, thereby obviating the need for further State-specific analysis. In those few cases where a State's law required an additional showing of intrastate impact on competition, the District Court found the requirement easily satisfied on the evidence at hand.

Having found Microsoft liable on all but one count, the District Court then asked plaintiffs to submit a proposed remedy. Plaintiffs' proposal for a remedial order was subsequently filed within four weeks, along with six supplemental declarations and over 50 new exhibits. In their proposal, plaintiffs sought specific conduct remedies, plus structural relief that would split Microsoft into an applications company and an operating systems company. The District Court rejected Microsoft's request for further evidentiary proceedings and, following a single hearing on the merits of the remedy question, issued its Final Judgment on June 7, 2000. The District Court adopted plaintiffs' proposed remedy without substantive change.

Microsoft filed a notice of appeal within a week after the District Court issued its Final Judgment. This court then ordered that any proceedings before it be heard by the court sitting en banc. Before any substantive matters were addressed by this court, however, the District Court certified appeal of the case brought by the United States directly to the Supreme Court pursuant to 15 U.S.C. § 29(b), while staying the final judgment order in the federal and state cases pending appeal. The States thereafter petitioned the Supreme Court for a writ of certiorari in their case. The Supreme Court declined to hear the appeal of the Government's case and remanded the matter to this court; the Court likewise denied the States' petition for writ of certiorari. *Microsoft Corp. v. United States*, 530 U.S. 1301 (2000). This consolidated appeal followed.

B. Overview

Before turning to the merits of Microsoft's various arguments, we pause to reflect briefly on two matters of note, one practical and one theoretical.

The practical matter relates to the temporal dimension of this case. The litigation timeline in this case is hardly problematic. Indeed, it is noteworthy that a case of this magnitude and complexity has proceeded from the filing of complaints through trial to appellate decision in a mere three years. See, e.g., *Data Gen. Corp. v. Grumman Sys. Support Corp.*, 36 F.3d 1147, 1155 (1st Cir. 1994) (six years from filing of complaint to appellate decision); *Transamerica Computer Co., Inc. v. IBM*, 698 F.2d 1377, 1381 (9th Cir. 1983) (over four years from start of trial to appellate decision); *United States v. United Shoe Mach. Corp.*, 110 F. Supp. 295, 298 (D. Mass. 1953) (over five years from filing of complaint to trial court decision).

What is somewhat problematic, however, is that just over six years have passed since Microsoft engaged in the first conduct plaintiffs allege to be anticompetitive. As the record in this case indicates, six years seems like an eternity in the computer industry. By the time a court can assess liability, firms, products, and the marketplace are likely to have changed dramatically. This, in turn, threatens enormous practical difficulties for courts considering the appropriate measure of relief in equitable enforcement actions, both in crafting injunctive remedies in the first instance and reviewing those remedies in the second. Conduct remedies may be unavailing in such cases, because innovation to a large degree has already rendered the anticompetitive conduct obsolete (although by no means harmless). And broader structural remedies present their own set of problems, including how a court goes about restoring competition to a dramatically changed, and constantly changing, marketplace. That is just one reason why we find the District Court's refusal in the present case to hold an evidentiary hearing on remedies—to update and flesh out the available information before seriously entertaining the possibility of dramatic structural relief—so problematic.

We do not mean to say that enforcement actions will no longer play an important role in curbing infringements of the antitrust laws in technologically dynamic markets, nor do we assume this in assessing the merits of this case. Even in those cases where forward-looking remedies appear limited, the Government will continue to have an interest in defining the contours of the antitrust laws so that law-abiding firms will have a clear sense of what is permissible and what is not. And the threat of private damage actions will remain to deter those firms inclined to test the limits of the law.

The second matter of note is more theoretical in nature. We decide this case against a backdrop of significant debate amongst academics and practitioners over the extent to which "old economy" §2 monopolization doctrines should apply to firms competing in dynamic technological markets characterized by network effects. In markets characterized by network effects, one product or standard tends towards dominance, because "the utility that a user derives from consumption of the good increases with the number of other agents consuming the good." Michael L. Katz & Carl Shapiro, *Network Externalities, Competition, and Compatibility*, 75 Am. Econ. Rev. 424, 424 (1985). For example, "[a]n individual consumer's demand to use (and hence her benefit from) the telephone network . . . increases with the number of other users on the network whom she can call or from whom she can receive calls." Howard A. Shelanski & J. Gregory Sidak, *Antitrust Divestiture in Network Industries*, 68 U. Chi. L. Rev. 1, 8 (2001). Once a product or standard achieves wide acceptance, it becomes more or less entrenched. Competition in such industries is "for the field" rather than "within the field." See Harold Demsetz, *Why Regulate Utilities?*, 11 J.L. & Econ. 55, 57 & n.7 (1968) (emphasis omitted).

In technologically dynamic markets, however, such entrenchment may be temporary, because innovation may alter the field altogether. See Joseph A. Schumpeter, Capitalism, Socialism and Democracy 81–90 (Harper Perennial 1976) (1942). Rapid technological change leads to markets in which "firms compete through innovation for temporary market dominance, from which they may be displaced by the next wave of product advancements." Shelanski & Sidak, at 11–12 (discussing Schumpeterian competition, which proceeds "sequentially over time rather than simultaneously across a market"). Microsoft argues that the operating system market is just such a market.

Whether or not Microsoft's characterization of the operating system market is correct does not appreciably alter our mission in assessing the alleged antitrust violations in the present case. As an initial matter, we note that there is no consensus among commentators on the question of whether, and to what extent, current monopolization doctrine should be amended to account for competition in technologically dynamic markets characterized by network effects. Compare Steven C. Salop & R. Craig Romaine, *Preserving Monopoly: Economic Analysis, Legal Standards, and Microsoft*, 7 Geo. Mason L. Rev. 617, 654–55, 663–64 (1999) (arguing that exclusionary conduct in high-tech networked industries de- serves heightened antitrust scrutiny in part because it may threaten to deter innovation), with Ronald A. Cass & Keith N. Hylton, *Preserving Competition: Economic Analysis, Legal Standards and Microsoft*, 8 Geo. Mason L. Rev. 1, 36–39 (1999) (equivocating on the antitrust implications of network effects and noting that the presence of network externalities may actually encourage innovation by guaranteeing more durable monopolies to innovating winners). Indeed, there is some suggestion that the economic consequences of network effects and technological dynamism act to offset one another, thereby making it difficult to formulate categorical antitrust rules absent a particularized analysis of a given market. See Shelanski & Sidak, at 6–7 ("High profit margins might appear to be the benign and necessary recovery of legitimate investment returns in a Schumpeterian framework, but they might represent exploitation of customer lock-in and monopoly power when viewed through the lens of network economics . . . . The issue is particularly complex because, in network industries characterized by rapid innovation, both forces may be operating and can be difficult to isolate.").

Moreover, it should be clear that Microsoft makes no claim that anticompetitive conduct should be assessed differently in technologically dynamic markets. It claims only that the measure of monopoly power should be different. [W]e reject Microsoft's monopoly power argument.

II. Monopolization

. . . .

B. Anticompetitive Conduct

A firm violates § 2 only when it acquires or maintains, or attempts to acquire or maintain, a monopoly by engaging in exclusionary conduct "as distinguished from growth or development as a consequence of a superior product, business acumen, or historic accident."

In this case, after concluding that Microsoft had monopoly power, the District Court held that Microsoft had violated § 2 by engaging in a variety of exclusionary acts (not including predatory pricing), to maintain its monopoly by preventing the effective distribution and use of products that might threaten that monopoly. Specifically, the District Court held Microsoft liable for: (1) the way in which it integrated IE into Windows; (2) its various dealings with Original Equipment Manufacturers ("OEMs"), Internet Access Providers ("IAPs"), Internet Content Providers ("ICPs"), Independent Software Vendors ("ISVs"), and Apple Computer; (3) its efforts to contain and to subvert Java technologies; and (4) its course of conduct as a whole. Upon appeal, Microsoft argues that it did not engage in any exclusionary conduct.

Whether any particular act of a monopolist is exclusionary, rather than merely a form of vigorous competition, can be difficult to discern: the means of illicit exclusion, like the means of legitimate competition, are myriad. The challenge for an antitrust court lies in stating a general rule for distinguishing between exclusionary acts, which reduce social welfare, and competitive acts, which increase it.

From a century of case law on monopolization under § 2, however, several principles do emerge. First, to be condemned as exclusionary, a monopolist's act must have an "anticompetitive effect." That is, it must harm the competitive process and thereby harm consumers. In contrast, harm to one or more competitors will not suffice. "The [Sherman Act] directs itself not against conduct which is competitive, even severely so, but against conduct which unfairly tends to destroy competition itself."

Second, the plaintiff, on whom the burden of proof of course rests, must demonstrate that the monopolist's conduct indeed has the requisite anticompetitive effect. In a case brought by a private plaintiff, the plaintiff must show that its injury is "of 'the type that the statute was intended to forestall,'"; no less in a case brought by the Government, it must demonstrate that the monopolist's conduct harmed competition, not just a competitor.

Third, if a plaintiff successfully establishes a prima facie case under § 2 by demonstrating anticompetitive effect, then the monopolist may proffer a "procompetitive justification" for its conduct. If the monopolist asserts a procompetitive justification—a nonpretextual claim that its conduct is indeed a form of competition on the merits because it involves, for example, greater efficiency or enhanced consumer appeal—then the burden shifts back to the plaintiff to rebut that claim.

Fourth, if the monopolist's procompetitive justification stands unrebutted, then the plaintiff must demonstrate that the anticompetitive harm of the conduct outweighs the procompetitive benefit. In cases arising under § 1 of the Sherman Act, the courts routinely apply a similar balancing approach under the rubric of the "rule of reason." The source of the rule of reason is *Standard Oil Co. v. United States*, 221 U.S. 1, 31 S. Ct. 502, 55 L. Ed. 619 (1911), in which the Supreme Court used that term to describe the proper inquiry under both sections of the Act. As the Fifth Circuit more recently explained, "[i]t is clear . . . that the analysis under section 2 is similar to that under section 1 regardless whether the rule of reason label is applied . . . ."

Finally, in considering whether the monopolist's conduct on balance harms competition and is therefore condemned as exclusionary for purposes of § 2, our focus is upon the effect of that conduct, not upon the intent behind it. Evidence of the intent behind the conduct of a monopolist is relevant only to the extent it helps us understand the likely effect of the monopolist's conduct.

With these principles in mind, we now consider Microsoft's objections to the District Court's holding that Microsoft violated § 2 of the Sherman Act in a variety of ways.

1. Licenses Issued to Original Equipment Manufacturers

The District Court condemned a number of provisions in Microsoft's agreements licensing Windows to OEMs, because it found that Microsoft's imposition of those provisions (like many of Microsoft's other actions at issue in this case) serves to reduce usage share of Netscape's browser and, hence, protect Microsoft's operating system monopoly. The reason market share in the browser market affects market power in the operating system market is complex, and warrants some explanation.

Browser usage share is important because . . . a browser (or any middleware product, for that matter) must have a critical mass of users in order to attract software developers to write applications relying upon the APIs it exposes, and away from the APIs exposed by Windows. Applications written to a particular browser's APIs, however, would run on any computer with that browser, regardless of the underlying operating system. "The overwhelming majority of consumers will only use a PC operating system for which there already exists a large and varied set of . . . applications, and for which it seems relatively certain that new types of applications and new versions of existing applications will continue to be marketed . . . ." If a consumer could have access to the applications he desired—regardless of the operating system he uses—simply by installing a particular browser on his computer, then he would no longer feel compelled to select Windows in order to have access to those applications; he could select an operating system other than Windows based solely upon its quality and price. In other words, the market for operating systems would be competitive.

Therefore, Microsoft's efforts to gain market share in one market (browsers) served to meet the threat to Microsoft's monopoly in another market (operating systems) by keeping rival browsers from gaining the critical mass of users necessary to attract developer attention away from Windows as the platform for software development. Plaintiffs also argue that Microsoft's actions injured competition in the browser market—an argument we will examine below in relation to their specific claims that Microsoft attempted to monopolize the browser market and unlawfully tied its browser to its operating system so as to foreclose competition in the browser market. In evaluating the § 2 monopoly maintenance claim, however, our immediate concern is with the anticompetitive effect of Microsoft's conduct in preserving its monopoly in the operating system market.

In evaluating the restrictions in Microsoft's agreements licensing Windows to OEMs, we first consider whether plaintiffs have made out a prima facie case by demonstrating that the restrictions have an anticompetitive effect. In the next subsection, we conclude that plaintiffs have met this burden as to all the restrictions. We then consider Microsoft's proffered justifications for the restrictions and, for the most part, hold those justifications insufficient.

a. Anticompetitive effect of the license restrictions

The restrictions Microsoft places upon Original Equipment Manufacturers are of particular importance in determining browser usage share because having an OEM pre-install a browser on a computer is one of the two most cost-effective methods by far of distributing browsing software. (The other is bundling the browser with internet access software distributed by an IAP.) The District Court found that the restrictions Microsoft imposed in licensing Windows to OEMs prevented many OEMs from distributing browsers other than IE. In particular, the District Court condemned the license provisions prohibiting the OEMs from: (1) removing any desktop icons, folders, or "Start" menu entries; (2) altering the initial boot sequence; and (3) otherwise altering the appearance of the Windows desktop.

The District Court concluded that the first license restriction—the prohibition upon the removal of desktop icons, folders, and Start menu entries—thwarts the distribution of a rival browser by preventing OEMs from removing visible means of user access to IE. The OEMs cannot practically install a second browser in addition to IE, the court found, in part because "[p]re-installing more than one product in a given category . . . can significantly increase an OEM's support costs, for the redundancy can lead to confusion among novice users." That is, a certain number of novice computer users, seeing two browser icons, will wonder which to use when and will call the OEM's support line. Support calls are extremely expensive and, in the highly competitive original equipment market, firms have a strong incentive to minimize costs.

Microsoft denies the "consumer confusion" story; it observes that some OEMs do install multiple browsers and that executives from two OEMs that do so denied any knowledge of consumers being confused by multiple icons.

Other testimony, however, supports the District Court's finding that fear of such confusion deters many OEMs from pre-installing multiple browsers. Most telling, in presentations to OEMs, Microsoft itself represented that having only one icon in a particular category would be "less confusing for end users." Accordingly, we reject Microsoft's argument that we should vacate the District Court's Finding of Fact 159 as it relates to consumer confusion.

As noted above, the OEM channel is one of the two primary channels for distribution of browsers. By preventing OEMs from removing visible means of user access to IE, the license restriction prevents many OEMs from pre-installing a rival browser and, therefore, protects Microsoft's monopoly from the competition that middleware might otherwise present. Therefore, we conclude that the license restriction at issue is anticompetitive. We defer for the moment the question whether that anticompetitive effect is outweighed by Microsoft's proffered justifications.

The second license provision at issue prohibits OEMs from modifying the initial boot sequence—the process that occurs the first time a consumer turns on the computer. Prior to the imposition of that restriction, "among the programs that many OEMs inserted into the boot sequence were Internet sign-up procedures that encouraged users to choose from a list of IAPs assembled by the OEM." Microsoft's prohibition on any alteration of the boot sequence thus prevents OEMs from using that process to promote the services of IAPs, many of which—at least at the time Microsoft imposed the restriction—used Navigator rather than IE in their internet access software. (Upon learning of OEM practices including boot sequence modification, Microsoft's Chairman, Bill Gates, wrote: "Apparently a lot of OEMs are bundling non-Microsoft browsers and coming up with offerings together with [IAPs] that get displayed on their machines in a FAR more prominent way than MSN or our Internet browser."). Microsoft does not deny that the prohibition on modifying the boot sequence has the effect of decreasing competition against IE by preventing OEMs from promoting rivals' browsers. Because this prohibition has a substantial effect in protecting Microsoft's market power, and does so through a means other than competition on the merits, it is anticompetitive. Again the question whether the provision is nonetheless justified awaits later treatment.

Finally, Microsoft imposes several additional provisions that, like the prohibition on removal of icons, prevent OEMs from making various alterations to the desktop: Microsoft prohibits OEMs from causing any user interface other than the Windows desktop to launch automatically, from adding icons or folders different in size or shape from those supplied by Microsoft, and from using the "Active Desktop" feature to promote third-party brands. These restrictions impose significant costs upon the OEMs; prior to Microsoft's prohibiting the practice, many OEMs would change the appearance of the desktop in ways they found beneficial. (March 1997 letter from Hewlett-Packard to Microsoft: "We are responsible for the cost of technical support of our customers, including the 33% of calls we get related to the lack of quality or confusion generated by your product.... We must have more ability to decide how our system is presented to our end users. If we had a choice of another supplier, based on your actions in this area, I assure you [that you] would not be our supplier of choice.").

The dissatisfaction of the OEM customers does not, of course, mean the restrictions are anticompetitive. The anticompetitive effect of the license restrictions is, as Microsoft itself recognizes, that OEMs are not able to promote rival browsers, which keeps developers focused upon the APIs in Windows. This kind of promotion is not a zero-sum game; but for the restrictions in their licenses to use Windows, OEMs could promote multiple IAPs and browsers. By preventing the OEMs from doing so, this type of license restriction, like the first two restrictions, is anticompetitive: Microsoft reduced rival browsers' usage share not by improving its own product but, rather, by preventing OEMs from taking actions that could increase rivals' share of usage.

b. Microsoft's justifications for the license restrictions

Microsoft argues that the license restrictions are legally justified because, in imposing them, Microsoft is simply "exercising its rights as the holder of valid copyrights." Microsoft also argues that the licenses "do not unduly restrict the opportunities of Netscape to distribute Navigator in any event."

Microsoft's primary copyright argument borders upon the frivolous. The company claims an absolute and unfettered right to use its intellectual property as it wishes: "[I]f intellectual property rights have been lawfully acquired," it says, then "their subsequent exercise cannot give rise to antitrust liability. That is no more correct than the proposition that use of one's personal property, such as a baseball bat, cannot give rise to tort liability. As the Federal Circuit succinctly stated: "Intellectual property rights do not confer a privilege to violate the antitrust laws." *In re Indep. Serv. Orgs. Antitrust Litig.*, 203 F.3d 1322, 1325 (Fed. Cir. 2000).

Although Microsoft never overtly retreats from its bold and incorrect position on the law, it also makes two arguments to the effect that it is not exercising its copyright in an unreasonable manner, despite the anticompetitive consequences of the license restrictions discussed above. In the first variation upon its unqualified copyright defense, Microsoft cites two cases indicating that a copyright holder may limit a licensee's ability to engage in significant and deleterious alterations of a copyrighted work. The relevance of those two cases for the present one is limited, however, both because those cases involved substantial alterations of a copyrighted work, and because in neither case was there any claim that the copyright holder was, in asserting its rights, violating the antitrust laws.

The only license restriction Microsoft seriously defends as necessary to prevent a "substantial alteration" of its copyrighted work is the prohibition on OEMs automatically launching a substitute user interface upon completion of the boot process. We agree that a shell that automatically prevents the Windows desktop from ever being seen by the user is a drastic alteration of Microsoft's copyrighted work, and outweighs the marginal anticompetitive effect of prohibiting the OEMs from substituting a different interface automatically upon completion of the initial boot process. We therefore hold that this particular restriction is not an exclusionary practice that violates § 2 of the Sherman Act.

In a second variation upon its copyright defense, Microsoft argues that the license restrictions merely prevent OEMs from taking actions that would reduce substantially the value of Microsoft's copyrighted work: that is, Microsoft claims each license restriction in question is necessary to prevent OEMs from so altering Windows as to undermine "the principal value of Windows as a stable and consistent platform that supports a broad range of applications and that is familiar to users." Microsoft, however, never substantiates this claim, and, because an OEM's altering the appearance of the desktop or promoting programs in the boot sequence does not affect the code already in the product, the practice does not self-evidently affect either the "stability" or the "consistency" of the platform. Microsoft cites only one item of evidence in support of its claim that the OEMs' alterations were decreasing the value of Windows. That document, prepared by Microsoft itself, states: "there are quality issues created by OEMs who are too liberal with the pre-install process," referring to the OEMs' installation of Windows and additional software on their PCs, which the document says may result in "user concerns and confusion." To the extent the OEMs' modifications cause consumer confusion, of course, the OEMs bear the additional support costs. Therefore, we conclude Microsoft has not shown that the OEMs' liberality reduces the value of Windows except in the sense that their promotion of rival browsers undermines Microsoft's monopoly—and that is not a permissible justification for the license restrictions.

Apart from copyright, Microsoft raises one other defense of the OEM license agreements: It argues that, despite the restrictions in the OEM license, Netscape is not completely blocked from distributing its product. That claim is insufficient to shield Microsoft from liability for those restrictions because, although Microsoft did not bar its rivals from all means of distribution, it did bar them from the cost-efficient ones.

In sum, we hold that with the exception of the one restriction prohibiting automatically launched alternative interfaces, all the OEM license restrictions at issue represent uses of Microsoft's market power to protect its monopoly, unredeemed by any legitimate justification. The restrictions therefore violate § 2 of the Sherman Act.

2. Integration of IE and Windows

Although Microsoft's license restrictions have a significant effect in closing rival browsers out of one of the two primary channels of distribution, the District Court found that "Microsoft's executives believed . . . its contractual restrictions placed on OEMs would not be sufficient in themselves to reverse the direction of Navigator's usage share. Consequently, in late 1995 or early 1996, Microsoft set out to bind [IE] more tightly to Windows 95 as a technical matter."

Technologically binding IE to Windows, the District Court found, both prevented OEMs from pre-installing other browsers and deterred consumers from using them. In particular, having the IE software code as an irremovable part of Windows meant that pre-installing a second browser would "increase an OEM's product testing costs," because an OEM must test and train its support staff to answer calls related to every software product preinstalled on the machine; moreover, pre-installing a browser in addition to IE would to many OEMs be "a questionable use of the scarce and valuable space on a PC's hard drive."

Although the District Court, in its Conclusions of Law, broadly condemned Microsoft's decision to bind "Internet Explorer to Windows with . . . technological shackles," its findings of fact in support of that conclusion center upon three specific actions Microsoft took to weld IE to Windows: excluding IE from the "Add/Remove Programs" utility; designing Windows so as in certain circumstances to override the user's choice of a default browser other than IE; and commingling code related to browsing and other code in the same files, so that any attempt to delete the files containing IE would, at the same time, cripple the operating system. As with the license restrictions, we consider first whether the suspect actions had an anticompetitive effect, and then whether Microsoft has provided a procompetitive justification for them.

a. Anticompetitive effect of integration

As a general rule, courts are properly very skeptical about claims that competition has been harmed by a dominant firm's product design changes. In a competitive market, firms routinely innovate in the hope of appealing to consumers, sometimes in the process making their products incompatible with those of rivals; the imposition of liability when a monopolist does the same thing will inevitably deter a certain amount of innovation. This is all the more true in a market, such as this one, in which the product itself is rapidly changing. Judicial deference to product innovation, however, does not mean that a monopolist's product design decisions are per se lawful.

The District Court first condemned as anticompetitive Microsoft's decision to exclude IE from the "Add/Remove Programs" utility in Windows 98. Microsoft had included IE in the Add/Remove Programs utility in Windows 95, but when it modified Windows 95 to produce Windows 98, it took IE out of the Add/Remove Programs utility. This change reduces the usage share of rival browsers not by making Microsoft's own browser more attractive to consumers but, rather, by discouraging OEMs from distributing rival products. Because Microsoft's conduct, through something other than competition on the merits, has the effect of significantly reducing usage of rivals' products and hence protecting its own operating system monopoly, it is anticompetitive; we defer for the moment the question whether it is nonetheless justified.

Second, the District Court found that Microsoft designed Windows 98 "so that using Navigator on Windows 98 would have unpleasant consequences for users" by, in some circumstances, overriding the user's choice of a browser other than IE as his or her default browser. Plaintiffs argue that this override harms the competitive process by deterring consumers from using a browser other than IE even though they might prefer to do so, thereby reducing rival browsers' usage share and, hence, the ability of rival browsers to draw developer attention away from the APIs exposed by Windows. Microsoft does not deny, of course, that overriding the user's preference prevents some people from using other browsers. Because the override reduces rivals' usage share and protects Microsoft's monopoly, it too is anticompetitive.

Finally, the District Court condemned Microsoft's decision to bind IE to Windows 98 "by placing code specific to Web browsing in the same files as code that provided operating system functions." Putting code supplying browsing functionality into a file with code supplying operating system functionality "ensure[s] that the deletion of any file containing browsing-specific routines would also delete vital operating system routines and thus cripple Windows . . . ." As noted above, preventing an OEM from removing IE deters it from installing a second browser because doing so increases the OEM's product testing and support costs; by contrast, had OEMs been able to remove IE, they might have chosen to pre-install Navigator alone.

Microsoft denies, as a factual matter, that it commingled browsing and non-browsing code, and it maintains the District Court's findings to the contrary are clearly erroneous. According to Microsoft, its expert "testified without contradiction that '[t]he very same code in Windows 98 that provides Web browsing functionality' also performs essential operating system functions—not code in the same files, but the very same software code."

Microsoft's expert did not testify to that effect "without contradiction," however. A Government expert, Glenn Weadock, testified that Microsoft "design [ed] [IE] so that some of the code that it uses co-resides in the same library files as other code needed for Windows." Another Government expert likewise testified that one library file, SHDOCVW.DLL, "is really a bundle of separate functions. It contains some functions that have to do specifically with Web browsing, and it contains some general user interface functions as well." One of Microsoft's own documents suggests as much. (Microsoft document indicating some functions in SHDOCVW.DLL can be described as "IE only," others can be described as "shell only" and still others can be described as providing both "IE" and "shell" functions)).

In view of the contradictory testimony in the record, some of which supports the District Court's finding that Microsoft commingled browsing and non-browsing code, we cannot conclude that the finding was clearly erroneous. Accordingly, . . . we conclude that such commingling has an anticompetitive effect; as noted above, the commingling deters OEMs from pre-installing rival browsers, thereby reducing the rivals' usage share and, hence, developers' interest in rivals' APIs as an alternative to the API set exposed by Microsoft's operating system.

b. Microsoft's justifications for integration

Microsoft proffers no justification for two of the three challenged actions that it took in integrating IE into Windows—excluding IE from the Add/Remove Programs utility and commingling browser and operating system code. Although Microsoft does make some general claims regarding the benefits of integrating the browser and the operating system, it neither specifies nor substantiates those claims. Nor does it argue that either excluding IE from the Add/Remove Programs utility or commingling code achieves any integrative benefit. Plaintiffs plainly made out a prima facie case of harm to competition in the operating system market by demonstrating that Microsoft's actions increased its browser usage share and thus protected its operating system monopoly from a middleware threat and, for its part, Microsoft failed to meet its burden of showing that its conduct serves a purpose other than protecting its operating system monopoly. Accordingly, we hold that Microsoft's exclusion of IE from the Add/Remove Programs utility and its commingling of browser and operating system code constitute exclusionary conduct, in violation of § 2.

As for the other challenged act that Microsoft took in integrating IE into Windows—causing Windows to override the user's choice of a default browser in certain circumstances—Microsoft argues that it has "valid technical reasons." Specifically, Microsoft claims that it was necessary to design Windows to override the user's preferences when he or she invokes one of "a few" out "of the nearly 30 means of accessing the Internet." According to Microsoft:

> The Windows 98 Help system and Windows Update feature depend on ActiveX controls not supported by Navigator, and the now-discontinued Channel Bar utilized Microsoft's Channel Definition Format, which Navigator also did not support. Lastly, Windows 98 does not invoke Navigator if a user accesses the Internet through "My Computer" or "Windows Explorer" because doing so would defeat one of the purposes of those features— enabling users to move seamlessly from local storage devices to the Web in the same browsing window.

The plaintiff bears the burden not only of rebutting a proffered justification but also of demonstrating that the anticompetitive effect of the challenged action outweighs it. In the District Court, plaintiffs appear to have done neither, let alone both; in any event, upon appeal, plaintiffs offer no rebuttal whatsoever. Accordingly, Microsoft may not be held liable for this aspect of its product design.

[The court affirmed the district court's findings that Microsoft's exclusive contracts with Internet Access Providers and its dealings with Apple and Intel concerning the development of Java were in violation of Section 2 of the Sherman Act.]

Notes & Questions

1. The Department of Justice's case against Microsoft was extensively litigated by the federal government in the late 1990s. A number of issues related to this case were also litigated in state claims against Microsoft and in the European Union. To give you a sense of the baroque drama of the case, here is a timeline of the major developments in the dispute:

1990:   The FTC begins investigation of Microsoft's pricing and exclusionary practices.

1993:   An evenly divided FTC board splits on bringing a suit against Microsoft. The Department of Justice takes over the investigation.

1994:   Microsoft and the Department of Justice enter into a settlement under which Microsoft agrees to alter its business practices. One of the terms of the settlement is that Microsoft will not distribute bundled versions of its software, but can distributed integrated products.

1995:   Judge Sporkin rejects the proposal settlement. The D.C. Court of Appeals overturns Judge Sporkin and orders a new judge assigned to review the settlement. Judge Penfield Jackson is assigned to the case and approves the settlement. Microsoft launches Windows 95 in the fall.

1996:   The Department of Justice initiates an investigation of Microsoft's practices with respect to Windows 95.

1997:   The Department of Justice brings a lawsuit claiming that Microsoft violated the terms of its settlement agreement in distributing Windows 95 by bundling the Internet Explorer browser with the operating system. Judge Jackson orders a preliminary injunction to keep Microsoft from requiring computer manufacturers to install Internet Explorer. Microsoft appeals the order.

1998:   The D.C. Court of Appeals reverses Judge Jackson's preliminary injunction order, finding that Internet Explorer and Windows were integrated, rather than bundled products. Since the products were integrated, Microsoft was not in violation of the settlement. The Department of Justice, along with several states attorney generals, file a suit claiming that Microsoft's conduct was exclusionary and monopolizing.

1999:   Judge Jackson issues his findings of fact against Microsoft, concluding that Microsoft had market power and had acted illegally. Judge Jackson orders Microsoft and the Department of Justice to mediate and appoints Judge Richard Posner as the mediator.

2000:   After the mediation fails, Judge Jackson issues his findings of law and orders Microsoft to be split into two companies.

2001:   The D.C. Court of Appeals overrules Judge Jackson's order to split the company, but does find violations of the law. The appeals court remands to a new judge for determinations of liability. [Note: The D.C. Court of Appeals' opinion is the one excerpted here and in the next section.] Microsoft and the Department of Justice enter into a settlement agreement.

2002:   Judge Colleen Kollar-Kotelly approves the settlement agreement, which requires Microsoft to disclose features of the Windows source code to make it easier for companies to create middleware and to allow computer manufacturers to decide which Microsoft features to include on equipment. The states opt out of the settlement.

Microsoft entered into settlement agreements with various states in 2003 and 2004. Many states and private companies continue to pursue the litigation. For a comprehensive discussion of the antitrust cases against Microsoft, *see* Andrew L. Gavil & Harry First, The Microsoft Antitrust Cases: Competition Policy for the Twenty-First Century (2014).

2. The European Union Competition Commission initiated an investigation of Microsoft's practices in the early 1990s and joined in the 1994 settlement agreement between Microsoft and the Department of Justice. The Competition Commission's investigation additionally addressed claims by Sun Microsystems Incorporated ("Sun"), a competing software developer, that Microsoft had illegitimately refused to disclose certain secret specifications of Microsoft products needed by Sun to produce competing software products. Based on its investigation, the Competition Commission concluded in 2004 that Microsoft violated EU laws in withholding this information, observing in its 2004 opinion that:

> Microsoft is abusing its dominant position by refusing to supply Sun . . . with the specifications for the protocols used by Windows work group servers in order to provide file, print and group and user administration services to Windows work group networks, and allow [Sun] to implement such specifications for the purpose of developing and distributing interoperable work group server operating system products.

European Union Competition Commission Decision of March 24, 2004 Relating to a Proceeding Under Article 82 of the EC Treaty, Case COMP/C-3/37.792 Microsoft. The timeline of the investigation leading up to the excerpted Competition Commission opinion from 2004 is as follows:

1998:   EU begins probe of Microsoft after a complaint is brought by Sun Microsystems asserting anticompetitive conduct in the licensing of Microsoft's operating system code.

2000:   EU launches investigation of Windows 2000.

2001:   EU issues a charge sheet to Microsoft, alleging that the company abused its dominant position in violation of Article 82 of the European Committee Competition Treaty. The charge sheet orders Microsoft to unbundle Media Player from its operating system.

2002:   Microsoft proposes concessions to the EU, such as including software of rival companies on a CD with sales of Windows. The EU rejects the proposals.

2003:   EU submits another charge sheet to Microsoft, ordering changes to Windows 2000.

2004:   EU Competition Chief Mario Monti issues the opinion, excerpted above, fining Microsoft 497 million Euros (613 million US dollars) and ordering the company to unbundle its Media Player from its operating system and to release portions of its source code and related software specifications to rival software companies as means to facilitate interoperability.

3. Microsoft's disputes with the EU concerning the company's compliance with the requirements of the opinion excerpted above continued for several additional years. Later developments in this case included the following:

2004:   Microsoft pays its fine of 497 million Euros in full. It creates and releases a version of its operating system without Windows Media Player. Microsoft reveals portions of its source code as ordered, but not the related software specifications.

2006:   A dispute with Neelie Kroes, appointed new European Commissioner for Competition in 2004, continues as to the scope of Microsoft's obligations under the Commission's order. Commissioner Kroes fines Microsoft 280.5 million Euros (448.58 million U.S. dollars) for the company's failure to comply with the Commission's 2004 order in a timely manner.

2007:   Microsoft loses its appeal to the European Court of First Instance challenging the Commission's 2004 ruling. The Court upholds the initial fine of 497 million Euros and the disclosure obligations imposed by the Commission but reverses portions of the Commission's order requiring that an independent trustee review Microsoft's internal operations in the future. Microsoft declines to appeal the Court's ruling. The company makes the disputed software specification information available to parties willing to pay a one-time access fee of 10,000 Euros (15,992 U.S. dollars).

2008:   The EU fines Microsoft an additional 899 million Euros (1.44 billion U.S. dollars) due to the company's delays in complying with the requirements of the March 2004 opinion excerpted in the text. This fine represents the largest penalty ever imposed under EU competition law up to that time. This fine is in addition to the prior 280.5 million Euro fine imposed for non-compliance during an earlier period of delay. Microsoft lodges an appeal in the European Court of First Instance seeking to overturn the 899 million Euro fine.

2011:   Microsoft presents arguments in the appeal of its 899 million Euro fine.

2012:   The General Court of the Court of Justice of the European Union (as the European Court of First Instance is now known) upholds the fine against Microsoft, but reduces it from 899 million Euros to 860 million Euros.

4. The *Microsoft* case illustrates the perils that may await a successful high technology company. Some critics of the case claim that Microsoft's only offense was being successful. Certainly, Microsoft's success and size put it on the radar screen of antitrust enforcers. Judge Jackson's decision to split the company into two (an operating system company and an applications company) is one possible response to concerns with company size. This approach, however, ignores some of the synergies that arise between operating systems and applications. Of course, these synergies could still be realized through joint ventures between the two companies. Since joint ventures receive relaxed treatment under antitrust law, the decision to split the company could potentially lead to even more problems in antitrust enforcement. For

this, and other reasons, the rejection of the divestiture remedy by the D.C. Court of Appeals was probably correct. What are the arguments in support of a split? What other remedies are responsive to the problems that the D.C. Court of Appeals identified?

5. While the Court of Appeals rejected the remedy imposed by Judge Jackson, the court did find that Microsoft monopolized the market for computer operating systems. Did the court define the market in a meaningful way? Microsoft made the argument that, given the dynamics of the software industry, its market size was continually threatened by competing systems. The Court of Appeals found this argument unpersuasive, partly because Microsoft's activities were found to shield the company from competitive threats. What were the bad acts that the court found? What are potential business justifications for these acts?

6. It might be helpful to think about the lessons that can be derived from the *Microsoft* case. The company's problems in that case stemmed from licensing and marketing practices that Microsoft engaged in during the 1990s. Do the 1995 Licensing Guidelines offer guidance on the legality or illegality of Microsoft's business practices? Is the Court of Appeals' analysis consistent with the 1995 Guidelines?

United States v. Microsoft

United States Court of Appeals for the District of Columbia

253 F.3d 34 (D.C. Cir. 2001)

[The court's analysis of Microsoft's practices continued:]

IV. Tying

Microsoft also contests the District Court's determination of liability under § 1 of the Sherman Act. The District Court concluded that Microsoft's contractual and technological bundling of the IE web browser (the "tied" product) with its Windows operating system ("OS") (the "tying" product) resulted in a tying arrangement that was per se unlawful. We hold that the rule of reason, rather than per se analysis, should govern the legality of tying arrangements involving platform software products. The Supreme Court has warned that "'[i]t is only after considerable experience with certain business relationships that courts classify them as per se violations . . . .'" While every "business relationship" will in some sense have unique features, some represent entire, novel categories of dealings. As we shall explain, the arrangement before us is an example of the latter, offering the first up-close look at the technological integration of added functionality into software that serves as a platform for third-party applications. There being no close parallel in prior antitrust cases, simplistic application of per se tying rules carries a serious risk of harm. Accordingly, we vacate the District Court's finding of a per se tying violation and remand the case. Plaintiffs may on remand pursue their tying claim under the rule of reason.

The facts underlying the tying allegation substantially overlap with those set forth in Section II.B in connection with the § 2 monopoly maintenance claim. The key

District Court findings are that (1) Microsoft required licensees of Windows 95 and 98 also to license IE as a bundle at a single price; (2) Microsoft refused to allow OEMs to uninstall or remove IE from the Windows desktop; (3) Microsoft designed Windows 98 in a way that withheld from consumers the ability to remove IE by use of the Add/Remove Programs utility; and (4) Microsoft designed Windows 98 to override the user's choice of default web browser in certain circumstances. The court found that these acts constituted a per se tying violation. Although the District Court also found that Microsoft commingled operating system-only and browser-only routines in the same library files, it did not include this as a basis for tying liability despite plaintiffs' request that it do so.

There are four elements to a per se tying violation: (1) the tying and tied goods are two separate products; (2) the defendant has market power in the tying product market; (3) the defendant affords consumers no choice but to purchase the tied product from it; and (4) the tying arrangement forecloses a substantial volume of commerce.

Microsoft does not dispute that it bound Windows and IE in the four ways the District Court cited. Instead it argues that Windows (the tying good) and IE browsers (the tied good) are not "separate products," and that it did not substantially foreclose competing browsers from the tied product market.

We first address the separate-products inquiry, a source of much argument between the parties and of confusion in the cases. Our purpose is to highlight the poor fit between the separate-products test and the facts of this case. We then offer further reasons for carving an exception to the per se rule when the tying product is platform software. In the final section we discuss the District Court's inquiry if plaintiffs pursue a rule of reason claim on remand.

A. Separate-Products Inquiry Under the Per Se Test

The requirement that a practice involve two separate products before being condemned as an illegal tie started as a purely linguistic requirement: unless products are separate, one cannot be "tied" to the other. Indeed, the nature of the products involved in early tying cases—intuitively distinct items such as a movie projector and a film. It was not until *Times-Picayune Publishing Co. v. United States*, 345 U.S. 594, 73 S. Ct. 872, 97 L. Ed. 1277 (1953), that the separate-products issue became a distinct element of the test for an illegal tie. Even that case engaged in a rather cursory inquiry into whether ads sold in the morning edition of a paper were a separate product from ads sold in the evening edition.

The first case to give content to the separate-products test was [*Jefferson Parish Hosp. Dist. No. 2 v. Hyde*], 466 U.S. 2, 104 S. Ct. 1551, 80 L. Ed. 2d 2. That case addressed a tying arrangement in which a hospital conditioned surgical care at its facility on the purchase of anesthesiological services from an affiliated medical group. The facts were a challenge for casual separate-products analysis because the tied service—anesthesia—was neither intuitively distinct from nor intuitively contained within the tying service—surgical care. A further complication was that, soon after the Court enunciated the per se rule for tying liability, new economic research began to cast doubt on the assumption, voiced by the Court when it established the rule, that "'tying agreements serve hardly any purpose beyond the suppression of competition.'"

The *Jefferson Parish* Court resolved the matter in two steps. First, it clarified that "the answer to the question whether one or two products are involved" does not turn "on the functional relation between them . . . ." In other words, the mere fact that two items are complements, that "one . . . is useless without the other," id., does not make them a single "product" for purposes of tying law. Second, reasoning that the "definitional question [whether two distinguishable products are involved] depends on whether the arrangement may have the type of competitive consequences addressed by the rule [against tying]," the Court decreed that "no tying arrangement can exist unless there is a sufficient demand for the purchase of anesthesiological services separate from hospital services to identify a distinct product market in which it is efficient to offer anesthesiological services separately from hospital service."

The Court proceeded to examine direct and indirect evidence of consumer demand for the tied product separate from the tying product. Direct evidence addresses the question whether, when given a choice, consumers purchase the tied good from the tying good maker, or from other firms. The Court took note, for example, of testimony that patients and surgeons often requested specific anesthesiologists not associated with a hospital. Indirect evidence includes the behavior of firms without market power in the tying good market, presumably on the notion that (competitive) supply follows demand. If competitive firms always bundle the tying and tied goods, then they are a single product. Here the Court noted that only 27% of anesthesiologists in markets other than the defendant's had financial relationships with hospitals, and that, unlike radiologists and pathologists, anesthesiologists were not usually employed by hospitals, i.e., bundled with hospital services. With both direct and indirect evidence concurring, the Court determined that hospital surgery and anesthesiological services were distinct goods.

To understand the logic behind the Court's consumer demand test, consider first the postulated harms from tying. The core concern is that tying prevents goods from competing directly for consumer choice on their merits, i.e., being selected as a result of "buyers' independent judgment." With a tie, a buyer's "freedom to select the best bargain in the second market [could be] impaired by his need to purchase the tying product, and perhaps by an inability to evaluate the true cost of either product . . . ." Direct competition on the merits of the tied product is foreclosed when the tying product either is sold only in a bundle with the tied product or, though offered separately, is sold at a bundled price, so that the buyer pays the same price whether he takes the tied product or not. In both cases, a consumer buying the tying product becomes entitled to the tied product; he will therefore likely be unwilling to buy a competitor's version of the tied product even if, making his own price/quality assessment, that is what he would prefer.

But not all ties are bad. Bundling obviously saves distribution and consumer transaction costs. This is likely to be true, to take some examples from the computer industry, with the integration of math co-processors and memory into microprocessor chips and the inclusion of spell checkers in word processors. Bundling can also capitalize on certain economies of scope. A possible example is the "shared" library files that perform OS and browser functions with the very same lines of code and thus may save drive space from the clutter of redundant routines and memory when consumers use both the OS and browser simultaneously. Indeed, if there were no efficiencies from a tie (including economizing on consumer transaction costs such as the time and effort involved in choice), we would expect distinct consumer demand for each individual component of every good. In a competitive market with zero transaction costs, the computers on which this opinion was written would only be sold piecemeal—keyboard, monitor, mouse, central processing unit, disk drive, and memory all sold in separate transactions and likely by different manufacturers.

Recognizing the potential benefits from tying, the Court in *Jefferson Parish* forged a separate-products test that, like those of market power and substantial foreclosure, attempts to screen out false positives under per se analysis. The consumer demand test is a rough proxy for whether a tying arrangement may, on balance, be welfare-enhancing, and unsuited to per se condemnation. In the abstract, of course, there is always direct separate demand for products: assuming choice is available at zero cost, consumers will prefer it to no choice. Only when the efficiencies from bundling are dominated by the benefits to choice for enough consumers, however, will we actually observe consumers making independent purchases. In other words, perceptible separate demand is inversely proportional to net efficiencies. On the supply side, firms without market power will bundle two goods only when the cost savings from joint sale outweigh the value consumers place on separate choice. So bundling by all competitive firms implies strong net efficiencies. If a court finds either that there is no noticeable separate demand for the tied product or, there being no convincing direct evidence of separate demand, that the entire "competitive fringe" engages in the same behavior as the defendant, then the tying and tied products should be declared one product and per se liability should be rejected.

Before concluding our exegesis of *Jefferson Parish*'s separate-products test, we should clarify two things. First, *Jefferson Parish* does not endorse a direct inquiry into the efficiencies of a bundle. Rather, it proposes easy-to-administer proxies for net efficiency. In describing the separate-products test we discuss efficiencies only to explain the rationale behind the consumer demand inquiry. To allow the separate-products test to become a detailed inquiry into possible welfare consequences would turn a screening test into the very process it is expected to render unnecessary.

Second, the separate-products test is not a one-sided inquiry into the cost savings from a bundle. Although *Jefferson Parish* acknowledged that prior lower court cases looked at cost-savings to decide separate products, the Court conspicuously did not adopt that approach in its disposition of tying arrangement before it. Instead it chose proxies that balance costs savings against reduction in consumer choice.

With this background, we now turn to the separate products inquiry before us. The District Court found that many consumers, if given the option, would choose their browser separately from the OS. Turning to industry custom, the court found that, although all major OS vendors bundled browsers with their OS's, these companies either sold versions without a browser, or allowed OEMs or end-users either not to install the bundled browser or in any event to "uninstall" it. The court did not discuss the record evidence as to whether OS vendors other than Microsoft sold at a bundled price, with no discount for a browserless OS, perhaps because the record evidence on the issue was in conflict.

Microsoft does not dispute that many consumers demand alternative browsers. But on industry custom Microsoft contends that no other firm requires non-removal because no other firm has invested the resources to integrate web browsing as deeply into its OS as Microsoft has. (We here use the term "integrate" in the rather simple sense of converting individual goods into components of a single physical object (e.g., a computer as it leaves the OEM, or a disk or sets of disks), without any normative implication that such integration is desirable or achieves special advantages.) Microsoft contends not only that its integration of IE into Windows is innovative and beneficial but also that it requires non-removal of IE. In our discussion of monopoly maintenance we find that these claims fail the efficiency balancing applicable in that context. But the separate-products analysis is supposed to perform its function as a proxy without embarking on any direct analysis of efficiency. Accordingly, Microsoft's implicit argument—that in this case looking to a competitive fringe is inadequate to evaluate fully its potentially innovative technological integration, that such a comparison is between apples and oranges—poses a legitimate objection to the operation of *Jefferson Parish*'s separate-products test for the per se rule.

In fact there is merit to Microsoft's broader argument that *Jefferson Parish*'s consumer demand test would "chill innovation to the detriment of consumers by preventing firms from integrating into their products new functionality previously provided by standalone products—and hence, by definition, subject to separate consumer demand." The per se rule's direct consumer demand and indirect industry custom inquiries are, as a general matter, backward-looking and therefore systematically poor proxies for overall efficiency in the presence of new and innovative integration. The direct consumer demand test focuses on historic consumer behavior, likely before integration, and the indirect industry custom test looks at firms that, unlike the defendant, may not have integrated the tying and tied goods. Both tests compare incomparables—the defendant's decision to bundle in the presence of integration, on the one hand, and consumer and competitor calculations in its absence, on the other. If integration has efficiency benefits, these may be ignored by the *Jefferson Parish* proxies. Because one cannot be sure beneficial integration will be protected by the other elements of the per se rule, simple application of that rule's separate-products test may make consumers worse off.

In light of the monopoly maintenance section, obviously, we do not find that Microsoft's integration is welfare-enhancing or that it should be absolved of tying liability. Rather, we heed Microsoft's warning that the separate-products element of the per se rule may not give newly integrated products a fair shake.

B. Per Se Analysis Inappropriate for this Case.

We now address directly the larger question as we see it: whether standard per se analysis should be applied "off the shelf" to evaluate the defendant's tying arrangement, one which involves software that serves as a platform for third-party applications. There is no doubt that "[i]t is far too late in the history of our antitrust jurisprudence to question the proposition that certain tying arrangements pose an unacceptable risk of stifling competition and therefore are unreasonable 'per se.'" But there are strong reasons to doubt that the integration of additional software functionality into an OS falls among these arrangements. Applying per se analysis to such an amalgamation creates undue risks of error and of deterring welfare-enhancing innovation.

The Supreme Court has warned that "'[i]t is only after considerable experience with certain business relationships that courts classify them as per se violations . . . .'" Yet the sort of tying arrangement attacked here is unlike any the Supreme Court has considered. The early Supreme Court cases on tying dealt with arrangements whereby the sale or lease of a patented product was conditioned on the purchase of certain unpatented products from the patentee. Later Supreme Court tying cases did not involve market power derived from patents, but continued to involve contractual ties.

In none of these cases was the tied good physically and technologically integrated with the tying good. Nor did the defendants ever argue that their tie improved the value of the tying product to users and to makers of complementary goods. In those cases where the defendant claimed that use of the tied good made the tying good more valuable to users, the Court ruled that the same result could be achieved via quality standards for substitutes of the tied good. Here Microsoft argues that IE and Windows are an integrated physical product and that the bundling of IE APIs with Windows makes the latter a better applications platform for third-party software. It is unclear how the benefits from IE APIs could be achieved by quality standards for different browser manufacturers. We do not pass judgment on Microsoft's claims regarding the benefits from integration of its APIs. We merely note that these and other novel, purported efficiencies suggest that judicial "experience" provides little basis for believing that, "because of their pernicious effect on competition and lack of any redeeming virtue," a software firm's decisions to sell multiple functionalities as a package should be "conclusively presumed to be unreasonable and therefore illegal without elaborate inquiry as to the precise harm they have caused or the business excuse for their use."

Nor have we found much insight into software integration among the decisions of lower federal courts. Most tying cases in the computer industry involve bundling with hardware. Just as Microsoft integrated web browsing into its OS, IBM in the 1970s integrated memory into its CPUs, a hardware platform. A peripheral manufacturer alleged a tying violation, but the District Court dismissed the claim because it thought it inappropriate to enmesh the courts in product design decisions. The court's discussion of the tying claim was brief and did not dwell on the effects of the integration on competition or efficiencies. Nor did the court consider whether per se analysis of the alleged tie was wise . . . .

. . . [T]he nature of the platform software market affirmatively suggests that per se rules might stunt valuable innovation. We have in mind two reasons.

First, as we explained in the previous section, the separate-products test is a poor proxy for net efficiency from newly integrated products. Under per se analysis the first firm to merge previously distinct functionalities (e.g., the inclusion of starter motors in automobiles) or to eliminate entirely the need for a second function (e.g., the invention of the stain-resistant carpet) risks being condemned as having tied two separate products because at the moment of integration there will appear to be a robust "distinct" market for the tied product.

The failure of the separate-products test to screen out certain cases of productive integration is particularly troubling in platform software markets such as that in which the defendant competes. Not only is integration common in such markets, but it is common among firms without market power. We have already reviewed evidence that nearly all competitive OS vendors also bundle browsers. Moreover, plaintiffs do not dispute that OS vendors can and do incorporate basic internet plumbing and other useful functionality into their OS's. Firms without market power have no incentive to package different pieces of software together unless there are efficiency gains from doing so. The ubiquity of bundling in competitive platform software markets should give courts reason to pause before condemning such behavior in less competitive markets.

Second, because of the pervasively innovative character of platform software markets, tying in such markets may produce efficiencies that courts have not previously encountered and thus the Supreme Court had not factored into the per se rule as originally conceived. For example, the bundling of a browser with OS's enables an independent software developer to count on the presence of the browser's APIs, if any, on consumers' machines and thus to omit them from its own package. It is true that software developers can bundle the browser APIs they need with their own products, but that may force consumers to pay twice for the same API if it is bundled with two different software programs. It is also true that OEMs can include APIs with the computers they sell, id., but diffusion of uniform APIs by that route may be inferior. First, many OEMs serve special subsets of Windows consumers, such as home or corporate or academic users. If just one of these OEMs decides not to bundle an API because it does not benefit enough of its clients, ISVs that use that API might have to bundle it with every copy of their program. Second, there may be a substantial lag before all OEMs bundle the same set of APIs—a lag inevitably aggravated by the first phenomenon. In a field where programs change very rapidly, delays in the spread of a necessary element (here, the APIs) may be very costly. Of course, these arguments may not justify Microsoft's decision to bundle APIs in this case, particularly because Microsoft did not merely bundle with Windows the APIs from IE, but an entire browser application (sometimes even without APIs, see id.). A justification for bundling a component of software may not be one for bundling the entire software package, especially given the malleability of software code. Furthermore, the interest in efficient API diffusion obviously supplies a far stronger justification for simple price-bundling than for Microsoft's contractual or technological bars to subsequent removal of functionality. But our qualms about redefining the boundaries of a defendant's product and the possibility of consumer gains from simplifying the work of applications developers makes us question any hard and fast approach to tying in OS software markets.

There may also be a number of efficiencies that, although very real, have been ignored in the calculations underlying the adoption of a per se rule for tying. We fear that these efficiencies are common in technologically dynamic markets where product development is especially unlikely to follow an easily foreseen linear pattern. When IBM first introduced [computer disk] drives in 1956, it sold an integrated product that contained magnetic disks and disk heads that read and wrote data onto disks. Consumers of the drives demanded two functions—to store data and to access it all at once. In the first few years consumers' demand for storage increased rapidly, outpacing the evolution of magnetic disk technology. To satisfy that demand IBM made it possible for consumers to remove the magnetic disks from drives, even though that meant consumers would not have access to data on disks removed from the drive. This componentization enabled makers of computer peripherals to sell consumers removable disks. Over time, however, the technology of magnetic disks caught up with demand for capacity, so that consumers needed few removable disks to store all their data. At this point IBM reintegrated disks into their drives, enabling consumers to once again have immediate access to all their data without a sacrifice in capacity. A manufacturer of removable disks sued. But the District Court found the tie justified because it satisfied consumer demand for immediate access to all data, and ruled that disks and disk heads were one product . . . .

These arguments all point to one conclusion: we cannot comfortably say that bundling in platform software markets has so little "redeeming virtue," and that there would be so "very little loss to society" from its ban, that "an inquiry into its costs in the individual case [can be] considered unnecessary." We do not have enough empirical evidence regarding the effect of Microsoft's practice on the amount of consumer surplus created or consumer choice foreclosed by the integration of added functionality into platform software to exercise sensible judgment regarding that entire class of behavior. (For some issues we have no data.) "We need to know more than we do about the actual impact of these arrangements on competition to decide whether they . . . should be classified as per se violations of the Sherman Act." Until then, we will heed the wisdom that "easy labels do not always supply ready answers," and vacate the District Court's finding of per se tying liability under Sherman Act § 1. We remand the case for evaluation of Microsoft's tying arrangements under the rule of reason.

Our judgment regarding the comparative merits of the per se rule and the rule of reason is confined to the tying arrangement before us, where the tying product is software whose major purpose is to serve as a platform for third-party applications and the tied product is complementary software functionality. While our reasoning may at times appear to have broader force, we do not have the confidence to speak to facts outside the record, which contains scant discussion of software integration generally. Microsoft's primary justification for bundling IE APIs is that their inclusion with Windows increases the value of third-party software (and Windows) to consumers. Because this claim applies with distinct force when the tying product is platform software, we have no present basis for finding the per se rule inapplicable to software markets generally. Nor should we be interpreted as setting a precedent for switching to the rule of reason every time a court identifies an efficiency justification for a tying arrangement. Our reading of the record suggests merely that integration of new functionality into platform software is a common practice and that wooden application of per se rules in this litigation may cast a cloud over platform innovation in the market for PCs, network computers and information appliances.

Notes & Questions

1. The issue facing the Court of Appeals in this part of the *Microsoft* opinion is whether Internet Explorer and Windows constitute one product or two products. If the web browser and operating system constitute one product, then Microsoft could not logically be tying the sale of one product to another. For example, an automobile is a product that consists of many elements. It would be absurd to say that the sale of an automobile constituted a tying sale of tires to the chassis of the car. To determine if a sale involves one product or two, a court must conduct an efficiency analysis to determine if there are identifiable benefits stemming from the combination of different elements into one product. It should be easy to see how an automobile would pass this efficiency test and be considered one product. The problem can become more complicated when services are involved. In *Jefferson Parish*, a case cited by the Court of Appeals, patients challenged a hospital's practice of requiring the use of certain designated anesthesiologists in surgical procedures. Patients reasoned that this practice restricted the supply of anesthesiologists and raised prices. The Supreme Court applied a market analysis in *Jefferson Parish* to conclude that anesthesiological services were a separate product from surgical services. Note, however, that the separate product analysis resolves only the first part of the overall analysis of liability for tying arrangements. If a court finds that there are separate products, the court will then need to consider whether tying the sale of the two products is anticompetitive.

2. How does the Court of Appeals apply the separate products inquiry to software? Keep in mind that, with appropriate reprogramming, software is often divisible into parts. Software with two functions can be divided in some situations into two pieces of software, each performing the separate functions. A previous Court of Appeals panel considered whether Internet Explorer and Windows were one product or two under the terms of the 1994 settlement agreement between Microsoft and the Department of Justice. The court was analyzing the term of the agreement that permitted

Microsoft to distribute integrated products, but not tied products. The Court of Appeals ruled that the combination of Internet Explorer and Windows constituted an integrated product, as defined in the agreement. In finding an integrated product, the court emphasized the functional interactions between Internet Explorer and Windows. How does the Court of Appeals analyze the separate products issue in the excerpted opinion? The court seems to be particularly sensitive to the unique features of software and the dynamics of high technology markets. Is there a meaningful way to determine whether individual pieces of software constitute one product or two?

3. The court concludes that per se treatment is not appropriate for analyzing tying claims in the software industry. What is the basis for this conclusion? Is the court basing its conclusion on the nature of software or the structure of software markets? Does the court provide a sense of how to apply the rule of reason to alleged tying agreements in the software industry? Is the analysis a technical one or an economic one? Notice that in *Jefferson Parish*, the analysis rested largely on the demand for the individual services at issue. In the Court of Appeals' review of the 1994 settlement agreement involving Microsoft, the court applied a technical analysis of how software functions. What approach is appropriate for the *Microsoft* case described in the opinion excerpted above?

4. The 1995 Licensing Guidelines state that a tying arrangement will be challenged if: (a) the seller has market power in the tying product, (b) the arrangement has an adverse effect on competition in the relevant market for the tied product, and (c) efficiency justifications do not outweigh the anticompetitive effects of the arrangement. Is this approach consistent with the Court of Appeals' analysis in the *Microsoft* opinion excerpted above? Would Microsoft's practices be challenged under the 1995 Licensing Guidelines as an illegal tying arrangement? Note that in 2006, the Supreme Court held that ownership of a patent does not create the presumption of market power for a tying claim. See *Illinois Tool Works Inc. v. Independent Ink, Inc.*, 547 U.S. 28 (2006). Presumably the Court's reasoning would apply to tying claims based on copyright, trademark, trade secret, or other types of intellectual property.

2. Downstream Licensing

Impression Products, Inc. v. Lexmark Intern., Inc.

United States Supreme Court

137 S. Ct. 1523 (2017)

CHIEF JUSTICE ROBERTS DELIVERED THE OPINION OF THE COURT.

A United States patent entitles the patent holder (the "patentee"), for a period of 20 years, to "exclude others from making, using, offering for sale, or selling [its] invention throughout the United States or importing the invention into the United States." 35 U.S.C. § 154(a). Whoever engages in one of these acts "without authority" from the patentee may face liability for patent infringement. § 271(a).

When a patentee sells one of its products, however, the patentee can no longer control that item through the patent laws — its patent rights are said to "exhaust." The purchaser and all subsequent owners are free to use or resell the product just like any other item of personal property, without fear of an infringement lawsuit.

This case presents two questions about the scope of the patent exhaustion doctrine: First, whether a patentee that sells an item under an express restriction on the purchaser's right to reuse or resell the product may enforce that restriction through an infringement lawsuit. And second, whether a patentee exhausts its patent rights by selling its product outside the United States, where American patent laws do not apply. We conclude that a patentee's decision to sell a product exhausts all of its patent rights in that item, regardless of any restrictions the patentee purports to impose or the location of the sale.

I

The underlying dispute in this case is about laser printers — or, more specifically, the cartridges that contain the powdery substance, known as toner, that laser printers use to make an image appear on paper. Respondent Lexmark International, Inc. designs, manufactures, and sells toner cartridges to consumers in the United States and around the globe. It owns a number of patents that cover components of those cartridges and the manner in which they are used.

When toner cartridges run out of toner they can be refilled and used again. This creates an opportunity for other companies — known as remanufacturers — to acquire empty Lexmark cartridges from purchasers in the United States and abroad, refill them with toner, and then resell them at a lower price than the new ones Lexmark puts on the shelves.

Not blind to this business problem, Lexmark structures its sales in a way that encourages customers to return spent cartridges. It gives purchasers two options: One is to buy a toner cartridge at full price, with no strings attached. The other is to buy a cartridge at roughly 20–percent off through Lexmark's "Return Program." A customer who buys through the Return Program still owns the cartridge but, in exchange for the lower price, signs a contract agreeing to use it only once and to refrain from transferring the empty cartridge to anyone but Lexmark. To enforce this single-use/ no-resale restriction, Lexmark installs a microchip on each Return Program cartridge that prevents reuse once the toner in the cartridge runs out.

Lexmark's strategy just spurred remanufacturers to get more creative. Many kept acquiring empty Return Program cartridges and developed methods to counteract the effect of the microchips. With that technological obstacle out of the way, there was little to prevent the remanufacturers from using the Return Program cartridges in their resale business. After all, Lexmark's contractual single-use/no-resale agreements were with the initial customers, not with downstream purchasers like the remanufacturers.

Lexmark, however, was not so ready to concede that its plan had been foiled. In 2010, it sued a number of remanufacturers, including petitioner Impression Products,

Inc., for patent infringement with respect to two groups of cartridges. One group consists of Return Program cartridges that Lexmark sold within the United States.

Lexmark argued that, because it expressly prohibited reuse and resale of these cartridges, the remanufacturers infringed the Lexmark patents when they refurbished and resold them. The other group consists of all toner cartridges that Lexmark sold abroad and that remanufacturers imported into the country. Lexmark claimed that it never gave anyone authority to import these cartridges, so the remanufacturers ran afoul of its patent rights by doing just that.

Eventually, the lawsuit was whittled down to one defendant, Impression Products, and one defense: that Lexmark's sales, both in the United States and abroad, exhausted its patent rights in the cartridges, so Impression Products was free to refurbish and resell them, and to import them if acquired abroad. Impression Products filed separate motions to dismiss with respect to both groups of cartridges. The District Court granted the motion as to the domestic Return Program cartridges, but denied the motion as to the cartridges Lexmark sold abroad. Both parties appealed.

The Federal Circuit considered the appeals en banc and ruled for Lexmark with respect to both groups of cartridges. The court began with the Return Program cartridges that Lexmark sold in the United States. Relying on its decision in *Mallinckrodt, Inc. v. Medipart, Inc.,* 976 F.2d 700 (1992), the Federal Circuit held that a patentee may sell an item and retain the right to enforce, through patent infringement lawsuits, "clearly communicated, . . . lawful restriction[s] as to post-sale use or resale." 816 F.3d 721, 735 (2016). The exhaustion doctrine, the court reasoned, derives from the prohibition on making, using, selling, or importing items "without authority." *Id.,* at 734 (quoting 35 U.S.C. § 271(a)). When you purchase an item you presumptively also acquire the authority to use or resell the item freely, but that is just a presumption; the same authority does not run with the item when the seller restricts post-sale use or resale. 816 F.3d, at 742. Because the parties agreed that Impression Products knew about Lexmark's restrictions and that those restrictions did not violate any laws, the Federal Circuit concluded that Lexmark's sales had not exhausted all of its patent rights, and that the company could sue for infringement when Impression Products refurbished and resold Return Program cartridges.

As for the cartridges that Lexmark sold abroad, the Federal Circuit once again looked to its precedent. In *Jazz Photo Corp. v. International Trade Commission,* 264 F.3d 1094 (2001), the court had held that a patentee's decision to sell a product abroad did not terminate its ability to bring an infringement suit against a buyer that "import[ed] the article and [sold] . . . it in the United States." 816 F.3d, at 726–727. That rule, the court concluded, makes good sense: Exhaustion is justified when a patentee receives "the reward available from [selling in] American markets," which does not occur when the patentee sells overseas, where the American patent offers no protection and therefore cannot bolster the price of the patentee's goods. *Id.,* at 760–761. As a result, Lexmark was free to exercise its patent rights to sue Impression Products for bringing the foreign-sold cartridges to market in the United States.

Judge Dyk, joined by Judge Hughes, dissented. In their view, selling the Return Program cartridges in the United States exhausted Lexmark's patent rights in those items because any "authorized sale of a patented article . . . free[s] the article from any restrictions on use or sale based on the patent laws." *Id.*, at 775–776. As for the foreign cartridges, the dissenters would have held that a sale abroad also results in exhaustion, unless the seller "explicitly reserve[s] [its] United States patent rights" at the time of sale. *Id.*, at 774, 788. Because Lexmark failed to make such an express reservation, its foreign sales exhausted its patent rights.

We granted certiorari to consider the Federal Circuit's decisions with respect to both domestic and international exhaustion, 580 U.S.——, 137 S.Ct. 546, 196 L. Ed.2d 442 (2016), and now reverse.

II

A

First up are the Return Program cartridges that Lexmark sold in the United States. We conclude that Lexmark exhausted its patent rights in these cartridges the moment it sold them. The single-use/no-resale restrictions in Lexmark's contracts with customers may have been clear and enforceable under contract law, but they do not entitle Lexmark to retain patent rights in an item that it has elected to sell.

The Patent Act grants patentees the "right to exclude others from making, using, offering for sale, or selling [their] invention[s]." 35 U.S.C. § 154(a). For over 160 years, the doctrine of patent exhaustion has imposed a limit on that right to exclude. See *Bloomer v. McQuewan,* 14 How. 539, 14 L.Ed. 532 (1853). The limit functions automatically: When a patentee chooses to sell an item, that product "is no longer within the limits of the monopoly" and instead becomes the "private, individual property" of the purchaser, with the rights and benefits that come along with ownership. *Id.*, at 549–550. A patentee is free to set the price and negotiate contracts with purchasers, but may not, "*by virtue of his patent,* control the use or disposition" of the product after ownership passes to the purchaser. *United States v.* Univis Lens Co., 316 U.S. 241, 250, 62 S.Ct. 1088, 86 L.Ed. 1408 (1942) (emphasis added). The sale "terminates all patent rights to that item." *Quanta Computer, Inc.* v. *LG Electronics, Inc.,* 553 U.S. 617, 625, 128 S.Ct. 2109, 170 L.Ed.2d 996 (2008).

This well-established exhaustion rule marks the point where patent rights yield to the common law principle against restraints on alienation. The Patent Act "promote[s] the progress of science and the useful arts by granting to [inventors] a limited monopoly" that allows them to "secure the financial rewards" for their inventions. *Univis,* 316 U.S., at 250, 62 S.Ct. 1088. But once a patentee sells an item, it has "enjoyed all the rights secured" by that limited monopoly. *Keeler v. Standard Folding Bed Co.,* 157 U.S. 659, 661, 15 S.Ct. 738, 39 L.Ed. 848 (1895). Because "the purpose of the patent law is fulfilled . . . when the patentee has received his reward for the use of his invention," that law furnishes "no basis for restraining the use and enjoyment of the thing sold." Univis, 316 U.S., at 251, 62 S.Ct. 1088.

We have explained in the context of copyright law that exhaustion has "an impeccable historic pedigree," tracing its lineage back to the "common law's refusal to permit restraints on the alienation of chattels." *Kirtsaeng v. John Wiley & Sons, Inc.,* 568 U.S. 519, 538, 133 S.Ct. 1351, 185 L.Ed.2d 392 (2013). As Lord Coke put it in the 17th century, if an owner restricts the resale or use of an item after selling it, that restriction "is voide, because . . . it is against Trade and Traffique, and bargaining and contracting betweene man and man." 1 E. Coke, Institutes of the Laws of England § 360, p. 223 (1628); see J. Gray, Restraints on the Alienation of Property § 27, p. 18 (2d ed. 1895) ("A condition or conditional limitation on alienation attached to a transfer of the entire interest in personalty is as void as if attached to a fee simple in land").

This venerable principle is not, as the Federal Circuit dismissively viewed it, merely "one common-law jurisdiction's general judicial policy at one time toward anti-alienation restrictions." 816 F.3d, at 750. Congress enacted and has repeatedly revised the Patent Act against the backdrop of the hostility toward restraints on alienation. That enmity is reflected in the exhaustion doctrine. The patent laws do not include the right to "restrain [ ] . . . further alienation" after an initial sale; such conditions have been "hateful to the law from Lord Coke's day to ours" and are "obnoxious to the public interest." *Straus v. Victor Talking Machine Co.,* 243 U.S. 490, 501, 37 S.Ct. 412, 61 L.Ed. 866 (1917). "The inconvenience and annoyance to the public that an opposite conclusion would occasion are too obvious to require illustration." *Keeler,* 157 U.S., at 667, 15 S.Ct. 738.

But an illustration never hurts. Take a shop that restores and sells used cars. The business works because the shop can rest assured that, so long as those bringing in the cars own them, the shop is free to repair and resell those vehicles. That smooth flow of commerce would sputter if companies that make the thousands of parts that go into a vehicle could keep their patent rights after the first sale. Those companies might, for instance, restrict resale rights and sue the shop owner for patent infringement. And even if they refrained from imposing such restrictions, the very threat of patent liability would force the shop to invest in efforts to protect itself from hidden lawsuits. Either way, extending the patent rights beyond the first sale would clog the channels of commerce, with little benefit from the extra control that the patentees retain. And advances in technology, along with increasingly complex supply chains, magnify the problem. See Brief for Costco Wholesale Corp. et al. as *Amici Curiae* 7–9; Brief for Intel Corp. et al. as *Amici Curiae* 17, n. 5 ("A generic smartphone assembled from various high-tech components could practice an estimated 250,000 patents").

This Court accordingly has long held that, even when a patentee sells an item under an express restriction, the patentee does not retain patent rights in that product. In *Boston Store of Chicago v. American Graphophone Co.,* for example, a manufacturer sold graphophones — one of the earliest devices for recording and reproducing sounds — to retailers under contracts requiring those stores to resell at a specific price. 246 U.S. 8, 17–18, 38 S.Ct. 257, 62 L.Ed. 551 (1918). When the manufacturer brought a patent infringement suit against a retailer who sold for less, we concluded that there was "no room for controversy" about the result: By selling the item, the manufacturer placed it "beyond the confines of the patent law, [and] could not, by qualifying restrictions as to use, keep [it] under the patent monopoly." *Id.,* at 20, 25, 38 S.Ct. 257.

Two decades later, we confronted a similar arrangement in *United States v. Univis Lens Co.* There, a company that made eyeglass lenses authorized an agent to sell its products to wholesalers and retailers only if they promised to market the lenses at fixed prices. The Government filed an antitrust lawsuit, and the company defended its arrangement on the ground that it was exercising authority under the Patent Act. We held that the initial sales "relinquish[ed] . . . the patent monopoly with respect to the article[s] sold," so the "stipulation . . . fixing resale prices derive[d] no support from the patent and must stand on the same footing" as restrictions on unpatented goods. 316 U.S., at 249–251, 62 S.Ct. 1088.

It is true that *Boston Store* and *Univis* involved resale price restrictions that, at the time of those decisions, violated the antitrust laws. But in both cases it was the sale of the items, rather than the illegality of the restrictions, that prevented the patentees from enforcing those resale price agreements through patent infringement suits. And if there were any lingering doubt that patent exhaustion applies even when a sale is subject to an express, otherwise lawful restriction, our recent decision in *Quanta Computer, Inc. v. LG Electronics, Inc.* settled the matter. In that case, a technology company—with authorization from the patentee—sold microprocessors under contracts requiring purchasers to use those processors with other parts that the company manufactured. One buyer disregarded the restriction, and the patentee sued for infringement. Without so much as mentioning the lawfulness of the contract, we held that the patentee could not bring an infringement suit because the "authorized sale . . . took its products outside the scope of the patent monopoly." 553 U.S., at 638, 128 S.Ct. 2109.

Turning to the case at hand, we conclude that this well-settled line of precedent allows for only one answer: Lexmark cannot bring a patent infringement suit against Impression Products to enforce the single-use/no-resale provision accompanying its Return Program cartridges. Once sold, the Return Program cartridges passed outside of the patent monopoly, and whatever rights Lexmark retained are a matter of the contracts with its purchasers, not the patent law.

B

The Federal Circuit reached a different result largely because it got off on the wrong foot. The "exhaustion doctrine," the court believed, "must be understood as an interpretation of" the infringement statute, which prohibits anyone from using or selling a patented article "without authority" from the patentee. 816 F.3d, at 734 (quoting 35 U.S.C. § 271(a)). Exhaustion reflects a default rule that a patentee's decision to sell an item "*presumptively* grant[s] 'authority' to the purchaser to use it and resell it." 816 F.3d, at 742. But, the Federal Circuit explained, the patentee does not have to hand over the full "bundle of rights" every time. *Id.,* at 741 (internal quotation marks omitted). If the patentee expressly withholds a stick from the bundle—perhaps by restricting the purchaser's resale rights—the buyer never acquires that withheld authority, and the patentee may continue to enforce its right to exclude that practice under the patent laws.

The misstep in this logic is that the exhaustion doctrine is not a presumption about the authority that comes along with a sale; it is instead a limit on "the scope of the *patentee's rights." United States v. General Elec. Co.,* 272 U.S. 476, 489, 47 S.Ct. 192, 71 L.Ed. 362 (1926) (emphasis added). The right to use, sell, or import an item exists independently of the Patent Act. What a patent adds—and grants exclusively to the patentee—is a limited right to prevent others from engaging in those practices. See *Crown Die & Tool Co. v. Nye Tool & Machine Works,* 261 U.S. 24, 35, 43 S.Ct. 254, 67 L.Ed. 516 (1923). Exhaustion extinguishes that exclusionary power. See *Bloomer,* 14 How., at 549 (the purchaser "exercises no rights created by the act of Congress, nor does he derive title to [the item] by virtue of the . . . exclusive privilege granted to the patentee"). As a result, the sale transfers the right to use, sell, or import because those are the rights that come along with ownership, and the buyer is free and clear of an infringement lawsuit because there is no exclusionary right left to enforce.

The Federal Circuit also expressed concern that preventing patentees from reserving patent rights when they sell goods would create an artificial distinction between such sales and sales by licensees. Patentees, the court explained, often license others to make and sell their products, and may place restrictions on those licenses. A computer developer could, for instance, license a manufacturer to make its patented devices and sell them only for non-commercial use by individuals. If a licensee breaches the license by selling a computer for commercial use, the patentee can sue the licensee for infringement. And, in the Federal Circuit's view, our decision in *General Talking Pictures Corp. v. Western Elec. Co.,* 304 U.S. 175, 58 S.Ct. 849, 82 L.Ed. 1273, aff'd on reh'g, 305 U.S. 124, 59 S.Ct. 116, 83 L.Ed. 81 (1938), established that— when a patentee grants a license "under clearly stated restrictions on post-sale activities" of those who purchase products from the licensee—the patentee can *also* sue for infringement those purchasers who knowingly violate the restrictions. 816 F.3d, at 743–744. If patentees can employ licenses to impose post-sale restrictions on purchasers that are enforceable through infringement suits, the court concluded, it would make little sense to prevent patentees from doing so when they sell directly to consumers.

The Federal Circuit's concern is misplaced. A patentee can impose restrictions on licensees because a license does not implicate the same concerns about restraints on alienation as a sale. Patent exhaustion reflects the principle that, when an item passes into commerce, it should not be shaded by a legal cloud on title as it moves through the marketplace. But a license is not about passing title to a product, it is about changing the contours of the patentee's monopoly: The patentee agrees not to exclude a licensee from making or selling the patented invention, expanding the club of authorized producers and sellers. See *General Elec. Co.,* 272 U.S., at 489–490, 47 S.Ct. 192.

Because the patentee is exchanging rights, not goods, it is free to relinquish only a portion of its bundle of patent protections.

A patentee's authority to limit *licensees* does not, as the Federal Circuit thought, mean that patentees can use licenses to impose post-sale restrictions on *purchasers* that are enforceable through the patent laws. So long as a licensee complies with the license when selling an item, the patentee has, in effect, authorized the sale. That licensee's sale is treated, for purposes of patent exhaustion, as if the patentee made the sale itself. The result: The sale exhausts the patentee's rights in that item. See *Hobbie v. Jennison*, 149 U.S. 355, 362–363, 13 S.Ct. 879, 37 L.Ed. 766 (1893). A license may require the licensee to impose a restriction on purchasers, like the license limiting the computer manufacturer to selling for non-commercial use by individuals. But if the licensee does so—by, perhaps, having each customer sign a contract promising not to use the computers in business—the sale nonetheless exhausts all patent rights in the item sold. See *Motion Picture Patents Co. v. Universal Film Mfg. Co.*, 243 U.S. 502, 506–507, 516, 37 S.Ct. 416, 61 L.Ed. 871 (1917). The purchasers might not comply with the restriction, but the only recourse for the licensee is through contract law, just as if the patentee itself sold the item with a restriction.

General Talking Pictures involved a fundamentally different situation: There, a licensee "knowingly ma[de] . . . sales . . . *outside* the scope of its license." 304 U.S., at 181–182, 58 S.Ct. 849 (emphasis added). We treated the sale "as if no license whatsoever had been granted" by the patentee, which meant that the patentee could sue both the licensee and the purchaser—who knew about the breach—for infringement. *General Talking Pictures Corp. v. Western Elec. Co.*, 305 U.S. 124, 127, 59 S.Ct. 116, 83 L.Ed. 81 (1938). This does not mean that patentees can use licenses to impose post-sale restraints on purchasers. Quite the contrary: The licensee infringed the patentee's rights because it did *not* comply with the terms of its license, and the patentee could bring a patent suit against the purchaser only because the purchaser participated in the licensee's infringement. *General Talking Pictures*, then, stands for the modest principle that, if a patentee has not given authority for a licensee to make a sale, that sale cannot exhaust the patentee's rights.

In sum, patent exhaustion is uniform and automatic. Once a patentee decides to sell—whether on its own or through a licensee—that sale exhausts its patent rights, regardless of any post-sale restrictions the patentee purports to impose, either directly or through a license.

. . . .

Notes & Questions

1. Patent exhaustion is the doctrine that indicates that even if a patent owner sells a patented product with only a limited license expressly stated for resale, that provision is ignored at least for the purposes of patent law. In the nineteenth century the Court had expressly stated that such a provision is to be ignored, *Keeler v. Standard Folding Bed*, 157 U.S. 659 (1895). Nevertheless, in *Mallinckrodt Inc. v. Medipart Inc.*, 976 F.2d 700 (Fed. Cir. 1992), the Federal Circuit expressly held that cases such as

Keeler were all overruled by *General Talking Pictures Corp. v. Western Electric Co.*, 304 U.S. 175, *aff'd on reh'g*, 305 U.S. 124 (1938). In *Lexmark*, the Court announced that there were limits on how far down the chain of distribution a patent owner could impose licensing restrictions on users of patented technology. How does the reasoning in *Lexmark* compare to the 1995 Licensing Guidelines? Would the downstream license at issue in *Lexmark* be appropriate under the Guidelines? The answers have to do with the relationship between patent and contract law. If a licensing restriction leads to exhaustion of the patent rights, then the patent owner must sue under contract law. The contract restriction must comply with antitrust law, such as the Licensing Guidelines.

2. When are patent rights exhausted? According to the Lexmark court, it occurs when the patented technology is sold. But what constitutes a sale? This question is the open one after the *Lexmark* decision. Early antitrust cases distinguished sales from other transactions such as a consignment or a license. *See, e.g., United States v. General Electric, Co.*, 47 S. Ct. 192 (1926) (distinguishing between a contract for sale and an agency contract). Courts have addressed the question of sale versus other transactions in the copyright context. *See UMG Recordings, Inc. v. Augusto*, 628 F.3d 1175 (9th Cir. 2011) (distribution of promotional CD was a sale, not a license). *But see Vernor v. Autodesk*, 621 F.3d 1102 (9th Cir. 2010) (customer of software distributor was licensee, not purchaser). For further analysis, see Shubha Ghosh, *Carte Blanche, Quanta, and Competition Policy*, 34 J. CORP. L. 1209, 1210 (2009).

3. The Supreme Court's decision in *Lexmark* seems to limit many business practices that involve the dissemination of intellectual property. The question is whether such interference with standard business practice is justified by legitimate policy concerns under the exhaustion doctrine.

One such concern is that of double-dipping, or the patent owner charging twice for the sale or use of a patented technology. The question of double dipping is at issue in a dispute involving Qualcomm and Apple, which is ongoing at the time of the writing of this Edition. Qualcomm has adopted a policy of "no license-no chips." Under this policy, Qualcomm sells chips covered by Qualcomm patents to equipment manufacturers for installation into chipsets and further requires mobile phone handset manufacturers who utilize the chipsets to license the patented technology.

The rationale for this policy is that two separate patent rights are implicated by installation of the patented technology in the chipsets and in the handsets. The first installation implicates the right to make; the second the rights to make and use. The problem is that once Qualcomm has sold the chips to the chipset manufacturers, the company arguably has exhausted its rights. Notice that the initial sale occurs through a subsidiary of Qualcomm while the license is to Qualcomm. This corporate structuring, however, is arguably not an appropriate way to get around the exhaustion doctrine since sale does originate from the patent owner.

Similarly, if Qualcomm structured the first transaction as a license, this would probably also be seen as a fiction as the chipset manufacturers effectively purchase the patented chips for installation into the chipsets. Qualcomm has only one bite at the patent royalty apple, so to speak, when its patented technology is integrated into downstream transactions. To understand this issue, consider the fact that when you buy a smartphone, you do not pay a separate license for the use of the patented technology. The costs of acquiring these rights are bundled into the sales price. Presumably, the patent owner can be compensated for that use upon the first sale.

Compare Qualcomm's business practice with that of LG Electronics, the subject of the *Quanta* decision discussed in the *Lexmark* opinion. LG transferred its patented processor technology to Intel for the manufacture of microprocessors. However, LG's agreement with Intel made it clear that no license was given to combine Intel's processors with other components such as in a laptop or desktop computer. The manufacturer of a laptop or desktop computer would have to obtain a separate license from LG. Quanta was one of many manufacturers who challenged LG's licensing practice, and the Supreme Court ruled in favor of the manufacturers. The Court held that LG's rights were exhausted upon the authorized sale by Intel of processors embodying the patented technology. LG lost the ability to control downstream uses of the patented technology once authorized units of products incorporating the technology were placed in the stream of commerce.

Does the exhaustion doctrine unnecessarily interfere with business practices? Or is there a legitimate interest in preventing downstream control by a patent owner of a patented product or process that has been distributed into the marketplace? Note the exhaustion doctrine applies only to the particular commodity that embodies the patented technology. Exhaustion does not mean the patent owner loses all its rights. The owner loses only rights as to the particular items sold. Furthermore, the patent owner still can obtain contract remedies if any apply to transactions affected by exhaustion. However, these contract remedies may be much less substantial than patent remedies. Is the exhaustion doctrine simply a matter of fairness or does it serve a purpose of making it easier and more efficient to distribute technology into the marketplace?

D. Standard Setting Organizations and FRAND

In re Innovatio IP Ventures, LLC Patent Litigation

District Court for the Northern District of Illinois

2013 U.S. Dist. LEXIS 144061 (N.D. Ill. Oct. 3, 2013), 2013 WL 5593609

James F. Holderman, District Judge.

Plaintiff and patent-owner Innovatio IP Ventures, LLC ("Innovatio") has sued numerous coffee shops, hotels, restaurants, supermarkets, large retailers, transportation companies, and other commercial users of wireless internet technology located throughout the United States (collectively, the "Wireless Network Users"). Innovatio alleges that the Wireless Network Users provide wireless internet access to their customers or use it to manage internal processes, and by doing so infringe various claims of twenty-three patents owned by Innovatio. (Dkt. No. 198; Dkt. No. 451.)

Cisco Systems, Inc., Motorola Solutions, Inc., SonicWALL, Inc., Netgear, Inc., and Hewlett-Packard Co. (collectively, the "Manufacturers") each manufacture electronic devices used by the Wireless Network Users. (Dkt. No. 819, Ex. A ¶ 10.) The Manufacturers have filed declaratory judgment actions against Innovatio seeking a declaration that the Manufacturers' products, and the networks or systems of which those products are a part, do not infringe Innovatio's patents, and that Innovatio's patents are invalid. (*See* Dkt. Nos. 431, 442; *see also* 12 CV 426, Dkt. No. 1; 12 CV 2773, Dkt. No. 1.) Innovatio, in turn, has alleged that the Manufacturers all infringe the same claims of the twenty-three patents Innovatio has asserted against the Wireless Network Users. (Dkt. Nos. 311–314.) All the pending cases and the parties thereto were transferred for pretrial coordination before this court by the Judicial Panel on Multidistrict Litigation in this MDL case, No. 2303. (Dkt. No. 1.) For ease of reference (and ignoring that some of them are also declaratory judgment plaintiffs), the court will refer to the Wireless Network Users and the Manufacturers collectively as the "Defendants."

Following discovery, but before claim construction, the parties and the court agreed that the best course toward resolving the parties' disputes would be to pause and evaluate the potential damages available to Innovatio if the Defendants are found to infringe the claims of Innovatio's patents. (*See* Dkt. No. 614 ("2/21/13 Tr.") at 24:6–26:18.) The court and all parties agreed to address damages at this stage of the litigation, before a determination on the questions of validity and infringement. The court hopes that by doing so, the possibility of settlement will be enhanced because the parties will be better able to evaluate the potential risks and benefits of expending additional resources in the litigation.

The damages available to Innovatio in this case turn on the determination of a single set of issues relating to the 802.11 wireless standard established by the Institute of Electrical and Electronics Engineers ("IEEE," pronounced "eye-triple-ee"). The prior owners of all of Innovatio's patents contractually agreed with the IEEE to license any patents that were essential to the operation of the 802.11 wireless standard on reasonable and non-discriminatory ("RAND") terms. According to the Defendants, Innovatio's recovery in this case is therefore limited to a RAND licensing fee for the patents-in-suit. The parties were entitled to a jury determination of damages, including the effect of Innovatio's RAND obligation, but both sides have waived their jury trial right and consented to this court's determination of the disputed damages questions. (*See* Dkt. No. 600, at 1.)

The parties agreed that many of Innovatio's asserted patent claims were essential to practice the 802.11 standard under the definition of essentiality provided in the IEEE bylaws. Following a two-day bench trial on July 18 and 19, 2013, the court determined in a Memorandum Opinion on July 26, 2013, that all of the other 168 patent claims Innovatio asserts, as to which the parties disputed essentiality, were also essential to the operation of the 802.11 standard. *In re Innovatio IP Ventures, LLC Patent*

Litig., MDL 2303, 956 F. Supp. 2d 925, 2013 U.S. Dist. LEXIS 105554, 2013 WL 3874042 (N.D. Ill. July 26, 2013) ("July 26 Order"). Accordingly, for purposes of this proceeding all of Innovatio's asserted patent claims are essential to the 802.11 standard, and all are therefore subject to the RAND obligation.

On September 9 through 12 and 17 through 20, 2013, the court held another bench trial at which the parties presented evidence regarding the RAND rate to which Innovatio is entitled, and limited, if it shows that its patents are infringed. The parties agreed at the beginning of the trial that the court would determine only a RAND rate for infringement of Innovatio's patents by the Manufacturers, and not by the Wireless Network Users. (Trial Tr. 8–10.) The court therefore severed any remaining issues regarding a RAND rate for infringement by the Wireless Network Users to address at a later time. (*Id.* at 10:8–10.) Accordingly, the RAND rate the court determines in this trial applies only to the Manufacturers. This Memorandum Opinion and Order constitutes the court's findings of fact and conclusions of law.

At the trial, Innovatio presented the testimony of five experts: Dr. David Teece, a professor at the University of California at Berkeley Haas School of Business, who testified regarding RAND policy; Dr. Raymond Nettleton, an electrical engineer and associate professor at the University of Colorado, who testified regarding 802.11 technology; Mr. Chris Bergey, a former Vice President of Marketing at Broadcom Corp. ("Broadcom"), who testified regarding the value of the 802.11 technology to consumers; Mr. Rick Bero, an accountant; and Mr. Larry Evans, a former president of the Licensing Executives Society-USA and the Licensing Executives Society-International, who testified regarding appropriate comparable licenses.

The Manufacturers presented the testimony of Mr. David Djavaherian, Associate General Counsel at Broadcom, who testified regarding the price of Wi-Fi chips, and the transaction in which Innovatio acquired the patents-in-suit; Dr. Matthew Shoemake, an electrical engineer who served as the chair of several working groups that developed the 802.11 standard and testified about that process; Dr. Stephen Wicker, a professor of Electrical Engineering and Computer Science at Cornell University, who testified regarding 802.11 technology; Dr. Gregory Leonard, an applied economist who testified regarding calculating a RAND rate and comparable licenses; and Dr. Matthew Lynde, an applied economist who also testified regarding calculating a RAND rate and comparable licenses.

After considering all of the evidence presented at the September 2013 trial, the court determines for the reasons stated herein that the RAND rate to be paid to Innovatio for licensing Innovatio's portfolio of nineteen 802.11 standard-essential patents[2] is 9.56 cents for each Wi-Fi chip used or sold by the Manufacturers in the United

---

2. Because the parties agreed during trial that the four patents in Innovatio's Mesh family of patents need not be considered as part of this proceeding to determine a RAND rate, the court's RAND rate applies only to Innovatio's nineteen non-Mesh family patents.

States, subject to the terms of the patents, the applicable statute of limitations, and a finding of infringement.

BACKGROUND

In the July 26 Order, the court explained the relevant background of the IEEE and the 802.11 standard:

> The IEEE is a professional association and developer of technical standards. (Dkt. No. 819, Ex. A ¶ 50.) Beginning in 1990, the IEEE formed a working group to establish the 802.11 standard for the operation of wireless local area networks ("WLANs"—also known as "wireless Ethernet," "Wireless Fidelity," or "Wi-Fi"). (*Id.* ¶ 51.) The IEEE continues to publish amendments to that standard periodically. (*Id.* ¶ 52.) Devices such as wireless routers, laptops, and cell phones that are compliant with the standard will be able to communicate effectively with one another in any WLAN. By establishing the 802.11 standard, the IEEE has ensured that the wireless devices of various manufacturers are interoperable, and that consumers are therefore able to purchase wireless devices from a variety of manufacturers without worrying about whether the devices will be compatible with each other. As a result, consumers experience no switching costs if they choose to buy wireless devices from different manufacturers, leading to greater price competition. *See Microsoft Corp. v. Motorola, Inc.*, No. C10-1823, 2013 U.S. Dist. LEXIS 60233, 2013 WL 2111217, at *5 (W.D. Wash. Apr. 25, 2013) (Robart, J.) (describing the role of standard-setting organizations).

> Although the standard-setting process has many potential benefits for consumers, there are dangers. After a standard is established, for example, every manufacturer of compliant products must use the technology stated in the standard. If one particular company owns a patent covering that technology, however, the standard will effectively force all others to buy that company's technology if they want to practice the standard. This requirement allows the company to charge inflated prices that reflect not only the intrinsic value of its technology, but also the inflated value attributable to its technology's designation as the industry standard.

Innovatio IP Ventures, 2013 WL 3874042, at *3.

The court also explained the genesis and nature of the RAND commitments to which Innovatio's patents are subject:

> To avoid this phenomenon (often called "patent hold-up," *see Microsoft*, 2013 U.S. Dist. LEXIS 60233, 2013 WL 2111217, at *10), standard-setting organizations like the IEEE often require owners of standard-essential patents to promise to license their patents on RAND terms before the establishment of the standard. Prior to being acquired by Innovatio, Innovatio's patents were owned by Intermec Technologies Corporation (a subsidiary of UNOVA) and Intermec IP Corporation (collectively "Internec"), Norand Corporation ("Norand"), or Broadcom Corp. ("Broadcom"). (Dkt. No. 819, Ex. A ¶ 53.)

Each of those previous owners of Innovatio's patents agreed to license any standard-essential technology covered by their patents on RAND terms. (*Id.* ¶ 54.) For example, on October 26, 1995, Intermec, wrote to the IEEE that

> [i]n the event that patents issue to, or are acquired by, Intermec in the future which Intermec believes will read on devices operating under the proposed IEEE 802.11 Standard, Intermec will (upon written request from any third party) grant a nonexclusive, nontransferable sole and personal license under any such issued patent on a nondiscriminatory basis, on terms and conditions which Intermec deems reasonable.

(Dkt. No. 709, Ex. 6.) Similarly, on October 17, 2006, Broadcom wrote to the IEEE that, "with respect to any patent(s) and/or patent application(s) that it may hold or control, the use of which would be essential to create a compliant implementation of either mandatory or optional portions of the [Proposed] IEEE Standard," it promised to "grant a license under reasonable rates to an unrestricted number of applicants on a worldwide, non-discriminatory basis with reasonable terms and conditions." (Dkt. No. 709, Ex. 7.) Broadcom and Norand wrote similar letters to IEEE on September 6, 2002, and June 20, 1997. (*See* Dkt. No. 709, Exs. 8–10.)

The parties do not dispute that the letters of Innovatio's predecessors in interest to the IEEE constitute binding contractual commitments to the IEEE and its members. *See Microsoft Corp. v. Motorola, Inc.*, 854 F. Supp. 2d 993, 999 (W.D. Wash. 2012) ("The court agrees with Microsoft that through Motorola's letters to both the IEEE and ITU, Motorola has entered into binding contractual commitments to license its essential patents on RAND terms."); *see also Apple, Inc. v. Motorola Mobility, Inc.*, 886 F. Supp. 2d 1061, 1083 (W.D. Wis. 2012) ("In this case, the combination of the policies and bylaws of the standard-setting organizations, Motorola's membership in those organizations and Motorola's assurances that it would license its essential patents oh fair, reasonable and nondiscriminatory terms constitute contractual agreements."). Moreover, this court has already held that those commitments are now binding on Innovatio, and that they can be enforced by the Defendants as potential users of the 802.11 standard and thus third-party beneficiaries of the agreements between Innovatio's predecessors and the IEEE. *See In re Innovatio IP Ventures, LLC Patent Litig.*, 921 F. Supp. 2d 903, 2013 WL 427167, at *17 (N.D. Ill. 2013) ("The longstanding rule in Illinois, and elsewhere, is that 'the promisee of a third-party-beneficiary contract may bring suit for a breach of that contract and recover damages therefor.'" (quoting *Carmack v. Great Am. Indent. Co.*, 78 N.E.2d 507, 511 (Ill. 1948))).

Innovatio IP Ventures, 2013 U.S. Dist. LEXIS 105554, 2013 WL 3874042, at *4.

As mentioned above, the twenty-three patents that Innovatio has asserted in this litigation were owned by other parties at various times. In 2002, all twenty-three patents were owned by Intermec. (Trial Tr. 130:1–5 (Djavaherian).) In 2002, Intermec sold the patents, [redacted] (*Id.* at 130:16–132:9.) [redacted]. (*Id.* at 136:18–24.) As part of the transaction, Innovatio also granted a license back to Broadcom for all of the patents that were a part of the deal. (*Id.* at 140:9–11.)

ANALYSIS

To the best of the court's knowledge and that of the parties, only one other court has previously undertaken a judicial determination of a RAND licensing rate for standard-essential patents: *Microsoft Corp. v. Motorola, Inc.*, No. C10–1823, 2013 U.S. Dist. LEXIS 60233, 2013 WL 2111217 (W.D. Wash. Apr. 25, 2013) (Robart, J.). The parties agree that Judge Robart's methodology is appropriate for the court to use here to set a RAND rate in this case. The court will first describe Judge Robart's methodology before discussing several modifications to it in light of the circumstances of this case.

I. Methodology for Determining RAND Rate

A. Judge Robart's Methodology in *Microsoft v. Motorola*

In *Microsoft v. Motorola*, Microsoft alleged that Motorola breached its contractual obligation to offer a RAND license through two offer letters to Microsoft. *Id.* at *1. The case was headed to a jury to determine Motorola's liability for breaching its contract. Judge Robart explained, however, that "[w]ithout a clear understanding of what RAND means, it would be difficult or impossible to figure out if Motorola breached its obligation to license its patents on RAND terms." *Id.* Moreover, a factfinder would need to compare Motorola's offers with a RAND rate and "because more than one rate could conceivably be RAND, a reasonable RAND royalty range." *Id.* at *3. Accordingly, Judge Robart first held a bench trial to set a RAND rate and range on Motorola's portfolio of standard-essential patents that could be provided to the jury as part of its deliberations on Microsoft's breach of contract claim. *Id.*

Judge Robart determined that the best way to perform the RAND valuation was to simulate a hypothetical bilateral negotiation between Motorola and Microsoft in the context of Motorola's RAND obligation. To that end, Judge Robart adapted the fifteen traditional *Georgia-Pacific* factors that courts consider to determine the outcome of a hypothetical negotiation. *See Georgia-Pacific Corp. v. U.S. Plywood Corp.*, 318 F. Supp. 1116 (S.D.N.Y. 1970).

The purpose of conducting such a hypothetical negotiation is "to ascertain the royalty upon which the parties would have agreed had they successfully negotiated an agreement just before infringement began." *Lucent Techs., Inc. v. Gateway, Inc.*, 580 F.3d 1301, 1324 (Fed. Cir. 2009). Accordingly, the court must try, "as best as possible, to recreate the *ex ante* licensing negotiation scenario and to describe the resulting agreement." *Id.* at 1325. For purposes of the hypothetical negotiation, the court assumes that the asserted patent claims are valid and infringed. *Id.*

Because of the unique circumstances of the RAND obligation, however, Judge Robart adapted the fifteen factors for evaluating a hypothetical negotiation by essentially eliminating three of them and modifying or combining others. The modified factors can be summarized as follows:

G-P Factor 1: The royalties received by the patentee for the licensing of the patent-in-suit in other circumstances comparable to RAND-licensing circumstances.

G-P Factor 2: The rates paid by the licensee for the use of other patents comparable to the patent-in-suit.

G-P Factor 3: The nature and scope of the license.

G-P Factor 6: The effect of the patented invention in promoting sales of other products of the licensee and the licensor, taking into account only the value of the patented technology and not the value associated with incorporating the patented technology into the standard.

G-P Factor 8: The established profitability of the product made under the patent, its commercial success, and its current popularity, taking into account only the value of the patented technology and not the value associated with incorporating the patented technology into the standard.

G-P Factor 9: The utility and advantages of the patent property over alternatives that could have been written into the standard instead of the patented technology in the period before the standard was adopted.

G-P Factors 10–11: The contribution of the patent to the technical capabilities of the standard and also the contribution of those relevant technical capabilities to the licensee and the licensee's products, taking into account only the value of the patented technology and not the value associated with incorporating the patented technology into the standard.

G-P Factor 12: The portion of the profit or of the selling price that may be customary in the particular business or in comparable businesses to allow for the use of the invention or analogous inventions that are also covered by RAND-committed patents.

G-P Factor 13: The portion of the realizable profit that should be credited to the invention as distinguished from non-patented elements, the manufacturing process, business risks, significant features or improvements added by the infringer, or the value of the patent's incorporation into the standard.

G-P Factor 14: The opinion testimony of qualified experts.

G-P Factor 15: The amount that a licensor and a licensee would have agreed upon (at the time the infringement began) if both were considering the RAND commitment and its purposes, and had been reasonably and voluntarily trying to reach an agreement.

See Microsoft, 2013 U.S. Dist. LEXIS 60233, 2013 WL 2111217, at *18–20. Judge Robart relied on each of these factors throughout his analysis. As a practical matter, however, Judge Robart's analysis proceeded in three steps which provide a framework for any court attempting to determine a RAND licensing rate for a given patent portfolio.

First, a court should consider the importance of the patent portfolio to the standard, considering both the proportion of all patents essential to the standard that are in the portfolio, and also the technical contribution of the patent portfolio as a whole to the standard. *See id.* at *20 ("Thus, a patent that is extremely important and central to the standard would reasonably command a higher royalty rate than a less important patent."). Second, a court should consider the importance of the patent portfolio as a whole to the alleged infringer's accused products. *See id.* ("[A] specific [standard-essential patent] may contribute greatly to an optional portion of a given standard, but if that portion is not used by the implementer, the specific [standard-essential patent] may have little value to the implementer."). Third, the court should examine other licenses for comparable patents to determine a RAND rate to license the patent portfolio, using its conclusions about the importance of the portfolio to the standard and to the alleged infringer's products to determine whether a given license or set of licenses is comparable.

B. Modifications to Judge Robart's Methodology

This court will generally follow a similar procedure to reconstruct a hypothetical negotiation over a RAND rate to license Innovatio's 802.11 standard-essential patents. The court notes, however, some of the distinct circumstances of this patent infringement case that will require some modifications to Judge Robart's approach. First, the purpose of the RAND evaluation in *Microsoft* was to define a RAND rate so that a jury could determine whether Motorola's licensing offers to Microsoft complied with its RAND obligations. Because under the RAND obligation, "initial offers do not have to be on RAND terms so long as a RAND license eventually issues" and "because more than one rate could conceivably be RAND" the court determined a reasonable RAND *range* to give to the jury for its comparison. *Id.* at *2–3. By contrast, the purpose of the RAND determination here is to set damages for infringement of the standard-essential patents. The court must therefore determine a single RAND rate for the purpose of calculating damages, rather than a range.

Second, the parties in *Microsoft* did not focus on the question of whether the allegedly standard-essential patents were in fact essential to the standard. Instead, whenever the essentiality of a patent was doubtful, the court concluded that "the implementer in a hypothetical negotiation would view [the allegedly standard-essential] patents with skepticism." *Id.* at *53. The court then concluded that the "parties to a hypothetical negotiation would sit down at the bargaining table and examine the[ ] patents for their importance" to the standard, and would conclude that "their value would be diminished by the lack of better evidence regarding their true relevance." *Id.* By contrast, this court has already held a separate proceeding to determine the essentiality of Innovatio's patents, and has determined that they are all standard-essential. The question therefore arises of whether the court should adjust the license rate for patents whose essentiality was questionable prior to the court's adjudication.

Making such an adjustment may seem reasonable, for "[t]he hypothetical negotiation tries, as best as possible, to recreate the *ex ante* licensing negotiation scenario and to describe the resulting agreement." *Lucent Techs.*, 580 F.3d at 1325. *Ex ante,* prior to infringement, the parties do not know whether a court would determine a given patent to be standard-essential, and so one might argue that the licensing negotiation should account for that uncertainty.

The problem with that argument is that the hypothetical negotiation is a counter-factual that the court usually relies on only after establishing liability. At the time of the hypothetical negotiation, the parties in actuality would not have known whether a given patent is valid or infringed, and the alleged infringer would have had the option of contesting these issues in court. Nonetheless, by the time the damages phase of an infringement suit arrives, the court has determined infringement and validity, thus foreclosing the hypothetical negotiator from benefiting from any uncertainty as to future court rulings. *See LaserDynamics, Inc. v. Quanta Computer, Inc.*, 694 F.3d 51, 76 (Fed. Cir. 2012) ("In considering the fifteen *Georgia-Pacific* factors, it is presumed that the parties had full knowledge of the facts and circumstances surrounding the infringement at that time."). Stated another way, the hypothetical negotiator could no longer leave the negotiating table to contest liability in court, and could no longer demand the benefit of uncertainty about a court's rulings. Accordingly, "[t]he hypothetical negotiation also assumes that the asserted patent claims are valid and infringed," *Lucent Techs.*, 580 F.3d at 1325, because no hypothetical negotiation would have taken place if it were otherwise. The patent infringer gets no discount on its licensing fee because of uncertainty about its liability that has since been cleared up by litigation.

Analogously, it would be inappropriate to adjust the RAND rate based upon pre-litigation uncertainty about the essentiality of a given patent. Now that the court has adjudicated essentiality, the patent owner cannot leave the hypothetical negotiation on the ground that it will contest essentiality in court. The RAND obligation requires that it grant a license. Thus, unlike Judge Robart, the court will not adjust the RAND rate in light of pre-litigation uncertainty about the essentiality of a given patent.

Finally, the court notes that in light of its conclusion in Part II, *infra*, that the appropriate royalty base in this case is the Wi-Fi chip, the small module that provides Wi-Fi capability to electronic devices in which it is inserted, steps one and two of Judge Robart's methodology effectively merge. Because the purpose of a Wi-Fi chip is, by definition, to provide 802.11 functionality, determining the importance of Innovatio's patents to the 802.11 standard also determines the importance of those patents to the Wi-Fi chip. Accordingly, the court's analysis does not include a separate section evaluating the importance of Innovatio's patents to the accused products, but instead merges that analysis into the inquiry about the importance of Innovatio's patents to the 802.11 standard.

C. The Date of the Hypothetical Negotiation

The Federal Circuit has stated that "in each case there should be only a single hypothetical negotiation date, not separate dates for separate acts of infringement." *LaserDynamics*, 694 F.3d at 76. Here, the parties agree that the appropriate date for the hypothetical negotiation is 1997, about the time of the initial adoption of the

802.11 standard, and therefore approximately the time when the Manufacturers began selling 802.11 compliant products that allegedly infringed the patents. (*See* Trial Tr. 1867:2–19, 1924:2–1925:2.) The parties agree that the negotiating parties would have negotiated a single license covering all subsequently obtained 802.11 standard-essential patents, and that it is therefore appropriate to use 1997 as the date of the negotiation for all of the patents, including those that were applied for and issued after that date.

D. Concepts Relevant to the RAND Determination

1. Avoiding Patent Hold-Up

As mentioned above, one of the primary purposes of the RAND commitment is to avoid patent hold-up, which occurs when the holder of a standard-essential patent demands excess royalties after standard implementers are already locked into using the standard. (*See* Trial Tr. at 189:21–190:21 (Teece).) After a standard is adopted, implementers of the standard invest significant resources to ensure that their devices comply with the standard. Following that investment, switching to an alternative technology would be prohibitively expensive, and in any case would take the implementer out of compliance with the standard. In that situation, the patent holder can demand excessive royalties far beyond the fair value of its technological contribution to the standard, merely because the implementer has no choice but to pay. The RAND commitment, which standard-setting organizations extract from patent holders prior to adopting their technology into the standard, prevents patent holders from demanding excessive royalties that capture value beyond the value of the patented technology itself. *See Microsoft*, 2013 U.S. Dist. LEXIS 60233, 2013 WL 2111217, at *10 ("The ability of a holder of [a standard-essential patent] to demand more than the value of its patented technology and to attempt to capture the value of the standard itself is referred to as patent 'hold-up.'"). If hold-up occurs, implementing the standard becomes excessively expensive for consumers, undermining the standard-setting process and jeopardizing further adoption of the standard. *Id.* at *10–*11.

The parties disagree about the seriousness of the concern of patent hold-up, although they agree that it is a potential problem. Dr. Teece testified that in his opinion, patent hold-up "is very rarely ever seen." (Trial Tr. 189:24–25 (Teece).) In addition, he noted that it is often difficult to distinguish the value of the underlying technology from the value of standardization, because the effectiveness of the technology at enabling interoperability often creates some of the value of the standard. (*See id.* at 217:18–20 ("Well, there's a recursive element which you're omitting, which is also the value that the . . . technology provides to the standard itself.").) By contrast, Dr. Leonard testified that hold-up is of significant concern, because it can jeopardize adoption of the standard, harm consumers, and even harm other holders of standard-essential patents who cannot recover all their patents are worth after other parties have extracted hold-up value from the market. (*Id.* at 1897:1–1898:12 (Leonard).) According to Dr. Leonard, "that's why it's important that the RAND royalty reach the right balance. It's both got to . . . appropriately reward the contributor, but it can't go beyond that, because then it's starting to get value for things it didn't do." (*Id.* at 1899:15–19.)

Moreover, Broadcom expressed the concern that patent hold-up is a significant problem in the industry in an August 5, 2011 letter to the FTC. (DTX-668.) As the letter explains, "Broadcom believes that many companies that have invented the technology incorporated into standards continue to feel the effects of patent holdup directly." (*Id.* at 1.) Moreover, "patent holdup means higher prices and fewer choices for the many millions of consumers of standards-based products." (*Id.* at 2; *see also id.* ("From Broadcom's perspective, far from being a 'rare disease,' patent ambush is widespread, and we believe that instances of patent ambush that are currently festering below the surface will continue coming to light as standards-based litigation continues to proliferate."). David Djavaherian, Associate General Counsel at Broadcom, testified that this concern was not merely theoretical for Broadcom, as it had seen a number of entities attempt to assert 802.11-essential patents, driving up costs in the industry. (Trial Tr. 145:14–146:10 (Djavaherian).) [redacted]

In light of all of the testimony, and particularly the evidence about Broadcom's real-world concerns about patent hold-up, the court concludes that patent hold-up is a substantial problem that RAND is designed to prevent. The court's RAND rate therefore must, to the extent possible, reflect only the value of the underlying technology and not the hold-up value of standardization. *Microsoft*, 2013 U.S. Dist. LEXIS 60233, 2013 WL 2111217, at *12 ("In the context of a dispute concerning whether or not a given royalty is RAND, a proper methodology used to determine a RAND royalty should therefore recognize and seek to mitigate the risk of patent hold-up that RAND commitments are intended to avoid.").

At the same time, the court finds Dr. Teece's testimony regarding the difficulty of distinguishing between the intrinsic value of the technology and the value of standardization to be persuasive. Part of the intrinsic value of a technology may precisely be the ease with which it can be adopted into a standard. For example, a technology may more easily interface with other extant technologies by making more efficient use of an existing infrastructure or requiring less modification to other technologies. Moreover, in a hypothetical negotiation occurring just prior to adoption of the standard (and before a patent holder knows whether its technology will be adopted into the standard), an inventor would be able to capitalize on this value by arguing that potential licensees should pay more for a technology that more easily integrates with the licensee's other technology. The court's analysis of the technical value of Innovatio's patents to the 802.11 standard will therefore take into account the ease of those patents' integration into the standard as a whole.

2. Royalty Stacking

Another concern of the RAND obligation is to prevent "royalty stacking." This concern arises because most standards implicate hundreds, if not thousands of patents, and the cumulative royalty payments to all standard-essential patent holders can quickly become excessive and discourage adoption of the standard. *See*

Microsoft, 2013 U.S. Dist. LEXIS 60233, 2013 WL 2111217, at *11. Therefore, the determination of a RAND royalty must "address the risk of royalty stacking by considering the aggregate royalties that would apply if other [standard-essential patent] holders made royalty demands of the implementer." *Id.* at *12; *see also, id.* at *11 (RAND commitments should be interpreted "to grant licenses on terms that are objectively commercially reasonable taking into account the overall licensing situation and including the cost of obtaining all necessary licenses from all other relevant patent holders for the technologies in the end product"). Mr. Djavaherian explained that Broadcom is also concerned about the problem of royalty stacking:

> [T]he concern is that if you don't take into account the whole gambit of patents that may potentially apply to a particular standard, in setting the rate of any patent within that standard, you can end up with a situation where the aggregate royalty stack is much, much higher than would seem to be reasonable and much, much higher than would be required for the standard to be successful and to allow companies to invest in, you know, exploitation of the standard.

*10 (Trial Tr. 145:5–13 (Djavaherian).)

On the other side, Innovatio's expert Dr. Teece expressed his view that stacking is only a concern if the stack does not accurately reflect the value of the patented technology. (Trial Tr. 175:22–176:14 (Teece) ("Bad stacking is if you're not adding value, but you're adding to the costs.").) If the technology is accurately valued, stacking the royalties for each invention merely reflects the value that is created by combining many inventions into a single product. *(Id.)* That synergy is good, according to Dr. Teece, and not of concern when setting a RAND royalty.

Based on the testimony of Mr. Djavaherian and Dr. Teece, the court concludes that royalty stacking may be a concern when setting a RAND rate to ensure that the asserted patents are not overvalued compared to the technological contribution they make to the standard. Practically speaking, that means that the court should consider royalty stacking as a way of checking the accuracy of a proposed RAND royalty's correspondence to the technical value of the patented invention. Imagine, for example, that the court has determined that a given patent portfolio provides 25% of the functionality of a standard, and that the court is considering a proposed RAND rate based on that determination. Logically, the other standard-essential patents outside of the portfolio should comprise 75% of the value of the standard, or three times the value of the asserted portfolio. If an independent evaluation of the technical merit of those other standard-essential patents would suggest a value greater than three times the royalty for the asserted patent portfolio, however, it would suggest that the court has overvalued the asserted portfolio.

In making this determination, the court notes that it is not appropriate to determine the value of the non-asserted standard-essential patents based merely on numbers. If a patent holder owns ten out of a hundred patents essential to a given standard, it does not automatically mean that it contributes 10% of the value of the standard. *See Microsoft*, 2013 U.S. Dist. LEXIS 60233, 2013 WL 2111217, at *11 (relating a "commonly understood principle of proportionality that [c]ompensation under [RAND] must reflect the patent owner's proportion of all essential patents" and noting that "[t]his is not simply a numeric equation but the compensation must, within reasonable bounds, reflect the contribution" (quoting a Motorola submission to the ETSI)). As a practical matter, therefore, this analysis will necessarily be imprecise, as the court cannot undertake a full technical evaluation of the hundreds or thousands of patents that sometimes comprise a standard. Nonetheless, the concern of royalty stacking requires that the court, to the extent possible, evaluate a proposed RAND rate in the light of the total royalties an implementer would have to pay to practice the standard.

Moreover, the court is sensitive to Mr. Djavaherian's concern that royalty stacking may push prices "higher than would be required for the standard to be successful." (Trial Tr. 145:11 (Djavaherian).) In evaluating a potential RAND royalty, therefore, the court will consider whether the overall royalty of all standard-essential patents would prohibit widespread adoption of the standard.

3. Incentivizing Inventors to Participate in Standard-Setting Process

Third, a RAND rate must be set high enough to ensure that innovators in the future have an appropriate incentive to invest in future developments and to contribute their inventions to the standard-setting process. As Judge Robart put it, "[t]o induce the creation of valuable standards, the RAND commitment must guarantee that holders of valuable intellectual property will receive reasonable royalties on that property." *Microsoft*, 2013 U.S. Dist. LEXIS 60233, 2013 WL 2111217, at *12.

Innovatio's expert Dr. Teece opined that one threat to this objective is "reverse hold-up," which is the concern that implementers of the standard will infringe standard-essential patents without taking a license, thereby forcing innovators to engage in costly litigation before realizing the value of their inventions. (Trial Tr. 190:10–21 (Teece).) The International Trade Commission recently expressed this concern in a final determination on an investigation:

> In reverse patent hold-up, an implementer utilizes declared-essential technology without compensation to the patent owner under the guise that the patent owner's offers to license were not fair or reasonable. The patent owner is therefore forced to defend its rights through expensive litigation. In the meantime, the patent owner is deprived of the exclusionary remedy that should normally flow when a party refuses to pay for the use of a patented invention.

Certain Elec. Devices, Including Wireless Commc'n Devices, Portable Music and Data Processing Devices, and Tablet Computers, Inv. No. 337-TA-794, at 63 (July 5, 2013) (Final). The court is not persuaded that the concern of reverse patent hold-up is relevant in this case, as there is no evidence before the court that Innovatio or its predecessors ever offered the Manufacturers a license, or that such an offer was rejected on the ground that it was not fair or reasonable. Moreover, the court is not

950 11 · ANTITRUST PERILS OF A DOMINANT IP POSITION

persuaded that reverse hold-up is a significant concern in general, as it is not unique to standard-essential patents. Attempts to enforce any patent involve the risk that the alleged infringer will choose to contest some issue in court, forcing a patent holder to engage in expensive litigation. The question of whether a license offer complies with the RAND obligation merely gives the parties one more potential issue to contest. When the parties disagree over a RAND rate, they may litigate the question, just as they may litigate any issue related to liability for infringement.

The ITC's decision suggests that a RAND situation is indeed unique because an injunction is unavailable to the holder of a RAND-obligated patent. Unlike in a typical patent case, therefore, the holder of RAND-obligated patents cannot halt infringement while it pursues monetary remedies in court. As this court has previously explained, however, the question of whether a RAND obligation precludes an injunction is "muddled" and "the subject of substantial, often contradictory, academic commentary." *In re Innovatio IP Ventures, LLC Patent Litig.*, 921 F. Supp. 2d 903, 916 (N.D. Ill. 2013). Even assuming that the holder of RAND-obligated patents cannot seek an injunction, however, it is plain that the injunction threat does not preclude all patent litigation. The court does not believe that the removal of the injunction threat in a RAND context would so significantly alter the balance of power in patent litigation as to put undue litigation burdens on the RAND-obligated party who, after all, voluntarily assumed the burdens of the RAND obligation.

Although the court is aware that alleged infringers may force RAND-obligated patent holders into court to enforce their patents, therefore, this reality does not present significant concerns unique to the RAND context. The court will therefore not give the ability of alleged infringers to force a lawsuit any special consideration in the RAND analysis beyond what it receives in a typical patent case. The court will, however, consider whether the proposed RAND rates provide a sufficient return to give innovators an incentive to invest in new technology and to make their technology available to standard-setting bodies.

. . . .

Notes & Questions

1. Concealment of relevant patent interests can support claims that companies have abused their patent rights in dealings with standard setting organizations. For example, in 1996 the Federal Trade Commission found that Dell Computer Corporation ("Dell") had engaged an unfair and deceptive business practice by not disclosing its patent interests in the VL-BUS standard set by the Video Electronics Standard Association. See In the Matter of Dell Computer Corporation Consent Order, 121 F.T.C. 616 (May 20, 1996). The Commission summarized Dell's actions as follows:

> 4. In February 1992 Dell became a member of the Video Electronics Standards Association ("VESA"), a non-profit standards-setting association composed of virtually all major U.S. computer hardware and software manufacturers.

5. At or about the same time, VESA began the process of setting a design standard for a computer bus design, later to be known as the VESA Local Bus or "VL-bus." Like all computer buses, the VL-bus carries information or instructions between the computer's central processing unit and the computer's peripheral devices such as a hard disk drive, a video display terminal, or a modem.

6. By June 1992 VESA's Local Bus Committee, with Dell representatives sitting as members, approved the VL-bus design standard, which improved upon then-existing technology by more quickly and efficiently meeting the transmission needs of new, video-intensive software. One year earlier, in July 1991, Dell had received United States patent number 5,036,481 (the "'481 patent"), which, according to Dell, gives it "exclusive rights to the mechanical slot configuration used on the motherboard to receive the VL-bus card." Nonetheless, at no time prior to or after June 1992 did Dell disclose to VESA's Local Bus Committee the existence of the '481 patent.

7. After committee approval of the VL-bus design standard, VESA sought the approval of the VL-bus design standard by all of its voting members. On July 20, 1992, Dell voted to approve the preliminary proposal for the VL-bus standard. As part of this approval, a Dell representative certified in writing that, to the best of his knowledge, "this proposal does not infringe on any trademarks, copyrights, or patents" that Dell possessed. On August 6, 1992, Dell gave final approval to the VL-bus design standard. As part of this final approval, the Dell representative again certified in writing that, to the best of his knowledge, "this proposal does not infringe on any trademarks, copyrights, or patents" that Dell possessed.

8. After VESA's VL-bus design standard became very successful, having been included in over 1.4 million computers sold in the eight months immediately following its adoption, Dell informed certain VESA members who were manufacturing computers using the new design standard that their "implementation of the VL-bus is a violation of Dell's exclusive rights." Dell demanded that these companies meet with its representatives to "determine . . . the manner in which Dell's exclusive rights will be recognized . . . ." Dell followed up its initial demands by meeting with several companies, and it has never renounced the claimed infringement.

9. By engaging in the acts or practices described in paragraphs four through eight of this complaint, respondent Dell has unreasonably restrained competition in the following ways, among others:

   (a) Industry acceptance of the VL-bus design standard was hindered because some computer manufacturers delayed their use of the design standard until the patent issue was clarified.

   (b) Systems utilizing the VL-bus design standard were avoided due to concerns that patent issues would affect the VL-bus' success as an industry design standard.

(c) The uncertainty concerning the acceptance of the VL-bus design standard raised the costs of implementing the VL-bus design as well as the costs of developing competing bus designs.

(d) Willingness to participate in industry standard-setting efforts have been chilled.

10. The acts or practices of respondent alleged herein were and are to the prejudice and injury of the public. The acts or practices constitute unfair methods of competition in or affecting commerce in violation of Section 5 of the Federal Trade Commission Act.

Id. The remedy was a compulsory license of Dell's essential patents to users of the standard. Dell was subjected to a consent decree providing for such licensing.

In dissent, Commissioner Mary L. Azcuenaga adopted a different interpretation of the meaning of an "unfair or deceptive trade practice" in this context. She felt that the key to establishing an illegal trade practice by Dell was in proving intentional misconduct, which she felt had not been proven. According to Commissioner Azcuenaga:

> By finding a violation of Section 5 in the absence of any allegation of a knowing or intentional misrepresentation, the Commission effectively imposes a duty of disclosure on Dell beyond what VESA required. The Commission may have the authority to do this but the question is whether it is advisable. VESA might have required, but did not, that each voting representative certify, on behalf of the entire company, that nothing in its entire patent portfolio overlapped with the standard and have made the certification binding regardless of any mistakes or subsequent, good faith discoveries. Had that been the standard, the process of collecting votes likely would have been quite prolonged and, perhaps, even impossible. Nevertheless, VESA could have structured its process in this more exacting way. Perhaps there is a good reason why it did not.

Id. For a discussion of the impact of antitrust laws on intellectual property issues faced by standard setting organizations, see Mark A. Lemley, *Intellectual Property Rights and Standard Setting Organizations*, 90 Cal. L. Rev. 1889, 1937–1948 (2002) (reviewing antitrust limitations on enforcement of intellectual property rights against standard setting organizations).

2. Review the provisions of the National Cooperative Research Act (NCRA) excerpted in Section A. How would that Act deal with Dell's actions with respect to VESA? How would the NCRA deal with VESA itself? Note that the NCRA establishes rule of reason treatment for antitrust claims against joint ventures. Would VESA be considered a joint venture under the NCRA?

3. Conduct by patent holders towards standard setting organizations has been the focus of several legal controversies in addition to the dispute leading to the Dell consent decree. In March 2003, the FTC brought a complaint against Union Oil of

California (Unocal) for its activities in persuading the State of California to adopt environmental standards for reformulated gasoline when the company had proprietary rights in emissions data and the gasoline. Unocal did not disclose its proprietary interests and subsequently enforced its patent rights against rival oil companies attempting to comply with the standard. The complaint against Unocal turned on the following allegations:

> The Complaint alleges that "Unocal's fraudulent conduct has resulted in Unocal's acquisition of market power in the following markets: the technology market for the production and supply of [California Air Resources Board (CARB) standard]-compliant "summer-time" gasoline in California, and the downstream product market for CARB-compliant "summer-time" gasoline in California." ¶ 91; see ¶¶ 73–75. Allegedly, "The extensive overlap between the CARB RFG regulations and the Unocal patent claims makes avoidance of the Unocal patent claims technically and/or economically infeasible." ¶ 92. Refiners, having "invested billions of dollars in sunk capital investments without knowledge of Unocal's patent claims to reconfigure their refineries in order to comply with the CARB Phase 2 RFG regulations . . . cannot produce significant volumes of non-infringing CARB-compliant gasoline without incurring substantial additional costs," ¶ 93, and "CARB cannot now change its RFG regulations sufficiently to provide flexibility for refiners and others to avoid Unocal's patent claims." ¶ 94. Had Unocal disclosed its proprietary interests and pending patent rights earlier, CARB would have been able to consider the potential costs imposed by the Unocal patents, and the harm to competition and to consumers would have been avoided. *Id.* Instead, Unocal allegedly "has exercised, and continues to exercise, its market power through business conduct by enforcing its patents through litigation and licensing activities."

See *In the Matter of Union Oil Company of California*, 138 F.T.C. 1, 2004 WL 5662245 (July 6, 2004). In November 2003, an administrative law judge made an initial ruling that Unocal's actions were protected by the Noerr-Pennington doctrine, which immunizes lobbying and political activities from antitrust scrutiny. However, in a later decision the Federal Trade Commission overruled the administrative law judge and found that the Noerr-Pennington doctrine provided no protection from the unfair trade practice claims raised in the case. *Id.*

The computer chip manufacturer Rambus also faced scrutiny for enforcing its patent rights in the design of a computer memory chip against rival company Infineon, which designed its memory board to conform to a standard established by the Joint Electronic Devices Engineering Council (JEDEC). Rambus had been involved with the standard setting process by JEDEC, and Infineon claimed that Rambus had failed to disclose its proprietary interest in the technology that was central to the standard, as required by the rules of JEDEC. After an initial victory at the district court level, Infineon saw its $3.5 million verdict overturned by the Federal Circuit, which held 2-1 that JEDEC's disclosure rules were too amorphous and vague to support a finding of fraud by Rambus. See *Rambus, Inc. v. Infineon Technologies*, 318 F.3d 1081 (C.A.F.C. 2003). In 2002, the FTC initiated a complaint against Rambus for deceiving JEDEC, a complaint that was reminiscent of the complaint in the Dell dispute. In 2004, an administrative law judge dismissed the complaint on the grounds that Rambus had not acted deceptively, that Rambus had not acquired monopoly power as a result of the standard adopted by JEDEC, and that Rambus' conduct did not have anticompetitive effects. See also, *Qualcomm, Inc. v. Broadcom Corp.*, 548 F.3d 1004 (Fed. Cir. 2008) (reading *Rambus* to impose a disclosure duty, under a purely objective standard, "when a reasonable competitor would not expect to practice the standard without a license under the undisclosed claims").

4. How would you counsel a standard setting organization in light of the materials presented? What other issues, in addition to the ones here, would you want to pursue? Would disclosure of a proprietary interest to a standard setting body under a confidentiality agreement be a wise and effective strategy? The *Innovatio* decision provides guidance on how a court would implement a FRAND (aka RAND) licensing agreement. For a comprehensive study of the issues surrounding the enforcement of FRAND licenses, see Jay P. Kesan & Carol M. Hayes, *FRAND's Forever: Standards, Patent Transfers, and Licensing Commitments*, 89 IND. L.J. 231 (2014). For a historical perspective, see Jorge Contreras, *A Brief History of FRAND*, 80 ANTITRUST L.J.___ (forthcoming 2014).

E. International Perspective from The European Union

Antitrust: Commission enforcement action in pharmaceutical sector following sector inquiry

European Commission Memo

Brussels, 31 January 2013

Following its competition inquiry into the pharmaceutical sector of 2008/2009 (see IP/09/1098 and MEMO/09/321) the European Commission has issued statements of objections against pharmaceutical companies in three major cases concerning citalopram, an antidepressant, (see IP/12/834), perindopril, a cardio-vascular medicine (see IP/12/835), and fentanyl, a pain-killer (see IP/13/81). In addition, the Commission's 3rd report on its monitoring of patent settlements in the pharmaceutical sector confirmed that, while the overall number of concluded settlements has significantly increased, the proportion of settlements that may be problematic for competition has fallen substantially compared to the levels observed at the time of the sector inquiry.

A. Main findings of the sector inquiry

The Commission's competition inquiry into the pharmaceutical sector, concluded in 2009, had indicated a number of structural shortcomings and problems in the companies' practices that potentially led to distortions of competition and delays to entry of new, innovative as well as cheaper generic medicines into the EU market (see IP/09/1098 and MEMO/09/321). In its final report, the Commission made a number of recommendations to address these problems. While these included policy steps, such as improving pricing and reimbursement procedures for medicines and creating a unified patent system, particular emphasis was put on stronger enforcement of competition rules and monitoring of pharmaceutical companies, especially with regard to patent settlements.

One of the main findings of the sector inquiry was that competitive pressure from generic producers, once the primary patent of the originator medicine had expired, was not as strong as expected. The conclusion of the inquiry was that this could be partly the result of so-called pay-for-delay transactions. With such agreements, an originator company removes generic companies' incentives to compete — or to challenge the patent — by transferring value to the generic company.

If an originator company eliminates or delays cheaper generic competition through significant payments or other benefits to a generic company for discontinuing or delaying the launch of generic medicine challenging the originator's patent (so-called reverse payment patent settlement), this can lead to substantial consumer harm. Such an agreement reduces the competitive pressure exercised by (potential) generic market entry in exchange of sharing the originator company's monopoly rents. Thus, it replaces competition by collusion, and is therefore considered a restriction of competition.

The sector inquiry also highlighted the competition problems linked to some unilateral practices of dominant companies, such as those aimed at shutting out generic competitors from the market. Such actions may consist of acquiring technology that is indispensable for potential competitors who want to enter the market or the conclusion of several reverse payment settlements by a dominant undertaking.

B. Antitrust investigations

On 25 July and on 30 July 2012 the Commission has sent statements of objections to more than 14 companies in two major cases of possible distortions of competition in the pharmaceutical sector through anticompetitive agreements and, in part, unilateral practices.

In the Citalopram case, Lundbeck and several generic competitors entered into agreements which may have hindered the entry of generic citalopram into markets in the European Economic Area. The companies concluded these agreements when generic entry became in principle possible, because certain of Lundbeck's citalopram patents had expired. The agreements foresaw substantial value transfers from Lundbeck to the four generic competitors. In turn, the generic companies abstained from entering the market with generic citalopram. Lundbeck's value transfers to the generic competitors included direct payments as well as other forms such as purchase of generic citalopram stock for destruction or guaranteed profits in a distribution agreement. The Commission takes the preliminary view that this may have caused substantial consumer harm, since generic entry was delayed and prices remained high as a result of the agreements (see also IP/12/834).

In the Perindopril case, Les Laboratoires Servier and several generic competitors entered into agreements which may have hindered the entry of generic perindopril into markets in the EU. In exchange for payments by Servier the generic companies agreed not to enter the market with their cheaper generic products and/or not to further challenge the validity of the patents that protected Servier's more expensive medicine. In addition, Servier may have implemented a comprehensive strategy to prevent market entry of cheaper generic versions of perindopril, when Servier's perindopril was about to reach the end of its patent protection. Among the practices used by Servier were patent acquisitions that could potentially shut out competitors from the market and patent settlements with other companies that included reverse payments. (see also IP/12/835).

Such practices, if established, would be likely to cause significant consumer harm as national health services or insurance schemes are then forced to continue paying for the more expensive patent protected versions of a medicine when, absent the practices, cheaper generic medicines would have been available earlier.

Today, with the Fentanyl case, the Commission is taking a new step against major pharmaceutical companies to fight against undue delay to generic entry. Rather than competing, the companies entered here into a so-called co-promotion agreement resulting in consumers being deprived of access to a cheaper pain killer medicine. The co-promotion agreement foresaw monthly payments from J&J to its close generic competitor for as long as no generic product was launched in the Dutch market. Consequently, Sandoz abstained from entering the market with generic fentanyl patches for the duration of the agreement. This behaviour, if established, would infringe Article 101 TFEU.

In addition to the Lundbeck, Servier and Fentanyl cases, the Commission has other ongoing antitrust investigations in the pharmaceutical sector. In particular, it has opened proceedings against Cephalon and Teva (see IP/11/511) for possible violations of EU competition rules, including practices involving generic companies.

C. Market monitoring

The continuous monitoring of patent settlements in the pharmaceutical sector was recommended by the Commission in its final report of the sector inquiry (see IP/09/1098 and MEMO/09/321).

The latest patent settlement monitoring report was published by the Commission on 25 July 2012. As in the two previous monitoring exercises (see IP/10/887 and IP/11/840), the aim was to identify potentially problematic settlements from an antitrust perspective, in particular those that limit generic entry against a value transfer from an originator to a generic company. The proportion of such potentially problematic settlements has stabilised at a low level of 11% vis-à-vis 21% in the findings of the sector inquiry.

At the same time the total annual number of concluded settlements during 2011 has reached 120, which is a significant increase compared to the findings of the sector inquiry (24 settlements p.a.). This shows that the Commission's action has not hindered companies from concluding settlements, contrary to fears expressed by certain stakeholders in that respect. At the same time the monitoring exercises may have generally increased stakeholders' awareness of competition law issues, given the lower number of potentially problematic settlements. The continuing existence of such settlements shows the need for the Commission to stay vigilant in this area.

Moreover, the Commission generally monitors and addresses market developments in terms of competition between pharmaceutical companies, such as originator and generic companies, but also companies' interactions with regulators, as confirmed in the AstraZeneca case (C-457/10 P, AstraZeneca v. European Commission). In this case, the Court of Justice of the EU recently (December 2012) upheld the EU General Court's judgement of July 2010 (see MEMO/12/956 and IP/05/737). The Court of Justice confirmed that the company had misused the regulatory framework to prevent or, at the very least, delay the market entry of competing generic products.

D. Policy initiatives following the sector inquiry

There were successful policy follow-ups to the sector inquiry to ensure speedy and less contentious market entry of medicines.

One of them is the review of Council Directive 89/105/EEC, which is commonly referred to as the "Transparency Directive" and which lays down harmonised procedural provisions to ensure the transparency of national provisions regulating the pricing and reimbursement of medicinal products. In March 2012, the Commission proposed faster access to medicines for patients by streamlining and reducing the duration of pricing and reimbursement (see IP/12/205). The Transparency Directive is now in first reading in the co-decision procedure that involves the Council of Ministers of the EU and the European Parliament.

The Commission had also recommended to introduce an EU patent and a unified specialised patent litigation system in order to improve the fragmented patent system which currently causes legal uncertainty in patent disputes all over the EU, particularly as regards medicines, thus possibly contributing to delays of generic market entry. The Commission welcomes the progress made in the creation of a unitary patent system as well as a corresponding patent court. The international agreement creating a unified patent court will enter into force on 1 January 2014 or after thirteen contracting states ratify it, provided that UK, France and Germany are among them.

Notes & Questions

1. The memo reproduced above represents the European Competition Commission's findings on structural problems inhibiting generic competition in the

pharmaceutical market. On June 19, 2013, coordinating with the announcement of the Supreme Court's ruling in *Actavis*, the Commission levied fines against Lundbeck and several generic manufacturers (Merck, Ranbaxy, Alpharma, and Arrow) for engaging in reverse payment settlements. The fine against the patent owner was for 93,766,000 euros and against all the generic manufacturers for 52,239,000 euros. The Commission is engaged in ongoing investigations of Servier, Cephalon, and Teva.

2. Article 82 of the EC Treaty reads as follows:

"Any abuse by one or more undertakings of a dominant position within the common market or in a substantial part of it shall be prohibited as incompatible with the common market insofar as it may affect trade between Member States.

Such abuse may, in particular, consist in:

(a) directly or indirectly imposing unfair purchase or selling prices or other unfair trading conditions;

(b) limiting production, markets or technical development to the prejudice of consumers;

(c) applying dissimilar conditions to equivalent transactions with other trading parties, thereby placing them at a competitive disadvantage;

(d) making the conclusion of contracts subject to acceptance by the other parties of supplementary obligations which, by their nature or according to commercial usage, have no connection with the subject of such contracts.

This provision is the counterpart in the EU to Section 2 of the Sherman Act. Compare the two provisions. Which seems to have more teeth?

3. An understanding of United States law is not sufficient in planning for the global marketplace. Assistant Attorney General Pate, in the speech discussed in the notes after the *Actavis* excerpt above, stated the need for harmonization of international competition law, especially with respect to the treatment of intellectual property. He also concluded that harmonization is occurring. After reading about the treatment of reverse payment settlements in the United States and the European Union, do you have a sense that the law is harmonizing?

Chapter 12

Acquiring and Using Intellectual Property in University and Governmental Contexts

Problem

Dr. See will be meeting with Henry Daimler, a professor of automotive engineering at the local public university. Dr. See is interested in learning about Dr. Daimler's research on ignition technology in electric vehicles. Dr. Daimler has been exploring improvements in this technology as part of his multi-million-dollar research project funded by several private car companies and the United States Department of Energy. Dr. Daimler is a tenured member of the faculty at the university and through the university technology transfer office has created a technology incubator where he tests new automotive technology and acquires patents and other intellectual property protections. One of the many projects within the incubator is the development of farm equipment (such as tractors and trucks) for developing countries. Dr. See would like to discuss the possibility of licensing Dr. Daimler's technology for use in electric commuter cars and in electric farm equipment. Dr. See seeks your advice on what issues to look out for in his negotiations with Dr. Daimler.

Focus of the Chapter

Intellectual property presents special transactional challenges that are distinct from other transactional issues. For example, inventions and expressive works protected by intellectual property are often created and developed within universities and through federally funded grants. Working with universities introduces questions of who owns university research and tensions between the implications of intellectual property protections for pure and applied research. Issues of ownership are even more complicated if the intellectual property involved in a transaction was created through federally funded research. The Bayh-Dole Act governs patent ownership in inventions that arose from federally funded research. The implications of this Act are just still being explored, especially as more universities pursue the commercialization of research and partnerships with for-profit entities.

Partnerships with public universities raise the possibility of state sovereign immunity for intellectual property infringement. A private company with a large intellectual property portfolio may be hesitant to license its technology to a public university since the university can (and very likely will) raise sovereign immunity as a defense should a dispute over intellectual property infringement arise. To avoid this problem, waivers of sovereign immunity have become a standard feature of negotiations with public universities. Furthermore, even if a transaction is with a non-profit entity that appears to be distinct from any state, as a practical matter courts may extend state sovereign immunity to a non-profit entity if there is a close tie with a state. For example, if a public university establishes a distinct non-profit entity for the purpose of commercializing intellectual property, this distinct entity may be treated as an extension of the state for sovereign immunity purposes. Therefore, the importance of state sovereign immunity may be broader than it first appears.

Finally, the last subsection in this chapter examines collaborative research agreements involving private and governmental entities. These agreements can establish frameworks for research projects and other joint efforts that serve the interests of both types of entities. Governmental agencies may use these agreements to set up research projects that would otherwise not be completed for lack of governmental funds or resources. These cooperative arrangements may also provide new revenues to governmental agencies if the projects lead to commercially successful products. Private entities may participate in projects initiated under these agreements to gain access to information or sites that would otherwise be unavailable to them. As a result of these agreements and the projects they promote, both public agency agendas and private commercial goals can sometimes be advanced, but with the result of granting some degree of private ownership control over information and intellectual property derived from public assets.

Readings

A. Commercializing University Research

1. Intellectual Property Ownership and Use within the University

M.J. Madey v. Duke University
United States Court of Appeals for the Federal Circuit
307 F. 3d 1351 (Fed. Cir. 2002)

In the mid-1980s [M.J.] Madey was a tenured research professor at Stanford University. At Stanford, he had an innovative laser research program, which was highly regarded in the scientific community. An opportunity arose for Madey to consider leaving Stanford and take a tenured position at Duke. Duke recruited Madey, and in 1988 he left Stanford for a position in Duke's physics department. In 1989 Madey moved his free electron laser ("FEL") research lab from Stanford to Duke. The FEL lab contained substantial equipment, requiring Duke to build an addition to its physics building to house the lab. In addition, during his time at Stanford, Madey had obtained sole ownership of two patents practiced by some of the equipment in the FEL lab.

At Duke, Madey served for almost a decade as director of the FEL lab. During that time the lab continued to achieve success in both research funding and scientific breakthroughs. However, a dispute arose between Madey and Duke. Duke contends that, despite his scientific prowess, Madey ineffectively managed the lab. Madey contends that Duke sought to use the lab's equipment for research areas outside the allocated scope of certain government funding, and that when he objected, Duke sought to remove him as lab director. Duke eventually did remove Madey as director of the lab in 1997. The removal is not at issue in this appeal, however, it is the genesis of this unique patent infringement case. As a result of the removal, Madey resigned from Duke in 1998. Duke, however, continued to operate some of the equipment in the lab. Madey then sued Duke for patent infringement of his two patents, and brought a variety of other claims.

A. The Patents and Infringing Equipment

One of Madey's patents, U.S. Patent No. 4,641,103 ("the '103 patent"), covers a "Microwave Electron Gun" used in connection with free electron lasers. The other patent, U.S. Patent No. 5,130,994 ("the '994 patent"), is titled "Free-Electron Laser Oscillator For Simultaneous Narrow Spectral Resolution And Fast Time Resolution Spectroscopy." The details of these two patents are not material to the issues on appeal. Their use in the lab, however, as embodied in certain equipment, is central to this appeal.

The equipment at the Duke FEL lab that practices the subject matter disclosed and claimed in the patents is set forth in the list below, which first lists the equipment and then the patent(s) it embodies.

- An infrared FEL called the "Mark III FEL," embodying the '994 patent and the '103 patent (by incorporating the microwave electron gun in the infrared FEL).

- A "Storage Ring FEL," embodying the same patents as the Mark III FEL because it incorporates a Mark III FEL.

- A "Microwave Gun Test Stand," embodying the '103 patent (by incorporating the microwave electron gun).

The three alleged infringing devices are the Mark III FEL, the Storage Ring FEL, and the Microwave Gun Test Stand. Although it is not clear from the record, perhaps because Duke defended by asserting experimental use and government license defenses, Duke seems to concede that the alleged infringing devices and methods read on the claims of the patents. Although the three devices were housed in Duke's physics facilities, the Microwave Gun Test Stand was not Duke's asset, but rather belonged to North Carolina Central University ("NCCU").

B. Duke's Relationship with NCCU

Madey and Duke built the Microwave Gun Test Stand as a subcontractor to NCCU after the government awarded NCCU a contract to study microwave guns (the "AFOSR Contract"). Professor Jones of NCCU was the principal investigator under this government project. The Microwave Gun Test Stand was built and housed in the Duke FEL lab. The AFOSR Contract listed the Microwave Gun Test Stand as NCCU's asset.

. . . .

D. The District Court's Summary Judgment Opinion

The Patent Motion and the Experimental Use Defense

The district court acknowledged a common law "exception" for patent infringement liability for uses that, in the district court's words, are "solely for research, academic or experimental purposes." The district court recognized the debate over the scope of the experimental use defense, but cited this court's opinion in *Embrex, Inc. v. Service Engineering Corp.*, 216 F.3d 1343 (Fed. Cir. 2000) to hold that the defense was viable for experimental, non-profit purposes.

After having recognized the experimental use defense, the district court then fashioned the defense for application to Madey in the passage set forth below.

> Given this standard [for experimental use], for [Madey] to overcome his burden of establishing actionable infringement in this case, he must establish that [Duke] has not used the equipment at issue "solely for an experimental or other non-profit purpose." More specifically, [Madey] must sufficiently establish that [Duke's] use of the patent had "definite, cognizable, and not insubstantial commercial purposes."

Summary Judgment Opinion at 10.

. . . .

Before the district court, Madey argued that Duke's research in its FEL lab was commercial in character. . . . Based on language in Duke's patent policy, Madey argues that Duke is in the business of "obtaining grants and developing possible commercial applications for the fruits of its 'academic research.'"

The district court rejected Madey's argument, relying on another statement in the preamble of the Duke patent policy which stated that Duke was "dedicated to teaching, research, and the expansion of knowledge . . . [and] does not undertake research or development work principally for the purpose of developing patents and commercial applications." The district court reasoned that these statements from the patent policy refute any contention that Duke is "in the business" of developing technology for commercial applications. According to the district court, Madey's "evidence" was mere speculation, and thus Madey did not meet his burden of proof to create a genuine issue of material fact. . . .

The District Court's Overly Broad Conception of Experimental Use

Madey argues, and we agree, that the district court had an overly broad conception of the very narrow and strictly limited experimental use defense. The district court stated that the experimental use defense inoculated uses that "were solely for research, academic, or experimental purposes," and that the defense covered use that "is made for experimental, non-profit purposes only." Both formulations are too broad and stand in sharp contrast to our admonitions in *Embrex* and *Roche* [*Products, Inc. v. Bolar Pharm. Co.*, 733 F.2d 858 (Fed. Cir. 1985)], that the experimental use defense is very narrow and strictly limited. In *Embrex*, we followed the teachings of *Roche* and *Pitcairn* [*v. United States*, 547 F.2d 1106 (Ct. Cl. 1976),] to hold that the defense was very narrow and limited to actions performed "for amusement, to satisfy idle curiosity, or for strictly philosophical inquiry." Further, use does not qualify for the experimental use defense when it is undertaken in the "guise of scientific inquiry" but has "definite, cognizable, and not insubstantial commercial purposes." The concurring opinion in Embrex expresses a similar view: use is disqualified from the defense if it has the "slightest commercial implication." Moreover, use in keeping with the legitimate business of the alleged infringer does not qualify for the experimental use defense. . . .

Cases evaluating the experimental use defense are few, and those involving nonprofit, educational alleged infringers are even fewer. In [*Ruth v. Stearns-Roger Mfg. Co.*, 13 F. Supp. 697, 713 (D. Colo. 1935)], the court concluded that a manufacturer of equipment covered by patents was not liable for contributory infringement because the end-user purchaser was the Colorado School of Mines, which used the equipment in furtherance of its educational purpose. Thus, the combination of apparent lack of commerciality, with the non-profit status of an educational institution, prompted the court in *Ruth*, without any detailed analysis of the character, nature and effect of the use, to hold that the experimental use defense applied. This is not consistent with the binding precedent of our case law postulated by [*Embrex, Inc. v. Service Engineering Corp.*, 216 F.3d 1343 (Fed. Cir. 2000), *Roche Prods., Inc. v. Bolar Pharm. Co.*, 733 F.2d 858 (Fed. Cir. 1984), and *Pitcairn v. United States*, 547 F.2d 1106 (Ct. Cl. 1976)].

Our precedent clearly does not immunize use that is in any way commercial in nature. Similarly, our precedent does not immunize any conduct that is in keeping with the alleged infringer's legitimate business, regardless of commercial implications. For example, major research universities, such as Duke, often sanction and fund research projects with arguably no commercial application whatsoever. However, these projects unmistakably further the institution's legitimate business objectives, including educating and enlightening students and faculty participating in these projects. These projects also serve, for example, to increase the status of the institution and lure lucrative research grants, students and faculty.

In short, regardless of whether a particular institution or entity is engaged in an endeavor for commercial gain, so long as the act is in furtherance of the alleged infringer's legitimate business and is not solely for amusement, to satisfy idle curiosity, or for strictly philosophical inquiry, the act does not qualify for the very narrow and strictly limited experimental use defense. Moreover, the profit or non-profit status of the user is not determinative.

In the present case, the district court attached too great a weight to the non-profit, educational status of Duke, effectively suppressing the fact that Duke's acts appear to be in accordance with any reasonable interpretation of Duke's legitimate business objectives. On remand, the district court will have to significantly narrow and limit its conception of the experimental use defense. The correct focus should not be on the non-profit status of Duke but on the legitimate business Duke is involved in and whether or not the use was solely for amusement, to satisfy idle curiosity, or for strictly philosophical inquiry.

Fenn v. Yale University

United States District Court for the District of Connecticut

283 F. Supp. 2d 615 (D. Conn. 2003)

I. Findings of Fact

A. Introduction

John B. Fenn ("Dr. Fenn") is a leading scientific expert in the field of mass spectrometry, which determines the masses of atoms and molecules. Mass spectrometry has important uses in the development of medicines and the mapping of genes. In 1967, Dr. Fenn joined the faculty of Yale University ("Yale") as a tenured full professor. In 1987, as required by Yale's then-mandatory retirement policy, Dr. Fenn retired from his position as a full professor, but continued his work at Yale for another seven years as a "Professor Emeritus" and "Senior Research Scientist." In 1994, Dr. Fenn left Yale and became a research professor at Virginia Commonwealth University.

This case concerns a dispute between Yale and Dr. Fenn over an invention in the field of mass spectrometry which he developed while at Yale. In the following findings of fact, the Court will first address the various Yale policies that concern the inventions of its faculty members such as Dr. Fenn, then the particular policy that applied to him for this invention, then the particular invention here.

B. Yale's Patent Policy

From before Dr. Fenn joined its faculty, Yale's administrative policies have provided that patentable inventions resulting from a faculty member's research conducted at Yale belong to Yale and not the faculty member unless Yale expressly releases its interest in such inventions. These policies have also provided, though, that licensing royalties resulting from such inventions would be shared by Yale and the faculty member/inventor. After Dr. Fenn came to Yale in 1967, Yale made changes to its patent policy in 1975, 1984, 1988, and 1989, but these changes dealt primarily with the division of net licensing royalties between Yale and the inventor. The policy that inventions belong to Yale and not the inventor remained unchanged throughout Dr. Fenn's employment at Yale.

In 1967, when Dr. Fenn began his employment at Yale, the Faculty Handbook, dated July 1, 1966, contained provisions about Yale's patent policy with regard to inventions by its faculty members (the "1966 policy"). Pursuant to that policy, a faculty member was required to report to the university any invention resulting from "research conducted under University auspices or with the use of facilities under its control" and Yale owned the invention. The patent policy further stated that Yale did not typically keep title to patents resulting from those inventions; Yale arranged with the "Research Corporation" to carry out the patenting and commercializing of the inventions and to retain title to the subject patents. The policy also indicated that an inventor's share of any net royalty income from such inventions was "usually" 15%. The policy further stated that the University could abandon its interest in an invention and that in such circumstances, "the inventor is free to handle or dispose of his invention as he wishes." Dr. Fenn does not dispute that this patent policy applied to him.

On July 1, 1970, Yale prepared and distributed an updated Faculty Handbook with a section setting forth a patent policy identical to the 1966 policy. Subsequently, Dr. Fenn wrote a letter to Yale's Provost expressing his opinion that the inventor's share of royalty income provided by that patent policy was inadequate.

In 1974, the Yale Provost appointed a committee of faculty and administrators, including Dr. Fenn, to review the patent policy. The committee's work resulted in the 1975 patent policy, which increased the faculty member/inventor's share of net licensing royalties from 15% to 50%. The policy reiterated that all discoveries and inventions which result from "teaching, research, and other intellectual activity performed under University auspices" must be reported to Yale and provided that:

> [t]he [Yale] Treasurer shall refer inventions to Research Corporation or make other arrangements for evaluation of them in accordance with this policy. . . . In addition, the inventor may propose, even though the invention is one in the patenting or licensing of which the University wishes to participate, that the patenting of the invention or the licensing of the patent shall be arranged by the inventor at the inventor's expense, and if his proposal is accepted by the University, he shall proceed in accordance with an agreement to be made between the inventor and the University providing for such patenting or licensing by the inventor. Finally, if the University decides that although patenting or licensing of an invention is not contrary to University policy or the University does not wish to participate in the patenting or licensing, the University shall release to the inventor the University's interest in the invention, and the inventor shall be free to dispose of the invention as he wishes.

The 1975 patent policy also provided that it was "subject to revocation or amendment by the [Yale] corporation at any time." Dr. Fenn concedes that he was contractually bound by this 1975 patent policy.

In the early 1980s, a committee headed by Yale Professor Clement L. Markert ("the Markert Committee") was convened and charged with the task of reviewing the 1975 patent policy, faculty research sponsored by private entities, and commercial activities of faculty members. The Committee also recognized a need to re-examine the patent policy in light of the Bayh-Dole Act's changes in federal law and a shift in responsibilities from the Research Corporation to the Yale Office of Cooperative Research. Dr. Fenn served on the Markert Committee.

The Markert Committee produced a "Report of the Committee on Cooperative Research, Patents, and Licensing" ("the Markert Report"), setting forth specific recommendations, including changes to Yale's 1975 patent policy. The report's recommendations were embodied in a revised draft of the Faculty Handbook and a revised draft patent policy. Among other things, the Markert Report recommended reducing the share of licensing royalties for faculty members set forth in its 1975 patent policy. In particular, the Markert Report provided that inventors should receive 30% of net royalty income up to $200,000 and 20% of net royalty income in excess of $200,000.

Professor Markert presented Yale's then-president, A. Bartlett Giamatti ("President Giamatti"), with a draft of the Markert Report by letter dated November 18, 1983. In that letter, Professor Markert indicated that the report "represents a consensus of diverse views held by members of the committee." In a reply letter dated November 28, 1983, President Giamatti thanked Professor Markert for the Committee's work and informed him that the Markert Report would be circulated to the faculty for their comments. President Giamatti wrote that "[a]s I receive comments, I will share them with you and the members of the committee. Sometime early in the next semester, having taken into account the advice of the faculty, I will take, with the Provost, the report to the [Yale] Corporation. My intention is to ask the Corporation to approve as university policy those relevant portions of the report." Subsequently, President Giamatti circulated the Markert Committee Report to faculty and research scientists. Dr. Fenn received a copy of the Markert Report.

On February 29, 1984, Dr. Fenn wrote to President Giamatti concerning the Committee's Report. Dr. Fenn wrote: "In the covering letter that accompanied the draft copy of the Report of the Committee on Cooperative Research, Patents and Licensing (CCRPL), Chairman Markert indicated that the views set forth comprised a consensus of the committee membership. Lest you harbor the illusion that this consensus was unanimous I write to record one member's dissent with respect to some of those views." Dr. Fenn's letter set forth his objections to the Markert Report, particularly taking exception to the Committee's recommendation to reduce the inventor's share of royalty income through licensing.

On March 10, 1984, the Yale Corporation "[v]oted, to accept in principle 'the Report of the Committee on Cooperative Research, Patent, and Licenses [the Markert Report].'" On March 23, 1984, President Giamatti responded to Dr. Fenn's February 29, 1984 letter in which he had objected to the Markert Report. In his letter, President Giamatti specifically told Dr. Fenn that "[t]he final draft has been approved by the Corporation in principle. The Report was modified in a few places, specifically with regard to copyright issues, in response to faculty comment." The draft patent policy dated March 6, 1984 became Yale's patent policy on March 10, 1984 through the approval of the Markert Report. As mentioned, that policy provided inventors with 30% of net royalty income achieved through licensing up to $200,000 and 20% of net royalty income in excess of $200,000. The policy also required that inventions be "reported promptly" to Yale and that Yale may release its interest to the inventor should it decide it does not wish and has no legal obligation to participate in the patenting or licensing of the invention. The 1984 policy, like the 1975 patent policy, specifically provided that it was "subject to revocation or amendment by the [Yale] corporation at any time."

In 1986, Yale prepared a revised edition of its Faculty Handbook which contained a section titled "Policy on Patents, Copyrights, and Licensing." The section indicated that a "full statement of the University policies on patent, copyrights, and licensing is available from the Office of the Provost, the Office of Cooperative Research, or the Office of Grant and Contract Administration." The section indicated that licensing royalties would be divided "in accord with the University patent policy," and reiterated that the patent policy required faculty to disclose "[a]ny potentially patentable invention or any potentially licensable computer program" to the Committee on Cooperative Research, Patent, and Licenses through the Office of the Director of Cooperative Research.

In June 1988, the Yale Corporation adopted a patent policy developed by the Committee on Cooperative Research, Patent, and Licenses and published the text of that policy in the October 10–17, 1988 Yale Weekly Bulletin and Calendar. The policy, consistent with the prior policies, stated that "all inventions . . . shall be reported promptly in writing to the provost through the director of the Office of Cooperative Research" and that "[i]f the University decides that it does not wish and has no legal obligation to participate in the patenting or licensing of an invention, the University may release to the inventor the University's interest in the invention, and the inventor shall then be free to dispose of the invention as he or she wishes." The 1988 policy continued the royalty sharing provisions set forth by the 1984 policy, providing 30% of net royalty income up to $200,000 to the inventor and 20% of net royalty income in excess of $200,000 to the inventor. The policy provided that it was effective as to "all inventions/discoveries made on or after June, 1988." It also provided that it was "subject to revocation or amendment by the [Yale] Corporation."

In October 1989, Yale published another patent policy which it indicated applied retroactively to "all inventions/discoveries made on or after June 1988." Like the policy set forth in the October 1988 bulletin, this policy stated that "all inventions . . . shall be reported promptly in writing to the Provost through the Director of the Office of Cooperative Research" and that "[i]f the University decides that it does not wish and has no legal obligation to participate in the patenting or licensing of an invention, the University may release to the inventor the University's interest in the invention, and the inventor shall then be free to dispose of the invention as he or she wishes." The 1989 policy changed the royalty sharing as follows: for the first $100,000, 50% to the inventor; for amounts between $100,000 and $200,000, 40% to the inventor; and for amounts exceeding $200,000, 30% to the inventor. Like all the policies since 1975, it provided that it was "subject to revocation or amendment by the [Yale] Corporation."

C. The Invention and Licensing of the '538 Patent

Prior to June 1988, Dr. Fenn, together with Matthias Mann and Chin-Kai Meng, Yale graduate students working with Dr. Fenn at Yale, invented a method for determining the molecular weight of particles through the use of multiply charged ions, which relates to the field of mass spectrometry. The research that led to that invention was conducted under Yale's auspices, on the Yale campus, and was funded by grants from the National Institutes of Health ("NIH") awarded to Yale.

Dr. Fenn first publicly disclosed this invention in San Francisco at the Annual Conference of the American Society for Mass Spectrometry ("ASMS") in June 1988. The paper he presented to the ASMS met the ASMS's novelty requirements because it demonstrated for the first time that the electrospray ionization process could produce ions from large molecules.

Fenn and others recognized the importance of the invention in medical diagnosis and treatment at the 1988 conference because it solved a "longstanding scientific problem" and was believed to "revolutionize the way that one could analyze peptides and proteins." Dr. Mann, Dr. Fenn's co-inventor, believed in 1988 that the invention was "revolutionary" and a "scientific breakthrough."

Dr. Fenn did not disclose the invention to Yale's Office of Cooperative Research ("OCR") in 1988. It was not until April 6, 1989 that Dr. Fenn submitted a completed invention disclosure form to the OCR regarding the invention. However, at least by the end of 1988, Dr. Fenn knew of the great importance of the invention and its commercial value. In his invention disclosure—which only generally and briefly summarized the invention—Dr. Fenn indicated that any patent application would have to be filed by June 1, 1989—within one year of the patent's public disclosure at the San Francisco conference. He also noted that co-inventor Mann would be out of the country until May 15, 1989.

After the Yale OCR received Dr. Fenn's invention disclosure, Dr. Robert Bickerton ("Dr. Bickerton"), the head of the OCR, telephoned Dr. Fenn to find out more about the invention. Dr. Bickerton specifically inquired as to the potential commercial value of the invention. Dr. Fenn stated to Dr. Bickerton that he did not believe the invention had the potential for much commercial value because any patent issued on it would be a "use" patent as opposed to an "apparatus" patent and, as such, it would difficult to protect against its infringement. Dr. Fenn did not disclose that Pfizer Corporation, colleagues at the Yale Medical School and others had previously expressed a strong interest in the commercial viability of the invention. Dr. Fenn also did not disclose his own view, and the view of others, that the invention was in fact "revolutionary" or "important" and that it would likely have substantial commercial value.

Dr. Bickerton asked Dr. Fenn if Analytica of Branford, Inc. ("Analytica"), a company founded in 1987 to pursue electrospray technology by Dr. Fenn and Craig Whitehouse, one of Dr. Fenn's former graduate students, would be willing to pay for a patent application in return for Yale's commitment to license the invention to

Analytica. As mentioned, Analytica was founded for the purpose of exploiting Dr. Fenn's two previous mass spectrometry inventions, which were owned by Yale, and Dr. Fenn was a 49% shareholder of Analytica. Though Dr. Fenn had already discussed the '538 invention with Mr. Whitehouse, also a 49% shareholder-owner of Analytica, he stated to Dr. Bickerton that he did not know if Analytica would be interested. Contrary to Dr. Fenn's representation to Dr. Bickerton, Dr. Fenn knew that Analytica was very much interested in the invention and its potential for commercial success.

On May 5, 1989, Dr. Bickerton called Dr. Fenn to discuss the invention again. When Dr. Bickerton noted that any patent application would have to be filed within a month, Dr. Fenn replied that he would be "up to his ears" preparing for several upcoming scientific conferences and that, beginning on May 20, 1989, he would be absent from the Yale campus for several weeks in Miami and Europe attending those conferences. Dr. Fenn stated that he was not scheduled to return from Europe until the end of June 1989, after the statutory deadline for filing a patent application had passed. Dr. Fenn did not tell Dr. Bickerton that co-inventor Meng was on the Yale campus during that same period of time and would be available to assist Yale with a patent application.

Dr. Fenn knew at that time that it would be difficult for Yale to prepare a patent application without his assistance in the limited time remaining. He also understood that he would have to assist Yale in preparing a patent application because information far beyond the inventors' disclosure document he gave the OCR would be needed for a proper patent application.

Yale did not file a patent application before the statutory deadline of June 1, 1989. In making this decision, Yale relied on Dr. Fenn's representations about the importance of the invention. Recognizing that Dr. Fenn was an expert in the technology, Yale accepted Dr. Fenn's statement that the invention and any resulting patent would have little commercial value. Dr. Fenn's representation that the invention was of limited value was very significant to the OCR staff and signaled that it should not expend its resources on a patent application.

In his own name and without Yale's knowledge, however, Dr. Fenn filed a patent application for the invention on May 19, 1989, which was financed by Analytica. In an October 19, 1989 letter to Provost Turner regarding the invention, Dr. Fenn continued to conceal from Yale that he had filed the patent application. Dr. Fenn testified that he did so in order to "let[] the scheme play out so the incompetence of [the OCR] would emerge." Dr. Fenn stated at trial:

> I ha[d] made a number of complaints to Yale, the fact that I thought that [OCR] was incompetent. And here was a case which I had filed a patent application, it had nothing further, and I thought we'll let it go because if it culminates in a patent this will be first rate evidence that I've been trying to convince Yale of for a long time that these guys over there weren't doing their

job. . . . And I knew that if I, from Bickerton's previous behavior, confirmed by subsequent behavior, that if I had told him that I had filed a patent application at that time he would have immediately said, well, that belongs to Yale. And there would have been a confrontation. And if no patent issued, the confrontation would have been pointless but, moreover, if the patent didn't issue, then he'd be off the hook in a sense because he could say, well, I knew it wasn't going to result in a patent. So I was essentially making my case.

Dr. Fenn stated that he "was trying to show up how [the OCR] handled its business which in my view was incompetent."

Also in the fall of 1989, Dr. Henry Lowendorf of the Yale OCR, not knowing of Dr. Fenn's pending patent application, wrote to the NIH that "Yale is reporting an invention which was disclosed to NIH on 17 May 1989 to be unpatentable. . . . The invention is not patentable because enabling information on this invention was published in an abstract, enclosed, at a conference in June of 1988 and Yale did not file a patent application between the time the invention was disclosed to this Office, 6 April 1989, and the one year anniversary of disclosure." Dr. Fenn received a copy of Dr. Lowendorf's letter to NIH. Dr. Fenn knew that this letter was untrue, but he did nothing to correct Dr. Lowendorf's unintentional misrepresentation to the NIH that no patent application had been filed.

Without telling Yale, Dr. Fenn licensed the invention to Analytica on July 31, 1991. On July 14, 1992, United States Patent No. 5,130,538 ("the '538 patent") issued to Dr. Fenn for the "Method of Producing Multiply Charged Ions and for Determining Molecular Weights of Molecules By Use of the Multiply Charged Ions of Molecules." Dr. Fenn also failed to let Yale known of the issuance of the patent.

Yale first learned about the '538 patent when Aldo Test, an attorney for the Finnigan Corporation, wrote to Dr. Bickerton on January 20, 1993 inquiring about the possibility of licensing the '538 patent. Mr. Test explained in his letter that he had tracked the patent to Yale through its NIH grant number. Mr. Test also indicated that the patent had issued to Dr. Fenn, that Analytica claimed control over the licensing of the patent through its assignment from Dr. Fenn, and that Analytica had refused to sub-license the invention to Finnigan. Dr. Fenn received a copy of Mr. Test's letter.

Upon receiving Mr. Test's letter, Dr. Bickerton spoke with Dr. Fenn and forwarded to him a form asking him to assign the patent to Yale pursuant to the patent policy. The form was attached to a letter dated March 2, 1993, in which Dr. Bickerton wrote:

> As we discussed last month, the University recently became aware that you had filed a patent application, and obtained one or more patents, on an invention disclosed by you to my office in 1989. The invention was made by you and your students in the course of research at Yale funded by NIH . . . We have looked into the matter and concluded that Yale's patent policy requires that the invention and the patents be assigned to the University. Enclosed is a standard assignment agreement for your signature.

Yale's Committee on Cooperative Research, Patents and Licensing had determined that Yale was the rightful owner of the invention and '553 patent, and that Dr. Fenn should assign the patent to Yale. Dr. Fenn, nevertheless, refused to assign the patent to Yale.

Concerned with its ability to pursue infringers of the '538 patent because of the question whether its assignment from Dr. Fenn was valid, Analytica then asked Dr. Fenn to also assign the patent to Yale so that Yale could then license the patent to Analytica. Although Dr. Fenn "thought Analytica had a legitimate concern," he refused to assign the patent to Yale. Analytica then asked Yale for a license to any rights Yale possessed. In a meeting with Dr. Bickerton, Mr. Whitehouse "emphasized the critical nature of the invention to his company and indicated that it was imperative that they have a license." In September 1993, Yale entered into a licensing agreement with Analytica granting Analytica a "worldwide exclusive license in and to any and all interest Yale has or may have in the licensed patents [i.e. '538 patent]."

Since January 30, 1997, Analytica has been paying into escrow amounts calculated pursuant to the royalty provisions of the Fenn-Analytica agreement to which Dr. Fenn would otherwise be entitled. Before Analytica began to deposit the royalties into the escrow accounts, it had paid out $302,435.16 in royalties to Dr. Fenn and his designees in accordance with the Fenn-Analytica license agreement. At the time of trial, the escrowed amounts through the third quarter of 2000 totaled $2,108,820.90. Analytica has been depositing in escrow only amounts calculated pursuant to the terms of the Fenn-Analytica agreement and has not also deposited additional amounts calculated pursuant to the Yale-Analytica agreement. Amounts calculated pursuant to the Yale-Analytica agreement total $1,717,975.92 of the $2,108,820.90 in escrow through the third quarter of 2000. Beginning in the first quarter of 1995, Analytica ceased making royalty payments to Yale. Up until that time, Analytica had paid Yale $43,011.30 pursuant to the Yale-Analytica license agreement. At the time of trial, the earned, but unpaid, royalties due Yale under the Yale-Analytica license amounted to $1,760,987.22.

[Based on these facts, Fenn alleged conversion, theft, tortious interference with business relationship, and violation of the Connecticut Unfair Trade Practices Act against Yale University. The University counterclaimed for breach of contract and fiduciary duty, fraud, negligent misrepresentation, conversion, theft, unjust enrichment, and unfair trade practice violations and sought an accounting of profits from Fenn on the '538 patent. The district court made the following determinations:]

Dr. Fenn's contributions to the science of mass spectrometry, including the invention that led to the '538 patent, are significant and beneficial to many. As evidenced by his receipt of the 2002 Nobel Prize for Chemistry, the invention that led to the '538 patent is one of far-reaching import and magnitude. Indeed, the Nobel Foundation stated that the invention has "revolutionized the development of new pharmaceuticals" and that "[p]romising applications are also being reported in other areas, for example foodstuff control and early diagnosis of breast cancer and prostate cancer." The Nobel Foundation, Press Release: The Nobel Prize in Chemistry

2002, at https://www.nobelprize.org/nobel_prizes/chemistry/laureates/2002/press
.html (accessed 12/1/2017).

However, Dr. Fenn failed to promptly disclose the '538 invention to Yale, misrepresented its importance and commercial viability, and actively discouraged Yale from preparing and filing a patent application by the statutory deadline. At the same time, Dr. Fenn secretly prepared a patent application in his own name and licensed the '538 invention to Analytica without notifying Yale and the NIH. Those actions not only violated Dr. Fenn's obligations to Yale, but also violated Connecticut state law. Moreover, his actions were intentional and without justification.

Accordingly, the Court finds for the defendant and counter-plaintiff, Yale University, as indicated above. However, in order to fashion a judgment consistent with this memorandum of decision, the Court directs the parties to file supplemental papers.

Specifically, the Court hereby orders the parties to file proposed findings of fact with factual support and proposed orders concerning the relief requested by Yale. The parties shall address: (1) Yale's request for an accounting/assignment of the patent; (2) the amount of damages under the 1989 patent policy and how they should be awarded; and (3) whether punitive damages should be awarded and their amount, including proof as to reasonable attorney's fees. Those proposed findings and orders are due within thirty days of the date of this order. Both parties are also ordered to file memoranda regarding Yale's theft and conversion claims within thirty days.

University of Colorado Foundation, Inc. v. American Cyanamid Co.

United States Court of Appeals for the Federal Circuit

196 F.3d 1366 (Fed. Cir. 1999)

Materna 1.60 (Materna) is a prenatal multivitamin/mineral supplement produced and sold by Lederle Laboratories, a division of Cyanamid. In 1981, Cyanamid began selling a reformulation of Materna. The reformulated product improved iron absorption over the previous version of the product. Cyanamid filed a patent application claiming the reformulation. The application named Dr. Leon Ellenbogen, a Cyanamid chemist, as the inventor. The '634 patent issued from this application in 1984.

[Doctors Robert H. Allen and Paul A. Seligman (the Doctors)] first learned of the '634 patent in 1993. The University and the Doctors then brought suit in federal district court against Cyanamid and Dr. Ellenbogen. That lawsuit alleged (1) that the Doctors (who were medical researchers at the University of Colorado Health Sciences Center) invented the reformulation of Materna covered by the '634 patent claims and communicated the invention to Dr. Ellenbogen, (2) that Dr. Ellenbogen intentionally omitted the Doctors as co-inventors in the patent application, and (3) that Cyanamid intentionally hid the patent from the Doctors.

In response, Cyanamid asserted that Dr. Ellenbogen hired the Doctors to perform research that convinced Cyanamid to reformulate Materna. According to Cyanamid, the Doctors transmitted the results of their research to Cyanamid with the intention that Cyanamid would reformulate Materna and thereby profit. Cyanamid further asserted that Dr. Ellenbogen was the true inventor. Consequently, Cyanamid argued that it had no duty to notify the Doctors of the patent and denied any liability to the University. The district court granted summary judgment to Cyanamid on the § 256 claim refusing to substitute the Doctors as the named inventors on the '634 patent. The district court also granted summary judgment to Cyanamid, denying the University's claims of patent infringement and ownership of equitable title to the '634 patent. The district court also granted summary judgment to the University on copyright infringement. Specifically, the district court found that four bar graphs and a table in the Doctors' published article were copyrightable subject matter and copied by Cyanamid into the patent application.

Following a bench trial, the district court found that the Doctors invented the Materna reformulation and that Dr. Ellenbogen was not an inventor of that composition. To determine inventorship, the district court applied state common law, rather than federal patent law. . . .

[The Federal Circuit reversed the district court on its finding of inventorship and addressed the issue as follows:]

Field preemption describes exclusive regulation of a legal subject by federal law. To preempt a field, federal law must evince "a scheme of federal regulation so pervasive" that no room remains for a state to supplement. Alternatively, federal law preempts a field by addressing a "federal interest . . . so dominant that the federal system will be assumed to preclude enforcement of state laws on the same subject."

A primary purpose of patent law is to reward invention. The law of inventorship, which has heretofore developed solely under federal law, supports this purpose by identifying the actual inventors of an invention eligible for patent protection. With its advent in Article 1 of the Constitution, patent law has developed under federal law to achieve the objective of national uniformity.

An independent inventorship standard under state law would likely have different requirements and give rise to different remedies than federal patent law. A different state inventorship standard might grant property rights to an individual who would not qualify as an inventor under federal patent law, or might grant greater relief to inventors than is afforded by federal patent law. Either situation might frustrate the dual federal objectives of rewarding inventors and supplying uniform national patent law standards.

The federal Patent Act leaves no room for states to supplement the national standard for inventorship. Title 35 contains explicit and detailed standards for inventorship. *See, e.g.,* 35 U.S.C. §§ 101–03, 116–20, 254–56, 261–62 (1994). Moreover, federal law has provided this court with jurisdiction to enforce these comprehensive provisions to provide a uniform national standard for inventorship. *See In re Snap-On Tools Corp.,* 720 F.2d 654, 655, 220 U.S.P.Q. 8, 9 (Fed. Cir. 1983). Therefore, the field of federal patent law preempts any state law that purports to define rights based on inventorship. Consequently, this court vacates the district court's conclusion that the Doctors were the inventors of reformulated Materna and that Dr. Ellenbogen was not the inventor. Upon remand, the court must apply federal patent law principles to determine whether the Doctors and/or Dr. Ellenbogen were inventors of the technology of the '634 patent.

[The Federal Circuit addressed a further copyright issue in the case as follows:]

The district court found that Cyanamid copied Figures 1–4 and Table 1 of the Doctors' journal article into the patent application. Because these depictions of data in the Figures and Table were protectable expressions under the copyright statute, the district court determined that Cyanamid infringed the Doctors' copyright in the article. However, the district court concluded that the University did not prove any damages from the copyright infringement.

The University argues that its proof of Cyanamid's gross revenues from sales of reformulated Materna shifted the burden of proof to Cyanamid under 17 U.S.C. § 504(b) (1994) to prove deductible expenses and to prove those elements of its profits that were attributable to factors other than copyright infringement. The University's argument presumes that the sales of reformulated Materna were due to Cyanamid's copyright infringement. The University had the burden to show this connection. See 4 Melville B. Nimmer and David Nimmer, Nimmer on Copyright § 14.03[A] (1999) (noting that plaintiff's claims for indirect profits rarely succeed). The district court found that the University did not meet this burden. This court detects no clear error in this finding. This court therefore affirms the district court's decision.

Notes & Questions

1. The three principal cases illustrate issues of ownership of intellectual property within universities. Compare the issues illustrated here with our discussion of employee inventorship in the for-profit context. Are the issues different? Review the materials discussed in Chapter 4. One question to consider is: Are professors employees or independent contractors with respect to a university employer? Why does this question matter?

2. Keep the issues raised by *Madey* and *Fenn* in mind when approaching the materials on the Bayh-Dole Act below, especially the *Stanford v. Roche* decision from the United States Supreme Court. Consider whether the issues are different when a university professor creates a patented invention outside the context of federally funded research, such as through privately funded research.

3. One way to address intellectual property ownership issues is through contracts, especially through the use of assignments. Would better contracting have changed the situations in *Madey* and *Fenn*? How would you have advised the universities or the professors on the contracting issues? How would you advise Dr. See or Dr. Daimler, in the principal problem of this chapter, on the drafting of a contract to clarify ownership issues?

4. The *University of Colorado* case illustrates some of the problems that can arise when university personnel collaborate with other individuals (either in industry or at other universities) in the creation of patentable technologies. In such endeavors, determinations of inventorship (that is, who is an inventor for patent law purposes) will control who has a potential ownership interest in the resulting patents. Do you think better contracting and internal policies would have avoided the dispute in *The University of Colorado* case? If so, how would you draft these policies? Would these policies run the risk of being pre-empted by federal law?

5. In light of these materials, consider the case of Dr. Joy Laskar, a successful engineering professor at Georgia Institute of Technology (Georgia Tech) in Atlanta, Georgia. Dr. Laskar's innovative work in chip design generated several millions of dollars in funding and sponsored research and produced a number of successful start-ups. He, however, found himself the subject of a significant dispute with Georgia Tech. The university accused Laskar of (1) misstating the extent of his involvement with a start-up company he founded, (2) allowing employees of the start-up to use university lab space, equipment, and resources without the university's authorization, and (3) misusing university funds to purchase items used to fulfill the start-up's contractual obligations to a Korean chip research institute. Laskar, in turn, contended that (1) his mistaken reporting of his role in the start-up was a result of sloppiness not deceit, (2) the start-up company had received authorization to use the lab and related resources, and (3) the university funds used to purchase the chips were applied to academic research purposes as the chips involved were used for research by the Korean entity and were returned to Georgia Tech for further research after personnel at the Korean institute confirmed that the chips worked. Laskar's activities were ultimately the focus of a criminal indictment for violations of state and federal laws based on misuse of funds. Stripped of tenure, he pursues his case as of this writing. His story illustrates the sometimes bitter and potentially devastating conflicts that can arise when academic culture, particularly at a state university, runs up against a culture of high stakes entrepreneurship. For further details, see Dr. Laskar's website at http://joylaskarstory.com/ (accessed 12/1/2017). A good journalistic account is provided by Nick Wingfeld, "Reaching for Silicon Valley, "The New York Times (November 16, 2013).

2. Transforming Federally Funded Research into Marketable Products: Goals of the Bayh-Dole Act

Wendy H. Schacht, The Bayh-Dole Act: Selected Issues in Patent Policy and the Commercialization of Technology

Congressional Research Service (October 5, 2007)

Changes to the patent laws embodied in the Bayh-Dole Act had as an objective the facilitation of collaborative ventures between and among academia, industry, and government. In 1980, universities performed 14% of the R&D undertaken in the

United States (similar to today); much of this the fundamental research basic to technological advance. The work is accomplished as part of the education process and provides training for scientists, engineers, and managers subsequently employed by the private sector.

Universities, however, generally do not have the means of production necessary to take the results of research and generate marketable products. Such activities are carried out by industry. Thus, the emphasis in the Bayh-Dole Act on the promotion of cooperative efforts between academia and the business community. By providing universities with intellectual property ownership with which to pursue and structure collaborative ventures, the legislation is intended to encourage the two sectors to work together to generate new goods, processes, and services for the marketplace. Such joint work allows for shared costs, shared risks, shared facilities, and shared expertise.

Prior to World War II, industry was the primary source of funding for basic research in universities. This financial support helped shape priorities and build relationships. However, after the war, the federal government supplanted the private sector as the major financial contributor and became the principal determinant of the type and direction of the research performed in academic institutions. This situation oftentimes resulted in a disconnect between the university and industrial communities. Because the private sector and not the government typically is involved in commercialization, the difficulties in moving an idea from the research stage to a marketable product or process appeared to have been compounded. Thus, efforts to encourage increased collaboration between and among the sectors through the Bayh-Dole Act were expected to augment the contribution of both parties to technological advancement.

Small Business

Special consideration concerning patent title was given to small businesses in part because of the role these companies were seen as playing in the generation of new jobs and in technological advancement. Research supported by several federal agencies concluded that small, high technology companies are the source of significant innovation. An often cited 1982 study financed by the Small Business Administration determined that small firms were 2.4 times as innovative per employees as large companies. Similar work performed at the time the legislation was being considered found that firms of less than 1,000 employees were responsible for more major innovations than large firms in the years 1953–1966 and for an equal number from 1967–1973. A study of national and regional data by the Federal Reserve Bank of Chicago concluded that "small firms—those with 20 or fewer employees—create a larger proportion of new jobs than their share of employment in the economy and continue to create jobs even during recession."

However, certain caveats need to be stated particularly within the context of small business, innovation, and technology development. Over the years, experts have argued that the contribution of small firms to the economy is overstated. Marc Levinson, writing in Dun's Business Month, maintained that small companies tended to produce fewer goods than larger ones because they are less capital intensive and, on the whole, add less to the gross national product because they offer lower salaries and often do not provide health insurance or pension plans. Professors Zoltan Acs and David Audretsch argued that the relationship between company size and innovation capacity varied by industry. Others maintained that there is no conclusive evidence that firm size affects the "success" of R&D.

An important factor affecting the ability of small companies to effect technological advance appears to be the relationship between these firms and large corporations, a concept that is reflected in the provisions of the Bayh-Dole Act. A study by the National Academy of Engineering concluded that "small high-tech companies play a critical and diverse role in creating new products and services, in developing new industries, and in driving technological change and growth in the U.S. economy." The reasons for this include the ability of these firms to rapidly develop markets, generate new goods and services and offer product diversity. Small businesses tend to be willing to take those technological risks that are not pursued by large firms and may be in a position to quickly exploit market opportunities. Yet, while small businesses can serve as the source of new products and processes, they often "cannot take advantage of their initial technological lead to establish a secure foothold in the key markets."

Bayh-Dole and Related Law

Provisions

In enacting P.L. 96-517, the Congress accepted the proposition that vesting title to the contractor will encourage commercialization and that this should be used to support innovation in certain identified sectors. The law states:

> It is the policy and objective of the Congress to use the patent system to promote the utilization of inventions arising from federally-supported research or development; . . . to promote collaboration between commercial concerns and nonprofit organizations, including universities; . . . to promote the commercialization and public availability of inventions made in the United States by United States industry and labor; [and] to ensure that the Government obtains sufficient rights in federally-supported inventions to meet the needs of the Government and protect the public against nonuse or unreasonable use of inventions. . . .

Each nonprofit organization (including universities) or small business is permitted to elect (within a reasonable time) to retain title to any "subject invention" made under federally funded R&D except under "exceptional circumstances when it is determined by the agency that restriction or elimination of the right to retain title to any subject invention will better promote the policy and objectives of this chapter." The institution must commit to commercialization within a predetermined, agreed upon, time frame. As stated in the House report to accompany the bill, "the legislation establishes a *presumption* [emphasis added] that ownership of all patent rights in government funded research will vest in any contractor who is a nonprofit research institution or a small business."

Certain rights are reserved for the government to protect the public's interests. The government retains "a nonexclusive, nontransferable, irrevocable, paid-up license to practice or have practiced for or on behalf of the United States any subject invention throughout the world. . . ." The government also retains "march-in rights" which enable the federal agency to require the contractor (whether he owns the title or has an exclusive license) to "grant a nonexclusive, partially exclusive, or exclusive license in any field of use to a responsible applicant or applicants. . . ." (with due compensation) or to grant a license itself under certain circumstances. The special situation necessary to trigger march-in rights involves a determination that the contractor has not made efforts to commercialize within an agreed upon time frame or that the "action is necessary to alleviate health or safety needs which are not reasonably satisfied by the contractor. . . ."

. . . .

Implementation and Results

The Bayh-Dole Act appears to have met its expressed goals of using "the patent system to promote the utilization of inventions arising from federally-supported research or development; . . . and to promote collaboration between commercial concerns and nonprofit organizations, including universities. . . ." In one of the earliest studies of the legislation, the General Accounting Office (now the Government Accountability Office, GAO) found agreement among university administrators and small business representatives that P.L. 96-517 had "a significant impact on their research and innovation efforts." While noting it was not correct to generalize about academia from the 25 universities studied, GAO did find that by 1987 all university administrators questioned indicated that the Bayh-Dole Act had "been significant in stimulating business sponsorship of university research, which has grown 74 percent . . ." from FY1980 to FY1985. According to the National Science Foundation (NSF), industry support for academic research grew faster than any other funding source until FY2002. Industry financing expanded from 3.9% of university R&D in 1980 to 7.2% in 2000, although by FY2006 industry support had dropped to 5.1% of academic R&D. In 1980, federal financing comprised 67.5% of the total academic undertaking; by 2000 federal support declined to 58.2% of university funding, yet increasing to 62.9% in FY2006. It should be noted, however, that the federal government still remains the major source of academic research funding.

The majority of the university personnel involved in the GAO study indicated that the increase in industry support for research at universities was "directly" attributed to the patent changes in P.L. 96-517 and P.L. 98-620. Academic faculty interviews conducted by GAO found that "since businesses knew that universities could take title to federally funded inventions, they no longer were concerned that their research efforts could be 'contaminated' by federal funding with the possibility that a federal agency could assert title rights to resulting inventions." All respondents agreed that the removal of licensing restrictions on nonprofit institutions (including universities) by P.L. 98-620 was of vital importance in promoting industry-university interaction. This was reinforced by the finding that 9 out of 10 business executives questioned identified the Bayh-Dole Act as an "important factor" in their decisions to fund R&D in academia.

Another GAO study published in May of 1998 reported that agency and university representatives believed the Bayh-Dole Act was meeting its goals as articulated by the Congress and the law had a positive impact on all involved. Academia was "receiving greater benefits from their inventions and were transferring technology better than the government did when it retained title to inventions." In addition, the report states that the increased commercialization of federally funded research that resulted from the implementation of the act positively affected both the federal government and the American people.

Other experts agree. Yale President Richard Levin argued that the purpose of the Bayh-Dole Act is to transition the results of government funded research "into practice for the benefit of humanity . . ." and that results indicate a "pretty emphatic positive answer that the Bayh-Dole Act has created public benefits" with minimal costs. As stated in an article in *The Economist*, the Bayh-Dole Act is "[p]robably the most inspired piece of legislation to be enacted in America over the past half-century. . . ."

One of the major factors in the reported success of the Bayh-Dole Act is the certainty it conveys concerning ownership of intellectual property. The Director of Stanford University's Office of Technology Licensing, Katherine Ku, noted that exclusivity is what motivates firms to invest financial and human resources in technology development. It provides an incentive for universities to take the time and effort to pursue a patent and to license those patents in its portfolio. This has led to a significant increase in academic patenting. In 1980, 390 patents were awarded to universities; by 2005, this number increased to 2,725.

Academia has become a major source of innovation for local and regional economic development. In the latest published survey (FY2005) performed by the Association of University Technology Managers (AUTM), universities identified 527 new products that were marketed that year based on academic R&D. In addition, the survey indicated that during FY2005 more than 628 new companies were created to commercialize university research, 4,932 new licenses/options were granted, with small businesses primarily responsible for the commercialization. Since 1980, more than 5,171 new companies have been established to develop and market academic R&D.

Notes & Questions

1. Wendy Schacht's summary of the Bayh-Dole Act provides important background to the cases presented in the next section on the impacts of the Act. Pay

particular attention to portions of her discussion indicating that a goal of the Act was to clarify patent ownership by vesting title to a federally funded invention in the contractor—that is, the recipient of a federal grant. The contractor is typically a university. After reading the *Stanford v. Roche* decision below, consider whether the Supreme Court's analysis is consistent with this purported goal of the Act.

2. Note that the Bayh-Dole Act applies to patented technologies. What would the implications be for other types of intellectual property, such as copyrights, trademarks, and trade secrets? Many universities are attempting to develop intellectual property policies. One needs to pay attention to these particular policies, especially when intellectual property not covered by the Bayh-Dole Act is concerned.

3. The Bayh-Dole Act has implications for small businesses as well as for universities. Small businesses can obtain federal funds through agencies like the National Science Foundation, but more often through the Small Business Administration. The Act purports to cover patents developed by small businesses through federal funds. It also aims to promote the founding of small businesses through the creation of start-ups, especially those arising from university-generated technologies.

4. Technology transfer offices are key players in the promotion of university-generated technology. The Association of University Technology Managers (AUTM) is a professional organization for persons working in technology transfer offices. The AUTM seeks to support and advance academic technology transfer globally. The organization's web site contains a wide variety of resources related to academic technology transfers. *See* Association of University Technology Managers, Home Page, https://www.autm.net/ (accessed 12/1/2017).

5. The importance of the Bayh-Dole Act in the United States has led to similar legislation in other countries. Questions of institutional capacity and the appropriateness of such legislation in less developed countries are the focus of policy and scholarly debate. For a discussion of these issues, see Arti Rai et al., *Is Bayh-Dole Good for Developing Countries?: Lessons from the US Experience*, 6 PLoS Biology 2078–2084 (October 2008). For an analysis of the effects of the Bayh-Dole Act, see David Mowery et al., Ivory Tower and Industrial Innovation: University-Industry Technology Transfer Before and After the Bayh-Dole Act (2004).

6. Universities often disseminate their technologies through auctions of exclusive licenses to the universities' patents. An auction of this sort allows a university to obtain commercial or defensive patenting value without actually engaging in product manufacturing and marketing in the field of technology involved in a patented invention. For an analysis of patent auctions in general with some discussions of the roles of universities, see Ron Laurie & Raymond Millien, *A Survey of Established and Evolving IP Monetization Models*, 1046 PLI/Pat 125 (2011); Adam Andrzejewski, *Patent Auctions: The New Intellectual Property Marketplace*, 48 U. Louisville L. Rev. 831 (2010). Additional issues raised by patent auctions are considered in Chapter 9.

3. Commercializing University-Generated Intellectual Property: Impacts of the Bayh-Dole Act

In thinking about the materials in this section, consider the following passage from *University of Rochester v. Searle*, 358 F.3d 916 (Fed. Cir. 2004) discussing the legislative history of the Bayh-Dole Act:

> Congress has determined that licensing of academia's inventions to industry is the best way to bring groundbreaking inventions to the public. *See* 35 U.S.C. § 200. By vesting in universities the patent rights to their federally funded research, the Bayh-Dole Act of 1980 encouraged "private industry to utilize government funded inventions through the commitment of the risk capital necessary to develop such inventions to the point of commercial application." H.R. Rep. No. 96-1307, pt. 1, at 3 (1980).

How does this commitment to commercialization and investment work in practice? The following two cases offer some insights.

Trinity Industries, Inc. v. Road Systems, Inc.

United States District Court for the Eastern District of Texas

235 F. Supp. 2d 536 (E.D. Tex. 2002)

[Trinity Industries, Inc. had worked with Texas A&M University ["TAMU"] to develop a patent method for treating highway guardrail ends. In an infringement suit brought against Road Systems, Inc., the defendant alleged that the patent on the method was invalid because of fraud on the patent office. The district court addressed the defense as follows:]

Defendants claim, and Plaintiffs admit, that TAMU did not disclose to the PTO that the federal government helped fund the research that led to the development of the '928 patent. . . . Therefore, the court must decide three issues: (1) whether TAMU was required to disclose the federal government's funding of the research leading to the '928 patent; (2) whether such funding and possible governmental rights were material to patentability; and (3) whether Defendants have presented sufficient evidence of TAMU's intent to deceive the PTO in order to prevail on the affirmative defense of inequitable conduct at the summary judgment stage.

The United States government has an interest in a patent developed under a "funding agreement". 35 U.S.C. § 202(c)(4) (also known as the "Bayh-Dole Act"). Defendants claim that the '928 patent was the product of a "funding agreement" and thus the federal government automatically had rights to the patent. Furthermore, Defendants claim TAMU had a statutory and contractual duty to disclose to the PTO the government's funding and consequential rights in the '928 patent. Plaintiffs contend that although federal funds were used to develop the '928 patent, there was no "funding agreement" to which TAMU was a party. Therefore, Plaintiffs argue that the federal government has no rights to the '928 patent and there was no duty to disclose the source of the funding. And, even if there were a duty to disclose, Plaintiffs' contend that the failure to do so is not inequitable conduct.

Within the specification of an application for a patent developed under a "funding agreement", there must be a statement specifying that the "invention was made with Government support and that the government has certain rights in the invention." 35 U.S.C. § 202(c)(6). In order to determine if there was a duty to disclose in the instant case, the court must first determine if federal funding went into the development of the '928 patent pursuant to a "funding agreement" as used in the Bayh-Dole Act:

> The term "funding agreement" means any contract, grant, or cooperative agreement entered into between any Federal Agency, other than the Tennessee Valley Authority, and any contractor for the performance of experimental, developmental, or research work funded in whole or in part by the federal government. Such term includes any assignment, substitution of parties, or subcontract of any type entered into for the performance of experimental, developmental, or research work under a funding agreement as herein defined. 35 U.S.C. § 201(b).

Under the Act, a "contractor" is "any person, small business firm, or nonprofit organization that is a party to a funding agreement." 35 U.S.C. § 201(c) (emphasis added). The Act grants the funding federal agency a "nonexclusive, nontransferable, irrevocable, paid-up license to practice or have practiced for or on behalf of the United States any subject invention throughout the world." 35 U.S.C. § 202(c)(4) (emphasis added). A "subject invention" is "any invention of the contractor conceived or first actually reduced to practice in the performance of work under a funding agreement." 35 U.S.C. § 201(e). Thus, if TAMU, a nonprofit organization, received funds from the Federal Highway Administration ("FHwA"), a federal agency, through the terms of a subcontract with the Texas Department of Transportation ("TxDOT"), in order to develop the '928 patent, a subject invention, the federal government automatically had an irrevocable license to the '928 patent, and TAMU had a statutory duty to disclose the existence of those rights during the patent application process.

FHwA, a federal agency within the United States Department of Transportation, provided money to the Texas State Department of Highways and Public Transportation in 1985 and 1986. The agreements under which the federal money was given by the federal agency to TxDOT are "funding agreements". *See* 35 U.S.C. § 201(b). TxDOT, in turn, used that federal money to fund research projects at the Texas Transportation Institute ("TTI") to develop guardrail end treatment technology. Between September 1, 1985 and August 31, 1987, TxDOT provided TTI with $216,608.92 for the guardrail end treatment project. The funding of the specific guardrail end treatment project described in the 1985 Study Proposal Agreement was made pursuant to the more general research agreement embodied in the 1985 Cooperative Research Agreement between TxDOT and TAMU.

Thus, funding was given by the federal government through its agency, FHwA, to TxDOT in order to conduct research. TxDOT forwarded a part of those funds to TAMU in order to develop new guardrail end treatment technology. The '928 patent resulted from the research. The 1985 Study Proposal Agreement and the 1985 Cooperative Research Agreement are "subcontracts" as used in 35 U.S.C. § 201(b). Therefore, a "nonexclusive, nontransferable, irrevocable, paid-up license" arose pursuant to the Bayh-Dole Act. See 35 U.S.C. § 202(c)(4). Furthermore, a contractual right to an interest in the patent arose from the 1985 Cooperative Agreement. The language of paragraph IV.(a) mirrors the language of the statute.

Because TAMU can accurately be labeled a "contractor" due to its status as a party to a "funding agreement", Section 202(c)(6) and the Manual of Patent Examining Procedures Section 310 issued by the PTO required the disclosure of the federal government's rights during the prosecution of the '928 patent. See 35 U.S.C. § 202(c)(6); Manual of Patent Examining Procedure § 310.

Plaintiffs did not disclose, as required, the government funding or the United States' rights in the '928 patent during the prosecution process. Defendants assert that this nondisclosure is "concealment" that amounts to sufficient inequitable conduct to preclude the Plaintiffs' ability to enforce the '928 patent against alleged infringement.

Parties before the PTO are charged with a duty to disclose information material to patentability:

> [I]nformation is material to patentability when it is not cumulative to information already of record or being made of record in the application, and (1) It establishes, by itself or in combination with other information, a prima facie case of unpatentability of a claim; or (2) It refutes, or is inconsistent with, a position the applicant takes in: (i) Opposing an argument of unpatentability relied on by the Office, or (ii) Asserting an argument of patentability. 37 C.F.R. § 1.56(b).

Information is "material" when there is a "substantial likelihood that a reasonable examiner would have considered the information important in deciding whether to allow the application to issue as a patent." To be material, the information must be the type that a reasonable examiner would consider in allowing the patent.

Although Defendants concede that most findings of inequitable conduct have involved the omission of prior art, they have failed to link the nondisclosure in the instant case to patentability. Even if TAMU had a duty to disclose the information, and it breached that duty by failing to disclose, Defendants have presented nothing more to show how the omission has affected the patent examiner's decision to accept or reject TAMU's patent application. Defendants have offered no evidence, other than the mere breach of a duty, to establish that Plaintiffs failed to disclose material information. Defendants have shown that Plaintiffs failed to disclose information, but the court finds the information to be less than material. Defendants have not even suggested that the information regarding funding and the government's subsequent rights would possibly cause an examiner to deny the patent. Had the information been disclosed, it would not have been considered by the examiner, because the funding information does not have a logical relationship to the decision on whether or not to issue the '928 patent.

Similarly, Defendants offer no proof to support their conclusory statement that Plaintiffs intentionally deceived the PTO. While Defendants do not need to present direct evidence of intent, they do need to present sufficient evidence to allow an inference of wrongful intent from the surrounding circumstances. [*Baxter Int'l, Inc. v. McGaw, Inc.*, 149 F.3d 1321, 1329 (Fed. Cir. 1998)]. There must be clear and convincing evidence that the Plaintiffs made a deliberate decision to withhold a known material reference. Due to the court's conclusion that the information in question was not material, it is impossible for the Defendants to clear the high burden required on this issue at the summary judgment stage.

Defendants have not presented sufficient evidence of materiality and intent to deceive the PTO to warrant summary judgment in their favor on the affirmative defense of unenforceability due to inequitable conduct.

Board of Trustees of Leland Stanford Junior University v. Roche Molecular Systems, Inc.

United States Supreme Court

131 S. Ct. 2188 (2011)

CHIEF JUSTICE ROBERTS DELIVERED THE OPINION OF THE COURT.

Since 1790, the patent law has operated on the premise that rights in an invention belong to the inventor. The question here is whether the University and Small Business Patent Procedures Act of 1980 — commonly referred to as the Bayh-Dole Act — displaces that norm and automatically vests title to federally funded inventions in federal contractors. We hold that it does not.

In 1985, a small California research company called Cetus began to develop methods for quantifying blood-borne levels of human immunodeficiency virus (HIV), the virus that causes AIDS. A Nobel Prize winning technique developed at Cetus — polymerase chain reaction, or PCR — was an integral part of these efforts. PCR allows billions of copies of DNA sequences to be made from a small initial blood sample.

In 1988, Cetus began to collaborate with scientists at Stanford University's Department of Infectious Diseases to test the efficacy of new AIDS drugs. Dr. Mark Holodniy joined Stanford as a research fellow in the department around that time. When he did so, he signed a Copyright and Patent Agreement (CPA) stating that he "agree[d] to assign" to Stanford his "right, title and interest in" inventions resulting from his employment at the University.

At Stanford Holodniy undertook to develop an improved method for quantifying HIV levels in patient blood samples, using PCR. Because Holodniy was largely unfamiliar with PCR, his supervisor arranged for him to conduct research at Cetus. As a condition of gaining access to Cetus, Holodniy signed a Visitor's Confidentiality

Agreement (VCA). That agreement stated that Holodniy "will assign and do[es] hereby assign" to Cetus his "right, title and interest in each of the ideas, inventions and improvements" made "as a consequence of [his] access" to Cetus.

For the next nine months, Holodniy conducted research at Cetus. Working with Cetus employees, Holodniy devised a PCR-based procedure for calculating the amount of HIV in a patient's blood. That technique allowed doctors to determine whether a patient was benefiting from HIV therapy.

Holodniy then returned to Stanford where he and other University employees tested the HIV measurement technique. Over the next few years, Stanford obtained written assignments of rights from the Stanford employees involved in refinement of the technique, including Holodniy, and filed several patent applications related to the procedure. Stanford secured three patents to the HIV measurement process.

In 1991, Roche Molecular Systems, a company that specializes in diagnostic blood screening, acquired Cetus's PCR-related assets, including all rights Cetus had obtained through agreements like the VCA signed by Holodniy. After conducting clinical trials on the HIV quantification method developed at Cetus, Roche commercialized the procedure. Today, Roche's HIV test "kits are used in hospitals and AIDS clinics worldwide."

In 1980, Congress passed the Bayh-Dole Act to "promote the utilization of inventions arising from federally supported research," "promote collaboration between commercial concerns and nonprofit organizations," and "ensure that the Government obtains sufficient rights in federally supported inventions." 35 U.S.C. § 200. To achieve these aims, the Act allocates rights in federally funded "subject invention[s]" between the Federal Government and federal contractors ("any person, small business firm, or nonprofit organization that is a party to a funding agreement"). §§ 201(e), (c), 202(a). The Act defines "subject invention" as "any invention of the contractor conceived or first actually reduced to practice in the performance of work under a funding agreement." § 201(e).

The Bayh-Dole Act provides that contractors may "elect to retain title to any subject invention." § 202(a). To be able to retain title, a contractor must fulfill a number of obligations imposed by the statute. The contractor must "disclose each subject invention to the [relevant] Federal agency within a reasonable time"; it must "make a written election within two years after disclosure" stating that the contractor opts to retain title to the invention; and the contractor must "file a patent application prior to any statutory bar date." §§ 202(c)(1)–(3). The "Federal Government may receive title" to a subject invention if a contractor fails to comply with any of these obligations. Ibid.

The Government has several rights in federally funded subject inventions under the Bayh-Dole Act. The agency that granted the federal funds receives from the contractor "a nonexclusive, nontransferable, irrevocable, paid-up license to practice . . . [the] subject invention." § 202(c)(4). The agency also possesses "[m]arch-in rights," which permit the agency to grant a license to a responsible third party under certain circumstances, such as when the contractor fails to take "effective steps to achieve practical application" of the invention. § 203. The Act further provides that when the contractor does not elect to retain title to a subject invention, the Government "may consider and after consultation with the contractor grant requests for retention of rights by the inventor." § 202(d).

Some of Stanford's research related to the HIV measurement technique was funded by the National Institutes of Health (NIH), thereby subjecting the invention to the Bayh-Dole Act. Accordingly, Stanford disclosed the invention, conferred on the Government a nonexclusive, nontransferable, paid-up license to use the patented procedure, and formally notified NIH that it elected to retain title to the invention.

In 2005, the Board of Trustees of Stanford University filed suit against Roche Molecular Systems, Inc., Roche Diagnostics Corporation, and Roche Diagnostics Operations, Inc. (collectively Roche), contending that Roche's HIV test kits infringed Stanford's patents. As relevant here, Roche responded by asserting that it was a co-owner of the HIV quantification procedure, based on Holodniy's assignment of his rights in the Visitor's Confidentiality Agreement. As a result, Roche argued, Stanford lacked standing to sue it for patent infringement. Stanford claimed that Holodniy had no rights to assign because the University's HIV research was federally funded, giving the school superior rights in the invention under the Bayh-Dole Act.

The District Court held that the "VCA effectively assigned any rights that Holodniy had in the patented invention to Cetus," and thus to Roche. But because of the operation of the Bayh-Dole Act, "Holodniy had no interest to assign." The court concluded that the Bayh-Dole Act "provides that the individual inventor may obtain title" to a federally funded invention "only after the government and the contracting party have declined to do so."

The Court of Appeals for the Federal Circuit disagreed. First, the court concluded that Holodniy's initial agreement with Stanford in the Copyright and Patent Agreement constituted a mere promise to assign rights in the future, unlike Holodniy's agreement with Cetus in the Visitor's Confidentiality Agreement, which itself assigned Holodniy's rights in the invention to Cetus. Therefore, as a matter of contract law, Cetus obtained Holodniy's rights in the HIV quantification technique through the VCA. Next, the court explained that the Bayh-Dole Act "does not automatically void ab initio the inventors' rights in government-funded inventions" and that the "statutory scheme did not automatically void the patent rights that Cetus received from Holodniy." The court held that "Roche possesse[d] an ownership interest in the patents-in-suit" that was not extinguished by the Bayh-Dole Act, "depriv[ing] Stanford of standing." The Court of Appeals then remanded the case with instructions to dismiss Stanford's infringement claim.

We granted certiorari.

Congress has the authority "[t]o promote the Progress of Science and useful Arts, by securing . . . to Authors and Inventors the exclusive Right to their respective Writings and Discoveries." U.S. Const. Art. I, § 8, cl. 8. The first Congress put that power to use by enacting the Patent Act of 1790. That Act provided "[t]hat upon the petition of any person or persons . . . setting forth, that he, she, or they, hath or have invented or discovered" an invention, a patent could be granted to "such petitioner or petitioners" or "their heirs, administrators or assigns." Act of Apr. 10, 1790, § 1, 1 Stat. 109–110. Under that law, the first patent was granted in 1790 to Samuel Hopkins, who had devised an improved method for making potash, America's first industrial chemical. U.S. Patent No. 1 (issued July 31, 1790).

Although much in intellectual property law has changed in the 220 years since the first Patent Act, the basic idea that inventors have the right to patent their inventions has not. Under the law in its current form, "[w]hoever invents or discovers any new and useful process, machine, manufacture, or composition of matter . . . may obtain a patent therefor." 35 U.S.C. § 101. The inventor must attest that "he believes himself to be the original and first inventor of the [invention] for which he solicits a patent." § 115. In most cases, a patent may be issued only to an applying inventor, or — because an inventor's interest in his invention is "assignable in law by an instrument in writing" — an inventor's assignee. §§ 151, 152, 261.

Our precedents confirm the general rule that rights in an invention belong to the inventor. See, e.g., *Gayler v. Wilder*, 51 U.S. (10 How. 477), 493, 13 L. Ed. 504 (1851) ("the discoverer of a new and useful improvement is vested by law with an inchoate right to its exclusive use, which he may perfect and make absolute by proceeding in the manner which the law requires"); *Solomons v. United States*, 137 U.S. 342, 346, 11 S. Ct. 88, 34 L. Ed. 667, 26 Ct. Cl. 620 (1890) ("whatever invention [an inventor] may thus conceive and perfect is his individual property"); *United States v. Dubilier Condenser Corp.*, 289 U.S. 178, 188, 53 S. Ct. 554, 77 L. Ed. 1114 (1933) (an inventor owns "the product of [his] original thought"). The treatises are to the same effect. See, e.g., 8 Chisum on Patents § 22.01, p. 22-2 (2011) ("The presumptive owner of the property right in a patentable invention is the single human inventor").

It is equally well established that an inventor can assign his rights in an invention to a third party. See *Dubilier Condenser Corp.*, supra, at 187, 53 S. Ct. 554 ("A patent is property and title to it can pass only by assignment"); 8 Chisum on Patents, supra, § 22.01, at 22-2 ("The inventor . . . [may] transfer ownership interests by written assignment to anyone"). Thus, although others may acquire an interest in an invention, any such interest — as a general rule — must trace back to the inventor.

In accordance with these principles, we have recognized that unless there is an agreement to the contrary, an employer does not have rights in an invention "which is the original conception of the employee alone." *Dubilier Condenser Corp.*, 289 U.S., at 189, 53 S. Ct. 554. Such an invention "remains the property of him who conceived it." *Ibid.* In most circumstances, an inventor must expressly grant his rights in an invention to his employer if the employer is to obtain those rights. See *id.*, at 187, 53 S. Ct. 554 ("The respective rights and obligations of employer and employee, touching an invention conceived by the latter, spring from the contract of employment").

. . . .

The Bayh-Dole Act's provision stating that contractors may "elect to retain title" confirms that the Act does not vest title. 35 U.S.C. §202(a) (emphasis added). Stanford reaches the opposite conclusion, but only because it reads "retain" to mean "acquire" and "receive." Brief for Petitioner 36 (internal quotation marks omitted). That is certainly not the common meaning of "retain." "[R]etain" means "to hold or continue to hold in possession or use." Webster's Third, supra, at 1938; see Webster's New Collegiate Dictionary 980 (1980) ("to keep in possession or use"); American Heritage Dictionary 1109 (1969) ("[t]o keep or hold in one's possession"). You cannot retain something unless you already have it. . . . The Bayh-Dole Act does not confer title to federally funded inventions on contractors or authorize contractors to unilaterally take title to those inventions; it simply assures contractors that they may keep title to whatever it is they already have. Such a provision makes sense in a statute specifying the respective rights and responsibilities of federal contractors and the Government.

The Bayh-Dole Act states that it "take[s] precedence over any other Act which would require a disposition of rights in subject inventions . . . that is inconsistent with" the Act. 35 U.S.C. §210(a). The United States as amicus curiae argues that this provision operates to displace the basic principle, codified in the Patent Act, that an inventor owns the rights to his invention. But because the Bayh-Dole Act, including §210(a), applies only to "subject inventions"—"inventions of the contractor"—it does not displace an inventor's antecedent title to his invention. Only when an invention belongs to the contractor does the Bayh-Dole Act come into play. The Act's disposition of rights—like much of the rest of the Bayh-Dole Act—serves to clarify the order of priority of rights between the Federal Government and a federal contractor in a federally funded invention that already belongs to the contractor. Nothing more.

The isolated provisions of the Bayh-Dole Act dealing with inventors' rights in subject inventions are consistent with our construction of the Act. Under the Act, a federal agency may "grant requests for retention of rights by the inventor . . . [i]f a contractor does not elect to retain title to a subject invention." §202(d). If an employee inventor never had title to his invention because title vested in the contractor by operation of law—as Stanford submits—it would be odd to allow the Government to grant "requests for retention of rights by the inventor." By using the word "retention," §202(d) assumes that the inventor had rights in the subject invention at some point, undermining the notion that the Act automatically vests title to federally funded inventions in federal contractors.

The limited scope of the Act's procedural protections also bolsters our conclusion. The Bayh-Dole Act expressly confers on contractors the right to challenge a Government-imposed impediment to retaining title to a subject invention. §202(b)(4). As Roche correctly notes, however, "the Act contains not a single procedural protection for third parties that have neither sought nor received federal funds," such as cooperating private research institutions. Nor does the Bayh-Dole Act allow inventors employed by federal contractors to contest their employer's claim to a subject invention. The Act, for example, does not expressly permit an interested third party or an inventor to challenge a claim that a particular invention was supported by federal funding. In a world in which there is frequent collaboration between private entities, inventors, and federal contractors, that absence would be deeply troubling. But the lack of procedures protecting inventor and third-party rights makes perfect sense if the Act applies only when a federal contractor has already acquired title to an inventor's interest. In that case, there is no need to protect inventor or third-party rights, because the only rights at issue are those of the contractor and the Government.

The Bayh-Dole Act applies to subject inventions "conceived or first actually reduced to practice in the performance of work" "funded in whole or in part by the Federal Government." 35 U.S.C. §§ 201(e), 201(b) (emphasis added). Under Stanford's construction of the Act, title to one of its employee's inventions could vest in the University even if the invention was conceived before the inventor became a University employee, so long as the invention's reduction to practice was supported by federal funding. What is more, Stanford's reading suggests that the school would obtain title to one of its employee's inventions even if only one dollar of federal funding was applied toward the invention's conception or reduction to practice.

It would be noteworthy enough for Congress to supplant one of the fundamental precepts of patent law and deprive inventors of rights in their own inventions. To do so under such unusual terms would be truly surprising. We are confident that if Congress had intended such a sea change in intellectual property rights it would have said so clearly—not obliquely through an ambiguous definition of "subject invention" and an idiosyncratic use of the word "retain." . . .

Though unnecessary to our conclusion, it is worth noting that our construction of the Bayh-Dole Act is reflected in the common practice among parties operating under the Act. Contractors generally institute policies to obtain assignments from their employees. Agencies that grant funds to federal contractors typically expect those contractors to obtain assignments. So it is with NIH, the agency that granted the federal funds at issue in this case. In guidance documents made available to contractors, NIH has made clear that "[b]y law, an inventor has initial ownership of an invention" and that contractors should therefore "have in place employee agreements requiring an inventor to 'assign' or give ownership of an invention to the organization upon acceptance of Federal funds." NIH Policies, Procedures, and Forms, A "20–20" View of Invention Reporting to the National Institutes of Health (Sept. 22, 1995). Such guidance would be unnecessary if Stanford's reading of the statute were correct.

Stanford contends that reading the Bayh-Dole Act as not vesting title to federally funded inventions in federal contractors "fundamentally undermin[es]" the Act's framework and severely threatens its continued "successful application." We do not agree. As just noted, universities typically enter into agreements with their employees requiring the assignment to the university of rights in inventions. With an effective assignment, those inventions—if federally funded—become "subject inventions" under the Act, and the statute as a practical matter works pretty much the way Stanford says it should. The only significant difference is that it does so without violence to the basic principle of patent law that inventors own their inventions.

Notes & Questions

1. The Bayh-Dole Act provided a major impetus for university-industry collaboration as the excerpted cases illustrate. What issues do you think a potential investor in the development of a university-generated technology will have in light of the Bayh-Dole Act? How does the Bayh-Dole Act affect the commercial potential of a technology that is subject to it?

2. The *Trinity Industries* case highlights some of the disclosure obligations of universities as they seek patents for inventions derived from federally funded research. What purposes do these required disclosures serve? What should be the consequences of a failure to make the required disclosures?

3. The *Stanford* decision is the only pronouncement by the Supreme Court on the Bayh-Dole Act since its passage in 1980. Notice how much the Court relies upon its precedents on employee ownership of inventions. Many of these cases are discussed in detail in Chapter 4. Are these precedents relevant to the university context? The Court may be relying on these precedents from the non-university context to provide predictability to for-profit entities that collaborate with universities or its employees. Should there be separate ownership rules for universities? Or are uniform ownership rules more appropriate? In considering these questions, keep in mind that universities are organized very differently from for-profit corporations and have a different mission.

4. Justice Breyer authored a dissent in the *Stanford* case, joined by Justice Ginsburg, which advocated a remand of the case for further argument before the Federal Circuit. The dissent pointed to open questions about university assignment practices and about the impacts of Federal Circuit precedents on the interpretation of patent assignments. Justice Sotomayor authored a concurrence, which also pointed to open issues about Federal Circuit jurisprudence on patent assignments. But since Stanford did not raise these issues in its petition for certiorari, Justice Sotomayor concluded that the Court need not address these open issues. Her concurrence does express skepticism about the Federal Circuit's decision in *FilmTec Corp. v. Allied Signal, Inc.*, 939 F.2d 1568 (Fed. Cir. 1991) (establishing principles for interpretation of patent ownership changes through assignments). At least one party has tried unsuccessfully to pursue the questions raised in Justice Breyer's dissent and to challenge the continued viability of the *FilmTec* principles. *See Shukh v. Seagate Tech., LLC*, 2011 U.S. Dist. LEXIS 120219, 2011 WL 4947608, at *2 (D. Minn. Oct. 18, 2011).

5. In light of the points mentioned in note (4) above, look closely at how the Federal Circuit interpreted the assignments at issue in the *Stanford* case. The result rests on one word: "hereby." Does the Federal Circuit overemphasize the formal language of the assignments? The Federal Circuit's approach may reflect the lack of statutory

guidance on the issue of priority. Section 261 of the Patent Act provides a rule of priority for recorded assignments: "An assignment, grant or conveyance shall be void as against any subsequent purchaser or mortgagee for a valuable consideration, without notice, unless it is recorded in the Patent and Trademark Office within three months from its date or prior to the date of such subsequent purchase or mortgage." Unfortunately, there is no requirement that assignments or grants be recorded, except for interests in patents held by federal governmental entities. See 37 C.F.R. 3.11(b) (2012), issued initially as Exec. Order No. 9424, 9 Fed. Reg. 1959 (Feb. 18, 1944). The Federal Trade Commission has recommended a mandatory recordation requirement for patent grants in order to facilitate public notice regarding the ownership of patents. *See* FTC: The Evolving IP Marketplace: Aligning Patent Notice and Remedies with Competition 131 (2011), available at: http://www.ftc.gov/sites/default/files /documents/reports/evolving-ip-marketplace-aligning-patent-notice-and-remedies -competition-report-federal-trade/110307patentreport.pdf (accessed 12/1/2017). Even with recording, there remain open questions about how to interpret an assignment as the Federal Circuit decision in the *Stanford* case demonstrates.

6. The Bayh-Dole Act applies only to patented inventions. Universities have to manage other types of intellectual property as well. The *University of Colorado* case in the previous subsection illustrates this point in its discussion of copyrights. Should Congress expand Bayh-Dole to include other types of intellectual property? Arguably, the Supreme Court's decision in *Stanford* supports the view that, with respect to ownership, the rules of patent law are the same for all entities. Perhaps the same view is true for other types of intellectual property absent a clear statement from Congress providing for special rules in the university context.

7. Recall Wendy Schacht's study of the Bayh-Dole Act excerpted in the previous subsection. She stated that one goal of the Act was to vest title in the contractor. Is the decision in *Stanford* consistent with her statement? In tension here are the intended goals of Congress and the language of the statute. Was too much riding on the word "retain" in the Act?

8. Do university patents pay off? Based on his research concerning university inventors in the fields of computer science and electrical engineering, Professor Brian J. Love says no. Professor Love finds that university patent programs collectively earn a negative rate of return, with an overall loss of three percent or more. Furthermore, Professor Love concludes that patent rights are not key motivators for university researchers and patent programs may reduce the quantity and quality of research in high-tech fields. According to Professor Love, university patent programs are of modest benefit to entrepreneurial professors and may hinder their efforts to obtain consulting arrangements with companies interested in sponsoring research. *See* Brian J. Love, *Do University Patents Pay Off?: Evidence from a Survey of University Inventors in Computer Science and Electrical Engineering*, 16 YALE J. L. & TECH. 285 (2014). In contrast, a June 2017 study commissioned by the Biotechnology Innovation Association and AUTM concluded that over 20 years academic licensors contributed (1) $320 billion to $1.33 trillion to industry output; (2) $148 billion to $591

billion in gross domestic product; and (3) 1.268 million to 4.272 million person years of employment. *See* Lori Pressman et al., *The Economic Contribution of University/ Nonprofit Inventions in the United States 1996–2015*, available at: http://www.autm .net/AUTMMain/media/Partner-Events/Documents/Economic-_Contribution _University-Nonprofit_Inventions_US_1996-2015_BIO_AUTM.pdf   (accessed 12/1/2017).

As you discuss these materials, consider some of the reasons for negative impacts of university patents. Are they due to poor implementation of particular university efforts to commercialize patents, a general disconnect between the goals of academia and the pursuit of commercial goals in business enterprises, or a poorly designed patent system?

9. Despite some continuing questions about the effects of university patenting on research and researchers, many universities are actively pursuing the development of start-ups to commercialize university-originated technologies. For example, in 2014, the University of California announced plans for a $250 million venture-capital fund to commercialize university research. *See* Erica E. Phillips, *University of California Plans Venture-Capital Fund for Campus Startups*, available at: http://www.wsj .com/articles/university-of-california-plans-fund-for-campus-start-ups-1410816743 (accessed 12/1/2017). Intellectual Ventures — a leading and sometimes controversial private specialist in commercializing and licensing patented technologies — has also been actively collaborating with universities to aid in commercializing university technologies. *See* Heidi Ledford, *Universities Struggle to Make Patents Pay*, available at: http://www.nature.com/news/universities-struggle-to-make-patents-pay-1.13811 (accessed 12/1/2017).

10. There are undoubtedly many success stories involving university start-ups and spin-offs, as Silicon Valley alone demonstrates. But what may be fueling university interest in patenting is a spate of high profile patent law suits brought by universities. In 2012, Carnegie Mellon University won a $1.17 billion verdict against Marvell Semiconductor. The verdict was enhanced by thirty-one percent before appeal. *See* Jonathan Stempel, *Marvell Patent Verdict Grows to $1.54 Billion*, REUTERS, Apr. 1, 2014, http://www.reuters.com/article/2014/04/01/marvell-carnegiemellon-lawsuit -idUSL4N0MT37L20140401 (accessed 12/1/2017) (noting that "the award is 31 percent more than the $1.17 billion previously awarded by a jury"). Some of the country's major research universities — including state universities — are highly active patent litigants. To get a sense of the number of patent law suits brought by universities, consider the following examples of cases brought in a ten-year period by patent holders associated with just two major research universities. These cases were initiated by the Wisconsin Alumni Research Foundation (WARF), holder of intellectual property interests generated by research at the University of Wisconsin, and the Board of Regents of the University of Texas System, owner of intellectual property interests generated by researchers at the University of Texas. WARF sued Creative Technology in 2002, Sony and Toshiba in 2003, and six more high-tech companies over the next five years. *See* WARF v. Intel Corp., 656 F. Supp. 2d 898 (W.D. Wis. 2009); WARF

v. Adv. Micro Dev., Inc., No. 3:06-cv-00726 (W.D. Wis. filed Dec. 12, 2006); WARF v. Cypress Semiconductor Corp., No. 3:05-cv-00336 (W.D. Wis. filed June 7, 2005); WARF v. Int'l Bus. Mach. Corp., No. 3:04-cv-00867 (W.D. Wis. filed Nov. 17, 2004); WARF v. Infineon Tech. AG, No. 3:04-cv-00394 (W.D. Wis. filed June 21, 2004); WARF v. Sony Corp., No. 3:03-cv-00595 (W.D. Wis. filed Oct. 20, 2003); WARF v. Creative Tech. Ltd., No. 3:02-cv-00570 (W.D. Wis. filed Oct. 15, 2002). The Texas Board of Regents filed three cases in 2005 claiming infringement by fifty-five high-tech companies. *See* Bd. Regents, Univ. of Tex. Sys. v. Mitsubishi Elec., No. 1:05-cv-00333 (W.D. Tex. filed May 6, 2005); Bd. Regents, Univ. of Tex. Sys. v. Alcatel, No. 1:05-cv-00198 (W.D. Tex. filed Mar. 22, 2005); Bd. Regents, Univ. of Tex. Sys. v. BenQ Am. Corp., No. 1:05-cv-00181 (W.D. Tex. filed Mar. 11, 2005).

B. Transacting with State and Federal Governments

Xechem Intern., Inc. v. Univ. of Tex. M.D. Anderson Cancer Center

United States Court of Appeals for the Federal Circuit

382 F.3d 1324 (Fed. Cir. 2004)

PAULINE NEWMAN, CIRCUIT JUDGE

Xechem International, Inc., a biopharmaceutical company, brought suit against the University of Texas M.D. Anderson Cancer Center and the Board of Regents of the University of Texas System (collectively "the University") in the United States District Court, raising several federal and state counts arising from a collaborative project between Xechem and the University. In response to the complaint the University asserted its Eleventh Amendment and state immunity from suit, and the United States District Court for the Southern District of Texas granted the University's motion to dismiss on the pleadings. . . . The only issue on appeal is whether the University is subject to suit in federal court to obtain correction of the inventorship of United States Patents No. 5,877,205 and 6,107,333, the patents flowing from the project.

We affirm the dismissal, for Supreme Court precedent controls the arguments raised by Xechem with respect to waiver or abrogation of the University's Eleventh Amendment immunity.

BACKGROUND

The basic facts are generally undisputed: Xechem and the University in 1995 entered into a Sponsored Laboratory Study Agreement, with financial and technical support by Xechem, for the purpose of developing a pharmaceutical formulation that would enhance the solubility and thereby the effectiveness of the cancer drug paclitaxel. The persons principally involved in the project were Dr. Ramesh C. Pandey, president and CEO of Xechem; Dr. Luben K. Yankov, a scientist employed by Xechem; and Dr. Borje S. Andersson and Dr. Elias Anaissie, scientists employed by the University.

The complaint states that a successful formulation was developed, and that Xechem prepared a patent application naming Dr. Pandey of Xechem and Dr. Andersson of the University as joint inventors, and in early 1996 sent the draft application to the University. The University objected to the designation of inventorship, and on June 28, 1996 the University filed a patent application in the United States Patent and Trademark Office, naming Dr. Andersson as sole inventor.

. . . .

On August 18, 1997 Xechem and the University entered into a Patent and Technology License Agreement whereby Xechem received the exclusive worldwide license to manufacture and market these paclitaxel formulations, and Xechem agreed to pay certain continuing sums and a royalty. Xechem also agreed to pay the costs of obtaining the patents in the United States and foreign countries. The University's patent application issued as the '205 patent on March 2, 1999, and a divisional application, also naming Dr. Andersson as sole inventor, issued as the '333 patent on August 22, 2000. Both patents were assigned by Dr. Andersson to the University.

On February 15, 2000 Xechem was notified that the University considered the License Agreement to have terminated automatically no later than December 31, 1998, due to Xechem's alleged insolvency, and that any use of this technology by Xechem was deemed to be patent infringement. Xechem then filed suit in federal court, presenting several counts sounding in tort and contract and also seeking correction of inventorship and a declaration of non-infringement. Xechem stated that Dr. Pandey made a mistake when he acquiesced in the naming of Dr. Andersson as sole inventor, and asked the court to determine the correct inventorship. Apparently upon the University's claim of sovereign immunity from state as well as federal action, the state law tort and contract counts were withdrawn by Xechem. This appeal relates only to the dismissal, on Eleventh Amendment grounds, of the inventorship correction claim.

DISCUSSION

The University of Texas is deemed to be an arm of the State of Texas, and Xechem does not dispute that the University is properly accorded Eleventh Amendment immunity.

The Supreme Court has addressed Eleventh Amendment immunity as it pertains to violation of federal patent and trademark laws. In *Florida Prepaid Postsecondary Education Expense Board v. College Savings Bank*, 527 U.S. 627, 119 S. Ct. 2199, 144 L. Ed. 2d 575 (1999) and *College Savings Bank v. Florida Prepaid Postsecondary Education Expense Board*, 527 U.S. 666, 119 S. Ct. 2219, 144 L. Ed. 2d 605 (1999), the Court invalidated the legislative abrogation of state immunity from suit under these laws. In *Florida Prepaid*, the Court ruled that the Eleventh Amendment was violated by the Patent and Plant Variety Protection Remedy Clarification Act of 1992). . . . The Court held that Eleventh Amendment immunity may be abrogated "only where the State provides no remedy, or only inadequate remedies, to injured patent owners for its infringement of their patent could a deprivation of property without due process result," thereby invoking the Fourteenth Amendment. The Court also referred to lack of a "pattern of patent infringement by the States," in suggesting that legislative remedy had not been shown to be necessary.

. . . .

Xechem argues that the University waived its Eleventh Amendment immunity when it entered into this collaborative research agreement, and further waived its immunity by contracting with Xechem in the License Agreement for purposes of commercial gain. Xechem argues that by entering into these contractual and commercial arrangements the University waived objection to federal court jurisdiction to secure constitutionally protected property rights, and for issues that can be decided only in federal court under preemptive federal statutes.

. . . .

In [*Parden v. Terminal Railway of the Alabama State Docks Department*, 377 U.S. 184, 84 S. Ct. 1207, 12 L. Ed. 2d 233 (1964)] the Court had relied on the Commerce Clause to hold that when a state voluntarily enters into federally regulated activity — in *Parden*, operating a railroad — the state is deemed to have consented to federal jurisdiction arising from that activity, in that case an action under the Federal Employers' Liability Act. In overruling *Parden*'s constructive waiver, the Court stressed in *College Savings* that a state's waiver of Eleventh Amendment rights cannot be imposed or implied based on a state's entry into commerce, but must be founded on a "clear declaration" by the state of its intent to submit to federal jurisdiction. Such a declaration was not made by the University in entering into its various relationships and contracts with Xechem.

Xechem also argues that the University constructively consented to federal jurisdiction by causing its employee Dr. Andersson to apply for United States patents. Xechem argues that the University made a clear and voluntary waiver of immunity when it entered the Patent and Trademark Office and sought its legal benefits, and that the University cannot both obtain patents and "hide behind the Constitution."

. . . .

Xechem also argues that a state's invocation of the authority of the PTO to grant patents is analogous to the state's invocation of federal authority to enforce its patent rights at state initiative, the latter clearly serving to waive Eleventh Amendment immunity. Such analogy does not withstand scrutiny, for waiver must be clear, explicit, and voluntary, and cannot be imposed on a state that has not voluntarily entered federal jurisdiction.

Thus the argument must be rejected that a state's entry into the patent system is a constructive waiver of immunity for actions in federal court against the state under the patent law.

Xechem also argues that the grant of a patent is a "gift or gratuity" by the government, whereby acceptance of the grant is a constructive waiver of immunity. The Court confirmed in *Petty* and again in *Dole* that Congress can condition receipt of federal funds on a commensurate waiver of state immunity. However, in *College Savings* the Court explained that such conditions on federal disbursements are "simply not analogous to *Parden*-style conditions attached to a State's decision to engage in otherwise lawful commercial activity."

. . . .

Patent activity is commercial activity, not governmental beneficence. The holdings of [*Seminole Tribe of Florida v. Florida*, 517 U.S. 44, 116 S. Ct. 1114, 134 L. Ed. 2d 252 (1996)], and the overruling of *Parden*, have foreclosed the broad ruling that by obtaining patents the state constructively waived its Eleventh Amendment immunity as to any federal proceeding involving those patents.

. . . .

AFFIRMED.

NEWMAN, Circuit Judge, additional views.

I write separately to state my concern lest the caveats and safeguards recognized by the Supreme Court in its rulings in *Florida Prepaid* and *College Savings* become submerged in generalizations of absolute state immunity. The Court observed in *Florida Prepaid* that if no state court remedy were available for patent infringement, such failure of recourse could raise the due process concerns of the Fourteenth Amendment. Although Xechem is here seeking judicial, not legislative, relief, its due process claims on the ground that there is no alternative remedy have not been fully explored.

In *Florida Prepaid*, the Court, discussing abrogation of Eleventh Amendment immunity, stated that "only where the State provides no remedy, or only inadequate remedies, to injured patent owners for its infringement of their patent could a deprivation of property without due process result." . . . Throughout the evolution of Eleventh Amendment jurisprudence the Court has stressed the rigor of the restraint imposed by the Fourteenth Amendment on the federal government as well as on the states. Thus the Court found in *Florida Prepaid* that patent infringement by states did not appear to be a sufficiently prevalent national problem to warrant § 5 abrogation. And in *College Savings* the Court held that unfair competition by a state based on false advertising did not raise a Fourteenth Amendment property issue; the Court observed that general business interests are not property rights, and held that while trademarks are constitutionally protected property, false advertising has no relation to the right to exclude and does not raise a constitutional issue. The Court recognized, however, that "the assets of a business . . . unquestionably are property, and any state taking of these assets is unquestionably a 'deprivation' under the Fourteenth Amendment."

Xechem has asserted that in this case inventorship controls ownership and the right to practice the patented invention—fundamentals of patent property. Xechem's claim on its face raises issues of property and due process. The Court explained in *Florida Prepaid* that "[i]n procedural due process claims, the deprivation by state action of a constitutionally protected interest . . . is not in itself unconstitutional; what is unconstitutional is the deprivation of such an interest without due process of law." However, the Court in *Florida Prepaid* required a showing—more than an allegation—of the unavailability of adequate remedy in state court. Although Xechem argues that only federal courts can order a change of inventorship, precedent has not dealt with whether state courts are precluded from resolving issues of ownership of patent property when ownership is based on inventorship.

In *Florida Prepaid* the Court noted that patent infringement by the state might be remedied in state court on the traditional state law grounds of taking of property or conversion, observing that a factor in the due process provision of the Fourteenth Amendment is whether any remedy is otherwise available. However, precedent establishes no ready rule as to when the nature of the wrong and remedy warrant recourse to the Fourteenth Amendment. On the record before us, and the premises of Rule 12(b)(6), the question of alternative remedy was not explored. We are told that various state law counts were withdrawn from the complaint in the district court; however, the potential presence of other issues does not avoid this dismissal on the pleadings. These questions are not resolved by today's decision. . . .

The circumstances of this case illustrate that when a state is charged with contravention of federal law in a way that directly affects private property, and if no remedy is indeed available within the state's tribunals—whether by the state's invocation of immunity or by federal preemption of the cause of action—there can arise an affront to the fundamentals of due process. Respect for the principles of federalism does not automatically immunize the state from due process considerations. The Court in *Florida Prepaid* kept this door ajar. I write to the same purpose, for there is an increasing urgency, as the states enter the private competitive arena governed by the laws of intellectual property, to establish fair relationships and just recourse.

Notes & Questions

1. The *University of Texas* case illustrates how sovereign immunity may affect university-industry-government collaborations. As Digital Ignition works with a public university or a related state entity in developing new technologies, the company needs to be aware of the possibility of potential uses of its intellectual property by the university, which would raise a sovereign immunity defense. Consider how this defense would arise in collaborations with university professors and researchers.

2. Why might Digital Ignition be concerned about any agreements between Dr. See and a university in connection with university personnel that Dr. See has spoken to or collaborated with? Does the Federal Circuit's decision in *Madey* alleviate any of these concerns? Do you think the narrow view of experimental use adopted by the Federal Circuit helps or hurts private industry? Do you think the Federal Circuit's decision reduces or increases incentives for university-industry collaboration? Does the court's decision in *Fenn* aid or hinder university-industry collaboration? How would you address the concerns of Digital Ignition's executives regarding inventions that arose from university-industry collaborations in light of *Madey* and *Fenn*?

3. State sovereign immunity from suits for intellectual property infringement clearly affects the balance between private industry and state governments in the innovation process. Discuss the arguments for and against waiver in *The University of Texas* case. As a legal matter, which side has the better argument? Which side is more persuasive as a matter of social or business policy? How does sovereign immunity affect the discussion of university-industry collaborations as illustrated by *Madey* and *Fenn*? Notice that private universities do not have sovereign immunity. Does this absence of immunity for private universities alter in any way the dynamics of university-industry collaboration discussed in note (2) above?

C. Collaborative Research and Development Agreements (CRADAs)

Edmonds Institute v. Bruce Babbitt, Secretary of the Interior

United States District Court, District of Columbia

93 F. Supp. 2d 63 (D.D.C. 2000)

LAMBERTH, DISTRICT JUDGE.

This matter comes before the court on the parties' cross-motions for partial summary judgment. Plaintiffs, three environmental advocacy organizations and a frequent visitor to Yellowstone National Park ("Yellowstone" or "Park"), challenge as arbitrary and capricious the Department of the Interior's ("Interior") entry into a research agreement with a private biotechnology company for the "bioprospecting" of microbial organisms from geysers and other thermal features in Yellowstone. Upon consideration of the motions, the oppositions thereto, the relevant record, and the applicable law, the court GRANTS defendants' motion for summary judgment and DENIES plaintiffs' motion for summary judgment.

I. BACKGROUND

. . . .

A. The Yellowstone-Diversa CRADA

Yellowstone is the nation's oldest national park. To commemorate its 125th anniversary, defendants hosted a ceremony on August 17, 1997, which was attended by top environmental policymakers, including Vice President Al Gore, Secretary of the Interior Bruce Babbitt, National Park Service Director Robert Stanton, and Yellowstone Superintendent Mike Finley. At the ceremony, it was announced that the federal government had entered into a novel contract with San Diego-based Diversa Corporation, by which Diversa would obtain a nonexclusive right to "bioprospect"[1]

---

1. As this court has previously explained, bioprospecting refers to a relatively new method of natural resource utilization that targets microscopic resources, such as the genetic and biochemical information found in wild plants. *Edmonds Institute v. Babbitt*, 42 F. Supp. 2d 1, 5–6 (D.D.C. 1999).

microbial organisms in Yellowstone, in exchange for an agreement to share with Yellowstone a portion of any financial returns generated by commercial applications or products developed from these research materials.

This novel agreement, officially termed a Cooperative Research and Development Agreement ("CRADA"), was the first of its kind to involve a national park. The Statement of Work in the CRADA explains how Yellowstone and Diversa will cooperate in researching and cataloguing the Park's biological diversity, primarily in the Park's thermal features such as geysers, hot springs, fumaroles, and mud pots, as well as in Yellowstone's "alpine tundra ecosystems, subalpine forests; riparian habitats, sedge marshes, bogs, swamps, streams and lakes." Following an initial survey, sites will be "prioritized and systematically sampled by [Diversa] scientists," using techniques to be "jointly selected by YNP and [Diversa] to ensure that there is no significant impact to park resources or other appropriate park uses." Once raw samples have been extracted from the selected sites, nucleic acids will be isolated, purified and used to create a library of genetic information. The resulting gene libraries will be the starting point for the discovery and cloning of biocatalytic and bioactive compounds, which will be evaluated for potential commercial applications. These libraries of genetic information will also be available to Park scientists for their own research. The CRADA and Statement of Work explicitly state that all activity carried on under the agreement will be in accordance with applicable law, including Yellowstone's management policy. According, to conduct the research under the CRADA, Diversa applied for and was issued a Research Authorization/Collection Permit, which authorized the Collection of certain biological materials from Yellowstone. Since 1994, prior to its entry into the CRADA, Diversa, under its previous name Recombinant Biocatalysis, Inc., had already been conducting the same sort of sampling from Yellowstone, pursuant to permits issued in accordance with Park regulations. The main difference, however, is that prior to the CRADA, the company was under no obligation to share any of the economic or other benefits that might result from its research on Park resources.

Thus, perhaps the most notable feature of the CRADA is the consideration that Yellowstone stands to receive in exchange for access to its biodiversity. Defendants have disclosed that Diversa will make annual payments of around $20,000 to the defendants, as well as provide research equipment and other support for Yellowstone's use and benefit. More importantly, however, Diversa will pay royalties to Yellowstone on any future commercial use or product derived from the company's bioprospecting activities in the Park. Although the specifics are not public, Yellowstone has indicated that it will receive royalties of between.5% and 10% depending upon the nature of the raw material and the final product. By virtue of the CRADA, Yellowstone will share in any revenues generated by future beneficial applications or products developed from Diversa's research at Yellowstone.

Bioprospecting is an extension of the field of biotechnology, which uses biological resources like genes and enzymes to develop beneficial pharmaceutical and industrial products and applications. *Id.*

B. Bioprospecting in Yellowstone

Notwithstanding the novelty of the Yellowstone-Diversa CRADA itself, this agreement is not the first time that the National Park Service has permitted scientific research and collection of microbial specimens from Yellowstone's thermal features. To the contrary, the earliest research permit authorizing collection of microbial samples from Yellowstone was in 1898. Indeed, in recent years, the number of annual requests by researchers for access to Yellowstone has averaged 1,500, with some 250–300 research permits issued each year (between 40 and 50 of which are for microbial research projects). National Park Service regulations govern this permit system and ensure that research activities are consistent with the Yellowstone and Interior's overall goals.

Prior to the CRADA, Diversa or other researchers were free to remove any specimen within the purview of their permit and develop it as they wished. If such development led to commercial uses, the Park Service never saw any proceeds from the derivative products. Thus, recognizing that resources yielding potentially valuable properties were being removed from Yellowstone with no remuneration to Yellowstone or the American people, officials at Interior began to consider a resource management scheme, patterned on the successes of Costa Rica and other nations, which would use bioprospecting to provide funds and incentives for the conservation of biological diversity. To that end, the defendants opened negotiations in 1995 with the Diversa Corporation and other biotechnology companies to explore possible bioprospecting contracts. These potential agreements would be drafted as cooperative research and development agreements (CRADA) under the Federal Technology Transfer Act of 1986, which authorizes federal laboratories to enter into CRADAs with nonfederal entities to facilitate the sharing of research developed in conjunction with government scientists. By the fall of 1996, Diversa and the defendants had begun drafting a CRADA that would permit the collection of raw environmental materials from Yellowstone. The final version of the CRADA was signed by National Park Service Director Robert Stanton and Yellowstone Superintendent Mike Finley on May 4, 1998.

C. Procedural History

Plaintiff Edmonds Institute is a nonprofit public interest organization based in Edmonds, Washington. The group advocates the regulation of biotechnology and the maintenance and protection of biodiversity. Plaintiff Alliance for the Wild Rockies is a nonprofit organization committed to the preservation and protection of the native biodiversity of the Northern Rockies Region. Plaintiff International Center for Technology Assessment (CTA) is a Washington, D.C.-based nonprofit corporation focused on the environmental, economic, and ethical issues surrounding the biotechnology industry (including bioprospecting), particularly as it relates to the national parks. Finally, plaintiff Phil Knight is a resident of Bozeman, Montana who allegedly visits Yellowstone some twelve times a year to hike, photograph, and otherwise enjoy its aesthetic and recreational qualities.

Defendants, of course, are Secretary of the Interior Bruce Babbitt, sued in his official capacity, and Robert Stanton, Director of the National Park Service, also sued in his official capacity only.

In 1997, plaintiffs filed a petition requesting that the agency not enter into the Yellowstone-Diversa CRADA (or similar agreements) because the agency had failed to provide public notice of its proposed change in policy and had not undertaken the environmental impact assessment required by law. The defendants denied plaintiffs' request in January of 1998. On March 5, 1998, plaintiffs filed this action, alleging that the Yellowstone-Diversa CRADA violated the Federal Technology Transfer Act of 1986, 15 U.S.C. § 3701 et seq., the National Park Service Organic Act of 1916, 16 U.S.C. § 1 et seq., the Yellowstone National Park Organic Act, 16 U.S.C. § 21, et seq., the National Environmental Policy Act, 42 U.S.C. § 4321 et seq., and the so-called public trust doctrine, as well as the Administrative Procedure Act, 5 U.S.C. §§ 702, 706.

. . . .

II. DISCUSSION

. . . .

[T]he parties agree that no genuine issue of material fact exists and that the central dispute concerns whether defendants acted in accordance with the FTTA, the National Park Service Organic Act, the Yellowstone National Park Organic Act, and Park Service regulations by entering into the CRADA with Diversa.

Under the Administrative Procedure Act, courts must set aside agency action found to be "arbitrary, capricious, an abuse of discretion, or otherwise not in accordance with law." 5 U.S.C. § 706(2)(A). As the Supreme Court has instructed,

> the 'arbitrary and capricious standard' is 'highly deferential' and presumes the validity of agency action. If the court can discern a rational basis for the agency's decision, the decision must be affirmed. Similarly, the court must uphold the agency's construction of the statute unless it is unreasonable.

United Transp. Union v. Lewis, 711 F.2d 233, 252 (D.C. Cir. 1983) (citations omitted); see also *American Horse Protect. Ass'n v. Yeutter*, 917 F.2d 594, 595 (D.C. Cir. 1990).

. . . .

The validity of this CRADA under the FTTA turns upon whether Yellowstone falls within the meaning of "laboratory" as that term is defined in the statute. By its terms, the FTTA defines "laboratory" as

> a facility or group of facilities owned, leased, or otherwise used by a Federal agency, a substantial purpose of which is the performance of research, development, or engineering by employees of the Federal Government.

15 U.S.C. § 3710a(d)(2)(A).

Plaintiffs object to the application of the FTTA to the Yellowstone CRADA because they assert that the plain meaning of "laboratory" forecloses application of that term to the research facilities in Yellowstone. Specifically, plaintiffs argue that Yellowstone is not a "facility" because Yellowstone's organic statute describes the Park only as a "tract of land." 16 U.S.C. § 21.

While the court agrees that a national park does not immediately conjure the term "laboratory," the court finds that defendants have provided a reasoned basis for concluding that the broad, statutorily-assigned definition encompasses Yellowstone's extensive research facilities. As a preliminary matter, the court notes that because the statute has specifically defined laboratory to include facilities owned or otherwise used by a federal agency, plaintiffs "plain meaning" argument with respect to the term "laboratory" is misplaced. As noted above, where Congress has assigned a particular definition to a term, courts may not simply cast such definitions aside in favor of the term's "ordinary" meaning. Thus, the specific definition of laboratory provided in the statute governs the court's review.

Yellowstone's research facilities fall within the definition of laboratory under the FTTA as a "facility owned . . . or otherwise used by a Federal agency," a "substantial purpose of which is the performance of research." While the term "laboratory" is defined in the statute, "facility" is not. Thus, the court must look to the ordinary meaning of that word. "Facility" is broadly defined as "something (as a hospital, machinery, plumbing) that is built, constructed, installed or established to perform some particular function or *to serve or facilitate some particular end*". Webster's Third New International Dictionary 812 (1961) (emphasis added). The extensive array of research facilities at Yellowstone plainly satisfy this definition. To begin with, as defendants correctly note, the statute makes no requirement that the entire facility be used exclusively for research. To the contrary, the only statutory restriction is that a "substantial purpose" of the facility be for "the performance of research, development or engineering by employees of the Federal government." 15 U.S.C. § 3710a(d)(2)(A). Defendants have adequately demonstrated that a substantial purpose of the facilities at Yellowstone is scientific research. Specifically, Yellowstone employs approximately 43 individuals engaged in scientific activities. Many of these scientific researchers possess doctorates or other advanced degrees, and are members of leading scientific societies. And, to coordinate scientific research at the Park, Yellowstone has established the Yellowstone Center for Resources ("YCR"), which oversees all aspects of research by Park scientists, including research concerning the Park's abundant mammalian wildlife such as bison or wolf populations, as well as the vast array of microorganisms contained in Yellowstone's hot springs and thermal features. Moreover, the plethora of scientific and research structures and equipment at Yellowstone plainly fall within the FTTA definition. For instance, Yellowstone maintains "wet" and "dry" laboratories at Yellowstone headquarters that are approved and regulated by the Occupational Safety and Health Administration, in addition to other scientific research facilities throughout the Park. And, many of the research facilities at Yellowstone are equipped with standard laboratory equipment. . . . Yellowstone's research facilities also include geographic information systems ("GIS") and a remote sensing facility, which collects, records and analyzes environmental data from satellites and aircraft. Thus, in light of these extensive scientific research facilities, the court finds that Yellowstone falls within the meaning of "laboratory" under the FTTA.

Legislation enacted subsequent to the Yellowstone-Diversa CRADA also reinforces the conclusion that application of the FTTA to this CRADA is consistent with Congressional intent regarding cooperative scientific research agreements with units of the National Park System. Notably, in 1998, Congress enacted the National Parks Omnibus Management Act ("Parks Management Act"), 16 U.S.C. §§ 5901–6011, for the purpose of "enhanc[ing] management and protection of national park resources by providing clear legal authority and direction for the conduct of scientific study in the National Park System and to use information gathered for management purposes" and "to encourage others to use the National Park System for study to the benefit of park management as well as broader scientific value." 16 U.S.C. § 5931. To achieve this end, the statute specifically authorizes the Secretary of the Interior to "solicit, receive and consider requests from Federal or non-Federal public or private agencies, organizations, individuals, or other entities for the use of any unit of the National Park System for purposes of scientific study." *Id.* at § 5935(a). Moreover, the statute further empowers the Secretary to "enter into negotiations with the research community and private industry for equitable, efficient benefits-sharing arrangements." *Id.* at § 5935(d). Under these broad terms, the CRADA at issue here plainly constitutes an "equitable, efficient benefits-sharing arrangement" with a private entity for the purposes of scientific study. *Id.* Had Congress wished to foreclose units of the National Park System from entering into cooperative scientific research agreements with private industry in the wake of the Yellowstone-Diversa CRADA, its subsequent enactment displays a contrary intent. Instead, the far-reaching terms of the Parks Management Act reinforce the conclusion that the Yellowstone-Diversa CRADA is proper.

. . . .

Finally, the court finds that defendants properly determined that the CRADA was consistent with the governing statutes because it would produce direct, concrete benefits to the Park's conservation efforts by affording greater scientific understanding of Yellowstone's wildlife, as well as monetary support for Park programs. . . . Agreements like the Yellowstone-Diversa CRADA would allow the Park to share in revenues generated by beneficial developments, and thus, provide a valuable source of funding to support the Park Service's ongoing wildlife preservation, protection, and study initiatives. Equally critical to the Park's conservation efforts as adequate funding, improved scientific knowledge and understanding of Yellowstone's habitat generated by these types of joint research projects would be shared with the Park and used to support its efforts to preserve the environment.

. . . .

Plaintiffs aver that because patent law allows scientists to obtain intellectual property rights over natural organisms, the CRADA at issue in this case necessarily involves the prohibited sale of natural materials. But this view of the scope of patent law ignores relevant precedent, which instructs that a substance occurring in nature may not be patented in that form. Instead, to obtain patent rights, a researcher must bring to a naturally-occurring substance a contribution that is non-obvious, novel and demonstrably useful. *See* 35 U.S.C. §§ 101–103. Thus, in accord with these fundamental principles, the Park Service has interpreted its regulations only to allow researchers to study, not sell, Park resources. The CRADA, in turn, accords with the regulations because any "commercial use" flowing from such research is limited to applications or products generated from the scientific study of the resources, not the resources themselves. Accordingly, the court finds that defendants reasonably construed Park regulations and concluded that the CRADA was consistent with their requirements.

Notes & Questions

1. The *Edmonds Institute* case provides a nice illustration of how private entities partner with agencies in order to further commercial interests and agency agendas. The case illustrates the use of a Cooperative Research and Development Agreement, or CRADA, a common tool for public-private partnerships. Do you think the court is adequately protective of the public interest? At the end of its opinion, the court identifies the goals of patent law and concludes that the CRADA is consistent with these goals. Does the court articulate the goals of patent law, and intellectual property law, correctly? How does patent law protect and promote social values? Are those social values consistent with the conservation ideals of the National Park System?

2. Often, bioprospecting arises in the context of developing countries. These countries provide rich sources of natural resources for multinational companies seeking strong intellectual property protections, such as pharmaceuticals or agribusiness concerns. Companies transact with the governments of developing countries, or groups representing the interests of indigenous groups within developing countries, to enter into agreements similar to the CRADA at issue in the *Edmonds Institute* case. For case studies illustrating these sorts of cooperative arrangements, see Centre for the Management of Intellectual Property in Health Research and Development, et al., IP Handbook of Best Practices, http://www.iphandbook.org (accessed 12/1/2017).

Chapter 13

Intellectual Property Influences on Resource Allocations: Four Case Studies

Problem

Digital Ignition continues to try to improve its practices for developing new IP. It is seeking lessons from the notable successes of several other companies in developing new technologies and in gaining profitable returns from these new technologies through IP controls. You are an attorney in the inside legal department of Digital Ignition. The General Counsel of the company has asked you to work with senior managers of Digital Ignition in suggesting business practices focusing on IP that will aid the company in future technology development projects. In particular, company managers wish to consider how IP interests might better be used in selecting innovation targets, in making resource allocation decisions regarding innovation efforts, and in involving outside parties (particularly parties in universities and start-up companies) in working on technologies of potential interest to Digital Ignition.

The General Counsel has identified four notable technology development success stories that she would like you to critique as possible sources of generally applicable strategies that Digital Ignition might use in its efforts. These four success stories are summarized in four case studies (reproduced in this chapter) that you have been asked to analyze. You have been asked to provide the General Counsel with a short description of how IP interests (particularly patents) served as key management tools in the projects profiled in these case studies, how similar techniques might be used to advance Digital Ignition's business interests, and what the limitations of these techniques may be.

Focus of the Chapter

The following readings describe four case studies of companies and individuals that produced several of the most important technological advances of the past few decades. In each of these cases, the promise of IP interests and controls had key impacts on decisions about initiating and continuing the innovation projects. IP interests also were key considerations in the allocation of extensive resources to these projects. These case studies provide clear examples of the roles that IP interests can play in the commitment of resources to innovation projects amidst strong contention for alternative uses of the same resources.

Highly rivalrous contention for needed resources has created significant barriers to innovation in some high-tech fields. Two trends have increased concerns over resource allocations in innovation efforts. First, resource needs for many types of research are growing. In some technology areas, such as pharmaceutical drug development or genetics research, the resources needed to complete successful research projects—including researchers, supporting staff, equipment, and research facilities—are enormously expensive. The resources committed to even one project in these fields must be large if the project is to have a chance to succeed. Each commitment precludes the use of the same resources for other large projects or other purposes. Second, management processes for resource allocations are becoming more thorough and demanding, giving ever-increasing voice and consideration to resource commitments competing with the support of research. In these processes, business managers must often choose between backing research (with uncertain prospects for technical success and commercial profitability) and backing other profit-making activities like increased marketing efforts or manufacturing efficiency. Non-innovative projects may easily win out in these contentious processes unless the projected rewards for successful innovation are clear and large. Patents help to clarify and increase these rewards and to shift resources toward innovation projects.

Amidst competing demands for resources, patents and the product development and marketing exclusivity that patents imply encourage business managers to take long-term views of investments in innovation. Patents tend to give business managers confidence about their ability to control the commercialization of patented technologies during the life of the applicable patents. This allows business managers to plan for the development and marketing of related products over this full period. In this way, patents serve a function much like that of property controls in other contexts, allowing potential patent recipients (much like holders of property interests in a building about to be built) to invest resources in the development of a new technology with confidence that the patent holders will gain the primary commercial returns from the new technology under patent controls (much like the initial owner of a building will control its commercialization when the building is built).

The four case studies presented here describe successful technological development projects in four very different contexts. These include (in the order presented in this chapter):

1. Large company technology development to complement and extend existing product lines (Monsanto)

2. Large company technology development to explore the commercial potential of a new technology (Cetus)

3. University technology development through commercially targeted and funded research (University of Edinburgh/Biogen)

4. Start-up company technology development with additional large company product production and testing (Julio Palmaz/Johnson & Johnson)

As described in the readings, patents played key roles in all of these projects and technology development contexts, but in somewhat different ways and at different project stages. The common theme present in all of these case studies is that, in times of extreme resource needs, the promise of patent protections encouraged new resource commitments to these projects that were critical to their successful completion.

As you consider how patents promoted long-term planning for technology development and the investment of additional resources in the four projects discussed in this chapter, keep the following questions in mind:

a. What were the respective roles of the individual innovators and supporting business or university organizations in the development of the technologies discussed in these case studies?

b. How did patents influence the decision making of the individuals and organizational managers involved in these projects?

c. At what stages were resource allocations made in these projects and with what information and objectives?

d. What information gathering and management practices might have helped the companies and institutions involved in these case studies to have considered their resource allocations more effectively?

e. What information gathering and management practices might have helped these entities to have considered the implications of potential patent interests more effectively?

f. How were the efforts of multiple parties combined in the innovation efforts described in these case studies?

g. What roles did patents play in combining these efforts?

h. What are some of the relative advantages of internal technology development by a company like Digital Ignition versus relying on outside sources of new technologies such as technological development projects completed in partnerships with university researchers or acquisitions of rights to partially developed technologies from start-up companies?

i. How might patents play roles in these strategies for technological development through university partnerships and outside acquisitions?

j. What are the limitations of patents in carrying out technology development through university partnerships and outside acquisitions?

Readings
A. Approaching the Case Studies
1. The Projects Profiled

The projects profiled here all led to patents identified by *IP Worldwide* magazine as among "10 Patents that Changed the World."[1] The patents reflect recent advances[2] with major social impacts. According to the magazine, "[i]nstead of picking patents that have made big bucks, the editors [of IP Worldwide] picked patents that have made a big difference—shaking up society for better or worse."[3] These are, in short, examples of patents and associated research projects with major social impacts.

All of the research in these diverse projects was fundamentally influenced and redirected by patents and the commercial opportunities that patents implied. The influences of patents were experienced at different stages of these projects, in some instances helping researchers to target what they would work on, in other instances justifying continuing projects despite early stage failures, and in further instances providing the funding for critical steps in product perfection and testing. These influences are briefly profiled here to illustrate several typical ways that patents can influence research commitments and decisions.

Taken together, the technology development processes described here illustrate why patent influences are important (and perhaps essential) tools in promoting and completing work on many types of socially important advances. While the research results achieved by these projects are definitely not typical—these are among the most significant technological advances of our time—the technology development processes that led to these advances and the impacts of patents on these processes are typical and serve to illustrate why we need to view patent-influenced environments as highly rivalrous resource allocation settings.

It is difficult to imagine any of the important advances described here resulting without the lure of patent-influenced commercial rewards, for reasons that are described in the project profiles that follow. These are, simply, cases where patents mattered and where patents brought critically needed resources to the service of highly valuable technology development. The loss of advances like these is the price we would pay for a weaker patent system and lesser patent rewards.

---

1. Alan Cohen, *10 Patents That Changed the World*, IP WORLDWIDE, Aug. 2002, at 27.

2. All of the patents selected by IP Worldwide were issued between 1985 and 2001 and reflected inventions made in the 1980s and 1990s. *Id.*

3. *Id.*

2. Analyzing Patent Influences at Individual and Organizational Levels

The accounts that follow focus on the scarcity of research resources at both individual and organizational levels and the probable impacts of patents in drawing these resources together in the projects leading to the patented advances under scrutiny.

For the individuals involved in these accounts, the probable scarcity of their knowledge and skills can be roughly gauged from their extensive educational backgrounds and their abilities to realize exceptional accomplishments and achievements in the remainder of their careers. Patents may not have influenced these individuals directly, as most worked in organizational environments where the terms of their employment called for them to assign their patent rights to their organizational employers. Hence, these individuals would have known that they would have no ownership stakes in the patents resulting from their work.

Yet, these individuals would have felt a number of real (albeit indirect) influences from patents. Their work incentives, conditions, and rewards were derived from patent considerations. These researchers were given salaries over extended periods, research labs, and the benefit of talented nearby colleagues, all of which reflected the commercial potential of the projects that they were working on and the potential for patenting of their research results as means to insure commercial returns from their work. In short, patents explain why the organizations involved in these projects were willing to take risks on highly costly research efforts by these individuals and to support these research endeavors with major resource commitments over extended periods. The individuals involved here, while not the primary beneficiaries of the patents described, were stakeholders in the research projects influenced by the patents. The individuals benefited significantly from the scientific results and reputational gains that they were able to realize through organizational backing of research projects that would not have existed without the patent rights flowing from the projects.

For the organizations participating in these projects, the implications of patents were both more direct and more fundamental. Patents (and the periods of market exclusivity that patents implied) were means to ensure that the organizations could gain substantial returns on investments of large amounts of research resources. Patent rights were the linchpins promoting technology development risk taking. With patents available, large commitments of salaries, equipment, and supporting staffs to new technology development made economic sense. Patents would ensure that the innovating companies would reap the gains resulting from commercially successful products emerging from the new research, at least for the life of the patents. Without patents, money spent on developing new technologies might just benefit the competitors of the innovating companies. These competitors could adopt the new technologies for free and then use the new technologies against the innovating companies in the marketplace. Few new technology development efforts of any magnitude would be funded in the face of these adverse implications. Hence, the quest for patents (and the redirecting of resources towards research that made obtaining commercially valuable patents more likely) was a fundamentally significant part of the research efforts pursued by the organizations profiled here.

B. The Patents and Inventions
Genetically Engineered Crops
Monsanto Corporation

Genetically engineered crops are traditional crops modified to insert genes that produce new plant characteristics.[4] For instance, genetically engineered crops have been produced to create plants that are more likely to survive and thrive in the settings where the plants will be grown by fighting off certain insects or by tolerating herbicides that kill weeds.[5] Other crops have been modified in ways that increase the nutritional content of resulting foods or that increase crop yields or growth rates. Genetically altered crops are dominant in some agricultural settings. For example, as early as 2002, altered crops accounted for 74 percent of soybean production and 32 percent of corn production.[6]

The first genetically engineered plants were developed by Monsanto researchers.[7] The company assembled a team of highly skilled researchers and set them out to use recently developed genetic engineering techniques to produce new discoveries and products that complemented Monsanto's prior weed killer products. The results were plants and engineering techniques that were both tailored to Monsanto's commercial goals and major scientific breakthroughs with much broader implications.

The research leading to the patent of interest in this case study was completed by a highly talented group of Monsanto employees that included inventors Steve Rogers, Robert Farley, Robert Horsch, and Dilip M. Shah. They developed several new, genetically engineered plant varieties that were resistant to "Roundup," a widely-used weed killer marketed by Monsanto. The Monsanto research team obtained a patent on the Roundup-resistant plants that they had newly engineered.[8] Roundup-resistant plants eventually included specially created versions of soybean, cotton, alfalfa, canola, flax, tomato, sugar beet, sunflower, potato, tobacco, corn, wheat, rice, and lettuce plants. Farmers growing these modified crops were able to use Roundup to kill weeds while not killing the nearby crops. The agricultural advantages of this practice were highly valuable and seeds for the Roundup-resistant plants were big sellers.

---

4. *See generally* Daniel Charles, LORDS OF THE HARVEST (2001).

5. Alan Cohen, *10 Patents That Changed the World*, IP WORLDWIDE, Aug. 2002, at 27; Robert Lengreth, *High Tech Harvest*, POPULAR SCIENCE, Dec. 1992, at 104, 108, 122.

6. Alan Cohen, *10 Patents That Changed the World*, IP WORLDWIDE, Aug. 2002, at 27.

7. For a description of the history of these efforts and their industry surroundings, see Daniel Charles, LORDS OF THE HARVEST (2001).

8. U.S. Patent No. 4,940,835 (Issued July 10, 1990).

Monsanto was not only able to gain considerable commercial success as the sole seller of Roundup-resistant plants during the life of its patent, it saw its sales of Roundup rise as well as this weed killer was increasingly used with the new Roundup-resistant plants.

The research team assembled by Monsanto to work on this project was a highly qualified group with rare technical knowledge and project management skills. The exceptional (and scarce) attributes of the inventors in this project were evidenced by the recognition they received for their work on genetically engineered plant research, as well as their selection for a number of technical and managerial leadership positions in the remainder of their careers. Their knowledge and skills were particularly rare and in demand at the time of their work on Roundup-resistant plants. In this period, the genetic engineering revolution was just underway and many universities and corporations were interested in recruiting persons with high-level training in genetic chemistry and related areas. Persons with this background were scarce because few persons with training in these areas had yet been educated by leading graduate schools.

The Monsanto research team included the following individuals with exceptional skills in genetic science, related experimental techniques, and high technology project management.

Robert T. Fraley: Fraley earned both his B.S. and Ph.D. degrees from the University of Illinois.[9] When hired by Monsanto, Fraley was a postdoctoral fellow at the University of California at San Francisco and a pioneer in techniques for transferring DNA into plants.

In a long career with Monsanto, Fraley held numerous engineering, engineering management, and business management posts. "Fraley's real skill proved to be organizing teams of scientists and driving them towards a common goal."[10] Another researcher noted that Fraley had "a big wide stripe of leadership right up the middle of him."[11] Over his career, Fraley held numerous research management positions at Monsanto, ultimately rising to be the Executive Vice President and Chief Technology Officer of Monsanto, overseeing all of Monsanto's crop and seed agribusiness technology research and facilities for conducting this type of research around the world.

Fraley was also a distinguished researcher and developer of commercially significant advances. He authored more than 100 publications and patent applications relating to technical advances in agricultural biotechnology. In 1999, Fraley was awarded

---

9. Robert T. Fraley, Biographical Profile, https://web.archive.org/web/20141114131016/http://www.monsanto.com/whoweare/pages/robert-fraley-bio.aspx (last visited 6/8/2018).

10. Daniel Charles, Lords of the Harvest: Biotech, Big Money, and the Future of Food 14 (2001).

11. *Id.*

the National Medal of Technology for his pioneering contributions to the genetic engineering of crops.

Robert B. Horsch: Horsch received his Ph.D. in genetics from the University of California, Riverside, in 1979[12] and completed postdoctoral work in plant physiology at the University of Saskatchewan. During his career, Horsch led a number of Monsanto's research projects involving plant tissue cultures and plant transformation efforts. In 1996, Horsch became Vice President and General Manager of the Agracetus Campus of Monsanto Company's Agricultural Sector in Middleton, Wisconsin, serving in that capacity until the end of 1999. Dr. Horsch also held the position of Vice President, Product and Technology Cooperation, at Monsanto. In this position, he was responsible for public-private partnerships that helped farmers in developing countries gain access to better agricultural products and technologies.

Horsch served on the editorial boards of several leading journals in the plant sciences field and as an advisor to the National Science Foundation and the Department of Energy. He published more than 50 articles on plant biology and plant biotechnology. In 1999 he was awarded the National Medal of Technology by President Clinton for contributions to the development of agricultural biotechnology.

Stephen G. Rogers: Rogers earned his M.A. and Ph.D. degrees in biology from the John Hopkins University.[13] When hired by Monsanto, Rogers was a newly appointed assistant professor at the Indiana University School of Medicine. Rogers led a group at Monsanto that developed new techniques for producing proteins in plants. These techniques remain standard and widely used research techniques in this field. Rogers eventually served as director of biotechnology projects for Europe at Monsanto's Cereals Technology Center in Cambridge, England. In 1999, Rogers was awarded the National Medal of Technology for his contributions to genetic engineering and crop development.[14]

Dilip M. Shah: Shah received his undergraduate education in India and his M.S. and Ph.D. degrees in genetics from North Carolina State University.[15] From 1976 to 1982, he held various academic research positions with the National Institute of Environmental Health Services, the University of Chicago, and the University of Georgia. He joined Monsanto in 1982 and later served as the Research and Development Director for Monsanto's agricultural research in India.[16] He subsequently joined the

---

12. Robert B. Horsch, Biographical Material, https://web.archive.org/web/20100116213251 /http://politicalfriendster.com/rateConnection.php?id1=6679&id2=2472 (last visited 6/8/2018).

13. Michael Hertz, Luna Magpili and Rob Smith, *Monsanto and Genetically Modified Seeds*, (Nov. 7, 1999) (unpublished manuscript), https://web.archive.org/web/20130108051256/http://cti. itc.virginia.edu/~meg3c/TCC401/A_Case.pdf (last visited on 6/8/2018).

14. MARQUIS WHO'S WHO IN SCIENCE AND ENGINEERING 1125 (2000–2001 edition).

15. Environmental Protection Agency, Nominations to the FIFRA Scientific Advisory Panel; Request for Comments, http://edocket.access.gpo.gov/2009/E9-19313.htm (last visited 6/8/2018) (including biographical information on Dilip M. Shah).

16. Dilip M. Shah, Biographical Material, https://web.archive.org/web/20100311231707/http:// www.danforthcenter.org/shah/bio.asp (last visited 6/8/2018).

Donald Danforth Plant Science Center (a public service research center in Saint Louis) as a Research Scientist and Principal Investigator.[17]

In addition to assembling and compensating this highly qualified team of researchers, Monsanto needed to support the team's research with extensive equipment and staff. The unexpected costs and duration of the needed research were enough to force many other firms out of similar technology development efforts. As recounted by one observer,

> Monsanto would outrace the large companies and outspend the small ones [in mastering the genetic manipulation of plants during the 1980s]. The trio of names [of three Monsanto researchers] — Steve Rogers, Robert Farley, and Robert Horsch — would become a familiar incantation, linked forever on a steady stream of scientific papers, and on patents giving Monsanto exclusive rights to new tools of genetic engineering and plants with unprecedented powers.

> The ultimate fate of this research would remain uncertain throughout the 1980s. There would be no products to sell for more than a decade. Most of the "nervous money" would run out of patience, sell out, and move on. But a small cadre at Monsanto would stick with their bet, and double it. In their own eyes, they had successfully caught a monster wave of technological innovation. . . . [18]

The size of Monsanto's ultimate resource commitment was enormous. The specificity of the commercial targeting of the research — aimed at creating Roundup-resistant plants — made successful results hard to achieve. Determining the genes needed to create Roundup resistance and identifying means to successfully inject these genes into plants both turned out to be highly difficult tasks. Successful results in both areas were developed only after numerous setbacks and extensive efforts. In the end, Monsanto researchers devoted 700,000 hours of researcher time and approximately $80 million dollars to the development of Roundup-resistant plants.[19]

The company's dedication to this research was clearly the product of patent influences. Shortly before the initiation of the project that led to Roundup-resistant plants, Monsanto's top executives had committed the company to an increased focus on commercially targeted products and research, with a particular focus on the development of patentable discoveries. Richard Mahoney, CEO of the company, noted at the time that: "We are not in the business of the pursuit of knowledge; we are in the business of the pursuit of products."[20] At Monsanto, "[t]he end had come for lavishly funded

---

17. Environmental Protection Agency, Nominations to the FIFRA Scientific Advisory Panel; Request for Comments, http://edocket.access.gpo.gov/2009/E9-19313.htm (last visited 6/8/2018) (including biographical information on Dilip M. Shah).

18. Daniel Charles, LORDS OF THE HARVEST: BIOTECH, BIG MONEY, AND THE FUTURE OF FOOD 8 (2001).

19. *Id.* at 140.

20. Marie-Monique Robin, THE WORLD ACCORDING TO MONSANTO 138 (2008) (quoting Richard Mahoney).

research on tinkering with petunias, and the aim was now clear: to create transgenic plants that brought in money."[21] Patent-influenced marketing opportunities and associated patent rewards were understood to be the means to realize company gains from new transgenic plants. Hence, patent incentives at the corporate level played a fundamentally important role in encouraging and targeting the research efforts and corporate risk taking that produced the patented discovery of Roundup-resistant plants.

Notes & Questions

1. Up to the time of the research described in this case study, Monsanto had focused primarily on chemical products (such as its highly successful Roundup brand weed killer). The research described here reflected a strong (and expensive) commitment of the company to genetics-based research in a period when this field was exploding with new technological breakthroughs and commercial potential. What would be the considerations that a company like Monsanto would want to address before committing large resources to a major shift in its technological focus (such as the shift from chemical research and products to genetics research and genetically engineered products)?

2. One of the advantages of Monsanto's new Roundup-resistant plants was that the marketing of these plants extended the commercial value of its Roundup product after the point when the composition of that product was no longer protected by patent rights. How could the company's patent-based controls over Roundup-resistant plants be used to establish product marketing and distribution channels that would promote sales of Roundup and sales of seeds of Roundup-resistant plants?

3. To what extent would trademark protections concerning the Roundup brand name aid in marketing of the new Roundup-resistant seeds or in marketing the combination of the new seeds and the original Roundup product? How could Monsanto's previous marketing programs revolving around the Roundup brand and trademark be evolved to promote sales of its new line of genetically engineered seeds?

4. While Monsanto's breakthroughs in creating genetically engineered plants solved a number of biotechnology research problems and produced a great deal of new understanding of genetic processes and related biochemical mechanisms, genetically engineered plants such as Monsanto's Roundup-resistant plants remain controversial. These plants generally have features (such as selective resistance to weed killers like Roundup) that appear to make them superior in some important ways to their naturally occurring predecessors. However, the full implications of use of the new plants are still unknown. Some commentators have expressed concerns over the large-scale agricultural production of these new sorts of plants without a better understanding of the ecological implications of introducing the new plants. Other parties have expressed concerns that the changes in genetically altered plants made

---

21. *Id.*

to achieve their desirable new properties may also have made the plants less wholesome food sources. Additionally, some observers have criticized the introduction of genetically engineered plants on the ground that the altered genetic material in these plants tends to spread throughout subsequent generations of related plants, potentially displacing the unmodified versions of the plants and precluding the option of going back to unmodified plant versions should the adverse consequences of genetically modified plants be recognized at a later point. Finally, some parties have criticized Monsanto and other vendors of genetically modified plants for the highly restrictive terms under which seeds for the new plants can be acquired. These terms—imposed upon farmers at the time of purchase of seeds—frequently restrict how the seeds can be used and require farmers to come back to the vendors season after season for new seeds and new payments if the farmers wish to continue planting crops using the patent-restricted seeds. For overviews of potential ecological, agricultural, and legal problems raised by genetically modified plants, *see generally* Keith Aoki, *Seeds of Dispute: Intellectual Property Rights and Agricultural Biodiversity,* 3 GOLDEN GATE U. ENVTL. L.J. 79 (2009); Kanchana Kariyawasam, *Legal Liability, Intellectual Property and Genetically Modified Crops: Their Impact on World Agriculture,* 19 PAC. RIM L. & POL'Y J. 459 (2010); Sophia Kolchmainen, *Precaution Before Profits: An Overview of Issues in Genetically Engineered Food and* Crops, 20 VA. ENVTL. L.J. 267 (2001); John Charles Kunich, *Mother Frankenstein, Doctor Nature, and the Environmental Law of Genetic Engineering,* 74 S. CAL. L. REV. 807 (2001).

5. Seed technologies raise special patent licensing issues because they are examples of self-replicating technologies. Seeds of many plants not only produce new crops of the plants, they produce more seeds. In this sense, the seeds are self-replicating—that is, they create more instances of the patented item. Indeed, this replication is not even limited to a one-to-one substitution process in which one set of seeds produces an equal number of seeds for future use. Rather, a few seeds initially purchased may produce numerous seeds for future use. This can allow a farmer who acquires seeds in small numbers to vastly expand his or her use in subsequent crop generations. It can also allow a farmer who acquires a limited number of seeds to become a supplier to other farmers for subsequent crop generations.

Patent holders have sought various ways to authorize farmers to make uses of patented seeds in crop production, while banning (or at least specially constraining) the use of patented seeds to produce more seeds. One way they have sought to accomplish this is to restrict the use of patented seeds under license agreements that purport to limit how the seeds, once acquired, can be used by the farmers that purchase them. In *Bowman v. Monsanto* Company, 133 S. Ct. 1761 (2013), the United States Supreme Court considered whether these sorts of attempted license restrictions on the subsequent or "downstream" use of patented seeds were barred by the first sale doctrine. That doctrine generally bars a patent holder that sells a patented item from imposing subsequent limitations on the use of the item sold. In *Bowman*, the Supreme Court held that the first sale doctrine does not bar a seed patent holder such as Monsanto from imposing licensing terms on a farmer who buys patented seeds that prevent the farmer from reproducing more of the patented seeds through planting and harvesting without the patent holder's consent. The Court was persuaded that upholding these restrictive licensing terms was necessary to ensure that Monsanto received the types of rewards for seed inventions that the patent laws were designed to provide. The first sale doctrine was interpreted narrowly to prevent an end run around patent controls via the self-replicating properties of seeds. According to the Court, allowing unlimited seed replication by farmers who had bought only one set of seeds from Monsanto would permit the farmers to "make and market replicas [of the patented seeds], thus depriving the company of the reward patent law provides for the sale of each article." *Id.* at 1769.

The scope of legitimate downstream licensing restrictions on the use of patented items is addressed further in discussions of the *Quanta* case in Chapter 11. For an assessment of the patent law and competition policy issues raised by attempts to restrict the downstream use of patented items through licensing terms, see Shubha Ghosh, *Carte Blanche, Quanta, and Competition Policy*, 34 J. CORP. L. 1209 (2009).

DNA Copying via Polymerase Chain Reaction (PCR)
Cetus Corporation

The polymerase chain reaction (PCR) method is a widely used process for producing large quantities of genetically identical material.[22] It allows parties starting with a very small amount of genetic material to multiply the amount of the material by millions of times in just a few hours.[23] The method has been fundamentally important as a tool in genetic research and medical testing processes.[24] PCR has aided scientists in producing advances in drug research and medical diagnostics by allowing researchers to find faulty genes and to identify viruses. PCR was also used extensively by scientists in mapping the human genome and in perfecting cloning technologies.

PCR was invented by Kary Mullis as an offshoot of other research he was performing for the Cetus Corporation. Cetus was engaged in a variety of research concerning biotechnology techniques and discoveries made possible by new knowledge regarding genetics and related chemistry. Mullis was one of many researchers engaged by Cetus as part of the company's exploration of the commercial potential of this new field of technology.

Mullis was a highly trained researcher, with a Ph.D. in biochemistry from the University of California, Berkeley, and two years of postdoctoral work in pharmaceutical chemistry at the University of California, San Francisco.[25] He initially worked as a

---

22. *See* Alan Cohen, *10 Patents That Changed the World*, IP WORLDWIDE, Aug. 2002, at 27.

23. U.S. Patent No. 4,683,202 (Issued July 28, 1987).

24. *See* Wikipedia, *Kary Mullis*, http://en.wikipedia.org/wiki/Kary_Mullis (last visited 6/8/2018).

25. Wikipedia, *Kary Mullis*, http://en.wikipedia.org/wiki/Kary_Mullis (last visited 6/8/2018).

biochemist at a medical school in Kansas City and served as a DNA chemist at Cetus for four years prior to his discovery of PCR.

Mullis conceived of the basic idea for PCR while trying to solve a research procedure problem. His research required replication of DNA, which was possible but highly laborious with techniques used prior to PCR. Mullis sought an easier means to produce copies of DNA material in substantial quantities. The PCR procedure was his proposed solution, but the original version of the process he proposed lacked many practical details.[26]

Working out the practical details turned out to be a considerable undertaking.[27] Many of Mullis' coworkers thought that the process was unworkable. As one coworker described:

> When Mullis first presented [the idea behind PCR] to people on paper, everyone was looking at it and trying to figure out why it wouldn't work. It was so simple it didn't take a lot of explanation. Once they understood it they thought there must be some reason that it didn't work.[28]

Indeed, many of the details in the process were critical and Mullis himself was unable to make it work for a considerable period. Corporate managers at Cetus were patient, however. Apparently recognizing the scientific and commercial significance of the PCR process if Mullis could prefect it, Cetus' managers committed Mullis' time to work on PCR. They relieved Mullis of other research duties and supported his full-time work on the PCR project. Finally, after more than a year of additional research beyond his initial idea about how PCR might work, Mullis was able to complete a version of the process that reproduced DNA material in substantial quantities.[29]

Mullis left Cetus in 1986 and later served for two years as director of molecular biology for Xytronyx, Inc., in San Diego.[30] His discovery of PCR was subsequently recognized as one of the great advances in the developing field of biotechnology. In 1993, Mullis received the Nobel Prize in Chemistry for his discovery of PCR.[31]

Patents were a key part of the business strategy underlying Cetus' contributions to the development of PCR. The company's business model was built on an expectation of commercialization of new advances in the developing field of biotechnology through the securing of patents on these discoveries and the subsequent use of the patents to obtain commercial rewards. Unlike the research at Monsanto to produce Roundup-resistant plants—which was undertaken in part to complement the company's preexisting commercial products and interests—Cetus' research was more

---

26. Mullis described his discovery of PCR and the process of making PCR workable in his autobiography. *See* Kary Mullis, Dancing Naked in the Mind Field 3–14 (1998).

27. Paul Rabinow, Making PCR 93 (1996).

28. *Id.* at 98.

29. *Id.* at 99–104.

30. Wikipedia, *Kary Mullis*, http://en.wikipedia.org/wiki/Kary_Mullis (last visited 6/8/2018).

31. Wikipedia, *History of polymerase chain reaction*, http://en.wikipedia.org/wiki/History_of_polymerase_chain_reaction (last visited 6/8/2018).

technology-driven, with an aim of exploring the new advances and commercial products made possible by a particular type of new scientific knowledge. Cetus was targeting research and commercial products incorporating new biotechnology advances made possible by new understanding of DNA and related biological processes. The company was a hotbed of research in this field, with a clear commercial focus.[32] Cetus' managers considered patent rights to be their preferred means to ensure commercial returns on the company's research successes.[33]

Cetus accounted for two important features of the development of PCR. First, it created a research environment that attracted and gave collegial and technical support to top researchers such as Mullis. Mullis described the attractions of working at Cetus as follows:

> [It] was an exciting time at Cetus. . . . They had just gotten enough money to start hiring a lot of people and doing a lot of things. It was the heyday of biotechnology. There were all kinds of bold ideas floating around all the time about what we were going to make, and there was absolutely no restraint in terms of imagination.[34]

Second, the company supported Mullis' work financially despite his early failures and the long period it took to make PCR work. The company expended the resources needed for this long program of research because of its willingness to back high-risk research with clear commercial potential. Henry Erlich, a researcher at Cetus when Mullis worked there, described the alignment of scientific and commercial interests at Cetus concerning research like Mullis' work on PCR:

> I really didn't know what Cetus was like—I really didn't know what directions they were taking. I thought about the fact that it could conceivably be very exciting to try to do biological research that lead to practical, useful things. . . . If you find a project that is of real fundamental passionate interest to you, and if it also has the possibility for having some real practical commercial outcomes, then you have the prospect of a company project that really satisfies a scientist.[35]

Cetus' bet on Mullis' research paid off handsomely. Mullis applied for a patent on the PCR process and the resulting patent was assigned to Cetus.[36] Mullis received a cash bonus of $10,000 for his invention, the largest bonus Cetus had paid for an invention to that time and an exception to the company's normal refusal to pay

---

32. *See* Paul Rabinow, Making PCR 79 (1996) (describing an "imperative to develop commercial products at Cetus" imposed by company management at the time of Mullis' work on PCR).

33. *Id.* at 119–122 (describing the views of Cetus' management as to the benefits of obtaining patents on PCR over a trade secret strategy (advocated by Mullis) for protecting and commercializing PCR).

34. *Id.* at 90.

35. *Id.* at 80.

36. U.S. Patent No. 4,683,202 (Issued July 28, 1987).

bonuses to scientists for inventions.[37] However, this bonus paid to Mullis was far less than Cetus' profits from PCR. In 1991, Cetus assigned its rights to its PCR-related patents to Hoffman-La Roche for $300 million.[38]

This extraordinary profit, secured through the exclusive rights afforded by patents and the ability of Cetus to transfer those rights to a large medical products supplier like Hoffman-La Roche, reflected the payoff for Cetus' research investment and risk taking. The payoff was a patent-influenced reward for the company's success in building an exceptional research enterprise and for the company's risk taking in backing Mullis' unusual project over its rocky path to completion. The results achieved by Cetus are indicative of how patents can encourage firms to make large research bets on developing new technologies with the expectation that successful results can be translated into high profits through patent rights.

Patent rights cannot only ensure that a company like Cetus gains the commercial returns on its research investment, these rights can also facilitate specialization in the development of new technologies and products.[39] In the case of PCR, Cetus was able to focus on research and gain much of the commercial value of PCR without actually developing all of the manufacturing and marketing capabilities needed to fully realize this commercial value. Cetus was able to gain a payment for its research results by transferring its rights to Hoffman-LaRoche. The latter was able to take over further commercialization steps and to realize the full commercial value of PCR through extensions of Hoffman-LaRoche's existing manufacturing and marketing activities. In this way, each company specialized in what it did best — Cetus in the support of research and Hoffman-LaRoche in the development of commercial products, in the production of those products, and in the marketing of the products through existing distribution chains.

Patent rights served as the bridge between these specialized activities because the rights allowed Cetus to pass on an exclusive commercial opportunity to Hoffman-LaRoche. Cetus was compensated in its patent assignment for the commercial value of its research results and for the specialized contributions that it made to the ultimate commercialization of PCR. The exclusive marketing opportunity Hoffman-LaRoche received in the patent assignment encouraged it to add its specialized resources and capabilities to the research results produced by Cetus. The profit potential associated with this exclusive opportunity induced Hoffman-LaRoche to devote additional resources to the commercialization of PCR. Hoffman-LaRoche could look to the market for PCR-related products and tailor its resource commitments to manufacturing and marketing of these products accordingly. In this way, patent rights concerning PCR (when held by Hoffman-LaRoche) attracted the allocation of

---

37. Paul Rabinow, MAKING PCR 133 (1996).

38. *Id.*

39. *See* Jonathan Barnett, *Intellectual Property as a Law of Organization* (June 10, 2010). USC CLEO Research Paper No. C10-10, available at: http://ssrn.com/abstract=1623565 (last visited 6/8/2018).

Hoffman-LaRoche's scarce resources to the development, production, and marketing of PCR-based products and assisted in these steps of bringing PCR into widespread use for public benefit.

Notes & Questions

1. Kary Mullis' insights into the PCR technique were among the most elegant and important scientific discoveries of the past century. In awarding Mullis the Nobel Prize in 1993, the Royal Swedish Academy of Sciences described Mullis' work and its implications as follows:

> The applications of Mullis' PCR method are already many. It is for example possible using simple equipment to multiply a given DNA segment from a complicated genetic material millions of times in a few hours, which is of very great significance for biochemical and genetic research. The method offers new possibilities particularly in medical diagnostics, and is used, for example, for discovering HIV virus or faulty genes in hereditary diseases. Researchers can also produce DNA from animals that became extinct millions of years ago by using the PCR method on fossil material.
>
> . . . .
>
> The PCR technique was first presented as recently as 1985 but is nevertheless already one of the most widespread methods of analyzing DNA. With PCR it is possible to replicate several million times, in a test tube, an individual DNA segment of a complicated genetic material. Mullis has described how he got the idea for the PCR during a night drive in the Californian mountains. Two short oligonucleotides are synthesized so that they are bound correctly to opposite strands of the DNA segment it is wished to replicate. At the points of contact an added enzyme (DNA polymerase) can start to read off the genetic code and link code words through which two new double strands of DNA are formed. The sample is then heated, which makes the strands separate so that they can be read off again. The procedure is then repeated time after time, doubling at each step the number of copies of the desired DNA segment. Through such repetitive cycles it is possible to obtain millions of copies of the desired DNA segment within a few hours. The procedure is very simple, requiring in theory only a test tube and some heat sources, even though there are now commercial PCR apparatuses that manage the whole procedure automatically and with great precision.
>
> [T]he PCR method has decisively improved the outlook for basic research. The sequencing and cloning of genes has been appreciably simplified.

Royal Swedish Academy of Sciences, Press Release: The Nobel Prize in Chemistry 1993 (October 13, 1993), available at: http://www.karymullis.com/pdf/pr-1993.pdf (last visited 6/8/2018).

2. Despite the fundamental nature of Mullis' discovery and the large commercial gains that Cetus realized from this discovery, Mullis' personal monetary gains from

this discovery were small. While his bonus of $10,000 for this discovery was large by the standards prevailing at Cetus at the time, this amount was a very small fraction of the amounts that Cetus gained from patents related to the discovery. What are the moral implications of this type of disparity between individual and organizational rewards for key discoveries? Is this a fair split of the profits from PCR given the respective contributions and risk taking of Mullis and Cetus? Does the actual insight of a researcher deserve a greater reward than occurred in the case of PCR, at least where large commercial profits are realized from a discovery?

3. How might a system of success-based rewards for individual inventors working in organizational contexts be implemented such that inventors of highly profitable advances like PCR are compensated more extensively? Should legal standards compel such rewards for individual inventors or is the present system of privately negotiated terms of employment for individual inventors sufficient to fully specify splits of patent-influenced rewards between employers and employees?

4. In private negotiations of employment terms providing for bonuses or profit sharing payments related to patented advances, are inventors and their employers similarly informed about the likelihood of technical and commercial success of projects such that they can effectively analyze the estimated value of bonuses and profit-sharing payments for individual inventors? What sorts of valuation errors are parties on each side of these negotiations likely to make in light of their information gaps? What types of uncertainties — technical or commercial — are likely to be most important in projecting the value of an innovation project and which side in these negotiations is better informed about these types of uncertainties and associated potentials for project successes and failures? If each side is only partially informed, should contractual negotiations amidst such information gaps and potentials for mistakes be seen as definitive or should legal standards guarantee an opportunity to renegotiate reward terms for individual inventors once the full commercial implications of their discoveries are known?

5. Assuming that private negotiations of employment terms for individual inventors are definitive and that these will specify the full rewards that individual innovators can expect when working for corporations, universities, or other organizational employers, what are the optimal bonus or profit-sharing terms that organizations should offer to key innovators? How can organizations adequately motivate individual researchers to devote diligent research efforts to patent-eligible advances while still retaining the primary patent-influenced commercial rewards for the organizations?

6. The research environment at Cetus in which PCR was discovered and perfected was one aimed at developing a number of products based on genetic engineering in a period when this technological field appeared to be very promising for new commercial products. However, the nature of the products that would result from the research was very ill defined. This led to some opportunistic research at Cetus—that is, research that was initiated or retargeted as unexpected opportunities became apparent. For example, PCR and processes like it were not targets of Mullis' original research efforts, but the development of PCR received considerable backing by Cetus

once Mullis' unexpected insights revealed a new commercial opportunity. Hence, PCR was really a product of Cetus' commitment to explore the various new commercial products and procedures that new scientific knowledge about genetics appeared to make possible. When will this type of somewhat open-ended exploration of a new field be commercially attractive? What types of fields are ripe for this type of commercial exploration of new technology and what features will indicate that a field is a good candidate for such exploration? What role will IP interests be likely to play in this type of exploratory technology development? How will patents, copyrights, trademarks, and trade secrets tend to influence project commitments by a company like Cetus that does not have many existing products, but that has assembled considerable expertise in a rapidly developing technological field?

Hepatitis Vaccine
University of Edinburgh/Biogen Corporation

Hepatitis B disease is a worldwide killer that claims as many as one million victims each year.[40] Since the late 1980s, effective vaccines for the disease have been available, due largely to research led by Kenneth Murray of the University of Edinburgh. Murray identified "intermediates" for hepatitis B—that is, molecules that aid in the production of hepatitis B virus antigens in the human body. Exposure to the intermediates in advance of exposure to the hepatitis B virus helps the body fight off hepatitis infections. Understanding of the relevant intermediates and their potential roles in preventing hepatitis led to the creation and widespread administration of several types of hepatitis B vaccines in the United States during the last two decades. As a result, deaths due to hepatitis B in the United States have dropped to a few thousand each year. The substantial numbers of hepatitis B deaths that still occur in the rest of the world are largely the result of limitations on the administration of hepatitis B vaccines.

Murray was a highly trained researcher and a leader in both academic and commercial enterprises that produced important discoveries in biotechnology. He was born in England and obtained his undergraduate and Ph.D. degrees from Birmingham University. In 1967, he took a faculty position at the University of Edinburgh in what was then the only Department of Molecular Biology in the United Kingdom. Murray subsequently led that department to a highly regarded reputation in its field. Murray pioneered in the development of methods for DNA sequencing[41] along with his wife, Noreen Murray, whose own distinguished career as a research geneticist led to her selection as a Commander of the Order of the British Empire (CBE) in 2002.[42]

---

40. *See* Alan Cohen, *10 Patents That Changed the World*, IP WORLDWIDE, Aug. 2002, at 27.
41. *See Kenneth Murray*, http://en.wikipedia.org/wiki/Kenneth_Murray_(biologist) (last visited 6/8/2018).
42. *See Noreen Murray*, http://en.wikipedia.org/wiki/Noreen_Murray (last visited 6/8/2018).

The Murrays were among the first researchers to use genetic engineering techniques to study the mechanisms for diseases like hepatitis and to develop related medical advances. By 1978, they had successfully produced hepatitis antigens in their laboratory. This work led to Kenneth Murray's later discoveries of hepatitis intermediates. Murray obtained a patent that claimed protection for several hepatitis B intermediate molecules. It also claimed protection for cellular hosts modified by the addition of the specified intermediates, chemicals resulting from the introduction of the intermediates, and methods of making and using the intermediates, hosts, and resulting chemicals.[43] Because of the breadth these claims, most subsequent hepatitis B vaccines have fallen under the patent and have generated enormous revenues for Biogen, the assignee of Murray's patent. As a co-founder and co-owner of Biogen, Murray reaped significant gains from the widespread use of his invention, as well as from other advances commercialized by Biogen. He used some of the wealth generated by his partial ownership of Biogen to establish the Darwin Trust, which supports educational and research activities in natural science. For his own discoveries and his further backing of scientific research, Murray was knighted by the British government in 1993.

Biogen was a major commercial contributor to Murray's research. Murray played a dual role as a co-founder of Biogen and as a beneficiary of the company's funding decisions in carrying out supported research at the University of Edinburgh. His dual role accounts for the extensive commercial considerations underlying the funding of Murray's research. Patents lay at the heart of Biogen's funding contributions and the decisions that led to Murray's research.

Biogen was founded with a heavy involvement of scientists in the targeting of research funding as well as in the research itself. Patents played a remarkably clear role in decisions about research directions meriting Biogen's support. In particular, these considerations were at the heart of the decisions leading to Biogen's funding of Murray's work on hepatitis B intermediaries. This funding choice resulted from analyses by Biogen company leaders of the business potential and scientific promise of various research alternatives. The background of Murray's decision to pursue research concerning hepatitis B intermediaries was explained by Murray as follows:

> Our involvement in research on hepatitis B virus (HBV) really began at a Microbiology Biology conference in Geneva in February, 1978. For the small group of academics involved this was not at all the sort of conference to which we were accustomed. It was an intensive discussion, convened by Dr. Raymond Schaeffer and Mr. Dan Adams of the venture capital group of the International Nickel Company of Canada (INCO), of the prospects for formation of a European biotechnology company and a review of research projects that such a company might pursue. The role model was Genentech Inc.,

---

43. U.S. Patent No. 4,710,463 (Issued December 1, 1987).

a company that had been formed two years previously and in which INCO had been a significant and well satisfied corporate investor.[44]

The factors affecting Murray's decision to go forward with hepatitis B research (and the impacts of commercial interests and patent objectives on this decision) are well documented in a line of opinions contesting the validity of one of the British patents stemming from Murray's research. In an opinion of the Lords of Appeal of the House of Lords in *Biogen Inc. v. Medeva PLC*, Lord Hoffman gave the following account of the actions leading to Murray's work on hepatitis B intermediaries:

> In February 1978 Professor Murray and a number of other molecular biologists of international repute, together with financial backers, met in Geneva and decided to found Biogen Inc., the patentee company ("Biogen"), for the purpose of exploiting the technology for commercial purposes. One of the first projects upon which they agreed was to try to make the antigens of [hepatitis B virus (HBV)]. Professor Murray began work in the spring of that year and in November reported that he had produced two of the known HBV antigens in colonies of cultured bacteria.[45]

This project reflected Biogen's typical mode of operation. Biogen's normal business approach was to fund and support projects under the direction of a member of its Scientific Board, who was usually the scientist who proposed the project. The actual research work was typically carried out in the proposing scientist's university laboratory.[46]

Writing at a distance of 20 years from the founding of Biogen, Murray noted that when the company was formed, its combination of scientific expertise and venture capital funding represented "a new avenue for funding research."[47] Changes in the needs of scientists over this 20-year period made these types of partnerships between scientists and business persons more common, according to Murray. He noted that:

> The recent advances in technologies and automation of many routine operations which have so effectively opened new opportunities in many areas of biological research and catalyzed the growth of the biotechnology industry, have also brought escalating costs that are changing the patterns of funding for basic research. Academics are now strongly encouraged to pursue the

---

44. Peter Hans Hofschneider & Kenneth Murray, *Combining Science and Business: From Recombinant DNA to Vaccines Against Hepatitis B Virus* in Recombinant Protein Drugs 43, 43 (P. Buckel ed. 2001).

45. Biogen Inc. v. Medeva PLC, [1996] UKHL 18, [1997] R.P.C.1 (appeal taken from U.K.), available at: http://www.bailii.org/uk/cases/UKHL/1996/18.html (last visited 6/8/2018).

46. Peter Hans Hofschneider & Kenneth Murray, *Combining Science and Business: From Recombinant DNA to Vaccines Against Hepatitis B Virus* in Recombinant Protein Drugs 43, 45 (P. Buckel ed. 2001).

47. *Id.* at 60.

commercial exploitation of their discoveries, sometimes to the extent that potential is a high impact factor that can compete with evaluation of basic scientific importance in the competition for research grant support.[48]

In short, Murray's work — even though undertaken in academic surroundings — was directly influenced by the commercially driven analyses of his business associates at Biogen. These assessments were, no doubt, strongly affected by the potential for discovering patent-eligible advances stemming from Murray's work. Patents based on Murray's findings were needed to fully realize the commercial potential of the discoveries. Commercial potential was a basic consideration in prioritizing Biogen's funding choices and in leading it to give top funding priority to Murray's research. Biogen's funding was, in turn, critically important in supporting that research and in producing a prompt solution to the problem of hepatitis B infections and deaths. Hence, the organizational importance of patents for Biogen (and the derivative importance of Biogen's patent-influenced funding decisions for the University of Edinburgh) accounted for Murray's research and the societal gains that it produced. In addition, due to his ownership stake in Biogen, Murray had personal, patent-influenced reasons to devote his attentions to hepatitis B research and to produce successful results. Thus, at the individual as well as the organizational levels, patents appear to have been significant influences in the allocation of scarce resources to the development of hepatitis B vaccines and to related disease prevention.

Notes & Questions

1. The targeting and funding of Kenneth Murray's research through the combined decision making of academic researchers and business executives represented an effort to serve both pure research and commercial ends in the resulting projects. What types of expertise would researchers and executives have each brought to this type of decision making? What types of fields would be especially suitable to this type of academic research funding with commercial goals and corporate involvement from the outset? When will it make sense to let academic figures pick commercially promising projects as occurred in targeting Biogen's funding? What may be the problems in having academic figures take the lead in this type of decision making about corporate funding?

2. University research is increasingly supported by corporate funding and retargeted to attract this sort of funding. To what extent is this consistent with the traditional missions of universities to expand knowledge through research and to educate students? When will these traditional university missions and the pursuit of commercial goals align and when will they diverge? How may intellectual property interests figure in processes whereby commercial entities support and reward university research? What are the limitations of using these interests as means of transferring valuable offshoots of university research?

---

48. *Id.*

3. Commercial influences and corporate funding may enter into university research and decisions about allocations of research resources in at least two ways.

First, as with the funding provided by Biogen, corporate sources may provide support from the outset for particular projects that have clear commercial potential. The business entities providing such funding will typically wish to be guaranteed exclusive opportunities to follow up on the commercial potential of project results (through mechanisms such as assignments of resulting patents or exclusive licenses under such patents). Universities and their corporate funding sources share risks of project failures in these funding arrangements since both have committed resources to the projects and both will stand to lose these resources if no results are produced. In addition, the business entities bear further risks that the projects will be academic successes (in that they produce useful research knowledge and increased understanding of some field) but commercial failures (because the results do not lead to commercially significant products).

Second, universities may pursue certain lines of research with expectations that the results will have commercial implications. University researchers will patent features of project results and these patents will serve as the basis for later attempts to interest commercial entities in developing products based on the patented technologies. Technology transfer offices in many universities have developed sophisticated analyses of the commercial potential of new patented technologies emanating from their universities. Some such offices construct basic business plans for commercial endeavors incorporating their patented technologies and use these business plans in presentations to convince businesses of the commercial potential of their universities' patented technologies. In these processes, the universities take the initial risks of technological or commercial failure of the projects, although once a company takes an assignment of a university patent or an exclusive license under such a patent and commits significant resources to the development, production, and marketing of related products, the company will take on significant business risks as well.

What types of technology development projects will be likely to be more successful if pursued with the involvement of university researchers and resources rather than through purely in-house development within companies? If the involvement of university researchers and resources would be advantageous, what types of projects will be best served by each of the above sorts of procedures for providing commercial support to university research efforts? What types of decision-making strengths do each of these funding and risk sharing procedures involve? What other mechanisms might be used to add commercial funding to university research efforts?

How would the provisions of a statute like the Bayh-Dole Act (discussed in Chapter 12) influence the development of collaborative efforts of universities and companies to fund and conduct new research? These provisions provide for private ownership and commercial development of offshoots of federally funded research. How would federal funding change, if at all, the research directions that companies and universities pursue through collaborative efforts?

4. If university research is to be conducted with commercial funding (and corresponding commercial goals) how should key researchers be motivated to keep the commercial features of project results in mind and to pursue those features diligently? To what extent will rewards to professors or other academic researchers for commercial success divert these individuals from other aspects of their university-related work?

5. To what extent should senior managers of institutions like the University of Edinburgh cooperate with the primarily commercial endeavors of faculty members like Kenneth Murray? Are these endeavors consistent with faculty members' primary attention to academic research and teaching? What versions of work by professors on commercial projects for individual gain might be seen by their universities as illegitimate and grounds for discipline or dismissal? What criteria might universities use to define illegitimate intellectual property development activities and transfers by university faculty members and other university researchers?

Cardiac Stents
Julio Palmaz/Johnson & Johnson Corporation

Cardiac stents are small devices used to repair clogged arteries.[49] The stents are inserted inside arteries when blockages are cleared and serve to prevent renewed blockages. At one time, the preferred procedure to repair clogged arteries was open-heart surgery, a practice that saved many lives, but that also involved substantial risks of infection and long recovery periods. Surgical procedures to repair arterial blockages with stents, by contrast, involve only small incisions and are typically completed on an outpatient basis, with small risks of infection and much less cost than comparable open-heart surgeries.[50]

The first cardiac stent design was developed and patented by Julio Palmaz, a physician working on cardiac stents as a solo inventor. He began to work on stent designs following a medical lecture describing an angioplasty procedure performed without a stent.[51] In the basic angioplasty procedure described in the lecture, a catheter attached to a small balloon is inserted into an artery far enough to position the balloon at the point of a blockage. The balloon is then expanded, thereby compressing and moving accumulated plaque out of the way and increasing blood movement. The balloon is then deflated and the catheter removed. While this procedure was often initially successful in reducing blockages, almost 50 percent of patients receiving this treatment suffered recurrences of arterial clogging when the balloon was removed.

---

49. *See* Alan Cohen, *10 Patents That Changed the World*, IP Worldwide, Aug. 2002, at 27.

50. *See id.*

51. Palmaz's work in developing his stent designs is described in Laura Lorek, *The Inventor of a Groundbreaking Stent Fought a Long Battle for . . . A Purpose of Heart*, San Antonio Express-News, February 27, 2005, at 1L.

Palmaz concluded that a rigid structure that was left behind following this type of balloon procedure might assist in preventing renewed blockages. He designed and patented a new stent that would provide this rigid structure, built an initial version, and tested it in animals. Palmaz's stent design involved a narrow cage-like element made of metal that enclosed a balloon catheter. In surgical use, the balloon and cage structure were both initially collapsed in a narrow form. The combined unit was threaded through an artery until it was positioned at the site of a blockage. The balloon was then inflated, causing the outer cage to expand. Once expanded, the cage was constructed so that it did not contract again when the balloon was deflated and the catheter removed. The expanded cage both pushed out the plaque at the site of the blockage and held the artery open at that point.

Palmaz's stents proved to be highly effective in surgical use and have transformed cardiac treatment. Within four years of their FDA approval, balloon-expandable stents of the type covered by Palmaz's patent were used in more than 80 percent of medical procedures concerning coronary blockages, a virtually unparalleled medical success.[52] More than one million stents of this type are implanted annually worldwide. Palmaz's designs have also led to many additional stent design improvements (some with features that are covered by additional patents). Palmaz's initial stents are now part of the medical collection of the Smithsonian Institution in Washington, D.C.

Palmaz's work on cardiac stents was initially a personal sidelight to his primary career as a physician and medical researcher. His extensive training was not in cardiac care, but rather in radiology. Palmaz received his M.D. degree from the National University of La Plata in Argentina in 1971 and practiced vascular radiology at the San Martin University Hospital in La Plata beginning in 1974.[53] He later received three additional years of radiology training at the University of California at Davis' Martinez Veterans Administration Medical Center. Palmaz was appointed Chief of Angiography and Special Procedures in the radiology department at the University of Texas Health and Science Center at San Antonio in 1983. Palmaz is currently the Ashbel Smith Professor at the Science Center.

Palmaz's story as an immigrant who achieved highly extraordinary scientific and financial success has a heroic quality. As noted by a colleague who served as a mentor early in Palmaz's career:

> Here's a young man who came to the United States in the early '70s, hardly speaking any English, and through a great deal of determination and imagination, he has created one of the better medical devices for helping people and has done well in the process. It's an amazing story.[54]

---

52. *See* Wikipedia, *Julio Palmaz*, http://en.wikipedia.org/wiki/Julio_Palmaz (last visited 6/8/2018).

53. *Id.*

54. Laura Lorek, *The Inventor of a Groundbreaking Stent Fought a Long Battle for . . . A Purpose of Heart*, San Antonio Express-News, February 27, 2005, at 1L (quoting Dr. Stewart Reuter, emeritus professor of radiology at the University of Texas Health and Science Center at San Antonio).

Palmaz indeed did well financially by virtue of the success of his stent designs. The patent that he obtained was the source of considerable personal income. While he has continued his medical research, Palmaz is also very wealthy. He operates a large vineyard and winery in Napa Valley, California that includes a 100,000-square-foot wine cave that is equivalent in size to an 18-story underground building. The wine cave includes an 8,000-square-foot car museum that contains Palmaz's collection of 17 rare racing Porsches.[55]

Aside from his financial success, Palmaz has achieved considerable success as a medical researcher and entrepreneur. He is named on more than 25 United States patents issued since the patent on his stent design. These additional patents cover several types of medical device designs, materials, methods of manufacturing, and methods of use. Palmaz has also participated in the founding of several business enterprises aimed at medical technology development. Palmaz formed Advanced Bio Prosthetic Surfaces (ABPS) in 1999, a private R&D enterprise to develop biomaterials suitable for implantable medical devices. In early 2008, Palmaz formed Palmaz Scientific to design, manufacture, and sell implantable bio prosthetic devices

Unlike the research projects profiled in the case studies to this point, Palmaz's work on his stent designs was not initially motivated by expectations of patents and patent rewards. Palmaz seems to have started his project out of scientific curiosity and a desire to help patients. He conducted some of his initial design efforts in his garage and was able to come up with some tentative designs without great expense.[56]

However, in order to conduct testing and to refine his stent designs to make them workable in surgical procedures, Palmaz needed help. At several stages in obtaining this help and in producing workable stent designs, patent rights played key roles.

Palmaz made initial inquiries to medical device companies about his stent designs, but got little interest. To continue his project, he formed a new business entity called the Expandable Graft Partnership with fellow partners Phil Romano (founder of several restaurant chains including Fuddruckers and The Macaroni Grill) and Dr. Richard Schatz (a cardiologist at Brooke Army Medical Center). Romano invested $250,000 in the partnership while Schatz contributed to the refinement of the stent designs from the perspective of a cardiologist who was familiar with the demands of heart surgery and treatment. The aims of the partnership were to both bring the stent designs to more finished states and to pursue commercial gains from the new stents.

Given the commercial goals of the partnership, a patent on Palmaz's discovery was a critical business feature. Romano, the experienced businessperson among the partners, immediately pressed Palmaz to obtain a patent on his stent designs. Romano

---

55. *See id.*

56. "Palmaz went to Radio Shack and bought some copper wire, a solder gun and other materials and began to tinker at a workbench in his garage. He came upon the inspiration for the stent's design from leftover construction material—a piece of wire mesh with a diamond-like pattern. Using that as his guide, he built the first stent prototype." *Id.*

noted that the lack of a patent would reduce the commercial value of Palmaz's invention. Palmaz then applied for and obtained a patent that claimed protection for several versions of his stent designs and for procedures for using the stents.[57] The patent was assigned to the partnership upon issuance, indicating that the partnership was the real party in interest.

Following additional work on the stent designs, the partnership was very successful in using its patent to attract the interest of a medical products company and in gaining favorable terms for a transfer of the technology to the company.[58] It also got the company to provide extensive funding for the final testing and FDA approval processes that were needed to transform Palmaz's designs into medical products available for use on humans. The partnership initially licensed the patented stent designs exclusively to Johnson & Johnson for $10 million plus royalties. Johnson & Johnson invested an additional $100 million in the development of the stents—again in reliance on the commercial potential of the designs as protected in part by the Palmaz patent. The company gained FDA approval for use of the stents in peripheral arteries in 1991 and for use in coronary arteries in 1994. Once the stents were approved for widespread use, Johnson & Johnson captured 90 percent of the early market for stents. The company bought out the stake in the patent held by Palmaz, Schatz, and Romano in 1998. Overall, payments for the patent transfer plus royalties netted the three partners $500 million.[59]

Although an expectation of patent protection was not a motivating force behind Palmaz's initial innovation efforts leading to his stent designs, his patent played several key roles in advancing his stent designs to completion and in bringing fully functional stents to the public. Palmaz's patent reassured various participants in the stent project of the commercial potential of his designs. This encouraged additional investments of resources in his project, first by members of the Expandable Graft

---

57. U.S. Patent No. 4,739,762 (Issued April 26, 1988).

58. *See* Laura Lorek, *The Inventor of a Groundbreaking Stent Fought a Long Battle for . . . A Purpose of Heart*, SAN ANTONIO EXPRESS-NEWS, February 27, 2005, at 1L. The "steady hand" in guiding the commercialization of Palmaz's designs was Romano, who was experienced with high stakes negotiations and large commercial transactions. In the negations between the partnership and Johnson & Johnson over a possible license for the designs, Romano's business experience and cool headedness played critical roles:

> In one meeting, Johnson & Johnson put $5 million on the table. It was more money than either Palmaz or Schatz had ever dreamed about, but not Romano.

> "I said no," Romano said. "And Julio and Richard [(the other Extendable Grafts partners)] were just about to take it. They were sweating bullets. We just kept going. We ended up at twice as much as they first offered."

> Johnson & Johnson agreed to pay $10 million to license the stent technology and 7 percent to 9 percent royalties on top of that.

> "We would have given this away for nothing," Palmaz said. "That's why having Philip [Romano] as the businessman helped us greatly."

Id.

59. *Id.*

Partnership and later by Johnson & Johnson. Palmaz's patent was a central commercial consideration to members of the Expandable Graft Partnership. The patent helping to draw the interest of the partners and to encourage them to provide the additional funding and research assistance that Palmaz needed to move his innovation project forward and to bring his stent designs to sufficiently complete states for effective presentation to Johnson & Johnson as candidates for large scale production. Palmaz's patent also provided the promise of market exclusivity and profit potential that Johnson & Johnson (as exclusive licensee of the patent) relied on in investing considerable additional sums to complete product perfection, testing, and regulatory approval steps needed to bring Palmaz's stents to market and into active surgical use. Hence, while an afterthought to Palmaz personally, his patent was a central consideration to other participants in the stent project and was probably essential in gaining the technical and financial backing needed to finalize the stent designs, to obtain FDA approval for the stents, to initiate large-scale production of the stents, and to bring the stents into widespread public use.

In using patents to fund and gain technical assistance for product development and testing steps, Palmaz was following a common approach for entrepreneurs in start-up companies. An initial founder, bringing a new but commercially unproven technology to the start-up enterprise, seeks initial assistance from a few associates who are willing to take high risks by investing money or labor in the future of the new technology. The initial funding generated in this manner is used to partially perfect the technology and to take steps needed to gain further funding to back the final commercialization of the technology. The promise of exclusive business opportunities as the result of patent rights is often a central requirement of this start-up business model. Absent this promise of exclusivity, early stage investors will be unlikely to provide significant amounts of financing, particularly where all of this funding may be lost if another party can freely copy the technology and reap most of the commercial rewards from the new technology. Hence, Palmaz's and his associates' use of his patent illustrates how patent rights can draw scarce resources to the development and popularization of a new technology after the point when that new technology is first invented in its raw form. Absent these sorts of attractions for commitments of scarce resources after the point of invention, new advances such as Palmaz's stent designs might be just missed opportunities, known to a few researchers but stalled in the product development process and never made available to the public.

Notes & Questions

1. Julio Palmaz conducted his initial research as a solo inventor. In what fields of research is this still possible? Are patents needed to encourage research in these fields where large-scale supporting resources are not needed for successful results? What roles may patents play in these fields?

2. In the course of testing and developing products based on his early research results, Palmaz formed the Expandable Graft Partnership. This business entity brought new investment, business management expertise, and scientific knowledge

to bear on the development of the stent technology originated by Palmaz. How did Palmaz's patent play a role in resource allocations and commitments achieved in this start-up business entity? How might the entity and its activities have been different if no patent were obtained for Palmaz's invention? What kinds of projects will typically need the boost of a patent to encourage the formation and operation of a related start-up company?

3. After some additional work on Palmaz's stent designs, the partnership interested Johnson & Johnson in further commercialization efforts. What sorts of preliminary project results would a large company like Johnson & Johnson be interested in seeing to consider a new technology like Palmaz's for additional investments and development into commercial products? How would patents affect the interest of a large company in these reviews? How would patents influence the resources that a company like Johnson & Johnson was willing to commit to expand on Palmaz's work and the early stage product development efforts of the Expandable Graft Partnership?

4. In what types of fields or business settings would the technology acquisition strategy used by Johnson & Johnson for heart stents be desirable for a company like Digital Ignition and in what contexts would in-house corporate development of new technologies be preferable? Does the answer turn in part on the stage of development of Digital Ignition as a company as well as on the characteristics of the technologies that Digital Ignition might acquire?

C. Lessons from the Case Studies

The four patents examined here all have had significant societal impacts and are doubtless "Patents That Changed the World" as contended by the commentator who selected the patents.[60] The advances underlying these patents were produced by highly trained and talented individuals, with the aid of large, well-supported corporate and university research organizations. These organizations supported work on the advances with substantial commitments of scarce resources—commitments that were directly influenced by potential patent rewards.

The work of the researchers themselves was one critically important scarce resource. This was a scarce resource because of the exceptional training and capabilities of the individuals involved. The researchers who accounted for the four advances examined here are a remarkable group of experts. They include a Nobel Prize winner (Mullis), a knight of the British Empire (Murray), and several winners of the National Medal of Technology (Fraley, Horsch, and Rogers). A very distinguished group, to say the least. These highly talented individuals—with many choices of action corresponding to their recognized talents—are the sorts of parties that patent rewards must attract (at least through the intermediaries of corporations

---

60. Alan Cohen, *10 Patents That Changed the World*, IP WORLDWIDE, Aug. 2002, at 27.

and universities that fund and conduct research) if patents are to influence state of the art research.

The organizations involved in the advances studied here also contributed other scarce resources beyond the time and efforts of highly talented researchers. Many modern types of research require vast amounts of supporting resources. The organizations that are large enough to conduct this sort of research are consequently scarce. Only a few large corporations or university organizations have the funds or physical resources needed to support the types of research seen in most of the projects described in this chapter. And these rare organizations can only support a few large projects, given that the organizations are typically the focus of many competing demands for their resources.

Amidst this contentious world of scarce organizational resources and scarce individuals capable of working at the frontiers of rapidly advancing and increasingly specialized fields, patents must often offer rewards that are very large. Patent rewards at these levels are often needed to trump the attraction of alternative activities and alternative resource allocations and to draw scarce individuals and organizational resources to work on the types of practical items and processes that the public seeks. Patent rights attaching high commercial values to successful inventions help to focus resource allocations and to encourage sufficient attention by researchers and supporting organizations to the full range of practical advances valued by the public.

The influence of substantial patent rights and rewards has the potential to align the interests of highly talented researchers and large research organizations with the public's interest in new inventions. Because the inventions that can result from this alignment can be highly valuable—as evidenced by the advances assessed in this chapter—the public's stake in this alignment and in the patent system is considerable. The public has a large stake in ensuring that the patent system continues to encourage our most talented individuals and largest organizations to pursue patent-eligible advances valued by the public. By causing the commercial potential of advances to reflect the public's views on the value of the advances, patents can serve important roles as key mediators of decisions about how to devote scarce resources to innovative projects.

Notes & Questions

1. In what circumstances will the special incentives and rewards of patents promote allocations of resources to the production of patentable innovations in ways that are in the public interest? To what extent does this depend on the public's need for intellectually distinctive innovations (that is, unusual and non-obvious inventions of the sorts that qualify for patents)? Is it enough that these inventions are conceptually unusual and departures from earlier technological designs? Or should patent protections (and the costs of the patent system) be limited to types of innovations with large and clear-cut public benefits?

2. If patents are means to encourage resource allocations toward work on patentable advances, what practical limitations on patent rights enforcement might suggest desirable exclusions from patentable subject matters? Should types of advances that are difficult to constrain through patent rights (and, therefore, difficult to attach to innovation rewards involving access limitations and access payments that will attract resource commitments) be excluded from the patent system because the resource allocations intended to be achieved by patent rights and enforcement are unlikely to occur for these advances?

Appendix

Introduction to Intellectual Property for the Nonspecialist

I. Types of Intellectual Property Interests[1]

A. Patents

A patent for an invention gives the inventor the ability to control the use and commercialization of the invention for a limited period. A United States patent is granted based on an application to and review for legal sufficiency by the United States Patent and Trademark Office (USPTO). Generally, the term of a new patent is 20 years from the date on which the application for the patent was filed in the United States. United States patents are effective only within the United States, U.S. territories, and U.S. possessions. Under certain circumstances, patent term extensions or adjustments may be available.

The right conferred by the patent grant is, in the language of the Patent Act, "the right to exclude others from making, using, offering for sale, or selling" the invention in the United States or "importing" the invention into the United States. What is granted is not the right to make, use, offer for sale, sell or import the invention, but rather the right to exclude others from making, using, offering for sale, selling, or importing the invention. Once a patent is issued, the patentee must enforce the patent without aid of the USPTO.

There are three types of patents:

(1) Utility patents covering new and useful processes, machines, articles of manufacture, or compositions of matter, or any new and useful improvements thereof;

(2) Design patents covering new, original, and ornamental designs for articles of manufacture; and

(3) Plant patents covering distinct and new varieties of asexually reproducing plants.

---

1. The material in this section is based on United States Patent and Trademark Office, "General Information Concerning Patents (2014)," https://www.uspto.gov/sites/default/files/inventors/edu-inf/BasicPatentGuide.pdf (accessed 11/17/2017).

B. Copyrights

Copyright is a form of protection provided to the authors of "original works of authorship" including literary, dramatic, musical, artistic, and certain other intellectual works, both published and unpublished. The 1976 Copyright Act generally gives the owner of copyright the exclusive right to reproduce the copyrighted work, to prepare derivative works, to distribute copies or phonorecords of the copyrighted work, to perform the copyrighted work publicly, or to display the copyrighted work publicly.

A copyright protects an author's particular form of expression rather than the subject matter of a protected writing. For example, a description of a machine could be copyrighted, but this would only prevent others from copying the description. It would not prevent others from writing a description of their own or from making and using the machine. Copyrights are registered by the Copyright Office of the Library of Congress.

C. Trademarks and Servicemarks

A trademark is a word, name, symbol, or device that is used in trade with goods to indicate the source of the goods and to distinguish them from the goods of others. A servicemark is the same as a trademark except that it identifies and distinguishes the source of a service rather than a product. The terms "trademark" and "mark" are commonly used to refer to both trademarks and servicemarks. This convention is also used in this Appendix.

Trademark rights may be used to prevent others from using a confusingly similar mark, but not to prevent others from making the same goods as the trademark holder or from selling the same goods or services under a clearly different mark. Trademarks which are used in interstate or foreign commerce may be registered with the USPTO.

D. Trade Secrets

A trade secret may consist of any formula, pattern, device or compilation of information which is used in secret in a person's business, and which gives him an opportunity to obtain an advantage over competitors who do not know or use it. The subject matter of a trade secret must be information that is not widely known or easily ascertainable. Matters of public knowledge or of general knowledge in an industry cannot be appropriated by a person as his trade secret. Matters which are completely disclosed by the goods which a party markets cannot be his trade secret.

Persons who have access to trade secrets in their work can be prevented by legal injunctions from disclosing these secrets to others and from using the trade secrets for purposes other than furthering the interests of the trade secret owner. Persons who acquire trade secrets through wrongful means — for example, by trespass or knowingly causing others to breach their obligations to keep trade secrets confidential — can also be precluded from using or disclosing the trade secrets. Persons who use or disclose trade secrets without the permission of the trade secret owners can be forced to compensate the trade secret holder for resulting damages.

II. Patent Laws[2]

The Constitution of the United States gives Congress the power to enact laws relating to patents, in Article I, section 8, which reads "Congress shall have power . . . to promote the progress of science and useful arts, by securing for limited times to authors and inventors the exclusive right to their respective writings and discoveries." Under this power Congress has from time to time enacted various laws relating to patents. The first patent law was enacted in 1790. United States patent laws most recently underwent a general revision in 1952, resulting in the present Patent Act which came into effect January 1, 1953. The Patent Act is codified in Title 35, United States Code. On November 29, 1999, Congress enacted the American Inventors Protection Act of 1999 (AIPA), which significantly revised the patent laws. The Leahy-Smith America Invents Act (AIA) additionally revised the patents laws effective March 16, 2013 to change the U.S. patent system from a "first to invent" system to a "first inventor to file" system.

The Patent Act specifies the subject matters that can be patented and the conditions for patentability. The law establishes the United States Patent and Trademark Office to administer the law relating to the granting of patents and contains various other provisions relating to patents.

A. What Can Be Patented

Three types of patents are authorized under the Patent Act: utility patents, design patents, and plant patents.

1. Utility Patents

Utility patents are granted for new inventions that are useful. These inventions can be in several forms, including new devices, new compounds or chemicals, and new procedures for undertaking a useful task. Utility patents are by far the most frequently issued type of patent and the form of patent the public is most familiar with. Indeed, when persons refer to a patent, they typically mean a utility patent. This convention will be used in this Appendix. Where the text refers to a patent, the interest involved should be presumed to involve a utility patent unless otherwise indicated.

In the language of the Patent Act, any person who "invents or discovers any new and useful process, machine, manufacture, or composition of matter, or any new and

---

2. The material on United States patent laws in this section is based on United States Patent and Trademark Office, "General Information Concerning Patents (2014)," https://www.uspto.gov/sites/default/files/inventors/edu-inf/BasicPatentGuide.pdf (accessed 11/17/2017).

useful improvement thereof, may obtain a patent," subject to the conditions and requirements of the law. The word "process" is defined by law as a process, act or method, and primarily includes industrial or technical processes. The term "machine" used in the statute includes artificially created assemblages that operate on some other subject matter, often transforming that additional matter. The term "manufacture" refers to articles that are made, and includes all manufactured articles. The term "composition of matter" relates to chemical compositions and may include mixtures of ingredients as well as new chemical compounds. These classes of subject matter taken together include practically everything that is made by man and the processes for making the products.

The Atomic Energy Act of 1954 restricts patentable subject matter in the atomic energy field, excluding the patenting of inventions useful solely in the utilization of special nuclear material or atomic energy in an atomic weapon.

The Patent Act specifies that patentable inventions must be "useful." The term "useful" in this connection refers to the condition that an invention has a useful purpose and operates to achieve its intended purpose. That is, a machine such as a perpetual motion device which will not operate to achieve its intended purpose would not be deemed useful, and therefore would not qualify for a utility patent.

Judicial interpretations of the Patent Act have defined the limits of the field of subject matter that can be covered by a utility patent. For example, it has been held that the laws of nature, physical phenomena, and abstract ideas are not patentable subject matter.

A patent cannot be obtained upon a mere idea or suggestion. A patent is only available for a new machine, manufacture, chemical or process with specific, implementable details and not for the idea or suggestion of the new invention. A complete description of the actual machine or other subject matter for which a patent is sought is required in a patent application and in the resulting patent if one issues.

2. Design Patents

The Patent Act provides for design patents granted to any person who has invented any new and nonobvious ornamental design for an article of manufacture. A design patent protects only the exterior ornamentation and appearance of an article, and not the article's structural or functional features. If the structural or functional features of an ornamented article are also new, the creator of the article can sometimes obtain a utility patent for these utilitarian aspects of the article in addition to gaining a design patent covering the ornamental features. A design patent has a term of 14 years from its grant, and no fees are necessary to maintain a design patent in force. A design patent is infringed by a party that makes, uses, sells, or imports, without the patent holder's permission, the type of article covered by the design patent augmented by ornamentation that is the same or similar to the design covered by the patent.

Both design patents and copyrights can apply to decorative features of useful items. Design patents cover ornamental features of articles of manufacture. By contrast, copyrights cover pictorial, graphic, or sculptural features of designs that can stand separate from useful articles as independent works of authorship.

The concept of an article of manufacture is changing with the emergence of new types of useful items. When a design covers only a portion of an article of manufacture (such as the face of an iPhone), problems arise about the aspects of the design that can be protected by design patents and how to separate the value of the design from the value of the entire article of manufacture. The Supreme Court has ruled that infringement of a design patent through sales of an infringing article generally does not entitle the design patent owner to recover the value of the entire article of manufacture. In wake of this Supreme Court decision, standards for identifying the value of the design features of an article of manufacture and for providing corresponding compensation to design patent holders upon design patent infringement are under development in emerging case law.

3. Plant Patents

The Patent Act also provides for the granting of a patent to anyone who has invented or discovered and asexually reproduced any distinct and new variety of plant, including cultivated sports, mutants, hybrids, and newly found seedlings, other than a tuber-propagated plant or a plant found in an uncultivated state.

Asexually propagated plants are those that are reproduced by means other than from seeds, such as by the rooting of cuttings, layering, budding, or grafting. Tuber-propagated plants, for which a plant patent cannot be obtained, include plants that are reproduced through a short, thickened portion of an underground branch such as an Irish potato or a Jerusalem artichoke. The term of a plant patent is generally 20 years from the date on which the application for the patent was filed in the United States. A plant patent is infringed by a party that reproduces, uses, sells, or imports the type of plant covered by the plant patent without the patent holder's permission.

Although not covered by the Patent Act, a second sort of intellectual property interest in new plant varieties is recognized under federal law. The Plant Variety Protection Act (PVPA) is a statute administered by the Department of Agriculture that provides intellectual property protection for sexually reproduced plants. Breeders of novel varieties of plants may apply for and obtain a plant variety protection certificate that allows the holder "to exclude others from selling the variety, or offering it for sale, or reproducing it, or importing it, or exporting it, or using it in producing (as distinguished from developing) a hybrid or different variety therefrom," 7 U.S.C. § 2483(a)(1). This protection extends for a term of 20 years from the date of issuance of a protection certificate (or 25 years for certificates related to vines and trees).

To secure a plant variety protection certificate, an applicant must show that the plant variety is:

(1) new, in the sense that, on the date of filing of the application for plant variety protection, propagating or harvested material of the variety has not been sold or otherwise disposed of to other persons . . . ;

(2) distinct, in the sense that the variety is clearly distinguishable from any other variety the existence of which is publicly known or a matter of common knowledge at the time of the filing of the application;

(3) uniform, in the sense that any variations are describable, predictable, and commercially acceptable; and

(4) stable, in the sense that the variety, when reproduced, will remain unchanged with regard to the essential and distinctive characteristics of the variety with a reasonable degree of reliability commensurate with that of varieties of the same category in which the same breeding method is employed.

7 U.S.C. §2402(a). Protection certificates issued under the PVPA are distinct from plant patents issued by the Patent and Trademark Office in that PVPA protection applies only to sexually reproduced plants, while plant patents protect only asexually reproduced plants.

In addition to qualifying for protection under a plant patent or a plant variety protection certificate issued under the PVPA, a variety of plant that is new and useful may qualify for protection by a utility patent as an innovative composition of matter.

B. Conditions for Obtaining a Patent: Novelty and Nonobviousness

The remainder of the discussion of patents here will address utility patents (although design patents and plant patents are subject to parallel rules in many respects). In order for an invention to be patentable it must be new as defined in the patent law, which provides that an invention cannot be patented if:

"(1) the claimed invention was patented, described in a printed publication, or in public use, on sale, or otherwise available to the public before the effective filing date of the claimed invention" or

"(2) the claimed invention was described in a patent issued [by the U.S.] or in an application for patent published or deemed published [by the U.S.], in which the patent or application, as the case may be, names another inventor and was effectively filed before the effective filing date of the claimed invention."

There are certain limited patent law exceptions to patent prohibitions (1) and (2) above. Notably, an exception may apply to a "disclosure made 1 year or less before the effective filing date of the claimed invention," but only if "the disclosure was made by the inventor or joint inventor or by another who obtained the subject matter disclosed . . . from the inventor or a joint inventor."

In patent prohibition (1), the term "otherwise available to the public" refers to other types of disclosures of the claimed invention such as, for example, an oral presentation at a scientific meeting, a demonstration at a trade show, a lecture or speech, a statement made on a radio talk show, a YouTube™ video, or a website or other online material.

Effective filing date of the claimed invention: This term appears in patent prohibitions (1) and (2). For a U.S. nonprovisional patent application that is the first application containing the claimed subject matter, the term "effective filing date of the claimed invention" means the actual filing date of the U.S. nonprovisional patent application. For a U.S. nonprovisional application that claims the benefit of a corresponding prior-filed U.S. provisional application, "effective filing date of the claimed invention" can be the filing date of the prior-filed provisional application provided the provisional application sufficiently describes the claimed invention. Similarly, for a U.S. nonprovisional application that is a continuation or division of a prior-filed U.S. nonprovisional application [created by amending or splitting the prior-filed application], "effective filing date of the claimed invention" can be the filing date of the prior filed nonprovisional application that sufficiently describes the claimed invention. Finally, "effective filing date of the claimed invention" may be the filing date of a prior-filed foreign patent application to which foreign priority is claimed provided the foreign patent application sufficiently describes the claimed invention.

Even if the subject matter sought to be patented is not exactly shown by the prior art, and involves one or more differences from the most nearly similar thing already known, a patent may still be refused if the differences would be obvious. The subject matter sought to be patented must be sufficiently different from what has been used or described before that it may be said to be nonobvious to a person having ordinary skill in the area of technology related to the invention. For example, the substitution in a publicly known product of one color for another, or changes in size, are ordinarily alterations with obvious functional implications and produce altered products that are not patentable.

C. The Role of the Patent Office

Congress established the United States Patent and Trademark Office (USPTO or Patent Office) to issue patents on behalf of the government. The Patent Office as a distinct bureau dates from the year 1802 when a separate official in the Department of State who became known as the "Superintendent of Patents" was placed in charge of patents. The revision of the patent laws enacted in 1836 reorganized the Patent Office and designated the official in charge as Commissioner of Patents. The Patent Office remained in the Department of State until 1849 when it was transferred to the Department of Interior. In 1925 it was transferred to the Department of Commerce where it is today. The name of the Patent Office was changed to the Patent and Trademark Office in 1975 and changed to the United States Patent and Trademark Office in 2000.

The USPTO administers the patent laws as they relate to the granting of patents for inventions, and performs other duties relating to patents. Patent examiners within the USPTO review applications for patents to determine if the applicants are entitled to patents under the law and the USPTO grants the patents when the applicants are so entitled. The USPTO publishes issued patents and most patent applications filed on or after November 29, 2000, at 18 months from the earliest filing date of the applications. The USPTO also issues various publications concerning patents, records assignments of patents, maintains a search room for the use of the public to examine issued patents and records, and supplies copies of records and other papers concerning patents. The USPTO also performs similar functions with respect to the registration of trademarks. The USPTO has no jurisdiction over questions concerning the infringement and enforcement of patents, except that persons wishing to challenge the validity of an issued patent can obtain post-grant reviews by the agency which may lead to invalidation of an issued patent.

The work of examining applications for patents is divided among a number of examining technology centers (TC), each TC having jurisdiction over certain assigned fields of technology. Each TC is headed by group directors and staffed by examiners and support staff. The examiners review applications for patents and determine whether patents can be granted. An appeal can be taken to the Board of Patent Appeals and Interferences from their decisions refusing to grant a patent, and a review by the Director of the USPTO may be had on other matters by petition.

D. Who May Apply for a Patent

Under United States patent law, only the inventor of a new item or process may apply for a patent, with certain exceptions. If a person who is not the inventor should apply for a patent, the patent, if it were obtained, would be invalid. The person applying for a patent who intentionally misstated that he was the inventor would also be subject to criminal penalties. If the inventor is dead, the application may be made by legal representatives, that is, the administrator or executor of the estate. If the inventor is insane, the application for patent may be made by a guardian. If an inventor refuses to apply for a patent or cannot be found, a joint inventor or, if there is no joint inventor available, a person having a proprietary interest in the invention may apply on behalf of the non-signing inventor.

If two or more persons make an invention jointly, they apply for a patent as joint inventors. A person who makes only a financial contribution is not a joint inventor and cannot be joined in the application as an inventor. It is generally possible to correct an innocent mistake in erroneously omitting an inventor or in erroneously naming a person as an inventor.

Officers and employees of the United States Patent and Trademark Office are prohibited by law from applying for a patent or acquiring, directly or indirectly, except by inheritance or bequest, any patent or any right or interest in any patent.

E. Contents of a Patent Application

1. Regular Patent Application

An application for a patent is made to the Director of the USPTO and must include:

(1) A written specification of the applicant's invention (a written description of the invention involved and further information on its use) and proposed claims delineating the legally operative scope of the patent rights being sought (a textual description of the critical elements making up the invention for which a patent is claimed);

(2) One or more drawings illustrating the elements of the claimed invention where these are required to understand the invention; and

(3) Filing fees (which are reduced if the party who will own the patent upon issuance is a "small entity" such as an independent inventor, a small business concern, or a non-profit organization).

2. Provisional Patent Application

Since June 8, 1995, the USPTO has offered inventors the option of filing a provisional application for a patent. This type of simplified application is designed to provide a lower cost first patent filing in the United States and to give U.S. applicants parity with foreign applicants. Patent claims are not required in a provisional application, but the invention for which a patent will be sought must be described in some clear way. A provisional application establishes a tentative filing date for the inventor's ultimate regular patent application. If a regular patent application covering the same invention is filed within 12 months of the filing of a provisional patent application, the filing date for the provisional application becomes the filing date for the regular application. However, if a regular application is not filed within 12 months, the provisional filing has no effect. Provisional applications may not be filed for new ornamental designs of the sort covered by design patents nor for new varieties of asexually reproduced plants of the sort covered by plant patents.

F. Patent Attorneys and Agents

The preparation of a proper patent application and the successful completion of proceedings in the USPTO to obtain a patent are undertakings requiring substantial knowledge of patent law and the rules and procedures of the USPTO. Inventors may prepare and file their own applications in the USPTO and conduct related proceedings themselves, but unless they are familiar with patent laws and USPTO procedures in detail, they may get into considerable difficulty. While a patent may be obtained in many cases by persons not skilled in this work, there would be no assurance that the patent obtained would have commercial value and adequately protect the particular invention involved. Most inventors employ the services of registered patent attorneys or patent agents to aid the inventors in drafting patent applications, in properly filing those applications and related materials, and in responding to rulings regarding the applications by USPTO officials.

Federal patent laws give the USPTO the power to make rules and regulations governing the conduct and registration of patent attorneys and agents. Persons who are not registered by the USPTO for this type of practice are not permitted by law to represent inventors before the USPTO. The USPTO maintains a list or "register" of authorized patent attorneys and agents. To be admitted to this register, a person must comply with the regulations prescribed by the Office, which require a showing that the person is of good moral character and of good repute and that she has the legal and scientific or technical qualifications necessary to render applicants for patents a valuable service. In addition, persons seeking to become patent attorneys or agents must pass a patent bar examination administered by the USPTO, which tests the individual's knowledge of patent laws and USPTO procedures.

The USPTO registers both attorneys at law who have already passed a state bar examination and persons who are not attorneys at law but who have gained specialized knowledge in the narrow area of patent law and USPTO procedure. The former persons are referred to as "patent attorneys" and the latter are referred to as "patent agents." Both patent attorneys and patent agents are equally entitled to prepare patent applications and represent clients before the USPTO. Patent agents, however, cannot conduct patent litigation in the courts or render other legal services since to do so would constitute the unauthorized practice of law. For example, a patent agent cannot draw up a contract relating to a patent, such as an assignment or a license agreement, if the state in which he works considers drafting contracts for other individuals to constitute practicing law.

G. Publication of Patent Applications

Publication of patent applications is required by the American Inventors Protection Act of 1999 for most plant and utility patent applications filed on or after November 29, 2000. On filing of a plant or utility patent application, an applicant may request that the application not be published, but only if the invention has not been and will not be the subject of an application filed in a foreign country that requires publication 18 months after filing. Publication occurs after the expiration of an 18-month period following the earliest effective filing date or priority date claimed by an application. Following publication, the application for patent is no longer held in confidence by the Office and any member of the public may request access to the entire file history of the application. For the rare patent application which is not published under these provisions, the USPTO will only disclose the patent application and its related file history upon the issuance and publication of a patent based on the application.

As a result of publication of a patent application, the applicant may assert provisional rights. These rights provide a patentee with the opportunity to obtain a reasonable royalty from a third party that infringes a published application claim provided actual notice is given to the third party by the applicant and a patent issues from the application with a substantially identical claim. Thus, damages for pre-patent grant infringement by another are now available.

H. Examination of Patent Applications

Applications, other than provisional applications, are generally reviewed or "examined" by patent examiners within the USPTO. The examination of an application consists of a study of the application for compliance with legal form requirements and a search through U.S. patents, publications of patent applications, foreign patent documents, and available literature, to see if the claimed invention is new, useful and nonobvious. If a patent examiner's decision on patentability is favorable, a patent is granted.

On the average, patents are granted based on about two out of every three applications for patents that are filed. However, in the course of examination, a patent applicant may have voluntarily limited his or her claims to avoid a disfavorable decision by a patent examiner. Hence, while some form of patent issues based on most patent applications, the resulting patents are sometimes relatively narrow in scope and not what the applicant sought in his or her initial filing.

I. Administrative Challenges to Patents

Under the Leahy-Smith America Invents Act (AIA), a party can challenge the patentability of an invention upon the issuance of a patent through three procedures. First, an inter partes review (IPR) allows a party to introduce prior art to challenge the novelty and nonobviousness of an invention, provided that the challenge is raised within nine months after the grant of a patent or upon the completion of a post-grant review (PGR). Second, through a PGR, a party can challenge the patentability of an invention on any grounds up to nine months after the grant of the patent. A third procedure for covered business method patents (CBM) allows challenges to business method patents. These procedures went into effect in 2012, with the provisions for CBM procedures set to expire in 2020.

J. Nature of Patent Rights

The owner of an issued patent — that is, the patent applicant or an assignee of the applicant's interest in the patent — has the right to exclude others from making, using, offering for sale, or selling the patented invention throughout the United States or importing the invention into the United States and its territories and possessions. Provided that relevant maintenance fees are paid as described below, these patent rights will generally extend for 20 years from the date on which the application for the patent was filed in the United States.

A patent right is essentially negative — that is, it allows the patent holder to bar others from certain actions — making, using, selling, or importing the patented invention—but does not give the patent holder the positive right to undertake these same activities. This is because the making, using, selling, or importing of the invention may be limited by government regulations or restricted by other parties' patent rights concerning components of the invention.

For example, an inventor of a new automobile who has obtained a patent thereon would not be entitled to use the patented automobile in violation of the laws of a state requiring a license, nor could the patentee sell an automobile adhering to the new design if the automobile failed to meet minimum safety standards imposed by law. Similarly, a party may not, by virtue of having a patent on an item, violate federal antitrust laws by selling the patented item through illegal means such as prohibited resale price agreements or entry into combinations in restraint of trade.

Even if the making, sale, use, or importation of a patented item by the patentee would otherwise be lawful, these actions may be restricted because they would infringe the rights of another patent holder having an interest in the same item. For example, if person A gains a patent on a particular design for a sewing machine and person B designs and patents an improvement adding computer controls to the same type of sewing machine, person B can only make, use, sell, or import sewing machines based on the new design upon obtaining the permission of person A so long as the new design still incorporates the patented features of A's original design. However, B will be able to prevent all other parties (including A) from making, using, selling, or importing sewing machines based on the new, improved design covered by B's patent.

K. Maintenance Fees

While the duration of rights stemming from a patent will generally be 20 years from the date on which the application for the patent was filed in the United States, in order for these rights to remain in force for this entire term, the patent holder must periodically pay maintenance fees. A maintenance fee is due 3 1/2, 7 1/2, and 11 1/2 years after the original grant for all patents issuing from the applications filed on and after December 12, 1980.

L. Patent Expiration

After a patent has expired anyone may make, use, offer for sale, sell, or import the formerly patented invention without permission of the patentee, provided that matter covered by other unexpired patents is not used. Free public access to a formerly patented invention is part of the public policy bargain under which a patent applicant discloses a patented invention (in a published patent application or issued patent) and ultimately dedicates the invention to the public in exchange for a temporary period of control over the invention during the life of a patent. Any attempt of a patent holder to extend the force or impact of a patent beyond the 20-year term of the patent will generally be seen as patent abuse or a violation of antitrust laws.

M. Relief for Patent Infringement

Patent infringement consists of the unauthorized making, using, offering for sale, or selling any patented invention within the United States or United States Territories, or importing into the United States of any patented invention during the term of the patent. The USPTO has no jurisdiction over questions relating to infringement of patents. In examining applications for patent, no determination is made as to whether the invention sought to be patented infringes any prior patent. An improvement invention may be patentable, but it might also infringe a prior unexpired patent for the invention improved upon.

If a patent is infringed, the patentee may sue for relief in the appropriate federal court — usually the federal district court where the infringement occurred or where the defendant resides. The patentee can typically obtain an injunction to prevent the continuation of the infringement, provided that the patent holder can show irreparable harm should the infringement continue. The patentee can also obtain an award of damages related to past infringement.

In such an infringement suit, the defendant may contest the validity of the patent in question. While patents are presumed valid once issued and the burden is on a defendant in an infringement suit to establish patent invalidity, patents are invalidated in litigation with substantial frequency. This sometimes results because a defendant threatened with extensive infringement liability uncovers evidence bearing on patentability that was not considered by the USPTO. For example, a defendant might find new evidence of prior knowledge in the field which indicates that the patented invention at issue was not new when created by the patent applicant or that the invention was merely an unpatentable, obvious extension of prior designs.

In addition to challenging the patent at issue, a defendant in a patent infringement action may claim that, even if the patent is valid, the defendant's conduct does not infringe the patent. The patent holder bears the burden of establishing patent infringement. This can be established by proof that the item or process made, used, sold, or imported by the defendant included all of the elements of the patented invention or, if one or more elements are missing, that the defendant's item or process included an equivalent of the missing element or elements. Infringement is determined primarily by the language of the claims of the patent. If the defendant's item or process does not involve the elements of the patented invention as defined in the patent claims (or equivalents of these elements), then there is no patent infringement.

Suits for infringement of patents follow the rules of procedure of the federal courts. The decision of a federal district court regarding patent infringement can be appealed to the Court of Appeals for the Federal Circuit. This court is highly experienced and knowledgeable concerning patent matters, hearing patent appeals from across the country. The rulings of the Court of Appeals for the Federal Circuit often constitute the final word on important patent issues, subject only to being overruled occasionally based on a rare successful appeal of a patent case to the Supreme Court. In addition to cases involving patent infringement which are heard by federal courts, suits turning on contracts for patent assignments and licenses can be decided in state courts, as can cases which are based primarily on state law claims, but which involve patent issues in counterclaims.

If the United States Government infringes a patent, a patentee has a remedy for damages in the United States Court of Federal Claims, but the patentee cannot stop the Government from using the patented invention at issue. The Government may use any patented invention without permission of the patentee, but the patentee is entitled to obtain compensation for the use by or for the Government.

N. Patent Marking and Notices of "Patent Pending"

A patentee who makes or sells patented articles or a person who does so for or under the authorization of the patentee will typically mark the articles with the word "Patent" followed by the number of the patent. If the patent holder does not mark articles in this way, the patentee may not recover damages from an infringer unless the infringer had actual notice of the applicable patent and continued to infringe after gaining such notice. There is no equivalent rule regarding the desirability of giving notice of an applicable patent when a patented process is carried out. The holder of a process patent can recover damages from an infringer of the patent regardless of whether the patentee gave notice of the patent before the infringement occurred.

Some persons mark articles sold with the terms "Patent Applied For" or "Patent Pending." These phrases have no formal legal effect, but do, if used honestly, give purchasers and users of the articles information that an application for patent has been filed in the USPTO and that patent rights concerning the article may arise in the future. The protection afforded by a patent does not start until the actual grant of the patent (or, in the case of published patent applications, upon the date of publication). False use of these phrases or their equivalents may constitute fraud or an unfair marketing practice providing a basis for recoveries by parties who are injured by the false message conveyed.

O. Patent Assignments and Licenses

1. Forms of Assignments

A patent is personal property and may be sold to others or mortgaged, bequeathed by a will, and passed to the heirs of a deceased patentee. The Patent Act provides for the transfer or sale of a patent, or of an application for patent, by an instrument in writing. Such an instrument is referred to as an assignment and may transfer the entire interest in the patent. The assignee, when the patent is assigned to him or her, becomes the owner of the patent and has the same rights that the original patentee had.

The Patent Act also provides for the assignment of a part interest, that is, a half interest, a fourth interest, etc., in a patent. A mortgage of a patent passes ownership of the patent to the mortgagee or lender until the mortgage has been satisfied. This will occur when the mortgagor—the borrower—pays the full amount of the loan secured by the mortgage. A conditional assignment also passes ownership of a patent and is regarded as absolute until canceled by the parties or by the decree of a competent court.

An assignment, grant, or conveyance of any patent or application for patent should be acknowledged before a notary public or officer authorized to administer oaths or perform notarial acts. The certificate of such acknowledgment constitutes prima facie evidence of the execution of the assignment, grant, or conveyance.

Sometimes a patent assignment is made before a patent has even issued. For example, it is common for employees of large companies who develop inventions as part of their jobs to be obligated by the terms of their employment to assign their rights in patent applications to their employers. An assignment agreement relating to an application should identify the application by its application number and date of filing, the name of the inventor, and the title of the invention as stated in the application. If an application for a patent has been assigned and the assignment is recorded on or before the date the issue fee for the patent is paid, the patent will be issued to the assignee as owner. If the assignment is of a part interest only, the patent will be issued to the inventor and assignee as joint owners.

2. Recording of Assignments

The USPTO records assignments, grants, and similar instruments in an official registry. The recording of these instruments serves as constructive (that is, legally presumed) notice to other parties of the assignment or other transfer. If an assignment, grant, or conveyance of a patent or an interest in a patent (or an application for patent) is not recorded in the Office within three months from its date and is still unrecorded when a second attempt to transfer the same interest is made, the first transfer is void against a subsequent purchaser of the same interest who takes the interest in exchange for valuable consideration and without notice of the first transfer. This means that if party A holds a patent and transfers it via an assignment to another party B, but B does not record the assignment, A's second assignment of the same patent to C in exchange for valuable consideration will be effective and C will hold the patent unless C had actual notice of the prior assignment to B. This type of impact of the recording statute is aimed at encouraging the recording of patent transfers and at protecting the interests of innocent purchasers such as C who have dealt with parties who appear, from the official records of issued patents and patent assignments, to be the owners of particular patents.

3. Patent Licenses

A patent license does not entail a transfer of patent ownership, but rather involves a grant of rights from a patent holder to another. Patent licenses are either exclusive or nonexclusive. An exclusive license grants the licensee the right to make, use, sell, or import a patented invention (or some portion of these rights) without fear of an infringement action by the patent holder and with the further guarantee that the patent holder will not grant equivalent rights to any other party. A nonexclusive license grants the licensee the right to undertake what would otherwise be infringing actions, but does not provide the licensee with any assurance that the patent holder will not grant equivalent rights to additional parties. In essence, an exclusive license conveys a unique opportunity to the licensee, while a nonexclusive license merely signifies a patent holder's permission for the licensee to proceed with a specified activity concerning a patented invention free from the risk of an infringement suit.

P. International Considerations

1. Foreign Patents and Patent Rights

Since the rights granted by a United States patent extend only throughout the territory of the United States and have no effect in a foreign country, an inventor who wishes patent protection in other countries must apply for a patent in each of the other countries or in regional patent offices (such as the European Patent Office) which can grant patents covering entire regions encompassing several countries.

The laws of many countries differ in various respects from the patent laws of the United States. Many foreign countries require that a patented invention must be manufactured in that country after a certain period, usually three years. If there is no manufacturing within this period, the patent involved will be void in some countries, although in most countries the patent will be subject to the grant of compulsory licenses to any persons who apply for licenses.

2. The Paris Convention

Several international treaties specify aspects of patent systems which the signatory countries have agreed to implement in order to create greater uniformity in the patent laws of various countries. One key treaty of this sort, adhered to by 175 countries as of 2014 (including the United States), is the Paris Convention for the Protection of Industrial Property. It provides that each country guarantees to the citizens of the other countries the same rights in patent and trademark matters that it gives to its own citizens. This means that, for example, a German inventor applying for a United States patent will have the same opportunity to gain a patent and have the same rights if a patent is issued as would a United States citizen. Similarly, a United States inventor seeking a German patent must be afforded the same opportunities and rights as a German citizen.

The Paris Convention also establishes important rules regarding the right of priority in the case of utility patents, and industrial designs (design patents). This right means that, once an applicant files a regular patent application on an invention or design in one of the signatory countries governed by the treaty, the applicant may, within a certain period of time, apply for utility or design patent protection in all the other member countries. The later applications will then be regarded as if they had been filed on the same day as the first application. This right is referred to as one involving "priority" because the applicant's second and subsequent applications, having an effective filing date of the first application, will have priority over patent applications of other parties for the same invention that may have been filed during the gap in time between the first and subsequent applications. Moreover, the later applications, having the benefit of the filing date of the first application, will not be invalidated by any acts accomplished in the intervals between the first and subsequent applications, such as, for example, publication or exploitation of an invention or the sale of copies of items bearing an industrial design. The period in which subsequent applications may be filed in the other countries and still gain the filing date of a first application is 12 months in the case of applications for utility patents and six months in the case of applications for industrial design or design patent protection.

3. The Patent Cooperation Treaty (PCT)

The Patent Cooperation Treaty (PCT) was negotiated in 1970 to streamline the process of securing patents in multiple countries. An application submitted in accordance with the PCT (sometimes called a "PCT application") reduces the cost and duplication of effort that would otherwise be involved in filing individual patent applications in multiple countries. The treaty, which came into force in 1978, is open to any country that has joined the Paris Convention and is administered by the United Nation's World Intellectual Property Organization (WIPO). As of 2013, over 148 countries (including the United States) adhere to the PCT.

The PCT facilitates filing for patents on a single invention in multiple countries by providing, among other things, for centralized filing procedures and a standardized application format. The timely filing of an international application affords an applicant an international filing date in each country which is designated in the international application and provides (1) a search of the invention and (2) a later time period within which the national applications for patents must be filed.

4. Foreign Filing License

Under United States law it is necessary, in the case of inventions made in the United States, to obtain a license from the Director of the USPTO before applying for a patent in a foreign country. Such a license is required if the foreign application is to be filed before an application is filed in the United States or before the expiration of six months from the filing of an application in the United States. The filing of an application for a patent constitutes the request for a foreign filing license and the granting or denial of such request is indicated in the filing receipt mailed to each applicant. After six months from the filing of a United States patent application, a license is not required unless the invention involved has been ordered to be kept secret. If the invention has been ordered to be kept secret, consent to a foreign patent filing must be obtained from the Director of the USPTO during the period when the order of secrecy is in effect.

5. Foreign Applicants for United States Patents

Under the patent laws of the United States, any inventor, regardless of citizenship, may apply for a patent on the same basis as a United States citizen. There are, however, a number of particular points of special interest to applicants located in foreign countries.

The application for a patent in the United States must be made by an inventor and the inventor must sign an oath or declaration confirming that he or she is the inventor of the claimed invention. This differs from the law in many countries where the signature of the inventor and an oath of inventorship are not necessary. If an inventor is dead, an application for a United States patent may be made by his/her executor or administrator, or equivalent, and in the case of mental disability it may be made by his/her legal representative (guardian).

A United States utility patent cannot be obtained if an invention was patented abroad before applying in the United States by the inventor or his or her legal representatives if the foreign application was filed more than 12 months before filing in the United States.

An application for a patent filed in the United States by any person who has previously filed an application for a patent for the same invention in a foreign country (provided the country affords similar privileges to citizens of the United States) shall have the same force and effect for the purpose of overcoming intervening acts of others as if filed in the United States on the date on which the application for a patent for the same invention was first filed in the foreign country. This is the case, provided the application for a United States utility patent is filed within 12 months (six months in the case of a design patent) from the earliest date on which any corresponding foreign application was filed.

III. Copyright Laws[3]

A. Copyrightable Works

Copyright is a form of protection provided by the laws of the United States to the authors of "original works of authorship," including literary, dramatic, musical, artistic, and certain other intellectual works. This protection is available to both published and unpublished works. In general, a copyright permits the holder to control how a protected work is copied, reused and modified as the basis for further works, and distributed or otherwise communicated to the public.

---

3. The material on United States copyright laws in this section is based on United States Copyright Office, Copyright Basics, http://copyright.gov/circs/circ01.pdf, and United States Copyright Office, Frequently Asked Questions About Copyright, http://www.copyright.gov/help/faq/ (accessed 11/17/2017).

Copyright protections arise automatically at the moment a work is created and fixed in a tangible form that is perceptible either directly or with the aid of a machine or device. Thus, for example, a person keeping a private diary gains copyright protection in this work as entries are made. A copyright notice is an identifier placed on copies of the work to inform the world of copyright ownership. This notice generally consists of the symbol "©" or word "copyright (or copr.)," the name of the copyright owner, and the year of first publication, e.g., "©2003 John Doe." While use of a copyright notice was once required as a condition of copyright protection, it is now optional. However, even though optional, the use of a copyright notice on a work is often desirable as a means to undercut assertions by persons reading and reproducing the work (or engaging in other infringing acts) that their conduct constituted unknowing or "innocent" infringement not warranting an award of statutory damages.

Copyrights do not protect ideas, concepts, systems, or methods of doing something. A person may express ideas in writing or drawings and claim copyright in the resulting description of the ideas, but copyright will not protect the ideas themselves as revealed in a written or artistic work.

In contrast to works protected by copyrights, many works are in the "public domain." A work of authorship is in the "public domain" if it was once copyrighted but is no longer under copyright protection or if it failed to ever meet the requirements for copyright protection. Works in the public domain may be used freely without the permission of the former copyright owner or any other party.

B. Copyright Registration

Registration of a copyright with the United States Copyright Office (an agency within the Library of Congress) is not needed to establish copyright protections. However, registration is often desirable for several reasons. The advantages of registration include the following:

- Registration establishes a public record of a copyright interest.

- Before an infringement suit may be filed in court, registration is necessary for works of United States origin.

- If made before or within five years of publication, registration will establish prima facie evidence in court of the validity of a copyright and of the facts stated in the certificate of registration received from the Copyright Office.

- If registration is made prior to an infringement of a work, statutory damages and attorney's fees will be available to the copyright owner in court actions. For published works, if the copyright owner registers within three months of publication, statutory damages and attorney's fees are available for any infringement that occurs after publication and before registration.

- Registration allows the owner of the copyright to record the registration with the United States Customs Service for protection against the importation of infringing copies.

To register a copyrighted work, a copyright holder must submit to the Copyright Office a completed application form, a nonrefundable filing fee of $30, and a nonreturnable copy or copies of the work to be registered. A person may register an initial work and then also register an altered version of the work provided that the changes are substantial and creative, something more than just editorial changes or minor alterations. For instance, simply making spelling corrections throughout a work does not warrant a new registration, but adding an additional chapter would.

C. Initial Copyright Ownership

Where a work is created by an independent author, the associated copyright in the work immediately becomes the property of the author. Only the author or those deriving their rights through the author can rightfully claim the copyright.

Different rules regarding initial copyright ownership apply to works produced by an author for another party—referred to as "works made for hire" in the federal copyright statute. One common type of work made for hire is a work created by an employee while working for a large corporation or other employer. In the case of such a work made for hire, the employer and not the employee is considered to be the author of the work and is recognized as the initial copyright holder.

Federal copyright laws define a "work made for hire" as:

"(1) a work prepared by an employee within the scope of his or her employment; or

(2) a work specially ordered or commissioned for use as a contribution to a collective work, as a part of a motion picture or other audiovisual work, as a translation, as a supplementary work, as a compilation, as an instructional text, as a test, as answer material for a test, or as an atlas, if the parties expressly agree in a written instrument signed by them that the work shall be considered a work made for hire . . . ."

In some instances, multiple authors will contribute to the creation of a single work—referred to as a "joint work." The authors of a joint work are co-owners of the copyright in the work, unless there is an agreement to the contrary. Co-owners of a copyright in a work will each be able to authorize copies of the work to be made and to authorize other normally infringing activities unless there is a contrary agreement among the co-owners.

The copyright covering each separate contribution to a periodical or other collective work—such as the copyright covering an individual article included in a magazine where the authors are not employees of the magazine—is distinct from the copyright in the collective work as a whole and vests initially with the author of the contribution.

D. Rights of Copyright Holders

The federal Copyright Act generally gives the owner of a copyright the exclusive right to do and to authorize others to do the following:

- *To reproduce* the work in copies or phonorecords;
- To prepare *derivative works* based upon the work;
- *To distribute copies or phonorecords* of the work to the public by sale or other transfer of ownership, or by rental, lease, or lending;
- To perform the work publicly, in the case of literary, musical, dramatic, and choreographic works, pantomimes, and motion pictures and other audiovisual works;
- *To display the copyrighted work publicly,* in the case of literary, musical, dramatic, and choreographic works, pantomimes, and pictorial, graphic, or sculptural works, including the individual images of a motion picture or other audio-visual work; and
- In the case of *sound recordings, to perform the work publicly* by means of a *digital audio transmission.*

Certain authors of works of visual art also have rights of attribution and rights to control the integrity of these sorts of works.

In addition to their control over copying of a protected work, copyright holders' exclusive right to authorize the making of derivative works from a protected original work gives these parties considerable control over how elements of a protected work are reused in subsequent works. A derivative work is one that is based or "derived from" a prior work protected by a copyright and that incorporates unchanged or modified versions of protected expression from the original work. Examples of derivative works include translations, musical arrangements, dramatizations, fictionalizations, art reproductions, and condensations.

The opportunity to create derivative works can be a highly valuable offshoot of an initial copyright. For example, the holder of the copyright in a movie such as "Star Wars" can control and license for considerable profit the opportunities to make action figures and other derivative works based on characters from the movie.

Any work in which the editorial revisions, annotations, elaborations, or other modifications represent, as a whole, an original work of authorship may qualify for a copyright as a new derivative work. This copyright interest concerning the derivative work is recognized in addition to the copyright covering the original work on which the derivative work was based. Where these separate copyright interests are held by different parties, all of these parties will need to approve the reproduction of the derivative work, but only the holder of the copyright on the original work needs to approve copying of that work.

Because copyright protections extend only to creative expression and not to the ideas conveyed by the expression, persons are free to reuse the ideas or information that are described in a publicly available copyrighted work so long as the persons do not reuse the particular words or other means of expression used to describe the ideas or information in the copyrighted work. Similarly, copyright protections do not extend to a procedure, process, system, method of operation, concept, principle, or discovery described or otherwise communicated in a copyrighted work.

For example, if an author writes a book explaining a new system for food processing, the copyright in the book, which comes into effect at the moment the work is fixed in a tangible form, will prevent others from publishing the text and illustrations describing the author's ideas for machinery, processes, and merchandising methods. But this copyright will not give the author any rights to prevent others from adopting the ideas for commercial purposes or from developing or using the machinery, processes, or methods described in the book.

A copyright holder generally does not have control over a particular copy of a copyrighted work (such as a single copy of a copyrighted book) once the copy has been sold in a manner authorized by the copyright holder. A buyer's legitimately obtained ownership of a single copy of a work generally gives the owner the right to make full private use of that copy (other than to make an additional copy or other reproduction of the work) and to sell the single copy to another owner. However, mere ownership of a book, manuscript, painting, or any other copy or phonorecord does not give the possessor an interest in the copyright concerning the contents. The law provides that transfer of ownership of any material object that embodies a protected work does not of itself convey any rights in the copyright.

E. Fair Use Limitations on Copyright Enforcement

The rights of copyright holders are limited by several important doctrines. For example, actions that would otherwise constitute copyright infringement are not a basis for liability where they involve "fair use" of copyrighted materials. The nature of a fair use of copyrighted materials is not defined in the Copyright Act. However, in general, uses that are commercially insignificant or that support socially valuable activities (such as political criticism or news reporting) are considered fair use and not infringing. In contrast, uses of materials in ways that are likely to have a negative impact upon the potential market for or value of a copyrighted work are not likely to be viewed as fair uses.

The Copyright Act indicates that the following factors should be considered in determining if a particular use of a copyrighted work is a fair use free from infringement liability:

1. the purpose and character of the use, including whether such use is of commercial nature or is for nonprofit educational purposes;

2. the nature of the copyrighted work;

3. the amount and substantiality of the portion used in relation to the copyrighted work as a whole; and

4. the effect of the use upon the potential market for or value of the copyrighted work.

There is no specific number of words, lines, or notes from a copyrighted work that may safely be reused without permission. Acknowledging the source of copyrighted material when the material is reused does not substitute for obtaining permission and does not automatically constitute fair use.

Examples of activities that courts have regarded as fair use include: quotation of excerpts in a review or criticism for purposes of illustration or comment; quotation of short passages in a scholarly or technical work, for illustration or clarification of the author's observations; use in a parody of some of the content of the work parodied; summary of an address or article, with brief quotations, in a news report; reproduction by a library of a portion of a work to replace part of a damaged copy; reproduction by a teacher or student of a small part of a work to illustrate a lesson; reproduction of a work in legislative or judicial proceedings or reports; incidental and fortuitous reproduction, in a newsreel or broadcast, of a work located in the scene of an event being reported; intermediate copying of protected software to understand unprotected systems and methods in hardware, like a videogame machine; and making intermediate copies of books to create a searchable database library displaying snippets of text. Home videorecording of over the air television broadcast for later viewing was held to be fair use by the Supreme Court in *Sony v. Universal Studios* in 1984. Later business disputes have revolved around the application of this precedent to digital video recording and other online systems for consumer time shifting of television programs.

F. Compulsory Licenses as Limitations on Copyright Enforcement

Holders of copyrights in certain types of works are also limited in their enforcement rights by "compulsory license" provisions of federal copyright laws. These provisions compel copyright holders to permit the use of certain works in exchange for a defined compensation. However, compulsory licenses apply only to specialized types of copyrightable works.

For example, a compulsory license is available to anyone wishing to record a musical work as soon as phonorecords of a nondramatic musical work have been distributed to the public in the United States under the authority of the copyright owner. This means that, once the holder of a copyright in a musical work authorizes one artist to initially record the work and the resulting recordings are distributed to the public, additional artists can rerecord their versions of the work without the permission of the holder of the copyright on the underlying musical work. However, to make these additional recordings, the second and subsequent recording artists must pay the copyright holder a licensing fee. Such provisions establish a "compulsory license" because the licensor has no choice but to allow the use covered by the compulsory license in exchange for the required royalty payment.

Thus, provided that a prior recording of the work by a singer such as Bing Crosby had been authorized and distributed to the public, a singer such as Elvis Presley would be entitled to record a song such as "White Christmas" regardless of whether Irving Berlin, the composer, agreed so long as the second recording artist paid the statutorily-defined royalty for use of the song. Such compulsory license provisions are included in United States copyright laws to encourage rerecording of musical works without allowing the original creators of the works to narrowly constrain how the works may be reused.

For companies involved in the cable or satellite industries, Congress created compulsory licensing rules for use of content from broadcast television stations. The impact of these compulsory licensing rules on online transmissions of television broadcasts is unclear and has produced significant litigation over the boundaries of these compulsory licensing rules.

G. Remedies for Copyright Infringement

As a general matter, copyright infringement occurs when a copyrighted work is reproduced, distributed, performed, publicly displayed, or made into a derivative work without the permission of the copyright owner. A copyright holder, through a legal action brought in a federal court, can obtain several types of remedies for past and future copyright infringement.

A federal judge can grant such an injunction as the judge deems reasonable to prevent or restrain infringement of a copyright. A judge can also order the destruction or other reasonable disposition of all copies or phonorecords found to have been made or used in violation of a copyright owner's exclusive rights, and of all plates, molds, matrices, masters, tapes, film negatives, or other items by means of which such copies or phonorecords may be reproduced.

For infringement already completed at the time of a suit, a copyright holder can recover either (1) the copyright owner's actual damages and any additional profits of the infringer, or (2) statutory damages.

If a copyright holder elects to seek actual damages, she is entitled to recover the monetary damages suffered as a result of the infringement, and any profits of the infringer that are attributable to the infringement and that are not taken into account in computing the actual damages. In establishing the infringer's profits, the copyright owner is required to present proof only of the infringer's gross revenues, and the infringer is required to prove his deductible expenses and the elements of profit attributable to factors other than the copyrighted work.

A copyright holder who elects to recover statutory damages for non-willful copyright infringement can obtain, instead of actual damages and profits, an award of statutory damages. Statutory damages for all infringements involved in a lawsuit with respect to any one work shall be not less than $750 or more than $30,000 as the judge in the case considers just. For willful infringement—that is, conduct known to infringe an outstanding copyright—statutory damages are authorized up to a limit of $150,000.

However, in a case where the infringer sustains the burden of proving, and the judge involved in the case finds, that the infringer was not aware and had no reason to believe that his or her acts constituted an infringement of a copyright, the judge in her discretion may reduce the award of statutory damages to a sum of not less than $200.

H. Duration of Copyright Protections

1. Works Originally Created on or after January 1, 1978

A work that is created (fixed in tangible form for the first time) on or after January 1, 1978, is automatically protected from the moment of its creation and is ordinarily given a term of copyright protection enduring for the author's life plus an additional 70 years after the author's death. In the case of "a joint work prepared by two or more authors who did not work for hire," the term lasts for 70 years after the last surviving author's death. For works made for hire, and for anonymous and pseudonymous works (unless the author's identity is revealed in Copyright Office records), the duration of copyright protections will be 95 years from publication or 120 years from creation, whichever period is shorter.

2. Works Originally Created before January 1, 1978, But Not Published or Registered by That Date

The duration of copyright in these works will generally be computed in the same way as for works created on or after January 1, 1978 — that is, the life-plus-70 or 95/120-year terms will apply to them as well. The law provides that in no case will the term of copyright for works in this category expire before December 31, 2002, and for works published on or before December 31, 2002, the term of copyright will not expire before December 31, 2047.

3. Works Originally Created and Published or Registered before January 1, 1978

Under the law in effect before 1978, copyright was secured either on the date a work was published with a copyright notice or on the date of registration if the work was registered in unpublished form. In either case, the copyright endured for a first term of 28 years from the date it was secured. During the last (28th) year of the first term, the copyright was eligible for renewal. The Copyright Act of 1976 extended the renewal term from 28 to 47 years for copyrights that were subsisting on January 1, 1978, making these works eligible for a total term of protection of 75 years.

Public Law 105-298, enacted on October 27, 1998, further extended the renewal term of copyrights still subsisting on that date by an additional 20 years, providing for a renewal term of 67 years and a total term of protection of 95 years.

Public Law 102-307, enacted on June 26, 1992, amended the 1976 Copyright Act to provide for automatic renewal of the term of copyrights secured between January 1,

1964, and December 31, 1977. Although the renewal term is automatically provided, the Copyright Office does not issue a renewal certificate for these works unless a renewal application and fee are received and registered in the Copyright Office.

Public Law 102-307 makes renewal registration optional. Thus, filing for renewal registration is no longer required in order to extend the original 28-year copyright term to the full 95 years. However, some benefits accrue from making a renewal registration during the 28th year of the original term.

I. Transfers of Copyright Interests

Transfers of copyright interests are normally made by contract. A contract providing for the transfer of ownership of a copyright interest is referred to as a copyright assignment. Any or all of a copyright owner's exclusive rights or any subdivision of those rights may be transferred, but the transfer of exclusive rights is not valid unless that transfer is in writing and signed by the owner of the rights conveyed or such owner's duly authorized agent. Transfer of a right on a nonexclusive basis does not require a written agreement.

A copyright may also be conveyed by operation of law and may be bequeathed by will or pass as personal property by the applicable laws of intestate succession. A copyright is a personal property right and is subject to the various state laws and regulations that govern the ownership, inheritance, or transfer of personal property.

Federal law includes provisions for the recording in the Copyright Office of transfers of copyright ownership. Although recordation is not required to make a valid transfer between the parties to an assignment agreement, it does provide certain legal advantages and may be required to validate the transfer as against third parties.

Advantages of recording contracts providing for transfers of copyright ownership include:

- Under certain conditions, recordation establishes priorities between conflicting transfers, or between a conflicting transfer and a nonexclusive license.

- Recordation establishes a public record of the contents of the transfer or document.

- Recordation of a document in the Copyright Office provides the advantage of "constructive notice," a legal concept meaning that members of the public are deemed to have knowledge of the facts stated in the document and cannot claim otherwise. The Copyright Act specifies that recordation of a document in the Copyright Office gives all persons constructive notice of the facts stated in the recorded document, but only if:

    (1) The document or material attached to it specifically identifies the work to which it pertains so that, after the document is indexed by the Register of Copyrights, it would be revealed by a reasonable search under the title (or registration number) of the work; and

(2) The copyright in the work has been registered.

- Recordation may be required to perfect a security interest in a copyright although case law on this point is mixed.

IV. Trademark Laws[4]

A. Characteristics of a Trademark or Service Mark

A trademark is a word, phrase, symbol or design, or a combination of these, that identifies and distinguishes the source of the goods of one party from those of others. A service mark is the same as a trademark, except that it identifies and distinguishes the source of a service rather than a product. For purposes of the following summary of trademark laws, the terms "trademark" and "mark" should be assumed to refer to both trademarks and service marks.

A broad range of items may serve as trademarks so long as they are capable of being associated with a particular source of goods or services. While most trademarks are comprised of words, phrases, graphic images, or some combination of these, more exotic items such as distinctive smells, colors, or sounds are capable of identifying the source of products and can qualify for trademark protections. Even the shape of a product package—referred to as the product's "trade dress"—can qualify for the equivalent of trademark protections if the shape is distinctive and associated with a particular product source.

Federal trademark laws provide for the registration of trademarks and nationwide protection against the use of confusingly similar marks by persons other than the registered trademark holder. Federal law also protects against trademark dilution—that is, the use of a famous trademark in a manner that weakens or "dilutes" the public's association of the mark with its owner or which entails a scandalous or otherwise distasteful use of the trademark that tarnishes the mark in the eyes of the public. State laws also provide for registration of trademarks within particular states and for the protection of unregistered trademarks within the areas of their actual use.

The summary which follows focuses on federal trademark laws and protections.

B. Items That May Serve as Trademarks

While other types of symbols or designs may also serve as trademarks, most marks are comprised of a distinctive word, phrase, or graphic work. The following

---

4. The material on United States trademark laws in this section is based on United States Patent and Trademark Office, Basic Facts About Trademarks, https://web.archive.org/web/20081218000417/http://www.uspto.gov/web/offices/tac/doc/basic//index.html, and United States Trademark Office, Frequently Asked Questions About Trademarks, https://web.archive.org/web/20140131052951/http://www.uspto.gov/faq/trademarks.jsp (accessed 11/17/2017).

are examples of each of these common types of marks along with typical information on the goods involved in the registration of these marks.

1. Textual Marks

If a mark is comprised of a word or phrase, does not depend on the use of a particular font to present the word or phrase, and does not incorporate any further graphical element, a registration may be sought for the word or phrase itself. If granted, the registration would apply to all forms of presentation as a trademark of the registered word or phrase. Since a merely descriptive term will be refused registration, a word or phrase granted registration will usually be made up or distinctively modified to be different from mere descriptive contents. The following registration material covers a typical textual trademark involving a single coined word.

Applicant's Name: A-OK Software Development Group

Correspondence Address: 100 Main Street, Any Town, MO 12345

Goods and Services: Computer services, namely on-line magazine in the field of business management

Date of First Use: January 15, 1995

Date of First Use in Commerce: May 15, 1995

Standard Character Claim: The mark is presented in standard character format without claim to any particular font style, size or color.

The Mark:

THEORYTEC

---

2. Graphical Marks

Where the appearance of a mark is one of its distinctive features — either because the mark includes a graphical element or because the mark involves letters or text presented in a particular font or with a particular appearance — protection should be sought for the mark's specific visual form. The following is an example of registration material for a mark which includes both a graphic work and a textual element:

Applicant's Name: Pinstripes, Inc.

Applicant's Address: 100 Main Street, Any Town, MO 12345

Goods and Services: Clothing, namely baseball caps and t-shirts

Date of First Use: Intent-to-Use Application

Date of First Use in Commerce: Intent-to-Use Application

The Mark:

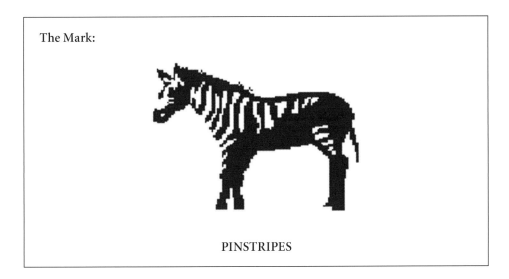

PINSTRIPES

C. Registering a Trademark

An application to the USPTO for registration of a trademark must include the following elements:

- the name of the applicant;
- a name and address for correspondence;
- a clear drawing of the mark;
- a listing of the goods or services for which registration is sought; and
- the filing fee for at least one class of goods or services.

The application must be filed in the name of the owner of the mark. The owner of the mark is the person or entity who controls the nature and quality of the goods identified by the mark or the services rendered in connection with the mark. The owner may be an individual, corporation, partnership, or other type of legal entity.

An applicant must list the specific goods or services for which registration is sought, regardless of the basis for the application. Most U.S. applicants base their application on their current use of a mark in commerce, or their intent to use their mark in commerce in the future. In addition, a party may base an application for registration of a trademark in the United States based on an application for trademark registration in another country.

1. Application Based on Use in Commerce

If a party has already started using a mark in commerce, the party may file an application for registration of the mark based on that use. For purposes of trademark registration application requirements, "commerce" means all commerce that the United States government may lawfully regulate, including interstate commerce and commerce between the United States and another country. A "use in commerce" is a bona fide use of the mark in the ordinary course of trade, and not a use simply made to reserve rights in the mark. Generally, acceptable uses include the following:

For goods: the mark must appear on the goods, the container for the goods, or displays associated with the goods, and the goods must be sold or transported in commerce.

For services: the mark must be used or displayed in the sale or advertising of the services, and the services must be rendered in commerce.

A "use" based application must include a sworn statement (usually in the form of a declaration) that the mark involved is in use in commerce, listing the date of first use of the mark anywhere and the date of first use of the mark in commerce. The applicant or a person authorized to sign on behalf of the applicant must sign the statement. The application should include a specimen showing use of the mark in commerce.

2. Application Based on Intent to Use

If a party has not yet used a mark when registration is sought, but plans to do so in the future, the party may file based on a good faith or bona fide intention to use the mark in commerce. An "intent to use" application must include a sworn statement (usually in the form of a declaration) that the applicant has a bona fide intention to use the mark in commerce. The applicant or a person authorized to sign on behalf of the applicant must sign the statement.

If a party files for a trademark registration based on an intent to use a mark, the applicant must begin actual use of the mark in commerce before the USPTO will register the mark. After filing an application based on an intent to use, the applicant must later file another form to establish that use of the mark has begun.

D. Role of the USPTO

The United States Patent and Trademark Office (USPTO) reviews trademark applications for federal registration and determines whether an applicant meets the requirements for federal registration. USPTO officials do not decide whether an applicant has the right to use a mark (which differs from the right to register).

After the USPTO determines that a party has met the minimum filing requirements for a registration application, the application is forwarded to an examining attorney. The evaluation of the trademark application by this attorney may take a number of months. The examining attorney reviews the application to determine whether it complies with all applicable rules and statutes and includes all required fees. A complete examination also includes a search for conflicting marks, and a review of the sufficiency of the written application, the drawing, and any specimen.

If the examining attorney decides that a mark should not be registered, the attorney will issue a letter describing the negative "office action" being taken based on the attorney's review and explaining any substantive or procedural deficiencies in the application. If only minor corrections are required, the examining attorney may contact the applicant by telephone or e-mail. If the examining attorney sends a notice of an office action, the applicant's response to the office action must be received in the USPTO within six months of the mailing date of the notice of the office action or the application will be declared abandoned.

If an applicant's response to a negative office action does not overcome all the examiner's objections to the registration of a proposed mark, the examining attorney will issue a final refusal to register the mark. To attempt to overcome a final refusal, the applicant may, for an additional fee, appeal to the Trademark Trial and Appeal Board, an administrative tribunal within the USPTO.

E. Bases for Rejection of a Trademark Registration Application

1. Likelihood of Confusion with an Existing Mark

As part of her review of a trademark application, an examining attorney will search the USPTO records to determine if a conflict—i.e., a likelihood of confusion—exists between the mark in the application and another mark that is registered or for which a registration application is pending in the USPTO. The principal factors considered by the examining attorney in determining whether there would be a likelihood of confusion are:

- the similarity of the marks; and
- the commercial relationship between the goods or services listed in the application and those associated with the potentially conflicting mark.

To create a conflict, marks do not have to be identical, and the goods or services associated with the marks do not have to be the same. It may be enough that the marks are similar and the goods or services are related.

If a conflict exists between a mark in a registration application and a registered mark, the examining attorney will refuse registration on the ground of a likelihood of confusion. If a conflict exists between a mark in a new registration application and a mark in a pending application that was filed before the new application, the examining attorney will notify the second applicant of the potential conflict. If the earlier-filed application results in the registration of the mark involved, the examining attorney will refuse registration of the mark covered by the second application on the ground of a likelihood of confusion.

2. Other Grounds for Rejection

In addition to refusing to register a proposed mark based on a likelihood of confusion with an existing mark, an examining attorney will refuse registration if the new mark is:

- primarily descriptive or deceptively misdescriptive of the goods or services associated with the mark;

- primarily geographically descriptive or deceptively misdescriptive of the goods or services associated with the mark;
- primarily used as a surname; or
- ornamental.

A mark also will be rejected for registration if the mark involves immoral or scandalous matter, deceptive matter, or matter that may disparage, or bring into contempt or disrepute, persons, institutions, beliefs or national symbols.

F. Impacts of Trademark Registration

Registration of a trademark is not necessary to establish rights in a trademark. However, registering a trademark generally provides the mark owner with several advantages, including establishing:

- constructive notice to the public of the registrant's claim of ownership of the mark;
- a legal presumption of the registrant's ownership of the mark and the registrant's exclusive right to use the mark nationwide on or in connection with the goods and/or services listed in the registration;
- the ability to bring an action concerning the mark in federal court;
- the use of the U.S. registration as a basis to obtain registration in foreign countries; and
- the ability to file the U.S. registration with the U.S. Customs Service to prevent importation of infringing foreign goods.

G. Use of Trademark Symbols TM, SM, and ®

Any time a party claims rights in a mark, the party may use the "TM" (trademark) or "SM" (service mark) designation to alert the public to this claim, regardless of whether the party has filed an application for registration of the mark with the USPTO. However, a party can only use the federal registration symbol "®" after the USPTO actually registers a mark, and not while an application is pending. Also, a party may use the registration symbol with the mark only on or in connection with the goods or services listed in the federal trademark registration.

H. Duration of Trademark Protections

Rights in a federally-registered trademark can last indefinitely if the owner continues to use the mark on or in connection with the goods or services specified in connection with registration of the mark and the owner files all necessary documentation in the USPTO at the appropriate times. In general, to keep federal trademark rights in force and avoid the cancellation of the registration of a mark, the owner of a registered mark must periodically file:

- Affidavits of Continued Use or Excusable Nonuse of a Mark; and
- Applications for Renewal of the Registration.

An affidavit of continued use or excusable nonuse of a mark must be filed on a date that falls on or between the fifth and sixth anniversaries of the registration of the mark (or, for an extra fee of $100.00 per trademark class, a trademark holder may file this affidavit within the six-month grace period following the sixth anniversary of registration of the mark). The failure of a trademark owner to file this affidavit in a timely manner will result in cancellation of the registration of the mark.

Between the ninth and tenth anniversaries of the registration of a trademark, and at the end of each successive ten-year period thereafter, a trademark owner must file both an affidavit of continued use or excusable nonuse of the mark and a registration renewal application (or, for an extra fee of $200.00 per class, the owner may file these two documents within the six-month grace period following the normal filing period). The failure to file either of these documents in a timely fashion will result in the cancellation of the registration of the mark.

I. Trademark Infringement and Remedies

Federal trademark laws provide that a person who, without the consent of the registrant:

(a) uses in commerce any reproduction, counterfeit, copy, or colorable imitation of a registered mark in connection with the sale, offering for sale, distribution, or advertising of any goods or services on or in connection with which such use is likely to cause confusion, or to cause mistake, or to deceive; or

(b) reproduces, counterfeits, copies or colorably imitates a registered mark and applies such reproduction, counterfeit, copy or colorable imitation to labels, signs, prints, packages, wrappers, receptacles, or advertisements intended to be used in commerce upon or in connection with the sale, offering for sale, distribution, or advertising of goods or services on or in connection with which such use is likely to cause confusion, or to cause mistake, or to deceive,

is liable to the registrant for trademark infringement. Remedies available to the registrant in these circumstances include the recovery of damages and the issuance of injunctions barring further infringement.

Damage recoveries for past trademark infringement generally extend to (1) the infringer's profits, (2) any further damages sustained by the trademark registrant, and (3) the costs of the legal action enforcing the registrant's rights. However, where liability is premised on a party's application of an imitation of a registered mark to items in commerce, the owner of a registered trademark will not be entitled to recover profits or damages unless the acts have been committed with knowledge that such imitation is intended to be used to cause confusion, or to cause mistake, or to deceive.

Once trademark infringement is established in a legal action, the court involved may also order that all labels, signs, prints, packages, wrappers, receptacles, and advertisements in the possession of the defendant, bearing the registered mark and all plates, molds, matrices, and other means of making the same, shall be delivered up and destroyed.

A trademark owner establishing trademark infringement is generally also entitled to an injunction barring the defendant from undertaking further infringing activities. The scope of this type of injunction will be determined in accordance with principles of equity and upon such terms as the court in the case deems reasonable.

A trademark owner may also obtain further relief against the attempted importation of goods bearing an unauthorized copy or simulation of a registered trademark. Such relief includes the barring of such goods from entry into the United States and is administered by United States customs officials.

J. Further Remedies for False Designations of Origin or False Descriptions

Section 43(a) of the Lanham Act codifies federal common law protection for trademarks and trade dress. Section 43(a) provides a federal civil cause of action against the "false designation of origin or false description" of a product or service as follows:

(a) Civil action.

(1) Any person who, on or in connection with any goods or services, or any container for goods, uses in commerce any word, term, name, symbol, or device, or any combination thereof, or any false designation of origin, false or misleading description of fact, or false or misleading representation of fact, which—

(A) is likely to cause confusion, or to cause mistake, or to deceive as to the affiliation, connection, or association of such person with another person, or as to the origin, sponsorship, or approval of his or her goods, services, or commercial activities by another person, or

(B) in commercial advertising or promotion, misrepresents the nature, characteristics, qualities, or geographic origin of his or her or another person's goods, services, or commercial activities,

shall be liable in a civil action by any person who believes that he or she is or is likely to be damaged by such act.

Lanham Act § 43(a), 15 U.S.C. § 1125(a) (2005). Note that registration of a mark is not a prerequisite for protection under § 43(a) of the Lanham Act. Most trade dress and product configurations are not registered and therefore depend on § 43(a) for protection.

K. Transfers of Trademark Interests

Federal trademark statutes specify that a registered mark or a mark for which an application to register has been filed shall be assignable with the good will of the business in which the mark is used, or with that part of the good will of the business which is connected with the use of and symbolized by the mark. An assignment agreement transferring a trademark interest must be in writing.

An assignment of a trademark interest can be recorded in the USPTO. While an assignment can be valid without such recording, a transferee gains several advantages from recording a trademark assignment. The recording of an agreement assigning a trademark interest provides prima facie evidence of proper execution of the agreement. In addition, the recording of an assignment provides the initial assignee with protections against an attempt by the assignor to transfer the same trademark interest to a second assignee. In general, a prior assignment shall be void against any subsequent assignee who is a purchaser for valuable consideration without notice of the first assignment, unless the first assignment is recorded in the USPTO within 3 months after the date of the first assignment or prior to the second assignment.

L. International Considerations

International trademark applications — meaning both applications by United States parties seeking protection for marks in other countries and applications by foreign parties seeking protection for their marks in the United States — are aided under the provisions of a key treaty called The Protocol Relating to the Madrid Agreement Concerning the International Registration of Marks ("Madrid Protocol"). This treaty allows a trademark owner to seek registration for a mark in any of the countries or intergovernmental organizations that are parties to the Madrid Protocol by submitting a single registration application, called an international application. The International Bureau ("IB") of the World Intellectual Property Organization ("WIPO"), in Geneva, Switzerland administers the international registration system. The Madrid Protocol became effective in the United States on November 2, 2003.

Under the Madrid Protocol, a party seeking international protection for a trademark starts by submitting an international application through the trademark office of the signatory country (the "Contracting Party") in which a basic application or registration is already filed (the "Office of Origin"). The Office of Origin must certify that the information in the international application corresponds with the information in the basic application or registration and forward the international application to the IB. If the IB receives the international application within two months of the date of receipt in the Office of Origin, the date of the international registration is the date of receipt in the Office of Origin. If the IB does not receive the international application within two months of the date it was received by the Office of Origin, the date of the international registration is the date the international application was received by the IB.

The international registration is dependent on the basic application or registration for five years from the international registration date. If the basic application or registration is abandoned, cancelled or expired during this five-year period, the IB will cancel the international registration.

The holder of an international registration may request protection in additional Contracting Parties by submitting a subsequent designation. A subsequent designation is a request by the holder of an international registration for an extension of protection of the registration to additional Contracting Parties.

Each Contracting Party designated in an international application or subsequent designation will examine the request for extension of protection as a national trademark application under its domestic laws. There are strict time limits (a maximum of 18 months) for the trademark office of a Contracting Party to enter a refusal of an extension of protection. If the Contracting Party does not notify the IB of a refusal within this time period, the mark is automatically protected. However, the extension of protection may be invalidated in accordance with the same procedures for invalidating a national registration, e.g., by cancellation.

The USPTO may be involved in an international application in any of three capacities:

- Office of Origin. The USPTO is the Office of Origin if an international application or registration is based on an application pending in or a registration issued by the USPTO.

- Office of a Designated Contracting Party. The USPTO is the Office of a Designated Contracting Party if the holder of an international registration requests an extension of protection under that registration to the United States.

- Office of the Contracting Party of the Holder. If the holder of an international registration is a national of, is domiciled in, or has a real and effective industrial or commercial establishment in the United States, the holder can file certain requests with the IB through the USPTO, such as requests to record changes of ownership and restrictions on the holder's right to dispose of an international registration.

V. Trade Secret Laws[5]

A. Characteristics of a Trade Secret

A trade secret is a design, practice, device, or compilation of information which is used in one's business and which gives the trade secret holder an advantage over competitors who do not know or use the trade secret. Common types of trade secrets

---

5. The material on state trade secret laws in this section is based on 29 C.F.R. § 1910.1200 (App. E).

include a commercially advantageous formula for a chemical compound, a process of manufacturing, a means of treating or preserving materials, a pattern for a machine or other device, or a list of customers.

A trade secret differs from other secret information in a business in that it is not simply information about a single action or ephemeral event in the conduct of a business, as, for example, the amount or other terms of a secret bid for a contract or the salary of certain employees. A trade secret is information about a process or device for ongoing use in the operation of a business. Generally it relates to the production of goods, as, for example, a machine or formula for the production of an article. It may, however, relate to practices used in the sale of goods or to other operations in a business, such as a code for determining discounts, rebates or other concessions in a price list or catalogue, or a list of specialized customers, or a method of bookkeeping or for undertaking other office management practices.

B. Secrecy

The subject matter of a trade secret must be secret. Matters of public knowledge or of general knowledge in an industry cannot be appropriated by one party as a trade secret. Matters which are completely disclosed by (or easily ascertained from) the goods which a party markets cannot be a trade secret. Likewise, information that can easily be obtained from customers or from other publicly available sources cannot be a trade secret.

The scope of proper knowledge of a trade secret within a business depends on the way the knowledge involved is used in business activities. It is not requisite that only the proprietors of a business or the senior managers know a trade secret. A trade secret may, without losing protection, be shared with those employees who can advantageously use the information. However, reasonable measures should be taken by a trade secret holder to release the trade secret to as few other parties as possible.

A trade secret holder may also communicate the information involved to others who are pledged to maintain the secrecy of the information. This type of transfer of trade secret information commonly occurs under trade secret licensing agreements in which a trade secret owner allows another party to use a trade secret and the second party agrees to maintain the secrecy of the information and, generally, to pay a royalty to the licensor for use of the trade secret.

Physical security measures should normally be maintained such that, absent improper means of access such as a trespass or theft, parties other than the authorized users of a trade secret will not gain access. Even if such security measures are in place, if a party can rediscover trade secret information through a modest amount of independent research, the information will probably be seen as available to the public and therefore not a proper subject for trade secret protections.

C. Other Significant Factors Indicating That Information is a Trade Secret

Because of the many variations in ways that information may be kept secret and have business significance, an exact standard for determining whether information is a trade secret has not yet been developed. However, courts have indicated that certain factors should be considered in determining whether a trade secret is present in a particular situation. Factors which should be considered in determining whether particular information is a trade secret include: (1) the extent to which the information is known outside of the business seeking trade secret protection; (2) the extent to which the information is known by employees and others involved in the business; (3) the extent of measures taken by the holder of the information to guard its secrecy; (4) the value of the information to the business and its competitors; (5) the amount of effort or money expended by the business in developing the information; and (6) the ease or difficulty with which the information could be properly acquired or duplicated by others.

D. Relationships Between Trade Secret and Patent Protections

1. Broader Subject Matter Covered by Trade Secrets

Trade secret protections are often available for secret designs of useful devices, materials, or processes, the same sorts of designs that can sometimes qualify for patent protections. However, trade secrets can cover many designs for useful devices, materials, and processes which are not patentable subject matter. For example, a trade secret may involve a device design which is unpatentable because it is not new but rather clearly anticipated in the prior design knowledge or "prior art" of the field. Alternatively, the trade secret may involve a design for a device which is new, but that is unpatentable because the design is merely a minor, obvious improvement over prior designs for similar devices and an average practitioner in the field could implement the improvement with modest effort. The fact that a business is relying on particular devices, materials, or processes and the advantages their use may gain for a business can qualify as trade secrets even though the same devices, materials, or processes would not be proper subject matters for patent protections.

Novelty and nonobviousness of useful designs are not requisites for trade secret protection as they are for patentability because the goals of these types of protection differ in fundamental ways. Trade secret protections are primarily aimed at maintaining confidential relationships while patent protections are primarily aimed at encouraging inventive efforts. Novelty and nonobviousness of inventions are essential to patentability because patent rewards and controls are reserved for inventions that are new to the public and not likely to be rediscovered through normal engineering processes. By contrast, trade secret protections are not primarily aimed at rewarding or otherwise encouraging the development of secret processes or devices. Trade secret protections are aimed at discouraging breaches of faith by persons entrusted with trade secrets and deterring reprehensible means of learning another's secret. In order for trade secret protections to act in this manner as a backstop to confidential relationships, it is not appropriate to limit those protections to only circumstances involving the kinds of novelty and nonobvious invention needed for patentability.

2. Reliance on Trade Secret Protections When Obtaining Patents

Where patentable subject matter is present in a new design for a useful device, material, or process, the inventor of the new design may rely on trade secret protections as a preliminary step in seeking patent protections. A developer of a patentable invention will typically rely on trade secret protections to prevent others from using the new design while a patent application is being prepared and while that application is pending in secret in the USPTO. Once a patent application is published (typically 18 months after filing) or a patent issues, the public disclosure of the design involved will preclude further trade secret protections. However, barring the failure to obtain a patent, the trade secret owner will typically be able to rely on patent protections as a substitute for the trade secret protections that are lost through these disclosures.

In most instances, the patent protections gained in this situation will be superior to the trade secret protections given up. In part, this stems from the fact that a patent holder need not be concerned about maintaining the secrecy of a useful design in order to keep control over use of the design. The holder of a patent can publicize the new availability of the patented invention without concern over maintaining the secrecy of the new invention and without the commercialization limitations such secrecy would otherwise entail. Furthermore, the holder of a patent on a given invention will be able to compel those who independently rediscover the same invention to stop making, using, or selling the invention during the life of the patent, whereas a holder of a trade secret can gain no relief against a party who independently rediscovers the design or information covered by the trade secret.

For many new designs of useful devices, patent protection is the only effective means of maintaining long-term control over the commercial value of the designs because the marketing of devices based on the new designs will disclose the design features and preclude subsequent assertion of trade secret protections. While trade secret laws will give the developer of a new design temporary control over the use of the design until disclosures through product marketing efforts or other public revelations disclose an initially secret design, this sort of brief opportunity to be the sole marketer of a new invention may not achieve enough benefit for the first offeror to offset the costs of developing the new invention. Once it is publicly disclosed, other businesses will be free to use an unpatented design in creating and marketing their own products, but will not be required to pay any of the development costs associated with producing the new design. In such settings, it may pay to be a copier rather than an innovator in manufacturing and marketing new products.

3. Strategic Choice of Trade Secret Protections Over Patent Protections

In some circumstances, businesses may choose to rely on trade secret protections for secret designs even though patent protections would probably be available if sought. This type of business strategy will typically only be advantageous if the commercial value of a trade secret can be realized without publicly revealing the trade secret. For example, a company that develops a new process for manufacturing an item might keep this process a trade secret rather than seeking a patent for the process. Provided that secrecy concerning the means of manufacturing can be maintained—for example, by only using the process in a secure work environment—the commercial value of the cost savings achieved by the new process or the marketing value of the superior product quality resulting from the process can be realized by the firm involved without disclosing and losing the trade secret.

This type of business strategy has one important potential advantage over obtaining a patent for the secret process involved—trade secret protections can be maintained indefinitely, while patent protections will expire with the patent involved, currently at a point 20 years from the date of the patent application leading to the patent. If the secrecy of a process or other trade secret can be maintained over time and the burden of securing such secrecy does not outweigh the advantages of the secret process to the business involved, a business strategy of relying on trade secret protections rather than seeking a patent may be an advantageous means to extend the business value of a new invention beyond the period that patent protections would cover.

Some trade secrets have been maintained over many years and have assertedly achieved significant value over such periods for the firms involved. The most famous example of this type of reliance on trade secret protection is the formula for "Coca-Cola," which was first developed in the 1800's and which is still limited to a few company employees today. The company is able to use this formula to create syrup for drinks in secret and the syrup is then distributed to bottlers for use in preparing Coca-Cola soda without revealing the formula.

E. Misappropriation of Trade Secrets

Misappropriation of a trade secret—the equivalent of infringement of a patent, copyright, or trademark—involves use of the trade secret in a manner that is not authorized by the trade secret owner. A trade secret can be misappropriated in either of two ways. First, a person who gains access to a trade secret through improper means may misappropriate the trade secret through use. Any use of the trade secret by such a party will be misappropriation since the trade secret owner has not authorized the party's access to the trade secret, much less the use. Second, a person who is given access to a trade secret for a specified use will misappropriate the trade secret if a different use is made. For example, an employee of a business who is given a secret list of store customers to contact them on behalf of the store to see if they would like to purchase additional items would not misappropriate the trade secret in making such calls but would misappropriate the trade secret if he took the information home and used the list to contact parties in conducting a personal business run by the employee.

Where a second business acquires the trade secret of another concern, whether the use of the information by the second business constitutes trade secret misappropriation may depend on whether the managers of the second business had reason to know that the information was a trade secret of another business. Thus if an individual A works for business B, takes a secret formula from B's files, and then goes to work for business C and uses the same formula for C's benefit claiming that A had developed the formula since coming to work for C, A's use of the trade secret would certainly constitute misappropriation by A since he made use of the formula beyond the scope of any use authorized by B. However, whether the use also constitutes misappropriation by C would depend on whether C had reason to doubt A's claim of having developed the formula and had grounds to believe that A must have brought the formula with him from his former employer. As this example suggests, potential trade secret misappropriation and liability can place significant limits on employee mobility in high-tech industries and constrain the ability to reuse information or techniques learned in one employer's secret work environment after an employee has transferred to a second employer.

F. Remedies for Trade Secret Misappropriation

If a trade secret is misappropriated (or will be misappropriated through reasonably anticipated future conduct), the proper relief will depend on whether the trade secret has been released to the public through the misappropriation or is still secret. If the information formerly constituting a trade secret has been fully disclosed, it is no longer a trade secret and the owner's loss is the full value of the trade secret. This value, if it can be proven, can generally be recovered from the party whose misappropriation led to the public release of the information.

If misappropriation of a trade secret has not produced a public disclosure, the owner of the trade secret can generally obtain an injunction barring further use of the trade secret by the misappropriator and a damage award compensating the trade secret owner for injury suffered due to the misappropriator's past use of the trade secret.

The nature of a trade secret is an important factor in determining the kind of relief that is appropriate against one who is subject to liability for improper use of the trade secret. Thus, if a trade secret consists of a device or process which is a novel invention, a party that acquires the secret wrongfully would ordinarily be enjoined from further use of the trade secret and required to account for the profits derived from the party's past use. If, on the other hand, the secret consists of modest improvements that a good mechanic could make without resort to the secret, the wrongdoer's liability may be limited to damages over the period in which independent research would have been needed to acquire similar information and an injunction against future use of the improvements made with the aid of the secret may be inappropriate.

G. Federal Trade Secret Protections

The federal Defend Trade Secrets Act (DTSA), which became effective on May 11, 2016, adds civil trade secret protections under federal law to existing state protections. The DTSA amends the Economic Espionage Act of 1996, 18 U.S.C. §§ 1831–1839, which provides for federal criminal penalties for foreign economic espionage and trade secret theft. The DTSA adds a federal civil cause of action for trade secret misappropriation, but does not preempt any state trade secrets acts. *See* 18 U.S.C. § 1836. Much of the DTSA is modeled on the longstanding Uniform Trade Secrets Act adopted by most states. The DTSA allows a trade secret owner to collect actual damages for trade secret misappropriation and, if the misappropriation is willful and malicious, a court may award exemplary damages of no more than two times the actual damages awarded, as well as attorneys' fees. The DTSA includes a seizure provision, which allows a court to take control of trade secret materials in the hands of an alleged misappropriator.

VI. Additional Intellectual Property Protections

A. Internet Domain Names

Domain names are the words that are used as part of an Internet address, such as www.intellectualproperty.com. The ".com" portion is referred to as the top-level domain name (TLD). Rights in a particular domain name are obtained by being the first to register the domain name with a registry sponsored by the Internet Corporation for Assigned Names and Numbers (ICANN), a private entity that regulates the registration of domain names. The rights obtained through registration are limited by trademark law. For example, if a company registers a domain name that is also a trademark owned by another company (such as www.mcdonalds.com), the domain name registrant very likely will be liable for trademark infringement if the domain name is used in commerce in a way that is likely to confuse consumers. In addition, a company that registers a domain name may be liable for cybersquatting under the Anti-Cybersquatting Consumer Protection Act (ACCPA) if the registration was done with a bad faith intent to profit from the trademark owned by someone else and the registrant has no bona fide rights in the domain name. Claims of trademark infringement or violations of the ACCPA are adjudicated in court. Alternatively, claims for cybersquatting can be settled through the Uniform Domain Name Dispute Resolution Process (UDRP) implemented by ICANN. The UDRP is a system of arbitration and is governed at the international and domestic levels by guidelines promulgated by the World Intellectual Property Organization (WIPO). In 2012, ICANN introduced the Uniform Rapid Suspension System as a streamlined, online system of dispute resolution to complement the UDRP. For more information, go to http://newgtlds .icann.org/en/applicants/urs.

B. Rights of Publicity

Rights of publicity protect a person's marketable image or persona. State laws specifying these rights create a form of intellectual property by granting an individual the exclusive ability to control the commercial use of his or her identity. Since state laws govern publicity rights, protection varies from state to state. Some states recognize common law rights of publicity while others have codified the rights in statutes. California recognizes both common law and statutory forms of protection for publicity rights.

Generally, rights of publicity protect elements that serve to identify a person, including one's name, voice, signature, likeness, and performance style. Celebrities are commonly the plaintiffs in suits alleging the infringement of rights of publicity. Infringement of publicity rights involves unauthorized commercial use of an element of an individual's identity in a way that identifies the individual. The typical remedy for infringement is an injunction against further unauthorized use of elements of the plaintiff's identity.

C. Protections Under the Semiconductor Chip Protection Act (SCPA)

In 1984, Congress passed the Semiconductor Chip Protection Act (SCPA), 17 U.S.C. §§ 901–914, which creates a distinct form of intellectual property protection for "mask works" used to create electronic circuitry on semiconductor chips. A mask work is a graphic work used to preserve or "mask" certain elements of semiconductor material from chemical processes in the production of highly sophisticated semiconductor chips. The details of a mask work define the physical layout of elements of a semiconductor chip and, in turn, the electronic characteristics of the chip. Hence, the ability to recreate and reuse a mask work in the production of semiconductor chips is an effective way to replicate the design of a chip. A new semiconductor chip typically costs $100 million to develop, but free riders can copy the chip by replicating and reusing a corresponding mask work for a fraction of the development cost. The SCPA was aimed at discouraging this type of free rider copying by granting the owner of a mask work the exclusive rights "to reproduce the mask work by optical, electronic, or any other means" as part of semiconductor production processes or otherwise and "to import or distribute a semiconductor chip product in which the mask work is embodied." 17 U.S.C. § 905.

The SCPA was enacted in response to concerns that existing patent and copyright laws did not adequately protect semiconductor chips. Designs for semiconductor chips often could not meet the novelty and nonobviousness requirements to secure patent protection. Copyright protections for images capturing patterns of electronic elements in semiconductor chips were also seen as inadequate because "it was uncertain whether the copyright law could protect against copying of the pattern on the chip itself, if the pattern was deemed inseparable from the utilitarian function of the chip." *Brooktree Corp. v. Advanced Micro Devices*, 977 F.2d 1555, 1561–62 (Fed. Cir. 1992). The Court of Appeals for the Federal Circuit has called the SCPA "an innovative solution to [the] problem of technology-based industry." *Id.* at 1563. The law drew from both copyright and patent law principles, but was "uniquely adapted to semiconductor mask works, in order to achieve appropriate protection for original designs while meeting the competitive needs of the industry and serving the public interest." *Id.*

D. Anti-Circumvention Protections Under the Digital Millennium Copyright Act (DMCA)

As content shifted towards the digital, online environment in the 1990s, Congress responded to copyright owners' concerns with rampant online infringement with the enactment in 1996 of the Digital Millennium Copyright Act (DMCA). These amendments to the Copyright Act provided enhanced protections for encrypted content by prohibiting the production and dissemination of devices or services aimed at circumventing encryption and other access controls applied to digital works. Provisions of the DMCA aided copyright holders by added anti-circumvention protections to traditional copyright protections, but may have gone too far by enforcing barriers to access even where the underlying works being restricted are uncopyrighted (and part of the public domain) and by limiting access to works where access would otherwise be non-infringing fair use of the works under copyright laws. The DMCA also created safe harbors for Internet Service Providers, which were largely protected from copyright infringement liability so long as they followed statutorily-defined procedures for responding to illegally uploaded copyrighted content. The scope of the DMCA and its protections are still controversial and being defined in extensive litigation, but anyone conducting business involving the Internet needs to be aware of the DMCA and its provisions.

Table of Cases

Table of Statutes

Code of Federal Regulations

Index

[References are to sections and appendices.]